SOCIOLOGY

IN FOCUS

PAUL TAYLOR • JOHN RICHARDSON
ALAN YEO • IAN MARSH
KEITH TROBE • ANDREW PILKINGTON

GORDON HUGHES • KEITH SHARP

Causeway Press

Acknowledgements

Cover design Andrew Allen
Cover illustration Tony Stone Images
Page design Andrew Allen
Graphic origination John A. Collins (Waring-Collins Partnership)
Graphics Elaine M. Sumner (Waring-Collins Partnership)
Author index Ingrid Hamer
Subject index Paul Taylor
Readers Linda J. Hick, Julie Rainford, Peter Withers

Picture credits

Advertising Archives 241 (r), 250, 458; Alan Hardman 231 (tr); Amnesty International 89 (l); Andrew Pilkington 698 (l and r), 699 (l); Andrew Allen 78 (mr and r), 244 (l and r), 307, 491 (t), 507 (bl), 522 (l), 667 (m); Bill Greensmith 635; Bookseller 17, Brick 12, 18, 64, 76 (r), 266, 392, 552, 588, 682; Bristol United Press 406 (t), 623; Bruce Coleman Ltd 692; Camera Press 109 (mr); Chris Garratt/Pierrot Productions 419; Conservative Central Office 109 (tl); David Gray 302 (bl); David Hoffman 82 (both), 406 (b), 478; Dorothea Heath 416; Ebony 100 (m); Financial Times 14; Format/Brenda Prince 19; Guardian 32, 175; House of Viz - John Brown Publishing Ltd 124 (b); Hulton Deutsch 52 (br), 79 (l and mr), 91, 93 (tr), 158, 194 (r), 205 (r), 213 (ml), 217, 274, 330, 368, 396, 427 (br), 442, 456 (mr), 496, 498 (r), 520 (t), 531, 546, 554, 684, 699 (r); Imperial War Museum 661; Institute of Agricultural History 246 (r); J. F. Batellier 363, 374; Jacky Fleming/Penguin Books 117, 137, 149 (bl); Joe Bloggs 113; John Kent 225; Kurdish Organisation for Culture and Education 220; Little, Brown and Company 138; Liverpool Daily Post and Echo 456 (bl); Mac/Stan McMurtry 481 (l); Mansell Collection 194 (l), 238 (ml), 384 (bl), 435; Mary Evans Picture Library 126, 173 (l), 238 (r), 398, 631 (br), 643 (m and b), 654, 664; Mike Haralambos 672 (tl); National Museums of Canada 649; Network 157, (and Mark Power) 449, (and John Sturrock) 539 (l); Observer 45; Oxo 241 (l); Peter Newark's Western Americana 8 (br), 494 (bl), 499 (l and r); Phil Evans 481 (r); Popperfoto 3 (bl and br), 36 (b), 47 (b), 52 (bl), 60 (l), 72 (r), 97 (tl), 102 (tl), 118, 121, 130, 138, 144 (mr), 147 (l), 185, 195 (m), 198 (l), 212, 214, 216 (l), 238 (tl), 281, 327, 384 (br), 413, 417, 423 (both), 477 (ml and mm), 479, 485, 494 (br), 520 (b), 525, 671 (br), 672 (m), 676 (l), 694; Posy Simmonds 68; Press Association 93 (tl), 108 (mr), 170 (r), 292, 400, 408, 687; Rex Features 4 (tl and mr), 8 (l), 35 (t and m), 44 (br), 60 (r), 78 (l and ml), 79 (ml), 80, 89 (r), 108 (ml), 109 (tr), 128, 129, 149 (m and br), 173 (r), 189, 205 (l), 208, 254, 264 (both), 290 (both), 311, 318 (mr), 321 (ml, mr and b), 341, 351 (b), 360 (m), 364, 366, 380, 388 (all), 390, 404, 433, 453, 456 (tl), 468 (both), 472, 477 (mr, bl and br), 491 (m), 498 (l), 511, 513 (tr), 515, 528, 573 (r and l), 579 (r), 592, 600, 603, 627, 667 (b), 671 (bl), 672 (tr); Sally and Richard Greenhill 2, 23, 36 (l and r), 39, 44 (mr and bl), 47 (t), 57, 79 (r), 133, 135, 144 (t and br), 162, 170 (l), 195 (tl), 198 (r), 209, 213 (tr and mr), 216 (r), 296, 334, 411, 456 (tr, ml and bl), 488, 507 (bl), 513 (bl), 539 (r), 560, 579 (l); SCRSS 13, 695; Times Newspapers Ltd 257; Topham Picture Source 3 (t), 4 (tr), 27, 37, 44 (ml), 60 (l), 97 (tr and br), 102 (b), 108 (b), 109 (tm), 124 (m), 144 (bl), 298, 318 (tl, tr and ml), 351 (t), 354, 360 (b), 370, 429, 503, 535, 575, 672 (r); Trog/Observer 45; United Nations/Ray Witlin 577.

Statistical data

Central Statistical Office for charts and tables from various issues of *Social Trends*. Crown Copyright. Reproduced by the permission of the Controller of HMSO and the Central Statistical Office.
Child Poverty Action Group for charts from C. Oppenheim *Poverty the Facts* (CPAG, London, 1993).

Every effort has been made to locate the copyright owners of material used in this book. Any omissions brought to the attention of the publisher are regretted and will be credited in subsequent printings.

British Library Cataloguing in Publication Data
A catalogue record for this book is available from the British Library.

ISBN 1 873929 21 8

Causeway Press Limited
PO Box 13, Ormskirk, Lancs L39 5HP

© Paul Taylor, John Richardson, Alan Yeo, Ian Marsh, Keith Trobe, Andrew Pilkington, Gordon Hughes, Keith Sharp

First impression 1995, reprinted 1996, 1997

Printed and bound by The Bath Press, Lower Bristol Road, Bath.

Contents

Chapter 1	**First Steps**	**1**
Part 1	What is sociology?	1
Part 2	Basic sociological ideas	5
Part 3	Sociological perspectives	11
Part 4	Sociological theories	14
Part 5	Sociological investigation	19

Chapter 2	**Class Stratification**	**25**
Part 1	Stratification	25
Part 2	Theoretical approaches	33
Part 3	Class matters	39
Part 4	Social mobility	46
Part 5	Class maps	50

Chapter 3	**Race and Ethnicity**	**66**
Part 1	Britain's minorities	66
Part 2	Racism	74
Part 3	Race and class	98

Chapter 4	**Gender**	**116**
Part 1	The feminist challenge	116
Part 2	Sex, gender and sexuality	121
Part 3	Ethnic minority women	128
Part 4	Women and work	134
Part 5	Women and stratification	141
Part 6	Men	148

Chapter 5	**Welfare and Poverty**	**154**
Part 1	The welfare state and social policy	154
Part 2	Poverty, inequality and the welfare state	171

Chapter 6	**Politics and Power**	**192**
Part 1	Power and political systems	192
Part 2	Pluralism and liberal democracy	199
Part 3	Inequalities of power	206
Part 4	Voting behaviour	222

Chapter 7	**Families**	**232**
Part 1	Families in different societies	232
Part 2	Theoretical perspectives on the family	235
Part 3	Social change and the family	244
Part 4	Husbands and wives	258

Chapter 8	Education	273
Part 1	The history of education in England and Wales	273
Part 2	Sociological theories of education	287
Part 3	Education and social class	293
Part 4	Gender and education	301
Part 5	Ethnicity and education	308

Chapter 9	Work and Non-work	317
Part 1	Work in industrial society	317
Part 2	Technological change and work	328
Part 3	Industrial relations	338
Part 4	Non-work	344

Chapter 10	Organisations	358
Part 1	Bureaucracy and organisations: the debate with Weber	358
Part 2	Organisation theory: beyond the debate with Weber	370

Chapter 11	Community	386
Part 1	What is community?	386
Part 2	Studying community	393
Part 3	Models of community	399
Part 4	Gender, race and age	402
Part 5	Spaces and places	411

Chapter 12	Health and Medicine	421
Part 1	The social construction of health and illness	421
Part 2	The history of disease	425
Part 3	Theories of disease	428
Part 4	Medicine's rise to preeminence	433
Part 5	Doctors and patients	436
Part 6	The social patterning of health and disease	442

Chapter 13	Crime and Deviance	455
Part 1	The nature of crime and deviance	455
Part 2	Representations of crime and deviance	458
Part 3	Crime statistics	461
Part 4	Explaining crime and deviance	466

Chapter 14	Religion	493
Part 1	The nature and interpretation of religion	493
Part 2	The variety of religious organisations	508
Part 3	The decline of religion?	521

Chapter 15	**Mass Media**	**533**
Part 1	The structure of the mass media	533
Part 2	Theoretical approaches to the mass media	538
Part 3	The content of the mass media: impartiality, politics and news	544
Part 4	Media representations of women and ethnic minorities	555
Part 5	The mass media and violence	560
Chapter 16	**Development**	**566**
Part 1	One world, divided	566
Part 2	Sociological theories of development	570
Part 3	The relationships of developed and less developed societies	580
Part 4	The demography of First and Third World countries	586
Part 5	Industrialisation and development	591
Part 6	Urbanisation and development	598
Part 7	Health as an aspect of development	601
Chapter 17	**Methodology**	**608**
Part 1	Primary sources	608
Part 2	Secondary sources	625
Part 3	Assessing research methods	633
Part 4	Sociology and science	636
Part 5	Interpretive methodology	641
Part 6	Sociology, methodology and values	644
Chapter 18	**Sociological Theory**	**651**
Part 1	What is sociological theory?	651
Part 2	Classical sociology and the advent of modernity	655
Part 3	The establishment of sociological theory	668
Part 4	Structure and action in sociology	682
Part 5	Challenges to sociological theory	689
Author Index		701
Subject Index		706

1 First Steps

Introduction

Taking first steps in anything is always difficult and sociology is no exception. One way of introducing sociology is to tell you what it is. A second way is to ask you to do sociology. The emphasis in this chapter is on doing. There are a number of activities which, after completion, should provide a basis for understanding the rest of this book. We hope you'll find this is the case - and that you'll enjoy 'doing sociology'.

Chapter summary

- This chapter starts by asking, '**What is sociology**?'
- It then looks at basic sociological ideas and introduces some key **concepts**.
- The main **sociological perspectives** are then

examined along with a number of **theories** which derive from those perspectives.

- The final part introduces the main **methods of sociological investigation**.

1 What is Sociology?

Key Issues

1 What do sociologists study?
2 What is a sociological approach?
3 Does sociology simply state the obvious?

1.1 'Private troubles, public issues'

One of the simplest and most common definitions of sociology is 'the study of people in social groups'. Although this is a limited definition, it nevertheless identifies the main concern of the subject. People are social beings, not just individuals with their own separate lives. Their lives are shared with others and shaped by the society in which they live. How different would your life be if you had been born a hundred years ago or brought up in another society? What if you had been born into an aristocratic family? How would this have affected your education, your family life, your political views, your job opportunities?

Describing sociology, the American social scientist C.Wright Mills makes the distinction between the 'private troubles' experienced by individuals and the 'public issues' of society as a whole. Mills argues that 'personal troubles' are events which happen to an individual and which affect only that individual and those immediately around them. 'Public issues' are the broader issues which are to do with large scale social institutions, social groups and whole societies. Mills illustrates this distinction using the example of unemployment.

'In these terms, consider unemployment. When in a city of 100,000, only one person is unemployed, that is their personal trouble, and for its solution we properly look to the character of the individual, their skills, and their immediate opportunities. But when in a nation of 50 million employees, 15 million people are unemployed, that is an issue, and we may not hope to find its solution within the range of opportunities open to any one individual. The very structure of opportunities has collapsed. Both the correct statement of the problem and the range of possible solutions require us to consider the economic and political institutions of the society, and not merely the personal situation and character of a scatter of individuals' (Mills, 1970, pp15-16).

Mills argues that to understand individual experiences we have to look beyond the personal circumstances in which they occur. We have to examine the structure of society by looking at those social institutions which reach down into these personal circumstances and which shape individual 'troubles'. It is not that sociologists are unconcerned about 'personal troubles'. Instead they argue that many 'personal troubles' can only be fully understood by an examination of broader 'public issues'. Mills concludes that this requires an awareness of social structure and the ability to trace the links between the wider society and the lives of individuals. 'To be able to do that is to possess the sociological imagination' (Mills, 1970, p17).

Activity 1   Private Troubles and Public Issues

Item A *'Private troubles'*

Living in poverty

Questions

1 How do Items A and B illustrate Mills' idea of 'private troubles'?
2 How do Items B and C illustrate the idea of 'public issues'?
3 Using Mills' idea of 'the sociological imagination', show the links between the 'private troubles' and 'public issues' of poverty.

Item B *Kelly*

Kelly lives in Birmingham. She is a single mother with a three year old daughter. She doesn't have a job (and couldn't afford the childcare if she did), and her income is £100 a week, including housing benefit. Kelly is typical of single parents, most of whom are on low incomes. Even those who are in work are relatively poor. This dramatically illustrates the poverty trap that exists because of the rate at which benefits are withdrawn from those who enter employment. For all too many single parents, work simply does not pay.

Adapted from S.Webb and R.Thomas 'Knowing Your Place in Society' *New Statesman and Society*, 30.7.93, p22

Item C *'Public issues'*

Income inequality has risen rapidly since 1979 as a result of rising unemployment and non-employment, a widening of the gap between the highest and lowest paid, and changes to the tax and benefit systems. Tax cuts in the 1980s gave the top 1 per cent of taxpayers, on average, £33,000 a year each, while the bottom half each gained only £400. The bottom half of the population receive only one quarter of all income (compared to a third in 1979) and the bottom tenth of the population saw a fall in their real incomes between 1979 and 1991. In 1993 almost two-thirds of the population, or 35 million people, live on an income below the average, three million more than in 1979.

Adapted from S.Webb and R.Thomas 'Knowing Your Place in Society' *New Statesman and Society*, 30.7.93, p22

1.2 'The sociological consciousness'

Sociologists study the social behaviour of people. But what kind of questions do they ask? Peter Berger suggests that sociology is based on a critical awareness of social life. Nothing is taken for granted and everything is open to question. This awareness challenges everyday explanations and understanding, asking why people think and behave in the way they do and digging deep to find hidden motives, causes and consequences. In Berger's words:

'It can be said that the first wisdom of sociology is this - things are not what they seem. This is a deceptively simple statement. It ceases to be simple after a while. Social reality turns out to have many layers of meaning. The discovery of each new layer changes the perception of the whole.

To ask sociological questions then, presupposes that one is interested in looking some distance beyond the commonly accepted or officially defined goals of human action. It presupposes a certain awareness that human events have different levels of meaning, some of which are hidden from the consciousness of everyday life. It may even presuppose a measure of suspicion about the way in which human events are officially interpreted by the authorities, be they political, juridical or religious in character. The sociological perspective can then be understood in terms of such phrases as "seeing through", "looking behind", very much as such

phrases would be employed in common speech - "seeing through his game", "looking behind the scenes" - in other words, "being up on all the tricks".

People who like to avoid shocking discoveries, who prefer to believe that society is just what they were taught in Sunday School, who like the safety of the rules and the maxims of what Alfred Schutz has called the "world-taken-for-granted", should stay away from sociology. People who feel no temptation before closed doors, who have no curiosity about human beings, who are content to admire scenery without wondering about the people who live in those houses on the other side of that river, should probably also stay away from sociology.' (Adapted from Berger, 1966, Chapters 1 and 2).

Berger argues that sociology is a distinctive way of thinking, a particular awareness of the nature of social life, an unwillingness to accept the superficial and the apparently obvious. In short, there is such a thing as the 'sociological consciousness'. What appears on the surface to be true may not, after sociological examination, actually be the full story. For example, on the surface, the law in our society exists to protect us all. But the sociologist is only too aware that other, alternative interpretations exist. Who makes the law? In whose interest are laws made? Are all laws equally enforced? Questions such as these probe the apparent reality and reveal all kinds of cross currents below the surface.

Sociological understanding is sceptical of the 'of

course!' statement. 'Is monogamy the natural form of marriage?' - 'Of course!'. 'Do families function for the benefit of their members?' - 'Of course!'. 'Do educational institutions work for the good of their students?' - 'Of course!'. Sociologists know that there are serious questions to be asked of every 'of course!' statement. This is an aspect of the 'sociological consciousness', part of what the philosopher Nietzsche called 'the art of mistrust'.

The following activity gives you an opportunity to apply Berger's 'sociological consciousness'. It looks at something we all have - a name. Most of us take our names for granted and rarely give them a second thought. But, adopting Peter Berger's 'sociological consciousness', can we in his words 'look behind' a name and discover whether names 'have different levels of meaning, some of which are hidden from the consciousness of everyday life'?

Activity 2 What's in a Name?

Item A *Malcolm X*

On joining the religious group known as the Black Muslims or the Nation of Islam, Malcolm Little changed his name to Malcolm X. He was later to become one of the most influential black American leaders. For Malcolm, his change of name had great significance. In his words, 'The Muslim's "X" symbolised the true African family name I could never know. For me, my "X" replaced the white slavemaster name of "Little" which some blue-eyed devil named Little had imposed upon my paternal forebears. The receipt of my "X" meant that forever after in the Nation of Islam, I would be known as Malcolm X.'

For Black Muslims, their change of name reflects a transformation of identity. Their 'old self' is dead and with it all the negative stereotypes associated with blacks. Their 'white' name, given by slaveowners, is wiped away. Their new name announces their new status to the world.

Adapted in part from *The Autobiography of Malcolm X*, 1966, p199

Malcolm X, 1925-1965

Item B *Numbers*

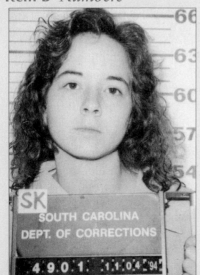

Prisoners are sometimes referred to by numbers. This also happens to soldiers in some armed forces.

Item C *'Gooks'*

Vietnamese prisoners led by US marines during the Vietnam war. The Americans referred to the Vietnamese as 'gooks'.

Item D *Marriage*

Miss Brown becomes Mrs Smith. Some women prefer to keep their 'maiden name' or combine their last name with their husband's.

Item E *Migration*

WORLD'S HIGHEST STANDARD OF LIVING

There's no way like the American Way

Many American immigrants changed their name to an English sounding name, eg Schmidt was often changed to Smith.

Item F *Nuns*

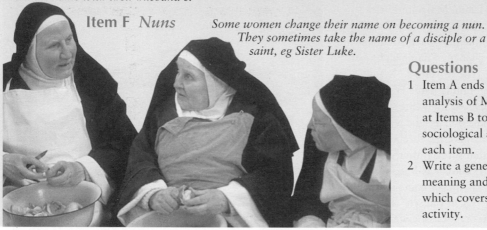

Some women change their name on becoming a nun. They sometimes take the name of a disciple or a saint, eg Sister Luke.

Questions

1 Item A ends with a brief sociological analysis of Malcolm X's name. Look at Items B to F. Write a short sociological analysis of the names in each item.
2 Write a general explanation of the meaning and significance of names which covers all the items in this activity.

1.3 Does sociology simply state the obvious?

Some critics have claimed that sociology has nothing new to say. Beneath all the jargon and theories, sociology simply states the obvious. We can explore this criticism by looking at a sociological study of the attitudes of United States soldiers during the Second World War. This 1,200 page work, *The American Soldier* by Samuel A. Stouffer, was criticised by a prominent historian Arthur Schlesinger as 'a ponderous demonstration of self-evident truths'. According to Schlesinger, it merely reported in a complicated form findings that were obvious to everyone.

Let's look at some 'obvious' statements about American soldiers.

1 Better educated men had more psychological problems, eg severe depression, than those with less education. This is because men with less education are more used to dealing with hardship.
2 Soldiers from the warmer southern states were better able to cope with the steamy heat of the South Pacific islands than those from northern states. Southerners were more accustomed to the heat.
3 White soldiers were more eager than black soldiers to become officers. This is because black soldiers had been deprived of opportunities before they joined the army and consequently had a lack of ambition.

4 Men were more eager to return home during the fighting than after the German surrender in 1945. This is understandable as there was a far greater chance of injury or death during the war.

These findings and explanations seem obvious and reasonable. They are in fact nonsense. Stouffer's research contradicted every one of these statements. It revealed that less educated soldiers had more psychological problems than those with more education, that men from the northern and southern states showed no difference in adapting to tropical heat, that black soldiers were more eager for promotion than whites and that men were more eager to return to the USA when the fighting ended than during the war itself. *The American Soldier* would seem to vindicate sociology and confirm Berger's claim that we should be careful of the 'of course!' statement. Just because something sounds reasonable or logical does not mean that it's true. One of sociology's most important contributions has been to challenge 'obvious' statements of apparent truth.

Those who criticise sociology for, as they see it, stating the obvious, often see the results of sociological research as largely insignificant. The following activity looks at the connection between social class and illness and death. You can judge for yourself whether the research is insignificant.

Summary

1 Sociology is the study of people in social groups.

2 Sociology is based on a critical awareness of social life. It attempts to see through and look beyond what seems obvious.

3 Sociology has been accused of stating the obvious. The results of sociological research do not support this view.

Activity 3 Illness and Death

Item A

Longstanding illness and social class (males, percentages, Great Britain, 1991)

Social class	16-44 years	45-64 years
1. Professional	19	33
2. Employers, managers	20	35
3. Intermediate and junior nonmanual	21	41
4. Skilled manual	24	45
5. Semi-skilled manual	22	45
6. Unskilled manual	26	51

Adapted from *General Household Survey* 1991, 1993, p156

Item B

Infant mortality and social class, 1990 (England and Wales)

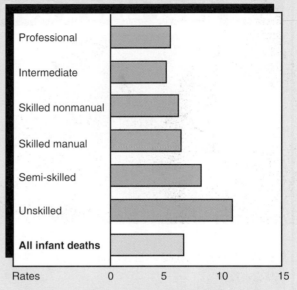

Infant mortality refers to deaths of infants under one year of age per thousand live births. Classes are based on the occupation of fathers.

From *Social Trends*, 1993, p96

Questions

1 What do Items A and B show?

2 Do you regard these findings as important?

3 Use your 'sociological imagination' to provide a brief explanation of the relationship between social class and longstanding illness and infant mortality.

2 Basic Sociological Ideas

Key Issues

1 What is social behaviour?

2 How is social life possible?

3 How do people learn to live in society?

4 What concepts do sociologists use to analyse social life?

2.1 Social behaviour and culture

What does the 'socio' in sociology mean? What are we talking about when we refer to 'social' behaviour? The answer is that human behaviour is not random but patterned and these patterns are shared with other people. In this sense our behaviour is social - we live in social groups, not as isolated individuals. Much of our behaviour is similar to that of other members of society and as such it is predictable and understandable.

For example, throughout the country, there will be thousands of students just like yourself starting a sociology course. Although you will not have met many of them, their behaviour will be broadly similar to your own, at least in respect to their studies. They will be in groups identifiable as 'classes' and in organisations exhibiting certain general similarities called 'schools' and 'colleges'. There is likely to be a teacher or tutor who has the basically similar task of 'getting you through the course'. And just like you they'll be reading sociology textbooks.

As members of society we have to learn social behaviour. We have no instincts to direct our actions. Through our membership of social groups, initially the family, later the school, community, workplace and other organisations, we acquire our understanding of the ways in which behaviour is patterned. We learn the language of our society, not just the sounds, but the meanings attached to those sounds, when and where to use particular words and how to communicate by non-verbal means. We develop an understanding of ourselves as social beings. In other words, we learn the unwritten rules of society.

The learned shared behaviour of members of society is known as *culture*. Culture is a social blueprint, a guide for living, the way of life of a society. Without culture it is difficult to see how human society could operate. The importance of culture can be seen from the following activity.

Activity 4 Horst

HE EVEN COCKED HIS LEG JUST LIKE A DOG

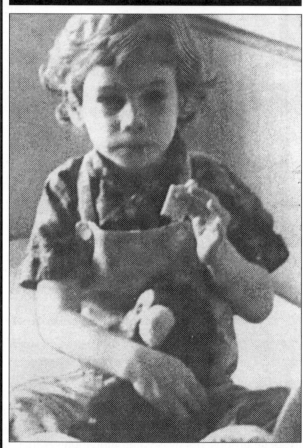

REBORN: Horst sits up, cuddling a soft toy, just like a normal child.

Shocking truth of the puppy boy

PUPPY boy Horst is three years old - and just beginning his life as a human being.

He is the child raised by a devoted pet Alsatian called Asta while his parents went out drinking.

He became so like a dog that he didn't know how to use a toilet - and cocked his leg against a bush instead.

Now, as Horst gradually learns the behaviour of a normal little boy, the full shocking story of his lost babyhood is being unravelled.

Alsatian Asta had a litter of eight puppies just before Horst was born and they were taken from her. Pining for her brood, the dog turned her affection to the new baby. Asta nuzzled him, licked his hands, face and bottom clean, kept him warm in a furry blanket under her tummy.

Horst's grandmother Elisabeth said: 'I saw how the dog's mothering instinct was transferred to the boy. She never left his side and growled when anyone came near.'

And the caretaker at the flats in Mettmenn, West Germany said: 'They touched and stroked each other. The dog was the only one who gave him anything like love.'

Meanwhile the parents left them in squalor. They gave Asta meat and water. They put out bananas, milk and porridge on a table for Horst. Then the door slammed on the two roomed flat and they were off out to the pub or a disco. They said: 'He had everything he needed. In fact he had more than most, he had Asta.'

Growled

It seems that they didn't notice that their son was growing more and more like a dog. He whimpered and growled instead of talked. He preferred crawling to walking. He slept curled up like a

DEVOTED: Horst's 'mum', Asta

puppy, his head between his 'paws'.

Horst and Asta were confined to one room. When they were discovered there, sharing a raw chicken, Horst's extraordinary existence came to light. The wallpaper was clawed to tatters. There was kennel stench. Scraps of old food were scattered around. Horst's cot was unused, a film of grime over the quilt while on the floor lay their blanket bed.

Now Horst is in a clinic in Wuppertal being reborn. He can keep down hot food - which he had never had - and he has added weight to his feeble frame, a third underweight. The staff are talking to him, slowly teaching him to accept and enjoy cuddles, smiling at him, showing him toys and encouraging him to explore his new world.

And he's learning that humans can be loving too.

Adapted from *Daily Mirror*, 24.3.88

Questions

1 Human behaviour is learned rather than based on instinct. Use examples of Horst's behaviour to support this statement.

2 How does the example of Horst show the importance of culture for human society?

2.2 Socialisation and social control

Socialisation The process by which we learn the culture of our society is known as socialisation. This is a lifelong process - we never stop learning - but the most important part probably takes place during a person's early years. As the example of Horst in Activity 4 shows, socialisation is vital if people are to play a normal part in human society.

In modern industrial society the main agencies of socialisation are the family, school, community, workplace and the mass media - TV, films, books and magazines. *Primary socialisation*, the first and probably most important part of the process, is usually centred on the family. In this context children learn many of the basic lessons for life from how to speak and use a knife and fork to the appropriate behaviour for a male and female. *Secondary socialisation* takes place as children grow up and move out into the wider world. For example, in the workplace they learn the basic disciplines of work.

Social control Socialisation is closely linked to social control. Every society has various methods for ensuring that its members conform to the accepted and approved ways of behaving. For example, in many traditional hunting societies such as the Inuit (Eskimo) the hunter has a moral duty to share his kill with other members of the community. If he does not he is ostracised - shunned by and cut off from the group. Without some form of social control it is difficult to see how the socialisation process could be effective and how standardised and predictable behaviour could be maintained. And without such behaviour human society could not operate.

In every society the family is a major agency of social control. Children are born helpless - they are totally dependent on adults. This gives parents enormous power both to teach and enforce what they teach. They are able to apply a battery of positive and negative sanctions - rewards and punishments - to ensure conformity. These range from words and expressions of approval and disapproval through to physical violence.

In every area of social life there is a variety of mechanisms of social control. For example, the promise of promotion or the threat of dismissal in the workplace and the encouraging smile or disapproving glance within a circle of friends. In many societies certain aspects of behaviour are defined as crimes. Officials are appointed to deal with such behaviour and apply punishment to those who have broken the law. However, most mechanisms of social control are much more subtle than the heavy hand of the law. For example, religion is a major instrument of social control in many societies. Religious beliefs often encourage people to conform to accepted ways of behaving. They may offer rewards such as an afterlife of everlasting happiness for those who follow the straight and narrow and punishments such as eternal damnation for those who do not.

The following activity looks at a very effective system of social control but one which every reader will hopefully find totally unacceptable. Known as the 'Jim Crow' system, it operated in the southern states of the USA to keep black Americans 'in their place'. The extracts are taken from the autobiography of Richard Wright, first published in 1937.

Activity 5   Social Control in Mississippi

Item A *'Black Boy'*

The back yard of Richard's house was paved with cinders. He and his friends used to have great fun throwing them at each other. One day Richard's gang got into a fight with a group of white boys. The black boys threw cinders but the whites replied with a barrage of broken bottles. One caught Richard behind the ear opening a deep gash which needed three stitches. He was furious. It wasn't fair to fight with broken bottles. All a cinder could do was leave a bruise. When Richard told his mother what had happened he was astonished at her reaction. She grabbed a barrel stave, dragged me home, stripped me naked and beat me, imparting gems of Jim Crow wisdom. I was never, never, under any circumstances, to fight white folks again.

One morning Richard was walking toward the center of town and passed the home of a classmate Ned Greenley. He was sitting on his porch looking glum.

'Hello, Ned. What's new?' I asked.

'You've heard, haven't you?' he asked.

'About what?'

'My brother, Bob'

'No, what happened?'

Ned began to weep softly.

'They killed him,' he managed to say.

'The white folks?' I asked in a whisper, guessing.

'Th-they t-took him in a car...Out on a country road... Th-they shot him,' Ned whimpered.

I had heard that Bob was working in one of the hotels in town.

'Why?'

'Th-they said he was fooling with a white prostitute there in the hotel,' Ned said.

Inside of me my whole world crashed. Bob had been caught by the white death, the threat of which hung over every black male in the South. The penalty of death awaited me if I made a false move. Things that influenced my conduct as a black person did not have to happen to me directly; indeed the white brutality that I had not seen was a more effective control over my behavior than that which I knew.

The white South said that it knew 'niggers' and I was what the white South called a 'nigger'. Well, the white South had never known me - never known what I thought, what I felt. The white South said that I had a 'place' in life. Well I had never felt my 'place', or rather, my deepest instincts had always made me reject the 'place' to which the white South had assigned me. It had never occurred to me that I was in any way an inferior being.

And no word that I had ever heard fall from the lips of southern white men had ever made me doubt the worth of my own humanity.

Adapted from R. Wright *Black Boy*, 1966 edition

Item B *The Ku Klux Klan*

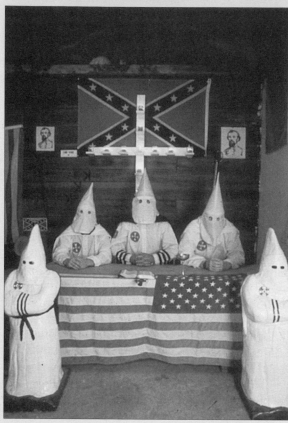

The Ku Klux Klan is a secret organisation dedicated to white supremacy. It claimed over one million members in the USA in the 1920s. Blacks who 'stepped out of line' were beaten, tarred and feathered, run out of town and even lynched by the Klan.

Item C *Civil rights*

A civil rights march in Mississippi, 1966. The initials of the Ku Klux Klan are painted on the road.

Questions

1 Why was the Jim Crow system of social control so effective?
2 No system of social control is completely effective. What evidence is contained in Items A and C to support this statement?

2.3 Norms and values

Norms Norms and values are important aspects of culture. A norm is a specific guide to behaviour in particular situations. Thus there are norms of dress which define appropriate clothing for work, play, school and so on.

Often we are unaware of the norms guiding our behaviour as the following example from the American anthropologist Edward Hall's *The Silent*

Language shows. Norms govern the distance between people when they are having a conversation. Hall observed that the norms for conversational distance in North and South America are different. This can cause problems when North meets South. In Hall's words, 'The result is that when they move close, we withdraw and back away. As a consequence, they think we are distant or cold, withdrawn and unfriendly. We, on the other hand, are constantly accusing them of breathing down our necks, crowding us and spraying our faces.' (Hall, 1959)

Often we are only aware of norms when they are broken and even then, as the above example shows, we would find it difficult to spell out exactly what the norm is.

Norms are essential to human society. They guide and direct our behaviour and allow us both to understand and predict the behaviour of others.

Values Values are much less specific than norms. They are general guides for behaviour. A value is a belief that something is important and worthwhile. A value is translated into behaviour by a range of norms. Take the value placed on human life in our society. It is reflected in a thousand and one aspects of normative behaviour from highway regulations to ways of settling an argument to rules for the preservation of food. In each case the norms are designed to protect human life.

Some sociologists see shared values as essential for the wellbeing of society. They argue that shared values produce social solidarity - the cohesion and unity necessary for society to run smoothly. Without shared values people would be pulling in different directions. The result may well be disruption and conflict.

2.4 Status and role

Status Every human society has a number of social positions which people occupy. They are known as statuses. In many pre-industrial societies the number of statuses is fairly small. For example in a hunting society most men will have the status of hunter along with family statuses such as father, son, husband, uncle and so on. By comparison the number of statuses in modern industrial societies is vast. For example, there are thousands of occupational statuses and the number is constantly growing as job requirements become more and more specialised.

In pre-industrial societies many statuses are *ascribed* - fixed, often at birth and largely unchangeable. Sons usually take on the occupational statuses of their father, daughters those of their mothers. In modern industrial societies there is more emphasis on *achieved* status. An achieved status involves some degree of choice and, as its name suggests, results partly from individual achievement. Thus to some extent a person achieves his or her job as a teacher, a plumber, a bank manager or a mechanic, on the basis of ability and effort.

In everyday speech status means prestige. It is also used in this way by sociologists. In every society social statuses are ranked in terms of prestige - some have more 'status' or social honour than others. In pre-industrial societies people are usually ranked in terms of age and gender with the old and men having more prestige than the young and women. In modern industrial society occupational statuses are accorded varying prestige - for example, professional occupations such as doctors and lawyers are usually more highly regarded than manual jobs such as labourers and window cleaners.

Role Each social status has an accompanying role. A role is a set of norms which defines appropriate and expected behaviour for those who occupy a particular status. They allow us to order our own behaviour and predict the behaviour of others. For example, when you visit a health centre to receive treatment, you do not expect the doctor to roar with laughter or pull silly faces as you describe your symptoms. Nor does the doctor expect you to lean forward and tweak his or her nose. These expectations are not based on a knowledge of doctors and patients as individuals but on an understanding of the social positions they occupy. So we would anticipate that all doctors, whether we have met them or not, will perform their role in a particular way. Like other aspects of culture, roles guide and direct behaviour in human society.

2.5 Cultural differences

Culture varies from society to society. It also varies over time within the same society. Thus behaviour regarded as normal in one society may be seen as abnormal in another. The same might be said of normative behaviour in today's society viewed from the perspective of our great grandparents. The following activity examines cultural differences. It provides an opportunity to appreciate the diversity of human behaviour. The examples are taken from the traditional culture of the Plains Indians of North America.

Summary

1 Culture is the learned, shared behaviour of members of society.

2 Socialisation is the process by which culture is learned.

3 Social control refers to the mechanisms in society which encourage conformity to accepted and approved ways of behaving.

4 A norm is a specific guide to behaviour.

5 A value is a belief that something is important and worthwhile.

6 A status is a position in society.

7 A role is a set of norms which defines appropriate behaviour for a particular status.

Activity 6 The Plains Indians

Item A *The shaman*

Shamans obtain their power from the spirits. Shamans have the power to cure the sick, discover the whereabouts of an enemy and recover lost or stolen property. Often the cause of illness was diagnosed as a foreign object in the patient's body. The Cree Indian shaman, Bull All The Time cured several patients by sucking at the afflicted parts and pulling out respectively a bone, a black beetle and a morsel of meat.

Adapted from R.H.Lowie *Indians of the Plains*, 1954, pp161-164

Sitting Bull, a shaman and chief of the Hunkpapa Sioux

Item B *'In-laws'*

The Cheyenne are not allowed to talk to their mothers-in-law or fathers-in-law. If a Cheyenne finds himself alone in a tipi with his mother-in-law he must cover himself with a buffalo robe and remain covered until his mother-in-law leaves. This rule saves a lot of trouble.

Adapted from John Stands In Timber and Margot Liberty *Cheyenne Memories*, 1967, p45

Item C *Wealth*

The Cheyenne believe that wealth - horses and weapons - should not be hoarded. Instead it should be given away. Generosity is highly regarded. Those who accumulate wealth and keep it for themselves are looked down upon. Those who give do not expect an equal amount in return. The greatest gift they can receive is prestige and respect for their generosity.

Adapted from E.A. Hoebel *The Cheyennes*, 1960

Item D *The sun dance*

The sun dance was the greatest religious ceremony of the Plains Indians. It was held every summer and lasted four days and four nights. The participants went without food and water and danced for many hours. Their purpose was to secure the help and support of the supernatural powers. Towards the end of the ceremony the dancers attached rawhide ropes through slits cut in their chest. The ropes were attached to a pole and the dancing continued until they were torn loose from the flesh. Any dancer who had a vision or heard voices was thought to be favoured by the spirits.

Adapted from John Stands In Timber and Margot Liberty *Cheyenne Memories*, 1967, pp91-94

Questions

1 Read Item A. What are the similarities and differences between a shaman and a modern doctor?

2 How might the values and norms outlined in Items B and C produce greater social harmony than those applied to similar situations in modern industrial society?

3 a) How might someone from contemporary Western society see the sun dance ceremony described in Item D?

   b) Should we judge other societies by our own standards? Give reasons for your answer.

A sun dancer

3 Sociological Perspectives

Key Issues

1 Do people shape society or does society shape people?
2 Is consensus or conflict the main characteristic of human society?

3.1 The individual and society

What shapes our behaviour? Do we control our own destiny or do social pressures determine our actions? Are we largely moulded by the wider society and forced to behave in certain ways or do we have the freedom to decide our own actions?

Let's look at a course of action many of you have taken - continuing your education beyond the age of sixteen. Was this your choice, a decision which was freely made, or was it the result of outside social forces such as parental pressure or a lack of employment opportunities? Or was it a combination of both?

In philosophical terms this is the distinction between 'determinism' and 'free will'. The former refers to our behaviour being determined by some external force, in this case, society, with little element of personal choice. The idea of 'free will' refers to an alternative view that the individual can exercise considerable choice and have a large degree of control over their behaviour. No one seriously argues that actions are totally determined by outside forces or totally directed by free will. Rather its a matter of emphasis. This tension between free will and determinism enables us to make our first categorisation of sociological perspectives. Those which emphasise the power of 'society' over the individual are referred to as 'social systems' or 'structuralist' approaches. Those which emphasise the ability of individuals to shape their own behaviour are known as 'social action' or 'interpretive' approaches.

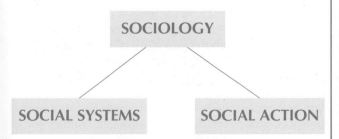

Social systems Social systems or structuralist approaches emphasise the way behaviour is constrained and structured by social forces. Society is seen as a system of interrelated parts, external to the individual, directing behaviour.

The individual is therefore a social construct, made and controlled by society, socialised into into pre-set roles and values - in other words, a product of the social system. We are what we are because of the expectations and pressures of the social groups to which we belong. 'Society' is in us, moulding our thoughts and directing our actions. We are socialised in terms of the culture of society, we are kept in line by mechanisms of social control, we learn roles, norms and values and act accordingly.

Social action Social action or interpretive perspectives, on the other hand, stress the ability of individuals to exert control over their own actions. The individual is no passive receptacle of society's directives, but an active creator of social behaviour. So it is society which is constructed by individuals, not the other way round. Human beings are capable of conscious thought and this enables them to be aware of themselves and others as social beings. They have their own motives and beliefs, their own interpretation of the meaning of a situation, they control their own actions. Social action perspectives are so called because of this emphasis on people taking action, on directing their own behaviour. This approach is also known as an interpretive perspective because it sees people interpreting and giving meaning to the situation and to the actions and motives of others.

Social action approaches do not necessarily deny the existence of roles, norms and values. However, they tend to see them as flexible guidelines rather than inflexible directives. Thus roles are open to interpretation and negotiation. For example, each doctor interprets his or her role somewhat differently. This will tend to vary depending on the meaning given to the situation. This in turn will be affected by the interaction between the doctor and patient which is seen as a process of negotiation rather than the acting out of prescribed roles.

Although we can differentiate between social systems and social action approaches, neither is quite so extreme as suggested here. Systems approaches do not see people as automatons totally controlled by society, nor do action perspectives view people as totally free agents completely unaffected by external constraints. Rather it is a matter of emphasis. Social systems approaches place more emphasis on the structure of society and its power to determine individual behaviour. Social action approaches place more emphasis on the freedom of individuals to direct their own actions. Thus the tension between free will and determinism outlined earlier is reflected in social systems and social action approaches.

Activity 7 Systems vs Action

Item A *Views of society*

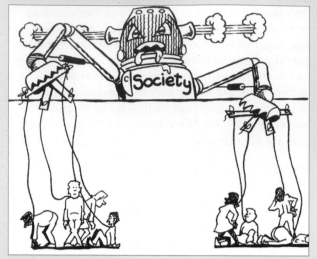

Social systems

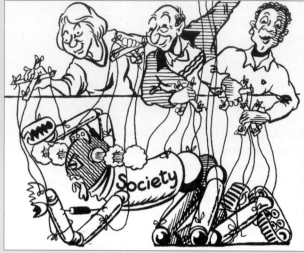

Social action

Item B *Defining situations*

People assign meanings to situations and to the actions of others and act in terms of the interpretation suggested by those meanings. Thus they may respond differently to what appears to be the same situation. For example, the same supervisory behaviour may be interpreted as a friendly act by one group of workers who see it as a reasonable measure taken by management to improve efficiency. However, a second group may define it as an illegitimate attempt to win their sympathy in order to accomplish objectives opposed to their own. The same individual may even, at different times or in different situations, assign varying

meanings to what appears to an observer to be the same act.

Berger (1966) has accused much sociology of viewing society as a 'prison' or as a 'puppet theatre'. According to the former position, society is external to people and constrains them through the operation of impersonal social facts; according to the latter, society enters into the minds of people through the process of socialisation which gives them their social roles and determines how they will respond in future. From a social action perspective both roles and structure provide a framework for action - they do not determine it. By comparison, the social systems

approach tends to regard behaviour as a reflection of the characteristics of a social system containing a series of impersonal processes which are external to actors and constrain them.

Adapted from D. Silverman *The Theory of Organisations*, 1970

Questions

1 Briefly outline the two views of human behaviour shown in the cartoons.
2 In support of which perspective - social action or social systems - does Silverman (Item B) use the example of the supervision of workers? Explain your answer.

3.2 Consensus and conflict in society

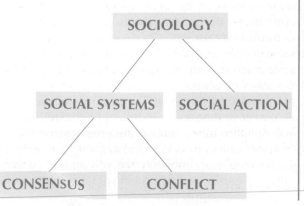

How would you describe society - is it based primarily on consensus (agreement) or on conflict? A brief glance through the newspapers, a review of family life or a glance through history books might well suggest that conflict prevails. But consider how we go about our daily lives. Most of us seem to agree with and accept the rules of our society and those of the social groups we live in. So although conflict might grab the headlines, it could be argued that social life is largely based on consensus and cooperation, not conflict.

So far we have distinguished between social systems and social action perspectives. The distinction between conflict and consensus allows us to make a further division. Social systems approaches can be divided into those which characterise society as based on conflict and those which see society as based on consensus.

Consensus Consensus approaches see agreement or consensus as the basis of social life. Without it society would collapse into anarchy with its members being unable to agree rules and norms of behaviour. Consensus provides the basis for cooperation and social unity. Unless there was general agreement about what was important and worthwhile - in other words, shared values - there would be no cooperation and unity in society. It would be replaced by conflict and division as individuals pursued their own interests which would often directly conflict with those of others. Value consensus provides a harmony of interests in society.

Conflict Conflict approaches see conflict as the essential characteristic of society. This does not mean that members of society are constantly at each others throats and on the brink of civil war. Rather it means that there are basic conflicts of interest in society with some groups gaining at the expense of others. Some groups are more powerful than others - usually as a result of their stronger economic position. In this situation, norms and values are not freely agreed by everyone but are imposed on the weaker sections of society by the more powerful groups. What appears on the surface as consensus is in fact coercion, what seems to be cooperation is in fact exploitation.

Summary

1 Social systems perspectives look at society as a system. They tend to see human behaviour as shaped by the system.

2 Some social systems perspectives see consensus, others see conflict, as the primary characteristic of society.

3 Social action perspectives place more emphasis on the freedom of individuals to direct their own actions.

Activity 8 Conflict or Consensus?

Item A *A social pyramid*

A Russian cartoon from 1900 giving one version of a conflict approach. The text on the cartoon clockwise from the top reads: 'We reign over you'; 'We fool you'; 'We eat for you'; 'We shoot you'; 'We rule you'. The banner reads: 'To live in freedom, to die in struggle'.

Item B *Social inequality - a conflict view*

In Western industrial societies there are two main classes - a small wealthy ruling class and a large, relatively poor subject class. The ruling class owes its position of dominance to its ownership and control of industry. It owns the factories in which members of the subject class work. Its wealth comes in the form of capital produced by its exploitation of the subject class.

There is a basic conflict of interest between the two classes since the ruling class gains at the expense of the subject class. Yet members of the subject class are largely unaware of this. In general they accept the situation as reasonable, or if not, as inevitable. This is because the values of society support the interests of the ruling class. The relationship between factory owner and worker is portrayed by government and the mass media as normal and reasonable. Workers are paid wages, owners receive profits - what's unreasonable about that?

Item C *Social inequality - a consensus view*

All societies have some system of social inequality. This system is based on value consensus. Those who perform successfully in terms of society's values will be ranked highly and will often receive a variety of rewards. In Western industrial society a high value is placed on successful economic activity. Thus the business person who runs an efficient and productive company will be highly regarded and well paid. Since society places a high value on their skills and achievements, the rewards of successful business executives will be seen as justified and deserved. And their success will not just benefit themselves - everybody will gain from an efficient business sector. In this way social inequality serves the interests of society as a whole.

Adapted from T. Parsons *The Social System*, 1951

Item D *Megawealth*

Garfield Weston

Garfield Weston is one of the richest people in Britain. In 1992 his wealth was estimated at £2,190 million. He is the major shareholder in Associated British Foods which manufactures foodstuffs such as bread and biscuits. In 1967, at the age of 23, he took over the chairmanship of the company from his father. His 'quiet and skilful management style' led to a rise in profits even during periods of recession.

Adapted from 'Britain's Rich' *The Sunday Times Magazine*, 10.5.92, p19

Questions

1 Look at Items A to C. How are social control and social order maintained in the face of social inequality from
   a) a conflict perspective
   b) a consensus perspective?
2 Read Item D. Explain Garfield Weston's wealth from
   a) a conflict perspective
   b) a consensus perspective.

4 Sociological Theories

Key Issues

1 What are the main sociological theories?
2 What are their differences and similarities?
3 What kind of explanations do they provide?

So far we have distinguished a number of broad perspectives within sociology. Social systems perspectives have been divided into conflict and consensus approaches and contrasted with social action perspectives. Part 4 of this chapter looks at specific sociological theories which derive from these broader perspectives.

A theory is a set of ideas which claims to explain something. Sociological theories claim to explain the social behaviour of human beings. Three sociological theories will now be briefly outlined. Each will be examined in terms of the basic assumptions it makes about people and society, the concepts it uses, the questions it asks and the general form its conclusions take.

Theories are sometimes seen as completely separate and distinct sets of ideas. As your awareness of sociology grows, you will find there is often an overlap between them. You will see that the boundaries are not clear cut. However, for the sake of simplicity sociological theories will be introduced as if they were separate and distinct.

Sociological theories

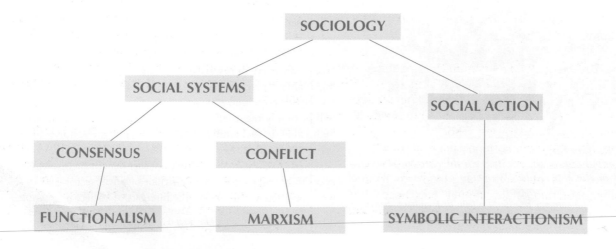

4.1 Functionalism

Consensus Functionalism sees society as a social system based on consensus. It begins from the assumption that society has certain basic needs which must be met if it is to survive. First and foremost is the need for social order. From this assumption derives questions such as: 'What is the basis of social order?' and 'How is social order possible?' It is assumed that social order requires a certain degree of cooperation and social solidarity (social unity). This is made possible by shared norms and values. This in turn requires some means of socialisation to ensure that norms and values are learned plus mechanisms of social control to ensure that norms and values are conformed to. In particular, value consensus is seen as essential since without it people would be pulling in different directions and the result would be conflict and disorder.

Society as a system Functionalists see society as a system - a set of parts which work together to form a whole. These parts are the institutions of society, for example the family, the education system and the political system. Based on the assumption that society is a system, the questions now become: 'How do the various parts work together to maintain social order?' and 'What is the contribution of each part to the maintenance and wellbeing of the social system?'

Let's look at some simple answers to these questions. When looking at any part of society, functionalists often ask, 'What is its function?' By function they mean its contribution to the maintenance of the social system. Thus a simple answer to the question 'What is the function of the family?' is that the family socialises new members of society and teaches them the norms and values which are essential for social life. Assuming that the various parts of the social system work together for the benefit of society as a whole, the next question is: 'What is the relationship between the family and other institutions such as the education system?' Again very simply, the educational system continues the process of socialisation begun in the family. In this way the institutions of family and education work together to maintain social order.

Social disorder It appears from this brief outline that society is a smooth running, well oiled system. What about conflict and social disorder? Functionalists obviously recognise their existence but see them as a temporary disturbance to the social system rather than inbuilt and permanent aspects of society. Functionalists accept that social groups have certain differences of interest but this usually results in competition rather than conflict. And these differences are minor compared to the values and interests they have in common.

Criticism Earlier in the chapter we made the distinction between determinism and free will. Functionalists have been criticised for presenting a deterministic view of social behaviour. Some versions of functionalism picture human beings as products of the social system, their behaviour determined by the social structure. As such they appear to lack free will, initiative and creativity. Hence Peter Berger's criticism that society is sometimes portrayed as a prison or a puppet theatre with people as prisoners of the system or puppets on the end of a string.

This has been a very brief and simplified outline of functionalism. There are varieties of functionalism and the theory is a lot more complex than this introduction suggests. However, the intention here is to provide a starting point. The final chapter examines functionalism in greater detail.

4.2 Conflict theory and Marxism

This section provides a brief introduction to conflict theory and to Marxism, the best known and most influential version.

Conflict theory has a number of similarities to functionalism. It sees society as a system and human behaviour, to some extent, as a response to that system. Some of the questions asked are similar, for example: 'How is social order maintained?' However, the type of social system and the kind of social order are very different. Conflict rather than consensus is the primary characteristic of society. Social groups are in conflict since their interests are fundamentally opposed. And social order tends to be imposed by the powerful rather than based on a consensus freely agreed by all.

Ideology Many conflict theorists replace the idea of value consensus with the concept of ideology. Used in this sense, ideology is a set of beliefs and values which disguises the truth and distorts reality. Thus members of society see their world in terms of ideology. They may be unaware of the conflicts of interest which divide them. They may not realise that some exploit and oppress others. This lack of awareness can help to maintain social order. People will not attempt to overthrow a system if they do not recognise its injustice. In terms of conflict theory, ideology is usually seen to justify and maintain the positions of both the rich and powerful and the poor and powerless.

Conflicts of interest Some conflict theorists identify a range of social groups whose interests conflict. These may include economic groups such as the 'haves' and 'have nots' who compete for income and wealth; ethnic groups who are prevented from equal opportunity by the racism of the dominant group in society; gender groups in which males jealously guard their power and privilege over females; religious groups in which one group attempts to dominate another (eg Protestants and Catholics in Northern Ireland); professional groups who go to great lengths to maintain their status and power (eg doctors claiming that only they have the right to diagnose and treat illness and who reject the claims of so-called 'fringe' or 'alternative' medicine). In each case, groups in a stronger position seek to maintain their supremacy and subordinate those in a weaker position. In each case someone is seen to gain at the expense of others.

The result is a conflict of interest which may or may not find direct expression. It may be suppressed by a variety of mechanisms of social control ranging from ideology through to force. Or it may find expression in a number of ways - a conflict of ideas, a war of words, industrial action, political protest, criminal behaviour, urban riots, through to revolution and civil war. Conflict may take place in the halls of government, in the classroom or workplace, on the street, in the home or on the battlefield.

Marxism

There a number of versions of conflict theory. Marxism - named after its founder Karl Marx (1818-1883) - is the most famous and influential.

Marx saw contradiction and conflict as the basic characteristics of all known human societies. He saw society as a structure divided into two major parts. The first and most important part is the economic base or *infrastructure*. The second major part, known as the superstructure, consists of the rest of society - the political, legal and educational systems, beliefs and ideas. Marx claimed that the infrastructure largely shapes the *superstructure*, in everyday language, the economic system largely shapes the rest of society.

Social classes All known human societies have two main social groups, a ruling class and a subject class. The power of the ruling class comes from its ownership of what Marx called the means of production. This includes the land, raw materials, machinery, tools and buildings used to produce goods. Thus in Western industrial society, capitalists - those who own private industry - form the ruling class. The subject class - the proletariat in capitalist society - is made up of workers who sell their labour in return for wages.

Contradictions Marx saw basic and fundamental contradictions in all class societies. For example, in capitalist society there is a contradiction between the collective nature of production - workers work together to produce goods - and the individual nature of ownership - companies are privately owned by individuals. This and other contradictions mean that society is inherently unstable. This instability can be

seen from the relationship between the classes. In capitalist society workers are exploited and oppressed by the ruling class. There is a basic conflict of interest between capital and labour. Workers produce wealth in the form of goods yet a large part of that wealth is taken in the form of profits by the capitalist class. Thus one group gains at the expense of the other.

Marx believed that these contradictions could not be resolved within the framework of capitalist society. They would eventually result in the overthrow of the capitalist class. A workers' revolution would lead to a communist society in which the means of production would be communally owned, classes would disappear and exploitation and oppression would end.

Ruling class ideology This, however, would only happen when workers became fully aware of their exploitation. But this awareness will not occur overnight because of the way society is structured. Since the infrastructure largely shapes the superstructure, the relationship of dominance and subordination between the ruling class and subject class will be reflected in the superstructure. Thus the political and legal systems will support ruling class power, for example laws will protect the rights of capitalists to own industry and take profits. In the same way the beliefs and values of society will support ruling class domination. Thus capitalism will be seen as reasonable and just rather than exploitive and oppressive. In this way beliefs and values will disguise and distort the true nature of society. In Marxist terms beliefs and values form a *ruling class ideology*. This produces a *false consciousness* which prevents people from seeing the reality of their situation. However, Marx believed that ruling class ideology can only slow down the eventual overthrow of capitalism. The contradictions of the capitalist system will inevitably lead to its downfall.

Marxism represents one version of conflict theory. In addition there are a number of versions of Marxism. Most versions of conflict theory take a structural or social systems approach. As such they have been criticised for being too deterministic, for portraying human behaviour as a product of the social system, for picturing people as largely unable to take initiatives and direct their own actions.

4.3 Social action and symbolic interactionism

Social action or interpretive perspectives offer an alternative view of social life. They focus on how people interact with each other in small group settings such as the classroom, police station, hospital ward or streetcorner. They are concerned with how people define themselves, each other and their situations and with the consequences of such definitions for their actions. There is an emphasis on negotiation - the meanings people give to situations are not seen as fixed but as negotiated by the actors concerned.

The difference between a social systems and a social action approach can be seen from the example of marriage. A functionalist analysis looks at marriage in terms of the social system. The emphasis is on the roles of husband/father, wife/mother which are seen as largely given by the system and shaped to meet the requirements of the system. Thus these roles are structured, for example, to provide a unit for the production and socialisation of children.

Social action theory would not necessarily reject the idea of roles. However, it would argue that when two people get married they have only a vague idea of how a husband and wife should behave. But, as a result of their day to day interaction, they gradually construct their own reality of married life. They give meanings to marriage, they define and redefine what it means to be a husband and wife and develop a shared view of their relationship. From a social action perspective marital roles are not prescribed by the social system, they develop from negotiated meanings during the process of interaction. This is a creative process with individuals directing their own actions rather than being constrained by the social system.

Symbolic interactionism

Symbolic interactionism starts from the idea that people interact in terms of symbols, the most important of which is language. To understand human action it is necessary to discover the meanings which people use to guide, interpret and make sense of their own actions and those of others.

Presentation of self Typical of the interactionist approach is the work of Erving Goffman. In *The Presentation of Self in Everyday Life* he analyses the techniques we use in order to influence how others see us. This process, which we all employ, he calls *impression management*. As social actors, we give more-or-less continuous 'performances' in that we present an 'appearance' of 'keen student', 'hard working, professional lecturer' or 'caring parent'. Our facial movements, body language, speech content, style and so on are coordinated in an attempt to create a particular impression. We create the proper 'setting' of office, classroom, doctor's surgery or whatever, equipping it with appropriate 'props' (desks, white coats, medical books etc) to reinforce this impression. As everyone else is also engaged in impression management, we become very skilled in interpreting the actions of others and at watching for discrepancies in their performances. For example, when cooking a meal for a friend, their polite response of 'what a lovely meal' will be checked by looking to see how much they've eaten, whether there are any facial signals of distaste or any whispered comments of a negative nature. When a performance fails, it can cause embarrassment or unpleasantness as a very different 'presentation of self' emerges from the shell of social convention.

Definition of the situation The American sociologist W.I.Thomas captured one of the main insights of symbolic interactionism when he wrote, 'If men define situations as real, they are real in their consequences'. By this he meant that people act in terms of the way they define situations. To give a rather flippant example - a person walks down a street swathed in bandages. This situation may be interpreted in a number of ways - fancy dress (the Invisible Man), a practical joke, a 'dare', a bet, someone who has serious injuries, or even a sociologist conducting an experiment. Each of these definitions is real in its consequences. People will act towards the bandaged figure depending on their interpretation of his or her behaviour. Whether or not their definition is 'really correct' is not the point. The point is that to understand their response, we have to understand their *definition of the situation*.

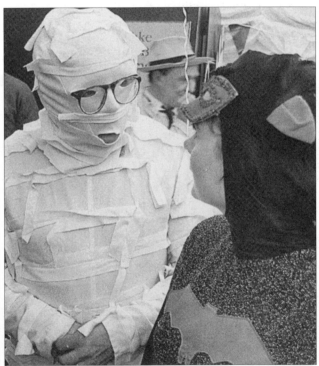

The 'Spooky Tea Party' given by Walker Books (publishers of children's books) at the Edinburgh Book Festival, 1993

Criticisms of symbolic interactionism and social action theory as a whole are in some ways a reversal of those of systems theory. Because they focus on small scale interaction situations, social action theorists tend to ignore the wider society. Critics argue that to some extent this wider social framework influences and even constrains interaction. They claim that social action theorists have gone too far - human action is not as free, creative, spontaneous and flexible as they seem to suggest.

Social action theory is a lot more complex and varied than this brief introduction implies. You will discover this as you read through the book. However, as with systems theories, the intention here is to provide a starting point.

Summary

1 Functionalism sees society as a social system based on consensus. It sees the various parts of society working together to maintain social order.

2 Marxism sees society as a social system based on conflict. The system is inherently unstable since it is based on contradictions which involve the exploitation of some by others.

3 Social action approaches focus on small scale interaction situations. They see social life as directed by negotiated meanings. Human action is not prescribed by the social system, it is a creative process directed by individuals in interaction situations.

Activity 9 Law and Society

Item A *Law and order*

Justice?

Item B *Whose law? What order?*

Injustice?

All societies have some form of law, written or unwritten, which defines certain kinds of acts as crimes. Emile Durkheim, one of the founders of sociology, saw crime as acts which 'offend strong and definite states of the collective conscience'. They are acts which are condemned in terms of society's shared values. Those who maintain the law, the police, judges and so on, are part of the social control mechanisms necessary to preserve social order.

Adapted in part from E. Durkheim, *The Rules of Sociological Method*, 1938 edition

Laws serve the interests of the powerful. Law enforcement is systematically biased in favour of the powerful. The heart of a capitalist economic system is the protection of private property, which is by definition, the cornerstone upon which capitalist economies function. It is not surprising then to find that criminal laws reflect this basic concern. Some laws do benefit other groups. But this is because the system needs a healthy and safe population of producers and consumers, and it needs their loyalty.

Adapted from W.J. Chambliss and M. Mankoff *Whose Law? What Order?* 1976

Item C *Negotiating justice*

How is a person charged with breaking the law? The following American study of delinquency - the criminal activity of young people - shows it is not a straightforward process.

When a young person is arrested, he or she is handed over to a juvenile officer who decides whether or not to prosecute. This decision is based on a process of negotiation between the juvenile officer, the person arrested and his or her parents. Crucial to the outcome of this negotiation is the picture juvenile officers have of the 'typical delinquent'. In their eyes the 'typical delinquent' is male, from a low income household in an inner city area, belongs to an ethnic group, comes from a broken home, rejects authority and is a low achiever at school. If the suspect fits this picture, he is more likely to be charged with an offence.

Middle class parents are often more skilled at negotiation than their working class counterparts.

They start with an advantage - their child does not fit the picture of a 'typical delinquent'. They present their child as coming from a stable home, as having a good background and a promising future. They promise cooperation, express remorse and define the 'offence' as a 'one-off' due to high spirits, emotional upset or getting in with the wrong crowd, all of which tends to remove blame from the young person. As a result the statistics show that delinquency is mainly a working class problem as young people from middle class backgrounds are typically 'counselled, cautioned and released'. Thus 'what ends up being called justice is negotiable'.

Adapted from A.V. Cicourel *The Social Organisation of Juvenile Justice*, 1976

Questions

1 The items are examples of social action, functionalist and Marxist approaches. Which is which? Give reasons for your answers.
2 Using the approach in Item A, give two examples of laws which reflect shared values. Briefly explain your choices.
3 Using the approach in Item B, give one example of a law which supports the interests of the powerful and one example of a law which helps to maintain a 'safe and healthy' population. Briefly explain your choices.
4 Using the approach in Item C, outline a possible negotiation with a juvenile officer in which a teenage girl from a wealthy background is released without charge after having been arrested for shoplifting.

5 Sociological Investigation

Key Issues

1 What is a sociological problem?
2 What research methods do sociologists use?
3 What is the difference between quantitative and qualitative research methods?

5.1 Sociological problems

All aspects of social behaviour are of interest to sociologists - everything from small scale situations, such as people queueing, to society wide issues like the nature of social classes. A glance through the contents of this book will give you some idea of the scope of sociological investigation. As you will have noted, sociology does not take things at face value but tries to see below the surface of social behaviour. Every aspect of social life is therefore seen as a *sociological problem*. As such, sociological problems are not the same as the *social problems* referred to in everyday language.

Put very simply, a sociological problem is a question that sociologists want an answer to. The question requires investigation and the answer will hopefully provide a better understanding of social life. The idea of a sociological problem becomes clearer whem we ask what it is not.

Objectivity In the first place, the investigation of 'sociological problems' is not carried out in order to establish whether a particular form of behaviour is 'right' or 'wrong'. Sociologists try to be objective and unbiased. They try to avoid making a moral judgement. Most people assume that crime is a 'bad' thing and is a danger to society. Sociologists do not necessarily assume this. They might argue that in some circumstances a limited amount of crime is beneficial to society because it allows for the punishment of an offender which reinforces our belief in the law. An alternative sociological perspective might question the basis on which laws are made and the way crime is defined. Who makes the laws? Do laws serve the particular interests of some groups? Are laws equally enforced on all sections of the population? These questions are sociological problems which require investigation.

Social problems Secondly, it is sometimes assumed that sociology is the study of 'social problems' such as poverty, unemployment and suicide. As social behaviour, these areas form part of the subject matter of sociology, but only part. And sociologists often look at them in very different ways than the person in the street or the government department which 'officially' defines them as a problem. Indeed, the very issue of why some groups and their activities get labelled as 'social problems' and others do not, is itself a 'sociological problem'. Why, for example, are the poor generally seen as a problem and not the rich? Inevitably some sociological problems do reflect social concerns, but most research is not directly connected to social problem solving. And, quite often, sociology challenges the official definition of 'social problems'.

Everyday explanations Thirdly, as we saw in the opening section of this chapter, sociology offers alternatives to commonsense, everyday explanations of social behaviour. The latter tend to be simplistic, uninformed judgements which often reflect a degree of personal prejudice. The opinions of individuals, the comments of journalists and others are interesting in their own right, but they are not sociological accounts. They are not answers to sociological problems. By clearing away ideas about right and wrong and by putting on hold commonsense and official definitions of problems, sociology is able to ask its own questions and define its own 'sociological problems'.

Defining terms Finally, sociological problems must be spelt out clearly and unambiguously. This in itself

raises further questions. Terms and ideas which have a vague and ill-defined meaning in everyday usage need redefining in a more precise way. For example, we probably all think we know the meaning of the term 'family'. Well just write down your definition and compare it with those of your classmates. It is very likely that the definitions will vary. Now imagine the range of different definitions if you asked people from other societies to define 'family'. It quickly becomes clear that all kinds of issues are involved in this apparently straightforward task. Does 'family' include people you are related to but never see? Is it about households? Is there a 'core family' and a 'fringe family'? And so on. By taking off the blinkers of official and commonsense ways of thinking, sociology opens up a real Pandora's Box of ideas about social behaviour.

Problems with sociology?

So far we have given the case for sociology. The picture presented is of an objective, unbiased discipline defining its terms in a clear, unambiguous way, looking beyond commonsense, taken for granted explanations of social life and uninfluenced by the often naive and largely unconsidered ideas of Mr and Ms Average. This is an ideal that many sociologists strive to attain.

But sociologists are people, they are members of society. Can they prevent their own beliefs and values from influencing research? Can they pose and solve sociological problems in a completely objective way? The short answer is no. But most do their best and their best is often better than the answers most people come up with.

Let's take a short example which is reflected in a number of studies. Two sociologists, a man and a woman, investigate family life. The woman is a feminist, the man does not support feminist ideals. They will probably ask different questions, look for different things, interpret what they find differently and reach different conclusions. In other words their values will influence their research. To some degree this is unavoidable no matter how hard sociologists try to guard against it.

Does this really matter? Possibly not. If sociologists can produce data which clearly backs up their beliefs then a strong case can be made in support of those beliefs. And the example of feminist sociologists is a case in point. Over the last twenty years they have made gender a central issue in sociology. They have produced masses of data to support their view that women are discriminated against in the home, at work, in law and in government and in society as a whole. Without a commitment to feminism the study of gender would have remained a backwater. And society and sociology would have been the poorer.

5.2 Sociological research methods

Sociologists do not just raise issues and talk about them in an abstract way. They research these issues in the real social world. They collect data which forms the evidence used to solve sociological problems.

Sociologists have developed various methods of data collection. To some extent these methods differ from those we use in our day-to-day life or which government officials or journalists employ in their accounts of events. When as an individual we answer a question we usually just give our opinion and then justify it in terms of something we have read in newspapers or seen on television, or perhaps we make reference to an experience that we or an acquaintance have had. Although our opinions are interesting enough and important to us, they fall a long way short of the detailed evidence and rigorous procedures demanded by sociological research.

These comments often apply to data produced by government officials and journalists. Official statistics and official versions of events may well say more about the government than what's really happening. Unemployment statistics are a case in point. Since 1982 British Conservative governments changed the method of calculating unemployment no less than 30 times. In nearly every case this resulted in a reduction of the numbers officially defined as unemployed. This can be seen as impression management on a massive scale. Journalistic accounts are also likely to fall short of the standards required for sociological research. Often produced at speed to meet publication deadlines, they may well have more to do with selling newspapers and appealing to a particular readership than with the accurate reporting of events.

Ideally data collection in sociology is rigorous and systematic, with care being taken to select the most appropriate methods. Sociologists take courses in research methods as part of their training. They have been taught to strive for objectivity and to avoid value judgements. There are two broad approaches to data collection in sociology, quantitative and qualitative.

Quantitative methods

In 1990 the most wealthy 1% of people in the UK owned 18% of privately owned wealth. In the 1991/2 season, the average attendance at Division 1 Football League matches in England and Wales was 21,600 (figures from *Social Trends,* 1993). These are examples of quantitative data - data presented in the form of numbers.

Some sociologists believe that quantitative research methods are essential. Unless human behaviour can be translated into numerical terms, it cannot be measured and compared. Without quantitative data conclusions are little better than impressions and opinions. Evidence must be collected in an organised, structured fashion by applying the principles of scientific enquiry to the study of social behaviour. This usually involves carrying out *social surveys* using *questionnaires* or *structured interviews*. A questionnaire is a set of written questions. People are asked to write down their answers. A structured interview is a set of written questions read out by an interviewer who writes down the answers people give.

A good example of a social survey is the General Household Survey produced annually by the Office of Population Censuses and Surveys. The 1991 survey was based on a 56 page structured interview given to a sample of 19,039 people over 16 years of age drawn from 9,955 households in Great Britain. The survey covers areas such as family life, housing, employment and health. Every person was asked exactly the same questions and the results were presented in a numerical form.

Sociologists rarely have the time or the money to conduct social surveys on this scale. And often the statistics produced by government bodies do not directly address sociological problems. Sociologists therefore design their own surveys to investigate particular areas of social life or to test specific hypotheses. A hypothesis is a supposition or a proposition - for example the proposition that there is a relationship or connection between social class and health or, more specifically, the lower a person's social class, the more likely they will be to suffer from ill-health. In terms of this example, a survey will be designed to measure people's health and social class, the results will be quantified and statistical tests applied to measure the strength of the relationship (if any) between health and social class.

Some sociologists argue that sociology should aim to become a 'science of society', adopting scientific research methods and approaching the study of human behaviour in the same way as scientists study the natural world. They claim that this can only be done by using quantitative research methods.

Qualitative methods

Other sociologists argue that quantitative approaches are unsuitable for the study of human behaviour. Questionnaires and structured interviews are based on questions which are relevant and important to sociologists - they may well be irrelevant and unimportant to those who answer them. Sometimes the questions give people little opportunity to say what they really mean - in some cases the required response is simply a tick in one of several boxes. The data may look neat, tidy and 'scientific' when quantified but its quality and validity may leave a lot to be desired.

Unstructured interviews Unstructured interviews provide one alternative to the above criticisms. They are more like a conversation than a structured interview. Although the sociologist usually identifies the general topic for discussion, the questions are not preset. The person being interviewed - the respondent - is given considerable freedom to express their views in their own way and to direct the interview into areas which interest them. Because of this there may be a better chance of obtaining data which accurately reflects respondents' views. However, such data is difficult to quantify and compare since all the interviews will be different and no respondent will be asked exactly the same questions.

Participant observation Sociologists who take a social action perspective are often among the strongest supporters of qualitative approaches. They argue that human action is directed by meanings negotiated in interaction situations. Since people may be unaware of these meanings they will be unlikely to spell them out in answer to a questionnaire. Since meanings are negotiated in interaction situations, it is often argued that they can only be discovered by directly observing those situations. This usually involves participant observation - the sociologist participates in the activities of a social group in order to observe its members' actions. Participant observation was used by Aaron Cicourel in his study of juvenile officers (outlined in Activity 9, Item 3, p19). He spent four years working as a juvenile officer in California. Much of Erving Goffman's research is based on participant observation. For example, he spent a year observing interaction in a mental hospital in Washington DC with the aim of understanding how the patients defined their situation and gave meaning to their experiences.

Those who support qualitative approaches claim that the data they produce is richer, has greater depth, offers more insight and is more likely to provide a true and valid picture of social life.

For many sociologists the question is not whether to use either quantitative or qualitative research methods. They use both. Each can be seen as suitable for particular kinds of research and for collecting particular types of data. Often both are used in the same research programme.

The following activity examines some of the issues raised in this part of the chapter. It looks at a study of family life in the early 1970s by Michael Young and Peter Willmott. This was a large scale social survey in which structured interviews were given to a sample of nearly 2,000 people. Among the sociological problems Young and Willmott wanted to investigate was the relationship between husbands and wives. Their previous studies of family life in London indicated that the roles of husband and wife were becoming increasingly similar. In particular, husbands were becoming more involved in domestic tasks and childrearing. There appeared to be a move towards greater equality in marriage. Was this trend continuing?

Activity 10 Husbands and Wives

Item A *Evidence*

Social class and husband's help in the home (married men working full time)

Reported help to wife at least once a week	Professional and managerial	Clerical	Skilled manual	Semi-skilled and unskilled manual	All
None	14%	13%	14%	24%	15%
Washing up only	16%	7%	13%	12%	13%
Other tasks (cleaning, cooking etc) with or without washing up	70%	80%	73%	64%	72%

Adapted from M.Young and P. Willmott *The Symmetrical Family*, 1975, p95

Item B *Interpreting the evidence*

The evidence suggests that marriage is becoming more equal. Husbands do a lot of work in the home, including many jobs which are traditionally women's tasks. There is now no work in the home strictly reserved for 'the wives'. Even washing clothes and making beds, still usually thought of as women's jobs, were frequently mentioned by husbands as things they also did. The extent of sharing is probably still increasing. What husbands did varied according to social class and taking all forms of help into account it was still true that fewer semi-skilled and unskilled workers contributed at all in this sort of way.

Adapted from M.Young and P. Willmott *The Symmetrical Family*, 1975, p94

Item C *Evidence*

An examination of the answers given in Young and Willmott's sample shows that fifteen per cent of the men do no domestic work at all. A further thirteen per cent only do washing up, while seventy-two per cent do what is vaguely and euphemistically termed 'other tasks'. The seventy-two per cent sounds impressive, but when one considers how it was arrived at it immediately becomes less so. This figure is based on only one question in the interview schedule: 'Do you/does your husband help at least once a week with any household jobs like washing up, making beds, helping with the children, ironing, cooking or cleaning?' A man who helps with the children once a week would be included in this seventy-two per cent; so would a husband who ironed his own trousers on a Saturday afternoon. The answers to this poorly worded question hardly holds up a convincing image of male domestication.

A typical modern husband?

And, of course, as Willmott and Young themselves comment, however much a man may help, the responsibility for domestic work remains with his wife. There is a long way to go before equality even appears on the horizon.

Adapted from A.Oakley *The Sociology of Housework*, 1974, pp164-5

Item D *Further research*

The following data is taken from the *British Social Attitudes Survey*, 1984. It is based on a sample of 1,120 married people. The categories do not add up to 100 per cent as some of the respondents answered 'don't know' or did not answer the question.

Household tasks of husbands and wives, Great Britain 1984 (percentages)

Allocation of tasks	Mainly men	Mainly women	Shared equally
Household tasks			
Washing and ironing	1	88	9
Preparation of evening meal	5	77	16
Household cleaning	3	72	23
Household shopping	6	54	39
Evening dishes	18	37	41
Organisation of household money and bills	32	38	28
Repairs of household equipment	83	6	8
Childrearing			
Looks after children when they are sick	1	63	35
Teaches the children discipline	10	12	77

Adapted from *Social Trends*, 1986, p36

Questions

1 Read Items A and B. Do you agree with Young and Willmott's interpretation of the evidence? Explain your answer.
2 Evaluate Ann Oakley's criticism in Item C. Why do you think she reaches different conclusions to those of Michael Young and Peter Willmott?
3 Read Item D.
   a) This survey gives a rather different picture of the allocation of domestic tasks. Suggest why the evidence is different.
   b) Young and Willmott make the following claim about husbands and wives: 'They shared their work; they shared their time'. Given the data in Item D, do you agree? Explain your answer.
4 This activity has looked at quantitative data on the roles of husbands and wives.
   a) What qualitative research methods could be used?
   b) What problems might arise by using such methods?
   c) How might qualitative data add to our understanding of the roles of husbands and wives?

5.3 Reading sociological research: a checklist

To understand and evaluate sociological research you should bear the following points in mind.

- What sociological problem is being addressed?
- Is a specific hypothesis being tested or is the research more concerned with a general investigation of an area of social life?
- Why have the researchers chosen to investigate this area? How is their study related to previous research?
- Which sociological perspective forms the framework for the study?
- How have the researchers defined the key terms in their study? How have they translated those definitions into a form which can be measured. Are there alternative definitions?
- What research methods did the investigators use? Did they try to obtain qualitative or quantitative data or both? How suitable were the research methods?

- How useful was the data produced by the research? What form did the data take? Was the interpretation of the data satisfactory? Could it be interpreted differently? Were the conclusions drawn from the data justified?
- Always approach sociological research critically. Question the research methods, the validity of the data, the interpretation of the data and the conclusions drawn from the research.

Summary

1 A sociological problem is a question which sociologists seek to answer.
2 Sociologists aim to be objective.
3 Research methods can be divided into quantitative and qualitative approaches.
4 Some sociologists favour one or other approach.
5 Many sociologists use both approaches. Each is seen as suitable for particular kinds of research and for collecting particular types of data.

References

Berger, P. *Invitation to Sociology* (Penguin, Harmondsworth, 1966)
Chambliss, W.J. and Mankoff, M. *Whose Law? What Order?* (John Wiley & Sons, New York, 1976)
Cicourel, A.V. *The Social Organisation of Juvenile Justice* (Heinemann, London, 1976)
Durkheim, E. *The Rules of Sociological Method* (The Free Press, New York, 1938)
Hall, E.T. *The Silent Language* (Doubleday, New York, 1973)
Hoebel, E.A. *The Cheyennes* (Holt, Rinehart and Winston, New York, 1960)
Lowie, R.H. *Indians of the Plains* (McGraw Hill, New York, 1954)
Malcolm X *The Autobiography of Malcolm X* (Grove Press, New York, 1966)
Mills, C.W. *The Sociological Imagination* (Oxford University Press,

New York, 1959)
Oakley, A. *The Sociology of Housework* (Martin Robertson, Oxford, 1974)
Parsons, T. *The Social System* (The Free Press, New York, 1951)
Silverman, D. *The Theory of Organisations* (Heinemann, London 1970)
Stands In Timber, J. and Liberty, M., *Cheyenne Memories* (Yale University Press, New Haven, 1967)
Young, M. and Willmott, P. *The Symmetrical Family* (Penguin, Harmondsworth, 1975)
Webb, S. and Thomas, R. 'Knowing Your Place in Society' *New Statesman and Society*, 30.7.1993
Wright, R. *Black Boy* (Harper & Row, New York, 1966)

2 Class Stratification

Introduction

The long running television series *Upstairs Downstairs* gave a potted view of the British class system in the early part of this century. Upstairs there lived the wealthy and aristocratic Bellamy family, distinguished by their refined tastes and prestigious social connections. Below stairs there was a small army of household staff, each with a precise position in the servant hierarchy (eg Mrs Bridges the cook ruled over the kitchen but Hudson the loyal butler was the main link between the ladies and gentlemen upstairs and the servants downstairs). The class structure of Britain today seems far removed from the rigid and deferential Edwardian world of *Upstairs Downstairs*. This is certainly the view of Dame Barbara Cartland, the grand socialite and romantic novelist. When a radio interviewer asked her if class barriers had broken down in modern Britain she replied disdainfully, 'Of course, otherwise I wouldn't be talking to someone like you!'.

In spite of Dame Barbara's amusing assertion, this chapter will present evidence that class differences are still important in British society. Sometimes people treat these differences as a matter of fun (something to laugh at), sometimes as a human interest story (isn't it *amazing* how some folks live!) and sometimes as an outrage (eg anger at the huge gulf in living standards between rich and poor). As for sociologists, they are often accused of being so obsessed with the class system that they use it to explain just about anything and everything that happens in society. That is taking things too far. But most sociologists are convinced that class is a strong influence on our lives. The class we belong to shapes such things as our income, housing conditions, attitudes and behaviour and even how long we are likely to live. That is why many sociologists regard it as the central issue in sociology.

Chapter summary

- The chapter starts by **defining** stratification and social class. It then deals with the **measurement** of class.
- This is followed by a review of **stratification theories**.
- The next two parts look at the **significance** of class and the nature and patterns of **social mobility**.
- The chapter concludes with a detailed investigation of the **class structure** of modern Britain.

1 Stratification

Key Issues

1 What is stratification?
2 What are the major systems of stratification?
3 How is social class measured?

1.1 Social strata

Social differences are found in every society. People vary in their personal qualities (eg intelligence, beauty), their social roles (eg occupations) and their general group characteristics (eg sex, age, religious or ethnic group). These differences mean that people have unequal chances of success when they compete for scarce and desirable resources such as food, material possessions or social respect. Some people may have *natural* advantages (eg the strong, athletic individual in a hunting society) while others may enjoy *social* advantages (eg being born into a rich family). Whatever the reasons, it is clear that societies distribute their rewards unequally between individuals and groups. These inequalities can be divided into three main types (sometimes called the 3 Ps): economic privilege, social prestige and power.

1 **Economic privilege** Some people have greater access than others to economic resources such as money, wealth and possessions. In some societies economic inequalities are quite small but in modern Britain there are large inequalities

income and wealth and they have been widening in recent years.

2 **Social prestige** Some personal or social qualities are valued more highly than others, although there is seldom a complete consensus. People may be accorded higher status because of their sporting ability, musical talent, spiritual wisdom, technical skills or whatever else their society happens to regard as important. In each case the people who have these qualities tend to be granted higher esteem and honour.

3 **Power** Some positions in society are more powerful than others and people who occupy these positions are able to exercise greater control over their own lives and over the lives of others. Their wishes are more likely to prevail when key decisions are taken in society. Also, they often use their superior power to advance their own positions (eg they try to boost their economic privileges and social prestige).

Strata Social inequality seems to be an ever present feature of societies. Beteille (1977) notes it has existed even among small tribes and groups based on hunting and gathering (eg Eskimos or Inuits, Bushmen, Andaman Islanders). But social inequality in these groups was traditionally a matter of inequalities between individuals or families. These societies were not organised into clearly defined levels or *strata* where whole groups are ranked in a more or less constant hierarchy of power and privilege. So social inequality is not always expressed in the form of *social stratification*.

Social stratification is the term sociologists use to describe the relatively enduring social divisions of inequality which appear in most societies. It suggests not only that social inequality exists but also that this inequality is structured in the form of strata. The idea of stratification is borrowed from geology where it describes how different types of rocks or minerals are arranged in successive layers (strata) in the earth's crust. Sociologists suggest that this image fits human societies too, since most societies contain a number of social groups organised in some sort of hierarchy, one on top of another (with the most privileged groups at the top). In Britain, for example, the class structure is often described in terms of an upper class perched above a middle class which rests in turn on the working class, with an underclass occupying the bottom rank or layer.

Comparisons between the physical world of rocks and the social world of human beings can be misleading. For one thing, human beings have attitudes and feelings (it is difficult to imagine a rock complaining about inequalities and injustices in the rock world!). Also, social divisions are not usually as fixed as layers of rock. For example, people often move from one level to another (this is called *social*

mobility). In spite of these differences, however, the idea of stratification is a useful starting point for discussing the structure of inequalities in society.

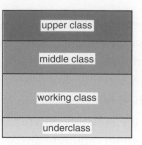

social strata

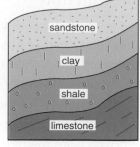

geological strata

1.2 Stratification systems

Stratification takes different forms in different societies and historical periods. It is common for sociologists to identify four major *systems* of stratification: slavery, feudalism, Hindu castes and the social class system of industrialised societies. These systems differ from each other in a number of respects.

1 **Criteria** What are the main criteria for ranking people?

2 **Ranks** How many major ranks or strata are there?

3 **Relationships** What are the social relationships between the strata? Is the system imposed by force or is there general consent?

4 **Mobility** Is membership of a stratum fixed and permanent? What are the prospects for people moving from one stratum to another?

These differences can be illustrated by looking briefly at some of these systems.

Slavery The prosperity of ancient Greece and Rome was based to a considerable degree upon slave labour. Under this system the major division was between free citizens and unfree slaves (obtained either by conquest or by purchase in the slave market). Slaves did not enjoy the civil, legal or political rights of citizens and they were regarded as the property of their owners. The status of slave was passed on to their children and their chances of becoming free were severely restricted (although some slaves were allowed to buy their freedom and some were granted freedom by their owners). Other examples of slavery are found in the societies of Central and South America, the West Indies and the southern states of the USA from the seventeenth century until the abolition of the transatlantic slave trade in the nineteenth century. During this period millions of black people were forcibly removed from Africa and compelled to work on plantations or in mines where they enjoyed very few rights (slaves were not even allowed to marry without the consent of owners). This slave system is explored further in Chapter 3, pp98-100.

Feudalism The feudal system of medieval Europe consisted of three 'estates': nobles, clergy, and commoners ('freemen'). Each of these estates had its own legally defined rights and duties. The positions were largely hereditary (with the exception of the clergy) and so there was little movement between strata. Feudalism was organised mainly around the ownership of agricultural land (even the clergy derived most of their income from land). The serfs who worked the land were not, strictly speaking, an estate but they too were bound into a system of mutual obligations. They gave economic 'tribute' (eg livestock, grain, eggs) and military and other services to the noble landowners who allowed them to farm the land. The landed nobles exercised control over their respective territories and in return they owed their tenants certain duties (eg protection from rival nobles). The nobles owed ultimate allegiance to the monarch but sometimes local lords entered into rival alliances.

Castes The Hindu caste system in India recognises four main castes (or Varnas).
1   Brahmins (priests and nobles)
2   Kshatriyas or Rajputs (warriors and rulers, landowners)
3   Vaishyas (merchants, traders, farmers)
4   Shudras (servants, labourers, manual workers)
The caste system is highly complex and the main castes are broken down into thousands of jatis (subcastes) based on occupations or village or kin groupings. A finely regulated system of etiquette governs social interaction between these groups and each group is anxious to avoid any 'pollution' or defilement which would result from close contact with members of a lower caste. This is especially true of contact with the outcasts or Untouchables (renamed as Harijans, or Children of God, by Gandhi). Traditionally these outcast groups have been responsible for menial tasks such as rubbish and sewage collection. Another feature of the caste system is its restriction on mobility. People cannot move out of their caste of birth although it is possible for a whole subcaste to improve its relative position in the hierarchy by following a stricter observance of 'pure' practices (a process known as Sanskritisation).

The caste system is supported by the religious beliefs and ideas of Hinduism. *Dharma* imposes a duty on Hindus to conduct themselves in a proper, moral manner (eg they should respect caste boundaries). And the doctrine of *karma* states that caste membership is a reflection of a person's moral worth (eg if you behave morally in this life you will be re-born into a higher subcaste in the next round of the reincarnation cycle). These doctrines provide religious justifications for the caste system. Nevertheless, in recent years the Indian government has attempted to relax and even remove caste barriers. For example, it has tried (not always successfully) to ban discriminatory caste practices in employment and housing.

Activity 1   Distinctions

Item A *India*

In India caste defines not only what you wear but where you live, what trade you follow, whom you marry, even the colour you paint your home. Every detail of life in the traditional Indian village, where 85% of Indians still live, is regulated. But if this is restrictive it can also be reassuring, a protection against anarchy. People know their places and what is expected of them. Moreover, it is divinely ordained. The Hindu doctrine of *karma* states that your caste in this life is determined by your actions in a previous existence. A good life is rewarded by high caste, a bad life punished by future untouchability. A good road sweeper can hope to be reincarnated next time round as a Brahmin and hence eventually to achieve *nirvana* (enlightenment, becoming one with the universe), so escaping the eternal cycle of suffering and rebirth.

Therefore, to rise out of your caste does more than just rock the foundations of society. It breaks the cosmic cycle, it defies 'nature'. So when the Indian government decided to raise the status of the lower castes, reserving government jobs for the hated untouchables, this sparked off violent caste wars.

Adapted from W.Dalrymple 'Caste Wars', *Observer Magazine*, 2.12.90, p27

Harijans, formerly known as untouchables, living on the pavement in New Delhi

Item B *Britain*

Commentators often remark on the importance of social class distinctions in British society. In Japanese factories it is the custom for managers and workers to take their meals and recreation together. In Britain, by contrast, such social mixing is unusual and unwelcome. People prefer not to bridge the gulf between 'us' and 'them'. The British display an awareness of class factors in their everyday lives which strikes foreigners, especially Americans, as very odd.

Adapted from P.Martin 'The Concept of Class', 1987, p67

Questions

1 Read Items A and B. Identify any similarities between the caste system of India and the social class system of Britain. Give examples where possible.
2 What are the main differences between the two systems?

Class in capitalist society

Social class is the dominant form of stratification within capitalist societies such as Britain, its Western European partners, the USA and the Scandinavian countries. The economic marketplace plays a major role in these societies, and basically it is people's positions in this market that determines their social class ranking. Class is a matter of economic inequalities and each class consists of people who share similar positions in the economic structure. Nevertheless, sociologists have different views on the best definition of class. 'Of all the concepts used by sociologists for describing and explaining social relationships, social class is probably the most ambiguous, confusing and ill- defined' (Scase, 1992, p1). For example, class can be defined in the 'narrow' sense as a matter of income, property and occupation. But class also has a much wider sense since the members of an economic class tend to develop similar social and cultural characteristics. Thus, we sometimes guess people's social class from their accents or lifestyles. So class can be defined more broadly as 'a group of people with certain common traits: descent, education, accent, similarity of occupation, wealth, moral attitudes, friends, hobbies, accommodation; and with generally similar ideas, and forms of behaviour, who meet each other on equal terms and regard themselves as belonging to one group' (Cooper, 1979, p14).

Every society is a 'class' society to the extent that it contains broad economic divisions. Nevertheless, there are some key differences between the social class system and the other stratification systems. In the class system there is generally much greater legal and political freedom (eg workers have contractual relationships with employers, quite unlike the feudal obligations of serfs or the forced labour of slaves). Secondly, the class hierarchy does not rely on religious justifications (unlike the caste system, or feudalism's notion of the divine right of kings). Thirdly, there are fewer barriers to social mobility in the class system and so there is greater movement between strata. And lastly, the economic marketplace assumes a much more central and dominant role in class based societies. This is especially true of capitalist societies.

Capitalism Capitalism can be defined as 'an economic system in which goods and services are produced for sale, with the intention of making a profit, in a large number of separate firms using privately owned capital goods and wage labour' (Jessop, 1987, p37). Its central mechanism is the market where numerous buyers and sellers pursue their own interests within a competitive framework. Producers compete with each other to provide the goods that consumers want, and the prices of goods are fixed according to how much producers are able to charge and what consumers are willing to pay (the laws of supply and demand). The means of production (machinery, factories, capital etc) are mostly privately owned and the owners have a profit motive to raise output. Workers sell their labour to employers in return for a wage and they are contractually free to change employers in the search for higher wages. However, there are limits to this freedom. For example, in recent years unemployment has become increasingly common in Western capitalist societies. This limits workers' ability to change employers.

Dimensions of inequality Social class clearly has a direct bearing on people's *life chances* - their opportunities and prospects, their likelihood of experiencing affluence or hardship. But class is not the only form of stratification in countries like Britain. Other major dimensions of inequality include those of race and ethnicity (see Chapter 3), gender (see Chapter 4) and age (Chapter 11, pp408-411). Each of these dimensions is important and deserves close attention in its own right. For example, women and racial minorities might be regarded as 'second class citizens' in the sense that they tend to have lower status and power than white males. Nevertheless, Westergaard (1995) insists that class is still the fundamental division in British society. He maintains that the disadvantages experienced by women and ethnic minorities are due more to their class position than to either their gender or ethnicity. For example, certain ethnic groups form lower strata because of class disadvantages such as high rates of poverty and unemployment. Westergaard's view is supported by Breen and Rottman (1995) who argue that racial and gender relations are shaped more by class than class relationships are shaped by gender and race.

Class in socialist society

Some sociologists (eg Kerr et al, 1962) argued that social classes were also a feature of the socialist societies of Eastern Europe (eg Hungary, Poland, USSR) in the decades following the Second World War. According to these sociologists the political differences between capitalist and socialist societies were less important than their structural similarities. They were *industrial* societies and the 'logic of industrialism' meant that they were increasingly becoming alike (the theory of *convergence*). But was this argument correct? Davis and Scase (1985) have identified some major flaws in convergence theory. First, the socialist states relied mainly on political planning rather than market forces. Decisions about investment and production were based on national plans, and social rewards were distributed in accordance with state priorities rather than market forces. Secondly, there were fewer extremes of income and wealth in the socialist societies. Certainly these societies had distinct social classes such as workers, peasants and 'intelligentsia' (professionals, administrators and managers). But production

resources were publicly rather than privately owned and therefore people could not inherit huge amounts of personal property and private wealth. So, although there were significant income inequalities, the range of income and wealth was narrower than that in the West.

However, recent years have witnessed dramatic changes in Eastern Europe. The dismantling of the Berlin Wall in 1989 signalled the general collapse of the socialist regimes. The 'satellite' states (eg East Germany) have won their political freedom from Soviet Union control, and the old USSR itself has fragmented and splintered into breakaway republics. The economic and political crisis in these countries has resulted in a move away from centrally planned economies towards Western style free markets. This transition to a market economy promises to be painful and difficult (poverty, crime and unemployment have increased) but many commentators predict an increasing convergence between East and West in the next few decades. Indeed, Fukuyama (1992) claims we have reached the 'end of history' or, more precisely, the end of major ideological conflicts. In his highly controversial opinion, the collapse of Soviet style communism signals the death of socialism and the permanent victory of Western style liberal democracy.

Activity 2 The End of Socialism?

Item A *A socialist economy*

A central principle behind the (former) Soviet economy was that everyone, no matter how poor, should have access to food, clothing and shelter. To this end, the central state in Moscow fixed the prices of goods and services. The state also provided subsidies to ensure that prices of products such as bread and milk were kept at levels that everybody could afford at the wages state firms were permitted to pay. Rents were kept low and unemployment was negligible.

Nevertheless, the Soviet economy had disadvantages. Many jobs were poorly paid and there was enormous inefficiency and waste. Also, individual freedoms were severely restricted. So recent political leaders (Gorbachev, Yeltsin) have introduced Perestroika (market reforms, privatisation) and Glasnost (political openness, democratic reforms).

Adapted from *Guardian Education*, 14.1.92, p2

Item B *The march of capitalism*

Dismantling the Berlin Wall

It is the end of the road for the communist system as we have known it: the central plan, the authoritarian state, the single-party system, the subjugated population. The Russian Revolution established socialism and capitalism as separate worlds, as different as chalk and cheese. That era is at an end. From now on, with gathering pace, there will be an interpenetration of the two systems. Eastern Europe will gradually acquire markets and international firms will operate there. The Berlin Wall must come down in our own minds.

Adapted from M.Jacques 'It's the End of the Road for Communism', *Sunday Times*, 26.11.89

Questions

1 Read Items A and B. The stratification systems of the socialist East and the capitalist West were shaped by their distinctive social and economic characteristics. Identify the main differences between them.

2 Suggest how the stratification systems of the former socialist countries will change as they move towards capitalism.

Definitions

Stratification

A system of structured inequality between social groups.

Life chances

Opportunities for obtaining material goods and cultural experiences (eg holidays, education); prospects for achieving certain living standards.

Social class

Class refers to differences in economic rewards and life chances which result from the unequal distribution of income and property. A class is defined by its command over material resources (S.Cotgrove, 1967).

Class is a set of social divisions that arise from a society's economic organisation (J.Westergaard, 1995).

Social status

The differing levels of prestige and honour attached to individuals or social groups. Status groups are ranked and organised by legal, political and cultural criteria. Slavery, feudalism and the caste system are examples of status based societies (G.Marshall, 1994).

Power

The probability of imposing one's will even against the resistance of others (M.Weber, 1948).

The set of resources people possess to enable them to pursue certain sorts of actions and the constraints they face in doing so (R.Breen and D.Rottman, 1995).

1.3 Measuring social class

How do sociologists decide on the social classes to which people belong? In order to do this they need a suitable measure or indicator of social class and they also need some idea of the overall number of classes and the position of the cut-off points between one class and the next. It is highly unlikely, however, that sociologists will ever agree on some final, 'correct' classification scheme. There is a wide variety of approaches and sociologists choose between them according to their particular theoretical and research interests.

Crompton (1993) states that class schemes are broadly divided into *theoretical* and *descriptive* approaches (although many sociologists draw on both). Theoretical approaches such as Marxism use class as an analytical tool in order to understand group behaviour and relationships and the likely direction of social change. The emphasis is on developing theoretical insights rather than describing the minute details of people's lives. Class theorists are usually more interested in underlying social forces (eg power struggles) than in 'surface' matters (eg class differences in leisure pursuits or the ownership of consumer goods). This perhaps explains why they often seem relatively unconcerned about defining class precisely or measuring the exact sizes of the various classes.

Descriptive approaches, on the other hand, attach a great deal of importance to the careful measurement of class. Precision is required because the descriptive approach is primarily designed to provide detailed empirical data on class patterns and inequalities. In sociological surveys for example, researchers often divide the sample population into classes in order to find out the extent to which class positions affect attitudes, behaviour and living standards. Also, government statisticians regularly collect data on changing patterns of social inequality (eg in health, educational achievements, income etc). These government surveys often allocate the general population to social classes in order to monitor the extent to which these inequalities run along class lines. This information can be useful in revealing the effects of government policies on different sections of the population.

Within the descriptive approach there is a broad division between studies which rely on 'subjective' ratings of class and those which use a more 'objective' form of assessment.

Subjective approaches

The subjective approach simply asks people to rate themselves. In a survey, for example, people might be asked to state their social class or they might be asked to select their class from a list prepared by the researcher. This approach relies on everyday, commonsense perceptions of social class. Marshall et al (1988) argue that this is quite a reliable method of measurement since class is still the most significant source of social identity for people in Britain. The majority of adults are aware of class differences and they usually feel quite comfortable in allocating themselves to a social class. Moreover, Reid (1989) found that there was relatively little disagreement between self-ratings and the more 'objective' assessments of social scientists. Also, the subjective approach has the added advantage that it allows people to discuss class in terms which are meaningful to them. It reveals how *they* see themselves, how *they* feel about class.

However, there are a number of difficulties with the

subjective approach. First, the choice of terms has to be handled with care. It is no use asking people if they are 'bourgeois' or 'proletarian' (they probably won't understand the terms). Second, people do not always attach a single, consistent meaning to terms like 'working class'. For example, when Mrs Thatcher was Prime Minister she claimed that 'In the world we now live in, divisions into class are meaningless. We are all working people now' (speech, 19.3.88). Other people might apply the term working class only to manual workers. Third, it is sometimes unclear whether respondents are stating their *own* views on their class position or simply reflecting how they think *other* people see them. Fourth, self-ratings sometimes result in absurd answers (eg a dustman insisting he is middle class, the millionairess who claims she is working class). And lastly, the subjective approach depends on the sociologist having the time, resources and means of access to discover self-ratings. In many types of research (eg using historical records) the information is just not available.

Objective approaches

Researchers usually find it convenient to measure class by some 'objective' indicator, one that derives from social science knowledge rather than individual opinion. The list of possible indicators is quite large since class is multi-dimensional (ie it covers many aspects of a person's life, including behaviour, values, accent, income and wealth). Obviously it would be a tall order to include all of these indicators and so normally only one is selected. The most popular measure is occupation since information on this is usually readily available. Besides, it is seen as a good predictor of lifestyles and life chances. 'In an industrial society, occupation is an excellent indicator of both levels of material reward and social standing, and over the years such indexes have been found to correlate with a range of factors, such as rates of infant mortality, access to education, voting behaviour, and so on' (Crompton, 1993, p13).

Occupation is the basis of the Registrar General's Social Class scheme (see Activity 3, Item B). The Registrar General supplies a handbook which lists the thousands of different occupations in Britain and arranges them into a few hundred groups which in turn are arranged into five 'social classes'. The split within class 3 is usually considered to represent the broad division between 'middle class' - classes 1, 2, 3NM(nonmanual) - and 'working class' - classes 3M(manual), 4 and 5. It should be noted that occupations are sometimes re-assigned to a different class (eg aircraft pilots were once in class 3 but are now in class 2). This means that comparisons over long time periods can be misleading.

Other schemes Sociologists and researchers have a wide choice of classification systems, and the final selection will depend on the particular requirements of the investigation. Ideally a classification should contain a sufficient number of classes to reflect the detailed differences in people's circumstances and lifestyles. Yet at the same time it should be reasonably simple to use (having too many social classes makes the data difficult to handle). Apart from the Registrar General's Social Class scheme, a number of other schemes have been developed. For example, the Registrar General also uses a Socio-Economic Groups scheme (based on occupation and employment status) which contains 17 different groups, each one containing people of supposedly similar social, cultural and recreational standards and behaviour. Modified versions of the Registrar General schemes are used in regular surveys such as the Family Expenditure Survey or the General Household Survey. Advertising agencies normally prefer to use a Market Research classification (A, B, C1, C2, D and E) which groups people along occupational lines which reflect consumption patterns, spending power and life styles (eg E people - old age pensioners, welfare claimants, casual workers - are those at 'the lowest level of subsistence'). And finally, some sociologists (eg Goldthorpe, 1980) have developed their own occupational scales to meet their particular sociological interests. Goldthorpe claims that his classification is not only convenient to use but also more sociologically informed than the 'official' classifications. In other words, it is more firmly based on sociological knowledge of social relationships, attitudes, behaviour and life chances.

Social class distribution, economically active persons, Great Britain, 1991 (percentages)

	(%)
1 Professional	5
2 Managerial & technical	28
3 Skilled nonmanual	23
Skilled manual	21
4 Partly skilled	15
5 Unskilled	6

(Figures do not include members of armed forces or respondents whose occupation was inadequately described).

Adapted from *1991 Census*, HMSO

People aged 16 and over in employment, by social class and sex, Great Britain, Spring 1991 (percentages)

	Men	Women
1 Professional	8	3
2 Intermediate	27	26
3 Skilled nonmanual	12	38
Skilled manual	34	8
4 Partly skilled	14	16
5 Unskilled	4	7

OPCS *Labour Force Survey* 1990 and 1991

Activity 3 Identifying Class

Item A *Class marks*

In one survey people were asked to pick two or three criteria they would use to judge a person's social class. Here are the results.

	%
The neighbourhood they live in	36
The job they do	31
How much money they earn	29
How much education they have	27
How wealthy they are	22
The way they talk	17
The clothes they wear	15
Who their parents are	13
How they spend their leisure time	11
The political party they support	11

Adapted from *The Scotsman*/ICM Research Ltd, September 1993, cited in G.Hadfield and M.Skipworth *Class*, 1994, p19

Item C *Extremes*

Item B *Social class*

Class 1 Professional
Accountant, architect, chemist, company secretary, doctor, engineer, clergyman, judge, lawyer, optician, scientist, solicitor, surveyor, university teacher, veterinarian.

Class 2 Intermediate
Aircraft pilot, chiropodist, farmer, laboratory technician, manager, proprietor, publican, Member of Parliament, nurse, police or fire brigade officer, schoolteacher.

Class 3NM Skilled nonmanual
Cashier, clerical worker, commercial traveller, draughtsman, estate agent, sales representative, secretary, shop assistant, typist, waiter, telephone supervisor.

Class 3M Skilled manual
Baker, bus driver, butcher, bricklayer, carpenter, cook, electrician, hairdresser, miner, policeman/woman, train driver/guard, upholsterer.

Class 4 Semi-skilled
Agricultural worker, barman/woman, bus conductor/conductress. fisherman, hospital orderly, machine sewer, packer, postman/woman, street vendor, telephone operator.

Class 5 Unskilled manual
Road sweeper, kitchen hand, labourer, car park attendant, driver's mate, messenger, railway porter, refuse collector, window/office cleaner, docker.

Adapted from I.Reid *Social Class Differences in Britain*, 1989, p56, and based on Registrar General's Social Class scheme.

Questions

1 Read Item A. How would you rank these indicators of class in order of importance? Give reasons for this ranking.

2 a) Why do you think the occupations in Item B have been ranked in this way?
  b) Do you agree with the rankings? Give reasons for your answer.

3 Item C suggests the extremes of the class system. What social inequalities does it reflect?

Summary

1 Social stratification refers to the structures of inequality in society.

2 The study of stratification helps us understand some of the basic operating principles of society.

3 The social class system is the dominant form of stratification in modern industrial societies.

4 Sociologists choose classification schemes according to their particular research purposes.

2 Theoretical Approaches

Key Issues

1 What are the main theories of stratification?
2 What are the strengths and weaknesses of these theories?

The main theories considered in this section are Marxism, Weberian theory and functionalism. Among contemporary British sociologists, some (eg Goldthorpe, 1987) work mainly within the Weberian tradition, some (eg Westergaard, 1995) within the Marxist perspective, while others (eg Giddens, 1979) draw on both traditions. These modern writers have developed the 'classical' theories and adapted them to present day society. It is less easy, perhaps, to find sociologists who openly declare themselves as functionalists but functionalist assumptions are far from unusual in British sociology!

Sociology is a self-critical discipline and so it is important to identify the limitations of these 'rival' theoretical models. But it is equally important to recognise their respective strengths. As Anderson et al (1985) point out, every model has something to offer in terms of its particular insights and preoccupations.

2.1 Marxism

Some sociologists claim that Karl Marx (1818-1883) still offers the most convincing approach to social class. But later generations of Marxists (neo-Marxists) have developed his ideas in different ways and so today there is no single Marxist viewpoint. Still, it is perfectly clear that Marx attached great importance to economic processes. Every social group must satisfy its material needs (eg food, shelter, clothing) and it does this by harnessing natural resources, producing goods, developing new technologies and establishing a division of labour in the workforce. And as people band together to perform these economic tasks, so they enter into social class relationships. According to Marx, the early era of *primitive communism* was reasonably egalitarian because it was based on very simple hunting and gathering techniques. But social classes started to emerge as soon as societies developed a more specialised division of labour and introduced private property. So history can be divided into a number of successive 'stages' (eg ancient slavery, feudalism, capitalism), each stage having a distinctive *mode of production* (this includes both the dominant technology of the society and its pattern of class relationships).

Marx was especially interested in capitalist societies with their advanced technology based on steam power, machinery and the factory system. Under capitalism, he argued, there are two major classes: the capitalists (*bourgeoisie*) and the workers (*proletariat*). These classes are defined by their relationship to the *means of production* (productive resources such as land, factories, machinery, raw materials). Capitalists (eg entrepreneurs, financiers and industrialists) own the means of production and so they are in a highly privileged and powerful economic position. The workers, on the other hand, do not own productive property and so they can survive only by selling their labour power to employers. It is this basic division, between the owners of capital and the workers, which creates major conflicts.

Class conflict

Marx confronted the paradox that capitalism had the technology to provide everyone with a good standard of living and yet it remained an oppressive and exploitive system. In Marx's view it is the workers who create wealth by their sweat and toil but most of the economic rewards are seized by employers and property owners (this is known as the labour theory of value). Thus, there is a basic conflict of interests between employers and workers (eg it is in the employer's interests to keep wages low in order to increase profits). This state of affairs creates all sorts of strains and tensions within capitalism. Marx attempted to explore these conflicts (or *contradictions*) in some detail.

Contradictions Marx identified the following contradictions.

1 **Polarisation of social classes** Marx expected capitalists to try to maintain their profits by driving down wages or by introducing machinery to replace workers. This would result in sharper contrasts between the living standards of the working class and the capitalist class. Marx's *immiseration thesis* predicted that the living standards of workers would fall further and further behind those of capitalists. Class divisions would become more polarised as *intermediate classes* merged with either capitalists or workers. For example, the *petty bourgeoisie* (eg small shopkeepers, self-employed craftsmen) would sink into the working class.

2 **Social alienation** Capitalism has an impressive ability to produce material goods but it does not seem to make people happy or contented. Instead it creates social *alienation*, an impoverishment of the human spirit. Capitalism is obsessed with the pursuit of profit and so it treats people simply as commodities to be bought and sold in the labour market. This prevents people from establishing

nourishing social relationships. Few people are able to control their own destinies and few people find any sense of fulfilment in their daily work.

3 **Economic crisis** Marx regarded capitalism as an erratic and uncontrollable system which frequently runs into deep economic crisis. Capitalists have no choice but to follow the competitive logic of capitalism but this intense competition simply creates further problems. Marx argued that there was a long term tendency for profit rates to fall and eventually this would cause the final collapse of the capitalist system.

According to Marx, these internal tensions would eventually lead to revolution and the replacement of capitalism with a classless communist society. However, this would happen only if workers first became aware of their 'true' class interests. This is difficult because many workers suffer from *false consciousness* (a flawed view of society and their position within it). They have been fooled into thinking that capitalism is fair and natural and so they are reluctant to challenge it. In a sense they have been brainwashed by the capitalists who have greater control over the social *superstructure* (the realm of ideas and social consciousness, including religion, law, politics and education). Any revolutionary movement would need to counteract this indoctrination and this is why Marx stressed the importance of political agitation and the creation of socialist ideas which would win the hearts and minds of workers.

Criticisms of Marx

A number of criticisms have been levelled at Marx's ideas.

1 Marx gave the impression that there were certain scientific 'laws of history'. This implies that the path of history is fairly predictable, with one historical stage leading to the next in some rigid and predetermined fashion. But critics insist that Marx underestimates the freedom of people to alter the course of history. Some neo-Marxists (eg Gramsci) eventually accepted that history involves genuine decisions and struggles and the outcome is by no means certain (see pp210;673).

2 Marx has been accused of attaching too much importance to economic factors since he took the view that the economic base shapes the superstructure of ideas and culture. For example, the laws of capitalist society protect private property, and the prevailing religious ideas (eg 'blessed are the poor') reconcile people to the massive inequalities of capitalism. So the dominant ideas of a society seem little more than ideologies which help to maintain the economic position of capitalists. Thus, Marx took the view that economic factors are 'primary' in the sense that they shape the ideas and culture of a society. But it is by no means clear that modern cultural issues (eg conflicts around gender, nationalism or ethnicity) can be adequately explained in economic terms (Parkin, 1979).

3 Many of Marx's apparent predictions have not been fulfilled. Instead of deeper poverty and misery, the living standards of workers in the major capitalist societies have risen. Instead of polarisation, the middle classes have steadily grown. And instead of revolution, workers seem to have reconciled themselves to capitalism. Indeed, it is the former East European socialist states which have been displaying the most spectacular crisis symptoms in recent years (eg the breakup of the former USSR, the collapse of communism).

4 Perhaps capitalism has survived because, for all its injustices and imperfections, it is still the best available system. It is certainly true that some capitalist societies (eg Nazi Germany, Brazil in the 1960s) have displayed appalling levels of brutality and cruelty. But Western liberal democracies have a strong track record (in terms of material progress, political freedoms and civil liberties) when compared with other types of system. In that case, workers might be perfectly sensible (rather than falsely conscious) in siding with capitalism.

Activity 4 Capitalism

Item A *Superiority*

There are two versions of modern capitalism: industrial capitalism (eg USA, Western European states) and East Asian industrial capitalism (eg Hong Kong, Taiwan, Japan). These can be contrasted with industrial socialism (the former East European bloc: USSR, Hungary, Poland etc). It is possible to survey the strengths and weaknesses of these systems scientifically, using empirical evidence.

The overall conclusion is that capitalism is morally superior and economically more effective.

- Capitalism is superior in bringing material wellbeing to large masses of people.
- Capitalism is a necessary basis for democracy.
- Capitalism is more tolerant of individual autonomy and the protection of human rights.
- Capitalism is more likely to generate social mobility and a fluid stratification system.

Adapted from P.Berger *The Capitalist Revolution*, 1987

Item B *Wants*

Capitalism has certainly improved the living standards of people in the postwar era. But it is a myth that markets can satisfy all our needs. Markets give people only a fraction of what they want. People want more compassion, less social cruelty, a more just distribution of wealth. People do not want so much violence, crime, fear, loneliness and addiction. They don't want child abuse, attacks on women, assaults on the elderly. They would prefer not to see such extensive emotional and psychological breakdown, such stress, despair and ruin of families.

Adapted from J.Seabrook *The Myth of the Market*, 1990, p159

Two sides of capitalism

Item C *Bias*

Sociology is substantially biased against capitalism. The syllabi for A level and university courses train students to be critical saboteurs of Britain. Sociology is contaminated by an ideological commitment which is prejudiced against capitalism, fails to see its good points and uncritically supports economic equality.

Adapted from D.Marsland *Seeds of Bankruptcy*, 1988, cited in *Guardian*, 18.3.88

Questions

1 Read Items A and B. To what extent do you agree with each account? Give reasons for your answer.
2 Read Item C. From your knowledge of sociology, do you think Marsland's statement is correct? Why might he have reached this conclusion?

2.2 Weberian theory

Max Weber (1864-1920) is another giant figure in the sociology of stratification. Just as there is a Marxist tradition in sociology, so many sociologists work within a Weberian framework. One of the key features of this Weberian tradition is the distinction between class, status and party. Weber treated these as separate (but related) sources of power and so they have direct effects on people's life chances.

Class Like Marx, Weber treated social class as basically an economic matter. He agreed that ownership (or non-ownership) of productive property is an important basis for class formation but Weber moved away from Marx's two class model. Instead, he chose to define class in terms of position in the economic marketplace. The market consists of a great many positions which vary according to source and amount of income, occupational skills and educational qualifications. A printer, for example, normally has greater skills and higher income than a casual labourer and so it is oversimplified to describe them both as 'working class'. So Weber's approach allows for a considerable number of finely graded occupational classes, each based on market position. All the people within each class share broadly similar life chances.

Status Status refers to the degree of honour or prestige which is attached to social groups in society. Different status groups compete with each other for a greater share of social esteem. Moreover, the members of a status group tend to share common values and lifestyles and so they resemble a community in many respects. They use 'status symbols' to announce their membership of this community (eg stockbrokers speed around in Porsches, skinheads wear Doc Martens and braces). Status, then, has more to do with social evaluation based on consumption styles (how people spend their money) than with production (how they earn it). So status groups are not quite the same thing as social classes. On the other hand, they are not always sharply separated. For example, the class position of a group might enhance its social status. Also, each status group adopts 'closure strategies' to enhance its material resources and improve its life chances. These strategies are examined in Chapter 3, p103.

Party When Weber talks about party he is referring to the exercise of power by pressure groups, political parties, trade unions and other organised interest groups. These groups compete for power which Weber defined as the probability of imposing one's will even against the resistance of others. Parties may form around social classes or status groups, a combination of these, or on some entirely different basis. Parties can use their power to enhance their economic wealth but Weber does not accept that economic wealth automatically confers power. For example, a bureaucrat or trade union leader might exercise greater power than a rich employer. Indeed, Weber suggested that power in modern society is increasingly concentrated in large bureaucracies rather than in the ownership of the means of production (see pp358-360).

Weber vs Marx

Many of the important debates in stratification involve clashes between the Marxist and Weberian perspectives. It is instructive, then, to look at some of their chief disagreements.

1 Crompton (1993) suggests the main difference is that Marxists view class relationships as grounded in exploitation and domination within *production* relations. Weberians, on the other hand, regard classes as reflecting positions in the *market* place.

2 Marxists maintain that the Weberian approach fails to appreciate the crucial importance of ownership of the means of production. They say that Weberians identify too many trivial market based classes and this merely distracts attention from the basic split between capitalists and workers.

3 Marx saw history as a long march towards the final goal of a communist society where class antagonisms would no longer exist. But Weber was sceptical about the possibility of a classless society and he regarded stratification as a more or less permanent source of conflict in every society.

4 Marxists usually portray class, status and power as 'matched' (eg the capitalist class not only has economic riches but also high status and decisive political power). Weber recognises that these three dimensions frequently overlap but he insists that they are sometimes less closely linked than Marxists suggest. For example, a penniless aristocrat might be high in status but low in class, while a market stallholder might earn good money but still be low in status.

5 Weber's market approach to class seems better equipped to deal with the existence of middle class groups. Marxists have great difficulty in fitting middle class groups into their basic model of capitalists and workers.

6 There are differences in emphasis in the way Marxists and Weberians treat divisions such as those based on gender, age or ethnicity. Marxists tend to see them as being rooted in class differences and class conflicts. But a Weberian approach is more likely to describe these divisions as status groups or status blocs (Turner, 1988) which are relatively independent of class.

Activity 5   Status

Item A *Status groups*

Sikhs

Skinheads

Wealthy at Ascot

Item B *Honour*

A reporter asked several people in a small town if they knew the mayor.
'He's a liar and a cheat' said the petrol pump attendant.
'He's a pompous ass' said the schoolteacher.
'Never voted for him in my life' said the chemist.
'Most corrupt politician I've ever known' said the barber.
When the reporter finally met the mayor he asked him what kind of salary he received.
'Good heavens, I don't get any salary' said the mayor.
'Then why did you take the job?'
'For the honour'.

Adapted from A.de Mello *The Heart of the Enlightened*, 1989, p102

Item C *Sloane Rangers*

Sloane Rangers are 'we' people, not 'me' people. Background means a lot to a Ranger. They want to establish it (name, rank and number) when they meet someone. Connections of family, school, university and job should all be made clear. Hence the eternal Ranger queries (eg 'You live in Shropshire...you must know the Sloane Rangers'). Sloane Rangers hesitate to use the term 'breeding' but that's what background means. Family is a magic word. Rangers think 'blood' and 'bloodstock' in a romantic way. It's ancestor worship. They enjoy references to grand roguish great-grandparents: 'It's her bad Percy blood coming out'.

Adapted from A.Barr and P.York *The Official Sloane Ranger Handbook*, 1982, p10

A Sloane Ranger. Sloane Rangers are a fashionable group, perhaps best represented by Lady Diana Spencer before she married Prince Charles.

Questions

1 a) Judging from the pictures in Item A, how do these groups identify themselves?
   b) How might they be ranked in terms of social honour?
   c) Are there any connections between their class and status positions? Explain your answer.
2 Read Item B. What serious sociological point about status is being made here?
3 Read Item C. Do you think this preoccupation with family and background is more pronounced in the upper class than in other classes? Give reasons for your answer.

2.3 Functionalism

Functionalist sociologists often draw a comparison between society and the human body. The body consists of separate but interdependent parts, each part playing a specialised role which contributes to overall physical wellbeing. Likewise, society is depicted as a more or less harmonious and integrated 'whole' with every social institution serving a particular *function*. The main task of the sociologist, then, is to discover the particular functions performed by each social institution. In the case of stratification, functionalists seek to reveal the contributions it makes to the survival and maintenance of society. This leads them to quite different conclusions from conflict theorists (whether Marxist or Weberian) who regard stratification as a source of conflict and tension. For functionalists, stratification is something which is beneficial and positive.

Davis and Moore

A long running debate on the functions of stratification was opened up by Davis and Moore (1945). They contend that stratification is a permanent and universal feature of human societies and conclude that this is because it is functionally necessary. Stratification is inevitable because every

society faces the task of 'placing' people (ensuring that its most important positions are filled by suitable people). Also, it needs to motivate these people (they must perform their duties in a responsible and conscientious manner). In order to achieve this, societies offer higher rewards (eg income, status) for the most important jobs. Davis and Moore offer certain guidance on how we can identify these jobs. Normally they are 'unique' (no other occupation can substitute for them). For example, a managing director is more important than a chauffeur because the director could drive the car but the driver probably could not direct a company. Also, the most important jobs tend to have other positions dependent on them (the managing director supervises many people, the chauffeur merely tends to the car).

But functional importance is not the only criterion which decides the distribution of rewards. Davis and Moore add a second criterion, the scarcity of personnel. This refers either to the shortage of people with innate ability (not everyone has the talent to become a brain surgeon) or to the necessity of a long period of job training. In order to tempt gifted people to acquire the necessary job qualifications, the stratification system compensates them by guaranteeing financial rewards and high social status at the end of the training period.

Evaluation The functionalist view of stratification has been heavily criticised (eg Tumin, 1967) but Davis and Moore have replied to many of these criticisms.

1 How easy is it to determine the functional importance of a job? Isn't a dustman just as important to our health as a doctor? (Davis and Moore say this criticism overlooks the 'scarcity of personnel' argument).

2 Davis and Moore assume that there is a general consensus on the pattern of rewards. How, then, do we explain the widespread resentment about the unequal distribution of income and wealth?

3 Davis and Moore seem to regard power as a social resource which is distributed throughout society in such a way that it works for the common good. They overlook the way power is used as a *weapon* by some groups to further their own material interests. So the distribution of rewards may be the result of fierce power struggles rather than something which emerges naturally from a consensus of values.

4 Some of the highest rewards go to wealthy people who do not really perform any 'function' at all but simply live off the interest and dividends on their wealth. (Davis and Moore accept this criticism).

5 Davis and Moore offer a dismal view of human nature which suggests that people will perform tasks only for monetary or status rewards. They overlook other motives such as altruism or sense of service or joy in work. (Davis and Moore reply that, unfortunately, these other motives are usually pretty weak!).

6 Davis and Moore neglect the *dysfunctions* (negative effects) caused by stratification. They assume that stratification is functional for *everyone*. But some people benefit more than others and some suffer greatly from stratification. The distribution of rewards is a major source of conflict in most modern societies.

7 Davis and Moore exaggerate the sacrifices involved in long periods of training. Student life, for example, is usually more enjoyable than slaving away at a lathe or working on an assembly line.

After this flood of criticism, many commentators concluded that the functionalist approach had been discredited. In recent years, however, some writers have returned to the debate. Saunders (1990) maintains that the arguments of Davis and Moore cannot be easily dismissed. Saunders believes they are correct in saying that stratification serves important functions (even if it creates dysfunctions at the same time). Also, even their critics agree that stratification is more or less universal.

The main disagreement arises over the claim that stratification is inevitable in all *future* societies. Here Saunders sides with the critics in accepting that stratification based on unequal material reward is not inevitable. But Saunders concludes that any alternative would probably require a coercive state willing and able to clamp down on any emerging inequalities: 'capitalist countries often turn out to be more unequal...but socialist countries are always more repressive' (Saunders, 1990, p66). Saunders also suspects that the abolition of unequal rewards would act as a disincentive to entrepreneurship and innovation.

Summary

1 Marxism, Weberian theory and functionalism represent three major traditions in class theory.

2 Each one of these models has strengths and weaknesses. Some sociologists draw on one or the other but many sociologists find something useful in all of them.

Activity 6 Class Injuries

Item A *Feelings*

Class is a matter of feelings as well as material resources. It causes massive injuries and emotional wounds, especially for manual workers. They sense from the 'hidden signals of class' that their worthiness is questioned and undermined by the system. Those who remain in the working class become part of the invisible mass, those who are sacrificed because attention is focused on the high-flyers. To be 'average' is to be condemned. Although manual workers sense that the system is unfair and unjust and robs them of human dignity, the system is so pervasive that it undermines their confidence to challenge it.

Instead of a class system which reduces human worth to the question of 'talent' or 'ability', we need to rediscover diverse concepts of human dignity. We need rituals and scales of value which transcend class dimensions.

Adapted from R.Sennett and J.Cobb *The Hidden Injuries of Class*, 1972

Item B *Hardships*

'I never go out now, never go nowhere. I can't afford sweets, don't have any entertainment, all I ever do is watch TV, read and listen to the radio.'

'I think the real problem of being on the dole is it destroys your self esteem, you know, and your ability to provide for yourself. If you're on the dole for a long period of time you tend to get lethargic.'

'I have had to swallow my pride till it hurts. It makes me feel like a complete failure. When I can't give my children the best it makes me feel like I'm failing.'

'We've got Christmas coming up. For me that's not any enjoyment, it's a nightmare. I look in the shops, looking at prices and it's a bloody nightmare.'

Transcripts from interviews with income support claimants, from R. Cohen et al *Hardship Britain*, 1992

A single parent in Hackney

Questions

1 Read Item A. What do you think Sennett and Cobb mean by 'rituals and scales of value which transcend class dimensions'?

2 Using Items A and B, suggest ways in which the functionalist view of stratification might be challenged.

3 Class Matters

Key Issues

1 What impact does class have on people's lives?

2 How are income and wealth distributed?

3 Is class diminishing in importance?

3.1 Life chances

'The social class into which we are born remains vastly influential in shaping our life course and life chances, even in the waning years of the twentieth century' (Breen and Rottman, 1995, p xi). Support for this statement can be found in research evidence which demonstrates the continuing link between social class and many aspects of social life (see box on right). This evidence firmly suggests there are substantial gaps between social classes in their lifestyles and life chances. Of course, the size of this gap is not the same in every sphere of social life and it can also change over time. Quite often the controversies surrounding class are not about whether a gap exists but rather whether the gap is closing or not. This is especially true of debates about trends in income and wealth.

Income

Income statistics are derived from the Inland Revenue or from sources such as the Family Expenditure Survey. In simple terms income is the 'flow' of money

Class patterns

Life expectancy
In Sheffield and Glasgow those who live in the most affluent communities can expect to live 8 years longer than those in the most deprived areas (*Commission on Social Justice*, 1994).

Health
Compared with class 1, class 5 are 2 times (men) or 2.5 times (women) more likely to report a long standing illness (Townsend and Davidson, 1980).

Social habits
In 1992, men and women in the unskilled manual group were three times more likely to smoke than those in the professional group (*Social Trends*, 1995). In 1993-94, 30% of households in market research groups D and E read *The Sun*, compared with 7% in groups A and B (*Social Trends*, 1995).

Education
In 1984, just 1% of those accepted into British universities were from the unskilled manual class, compared with 6% from semi-skilled manual and 70% from the top two classes (Wicks, 1987).

Housing
In 1993, 90% of professional households were owner-occupiers, compared with 72% of skilled manual and 42% of unskilled manual (*Social Trends*, 1995).

Divorce
Divorce rates for unskilled manual families are 2 times higher than those for skilled manual and 4 times higher than those for professionals (Haskey, 1984).

Leisure
In 1988, 55% of adults in classes D and E did not have a holiday, compared with only 20% in classes A and B (*Social Trends*, 1990).

a person (or family or household) receives within a given time period. But economists make a distinction between 'original income' and 'disposable income'. Original income refers to earnings from employment and self-employment, occupational pensions and interest on savings and investments. Disposable income allows for flows to and from the state by taking original income and adding any state benefits (eg income support) and deducting direct taxes (eg income tax).

The Royal Commission on the Distribution of Income and Wealth (1979) reported that there is no simple and direct link between income and social class. For example, it found that there was a wide spread of earnings among people doing similar kinds of work. Nevertheless, it is broadly true that income is related to social class (eg for both males and females, nonmanual workers earn more than manual workers). According to Family Expenditure Survey data the weekly disposable income of households tends to decline as we descend the social class scale.

Trends Income inequalities slowly narrowed in the postwar period up until the late 1970s. But although the very rich lost some of their share of income, most of the gains were made by those immediately below them in the income league. The bottom half of the population did not manage to increase their modest share of the national income (although, like most of the population, their *absolute* living standards improved considerably). Then society became much more unequal in the 1980s when there was a reversal of the trend towards income redistribution. The rise in top salaries and the cuts in income tax meant that richer groups gained significantly, while the poorest 10% of households actually suffered a reduction in their absolute incomes (Commission on Social Justice, 1994). Between 1971 and 1992 the percentage of the population below half average income increased from 11% to 21% (*Social Trends*, 1995).

Pay power

Occupation	Typical annual earnings
Commercial QC	£750,000
Senior director (big firm)	£500,000
Top footballer	£500,000
Leading hospital consultant	£300,000
National newspaper editor	£160,000
Solicitor (partner)	£100,000
Public school headmaster	£60,000
General practitioner	£40,000
Head of state school	£40,000
Police chief superintendent	£38,000
London Underground driver	£23,000
Primary teacher	£20,000
Lorry driver	£15,000
Nurse	£15,000
Social worker	£14,500
Bricklayer	£11,000
Cleaner	£9,000
NHS porter	£6,500

Adapted from G.Hadfield and M.Skipworth *Class*, 1994, p114

Household incomes

Disposable household income before housing costs, United Kingdom (percentages).
(Quintiles are formed by dividing the population into five groups of equal size.)

	Quintile groups				
	Bottom	next	middle	next	top
1979	10	14	18	23	35
1987	9	13	17	23	39
1991-92	7	12	17	23	41

Adapted from *Social Trends*, 1995, p94

Inquiry into Income and Wealth
Joseph Rowntree Foundation ,1995

Key findings
- Income inequality in the UK grew rapidly between 1977 and 1990, and the gap between rich and poor is now greater than at any time since World War 2 (1939-45).
- The pace at which inequality increased in the UK was faster than in any other country apart from New Zealand.
- Over the period 1979 to 1992 the poorest 20-30% of the population failed to benefit from economic growth. Income grew by 36% for the population as a whole but the income for the poorest tenth fell by 17% (after deducting housing costs).
- Since 1977 the proportion of the population with less than half the average income has more than trebled (from 7% to 24%, after allowing for housing costs).

Main causes
- During the 1980s more people became dependent on state benefits like Income Support as a result of both higher unemployment and demographic factors like the increase in the numbers of lone parents. The income gap widened between those dependent on benefits and the population with earnings.
- Differences in income from work have grown rapidly. Between 1978 and 1992 hourly wages for the lowest paid men hardly changed while median wages grew by 35% and high wages by 50%.
- The tax system failed to redistribute incomes in any significant way.
- The socioeconomic changes of the 1980s have not had a uniform effect. For example, pensioners with occupational pensions have done better than those who rely on state pensions. Some ethnic minorities and some regional groups have suffered disproportionately.

Dwarves and giants

The Dutch economist Jan Pen invented a way of describing income distribution based on the idea that people's heights are proportional to their incomes (eg someone with average height would have average income). Then Pen imagined that the population would parade past an observer in an hour, with those on lowest income (dwarves) coming first and those on highest incomes (giants) coming last. What would an income parade in 1990/91 look like? If average height is 5ft 8 ins, then 62% of the population would have below average height. The bottom fifth of the population would have heights of less than 2ft 10ins, while the top fifth would have heights from 7ft 8ins upwards. As Pen put it, in the final seconds of the hour long parade the scene is dominated by colossal figures: people like tower flats, giants whose heads disappear into the clouds. The richest man would be over 4 miles high.

Adapted from Joseph Rowntree Foundation *Inquiry into Income and Wealth* vol 2, 1995, pp6-9

Activity 7 It's Only Money

Item A *Distribution of income*

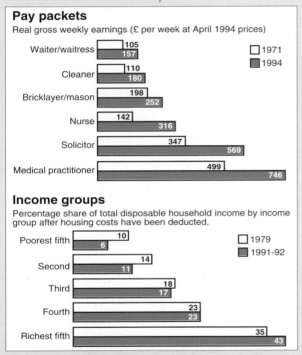

Pay packets
Real gross weekly earnings (£ per week at April 1994 prices)

☐ 1971 ■ 1994

	1971	1994
Waiter/waitress	105	157
Cleaner	110	180
Bricklayer/mason	198	252
Nurse	142	316
Solicitor	347	569
Medical practitioner	499	746

Income groups
Percentage share of total disposable household income by income group after housing costs have been deducted.

☐ 1979 ■ 1991-92

	1979	1991-92
Poorest fifth	10	6
Second	14	11
Third	18	17
Fourth	23	23
Richest fifth	35	43

Adapted from *Guardian*, 26.1.95 (based on figures from Department of Social Security)

Questions

1 a) Briefly summarise the trends shown in Item A.
   b) Suggest reasons for these trends.
2 a) Read Items B and C. Using these items, describe what is meant by 'market forces'.
   b) Do you agree that the condemnation of the chief executive's pay rise was based purely on envy? Give reasons for your answer.

Item B *Privatisation*

Since being privatised a few years ago British Gas has shed 22,100 jobs. In 1994 its chief executive was awarded a salary increase of 75%, taking his annual salary to £475,000 (not including generous share options). A few weeks later British Gas announced that its 2,600 showroom workers must take cuts in their holiday entitlements and cuts of 16% in their pay (before the pay cut, their annual average pay was £13,000). The increase in the chief executive's salary and the cuts in the pay of showroom workers were both justified on the grounds of 'market forces'.

Adapted from *Guardian*, 16.12.94

Item C *Envy?*

The fuss over the salary of Mr Brown, the chief executive of British Gas, is a classic case of socialist envy. We should be celebrating his good fortune, not condemning it. Mr Brown has got to the top on merit. His salary is not unreasonable for our seventh largest public company.

There is no comparability between Mr Brown's situation and those of his showroom workers. The pursuit of greater efficiency, for which a top manager should be justly rewarded, sometimes involves the cutting out of surplus staff and the suppression of wage increases. A wage increase for many thousands of British Gas workers would take a slice straight out of the company's profits, whilst the size of Mr Brown's pay package makes no real difference at all. His pay rise has cost gas customers less than two pence each, but Mr Brown's skill in cost control may save them several pounds per year and at the same time add significantly to returns to shareholders.

Adapted from leader article, *The Spectator*, 28.1.95, p5

Wealth

Wealth refers to the total 'stock' of economic resources and possessions. It is a measure of the monetary value of assets such as stocks and shares, savings, land, buildings and consumer goods. Economists use the term 'marketable wealth' to describe those assets (eg house, car, shares, money) which can be disposed of or sold. Another measure, 'marketable wealth plus pensions', adds on the estimated cash value of pension entitlements. Occupational and state pensions usually cannot be cashed in or marketed but they are genuine assets as far as income is concerned.

The Inland Revenue calculates wealth on the basis of the income people receive from their assets, but wealthy people sometimes try to conceal their true wealth. Inland Revenue statistics also include wealth calculations based on the estate duty paid when people die. However, many people do not leave enough wealth to qualify for estate duty and those who do are an older group who are not necessarily representative of the rest of the population. Another difficulty is that the figures do not usually list the social class of the people concerned. But wealth and class are certainly related. 'While it is not possible to demonstrate by data a relationship between personal wealth and social class, one may be safely assumed. Such wealth is the result of inheritance, creation, saving or accumulation, the legal opportunities for which are clearly related to class' (Reid, 1989, p176).

Trends Wealth is much more unevenly distributed than income (partly because of the concentration of wealth among older age groups and partly because of the cumulative effects of inheritance). However, wealth inequalities have certainly narrowed this century (eg in 1911 the top 1% of the population owned 69% of the country's wealth but by 1991 this had dropped to 18%). This broad trend to redistribution continued for some time into the postwar period but there has been little change in the overall distribution of marketable wealth since 1976 (*Social Trends*, 1993). Nevertheless, a number of gains have been made by the middle 40% 'slice' of the population (Scott, 1994). They have become wealthier because of the spread of pension schemes and the rise in home ownership (owner occupation increased from 30% of households in 1951 to about 68% in the 1990s). Another factor is the spread of share ownership (eg the general public has been urged to buy shares in privatised utilities like British Telecom or British Gas). The number of adults owning shares increased from two and a half million in 1980 to nine and a quarter million in 1992. However, shares are still heavily concentrated in numbers and value. For example, in 1986 2% of the adult population owned 82% of all (personal) company shares (Fielding, 1990). And the higher the social class the more likely people are to own shares (*Social Trends*, 1994).

3.2 Classlessness?

Some commentators claim that Britain is becoming a 'classless' society, one where the stamp of class leaves only a faint impression on people's lives. But classlessness has a number of contrasting meanings.

Equal opportunity One view is that a classless society is simply one where there is equality of opportunity, where everybody has a fair chance to compete for the major prizes. This is what the Prime Minister, John Major, had in mind when he proclaimed his goal of making Britain 'a genuinely classless society in which people can rise to whatever level that their own abilities and good fortune may take them, from whatever their starting point' (speech 28.11.90). In this type of society there are still large differences between groups in terms of wealth and living standards. The hierarchy of class still remains, with a steep gradient from top to bottom. It can be regarded as classless only in the limited sense that it provides certain opportunities for people in the lower social classes to move upwards. (For evidence on mobility, see Section 4.2).

Levelling A contrasting version of classlessness claims that the massive inequalities of the old class system have more or less been eliminated. General improvements in living standards are said to have resulted in a levelling out of social classes, giving the working class access to rewards previously reserved for the privileged middle class. The most obvious examples of this are the rise in car and home ownership and the spread of consumer durables (eg videos, washing machines). Consequently, some theorists claim that the boundaries between classes have become increasingly blurred. (For evidence on this, see the embourgeoisement debate in Section 5.3).

New divisions A third version of classlessness maintains that new social divisions have become equally or even more important than class. This is why many sociologists are turning their attention to the divisions of gender, race and ethnicity and age. Also, stratification theorists have developed new

Distribution of wealth, United Kingdom (percentages)

Marketable Wealth

	1971	1981	1991
% of wealth owned by			
most wealthy 1%	31	18	18
most wealthy 5%	52	36	37
most wealthy 10%	65	50	50
most wealthy 50%	97	92	92

Marketable wealth plus occupational and state pension rights

	1971	1981	1991
% of wealth owned by			
most wealthy 1%	21	12	11
most wealthy 5%	37	24	26
most wealthy 10%	49	34	37
most wealthy 50%	87	79	84

Adapted from *Social Trends*, 1990, 1993, 1994

ideas around the related concepts of *consumption cleavages* and *lifestyles*.

Dunleavy (1979) divides the population into 'sectors' which are based on distinctive consumption patterns. For example, car or home owners are in a different consumption sector from non-owners. These consumption cleavages (splits) cut across the horizontal divisions of class: 'Basically, sectors are lines of vertical division in a society, such that certain common interests are shared between social classes in the same sector, while within a social class, sectoral differences reflect a measure of conflict of interests' (Dunleavy, 1979, p419). This idea has been used by Crewe (1985) to explain voting patterns (eg among the working class, home owners are more likely than non-owners to vote Conservative). It has also been developed by Saunders (1986) who identifies consumption sectors in fields such as housing, transport, education, medical and welfare services and leisure. The major division is between those who rely on the 'market' and those who rely on the 'state' for their consumption of goods and services. According to Saunders these consumption cleavages do not always coincide with class divisions, although they are interrelated. Moreover, they can be just as important as class in shaping life chances, values, lifestyles and cultural identities.

In recent years a number of sociologists have singled out *lifestyles* for particular attention. They argue that these lifestyles are a central organising feature of people's lives and a major source of social and personal identity. Clarke and Saunders (1991) argue that class identity is being eroded and replaced by identities based on consumer lifestyles. At one time, perhaps, lifestyles were a more or less direct expression of class membership and so people followed rigid and 'traditional' class based pursuits. In the modern age, however, lifestyles seem to be much more flexible and varied and based on individual choices. Personal lifestyles replace class lifestyles. 'As the importance of tradition

declines, more and more issues become matters of personal decision. What we wear, how we vote, what we eat, what job we do, where we live - these are no longer determined by birth' (*Commission on Social Justice*, 1994, p81).

The end of class analysis?

Is Britain really becoming classless? If so, this implies that class analysis has lost much of its relevance and explanatory power. Indeed, some sociologists claim that class analysis is no longer a valuable source of sociological insights. According to one of these sociologists, 'class as a concept is ceasing to do any useful work for sociology' (Pahl, 1989, p710). Although Pahl recognises that capitalism produces class divisions, he nevertheless thinks that class analysis has declined into mere 'dogma' and has very little explanatory value.

However, there are a number of reasons why it would be premature to announce the end of class analysis.

1 **Classlessness is exaggerated** Evidence has already been presented (Section 3.1) that class remains a major influence on life chances. As far as income and wealth are concerned, the class gaps are widening rather than closing. Ironically, Westergaard (1995) notes that the current debate about classlessness has arisen at a time when class divisions are actually hardening!

2 **'New divisions' are class related** The new divisions in society certainly demand the serious attention of sociologists. But as Westergaard (1995) points out, many of these divisions run along class lines. For example, the affluent middle class are far more likely to buy their homes or to engage in expensive lifestyle pursuits.

3 **Consumption explanations are weak** Pahl (1989) is critical of class analysis but he is equally critical of the recent sociological emphasis on consumer lifestyles. Where do poor people fit in to the new consumption oriented society? Are consumer lifestyles stable and fundamental or merely fleeting fashions? If consumption patterns are not based on class positions then where do they come from? Consumption analysis has hardly fulfilled its early promise as a serious rival to class analysis.

4 **Class identity is strong** A survey by Marshall et al (1988) found that class is still the most common and powerful source of social identity. This finding is echoed by a *British Social Attitudes Survey* (Young, 1992) which shows the remarkable persistence of a 'sense of class' (eg respondents declared they felt 'closer' to someone of the same class than someone of the same age, religion or political views).

5 **Role of class analysis** Goldthorpe and Marshall (1992) have replied to critics like Pahl by putting

---

Consumption cleavages

Home-owners	Consumption cleavage	Non home-owners
middle class (1)		middle class (3)
Class		
cleavage		
working class (2)		working class (4)

Class cleavage: 2 and 4 have common class interests which set them apart from 1 and 3.
Consumption cleavage: 1 and 2 have common consumption interests which set them apart from 3 and 4.

up a stout defence of class analysis. First, they argue that many criticisms are misplaced (eg class analysis does not necessarily commit sociologists to dogmatic views about the inevitability of class consciousness or class conflict). Furthermore, research programmes on class have many attractions. For example, they allow sociologists to connect 'personal troubles' with 'public issues' and they provide handy explanations (eg concepts such as class position or class mobility help to explain a good deal of what happens in society). At the same time, Goldthorpe and Marshall concede that class analysis must remain self-critical (eg it cannot simply assume that class is the most important factor in social life).

Summary

1 Some sociologists claim there has been a trend to a more classless society. But classlessness means a number of different things (opportunity, levelling, or new divisions).

2 The study of social class still plays a valuable role in sociology. It draws attention to differences in lifestyles, behaviour, income and wealth.

Activity 8 Lifestyles

Item A *Styles*

Elvis Presley lookalikes

Rastafarians

Punks

Chelsea fan

Item B *Identities*

Social identity is no longer crucially defined by our occupations. There is no automatic link between the job you do and the life you lead, your possessions, your tastes or cultural pursuits.

- We live in an affluent, materialistic society and so we are judged by the quantity and quality of our possessions.
- We live in a media culture and so we are judged by the newspapers we read, the television we watch, the films we see and the celebrities we admire.
- We live in a consumer society and so we are judged by our consumer lifestyles.

Lifestyle is an invention of the late twentieth century. It is shaped by personal wealth and a seemingly infinite number of individual choices. People are grouped according to what they wear, where they shop, what they eat and drink, how they speak, even their attitudes and sense of humour.

Adapted from G.Hadfield and M.Skipworth *Class*, 1994, pp8, 24, 137, 140

Item C *Diversity*

British society used to be based on hierarchy and deference with class as the foundation stone. But that world has slowly been replaced by market driven egalitarianism, where rank and title matter little. Homogeneity and class have been replaced by diversity and multi-identity. Look at a football crowd in the early 1950s: male, working class and all wearing cloth caps. Now take a walk through any city centre, or saunter down a suburban street: we are confronted with a profusion of styles, ethnicities, identities. This is the pick-and-choose society. From food to holidays, from sport to fabrics, from sexual identity to clothes, we can choose like never before.

Adapted from M.Jacques 'The End of Politics', *Sunday Times*, 18.7.93, p8

Item D *A classless society?*

Observer, 1.2.91

Questions

1 Use the photos in Item A to illustrate the points made in Item B.
2 Read Item C. Suggest ways in which a 'class' theorist might disagree with this passage. Refer to Item D in your answer.

4 Social Mobility

Key Issues

1 What are the main types of social mobility?
2 What are the causes and effects of mobility?
3 What are the rates and patterns of mobility?

Social mobility occurs whenever people move across social class boundaries or from one occupational level to another. The direction of mobility may be *upwards* (eg the cleaner's daughter who qualifies as a doctor) or *downwards* (eg the stockbroker's son who becomes a train driver). Another distinction is between *intergenerational mobility* (differences between the levels of parents and their children) and *intragenerational mobility* (career shifts within a person's working life, such as promotion from the shop floor to the company boardroom).

The study of social mobility is important for a number of reasons.

1 Social mobility matters to people in their everyday lives.'Getting on in life' is a common concern of many people (Payne,1987).
2 Mobility studies draw attention to people's pasts (life histories) and futures (career trajectories) as well as their current class positions. This gives a much more rounded picture of class since it takes account of people's backgrounds and ambitions (Hadfield and Skipworth, 1994).
3 Mobility is a test of fairness. A class society is seen as more legitimate and fair if it offers plenty of opportunities for mobility. So social mobility can act as a 'safety valve' which eases some of the pressures in a class system.
4 Mobility affects the way classes are formed, their size and shape and the firmness of the boundaries between them. It also has implications for class consciousness. Giddens (1979) argues that where mobility is restricted, class boundaries become sharper and each of the classes becomes more cohesive.

4.1 A mobile society

In certain types of society there are only limited prospects for social mobility. Under feudalism or the caste system a person's position is largely fixed on the basis of ascribed characteristics (features inherited at birth, such as family of origin, gender or ethnic group). These ascribed characteristics are still socially significant in modern societies but these societies tend to place greater emphasis on achievement (what people can do rather than their social origins). Thus, modern Britain has some of the features of a *meritocracy* where position in the hierarchy is determined by individual merit. In a perfect meritocracy the social origins of people are unimportant because people compete under the same fair conditions. Therefore the positions people achieve and the rewards they enjoy are based solely on their individual talents and effort.

It would be far fetched, however, to claim that Britain is a pure meritocracy. The social origins of people still continue to shape their opportunities. As long as there are marked differences in the social circumstances of classes, of men and women, and of different ethnic groups, then it is difficult to argue that people start off on an equal footing in the race for social prizes. So equality of opportunity has not yet been achieved. But even if Britain is not a perfect meritocracy, at least it offers some genuine opportunities for mobility.

Social changes In postwar Britain the opportunities for mobility have improved for a number of reasons.

1 **Occupational changes** The changing occupational structure has created more room at the 'top'. With computerisation and automation, there is less demand for manual labour and greater demand for nonmanual skills and a better educated workforce. This applies within each industrial sector.

2 **Industrial changes** There has been a shift away from the older 'smokestack' industries (eg foundries) towards the new, high technology 'sunrise' industries (eg computers). These new industries have a higher proportion of nonmanual jobs. In addition, there has been a shift from manufacturing industries with their largely manual workforce towards the (mainly white collar) service sector.

3 **Ladders** In the past, ambitious people might have relied on marriage to the boss's daughter, 'connections' (knowing the right people), working one's way up from the shop floor, or sheer luck (being in the right place at the right time). These ladders to mobility are still available but education is increasingly recognised as the most important step to a good career. Of course, middle class people still tend to be more successful in gaining educational qualifications. But the emphasis on credentials and qualifications is probably more meritocratic than a system where people are appointed simply because of their social origins.

Activity 9 Class Merits

Item A *Meritocracy*

(Michael Young's satire looks ahead to the year 2034 and imagines a society based on meritocractic principles).

The ruling class is no longer selected on the basis of kinship or wealth but on merit (IQ + Effort). Also, IQ is no longer randomly distributed. The most capable people intermarry and produce the most intelligent children. So the ruling class has taken on a hereditary character, but one based on talent rather than birth. The ruling class are smug and they lack sympathy with those they govern. And the masses can no longer pretend that their lowly position is simply a matter of luck or lack of opportunity.

In this society a protest group emerges which calls for the overthrow of the meritocracy and its replacement with a truly classless society which would run along the following lines: 'The classless society would be based upon plural values. It would evaluate people not just according to their intelligence or education but also according to their kindliness and their courage, their imagination and sensitivity, their sympathy and generosity. It would encourage individual differences and it would respect the dignity of every human being.'

Adapted from M.Young *The Rise of the Meritocracy*, 1961

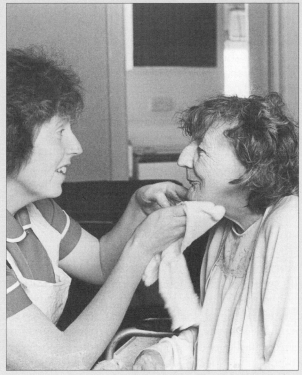

Kindness

Item B *Opportunities*

What every sensible Tory should want is not classlessness but equality of opportunity. Usually this is taken to mean doing away with hereditary privileges, eg abolishing Eton and the other public schools. But that would be a foolish policy. Egalitarians must not be allowed to destroy the agreeable and civilised lifestyles of those at the top. It is hardly worth getting to the top if that lifestyle has already been destroyed. The bourgeois lifestyle is about more than money. It is about culture, values, responsibility, respectability and so on. These qualities have been bred in to the top families over many generations.

A pure meritocracy would result in a yobbocracy (rule by yobs). Meritocracy without class makes for an uncivilised society, one stratified only by money. The way to avoid this is to ensure that there are enough bourgeois families left in charge of the social high ground to be able to impose superior standards in manners and in morals.

Adapted from P.Worsthorne 'The Grace of Class', *Sunday Telegraph*, 2.12.90

Eton

Questions

1 Read Items A and B. Young and Worsthorne both criticise meritocracies but on different grounds. Identify the key differences in their arguments.
2 What arguments can be used in defence of meritocracies?

4.2. Measuring social mobility

Mobility studies

How many people move up or down the social scale? How far do they move away from their class of origin? Do some social groups have better chances of mobility than others? These are the sorts of issues considered by mobility studies. The measurement of social mobility presents lots of technical difficulties but the basic procedure is to select a sample of people and identify their occupations. These occupations can then be compared with their previous occupations (to measure intragenerational mobility) or with the occupations of their fathers (to measure intergenerational mobility). This approach was followed by the large scale Oxford mobility study (Goldthorpe, 1980).

Oxford mobility study This was based on interviews with over 10,000 men (aged twenty to sixty-four) in England and Wales in 1972. Using his own class scheme, Goldthorpe allocated these men to seven social classes which were based on market situation (source and level of income, security of employment, promotion prospects) and work situation (degree of control and authority in the job). For purposes of

---

Goldthorpe's social class scheme

Service class
Class 1 (13.6% of sample)
Higher grade professionals, administrators and managers, large proprietors.

Class 2 (11.5%)
Lower grade professionals, administrators and managers; higher grade technicians and supervisors.

Intermediate class
Class 3 (9.2%)
Routine nonmanual (eg clerical, sales personnel), rank and file service employees.

Class 4 (9.4%)
Small proprietors, self employed artisans (non-professional workers).

Class 5 (11.6%)
Lower grade technicians, supervisors of manual workers.

Working class
Class 6 (21.2%)
Skilled manual workers.

Class 7 (23.5%)
Semi-skilled and unskilled manual workers, agricultural workers.

Adapted from J.Goldthorpe, *Social Mobility and Class Structure in Modern Britain*, 1980

---

simplification these classes are usually grouped into three clusters: service class, intermediate, and working. The service class includes experts and specialists who fill important positions in the dominant institutions of society. This class acts as a sort of bridge between the top decision makers and the mass of the people. It consists of a broad range of people and so it is certainly not the same thing as a 'ruling class' or 'elite' (which is more exclusive, more closed to outsiders). Nevertheless, Goldthorpe argued that the service class was a highly privileged group and so he felt justified in regarding the service class and the working class as representing opposite ends of the hierarchy of privilege. The intermediate class occupies a much more ambiguous position somewhere in the middle of the hierarchy.

Patterns of social mobility

Goldthorpe's findings challenge the conventional wisdom on mobility. This conventional view was largely derived from empirical research (eg Glass, 1954) and various sociological theories. It consisted of three main statements.

1 **Closure thesis** This argues that the service class is largely self-recruiting, reserving its privileged positions for its own offspring. It does this by closing its ranks to newcomers from lower social classes. But Goldthorpe found that only a minority of the service class had been born into it, so this class was only partly successful in guarding its privileges.

2 **Buffer zone thesis** This argues that the occupations clustered tightly around the manual/nonmanual zone act as a kind of brake which prevents long range mobility. People who are mobile across the manual/nonmanual line are usually 'absorbed' into this zone (eg people downwardly mobile from nonmanual classes often end up in the skilled manual class, while people upwardly mobile from manual classes usually end up in the lower ranks of white collar occupations). In Goldthorpe's survey, however, the newcomers to the service class had been drawn from all the other social classes. As many as 28.5% of those currently in class 1 had been born in classes 6 and 7, so long range mobility was not so unusual after all.

3 **Counterbalancing thesis** This argues that, in the postwar period, the chances of intergenerational mobility have increased but the chances of intragenerational mobility have declined. Goldthorpe found only limited support for this. Certainly there were signs that employers were increasingly relying on the direct recruitment of highly qualified and educated individuals (rather than recruiting people who had worked their way up through the ranks). But intragenerational

mobility had been just as important as intergenerational mobility for the men in the Oxford study sample.

Absolute and relative mobility Absolute mobility refers to the total mobility which takes place in a society (Crompton, 1993). It is measured by figures in a mobility table (see Activity 10) which reveal the numbers of individuals within each class who have been socially mobile. Goldthorpe's survey found surprisingly high rates of absolute mobility and the main reason for this was the transformation of the occupational structure of postwar Britain. There had been an enormous expansion in the number of service class and intermediate jobs and this had created more room at the 'top'. So, compared with previous generations, working class people now had a better chance of moving upwards. For example, in 1900 the sons of miners had a slim chance of becoming middle class but by 1970 their chances of upward mobility had improved considerably. Thus, absolute mobility rates had increased.

Relative mobility rates, on the other hand, are calculated by comparing the mobility prospects of different social groups at the same point in time. In the year 1970, for example, there may have been room at the 'top' but some social groups were more likely than others to fill these places. Someone born into the middle class had a good chance of getting a middle class job but someone born into an unskilled manual family had a slimmer chance of becoming middle class. This can be expressed in terms of the 1:2:4 rule - whatever the chance of a working class boy reaching the service class, a boy from the intermediate class has twice the chance and a boy from the service class four times the chance. So relative mobility rates measure the chances of one group *relative* to other groups. And whereas Goldthorpe argued that absolute mobility prospects had improved, he suggested there had been little change in relative mobility rates. The odds were still weighted in favour of those from the higher classes and so equality of opportunity had not been achieved. Britain was no more 'fluid' or 'open' than it had been in the interwar period. Goldthorpe concluded that 'No significant reduction in class inequalities has in fact been achieved' (Goldthorpe, 1980, p252).

Goldthorpe's original study was conducted in 1972 but in a second edition (Goldthorpe, 1987) he was able to update it by drawing on data from the *British General Election Survey* of 1983. Goldthorpe concluded that the mobility chances of the working class had become more polarised. On the one hand, their chances of moving into the service class had improved (both in absolute and relative terms). On the other hand, the economic recessions since 1972 had created a higher risk of unemployment.

Debates

The Oxford mobility study sparked off a number of controversies and debates (for feminist criticisms see pp145-147). For example, Goldthorpe has been accused of offering an exceptionally gloomy and pessimistic picture of social mobility in Britain. The Scottish mobility study (Payne, 1987) placed more emphasis on mobility between *occupations* rather than between *social classes*. This investigation resulted in even higher estimates of absolute mobility rates. Also, it concluded that *relative* class inequalities had been 'modified' to a certain extent. According to Payne, British society is less 'closed' and static than Goldthorpe believes.

Likewise, Saunders (1990) takes issue with Goldthorpe's view that nothing has really changed. Saunders claims that Goldthorpe 'moved the goalposts' in an unjustifiable way. After discovering that mobility rates were higher than expected, Goldthorpe proceeded to dismiss their significance by insisting that only relative rates really mattered. But Saunders argues that improvements in absolute rates cannot be dismissed quite so easily. Capitalism may not have eliminated class inequalities but it has certainly opened up new opportunities for advancement. If this has brought benefits to the middle class as well as the working class, then this is a matter for further celebration (it would be petty to insist that the only gains that count are where some group loses while another group wins). In addition, Saunders challenges Goldthorpe's assumption that abilities and talents are randomly distributed across all social groups. Goldthorpe seems to deny that 'natural' inequalities play a part in deciding class destinies. 'If, for example, the working class accounts for half of the population, then for Goldthorpe...we should expect half of all doctors, managers and top civil servants to have originated in the working class' (Saunders, 1990, p83). Against this, Saunders maintains that talents are unevenly distributed across social classes. The most talented usually end up in the higher social classes and they tend to pass on some of their genetic advantages to their offspring. So differences in relative mobility rates cannot be totally attributed to class 'injustices'.

Summary

1 There are different types of social mobility: upward and downward, intergenerational and intragenerational.

2 Changes in the occupational structure have created greater chances of (absolute) mobility.

3 Sociologists disagree about whether Britain is now a 'fairer' society. Relative mobility rates show that social groups have varying prospects for getting the best jobs.

Activity 10 Ups and Downs

Item A *Outflows*

This 'outflow' table (of intergenerational mobility) shows the eventual class destinations (horizontal rows) of people born into a given social class (left hand vertical column). Thus, of all sons originating in social class 1, 46% landed occupations in the same class whereas 5% ended up in class 5.

| Father's class | | | | Son's Class (%) | | | |
	1	2	3	4	5	6	7	Total
1	46	19	12	7	5	5	6	**100**
2	29	23	12	6	10	11	9	**100**
3	19	16	13	7	13	16	17	**100**
4	14	14	9	21	10	15	16	**100**
5	14	14	10	8	16	21	17	**100**
6	8	9	8	6	12	31	26	**100**
7	7	8	9	6	13	25	32	**100**

Item B *Inflows*

This 'inflow' table (of intergenerational mobility) shows the social class origins of people within each social class. Thus, if we take class 4 (top row), then we find that 7% of the people in this class had fathers from class 1, 27% from class 4.

| Father's class | | | | Son's Class (%) | | | |
	1	2	3	4	5	6	7
1	25	12	10	7	3	2	2
2	13	12	8	5	5	3	2
3	10	10	11	7	9	6	6
4	10	12	10	27	9	7	8
5	13	14	13	12	17	12	10
6	16	22	26	24	31	42	35
7	12	17	23	18	27	28	37
Total	**100**	**100**	**100**	**100**	**100**	**100**	**100**

Both tables adapted from J.Goldthorpe *Social Mobility and Class Structure in Modern Britain*, 1980

Questions

1 Read Item A.
  a) Describe the upward mobility patterns of people born into classes 6 and 7.
  b) Describe the downward mobility patterns of people born into classes 1 and 2.
2 Read Item B.
  a) Describe the class origins of people in the service class (classes 1 and 2).
  b) Describe the class origins of people in the intermediate class (classes 3, 4, 5).
  c) Which class is the most self-recruiting?
3 On the basis of Items A and B, would you describe Britain as a meritocratic society? Give reasons for your answer.

5 Class Maps

Key Issues

1 What are the main divisions in the class structure?
2 Does an upper class still exist?
3 Where are the boundaries of the middle class?
4 Is the working class becoming middle class?
5 What are the characteristics of the underclass?

How many social classes are there? What makes one social class different from another? What are the relationships between them? Some answers to these questions have already been given but this section attempts to set out a more detailed map of Britain's class structure. Crompton (1993) points out that there is no single 'correct' map of the class terrain. Rather, sociologists take particular views according to their individual research interests and theoretical loyalties. But for many purposes it is convenient to use a simple model of four classes: upper, middle, working and underclass. This is the basic approach which has been adopted by a number of sociologists including Giddens (1979) and Runciman (1990).

5.1 Upper class

The top group in the class hierarchy is known by a variety of names: upper class, ruling class, the rich, the Establishment, the elite or the capitalist class. It is not usually given a special listing in occupational scales and Saunders (1990) contends it is really too small to be regarded as a separate, distinct class. However, many sociologists believe it is an exceptionally important social group because of its immense influence and power.

The changing upper class Scott (1982, 1986) states that the origins of the upper class lie in early capitalist development when a landed class was formed. This consisted of landed magnates (large estate holders who lived mainly off the rent from their land) and landed gentry (those who either rented land from others or owned modest estates, and whose income derived from farming the land). By the eighteenth century this landed class was faced with new and powerful rivals in the commercial and manufacturing classes. A commercial class had emerged in the fifteenth and sixteenth centuries as urban centres grew and trade expanded and this class eventually became internally specialised into merchants and financiers. Alongside these commercial groups were the manufacturing capitalists, the industrialists and factory owners, who rose to prominence with the Industrial Revolution. So by the nineteenth century there were three relatively distinct upper classes: landed, commercial and manufacturing. But gradually these groups came together. 'By the early years of the twentieth century it was possible to speak of a unified upper class with its roots in the increasingly intertwined areas of land, commerce and manufacturing' (Scott, 1986, p4). They were united not only by shared economic investments but also by social, cultural and marital ties which resulted in similar lifestyles and values.

But does an upper class still exist in modern Britain? According to some commentators the upper class has more or less disappeared, its exclusiveness eroded by a tide of democracy and its wealth fragmented by inheritance taxes and estate duties. Against this both Scott (1986) and Giddens (1979) maintain that there is still a recognisable and socially cohesive upper class. This class manages to reproduce itself across the generations so that its members continue to enjoy massive economic privileges.

The rich The rich are a constant source of fascination for many people who follow their exploits in the gossip columns and glossy magazines. At present there are over 20,000 millionaires in Britain and at least 500 of them are worth £20m or more. Many of these rich people have origins in the upper class although each generation is joined by some newcomers. Giddens (1976) divides the rich into three main groups.

1 **Jet set or pop aristocracy** This refers to people who have earned vast amounts of money in the fields of media, sport or entertainment (eg Elton John, Andrew Lloyd Webber). This type of income is unpredictable and so the wiser ones invest their earnings in capital assets such as land or stocks and shares.

2 **Landowning aristocracy** Some irate members of the aristocracy claim that savage inheritance taxes have either destroyed their great estates or turned them into heritage museums for the fee paying public. But while it is true that the landed rich have lost some of their prominence they have hardly been taxed out of existence. The Duke of Buccleuch, for example, still owns 277,000 acres, mainly in Scotland. And 'old money' is still well represented in the *Sunday Times* 1990 list of the richest 200 which includes one sovereign, 8 dukes, 4 marquesses, 9 earls, 7 viscounts, 16 lords and 21 knights.

3 **Entrepreneurial rich** A common image of the rich is that of an idle, feckless group who live a life of unbridled pleasure and self-indulgence. But many of them are actively involved in business enterprise, management and directorships. The top 200 rich people are involved in fields such as retailing (eg Anita Roddick's Body Shop); property development (eg McAlpines); publishing and communications (eg Paul Hamlyn); banking and finance (eg Rothschilds); brewing and distilling (eg Guinness); and manufacturing (eg Pilkington). The fields of property development and retailing offer especially promising paths to the top riches but in recent years industrialists have been making a comeback (Beresford, 1993).

Upper class assets

The privileges of the upper class are preserved largely through the mechanisms of inheritance and culture.

Inheritance The laws of inheritance allow upper class families to retain much of their wealth and this gives their children an enormous advantage in life. It is difficult to move from rags to riches but those who inherit significant wealth find it far easier to maintain or improve their fortunes. Harbury and Hitchens (1979) concluded that inheritance is the major determinant of wealth inequality. In the sample of wealthy people they studied over 60% had inherited considerable fortunes from their parents. On the other hand there are some signs that inheritance is becoming less significant at least as far as millionaires are concerned. In 1994 the *Sunday Times* list of the 500 richest people in Britain reported that 'old wealth' accounted for only 28% while the remainder had inherited very little wealth.

Culture As well as passing on financial wealth to their children the upper class also transmit 'cultural capital' (cultural resources that help people to make money or get ahead). Children born into this class learn to adopt its language, mannerisms, attitudes and values and this makes it easier for them to move in upper class circles. They are 'accepted' and sponsored by powerful people who share the same values. According to Scott (1991) the upper class consists of a series of intersecting status circles. What they have in common is a remarkable level of self confidence and a well developed sense of their exclusiveness and social superiority. This exclusiveness is reinforced by their close kinship links - not surprisingly, they tend to marry 'people like us' and people with 'money'. They are also connected by a network of prestigious social institutions: the public schools, Oxbridge (the universities of Oxford and Cambridge), gentlemen's clubs, fashionable haunts (night clubs, country house weekends), the social 'season' (Royal Ascot, Henley), favourite pursuits (riding, shooting) and influential magazines (eg *Tatler*).

Newcomers sometimes succeed in breaking into upper class circles but many of these newcomers are recruited from the public schools or Oxbridge and so they have already been socialised into the appropriate climate of values. And even if the newcomers are vulgar rich (*nouveaux riches*) they usually ensure that their children get an expensive education so that they can move effortlessly in the upper class world.

Gentlemen

Successful British capitalists, politicians and officials have always been driven by the social goal of becoming *gentlemen*, apeing the lifestyle of the English aristocrat. A gentleman does not try too hard; is understated in his approach to life; celebrates sport, games and pleasure; he is fair-minded; he has good manners; is steady under fire. A gentleman's word is his bond; he does not lie; takes pride in being practical; distrusts foreigners; is public spirited; and above all keeps his distance from those below him.

W.Hutton *The State We're In*, 1995, p114

Activity 11 Rich and Famous

Item A *Pop aristocracy*

Paul McCartney, pop star, age 51. Worth £400m (24th richest in Britain).

Ex-Beatle McCartney has earned a fortune in royalties from his hit songs. He owns substantial interests in music and entertainment companies. But he prefers a simple life. His children are state educated and he commutes to London by train. He rarely goes out, preferring home cooked vegetarian stews and mineral water. He drives a Range Rover and lives in a Sussex farmhouse, with another house in London and an estate on the Mull of Kintyre. His wife Linda Eastman is a substantial heiress in her own right.

Paul McCartney

Item B *Landowning aristocracy*

Duke of Westminster, landowner, age 42. Worth £1,500m (7th richest in Britain). Gerald Grosvenor, sixth Duke of Westminster, owes much of his wealth to the 300 acres of Mayfair owned by the Grosvenor estate. The family estate also includes 13,000 acres near Chester, the family home (Eaton Hall),

Duke of Westminster

100,000 acres of Scottish forest, a huge tract of County Fermanagh in Northern Ireland, 12,000 acres of Vancouver, Hawaii office blocks and a 10,000 acre Australian sheep station. Despite gaining only two O levels at Harrow, the Duke has shown a shrewd business brain in handling his empire. He commutes from Eaton Hall to London by his own executive jet. He supports over 150 charities and his wife, Natalia, is godmother to Prince William.

Elites

One way of assessing the power of the upper class is through the study of elites (people who fill the top positions in each of the major institutions of society). Most of the sociological debates have centred around economic elites and political elites.

Economic elites The wealth of the upper class may appear to give it tremendous economic power but some social scientists argue that in the modern age it has lost control of industry and the economy. This view is called the *managerial revolution* thesis (Berle and Means, 1932) and its basic argument is that 'ownership' and 'control' have been separated. The day to day running of the economy has passed from wealthy owners to technically qualified experts and managers. This thesis gained fresh popularity in the postwar period (eg Dahrendorf, 1959). It was argued that economic power had effectively been 'democratised' and that the new managers were less concerned with the ruthless pursuit of profits and more concerned with social responsibility. More recently, the thesis was updated by Abercrombie and Urry (1983) who suggest that a new 'service class' (based on knowledge) is taking over the functions of controlling and directing capital.

The thesis seems to be supported by the growth of huge organisations and transnational companies which require large management teams. Moreover, these companies have had to raise enormous amounts of capital through the share market and so this has led to ownership becoming more dispersed. For example, many members of the general public bought shares in privatised utilities (eg gas, electricity, water) in the 1980s and 1990s. More significant, however, is the steady rise of institutional shareholders (eg pension funds, insurance companies and banks). This signals a corresponding decline in firms where a dominant family owns all, or a large majority, of the company shares. In modern large companies the wealthy private investors tend to own only a minority of shares and control is passed to professional managers who act on behalf of all shareholders. (See also pp322-323).

Criticisms A number of criticisms have been levelled at the managerial revolution thesis. First, there are a number of large companies (eg Guinness, Sainsbury, Laing) where families still hold high concentrations of shares. Scott (1986) estimates that over half of the top 250 enterprises in Britain have 'dominant' shareholders and in almost half of these cases this shareholder is an individual or family. Secondly, even when private shareholders own only a minority of shares this may be enough to give them effective control of strategic company decisions since the rest of the shareholders are often unorganised or apathetic. Thirdly, it is unlikely that managers can be totally indifferent to market forces or the wishes of wealthy shareholders. Besides, these managers usually own shares in the company they work for and so they are strongly motivated to increase company profits.

Scott (1986) recognises that there has been a fundamental transformation of property ownership towards more impersonal forms of shareholding. But he concludes that the managerial revolution thesis is flawed and he offers an alternative model. He suggests that the control of business enterprises is now exercised by a 'constellation of interests' which includes large shareholders (entrepreneurial capitalists) and managers (internal capitalists). It also includes finance capitalists, those who hold top posts in important financial institutions (banks, pension funds etc). All these interests come together in the company board of directors where the strategic decisions are made. Moreover, this control is reinforced by a system of interlocking directorships (directors in one company are often directors in other companies as well) which allows the key participants to exert widespread influence in the economy as a whole. The individuals who form this network (Scott calls them the 'business class') are few in number and Scott estimates that the core is a tiny 0.1% of the population. They are recruited largely from the upper class or, if they were originally 'outsiders', they soon become members of it. (For further discussion of elite theories, see pp206-209).

Political elites

Pluralism Pluralists (eg Hall et al, 1975) argue that Britain is a representative democracy in which power is widely dispersed rather than monopolised by a dominant group. They claim that democracy is safeguarded by the prevailing culture of political liberty (which encourages freedom of speech) and by the regular provision of free elections (which ensures that public opinion is ultimately respected). People are relatively free to form pressure groups or political parties to represent their particular interests. Admittedly some groups are more powerful than others. But there are many different elites (eg political parties, trade unions, business associations, pressure groups, voluntary organisations) and they must compete with each other for power and influence. Since no single group consistently emerges as the victor in these contests, power is never concentrated in one set of hands.

The pluralist model has been heavily criticised by many sociologists (eg Scott, 1986). It underestimates the extent to which social class is still a major factor in determining who wins and who loses. Powerful economic groups may not win on every issue but they often seem to win on key issues. Some issues (eg whether capitalism should be abolished, whether wealth should be radically redistributed) are not even treated as serious topics for discussion. (For further discussion of pluralist theories, see pp199-202).

Ruling class The orthodox Marxist position is that the capitalist class is also a ruling class (ie its economic power allows it to control the political state). For Marxists, the notion of a more or less 'neutral' state responding in a fair fashion to public wishes is merely a delusion. Rather, capitalists ensure the state protects their own economic interests. They enforce their will on the state either directly (by taking up the top political offices) or indirectly (through manipulation and threats). The state, then, is little more than the 'executive committee' or 'tool' of the bourgeoisie. Miliband (1973) identifies three main reasons why political power is usually exercised in a way that benefits capitalists. First, the common class origins of the top economic and political groups mean they usually share similar values and economic interests. Secondly, the economic power of the capitalist class means they can manipulate governments (eg by threatening to withdraw investment, by giving generous 'donations' to political parties or by using the media to circulate propaganda). Finally, Miliband argues that Britain still operates within a capitalist framework and therefore this sets limits on the extent to which governments can interfere with the privileges of the capitalist class. Just by following the 'logic' of capitalism, the government cooperates with, rather than challenges, capitalist interests. (For further discussion of Marxist theories, see pp209-214).

Power blocs Scott (1986) is critical of the cruder Marxist views on the ruling class. For example, he argues that 'not all capitalists are politically active, and not all leading holders of political power are drawn from a business background' (Scott, 1986, p7). Scott further refines the model of a ruling class by describing it in terms of a *power bloc*: an informal coalition of social groups (eg capitalists, government, trade unions) which is based on concessions and compromises between the different partners. The capitalist business class increasingly finds it can exercise power only by working through these coalitions. Nevertheless, it still manages to retain its dominant position, both economically and politically. In a later work Scott concludes that 'there is in Britain today a ruling class' (Scott, 1991, p3). He maintains there are two main grounds on which the capitalist class can also be regarded as a ruling class. First, its economic dominance is maintained by the operations of the state (ie the state does little to disturb the economic status quo). Secondly, its members are still heavily represented among the top political elite (and the power bloc).

5.2 Middle class

There has been a spectacular growth of nonmanual groups (Registrar General's classes 1, 2 and 3NM) in the postwar period. They accounted for 25% of the population in 1901 but this rose to 30% by 1951 and increased still further to about 51% by the 1991 census. However, it might be misleading to describe all nonmanual groups as middle class since there are significant differences among them in terms of pay, status, wealth and power. Runciman (1990) divides them into three main groups: *upper middle class* (higher grade professionals and managers, small business proprietors); *middle middle class* (lower grade professionals and managers, technicians); and *lower middle class* (routine nonmanual, clerical and sales occupations).

Roberts et al (1977) divide the middle class into two sectors of activity: the *old* and the *new*. At one time the (old) middle class consisted largely of the established professions (eg law, medicine) and the commercial classes (eg entrepreneurs, manufacturers, traders, shopkeepers). But the period after World War 2 saw an enormous expansion in the new 'salariat' (salaried public sector employees such as teachers, social workers and civil servants). Of course, this does not mean that the older groups have entirely disappeared. Elliott et al (1988) note the recent revival of 'traditional entrepreneurs' (small and medium sized employers and self-employed workers) and suggest this expansion is a sign of the difficulties of the economy. In many cases these businesses are a result of government incentive schemes or workers ploughing their redundancy money into new enterprises. Typically the hours are long and the rewards modest and many of these businesses suffer bankruptcies. Consequently, Elliott et al describe the modern petty bourgeoisie as an insecure group which is anxious about its declining power and status.

Drawing lines

Where exactly are the dividing lines between the middle class and other classes? This question has stimulated a number of sociological discussions including the *boundary debate* and the *proletarianisation thesis.*

Boundary debate Marxists have always found it difficult to fit the middle classes into their largely dichotomous model of capitalists (bourgeoisie) and workers (proletariat). As one critic points out, 'Either people own the means of production, or they do not' (Saunders, 1990, p17). However, one modern Marxist, Erik Olin Wright (1976), has tried to set out the boundaries of the middle class. Wright argues that the tiny capitalist class (only about 1-2% of the population) is characterised by its high degree of control in three areas: ownership, investment (direction of resources) and control over the way work is performed. This contrasts with the working class (50% of the population) who lack control in these areas. Within this basic capitalist-worker scheme, however, Wright identifies groups which fill *contradictory class locations* (contradictory in the sense that they do not fit neatly into the category of capitalists or workers). They are mixed types and they do not normally share the social cohesion of a more fully developed class. They may enjoy reasonably high degrees of control in one or other of the three areas Wright describes, but not in any uniform way. These contradictory class locations are small employers (between bourgeoisie and petty bourgeoisie ie the self-employed); semi-autonomous wage earners, eg university lecturers (between petty bourgeoisie and proletariat); and managers and supervisors (between bourgeoisie and proletariat).

Most sociologists remain unconvinced by Wright's classification. Marshall et al (1988) point out that Wright's 'semi-autonomous' group covers a bewildering range of occupations from lawyers and doctors right through to caretakers and cleaners! Wright introduced a later version (1985) containing twelve social classes based on types of 'exploitation' but this is just as complex and problematic as the earlier scheme. Moreover, Parkin (1979) criticises boundary theorists for emphasising 'structure' rather

than 'action'. They concentrate on class 'positions', 'locations' and 'boxes' and show little interest in how people act or in how they see their situations. We might reasonably ask whether small employers really regard themselves as being in a contradictory situation.

Proletarianisation What about the lower ranks of nonmanual workers? Are they middle class or working class? At one time the line between nonmanual and manual workers represented significant differences in career prospects, pay and status. Nowadays, however, it is doubtful whether, say, a shop assistant is really regarded as being in a higher class than a skilled or even a semi-skilled manual worker. The *proletarianisation thesis* (Braverman, 1974) goes even further. It suggests that an increasing number of nonmanual workers are suffering deskilling. Their skills are being eroded by automation, computerisation and the fragmentation of work tasks into simpler routines. So large sections of the middle class are becoming working class or 'proletarian'.

It is difficult to evaluate the proletarianisation thesis. Lockwood (1958) points out that every occupation can be ranked along three dimensions: *market situation* (pay, working hours, career prospects, job security, fringe benefits); *work situation* (authority relations at work, social relations with employers, extent to which job is supervised); and *status situation* (social prestige). Any verdict on proletarianisation requires a detailed look at trends in all three spheres so perhaps it is not surprising that British sociologists have arrived at differing conclusions. The thesis is supported by Abercrombie and Urry (1983) who argue that the main class division is no longer between nonmanual and manual but between the upper middle class and an increasingly proletarianised lower middle class. Also, Crompton and Jones (1984) discovered empirical evidence for the deskilling of female clerks. On the other hand Marshall et al (1988) reject the thesis as

Contradictory class locations

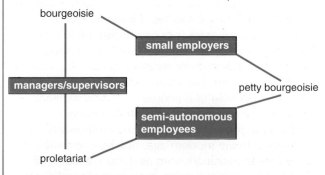

Adapted from E.O. Wright, 1976. The boxed classes are the contradictory locations.

far as routine white collar workers are concerned. In their large middle class sample they found that very few people had suffered deskilling. Moreover, compared with working class employees the majority of the sample continued to enjoy much greater autonomy in the way their jobs were performed. They tended to see themselves as middle class and they largely adopted middle class voting patterns. However, Marshall et al admit that it is not realistic to classify 'personal service' jobs (shop assistants, receptionists, supermarket check-out staff) as middle class. (For further discussion of the deskilling debate see pp328-331).

Service class

The 'service class' refers to the more privileged sectors of the middle class, a category which excludes routine nonmanual workers. The service class has expanded considerably in the postwar period and this growth reflects profound transformations in the economic and occupational structure (see Section 4.1). Indeed, in the 1960s and 1970s a number of social scientists (eg Bell, 1976) claimed that a 'post-industrial society' was emerging, based not so much on manufacturing as on the expansion of the service sector (eg financial and banking services, health and education, administration). Knowledge and information were the most valuable assets and therefore there was a greater demand for white collar workers and professional and technical experts.

Lifestyles Britain's middle classes get plenty of attention from novelists but surprisingly little attention from sociologists. One recent exception is the study by Savage et al (1992). These researchers claim that the service class is fragmenting into three main groups based on different types of 'asset'. *Professionals* rely mainly on cultural assets (eg knowledge, qualifications, values). They are successful in passing this 'cultural capital' on to their children who usually do well in education and proceed to the better jobs in society. *Managers*, on the other hand, depend on bureaucratic assets (organisational positions) which are more precarious (eg quite often their expertise is based on particular firms and so their asset is not so 'transferable'). The third group, the *petty bourgeoisie* (entrepreneurs, traders) is based on property assets (economic capital) which can be stored and transferred.

Savage et al note that people have contrasting images of the middle classes. The traditional image is that they are respectable, traditional and deeply conformist. In the modern age, however, the middle classes are increasingly seen as daring pioneers of exciting new cultural styles. Savage et al used survey data gathered by the British Market Research Bureau

in order to find out how the middle classes actually lived. They discovered three distinctive (but overlapping) patterns.

1 **Postmodern** This is the innovative pattern adopted by artists, advertising executives, stockbrokers and 'yuppies' (young upwardly mobile professionals). In some ways it is a contradictory lifestyle. They are interested not only in opera and skiing but also in stock car racing and 'street culture'. They have extravagant, self-indulgent tastes (eg Porsches, champagne, exotic holidays, expensive restaurants) but they are also influenced by health and fitness cults (eg dieting, rigorous exercise).

2 **Ascetic** This is the lifestyle favoured by people employed in education, health and welfare sectors. Typically they have high cultural capital (they are knowledgeable about art and 'high culture') but modest economic capital. They are ascetic in their tastes (eg their consumption of alcohol is low) and their leisure pursuits tend to be intellectual (eg classical music) and individualistic (eg hill walking).

3 **Managerial** Managers and government bureaucrats tend to be the least distinctive group as far as cultural tastes are concerned. They follow more staid and conventional middle class activities such as golf or fishing. They are also keen on the countryside and heritage matters (eg they visit National Trust houses, heritage museums).

Professions Sociologists usually define professions in terms of three criteria: a systematic knowledge base (which requires prolonged study), a service ideal (a strong commitment to the client's welfare) and a high degree of autonomy and control (eg over recruitment and standards). These characteristics are most pronounced in the traditional professions such as the church, medicine and law. But the twentieth century has witnessed a huge rise in the numbers of occupations which call themselves professions. Etzioni (1969) suggests that many of these new professions (eg teachers, nurses, social workers) are better described as 'semi-professions'. He claims that they are not entitled to full professional status (eg perhaps their training period is too short or they have not won sufficient trust from the general public). Nevertheless, it is clear that many occupations actively seek recognition as 'true' professions. Sociologists use the term *professionalisation* to describe this process. Aspiring professions (eg personnel managers, estate agents) typically set up advanced training courses, develop codes of ethics, declare their special concern for standards and ask for greater autonomy in their work. While this strategy may succeed in some cases, there are forces acting in the opposite direction (ie towards *deprofessionalisation*). For example, professionals are increasingly being employed in large organisations which sometimes restrict their autonomy and fragment their work into simpler sub-tasks. Also, the service ideal is slowly being eroded by 'market' forces (eg market oriented managers are becoming more powerful than doctors in the National Health Service).

Some sociologists argue that professions are altruistic bodies which perform valuable social functions (eg they serve the community and they protect the weaker members of society). Thus, Halmos (1978) celebrates the humanitarian achievements of the 'personal service' professions (eg doctors, nurses, social workers, teachers, clergy). He argues that these professions have a distinctive ideology based on compassion, a sense of service and faith in the goodness of people. This ideology inspires them to act in a dedicated and responsible manner which sets a fine example for the rest of society.

On the other hand, critics (eg Dale and Foster, 1986, Esland, 1980) accuse the professions of building up their own power and privileges rather than genuinely serving their clients. The service ideal is little more than a smokescreen which disguises the way professions advance their own material rewards and status. Professions have gathered excessive powers far and above those strictly required for the performance of their duties. Wilding (1982) declares that welfare professions have too many powers in policy making, in defining client needs and problems, in resource allocation, and in control over people's lives. Although the professions regard themselves as politically neutral, they fail to challenge the social system which creates most of their clients' problems. In this sense, professions are conservative bodies which simply prop up an unjust social order.

Activity 12 The Professional Classes

Item A *Mystique*

This is the Age of Disabling Professions when monopolistic professions have gained the power to decide our needs, shape our desires and undermine our confidence to handle our own lives. Ordinary citizens feel bamboozled by the mystique of professions and so we foolishly delegate responsibility for our lives to these so-called experts. Mothers do not feel they are truly capable of looking after a baby unless they have read the latest bestselling baby care book; people do not feel they really 'know' something unless they have an educational certificate to prove it.

Yet these professions have not improved our lives. Even after many years of compulsory schooling, people are unable to guide their own learning; doctors create as many illnesses as they cure; scientific advances such as the motor car simply mean that we spend more time in traffic jams.

Adapted from I.Illich *Disabling Professions*, 1977

The legal profession

Item B *Death*

A natural death centre, offering midwives for the dying, death exercises, recyclable coffins and a DIY guide to getting bodies to graveyards, is to open in London this month. Nicholas Albery, the founder, says his idea came from natural childbirth. 'There could be that same feeling of expectation, of transition, as at birth. Dying could be an ecstatic experience'.

Ms Speyer, a psychotherapist, said the centre aimed to bring in a new profession, a nurse-cum-midwife for the dying, trained in counselling, rituals and wisdoms of many cultures. She said regular death exercises, taken at any age, can help people live more fully because they will value every second.

Exercises will include meditation, breathing and 'visualising' one's own death. Tibetan and other techniques could help people to let go. Mr Albery said death exercises could be half a lifetime's work. 'We aim at all those who have just begun to get the first whiff of thinking about death, say those from 35 upwards.'

Adapted from W.Schwartz, *Guardian*, 16.4.91

Questions

1 Read Item A. Select one profession and show how it can be seen as 'disabling'.

2 Use Item B to support the following propositions. Professions are
   (i) disabling
   (ii) self-serving
   (iii) valuable to the community.

3 What aspects of professionalisation are indicated by Item B?

5.3 Working class

In the Registrar General's scheme the working class is represented by 'manual workers' (classes 3M, 4 and 5). Using this definition, it is clear that the working class has been getting relatively smaller. It accounted for 75% of the total population in 1951 but declined to less than half by 1991. Its absolute size, too, has declined (eg there were 15.25 million manual workers in Great Britain in 1951 but this dropped to 10.92 million in 1991). Roberts et al (1977) believe that the working class has become not only smaller but also more homogeneous. Internal differences in pay and status have declined and so it now contains fewer clear 'ranks'. Runciman (1990) identifies only two working class strata, the skilled and unskilled. On the other hand, some sociologists claim that new kinds of cleavages have opened up. Crewe (1985) draws important distinctions between the dwindling 'old' working class (council tenants, employed in manufacturing and the public sector and based mainly in Scotland and the North) and the 'new' working class (home owners, employed in the private sector, unlikely to belong to unions, and based mainly in the Midlands and the South). A more complex scheme is offered by Hobsbawm (1983) who suggests that the working class is dividing into 'sections' according to ethnicity, gender, region, housing tenure and consumption styles.

The working class has always been a major focus of sociological attention. The most celebrated example of this is the long running debate over the decline of the 'traditional' working class (see Chapter 11, pp394-395). In this section, however, attention is concentrated on two other sociological debates: the embourgeoisement thesis and debates about class consciousness.

Embourgeoisement

In 1958 the Prime Minister, Harold MacMillan, boasted with some justification that Britain had 'never had it so good'. Britain was leaving the era of postwar rationing and hardship and entering a new age of prosperity. Over the next few decades the rising incomes of workers allowed them to enjoy better living standards (eg car and home ownership, possession of consumer durables such as washing machines and fridges) and wider opportunities (eg foreign holidays). Indeed, certain sections of the working class seemed to be catching up with and even surpassing some middle class groups. This was called *embourgeoisement*, the process by which members of the working class seemed to be adopting middle class lifestyles and living standards. According to this view the working class were being upgraded (whereas the proletarianisation thesis had described the middle class as being *down*graded). If true, this had important social, political and economic

implications. Had workers finally settled their disputes with capitalism? Had class distinctions become irrelevant in the new 'democratic' age?

Affluent workers Goldthorpe et al (1969) tested the embourgeoisement thesis by studying affluent workers in Luton, an economically prosperous area with reasonably high wages based on growth industries. If embourgeoisement did not apply to Luton workers then it was unlikely to apply anywhere. The research sample consisted mainly of male manual workers in the Vauxhall car works and a chemicals factory, along with a smaller sample of nonmanual (mainly clerical) employees. This intensive study used a variety of methods (eg interviewing, observation) to gather data on things like political attitudes, work routines and community lifestyles. The findings were grouped according to the three main 'dimensions' of embourgeoisement: economic, relational and normative.

1 **Economic differences** The manual workers in Luton had relatively high earnings compared with other members of the working class but they did not earn as much as middle class groups (with the exception of clerks). Middle class groups had the additional advantage of greater job security and considerable fringe benefits. In Britain as a whole there had been very little redistribution of income and wealth between social classes.

2 **Class relationships** There was little social mixing between the classes in Luton. They were residentially and socially segregated and they were keenly aware of the status differences between them.

3 **Normative differences** This refers to differences in attitudes, values and outlook. The Luton researchers were particularly interested in attitudes to politics, careers and community.

   a) *Politics* Most of the manual workers still supported the Labour Party and the trade unions. Unlike 'traditional' workers (eg miners), however, their support was largely 'conditional' rather than unswerving. They were more willing to consider switching allegiance to the Conservative Party if it offered them a better economic deal (eg the prospect of higher wages).

   b) *Careers* The Luton workers were typically employed in routine assembly line work. Unlike traditional workers, their jobs provided them with little sense of pride or craftsmanship. Unlike middle class groups, they did not see themselves following a progressive 'career' involving a series of promotions.

   c) *Community* Traditional workers had a pattern of socialising with workmates outside of work and they had an active community life. In contrast, the affluent workers in Luton adopted a 'privatised' lifestyle based on the home and family (see pp396-397).

The Luton researchers concluded that the embourgeoisement thesis was deeply flawed, especially as far as economic conditions and class relationships were concerned. Class relationships are not fundamentally changed by a small rise in the pay packet or by the mere purchase of a washing machine. The thesis was more convincing in terms of normative changes (eg the attitudes of the 'new' working class differed in certain respects from those of traditional workers). But the affluent workers were not deliberately modelling themselves on the middle class or actively seeking to emulate them. Rather, there was a process of 'independent convergence' whereby sections of the working class happened to be moving closer to middle class lifestyles (eg home centred rather than community oriented). At the same time, the middle class was moving closer to certain working class styles (eg they were becoming more 'collectivist' in the sense of joining middle class trade unions).

Evaluation *The Affluent Worker* was a landmark study but it did not entirely escape criticism. A number of reviewers took issue with the researchers' apparent defence of the attitudes of the Luton workers. The typical worker seemed contented rather than militant and Goldthorpe et al felt this was a sensible attitude in the circumstances. Admittedly the Luton worker found little immediate satisfaction in his job but he was willing to tolerate this it in return for a wage packet which permitted a reasonably high standard of living. The car worker was able to find compensations outside the job which made it all worthwhile. But Marxist critics insisted that this was exactly what Marx meant by alienation! Westergaard (1970) argued that the only bond the affluent worker had with his work was through the 'cash nexus' (ie his reward was purely a monetary one and he derived little social or creative pleasure from his work). Westergaard speculated that affluent workers might turn radical if their wages were to fall. In fact, there was a strike at the Vauxhall car works shortly after the conclusion of the study! But Goldthorpe et al observed later that this strike was of short duration and workers very quickly resumed their normal relationship with their employers.

Regardless of these criticisms, the Luton study helped to discredit the embourgeoisement thesis and many sociologists concluded that the debate was more or less finished. However, more sophisticated versions of the embourgeoisement thesis have been developed since the original study was conducted. For example, Young and Willmott (1975) introduced the notion of 'embourgeoisement with a time lag' (what the middle class have today, the working class will have tomorrow). And Pahl's (1984) research on the Isle of Sheppey identified the emergence of a 'middle mass' in which the boundaries between lower middle class and the skilled manual class have become increasingly blurred. So it would be premature to declare that the embourgeoisement debate has finished.

Class warriors?

Is there a fundamental class struggle in Britain? Are the workers firmly opposed to capitalism? The history of the working class provides plenty of examples of collective resistance and protest. This class struggle includes trade union organisation, strikes, marches and demonstrations, Labour Party and left wing politics as well as 'everyday resistance' (eg sabotage, slowing down the pace of work) in factories and workplaces (see pp338-341 for a discussion of industrial conflict). The protracted miners' strike of 1984-85 is one of the most dramatic examples. Yet even in the most bitter struggles it often seems that workers are more interested in *reform* than *revolution*. For many sociologists, and especially Marxists, this poses a mystery. Why is the working class not more radical? These sociologists usually work with a model which links *structure* to *consciousness* to *action*. The line of argument runs as follows: since the working class is in a *structural* position of economic disadvantage it will gradually become *conscious* that it is being exploited and this will lead to political *action* in the form of open conflict and an attempt to overthrow the system. But British workers have failed to take all the steps in this model. They do not seem to have developed a particularly militant consciousness and they have not formed a popular movement which presents a truly radical challenge to capitalism. Consequently, many social scientists have hunted for explanations for this apparent compromise with capitalism. Marshall (1988) describes these explanations as falling into two broad camps, *instrumentalism* (or what Marxists call *economism*) and *ambivalence*.

Instrumentalism The argument here is that workers calculate that capitalism serves their long term interests. They willingly accept it because they recognise that it is an effective instrument for raising their living standards. So the occasional outburst of militancy (eg a strike) merely indicates a desire for a slightly larger slice of the economic cake rather than a desire to overthrow the entire social system. Marxist sociologists despair of this instrumental attitude because they are convinced that capitalism is a system which exploits labour and so it can hardly be in the workers' long term interests. But Parkin (1979), a Weberian sociologist, accuses Marxists of making arrogant claims to privileged insight (ie they claim to know better than the working class itself what is in its best interests). Parkin maintains that workers are perfectly sensible to side with capitalism because it really does offer them better prospects than any alternative system (the economic and political collapse of East European socialist systems perhaps lends some support to Parkin's views). Nevertheless, Parkin does accept that limited class struggles still take place *within* capitalism because of resentment at the unequal distribution of rewards.

Ambivalence Some sociologists (eg Newby, 1979) regard 'ambivalence' as the most accurate term to describe working class consciousness. Workers may criticise some features of capitalism, approve of others and remain largely indifferent to the rest. Their attitudes are seldom consistent and so they switch between contradictory viewpoints in confusing ways. The main point, however, is that the working class is neither fully committed to capitalism nor fully opposed to it. This has important implications.

1 **Dominant ideology** The ambivalence model casts doubt on the idea that there is a single 'dominant ideology' which successfully incorporates the working class into capitalism. Abercrombie et al (1980) argue that it is difficult to identify such an ideology in the modern world where there are so many different viewpoints and plural meaning systems. Thus, it is unlikely that the ruling class have really managed to brainwash the working class into an uncritical acceptance of capitalist values. This means that the Marxist concept of false consciousness needs to be questioned. Indeed, many Marxists now prefer the concept of *hegemony*. Hegemony is a matter of dominance by cultural and political means. It refers to the way capitalists use their superior resources (eg control of mass media and education) to win the hearts and minds of workers. They try to convince workers that the capitalist system is legitimate, normal and a matter of commonsense. But Gramsci (1971) notes that hegemony is a precarious thing since it is usually contested by rival groups with competing ideologies. The attitudes of workers are not usually fixed and so they can be 'won over' to different political positions.

2 **Informed fatalism** The Conservative Party has been successful in the last four general elections and so the long term prospects for socialism might seem rather bleak. However, if the ambivalence model is correct then the working class has not totally rejected socialist values. Indeed, survey evidence (Marshall et al, 1988) indicates that there is still a great deal of sympathy for the Labour Party. Marshall et al describe the prevailing mood as one of 'informed fatalism'. Many people have taken the realistic (informed) view that there was little immediate prospect for a change of government or of policies. To that extent they have resigned themselves to the status quo. But this 'fatalism' could be readily abandoned if a viable and electable Labour Party sets out attractive socialist alternatives. So Marshall et al's analysis shifts the emphasis away from class *consciousness* towards the issue of the most effective means of class *organisation*. They argue that the Labour Party needs to develop effective leadership and a coherent package of reforms in order to win back electoral support.

Activity 13 What About the Workers?

Item A *Working class action*

Demonstration against the poll tax (replaced by the council tax)

Strike by dustmen in Liverpool

Item B *Affluence*

Images of the working class include the unemployed teenager drifting about the inner city and the redundant miner from South Wales. But most members of the working class have seen their living standards rise markedly since the end of the war. Employed workers enjoy a middle class lifestyle and they have middle class aspirations. The spread of home ownership has brought more autonomy and choice and it has reduced collectivist attitudes. The accent now is on bettering oneself. The 1980s have seen videos, cars, holidays abroad and share ownership dominating the ambitions of the working class. Granted, the working class has kept its essential characteristics: the source of its income is wages (or social benefits); income levels are relatively low; and individual members of the working class have limited power and influence. However, the bulk of the working class does not share the squalor, insecurity and hopelessness of the poor, elderly or the unemployed teenager.

Adapted from E.Cashmore *United Kingdom?* 1989, p73

Item C *Insecurity*

Society is dividing before our eyes, opening up new fissures in the working population. 40% are *privileged* (this includes those in full time employment and secure self-employment; those represented by trade unions) 30% are *insecure* or *marginalised* (this includes people forced into part time or casual or temporary work; those with precarious or low incomes) 30% are *disadvantaged* (this includes the unemployed or economically inactive; people on government training schemes).

It is this segmentation of the labour market that is creating the new and ugly shape of British society. The fact that more than half the people in Britain who are eligible to work are living either on poverty incomes or in conditions of permanent stress and insecurity has had dreadful effects on the wider society. It has become harder and harder for men and women in these circumstances to hold their marriages together, let alone parent their children adequately, as the hours of work in which a decent wage can be earned grow longer and longer. Britain has the highest divorce rate and the most deregulated labour market in Europe, and these two facts are closely related.

Adapted from W.Hutton *The State We're In*, 1995, pp106-109

Item D *Respect*

Andrew Cavendish, Duke of Devonshire, age 73
A lot of people try and pigeonhole people by class. But class is like beauty, it's all in the eye. I think the class system is breaking down. Mrs Thatcher came from what used to be called the working class, and the aristocracy has ceased to be any force in the country. We are lucky here at Chatsworth (the family home, which has 175 rooms and is set in an estate of 11,000 acres). I have been described as paternalistic but the employees (175 in total) can see me on request with no difficulty. The forelock stuff has gone out and I like to think what binds us together is mutual respect.

Adapted from A.Cockburn 'Class of '93', *Observer Life*, 12.12.93, p10

Questions

1 a) How can the working class actions shown in Item A be interpreted?
   b) Evaluate the interpretations you have outlined.
2 Read Items B and C. What light do these items shed on the debate about embourgeoisement?
3 Read Item D. How would this passage be interpreted by the 'instrumental' and the 'ambivalence' models?

5.4 The underclass

The have-nots

The underclass is a disadvantaged and marginalised group at the bottom of society. The idea of an underclass is not exactly new but different terms (often moral in tone) were used in the past. For example, Marx referred to the lumpenproletariat (dregs, misfits, vagrants and thieves) while Victorian society expressed its disapproval of the disreputable poor. But the term underclass became popular with some social scientists in the 1980s. They saw it as a useful way of describing a group which is excluded from the prosperity enjoyed by the general population. In the USA the underclass was largely associated with racial and ethnic minorities (see pp103-106) but in Britain it was seen as more general. Dahrendorf (1987) estimated that the underclass comprised about 5% of the total British population but he warned that it was growing rapidly.

The idea of an underclass is controversial. Some sociologists claim that the underclass is really an integral part of the working class rather than a separate class in its own right. Moreover, they argue that the idea of an underclass diverts attention from the disadvantages experienced by the working class as a whole. The idea has also been criticised for stigmatising members of the so-called underclass by implying that they are to blame for their lowly position. Despite these criticisms, a number of sociologists still maintain that the concept is useful. They claim that there is an identifiable underclass and they argue it is foolish to deny its existence simply because of the dangers of unfairly stigmatising its members.

Features The underclass is defined by its economic, social and cultural features. In *economic* terms the underclass is materially deprived and impoverished. Oppenheim (1993) lists some of the reasons for the increase in poverty over the last decade or so. First, there has been an enormous increase in unemployment (between 1979 and 1986 unemployment tripled to over 3 million people). Second, the nature of employment has changed dramatically due to the increase in part time work and the rise of a low pay 'flexible' workforce, often engaged in temporary or casual work. Third, the number of single parent families has risen from 900,000 in 1981 to 1,300,000 in 1991. Most of these families are headed by women and they are highly likely to be low paid or unemployed, largely because of difficulties in finding adequate and cheap childcare. Fourth, the social security system has failed to provide adequate levels of benefits for the rising numbers of claimants.

The *social* features of the underclass are identified by Field (1989) who suggests it consists of three main groups: the long term unemployed (with ethnic minorities and women over-represented), single parent families and elderly pensioners. Of course, not everybody within these categories is automatically a 'member' of the underclass. Field adds that various psychological and social characteristics are important. For example, if poor people receive strong support from family and community then they are less likely to be trapped in the underclass and they will have a better chance of improving their situation.

It is the *cultural* features of the underclass which are the most controversial. Most social scientists agree that there is an extremely disadvantaged group at the bottom of the class pyramid but they disagree over whether its members have markedly different *attitudes* and *values* from the rest of society. This issue is explored in the following section.

Explanations

The debate about the underclass closely resembles the one on the 'culture of poverty' (see pp182-183). In both cases a decision has to be made on whether the main reasons for the problem are 'structural' or 'cultural' or some combination of the two.

Blaming the victim Some social scientists argue that the underclass are poor because they hold 'pathological' values (eg laziness, lack of self respect) which do not equip them for success in a competitive society. The members of the underclass are seen as victims of their own distinctive cultural values.This view is associated with the American political scientist Charles Murray (1984), but in some ways this is a misinterpretation of his position. Although he deplores the characteristics of the underclass he feels

that its members are behaving quite 'rationally' (rather than pathologically) by taking full advantage of an over generous welfare state. Murray directs most of the blame at misguided governments which provide too many benefits for the underclass. This encourages dependency and allows them to continue their unattractive and unproductive lifestyles. Murray advocates a policy of withdrawing or sharply reducing welfare benefits in order to force members of the underclass to take responsibility for their own lives.

According to Field (1989) a succession of Conservative governments has managed to persuade a large section of the British public that the problems of the underclass are due to the personal inadequacies and inferior cultural values of its members. Many people seem to believe that Britain is a land of genuine opportunity for everyone who is willing to work hard. The casualties of this society (the underclass) are therefore condemned as 'misfits' or 'failures' who do not really try to help themselves. Indeed, Oppenheim (1993) detects a revival of the Victorian distinction between the 'deserving' and the 'undeserving' poor. Members of the underclass are stigmatised and treated as undeserving because of their 'deviant' cultural values.

Blaming society Some social scientists reject the underclass concept because it is so closely associated with right wing views such as those of Murray. As a result, it is difficult to use the term without appearing to blame and stigmatise the victims. Nevertheless, a number of liberal and radical writers do accept that the concept of underclass is useful for exploring issues of social inequality. But they insist that the main reason for the existence of the underclass lies in the structural inequalities of society rather than the cultural values of the poor. The underclass share much the same values as everyone else but unfortunately their opportunities are severely restricted. In this view, the underclass suffers from an unjust or inefficient social order which fails to ensure a fair distribution of opportunities and resources. Thus, Field (1989) attributes the rise of the British underclass to the Thatcherite policies and economic failures of the 1980s.

Dahrendorf (1987), too, places most of the blame on structural factors, especially large scale unemployment and economic recession. Nevertheless, he allows for a combination of structural and cultural explanations. Structural factors explain the emergence of the underclass but after a while this underclass seems to develop its own cultural style. The longer people are part of the underclass, the more likely it is that they will become attached to its cultural values. They become accustomed to dependency and powerlessness and they slowly lose the motivation and discipline to improve their living standards. This view is echoed by another writer: 'Inactivity breeds apathy. Empty hours are filled with sleep, and days go by in a dull haze of television programmes and signing on. Sooner or later the unemployed become unemployable, and even when jobs are found they are swiftly lost' (Saunders, 1990, p124).

Citizenship

In many respects the underclass is excluded from full citizenship rights. This places its members at a considerable disadvantage since citizenship is one of the most important features of modern society. Marshall (1950) was one of the first sociologists to demonstrate its social significance. He argued that the previous couple of centuries had seen the slow but progressive establishment of citizenship rights in Britain. In the eighteenth century there was progress in civil rights (eg freedom of speech, property rights). In the nineteenth century the battle was successfully fought for political rights (although the vote was not fully extended to women until the early twentieth century). In the present century attention has swung towards social rights which are largely concerned with decent living standards and the provision of social services such as education and health. Social rights include 'the right to share to the full in the social heritage and to live the life of a civilised being according to the standards prevailing in the society' (Marshall, 1950, p11).

According to Marshall citizens are full members of a community and they enjoy common rights and duties. But is this kind of citizenship really possible in a class divided society? Marshall felt it was, as long as market based inequalities did not become too large. However, his optimism was challenged in the 1980s when the tensions between market forces and citizenship rights became more visible. Field (1989) argues that the long march of citizenship has been thrown into reverse with the recent expulsion of the underclass from the mainstream of society. Economic and tax policies have resulted in rising unemployment and a massive redistribution of income and wealth in favour of the rich. As a result there has been a considerable widening of class differences (eg in health and in educational achievement). The underclass now live under a subtle form of political, social and economic 'apartheid' and their severe problems are ignored by politicians and the general public.

Social justice Many of these themes are repeated by the Commission on Social Justice (1994) which declares that the foundation of a free and just society is the equal worth of all citizens. Citizenship is about giving everyone a reasonable share of income, wealth, food, shelter, health and education. But the Commission feels that too many people in Britain are being denied decent opportunities: 'Our survey of life chances reveals that opportunities are too often distributed not on the basis of ability, but of ability to pay; not on who you are but who your parents were; not on what you can offer but on where you live; not on the basis of merit, but on grounds of race or gender' (p30). Admittedly the government has recently introduced a Citizens Charter aimed at making public services (health, transport, Post Office etc) more responsive to public needs. But this limited conception of citizenship does little to help the more marginalised and vulnerable groups such as homeless or unemployed people. What they really need is a widening of social and economic opportunities so they can gain self respect and personal autonomy. So the Commission puts the case for a bold strategy for national renewal in order to ensure social justice for all.

Summary

1 The class structure of modern Britain consists of an upper class, middle class, working class and underclass. But there are important subdivisions within these classes.

2 In some respects the class structure has not changed very much (eg persistent inequalities of property and power). In other respects important changes have taken place (eg rise of more 'democratic' attitudes).

3 Class is *controversial*. There are fierce debates about the 'facts' and 'interpretations' of class structure. Nevertheless, these debates sharpen our understanding of important social issues.

Activity 14   It's the Poor Wot Gets the Blame

Item A   *Underclass or underfoot?*

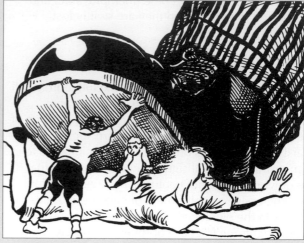

Item B   *The 'New Rabble'*

Characteristics of the New Rabble (the underclass).

- Low skilled working class, poorly educated
- Single parent families are the norm
- Dependent on welfare and 'moonlighting' (informal economy)
- High levels of crime, child abuse and drug abuse
- Great resistance to changing their behaviour
- Exploit welfare benefit system
- Unwilling to get a job
- Children have truancy and discipline problems
- Keen on violent and pornographic films

Adapted from C. Murray 'The New Victorians and the New Rabble', *Sunday Times*, 29.5.94

Item C   *Lower class*

(Judith Gardam, age 28, single mother who lives on state benefits)

It's just not fair being branded a scrounger.
It is a class war, they've got the money, they've got the education, they've got the jobs and they simply don't understand the life single parents lead. I'm sure if the Government sat down and spoke to me and had a cup of tea with me they'd get to like me. I have learnt about life, I know how to love, I have got compassion, I have feelings for people. But do they have any feelings for anybody but themselves? I want something better for the kids and I am attending college part time. But at the moment I feel I am lower than lower class. I am a single parent, a nobody.

Adapted from A.Cockburn 'Class of '93', *Observer Life*, 12.12.93, p7

Questions

1 What does the cartoon in Item A imply is the reason for the woman's situation?
2 Read Item B. Compare and contrast the ways in which 'cultural' and 'structural' theorists might interpret this list of characteristics.
3 Read Item C. What light does this passage shed on debates about the underclass?

References

Abercrombie,N., Hill,N. and Turner,B.S. *The Dominant Ideology Thesis* (Allen & Unwin, London, 1980)

Abercrombie,N. and Urry,J. *Capital, Labour and the Middle Classes* (Allen & Unwin, London, 1983)

Anderson,R.J., Hughes,J.A. and Sharrock,W.W. *The Sociology Game* (Longmans, Essex, 1985)

Barr,A. and York,P. *The Official Sloane Ranger Handbook* (Ebury Press, London, 1982)

Bell,D. *The Coming of Post-Industrial Society* (Penguin, Harmondsworth, London, 1976)

Beresford,P. 'Britain's Rich' *Sunday Times Magazine* 7.4.1989 and 8.4.1990

Berger,P. *The Capitalist Revolution* (Gower, Aldershot, 1987)

Berle,A.A. and Means,G.C. *The Modern Corporation and Private Property* (Macmillan, London, 1932)

Beteille,A. *Inequality Among Men* (Basil Blackwell, Oxford,1977)

Braverman,H. *Labour and Monopoly Capitalism* (Monthly Review Press, New York, 1974)

Breen,R. and Rottman,D. *Class Stratification* (Harvester Wheatsheaf, London, 1995)

Cashmore,E. *United Kingdom?* (Unwin Hyman, London, 1989)

Clarke,J. and Saunders,C. 'Who Are You and So What?' *Sociology Review* vol1 no1, 1991

Cohen, R., Coxall, J., Craig, G. and Sadiq-Sangster, A. *Hardship Britain* (Child Poverty Action Group, London, 1992)

Cooper,J. *Class* (Eyre Methuen, London, 1979)

Cotgrove,S. *The Science of Society* (Allen & Unwin, London, 1967)

Crewe,I. 'Can Labour Rise Again?' *Social Studies Review* vol1 no1, 1985

Crompton,R. and Jones,G. *White Collar Proletariat* (Macmillan, London, 1984)

Crompton,R. *Class and Stratification* (Polity Press, Cambridge, 1993)

Dahrendorf,R. *Class and Class Conflict in an Industrial Society* (Routledge, London, 1959)

Dahrendorf,R. 'The Erosion of Citizenship and its Consequences for Us All' *New Statesman and Society* 12.6.1987

Dale,J. and Foster,P. *Feminists and State Welfare* (Routledge Kegan Paul, London, 1986)

Dalrymple,W. 'Caste Wars' *Observer Magazine* 2.12.1990

Davis,K. and Moore,W.H. 'Some Principles of Stratification' *American Sociological Review* vol10, 1945

Davis,H. and Scase,R. *Western Capitalism and State Socialism* (Basil Blackwell, Oxford, 1985)

Dunleavy,P. 'The Urban Basis of Political Alignment', *British Journal of Political Science*, vol 9, 1979

Elliott,B., McCrone,D. and Bechofer,F. 'Anxieties and Ambitions' in D.Rose (ed) *Social Stratification and Economic Change* (Hutchinson, London, 1988)

Esland,G. 'Professions and Professionalism' in G.Esland and G.Salamon (eds) *The Politics of Work and Occupations* (Open University Press, Milton Keynes, 1980)

Etzioni,A. *The Semi-Professions* (The Free Press, New York, 1969)

Field,F. *Losing Out* (Basil Blackwell, Oxford, 1989)

Fielding,N. 'The Thatcher Audit' *New Statesman and Society* 21.12.1990

Fukuyama,F. *The End of History* (Hamish Hamilton, London, 1992)

Giddens,A. 'Elites', *New Society* 16.11.1972

Giddens,A. *The Class Structure of the Advanced Societies* (Hutchinson, London, 1979)

Giddens,A. 'The Rich', *New Society* 14.10.1976

Giddens,A. 'An Anatomy of the British Ruling Class', *New Society* 4.10.1979

Giddens,A. *Sociology* (Macmillan, Basingstoke, 1986)

Glass,D.V. (ed) *Social Mobility in Britain* (Routledge, London, 1954)

Goldthorpe,J.H., Lockwood,D., Bechofer,F. and Platt,J. *The Affluent Worker in the Class Structure* (Cambridge University Press, Cambridge, 1969)

Goldthorpe,J.H. *Social Mobility and Class Structure in Modern Britain* (Oxford University Press, Oxford, 1980)

Goldthorpe,J.H. *Social Mobility and Class Structure in Modern Britain* 2nd edition (Oxford University Press, Oxford, 1987)

Goldthorpe,J.H. and Marshall,G. 'The Promising Future of Class Analysis', *Sociology* vol 26 no 3, 1992

Gramsci,A. *Selections from the Prison Notebooks* (Lawrence and Wishart, London, 1971)

Hadfield,G. and Skipworth,M. *Class* (Bloomsbury Publishing, London, 1994)

Hall,P., Land,H., Parker,R. and Webb,A. *Change, Choice and Conflict in Social Policy* (Heinemann, London, 1975)

Halmos,P. *The Personal and the Political* (Hutchinson, London,1978)

Harbury,C.D. and Hitchens,D.M.W. *Inheritance and Wealth Inequality in Britain* (Allen and Unwin, London, 1979)

Haskey,J. 'Social Class and Socio-Economic Differentials' *Population Studies* vol 38, 1984

Hobsbawm,E. 'Labour's Lost Millions' *Marxism Today* Oct 1983

Hutton,W. *The State We're In* (Jonathan Cape, London, 1995)

Illich, I. *Disabling Professions* (Marion Boyars, London, 1977)

Jessop,B. 'The Future of Capitalism', in R.J.Anderson et al (eds) *Classic Disputes in Sociology* (Allen Unwin, London, 1987)

Joseph Rowntree Foundation *Inquiry into Income and Wealth* (Joseph Rowntree Foundation, York, 1995)

Kerr,C., Dunlop,J.T., Harbison,F.H., and Mayers,C.A. *Industrialism and Industrial Man* (Heinemann, London, 1962)

Lockwood,D. *The Blackcoated Worker* (Allen and Unwin, London,1958).

Marshall,G., Rose,D., Newby,H. and Vogler,C. *Social Class in Modern Britain* (Unwin Hyman, London, 1988)

Marshall,G. 'Some Remarks on the Study of Working-Class Consciousness' in D.Rose (ed) *Social Stratification and Economic Change* (Hutchinson, London, 1988)

Marshall,G. (ed) *Concise Oxford Dictionary of Sociology* (Oxford University Press, Oxford, 1994)

Marshall,T.H. *Citizenship and Social Class* (Cambridge University Press, Cambridge, 1950)

Martin,P. 'The Concept of Class' in R.J.Anderson et al (eds) *Classic Disputes in Sociology* (Allen & Unwin, London, 1987)

de Mello,A. *The Heart of the Enlightened* (Fontana, London, 1989)

Miliband,R. *The State in Capitalist Society* (Quartet, London, 1973)

Murray,C. *Losing Ground* (Basic Books, New York, 1984)

Newby,H. *The Deferential Worker* (Penguin, Harmondsworth, 1979)

Oppenheim,C. *Poverty: The Facts* (Child Poverty Action Group, London, 1993)

Pahl,R.E. *Divisions of Labour* (Basil Blackwell, Oxford, 1984)

Pahl,R. 'Is the Emperor Naked?' *International Journal of Urban and Regional Research*, vol 13, 1989

Parkin,F. *Marxism and Class Theory* (Tavistock, London, 1979)

Payne,G. *Mobility and Change in Modern Society* (Macmillan, London, 1987)

Reid,I. *Social Class Differences in Britain* (Fontana, Glasgow, 1989)

Roberts,K., Cook,F., Clark,S. and Semeonoff,E. *The Fragmentary Class Structure* (Heinemann, London, 1977)

Royal Commission on the Distribution of Income and Wealth *An A to Z of Income and Wealth* (HMSO, London, 1979)

Runciman,W.G. 'How Many Classes Are There in Contemporary British Society?' *Sociology* vol 4 no 3, 1990

Saunders,P. *Social Class and Stratification* (Routledge, London,1990)

Saunders,P. *A Nation of Home Owners* (Unwin Hyman, London,1990a)

Savage,M., Barlow,J., Dickens,P. and Fielding,T. *Property, Bureaucracy and Culture* (Routledge, London, 1992)

Scase,R. *Class* (Open University Press, Buckingham, 1992)

Scott,J. *The Upper Classes* (Macmillan, London, 1982)

Scott,J. 'Does Britain Still Have a Ruling Class?' *Social Studies Review* vol 2 no 1, 1986

Scott,J. 'The Debate on Ownership and Control' *Social Studies Review* vol 1 no 3, 1986a

Scott,J. *Who Rules Britain?* (Polity, Cambridge, 1991)

Scott,J. *Poverty and Wealth* (Longman, Harlow, 1994)

Sennett,R. and Cobb,J. *The Hidden Injuries of Class* (Cambridge University Press, Cambridge, 1972)

Townsend,P. and Davidson,N. *The Black Report* (Penguin, Harmondsworth, 1982)

Tumin,M. *Social Stratification* (Prentice-Hall, New Jersey,1967)

Turner,B. *Status* (Open University Press, Milton Keynes, 1988)

Weber,M. 'Class, Status, Party', in H.Gerth and C.W.Mills (eds) *From Max Weber* (Routledge, London, 1948)

Westergaard,J. 'The Rediscovery of the Cash Nexus' in R.Miliband and J.Saville (eds) *The Socialist Register* (Merlin Press, London, 1970)

Westergaard,J. *Who Gets What?* (Polity Press, Cambridge, 1995)

Wicks,M. 'The Decade of Inequality' *New Society* 6.2.1987

Wilding,P. *Professional Power and Social Welfare* (Routledge Kegan Paul, London, 1982)

Wright,E.O. 'Class Boundaries in Advanced Capitalist Societies', *New Left Review* no 98, 1976

Wright,E.O. *Classes* (Verso, London, 1985)

Young,K. 'Class, Race and Opportunity', in R.Jowell et al (eds) *British Social Attitudes 9th Report* (Dartmouth Publishing, Aldershot, 1992)

Young,M. *The Rise of the Meritocracy* (Penguin, Harmondsworth, 1961)

Young,M. and Willmott,P. *The Symmetrical Family* (Penguin, Harmondsworth, 1975)

3 Race and Ethnicity

Introduction

The headline in today's newspaper announces new laws to ban discrimination between *races*. On page two there is a story about Britain's growing *ethnic* diversity. Turning to the middle pages we find the editor discussing government plans to reduce the numbers of *immigrants*, while the main feature covers the high unemployment rate among Britain's *minorities*. Finally, the sports pages report some recent victories by *black* athletes.

This quick scan of the newspaper reveals a number of things. First, it shows that Britain is now a multicultural, multiracial society (even if there is still some confusion over the precise labels we use to describe the various groups). Secondly, the presence of minority groups has considerably enriched our social and cultural life. Just look at the way we support black sports stars, dance to 'black' music or eat 'ethnic' foods, and think of the benefits we get from minority enterprise in the fields of commerce, industry and retailing. But thirdly, and less happily, there is still a disturbing level of racial tension and racial inequality in modern Britain. Indeed, some sociologists say that the main reason for looking at race relations is because of the *problems* they involve. *Racism* is an important force in our society. It is one of the main reasons why stratification tends to run along racial lines, with minority groups losing out in terms of wealth, status and power.

Yet for a long time sociology was accused of neglecting these problems. Just as feminists criticise 'malestream' sociology, so black people sometimes complain that sociology either ignores them or stereotypes them in harmful ways. Fortunately, this is less true nowadays and sociologists are starting to pay far more detailed attention to racial and ethnic issues.

Chapter summary

- The chapter starts with a profile of Britain's **minorities**: their names, composition and size.

- Attention then shifts to the issue of **racism**: its definition, extent, causes and solutions.

- The final part explores the relationship between **race** and **class** by introducing relevant stratification theories and concepts.

1 Britain's Minorities

Key Issues

1 What are the most suitable terms for describing and classifying Britain's minorities?
2 What are the main ethnic minority groups?
3 Why are numbers so important?

1.1 Getting the name right

It is not only newspaper editors who are puzzled by the wide choice of terms and classifications in the field of race relations. Sociologists, too, find it difficult to settle on an agreed set of labels. They use a number of overlapping classifications, each giving a different breakdown of the population. This lack of consensus can be a problem since it causes sociologists to disagree about the precise number of groups, the exact position of the dividing line between them and other related issues. On the other hand, Banton (1987) feels this flexibility is actually a good thing. It gives members of minority groups some freedom to choose the labels they prefer rather than having a single set of terms imposed on them. So, at different times and in different contexts, a person might choose the label 'black' or 'British' or 'black British' or some other term altogether. Banton feels that using a variety of names helps to reduce racial tensions by softening the boundaries between groups. However, Banton also recognises that rival classifications are based on rather different sets of assumptions, many of which are highly suspect. This can be illustrated by looking at the most common terms: races, black- white groups, ethnic groups, immigrants and minorities.

Races

Biological definitions In the nineteenth century a number of scientists hit on the idea of classifying humans into separate 'racial' types on the basis of their inherited biological and physical features (eg nasal shape, hair type, eye slant, lip form and skin colour). Different schemes were proposed, including the now familiar one based on Mongoloid, Negroid and Caucasoid groups (see illustrations). These scientists assumed that racial characteristics were more or less 'fixed' and so the boundaries between 'pure' races were permanent and rigid. Moreover, they believed that the biological properties of races were the main cause of their different moral, cultural and intellectual achievements. So they proceeded to rank the races in a hierarchy of superiority-inferiority. Not surprisingly, the rapid strides of Western European nations at that time made a convincing case for placing 'white' races at the 'superior' end! The spectacular growth of the British Empire apparently demonstrated the truth of Darwin's theory of evolution and the 'survival of the fittest'.

But these classifications were developed before the discoveries of modern genetics which have transformed our understanding of biology and heredity. Modern research now reveals that the assumptions behind the race classifications were severely flawed. For instance, it makes little scientific sense to talk about separate races: there is great genetic diversity *within* these so-called races, and a great deal of genetic overlap and continuity *between* them. Besides, they can hardly be fixed or pure since genetic characteristics are constantly altering (eg through mutations, interbreeding etc). Most importantly, modern genetics undermines the notion of 'innate' racial superiority since there is no evidence that racial differences have a direct effect on behaviour and culture. In fact, the race concept has been described as 'pre-scientific and pseudo-scientific...Skin pigmentation has nothing at all to do with

The Caucasoid group covers the white inhabitants of Europe but it also includes Arabs and the brown-skinned people of India.

The Negroid group includes black people from sub-Saharan Africa and the West Indies.

"civilisation", or intelligence, or energy, or creativity, or any kind of skill' (Fryer, 1988, p61).

Social definitions Racial differences in the *physical* sense have little explanatory value for sociologists. Indeed, there is absolutely no need to refer to biological evidence in order to understand race relations. These relations are shaped by *social* factors. The physical features of race are not important in themselves - they enter into social life only if people *think* they are important and act on that belief. This is why sociologists are more interested in the *folk* or social meanings of race (Banton, 1979). What do people think and feel about the physical differences of race? How does it fit into their commonsense views? Both Banton and Miles (1982) use the term *racialisation* to describe the way people 'frame' the social world in racial terms. People *construct* racial categories which they then impose on their own and other groups. They use physical appearance to mark out the social boundaries between groups. And they draw the false conclusion that the moral and intellectual achievements of groups are a result of their physical features.

These commonsense views on race may be unscientific but clearly they have very real consequences for the groups concerned. When sociologists refer to races, therefore, they are normally using the term in the social rather than biological sense. But there is a danger of confusing the two meanings, and some sociologists put the term in inverted commas as a way of distancing themselves from the older, pseudo-scientific assumptions. Miles (1982) prefers the even bolder solution of abandoning the term altogether because it is unscientific and because of its dangerous association with outdated notions (eg racial superiority). But it is difficult to see how we can talk

The Mongoloid group includes American Indians, Tibetans, Eskimos, Polynesians and people from North and East Asia.

about 'racism' (or even 'racialisation') without implying the existence of some sort of (socially constructed) 'race' categories. Besides, the term is well established and widely used (eg in the Race Relations Acts) and so it is unlikely that it will vanish overnight. As Banton and Harwood (1975) observe, it is not so much the *term* that is important as the *assumptions* which lie behind it.

Activity 1   Mind Your Language!

Item A *P.C. 43*

© Posy Simmonds 1992

Item B *Political Correctness*

Political Correctness (PC) is a movement which first emerged in colleges in the United States in the 1980s. It regards all minorities as oppressed and places much of the blame for this on insensitive language. It seeks to 'empower' minorities by introducing new terms which treat them with greater respect.

Some PC examples (old terms in brackets):
  'chemically inconvenienced' (drunk)
  'horizontally challenged' (fat)
  'differently interesting' (boring)
  'follicularly challenged' (bald)

PC substitutes for 'white' and black':

whites	blacks
melanin-impoverished	African-American
person of non-colour	person of colour
'ice people'	'sun people'
(materialistic,	(humane,
exploitative,	communal,
egotistical)	caring)
genetically oppressive	genetically oppressed

Adapted from H.Beard and C.Cerf *The Official Politically Correct Dictionary*, 1992

Questions

1 Take two examples of PC language from Item B and consider whether they are an improvement on 'older' terms.
2 Give two examples of 'politically incorrect' terms not included in Item B which you consider offensive. Suggest some substitutes for them.
3 PC is very controversial. Give some reasons why people might object to it. Use Items A and B in your answer.

Black-white groups

Two worlds 'Britain is now two entirely different worlds, and the one you inherit is determined by the colour of your skin' (Rushdie, 1982, p418). This dramatic quote draws attention to the social significance of physical appearance. People tend to be *treated* differently according to social stereotypes about skin colour. Britain's cultural legacy includes many negative images of black people and so people with a dark skin are likely to be selected as targets for prejudice and discrimination. The black-white distinction also has strong *political* significance. Britain's minorities are really quite diverse and fragmented and this means each one is relatively powerless. So political activists have urged the various minorities to rally around the 'black' banner (after all, the wider society treats them all the same!). The hope is that this will create an effective and united movement to tackle the problem of racism.

Criticisms In spite of its popularity, this black-white terminology presents a number of problems. First, it is not always clear which groups are included in the 'black' category. What about 'yellow' groups (eg Chinese, East Asians)? What about people of 'intermediate' appearance (eg Cypriots, Maltese, Arabs)? And what about people of *mixed* parentage - are we to assume they are always black or *only* black? One particular source of confusion is the dual meaning of 'black': sometimes it refers to *all* minority groups, and at other times it refers much more narrowly to Afro-Caribbean groups. Secondly, the black-white distinction rests mainly on the way black people are *treated*, on their common experiences as victims of racism and discrimination. A contrast is drawn between the oppressed black minority and the dominant white majority. But maybe it makes more sense to classify minorities according to how they see themselves. Modood (1988) argues that people from the Indian sub-continent do not define themselves as 'black' - they have their own identity, history and tradition which separates them from, say, the Afro-Caribbean groups. And we cannot even assume that everybody from an Afro-Caribbean background shares the same social experiences or cultural identities (Gilroy, 1987; Hall, 1992). Thirdly, some critics claim that the black-white distinction is unlikely to improve race relations. Instead of creating harmony, it polarises the population into two factions and exaggerates their conflicts of interest.

In spite of these criticisms, 'black' is still widely used, both as a general term for *all* minorities and in a more restricted sense (eg the 1991 census used a 'black' category to identify African and Caribbean groups).

Activity 2 Black, White or Something Else?

Item A

**LABOUR SAYS HE'S BLACK.
TORIES SAY HE'S BRITISH.**

CONSERVATIVE X

A Conservative Party election poster (1983)

Item B *Mixed parentage*

Many people in Britain have a 'white' and a 'black' parent. But what do we call them? Research suggests that children of mixed parentage have positive views of their backgrounds and they usually classify themselves as 'mixed parentage', 'coloured', 'brown', 'half and half' or even 'half-caste'.

Adapted from B.Tizard and A. Phoenix 'Black Identity and Transracial Adoption', *New Community*, April 1989

Item C *Defining 'blackness'*

Elaine: 'I've noticed that some people give me and my mum dirty looks when we're out together - she's white. And a lot of Black men have said to my dad that he should stick to his own kind, and they've been really nasty about white people.'
Marcia: 'For me, as a Black person, when I see a mixed race person I treat them as a Black person. I can't really push them aside and say, "Oh, you're white or you're half caste." Elaine or anyone else, I treat them as Black people.'
Cynthia: 'There are some mixed race people who don't like to be classed as black. They say, "I'm not Black, I'm brown." The same is true of some Asians. They are Black but they don't want to admit that they're Black. It's because of some kind of fear of saying, "I'm Black". We live in a racist society.'

Discussion between some 16 year olds, in A.Osler *Speaking Out*, 1989, pp82-3

Questions

1 Why do you think the poster in Item A caused controversy?
2 Suggest reasons why the young people in Item B
   i) take a 'positive view' of their mixed parentage
   ii) are reluctant to classify themselves as 'black'.
3 a) Why are people nasty to Elaine and her mum? (Item C)
   b) Why do Marcia and Cynthia want to describe people with mixed parentage as 'black'?

Ethnic groups

Ethnicity and culture Ethnic groups are identified according to their distinctive *cultural* features (*ethnos* is the Greek word for 'tribe'). Jeffcoate (1984) defines an ethnic group as a comparatively small and powerless community whose culture differs in significant respects from that of the majority. Its members often have a strong sense of 'belonging' based on their shared culture and regular social interaction. Some of the *legal* requirements for a group to qualify as an ethnic group have been spelled out in an important House of Lords judgement (1983 Mandla vs Dowell Lee). This specified two fundamental criteria: a long, shared history and a cultural tradition of its own. This legal ruling also mentioned some additional 'requirements': a common geographical origin or common descent, a common language, a common literature peculiar to the group, a common religion, and minority or 'oppressed group' status. Under these criteria, Sikhs legally constitute an ethnic group but Rastafarians are only a religious sect.

Ethnicity is an attractive concept for sociologists because it draws attention to significant cultural and social features. This is important in a country like Britain where cultural diversity is quite marked. For example, an estimated 160 languages and dialects are spoken by children in London schools (*Ethnic Minorities*, HMSO, 1991). Also, the ethnic model opens up some interesting avenues for sociological research. It treats minorities as groups with their own independent values and preferences. When they try to set their own goals they sometimes clash with other groups, and many so-called 'race' conflicts are basically disputes over cultural disagreements (Ballard and Driver, 1977).

Mapping ethnic groups It is not easy to allocate people to ethnic groups. Culture is sprawling and untidy and so it is difficult to map the boundaries where one culture ends and another begins. Ethnic cultures change and develop and they 'borrow' from one another. So their boundaries are always shifting. Moreover, we cannot assume that each ethnic culture is internally uniform, with every member equally committed to the 'core' values of the group. Gilroy (1987) warns against the fallacy of 'ethnic absolutism': the assumption that once we know which ethnic group someone 'belongs' to we can totally predict that person's values and behaviour. Ethnicity is dynamic and flexible, not some sort of fixed 'essence' which we all carry around.

In practice, researchers are faced with a choice of 'marker' for mapping the boundaries of ethnic groups. Some choose to classify according to territory on the assumption that people from the same place will normally share a common culture. On this basis, figures are gathered on the numbers of people connected - through birthplace or descent - with 'New Commonwealth' (NC) countries (see Table 1). This is usually broken down further into regional groupings (eg 'West Indies') or particular countries (eg Jamaica). But many of these units are culturally diverse. For example, Trinidad and Guyana contain 'Asian' as well as 'Afro-Caribbean' populations; 'East Africans' may be 'Asian' rather than 'African' in origin; and 'Indians' may be Hindus, Sikhs, or Muslims. Consequently, some sociologists think it is more sensible to classify according to dominant *culture* or *religion* rather than territory (see Table 2). For example, Punjabi Muslims might have far more in common with Bangladeshi Muslims than they have with Punjabi Hindus.

Table 1 New Commonwealth (NC) countries

Eastern Africa:	Kenya, Malawi, Tanzania, Uganda, Zambia
Southern Africa:	Botswana, Lesotho & Swaziland, Zimbabwe
Western Africa:	Gambia, Nigeria, Sierra Leone
Caribbean:	Barbados, Jamaica, Trinidad & Tobago, Antigua, St.Kitts-Nevis, Anguilla, Belize, Guyana
South Asia:	Pakistan, Bangladesh, India, Sri Lanka
South East Asia:	Hong Kong, Malaysia, Singapore
Mediterranean:	Cyprus, Gibraltar, Malta
Remainder:	Mauritius, Seychelles, Falkland Isles, other islands and territories

Commission for Racial Equality *Ethnic Minorities in Britain*, 1985, p1

Table 2 Religions in the United Kingdom

**Estimates of numbers of people who
consider themselves within each faith:**

Christians	37.6m
Muslims	1.0m
Hindus	0.25m
Sikhs	0.25m
Jews	0.25m
Jains	0.02m
Baha'is	0.006m
Parsees	0.005m

Guardian, 30.4.1991

Minorities

A minority is 'a group of people distinguished by physical or cultural characteristics, subject to different and unequal treatment by the society in which they live and who regard themselves as victims of collective discrimination' (Wirth, 1945, p347). In any society we will find a number of minorities, based on such things as gender, age, religion, sexual orientation, physical handicap or 'deviant' behaviour. In this chapter, of course, we are concerned with ethnic or racial minorities. Sometimes these racial minorities are actually a numerical majority, as in the case of the black population in South Africa. So we are dealing with issues of *power* as much as numbers. The idea of a minority implies the existence of a more powerful 'majority' which manages to impose its will by marginalising the minority and preventing it from running its own affairs.

Policies Majority-minority relationships vary according to the sizes of the groups, their relative power and the policies they pursue. For example, the dominant group might follow a policy of assimilation (trying to incorporate the minority so that it loses its distinctiveness), pluralism (peaceful coexistence), or, in extreme cases, extermination. For its part, the minority might willingly adopt a policy of assimilation or pluralism, it might opt for secession or it might even try to gain dominant power for itself.

In Britain the term 'minority' is normally used in a loose, imprecise way and it is usually interchangeable with other terms (black, ethnic group etc).

Immigrants

History The British nation was shaped by successive waves of migrants including Romans, Angles, Saxons, Vikings, Danes, Jutes, Normans, Jews, Huguenots and Irish. These migrants were by no means exclusively white and Fryer (1984) states that black soldiers arrived in Britain with the Roman army even before the English (Angles) came here. Also, Walvin (1984)

notes there has been a continuous black presence in Britain for the past 500 years or so. As the British Empire expanded its economic, political and military links with the rest of the world, so the people of Britain came into closer contact with other racial and ethnic groups. Small communities of black people were gradually established within Britain itself. This was made possible by regular trading and shipping links or, more brutally, as a result of the slave trade. But these black communities were relatively modest in size until the post-World War 2 period when migration from New Commonwealth countries increased in scale. In the 1940s and 1950s most of these migrants were from the West Indies but in the 1960s their numbers were exceeded by groups from the Asian subcontinent. Later, in the 1960s and early 1970s, they were joined by 'East African Asians', a group of Asian refugees from the 'Africanisation' policies of Uganda, Kenya, Tanzania and Malawi.

Criticisms 'Immigrant' is a controversial term. It is often restricted only to black people or ethnic minorities. Yet most migrants to this country are white and this has been the pattern for a long time. Walvin (1984) estimates that something like 457,000 European refugees came to Britain in the years 1945-1950. By the time of the 1981 census, an estimated 3.4 million people were 'born overseas', and out of this total some 1.89 million were white (mainly from Eire, Europe, the United States and the 'Old Commonwealth' countries of Canada, Australia and New Zealand). In 1989 the International Passenger Survey recorded some 250,000 'immigrants' to Britain but only 23% of these were from New Commonwealth countries. Another problem with the term 'immigrant' is the way it is extended to *all* members of racial and ethnic minorities. This is misleading, since about 1,245,000 of them were born in this country (*Labour Force Survey* 1990-91). Overall, about 45% are British-born although the exact percentage for each ethnic group varies (see Table 3). It depends on the group's particular

Table 3 Population by ethnic group, country of birth, Great Britain 1984-86

Ethnic group	UK-born (%)
White	96
West Indian/Guyanese	53
Indian	36
Pakistani	42
Bangladeshi	31
Chinese	24
African	35
Arab	11
Mixed	74
Other	28

Labour Force Survey, 1985, 1986

migration pattern (the earlier the 'peak' of migration, the higher the proportion of British-born) and its age structure (the vast majority of those under the age of 16 are British-born, but older people are more likely to have been born overseas). Finally, some sociologists argue that the term 'immigrant' is increasingly irrelevant, now that we are in to 'second' and even 'third' generations of black Britons. It is also divisive and dangerous: calling people 'immigrants' might suggest that they do not really 'belong' here. This encourages hostility and resentment by portraying minorities as 'outsiders'.

1.2 The 'numbers game'

Why count?

Abuses of statistics Some sociologists question the wisdom of collecting statistics on Britain's minorities. After all, these statistics are not gathered within a neutral, impartial context where people have nothing to fear. New Commonwealth migration triggered a sharp reaction in Britain right from the beginning. The mass media and various politicians created a moral panic about the country being 'swamped' by 'alien' black intruders (Solomos, 1989). In such a low-trust situation, black people have every reason to fear that statistical data will be used *against* them (eg to justify further restrictions on immigration). Indeed, some researchers say that 'counting' black people already implies that they are a problem and that their numbers must be curtailed. When politicians reassure the white electorate that the black population is really quite small, they are in effect branding black people as undesirable. Yet it is unlikely that racists will be appeased by statistical proof that minority numbers are modest - they are far more likely to raise the stakes by demanding further restrictions or even repatriation.

Uses of statistics On the other hand, accurate statistics help to correct public ignorance. Surveys suggest that many white people regularly overestimate the size of Britain's minorities. For example, in one national opinion poll (Runnymede, 1991) half the sample thought it was more than double the actual figure and one third thought it was over four times the true figure. Without the routine collection of statistics it would not be easy to challenge such exaggeration. Also, statistics are needed in order to monitor the progress of ethnic minorities in fields such as housing, education, health and employment. If we wish to find out whether minorities are getting a fair deal in these areas then we have to identify them and follow their progress (or lack of it). Admittedly, the 'facts' of racial disadvantage have been known for a long time and yet there are very few signs of any political will to remedy the situation. Indeed, cynics say that the collection of data simply lends bogus 'respectability' to governments by pretending they really care about racial inequalities. While there may be some truth in this view, it must be said that there is still a shortage of *detailed* information about the socioeconomic fortunes of Britain's minorities. Besides, statistics *do* influence the development and implementation of social policies. Haskey (1991) reports that ethnic estimates have been used by local authorities in a number of ways: in policymaking and resource allocation in education and housing; in targeting of language programmes for minority populations; in allocation of grants under the Urban Programme; and in assessing whether authorities are fulfilling their responsibilities as equal opportunity employers under the Race Relations Act. And Gordon (1992) points out that statistics played a major role in revealing that young blacks were over-represented among those arrested under the controversial 'sus' laws (where people could be arrested on suspicion that they were about to commit a crime). This led to the repeal of these laws.

Activity 3 Swamped?

Item A

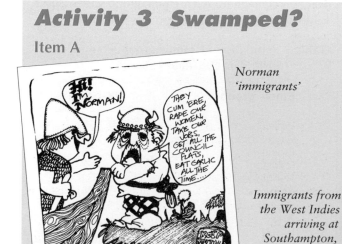

Norman 'immigrants'

Immigrants from the West Indies arriving at Southampton, 1962

Item B *Swamped!*

'There was a committee which looked at it and said that if we went on as we are, then by the end of the century there would be 4 million people of the New Commonwealth and Pakistan here. Now that's an awful lot and I think it means that people are really rather afraid that the country might be rather swamped by people with a different culture. And you know...if there is any fear that it might be swamped, people are going to react and be rather hostile to those coming in.'

Mrs Thatcher, interviewed on *World in Action*, Granada TV, and reported in *Daily Mail* 31.1.78

Item C *Cheated!*

Following Mrs Thatcher's speech, the *Daily Mail* published an article ('They've taken over my home town') on Roger Coultras, returning to his home area of Harlesden after many years living in Australia, only to find that it had a 'massive' 24% black population:

'He slumped against an old Victorian statue and said: "We used to have a community singsong round here on New Year's Day, whole families of people. We'd end up with a chorus of Auld Lang Syne." He shook his head, said he'd been robbed of his birthright, his roots. "I wonder how many thousands of Britons have been cheated in just the same way. And more to the point, how many millions are going to suffer the same fate in the future?".'

Daily Mail, February 1978, quoted in Barker, 1982, pp24-5

Questions

1 Look at Item A. Do *all* immigrants meet a hostile reception in Britain? Give reasons for your answer.
2 Do you think Mrs Thatcher (Item B) was right to use the word 'swamped'? Give reasons for your answer.
3 Do you think the *Daily Mail* article (Item C) is a 'responsible' piece of journalism? Give reasons for your answer.

Sources of data

1 Census Until recently, minority groups have resisted any question which asks directly about their ethnic origins. But the 1981 census included a question on the 'birthplace of the head of household'. This allowed an estimate of Britain's black minority population by counting heads of households born in New Commonwealth countries, along with the other members of their households. This was an unsatisfactory measure since it both over-counted (by including whites born in the New Commonwealth) and under-counted (by omitting those minority heads of households born in Britain). Haskey (1991) feels that these errors usually cancelled each other out. But he argues that birthplace is an increasingly unreliable measure now that a greater proportion of Britain's black population are British born. Fortunately, recent census tests have shown more favourable attitudes towards a direct 'ethnic question' and so this was included in the 1991 census. The 'ethnic group' categories (see Table 5) are a bit crude but the census is likely to become the most comprehensive source of detailed data on Britain's minority populations.

Table 4 Ethnic minorities as % total population

	1951	1961	1971	1981	1991
all ethnic groups	0.4	1.0	2.3	3.9	5.5

Office of Population Censuses and Surveys, 1993

2 Labour Force Survey (LFS) This is a random survey of private households in Great Britain and Northern Ireland. The sample is relatively small and it tends to under-represent people from minority groups.

Because of this, results are normally averaged over a three-year period in order to reduce sample error. But in 1992 some changes were introduced: quarterly (rather than annual) sampling, an increase in sample size (to about 250,000 respondents) and improvements in interview procedures.

Table 5 Ethnic population (Great Britain, 1991 Census)

Ethnic group	Numbers (thousands)	Percentage
White	51,843	94.5
Black Caribbean	499	0.9
Black African	207	0.4
Black other	178	0.3
Indian	840	1.5
Pakistani	475	0.9
Bangladeshi	160	0.3
Chinese	157	0.3
Other-Asian	196	0.4
Other-other	290	0.5
all minorities	3,006	5.5
Total population	54,860	

Derived from Owen, 1992

These changes should result in greater accuracy. The survey includes questions on country of birth, nationality and ethnic group. Members of the sample choose their ethnic group from a list of ten possibilities shown on a card (from 1992, this list was the same as the census classification). The LFS estimate for 1990/91 - an ethnic minority population of 2,677,000 - is not hugely different from the figure given by the 1991 census. But the LFS is useful for providing relatively up to date information in the ten year gap between censuses. Although it is concerned mainly with employment characteristics, it also covers things like birth rates, family size and age structure (see Figure 1).

Figure 1 Ethnic minority groups as a percentage of each age group of the population

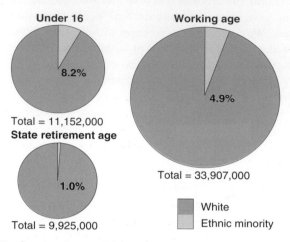

Under 16
8.2%
Total = 11,152,000

Working age
4.9%
Total = 33,907,000

State retirement age
1.0%
Total = 9,925,000

White
Ethnic minority

Employment Gazette, February 1993, p26

3 International Passenger Survey (IPS) This survey is based on a sample (between 0.1% and 0.4%) of passengers interviewed at principal sea and air ports in Britain. But it excludes the well-travelled route between the Irish Republic and the United Kingdom. Passengers are asked about citizenship (nationality), country of birth and country of last/next residence. It provides a count of 'immigrants' - those who, on arrival, have lived abroad for a year or more, and intend to stay in the UK for a year or more (and vice versa for 'emigrants'). This definition of immigrants is very broad and it includes au pairs, students and British citizens returning from a stay overseas. But at least the IPS reminds us that Britain also 'exports' population. In 1989, for example, there were 205,000 emigrants: 27% of these were bound for Australia, New Zealand and Canada; 22% for EU countries; and 15% for the United States.

Table 6 UK immigration and emigration (thousands)

	Old Commonwealth	India, Bangladesh, Sri Lanka	Pakistan	Caribbean
inflow				
1966	36	27	..	15
1971	52	24	..	5
1976	40	15	12	4
1981	20	18	9	3
1986	30	16	10	5
1990	57	13	9	7
outflow				
1966	166	9	..	9
1971	99	8	..	8
1976	63	4	2	3
1981	79	2	1	3
1986	50	4	2	2
1990	59	2	3	4

International Passenger Survey figures, reported in *Population Trends*, Winter 1991

Summary

1 There are several schemes for classifying Britain's racial and ethnic minorities. The choice of scheme determines the number and sizes of the groups.

2 Each of these classifications rests on special assumptions which are open to challenge.

3 There are dangers in collecting race-related statistics but they play a useful role in monitoring racial discrimination and disadvantage.

4 Sources of data vary in their reliability and scope but it is clear that Britain's minorities are both diverse and relatively small.

2 Racism

Key Issues

1 What forms does racism take?

2 Is racism a big problem in Britain?

3 What are the main causes of racism?

4 What steps have been taken to combat racism?

Racism is probably the central concept in the sociology of race relations. Yet Miles (1989) observes that it is a *contested* concept, with fierce disagreements over its *definition* and its *extent*. In this part, racism is defined in three senses: cultural racism, racialism and institutional racism. This framework is used to explore some important debates and issues.

2.1 Cultural racism

'Cultural racism' refers to cultural attitudes, beliefs and ideologies which are based on mistaken notions about 'racial' groups (Richardson and Lambert, 1985). In simple terms, it can be regarded as a cultural form of prejudice.

Table 7 Definitions

Prejudice
A negative or hostile attitude towards a person who belongs to a group, simply because s/he belongs to that group and is therefore presumed to have the objectionable characteristics attributed to the group (Allport, 1958).

Discrimination
The unequal treatment of groups (or individuals within them) in a way that is unfair and against the wishes of those who are disadvantaged by this treatment.

Stereotype
A mental image held about particular groups of people and constructed on the basis of simplified, distorted or incomplete knowledge of them (Cashmore and Troyna, 1983).

Ethnocentrism
Cultural short-sightedness: the uncritical assumption that one's own culture is 'natural' and 'best', and the rejection or misrepresentation of 'foreign' cultures.

Racism
There are certain routine practices, customs and procedures in our society whose consequence is that black people have poorer jobs, health, housing and life chances than do the white majority...These practices and customs are maintained by relations and structures of power and are justified by centuries-old beliefs and attitudes which hold that black people are essentially inferior to white people - biologically, or culturally or both. Racism is a shorthand term for this combination of discriminatory practices, unequal relations and structures of power, and negative beliefs and attitudes (Inner London Education Authority, 1983).

Prejudice

As Allport (1958) pointed out in a classic work in social psychology, prejudice is a style of thinking which relies heavily on *stereotypes*: sweeping generalisations which are highly selective and over-simplified. These stereotypes are usually factually incorrect, exaggerated or distorted, and this is why prejudice is unfair - it not only prejudges people, it also *mis*judges them. Allport divided racial prejudices into two components: unfavourable *attitudes* and mistaken *beliefs*. Attitudes are *evaluative* (eg 'I don't like Pakis') while beliefs are supposedly *factual* (eg 'All West Indians are work-shy'). Sociologists share this interest in attitudes and beliefs, but they are more likely to locate them in the wider *culture* of society rather than in the personalities of 'individuals'. Racial prejudices are not just something that individuals invent in their own private worlds. Rather, they are part of the cultural heritage of the society and they are transmitted across the generations. People are exposed to these attitudes and beliefs from an early age and so they can easily start to regard them as 'commonsense'.

Surveying prejudice Racist attitudes are not uniformly distributed across the British population. Some groups (eg extreme right-wing groups like the British Movement) willingly endorse racist views. But

many other people reject racism because of their religious, political or humanitarian beliefs. These differences are sometimes revealed by attitude surveys which take a sample of the population, give them questionnaires to tap their racial attitudes and then assign them a 'score' according to their replies. The sample can then be sorted into various categories (eg 'very prejudiced', 'neutral', 'tolerant'). Some sociologists criticise these surveys because of the way they focus on the 'free-floating' attitudes of individuals. Critics say they only offer a snapshot picture which does not tell us much about behaviour, group interaction, power or the social structure. On the other hand, sensitive surveys do provide valuable data (Cashmore, 1987). For example, they allow us to examine interesting attitude differences within and between social groups.

Racial ideologies

Scientific racism Cultural racism has a long history but it takes different forms according to time and place. The earlier section on 'races' contained one example, the 'scientific' racism of the nineteenth century. Banton (1969) says this doctrine assumed the existence of separate racial 'stocks' ranked in a hierarchy of superiority-inferiority. Obviously, this kind of assumption was politically convenient at a time of colonial expansion. After all, if black people are 'savages' or 'childlike', then white people are justified in colonising them and introducing them to 'civilisation'! This illustrates the *ideological* nature of cultural racism. Racist ideas are more than a simple matter of innocent 'errors': they are sometimes used as 'weapons' to promote the economic and political interests of particular social groups. Of course, people do not always realise that they are using ideas in this fashion. Ideologies help people 'make sense' of the world but they also tend to distort the reality (eg the notion of the 'white man's burden' disguised the considerable material benefits of the Empire for Britain). These distortions allow dominant groups to 'rationalise' exploitation in a way which reduces their sense of guilt.

Racist belief systems Nowadays scientific racism stands largely discredited but Rex (1986) notes that cultural racism can be expressed in other ways. For Rex, a typical race relations situation usually involves two or more groups locked in conflict (exploitation, oppression, discrimination etc). The dominant group tries to justify its privileges by circulating racist ideologies which present group characteristics as rigidly 'fixed'. This serves a dual function: it portrays the status quo as 'natural' (and therefore not to be meddled with) and it discourages movement between groups (which would dilute the privileges of the dominant group). In the case of scientific racism, the belief system was based on the false claim that the physical features of a race determine its moral and cultural achievements. But Rex identifies other kinds of belief system. For example, South African apartheid was partly based on 'religious' arguments (eg 'God created many mansions', 'slavery is the curse of Ham'). Racist beliefs do not even need to be gathered into a systematic doctrine - they may just exist at the rather confused and contradictory level of 'commonsense' and 'folk wisdom'. In recent years, however, sociologists have identified the emergence of a new and coherent form of racism: *new racism*.

Activity 4   Attitude Problems

Item A   *Cartoons*

THE BLACK BABY.

Mr. Bull. "What, another!! - Well, I suppose I must take it in !!!"

Mr. Bull. "What, another!! - Well, I suppose I must take it in !!!"
A 19th century cartoon showing Britain, represented by John Bull, and the new African colony of Uganda

'Yes, I'm on Social Security...No, I've never done a day's work in my life...Yes, I'm of Irish extraction...'

Isn't it lovely to see the kids playing with Josephine's little boy!

Gives you hope for the country, doesn't it?
Certainly does.

Right, let's play Mummies, and Daddies and servants.

A South African cartoon

Item B   *Survey data*

Data from the 1991 British Social Attitudes survey (Jowell et al, 1992)

Data 1 *How would you describe yourself?*

	(%)
very prejudiced	2
a little prejudiced	29
not prejudiced at all	68

Data 2 *How much prejudice do you think there is against Asians?*

	(%)
a lot	58
a little	35
hardly any	4
don't know etc	3

Data 3 *Respondents who would object to a West Indian:*

	(%)
as boss	12
in the family	44

Questions

1 a) Identify the racist attitudes shown in the cartoons in Item A.

   b) How can the John Bull cartoon be seen as an ideology justifying colonialism?

2 a) Look at Item B. Can you see any contradictions here? Try to explain this.

   b) The *British Social Attitudes* survey suggests that prejudice is more likely among men, Conservative voters and older people. Suggest possible reasons for this pattern.

   c) Data 3 indicates that white people are more willing to accept a 'West Indian' as a boss than as a family member. Suggest possible reasons for this.

   d) Can we trust attitude surveys to measure the 'real' level of prejudice? Identify the research problems involved.

'New racism'

Cultural differences Barker (1982) maintains that 'new racism' is the major form of cultural racism in contemporary Britain. It was developed over a long period by the 'New Right' (intellectuals, politicians and activists who wish to introduce revitalised right wing policies). The New Right have tried to exploit genuine fears about social problems (eg racial tensions, unemployment) in order to pursue their own political agenda. But they are aware that older forms of racism have unpleasant associations with Nazism. So they have been careful to avoid any talk of racial 'superiority' and they do not use racist terms of abuse (eg wog, nigger, coon). Instead, they rest their case on *cultural differences.* They draw a sharp contrast between 'traditional' British (or English) culture and the cultures of racial and ethnic minorities. The 'traditional' culture which the New Right are so keen to defend is presented in highly stereotypical and selective terms (eg Shakespeare, the 'natural' birthrights of free-born Englishmen etc). It owes as much to the imagination of the New Right as it does to historical reality.

Nevertheless, they try to lend it credibility by manipulating potent symbols (flags, anthems) and by appealing to a sense of 'history', 'patriotism' and 'community'. This narrow model of traditional British culture leaves very little room for black minorities who are seen as 'alien' and 'foreign'. (In the words of one Tory politician, minorities fail the 'cricket test' because they support teams playing against England!). According to the New Right, the cultures of black people are radically and permanently *different.* So the arrival of ethnic minorities is presented as a threat to the 'British way of life', destroying its homogeneity and cohesiveness.

The New Right think they are merely expressing a commonsense view of human nature. According to one critic, they believe that, 'It is only natural that, given the choice, people should prefer to live with their *own kind* and not in a multiracial society' (Solomos, 1990, p76). But Gilroy (1987) observes that new racism is based on the unreliable assumptions of 'ethnic absolutism'. It mistakenly portrays cultural boundaries as fixed and permanent and treats each culture as a homogeneous community. Consequently, it offers an over-simplified description of traditional British culture and it exaggerates the 'strangeness' of other cultures. For Gilroy, culture is never 'fixed, finished or final', and this means that different cultures can and do interact in mutually nourishing ways.

The New Right and racism Sociologists also criticise the 'racist' components of new racism. Admittedly, the New Right do not always regard themselves as racist and some of them object to the term 'new racism' being applied to their ideas. They defend themselves by saying that minorities are just as concerned about protecting their own cultures (compare the Rushdie affair, pp407-408). Nevertheless, many sociologists are convinced that the New Right fall into the racist trap. They might not use blatantly racist language, but Reeves (1983) points out that they pursue racist ends by adopting a 'sanitary code'. This code uses non-racial metaphors (eg talk about being 'swamped', or fears about the 'strain on social services'). It may appear reasonable but really it acts as a smokescreen to hide the underlying racist implications (eg Why do we single out *black* people for the 'cricket test'? What about Britain's Australian population? Do we expect Scots to support England's football team?). Also, the New Right generally play down the problem of racism in Britain and to that extent they help perpetuate the problem. Indeed, they direct their anger not at racism but at *anti-racists* whom they blame for stirring up trouble and destroying racial harmony. Lewis (1988), for example, attacks the 'mania' of the 'race relations industry' and he accuses anti-racists of intolerance, coercion and naivety.

It is not even clear that new racism really represents a distinct break from older versions of racism. Like 'scientific' racism, it still refers to 'biological' arguments (eg it draws on sociobiology to support its claims that it is 'natural' to maintain culturally exclusive barriers). And perhaps it is not even very *new*, since these ideas have been around a long time (eg the apartheid system was based on the different cultures and histories of blacks and whites). But the concept of new racism is certainly helpful in drawing attention to the very important cultural tensions which surround race relations in modern Britain. Many sociologists would agree that, 'The most resonant themes in contemporary racial discourses are not concerned with absolute notions of racial superiority, but with the threats which black communities are seen to represent to the cultural, political and religious homogeneity of white British society' (Solomos, 1989, p127).

Ethnic minority cultures

New ethnicities The New Right tend to exaggerate the 'exotic' or 'alien' nature of ethnic minority cultures but at least they acknowledge the existence of cultural differences. A surprisingly large number of sociologists have shown comparatively little interest in these differences. But Hall (1992) argues that there is now an urgent need to study the 'new ethnicities' in Britain. And this includes not just the differences between the ethnic minorities and the white majority, but also the cultural differences *between* minorities. At one time, perhaps, it was important to maintain the 'necessary fiction' that the cultural divisions between minorities were relatively insignificant. An emphasis on the *common* 'black experience' was helpful in mobilising an effective 'politics of resistance' against racism. But Hall believes it is no longer possible to ignore the diverse outlooks, social experiences and cultural identities of Britain's various ethnic minorities. However, he adds that any examination of ethnicity must be 'decoupled' from its association with New Right notions of nationalism and new racism. Otherwise, sociologists run the risk of seeing their research findings used (or misused) for political ends by the New Right. In order to avoid this, Hall calls for the development of a new 'politics of difference' which challenges dogmatic and inflexible views on cultural differences.

Ethnographies Hall seems to underestimate the major contributions already made by ethnographers in studying the 'new ethnicities'. Ethnographers and anthropologists have attempted to map the cultural values and lifestyles of ethnic minorities in postwar Britain (eg Watson, 1977). Admittedly, radical sociologists such as Hall are usually very critical of this ethnographic approach. They say it focuses too narrowly on 'culture' and therefore neglects important political and economic issues such as exploitation and class conflict. Nevertheless, there is little doubt that the cultural features of minorities deserve detailed attention and this is where ethnography provides useful insights. Some examples of these insights are included in Chapter 4 Gender and Chapter 11 Community. But for the moment it is worth looking at some general features of minority cultures, as revealed by ethnographic research.

1 **Cultures are dynamic rather than static** Minorities sometimes appear highly conservative, forever looking to the past and clinging to 'traditional' cultural values. But this impression is misleading, because cultures are always evolving. Younger generations are attracted to 'new' cultural movements such as Rastafarianism (Cashmore, 1979). And the 'old' traditions are re-interpreted in response to changing circumstances. For example, Asian groups in Britain have developed more flexible forms of the arranged marriage system (Bhachu, 1985).

2 **Cultures are formed in social situations** The culture of a group develops partly as a response to its *structural* position. Pryce's (1979) study of St Paul's in Bristol shows how the 'endless pressure' in this area had a marked effect on black lifestyles and values. Also, the culture of a group is affected by its relationships with other groups. If a minority group is not 'accepted' by others, then this can drive it back to re-asserting its 'traditional' values. This is called 'reactive ethnicity' (the renewed emphasis on ethnic culture is a reaction to racism or hostility).

3 **Cultures are not uniform** Each minority culture may be identified by certain 'core' values but its members are not equally committed to these values. Individuals make different selections from the available range of values and meanings within the culture. The group's own internal divisions (eg age, gender, social class) ensure a certain amount of cultural diversity. For example, the Asian custom of *purdah* (which stresses the 'seclusion' of women) lays down different cultural expectations for males and females.

4 **Cultures borrow from one another** Gilroy (1987) describes minority cultures as 'syncretic': they pick values and lifestyles from other cultures and incorporate them into their 'own' cultures. And, of course, the 'majority' culture raids the minorities for ideas (note the popularity of reggae and rap in 'mainstream' pop culture). So cultures are constantly being redefined and improvised and there is usually a great deal of overlap between them.

Activity 5 Cultural Differences

Item A

Item B

Scottish piper

Rastafarian

Anglican church

Muslim mosque

Item C

Welsh Eisteddfod

Notting Hill carnival

Item D

Morris dancers

Chinese New Year celebrations

Questions

1 Compare the two pictures in each of the items. Is one any more 'strange' or 'different' than the other? Explain why.
2 Why are the pictures on the right in each of Items A to D sometimes seen as a 'threat' to British culture, whereas those on the left are not?

Media and racism

Media messages The mass media help set the 'tone' of a culture, creating and sustaining many of its popular stereotypes, images and taken-for-granted assumptions. So the media (and especially the tabloid press) must share some of the blame for the state of race relations in Britain (see pp557-560). Sociologists regularly accuse the media of failing to address the serious difficulties and problems faced by racial and ethnic minorities. The evils of racism are just not given sufficient attention. Indeed, it is black people themselves who are seen as the 'problem': 'The main way in which black people are treated in newspapers is as a social problem. Black people are portrayed as constituting a threat to white British society, first through their immigration to this country and then, when settled here, as posing a law and order problem' (Gordon and Rosenberg, 1989, p3). Gordon and Rosenberg cite the way the media reported Metropolitan Police statistics, released in 1982, which claimed that 80% of all muggings in London were committed by black people. The press responded with sensational headlines: 'Black crime: the alarming figures' *(Daily Mail)*; 'The Yard blames black muggers' *(Sun)*; 'London's streets of fear' *(Daily Mirror)*. But the tabloids did not challenge the highly suspect basis for these figures (How was the race of the muggers determined? What proportion of muggings was reported to the police?). And they did not ask why race-related figures were released only for muggings (a very small proportion of all crimes) but not for other offences (How many burglars or fraudsters are black?).

Media and the New Right The tabloid press also have a special relationship with the gurus of the New Right. Using the authoritative platforms of newspaper columns, right wing commentators gain huge publicity for their new racism views: 'Although Britain is a multiracial society, it is still very far from being a multiracial nation. Its heart does not beat as one...Birds who are not of the same feather do not flock together at all easily' (Peregrine Worsthorne, *Sunday Telegraph* 27.6.82). They also whip up hysterical fears about anti-racism: 'How would you fancy a race relations inspector, armed with a search warrant, entering your home and demanding to see what books you read?... Would you relish getting your favourite newspaper with blank spaces, where the race relations censor has been at work? Impossible in Britain? Just you wait' (Paul Johnson, *Daily Mail* 17.6.85).

Media effects It is small wonder, then, that sociologists tend to regard newspapers, magazines and television as key agents of racism. Deliberately or unwittingly, the media trade in racist myths and fears, they exaggerate immigration figures, they highlight minorities as a 'problem', they create or recycle harmful stereotypes of black people, and they repeatedly give credibility to unreliable stories ('40 Pakistanis sleeping in a loft' etc). On the other hand, media messages are highly complex. The 'racist' messages are often couched in subtle codes rather than outright abuse. Also, media content is hardly consistent or one-dimensional (eg the quality newspapers are more likely to challenge racism). Alongside the 'negative' and sensationalist coverage we are quite likely to find 'positive' images of black people as sports stars, celebrities, economic 'success stories' or just plain 'decent' people. Moreover, we cannot just assume that the media have predictable and uniform 'effects', since audiences select and interpret media content according to their own values, interests and assumptions (see pp538-539).

2.2 Racialism

In the mid-1960s a white man, John Griffin, used medication and dyes to disguise himself as black and then wandered around some southern states of the USA. Although he behaved in his normal manner, he found that other people reacted to him in a completely different way. Every day he endured insults, hostility, off-hand treatment and enforced segregation. He had become discredited, an inferior. In 1988, a television programme *(Black and White)* arranged some experiments in Bristol. Two journalists - one black, one white - applied separately for housing, employment and access to entertainment facilities and the results were secretly filmed on camera. These journalists had been given identical 'backgrounds' yet the black person received a far higher number of refusals from landlords, employers and night clubs.

These two undercover experiments reveal the impact of racial discrimination, or *racialism*. If prejudice is a matter of *attitudes*, then discrimination is about

behaviour: treating people differently simply because of their social group, even when group membership is not strictly relevant. Thus, if an employer refuses to give a job to a suitably qualified black person simply because of skin colour, then that is an example of direct racial discrimination. The 1976 Race Relations Act bans not only *direct discrimination* but also *indirect discrimination*: treatment which is 'equal' in a formal sense but which results in unjustifiable discrimination against particular racial groups (eg a severe 'language' test is not strictly necessary for a labouring job and it may handicap those whose first language is not English).

We cannot assume that there is always a neat fit between cultural racism and racialism. People who hold racist attitudes may not act upon them for fear of social condemnation or legal prosecution. Conversely, people who are not especially prejudiced may be bullied or pressurised into discriminating. But it seems reasonable to assume that prejudice and discrimination usually reinforce one another. Prejudices serve to 'justify' inferior treatment, and if black people are continually *treated* as inferior it becomes easier to *regard* them as inferior and so the cycle continues. But for independent evidence of racialism we need to turn to specialised studies which explore the problem in detail. Unfortunately, this evidence 'shows that racial discrimination remains rampant in virtually all aspects of life in Britain' (Ouseley, 1990).

Activity 6   Stop That Car!

Item A   *A fair cop?*
Barry Coy, a professional ice hockey player, has made a formal complaint of harassment against Merseyside police after being stopped more than 100 times since he bought a high performance rally car in January. Mr Coy, who is aged 20 and looks 'West Indian' (he has a white mother and Jamaican father), says that he has been stopped as many as five times in one evening. One time he had 14 police officers surrounding his house in the belief that he and his friends had stolen their cars. Despite all the police checks he has not been charged with any offence. 'At first I just laughed it off and the police made a joke when they realised they had stopped me before, but now I want it to stop.'

Guardian, 24.8.82, cited in Bygott, 1992

Item B   *I've got your number*
The Chief Constable of Staffordshire, Mr Charles Kelly, started an inquiry yesterday into a crime prevention leaflet which urged villagers to note the registration numbers of cars driven by coloured people. Staffordshire police have said the leaflet was never intended to be racist.

Guardian, 13.10.87, cited in Bygott, 1992.

Questions
1   Briefly explain why Items A and B are examples of *racialism*.
2   Identify the racial stereotypes which are being employed to justify this discriminatory treatment.
3   Comment on the statement (Item B) that 'the leaflet was never intended to be racist'.
4   Why might the man in the photograph have problems with the police?

PEP/PSI

Valuable information on racial discrimination is provided by the major series of studies conducted by Political and Economic Planning (PEP), later renamed the Policy Studies Institute (PSI).

1960s Daniel (1967) conducted a study in England with a sample of some 1,000 immigrants (West Indian, Pakistani, Indian and Cypriot) and 500 potential discriminators (employers, landlords, insurers etc). As well as interviews and questionnaires, he also used the imaginative device of 'situation tests' along the same lines as the *Black and White* television experiment. In each case, a 'matched' non-white migrant ('West Indian', 'Asian'), white migrant (eg Hungarian) and white Englishman applied independently for some post or service. The findings revealed that discrimination ranged from 'the substantial to the massive' in the fields of employment, housing and services (eg motor insurance, bank loans, mortgages). This landmark study created pressure for the introduction of anti-discrimination legislation.

1970s Smith (1977) continued the PEP series by interviewing a random sample of 3,292 Asians and West Indians and 1,239 whites in England and Wales during 1972-75. As well as situation tests, Smith took a detailed look at a sample of key organisations (firms, trade union head offices, local authority housing departments). Based on this research, Smith concluded that discrimination had lessened a little (perhaps the effect of new anti-discrimination laws) since Daniel's study. But it still occurred. In employment, for example, black workers met discrimination when applying for nonmanual jobs and unskilled manual jobs and this could not be explained away simply by lack of qualifications. In housing, black people still encountered substantial discrimination in obtaining private rented accommodation. And although the West Indian population had a high percentage of manual workers, they were under-represented in council housing and if they did occupy council housing it was usually of inferior quality or location.

1980s The third major study, again based in England and Wales, was conducted in 1982 by Brown (1984). One criticism of the earlier PEP studies was that they relied mainly on inner city samples in order to reach large numbers of black people. The effect of this was to exaggerate the socioeconomic gap between blacks and white people in general. Brown claimed his PSI sample avoided this bias since it was based on a nationally representative sample of 5,000 blacks and 2,305 whites. Nevertheless, the findings confirmed those of earlier studies, in that black people suffered greater *disadvantage* than whites. But how much of this disadvantage was due to racial discrimination rather than other causes? Brown did not measure discrimination directly through situation tests but relied on the weaker evidence provided by what people told the interviewers. But he concluded that, 'It is clear that racialism and direct racial discrimination continue to have a powerful effect on the lives of black people' (Brown, 1984, p318).

Racial attacks

Defining the problem It is not easy to define a 'racial attack'. How do we know if an attack was racially motivated? Recognising this problem, the Commission for Racial Equality (CRE) offers a broad definition: 'Racial attacks are those which are perpetrated against individuals or groups because they are perceived as belonging to a particular racial group and which the victim believes to have been racially motivated or for which there is direct evidence of racism' (CRE, 1987, p7). There is no specific crime of 'racial attack', but the term covers crimes against property (eg vandalising houses) as well as crimes against the person (assault, abuse, murder). Police forces usually keep records on 'inter-racial incidents' (where some racial motive is inferred). This seems to allow for cases of attacks by blacks on whites and also attacks *between* minorities (eg the outbreak of Hindu-Muslim violence in Blackburn in 1992). But Gordon (1990) insists that 'racial attacks' can mean only one thing: attacks by whites on blacks. He believes that few attacks by blacks on whites are racially motivated. Certainly black minorities are much more likely than whites to be selected as targets. One Home Office Report (1981) concluded that, compared with whites, Asians were 50 times more likely, and West Indians 36 times more likely, to be victims of a racially motivated attack.

Types of attack The CRE definition covers a wide variety of behaviour, including *racist name-calling*. Troyna and Hatcher (1992) say this is more common in schools than most teachers care to admit. It is sometimes used in 'hot' contexts where there is an emotionally charged encounter between children (often friends!), usually leading to feelings of guilt and apologies afterwards. But it is also used in 'cold', calculating ways when children deliberately tease or torment other children for malicious pleasure. Another category of racial attack is *street violence*. Moral panics about mugging have created the misleading impression that street violence is predominantly carried out by young blacks (Hall et al, 1978) but it is often the minorities who are the main victims. There is a long history of racially motivated attacks in Britain's streets, including the 1919 race riots in Cardiff, Liverpool and other ports, and the 1960s wave of 'Paki-bashing' by skinheads. In recent years there are signs that the problem is growing. Home Office figures suggest there are some 8,000 attacks per year in England and Wales but this is likely to be a gross underestimate (Runnymede, 1991a). A significant number of these attacks end in fatalities, and Gordon (1990) estimates 74 deaths in the period 1970 to 1989. Moreover, several observers say it is becoming a more serious problem throughout the European Union as right wing movements grow in strength.

Activity 7 A Safe Place to Live?

Item A *Their home is their castle*

A British Sikh, Hindu, Muslim, Bengali, Tamil or Barbadian is as welcome as a British Jew, Pole or Irishman. All who accept our public traditions are guaranteed the safety of their private traditions in their own homes, because their home is their castle.

Adapted from R. Lewis *Anti-Racism*, 1988, p16

Five members of an Asian family were killed in this racist arson attack on their home in London.

Item B *Beseiged*

Moyna Meah's troubles started when the rest of his family arrived from Bangladesh and they all moved into an Islington council flat. Years of intense and persistent racial harassment followed and they became prisoners in their own home. The harassment began with his daughters being hit and spat at by white teenagers - boys and girls - on the estate. Their front door was always being kicked, smoke bombs were put through the letterbox and rubbish was dropped on to their balcony. The teenage tormentors then took to blocking the tenement passageway so that visitors could not reach the Meah home and the Meahs could not go out. Some of the neighbours were supportive and agreed to act as witnesses, and two years ago the Meah family succeeded in having one of the ringleaders bound over. Since then the family has been left alone to get on with their life.

Adapted from *Observer*, 14.5.89

Item C

'Black people's reality'

As a boy sleeps, a pig's head, its eyes, ears, nostrils and mouth stuffed with lighted cigarettes, is hurled through the window of his bedroom. A youth is slashed with a knife by an older white boy as he walks along a school corridor between classes. A family home is burned out and a pregnant woman and her three children killed. A ticket collector is stabbed in the eye with a metal stake and killed simply because he refused to take racial abuse from some white passenger. These cases, all reported in the last few years, are part of the black experience of Britain in the 1980s, part of black people's reality.

Adapted from P.Gordon *Racial Violence and Harassment*, 1990, pv

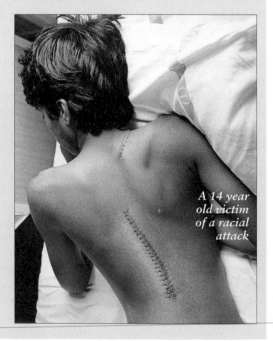

A 14 year old victim of a racial attack

Questions

1 What do you think Lewis (Item A) means by 'public traditions' and 'private traditions'?

2 State briefly whether Items B and C support Lewis's views.

3 In the Meahs' case (Item B) some action was taken against the offenders. Suggest reasons why this does not happen in every case.

2.3 Institutional racism

Some sociologists argue that racism is a basic feature of Britain's social institutions (eg the legal system, central and local government, employment and housing markets). According to this view, racist assumptions are built in to the rules and routines of these institutions. Consequently, racial and ethnic minorities are systematically discriminated against and their particular needs are neglected. Now, this does not necessarily mean that every individual working within these institutions 'supports' racist attitudes and behaviour. But regardless of their personal views on racism they tend to reinforce it just by going about their 'normal' business. Racism is taken for granted and habitual - it has become so 'institutionalised' that it is not even recognised as racism. Yet it has serious consequences for racial and ethnic minorities. If they receive a raw deal from the major social institutions then it is highly likely that they will suffer socioeconomic *disadvantage*. This is confirmed by a long line of research, including the PEP/PSI studies. These investigations show that minorities suffer relative disadvantage in areas such as jobs, housing and educational qualifications.

Criticisms The concept of institutional racism rests on two main arguments: that Britain's social institutions are racist and that this results in distinct patterns of racial disadvantage. But these arguments are very controversial.

1 Is it sensible to describe *institutions* as racist? Jeffcoate (1984) suggests that the term 'institutional racism' may be applicable to South Africa, where the state has enforced racial discrimination, but not to Britain, where the state has passed laws *against* racial discrimination! And perhaps we need proof of some conscious *intention* to discriminate. Scarman (1983) maintained it was unfair to apply the term to police in Britain since there was little direct evidence that they really intended to victimise black people. However, some sociologists prefer to place the stress on *effects* rather than intentions. For example, the 'waiting list' system for allocating council houses seems reasonably fair and non-racist but in the 1960s it had the effect of excluding newly arrived black migrants from council housing (Rex and Moore, 1967). In this view, even 'colour blind' policies are racist if they neglect the special needs of black people.

2 Are institutions *equally* racist? Some discussions create the impression of a uniform degree of racism across the whole range of state institutions. But that is far too sweeping. It might be reasonable to accuse Britain's immigration laws (see p85) of racial discrimination. But the British state system is not consistently racist. Much more attention needs to be given to the detailed differences *between* and *within* institutions and to *changes* over time. Within schools, for example, there are various initiatives (such as multicultural education) which actively *challenge* racism.

3 Is it wise to stretch the meaning of racism beyond racist *attitudes* (cultural racism) and *behaviour* (racialism) to include socioeconomic *outcomes* (institutional racism) as well? Miles (1989) feels this 'conceptual inflation' results in racism losing any precise meaning since it is applied too loosely to quite different kinds of things. Moreover, our understanding of racial disadvantage is not really helped by calling it institutional racism. So Miles prefers to restrict the definition of racism to the level of attitudes and behaviour.

4 What is the connection between racism and racial disadvantage? In some cases we can safely say that racism is a major 'cause' of racial disadvantage (eg where council officials give black people inferior accommodation and 'justify' this in terms of racist stereotypes). But disadvantage is also caused by other, non-racist factors, eg the higher unemployment rate among blacks may be *partly* due to their age structure, geographical location, skill levels or language problems. The concept of institutional racism tends to overlook these alternative explanations.

5 Is the concept of institutional racism based on an oversimplified model of stratification? Miles (1990) observes that not all blacks are 'victims' (some are quite prosperous and powerful) and not all whites are powerful or privileged (eg Irish have suffered in similar ways to blacks). Although racial and ethnic minorities *tend* to be relatively disadvantaged there is no sharp dividing line between them and the white majority. Patterns of disadvantage change over time and they vary between different minority groups. In the most recent PSI study, for example, Jones (1993) uses Labour Force Survey data to show that certain ethnic groups have made substantial socioeconomic progress over the past decade while other groups continue to suffer high levels of deprivation (see Activity 8).

In light of these criticisms and debates, institutional racism remains a controversial idea. In this respect it is very like a closely related term, the 'underclass' (see pp103-106). Nevertheless, it is useful in directing our attention away from 'individual' racism towards the way society is organised, its basic operating principles and the unequal distribution of power and privilege.

Activity 8 Racial Disadvantage

Item A *Patterns of racial disadvantage*

HOUSING

The quality of housing of black people tends to be poor. They are more often found in flats (and at higher floor levels) and those with houses are less likely to have detached or semi-detached property. Black families tend to have smaller property and larger household sizes and so their density of occupation is much higher. They more often share rooms or amenities with other households, their properties are older and they are less likely to have a garden.

Adapted from C. Brown *Black and White Britain*, 1984, p93

JOBS

There is increasing diversity within the ethnic minority population:
The East African Asian, Indian and Chinese populations are the most successful - they have higher proportions of well qualified people, comparable (or better) job levels to whites and similar unemployment rates to whites.
The Pakistanis and Bangladeshis are least successful - they have the lowest proportion of people with formal qualifications, lower job levels than other minority groups and the highest rates of unemployment.
The Afro-Caribbean population falls somewhere between the two extremes above.

Adapted from T. Jones *Britain's Ethnic Minorities*, 1993, p151

POVERTY

Poverty is not even-handed. The chances of experiencing poverty are far higher for people from ethnic minorities than for white people. Moreover, the way in which poverty is experienced by ethnic minority communities may be more acute, as low income is compounded by discrimination and exclusion.

Adapted from K. Amin *Poverty in Black and White*, 1992, p1

Item B *'Institutional terrorism'*

When white terrorists bomb a black church and kill five black children, that is an act of individual racism, widely deplored by most segments of the society. But in that same city - Birmingham, Alabama - five hundred black babies die each year because of the lack of proper food, shelter and medical facilities. That is a function of institutional racism - it is institutional racism that keeps black people locked in dilapidated slum tenements.

Adapted from S. Carmichael and C. Hamilton *Black Power*, 1969, p20

Item C *Race and poverty - vicious circles*

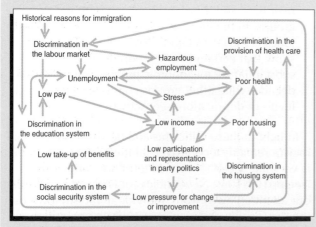

Adapted from *Runnymede Trust Annual Report 1992-93*, p9

Questions

1 Read Item A.
   a) Brown describes racial disadvantage in the housing sector. How might this be regarded as an example of institutional racism?
   b) Jones describes the 'diversity' of economic circumstances between ethnic groups. Does this undermine the notion of institutional racism? Give reasons for your answer.
   c) Amin states that black poverty is made worse by 'discrimination and exclusion'. Give some examples of this.
2 Carmichael and Hamilton (Item B) make a basic distinction between 'individual' and 'institutional' racism. State how we can distinguish between these two forms of racism and give some examples.
3 How can Item C lend support to the idea of institutional racism?

Immigration laws

Racist laws Britain's immigration laws are often cited as a dramatic example of institutional racism. According to one expert, 'The most brutal and wide-ranging racism which occurs day after day is not the work of fascist minority parties but of Her Majesty's Government. It is the racism written into, and demanded by, Britain's immigration laws' (Wilson, 1984, p72). Britain followed a reasonably laissez-faire ('open door') Commonwealth immigration policy in the 1940s and 1950s but an increasingly restrictive set of laws were passed during and after the 1960s. Sivanandan (1982) interprets this change in terms of the economic 'system needs' of capitalism: in the 1950s there had been a labour shortage, but later economic difficulties meant there was a decreasing need for cheap immigrant labour (especially since transnationals were moving their manufacturing operations to the Third World). But Layton-Henry (1984) insists that economic factors were not the sole reason for changes in the immigration laws. He makes a case for the powerful influence of cultural and political debates about 'race'. The mass media had started broadcasting scare stories about black immigration, and political constituencies were pressing for strict limitations on the numbers of black immigrants.

Effects on race relations Whatever the reasons for the new restrictions, they have had a profound effect on race relations.

1 It seems the laws are *intended* to restrict the entry of black people while keeping the door open for white migrants. Solomos (1989) observes that black migrants were seen as a 'problem' throughout the postwar period and successive British governments resorted to stealthy 'administrative' measures to control their numbers. More blatantly, the 1968 Immigration Act was hastily passed in order to prevent the entry of Kenyan Asians even though they held British passports. But the targeting of black people was partly disguised by the 'patrials' clause in the 1971 Immigration Act. This gave greater migration rights to people who had a close connection with United Kingdom through birth, adoption, or having a parent or grandparent born or naturalised here. These patrials, of course, were more likely to be white people from the 'Old Commonwealth'.

2 Quite apart from the actual legislation, there is evidence that the laws have been *implemented* in a racialist manner (CRE, 1985). According to the CRE report, the system involves long queues and intolerable delays in those New Commonwealth countries where applicants apply for permission to come to Britain. The dependents of people already settled in this country have complained of severe

Table 8 Commonwealth Immigration Acts

1948 British Nationality Act Divided 'British subjects' into two groups: citizens of UK and Colonies (UKC), and Commonwealth citizens (ie citizens of independent Commonwealth countries). The Act confirmed rights of both groups to enter Britain, find work and bring their families to settle.

1962 Commonwealth Immigrants Act Introduction of first major controls for Commonwealth citizens. Automatic right of entry only for those who held UKC passports. Others had to apply for an employment voucher (issued in limited numbers).

1968 Commonwealth Immigrants Act People holding UKC passports subjected to controls. This was used to bar entry of Kenyan Asians who had chosen not to take out independent Kenyan citizenship. (After protests, the government made special concessions to allow phased entry).

1971 Immigration Act Distinction between patrials and non-patrials. Patrials clause (first introduced in 1968 Act) was extended to those holding Commonwealth citizenship. So more white people (eg patrial Canadians, Australians) were eligible to enter Britain. But all non-patrials were subjected to more severe restrictions (eg work permits on much the same legal footing as 'aliens').

1981 British Nationality Act Not an immigration act so much as a clarification of 'nationality' and its attendant rights. Patrials clause had created confusing system: some UKC citizens had no right of entry, while some Commonwealth citizens did. So this act introduced three classes of citizenship, each with clearly defined immigration status:

British citizenship (includes most patrials) - full right of abode in Britain.
British Dependent Territories citizenship (eg Hong Kong, Belize)- no right of entry (with exception of Falklands and Gibraltar).
British Overseas citizenship (non-patrial citizens of colonies with no other citizenship) - a category destined to fade away; no rights of entry.

and heartless treatment which keeps families apart for many years (or even permanently). In Britain's ports, black visitors are much more likely than white people to be stopped for questioning. Some immigration officers seem to take delight in refusing black people permission to enter.

3 The tight controls are often defended on the grounds that they *improve* race relations by reassuring white people that the numbers of blacks will be kept to a modest level. However, critics argue that these laws make racial harmony more difficult, since they are a symbolic statement that black people are unwanted in this country.

Immigration and Europe A number of commentators have speculated on the impact that closer European Union integration will have on migration laws and procedures. Gordon (1992a) predicts that it will become easier for EU citizens to travel and establish themselves in other EU countries. But millions of others, both inside the Union and outside, will find their movements more restricted. As internal movement becomes easier, so the external borders of the EU will be made more secure in order to prevent the entry of illegal migrants and bogus asylum seekers. The prospects for the emergence of 'Fortress Europe' are reinforced by current British Government plans for tighter asylum and visa laws.

2.4 Explanations of racism

The story of racism is also the story of European and world history. If we wish to understand it fully we need to look at all the forces - cultural, political, economic, geographical - which have shaped that complex history. Even within sociology there is no single explanation for racism. Rather, there are a number of approaches or models, some of them in direct competition and some of them simply looking at the problem from different angles. In a sense we learn something from all of them but they are not equally convincing (and some are perhaps not convincing at all!). This section takes a critical look at three distinctive approaches: sociobiology, cultural models and structural models. It also includes 'case studies' of Bosnia and the Isle of Dogs.

Sociobiological explanations

Natural selection Sociobiologists (eg Wilson, 1975; van den Berghe, 1981) claim that human behaviour is the result of a long process of evolution in which genetic, environmental and sociocultural factors interact. The key to this evolution is the mechanism of 'natural selection' (or 'maximisation of fitness'). At its simplest, this means that the most successful or fittest people will have higher survival rates and so they will manage to pass on their genes to their offspring. Over time, these successful genes will predominate in the population. Indeed, sociobiologists argue that people are genetically programmed to ensure the reproduction of their own 'selfish genes' (Dawkins, 1976). People who act in such a way will win through and their descendants will share the same drives.

Racism and the 'selfish gene' So how do sociobiologists explain racism? They tend to see racism as a basic ('primordial') feature of human nature, rooted in deep human instincts. Humans are genetically programmed to pass on the 'selfish gene' but this can be achieved at 'kin' as well as individual levels. If people help those kinfolk who share similar genes, then this 'kin selection' enhances the prospects of their common genes surviving. So people are genetically predisposed towards 'nepotism' (favouring their relatives) and this can even stretch beyond immediate kin towards a wider circle ('inclusive fitness') as long as they share similar genes. On the other hand, there is little to be gained by cooperating with people of strikingly dissimilar

appearance, such as those of other races or tribes or ethnic groups (although sociobiologists do allow for occasional 'reciprocal altruism' on a calculating, self-interested basis). So sociobiology offers a biological argument to explain why people act in a kindly fashion towards their 'own' groups and in a hostile (racist) fashion towards 'other' groups.

Criticisms Critics (eg Bleier, 1984) have identified several weaknesses in this approach.

1 It has an 'unfalsifiable' character, partly because many of its basic terms are so poorly defined that it is sometimes difficult to decide just exactly what is being argued. Sociobiology frequently indulges in bold, sweeping generalisations which are based on highly selective cross-cultural evidence. Yet when it is challenged it often retreats to looser and 'weaker' arguments (eg it is only speculating about broad 'tendencies' rather than claiming that genes 'dictate' behaviour).

2 It is a *reductionist* approach - everything is reduced to genes. In spite of their declared interest in sociocultural as well as biological factors, sociobiologists tend to explain most things in terms of genetic codes rather than the *interaction* between biology and culture. Yet they have not succeeded in identifying the precise genetic codes which are capable of explaining the enormous complexity of race relations through the centuries (indeed, much of their 'evidence' is actually derived from studies of animal behaviour).

3 Its explanations are limited and unsatisfactory. Why do race relations vary so much over the centuries and between societies? Why do black and white people sometimes live harmoniously and even intermarry? Why should people help those members of their 'own' race who are *not* blood relatives? Some critics say sociobiology offers only a very trivial truth: that there is a 'consciousness of kind' based on physical appearance.

4 Sociobiology is itself racist. This criticism is actually very unfair on liberal sociobiologists like van den Berghe. Nevertheless, sociobiology does offer a profoundly pessimistic message: it seems to ask us to resign ourselves to racism rather than fight it. And regardless of the particular values of sociobiologists themselves, their ideas have been enthusiastically adopted by the New Right and incorporated in 'new racism'.

On the other hand, Stone (1985) concludes that, for all its faults, it would be too harsh to describe sociobiology as 'racist, reductionist and ridiculous'. And Sharp (1991) argues that sociobiology raises very serious issues for sociology: if it is true that humans, like other species, are the products of evolution, then we do have to pay some attention to genetic predispositions.

Cultural explanations

Cultural approaches are popular with sociologists because they deal with the familiar territory of values, attitudes and beliefs. The hallmark of these approaches is their emphasis on cultural origins and cultural stereotypes. But they are applied to the problem of racism in a number of different ways. In the section on 'cultural racism' we saw how people may be fooled into accepting negative stereotypes of blacks. Many of these stereotypes originated in the colonial past but they are handed down as part of the 'conventional wisdom' of British culture. People pick up these stereotypes in the course of normal socialisation. A great deal of cultural racism can therefore be explained in terms of faulty stereotypes and a lack of accurate information about the true nature of black people.

In the section on 'institutional racism' we noted that black people tend to suffer socioeconomic disadvantage. Much of this results from racial discrimination, but it is possible that *some* of the disadvantage stems from the cultural characteristics of minority groups. Krausz (1971) says that first generation migrants sometimes had language problems or lacked appropriate industrial skills or qualifications and this accounted for some of their early socioeconomic problems. Also, Dahya (1974) argues that cultural choices are important: many Pakistani migrants actually chose to live in inner-city areas because the geographical concentration helped keep their cultural groups intact (ie segregation was *voluntary*).

In the section on 'new racism' we noted that many of the fiercest 'race' clashes in modern Britain revolve around issues of cultural conflict and cultural incompatibility. New racism often relies on sociobiological assumptions, but we can recognise the importance of cultural conflicts without necessarily accepting that they are 'natural' or inevitable. And not all cultural conflicts are necessarily 'racist' in character. 'Legitimate' cultural conflicts arise when groups - even with the best will in the world - find that the collision of their different value systems causes difficulties (eg some Muslim parents worry about their children being 'seduced' by Western values).

The host-immigrant model A good example of an approach which stresses the importance of culture is the *host-immigrant model* (Patterson, 1965). Originally developed in the USA, this model was borrowed and modified by sociologists trying to understand the 'race' situation in Britain in the 1950s and 1960s, a time of increasing alarm over New Commonwealth immigration. The host-immigrant framework shared many of the assumptions of functionalist sociology. It depicted Britain as a

basically stable, homogeneous and orderly society with a high degree of consensus over values and norms. But this tranquil equilibrium was disturbed by the arrival of immigrant 'strangers' who subscribed to quite different sets of values. Patterson described the culture clash between West Indians (boisterous and noisy, and not in the habit of queuing at bus stops!) and the English hosts (who valued privacy, quiet and 'keeping oneself to oneself'). Other commentators have described similar clashes between Asians and whites: 'The British put much value on restraint in speech and behaviour, reserve and formality; the Asian was used to informality, openness and loud speech often accompanied by gesticulation...early immigrants continued to live and act as if they were still in their villages...the British were offended and scandalised' (Hiro, 1992, p149).

The host-immigrant model interpreted these clashes in terms of understandable fears and anxieties on the part of the puzzled hosts. The hosts were not actually 'racist', but they were very unsure about how to act towards the newcomers. Their confusion sometimes spilled over into suspicion and resentment (especially since the migrants competed with hosts for jobs and houses). But for Patterson the main problem was not so much racism or black-white hostility but cultural 'strangeness'. She was reasonably optimistic about the long-term prospects for racial harmony. She thought Britain's black migrants would eventually follow the path of previous waves of migrants (eg Irish, Jews) as they slowly moved towards full cultural 'assimilation' by shedding the 'old' ethnic values and taking on the dominant values of the host society.

Criticisms The host-immigrant model illustrates a common weakness in cultural approaches. By concentrating so much on culture it can easily lead to 'blaming the victim' (unfairly attributing the difficulties of ethnic groups to their 'strange' cultures). Critics of the model say it is the *structure* of British society which provides the main clues as to why racism exists. After all, racial hostility has not declined to the extent 'predicted' by the host-immigrant model and perhaps this is because the basic structure of British society remains unchanged. There is a constant struggle over jobs, housing and money and this causes frustrations which can easily result in racial tensions. Also, the cultural approach tends to treat culture as 'free-floating' rather than something which is formed within particular social structures and situations. Structural theorists say that it is structure which 'shapes' culture - cultural choices are not free and unimpeded but take place within particular social situations which make some choices more likely than others.

Nevertheless, culture is an important consideration for sociologists. If the host-immigrant model underestimated the persistence of racism, it also underestimated the persistence of ethnic minority cultures. Indeed, the continued vitality of ethnic cultures has forced policymakers to revise their previous goal of 'assimilation' in which ethnic minorities were expected to adopt the culture of the majority. Nowadays there is far greater acceptance of 'cultural pluralism' where ethnic minorities retain their own cultures while adjusting to a society which accepts cultural diversity. But this 'acceptance' of cultural diversity is a precarious affair and the potential for cultural conflict still exists.

Structural explanations

Structural approaches claim that racism is mainly a result of the way society is organised. Western capitalist societies are based largely on market principles and the profit motive and so their populations are locked in competition for desirable social resources. Social groups struggle for control over goods and services and this struggle creates a great deal of anxiety and frustration. Structural theorists say this kind of conflict situation is highly likely to breed racist attitudes and behaviour. Also, the structure of capitalist society ensures that racial minorities suffer socioeconomic disadvantage (institutional racism). In the 1950s and 1960s many Western European societies faced a labour shortage which was eased by the recruitment of black people from the New Commonwealth. This 'replacement population' of black migrant labour made a valuable contribution to the British economy but the jobs they filled were typically low in skill, pay and status. And once racial minorities were trapped in the lower strata of society, the unequal opportunity structures of capitalism made it difficult for them to improve their situation and so their disadvantage was handed down to their children.

Functions of racism Those sociologists who adopt structural explanations of racism are mostly 'conflict' theorists but they often employ 'functionalist' arguments. They say that racism exists in capitalist societies because it fulfils certain 'functions'.

1 **Legitimisation** If black people are regarded as 'inferior', then this makes it easier to exploit them. This happened under colonialism and slavery when racist theories 'dehumanised' blacks - this legitimised what otherwise might have seemed a ruthless and greedy venture by Western nations. Another example, from modern Britain, is the way the low pay and poor working conditions of black employees are widely tolerated because blacks are seen as 'second class' citizens. This suits the economic interests of employers who benefit from the cheap labour provided by black workers.

2 **Divide-and-rule** If black and white workers unite then they are in a stronger position to campaign for better wages and conditions. But employers might prefer them to be divided by racism so they can be played off against one another (eg employers might hope to use blacks as a 'reserve army' to prevent white workers from pressing for higher wages). White workers might be tempted to exclude blacks because they fear their presence will drag down their wage levels. More generally, white people may feel they are in direct competition with blacks and in this respect it is 'rational' for them to try to gain an 'edge' by supporting racial discrimination. In conflict situations, racism sometimes has a perverted 'logic' (Cashmore, 1987).

3 **Scapegoating** If a society is troubled by severe social and economic problems then this can create widespread frustration and aggression. Instead of directing this anger at the powerful groups who run the system, whites are sometimes tempted to pick on relatively vulnerable groups. They use black people as scapegoats: it is blacks (rather than the social system) who are blamed for unemployment, housing shortages and the breakdown of social consensus. For instance, Cashmore (1987) says that many white people in his Birmingham sample felt bewildered and threatened by rapid social change. They tried to make some sense of this by blaming it on the presence of blacks. Clearly, scapegoating is in the interests of the richer and more powerful groups because it protects them from direct criticism and reduces pressures for radical change. Indeed, Hall et al (1978) suggest that the capitalist state tried to overcome its serious crises in the 1970s by launching a moral panic about black 'muggers'. This distracted attention from the failure of capitalism to solve its problems (eg industrial decline) and it helped to win public consent for a 'stronger' state which then cracked down on the mounting social unrest (see pp482-483).

Criticisms The structural conflict approach has a number of different versions (see Part 3 for details of Marxist and Weberian models). But it is possible to identify some general criticisms of structural explanations.

1 Solomos (1989) observes that much of the 'radical' literature is pitched at a very general theoretical level. In many cases it fails to integrate theory with empirical research. A more detailed inspection of empirical evidence might reveal that the structural models are oversimplified (eg it is not true that all black people are economically disadvantaged).

2 There are certain problems with functionalist arguments, even in their conflict form. Just because racism is 'functional' for capitalism, this does not necessarily mean that it was deliberately *created* for that purpose. So 'functions' are not the same thing as 'causes'. We need independent evidence on the causes and origins of racism. Besides, it is

perfectly possible that racism is also *dysfunctional* for capitalism (eg it may create social unrest which threatens the stability of the capitalist system). So racism has *contradictory* effects and we cannot assume that it always dances to the tune of capitalism.

3 Marxist versions usually claim that racism is much more intensive under capitalism or even that it is found only in capitalist societies. But critics of this view say that it is 'true' only because Marxists have defined 'racism' and 'capitalism' in very selective ways in order to make it true. Racist beliefs and doctrines probably predated capitalism and they also exist in present day non-capitalist societies. Also, it is not at all clear that there is a single 'logic of capitalism' which makes racism necessary and inevitable - it is quite possible to imagine capitalism working without any racism at all.

Activity 9 Ethnic Cleansing

Item A *Bosnia*

'Ethnic cleansing' is a sinister term recently introduced into everyday language in Europe. It arose from the breakup of Yugoslavia and its disintegration into feuding territories and states, especially those of Serbia, Croatia and Bosnia. A bloody civil war is currently raging in Bosnia, which has an ethnic mix of Serbians (Orthodox Christians), Croatians (Catholic) and Bosnian Muslims. There is a historical legacy of ill-feeling which stems from the German occupation of Yugoslavia during the Second World War when Croats and Muslims sided with the German forces and an estimated two million Serbs were killed in the country as a whole. So there are plenty of old scores to settle.

The present violent conflict revolves around Serbian and Croatian claims to Bosnian land and Muslim demands for political independence. Each group is staking claims on territory and trying to 'cleanse' this territory of other ethnic groups. But the term 'ethnic cleansing' mainly refers to Serbian aggression against the Bosnian Muslims (who are the largest single group in Bosnia - some 40% of the population - and also the wealthiest). The obscene spectacle of slaughter and atrocities led the UN to intervene in order to provide humanitarian aid and attempt to establish peace in the region.

Adapted from *Runnymede Bulletin* October 1992 and from P. Nitzova 'The Bosnian Crisis', *New Community*, April 1993

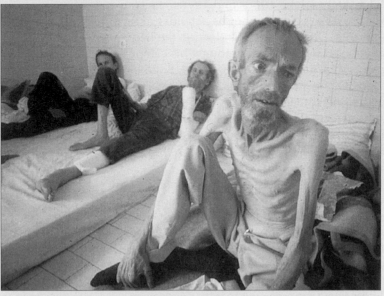

A Bosnian Muslim in a Serb prison camp

Item B *Iraq*

One of the thousands of Kurds killed by chemical weapons in 1988 in Northern Iraq on the orders of Saddam Hussein

Questions

1 a) Briefly outline a structural conflict explanation of the Bosnian crisis.

   b) Briefly outline a cultural explanation of the Bosnian crisis.

   c) Which of the following do you prefer: (i) a structural explanation (ii) a cultural explanation (iii) a combination of the two? Give reasons.

2 Analyse the term 'ethnic cleansing'. What does it suggest about the way the group doing the 'cleansing' sees both itself and the group being 'cleansed'? Illustrate your answer with other examples of ethnic cleansing.

Explaining 'racist' elections

Rights for whites In September 1993 the right wing British National Party (BNP) won a council by-election in the Millwall ward of the Isle of Dogs, Tower Hamlets. Although only 44% of the electorate turned out, the BNP got 33.9% of the votes cast and beat Labour by 7 votes. Some observers explained the result in terms of the long tradition of racism in London's East End. The East End has been an important recruiting area for a succession of right wing extremist groups such as Sir Oswald Mosley's British Union of Fascists in the 1930s. Later, in the 1960s and 1970s, the National Front concentrated many of its activities in the Brick Lane area. During the 1993 election the BNP candidate, Derek Beackon, fought his campaign under the slogan 'Rights for Whites'. But the local Liberal Democrats and Labour Party were also accused of pandering to racism in their campaigns. And since the BNP victory the already high level of racial attacks in Tower Hamlets has increased significantly (Mann, 1994).

Isle of Dogs life Other observers maintained that right wing groups have never really enjoyed popular support in the East End and they challenged the assumption that most whites in the area are truly 'racist'. According to this view, the election result was not a straightforward expression of racism but rather a protest vote against the deprived conditions on the Isle of Dogs. The area suffers from widespread poverty and high unemployment (following the decline of the docks). In the 1980s City developers arrived and erected luxury apartment blocks and spectacular offices (eg Canary Wharf) but this was of little direct benefit to the local population (see p400).

Many of their houses are unfit and in need of repair and there is an acute housing shortage. Local people are especially sensitive about the allocation of council houses. The Liberal Democrats, the ruling party in Tower Hamlets, have operated a controversial housing policy which gives preference to the 'sons and daughters of locals' (in effect, 'whites'). But in the few years before the election the local authority started to house some homeless Bangladeshi families in the Isle of Dogs. Rumours circulated that all vacant council houses were being allocated to these families (in reality, fewer than one fifth of the 105 families housed in Millwall between April and August 1993 were Bangladeshi). It was against this background that the election took place. The mounting frustrations of the white population resulted in the scapegoating of Bangladeshis. Just like East End Jews in the late nineteenth century or the 1930s, the new arrivals were blamed for 'stealing' homes and jobs.

Community A third explanation of the election result places emphasis not so much on *material* conditions but on the decline of *community* on the Isle of Dogs. The area is formed by a 'loop' in the Thames and it is quite isolated geographically from the rest of the East End. Moreover, the area experienced very little immigration until the recent arrival of Bangladeshis. Consequently, the white population were reasonably cohesive and homogeneous and they had an unusually strong sense of collective identity. But this sense of community was being undermined, partly because of the 1970s migration of Islanders to Essex and partly as a result of the more recent 'yuppie' redevelopment of the area. So the vote for the BNP can be seen as a desperate 'defence' of community against the most visible 'outsiders', the Bangladeshis.

Activity 10 Scapegoating

Item A

Unemployment
Male / Female
(%) Greater London, Inner London, Newham, Southwark, Tower Hamlets

Item B

Ethnic origins
Ethnic origin of residents as a percentage of all residents

Inner London / Tower Hamlets

White 74.4% / 64.4%, Black Caribbean, Black African, Black Other, Indian, Pakistani, Bangladeshi, Chinese, Other Asian, Other Groups

Item C

Tenure and transport
Greater London / Tower Hamlets

(%) Owner Occupied, Rented from Housing Assoc., Rented from Local Authority, Overcrowding, No car

Item D

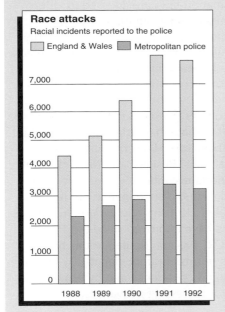

Race attacks
Racial incidents reported to the police

☐ England & Wales ■ Metropolitan police

Items A–D adapted from *Guardian*, 28.9.93

Item E *Dirty pigs*

Pensioner Gladys Lawrence said she voted Labour, but added that the Bangladeshis were 'dirty pigs who bring disease and spit everywhere. I'm not prejudiced, but they've got two wives and get about £300 per week. We have to pay. We work all these years and it is for them. This country is finished.'

Adapted from D. Nelson 'Local Democracy Goes to the Dogs' *Observer*, 19.9.93

Item F *Celebrating*

British National Party supporters celebrate the BNP victory in Millwall.

Item G *No problems in Millwall*

'The British people are no longer prepared to be second class citizens in their own country. We've had enough. We are going to take our country back. Yes, I am a racist. I prefer to live with my own race. I support repatriation. There were no problems in Millwall until the blacks came in.'

Derek Beackon (BNP elected councillor) quoted in *Runnymede Bulletin*, October 1993, pp3–4

Item H *Community*

It is ironic that ethnic minorities are accused of 'destroying' communities, because it is these minorities which best express the spirit of community. What have immigrants to do with the destruction of family, the ruin of relationships, the erosion of neighbourhood? The 'British way of life' would stand a better chance of being restored if we were to take instruction from ethnic minorities: instruction in social cohesion, family solidarity, abiding by the law, hard work. Is it because they remind us of the qualities we have lost that we are so eager to make scapegoats of them?

Adapted from J. Seabrook 'Tabula Rasa', *New Statesman and Society*, 4.6.93, p16

Questions

Look at Items A to H

1 Use relevant items to illustrate
  a) the racism of East Enders
  b) the scapegoating function of racism.
2 Seabrook (Item H) attaches greater importance to 'community' factors than to 'material conditions'. Do you agree? Give reasons for your answer.

2.5 Anti-racism

This section examines some strategies for reducing or eliminating racism in Britain and the United States. Most anti-racism strategies fall into 'liberal' or 'radical' camps although this is not a hard and fast distinction. Broadly speaking, liberals feel that 'race' problems are due to cultural misunderstandings, blocked opportunity structures and the misbehaviour of some foolish or evil people. Successive British governments have followed this 'liberal' route by introducing multicultural education in schools (to remove misunderstandings), by supplying grants (eg under the Urban Programme or Inner City Programme) to create 'opportunity ladders' for ethnic groups, and by enforcing anti-discrimination laws (to curb racialist behaviour). Radicals, on the other hand, usually stress that racism is deeply rooted in society and so they favour more robust political and structural measures. These include physical confrontation with racists, grass-roots organisation and political action to transform the power structure.

Anti-discrimination legislation

Legal measures British governments have introduced a series of Race Relations Acts to prohibit racial discrimination. The 1965 Act covered direct discrimination in public places (hotels, restaurants etc) but the 1968 Act extended its powers to cover important areas like housing and employment. The 1976 Act incorporated 'indirect' as well as 'direct' discrimination and it set up the Commission for Racial Equality (CRE). This signalled a greater stress on prevention and on establishing machinery for 'strategic' investigations (rather than simply responding to individual complaints). Although these acts were accused of 'favouring' black people, it is worth noting that they do not permit 'reverse discrimination' or 'positive discrimination' (eg giving a person a job simply because that person is black). But they do allow employers to maintain a 'reasonable' racial balance in the workforce and they do allow some forms of 'positive action' (eg special training schemes to allow black people to compete on equal terms with whites).

Criticisms A number of criticisms have been levelled at the Acts themselves and also at the way they have been implemented. They have been described as 'toothless', since very few cases are actually taken up and only a small proportion result in successful prosecutions against discriminators. Banton (1992) reports that, out of 1,020 employment cases dealt with at the end of the 1980s, 250 were settled by ACAS (an advisory and conciliation service), 410 by an industrial tribunal, and 360 were withdrawn by the applicants (some of whom may have reached private settlements). And out of the 410 cases presented to tribunals, only 80 reached a finding of discrimination (225 were dismissed and the rest were either outside the tribunal's powers or some other action was taken). Although these prosecution figures seem low, it is worth remembering that CRE places as much emphasis on conciliation and persuasion as on 'punishment'. And there is some evidence that personnel managers and similar groups do indeed fear the scrutiny of CRE investigators (McCrudden et al, 1991).

A second criticism is that the CRE works with an inadequate budget. This suggests a lack of commitment on the part of government. Sivanandan (1982) claims the real purpose of CRE is to create 'tame' black leaders rather than eliminate racism. A third criticism is that, even allowing for its slim budget, the policies of the CRE have been incoherent, reaching out in every direction without having a sufficiently clear sense of purpose. The 1981 Report of the Home Affairs Committee accused the CRE of operating without any obvious sense of priorities or any clearly defined objectives. But the CRE has responded to these criticisms and in the 1980s it developed longer term strategies (eg a Code of Practice for employers). Finally, a frequent criticism is that anti-discrimination laws are doomed to failure because laws cannot change attitudes. But this perhaps misses the point that the laws are primarily intended to change *behaviour* (and if this helps black people to succeed, then indirectly this may start to change attitudes).

Successes Parekh (1991) rescues the reputation of the CRE by pointing out that it has won several important test cases which have forced discriminators to reconsider their actions. Besides, anti-discrimination laws have an important symbolic value: they state that racial prejudice and discrimination are not morally acceptable in British society. Parekh believes that race relations have improved since the 1960s and he feels the CRE has contributed to this by helping to set the norms of public debate, by building a climate of trust and confidence and by providing a peaceful means for redressing grievances.

Table 9 Race Relations Acts

1965 Race Relations Act Banned discrimination in public places (eg hotels, public transport, cinemas). Set up the Race Relations Board.

1968 Race Relations Act Banned discrimination in employment, housing, trade unions, provision of goods and services, and advertising. Set up the Community Relations Commission to foster harmonious community relations at national and local level.

1976 Race Relations Act Extended legislation to include indirect discrimination. Replaced the Race Relations Board and the Community Relations Commission with the Commission for Racial Equality. Powers to launch 'strategic' investigations. Different procedures for complaints - employment cases handled by industrial tribunals; individual complainants given direct access to courts or tribunals.

'Direct action' approaches

Black people (and sympathetic whites) have actively resisted racism in a number of ways - through trade union and political organisation, strikes, demonstrations and civil rights campaigns. One of the most dramatic (and dangerous) anti-racist activities is face to face confrontations with members of right wing and fascist organisations such as the British National Party and the National Front. Although these right wing groups normally attract very few votes when they field candidates in elections, they have built up significant support in certain localities. They have a 'nuisance value' in stirring up racial hatred and creating insecurity among ethnic minorities. Also, some right wing fringe groups are suspected of involvement in racial attacks. In recent years there has been an alarming upsurge in extreme right wing movements throughout Europe and this has been accompanied by an escalation in attacks on 'immigrants'. In Britain, one response to these developments is the revival of anti-racist organisations such as the Anti-Nazi League and the Anti-Racist Alliance. These organisations continue a long tradition of physical challenge to racism: they campaign against right wing electoral candidates and they organise counter marches and demonstrations whenever fascist groups parade through the streets. Defence teams have been formed in some localities to protect minorities and to establish a street 'presence'.

Activity 11 Fighting Back

Item A *Right wing street march*

British National Party, 1993

Item B *A counter-demonstration*

Black People's Alliance march against racism

Item C *New kids on the block*

'Bengalis Rule!'

The 50,000 strong Bangladeshi community in London's Brick Lane are the victims of poverty, deprivation and frequent racist attacks. But the new generation of Asian East Enders are no longer willing to turn the other cheek to white violence and bullying and they are now claiming back the streets. These youngsters are willing to fight back in order to defend their community. 'Take a look at this', chimes "Wally", 'Five years ago no Bangladeshi would have walked down here this time of night. But here we are in Bow, quarter to one, the heart of white man's country, walking nice and easy. Most people aren't going to start with us any more. A few might but they know what they can expect back in return.'

This vigilante action frightens white residents in the area and it also worries Bangladeshi parents who are alarmed at the anger of their children. These parents complain about Asian teenagers being corrupted by the West and they condemn the rise in criminal activity (much of it directed against local Bangladeshi business people). But there are more constructive signs, such as the formation of 'progressive' organisations and youth clubs.

Adapted from 'New Kids on the Block', *Sunday Correspondent*, 5.8.90

Questions

1 Suggest reasons why some people are attracted to right wing groups such as that depicted in Item A.
2 Item B depicts a peaceful anti-racist demonstration, while Item C discusses a 'vigilante' approach. Compare these two approaches, identifying their 'good' points and 'bad' points.

Municipal anti-racism

In the 1970s and early 1980s a number of Labour controlled local authorities (especially in London) began to tackle racism in a vigorous manner. They 'developed positive action programmes, established race relations units, improved training schemes and introduced monitoring of recruitment and employment practices' (Skellington, 1992, p133). Authorities such as the Greater London Council were anxious to ensure that their own policies were in line with their anti-racist public statements. So they introduced Anti-Racism Training (ART) for council staff and they tried to make sure that black people were represented at all levels of the organisational hierarchy. Sometimes they used the tool of 'contract compliance', where they offered council contracts to outside firms only if those firms had a good track record on anti-racism and an acceptable racial balance in their labour force. The councils were also concerned to educate the general public about racism and they ran publicity and information campaigns to that end.

Tabloid images The tabloid press were almost uniformly hostile to these efforts and they missed few opportunities to expose what they saw as the foolish antics of the 'loony left'. They manufactured all sorts of scares and rumours, some of which were plainly untrue (eg councils were planning to abolish 'black' bin liners and ban 'Baa Baa Black Sheep' from council nursery schools). Other stories were exaggerated or distorted (eg Brent was planting 'race spies' in its classrooms - these 'spies' were actually teachers or advisers). The media gave plenty of space to the pundits of the New Right who condemned anti-racism as illiberal, coercive and sinister (eg they complained that contract compliance interfered with the 'natural' workings of the market). Councils were described as 'thought police' who were so obsessed with 'political correctness' that they even cracked down on innocent language (coffee was no longer black or white - it had to be with or without milk!). According to Gordon and Rosenberg (1989), the press questioned the *motives* and *methods* of anti-racists but glossed over the important underlying issue of racism. This had the unfortunate effect of discrediting race equality initiatives.

The end of anti-racism? It is true, however, that some liberals and radicals share media misgivings about these council campaigns. At times the councils appeared very high-handed and they sometimes invited ridicule by trivialising issues (eg a tremendous fuss was created over the golliwog on Robertson's jam jars). Gilroy (1990) says that the campaigns were rather unimaginative and crude, portraying issues mainly in terms of black 'victims' and white

'oppressors' without any consideration of other important factors such as class and gender. Anyway, Gilroy considers that municipal socialism is no longer suitable as the main vehicle for anti-racism, because Conservative governments in the 1980s have progressively weakened the power of local authorities. Moreover, he states that 'direct action' approaches are too preoccupied with fighting 'Nazis' and so they fail to tackle the more subtle problems of 'new racism'. For Gilroy, we have reached the 'end of anti-racism' in its old forms. Nevertheless, he hopes that anti-racists will develop more imaginative 'cultural' and 'political' strategies in the future.

USA: the melting pot

There are obvious social, cultural and historical differences between Britain and the United States. The black minority in the US is larger (over 10% of the population), more homogeneous and longer 'settled' (due to the slave trade). Also, the US has an established tradition of 'ethnic politics', one feature of which is the important leadership role provided by black churches. Because of these differences, it cannot be assumed that the 'lessons' of one country apply to the other. Nevertheless, connections do exist. British policymakers have copied some US anti-racist strategies and Britain's blacks have been influenced by the 'Black Consciousness' movement across the Atlantic. Besides, the US experience is interesting because of the energy and range of its anti-racist approaches. It provides models of bold strategies to combat racialism (civil rights), institutional racism (riots/Black Power) and cultural racism ('soul'/Black is Beautiful).

Civil rights Although black slaves were emancipated after the American Civil War of 1861-65, black people continued to be denied full civil rights. 'Jim Crow' legislation was gradually introduced in many states to enforce racial segregation (eg in restaurants, buses, toilets, housing) and to restrict voting rights (by means of registration rules or taxes). In 1954 the Supreme Court ruled that 'separate but equal' provisions in education were unlawful (and seldom equal), but the process of desegregation seemed to be painfully slow. Racial discrimination was still widespread, especially in Southern states such as Alabama. So the civil rights movement of the 1950s and 1960s decided to challenge this in a very dramatic way. It gained worldwide publicity through its 'direct action' tactics of boycotts, sit-ins, 'freedom rides', marches and campaigns of civil disobedience. A major inspiration for the movement was Martin Luther King, a Christian who urged protesters to remain non-violent and dignified even when severely provoked by racists and police. The early activists were often middle class and included white sympathisers, but by the 1960s the civil rights crusade had turned into a mass black movement. Key victories came with the 1964 Civil Rights Act and the 1965 Voting Rights Act which finally ended the 'Jim Crow' system.

Riots Civil rights legislation failed to provide a solution to the plight of the black urban ghettoes of the north and west. These 'internal colonies' (Blauner, 1972) had deep social and economic problems and they were the most visible expression of institutional racism within US society. The mounting tensions exploded in a series of disturbances and riots in many US cities in the 1960s. Harlem, Chicago, Detroit and Newark witnessed serious eruptions but the greatest 'shock' to US society was the 1965 riot in the Watts district of south Los Angeles. This 6-day rampage stunned the nation with its spectacle of pitched battles between rioters and police, destruction of cars and shops, and arson ('Burn, baby, burn!'). The Kerner Report (1968) on Watts identified a long list of community grievances: police racism, poverty, unemployment, poor housing and education, lack of recreational facilities and an unresponsive political system. 'What the rioters appeared to be seeking was fuller participation in the social order and the material benefits enjoyed by the majority of American citizens' (Kerner, 1968, p7).

Black Power The Black Power movement emerged from the ghetto unrest of the mid-1960s. Its leaders (eg Stokely Carmichael, Malcolm X) were young and militant and impatient for change. They accepted the Kerner Report's conclusion that white racism was responsible for the problems of the ghettoes but they scorned its faith in 'reform' and they rejected the 'integration' of black people into white society. 'Integration' implied accepting the terms imposed by whites, terms which would ensure the continued dehumanisation and degradation of black people. Instead, Black Power aimed for self-determination and this meant black people taking control of their own communities and building their own businesses and political organisations. If black people were to prosper, they would have to 'separate' from white society. Once they had developed their own power structure they could then negotiate with white people as 'equals' from a position of strength. The movement achieved notoriety because of this separatist stance and because of its willingness to resort to armed struggle. Its public image was epitomised by Huey Newton and Bobby Seale, founders of the Black Panthers, who posed with guns, black berets and clenched fists. They were accused of being 'racists in reverse' but they insisted their aim was not to subjugate whites. 'The black people of this country have not lynched whites, bombed their churches,

murdered their children and manipulated laws and institutions to maintain oppression. White racists have' (Carmichael and Hamilton, 1968, p61).

Say it loud, I'm Black and I'm proud This James Brown song expressed the new mood of 'Black Consciousness' in the mid-1960s. The Kerner Report noted that the alienation and apathy of the ghettoes had been transformed into a growing sense of racial pride. Black people no longer suffered from low self-esteem. They proclaimed that 'Black is Beautiful', they adopted 'Afro' hairstyles and ethnic dress, and they set up courses in 'black studies' and 'black culture'. They proudly claimed that black people possessed 'soul'. Soul is not easy to define, but Keil (1966) suggests it includes the following components: a warm emotional spirit; physical accomplishments ('walk that walk'); perseverance and staying power ('survival'); shared experiences and strong bonds ('brotherhood'); a rich, earthy vocabulary ('rap'); a sense of timing and rhythm; and the wisdom of experience ('tell it like it is'). Haralambos (1994) describes how 'soul music' became the dominant style of black musical expression in the 1960s. Whereas 'blues' music reflected misery and suffering, soul mirrored the new buoyant mood of optimism and hope. Above all, it offered blacks a positive identity: 'Soul associates those aspects considered essentially black and stamps them with a seal of approval. Black is no longer inferior, no longer a poor copy of white' (Haralambos, 1994, p130). By overturning racist stereotypes, Black Consciousness issued a clear challenge to the cultural racism of US society.

Progress? The 1960s riots led to major policy changes in US society. These included civil rights legislation, police recruitment of more blacks, and the reform programmes of President Johnson (eg schemes to promote minority businesses, the War Against Poverty). The US also moved towards 'affirmative action' policies which set targets and quotas for minority representation in education and employment. But have these policies been effective?
1 Cultural racism Clairborne (1970) claims there has been a gradual 'revolution of attitudes' so that it is no longer acceptable (at least in public) for whites to allege that blacks are 'inferior'. However, Blauner (1989) notes the irony that many blacks seem to have rejected the racial consciousness which was expressed in the 1960s by Black Power, black pride and black culture.
2 Racialism Powerful legal remedies now exist to punish the more blatant forms of discrimination. Moreover, black people have improved their political representation (although they are still under-represented in Senate) and black mayors have been elected in many US cities. This gives them greater

power to resist racial discrimination.

3 Institutional racism Most black people have enjoyed absolute improvements in education, housing and jobs. But Wilson (1978, 1987) argues that middle class blacks and ghetto blacks have become polarised. Confident middle class blacks (eg as shown in the *Cosby Show*) have taken full advantage of the new opportunities created by affirmative action and civil rights legislation. But very little of their new prosperity trickles down to the working class blacks left in the inner city areas. These ghettoes have become far less pleasant places. Quite apart from increases in violence, unemployment, drug use, crime and family instability, the sense of 'community' has been lost. The flight of the successful, 'respectable' blacks to the suburbs has left the ghettoes without role models and community organisers. Wilson (1987) maintains that 'race' policies do not provide an effective solution for the ghetto, since it is wider economic trends which have created the present problem. For Wilson, the main solution lies in reducing the high unemployment rates among working class blacks.

It is clear that the problems of the ghetto have not been resolved. Films such as *Boyz n the Hood* (set in Los Angeles) reveal the high levels of violence and help us understand why black leaders have called for the ending of 'black genocide' in the ghettoes. Sadly, the Watts riot of 1965 was eclipsed by the Los Angeles riots of 1992, sparked off when a jury acquitted four policemen although video evidence revealed their brutal beating of a black suspect. This riot left 50 people dead and caused one billion dollars of damage.

Summary

1 Racism can be defined in terms of ideologies (cultural racism), practices (racialism) or outcomes (institutional racism). 'New racism' is an exaggerated expression of cultural *differences*.
2 Evidence suggests that racism is a significant problem in modern Britain.
3 There is no single or simple explanation for racism but sociologists usually adopt 'cultural' and 'structural' models.
4 Anti-racist 'solutions' have enjoyed varying amounts of success.

Activity 12 The American Dream

Item A *Watts*

As we assembled in the prison yard we met a group of 'low riders' (ghetto youth) from Watts. They were wearing jubilant, triumphant smiles, as if they, too, were in the thick of the uprising taking place hundreds of miles away to the south in the Watts ghetto. They slapped each other's outstretched palms and burst out laughing with joy. 'Them brothers is taking care of business!', shrieked one ecstatically.

Then one low rider stepped into the centre of the circle. 'Baby', he said, 'they walking in fours and kicking in doors, drinking wine and committing crime, shooting and looting; setting fires and slashing tyres; turning over cars and burning down bars; putting an end to that go slow crap and putting sweet Watts on the map - my black ass is in Folsom prison this morning but my black heart is in Watts!' Tears of joy were rolling from his eyes.

It was a cleansing, revolutionary laugh we all shared. Watts used to be a place of shame. But now blacks are saying, 'I'm from Watts, baby!'

Adapted from E. Cleaver *Soul on Ice*, 1968, pp37-8

Item B *Black males*

Black males have the lowest life expectancy of any group in the United States. Their unemployment rate is more than twice that of white males; even black men with college degrees are 3 times more likely to be unemployed than their white counterparts. About 1 in 4 black men between the ages of 20 and 29 is behind bars. Blacks receive longer prison sentences than whites who have committed the same crimes. Nearly one third of all black families in America live below the poverty line. Half of all black children are born in poverty and will spend all their youth growing up in poor families.

Adapted from a 1991 report of the 21st Century Commission on African-American Males, quoted in preface of S.Terkel *Race*, 1993

Item C *Progress?*

Median school years completed for people aged 25-29

	All Persons (Years)	Blacks (Years)
1940	10.3	7.0
1950	12.0	8.6
1960	12.3	9.9
1970	12.6	12.1
1980	12.9	12.6
1985	12.9	12.7
1986	12.9	12.7
1987	12.8	12.7

High-school dropouts, as a percentage of the 14-24 population

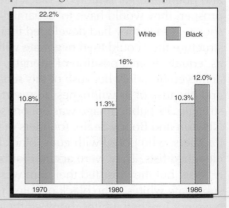

Watts riots, 1965

Watts riots, 1992

Comparative unemployment rates

	1972 %	1975 %	1980 %	1982 %	1983 %	1984 %	1985 %	1986 %	1987 %
White	5.1	7.8	6.3	8.6	8.4	6.5	6.2	6.0	5.3
Black	10.4	14.8	14.3	18.9	19.5	15.9	15.1	14.5	13.0
Ratio Black: White	**2.0**	**1.9**	**2.3**	**2.2**	**2.3**	**2.4**	**2.4**	**2.4**	**2.4**

Comparative median weekly earnings of full time workers

	1980 %	1982 %	1983 %	1984 %	1986 %	1987 %
Black males as % of white males	76.6	74.6	75.3	75.4	73.4	72.4
Black females as % of white females	90.6	88.1	91.3	91.7	89.5	89.6
Black females as % of white males	57.3	57.2	58.2	60.0	60.7	61.1

Changes in occupational distribution of black workers

Occupational group	Blacks 1960 %	1970 %	1975 %	1979 %	1980 %	Whites 1980 %
White collar	16.1	27.9	34.7	37.9	39.2	53.9
Blue collar	40.1	42.2	37.4	36.7	35.8	31.1
Service workers	31.7	26.0	25.8	23.2	23.1	12.1
Farm workers	12.1	3.9	2.6	2.2	1.8	2.9

Black elected officials in southern states

	1968 Numbers	1970 Numbers	1980 Numbers	1988 Number	1988 Black % of total offices	1988 Black % of state's population
Alabama	24	83	283	442	10.6	24.5
Georgia	21	42	249	458	6.9	26.2
Louisiana	37	64	363	524	11.1	29.6
Mississippi	29	78	387	578	11.0	35.1
North Carolina	10	58	247	428	8.1	21.5
South Carolina	11	34	238	352	11.0	31.0
Virginia	24	28	91	126	4.1	18.7
Total	**156**	**387**	**1858**	**2908**	**9.0**	**26.6**

Note: The seven states shown are those covered by the Voting Rights Act.

Statistical data adapted from D. Mervin ' Black Progress in the USA' *Social Studies Review*, vol 5 no4, 1990

Watts riots, 1992

Questions

1 Explain the reactions of the black prisoners (Item A).

2 Using Items B and C, describe the 'progress' of black people in the USA.

3 Race and Class

Key Issues

1 What are the main features of racial stratification?
2 How do Marxist and Weberian models differ?
3 Is there a black underclass?
4 How do racial and ethnic minorities fit in to the labour market?

Stratification refers to the hierarchical arrangement of social groups, where the position of each group reflects its relative wealth, status and power. Sociologists usually discuss stratification in terms of 'economic' categories such as social class, occupations and the market-place. But this does not mean that 'race' and 'ethnicity' are irrelevant. Indeed, a number of sociologists use the term 'racial stratification' to stress the close connections which sometimes exist between race and class. The basic idea is that the stratification hierarchy represents racial divisions as well as social class divisions. In some societies the boundaries of class and race broadly coincide, with racial minorities forming a more or less distinctive and subordinate class. Slavery and apartheid offer the clearest examples of this kind of racial stratification. In modern Britain the connection between race and class is not quite so clear cut, since minorities are found at different levels within the stratification pyramid. Nevertheless, even here race has a significant effect on class, status and power. For example, racial discrimination increases the chances that racial minorities will be concentrated in the lower social strata.

Part 3 explores these relationships between race and class. It looks at historical examples, contemporary evidence and relevant theories. The theories fall into two main camps: Marxist and Weberian models. These models are based on different assumptions and arguments and they employ distinctive concepts. But it is easy to exaggerate their disagreements. In spite of all the shadow-boxing which goes on, there is a considerable degree of consensus on many issues.

3.1 Slavery

The transatlantic slave trade The transatlantic traffic in slaves lasted from the sixteenth to the nineteenth century. During this period, millions of black Africans were forcibly uprooted from their homelands and transported to the Americas and West Indies. Some African societies already had a tradition of slavery even before this traffic began. People in these societies sometimes became slaves through conquest or as punishment for crimes or debt, but it was not the normal custom to sell slaves. However, this changed when Arab traders began to develop a flourishing trans-Saharan slave trade (Fryer, 1988). Long before Europeans started to ship Africans across the Atlantic, Arab traders had already transported some 4 million black slaves to the Mediterranean and the Middle East (Walvin, 1992). But the transatlantic trade was on an even larger scale. Estimates for the total number of slaves transported across the Atlantic vary between 10 and 20 million, with perhaps 10-20% perishing during the voyage.

The transatlantic slave trade was started by the Spanish and Portuguese and they were soon joined by French and Dutch traders. But British ships played a leading role in the 'triangular slave trade' between Britain, Africa and the Caribbean. The first passage of this triangle was from the ports of Britain to the western coast of Africa. The ships carried metalware, cutlery, silks, textiles, spirits and firearms and these goods were exchanged for black slaves. Captains of slave ships colluded with African rulers and merchants whom they usually depended upon to organise slave-raiding operations and escort the captives to the coastal ports. These slaves were often bewildered and terrorised after being marched long distances, usually linked together by neck collars ('coffles'). The slave cargo then endured the gruelling 'middle passage' to the Caribbean (mainly Jamaica) in shipboard conditions which were cramped, filthy and insanitary. Not surprisingly, disease was rife and there were high death rates among the white crews as well as the black slaves (Banton, 1987a). On arrival in the Caribbean the slaves were auctioned off and the ships loaded up with sugar, tobacco, rum, molasses or cotton before setting off on the third passage back to Britain.

Plantation economy The main reason for the growth in the slave trade was the increasing demand for labour in the New World colonies. Workers were needed for the profitable mines and plantations of Latin America, the tobacco and cotton fields of North America and the sugar plantations of the West Indies. At first the European colonial powers relied on forced labour by the local populations but the original inhabitants were soon depleted by disease, overwork and violence (eg in the West Indies the Caribs and Arawak Indians were wiped out). The resultant labour shortage was partly filled by indentured whites, including paupers, convicts or deportees, and these 'servants' were often treated with great cruelty (Patterson, 1967). But these sources were not sufficient to satisfy the labour needs of the developing colonies and so African slaves were forced to fill the gap.

In Jamaica most slaves were set to work in the cane fields and in the sugar distilleries and boiling houses. Women were normally expected to work alongside men but they were also used as domestic servants or cooks in the houses of the landowners. Indeed, it would be wrong to think that slaves comprised a uniform mass. Different skills were required to run plantations efficiently and so there was a move towards occupational specialisation: 'a large labouring majority at the base, above which was a smaller number of semi-skilled slaves (craftsmen, domestics) with a small elite of drivers and headmen at the top' (Walvin, 1992, p105). Black overseers ('slave drivers') and those with skills (eg smiths, masons, carpenters, shoemakers, seamstresses) usually had a few more privileges than labourers and field hands. Domestic servants who misbehaved were typically punished by being sent back to work in the fields.

Slavery and stratification Even though slaves performed essential tasks in plantation society, they were clearly at the bottom of the social ladder. The top of Jamaican society was occupied by the 'plantocracy', a small elite group of wealthy whites who owned the large estates and sugar plantations. Once they had established their fortunes they often grew bored with life in the West Indies and many of them became absentee landlords, returning to their grand mansions in Britain and leaving their Jamaican plantations in the hands of agents and overseers (Walvin, 1992). Below the plantocracy there were other small groups of whites - those who owned more modest amounts of land and slaves, those who filled specialised occupations (eg , colonial officials, agents, soldiers) and a sprinkling of adventurers and sailors. Patterson (1967) notes that sailors and black slaves often mixed freely and treated each other as social 'equals'. But this was deceptive. Whatever their station in life, whites enjoyed more 'rights' than the black slaves who formed the great majority of the population. Slaves were disadvantaged in terms of property, status and power.

1 Property Instead of being paid for their work, slaves were normally 'rewarded' by their masters giving them food, shelter and clothing. Only a very few (eg blacksmiths) were allowed to earn a little money by hiring out their skills. Consequently, slaves generally had little property of their own. In fact, slaves *were* property. They were bought and sold and even their children became the property of the slaveowner. Members of a family could be separated at the whim of the owner.

2 Status Slaves were not regarded as fully 'human'. Although some limited legal 'protection' was gradually extended to them, they were denied the normal legal, civil and political rights enjoyed by free citizens. Occasionally, slaves were granted their freedom, usually as a reward for long service or to save the owner the cost of keeping slaves who were too old to work. But even freed slaves found that they were not treated as equals by white society. The stigma of slavery rubbed off on all black people, slave or free, and it also attached to children of 'mixed' race (although, in the West Indies, mixed offspring and slaves with 'lighter' skin had higher status than 'black' slaves).

3 Power Slaveowners were legally entitled to inflict brutal punishments (eg branding, flogging, maiming) in order to maintain tight control over slaves. They forced slaves to work long hours in exhausting conditions, and an estimated 1 in 3 died within three years of arrival in the West Indies. Moreover, female slaves were sexually exploited on a regular basis by whites. Usually it was too risky for black slaves to complain about their treatment and so they mostly had to develop 'secret' strategies of resistance (eg slowing down the pace of work, or deliberately 'playing dumb'). But sometimes slaves ran away to escape the harsh conditions, risking heavy punishment if they were caught. Violent insurrections were quite frequent in the West Indies, even after slavery was abolished. But the famous 'Maroon' rebellion of 1865 was ruthlessly suppressed by the troops of Governor Eyre.

The legacy of slavery Historians dispute the main reasons for the abolition of slavery. Some credit the activities of anti-slavery campaigners (such as Wilberforce) who attacked the violent and dehumanising nature of the slave system. Others claim the main factor was the long term economic decline of the plantations. Whatever the reason, slavery in the West Indies was ended in the 1830s. By that time, however, the slave plantations had already made a significant contribution to Britain's prosperity (sugar was called 'white gold' or 'King Sugar'). Historians argue about the scale of the profits and whether these profits financed the Industrial Revolution or were spent mostly on 'conspicuous consumption' (eg large mansion houses and estates in Britain). But there is little doubt that Britain made great economic gains. For example, the slave trade boosted the fortunes of ports like Bristol and Liverpool.

But slavery also left a bitter legacy. Rodney (1972) argues that the slave trade had a disastrous effect on the economic fortunes of Africa. He maintains that the massive depopulation of the African continent severely hindered its prospects for economic development. Also, the historical tragedy of slavery has had a lasting effect on race relations. Even today many white people associate black skin with the stigma of slavery (although Walvin, 1992, shows that many racist stereotypes pre-dated the slave trade). Not surprisingly, the memory of the African 'diaspora' (forcible scattering) still has deep significance for many black people in the present day (Gilroy, 1987).

Activity 13 Slave Conditions

Item A 'Slave Driver'

Every time I hear the crack of the whip
My blood runs cold
I remember on the slave ship
How they brutalised my very soul
  (Bob Marley and the Wailers)

Item B *The slave 'business'*

I know I speak for all of us when I say that we're delighted to have you people join us, and that we look forward to working with you on many interesting projects in the days and years to come

$1200 TO 1250 DOLLARS! FOR NEGROES!!

NEGROES

LEXINGTON, JULY 2, 1853.   WM. F. TALBOTT.

Item C A *slave's viewpoint*

My mother and I were separated when I was an infant. She was taken away and hired out to a distant farm. My first master, Anthony, took great pleasure in whipping slaves. I was often awakened at dawn by the heart-rending shrieks of my aunt who he would whip until she was literally covered with blood.

Very soon I went to live with Mr and Mrs Auld. She very kindly started teaching me the ABC. But Mr Auld found out what was going on and forbade her to instruct me, telling her that, 'A nigger should know nothing but to obey his master - to do as he is told to do. Learning would spoil the best nigger in the world.'

Adapted from Frederick Douglass *Autobiography of a Black Slave*, 1867

Questions

1 Using all the items, examine the position of slaves in the 'racial stratification' system. Use the concepts of power, status, wealth, life chances and social mobility in your answer.
2 Using Items C and D, briefly describe
  a) slavery as a form of social control
  b) the arguments white people used to 'justify' slavery.

Item D *Slavemasters' viewpoints*

The state gave the slaveowner the right to punish his slaves. Whipping was the most common punishment on the plantations in the USA. However, in the words of a Louisiana slaveowner, it must never be 'cruel or severe' though it must be repeated at regular intervals 'until the most entire submission' was achieved. And this was good for a slave. According to a Georgian slaveowner, it tended 'to win his attachment and promote his happiness and wellbeing'. Many used whipping to 'break in' a young slave and to 'break the spirit' of an older, insubordinate slave. And some masters got quite upset about having to punish their slaves. A slaveowner from Tennessee wrote, 'Had to whip my man Willis for insolence to the overseer. This I done with much regret as he was never whipped before.'

Adapted from K.M.Stampp *The Peculiar Institution*, 1956, pp171-191

3.2 Apartheid

The South African system of apartheid ('separate development') is a striking example of stratification along racial lines. The doctrine of apartheid states that the main racial groups have radically different cultures and histories and so they should lead a separate existence as far as possible. This doctrine was formally introduced by the National Party in 1948, but racial segregation was a persistent feature of the troubled history of South Africa since the Dutch first established a settlement in the Cape of Good Hope in 1652 (Lapping, 1986). The new settlers pushed the local populations (nomadic Khoi Khoi and San) to the fringes and they also brought Malay slaves to the Cape area. Nearly a hundred years later the British occupied the Cape and by 1806 they had established local control. This prompted the disaffected Dutch Boers ('farmers') to start the 'Great Trek' which lasted from 1835 to the early 1840s. This trek to the north and east brought the Boers into armed conflict with the highly organised Bantu populations. (Bantu means 'people' but generally it refers to the language group to which most black South Africans belong). The Boers (or Afrikaners) managed to establish independent republics in the Orange Free State and the Transvaal but the British followed them north after the discovery of diamonds in 1867 and gold in 1887. Tensions increased between the Boer republics, the British controlled areas (Cape and Natal) and the independent black states which still existed. The British emerged as victors of the Zulu Wars in 1887, but soon after they were locked in combat with the Afrikaners in the Boer Wars of 1899-1902. The Union of South Africa was finally formed in 1910, with a joint British-

Afrikaner government (which denied full voting rights to non-whites).

Apartheid laws The basic trappings of apartheid were slowly assembled in the ensuing years. In 1913, for example, a Land Act was passed to allocate blacks to 'tribal lands' (later called homelands or Bantustans). But it was the period following the 1948 elections that saw the most rigorous legislation to enforce apartheid. The Population Registration Act (1950) formally divided the population into distinct racial groups: *whites* (Afrikaans and English-speaking), *coloured* (mixed-race, mainly descendants of white-black relationships in the Cape area), *Indian* or *Asian* (originally indentured labourers recruited around 1860 for the Natal sugar plantations) and African or Black (Bantu-speaking tribal groups eg Zulu, Xhosa, Swazi). The government specified the geographical areas where each of these groups was entitled to live (see Table 10). Blacks were supposed to live in the allegedly 'independent' homelands (eg Ciskei, Transkei) or in one of the six non-independent homelands. But the white-designated areas (Cape, Natal, Orange Free State and Transvaal) still needed black labour and so many blacks continued to live there, mainly in municipal townships (eg Soweto) which remained under white control. The Coloured and Indian populations (who were not given separate land) were usually found in zones within 'white' towns and cities.

The apartheid system used tight controls in order to maintain racial separation. Pass Laws restricted the movement of blacks within white areas, while the Job Reservation Act specified the type of work which each racial group could legally perform. Blacks and whites attended different schools, colleges and hospitals and there was rigid segregation even in public spaces such as beaches, waiting rooms or public transport. Sexual relations between white and non-white were prohibited by the Immorality Act. So apartheid required a very complicated system of regulations and provisions to enforce racial divisions.

Social inequalities Defenders of apartheid sometimes claimed that it gave each racial group the 'freedom' to develop its own way of life. Against this, critics argued that apartheid was a single, inter-linked system, and one in which the more powerful whites were able to pursue their own interests by exploiting other groups. Apartheid has been described as 'a rationalisation for racial oppression dressed up in the language of group rights' (Stone, 1985, p16). Although blacks are the largest population group, they have only 13% of the land. There are massive inequalities in living standards between the racial groups, with many blacks living in appalling squalor in the townships. It is the scale of these inequalities,

as well as the offensive nature of racial segregation, that explain the international condemnation of apartheid. In 1962 South Africa left the Commonwealth and after that it was subject to international sanctions and boycotts. Moreover, the system's internal strains and conflicts resulted in tragic violence (eg the massacre at Sharpeville in 1960, when 69 black demonstrators were killed).

Dismantling apartheid Because of the mounting pressures, the apartheid system is slowly being dismantled. The 1980s witnessed a number of important reforms: the Dutch Reformed Church in South Africa declared that apartheid was 'sinful' and unacceptable to Christians; mixed marriages were legalised; the Pass Laws were abolished; and coloured and Indian politicians entered the government as junior partners. In the 1990s, President de Klerk ended segregation in public places, legalised the African National Congress (ANC) and freed the black leader Nelson Mandela, who had been imprisoned from 1962 till 1992 for his resistance to apartheid. The laws of apartheid have now been repealed but the move towards constitutional reform and full voting rights for all groups was painful. Fighting between the rival black parties of the ANC and (mainly Zulu) Inkatha resulted in many deaths (eg the 1992 massacre in Boipatong, a township south of Johannesburg, where 51 people were killed by Zulu raiders). Some observers say these violent incidents were deliberately triggered by sinister white groups (eg covert security forces, or right wing extremist groups such as the Afrikaner Resistance Movement).

In 1994 South Africa had its first non-racial elections. Nelson Mandela was appointed president and the country is now governed by a multi-racial assembly. However, the legacy of apartheid remains. It will take many years and concerted action at every level of society to remove the harsh and brutal inequalities which apartheid created. But, for the first time in centuries of white rule, there is hope for the possibility of a society without racism.

Table 10 South African population, 1991 (thousands)

	African	Asian	Coloured	White
white-designated areas	12,266	984	3,272	5,068
'independent' homelands	7,239	5	22	17
other homelands	9,558	4	7	6
(total)	29,063	993	3,301	5,091

Adapted from *The Economist* (South Africa supplement), 20.3.93, p8

Activity 14 Separate Lives

Item A *Segregation*

Whites and blacks have to live in different areas. Education and health services are segregated - black people have to use separate buses, trains, beaches, restaurants, hotels, bars, cinemas, toilets, sports grounds and even separate taxis and ambulances. In every case the services for whites are much better than those for blacks.

Adapted from *International Defence and Aid Fund for Southern Africa*, 1978, p6

Nelson Mandela

Item B *Life chances*

Living standards in South Africa (1988)

	whites	blacks
Income per head	$6,500	$670
life expectancy	73 years	57 years
adult literacy	100%	80%
infant mortality	13 per 1,000	57 per 1,000
patient/doctor ratio	400/1	9,000/1

Adapted from *The Economist* (South Africa supplement), 20.3.93, p3

Item C *Makeba's story*

The whites have to justify the rape of our land, and so they claim that we are inferior. They say we are ignorant children. Our salvation and welfare are - alas! - 'the white man's burden'. The message begins to sink in. First, your self- respect disappears. You begin to hate everything that is black...

   Now that I am going out into the white world, I must be careful how I act. I do not know any white people, but I have learned how to speak to them. If a man or woman addresses me, I must answer 'Ja, baas', which is Afrikaans for 'Yes, boss'. If a white child addresses me, I must say 'Ja, klein baas', which is 'Yes, little boss'. I must be very careful if I want to survive.

Adapted from Miriam Makeba *Makeba, My Story*, 1988

Item D *Nelson Mandela*

Prisons, torture and even death will never cow us into submission. We will pursue the struggle until we have transformed South Africa into a united, nonracial, nonsexist democratic country. We are on the brink of major changes. But before we reach that promised land we still have to travel a tortuous road. Apartheid is still in place. Apartheid continues to imprison, brutalise, maim and kill our people. Apartheid continues to destroy the future of our children. Apartheid remains a crime against humanity.

Adapted from a speech by Nelson Mandela, 1990, in G.Carson et al *The Eyes on the Prize*, 1991, pp721-722

Item E *Non-racial elections*

'Today I became a human being.'
An old black man waiting to vote in the first non-racial election in South Africa.

Quoted on *Today*, Radio 4, 26.4.94

Questions

1 a) Identify any similarities in the race relations situations in Britain and South Africa.
   b) Identify the main differences in the race relations situations in Britain and South Africa.
2 Why has apartheid been called a system of 'racial stratification'?
3 Compare Makeba's 'personal' story (Item C) with Mandela's 'political' statement (Item D). Identify the similarities and differences in their accounts.
4 Explain the comment in Item E.

3.3 Weberian models

Class and status In order to understand Weberian ideas on racial stratification we first have to recall their general views on class and status. For Weberians, social class is defined in terms of positions in the economic market-place. And whereas Marxists stress the basic dichotomy between the ruling class and working class, Weberians recognise a much greater variety of economic positions and social classes. So where do racial and ethnic minorities fit in to the British class system?

Weberians suggest that, although members of minorities may be distributed across a number of social classes, they are usually concentrated in 'lower' economic groups and they may even constitute an 'underclass' (see below). In addition to treating racial and ethnic groups as members of 'classes', Weberians also describe them as members of 'status' groups or communities. Minority groups in Britain are usually ranked lower than white people in terms of prestige and respect and so they suffer from status inequality as well as class inequality. For example, even middle class 'Asians' in Britain are likely to be regarded as 'low status' by whites. In Weberian terms, then, races can be treated as groups which occupy particular market positions ('classes') or as members of stigmatised communities ('status groups').

The 'status group' approach involves paying special attention to the 'cultural' features of race relations. And these features need to be studied at their own level rather than always 'reducing' them to economic explanations. 'Race' and 'culture' are not merely 'surface' matters which are better explained at the 'deeper' level of class and the economy. So racial and ethnic conflicts cannot just be brushed aside in order that the 'real' task of class analysis can begin. For example, Parkin (1979) contends that ethnic conflict is just as important as class conflict and he urges sociologists to pay more attention to 'ethnic cleavages' in Western societies.

Nevertheless, while most Weberians recognise the 'autonomy' of race they usually accept that it is only partial. It makes little sense to study race and culture in total isolation from class analysis, because racial and ethnic groups participate alongside every other group in the class struggle. Thus, Parkin shows how ethnic groups frequently engage in power struggles not just for status but also for material goods. They mobilise themselves to protect their existing privileges by 'excluding' other groups and they also try to 'usurp' the privileges of groups which are better off. So racial and ethnic groups use their power to maintain or challenge the distribution of social privileges and rewards.

The underclass

The underclass - definitions

That massive population at the very bottom of the social class ladder, plagued by poor education and low-paying unstable jobs (W.J.Wilson, 1978, p1).

The class structure of industrial societies, including Britain, is developing an underclass of those who cannot be placed in the stable workforce of the formally employed...They suffer a cumulation of social pathologies - educational failure, illiteracy, broken families, high crime rates, poor housing, and spatial concentration in the inner city. They are disproportionately recruited from the young and the ethnic minorities, and they tend to adopt a ghetto existence outside the normal social contract of citizenship and with little or no stake in official society. (A.H.Halsey, 'Britain's Class Society', *Guardian* , 13.7.87)

Features of the underclass Glasgow (1981) describes the underclass as a more or less permanently trapped population at the very bottom of the stratification pyramid. Basically, then, it refers to poor and powerless people, the 'losers' in the system. This includes white people but Rex and Tomlinson (1979) feel that the 'underclass' is an especially suitable term for describing the collective plight of Britain's racial and ethnic minorities. This can be illustrated by looking at the characteristic features of the underclass as described by Dahrendorf (1987) and Saunders (1990).

1 Multiple deprivation The underclass suffers from a host of social ills including low income, unemployment, poor housing and education. In the case of black people, their disadvantage is even more severe because they are the victims of racial discrimination as well. Indeed, Rex and Tomlinson (1979) say there is a 'structural break' between black people and the white working class. In the 1950s and 1960s immigrants filled the menial jobs which white people had deserted. To a large extent this black 'replacement population' has remained concentrated in the same jobs and industries. In housing, too, they have been forced into quasi-ghetto conditions and disadvantaged 'housing classes'. In general, black people do not share the same privileges and experiences as the white working class.

2 Social marginality The underclass is marginalised in terms of power and so it is unable to organise effectively to improve its situation. Rex and Tomlinson argue that minorities may be members of 'traditional' working class institutions such as the Labour Party or trade unions but these bodies do not represent or promote their interests. This means they are denied the normal channels for expressing and resolving grievances. Indeed, in a later work, Rex (1988a) developed the idea that the underclass is excluded from full *citizenship* rights in the welfare state. Historically, class conflict in Britain was resolved by means of a postwar 'truce' or 'welfare deal' which guaranteed the 'mainstream' working class certain fundamental citizenship rights (eg employment, welfare services, police protection). But black people have not been 'incorporated' to the same extent and they tend to get a raw deal from the welfare state.

3 Culture of fatalism and despair Members of the underclass feel alienated from the wider society and they lack a sense of hope or purpose in life. Field (1981) found little empirical evidence for the view that young blacks are significantly more cynical or critical of British society. Nevertheless, a National Opinion Poll survey in 1991 found that there was considerably more dissatisfaction and disaffection among Afro-Caribbean people than among Asians or whites (Runnymede, 1991). They were much more suspicious of employers, police and the education system and they felt that they received far worse treatment from the major institutions of society. Also, Pryce's (1979) ethnographic study charted the sense of despair of blacks located in the inner city ghettos or 'internal colonies' of Britain. Sometimes these resentments and frustrations erupt into violence. Thus, Young and Lea (1982) argue that urban riots can be partly explained by the political marginalisation of black people.

4 Welfare state dependency Saunders (1990) describes the underclass as almost entirely dependent on state welfare provisions. It is a client class locked into state patronage. And Dahrendorf (1987) fears that members of the underclass may lose the work habit as they become accustomed to life on the dole. But does this apply to racial minorities? Although minority groups are more likely to receive certain welfare benefits (with the exception of retirement pensions), Oppenheim (1993) shows that this is a direct result of their greater poverty rather than any 'welfare mentality'. Indeed the evidence suggests that they *under*-claim benefits to which they are entitled. Also, research suggests that many black youngsters try very hard to get jobs but find it difficult because of racial discrimination (Lee and Wrench, 1981). Finally, although minority groups have higher unemployment rates it is worth remembering that most adults in these groups are employed.

Criticisms So, while the concept of underclass appears relevant to Britain's minorities, it is not applicable in every respect. It has to be handled with a great deal of care, especially in light of the general criticisms which have been levelled at it. These criticisms fall under three main headings.

1 Lack of clarity The term 'underclass' is so flexible that it is not always clear just exactly what is being argued. Does it refer only to racial minorities or does it include white people as well? Does it apply to all ethnic minorities or only to certain ones? Is the underclass a homogeneous group, or are there important divisions *within* it? Also, Williams (1989) says Rex and Tomlinson's approach is theoretically weak since it does not really clarify the relationship between race and class.

2 Blaming the victim Some writers stigmatise and blame the members of the underclass as if their poverty was the direct effect of their own moral failings and shortcomings (compare some of the 'culture of poverty' arguments, p182). Murray (1984), for example, highlights their 'deviant' lifestyles (violent crime, drugs, welfare scrounging, unstable family life). However, Murray attaches most blame not to the underclass but to an allegedly 'over-generous' welfare state system which, he claims, wraps them in a permanent state of dependency. This 'right-wing' interpretation of the underclass is one reason why many social scientists are wary of using the term. Lister (1990) says that underclass debates frequently use the language of 'contamination' and 'disease' when discussing the supposedly 'pathological' features of the poor. This takes attention away from the major structural and political causes of poverty and powerlessness. On the other hand, the term 'underclass' is used right across the political spectrum and some liberals (eg Field, 1989) and radicals (eg Sivanandan, 1990) employ the term without implying that the poor are at fault.

3 Structural break? Is there really such a total and complete separation between a black underclass and the rest of society? After all, there are important socioeconomic differences between ethnic groups and a wide range of circumstances *within* each group: 'there are substantial numbers of well-qualified persons within the black community, and the overall picture of black employment patterns is one of great diversity rather than of a uniformly low economic status, so that "average" levels are potentially misleading' (Ely and Denney, 1987, p57). Even Rex and Tomlinson admitted there was 'considerable overlap' between black minorities and the white population, although they cautioned that such overlap is often 'deceptive' (eg broad occupational categories conceal the fact that, *within* each category, black people occupy the least desirable jobs in the less attractive industries). In a later work Rex (1986) repeated his claim that immigrant minorities have a much higher statistical risk of disadvantage but he accepted that the underclass model overstated the case and so he added a 'separate pyramid'. This revised model recognises the scope for successful mobility *within* ethnic communities and it allows for gradual convergence *between* the 'white' and 'ethnic' pyramids (eg 'Asian' businesses are increasingly likely to employ white staff and cater for a white clientele).

It makes little sense, then, to regard blacks as a whole as an underclass. Nevertheless, the concept is useful for showing how certain groups are trapped in situations where they face a high risk of becoming poor, unqualified or unemployed. As Pilkington (1992) points out, most people agree that minorities are relatively disadvantaged in class terms. And the constant threat of racism does suggest some sort of 'break' with the interests of the white working class.

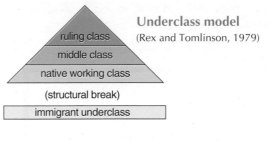

Underclass model
(Rex and Tomlinson, 1979)

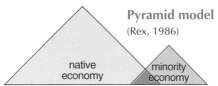

Pyramid model
(Rex, 1986)

(shaded area - area of overlap representing minority trade with, or employment of, whites)

Activity 15   The Underclass

Item A   *Class distribution*

Socioeconomic groups, Great Britain 1989-91
People aged 16 and over in employment (percentages)

	Whites	West Indian	Indian	Pakistani/ Bangladeshi
Men				
professional	7	4	12	5
employers, managers	21	8	18	15
other nonmanual	18	18	20	14
skilled manual	36	42	30	33
semi-skilled manual	13	20	14	27
unskilled manual	3	5	3	4
Women				
professional	2	0	5	0
employers, managers	11	9	9	4
other non-manual	52	51	42	48
skilled manual	8	5	12	14
semi-skilled manual	19	22	28	26
unskilled manual	6	9	2	1

Adapted from *Labour Force Survey*, 1990-91, table 6.35

Item B   *Unemployment*

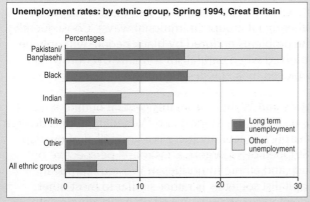

Unemployment rates: by ethnic group, Spring 1994, Great Britain

Adapted from *Social Trends*, 1994, p63

Item C   *Qualifications*

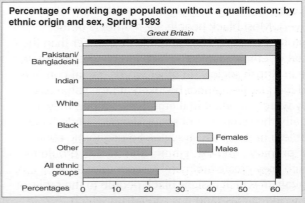

Percentage of working age population without a qualification: by ethnic origin and sex, Spring 1993

Adapted from *Social Trends*, 1994, p52

Item D *Housing*

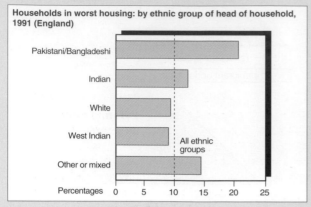

Households in worst housing: by ethnic group of head of household, 1991 (England)

- Pakistani/Bangladeshi
- Indian
- White
- West Indian
- Other or mixed

All ethnic groups

Percentages 0 5 10 15 20 25

Adapted from *Social Trends*, 1994, p112

Item F *Imprisonment*

Prison population rates: by ethnic origin, June 1992

England & Wales	Rate per 10,000 population		
	Males	Females	All
White	19.4	0.5	9.6
West Indian, Guyanese, African	144.0	9.9	76.7
Indian, Pakistani, Bangladeshi	24.3	0.4	12.4
Other/not disclosed	72.1	5.4	38.3
All ethnic origins	22.0	0.7	11.0

Adapted from *Social Trends*, 1994, p162

Item E *Victimhood*

Victims of one or more crimes: by ethnic origin and type of offence, 1991

England & Wales	Percentages		
	Ethnic origin of victim		
	White	Afro-Caribbean	Asian
Percentage who were victims of each offence			
Assault	3	5	4
Threats	3	3	4
Robbery/theft from the person	1	3	3
Burglary	6	12	9
Other household theft	7	6	4
Household vandalism	4	4	5
Vehicle (owners)			
Vandalism	9	11	10
All thefts	20	28	22
Bicycle (owners) theft	6	10	7

Adapted from *Social Trends*, 1994, p155

Questions

1 Look at Item A. Briefly describe how occupational distribution varies according to racial/ethnic group
   a) among males
   b) among females.
2 Does the data in Items A-F support the notion of a 'black underclass'? Give reasons for your answer.

3.4 Marxist and radical approaches

Capitalism and racism Marxist analyses of racial stratification are based on a distinctive view of capitalism and the class system. In this view, capitalism creates a deep rift between the privileged ruling class (who own the means of production) and the oppressed working class (who sell their labour power). Most black people are members of the exploited working class and it is this, rather than their racial or ethnic features, which largely dictates their fate in British society. In other words, racial conflicts and inequalities cannot be taken at face value as if they were important in themselves. Rather, they are usually the symptoms of some 'deeper', underlying problem (ie the class struggle). So economic conflicts are 'primary', and the 'ethnic' and 'racial' problems which they create are merely 'secondary'. It is capitalism which assigns black people to the ranks of the working class and it is capitalism which 'racialises' their situation by encouraging racial

divisions and racial hostility. Thus, Miliband (1987) argues that white workers resort to racial discrimination in a desperate attempt to improve their bargaining power in the competitive climate of a capitalist economy. Miliband suggests that racial prejudice is also a pathological expression of the deep 'injuries of class' (ie the cruelty of the capitalist system brutalises people and so they strike out at other racial groups in irrational ways). Consequently, the problems endured by black people will only be resolved when capitalism is finally overthrown and replaced by a classless, egalitarian society.

Marx and Weber From this general outline it might appear that the Marxist and Weberian models diverge sharply but actually there is a good deal of overlap: 'Stripped of its jargon, a "Marxist" perspective on race and ethnic minorities in Western European, capitalist societies is rather similar to most other sociological analyses based on a broadly flexible theory of stratification' (Stone, 1985, p71). The two models may start from contrasting theoretical positions but they often converge in terms of research interests and empirical findings (eg they agree that black people are relatively disadvantaged). Furthermore, some radical writers have modified the basic Marxist model in a way that has brought them much closer to Weberians. It is easy to regard Marxists or 'radicals' as a single school of thought but in fact they span quite a wide range of views on race and class. We can see this when we consider the issue of economic 'reductionism' (explaining race in terms of class, and racism in terms of capitalism).

Autonomy and reductionism Marxists are often accused of taking reductionism to extremes. Some sociologists take the opinion that 'the most distinctive contribution of Marxism to the study of race relations is to deny the existence of race relations at all' (Stone, 1985, p62). Now, this might be fair comment on Sivanandan (1982) who places great emphasis on the economic 'logic' of capitalism. But it hardly applies to Gilroy (1987) who takes a *relative autonomy* approach. For Gilroy, race and class are 'separate yet connected': they have their own 'independent' effects but they can be fully understood only in relation to one another. Like other radical writers connected with the Centre for Contemporary Cultural Studies (eg Hall et al, 1978), Gilroy is especially interested in how racist ideologies are produced and reproduced. But he points out that racism also has effects on the class struggle. For instance, if black people choose to form their own cultural or political organisations then they are quite likely to use these organisations to challenge general class inequalities in society.

Within the repertoire of radical approaches we can even find writers who stress the *autonomy* of race. Thus, Ben-Tovim and Gabriel (1979, 1986) insist that the 'relative autonomy' approach is still guilty of reductionism because it usually regards economic factors as decisive 'in the final analysis'. The danger of this, they say, is that it treats race as a mere sideshow and underestimates the significance and strength of racial conflicts. Ben-Tovim and Gabriel do not deny that race is linked to class in some way but they find no compelling reason to assume this is the case. Their central point is that most Marxists entangle race and class analysis so closely that it becomes almost impossible to discover the separate influence of racial (or cultural) factors. The solution, they suggest, is to treat racial matters as fully 'independent' by erecting a 'fence' around them. They should be studied in their own right rather than explaining them in terms of other types of social relationship. And this, they feel, is best done by conducting detailed studies at the local level. In their own work, Ben-Tovim and Gabriel have investigated local authority politics as a means of exploring racist ideologies, racial inequalities and the politics of racial struggle.

Marxist models of racial stratification

The 'autonomy versus reductionism' debate is usually pitched at a highly abstract level. But Marxists have also offered much more specific 'models' to describe how racial minorities fit into the stratification system. The three main models are outlined below.

1 Unitary working class This model has a simple message: racial and ethnic minorities are just 'normal' members of the working class. Class is the key division in society and race is really quite insignificant. Therefore those sociologists who say that race involves 'extra' burdens or disadvantages are guilty of exaggeration: 'Preoccupied with the disabilities that attach to colour, liberal reformers and research workers have been busy rediscovering what in fact are common disabilities of class: widespread and longstanding conditions inherent in the workings of capital, market and state in a divided society' (Westergaard and Resler, 1976, p359). So Westergaard and Resler treat race as a distraction from the main issue which is the grossly unequal character of capitalism. It is this which condemns all members of the working class (black and white) to an exploited and deprived existence. But this unitary model can be criticised on two counts: it neglects racial conflicts within the working class and it ignores the existence of middle class blacks.

2 Divided working class This model, like the previous one, proposes that class location is the dominant influence in the lives of black people. It also shares the view that capitalism is an exploitive system: 'Western European societies are class societies based on the ownership and control of the means of production by a small minority and on the concomitant domination and exploitation of the masses. Social relationships are characterised not by harmony and free will but by conflict and coercion' (Castles and Kosack, 1973, p6). Castles and Kosack draw parallels between Britain's black immigrants and Continental 'guestworkers' (the Slavs, Turks, Greeks, North Africans etc who migrate to find temporary and insecure work in the factories and service industries of the more prosperous Western European economies). Castles and Kosack are not convinced that we discover much by looking at the cultural and ethnic characteristics of these groups, since it is their class position which rules their lives. Black people are firmly located in the ranks of the working class. But Castles and Kosack break from the 'unitary' model by conceding that racism does make some difference: objectively, black people tend to fill the less desirable jobs; and subjectively, they are ranked lower in status than white workers. So Castles and Kosack prefer to talk about the divided working class. They regard this internal racial division as a major factor in preventing the working class from mounting effective opposition to capitalism.

3 Racialised class fraction Miles (1989) regards the concept of 'race' as a non-scientific and irrelevant nonsense, since it mistakenly implies that the physical features of race directly affect social behaviour and cultural achievement. It makes little sense, therefore, to talk about 'race relations'. Miles prefers to describe racial minorities as a form of 'migrant labour'. He believes their problems can be explained largely in terms of production relations, using the traditional concepts and categories of Marxist political economy. Nevertheless, he does recognise that the class position of black people is complicated by the process of 'racialisation' (ie 'racial' categories are imposed on them and they are treated as socially, culturally and morally inferior). Thus, black people are the victims of racist ideologies. Miles is especially interested in how these ideologies are generated and reproduced and in how they operate at political and cultural levels as well as the more fundamental economic level.

Phizacklea and Miles (1980) pursued these interests in an empirical study of workers in northwest London and it was here that they introduced the idea of a 'racialised class fraction'. The basic idea is that black people ('migrant labour') are members of the working class but within this class they have been singled out as a racialised 'fraction'. These fractions or divisions are significant, since they increase the possibility that black people will choose to develop their own forms of political action. In later works, Miles recognised that black people are not confined to the working class and he gave more attention to the existence of a black middle class (*petty bourgeoisie*) who might side with their 'class' interests rather than with their 'racial' groups. But he maintains that black people still constitute a racialised fraction at each class level. However, Miles has not yet given many details about the nature of 'fractions' and it is not clear how the concept might be developed further. Also, we might question whether the term 'migrant labour' is still appropriate now that so many of Britain's black population were born in this country.

Activity 16 Race or Class?

Item A *Black Labour MPs*

Piara Khabra (Ealing Southall)

Diane Abbott (Hackney North)

Left-right: Keith Vaz (Leicester East), Bernie Grant (Tottenham) and Paul Boateng (Brent South)

Item B *Black Conservatives*

Nirj Deva (MP for Brentford and Isleworth)

John Taylor - a black barrister who stood unsuccessfully as Conservative candidate for the 'safe' Tory seat of Cheltenham

Item C *Trade unions*

Bill Morris, General Secretary of TGWU, Britain's largest trade union

Item D *Political views*

Between 1974 and 1987, 4 out of every 5 black voters supported the Labour Party. But a small number of (mainly middle class) Asian electors have recently shifted their allegiance to the Conservatives and Liberal Democrats.

Survey evidence suggests that class membership is the most important reason for black people identifying with the Labour Party. A less important reason is the 'pro-minority' credentials of the Labour Party.

Black people are certainly influenced by a 'race agenda' (ie interest in race-related issues). But the majority of the black electorate are interested in the same range of political issues as their white counterparts (eg unemployment, the welfare state). 'Black opinion' tends to mirror 'white opinion'.

Adapted from S. Saggar 'Black Participation and the Transformation of the Race Issue in British Politics', *New Community*, vol 20 no 1, 1993, pp29-30

Item E *Street clashes*

Brixton riots

Questions

1 Look at Items A to E. Which Marxist model do they support - a unitary working class, a divided working class or a racialised class fraction? Give reasons for your answer.
2 Identify arguments for and against the proposition that the Labour Party is the 'proper' and 'genuine' choice for racial and ethnic minorities.

3.5 Racial minorities in the labour market

This sporting life: the labour market

The labour market can be likened to a long-running sports contest where the 'trophies' are higher income and status, more interesting jobs and better working conditions. Members of the ethnic minorities try to take part as 'players' (participants), although they are not always 'selected' (recruited) by team managers and even when they do play they are more likely to be 'sent off' (made unemployed). Also, they usually play in less attractive 'positions' (jobs) in less glamorous 'teams' (industrial sectors). This reduces their chances of winning medals, although a number of the outstanding (or lucky) players do gain 'promotion' to star (middle class) positions or better teams.

Players: competitors in the labour market

Ethnic minorities are usually active competitors in the labour market. Participation levels are normally expressed in terms of 'economic activity' rates which count the percentage of each group who are in work or, if unemployed, looking for work. From the available figures (see Table 11) it is clear that Afro-Caribbean groups have reasonably high participation rates but the rates are much lower for Pakistani/Bangladeshi groups (especially women). Among young people aged 16-19, the activity rates for ethnic minorities vary between 35% and 42% compared with 62% of the equivalent white population, but this is mainly because the minority groups have a larger proportion of young people in full-time education.

Table 11 Economic Activity Rates, 1993 (as % of people of working age, males aged 16-64, females aged 16-59)		
	males	females
White	86	72
Afro-Caribbean	80	66
Indian	81	61
Pakistani/ Bangladeshi	72	25

Social Trends, 1994, p57

Selection: getting a job

Black people are not always 'signed up', as Jenkins (1986) found in his interviews with managers and personnel officers in the West Midlands. These managers assessed job applicants according to two main criteria: 'suitability' (eg relevant skills and qualifications, ability to do the job) and 'acceptability' (eg whether they would fit in with the prevailing ethos; their 'manner', 'appearance', 'attitude' and predictability). Even if black candidates passed the suitability hurdle, they were likely to be disqualified on the grounds of acceptability. This seemed to be largely based on the managers' gut feelings and racial stereotypes (eg 'Asians are clannish', 'West Indians are aggressive and excitable', 'whites won't accept black workers'). Also, the 'routine ethnocentrism' of the managers meant they were likely to misinterpret signs (eg a white recruitment officer might see avoidance of direct eye contact as a sign of shiftiness, whereas it could be a gesture of respect by an Asian candidate). Black people were also put at a disadvantage because these organisations often hired staff by means of 'internal recruitment' and 'word of mouth' recommendations.

If these workforces were already predominantly white, this meant blacks were unlikely to hear of job opportunities. But Jenkins did find that public sector organisations were more likely than retailing firms to advertise posts openly.

Teams: sectors of the labour market

Ethnic minorities are still concentrated in those 'teams' (sectors of the economy) which they joined as migrant workers in the 1950s and 1960s. So their pattern of industrial distribution differs from that of whites. The 1989-91 *Labour Force Survey* revealed the following patterns (figures in brackets refer to white males): 5% of minority males work in construction (13%); 29% in distribution, hotels and catering (16%); 13% in metal goods, engineeering and vehicles (14%); 11% in transport and communications (8%); and 5% in health services (2%). The differences betweeen whites and minorities are much less marked among women, because women in general tend to be concentrated in certain areas of the labour market. So similar proportions (about 25%) of white and minority women are found in distribution, hotels and catering. But minority women are more likely to be working in health services (15% compared with 9%) and in footwear and clothing (5% and 2%). Of course, there are also differences between particular minority groups. Owen and Green (1992) report that West Indians and Africans are over-represented, and Asians under-represented, in 'other services' (eg local government and health services). It is worth remembering that industrial classifications are very broad and so they may conceal important differences between whites and minorities. For example, minorities are more likely to be found in older 'smokestack' industries such as foundries rather than the newer 'sunrise' industries such as microchip technology.

The red card: becoming unemployed

Ethnic minorities are more likely than whites to be shown the 'red card' ie become unemployed. Their chances of staying on the field are quite good during times of economic prosperity but economic recession increases their chances of an early bath. That is why their unemployment rates soared above those of whites in the late 1970s and early 1980s. But between 1984 and 1990 the unemployment rates for all groups of working age fell back: those for the white population declined by two fifths to 6.5%, while those for all minority groups halved to 11.2% (Labour Force Survey, 1989-91). Nevertheless, the 1989-91 data clearly shows that rates for minorities remain higher than those for whites and this is true even for the 'high risk' groups aged 16-24 (12% minorities, 8% whites). And this pattern is not entirely explained by lack of qualifications, since blacks have higher unemployment rates than whites at each and every qualification level. Since 1990, moreover, the unemployment rates have risen once more (by about 1.5% for whites and 4% for minorities).

Activity 17 Employment Patterns

Employment status, Great Britain 1989-91
Economically active people aged 16 and over, by sex, employment status and ethnic group (percentages)

	Whites	West Indian	Indian	Pakistani/ Bangladeshi
Men				
in employment	93	84	90	79
(employee	75	72	65	58
full time	71	68	62	53
part time	4	3	3	5
self-employed	16	9	23	19
on govt.scheme)	2	3	1	2
unemployed	7	16	10	21
Women				
in employment	93	88	90	77
(employee	85	83	78	58
full time	48	60	56	37
part time	38	23	22	21
self-employed	7	2	10	12
on govt.scheme)	1	2	2	8
unemployed	7	12	10	24

Adapted from *Labour Force Survey* ,1990-91, table 6.33

Questions
Use the information from the above table to answer the following:
1 What impact does ethnicity have on unemployment rates? Suggest reasons for this.
2 What impact does gender have on the patterns of full time and part time employment? Suggest reasons for this.
3 What impact do gender and ethnicity have on self-employment? Suggest reasons for these patterns.

Trophies: status and pay

Minorities often find that the labour market is not a level playing field: 'Ethnic minority groups in Great Britain have fared relatively badly in the labour market, tending to be employed in low status and poorly paid jobs in declining industrial sectors' (Owen and Green, 1992, p7). Of course, the patterns of disadvantage are not uniform and we have to consider complicating factors such as gender, region, economic sector and variations between particular ethnic groups. For example, Oppenheim (1993) states that although white women earn more than Asian women they earn less than West Indian women (because the latter are more likely to work full time, to do shift work and to be based in large unionised public sector workplaces where wages tend to be higher). But generally speaking it is hard to disagree with the conclusion that 'ethnic minorities are more likely to work in sections of the economy with greater risk of low pay, doing shift work, with longer hours of work and with less access to training and occupational benefits' (Amin, 1992, p14). Moreover, Amin (1992) reckons that recent changes in the labour market mean that the immediate prospects for ethnic minorities are not all that bright. The continued decline of 'old' manufacturing industry (eg textiles, metal manufacturing industries) deprives them of jobs, and the 'new' industries are being located away from the towns and cities where most ethnic minorities live. This is partly offset by the rise of the service sector (eg retail sector, NHS, financial services) but this sector tends to reinforce racial divisions (eg minorities are relegated to the lower level jobs and they miss out on financial services and computer related jobs). It is more difficult to speculate on the likely effects of other labour market changes such as 'restructuring', privatisation and greater 'flexibility' (eg growth in part time work, self-employment and 'casual' and temporary jobs). But Amin believes there are good grounds for expecting a deterioration in employment conditions (eg privatisation might remove some of the 'protection' of public sector employment and inflict poorer pay and conditions on black employees).

Promotion: upward social mobility

It would be a mistake to think that all black people are 'losers'. Owen and Green (1992) cite Indians and Chinese as two ethnic groups which have made significant economic progress in the British labour market in the 1980s. More generally, evidence suggest that increasing numbers from the minorities are being 'promoted' into the ranks of the professional middle class (eg Bhachu, 1991; Jones, 1993). Moreover, sociologists are starting to notice the growth of 'black businesses' and the spread of self-employment among minority groups. This growth is not uniformly distributed among the minorities and some sociologists explain this in terms of the 'cultural' predispositions of ethnic groups. Some Asian groups (eg East African Sikhs) are described as having a 'spirit of enterprise' and a supportive family network which favours economic success. Afro-Caribbean groups have a good business reputation in the United States but Cashmore (1991) reports that successful black entrepreneurs are treated with suspicion in Britain. The black community often accuses them of 'selling out' or adopting 'white' values. But culture is only part of the explanation for the expansion of black businesses, and an alternative approach focuses on 'ecological' factors (eg the decline of corner grocery shops once owned by whites creates an 'opportunity gap' for minorities to fill).

Rafiq (1992) estimates there were about 61,000 Asian-owned businesses in Britain in 1990. Taking Muslim-owned businesses in Bradford as an example, Rafiq says these are concentrated mainly in retailing (groceries, newsagencies, clothes shops) and in restaurants and takeaways, although there are growing numbers of wholesalers (mainly in the food sector) and manufacturers (mainly in textiles and clothes manufacturing). As for Afro-Caribbean businesses, Ward's (1988) study in Brent suggests that, unlike Asian businesses, these are more likely to be in 'services' (hairdressing, repairs etc) than in retail. And within the retail sector, Afro-Caribbean businesses do not usually 'buy and sell' standard items; rather, they specialise in 'make-and-sell', producing tailored items (breads, records, designer fashions etc) which require very detailed knowledge of their likely markets.

Assessing progress While any signs of economic progress among minority groups are to be welcomed, it is possible that some of the success is illusory. First, those who are upwardly mobile often end up in the lower middle class where status and pay are not particularly high. Secondly, broad social class categories might mask important differences between whites and minorities. Thus, even if there are similar percentages in, say, the 'other nonmanual' category, it is quite possible that whites fill the better paid and higher status positions within this level. And thirdly, some sociologists have questioned whether self-employment is really such a privileged sector of the economy. Minorities may be forced into setting up their own businesses because racial discrimination prevents them from getting employment. Sometimes these businesses are precarious ventures in extremely competitive markets, offering small returns for long hours and managing to survive only because they exploit cheap family labour. They may be 'dead-end' enterprises which offer few chances for further expansion. Ward and Jenkins (1985) conclude that many Asian businesses are marginal, relying on a very limited, segregated ('ethnic niche') market where they cater for the specialised needs of their own ethnic groups.

On the other hand, Srinivasan (1992) reports that Asian small shopkeepers and restaurant owners in Oxford were reasonably secure and prosperous and they appreciated the independence and social status which their enterprises brought them. Likewise, Rafiq (1992) challenges the assumption that Asian businesses always bring in low financial returns. Admittedly, a great deal depends on the prosperity of the local economy and the surrounding population and also on the skills and capital of the entrepreneurs concerned. But Rafiq believes there are significant opportunities for developing larger and more ambitious enterprises. This usually means moving away from an 'ethnic niche' market towards catering for the tastes of the wider public. But Cashmore (1991) points out that these larger businesses tend to take on increasing numbers of white management and personnel because of the widespread belief that this is necessary in order for the business to be socially 'accceptable' and successful.

Summary

1 There is a direct connection between 'race' and 'class' under slavery and apartheid but the relationship is more complex in modern Britain.

2 Models of racial stratification (eg 'underclass') are usually over simplified and controversial.

3 The labour market and social class profiles of Britain's minorities differ from those of whites. Minorities are relatively disadvantaged.

Activity 18 High Income, Low Profile

Item A *Rapport*

Rapport is a new networking organisation for black professionals (successful young blacks, or 'buppies'). 'Us second-generation blacks are not going to settle for working for the National Health Service like our parents', says Ron, fiddling with his bow-tie. 'We're trying to show that black people are not just junkies, criminals, musicians and athletes'. That entails showing blacks enjoying their hard earned success, flaunting material wealth, exhibiting little guilt over conspicuous consumption. Valerie claims that Rapport was set up to respond to the resentment and despair felt by black professionals - 'We want advertisers, marketing people and the host community to recognise us as honest, successful blacks, as role models who aren't just rappers or sprinters.'

Adapted from A. Kershaw 'Buppies on the Up and Up', *New Statesman and Society*, 30.11.90

Questions

1 Why are 'role models' important for the black community?
2 Cashmore (1991) says that successful blacks are regarded with suspicion by other blacks. Suggest reasons for this.
3 What do you think are the main reasons for the success of Asian millionaires?

Item B *Asian millionaires*

Shami Ahmad, founder and managing director of Joe Bloggs, the Manchester based clothing firm

The dinner held at Kensington Palace was one of those occasions when businessmen pay dearly for the pleasure of socialising with the Prince of Wales. The two notable features about the businessmen were that they were all Asian and included some of the richest people in Britain. Many of the Asian millionaires came to Britain 20 years ago with virtually nothing and have built multi-million pound companies which employ thousands of people, mostly non-Asian. Though many from the first generation began with the corner shop, they have branched out into many fields - cash-and-carry stores, textiles, fashion, banking, newsagents, grocery and retail chains, electronics and even manufacturing. One estimate is that Britain has at least 300 millionaires in its 1.5 million strong Asian community.

Adapted from 'The Quiet Millionaires' *Telegraph Weekend Magazine*, 25.8.90, pp21-24

References

Allport,G. *The Nature of Prejudice* (Doubleday Anchor, New York, 1958)

Amin,K. *Poverty in Black and White* (CPAG/Runnymede Trust, London, 1992)

Ballard,R. and Driver,G. 'The Ethnic Approach', *New Society* 16.6.1977

Banton,M. 'What Do We Mean By Racism?', *New Society* 10.4.1969

Banton,M. 'Analytical and Folk Concepts of Ethnicity', *Ethnic and Racial Studies* vol 2 no 2 April 1979

Banton,M. 'The Battle of the Name', *New Community* vol 14 no 1/2, 1987

Banton,M. *Racial Theories* (Cambridge University Press, Cambridge, 1987a)

Banton 'Research and the Race Relations Act', *Sociology Review* vol 2 no 1, September,1992

Banton,M. and Harwood,J. *The Race Concept* (David & Charles, Newton Abbott, 1975)

Barker,M. *The New Racism* (Junction Books, London, 1982)

Ben-Tovim,G. and Gabriel, J. 'The Conceptualisation of Race Relations in Sociological Theory', *Ethnic and Racial Studies* vol 2, 1979

Ben-Tovim,G. and Gabriel, J. *Local Politics of Race* (Macmillan, London,1986)

Bhachu,P. *Twice Migrants* (Tavistock, London, 1985)

Blauner,R. 'Black Culture: Myth or Reality?' in D.Bromley and C.Longino (eds) *White Racism and Black Americans* (Schenkman, Cambridge, Mass., 1972)

Blauner,R. *Black Lives, White Lives* (University of California Press, 1989)

Bleier,R. *Science and Gender* (Pergamon, New York, 1984)

Brown,C. *Black and White Britain* (Heinemann, London, 1984)

Bygott,D. *Black and British* (Oxford University Press, Oxford, 1992)

Carmichael,S. and Hamilton,C. *Black Power* (Jonathan Cape, London,1968)

Cashmore,E. *Rastaman* (George Allen & Unwin, London, 1979)

Cashmore,E. *The Logic of Racism* (Allen & Unwin, London, 1987)

Cashmore,E. 'Flying Business Class', *New Community* vol 17, 1991

Cashmore,E. and Troyna,B. *Introduction to Race Relations* (Routledge, London, 1983)

Castles,S. and Kosack,G. *Immigrant Workers and Class Structure in Western Europe* (Oxford University Press, Oxford, 1973)

Clairborne,L. *Race and Law in Britain and the United States* (Minority Rights Group, London, 1979)

Commission for Racial Equality *Report on Immigration Procedures* (CRE, London, 1985)

Commission for Racial Equality *Racial Attacks* (CRE, London,1987)

Dahrendorf,R. 'The Erosion of Citizenship', *New Statesman* 12.6.1987

Dahya,B. 'The Nature of Pakistani Ethnicity', in A.Cohen (ed) *Urban Ethnicity* (Tavistock, London, 1974)

Daniel,W.W. *Racial Discrimination in England* (Penguin, Harmondsworth, 1968)

Dawkins,R. *The Selfish Gene* (Oxford University Press, Oxford,1976)

Ely,P. and Denney,D. *Social Work in a Multi-Racial Society* (Gower, Aldershot, 1987)

Field,S. *Ethnic Minorities in Britain Today* (HMSO, London,1981)

Field,F. *Losing Out* (Basil Blackwell, Oxford, 1989)

Fryer,P. *Staying Power* (Pluto Press, London, 1984)

Fuller,M. 'Young, Female and Black', in E.Cashmore and B.Troyna (eds) *Black Youth in Crisis* (Allen & Unwin, London, 1982)

Gilroy,P. *There Ain't No Black in the Union Jack* (Hutchinson, London, 1987)

Gilroy,P. 'The End of Anti-Racism', *New Community*, vol 17, 1990

Glasgow,D. *The Black Underclass* (Vintage Books, New York, 1981)

Gordon,P. *Racial Violence and Harassment* (Runnymede Trust, London, 1990)

Gordon,P. 'The Racialisation of Statistics', in R.Skellington (ed) *'Race' in Britain Today* (Sage, London, 1992)

Gordon,P. 'Unfreedom of Movement', *Runnymede Bulletin* no 252 February 1992a

Gordon,P. and Rosenberg,D. *Daily Racism* (Runnymede Trust, London,1989)

Griffin,J. *Black Like Me* (Panther, London, 1964)

Hall,S., Critcher,C., Jefferson,T., Clarke,J. and Roberts,B. *Policing the Crisis* (Macmillan, London, 1978)

Hall,S. 'New Ethnicities', in J.Donald and A.Rattansi (eds) *'Race', Culture and Difference* (Open University/Sage, London, 1992)

Hall,S. 'The Question of Identity', in S.Hall, D.Held and T.McGrew (eds) *Modernity and Its Futures* (Polity Press, Cambridge, 1992a)

Haralambos,M. *Right On: From Blues to Soul in Black America* (Causeway Press, Ormskirk, 1994)

Haskey,J. 'The Ethnic Minority Populations Resident in Private Households', *Population Trends* no 63 Spring 1991

Hiro,D. *Black British, White British* (Paladin, London, 1992)

Home Office *Racial Attacks* (HMSO, London, 1981)

Inner London Education Authority *Race, Sex and Class* (ILEA, London, 1983)

Jeffcoate,R. *Ethnic Minorities and Education* (Harper & Row, London, 1984)

Jenkins,R. *Racism and Recruitment* (Cambridge University Press, Cambridge, 1986)

Jones,T. *Britain's Ethnic Minorities* (Policy Studies Institute, London, 1993)

Jowell,R. et al *British Social Attitudes* 9th Report (Social and Community Planning Research, Dartmouth Publishing, 1992)

Keil,C. *Urban Blues* (University of Chicago Press, Chicago,1966)

Kerner Commission *Report of the National Commission on Civil Disorders* (US Government Printing Office, Washington DC,1968)

Krausz,E. *Ethnic Minorities in Britain* (Paladin, London, 1971)

Lapping,B. *Apartheid* (Paladin, London, 1986)

Layton-Henry,Z. *The Politics of Race in Britain* (Allen & Unwin, London, 1984)

Lee,G. and Wrench,J. *In Search of a Skill* (CRE, London, 1981)

Lewis,R. *Anti-Racism* (Quartet, London, 1988)

Lister,R. 'Concepts of Poverty', *Social Studies Review* vol 6 no 5, May 1990

Mann,N. 'Fighting talk', *New Statesman and Society* 18.2.1994

McCrudden,C., Smith,D. and Brown,C. *Racial Justice at Work* (PSI, London, 1991)

Miles,R. *Racism and Migrant Labour* (Routledge, London, 1982)

Miles,R. *Racism* (Routledge, London, 1989)

Miles,R. 'Racism, Ideology and Disadvantage', *Social Studies Review* vol 5 no 4 1990

Miliband,R. 'Class Analysis', in A.Giddens and J.Turner (eds) *Social Theory Today* (Polity Press, Cambridge, 1987)

Modood,T. 'Black, Racial Equality and Asian Identity', *New Community* vol 14 no 3 1988

Murray,C. *Losing Ground* (Basic Books, New York, 1984)

Ouseley,H. 'Resisting Institiutional Change' in W.Ball and J.Solomos (eds) *Race and Local Politics* (Macmillan, Basingstoke, 1990)

Nitzova,P. 'The Bosnian Crisis', *New Community* vol 19 no 3 1993

Oppenheim,C. *Poverty: the Facts* (Child Poverty Action Group, London, 1993)

Owen,D. *Ethnic Minorities in Great Britain: Settlement Patterns* (Centre for Research in Ethnic Relations, University of Warwick, 1992)

Owen,D. and Green,A. 'Labour Market Experience and Occupational Change among Ethnic Groups in Great Britain', *New Community* vol 19 no 1, October 1992

Parekh,B. 'Law Torn', *New Statesman and Society* 14.6.1991

Parkin,F. *Marxism and Class Theory* (Tavistock, London, 1979)

Patterson,O. *The Sociology of Slavery* (MacGibbon & Kee, London,1967)

Patterson,S. *Dark Strangers* (Penguin, Harmondsworth, 1965)

Phizacklea,A. and Miles,R. *Labour and Racism* (Routledge Kegan Paul, London, 1980).

Pilkington,A. 'Is there a British Underclass?', *Sociology Review* vol 1 no 3 1992

Pilkington,A. 'Race and Ethnicity', in M.Haralambos (ed) *Developments in Sociology* vol 9, 1993

Pryce,K. *Endless Pressure* (Penguin, Harmondsworth, 1979)

Rafiq,M. 'A Comparison of Muslim and non-Muslim Owned Asian Businesses in Britain', *New Community* vol 19 1992

Reeves,F. *British Racial Discourse* (Cambridge University Press, Cambridge, 1983)

Rex,J. *Race and Ethnicity* (Open University Press, Milton Keynes, 1986)

Rex,J. and Moore,R. *Race, Community and Conflict* (Oxford University Press, Oxford 1967)

Rex,J. and Tomlinson,S. *Colonial Immigrants in a British City* (Routledge & Kegan Paul, London, 1979)

Richardson,J. and Lambert,J. *The Sociology of Race* (Causeway Press, Ormskirk, 1985)

Rodney,W. *How Europe Underdeveloped Africa* (Bogle-L'Ouverture, London, 1972)

Runnymede Trust Bulletin no 247, July/August 1991

Runnymede Trust Bulletin no248, September 1991a

Rushdie,S. 'The New Empire Within Britain', *New Society* 9.12.1982

Saunders,P. *Social Class and Stratification* (Routledge, London,1990)

Scarman Report *The Brixton Disorders* (Penguin, Harmondsworth,1983)

Sharp,K. 'Sociobiology' in *Sociology Review*, vol 1 no 1 1991

Sivanandan,A. *A Different Hunger* (Pluto Press, London, 1982)

Sivanandan,A. 'The Common Hurt of the Underclass', *New Statesman and Society*, 16.2.1991

Skellington,R. *'Race' in Britain Today* (Sage/Open University, London, 1992)

Smith,D. *Racial Disadvantage in Britain* (Penguin, Harmondsworth, 1977)

Solomos,J. *Race and Racism in Contemporary Britain* (Macmillan, London, 1989)

Solomos,J. 'Changing Forms of Racial Discourse', *Social Studies Review* vol 6 no 2, 1990

Srinivasan,S. 'The Class Position of the Asian Petty Bourgeoisie', *New Community* vol 19 1992

Stone,J. *Racial Conflict in Contemporary Society* (Fontana, London, 1985)

Troyna,B. and Hatcher,R. *Racism in Children's Lives* (Routledge, London, 1992)

Van den Berghe,P. *The Ethnic Phenomenon* (Elsevier Press, New York, 1981)

Walvin,J. *Black and White* (Allen Lane, London, 1973)

Walvin,J. *Passage to Britain* (Penguin, Harmondsworth, 1984)

Walvin,J. *Black Ivory* (Harper Collins, London, 1992)

Ward,R. 'Caribbean Business Enterprises in Britain', in M.Cross and H.Entzinger (eds) *Lost Illusions* (Routledge, London,1988)

Ward,R. and Jenkins,R. (eds) *Ethnic Communities in Business* (Cambridge University Press, London, 1985)

Watson,J. *Between Two Cultures* (Basil Blackwell, London, 1977)

Westergaard,J. and Resler,H. *Class in a Capitalist Society* (Penguin, Harmondsworth, 1976)

Wilson,A. *Finding a Voice* (Virago, London, 1984)

Wilson,E.O. *Sociobiology* (Harvard University Press, Mass., 1975)

Wilson, W.J. *The Declining Significance of Race* (University of Chicago Press, Chicago, 1978)

Wilson,W.J. *The Truly Disadvantaged* (University of Chicago Press, Chicago, 1987)

Wirth, L. 'The Problem of Minority Groups' in R.Linton (ed) *The Science of Man in the World Crisis* (Columbia University Press, New York, 1945)

Young,J. and Lea,J. 'Urban Violence and Political Marginalisation', *Critical Social Policy* vol 1 no 3, Spring 1982

4 Gender

Introduction

You hear the sound of footsteps in the corridor. The door handle turns. Someone is about to enter the room. Now, what piece of advance information would give you most clues about the sort of person coming in? The person's social class, age, race or gender? Each of these dimensions of stratification has a significant influence on people's lives. We recognise this when we make broad predictions about people on the basis of their social characteristics. This chapter examines one of these dimensions - gender - in some detail.

The sociological study of gender was boosted by the emergence of the modern women's movement. Feminists in the 1960s and 1970s pointed out that 'malestream' sociology either neglected women altogether or, even worse, reduced them to narrow stereotypes. Nowadays, however, sociology gives gender much closer attention. First, women are now more likely to be *added in* (ie conventional sociological analyses are applied to women as well as men). Secondly, the range of sociology is being *extended* into relatively new areas such as housework, domestic violence and masculinity. And thirdly, mainstream sociological ideas are being *reconceptualised* to take account of gender. Clearly, gender is not just a trivial afterthought: 'the study of gender is an important means through which sociology itself is being re-shaped' (Maynard, 1990, p269).

Chapter summary

- The chapter begins by examining **feminism** and the **women's movement**.
- This is followed by a discussion of the distinctions between **sex**, **gender** and **sexuality**.
- The chapter then turns to the special

features of **ethnic minority women**.
- The next two parts concentrate on women's **employment** and **social class** profiles.
- Finally, the chapter rounds off with a look at the way gender studies are being extended to include **men**.

1 The Feminist Challenge

Key Issues

1 What are the main reasons for the emergence of the modern women's movement?
2 What are the main perspectives within feminism?

1.1 The modern women's movement

The second wave The 'first wave' of feminism refers to events between about 1890 and 1920 when women in many Western countries mobilised to win the vote. This period conjures up dramatic images of suffragettes marching in the streets, chaining themselves to railings or going on hunger strike. Even if some of their tactics were highly controversial, the early feminists seemed to have achieved their major goals when full voting rights were gradually extended

to women. Yet, some fifty or so years later, a 'second wave' of feminism broke on the shores of Britain and other Western societies. Journalists and other social commentators sometimes found it difficult to understand this renewed feminist activity. They tended to dismiss it with jokes about 'ugly' demonstrators disrupting beauty contests or burning their bras. However, it soon became clear that the modern women's movement had the serious task of attending to unfinished business. Women were still disadvantaged in many respects, even in affluent postwar societies, and so there was a need for a revived women's movement.

Mitchell (1971) suggests three reasons for the resurgence of feminist activity in the 1960s. First, these were times of political turmoil and many women gained valuable experience in student countercultures, peace groups and the black power movement. As women developed political confidence within these movements, they increasingly resented the patronising attitudes of males who expected them to make the tea and defer to male leaders. This convinced many female activists that true liberation required a struggle against male power. Secondly, Mitchell points to the contradictions and tensions in women's lives. They enjoyed new sexual freedoms in the 'permissive' age yet at the same time they were still treated as little more than sex objects. They were also pulled between work and home: more married women were joining the workforce but the attitude still prevailed that a woman's place is in the home. Tensions such as these created the need for a movement to help women make sense of their situation. Finally, Mitchell notes the effects of general social trends on women's lives. Women were entering higher education in greater numbers and they were much more interested in developing careers. Moreover, the contraceptive pill gave them better control over family size and the spacing of children. So the new opportunities of the 1960s challenged the 'traditional' roles of women.

Dale and Foster (1986) identify some broad differences between the first and second waves of feminism. The earlier feminists were concerned mainly with the public sphere but the modern movement added that the 'personal is political': the fight is not just about legal and political rights but also about more intimate and 'private' spheres (eg family, motherhood, personal identity). Another difference lies in the preferred forms of organisation. Although the early movement occasionally resorted to 'direct action', it tended to rely on hierarchical organisations to promote its aims. However, the modern movement preferred a 'grassroots' approach.

The British women's movement modelled itself as a loose federation of small, leaderless groups, each with a high degree of autonomy.

Inspirations Certain books - Germaine Greer's *The Female Eunuch* and Betty Friedan's *The Feminine Mystique* - were extremely influential in shaping views and stimulating debate. Friedan's book was a powerful catalyst for the US movement and its opening passage is frequently quoted: 'The problems lay buried, unspoken for many years in the minds of American women. It was a strange stirring, a sense of dissatisfaction, a yearning that women suffered in the middle of the twentieth century in the United States. Each suburban wife struggled with it alone. As she made the beds, shopped for groceries, matched slip cover material, ate peanut butter sandwiches, chauffeured Cub Scouts and Brownies, lay beside her husband at night, she was afraid to ask even of herself the silent question: is this all?' (Friedan, 1971, p1).

Friedan called this the 'problem that has no name' and she tried to describe the vague feeling of discontent that affected so many women. She saw it largely in terms of a struggle for 'personhood': women were treated as pale reflections of men rather than fully rounded persons in their own right. Whatever a woman's social class, age, race or occupation, she was likely to be belittled simply because of her sex. It was this kind of problem that the women's movement resolved to combat. In Britain, this struggle has been pursued in many different ways: consciousness raising groups, pressure groups for changes in legislation, and practical activities such as establishing hostels for battered women.

Activity 1   Revolting Women

Item A   *The 7 demands*

In a series of meetings in the 1970s the British women's movement drew up the following list of 'demands'.
1 Equal pay for equal work
2 Equal job and educational opportunities
3 Free contraception and abortion on demand
4 Free, community controlled child care facilities
5 Legal and financial independence for women
6 An end to discrimination against lesbians
7 Freedom for all women from intimidation by the threat or use of violence or sexual coercion.

Item B   *Because you're a boy*

Cartoon: Jacky Fleming *Be a Bloody Train Driver*, 1991

Item C *Women speaking out*

Questions

1 Look at Item A.
   a) Choose two of these demands and
       suggest reasons why the women's
       movement urged change.
   b) What progress has been made in
       meeting these 7 demands? Which have
       been the most and the least successful?
2 What point is the cartoon (Item B)
   making?
3 What points are being made on the
   placards in Item C?

1.2 Feminist perspectives

What is feminism? Feminism means different things
to different people. For some, feminism and the
women's movement are more or less the same thing.
Others choose to separate them, arguing that the
movement is a form of practical action while
feminism is the ideology or outlook which guides this
action. But what exactly are the defining features of
this feminist outlook? The basic assumption shared by
all feminists is that women suffer certain injustices on
account of their sex. Feminist sociology, for example,
stresses the importance of gender divisions in society
and it portrays these divisions as working to the
overall advantage of men. Beyond this broad
agreement, however, there are quite striking
differences in theories and values.

  Some writers set out lists of supposedly 'essential'
feminist policies. For them, 'true' feminists support
legal abortion, disapprove of nuclear weapons, avoid
marriage and so on. The trouble with these lists is that
they ignore changing circumstances and shifts in
policy. For example, 'first wave' feminists *opposed*
abortion and contraception and *supported* the family
and motherhood (Dale and Foster, 1986). Also, these
lists ignore differences of opinion among present day
feminists (eg many feminists support the peace
movement but some feminists in the USA have used
sexual equality legislation to join combat units in the
armed forces). It is for these sorts of reasons that
Radcliffe Richards (1982) prefers a 'non-ideological'
definition of feminism, one which avoids attaching it
to a narrow range of policies. In her view, feminism is
best described simply as a movement for the
elimination of sex-based injustices.

  Although feminists are united by their common

desire for sexual justice and their concern for
women's welfare, there is actually quite a wide
spectrum of 'feminisms' (Mitchell and Oakley, 1986).
At the risk of oversimplification, these can be divided
into four broad 'tendencies': liberal, radical,
Marxist/socialist and Black.

Liberal feminism

Equal rights Liberal feminists seek equal rights with
men. They argue that people should be treated
according to their individual merits (talents, effort etc)
rather than on the basis of their alleged 'sexual'
characteristics. So, instead of society imposing
separate roles for women, they should be allowed to
compete freely with men and they should enjoy the
same privileges and opportunities. This does not
happen at present because of prejudice (eg cultural
stereotypes about the 'proper' roles for males and
females) and discrimination (eg the exclusion of
females from 'male' roles). So liberal feminists
campaign for the removal of all those social,
economic, political or legal obstacles which deny
women the same freedom of choice as men. This task
includes grass roots struggles and, at a more 'official'
level, the work of organisations such as the Equal
Opportunities Commission which monitors sexual
discrimination in Britain.

Evaluation The liberal approach has exposed
discriminatory practices and it has had legislative
successes (eg the Equal Pay Act of 1975), so it is not
surprising that it has the support of most feminists.
But some critics say that it does not go far enough. It
seems to imply that a society like Britain is basically
sound and good and all that is required is the
removal of several discriminatory barriers so that

women can achieve the rights that men already possess. Socialist and radical feminists insist that the problem is deeper than this and so a more critical analysis is needed.

Radical feminism

The sex war Radical feminists stress the basic conflict between all men and all women. The main enemy of women is 'patriarchy': 'the combination of social, economic and cultural systems which ensures male supremacy' (Coote and Campbell, 1982, p32). Men use their collective power to ensure that society is run in their interests. They seize most of the material rewards and social privileges and they inflict physical and sexual violence on women. Men also exercise control over cultural attitudes and this means they are able to 'justify' their dominance by convincing people that it is 'natural' - it is just 'the way things are'. Many radical feminists agree that there are natural differences between the sexes (ie males and females think, feel and act differently) but they do not accept that male domination is inevitable.

Separatism The main goal for radical feminists is not to introduce 'equal rights' (they don't want women to become like men) but to free women from patriarchal control. To announce their more militant intentions, some American groups adopted fierce titles such as SCUM (Society for Cutting Up Men) and WITCH (Women's International Terrorist Conspiracy from Hell). But the main challenge to patriarchy is through 'separatism', the policy that women should cut themselves off (sexually and socially) from men. For example, Shulamith Firestone (1979) believes that it is the burden of childbearing which has placed women at a considerable disadvantage in the past. She looks to the new reproductive technology ('test tube fertilisation', 'artifical wombs' etc) to free women from continued dependence on, and contact with, men.

Marxist/socialist feminism

Capitalism Socialist feminists stress that women, like men, are members of social classes and this has a significant effect on their life chances and experiences. And social class is the principal factor affecting the relations *between* men and women. These relations alter as the class structure changes, and the emergence of capitalism has led to an intensification of sexual conflicts. Under capitalism, men try to gain control over the labour power of women in various ways: male employers treat women as a 'reserve army of labour' to be hired and fired at will; male workers try to exclude females from their trades and crafts; and husbands exploit their wives' unpaid housework.

Solutions Socialist feminists say that egalitarian relationships will be established only when capitalism is abolished and replaced by a non-exploitive socialist system. However, as feminists they recognise that the struggle is not just against capitalism but also against sexism and patriarchy. Although conventional Marxism explains why there is a hierarchy of workers in capitalist society, it does not provide a convincing explanation of why the lower positions are filled by women or why sexual discrimination persists (indeed, some early Marxists thought patriarchy would fade away as capitalism developed). So socialist feminists stress the need to look at 'sex' as well as 'class' factors. (See pp239-240 for Marxist/feminist theories of women's role in the family).

Black feminism

Sisterhood Mainstream feminists stress the importance of 'sisterhood'. All women suffer discrimination and so it is in their interests to organise collectively and remain loyal to their sisters. Consequently, these feminists concentrate on 'universal' woman and they neglect those things (eg age, social class) which separate one woman from another. In recent years, however, the women's movement has been fractured by the decision of many black women to form their own splinter groups (Murphy and Livingstone, 1985). This development has led to new analyses which recognise the importance of race and ethnicity.

Racism Bourne (1983) comments that the feminist neglect of racism is ironic since it was black culture which provided the women's movement with many of its ideas, slogans, organisational blueprints and consciousness raising techniques. Bourne also contends that white feminists have only paid lip service to the anti-racism struggle. White feminists are lukewarm about tackling racism since this would require a direct challenge to the power structure which grants them so many social, political and economic privileges. In effect, 'white women stand in a power relation as oppressors of black women' (Carby, 1982, p214).

Ethnicity Anthias and Yuval-Davis (1983) feel that the racism model overlooks Britain's 'non-black' minority women (eg Greeks, Cypriots, Chinese, Iranians and Filipinos). The lives of these women are affected not just by racism but also by their cultures: 'Such aspects as mothering, housework, sexual obligations, obedience and submissiveness to male commands...will differ according to ethnicity' (Anthias and Yuval-Davis, 1983, p68). So the 'ethnicity' framework is just as valuable as the 'racism' model for understanding the special interests and problems of minority women.

Reactions

Post feminism Mitchell and Oakley (1986) state that internal divisions and disagreements have become more pronounced in recent years as the women's movement has become more fragmented. Cashmore (1989) sees this trend as a healthy sign: the movement is now confident enough to air its differences. At another level, however, there has been a reaction to feminism, especially in the emergence of 'post feminism' (Stacey, 1986). This is a term which is used very loosely but usually it refers to the new mood of the 1980s and 1990s when a number of women openly resisted defining themselves as feminists. Partly they felt that feminism had gone 'too far' in criticising men, family and femininity. Besides, they believed that the really important battles - legal, political, economic - had already been won. But Faludi (1992) insists that sexual equality is still largely an illusion. Moreover, she argues that women's progress is threatened by a media 'backlash' which spreads scare stories about feminism (eg career women are alleged to miss out on the joys of marriage and motherhood). Partly because of this backlash, the women's movement appeared to lose its momentum and sense of direction in the cold economic and social climate of the 1980s (a period dominated by right wing policies and market forces). There was increasing uncertainty about exactly where feminism was heading.

The feminist mystique Friedan (1983) warns of the dangers of feminism becoming locked in reaction (people know what it is against but what is it for?). In an earlier book (Friedan, 1971) she had criticised the 'feminine mystique', the ideal of femininity that restricted so many women's lives. But in her later work Friedan is equally critical of the 'feminist mystique', the notion that female fulfilment lies in attacking love, men, children, family and fidelity. Back in the 1970s it was tactically necessary for feminists to challenge conventional values but

Friedan now felt that the time had arrived for feminism to develop more positive attitudes. Things like family, love and motherhood are still valued by most women and so feminists cannot afford to ignore their attractive features. Friedan thought there was a specially pressing need for women to enter into new forms of 'partnership' with men. In the 1990s there are increasing signs that feminism is moving in the direction that Friedan recommends.

Power feminism More recently, commentators have remarked on the emergence of 'power feminism' in the United States. Writers such as Camille Paglia accuse other feminists of popularising a 'victim mentality' which traps women into thinking of themselves as helpless, downtrodden and oppressed. Instead of this, power feminism invites women to recognise their new found power and opportunities. This new air of confidence is expressed by Wolf (1993) who urges women to celebrate and enjoy their formidable powers. Another example is the work of Roiphe (1994) who is particularly critical of allegations of 'date rape' (eg where a date ends in drunken intercourse and the 'morning after' the woman feels that she was coerced into sex). Roiphe criticises this broad definition of 'rape' and asserts that women should take more responsibility for their actions and decisions.

Summary

1 The women's movement has challenged many cultural assumptions and social practices which have held women back.

2 Feminism is not a uniform body of thought or action. The internal divisions have become more visible in recent years.

3 Feminism consists of a number of 'tendencies': liberal, radical, Marxist/socialist and Black.

Activity 2 Patriarchy

Item A *A useful concept?*

Is patriarchy a useful concept for exploring the disadvantages suffered by women? Here are two sides of the argument.

The trouble with patriarchy

1 It implies that nothing has really changed (men have always ruled), yet there have been significant historical shifts in male-female relationships.

2 It is too one sided, suggesting that men exercise fixed power over women in all areas. Yet, within any society, there will be a 'kaleidoscope' of forms: in some areas (eg family) women may have considerable power and in other areas there may be cooperation rather than male domination.

3 It presents a bleak and unchanging picture of men dominating women. This is likely to create a sense of hopelessness and helplessness rather than encouraging women to change things.

4 It suggests one cause (male power) for women's subordination and a separate cause (capitalism) for men's exploitation. But gender and class (and race) cannot be separated in this way.

5 It depicts a 'war' between men and women. Yet males (unlike capitalists) cannot be abolished and so some form of reconciliation is necessary.

Adapted from S. Rowbotham 'The Trouble with Patriarchy', *New Statesman* 21.12.79

In defence of patriarchy

1 Women need a general *theory* which explains their subordination. Patriarchy provides the basis for this.

2 Women may cooperate with, and even love, men. But male domination still exists.

3 It is a useful rallying symbol for women. It helps bring women together for necessary action.

4 The theoretical 'integration' of class, sex and race is possible only after a separate theory of gender relations has been developed.

5 The aim is not to eliminate men but rather those forms of *male power* which oppress women.

Adapted from S.Alexander and B.Taylor 'In Defence of Patriarchy', *New Statesman*, 1.2.80

Item B *Greenham Common*

Women protesting against a nuclear weapons base at Greenham Common - thousands linked arms to encircle the 9 mile perimeter of the American base in 1982.

Questions

1 Examine the two main arguments in Item A. Which do you find more convincing? Give reasons for your answer.

2 Look at Item B. Which group is most likely to support this kind of all-women action: those who find the concept of patriarchy useful or those who don't? Explain your answer.

2 Sex, Gender and Sexuality

Key Issues

1 What is the distinction between sex and gender?

2 What are the main explanations for gender differences?

3 How do sex and gender stereotyping operate?

2.1 Sex and gender

Sex This refers to the biological differences between 'males' and 'females'. These include variations in chromosomes, hormones, genitals and secondary sexual characteristics (breasts, hairiness of body etc). Most people can be clearly assigned to one sex or the other, although some individuals have androgynous (both male and female) characteristics. But it is perhaps too simple to regard sex as something totally fixed and permanent, since biology and culture interact. For example, shifting social fashions dictate the 'ideal' body (eg currently a muscular physique for men, a slim figure for women).

Gender This refers to cultural classifications of people as 'masculine' or 'feminine'. Societies set down expectations for males and females, and people are encouraged to think, feel and act in the manner 'appropriate' to their sex. Gender is one of the most pervasive and taken for granted features of our lives (Hearn and Morgan, 1990). But views on what is 'masculine' and 'feminine' vary from one society to the next and over time as cultures change.

Consequently, many sociologists argue that gender is socially *constructed* rather than *biologically determined*. But this debate - about the relationship between sex and gender - is highly controversial.

Social construction of gender

Socialisation According to this view, gender is socially constructed rather than genetically programmed. Genes do not determine the way men and women behave or think and genes do not force us into 'masculine' and 'feminine' pigeonholes. Rather, our gender characteristics are shaped by our social and cultural environment. Societies *create* these gender patterns and transmit them through the process of socialisation. From an early age, people are trained to conform to social expectations of how males and females should behave. For example, parents use different terms of endearment for boys and girls, dress them differently ('blue' and 'pink') and encourage different types of behaviour (boys can be boisterous but girls should be 'sweet'). And these gender differences tend to be reinforced throughout society by media, teachers and peer groups.

Gender expectations are *flexible*: they vary within and between societies and they change over time. Oakley (1972) observes that societies diverge in what they see as the 'natural' roles for males and females. In one society women are given 'gentle' tasks, while in another they do all the heavy work; something that is a man's task in one society will be reserved for women in another. So cross-cultural evidence suggests that the behaviour of the two sexes is fashioned by society. Margaret Mead (1935) identified the broad range of possibilities in her famous study of three New Guinea tribes. The Arapesh made little distinction between men and women, and the character of both sexes was gentle and submissive (ie 'feminine'). Similarly, few distinctions were made between Mundugamor men and women, but this tribe bred aggressive, rough, competitive ('masculine') personalities. Finally, among the Tchambuli the gender roles seemed the reverse of Western stereotypes: women were the main providers and made the sexual advances, while the vain but insecure men adorned themselves and enjoyed a good gossip. Mead's study supports the argument that gender differences are a matter of cultural *choice* rather than the predictable outcome of innate tendencies.

Biological determinism

This approach argues that genes ultimately control behaviour, temperament, abilities and social relationships. And since there are marked genetic differences between males and females, this sets tight limits on the cultural roles which they are suited to fill. Some radical feminists (eg Daly, 1979) seem to share these assumptions, especially when they assert that men are 'naturally' aggressive and women are morally and spiritually superior. But genetic explanations are most commonly associated with sociobiology.

Sociobiology In this approach gender differences are seen as evolutionary adaptations which improve the survival capacities of the human race. Thus, if men act in a 'masculine' way and women in a 'feminine' way, then they are more likely to survive and pass on their genes to future generations. Over long stretches of time the 'successful' genes will dominate, and these genes will programme people to behave in masculine or feminine ways. Wilson (1976) uses this idea to explain differences in sexual behaviour. A man is promiscuous because it is in his own 'selfish' interests to produce as many offspring as possible and thereby ensure the survival of his genetic line. But a woman can produce only a limited number of offspring (because of the nine months gestation period) and therefore she has a greater individual investment in each of her children. So she takes great care in choosing the father of her child and she is more faithful to him since she depends on his protection.

Male dominance Some biological determinists do not rely on evolutionary arguments. Goldberg (1979), for example, simply argues that male dominance is found in every known society and therefore must have some biological basis. Goldberg believes that

the male hormone, testosterone, interacts with the central nervous system at an early age to create a dominance tendency in men. This dominance is not the result of men's superior abilities (since there is little evidence for this) but derives from their greater determination to achieve power and control. As for apparent exceptions to male dominance, Goldberg insists that these are based on flawed evidence (eg Mead's 'effeminate' Tchambuli men were actually ex-headhunters!).

Between the extremes

Many social scientists adopt a position somewhere between the two extreme poles.

Biological determinists normally admit that sociocultural factors play some part in shaping gender patterns. For example, Goldberg allows that some cultures are more 'masculine' or 'feminine' than others. Also, within any society males and females are socialised into different roles and these roles change over time. Nevertheless, Goldberg still insists that men dominate in every known society. Real (biologically based) gender differences exist and they are bound to emerge eventually in social behaviour. So, when societies socialise males and females into different roles they are simply helping the 'natural' process along.

Social constructionists sometimes accept that biological factors are socially significant. After all, the argument that gender is solely a matter of socialisation seems to treat men and women as if they were nothing more than the passive recipients of cultural messages. Is it realistic to deny that males and females enter the world with different, biologically influenced, *predispositions?* Certainly some feminists are uncomfortable with the notion that men and women are totally interchangeable in terms of social and cultural characteristics. But they are understandably hesitant about identifying the mysterious *something*, the 'natural' difference, that sets men and women apart.

Political motives Feminists are suspicious of 'natural' arguments because these are frequently used to justify male privileges. Take Wilson's (1976) sociobiological explanation for women's maternal role: a man is seldom sure that 'his' baby is really his and so he does not take much interest in raising it; but a woman is confident that her baby shares her genes and so she will devote herself to it. It is easy to see how this argument could be used against women, as it implies it is their 'destiny' to be mothers and housewives. This is why some feminists say it is vital to treat men and women as basically the same - otherwise, the social disadvantages of women will be passed off as 'natural' differences. But Radcliffe Richards (1982) sees no need to deny 'real' differences between men and women. She says the case for feminism does not rely on men and women being strictly identical since societies still have a wide range of choice in deciding what to do about any differences that do exist.

Activity 3 Gender Differences

Item A *Gender ideals*

According to an American psychologist, most people see the following as the desirable characteristics for men and women.

Masculine Ideals	Feminine Ideals
aggressive	affectionate
ambitious	compassionate
assertive	soft spoken
athletic	gentle
competitive	conciliatory
dominant	yielding
forceful	understanding
leadership qualities	childlike
independent	sensitive
self reliant	easily flattered
strong personality	shy
individualistic	loyal

Adapted from S. Bem 'The Measurement of Psychological Androgyny' *Journal of Clinical Psychology*, vol 42, 1974

Item B *The boy can't help it*

Here is an excerpt from a teen magazine article which attempts to 'explain' some differences between boys and girls.

She says: 'He won't ever talk to me!'
He says: 'She wants to analyse everything.'
(Boys have trouble expressing themselves, especially about personal and emotional things. They're brought up to be the strong, silent type. Girls love to talk and often want to go over every detail of a relationship. Girls' friendships are based on intimacy - they like to trade personal, private feelings and secrets with each other.)

She says: 'He never tells me he loves me.'
He says: 'Of course I love her, but do I have to keep telling her?'
(Boys are frightened of committing themselves. They think that by admitting how much they feel for you, they are giving you power over them.)

She says: 'He sulks and that really upsets me.'
He says: 'Sometimes I just want to be alone. But it's nothing personal.'
(Boys are brilliant at withholding warmth and affection - sulking is their way of showing they are fed up. But a wise girl will let him get on with it and will then welcome him back when he's finally ready for company again.)

She says: 'He's only interested in watching Manchester United and tinkering with his car.'
He says: 'She doesn't understand any of the things I care about.'
(Men are tuned into things while women are tuned into people.)

Adapted from *19* magazine, April 1991, pp15-16

Questions

1 Look at Item A. How do these gender 'ideals' serve to reinforce patriarchy?
2 Look at Item B.
   a) How would these differences be explained in terms of the 'social construction of gender'?
   b) How would these differences be explained in terms of 'biological determinism'?

2.2 The sex-role system

Most societies treat men and women as quite distinct kinds of people. Hartnett (1978) calls this the *sex-role system*: the network of attitudes, feelings and behaviour which results from the pervasiveness of sex-role stereotyping within a culture. Hartnett uses the term 'sex-role' but it could just as easily be called 'gender-role'. The key point is that 'gender' roles are largely allocated on the grounds of 'sex'. Hartnett describes three main features of the sex-role system.

1 Males and females are assigned personality traits (masculine and feminine) which are viewed as polar opposites.
2 They are allocated different tasks and activities.
3 Males are given a higher social value than females, regardless of the specific tasks involved.

Roles, stereotypes, ideals The concept of a 'sex-role system' is useful for describing gender divisions in society. But it needs to be handled with care. After all, the social gaps between men and women are neither permanent (eg note the impact of equal opportunities legislation) nor uniform (eg they are probably more rigid in housework than in employment or education). Also, there is a danger of confusing the reality with what people *think* is the case. Here Clatterbaugh (1990) makes a helpful distinction between roles, stereotypes and ideals. *Gender roles* are the sets of behaviour, attitudes and conditions that are empirically observed among particular groups of men and women. But this 'real' state of affairs is not the same thing as *gender stereotypes*: general ideas of what most people *consider* (often mistakenly) to be typical masculine or feminine gender roles. And finally there is the *gender ideal*: widespread notions as to what the gender roles *should* be. Roles, stereotypes and ideals are interlinked (eg ideals and stereotypes act as guides for gender roles). But they do not always coincide.

Activity 4 Sex Roles

Item A *Becoming a woman*

The following passage is from a writer who was born a male but later in adult life had an operation to change sex.

'We are told that the social gap between the sexes is narrowing but I can only report that, having experienced life in both roles, there seems to me no aspect of existence, no moment of the day, no contact, no arrangement, no response, which is not different for men and for women. The very tone of voice in which I was now addressed, the very posture of the person next in the queue, the very feel in the air when I entered a room or sat at a restaurant table, constantly emphasised my change of status.

And if others' responses shifted, so did my own. The more I was treated as a woman, the more woman I became. If I was assumed to be incompetent at reversing cars, or opening bottles, oddly incompetent I found myself becoming. If a case was thought too heavy for me, inexplicably I found it so myself. I began to find women's conversation more congenial. Women treated me with frankness. Men treated me more and more as a junior. I discovered that men prefer women to be less informed, less able, less talkative and certainly less self-centred than they are themselves, so I generally obliged them.'

Adapted from J. Morris *Conundrum*, 1987, p140

Item B *Tootsie*

Dustin Hoffman in the film 'Tootsie', where he played an out of work male actor who passes as a woman in order to get acting roles.

Item C *Fat slags*

© House of Viz - John Brown Publishing Ltd

Questions

1 Read Item A.
   a) What does this passage reveal about the 'sex-role system'?
   b) Morris shows how males and females are treated differently. Give some other examples of this.
2 Look at Item B. How easy is it for someone to 'pass' as a member of the opposite sex? Give reasons for your answer.
3 Why might some people be shocked by the behaviour of the 'Fat Slags' in Item C?

2.3 Sexuality

Sex-roles and sexuality Sexuality refers to sexual attitudes, emotions, desires and behaviour. Although this is a very intimate and personal matter, it is regulated by the wider sex- role system. First, males and females are assumed to have different sexual 'personalities' (eg the promiscuous man with a high sex drive; the chaste woman who is more interested in love than sex). Secondly, they are given detailed sexual 'scripts' (eg man is the active predator and woman is the passive object of male attentions). And thirdly, men usually have higher status and power (note the 'double standard' in sexual infidelity: it can add to a man's reputation as a 'red-blooded' male but it stigmatises a woman as 'loose'). Again, it is important to remember the distinction between 'reality' and 'stereotype'. For example, Gathorne-Hardy (1981) suggests that the 'sexual revolution' in recent decades has led to more liberal attitudes to sex and this has resulted in a convergence in male and female sexual behaviour. Nevertheless, there is still a 'sex-role system' in sexual relations, and this can be seen in the way men try to control women's sexuality.

Male control Feminists argue that men shape sexual behaviour to suit their own interests. Women are not respected as autonomous individuals but are treated as dehumanised sex objects, the mere sexual playthings of men. This was vividly illustrated in the film *The Stepford Wives,* where the men of the community created beautiful life-like robotic wives whose sole function was to please their husbands. Although that is an extreme example from fiction, some feminists suggest it is not so far-fetched as far as its sentiments are concerned. Consequently, they have urged women to break away from conventional sexual roles and embrace either 'heterosexual chauvinism' (ie the promiscuous woman in search of the perfect orgasm) or 'separatism' (ie lesbianism). But Coote and Campbell (1982) believe this just forces women into yet another set of rigid roles. They prefer the more flexible model of 'self-determining sexuality' where women are free to decide for themselves their sexual preferences and lifestyles. A different view is taken by Greer (1985). At one time she supported sexual 'liberation' but in her later work she questioned the benefits of sexual licence and recommended instead a life of chastity or fidelity.

The beauty myth Females are under great pressure to evaluate themselves in terms of their physical attractiveness to men. This preoccupation with appearance has damaging effects. For example, the 'beauty myth' (Wolf, 1990) encourages women to worry about their looks and spend far too much time cultivating a 'Barbie Doll' image. For the older woman, especially, this is likely to induce a sense of inferiority, as it is increasingly difficult to compete with the glamorous young models in the glossy magazines. But even on this issue we find debates *within* feminism. For instance, Radcliffe Richards (1982) declares that feminists should celebrate beauty and adornment. She reckons that it is just as reasonable to value people for their looks as for, say, their musical gifts or personality. 'Fashion' can be pleasurable and life-enhancing. Perhaps this is why the modern male is taking an increasing interest in appearance and fashion! (Willis, 1990).

Pornography Many women are offended by the way females are represented in pornography, ranging from Page 3 pin-ups through to 'hard-core'. Dworkin (1981) lists a number of criticisms of pornography: it exploits and harms the women who take part; it reinforces the myth that women like to be dominated by men; it projects highly degrading and humiliating images of women; and it probably has a causal link with sexual violence against women (either by de-sensitising men to the brutality of violent domination, or by encouraging direct imitation of pornographic scenes). In Britain, Clare Short MP has run a parliamentary campaign to restrict public displays of nude pin-ups in newspapers, magazines and advertising. Some feminists, however, have made a case for male pin-ups ('soft porn') for women, on the grounds that women, too, enjoy erotic displays. Also, Feminists Against Censorship believe that censorship simply plays into the hands of conservative forces who may wish to extend it to other social, moral and political issues.

Sexual violence One area where feminists are united is their condemnation of sexual violence against women. Sexual harassment (eg unwelcome sexual comments, teasing or touching) is a common hazard for females in workplaces and other public spheres. (Some Japanese night clubs have even introduced 'sexual harassment' areas where paid 'secretaries' walk around and customers can fondle and grab them at will). Other forms of sexual violence range from sexual molestation and beatings right through to rape and murder. Estimates of the prevalence of these types of violence are usually rough and ready and they do not always distinguish adequately between different types of violence. However, some government research (HMSO, 1989) suggests that in Britain as many as half a million women are affected annually by domestic violence ('threatening, violent or sexually harassing behaviour'). And Pahl (1985), reviewing British and American surveys, refers to estimates that 10% of married women will experience marital rape, while 20-30% of all females (over the age of 12) will suffer a violent sexual attack at some time in their lives. Brownmiller (1975) sees these problems as part of a wider pattern of coercive sexuality and she regards rape as a conscious conspiracy by which all men keep all women in a state of fear. Females are constantly faced with the threat of sexual abuse, ridicule or violence and this effectively limits their movements and freedom.

Debates Sexuality is pleasurable and fulfilling for most people. But the preceding sections show that it can be a dangerous and disturbing area, especially for women. However, it is also clear that there is no single feminist 'line' on many of these issues. Some of the fiercest debates are not between men and women but between different feminist camps.

Activity 5 Asking For It

Item A *A normal beating?*

The following passage is based on transcripts of interviews with fifth formers in a Birmingham comprehensive school.

Deb: Did you see that film about battered women on the telly the other night?

El: Yeh, it's terrible. She could have fought back like my mam does. She hits him back.

Penny: Don't you think she might get beat up worse then?

Sue: When my dad hits my mum and we think he shouldn't, we have a go at him and stop him. But sometimes when she goes on and on at him we don't 'cos she deserves it.

Researcher: You mean she deserves to get beaten up for just talking to him?

Sue: Yeh, well not really I suppose.

Penny: If he beats you up does it mean he loves yer?

Deb: When I first went with blokes I thought that getting beat up was just normal 'cos it happens all the time. I thought I had to put up with it 'cos that was what women was supposed to expect. Then I realised that it was wrong to have to put up with it.

Adapted from C.Griffin *Typical Girls*, 1985, pp48-49

Item C *Safety after dark*

72% of women feared for their safety after dark, as opposed to 27% of men. Women generally, and particularly older women and black and Asian women who are subject to racial attack, feel that they must restrict their behaviour as a precaution against crime. For example, 37% of women in the borough never go out unaccompanied after dark and 50% usually or always went out with someone rather than alone. 60% of young white women and 72% of young black women experience street harassment - kerb crawling, lewd suggestions, threats etc.

Islington Crime Survey, quoted in *New Society*, 25.10.91

Item B *Wife beating*

THE ADVANTAGES OF MATRIMONY.
" What's the matter with your face, ma?"
" Your ma's got a black eye, dear."
" Can't I have one, too, ma?"
" Wait till you're old enough to get married, pet."

A cartoon from 1896

Item D

Mr & Mrs Punch

Questions

1 Read Item A.
   a) Suggest reasons why some people might think that beating women was 'just normal'.
   b) Suggest some reasons why battered women might be reluctant to leave home.
2 Look at the pictures in Items B and D. What do they suggest about attitudes to wife beating?
3 Read Item C. Do you think this 'fear of crime' is justified? Give reasons for your answer.

Sexuality and adolescents

Slags When Lees (1986) interviewed 16 year old girls in three London comprehensives, she was struck by their fear of being labelled a 'slag' (someone who is 'flighty', 'tartish', or 'cheap'). It was not always clear what qualified a girl as a 'slag' and so this created a great deal of anxiety and uncertainty. Concerned to protect their reputations, girls became preoccupied with their appearance: 'Appearance is crucial: wearing too much make-up; having your skirt slit too high; not combing your hair; wearing jeans to dances or high heels to school; having your trousers too tight or your tops too low...Is it any wonder that girls have to learn to make fine discriminations about appearances and spend so much time deciding what to wear?' (Lees, 1986, p37). The girls were also confused about appropriate behaviour. If they were too free with boys they were likely to be condemned as a 'slut'; yet if they refused to go out with certain boys they ran the danger of being called a 'tight bitch'.

Lees also identified the operation of double standards. The sexual licence of boys was seen as 'natural' and it enhanced their reputations as 'studs'. Yet girls were subject to constant verbal and sexual abuse which constrained their behaviour and freedom. And what made it even worse was that girls colluded with the system - instead of challenging the language of abuse, they even used it themselves against other girls. In a later work, however, Lees suggested that girls are starting to develop strategies of resistance: 'There may be little collective protest but some girls are questioning sexism. Girls tease each other for playing up to boys, girls are having fun, and can be humorous, self-assured and full of spark. Girls do not passively accept their subordination' (Lees, 1993, p65).

Changing attitudes Sex-role systems can change, and one example of this is adolescent attitudes towards romance. McRobbie (1982) found from her field study that many teenage girls retreated into the world of 'romance' and the 'culture of femininity' and they were desperate to find a 'steady'. Nevertheless, in a later work (McRobbie, 1991) she identifies certain changes in teenage magazines. Where magazines like *Jackie* used to favour sentimental, romantic stories about boy friends, the magazines of the late 1980s and 1990s (eg *Just Seventeen*) adopt different themes. They are far more interested in fashion, pop and personal problems, and they are far franker and more realistic in their content. The reader of these magazines is visualised as someone who is confident, fun-oriented and far less obsessed with getting a 'steady'. Teenage girls are treated as intelligent and they are recognised as future workers. There are clearer signs of gender equality (eg having friends of both sexes) and of informed consumerism (make-up, fashion). McRobbie credits certain TV programmes such as *Grange Hill*, *Brookside* and *Neighbours* for helping to overturn rigid gender stereotypes. Girls are now portrayed as strong-minded, independent and assertive, and boys are seen as capable of having 'feelings'.

Summary

1 The 'real' differences between men and women are a matter of dispute. It is not easy to specify the relative importance of 'biology' and 'society'.
2 Nevertheless, societies have considerable 'choice' in deciding what cultural roles they allocate to males and females.
3 Societies operate sex-role systems. In the case of sexuality we can find some evidence for both change and continuity in these systems.

Activity 6 Selling Sex

Item A *Advertising*

Pictures of women plaster the environment. Legs, breasts, hands, bottoms and smiles are displayed on advertising hoardings, in magazines, calendars and TV commercials. They belong to Ms Perfection and are used to sell a variety of objects - car tyres, lawnmowers, deodorants, diamonds, videos and hair dyes.

Adapted from D. Souhami *A Woman's Place*, 1986, p8

Wonder Bra ad

Item B *Male fantasies*

Practically all advertising is on behalf of the masculine image, either showing him what kind of status he can hope to attain, or showing a woman what kind of man she can hope to attract.

Advertising addressed to women always promises love: someone wonderful will canter up on a white horse if she uses the right soap, her husband will never leave her if she gives him the right coffee, and if she wears the swimsuit on page 98, she will magnetise muscular males like those who are prowling around the model in the photograph. Advertising aimed at men promises that if he buys the right razor he will be as daring as hang-gliders who sail the wind; if he drinks one brand of vodka, he will be among the rich smoothies who frequent the best hotels in Europe; if he buys the right car, he will pull women and also, it goes without saying, his erection will never wilt. Advertising demeans men. It turns their longings for triumph, freedom and sex into four wheels, a floozy and a Havana cigar.

Adapted from I.Kurtz *Malespeak*, 1986, p80

Questions

1 What criticisms can be levelled at these media images? Can you suggest some counter arguments to the criticisms?
2 Give some other examples of the different ways males and females are portrayed in advertising and the media.
3 Is there any evidence that advertising images of males and females are changing (eg 'role reversals')?

3 Ethnic Minority Women

Key Issues

1 Why were ethnic minority females 'invisible' for such a long time in sociology?
2 What are the connections between race and gender?
3 Are feminist theories and policies applicable to ethnic minority women?

3.1 Invisible women

History Until recently ethnic minority women in Britain were relatively invisible to researchers. Historically, of course, Britain's black communities were small and sexually imbalanced, with males greatly outnumbering females (Walvin, 1973). But Indian *ayahs* (nannies, female servants) were brought to Britain as far back as the eighteenth century. By the beginning of the twentieth century they had formed a small community in London (Visram, 1986). Also,

some Afro-Caribbean women played important roles in Britain's past. For example, Mary Seacole deserved perhaps as much credit as Florence Nightingale for improving nursing services during the Crimean War. But black women did not establish any significant numerical presence in Britain itself until the postwar period of New Commonwealth immigration. Even then, they were unevenly represented among the various ethnic groups. Among migrants from the Indian subcontinent, men initially outnumbered women. Some balance was restored as female dependents joined the original 'primary' migrants but there is still a marked sexual imbalance among Pakistani and Bangladeshi communities (see Table 1).

Stereotypes As the numbers of ethnic minority women rose in the 1960s and 1970s, so social scientists started to explore their lives in greater detail. But this study was still very patchy. Ethnographers studied 'ethnicity' but neglected 'gender', while feminist scholars highlighted 'gender' and overlooked 'ethnicity'. Moreover, researchers were frequently accused of resorting to crude stereotypes when describing minority women. For example, Bryan et al (1985) claim that Afro-Caribbean women are usually portrayed in terms of the 'matriarchal myth'. This depicts them as strong, self-reliant 'survivors' who are largely independent of men. Asian women, in contrast, are typically presented as passive victims who meekly submit to the cruel treatment inflicted on them by patriarchal males. According to critics, these stereotypes are based on ethnocentric (and possibly racist) misreadings of the lives of ethnic minority women.

Table 1 Sex distribution by ethnic group, 1988-90

Males per 100 females:

White	Afro-Caribbean	African Asian	Indian	Paki-stani	Bangla-deshi	Chinese
95	98	105	103	111	113	105

Adapted from T. Jones *Britain's Ethnic Minorities*, 1993, p24, and based on Labour Force Surveys

3.2 Making connections

Multidimensional lives Minority women are not just women - they are also members of racial or ethnic groups and they belong to social classes. Each of these factors has an effect on their lives. As women, they find that their lives are affected by gender expectations. As black women, they suffer the additional problem of racism. Also, the fine details of their lives are shaped by the cultural norms of their particular ethnic groups. Finally, women are located in different positions in the class structure and this means their lifestyles and life chances differ: 'Women's lives are affected by class and work relationships in ways that give some women power over others, in which some women benefit from the exploitation of others and in which women have different interests' (Ramazanoglu, 1989, p112).

Most sociologists agree that race, class and gender are interconnected but there is less agreement on their relative importance. Which of these dimensions has the greatest influence on a black woman's life? As a rough guide, radical feminists lay stress on 'gender', Marxists on 'class' and black activists on 'race' (or, more accurately, racism). But it seems unwise to present bold claims at this stage of knowledge. Perhaps the best way forward lies with detailed empirical studies which show the *interaction* of these factors in specific situations. Certainly this seems better than the crude 'additive' approach which simply assumes that black women lose out in all three spheres (the 'lowest' social class, the 'subordinate' race and the 'oppressed' sex). This additive approach falsely reduces them to constant 'losers' and it takes little account of their creative responses. Fuller's (1982) study of a London comprehensive found that racism and sexism certainly caused difficulties for black girls but they were resilient and managed to develop strategies which ensured educational success. And Maynard (1990) challenges the idea that 'race' simply increases the inequality and oppression which black women experience as women. For Maynard, race cannot just be 'added in' to existing analyses of women, because race qualitatively changes the nature of women's subordination. This means that new forms of analysis need to be developed.

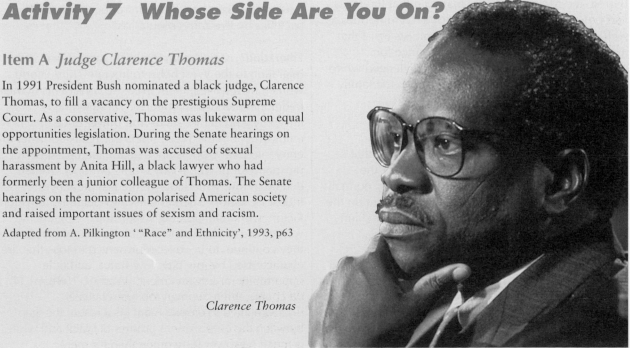

Activity 7 Whose Side Are You On?

Item A *Judge Clarence Thomas*

In 1991 President Bush nominated a black judge, Clarence Thomas, to fill a vacancy on the prestigious Supreme Court. As a conservative, Thomas was lukewarm on equal opportunities legislation. During the Senate hearings on the appointment, Thomas was accused of sexual harassment by Anita Hill, a black lawyer who had formerly been a junior colleague of Thomas. The Senate hearings on the nomination polarised American society and raised important issues of sexism and racism.

Adapted from A. Pilkington ' "Race" and Ethnicity', 1993, p63

Clarence Thomas

Item B *Choices*

What exactly went on between Thomas and Hill we shall never know. No hard evidence, no witnesses - just his word against hers. This was why the televised hearings had such high ratings. Here was a story that had it all: race, sex, ambition, power. Yet ultimately it all hinged on a simple choice. Who do you believe, him or her?

Adapted from S. Moore *Guardian*, 21.5.93

Item C *Identities*

The Thomas-Hill scandal illustrates the fragmentation and dislocation of identities in modern society. It was not just that people took up different positions according to the priority they attached to racism, sexism and liberalism. The arguments also went on inside the head of each individual. People found they were pulled in different directions by their competing identities - should their sympathies be decided by their sex, race or political attitudes? Identity is not something 'fixed' - it can shift and it can be 'won' or 'lost'.

Adapted from S. Hall *The Question of Identity*, 1992, pp279-280

Anita Hill

Questions

1 Thomas accused the Senate hearings of racism (a 'hi-tech lynching for uppity blacks'). In what ways was racism a factor in the debate?
2 Hill accused the (all male) Senate committee of sexism. In what ways was sexism a factor in the debate?
3 Item C draws attention to people's competing loyalties. Select one social group (eg black females or white liberals) and show how its loyalties might be divided over the Thomas appointment.
4 Thomas's appointment to the Supreme Court was eventually confirmed (although public opinion on the honesty of Thomas and Hill remained divided). Do you think this was the right decision? Give reasons for your answer.

3.3 New analyses

Barrett and McIntosh (1985) maintain that the ideas and policies of feminism apply to racial minorities as well as whites. But some black feminists insist that mainstream feminism has little relevance for minorities. In particular, they have challenged white feminist views on capitalism, patriarchy, the family and reproduction.

Capitalism

Traditional cultures Many feminists believe that capitalism carries a heavy responsibility for the subordination of women. Nevertheless, they normally regard Western capitalism as an improvement on the traditional cultures of the Third World. They claim that the backward, primitive nature of these traditional cultures is revealed by their harsh treatment of women (eg female circumcision, forced marriages). But these feminist attitudes have been criticised as patronising and misleading (Carby, 1982). The so-called 'traditional' ethnic cultures were never uniformly patriarchal. For example, women in West African societies had high status and important

social, cultural, political and economic roles (Bryan et al, 1985). Indeed, far from being 'traditional', patriarchy might have been introduced into these societies by Western colonialists!

Liberation? Mainstream feminists suggest that migration to the West helps to liberate Third World women by releasing them from the constraints of their traditional patriarchal cultures. These women allegedly gain higher status and power once they find employment in the West. But is this really so? After all, entry into paid work is not a guaranteed passport to prosperity or power. Many ethnic minority women end up in low skilled jobs in the less attractive industrial sectors (such as catering, cleaning, transport, factory work and clothing sweatshops). Migrant women are 'a cheap and flexible source of labour and they continue to be over-represented in jobs that are characterised by low pay, low status, and little opportunity for advancement' (Warrier, 1988, p134). Of course, white women too are relatively disadvantaged in employment (as a result, the 'gap' between the employment profiles of black and white is much narrower for women than for men).

Bargaining power Bhachu (1991) found that the bargaining power of British Sikh women was strengthened by wage earning. It allowed them to spend more on themselves and gave them much more influence in domestic affairs. But it is not always easy to decide whether entry into paid work empowers minority women. Anthias (1983) illustrates some of the complexities in her study of Greek Cypriot women in London. These women usually end up working for menfolk within their rather self-enclosed community. They find a niche in low paid and insecure employment in clothing workshops, cafés and homeworking (where they do piece-work for low pay without any job security or employment rights). In many ways this pattern fits their cultural tradition, which sees women primarily as mothers and housewives rather than people with careers. To this extent their culture facilitates their 'exploitation'. Nevertheless, the women were reasonably happy with their wages which they felt gave them greater bargaining power and status. And the women remained firmly loyal to their community, even although they were subordinate to men.

Patriarchy

Cultural relativism Is it accurate to describe Britain's minority cultures as patriarchal? The stereotypical image of 'Asian' cultures - one of downtrodden women who are bossed about by dominant males - suggests this is the case. But is this image based on ethnocentrism (ie interpreting one culture from the standpoint of an 'outside' culture which is based on a quite different set of values)? Sociologists employ the concept of 'cultural relativism' to stress that cultural practices and beliefs are sometimes best understood from the point of view of 'insiders' (ie relative to the society and culture concerned). Things often seem very different when we try to understand cultures in their own terms and in their proper context. Thus, many Asians claim that their religious and cultural values do not treat women as inferiors. Rather, the culture simply allocates men and women to roles which are 'different' but of 'equal' status.

Muslim females Ethnocentric approaches often end up placing too much 'blame' on minority cultures. Take the case of Muslim women in Britain. These women have very low economic activity rates and this is often attributed to their patriarchal culture which lays heavy stress on *purdah* (seclusion of women). But purdah is not confined to Muslim women and anyway there are a number of other reasons which help account for their low participation rates. It is partly explained by the 'historical' background (many Muslim women came here as dependants rather than primary workers), date of arrival (Pakistani and Bangladeshi women

came to Britain later than most other groups, so they have had less time to adjust) and language problems (Brown, 1984, found this was an important obstacle). Also, the economic activity rate of Muslim females varies according to their socioeconomic skills (the better educated groups from East Africa have higher rates) and the area of settlement in Britain (this affects local employment opportunities). Finally, the ever present threat of racism may restrict their job opportunities or even deter them from joining the workforce in the first place.

Matrifocal culture For Afro-Caribbean (or 'West Indian') groups, the issue of patriarchy is not clear cut. For example, the West Indian 'matrifocal' (woman centred) tradition is one where women have a great deal of experience organising themselves independently of men. Women in the Caribbean have a long history of running their own lives and providing for themselves (eg high levels of female-headed households). This is not quite the same thing as a 'matriarchal' culture, since West Indian women do not 'rule' men. When the man is present in the family he can exert a great deal of influence and power. However, some historians argue that colonialism and slavery had the effect of stripping power from black men. Even in present day Britain, black men are a disadvantaged group. Their daily lives are disfigured by racism. Consequently, Afro-Caribbean women often distance themselves from the 'anti-man' bias of some white feminists. They prefer to view black men as allies in a common struggle against racism. Moreover, they accuse feminists of reinforcing racist stereotypes of black men. When feminists run campaigns to 'reclaim the streets' or when they treat men as 'potential rapists', this risks resurrecting the 'myth of the black rapist'. This racist image portrays black men as sexual predators and it has been used in the past to oppress these men.

Black patriarchy It would be far-fetched to claim that there are no problems of sexism or patriarchy in minority cultures. After all, black feminist groups have been formed to fight these problems. These groups have challenged male violence and they have set up women's refuges and campaigned for equal rights. This causes a number of tensions within minority communities. Mama (1990) found that battered black women were often reluctant to seek police help because this was seen as a 'betrayal' of black men. Black women were expected to tolerate their beatings (which were explained away as a 'natural' and inevitable result of the oppression and frustration suffered by black men!). As for Asian women, they can be intimidated into silence by powerful traditions of family loyalty and by threats of exclusion from their close knit communities.

Family

Family variations Minority families differ in size and composition from those of the wider society and from each other. In 1989-91 the average size of household was 2.4 for whites, 4.7 for Pakistanis and Bangladeshis, 3.6 for Indians and 2.4 for West Indians (*Labour Force Survey*, 1989-91). Ethnic minority groups have a 'younger' age profile than the white population and this helps to explain why they have higher proportions of households with dependent children (see Figure 1). Among families with dependent children, figures for 1989-91 reveal that 15% of white families were lone parent, compared with 49% of West Indian, 6% of Indian, and 8% of Pakistani and Bangladeshi families (Haskey, 1991). Minority groups also differ in terms of family norms and customs (eg the Asian pattern of arranged marriages and the dowry system). Also, there are variations in family styles *within* minority communities, according to social class or individual choice (Westwood and Bhachu, 1988). For example, middle class West Indian families are less likely to fit the matrifocal pattern.

Values The family is a favourite target for feminist critics who often condemn it as 'anti-social' and oppressive (Barrett and McIntosh, 1982). But does this apply to racial and ethnic minorities? Values obviously influence people's opinions on this issue. The matrifocal family may appear disorganised and 'pathological' to people who cherish the traditional 'British' nuclear family. But Afro-Caribbeans might reply that the matrifocal family is a positive resource and a valid lifestyle. A similar value clash is visible in the case of Asian groups. Western feminists usually hold 'individualistic' values (freedom, independence, privacy, choice etc) and so they tend to look disapprovingly on the 'collective' values of Asian cultures. These cultures place high value on the

extended family, the village and the religious community. To the Asian, 'the Westerner's stress on independence and individuality appears immoral, selfish and irresponsible' (Saifullah-Khan, 1976, p241).

The good family Some black writers declare that, far from being 'anti-social', minority families offer many rewards for their members. Families certainly sustain them in the fight against racism: 'the black family is a source of support in the context of harassment and attacks from white people' (Bhavnani and Coulson, 1986, p88). Indeed, the problem for many black people is not the need to escape from family life but the difficulty in bringing families *together*: 'In identifying the institution of the family as a source of oppression for women, white feminists have again revealed their cultural and racial myopia, because for Asian women in particular, the British state through its immigration legislation has done all it can to destroy the Asian family by separating husbands from wives, wives from husbands and parents from children' (Amos and Parmar, 1984, p15).

Family problems Nevertheless, there is a danger of romanticising black family life. It is extremely unlikely that black families are shielded from the severe problems which currently afflict family life in the West. Moreover, the problems of minority families are likely to be made harsher because of the greater risk of poverty and the ever present threat of racism. And this is why some white feminists insist that their analyses of the family also apply to black women: 'We would argue forcefully that nothing has so far emerged that would lead us to modify our general critical stance towards the family' (Barrett and McIntosh, 1985, p42).
(See pp256-257 for further material on ethnic minority families).

Figure 1 Households with dependent children: by ethnic group of head, 1989 and 1991 average (Great Britain)

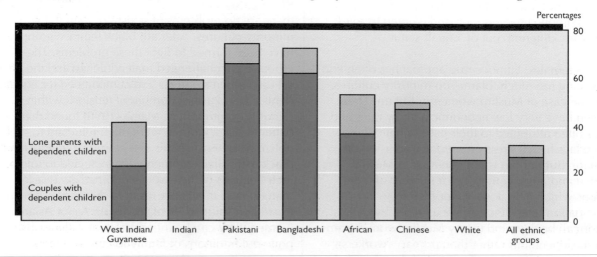

Activity 8   Asian Cultures

Item A   *Blame it on the girls*

Nazrah (a 16 year old): With Asian families reputation is the first thing. If you've got a bad reputation nobody wants to know you. It's very important for girls. If you behave well then that helps when you want to get married to a particular person. *Izzat* means 'reputation', 'honour'. The woman takes more responsibility for *izzat* than the man.

If you get followed by boys, most Asian parents are likely to blame it on the girls not the boys.

A lot of white people think Asian men are sexist and don't treat women fairly. I expect white men are equally sexist but perhaps it shows in different ways. Many Asian men have been brought up in a culture where the wife does all the housework and doesn't go out for a

job. But in the modern parts of Pakistan and India men are brought up differently, and so they have different attitudes. Asian culture is developing. Here in Britain many Asian men accept their wives going out to work.

Adapted from A.Osler *Speaking Out*, 1989, pp96-98

Item B   *Foolish romance?*

'Western' romantic love and 'Asian' arranged marriages are based on different sets of assumptions and expectations. Romantic love is a mating system which relies on the emotions of two individuals, their passions, lust and a kind of burning love which may soon fade. Arranged marriages, on the other hand, are based on the responsibility, stability and maturity that a marriage demands; people look for wisdom, patience and good sense rather than 'exciting' qualities. The marriage is seen as a union of two families and so parents engage in painstaking research on the background of potential spouses in order to ensure the happiness of their children.

Forced marriage - found among some Muslim Mirpuris in the north of England and many deeply conservative Sikh and Hindu groups - is indefensible, since women are subjected to emotional blackmail, guilt, shame and even violence. But arranged marriages are voluntary and the couple have the final choice. Many young Asians choose not to join the romantic 'circus' which involves degrading competition and so much pain and risk. They appreciate the greater stability of Asian family life. Yet, because of the cultural arrogance of British society, many people do not consider that arranged marriages might be a more reliable and dignified way of finding a partner than following the fluttering of your heart or the alluring calls of a smooth-talking man.

Adapted from Alibhai-Brown, 'Marriage of Minds not Hearts', *New Statesman and Society*, 12.2.93

Hindu wedding

Questions

1 Read Item A.
   a) Are Asian girls any different from white girls as far as responsibility for 'reputation' is concerned?
   b) Do you agree that white and Asian males are 'equally sexist'? Give reasons for your answer.
2 Read Item B.
   a) Do you think Alibhai-Brown's description of Western romantic love is accurate?
   b) Do you agree that the 'stability' of Asian family life is mainly due to the arranged marriage system? Give reasons for your answer.

Reproduction

Religion Feminists attach great importance to women's control over reproduction and this is why they press for abortion rights and easy access to contraception. However, reproductive rights pose particular problems for some minorities. For one thing, contraception is disapproved of in certain cultures and religions (eg Roman Catholicism, Islam, Ras Tafari). Ramazanoglu (1989) notes that feminism has shown very little interest in religious affiliations, yet religion is a dominant factor in the identities and behaviour of many ethnic minority women.

Contraception The problem is not always one of lack of access to contraception; quite the contrary. Some ethnic minority women complain that they have been actively *encouraged* by the state and by doctors to limit their family size. The underlying (racist) assumption seems to be that it is especially desirable to reduce the size of the minority population. In some cases women have been given Depo Provera (an injectible contraceptive which lasts for about six months) without their full knowledge or consent. Consequently, minority women are suspicious of reproductive campaigns: 'When the women's movement demanded free, safe and available contraception for all women, we had to remind them that for black women this often means being used as guinea pigs in mass birth control programmes, or as objects of research when new forms of birth control need to be tested' (Bryan et al, 1985, p105).

Abortion Abortion, too, has been pressed on black women: 'When the women's movement took up the issue of "Abortion on Demand" in the early seventies, black women had to point out that we have always been given abortions more readily than white women and are indeed often encouraged to have terminations we didn't ask for' (Bryan et al, 1985, p105). Given the long history of attempts to limit the black population (because they were seen as 'unfit' and undesirable), black women are insistent on their rights to choose to have their babies.

Family planning With the development of reproductive technology, it is now possible to exercise greater choice over the sex of children. But this raises alarming prospects for some Asian groups where there is a marked cultural preference for male children. This preference exists partly because of the burden of dowries and partly because a bride is seen as 'belonging' to her husband's family (so this limits the help she can give her own parents in their old age). Some observers predict there will be increasing pressures on Asian women to abort simply on the grounds of the sex of the foetus: 'Already some women in India have had to abort a perfectly healthy female foetus after an amniocentesis test has revealed that the desired male child will be a girl' (Dale and Foster, 1986, p91).
(For further discussion of ethnicity and families see pp256-257).

Summary

1 Ethnic minority women have become less 'invisible' within sociology and feminism.
2 Gender interacts with race and social class.
3 Ethnic minority women share certain problems with white women but their goals and interests do not always coincide.

4 Women and Work

Key Issues
1 How do the employment patterns of males and females differ?
2 What are the explanations for these differences?
3 How do the work experiences of women vary?
4 What are the main features of housework?

4.1 Employment patterns

Employment is 'gendered' insofar as there are different expectations of males and females. For example, the attitude still persists that a woman's true place is in the home. A major survey of female employment in Britain (Martin and Roberts, 1984) found that most married women regarded their 'real' job as home and children. Paid work was not as 'central' to their lives as it was for men. Employment is also gendered in the sense that men and women occupy different positions in the labour market. Nevertheless, employment patterns and attitudes are slowly changing.

Women in the labour force

Females have never dropped below 30% of the labour force this century. But since the 1950s there has been a marked trend towards the increasing 'feminisation' of the workforce and this is clearly documented by Labour Force Surveys. For the years 1969-89, the number of female workers rose by 2.25m (and males only by 0.5m). By 1993 women comprised about 44% of the workforce. In the same year, 71% of women of working age (16- 59) were 'economically active', compared with 86% of men (aged 16-64). The increase in the female workforce is partly a result of labour market trends (eg growth of the service sector) but it is largely due to the increased economic activity of married women. The proportion of married women in paid employment increased from 47% in 1971 to 68% in 1993. Demographic changes suggest that this trend will continue. The 'demographic timebomb' refers to the possibility that a declining birthrate may eventually lead to a shortage of labour. This has created the expectation that employers will be more willing in future to recruit from underused pools of labour, including ethnic minorities and women.

Part time work

The 1991 Labour Force Survey reported that 40% of female employees (and 48% of married women employees) worked part time, compared with only 4% of male employees. Beechey (1987) identifies two main reasons for women's over-representation in part time work. First, they still carry major domestic and childcare responsibilities. This helps account for their 'bimodal pattern' (full time work before marriage and children, then a withdrawal from the workforce while the children are young, followed by an eventual return to work). But Martin and Roberts (1984) report that women are returning to work earlier than in the past (and between births). Nevertheless, many women returners take up part time work so they can cope with their domestic responsibilities. The second reason Beechey cites is that many part time jobs have been 'designed' especially for married women. Although the number of people in full time work has been falling in recent years, the number in 'flexible' and part time work has been increasing, especially in the service sector (Crompton and Sanderson, 1990). (See also pp331-332).

Segregation in the workforce

Horizontal segregation This refers to the way men and women are located in different sorts of industries and occupations. According to the EOC (1990), women are under-represented in the 'primary' sector (agriculture, mining, fisheries, energy and water) and in the construction industry, transport and manufacturing (with certain exceptions such as clothing, textiles, footwear and food processing). They are over-represented in distribution, hotels and catering, in banking, finance and insurance, and in 'other services' (education, health, the public sector and personal services such as hairdressing). There is some evidence that horizontal segregation has been declining this century, although this often takes the form of men entering women's 'traditional' fields (eg nursing) rather than vice versa. However, Crompton and Sanderson (1990) speculate that, with the decline in manual occupations and traditionally 'male' industries (mining, shipbuilding etc), we might expect to see further decline in sex-typed occupations (especially since anti-discrimination laws now exist). Moreover, they feel that recent trends in education are helping break down occupational segregation for a growing number of women.

Vertical segregation This refers to the way men and women are found at different job levels within each industry or occupational group. Women tend to be over-represented at the lower levels and under-represented in the most senior or higher status positions. Middle class women often proceed so far and then encounter the 'glass ceiling' (they can see where they would like to go next but the ceiling impedes further progress). For example, women have comprised between 60-70% of all teachers for most of this century yet they were only 16% of secondary school heads in 1983 (Rees, 1991). Some observers believe that vertical segregation has actually widened this century, but Crompton and Sanderson (1990) predict that the occupational profiles of males and females will increasingly converge.

Employment disadvantage

1 Women are more likely than men to be employed in temporary or casual work. In the early 1990s women made up about 63% of the temporary workforce (Oppenheim, 1993).

2 Women earn less than men. In 1992, women's average gross hourly earnings including overtime were 80% of men's (Oppenheim, 1993).

3 Women are more likely to be low paid. In 1991, 6.53 million women were low paid (ie earning less than two thirds of median male earnings). Mostly engaged in part time work, they comprised 65% of all low paid workers (Oppenheim, 1993).

4 According to Labour Force Survey figures for spring 1993, the unemployment rate for women of working age was 8%, compared with 12% for men. But it is not easy to decide on 'true' unemployment rates, because women are less likely to register as unemployed. Chignell (1990) reports that between 1979 and 1986 male unemployment rose by 143% and female unemployment by 189%. However, the faster rise in female unemployment was partly due to the increasing tendency of women to register as available for work. In recent years, women have 'gained' more jobs than men. The number of women in employment increased by 1.47 million (16%) between 1984 and 1993, while the number of men in work remained more or less unchanged.

Activity 9 Pin Money?

The following excerpts are taken from a study of factory workers.

Steven (chargehand): With this equal pay, women are talking themselves out of work. Now, a man's got a family to keep, he's more reliable. Men don't leave to have babies do they? But the women do! It's not fair! If a firm had any sense they wouldn't train a woman for a responsible job. Not unless she can't have any children - that's fair enough then. Some women have to work. But for 90% it's pin money. They don't have to work, they just say (whining), 'I shall miss the company'. All that type of tommy rot.

Anna (researcher): What's it like here?
Jenny (worker): Hateful. I can't stand it.
Anna: How much longer do you think you'll stay?
Jenny: Till I get married. As soon as I get married, I won't come back in here.
Anna: What'll you do?
Jackie (worker): Stay home.
Anna: What'll you do at home?
Jackie: Have a couple of kids.
Val (worker): Anything's better than working here. Well, most women get married, don't they? Not all of them work all their lives like a man. I don't really believe in married women working. There's not much work anyway, and they ought to make room for people who've got to lead their own lives.

Adapted from A. Pollert *Girls, Wives, Factory Lives*, 1983, pp101,103

Questions

1 Suggest some criticisms of Steven's views.
2 Why do you think the female factory workers seem to accept that a woman's place is in the home?
3 Do you think that middle class women would agree with the factory workers? Give reasons for your answer.

4.2 Labour force explanations

Why are women under-represented in the workforce and why are they concentrated in lower status, lower paid jobs? Explanations generally fall into two broad camps: 'supply side' and 'demand side'.

Supply side These explanations point to factors which restrict the supply or quality of female labour. For example, men (and the state) still expect women to shoulder the main burden of childcare and domestic responsibilities. This reduces women's opportunities to obtain satisfactory employment. 'Men and women cannot be equal partners outside the home if they are not equal inside it' (Oakley, 1979, p393). And when women do find employment, they usually work a 'double day', managing the dual responsibilities of employment (often part time) and housework. Another supply side explanation concerns women's educational qualifications and skills. Although girls are catching up with boys in terms of A level results, they are more likely to specialise in arts subjects rather than more technical, mathematical and scientific subjects. This can be a handicap in getting high paid and prestigious jobs.

Demand side Alternatively, employment patterns might be explained by those features of the labour market which determine the demand for female labour. Women's employment prospects depend on things like changing technology (this affects the types of jobs which are available and the skill levels needed). Also, the attitudes of male employers and workers are important. If a male employer insists on recruiting or promoting through the 'old boy network' then this works to the disadvantage of women. Likewise, if the top jobs are organised in a 'malestream' way - requiring long hours of work, expecting employees to 'fit in' with the dominant male ethos of sociability - then this handicaps women. Another demand side explanation is the theory of the *dual labour market* (Barron and Norris, 1976). This suggests that men are concentrated in the

primary sector (skilled labour, sound training, high job security, good pay and promotion prospects) while women are mainly confined to the *secondary sector* (with opposite characteristics). Barron and Norris claim that the primary sector emerges because employers need to provide superior conditions if they are to attract and retain skilled workers. But the model is rather weak in explaining why it is women who come to fill the positions in the secondary sector (although Barron and Norris suggest it might have something to do with their alleged lack of trade union solidarity). Also, critics accuse the model of exaggerating the extent to which market divisions (primary and secondary) coincide with sexual divisions (male and female).

4.3 Working lives

Women are not a uniform mass stuck at the very bottom of the work hierarchy. They are spread across a wide range of job levels and this affects their pay, status and job autonomy. So the 'experience' of work varies according to particular circumstances. This is illustrated in the following brief sketches.

Factory life

The factory Factory work for women usually involves semi-skilled or unskilled work on low pay. Several ethnographic studies (eg Pollert, 1981, Westwood, 1984) describe factory work as boring and monotonous, requiring long and tiring stretches of repetitive tasks. Moreover, the women are often subject to patronising remarks and unfair treatment by male workers and supervisors. Nevertheless, they are sometimes able to get their own back through humour, sexual innuendo and 'pranks', and this provides some light relief from work pressures. These research studies also indicate that, although women's main motive is financial (the pay packet), they get some additional rewards in the form of the companionship and cultural life of the factory floor. They enjoy celebrating each other's birthdays with special treats and they talk eagerly about forthcoming weddings and other events connected with their home lives.

The home 'Work' and 'home' are not strictly separated. The home lives of the women are a central part of their identities and the world of the home keeps intruding into the workplace (eg they 'soften' the work environment by wearing slippers or adorning their machines with family snapshots). On the other hand, the experience of working in a factory also has an effect on home life (eg Westwood notes how some workers started introducing 'time out' at home, along the lines of rest breaks in the factory). Both Pollert and Westwood describe the women's outlooks as inconsistent and fragmented. The women accept that family and home are their main responsibilities, and it is clear that factory work does not provide them with a high status 'career' (indeed, it reinforces their image as second class citizens). At the same time they reject the idea that a woman's place is in the home and they are resentful of male privileges at work.

Secretarial and clerical work

Feminisation Clerical work was dominated by middle class males until the late nineteenth century when 'mechanisation' (eg typewriters) and compulsory education opened it up to people of working class origins (Griffin, 1985). This resulted in a decline in the status of clerical work and it was only then that women started entering the occupation in large numbers. In 1911, only 21% of clerks were women but by 1980 women comprised 70% of all 'office staff' and 99% of 'typists and secretaries' (Griffin, 1985). In 1982, 17,000 young women embarked on secretarial training, in contrast to only 300 boys (Crompton and Sanderson, 1990).

A glamorous life? Office work is often seen as a 'nice job for a girl' and it has a rather glamorous image. It is relatively clean and the work conditions are usually superior to those found in the factory. Besides, secretarial work covers a wide range (from filing clerks through to personal assistants) and the top ranks can provide challenge, variety and handsome financial rewards. But Griffin's research indicates that the typical situation is far from glamorous. For many females secretarial work involves menial, routine work within rigidly hierarchical settings where female promotion prospects are low (only 14% of office managers are women). Offices may be less 'vulgar' than factories but secretaries frequently have to deal with sexist (and racist) comments and harassment. The work frequently involves 'feminine' obligations (eg making tea for the boss). Secretaries are sometimes described as the 'underclass' of the middle class: the status and pay are quite low and job autonomy is limited. As for the future, Souhami (1986) predicts that electronic data processing will reduce the demand for clerical workers. But Griffin is sceptical about this - male managers will still want female secretaries as status symbols, decorative sex objects, waitresses and even mistresses!

Activity 10 The Ideal Secretary

Item A *Likes and dislikes*

In 1975 the Alfred Marks Bureau conducted a survey of 650 male managers to discover their ideal secretary. The desired attributes included 'personality', good grooming, clear speech and a sense of humour. The list of dislikes was longer, including body odour, bad accents, bad grooming, poor personality, heavy make-up, flashy clothes and sticky hands. Their personal dislikes included strident laughter, spots, gossipers, self-assertion, rudeness, bad manners, no sense of humour and women with more than three children. The overwhelming emphasis in these lists was on the appearance and manner of the ideal secretary, with little reference to technical skills.

Cited in C. Griffin *Typical Girls?*, 1985 , p127

Item B *Looking good*

Cartoon: Jacky Fleming *Be a Bloody Train* Driver, 1991

Questions

1 Look at Item A.
   a) What sorts of assumptions lie behind these lists?
   b) Suggest a similar list for males in office jobs and compare this with the Alfred Marks list.
   c) Suggest a similar list for females in factory work and compare this with the Alfred Marks list.
2 Do you have any sympathy for the woman shown in Item B? Give reasons for your answer.

Professions

Professions usually enjoy a number of privileges (eg high status, pay, autonomy and opportunities for self-fulfilment). But women are under-represented in the 'higher professions' such as medicine, law, clergy, university teaching, professional engineering, accountancy and banking. During the inter-war period some professions introduced 'marriage bars' which forced women to leave employment on marriage, and some of these bars were not formally removed until the 1950s. On the other hand, women are over-represented in what Etzioni (1969) calls the 'semi-professions' (eg nursing, teaching and social work), which normally carry less status, power and material rewards. However, within all professions there is a tendency to vertical segregation which results in women being more thinly represented at the most senior levels. In 1988 women were 43% of all university undergraduates but only 14% of lecturers, 6% of senior lecturers and 3% of professors (*Hansard*, 1988).

Changes There are signs that the professions are becoming less 'gendered'. For example, about half of all new recruits to accountancy in the 1980s were female (*Times*, 12.12.90). In 1987 more women than men passed the final solicitors' examinations (Hansard Society, 1990). Crompton (1986) reports that an increasing number of younger women are getting the necessary qualifications for professional success (eg in pharmacy, insurance, banking), although she is not certain that their promotion prospects will expand significantly. They are still constrained by domestic responsiblities which interrupt their careers and restrict their geographical mobility.

Activity 11 Careers

Item A *Life at the top*

Ruth Lister's first job after graduation was as legal research officer with the campaigning organisation, Child Poverty Action Group. She eventually became director of CPAG and manages a staff of about 20 people.

Ruth Lister: Because I am an only child it was always assumed by my parents that I would go to university, so I didn't have that initial handicap that many women have that they are just filling in time until they get married. The obstacles I have experienced have been more internal than external. I find discipline and management extremely difficult. Perhaps women worry more about such things than men do.

I don't have any domestic responsibilities so I am in a different position from many women and I don't really know if I could do the job if I had children. There is a slight macho pressure applied in voluntary organisations. You work yourself to the bone to show you are committed and you feel guilty if you are not working all the time.

When I took over I was very conscious of being a woman. I imagined people thought, could I do the job? That feeling made me work very much harder than perhaps I needed to. In this job, you need to constantly push yourself on the media and on MPs - that's something I find difficult. But I sometimes wonder whether the fact that I am a woman is an advantage in that it makes me less threatening.

Adapted from *Community Care Supplement*, 18.9.86

Item B *Talking it over*

It is essential that your relatives understand how important having a career is to you. Sit down with them, explain it, reveal your feelings, answer their questions, let them really see how much it means to you. If that doesn't work, buy each of them an expensive gift with the money you earn!

Adapted from B. and J. Dale *The Working Woman*, n.d., p46

THIS IS MY DAUGHTER WHO STARTED AT THE BOTTOM OF HER COMPANY AND ROSE TO BECOME A SUPERVISOR IN ONLY TWO YEARS, SET THE NATIONAL SALES RECORD THIS YEAR, HAS BEEN ASKED TO JOIN THE BOARD OF DIRECTORS, AND WHOSE HOUSE IS A MESS. I DON'T KNOW WHERE I WENT WRONG.

Item C *Professions*

Women as % of membership of professional bodies

	1971-2	1980	1987
Law Society	3	12	15
Institute of Bankers	1	13	18
Inst. of Chartered Accountants	2	4	8
Institute of Building	0	0.4	0.7
British Medical Association	18	22	25
Inst. of Personnel Management	n.a.	30	46
British Inst. of Management	n.a.	2	3
Inst. of Mechanical Engineers	0.1	0.3	1

Adapted from I. Reid and E. Stratta *Sex Differences in Britain*, 1989, p149

Questions

1 Using Item A, identify some typical difficulties professional women face in developing their careers.
2 Expand on Ruth Lister's comment that being a woman is sometimes an 'advantage'.
3 Item B is a humorous piece of advice. But what serious point is it making?
4 What are the main points of interest in Item C?

4.4 Housework

Politics of experience One of the key ideas of the women's movement is the 'politics of experience': an invitation to look at 'everyday life' in an attempt to make sense of oneself and the surrounding society. Sometimes it is only by looking more closely at these apparently trivial personal areas that we realise how important they really are and how they give us clues about what is wrong with the wider society. The study of housework is a good example of this.

Domesticity It appears that housework is a relatively modern invention. In preindustrial times, household tasks were not clearly distinguished from more general economic tasks, such as working on the farm, tending to the animals, baking and the various activities of cottage industries (Pahl, 1984). Also, Garrett (1987) states that domestic tasks in preindustrial Britain were not the exclusive responsibility of women. During the Industrial Revolution, however, men became increasingly identified with the public world of production and wage labour, while women were confined to the private sphere of consumption and the home. By the end of the nineteenth century, most women left the labour force on marriage (Gavron, 1983). This period also saw the rise of 'domestic science' or 'home economics', which reflected the prevailing social concern with preserving the 'maternal' and 'feminine' instincts of women. Even middle class women were expected to cultivate domestic skills, because there was no longer a steady supply of domestic servants. In the present century, housework continues to be regarded as a specialised task and a 'natural' role for women.

Modern housework

What are the main features of housework in the present day?

Work Housework is not normally regarded as 'real' work, since there is no wage for it and it is not included in figures for the Gross National Product. Yet it makes a major contribution to the economic welfare of a country (imagine what it would cost if a 'price' were placed on the services given freely in housework). Moreover, housework is work in the sense that it is demanding and time consuming.

Oakley (1974) estimated (on the basis of a small and unrepresentative sample) that full time housewives spent an average of 77 hours per week on housework. Young and Willmott (1973) claimed a lower figure of 45.5 hours per week (but their sample contained a higher proportion of older women who were therefore less involved with childcare). Convenience foods and new labour saving gadgets (washing machines, microwaves etc) have taken some of the drudgery out of housework but Garrett (1987) suggests that housework expands to fill the time available. In some respects the standards of housework have become more demanding (eg in the areas of cleaning, home decoration and cooking).

Men Responsibility for housework usually falls on women. Young and Willmott (1973) found that men spent an average of only 9.9 hours per week on housework. Perhaps there is a slow trend towards the 'symmetrical family', with household tasks being shared less unequally (see p248). Certainly men seem to be getting involved in things like washing up, supermarket shopping and childcare. But often this is a form of 'helping out' (when convenient) rather than a regular and normal role. Also, men tend to do specialised tasks (household repairs, DIY) and the more pleasant tasks (playing with children rather than changing nappies). Husbands sometimes adopt strategies in order to dodge housework: 'Determinedly Hopeless Husbands break glasses when washing up, singe the ironing, burn saucepans and ask for instructions at every stage of cooking until their wives decide it is quicker and easier to do it themselves' (Holdsworth, 1988, p35).

Household circumstances The special circumstances of particular households affect the distribution of housework tasks.

1 Cohabiting couples seem more likely to share household tasks. In one newspaper survey of 11,000 readers (*Guardian*, 7.3.91), it was reported that 49% of cohabiting women shared the household chores 'equally' with their partner.
2 When a woman takes on paid employment there is normally only a marginal reduction in the time she spends on housework (Martin and Roberts, 1984).
3 Women still carry the main burden of housework even if their husbands are unemployed. However,

there is some evidence that males vary in their response to unemployment: 'Men who place little importance on the companionship of a male peer group and who have a fairly restricted social life tend to be home-centred and to have a flexible approach to domestic labour' (L. Morris, 1987, p18).

(For further discussion of housework and the role of women in the family, see pp258-264).

Summary

1 Sex-role systems operate within the fields of employment and housework. These systems are changing very slowly.

2 The employment profiles of females still differ from (and are generally inferior to) those of males.

3 There is no single adequate explanation for the patterns of female labour.

4 There are important differences between women in their employment situations.

Activity 12 Happiness is...Housework?

Item A *Conversations*

A: I don't understand why everyone talks as though all housewives have a miserable time. Lots of women like being housewives.

B: It's ridiculous to pretend that anyone actually likes cleaning floors and washing dishes - how can they? Housework is awful work. It's lonely and boring. There's nothing to show for it - it's all got to be done the next day. You don't get paid for it, either.

A: That may be your view, but the plain fact is that most women want to get married and become housewives. They don't complain about it - it's very important to them to look after their homes and their children and they don't really have any other ambition. It's only a small minority of militant women who put your point of view. You're degrading the housewife. There's nothing wrong with being a housewife and liking it. Running a home is more satisfying than doing a dreary office or factory job.

B: But being a housewife is the only option open to many women. It's because there's no alternative that they say they like being housewives - that they like housework. If things were different they might declare their real feelings.

Adapted from an imaginary conversation in A.Oakley *Sociology of Housework*, 1974, p186

Item B *Glamour*

Univac. The Ultimate Cleaning Machine.

Item C *No job for a man?*

Allocation of household tasks between married people, 1989 (%)

	mainly man	mainly woman	shared equally
Shopping	7	50	43
Making evening meal	6	77	17
Cleaning	4	72	24
Washing and ironing	2	88	10
Repairing household equipment	82	6	12
Looking after sick child	2	67	31

Adapted from *British Social Attitudes Survey*, 1989

Questions

1 Read Item A. Which side of the argument do you find more convincing? Give reasons for your answer.

2 Item B presents housework as a 'glamorous' activity. Give other examples of adverts which do this. Give examples of adverts which present a more 'realistic' view of housework.

3 Suggest explanations for the pattern of tasks in Item C.

5 Women and Stratification

Key Issues

1 What is the position of women within the stratification system?
2 Do occupational classifications take proper account of women's work?
3 What are the social mobility patterns of women?

5.1 Women in the class structure

Class awareness People's life chances - their living standards, experiences, opportunities etc - depend to a large extent on their positions in the class structure. Of course, they are not always aware of the extent to which class shapes their lives. Females are supposedly less 'class conscious' than males. For example, McRobbie (1982) found that class seldom figured as a conversational topic among the working class female adolescents she studied. They were far more conscious of their gender than their social class. But Frazer (1988) found greater class awareness among upper middle class and upper class girls in a public school. Class was a central factor in their self-identities and lifestyles. They were keenly aware of their class 'superiority' and they were proud to display their privileged class status (although they also felt threatened by the 'lower classes').

Class and gender Even if people do not fully realise the significance of class, their lives are still structured along class lines. That is why sociologists of gender have paid increasing attention to the relationship between class and gender. Certain themes emerge from this literature. First, men and women have different class profiles. In the Registrar General's breakdown (see Table 2), women are over-represented in some occupational classes (eg 3 nonmanual) and under-represented in others (eg 3 manual). Secondly, there are class divisions *among* women and this means they do not share the same lifestyles or aspirations. For example, Lees (1986) found that middle class girls were more career oriented, while working class girls were more likely to be involved in domestic chores at the expense of schoolwork. A third theme concerns the way stratification approaches often fail to take full account of gender. Indeed, feminists accuse mainstream class analysis of a sex blind or even sexist approach. In response to these shortcomings, sociologists have started to develop new frameworks to handle class and gender.

Table 2 Social class distribution by sex, Great Britain, 1991 percentages

	Males	Females
1 Professional	6.5	1.8
2 Managerial & technical	26.2	26.5
3 NM (Skilled nonmanual)	10.4	37.5
3 M (Skilled manual)	30.7	6.9
4 Partly skilled	14.7	16.1
5 Unskilled	5.1	7.0
(economically active)	(93.6)	(95.8)

Adapted from *Census of Population*, 1991

Activity 13 Class Locations

People aged 16 and over in employment, by socioeconomic group, ethnic group and sex, Great Britain 1987-89 (percentages)

Men	White	West Indian	Indian	Pakistan/Bangladesh
professional	7	3	11	5
employers/managers	20	8	19	16
other nonmanual	18	17	16	11
skilled manual	37	43	35	32
semi-skilled manual	13	21	16	31
unskilled manual	4	7	3	6
Women				
professional	2	1	4	-
employers/managers	10	6	7	-
other nonmanual	52	54	45	-
skilled manual	8	5	14	-
semi-skilled manual	21	24	27	-
unskilled manual	7	9	3	-

Adapted from *Labour Force Survey 1988* and *1989*, 1991

Questions

1 Use this table to describe the main differences in the class distribution of
   a) white males and white females
   b) ethnic minority males and ethnic minority females.
2 Suggest reasons for these patterns.

5.2 Weberian approaches

Class and status   Many sociologists (eg Dale et al, 1985) use a Weberian perspective to make sense of the stratification position of women. In this approach, a woman's social class depends on her particular position in the economic market place. Since women occupy different occupational positions, they are spread across a number of social classes (although they tend to be bunched in certain locations).

Alternatively, women can be classified according to Weber's notion of a 'status group'. Women resemble a status group in the following ways: membership is 'ascribed' (fixed at birth) rather than 'achieved'; they are normally accorded less status or prestige than men; they tend to be 'segregated'; and to a certain extent they share common values, lifestyles and consumption patterns. In Weberian terms, then, women can be considered in terms of 'social class' or 'social status'. But these are not mutually exclusive. Weber pointed out that class and status interact (eg privileged economic groups acquire high status; and status groups attempt to gain economic privileges).

Social closure   Parkin (1979) regards Weber's concept of 'social closure' as especially useful for exploring gender stratification. Social closure refers to strategies for creating and maintaining group privileges. The 'exclusion' strategy (placing restrictions in the paths of others) is used by groups anxious to protect their existing privileges. They may insist that new recruits to their ranks possess the right educational 'credentials' or an acceptable 'culture'. Or they may simply use their economic and political power to keep others out. The 'usurpation' strategy, on the other hand, is a matter of grabbing some of the privileges enjoyed by others. For example, workers sometimes attempt to improve their position by going on strike for better pay or conditions.

Parkin applies this closure framework to gender inequalities. Men use exclusion strategies against women: male workers resist female entry into their skilled trades, and employers use 'cultural' arguments ('it's not woman's work'). On the other hand, females have tried to usurp male privileges by mounting campaigns and protests and by pushing for legislative reform (eg Sex Discrimination Act and Equal Pay Act).

5.3 Occupational classifications

Sociologists (especially Weberians) find it convenient to use occupational scales which sort people into social classes on the basis of their particular occupations. But this approach presents certain difficulties as far as women are concerned.

1   What counts as 'work'? Full time housework or childcare are not regarded as 'occupations' and so this creates problems. Should a full time housewife be classified according to her previous occupation, her husband's occupation or what? Even part time female workers pose a problem, because their domestic responsibilities may have forced them to take a job at a lower level than they would otherwise have achieved.

2   Sexual segregation in the workforce means that men and women do different types of jobs. So, even if they are classified in the same broad 'social class' they may not share the same work and market situations. Within any given class, women's jobs tend to be rated as lower in status than men's.

3   Occupational classifications make finer distinctions among men's jobs than women's. For example, the Registrar General's scheme lumps together different levels of nurse (from untrained auxiliaries to ward sisters) in class 2. Moreover, the skill levels of women's jobs tend to be under-estimated (Pahl, 1984). New occupational schemes are currently being developed to deal with these problems and there are plans to replace the Registrar General's classification with the 'Standard Occupational Classification'.

4   Do occupations have the same 'meaning' for men and women? Stewart et al (1980) cite clerical work: male clerks often see their present position as a stepping stone to management, whereas female clerks are much less likely to entertain ambitions of promotion. So the two sexes have different career 'trajectories'. Also, Arber et al (1986) suggest that the manual/nonmanual divide is less significant for women, since they are mostly in service work.

5   In most research the household or family is taken as the basic unit of class analysis. It is assumed that everyone in a household shares the same class position as the 'head' of the unit. Now, this is entirely reasonable if the 'head' is a single parent or if the adult couple share the same occupational class. But it is less satisfactory in the case of 'cross-class families' where male and female partners have different occupational classes. In one survey (Marshall et al, 1988), only half the families had husband and wife in the same 'class' (defined in terms of Goldthorpe's 'service class', 'intermediate' and 'working class' categories). This problem has led to a sharp debate between 'conventional' and 'revisionist' approaches.

The conventional approach

The conventional view maintains, firstly, that the family is the basic unit of stratification. Secondly, the social class of family members is determined by the 'head' (usually male). In effect, women derive their class position from men.

Defence Goldthorpe (1983) rests his defence of the conventional approach on three main arguments.

1. The family is a 'unit' because it has great demographic significance (families 'place' people in the class system) and sociopolitical importance (household members tend to share voting patterns and political identities).

2. It makes sense to measure class by the occupation of the 'head of the household'. The head is the one with the 'greatest commitment to, and continuity in, labour market participation' (1983, p470). This head might be a woman, if she is a lone parent, or (in the case of couples) if the woman's occupation is more 'salient'. Salience is measured along two dimensions - *work time* (whether full or part time, and number of hours) and *dominance* (indicated by educational level, status, and pay). But these criteria usually result in the man being classified as the 'head'. In terms of 'work time', women's participation in labour markets is more likely to be intermittent and part time. In terms of 'dominance', women's work tends to carry 'secondary status' (feminists agree this is the case, otherwise they would not complain about sexism in employment markets!). Goldthorpe notes further that a man's occupational level exerts considerable influence on his partner's employment opportunities (eg working class women have less 'freedom' than the wives of professionals to decide whether to work or not).

3. The incidence of cross-class families has been grossly exaggerated. In most cases it consists of a lower middle class woman married to a skilled manual worker and really there is little to distinguish between them in terms of status or skill levels.

Support Scott (1987) agrees that the household is still the most appropriate unit of class analysis. He believes this is so because of two factors: the continued dominance of the patriarchal family and the continued effect of husbands' occupations on wives' employment. Scott feels that critics of the conventional approach have not provided the necessary evidence to contradict Goldthorpe: 'such evidence would depend upon there having been a much greater change in patterns of female employment and in the position of women in the family than most researchers have been able to observe' (1987, p66).

The revisionist approach

Revisionists state that conventional classifications need to be modified if they are to take due account of gender and avoid 'intellectual sexism' (Acker, 1973).

They suggest that the unit of class analysis should be either the 'individual' or a 'joint' measure.

Individual classifications Stanworth (1984) sets out the following criticisms of Goldthorpe.

1. Goldthorpe asserts that husbands have a more extensive involvement with labour market but this underestimates the increasing work commitments of women (eg the 'feminisation' of the workforce).

2. It is not always true that a wife's experiences are strongly influenced by her husband's employment. Admittedly, a survey by Marshall et al (1988) found that a woman's 'class actions' are influenced by her husband's occupation (eg a middle class woman is much more likely to vote Labour if she is married to a working class man). But her 'class fate' (promotion opportunities, pay levels etc) is decided mainly by her own occupational credentials rather than those of her husband.

3. Goldthorpe states that there are very few 'true' cross-class marriages. Stanworth disagrees. If we accept Goldthorpe's view that social class 3 nonmanual is 'really' working class then we actually end up with far *more* cross-class marriages!

Stanworth concludes that it makes better sense to take the 'individual' (rather than household) as the basic unit for occupational classifications. This means that certain families will be 'dual class' if the male and female partners have different occupational classes.

Joint classifications Another revisionist solution is offered by Britten and Heath (1983, 1984), who examine the particular problems posed by cross-class families. They say that survey data (eg General Household Survey) shows that these families are different in many ways from families where adults share the same occupational class. Families where a 'working class' male is married to a 'middle class' female tend to have higher income and higher educational levels than 'homogeneous' working class families, and the man is more likely to vote Conservative. But the special circumstances of cross-class families are ignored by 'head of household' and 'individual' approaches. So Britten and Heath propose a 'joint' classification which combines the occupations of husband and wife into a composite measure. They retain the 'household' as the basic unit, but the class of this household is decided by the occupations of both partners. They say this will not necessarily lead to too many additional permutations, since most women are concentrated in Registrar General's class 3 nonmanual and class 4.

Activity 14 Classifying Women

Item A *New Scales*

Here are some recent attempts to devise more suitable occupational scales. Dex's (on the left) is intended for women only, while the other one - the 'Surrey Occupational Class Scale' - is intended to be used for both men and women.

1 Professional occupations	1 Higher professional
2 Teachers	2 Employers and managers
3 Nursing, medical and social	3 Lower professional
4 Other intermediate and nonmanual	4 Secretarial and clerical
5 Clerical	5 Foremen and self-employed manual
6 Shop assistants and related sales	6 Sales and personal service
7 Skilled occupations	7 Skilled manual
8 Childcare occupations	8 Semi-skilled
9 Semi-skilled factory work	9 Unskilled
10 Semi-skilled domestic work	
11 Other semiskilled occupations	
12 Unskilled occupations	

From S. Dex *Women's Occupational Mobility*, 1987

From S. Arber, A. Dale and G. Gilbert 'The Limitations of Existing Social Class Classifications for Women', 1986

Item B *Working women*

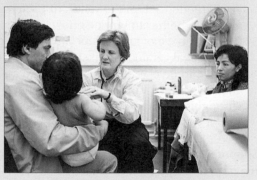

Questions

1 Using the occupational scales in Item A, place the female workers in Item B in their appropriate social classes. Note any problems that arise.

2 What are the advantages and disadvantages of using a separate occupational scale for women?

5.4 Radical views

Gender stratification According to Maynard (1990), the radical approach seeks to broaden the range of stratification analysis. Radicals complain that stratification theory is so preoccupied with social class divisions that it neglects other dimensions of stratification such as age, gender or race. In reaction to this, Delphy and Leonard (1986) challenge the assumption that social class is the 'primary' system of stratification. Moreover, they insist that gender divisions constitute a major axis of stratification in society. Given the influence of patriarchy, women can even be regarded as a separate class: 'radical feminists argue that women have shared interests

because they are all exploited and oppressed by men. Women, then, are said to form a class that is in conflict with another class - men' (Abbott and Wallace, 1990, p13). However, Lockwood (1986) questions whether gender relations really represent a 'system' or 'structure' in quite the same way that class does (eg he does not think that women have *systematically* organised against men, with the exception of certain short-term campaigns).

Gender and class Stanworth (1984) notes that gender and social class interact: the shape of the class system depends on the position of women within it, and gender inequalities are themselves partly the outcome of the operation of the class system. But radicals say that class analysis takes insufficient account of gender: the *conventional* approach underestimates its importance, while revisionists simply 'add in' women or make minor alterations to occupational classifications. This is why radicals press for a more fundamental *transformation* of class concepts and theories.

Dual class The radical approach is illustrated by the work of Walby (1986), who argues that married women occupy a 'dual' class position. One class position is formed in the 'domestic mode of production', where husbands and wives constitute separate classes (since husbands exploit the domestic labour of their wives). But women also work in the 'capitalist mode of production', where class is determined by particular work and employment situations. And whereas 'husbands' and 'wives' form separate classes (in the domestic mode), this is not true of 'men' and 'women' (in the capitalist mode). The capitalist system *divides* women according to their respective social classes. It also *unites* men and women within each class (although Walby does allow that, within each class, men and women can be regarded as 'status groups'). These two systems - domestic and capitalist - interact in the lives of women.

Triple system In a later work, Walby (1990) identifies three interacting systems: racism, capitalism and patriarchy. The inclusion of racism marks this approach as different from the earlier 'dual' model. Also, she places the major emphasis on patriarchy, which she defines as 'a system of social structures and practices in which men dominate, oppress and exploit women' (Walby, 1990, p20). Patriarchal relations are found in six interacting 'structures': the patriarchal (or 'domestic') mode of production, employment, state policies, male violence against women, sexuality and cultural institutions (eg media, education, religion). Walby dismisses some of the criticisms which have been levelled at the concept of patriarchy. She insists it can take account of class and race variations and she recognises that it changes over time. In recent decades it has changed in *degree* (eg improvements in women's educational and employment opportunities have lessened the intensity of patriarchy). It has also changed in *form*: the main site of women's oppression has shifted from the 'private' household to the more 'public' spheres of employment, culture and the state.

5.5 Social mobility

Missing women

Women are usually missing from mobility studies. Researchers tend to concentrate on the mobility patterns of men rather than women. Even where women have been included, as in the *Scottish Mobility Study* (G.Payne, 1987), the results have received little publicity. Why have women been so neglected by mobility researchers? Goldthorpe and C.Payne (1986) identify three main reasons. First, the inclusion of women as well as men requires larger research samples and that would prove time consuming and expensive. Secondly, researchers normally prefer all male samples so that they can make comparisons with previous studies (which share the same bias towards males). And thirdly, women present certain technical difficulties. For example, should the occupation of a woman be compared with that of her father or mother; what is the occupational classification of full time housewives?

Sociologists disagree about the consequences of this neglect of women. According to some researchers, the omission of women makes little difference to the general conclusions of mobility studies. Goldthorpe and C.Payne (1986) claim that all-male samples provide a more or less reliable guide to general mobility patterns. They argue that since a woman normally takes her 'class' from her husband or partner (see Goldthorpe's defence of this 'conventional' approach in Section 5.3), there is little need for an independent study of women's mobility patterns.

Bringing women in An opposing view is taken by G.Payne and Abbott (1990). They argue that generalisations derived from male samples do not apply to women, because women have a different occupational distribution and different patterns of movement between occupations. So men and women have different absolute mobility rates (statistical chances of moving up or down the occupational hierarchy). Since mobility rates are a key measure of social justice, it is essential that sociologists pay attention to these differences. Besides, it is not really possible to understand men's mobility patterns without taking account of the patterns for women. We can make sense of them only in relation to one another. For example, the limited mobility prospects of women actually enhance men's opportunities: if women find it difficult to enter service class occupations, then men have an increased chance of filling these positions (Marshall et al, 1988).

Women's mobility patterns

Researchers have started to build a clearer picture of women's mobility patterns. Recent major investigations include the Scottish Mobility Study (G.Payne, 1987; Chapman, 1990) and the Open

University People in Society survey (Abbott and Sapsford, 1987). These studies reveal differences in the mobility patterns of males and females.

Upward mobility Women apparently have less chance than men of upward mobility (ie moving up the occupational hierarchy to 'better' jobs). The Scottish Mobility Study reported that only 32% of women had been upwardly mobile, compared with 42% of men. Similarly, the People in Society survey found that the daughters of manual workers were less likely than sons to be upwardly mobile.

Downward mobility The Scottish study reported that 49% of women had been downwardly mobile, compared with 30% of men. And the People in Society survey found that daughters of professional and managerial fathers were more likely than sons to be downwardly mobile. Career interruptions (eg to have babies) are an important factor, according to Martin and Roberts (1984). Their interviews with 5,320 women revealed that 37% of women who returned to work after a break had been downwardly mobile, while only 14% had been upwardly mobile.

Oxford Mobility Study This landmark study (Goldthorpe, 1980) examined three major theses on social mobility. But to what extent are Goldthorpe's findings applicable to women?

1 The closure thesis concerns the privileged 'service class' at the top of the class hierarchy. The thesis states that this service class effectively closes its ranks to 'outsiders'. It adopts strategies (eg insistence on academic or 'cultural' credentials) which make it difficult for outsiders to get service class jobs. This ensures that these jobs are reserved for the sons and daughters of the service class. Goldthorpe concluded there was little evidence for this thesis, since many members of the service class were originally from lower social classes.

The mobility patterns of women cast further doubt on the closure thesis. For example, the Scottish Mobility Study found that only 12% of the daughters of professional/managerial fathers stayed in that class. This shows that many high status fathers did not manage to reserve service class places for their daughters. However, Abbott and Sapsford (1987) note that males born into the service class are much more successful than females in remaining there.

2 The buffer zone thesis is based on those occupations (routine nonmanual and skilled manual) which cluster around the manual/nonmanual divide. The thesis claims that this zone acts as a kind of 'brake' on social mobility. It limits the amount of long range mobility in society, since many mobile people are 'absorbed' into the buffer zone. The Registrar General's social class categories can be used to illustrate this. Long range mobility from class 5 to class 1 (or vice versa) is less likely than movement from, say, class 4 to class 3NM (routine nonmanual), or from class 2 to class 3M (skilled manual). So, even when people are mobile across the manual/ nonmanual divide, they do not normally progress very far beyond the buffer zone. However, Goldthorpe's research on men's mobility patterns led him to conclude that there was little empirical evidence for this thesis.

But the idea of a buffer zone is perhaps more convincing when applied to women. The People in Society survey found that women who were upwardly or downwardly mobile tended to end up in routine nonmanual occupations. This buffer zone 'arrested' further movement up or down the occupational scale. Furthermore, a great deal of female mobility takes place *within* the buffer zone. For example, Chapman (1990) suggests that a great deal of female upward mobility is from skilled manual to routine nonmanual. He questions whether this signifies any real advancement in status, pay, career prospects or employment security.

3 The counter-balancing thesis notes the long term increase in *intergenerational* mobility (ie the occupational levels of individuals are generally higher than those of their parents). Nevertheless, it claims that this has been counter-balanced by a decline in *intragenerational* mobility. There are fewer opportunities now for people to improve their occupational positions within their own working lifetimes (eg working one's way up from the shop floor to the boardroom). But Goldthorpe cast doubt on this thesis, since he found no clear evidence that intragenerational mobility had declined significantly for men.

However, there is evidence that women have fewer opportunities than men for *upward* intragenerational mobility. The People in Society study suggests that women 'are much less likely to experience intragenerational upward mobility - that is, to be promoted on the basis of work experience as opposed to initial qualification' (Abbott and Sapsford, 1987, p87). Also, women are more likely to experience *downward* intragenerational mobility. The Scottish study found that 77% of women had suffered downward intragenerational mobility (mainly because of career interruptions). Many of them were unable to recover their former occupational levels.

Summary

1 The class system is 'gendered'. Men and women are concentrated in different occupational positions and they have distinctive mobility patterns.

2 Conventional stratification approaches have been criticised for underestimating gender differences and for perpetuating gender stereotypes.

3 In order to take account of gender, sociologists have proposed modest 'revisions' or radical changes to stratification theories and classifications.

Activity 15 Going Places

Item A *Outflow tables*

Social mobility, by sex and class (percentages)

Males		1	2	Class of respondent 3	4	5	6	7	Total
Class	1	28	32	13	6	4	11	6	100
of	2	21	40	4	11	2	13	9	100
origin	3	25	22	0	6	9	31	6	100
	4	14	16	6	29	10	11	14	100
	5	14	19	5	7	13	14	28	100
	6	8	12	10	7	15	23	25	100
	7	12	8	4	12	10	19	35	100

Females		1	2	Class of respondent 3	4	5	6	7	Total
Class	1	14	28	48	3	0	0	7	100
of	2	14	43	32	0	0	0	11	100
origin	3	4	38	38	4	0	4	12	100
	4	9	26	31	9	4	2	20	100
	5	0	28	43	6	1	6	16	100
	6	4	15	44	3	5	8	21	100
	7	2	8	31	8	6	5	40	100

Adapted from G. Marshall et al *Social Class in Modern Britain*, 1988, p77

Item B *Rising women*

Helen Sharman, Britain's first astronaut - but men were there first.

Margaret Thatcher - Britain's first female Prime Minister

Questions

1 Use Item A to answer the following questions.
   a) Are males or females more likely to experience downward mobility from social class 1?
   b) Identify the main 'destinations' of males and females who are downwardly mobile from class 1.
   c) Are males or females more likely to experience upward mobility from the skilled manual group (social class 6)?
   d) Identify the main 'destinations' of males and females who are upwardly mobile from class 6.

2 Look at Item B. Are there any reasons why it might be unwise to get excited about female astronauts, female Prime Ministers etc?

6 Men

Key Issues

1 Are men included in 'gender studies'?
2 What is 'masculinity'?
3 What are the main theoretical perspectives on men?

6.1 Bringing men back in

Gender studies According to many feminist critics, 'malestream' sociology has focused almost exclusively on men, as if men somehow represented all humanity. But this does not mean that sociology has mapped in detail all the important features of men's lives. Ironically, one of the last great uncharted territories is the way 'masculinity' structures men's attitudes and behaviour. Feminist sociology certainly made some attempts at studying masculinity, but mostly for its effects on women. Until recently, 'gender studies' nearly always meant the study of women. Nevertheless, 'it is beginning to be recognised in many areas of sociology that emphasising gender no longer means talking only about women' (Maynard, 1990, p271). So gender studies are being broadened to include men and men's studies (eg Hearn and Morgan, 1990; Morgan, 1992). Walby (1988) argues that this inclusion is necessary. Otherwise, men will be regarded as 'gender neutral' and women alone will be viewed as 'gendered' subjects. This would have the effect of turning women into an apparently 'deviant' minority.

Studying men Many of the pioneers in men's studies are anxious to acknowledge their debt to feminism and they sometimes state that they are *following* feminist ideas rather than challenging them. They are also aware of the sensitive issue that men's studies may attract scarce resources (funding, grants etc) away from women's studies. Nevertheless, they feel that the study of men and masculinity deserves sustained attention. Maynard (1990) points out that much of the emerging literature is preoccupied with what men *are* rather than what they *do* or even the *power* they exercise over women. It is often pitched at a social psychological level, looking at men's feelings, identities and self-images and the way they handle personal relationships. Still, the literature is growing both in quantity and in the range of topics covered.

6.2 Making sense of men

Masculinity

Social construction of masculinity Most writers on masculinity regard it as something which is socially constructed rather than natural or innate. So attention is given to the way boys are *socialised* into dominant patterns of masculinity which emphasise such things as toughness, competition, hierarchy and aggression. However, if masculinity is shaped by culture rather than biology, then this means that males can be resocialised into gentler and more sensitive ways. Many contributors to men's studies are actively concerned with this task. But Seidler (1990) thinks it is misleading to regard human behaviour as completely flexible and 'open', as if 'bad' characteristics can be totally eliminated. He suggests that Freudian theory is useful in encouraging men (and women) to confront the 'darker' side of their natures. The existence of this darker side needs to be recognised if more realistic methods of controlling it are to be developed.

New men According to the social construction approach, masculinity is something which varies historically and cross-culturally. Compare, for example, the stereotype of the stiff upper-lipped Englishmen with that of the supposedly more volatile and expressive Italian or Frenchman. Even within one country there may be important historical shifts. Since the 1970s, various commentators claim to have spotted the appearance of 'New Man' in Britain. This new (mythical?) 'model' is described as an anti-sexist, non-aggressive male who is much more considerate, respectful and faithful than his predecessor. He is in touch with his 'feminine' side and he is quite different from the yobbish 'lads' who give masculinity such a bad name.

Everyday masculinity Another theme is the ordinary, everyday nature of masculinity. This emphasis on the 'man next door' stands in sharp contrast to the extreme stereotypes which are sometimes bandied about. In radical feminism, for example, men tend to be depicted either as 'monsters' (rapists, wife beaters, child molesters) or as 'oppressors' (a privileged, powerful elite). Some contributors to men's studies endorse these stereotypes but others try to balance these negative images with a more representative description. Most men, in this view, are just ordinary, confused, unheroic human beings, no better or worse than women. For the most part they lead mundane lives. A number of them do behave badly but it is far too sweeping to label them all as brutes (and this might even create a self-fulfilling prophecy!).

Crisis of masculinity Masculinity suffers from contradictions and tensions. For example, Ehrenreich (1983) believes that males in the United States started 'revolting' about ten years before the rise of the women's movement in the 1960s. These men felt trapped by their breadwinner roles which enslaved them to the 'rat race' and marked them out as likely victims of heart attacks. So they began to reject 'maturity' and 'responsibility' and sought escape in 'fun morality' and 'personal growth' movements. In Britain, too, Tolson (1977) identifies a general 'crisis of masculinity'. He argues that the 'heroic' image of the male breadwinner is less convincing in an age of high male unemployment. Faced with rising challenges to their traditional privileges and responsibilities, many males are confused and unsure of their 'proper' roles and identities. In some respects they are to be pitied, because masculinity is 'limiting'. According to Tolson, it is developed at the expense of a rich emotional life, close relationships with children and intimate friendship with other males.

Masculinities It is perhaps more accurate to talk about 'masculinities', since there is no single male 'type'. Not every male resembles the macho Rambo-style figure! Carrigan et al (1985) make an important distinction between 'hegemonic' and 'subordinate' masculinities. Hegemonic masculinity is the dominant image of masculinity in twentieth century Western society - white, heterosexual and middle class. But this coexists with subordinate forms, including those of gays, black men and the working class. For example, black males in Britain have less power than white men: 'What affects the lives of black men on a day to day basis is the level of routine harassment where they are stopped, searched, intimidated, and subjected to racially abusive name calling and physical duress' (Westwood, 1990, p64).

Activity 16   Doing the Right Thing

Item A *Contradictions*

Men are told to be gentle, while gentle men are told they are wimps. Men are told to be vulnerable, but vulnerable men are told they are too needy. Men are told to be less performance oriented, but less successful men are rejected for lack of ambition. The list of contradictions is seemingly endless.

F. Hayward 'A Shortage...of Good Women' *Single Scene Magazine*, September 1987, cited in Clatterbaugh, 1990

Item C *Changing men*

Current demands make it almost impossible for a man to do the right thing without sacrificing freedom, independence, male robustness and pleasure to the female's cry for fidelity, eternal love and security. I am tired of the easy assumption that men do not feel because they don't feel the same things women do. It isn't fair. We condemn them for not being all sorts of things we have decided we want them to be. We keep hearing that men should be more emotional by which it is meant that they should react as brainlessly as many women do.

Adapted from I. Kurtz *Guardian*, 21.5.86

Item D *Why change?*

Item B *New men?*

Gazza's tears - a footballer weeps

An au pair

Cartoon: Jacky Fleming *Be a Bloody Train Driver*, 1991

Questions

1 Give examples of the 'contradictions' men face. Use Items A, B and C in your answer.
2 Kurtz (Item C) says that men do feel, but they don't feel the same things as women. Give some examples.
3 The cartoon (Item D) depicts one way of changing men. How would you change men (if at all)? Give reasons for your answer.

Men's reactions

Surprise How did men react to the challenges posed by feminism and the women's movement? Goode (1982) believes that most men were genuinely surprised by the discontent expressed by women, especially since men thought *they* were the ones making the sacrifices! Also, men (and women) are usually far more aware of the trials and tribulations endured by their own sex and they find it difficult to appreciate the problems of the opposite sex. Consequently, many men reacted in a hostile fashion and jeered at the standard bearers of feminism. Others expressed their enthusiastic support for the women's movement, although sometimes they dragged their feet when it came to practical action. But Goode reckons that most men fell somewhere in the middle: surprised and confused rather than hostile or enthusiastic. Slowly, they started adjusting to changing gender roles.

Change In Goode's opinion, it is too crude to portray men as 'oppressors' who will resist any threat to their privileges. Indeed, there are sound reasons for predicting that they will accommodate to change. First of all, women are now too well organised to allow men to turn back the clock. Secondly, Western societies have a wide range of male 'types', at least some of whom will lend support to women's campaigns. Thirdly, most men prefer the women close to them - wives, daughters, lovers, sisters - to be happy. This will motivate men to accept reforms which allow women a fairer share of power and privileges. They will be especially anxious to protect their wives, sisters etc from gender discrimination by *other* men.

Perspectives

Men's movements and men's studies are are still far more prominent in the USA than in Britain, but there are important lessons to be learned from the American experience. Mainly, it shows the wide range of theoretical perspectives and social movements which are possible. For instance, Clatterbaugh (1990) identifies six main perspectives on masculinity.

Conservatives There are two main groupings here. *Biological conservatives* defend 'traditional' gender roles on the sociobiological grounds that these have been determined by evolution. *Moral conservatives* (eg Gilder, 1973) see men as 'barbarians' who need their traditional roles in order to be 'civilised'. Masculinity is created by society in order to control men's natural anti-social tendencies and channel them into the safer roles of father, protector and provider. Therefore Gilder argues that the feminist inspired erosion of traditional family values poses a great threat to society.

Profeminists This school of thought sympathises with many of the feminist criticisms of masculinity (eg that it is a form of male privilege based on hostility to women). *Radical profeminism* is fiercely critical of the way men behave and is perhaps best represented by what Landesman (*Guardian*, 20.6.90) calls Masochismo Man, a male who subscribes to the view that 'all men are bastards'. But *liberal profeminists* prefer to describe men and women as joint victims of gender stereotypes and roles.

Men's rights This group maintains that men are the principal victims of gender divisions. For example, separated or divorced men are expected to maintain their families yet they are restricted in terms of custodial or access rights. Men's rights groups argue that males merely enjoy the *illusion* of power - in reality they are overworked and guilt laden and the male role is a 'lethal' one. Men do not live as long as women and their lives are valued less than women's (eg men are expected to lay down their lives in war).

Spiritual approach This approach is 'therapeutic' and 'personal' rather than 'theoretical' and 'political'. The basic argument is that masculinity is currently an unhealthy, spiritually impoverished conditon, since males are out of touch with their deepest instincts ('archetypes'). Bly (1991) says this is partly because of the lack of older male mentors who can initiate and guide young men into manhood. Bly has established a movement which uses myths, rituals and adventure weekends so men can re-establish contact with the wild and primitive part of their natures (which includes a feminine part as well). This 'wild man' is fierce in defending his rights but he is also honest, sociable and life enhancing. He is not to be confused with the anti-social (macho) 'savage man' or the dangerous 'soft male' (a frustrated male who has repressed his true instincts and is therefore, according to Bly, likely to erupt into violence against women).

Socialists Socialist men's groups start from the premise that capitalism is a ruthless system which breeds conflicts between social groups and prevents people from relating to one another in an open, trusting and non-exploitive way. Such a system brutalises men's feelings and teaches them to 'use' others in order to serve their own interests. So masculinity can be regarded as a form of 'alienation' which will be ended only when capitalism is replaced by socialism. Socialists also state that masculinity is not the same from class to class (eg working class men place more value on physical strength and less on 'talking things through').

Group-specific Rather than discuss 'men in general', certain groups have developed perspectives to take account of their specific interests and characteristics. Gay groups, for example, identify ways in which they differ from heterosexual men: they do not dominate women sexually and they do not benefit from patriarchy (indeed, they say the dominant culture of heterosexual masculinity victimises or ridicules gay men). Similarly, black men's groups have stressed that their masculinity has been formed within the context of poverty, slavery and racism, so black manhood has been associated with the status of 'victim' rather than 'oppressor'.

Summary

1 Gender studies has broadened out to include men as well as women.
2 Patterns of masculinity (or 'masculinities') are socially shaped and constructed.
3 There are a number of competing perspectives on men and masculinity. Some call for a 'return' to male roles, some urge change and others describe men as victims.

Activity 17 Men as Victims

Item A   *World War 1 recruiting poster from USA*

These Men Have **COME ACROSS** They Are at the Front **NOW** **JOIN THEM ENLIST** *in the* **NAVY**

Item B   *Conventional men*

What does patriarchy do to each new generation of men (who cannot possibly be accused of inventing it)? The surface answer is that young men grow up privileged. The far bigger answer is that they are put upon. They are denied their individuality. Patriarchy assumes men will be conventional, proper men. It still does not encourage boys to become ballet dancers or readers of poetry. Neither does it encourage most men to become more than minimally successful. For patriarchy is hierarchical. It relies upon system of bosses and workers. There is only so much room at the top.

Adapted from C. Lee *Talking Tough*, 1993, p22

Item C   *Not guilty*

There is a double standard. Men are expected to remain silent about their problems. But women are encouraged to complain. Yet unhappiness and oppression are far more evenly distributed than we assume. Certainly there is a positive side to being male: it is possible to be strong without being oppressive, assertive without being domineering, to possess energy without bullying. But there is also a negative side:

• In Britain in 1991, 3,007 men committed suicide (compared with 886 women).

- Men live, on average, lives that are about 7% shorter than those of women.
- Men often feel alone. We talk a lot, but from a distance.
- Men's feelings are not valued - people feel free to say disparaging things about men (eg 'all men are potential rapists').

Adapted from D.Thomas *Not Guilty*, 1993

Questions

1 a) What picture of a man does Item A give?
   b) How might this place limits on masculinity?
2 Read Item B. Give some further examples of the pressures on men to be 'conventional'.
3 The work of Thomas (Item C) and Farrell (Item D) has been described as a 'backlash' against feminism. State (giving reasons) whether you think this is a fair assessment of their arguments.

Item D *Myth of male power*

Women often feel a greater sense of powerlessness (eg fear of pregnancy, rape, parental pressure to marry, pressure to interrupt a career for children, less freedom to walk into bars). But it is a myth that males monopolise power. The world is both patriarchal and matriarchal.

It has been mainly men who have died for their country - and they have had little choice in the matter. Men do the worst jobs; they die sooner; their lives are given less value (women and children come first); they suffer legal discrimination (eg custody of children); their traditional role of breadwinner is misleadingly called 'power' (power is about the ability to control one's life, not the obligation to earn money). Men have been oppressed and damaged by gender roles. The wound that unifies all men is their disposability: as soldiers, workers, fathers.

What we need is not a women's movement or a men's movement but a gender transition movement.

Adapted from W. Farrell *The Myth of Male Power*, 1993

References

Abbott,P. and Sapsford,R. *Women and Social Class* (Tavistock, London, 1987)
Abbott,P. and Wallace,C. *An Introduction to Sociology* (Routledge, London, 1990)
Acker,J. 'Women and Social Stratification', *American Journal of Sociology* vol 78 no 4, 1973
Amos,V. and Parmar,P. 'Challenging Imperial Feminism', *Feminist Review* no 17, 1984
Anthias,F. 'Sexual Divisions and Ethnic Adaptation' in A.Phizacklea (ed) *One Way Ticket* (Routledge, London, 1983)
Anthias,F. and Yuval-Davis,N. 'Contextualising Feminism', *Feminist Review* no 15, 1983
Arber,S., Dale, A. and Gilbert,G. 'The Limitations of Existing Social Classifications for Women', in A. Jacoby (ed) *The Measurement of Social Class* (Social Research Association,1986)
Barrett, M. and McIntosh, M. *The Anti-Social Family* (Verso, London,1982)
Barrett, M. and McIntosh, M. 'Ethnocentrism and Socialist-Feminist Theory', *Feminist Review* no 20, 1985
Barron,R. and Norris,G. 'Sexual Divisions and the Dual Labour Market', in D.Barker and S.Allen (eds) *Dependence and Exploitation in Work and Marriage* (Longman, London, 1976)
Beechey,V. *Unequal Work* (Verso, London, 1987)
Bhachu,P. 'Culture, Ethnicity and Class among Punjabi Sikh Women', *New Community* vol 17, 1991
Bhavnani,K. and Coulson,M. 'Transforming Socialist-Feminism', *Feminist Review* no 23, 1986
Bly,R. *Iron John* (Element Books, Shaftesbury, 1991)
Bourne,J. 'Towards an Anti-Racist Feminism', *Race and Class* vol 25 no 1, 1983
Britten,N. and Heath, A. 'Women, Men and Social Class' in E.Gamarnikow et al (eds) *Gender and Stratification* (Polity Press, London, 1983)
Brown,C. *Black and White Britain* (Heinemann, London, 1984)
Brownmiller,S. *Against Our Will* (Penguin, Harmondsworth, 1975)
Bryan,B., Dadzie,S. and Scafe,S. *The Heart of the Race* (Virago, London, 1985)
Carby,H. 'White Woman Listen!', in Centre for Contemporary Cultural Studies *The Empire Strikes Back* (Hutchinson, London, 1982)
Carrigan,T., Connell,R. and Lee,J. 'Towards a New Sociology of Masculinity', *Theory and Society* vol 14, 1985
Cashmore,E. *United Kingdom?* (Unwin Hyman, London, 1989)
Chapman,T. 'The Mobility of Women and Men' in G.Payne and P. Abbott *The Social Mobility of Women* (Falmer Press, London, 1990)
Chignell,H. *Data in Sociology* (Causeway Press, Ormskirk, 1990)
Clatterbaugh, K. *Contemporary Perspectives on Masculinity* (Westview Press, Colorado, 1990)
Coote, A. and Campbell,B. *Sweet Freedom* (Pan, London, 1982)
Crompton,R. 'Women and the Service Class', in R.Crompton and M.Mann (eds) *Gender and Stratification* (Polity, Oxford, 1986)
Crompton,R. and Mann,M. *Gender and Stratification* (Polity, Oxford, 1986)
Crompton,R. and Sanderson,K. *Gendered Jobs and Social Change* (Unwin Hyman, London, 1990)
Dale, A., Gilbert,G. and Arber,S. 'Integrating Women into Class Theory', *Sociology* vol 19 no 3, 1985
Dale, J. and Foster,P. *Feminists and State Welfare* (Routledge, London, 1986)
Daly, M. *Gyn/Ecology* (Women's Press, London, 1979)
Delphy, C. and Leonard,D. 'Class Analysis, Gender Analysis and the Family', in R.Crompton and M.Mann (eds) *Gender and Stratification* (Polity, Oxford, 1986)
Dex,S. *Women's Occupational Mobility* (Macmillan, London, 1987)
Dworkin, A. *Pornography* (Women's Press, London, 1981)
Ehrenreich, B. *The Hearts of Men* (Pluto, London, 1983)
EOC *Women and Men in Britain 1990* (HMSO, London, 1990)
Etzioni,A. *The Semi-Professions* (Free Press, New York, 1969)
Faludi,S. *Backlash* (Chatto & Windus, London, 1992)
Farrell,W. *The Myth of Male Power* (Fourth Estate, London, 1993)
Firestone,S. *The Dialectic of Sex* (Women's Press, London, 1979)
Frazer,E. 'Teenage Girls Talking About Class', *Sociology* vol 22 no 3, 1988
Friedan,B. *The Feminine Mystique* (Gollancz, London, 1971)
Friedan,B. *The Second Stage* (Abacus, London, 1983)
Fuller,M. 'Young, Female and Black', in E.Cashmore and B.Troyna (eds) *Black Youth in Crisis* (Allen & Unwin, London,1982)
Garrett,S. *Gender* (Tavistock, London, 1987)
Gathorne-Hardy,J. *Love, Sex, Marriage and Divorce* (Cape, London, 1981)
Gavron,H. *The Captive Wife* (Routledge, London, 1983)
Gilder,G. *Sexual Suicide* (Bantam Books, New York, 1973)

Goldberg,S. *Male Dominance* (Abacus, London, 1979)

Goldthorpe,J.H. *Social Mobility and Class Structure in Modern Britain* (Oxford University Press, Oxford, 1980)

Goldthorpe,J.H. 'Women and Class Analysis', *Sociology* vol 17 no 4, 1983

Goldthorpe,J.H. and Payne,C. 'On the Class Mobility of Women', *Sociology* vol 20 no 4, 1986

Goode,W. 'Why Men Resist', in B.Thorne and M.Yalom (eds) *Rethinking the Family* (Longman, New York, 1982)

Greer,G. *The Female Eunuch* (Paladin, St Albans, 1971)

Greer,G. *Sex and Destiny* (Picador, London, 1985)

Griffin,C. *Typical Girls?* (Routledge, London, 1985)

Hall,S. 'The Question of Identity', in S.Hall, D.Held and T.McGrew (eds) *Modernity and Its Futures* (Polity Press, Cambridge, 1992)

Hansard Society Commission on Women at the Top *Report 1990*, (Hansard Society, London, 1990)

Hartnett,O. 'Sex Role Stereotyping at Work', in J.Chetwynd and O.Hartnett (eds) *The Sex Role System* (Routledge, London 1978)

Haskey,J. 'Estimated Numbers and Demographic Characteristics of One-Parent Families in Great Britain', *Population Trends* no 65, 1991

Hearn,J. and Morgan,D. *Men, Masculinities and Social Theory* (Unwin Hyman, London, 1990)

Heath,A. and Britten,N. 'Women's Jobs Do Make a Difference', *Sociology* vol 18 no 4, 1984

HMSO *Domestic Violence* (London, 1989)

Holdsworth,A. *Out of the Doll's House* (BBC Books, London,1988)

Jones,T. *Britain's Ethnic Minorities* (Policy Studies Institute, London, 1993)

Kurtz,I. *Malespeak* (Jonathan Cape, London, 1986)

Lee,C. *Talking Tough* (Arrow, London, 1993)

Lees,S. *Losing Out* (Hutchinson, London, 1986)

Lees,S. *Sugar and Spice* (Penguin, Harmondsworth, 1993)

Lockwood,D. 'Class, Status and Gender', in R.Crompton and M.Mann (eds) *Gender and Stratification* (Polity, Oxford, 1986)

Mama,A. *The Hidden Struggle* (Runnymede Trust, London, 1990)

Marshall,G., Rose,D., Newby,H. and Vogler,C. *Social Class in Modern Britain* (Unwin Hyman, London, 1988)

Martin,J. and Roberts,C. *Women and Employment* (HMSO, London, 1984)

Maynard,M. 'The Re-Shaping of Sociology?', *Sociology*, vol 24 no 2, 1990

McRobbie,A. 'The Politics of Feminist Research', *Feminist Review* 12, 1982

McRobbie,A. *Feminism and Youth Culture* (Macmillan, London,1991)

Mead,M. *Sex and Temperament in Three Primitive Societies* (Morrow, New York, 1935)

Mitchell,J. *Woman's Estate* (Penguin, Harmondsworth, 1971)

Mitchell,J. and Oakley,A. *What is Feminism?* (Basil Blackwell, Oxford, 1986)

Morgan,D. *Discovering Men* (Routledge, London, 1992)

Morris,J. *Conundrum* (Penguin, Harmondsworth, 1987)

Morris,L. 'The No-Longer Working Class', *New Society* 3.4.1987

Murphy,L. and Livingstone,J. 'Racism and the Limits of Radical Feminism', *Race and Class* vol 26, 1985

Oakley,A. *Sex, Gender and Society* (Temple Smith, London, 1972)

Oakley,A. *The Sociology of Housework* (Martin Robertson, Oxford,1974)

Oakley,A. 'The Failure of the Movement for Women's Equality' *New Society* 23.8.1979

Oppenheim,C. *Poverty:The Facts* (CPAG, London, 1993)

Pahl,R. *Divisions of Labour* (Basil Blackwell, Oxford, 1984)

Pahl,J. 'Violence Against Women', in N.Manning (ed) *Social Problems and Welfare Ideology* (Gower, Aldershot, 1985)

Parkin,F. *Marxism and Class Theory* (Tavistock, London, 1979)

Payne,G. *Mobility and Change in Modern Society* (Macmillan, London, 1987)

Payne,G. and Abbott,P. *The Social Mobility of Women* (Falmer Press, London, 1990)

Pilkington,A. 'Race and Ethnicity', in M.Haralambos (ed) *Developments in Sociology* vol 9, 1993

Pollert,A. *Girls, Wives, Factory Lives* (Macmillan, London,1981)

Pollert,A. 'Women, Gender Relations and Wage Labour', in E.Gamarnikow et al (eds) *Gender and Stratification* (Polity Press, London, 1983)

Radcliffe Richards,J. *The Sceptical Feminist* (Penguin, Harmondsworth, 1982)

Ramazanoglu,C. *Feminism and the Contradictions of Oppression* (Routledge, London, 1989)

Rees,T. *Women and Top Jobs in Wales* (Report for HTV Wales, 1991)

Reid,I. and Stratta,E. *Sex Differences in Britain* 2nd edition (Gower, Aldershot, 1989)

Roiphe,K. *The Morning After* (Hamish Hamilton, London, 1994)

Saifullah-Khan,V. 'Purdah in the British Situation', in D.Barker and S.Allen (eds) *Dependence and Exploitation in Work and Marriage* (Longman, London, 1976)

Scott,J. 'Women and Class Theory', *Social Studies Review* vol 3 no 2, 1987

Seidler,V. 'Men, Feminism and Power', in J.Hearn and D.Morgan (eds) *Men, Masculinities and Social Theory* (Unwin Hyman, London, 1990)

Souhami,D. *A Woman's Place* (Penguin, Harmondsworth, 1986)

Stacey,J. 'Are Feminists Afraid to Leave Home?' in J.Mitchell and A.Oakley (eds) *What is Feminism?* (Basil Blackwell, Oxford, 1986)

Stanworth,M. 'Women and Class Analysis', *Sociology* vol 18 no 2, 1984

Stewart,A., Prandy,K. and Blackburn,R. *Social Stratification and Occupations* (Macmillan, London, 1980)

Thomas,D. *Not Guilty* (Weidenfeld & Nicolson, London, 1993)

Tolson,A. *The Limits of Masculinity* (Tavistock, London, 1977)

Visram,R. *Ayahs, Lascars and Princes* (Pluto, London, 1986)

Walby,S. 'Gender, Class and Stratification', in R.Crompton and M.Mann, (eds) *Gender and Stratification* (Polity, Oxford 1986)

Walby,S. 'Gender Politics and Social Theory', *Sociology* vol 22, 1988

Walby,S. *Theorising Patriarchy* (Blackwell, Oxford, 1990)

Walvin,J. *Black and White* (Allen Lane, London, 1973)

Warrier,P. 'Taking and Giving', in S.Westwood and P.Bhachu (eds) *Enterprising Women* (Routledge, London, 1988)

Westwood,S. *All Day, Every Day* (Pluto, London, 1984)

Westwood,S. 'Racism, Black Masculinity and the Politics of Space', in J.Hearn and D.Morgan (eds) *Men, Masculinities and Social Theory* (Unwin Hyman, London, 1990)

Westwood,S. and Bhachu,P. *Enterprising Women* (Routledge, London,1988)

Willis,P. *Common Culture* (Open University, Milton Keynes, 1990)

Wilson,E.O. *On Human Nature* (Harvard University Press, Cambridge, Mass.,1976)

Wolf,N. *The Beauty Myth* (Vintage Books, London, 1990)

Wolf,N. *Fire with Fire* (Chatto & Windus, London, 1993)

Young,M. and Willmott,P. *The Symmetrical Family* (Penguin, Harmondsworth, 1973)

5 Welfare and Poverty

Introduction

Who will take care of us if we have the misfortune to be seriously ill or unemployed? Who will take responsibility for our education? Who will provide financial support for our old age? At least in part, the answer is the welfare state. However, the National Health Service, training and financial support for the unemployed, free state education and old age pensions are fairly recent developments in Britain. In the past these services were either unavailable or provided by individuals, families or the local community. And in many societies today, the welfare state as we know it does not exist.

Many of us take the welfare state for granted, assuming that it is a good thing and here to stay. But how effective is it in dealing with areas such as poverty, health and housing? For example, in Britain in the 1990s there is a chronic housing shortage despite some forty years of the welfare state. Some have questioned the very idea of state welfare. Should the state take on this range of responsibilities for its citizens? Does it do more harm than good by making people dependent on the state and unable to stand on their own feet? These are some of the issues which provide the focus of this chapter.

Chapter summary

- The chapter starts with a critical review of the main **theoretical perspectives** on the **welfare state** and **social policy**.
- The role of the welfare state in relationship to **other sources of welfare** in society is then considered.
- This is followed by an examination of the **origins** of the welfare state in Britain and its **development** in recent years.

- The second half of the chapter looks at **poverty**, its definition, measurement and extent and theories which claim to explain poverty.
- The final part examines the extent to which the welfare state has succeeded in reducing **social inequalities** in areas such as income, health, housing, gender and ethnicity.

1 The Welfare State and Social Policy

Key Issues

1. How do different perspectives on social policy view the role of the welfare state and other welfare agencies in capitalist societies?
2. What is the relationship between the welfare state and other sectors of welfare? How is this changing?
3. What social influences have shaped the historical development of the British welfare state?
4. How and why has welfare provision in the United Kingdom changed in recent years?

1.1 Perspectives on welfare

This section considers some of the main theoretical perspectives on the welfare state and social policy.

Each perspective reaches different conclusions about the development of the welfare state, whose interests it serves and how it should develop. The issues with which the welfare state is concerned - poverty and inequality, education, provision of health care, housing and other services - are inevitably political and therefore many of the theories of welfare are linked to values and beliefs about how society should be organised.

Social democratic theories

Social democratic approaches to welfare are based on the belief that a certain degree of collective welfare provision, organised by the state, is necessary to regulate the more undesirable features of a capitalist free market economy. These features include unemployment and low wages. Social democratic theories support gradual and piecemeal social reform rather than revolutionary or radical social change. A good example of this type of approach is the work of William Beveridge whose ideas provided the framework of the modern welfare state. Social democratic theories vary in detail but share a number of general assumptions.

1 **Capitalism is not self-regulating**. Unlike market liberals (see below), social democrats do not see market forces alone allowing the economic system to run smoothly. Some element of state intervention is necessary to eliminate problems such as unemployment and poverty. (See for example discussion of Keynes's theories p345).

2 **Capitalism is wasteful and inefficient**. Problems such as unemployment mean that resources such as labour are wasted. Also some needs are not dealt with adequately by market forces, for example care of the disabled and elderly and support for those in poverty, since these are not profitable to private enterprise.

3 **Economic development under capitalism does not automatically lead to the abolition of poverty and injustice.** If growing wealth in society is not redistributed, it may leave certain groups in poverty and widen social divisions.

4 **Unrestrained capitalism leads to conditions which threaten social stability**. A stable society requires loyal citizens. This loyalty can only exist if the state is seen to care for their welfare. T.H. Marshall (1963) emphasised the importance of the development of what he called 'citizenship rights', for example the right to social security and health care. He argued that the universal provision of such rights would help to encourage individuals to feel a sense of citizenship and loyalty to the state. He believed that a welfare state providing benefits for all would help to reduce the conflicts created by social inequality. Marshall's views echo functionalist sociologists' assumptions about the need for consensus and equilibrium in society.

The institutional model of welfare Social democratic models of welfare first began to have some influence at the end of the nineteenth century when the drawbacks of an unrestrained free market economy were being demonstrated. Social reformers, like Booth and Rowntree, collected detailed evidence of widespread poverty. They showed that poverty, poor housing, unemployment and other social problems were not due simply to personal inadequacy but were created by circumstances beyond individual control. This provided support for the view that only the state was able to coordinate the extensive welfare services required to tackle these problems.

This view is extended in the *institutional model* of welfare which sees the welfare state as existing not just for the less fortunate minority but for all citizens. Beveridge, for example, argued that the welfare state should care for all citizens 'from the cradle to the grave'. Social democratic theories usually favour *universal* benefits and services that are available to all as of right. The alternative approach is a *selective* system whereby benefits and services are targeted at those regarded as in greatest need. They are often based on a *means* test, a test of whether an individual or household actually needs help from the state. Services such as the National Health Service and Child Benefit (formerly Family Allowance) are examples of universal benefits since they are available to all. Some aspects of the health service have, however, become more selective in recent years. For example, charges are now made for adults of working age for prescriptions, eye tests and dental treatment, except where they are exempted by passing a means test.

Social democratic approaches are generally critical of means testing and selectivity, arguing that they are humiliating since claimants are treated as a separate group and often stigmatised (made to feel different and inferior). They also point out that means tested benefits can lead to a poverty trap since those with incomes just above the threshold for benefits may lose out on a range of benefits (like the free medical services noted above). This can be a disincentive to take jobs with wages just above the poverty line.

Market liberal theories

Market liberal or 'anti-collectivist' theories have their origins in the ideas of nineteenth century thinkers such as Adam Smith and John Stuart Mill. They argued that a free market in both goods and labour was necessary for a capitalist economy to operate effectively. Any state intervention beyond the bare minimum would upset the free play of market forces. More recently market liberal ideas have been developed by monetarist economists, most notably Milton Friedman, and political thinkers of the New Right, such as F. A. Hayek.

Market liberals are opposed to state intervention in social policy for both philosophical and practical reasons. Writers such as Hayek (1976) argue the state does not have the right to force people to contribute to the welfare of others. Individuals may contribute if they wish, for example by charitable donations or voluntary work. Market liberals also argue that state provision is excessively bureaucratic and therefore inefficient. Most market liberals are not totally opposed to state provision. They believe it should be based on a *residual model*, whereby help is given selectively to those who truly cannot help themselves rather than to all as a right.

George and Wilding (1985) suggest that market liberals are critical of state welfare provision beyond a bare minimum for the following reasons.

1 **The welfare state interferes with individual freedom**. Individuals are forced to contribute to benefits and services they may not want.

Minorities may be forced to pay for what has been decided by the majority even if they would prefer their money to be spent in other ways.

2 **Overloaded government**. Governments are weakened by constantly having to make concessions to a whole variety of interest groups who feel more should be spent on their area of concern. Interest groups are encouraged to compete for a bigger share of government resources. Governments increase spending in response to this pressure as a means of 'buying votes'.

3 **The inefficiency of planning**. In a welfare state politicians, planners and officials decide what clients want and need, often incorrectly. Providing services through the market gives consumers choice and ensures that only services which are wanted are provided (otherwise no one will pay for them).

4 **State run services are inefficient and inflexible**. Milton Friedman (1980) argues that because those responsible for government spending are spending other people's money they are less concerned with efficiency and value for money. Also, because of lack of competition, state services are not responsive to the needs of consumers. Often it is the more powerful and vocal groups in society who gain most from the welfare state rather than those in greatest need. A universal approach means that many who can afford to pay for services get them for nothing and those who do not need benefits still receive them.

5 **Other sources of welfare are insufficiently developed because of the activities of the state**. High taxation to pay for state services means that many people cannot afford private welfare provision or provide financial support for voluntary organisations.

6 **The welfare state creates dependency**. It undermines people's capacity and willingness to take responsibility for their own welfare. Segalman and Marsland (1989) argue that in a democracy citizens not only have rights but also duties. These duties include responsibility for the welfare of themselves and their families. However, many recipients of welfare benefits simply pass this responsibility on to the state.

While market liberal or New Right theories have gained only limited support from sociologists in Britain, they provided the ideological basis for many of the policies of both the Thatcher and Major Conservative governments since 1979. These governments pursued policies aimed at cutting government expenditure on welfare benefits and services, increasing selectivity and means testing and privatising a variety of state run services. They also emphasised the responsibility of the individual and the family for welfare and called for a reduction in dependency on the state.

Marxist theories

While market liberals see the welfare state as detrimental to the free market, Marxists usually take the opposite view. They see the welfare state as serving the needs of the capitalist system and the interests of the capitalist class. Marxist theories argue that the state in capitalist societies inevitably serves the interests of the ruling capitalist class in the long run. However, in the short term, it may take decisions which are opposed by sections of the ruling class (see pp209-214). Marxists are divided over how the welfare state came into being, since it seems to contradict the argument that capitalist societies operate in the interests of property owners rather than the working class. Three main types of explanation have been put forward.

1 **The welfare state has emerged as the result of the class struggle**. Writers such as Ralph Miliband (1969) have argued that the welfare state represents a concession by the ruling class in the face of pressure from the working class. By granting such concessions the working class is 'bought off' and the capitalist system preserved.

2 **The welfare state is an attempt by the ruling class to manipulate the working class**. This is closely related to the first explanation. For example the early welfare reforms in Germany in the 1880s, introduced by Bismarck, are often seen as an attempt to undermine the influence of trade unions and socialist parties and weaken their hold on the working class.

3 **The welfare state serves the demands of capitalism for increased efficiency**. For example, Ernest Mandel (1968) argues that as capitalism has developed, governments have been forced to intervene in economic and social affairs, since free market policies tend to lead to economic stagnation, as in the 1930s.

In practice many Marxists like John Saville (1975) see the emergence of the welfare state as a result of all three factors.

Some Marxists such as J.O'Connor and Klaus Offe argue that the welfare state fulfils contradictory functions in advanced capitalist societies. O'Connor (1973) suggests that the capitalist state is concerned both with *accumulation* - assisting capitalists to create profits - and with *legitimation* - making the system appear fair and just to all. These two functions conflict. In raising revenue for public services the state threatens profitability through excessive taxation which leads to a 'fiscal crisis'. However, responding with cuts in expenditure leads to a 'legitimation crisis', whereby citizens begin to question whether the state is acting in their interests as benefits and services are cut back. Offe (1982) sums this up: 'The contradiction is that while capitalism cannot coexist with the welfare state, neither can it exist without the welfare state'.

Since Marxists see the welfare state as closely linked to the needs of capitalism there is little prospect of it overcoming problems such as poverty, ill health and unemployment, which they see as being created by the capitalist system itself.

Feminist theories

Feminists, like Marxists, question the view that the welfare state acts equally in everyone's interests. Like Marxists they see the welfare state as primarily existing to maintain the status quo and to support the interests of powerful groups in society. But, where Marxists emphasise the dominance of the ruling class, feminists emphasise male dominance or *patriarchy*.

Feminists point to the support given by the welfare state to the conventional family which they argue helps to reinforce the existence of patriarchal structures. One example of this is the emergence of the idea of the *family wage* at the end of the nineteenth century. This was based on the assumption that the male head of the family should be the wage earner and that his wage should be sufficient to support a wife and children.

Feminists argue that this notion of *female dependency* was built into the welfare state from its outset. Hilary Land (1978) points out that the 1911 National Insurance Act was largely concerned with insuring male workers against sickness, injury and unemployment, rather than their wives and children. The assumption of female dependency was reflected in the Beveridge Report of 1942, which allowed married women to opt out of full national insurance cover and to rely on their husbands' instead. Land argues that the current social security system perpetuates such assumptions. For example, a woman who 'cohabits' with a man may lose her entitlement to Income Support since he is deemed to be responsible for supporting her.

Feminists influenced by Marxism, such as Michele Barrett (1980), argue that in supporting the ideal of a nuclear family in which the father is the breadwinner and the mother and children are economically dependent, the state not only reinforces male dominance in the family but helps to serve the interests of the capitalist class. Thus low pay for women, which increases profits, is justified by the ideology of the family wage. Moreover, the assumption that unpaid domestic labour is a natural part of women's role justifies both the state and the employer absolving themselves of much of the responsibility for the care of children, the sick, the disabled and the elderly.

Values and social policy

The study of welfare is influenced by values as much, if not more, than other areas in sociology. Ideas about what approach the state should adopt towards the welfare of its citizens inevitably start from value judgements about what kind of society is desirable. For example, those who are critical of capitalist society and the social inequality it generates will take a very different view of state welfare from those who believe in a free market economy. In this sense no perspective on the welfare state can be seen to be 'correct'. Values are an integral part of the social policy theories which have shaped and continue to shape the welfare state.

Activity 1   Perspectives on Welfare

Item A *Disservice and diswelfare*

The emphasis today on 'welfare' and the 'benefits of welfare' often tends to obscure the fundamental fact that for many consumers the services used are not essentially benefits at all. They represent partial compensations for disservices, for social costs and social insecurities which are the product of a rapidly changing industrial urban society. They are part of the price we pay to some people for bearing part of the costs of other people's progress - the obsolescence of skills, redundancies, premature retirements, accidents, many categories of disease and handicap, urban blight and slum clearance, smoke pollution, and a hundred and one other socially generated disservices. They are the socially caused diswelfares; the losses involved in overall welfare gains.

Adapted from R. Titmuss *Commitment to Welfare*, 1968

Item B *Social costs (1)*

Remains of a factory in Walsall

Item C *Social costs (2)*

Living in the shadow of a steelworks in South Wales

Item F *Women and housing policy*

Women without men are much less likely to be able to buy houses. Although the number of successful women mortgage applicants has gone up, in 1981 the proportion of females to males was 1:10 in the UK. The decline of the privately rented sector - once the resort of those outside standard families - has severely cut back housing access for women alone and for women with children. Local authority policies are now crucial for women without men. But here again such women are disadvantaged. Council house waiting lists which stress length of residence and allocate points according to family size tend to disadvantage women alone with children (because they tend to move often and lack one adult member compared with other families), and virtually to exclude women alone (unless they are elderly).

Adapted from G. Pascall *Social Policy: A Feminist Analysis*, 1986, pp133-134

Item D *Against the welfare state*

The welfare state should be scrapped according to a report by the right wing Adam Smith Institute. It claims the benefits system is turning some neighbourhoods into 'factories of crime and violence'. Welfare benefits cost the country £79 billion in 1994 - one third of the Government's total expenditure. But ministers have shied away from big cutbacks for fear of provoking public outrage. The institute, in one of its hardest hitting studies, maintained the handouts not only cost more than the country could afford, but they were eroding the will to work and creating a crime culture. People were caught in a poverty trap in which the high level of benefits made getting a job not worthwhile. Institute President Madsen Pirie suggested a dramatic scaling down of automatic benefits with private provision for things such as health care and pensions taking over. Help should be based on needs, not rights, and any given should be temporary, in the form of carefully monitored loans, repayable once the recipient had recovered financially.

Adapted from D. Norris 'Time to Abolish the Welfare State' *Daily Mail*, 28.2.94, p11

Item E *The welfare 'bribe'*

One may argue that state welfare represents a 'bribe' offered to the working class in exchange for political quiescence and industrial peace. This was certainly Bismarck's view of his social insurance schemes, Lenin's view of Lloyd George's welfare legislation and a common interpretation of the reforms initiated by the Beveridge Report. It captures the political importance of capitalist state welfare, which is correctly considered by working class consumers as a 'piece of cake' sacrificed by capital to secure their wider cooperation. The Welfare State indeed exerts an important cushioning effect on working class experience, actively diverting attention from the structure of class inequality.

Adapted from N. Ginsberg *Class, Capital and Social Policy*, 1979, p12

Questions

1 Use evidence from Items B, C and elsewhere to support the argument in Item A.
2 What value judgements underlie the views in Items D and E?
3 Read Item F. What assumptions does it suggest underlie the welfare state's treatment of women and men?
4 a) Evaluate the four perspectives on the welfare state represented by the extracts above.
   b) Which comes closest to your own view. Briefly explain why.

1.2 Types of welfare provision

A comprehensive welfare state emerged in Britain in the period 1945-50 largely shaped by the principles of the Beveridge Report. Beveridge argued that there

were five giant evils in society which needed to be overcome in order to ensure the welfare of all. These were want, disease, ignorance, squalor and idleness.

Before the development of the modern welfare

state other agencies were responsible for dealing with these problems. Today other providers continue to work alongside the statutory sector. Some commentators, for example Norman Johnson (1987), have argued that we are moving into an era of *welfare pluralism*, in which the state is only one amongst a number of institutions concerned with welfare. Apart from the state sector there are three other sectors of welfare - the informal sector, the voluntary sector and the private sector.

The state sector

The state is by far the largest provider of welfare services in most industrial societies, though the extent of state involvement and the way in which welfare is provided varies considerably between countries. Many sociologists see the welfare state as a result of the growth in the scale and complexity of industrial societies and the need for some central agency to plan and coordinate welfare provision. In Britain today the state sector comprises both services organised by central government and those organised by local authorities. The table below summarises the main services and who provides them. In recent years the division of responsibility between local and central government has become less clear. Certain services have been removed from the control of local authorities and are now funded by central government, for example grant maintained schools and further and higher education.

Central government welfare services

Department of Social Security
Social Security benefits, the Social Fund, old age pensions, child benefits.

Department of Health
National Health Service, including: general and psychiatric hospitals, general practitioner services, dental services, NHS prescriptions, family planning and maternity services.

Department for Education
Coordination of Local Education Authority provision, funding universities, further and higher education and grant maintained schools.

Department of Employment
Job centres, training schemes for the unemployed, Training Enterprise Councils.

Department of the Environment
Central government funding for local authorities, coordinating town and country planning, environmental protection.

Department of Transport
Motorways and trunk roads, subsidies to rail services, transport safety standards.

Home Office
Prisons, special hospitals, probation service, Metropolitan Police Service, coordination of police forces nationally, Commission for Racial Equality.

Local authority welfare services

Social Services Departments
Residential homes for elderly and children, social work services, fostering and adoption, home helps, community care services.

Environmental Health Departments
Maintenance of statutory standards in housing, food hygiene in restaurants and shops etc.

Local Education Authorities (LEAs)
LEA controlled schools, adult education, youth and community services, careers services.

Housing Departments
Local authority (council) housing provision.

Other local services
Police and fire services, waste disposal and recycling, libraries, parks and playing fields, swimming pools, sports and leisure centres, roads and streetlighting, town and country planning.

The informal sector

Before the welfare state most people relied on what is now termed the informal sector of welfare - family, friends and neighbours. Some sociologists have argued that the welfare state has taken over many functions of the family. However, there is considerable evidence that for many people both nuclear and extended families continue to provide help and support not only in crises but in coping with daily life (see pp247-250).

Community care In recent years there has been growing support for the policy of removing welfare clients such as the elderly, disabled, mentally ill and mentally handicapped from institutional care to 'care in the community'. In the nineteenth century most welfare provision was provided in large institutions such as workhouses, orphanages and asylums. During this century there have been moves to care for groups such as the elderly, disabled and mentally ill in the community.

Supporters of community care policies, including recent governments, have argued that it offers a number of advantages. Institutional care can have adverse effects. Erving Goffman's famous study *Asylums* (1968) demonstrated the disadvantages to mental patients of being treated in an institution largely cut off from friends, relatives and everyday life (see pp380-381). Care in the community by contrast is seen as allowing people to lead as normal a life as possible. Many prefer to be cared for by family or friends. And many carers value the opportunity to contribute something to family members or to the wider community. Community care is also much cheaper than institutional care - government estimates in 1986 suggested that support for a frail elderly person in their own home would cost around £100 a week, a bed in a NHS geriatric ward would cost £295 a week.

Criticisms of community care Critics argue that saving money rather than improving services is the real motive for community care. The neo-Marxist writer, Andrew Scull (1984) prefers the term *decarceration* to community care. He argues that there is little evidence that people ejected from institutions receive any real care from the community. Instead they end up prey to unscrupulous landlords and nursing home operators. Other ex-inmates simply join the homeless and poor in the run down neighbourhoods of inner city areas.

Feminist writers have also criticised community care policies. Finch and Groves (1983) point out that community care usually means care by the family which usually means care by women. Gillian Parker (1985) in a review of research in this area claims that 'at the most conservative estimate, there are 1.3 million people in Britain acting as principal carers for elderly relatives, children with disabilities or chronically sick and disabled adults'. She suggests that while 20% of women aged between 40 and 59 were providing such care, it is probable that half of all women will do so at some stage in their lives. A survey conducted by the Equal Opportunities Commission (1980) found that three times as many women as men were looking after elderly and handicapped relatives. Another Equal Opportunities Commission report suggested:

'Whilst this policy [community care] may be economically expedient for local authorities, its implications can be severe for families caring for dependents who, without adequate support, may find it very difficult to cope. In this light the government's 'community care' policy is revealed as a euphemism for an under-resourced system which places heavy burdens on *individual* members of the community, most of them women. It represents care 'on the cheap'(1982, p3).

Market liberal theorists have applauded attempts by governments in the 1980s and 90s to give greater responsibility to the family rather than the state. However, Graham Allan (1985) argues that the belief that the family could take on more responsibility for welfare suggests ignorance of the reality of family life for many people. More married women work outside the home and greater geographical mobility has made it harder for extended families to give their members continuous support. He suggests that this policy means that women will continue to bear the brunt of responsibility for informal care.

The voluntary sector

The voluntary sector is made up of organisations such as the NSPCC, MIND, the Howard League for Penal Reform, Barnardos, the Salvation Army and the Samaritans. Statutory organisations - the state sector - are set up by acts of Parliament. Voluntary organisations are formed by people who join together for a common purpose. The voluntary sector also includes unpaid work in the state sector, for example parents helping teachers in primary schools, and prison visitors.

Some voluntary organisations provide services which the welfare state does not perform, others supplement statutory services. Some are based on self-help. Organisations such as Alcoholics Anonymous encourage those with a problem to help themselves or others with the same problem. Many voluntary organisations also act as pressure groups, lobbying for more resources from the state. For example Shelter which campaigns on behalf of the homeless and Child Poverty Action Group are well organised pressure groups.

Robert Page (1993) suggests that voluntary organisations can offer a number of advantages as welfare providers.
1 They are cost effective because they often use a high proportion of unpaid volunteers and tend to have less costly administrative structures.
2 The voluntary sector has more freedom to innovate and experiment and can respond quickly to new or neglected problems such as HIV/AIDS and domestic violence against women.
3 It can supplement state provision where statutory services are unable to cope because of increased demand, for example services for the elderly.
4 It provides an opportunity for a substantial minority of the population (25% of women and 20% of men) to care for each other and contribute to the welfare of their communities by participating in voluntary work.

Recently governments concerned to reduce the

involvement of the state in welfare have given more priority to the voluntary sector. In 1984 the Secretary of State for Social Services suggested that local authorities contract out services for children, the elderly and handicapped people to private and voluntary organisations. Not all voluntary organisations were enthusiastic about this. In 1986 the Voluntary Organisations Personal Social Services Group (an umbrella organisation representing many voluntary organisations) called for a continuing role for local authority social service departments. It argued that an inadequately funded voluntary sector could not cope with providing the services presently given by the state.

Arguably voluntary organisations could play a more important role if they received adequate financial support from government. This is certainly the argument of those who favour 'welfare pluralism'. However, this would require planning to ensure that funds were distributed fairly. Also since voluntary organisations are not under the same democratic control as statutory bodies it would not be clear to whom they were accountable. In the end a state funded voluntary sector might become just as bureaucratic and inefficient as critics claim the state sector is. However, few would deny that the voluntary sector is an important supplement and alternative to the state as well as a source of innovation and criticism. This suggests that it will always have a role alongside statutory provision.

The private sector

Private sector welfare refers to welfare services provided by private businesses. It includes private hospitals and schools, private pensions and medical insurance and privately owned homes for the elderly. These services are usually paid for by individuals rather than being funded through local or national taxation. Sometimes the state sector subcontracts services to commercial organisations in which case they are funded by taxes. For example, hospitals may subcontract laundry services to private businesses. The state sometimes assists private welfare organisations by tax exemptions, for example private schools are normally treated as charities. Contributors to private pension schemes can in some cases claim exemptions from income tax on part of their contributions.

Evidence from Britain indicates that private sector welfare is increasing. There has been a steady growth in private education over the past twenty years. Over the same period the number of people covered by private medical insurance has more than doubled. The growth in private nursing homes, hospitals and clinics has been dramatic, from 25,300 in 1971 to 147,200 in 1991-92 (*Social Trends*, 1994, p105).

Market liberal views Market liberal theorists such as Milton Friedman (1980) argue that welfare services based on market principles have a number of advantages over public provision. Firstly they see the commercial sector as more *efficient* and *effective*. They claim that private services are cheaper, since they need to compete over price, and they serve their clients needs more effectively, otherwise they would go out of business. Whether private provision is actually cheaper and more effective is debatable. Savings from reducing bureaucracy may be lost by greater expenditure on advertising and marketing. Services may be duplicated causing more expense. The need to make profits may be given priority over quality of service to the consumer.

Supporters of private welfare argue that it offers greater *freedom* and *choice*. Market liberals argue that people are only truly free when they can choose how to spend their money. State provision only allows choice through the ballot box for a package of measures. It does not allow individuals to spend more on one service and less on another or to choose between competing welfare services. Against this social democrats like Titmuss (1963) argue that only those with money have freedom and choice in a market based system, while those without money may receive no services at all.

Finally market liberals argue that private provision allows greater *equality of opportunity* providing everyone with the same opportunity to compete with others both as consumers and providers of welfare services. Some supporters of this approach, however, recognise that equality of opportunity is a problem when individuals have unequal resources to start with. Critics of market liberalism go further arguing that the growth of the private sector may result in widening inequalities as poorer and more vulnerable groups are left to fend for themselves.

Conclusion

This section has examined four areas of welfare provision - the state sector, the informal sector, the voluntary sector and the private sector. Supporters of the idea of welfare pluralism see welfare provision as ideally a combination of the four sectors. Indeed many commentators see welfare pluralism as the most likely direction for social policy in the future. As the state struggles to fund an increasingly wide range of services and benefits, one solution has been to pass more responsibility to other sectors. However, this view is not without its critics as Activity 2 illustrates.

Activity 2 Welfare Pluralism

Item A *Formal and informal welfare*

My own experience of social work in Liverpool has shown that it is not easy for statutory services to effectively link together at the local level. It is even more difficult to link the statutory services with the informal care provided by friends, relatives and neighbours. Some elderly people may need a combination of services such as home helps, mobile meals, a good neighbour scheme visitor, a social worker, a health visitor, nursing and other health services. If these services themselves do not always work effectively together, it does not require much imagination to see why interweaving of formal and informal care is often difficult to achieve.

Adapted from P. Sharkey 'The Sociology of Welfare' in M. Haralambos (ed) *Developments in Sociology*, vol 3, 1986, p150

Item B *A lack of community care*

In December 1992, Christopher Clunis, a schizophrenic with a long history of mental instability and violence, walked up to Jonathan Zito, a complete stranger, and stabbed him to death. The murder took place in broad daylight, in front of horrified bystanders at Finsbury Park Tube Station. Clunis had passed through ten hospitals including psychiatric units at four major London hospitals. His records were rarely passed on and there was little or no coordination between doctors, social workers and police. In the words of the official inquiry, 'Clunis's after-care plan was virtually non-existent. No one was coordinating his psychiatric care and treatment in the community.'

Adapted from *Daily Telegraph* and *Guardian*, 25.2.94

Item C *Women as carers*

In recent years, feminists have highlighted the true meaning of 'community care' as it applies to elderly and handicapped people. For community read family, and for family read women! Feminists are suspicious of attempts to increase such 'community' provision, seeing them as part of the political agenda of getting women out of the labour market and back to the home, to provide unpaid health and welfare services for members of their own families.

Adapted from J. Finch 'Community Care: Developing non-Sexist Alternatives' *Critical Social Policy*, no 9, 1984, p6

Item D *Towards private welfare?*

The underlying ideology of welfare pluralism is anti-statist - it wishes to see a substantial shift in the balance of provision from the state to the other three sectors. But even with statutory finance and regulation, serious doubts arise as to the willingness and capacity of the voluntary and informal sectors to substitute for the state. If they cannot respond in the ways and to the extent expected of them by welfare pluralists then welfare pluralism will merely serve to legitimate cuts in public expenditure and the development of market provision.

Adapted from N. Johnson *The Welfare State in Transition: The Theory and Practice of Welfare Pluralism*, 1987, p200

Item E *Child care*

Nearly 50% of under threes in Denmark and 20% in France are in publicly funded childcare. In the UK, the figure is just 2%. Private sector day nursery places for our under fives, which parents pay for at market rates, are increasing while local authority places, which are free or subsidised, are diminishing. Because of lack of affordable childcare most working mothers rely on friends and family, but where they do have to pay, childcare costs on average a quarter of their earnings. The proportion of earnings paid is highest for the poorest paid and for part time workers.

Wealthier parents have more options - a nanny or private day nursery, perhaps. Many others do not. The only affordable childminder is often an hour's walk away, and childcare can cost between £50-£100 a week. The cost or lack of quality childcare can force a parent to give up work altogether, or reduce working hours and impoverish the family. Trade unions, childcare charities and employers all agree that a government led national childcare strategy, funded by parents, employers and government is essential.

Adapted from *Poverty* no 86, 1993, p6

Questions

1 What problems of welfare pluralism are highlighted by Items B and C?
2 Community care can be seen as a partnership between the state and other welfare sectors.
   a) How is it seen in Item A?
   b) What solutions can you suggest for the problems raised in Item A?
3 Read Items D and E.
   a) To what extent are Johnson's fears in Item D reflected in Item E?
   b) Who will suffer most from cuts in the state sector and the expansion of the private sector?   Provide evidence to support your answer.

1.3 Historical changes in welfare

Welfare provision in England has changed considerably over the last five hundred years, reflecting social and economic changes as well as changing views. There have been two main views of welfare. Firstly, that help for those in need must be linked to deterrents to put off undeserving claimants and encourage self-help and individual enterprise. Secondly, that help must be widely available in order to ensure that those in need obtain assistance. Linked to these views are different explanations of individual misfortune. The first view tends to see people as responsible for their own situation. The second approach argues that social factors, over which individuals have little or no control, create problems such as poverty, homelessness and unemployment. Changes in the state's attitude towards welfare provision have often reflected changes in the influence of one or the other of these views.

The origins of the Poor Law

In the Middle Ages help for the poor, the sick and the elderly was provided primarily by family and friends and to a lesser extent the church. The state did not become involved in welfare provision until the Poor Law Act of 1601 which made local parishes responsible for providing poor relief paid for by local rates. By the beginning of the nineteenth century the Poor Law was coming under increasing strain. The upheavals brought about by the industrial revolution and urbanisation made it increasingly difficult to administer a system based on local parishes and an agricultural economy. By 1800 around 10 per cent of the population was receiving poor relief creating a considerable burden for rate payers. And there was widespread social unrest amongst the poor because of rising food prices and high levels of unemployment.

Welfare in the nineteenth century

In 1832 a Royal Commission was set up to investigate the Poor Law. Its conclusions reflected the influence of market liberal theories about welfare. State intervention was seen as interfering with market forces. For example, the Poor Law required the unemployed to stay in their home village to be eligible for relief. This prevented the free movement of labour necessary for a modern industrial economy.

The result of the Royal Commission's work was the passing of the Poor Law Amendment Act in 1834. This made the provision of poor relief subject to much more stringent conditions. Only the old and sick were able to claim 'outdoor relief', whereby they were supported in their own homes. All other relief was to be given in workhouses where conditions were to be less desirable than those afforded by the lowest paid employment on the outside. The workhouse was supposed to be a deterrent to drive the able bodied poor back to work. This assumed that jobs were available - often they were not. It also assumed that poverty was the result of idleness - often it was not.

The Victorian era in many ways represented the triumph of market liberal ideas of laissez faire - non-intervention by the state. Yet the social problems created by urbanisation and industrialisation meant that the state was eventually forced to take action. The high death rate from infectious diseases led to public health provision in the form of municipal sewers and uncontaminated water supplies. The 1848 and 1875 Public Health Acts established local health authorities which probably had more effect than the modern National Health Service in reducing death rates. The 1870 Education Act meant that for the first time the state accepted responsibility for elementary education. The development of modern local government from the 1880s onwards led to municipal provisions such as parks, libraries, swimming pools and other recreational amenities.

Alongside the limited but slowly growing involvement of the state, charitable and voluntary organisations remained a major source of welfare provision. For example, many schools and hospitals were provided for the poor by charities. For many working class people self-help networks based on the family and the local community were also important when poverty was ever present and the alternative was the workhouse. Some working class people also subscribed to friendly societies, a form of cooperative insurance which provided benefits in the event of crises such as sickness and death.

In many respects the nineteenth century saw the beginning of the battle between *individualist* and *collectivist* views of welfare which continues today. The 1834 Act was strongly influenced by market liberal ideas. Writers such as Samuel Smiles were preaching the virtues of 'self help' and individual responsibility. These ideas were strongly supported by the newly emergent capitalist class with its belief in a free market economy and minimal state intervention. Many reforms, however, represent a gradual acceptance of the social democratic argument that a certain degree of state intervention is necessary to relieve the worst excesses of a market economy. This can be seen in the development of collective provisions in areas such as education and public health.

The origins of the welfare state

Towards the end of the nineteenth century pressure for social reform was growing stronger. A number of factors encouraged the state to assume greater responsibility for the welfare of its citizens.

1 **The growing power and influence of working class organisations** such as trade unions and the fact that a significant section of the working class had gained the vote. This led to concern among the dominant groups in society that working class discontent might lead to social disorder or even revolution. The Prussian Chancellor, Bismarck, introduced welfare reforms in the 1880s for precisely this reason. He believed that state education and a comprehensive national insurance system would win the loyalty of the German working class.

2 **Concern about declining national efficiency** The success of German industry compared to Britain was seen to be the result of a better educated workforce.

3 **The Boer War** (1899-1902) revealed the extent of ill health in the population. Many young volunteers were rejected as unfit for military service.

4 **The extent of poverty** was clearly documented for the first time. Charles Booth and Seebohm Rowntree carried out their famous studies at the end of the century. They revealed that around one third of the populations of London and York were living in poverty.

The Liberal reforms Largely as a result of such pressures the Liberal government of 1906 introduced a number of important measures which have been seen as the beginnings of the modern welfare state. These included the first school meals (1906) and school medical inspections (1907). Old age pensions were introduced in 1908 for those over 70, providing the first alternative to the hated workhouse for elderly people without incomes. The National Insurance scheme was introduced in 1911, providing health insurance for most workers (though not for their families) and unemployment benefits for workers in industries with a high risk of unemployment.

The Liberal reforms did not lead to the creation of a welfare state in the modern sense. However, they marked an important move away from the Victorian view of welfare based on very limited selective help, such as the workhouse, for specific groups, to a more modern view where universal benefits, such as National Insurance and old age pensions, are provided for all citizens as a right.

The limited welfare provisions set up before the First World War were severely tested by the economic depression of the 1920s and 1930s. Widespread and long term unemployment meant that the National Insurance scheme was paying out more than it received in contributions. Benefits were cut and a humiliating means test was enforced. The inadequacy of the existing provision was revealed by evidence of widespread poverty, especially among the families of the unemployed.

The Beveridge Report and the establishment of the welfare state

The 1942 Report on Social Insurance and Allied Services or Beveridge Report was a landmark in the development of the welfare state. It provided the basis for much of the postwar legislation which set up the welfare state. Its publication during the Second World War was significant. Richard Titmuss (1963) argues that the changes brought about by total war helped to create the conditions for the establishment of a welfare state. The sense of national identity and common purpose increased support for collectivist policies designed to give universal rights to all. Evacuation of poor working class children from the slums brought home to middle class families the reality of poverty in the cities. The greater control by the state over people's lives necessitated by the war, and the need to ensure the efficiency and health of both the military and civilian populations, paved the way for further state intervention.

While many government ministers and civil servants expressed reservations about Beveridge's proposals, the Report received widespread public support. Beveridge hoped to abolish the 'five giant evils' of Want, Disease, Ignorance, Squalor and Idleness by means of a comprehensive system of national insurance and social services. His main proposals are summarised below.

Want In order to abolish 'want' or poverty Beveridge proposed a universal system of National Insurance for all adults. This would alleviate poverty during periods of sickness and unemployment and provide old age

WELFARE AND POVERTY 165

pensions for all. As a safety net Beveridge also proposed the introduction of National Assistance, a means tested benefit to replace the Poor Law. In practice because insurance benefits were not set at subsistence level an increasing proportion of claimants have had to rely on National Assistance and its successors, Supplementary Benefit and Income Support. Finally Beveridge proposed a universal system of family allowances, for second and subsequent children, to help with the cost of raising children.

Disease Beveridge proposed a National Health Service providing free health care to all citizens. Existing hospitals, general practitioners as well as auxiliary medical services, for example dentists and maternity services, were to be organised and funded by the state.

Ignorance Beveridge called for free education provided by the state at all levels so that access to educational opportunities would no longer be dependent on ability to pay.

Squalor Although a series of Acts had extended the powers of local authorities to provide rented housing, Beveridge called for a growth in the public sector in order to provide cheap housing of a good standard for all who needed it.

Idleness One of the main assumptions of the Beveridge Report was that the state would maintain full employment through economic intervention in line with the theories of the economist J. M. Keynes. This would prevent the return of the mass unemployment of the 1930s and mean that only the sick, disabled or temporarily unemployed would need benefits.

The election of a Labour government in 1945 was followed by the implementation of most of the recommendations of the Beveridge Report. R.A. Butler's 1944 Education Act had already established the universal state education system outlined in the Report. This was followed by a series of other acts such as the 1945 Family Allowances Act and the 1946 National Insurance Act. On 5th July 1948, 'the appointed day', both the National Assistance Board and the National Health Service came into operation. This is usually regarded as the start of the modern welfare state.

The welfare state 1950-79

The Labour government of 1945-51 established the modern welfare state within a very short time. However, it developed from legislation and built on ideas from a much longer period. The extent of state intervention can be seen from the growth in welfare expenditure per head which increased twelve fold in real terms between 1900 and 1950 (Saville, 1975).

During the 1950s there was a degree of consensus about the welfare state. The Conservative governments of 1951-64 largely continued Labour's welfare policies. This was a period of economic growth and virtually full employment and many felt that poverty had been virtually eradicated.

During the 1960s and 70s there was a move towards selective benefits and services under both Labour and Conservative governments. This was partly influenced by a desire to save money because of problems in funding welfare services. However, it also reflected a wish to target funds on the worst off. Despite this erosion of Beveridge's principle of universality in welfare, both major parties shared a commitment to public provision through the welfare state. They differed over specific issues, for example Labour governments gave more emphasis to council housing and Conservatives to home ownership. However, both were committed to the basic framework established by Beveridge and the essentially social democratic approach embodied within it. The election of Margaret Thatcher's Conservative government in 1979, with its explicit commitment to anti-collectivist free market principles, was the first time this consensus had been seriously questioned.

Activity 3   Self Help versus State Intervention

Item A *Self help*

The spirit of self help is the root of all genuine growth in the individual. Help from without is often weakening in its effects, but help from within invariably strengthening. Whatever is done for men or groups to a certain extent takes away the stimulus and necessity of doing for themselves. And where men are subjected to over-guidance and over-government, the inevitable tendency is for them to become comparatively helpless.

From S. Smiles *Self Help*, 1859

Item B *Freedom from state control*

We prefer to take our chance with the cholera than be bullied into health. There is nothing a man hates so much as being cleansed against his will or having his floor swept, his hall whitewashed, his dungheaps cleared away and his thatch forced to give way to slate. It is a fact that many people have died from a good washing. The truth is that Mr Chadwick has a great many powers but it is not so easy to say what they can be applied to.

[Edwin Chadwick was a leading public health campaigner of the day and a member of the General Board of Health set up by the Public Health Act of 1848]. From *The Times*, 1854

Item C *Municipal provision*

The Town Councillor who supports 'self help' will walk along the municipal pavement provided by town council, lit by the municipal gas and cleansed by the municipal brooms with municipal water, and seeing by the municipal clock in the municipal market that he is too early to meet his children from the municipal school close by the County lunatic asylum and municipal hospital, will use the national telegraph system to tell them not to walk through the municipal park but to come by the municipal tramway, to meet him in the municipal reading room by the municipal art gallery, museum and library. 'Socialism sir', he will say, 'don't waste the time of a practical man by your fantastic absurdities. Self help sir, individual self help, that's what made this city what it is.'

From S. Webb *Socialism in England*, 1889

Item D *'Punch' cartoon, 1858*

DIPTHERIA ⁓ SCROFULA   CHOLERA

FATHER THAMES INTRODUCING HIS OFFSPRING TO THE FAIR CITY OF LONDON.

In England in 1831, an outbreak of cholera (a water borne disease) killed over 30,000 people in industrial towns. A further outbreak in 1847-48 killed over 50,000.

Item E

Orphans in 1880

Item F

Glasgow, 1868. Housing conditions such as these were common in working class urban areas in the 19th century.

Questions

1 a) How does Item C ridicule the arguments put forward in Item A?
   b) Do you think this ridicule in justified? Explain your answer.
2 Do you think the views in Item B are justified given the information in Item D?
3 Assess the merits of self help and state intervention as solutions to the problems in Items E and F.

1.4 Recent changes in welfare

The election of a Conservative government in 1979 has been seen as the first serious challenge to the social democratic consensus on the welfare state. Margaret Thatcher and many of her leading supporters were firmly committed to a market liberal approach, involving a radical reduction in the responsibilities of the state. Under Mrs Thatcher's successor John Major similar policies have been pursued.

These policies reflect not only a commitment to market liberalism but also a concern with the rising costs of welfare. Recent changes in the welfare state can be seen as cost cutting measures designed to deal with what many believe is a 'crisis' in social security spending. Whether or not such a 'crisis' exists will be considered at the close of this section.

New right policies and the welfare state

Since 1979 Conservative governments have introduced a variety of changes in welfare benefits and services.
These changes include:

1 **Increased selectivity and means testing** In a number of areas formerly universal benefits have become selective. For example, eyesight tests are no longer free for all but means tested. Cuts in other benefits, for example Unemployment Benefit (now Jobseekers Allowance), have meant that claimants have to rely more on means tested benefits such as Income Support to supplement their income.

2 **Greater use of discretionary payments and loans rather than benefits as a right** Social Security claimants were formerly entitled to a variety of grants to cover items over and above normal weekly expenditure. These grants were replaced in 1986 by the Social Fund which gives discretionary payments (dependent on how much money is left in an office's allocation and the priority given by officials to a particular claim). Most payments under the Social Fund are loans rather than grants and consequently have to be repaid out of claimants' benefits.

3 **Cuts in benefits** Few benefits have been directly cut. Some, despite being raised, have not kept up with inflation. Others, formerly increased annually, have simply not been raised at all in some years, for example Housing Benefit and Child Benefit. Some benefits have kept pace with inflation but have fallen behind the general increase in wages, for example old age pensions and Income Support.

4 **Privatisation** A number of areas of welfare have been contracted out to the private sector. For example cleaning in hospitals and schools, and, in some local authorities, refuse collection. Another major area of welfare privatisation has been the right of council house tenants to buy their properties.

5 **Competition and local management of services** While many areas of welfare have remained state funded, the government has attempted to introduce elements of 'market forces' into their operation. In a number of areas local managers have been encouraged to take control of their own spending in order to improve flexibility and efficiency and to compete with other providers of the same service. This has developed furthest in the health service with trust hospitals and in education with grant maintained schools.

6 **Decarceration and community care** Institutional care for the elderly, disabled and mentally ill has increasingly been replaced by a policy of 'care in the community'. Many psychiatric and geriatric hospitals have been closed down and local authorities, voluntary organisations and families have been expected to care for former inmates (see pp159-160).

7 **Encouragement of welfare pluralism** In attempting to reduce the state's responsibility for welfare, Conservative governments since 1979 have encouraged welfare pluralism. They have done this in two main ways. Firstly, by inviting other welfare sectors, in particular the private sector to take on responsibilities formerly undertaken by the state. This can be seen from the examples of privatisation noted above. Secondly, by lack of government action - for example, voluntary organisations have attempted to provide a safety net in the form of 'soup kitchens' and night shelters for the growing number of homeless people living on city streets. Such organisations have felt morally obliged to offer this help because of government inaction.

Peter Saunders: the privatisation of welfare

Some sociologists have seen changes in patterns of welfare provision as part of broader changes in patterns of consumption in Western societies. Housing provides an example of these changes. Peter Saunders (1989) argues that housing provision in Britain has followed three distinct phases.

1 **The market mode** Housing (and other services) were mostly provided through the market. Consumers had to pay for them at market rates.

2 **The socialised mode** Because many consumers were unable to afford decent housing and other services the state began to provide these free or at subsidised rates.

3 **The privatised mode** The socialised mode, however, generated new contradictions, in particular between the cost of welfare provision and government's desire to control expenditure. This led to the third phase, the privatisation of

consumption. As living standards rise more people can afford private services and the state is able to reduce collective provision.

Saunders suggests that large scale collective provision may only be a temporary phase before the development of privatised consumption. While he acknowledges that changes in welfare are partly a response to the 'fiscal crisis' in the state, he also stresses the importance of individual choice and the growing preference for private rather than state run services. Saunders does point out that this is a choice which to some extent has been forced on many people. The worse state provision becomes, due to underfunding, the more pressure there is to turn to the private sector. For example, the number of beds in private sector hospitals increased by 50% between 1979 and 1986, due in part to long waiting lists for the NHS. Private education became more popular during the 1980s and early 90s because of perceived inadequacies in the state system.

Criticisms of Saunders Other sociologists have questioned whether there has been or will be a large scale move to private welfare. They note that:

1 **Overall government expenditure on welfare provision has continued to increase throughout this century**. Forrest and Murie (1989) argue that what has in fact occurred is a reorientation of state expenditure. For example, the reduction in universal benefits has necessitated more spending on means tested benefits.

2 **Moves towards privatised welfare may not be simply a response to the fiscal crisis of the state**. Forrest and Murie argue that a belief in monetarism and anti-collectivism may have been more significant as an influence on the Conservative governments of the 1980s than the pressures created by a fiscal crisis. Given this, the trend towards privatised welfare might be reversed by a future government more committed to collectivist policies.

3 **The extent of privatisation varies widely between services**. Harloe and Paris (1989) point out that the example of housing may be unrepresentative. It is in fact the area in which government expenditure on welfare in Britain declined fastest in the 1980s. In other areas the state remains the major provider. In 1987 only 10% of the population were covered by private health care and only 8% of children were educated privately.

Continuities in state welfare provision

Changes in welfare provision over the past 25 years have been seen by some as the beginning of the end of the welfare state. Phrases like 'creeping privatisation' and the 'dismantling of the welfare state' have been used to describe the recent history of welfare provision. However, many argue that the continuities outweigh the changes. They see the move to privatisation as limited. They note that state expenditure on welfare increased during the Thatcher and Major administrations as it has done throughout this century. Peter Sharkey (1986) suggests a number of reasons for this, including the growth in unemployment leading to increased social security expenditure; public opinion and pressure group activity, for example concern by parents, teachers and schools inspectors over the effect on educational standards of underfunding; and opposition by local authorities (especially those under Labour control) to cutbacks in public services.

Some right wing commentators argue that Conservative governments should have pursued a more radical market liberal policy. Green and Lucas (1992) conclude that despite increases in private health care, private pension schemes and the sale of council houses, they failed to significantly reduce the state's involvement in areas such as health and education

Despite their influence on Conservative governments, market liberal ideas seem to have limited public support. Surveys show no major shift of public opinion towards anti-collectivist welfare policies. The British Social Attitudes Surveys suggest that most people support the welfare state and existing or increased public spending. In 1989 only 3% of respondents felt the government should reduce taxes and spend less on education, health and social benefits

The welfare state in crisis?

Can we afford a welfare state? Has the universal welfare system established by Beveridge created a 'fiscal crisis'? Is social security spending out of control? In 1993, Peter Lilley, the Secretary of State for Social Security echoed the views of many on the right when he stated,

'The underlying growth in social security has exceeded and will continue to exceed growth in the economy... The underlying growth is above the growth that can be afforded for public expenditure as a whole... There is no escaping the need for structural reform of the social security system to contain spending' (quoted in Oppenheim, 1994, p7).

Many of the measures referred to in this section can be seen as a response to this growing 'crisis'. And many believe it will get worse as an aging population makes increasing demands on the National Health Service (to treat the ailments of old age) and the Treasury (to pay for state pensions).

Expenditure on the welfare state has increased both in real terms and as a proportion of GDP (gross domestic product). However, this does not mean it will continue to do so. Carey Oppenheim attacks the idea of a 'crisis in welfare' arguing that 'to talk of a "crisis" is alarmist and has fostered the myth of "unsustainable spending"' (1994, p1). She notes that the rise in social security payments has been primarily due to the rise in unemployment. A concerted attack on unemployment could significantly reduce this area of welfare expenditure. If this were combined with a growth in the economy then social security spending as a proportion of GDP could decrease rather than increase in future years. And the financing of state welfare could be further supported by more progressive taxation - proportionately higher taxes for the better off. Oppenheim concludes that, 'we *can* afford our social security system for years to come if the economy continues to grow and unemployment continues to fall. The case for cuts has not been made' (1994, p33).

Lois Bryson (1992) points out that a similar questioning of the necessity for comprehensive welfare systems has occurred in most Western industrial societies. She argues that the 'crisis' of the welfare state represents part of the ongoing struggle over the distribution of power and resources in capitalist societies. The development of welfare states represented gains for various subordinate groups such as the working class, women and ethnic minorities. She suggests that the swing to the right in welfare policies in Britain and other countries can be viewed as a fight back by privileged groups who feel they have lost ground in this struggle over the distribution of resources. As the previous section shows struggles over welfare are not new - they have been going on for centuries.

Summary

1 Different theoretical perspectives on social policy reflect different value positions on issues such as the desirability of state intervention in welfare.

2 The relationship between the statutory, informal, voluntary and commercial sectors of welfare has changed and is continuing to change.

3 The welfare state developed in response to the social problems created by urban industrial society. It was also shaped by the influence of conflicting political views and interest groups.

4 The welfare state has undergone important changes since 1979 resulting from the influence of market liberal theories and an apparent crisis in state funding of welfare provision. This has affected the nature of statutory welfare provision and given greater significance to the role of other welfare sectors. Many sociologists see this as a significant challenge to the postwar social democratic consensus on welfare.

Activity 4 The Contemporary Welfare State

Item A

General government expenditure

United Kingdom	Percentages	
	1981	1992
Defence	10.8	9.7
Public order and safety	3.7	5.5
Education	12.2	12.7
Health	11.4	13.8
Social Security	26.6	33.1
Housing and community amenities	6.1	4.3
Other expenditure	29.2	21.0

Adapted from *Social Trends*, 1994, p91

Item B

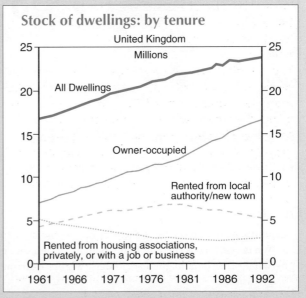

Stock of dwellings: by tenure

From *Social Trends*, 1994, p110

Item C

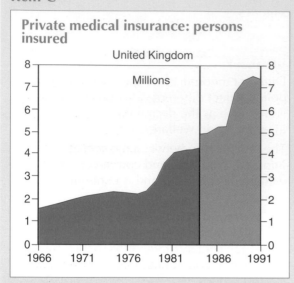

Private medical insurance: persons insured

United Kingdom

Millions

Figures from 1984 are from a different source than those before 1984.

From *Social Trends*, 1994, p105

Item D *Return of the 'five giant evils'*

The socialist writer Jeremy Seabrook argues that Beveridge's 'five giant evils' have returned to Britain. Idleness has returned with mass unemployment and want still exists with seven million people dependent on Supplementary Benefit (now Income Support). While the health service seems to have tackled disease, new epidemics, such as the plague of heroin have arisen to replace those of the nineteenth century, such as cholera. Ignorance seems unlikely to exist in an 'information rich society' but industries such as advertising are based on the manufacture of ignorance. Consumers' attention is drawn away from awkward questions about the suffering and exploitation involved in the production of commodities. Squalor has partly been dealt with by the clearance of slums. But 'the ugly graffiti of the poor estates, the violation in the marketing images of women, and the ruined relationships of people caged and goaded by poverty until they tear each other apart' are new forms of squalor.

Based on J. Seabrook 'Beveridge's Five Evils Return' *New Society*, 28.2.85

Item E *Homelessness*

Item F *Unemployment*

A growing number of homeless people have been sleeping on the streets of big cities in the 1980s and 90s.

In the 1980s unemployment reached its highest level since the 1930s. This picture shows unemployed men and women displaying the latest unemployment figures in 1993.

Questions

1 Examine Item A. How have patterns of government expenditure changed? Suggest reasons for these changes.

2 a) What evidence is there in Items B and C to indicate a move towards the privatisation of welfare?

   b) What other data might a sociologist wish to examine in order to assess the extent to which welfare had become privatised?

3 Using Items D, E and F and any other data evaluate Seabrook's view (Item D) that Beveridge's 'five evils' have returned.

2 Poverty, Inequality and the Welfare State

Key Issues

1 How should poverty be defined and measured?
2 How do definitions of poverty affect conclusions about the extent of poverty in society?
3 How can the persistence of poverty in industrial societies like Britain be explained?
4 To what extent does the welfare state help to reduce social inequalities?

Poverty is one of the major problems which the welfare state was set up to deal with. Much of the research into welfare has been concerned with the state's effectiveness in combatting poverty. In order to measure the extent of poverty social scientists must begin with a definition of poverty. The fact that different definitions have been used results in widely varying estimates of the extent of poverty and indeed the kind of social groups most affected by poverty. This in turn influences the kind of theories put forward to explain the persistence of poverty.

Social inequality and poverty A distinction is often made between social inequality and poverty. Social inequality exists in all societies. But does this mean that poverty exists in all societies? Do those at the bottom who have least, necessarily live in poverty? Some researchers would say yes. They would argue that social inequality automatically generates poverty since those at the bottom are poor compared to the rest of society.

Others would argue that this merely confuses poverty with social inequality. Just because people are at the bottom of a system of social inequality doesn't necessarily mean they are poor. Real poverty - the hunger, the inadequate clothing and the damp, overcrowded housing of Victorian times - has all but disappeared in modern Britain. Today's so-called poverty is simply an aspect of social inequality and must not be confused with 'real poverty'.

The distinction between poverty and social inequality is important. It underlies many of the debates on poverty which form the second part of this chapter.

2.1 Absolute definitions of poverty

Social scientists have used two main ways of defining poverty, *absolute poverty* and *relative poverty*. Within each of these broad definitions a wide variety of methods of actually operationalising definitions for research purposes has been developed.

Absolute definitions of poverty are based on the belief that all human beings have the same basic needs. Poverty involves a lack of the resources to meet such needs. Physical needs are usually seen as the most important - individuals need essentials such as food, clothing and shelter in order to stay alive and healthy. Researchers have attempted to develop scientific ways of measuring the minimum requirements necessary to meet basic human needs.

Rowntree and the scientific measurement of poverty

One of the first systematic studies of poverty was conducted by Seebohm Rowntree in York in 1899. For Rowntree poverty existed when 'total earnings are insufficient to obtain the minimum necessities for the maintenance of merely physical efficiency' (1901). Rowntree worked out a family budget based on the cost of the cheapest food and clothes which would meet these basic requirements. He obtained expert medical advice on nutritional requirements and the cheapest foods which could provide these. To this he added allowances for rent, fuel and a small amount for other 'sundries'. Using this information Rowntree worked out an allowance, according to the size of family, which was his 'poverty line'. Households whose total income fell below this line were defined as being in poverty.

Rowntree introduced a distinction between *primary poverty* and *secondary poverty*. People in primary poverty were those who spent all their income on basic essentials but still had to go without some necessities. For example, some mothers went without food to pay for new clothes or shoes for their children. Those in secondary poverty had just enough to pay for the essentials but because of buying non-essential items, or not buying the cheapest food, clothing and so on, they lacked certain necessary items. Many men, for example, spent money on alcohol or tobacco, resulting in a shortage of money for essentials. Wives did not always have the expert knowledge needed to buy the cheapest and most nutritious foods.

It has been argued that absolute definitions of poverty have the merit of providing a fixed and universal definition which can be used for measuring and comparing poverty in all societies. They can also reveal changes in living standards in a society over time. For example, Rowntree calculated that 33% of York's population were in poverty in 1899 but only 1.5% in 1950, a change he attributed to higher living standards and the provisions of the welfare state.

However, the fixed nature of absolute definitions has been criticised by many sociologists.

Criticisms of absolute definitions of poverty

Supporters of relative definitions of poverty argue that universal definitions are meaningless since what counts as poverty varies from time to time and from place to place. They make the following criticisms.

1 **Human needs cannot be objectively measured**. This even applies to physical needs. For example, 'scientific' views of an adequate diet vary considerably. Given this, an objective measurement of human nutritional requirements is not possible.

2 **Physical needs are affected by age, sex, occupation and other social factors**. For example, a labourer on a building site will require much more food than an office worker. Thus nutritional requirements are not fixed and absolute, they must be related to a range of social factors.

3 **What counts as 'necessities' and 'essentials' varies from time to time and place to place**. In this respect human needs are culturally defined. Normal and reasonable standards of housing, diet and clothing in Britain today differ form those in other societies and from Britain a hundred years ago. Thus Income Support recipients in the 1990s may be seen as fairly well off by the standards of the 1890s. However, by today's standards they may be seen as poor since they are deprived of many of the things taken for granted as part of normal life in modern Britain. In this respect poverty is relative, it is measured in relation to the standards of a particular society at a particular time. And these standards are not fixed, they change.

To some extent this is recognised even by those who try to use absolute definitions of poverty. For example, in his second survey of York in 1936, Rowntree extended his view of 'human needs' to include items such as a radio, books and a holiday.

Income Support level as a poverty line

Rowntree's surveys were very influential in Britain. Beveridge used them as a basis for his proposals for National Assistance. Like Rowntree, Beveridge drew a poverty line below which he argued nobody should fall. National Assistance Benefit (the precursor of Supplementary Benefit and Income Support) was designed to provide a minimum income for those unable to cover the cost of essentials similar to those identified by Rowntree. While there is no official 'poverty line' in Britain, many researchers argue that Income Support levels provide a convenient measure of absolute poverty. However, there is considerable evidence to suggest that this unofficial absolute poverty line is unduly stringent as it leaves out many who are unable to afford basic necessities.

A recent study by Nina Oldfield and Autumn Yu (1993) undertaken for Child Poverty Action Group attempted to calculate low cost budgets for different types of families. Like Rowntree, they relied on the advice of experts about what items should be included. They devised a 'modest but adequate family budget' and a more stringent 'low cost budget' which included only the bare necessities. Even compared to this low cost budget Income Support scales were found to be inadequate. In April 1993 they calculated that a family of two adults and two children under 11 would require £142.56 on the low cost budget but would receive only £108.75 in Income Support - a shortfall of £33.81. Evidence from such studies suggests that even in terms of absolute definitions of poverty, Income Support level is an inadequate poverty line.

Activity 5   Absolute Poverty

Item A   *Defining absolute poverty*

An absolute standard is defined by reference to the actual needs of the poor and not by reference to the expenditure of those who are not poor. A family is poor if it cannot afford to eat. A person who enjoys a standard of living equal to that of a medieval baron cannot be described as poor for the sole reason that he has chanced to be born into a society where the great majority live like medieval kings. By any absolute standards there is very little poverty in Britain today.

Adapted from K. Joseph (formerly Secretary of State for Social Services) *Stranded on Middle Ground*, 1976

Item B   *Poverty as exclusion*

Poverty means exclusion from the living standards, the lifestyles and the fellowship of one's fellow citizens. We constantly manufacture new forms of poverty as we drive forward the living standards of the majority without thinking what we are doing to those who cannot keep pace.

Adapted from D. Donnison (formerly Chairman of the Supplementary Benefits Commission) *The Politics of Poverty*, 1982, p226

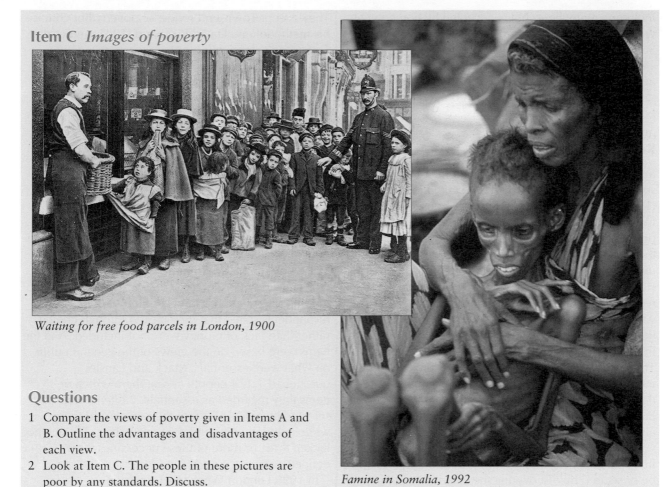

Item C *Images of poverty*

Waiting for free food parcels in London, 1900

Famine in Somalia, 1992

Questions

1 Compare the views of poverty given in Items A and
   B. Outline the advantages and disadvantages of
   each view.
2 Look at Item C. The people in these pictures are
   poor by any standards. Discuss.

2.2 Relative definitions of poverty

Relative definitions of poverty advocate a poverty line
which moves in response to changing social
expectations and living standards. For many
researchers freedom from poverty involves the ability
to participate in the accepted lifestyle of the majority
of the population. For example Peter Townsend
(1979) states:

> 'Individuals can be said to be in poverty when
> they lack the resources to obtain the types of
> diet, participate in the activities and have the
> living conditions and amenities which are
> customary, or at least widely encouraged or
> approved, in the societies to which they belong.'

Such approaches emphasise that people's needs are
not simply shaped by physical necessity but also by
cultural expectations. For example, buying Christmas
presents is not a physical necessity but it is an
important tradition in Western culture. In terms of
relative definitions, poverty is not fixed but changes
in line with society's expectations. For example,
inside toilets, televisions and central heating, once
regarded as luxuries available to the few, have now

become accessible to the majority of the population
in the United Kingdom. Today households unable to
afford such items can be seen as poor relative to the
majority of the population.

Relative definitions based on income levels

One of the earliest attempts to develop a relative
definition of poverty was by Brian Abel-Smith and
Peter Townsend in *The Poor and the Poorest* (1965).
They argued that National Assistance Benefit levels
(which were close to Rowntree's poverty line) were
too low to represent a realistic poverty line. They
claimed that both people on National Assistance and
those just above it were excluded from enjoying the
living standards of the majority. Abel-Smith and
Townsend therefore proposed that a line based on
140% of a household's entitlement to National
Assistance plus their rent or housing costs was a more
realistic poverty line.

While the 140% of NationalAssistance/Supplementary
Benefit poverty line has been widely used by
researchers it has been criticised for being over-
generous and arbitrary. Paul Ashton (1984) argues
that if this definition were used, 14 million people
would have been in poverty in Britain in 1984,

including many households occupied by homeowners with almost average incomes. 140% of Supplementary Benefit also seems somewhat arbitrary - why not 130% or 150%? Peter Townsend himself acknowledges this deficiency and in his subsequent research attempts to move away from a definition of poverty solely based on income.

Relative deprivation

In 1968-69 Townsend carried out a major national survey of poverty, *Poverty in the United Kingdom* (1979), based on a sample of 2,052 households. In this study he used three different definitions of poverty but claims the most objective definition was the *deprivation standard*. Townsend argued that income alone is not a satisfactory measure of poverty since households may have a variety of other resources at their disposal. For example, growing vegetables in a garden or allotment or receiving help in kind from relatives or social services may be ways in which a family's living standard can be improved. This would not be apparent from measures of income. Similarly poor standards of housing or deprivations at work (such as working anti-social hours) are dimensions of poverty which are not always revealed in surveys based on income.

Townsend argues that poverty involves exclusion from the accepted lifestyle of the community. It can be measured by discovering the extent to which people are deprived of the amenities and activities seen as normal by the majority. Townsend asked detailed questions on 60 indicators of deprivation. From these he chose 12, which he regarded as particularly revealing indicators of lifestyles, and used them to compile his deprivation index (see Activity 6, Item B). They include not having a refrigerator and lack of an annual holiday. Households deprived of a significant number of these items were judged to be poor.

To support this judgement Townsend showed that there was a correlation (relationship) between relative deprivation (as measured by the deprivation index) and income. Below a particular income level (around 150% of Supplementary Benefit levels) the amount of deprivation increased rapidly. Townsend argues that this represents an objective relative poverty line and classifies all households below 150% of SB as poor. On this basis 22.9% of the population (12.46 million people) were in poverty in 1968-9.

Criticisms The main criticism of Townsend's work has come from those on the right. They argue that his research measures inequality rather than poverty. Since they see inequality as inevitable they regard the concept of relative poverty as meaningless (see Item D in Activity 6).

Some sociologists have been more sympathetic.

They accept Townsend's view of poverty but criticise his methodology. David Piachaud (1981) argues that Townsend's deprivation index represents a rather arbitrary choice of indicators of deprivation. For example, not eating a cooked breakfast may be due to taste rather than lack of money.

Townsend has also been criticised for not finding out what people consider to be a normal and acceptable lifestyle. Given his definition of poverty, this is a strange omission from his research.

A social consensus definition of poverty

Joanna Mack and Stewart Lansley attempted to overcome some of these problems when they carried out a survey in 1983 on behalf of London Weekend Television for the programme *Breadline Britain* (1985). Like Townsend they drew up a list of items to measure deprivation. However, items which respondents stated that they lacked through choice rather than lack of money were not included. And the items were based on the views of the general public on what were essentials. Mack and Lansley questioned 1,174 people asking them which of 35 items they regarded as essentials. 22 items were selected by at least 50% of the sample and these were included in the index of necessities. Those who lacked three or more of these necessities were defined as poor.

In 1990 London Weekend Television commissioned a new survey, *Breadline Britain: 1990s*. The survey used much the same methodology as the original *Breadline Britain*. A questionnaire which included a number of new items was given to a sample of 1,319 people (see Item C in Activity 6). As before items classified as 'necessities' by 50% or more of respondents were included in the list of essentials. In the 1990 survey the list of essential items increased from 22 to 32. Mack and Lansley argue that this increase is justified since it reflects changing social expectations about living standards in the period between the surveys. Comparison of the two surveys certainly supports the view of many sociologists that poverty increased in the 1980s. While the first survey in 1983 estimated that 7.5 million people were in poverty in Britain, this had increased to 11 million in the 1990 survey.

Criticisms The items in Mack and Lansley's list of essentials were selected by their respondents. However, the authors themselves constructed the working definition of poverty - a lack of three or more essentials - after the survey was completed. In view of this, Paul Ashton (1984) questions whether the Breadline Britain poverty standard can be regarded as 'society approved'. In other words would the public regard a lack of three or more essentials as constituting poverty.

The LWT researchers, however, justify their definition by showing that many households lacking one or two items do not seem to be deprived in other ways while 'those who lack three or more are heavily concentrated among those with the lowest incomes and who are deprived in other ways' (Frayman, 1991, p9). They also argue that their definition represents an attempt to define poverty according to the views of a representative cross section of the population. As such it may represent a social consensus view of poverty.

Political views and definitions of poverty

Academics and politicians influenced by market liberal theories argue that we should return to absolute definitions of poverty. On this basis it makes no sense to talk of widespread poverty in contemporary Britain (see for example Activity 5, Item A). Researchers and politicians influenced by social democratic perspectives have tended to favour relative definitions. They believe that social justice requires that the poor are not simply maintained at some absolute level of subsistence but given the opportunity to enjoy the living standards of the majority.

Some Marxist sociologists like John Westergaard and Henrietta Resler have gone even further, claiming that the whole idea of drawing a line (whether absolute or relative) below which people are defined as poor diverts attention from the wider pattern of inequality in society. And since it is the class system as a whole which generates poverty, it diverts attention away from the real causes of poverty.

There is no objective definition of poverty. There is no consensus about what constitutes poverty. Defining poverty is essentially a political issue. Underlying the debates about definitions of poverty are important questions about the desirability and necessity of social inequality in general.

Activity 6 Poverty or Inequality?

Item A *Social inequality*

Going to Ascot - a view from the other side of the fence

Item B *Townsend's deprivation index*

1. Has not had a week's holiday away from home in the last twelve months.
2. (Adults) Has not had a relative or a friend to the home for a meal or snack for the last four weeks.
3. (Adults) Has not been out in the last four weeks to a relative or friend for a meal or snack.
4. (Children under fifteen) Has not had a friend to play or to tea in the last four weeks.
5. (Children) Did not have a party on last birthday.
6. Has not had an afternoon or evening out for entertainment in the last two weeks.
7. Does not have fresh meat (including meals out) as many as four days a week.
8. Has gone through one or more days in the last fortnight without a cooked meal.
9. Has not had a cooked breakfast most days of the week.
10. Household does not have a refrigerator.
11. Household does not usually have a Sunday joint.
12. Household does not have sole use of four amenities indoors (flush WC; sink or washbasin and cold water tap; fixed bath or shower; and gas or electric cooker).

From P. Townsend *Poverty in the United Kingdom*, 1979, p250

Item C *Breadline Britain*

Respondents deeming items to be necessary in *Breadline Britain* surveys, 1983 and 1990

	1990 %	1983 %	Change % +/−
A damp-free home	98	96	+2
An inside toilet (not shared with another household)	97	96	+1
Heating to warm living areas of the home if it's cold	97	97	0
Beds for everyone in the household	95	94	+1
Bath, not shared with any other household	95	94	+1
[2] A decent state of decoration in the home	92	-	-
Fridge	92	77	+15
Warm waterproof coat	91	87	+4
[1] Three meals a day (for children)	90	82	+8
[4] Two meals a day (for adults)	90	64	+26
[2] Insurance	88	-	-
[2] Fresh fruit	88	-	-
[1] Toys for children eg dolls or models	84	71	+13
[1] Separate bedrooms for every child over 10 of different sexes	82	77	+5
Carpets in living rooms and bedrooms in the home	78	70	+8
[3] Meat or fish or vegetarian equivalent every other day	77	63	+14
Celebrations on special occasions such as Christmas	74	69	+5
Two pairs of all-weather shoes	74	78	−4
Washing machine	73	67	+6
Presents for friends or family once a year	69	63	+6
[1,2] Out of school activities eg sports, orchestra, Scouts	69	-	-
[2] Regular savings of £10 a month for 'rainy days' or retirement	68	-	-
Hobby or leisure activity	67	64	+3
New, not secondhand, clothes	65	64	+1
[3] A roast joint or its vegetarian equivalent once a week	64	67	−3
[1] Leisure equipment for children eg sports equipment or bicycle	61	57	+4
A television	58	51	+7
Telephone	56	43	+13
An annual week's holiday away, not with relatives	54	63	−9
A 'best outfit' for special occasions	54	48	+6
[1] An outing for children once a week	53	40	+13
[1] Children's friends round for tea/snack fortnightly	52	37	+15
A dressing gown	42	38	+4
A night out fortnightly	42	36	+6
[2] Fares to visit friends in other parts of the country 4 times a year	39	-	-
[1,2] Special lessons such as music dance or sport	39	-	-
Friends/family for a meal monthly	37	32	+5
A car	26	22	+4
Pack of cigarettes every other day	18	14	+4
[2] Restaurant meal monthly	17	-	-
[2] Holidays abroad annually	17	-	-
[2] A video	13	-	-
[2] A home computer	5	-	-
[2] A dishwasher	4	-	-

The descriptions of items have been abbreviated

[1] For families with children
[2] Not included in the 1983 survey
[3] Vegetarian option added 1990
[4] Two hot meals in the 1983 survey

Adapted from H. Frayman *Breadline Britain 1990s: The Findings of the Television Series*, 1991, p4

Item D *Poverty or inequality?*

Townsend's extremely voluminous *Poverty in the United Kingdom* contends that about one quarter of the British population lives in a state of actual or near poverty. However, much of what Professor Townsend describes as poverty does not deserve this dread word at all.

In his view poverty means relative deprivation. Thus anyone whose income falls below the average runs the risk of being described as poverty-stricken. If that is how Professor Townsend wishes to use the term he is obviously at liberty to do so. But where I take issue with him is in the assumption that poverty so described should provoke moral outrage. To my way of thinking poverty can be morally outrageous only if the condition contravenes some absolute yardstick as to what is morally acceptable. Compared to most human beings in the world today, Professor Townsend's victims are rich beyond the dreams of avarice. They are only poor in relation to contemporary British standards of affluence. What is offensive to Professor Townsend, in short, is not so much the existence of poverty in Britain as the existence of inequality. To pretend that one is interested in curing poverty, when one is really concerned about rectifying inequality, is intellectually dishonest, since it is to exploit feelings that are common to everybody for a purpose that is highly partisan [one-sided]. Short of imposing a uniform standard of living, there is no way of eradicating relative deprivation. However much the lot of the poor is improved, there will always be a superior standard of living by comparison with which the poor remain underprivileged.

Adapted from P. Worsthorne *Daily Telegraph*, 27.10.79

Questions

1 Using the picture in Item A, briefly discuss the distinction between poverty and social inequality.

2 Study Townsend's deprivation index (Item B).
   a) How many of the items do you go without? Is this through choice or lack of money?
   b) Which items do you feel are useful as indicators of deprivation and which are not? Give reasons for your answer.
   c) Draw up your own deprivation index. Compare your list with those of other students and discuss the advantages and disadvantages of including various items.

3 Examine Item C.
   a) Suggest reasons for the percentage changes between 1983 and 1990.
   b) In the 1990 *Breadline Britain* survey, the list of 'essential' items was increased from 22 to 32. Do you think that this was justified. Give reasons for your answer.

4 Are Worsthorne's criticisms of Townsend in Item D justified? Explain your answer.

2.3 Measuring poverty

Questions about the extent and distribution of poverty are inseparable from the debates about the definition of poverty. If we define poverty in stringent subsistence terms using some sort of absolute definition, then comparatively few people in Britain are in poverty. However, if poverty is defined as relative deprivation a much larger proportion of the population is defined as poor.

The extent of poverty in Britain

Whether or not poverty is a serious social problem has been a matter of much political debate in recent years. Critics of Conservative governments since 1979 have argued that their policies have led to a widening gap between the rich and poor and a consequent increase in relative poverty. Government ministers maintain that absolute poverty has been virtually eradicated and that the remaining social inequalities are necessary to encourage wealth creation. They see the long term consequence of this as higher living standards which will 'trickle down' from the top to all income groups in society.

There is certainly evidence that for most of this century higher living standards have led to a reduction in absolute poverty. Seebohm Rowntree's famous studies of York showed a sharp decline in the extent of poverty from 33% of the population in 1899 to 18% in 1936 and 1.5% in 1950. However, in the 1960s sociologists using relative concepts of poverty rejected this optimistic view. On the basis of his 1969 survey, Townsend (1979) argued that 21.8% of the population were below the 140% of Supplementary Benefit line and 22.9% below his deprivation standard. Such findings challenged the widely held belief that the welfare state had eradicated poverty. Moreover, they suggested that far from poverty declining, the numbers in poverty were actually increasing.

Poverty in the 1980s and 90s

Since 1979 there has been renewed debate over poverty. Although no consensus has emerged on the definition of poverty, there is considerable evidence to suggest that, however it is defined, poverty has increased in recent years. A number of factors may account for this increase. Firstly, many of the groups most vulnerable to poverty have grown larger in recent years. As people live longer there are more old age pensioners; as people divorce more often there are more lone parent families; and there were more unemployed people in the early 1980s than at any time since the

1930s. In the early 1990s unemployment increased again after a brief decline. Such changes help to explain why an increasing number of people are dependent on welfare benefits such as Income Support. But poverty also seems to be increasing among groups who do not depend on the welfare state, such as families dependent on the income of a low wage earner. The difference in earnings between those in well paid, secure jobs and those in low paid, often insecure or casual employment has widened greatly since 1979.

Critics of government policies argue that the main reason for the increase in poverty is the fact that the incomes of the poor have not kept pace with those of the majority. There is therefore a widening gap between rich and poor. Using the government's own statistics, Child Poverty Action Group point out that the income of the poorest tenth of the population actually fell by 6% in real terms (after housing costs) between 1979 and 1988/9, while the average income rose by 30%. Similarly in 1988/9 around 12 million people were living on less than 50% of average income after housing costs - over a fifth of the population - compared to around 5 million in 1979 - 9% of the population (Oppenheim, 1993).

Many benefits have in fact fallen behind both prices and average earnings. For example in 1992 a married man previously on average earnings with two children would have received £87.10 per week in unemployment benefit and child benefit. If benefits had risen in line with prices since 1979 his benefits would be worth £127.70, and £166.55 if they had risen in line with earnings (*New Statesman and Society*, 27.11.1992, p15).

Government supporters argue that relative measures of poverty give a misleading picture. If more stringent definitions are used then poverty is far less widespread. They point to the improvement in living standards for the population as a whole and argue that in absolute terms lower income groups are much better off than in the past. Once again debates on whether poverty is increasing or decreasing hinge on how poverty is defined.

The distribution of poverty

Studies have consistently identified certain groups of people as likely to be poor. These groups are much the same as those identified by Rowntree in 1899. Poverty is unevenly distributed in society. It is no coincidence that it tends to hit precisely those groups who are socially disadvantaged in other ways. Some of the main groups are identified below.

The unemployed Official statistics estimated there were 2.9 million unemployed at the end of 1992 (compared to 1 million in 1979).

Low wage earners According to the Low Pay Unit (1990) the number of workers on low pay (defined as below two-thirds of median male earnings) increased from 36% of the workforce in 1979 to 41% in 1989 ie 8.88 million workers.

Families Despite the provisions of the welfare state people with children tend to be worse off than childless couples. The main benefits available are Child Benefit and Family Credit. Child Benefit was frozen from 1987 to 1990 (though it was increased in 1991). This means its real value went down. Family Credit has been increased but only has about a 40% take up rate. Families with the lowest income of all are lone parent families, most of them headed by women. According to the 1990 *Family Expenditure Survey* the average income of the poorest quarter of the single population without children was £155 a week while the poorest quarter of lone parents with one child had an average income of only £74 a week.

Disabled people Official estimates suggest that there are over 6 million disabled adults and around 360,000 disabled children in Britain today. People with disabilities are disproportionately represented among those with low incomes.

Old people In 1988 those over pensionable age numbered 10.4 million or 18% of the population. Women make up about two thirds of the elderly population and constitute an even larger proportion of the elderly poor. Not all elderly people live in poverty. Those formerly in low paid jobs are most at risk since their wages offered little chance to save and state pensions can hardly be described as generous. According to the Department of Social Security the retirement pension for a single person was 20.4% of male average earnings in 1979 but only 16.3% in 1989.

Social class and poverty

Most poor people have one thing in common, their social class position. Peter Townsend (1979) notes that most of the low paid, unemployed, elderly, sick or disabled poor, hold or have held unskilled or semi-skilled manual jobs. Not only do such jobs have the lowest rates of pay, they are also less secure with greater risks of redundancy and short time working, they have higher rates of accidents and industrial diseases and are less likely to benefit from occupational pensions and other fringe benefits.

Westergaard and Resler (1975) take this even further and argue that to see the characteristics of the poor - such as old age and unemployment - as the causes of poverty ignores their common class position and the fact that class inequalities generated by the capitalist system are the fundamental reason for the persistence of poverty.

Women and poverty

62% of adults who receive income support are women. There is considerable evidence that women are more likely to experience poverty than men. Comparing the extent of poverty among women and men is difficult since statistics are normally based on households. This implies that household resources are equally shared by all adult members. Caroline Glendinning and Jane Millar (1987) claim that men usually get a greater share. This may reflect their higher earning capacity and the fact that in many households men still have more power than women to determine the way money is spent.

In general women are paid less than men. The Low Pay Unit estimated that in 1989 6.34 million women were low paid (71% of the total number on low wages). Low pay is particularly prevalent among part time workers, most of whom are women. Apart from the low paid, women constitute a large proportion of other groups in poverty. For example, 96% of lone parents on income support are women and over three times as many women as men over pension age receive income support.

Peter Townsend et al (1987) argue that there has been a *feminisation of poverty*. This has been accentuated by government policies in the 1980s aimed at reducing social security costs and removing protection from groups of low paid workers such as part timers. Townsend identifies four main groups which make up the majority of the female poor.

1 Women who look after children or other dependents. They are unpaid and unable to take paid employment.
2 Lone women with children, whether or not in employment.
3 Elderly women pensioners, especially those who live alone.
4 Women with low earnings where the earnings or income of others does not enable total household income to exceed the poverty line.

Ethnicity and poverty

There is no recent national data on income and ethnicity. However, there is considerable evidence to suggest that poverty is more common among ethnic minorities than whites. Firstly, unemployment is higher among ethnic minorities - the male unemployment rate for ethnic minorities was 21% in 1993 compared to 10% for whites. Secondly, black people are disproportionately concentrated in low paid jobs. The third PSI survey (Brown, 1984) found that while average weekly earnings for full time male white workers were £129.00 in 1982, the comparable figures were £110.70 for Asians and £109.20 for Afro-Caribbeans.

Ethnic minorities are also disadvantaged by the way the social security system operates. For example, to claim severe disablement allowance or certain types of old age pensions a person must prove residence in Britain for 10 out of the preceding 20 years. This may exclude many immigrants. There is also evidence that some black people are afraid to claim means tested benefits in case this jeopardises their chances (or those of their relatives) of being allowed to settle in Britain (Oppenheim, 1990).

(For further discussion of ethnic inequality see pp103-113).

Region and poverty

Poverty is not only unequally distributed socially but also geographically. This is reflected in the phrase 'the North-South divide'. A higher proportion of people on low incomes (defined as less than 50% of average income) live in Northern England than in the South. Poverty is also more widespread in Wales and Scotland. The poorest region is Northern Ireland while Southeast England is the most affluent. These variations are associated with other kinds of regional inequalities such as levels of unemployment and measures of health and mortality.

However, during the recession of the early 1990s the gap between regions in the South of England and other parts of the UK has narrowed . House prices in the South fell much faster in the early 90s than elsewhere and unemployment began to affect the South East, especially London, far more severely. For example, in 1988 unemployment in the South East stood at 5.3% but at 11.8% in the North. By 1993 it had increased to 10.2% in the South East but remained virtually the same at 11.9% in the North (*Regional Trends*, 1994).

But regional averages conceal wide variations within regions. Poverty is often concentrated in certain urban and rural areas where it is linked to other forms of social deprivation. Townsend et al (1987) in their study of Greater London showed that low income households are concentrated in inner city London boroughs. High levels of poverty are associated with other forms of deprivation such as high levels of unemployment, high mortality rates, poor housing and overcrowding. According to the Department of the Environment's official scores of multiple deprivation, the ten local authorities with the highest scores in the country were all inner London boroughs.

Activity 7 Counting the Poor

Item A

Numbers of people living in or on the margins of poverty in 1979 and 1989 (defined as 140% of supplementary benefit/income support and below)

(bar chart)

1979:
- 3,170,000 (6%)
- 7,740,000 (14%)
- 13,010,000 (24%)

1989:
- 4,350,000 (8%)
- 11,330,000 (20%)
- 16,520,000 (29%)

Legend: ■ 140% of SB/IS and below ■ On and below SB/IS □ Below SB/IS

The bar chart above shows the number of people in households defined as in poverty according to three definitions:

a) those living on an income equivalent to or below 140% of supplementary benefit/income support;

b) those living on an income equivalent to or below supplementary benefit/income support;

c) those living on an income below supplementary benefit/income support.

From C. Oppenheim *Poverty: The Facts*, 1993, p33

Item C *Are the poor better off?*

John Moore, Secretary of State for Social Security, yesterday accused the poverty lobby of manipulating the facts to produce 'arbitrary and exaggerated' estimates of the number of poor people. What was being defined as poverty, he told a conference of the Greater London Conservative Party, was only inequality. He said: 'Not only are those on lower incomes not getting poorer, they are substantially better off than they have ever been before'. More and more people even in the bottom fifth of households had cars, colour television sets, and washing machines. 'It is hard to believe that poverty stalks the land when even the poorest fifth of families spend nearly a tenth of their income on alcohol and tobacco', Mr Moore said.

Adapted from N. Timmins 'Moore Says Poverty Levels are Exaggerated' *Independent*, 12.5.89

Item B

The growing ranks of the poor...

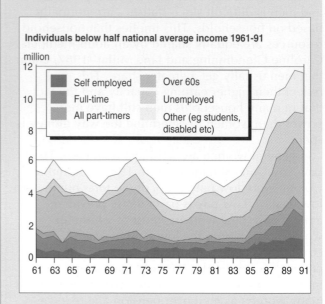

Individuals below half national average income 1961-91

Legend: Self employed, Full-time, All part-timers, Over 60s, Unemployed, Other (eg students, disabled etc)

...and the growing incomes of the rich

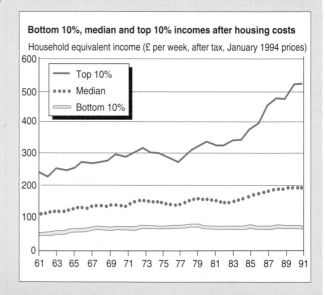

Bottom 10%, median and top 10% incomes after housing costs

Household equivalent income (£ per week, after tax, January 1994 prices)

Legend: Top 10%, Median, Bottom 10%

The Council of Europe defines poverty as below 50% of average national income.

Taking into account the effects of housing costs can greatly affect assessment of changes in real living standards. The real incomes of the poorest tenth ranked by income after housing costs actually fell sharply from the peak in 1979 of £73 per week to just over £61 per week in 1991 (both at 1994 prices). This represented a return to living standards of a quarter of a century ago.

Adapted from Institute for Fiscal Studies *For Richer for Poorer: the Changing Distribution of Income in the UK 1961-1991*, 1994, pp15, 44, 66

Item D *The benefits of income inequality?*

Conservative governments have justified income inequality in the following ways. The growing income of the rich will benefit the whole community as income will steadily trickle down from the top. We will all be better off because the rich are the wealth creators. Tax them less and let them keep more. This will provide incentives. They will work harder, the economy will grow and everybody will benefit.

Obviously there will still be social inequality but that's all to the good. We will all be better off. What matters is how well each person is, compared with their position 5, 10, 20 years ago.

Adapted from *Guardian*, 3.6.94

Item F *Comment*

On becoming Prime Minister John Major said be hoped to create 'a society at ease with itself'. The following comments were made on the publication of *For Richer, For Poorer* (Item B).

'This is not a recipe for a society at ease with itself' Editorial *Financial Times*, 3.6.94

'This is a society gravely at odds with itself - and finding a community of interest becomes increasingly difficult.' Will Hutton *Guardian*, 3.6.94

Item E

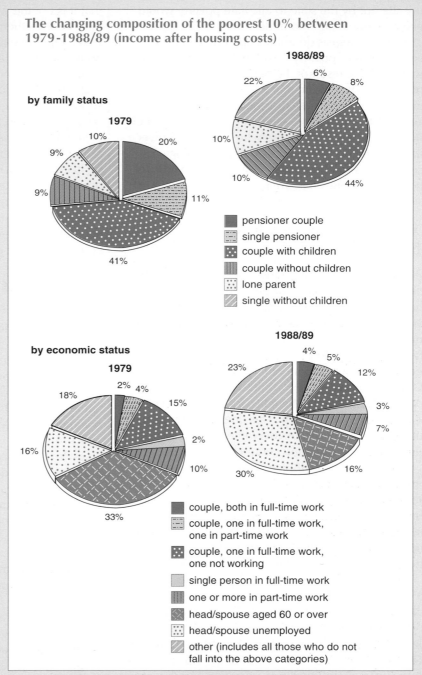

The changing composition of the poorest 10% between 1979-1988/89 (income after housing costs)

From C. Oppenheim *Poverty: The Facts*, 1993, p47

Questions

1 Summarise the trends shown in Items A and B.
2 Comment on Items C and D in the light of your previous answer.
3 a) Summarise the changes shown in Item E.
   b) Suggest reasons for these changes.
4 Do you agree with the comments in Item F? Give reasons for your answer.

2.4 Explaining poverty

The poor have only themselves to blame. This was probably the most popular explanation for poverty in the 19th century. Poverty was seen as the result of idleness, drunkenness and moral degeneracy. If people got themselves into poverty, then it was their responsibility to get themselves out of it. The belief that the poor are responsible for helping themselves is still an important part of market liberal thinking about welfare. However, few would go as far as the 19th century sociologist Herbert Spencer and argue that *any* attempt by the state to alleviate poverty would lead to laziness and moral decline.

Most sociologists do not accept individualistic explanations of poverty - explanations which see poverty as the result of the behaviour of the individual. They argue that the way in which incomes and other resources are distributed is the result of social factors which are often beyond the control of individuals, especially those who have little power like the poor. This section examines sociological explanations for the existence of poverty in affluent industrial societies like Britain.

Dependency theories: the welfare state as the cause of poverty

Market liberal theorists argue that the poor need to take responsibility for their own situation. They see the main obstacle to this as their dependency on the welfare state. As long as the state continues to maintain the poor they have no incentive for helping themselves. Indeed the 'poverty trap' means that recipients of benefits are often better off not working. As paid employees they would be taxed and would loose certain selective benefits, for example free school meals for children. This line of argument has influenced Conservative governments' policies for reducing income tax and certain benefit levels.

David Marsland (1989) argues that state welfare provision should be kept to a minimum and provided on a selective basis as a last resort. Marsland believes that the welfare state has undermined other welfare agencies, for example the family, local communities and voluntary organisations, agencies which allow the poor to help themselves and each other.

Some New Right thinkers, such as Charles Murray (1990) in the USA and Digby Anderson (1990) in the UK, have argued that a new *underclass* is emerging - a social class below the working class which is dependent on welfare benefits. According to Murray it is characterised by family instability, violent crime, drug abuse, dropping out of education and the labour market and irresponsible 'scrounging' off welfare benefits. Murray claims that what distinguishes members of the underclass is their refusal to take responsibility for their own welfare, for example by failing to seriously look for work when they are unemployed. And state benefits are again seen as causing social problems. They support the underclass and create a culture of dependency which saps people's initiative.

(For further discussion of the underclass see pp61-64).

Criticisms Dependency theory has been strongly criticised by social democratic thinkers who support

the philosophy of the welfare state. Labour MP, Frank Field (1989) sees the poor as an underclass but argues that it is not the welfare state but lack of resources that prevents them from participating fully in society. Carey Oppenheim of the Child Poverty Action Group points out that many groups in society which depend on the state are not seen as a social problem by New Right thinkers. Home buyers whose mortgages are subsidised by tax relief are an example. Moreover, reducing support from the welfare state may simply create other forms of dependency on agencies such as the family, friends and private charities which may be ill equipped to help those in poverty. Social democratic thinkers reject the argument that dependency is created by the welfare state. They believe that the state has a duty to enable vulnerable and dependent groups to participate in society on equal terms with other citizens.

The culture of poverty: culture as the cause of poverty

New Right theories see the underclass as characterised by a way of life and attitudes which create dependency and so prevent the poor from escaping from poverty. This idea of a *culture of poverty* has its origins in the work of the American anthropologist Oscar Lewis who studied poor communities in Mexico and Puerto Rico in the 1950s and 1960s.

Lewis (1968) argued that in Third World societies the poor have a distinctive culture with attitudes, norms and values which differ from those of the mainstream culture. This culture of poverty includes attitudes of resignation and fatalism which lead the poor to accept their fate rather than attempting to improve their lot. This can be seen as their failure. The culture of poverty emphasises immediate gratification and a concern with the present. This makes it difficult for poor people to plan or save for the future, join trade unions, political organisations and community groups which might help them to improve their situation.

Lewis saw the culture of poverty as a way of life which is passed on from generation to generation. Children learn the culture from an early age. It helps them to cope with day to day life in poverty, but means they are ill-equipped to take advantage of opportunities such as education which might help them to escape from poverty. In this way the poverty of the parents is passed on to children.

Criticisms The idea of a culture of poverty has been criticised by a number of anthropologists who have studied communities in Latin America similar to those studied by Lewis. For example, William Mangin's (1968) research in the slums of Peru suggests that the poor are far from apathetic or resigned but often show a remarkable capacity for community organisation and self help.

Sociologists studying industrial societies have also questioned whether the culture of poverty explains why the poor are poor. Ken Coates and Richard Silburn (1970), in their study of the slum area of St Ann's in Nottingham, found that many poor people did exhibit a degree of resignation and hopelessness but that this was a consequence rather than a cause of being poor (see Activity 8, Item E). Similarly Michael Rutter and Nicola Madge in a review of the research concluded that 'there is little documentation of any communities in this country [the United Kingdom] which might correspond with the descriptions of a culture of poverty given by Lewis' (1977, p30).

The cycle of deprivation: situational constraints as the cause of poverty

Situational constraints Those who reject cultural explanations of poverty point to the fact that there are many social, economic and environmental factors which prevent the poor from behaving in the same way as other members of society. Such *situational constraints* might include lack of educational and employment opportunities, poor housing conditions and greater chances of long standing illness and disability. From this perspective the behaviour of the poor is a reaction to their disadvantaged social situation rather than being directed by alternative norms and values. The poor have the same norms and values as the rest of society. It is simply that situational constraints often prevent them from translating these norms and values into behaviour.

Ken Coates and Richard Silburn (1970) showed in their study of St Ann's in Nottingham that poverty resulted from a series of multiple deprivations. Not only did poor people suffer from low incomes, they were also likely to live in seriously substandard housing, they often had poor diets, their children went to a primary school which lacked modern amenities and they lived in an area which could be best described as a slum. Coates and Silburn argue that in such circumstances it was difficult for people to escape from poverty. They needed all their energy and what little money they had just to survive. And faced with similar situational constraints, children were likely to experience the same poverty as their parents.

Cycle of deprivation Some researchers argue that there is a cycle of deprivation, whereby the poverty of parents is passed on to their children. Michael Rutter and Nicola Madge reviewed the evidence for this view in their study *Cycles of Disadvantage* (1976). They found that a variety of factors may create cycles of disadvantage. For example, children from poor backgrounds were more likely to underachieve at school, become unemployed or end

up in unskilled jobs, be convicted of juvenile offences and suffer from certain types of psychiatric disorder. Rutter and Madge acknowledge that some of these disadvantages may be the result of children from low income families being 'labelled' as a problem. However, they conclude that there is some evidence that cycles of disadvantage do exist, that they are caused in part by poverty, and that to some extent they are a cause of poverty.

Criticisms Rutter and Madge, however, qualify their support for the cycle of deprivation model by pointing out that:

'At least half of the children born into a disadvantaged home do not repeat the pattern of disadvantage in the next generation. Over half of all forms of disadvantage arise anew in each generation. On the one hand, even where continuity is strongest many individuals break out of the cycle and on the other many people become disadvantaged without having been reared by disadvantaged parents. In short, familial cycles are a most important element in the perpetuation of disadvantage but they account for only a part of the overall picture' (1976, p304).

The argument that poverty is created by situational constraints and perpetuated by cycles of disadvantage has been criticised for providing only a partial explanation. Why does poverty exist in the first place? How can we explain the situational constraints which are seen to generate poverty? Many sociologists argue that to answer such questions we must turn to theories of social stratification. From this point of view, poverty is an aspect of class, gender and ethnic stratification .

Social democratic structural explanations of poverty: class inequality as the cause of poverty

Many of those who support social democratic theories see the existence of poverty as a part of the inequality created by the labour market in capitalist economic systems. They point out that most of the groups in poverty are either excluded from the labour market - for example unemployed people, people over retirement age and people unable to work because of sickness or disability - or they are in a weak position in the labour market and thus tend to be restricted to low paid, often casual and insecure work - for example, workers with few skills and those who experience discrimination, such as women, black people and people with disabilities.

This line of argument has been developed by Peter Townsend (1979, 1987). Townsend argues that poverty is closely related to class. The majority of the poor occupy (or have occupied) unskilled or semi-skilled jobs. In his more recent work Townsend points to the large numbers of women and black people who also suffer from poverty because of the disadvantages they face in the labour market. He argues that the concept of the poor forming an *underclass* has some validity. However, unlike Murray, Townsend argues the poor are an underclass not because of their personal inadequacy or the 'over-generosity' of the welfare state, but because they are excluded from the opportunities for employment available to others. For most people in capitalist society, well paid employment offers the best opportunity to escape poverty.

For Townsend (1987) the growth of poverty in cities like London in the 1980s is directly linked to widening inequalities in the labour market encouraged by government free market policies. For example, the abolition of Wages Councils which set minimum wages in certain industries has resulted in lower wages for many workers. This has had an impact on groups outside the labour market such as those dependent on state benefits since benefits are generally set at a rate below the lowest earnings.

For writers like Townsend poverty will only be tackled effectively by radical social policies. The state must redistribute resources from the rich to the poor and direct investment towards social priorities such as housing and education. State intervention can change the system of social inequality which causes poverty.

Townsend's view of class, power and poverty is largely Weberian (see pp35-36 for Weber's view of class). He sees a number of powerful groups ranging from capitalists to professionals whose rewards and privileges are gained in part at the expense of others. He sees the possibility of the state acting independently of such groups and reshaping the class system for the benefit of those at the bottom.

Criticisms Marxists have criticised these views. They argue that the capitalist class is the dominant group in capitalist society and that the state will inevitably represent its interests. Given this, it is naive to even hope that the state will make significant reductions in social inequality.

Marxist structural explanations of poverty: capitalism as the cause of poverty

Marxists argue that poverty in capitalist society can only be understood in terms of the economic system. Money is the main motivation for work. Unequal monetary rewards motivate workers to compete for higher wages. And capitalism requires highly motivated workers.

Jack Kincaid (1973) develops this argument. He sees the low wage sector as an inevitable feature of a capitalist society. This benefits employers in a number of ways. It provides a pool of cheap labour. It creates divisions within the working class - a united working class might threaten capitalism. It drives down the level of benefits available to those outside the labour force. Benefits for groups such as the unemployed must be kept low or there would be no incentive to work. Given the importance of the low wage sector to capitalism, it is unrealistic to hope for its abolition by the state.

Marxists argue that to focus on the poor can divert attention from the real cause of poverty - the social inequality generated by the capitalist system. It follows that any solution to poverty must involve the abolition of capitalism.

Criticisms Critics of Marxism argue that it fails to explain why some groups are more prone to poverty than others, for example the particular vulnerability of women and black people. Moreover, writers like Townsend point out that the state can influence the operation of the labour market, often in opposition to capitalist interests. For example, employment protection legislation provides workers with protection against unfair dismissal and the Equal Opportunities Commission attempts to ensure equal pay for women.

Activity 8 Explaining Poverty

Item A *The labour market and poverty*
A major reason for the existence of poverty lies in the inequalities in occupational rewards, created by a highly stratified labour market. Large sections of the population are denied access to work which has good pay, security, and otherwise good conditions. The existence of poverty is thus related to the fact that Britain is a hierarchically organised society. The direct implication of this is that, if poverty is to be reduced, Britain must become a less hierarchical society with a smaller proportion of national resources devoted to higher groups in society.

The fact that the majority of national resources are channelled through the individual wage system rather than say through the child benefit and social security systems also means that groups who are not part of the paid workforce or of the households of that workforce are put at a disadvantage. This would include people who are retired, disabled, chronically sick, long term unemployed and those in one parent families. They have been denied access to paid employment, conceded incomes equivalent in value to bare subsistence, attracted specially defined social status as minority groups, and accommodated, as a result, within the social structure as a kind of modern underclass.

Adapted from P. Townsend *Poverty in the United Kingdom*, 1979, pp916-922

Item B *Welfare and dependency*

Universal Welfare Provision (UWP) works its damaging effects on everyone, not just the poorest. However, the most unpardonably destructive effects are on those its supporters claim they want to help, the people at the bottom of the pile. Instead of encouraging them to aspire and struggle to improve their lives, UWP locks them tight into under-caste dependency. For example:

- It offers incentives for staying unemployed or underemployed, though work is the major source of independent dignity.
- It imposes on the most deprived, housing and neighbourhood conditions calculated to pen them in inhuman subjection and prevent privacy, pride and mobility.
- It facilitates the growth of fractured, fatherless families, depriving children of the disciplined, loving environment they need if they are to achieve personal autonomy.
- It encourages street-wise trickiness and short-term gratification incompatible with genuine freedom and self-improvement.
- By ridiculing competition and excellence, it deprives children of the welfare-dependent underclass of self-improvement through education - in the past the salvation of even the most disadvantaged.

I cannot emphasise too much that this is not their fault. Critics of UWP are not blaming the poor, as welfarist ideologies allege. On the contrary, these are the foremost victims of erroneous ideas and destructive policies imposed upon them by the paternalists, socialists and privileged members of the professional New Class. They deserve, and Britain needs, a radically different approach.

Adapted from D. Marsland 'Universal Welfare Provision Creates a Dependent Population' *Social Studies Review*, November 1989, p55

Item E *Attitudes of poor people*

In a number of important respects there seems to be a parallel between the description of Lewis of the culture of poverty, and our own first impressions of slum life in Nottingham. Certainly we observed the hopelessness and despair, we saw that our respondents did not participate to any significant degree in the 'major institutions' of the larger society, even in such organisations as trade unions where a basic self-interest might be assumed. However, except for the so-called 'problem families', the poorer households could not be said to be culturally distinct from the richer. They appeared to respond to the same values, to share the same basic assumptions, to accept similar restraints. Their hopes for the future may not have been as high as those in mainstream society but there was no indication that this was due to a culture of poverty. More probably it was simply a 'realistic' appraisal of their possibilities, given that they had so little power at their disposal to change them.

Adapted from K. Coates and R. Silburn *Poverty: the Forgotten Englishmen*, 1970, pp153, 167

Item C *The 'uses' of poverty*

The existence, even the creation, of a group identified as the poor serves to set them apart from the rest of the population. The result is not just that the working class is divided and thereby weakened. Rather, the use of the poor as a reference group persuades those sections of society (which are neither wealthy nor poor) that their lot in terms of status, resources and power is acceptable. Consequently, the possibility that they will strive to change the position of the elite is reduced. Further, the poor act as a warning. They demonstrate the fate of those who do not conform to prevailing work and social standards. Their plight is needed to reinforce the will of others to work for low returns in unpleasant and even degrading conditions from which the economic output gives a disproportionate financial reward to a minority of existing reward holders. Not least, those in poverty act as scapegoats, a vulnerable group on whom the blame for social problems can be placed, so diverting attention away from that minority which has some control over social affairs.

Adapted from R. Holman 'Another Model of Poverty' in E. Butterworth and R. Holman (eds) *Social Welfare in Modern Britain*, 1975, p411

Item D *Growing up in poverty*

Questions

1 a) How and why would Townsend (Item A) and Marsland (Item B) differ in their solutions to poverty?
   b) Which of these theories of poverty do you find more convincing? Give reasons for your answer.
2 Whose interests does Holman (Item C) imply are served by the existence of poverty? Do you agree with him?
3 Look at Item D. How might children such as these be disadvantaged by growing up in poverty?
4 To what extent do the findings of Coates and Silburn in Item E support the theory of a culture of poverty?

2.5 The welfare state and social inequality

It is generally assumed that the welfare state represents the main means by which poverty and the more extreme forms of social inequality are dealt with in societies like the United Kingdom. This section examines the extent to which the British welfare state does in fact reduce social inequalities.

The welfare state and class inequalities

Many advocates of the welfare state hoped that it would lead to greater social equality by redistributing resources from the rich to the poor. For example, the social democratic thinker R.H. Tawney (1931) described the welfare state as a 'strategy for equality'. Studies from the 1960s onwards show that in relative terms the gap between the top and bottom of society has not narrowed. In fact there is evidence that since 1979 the gap has widened and relative poverty has increased. Two major studies showed that the real incomes after housing costs of the poorest 10% had actually fallen between 1979 and 1991 (see pp180; 188). Though the welfare state may have prevented an even greater widening of income inequality, it does not appear to have been successful as a 'strategy for equality'.

John Westergaard and Henrietta Resler question the view that the welfare state has any real impact on class inequalities. In a detailed analysis of data on taxation and welfare benefits, they argue that:

'Taken together the various social services result in some narrowing of inequalities of real income. But they reshuffle resources far more *within* classes - between earners and dependents, healthy people and the sick, households of different composition, from one point in an individual's life cycle to another - than they do *between* classes' (1976, p176, italics added).

The benefits of groups in the working class such as the elderly, unemployed and lone parents are largely paid for by other tax payers in the working class. The result is a redistribution of resources within rather than between classes.

Julian Le Grand's *The Strategy of Equality* (1982) provides a wide ranging review of the effects of taxation and welfare on social inequality. Le Grand finds little evidence of a redistribution of resources from rich to poor. In fact in a number of areas the state appears to spend more on the rich.

Health care In his examination of spending on health from 1978-79, Le Grand argues that:

'There is no consistent pattern favouring either the higher or the lower socio-economic groups in so far as expenditure per person is concerned. But if differences in need are taken into account a rather different picture emerges ... with the highest group (professional employers, managers and their families) receiving over 40% more than the lowest group (semi-skilled and unskilled manual workers and their families)' (1982, pp25-26).

Evidence of reported illness indicates that manual workers have a greater need for health services than non-manual workers. On this basis the lowest socioeconomic groups have least spent on them in proportion to their need.

Le Grand argues that the National Health Service has done little to reduce the differences in health chances between the classes. Support for this view comes from the *Black Report* (see pp442-443). Evidence from the *Black Report* indicates that while mortality rates have fallen for all social classes, they have fallen fastest in the higher classes, leading to a widening of inequalities in health.

Education Le Grand argues that education provides a clearcut picture of greater state expenditure on the higher socioeconomic groups. The top group in fact receives about one and a quarter times the average public expenditure, and one and a half times as much as the lowest group. This is because, 'although people in the top socioeconomic group received slightly less state expenditure on primary and secondary education for pupils under 16 (presumably because they made greater use of private education), they receive substantially more expenditure in all other sectors' (for example further education and universities) (1982, p58). Middle class children are more likely to stay on in education after the age of sixteen and in particular go on to higher education, the most expensive sector.

Again there is support from other research for Le Grand. The findings of the Oxford Mobility study (Halsey et al 1980) showed that an increasing proportion of men from all classes had attended universities after 1944. However, the relative proportions of each class had remained much the same with the largest proportion of places still being taken by the sons of the service class (professionals, employers and managers).

Housing In terms of state expenditure on housing, Le Grand's evidence indicates that the lower socioeconomic groups benefit most. In particular, they are helped by subsidies for council housing and rent rebates (now housing benefits). However, if we look at home buyers it is those with the largest mortgages who gain most from tax concessions. And these people are usually better off.

Recent government policies have, however, reduced subsidies to council tenants and reduced public sector housing stocks. This has worsened the housing position of many low income families. For example, official statistics on unintentionally homeless households show that their numbers increased from 70,010 in 1981 to 167,000 in 1992. On the other hand the right to buy for council tenants has meant that many more working class people have become owner occupiers. Supporters of privatisation of housing argue that this has led to a reduction in inequality in access to home ownership.

Transport It is commonly believed that private cars are used more by the middle class and public transport by the poorest groups. However, Le Grand's research reveals that it is the middle class who make greatest use of public transport, for example in commuting to work. Poor people are not only unlikely to own cars and benefit from government expenditure on roads but also benefit less from subsidies to rail and bus transport since they cannot afford to travel much. Le Grand thus claims that state subsidies to all forms of transport disproportionately benefit the higher social classes.

The welfare state and gender inequalities

The state has attempted to reduce inequalities between men and women. The Equal Pay Act (1970) and the Sex Discrimination Act (1975) aimed to provide equal opportunities in the labour market. It is difficult to measure the effects of such legislation. However, since 1975 women's earnings have remained on average 75% of those of men and women are still concentrated in low pay, low status 'women's jobs'.

The picture in education is brighter. State policies of equal opportunity may have helped to close the gap between males and females in terms of public examination results and access to higher education (see p304).

But in other ways the welfare state is seen to promote gender inequality. According to Linda McDowell, women provide a large proportion of the workforce in many welfare occupations often in part time and low paid jobs, such as nursing, health service ancillaries and social work. Women also make up most of the workforce in the informal sector of welfare, as carers in the family. McDowell argues that 'attributes that are used to define femininity such as patience, dexterity, sympathy and tolerance for others' weakness are all used to construct these occupations as "women's work" and to justify their low pay' (1989, p187). McDowell goes on to argue that since 1979 the government's emphasis on the family as a source of welfare and on the need for a return to 'Victorian values' has placed even greater pressure on women to act as carers.

The welfare state and racial inequalities

The contradictions in the approach of the welfare state towards sexual inequalities are also apparent in its policies on race. British governments have passed a series of Race Relations Acts (in 1965, 1968 and 1976) which have attempted to outlaw racial discrimination in areas such as housing and employment.

Have these measures reduced social inequalities between ethnic minorities and the mainstream population? As Chapter 3 shows, it is difficult to measure the effects of the Race Relations Acts. On the one hand a survey of available evidence shows that 'racial discrimination remains rampant in virtually all aspects of life in Britain' (Ouseley, 1990). On the other hand the Commission for Racial Equality has won some important test cases which have at least forced those who discriminate to reconsider their actions (see p92).

Despite the apparently liberal approach of the Race Relations Acts, Andrew Pilkington (1984) points out that state policies in other areas - such as immigration control - have discriminated against ethnic minorities. He suggests that a series of increasingly tight controls on immigration from the New Commonwealth since 1962 have been influenced as much by public fears about Britain being 'swamped' by black immigrants, as by any economic problems caused by immigration. In addition the complexity of immigration rules means that members of some ethnic minorities fear that they may be defined as illegal immigrants and this may deter them from claiming social security benefits to which they are entitled (Tarpey, 1984).

A report by the Commission for Racial Equality (1984) suggests discrimination may also take place in local authority housing provision. An investigation of the London borough of Hackney's policies revealed that black people tended to be allocated to less desirable council properties than whites. For example, black families were more likely to be in flats rather than houses, in older properties and on less desirable estates. Critics have pointed out the contradictions of a state which on the one hand promotes racial equality while on the other allows discrimination to occur in its own practices.

Social inequalities in the UK: the 1980s and 90s

In 1994 two major studies on the distribution of income were published (Goodman and Webb; Jenkins). Both showed a widening of income inequality throughout the 1980s and early 90s. In other words the gap between rich and poor increased. Both showed a reduction in real income after housing costs for those on the lowest income levels. In other words the living standards of the poor had fallen. In the light of this evidence the welfare state as a 'strategy for equality' had failed.

More than this, the state may well have contributed to this growth in social inequality by:

1 **Changes in benefits** Greater selectivity in benefits, tighter tests of eligibility and the fact that benefit levels have not kept pace with earnings have hit those most dependent on the welfare state.

2 **Changes in taxation** There were major tax reductions for high earners in the 1980s but lower income groups have suffered an increased tax burden (see Activity 9).

3 **The labour market** High levels of unemployment and the growth of part time and casual employment, combined with the weakening of trade union rights and of employment legislation protecting workers have all tended to increase the number of low paid and unemployed workers.

The role of the welfare state

This section has examined the extent to which the welfare state has reduced social inequality in Britain. It has argued that since many aspects of social inequality have grown, particularly during the 1980s and 90s, that the welfare state as a 'strategy for equality' has failed. However, to judge the welfare state simply on this basis reflects the values of the researcher.

It could be just as easily argued that it is not the job of the welfare state to promote social equality. Instead its job is to provide a safety net below which no one should be allowed to fall. And this may lead

to a very different judgement of its effectiveness. But again, to judge the welfare state on this basis reflects the values of the researcher. Whatever the values involved, one thing is clear. Judging from the experience of those at the bottom of the stratification system, poverty is a social evil. It can lead to desperation and despair, it can destroy families and ruin lives. In view of this, debates about the welfare state are not just academic, they are vital to the lives of millions of people.

Summary

1 Sociologists differ over how poverty should be defined and measured. Support for different definitions of poverty is related to different views about welfare provision and social inequality.

2 The definitions used to measure poverty are of crucial importance in answering questions about the extent of poverty. In general, measurement in terms of relative concepts suggests that poverty is far more widespread in the United Kingdom than measurement in terms of absolute concepts. Sociologists using a variety of relative definitions claim that the numbers in poverty in the UK have increased in the last decade.

3 Research indicates that some groups are more vulnerable to poverty than others, especially those who are excluded from the labour market by old age, sickness, disability and unemployment and those in a weak position in the labour market such as the low paid. Poverty is also related to class, gender and racial inequalities.

4 Different sociological perspectives provide different explanations for poverty in capitalist societies. Some emphasise cultural factors, others see economic factors as more significant. Most sociologists argue that the causes of poverty are to be found in the structure of society rather than the behaviour of individuals.

5 Most evidence suggests that the welfare state does little to reduce economic inequalities in society and its impact on gender and racial inequalities has been limited. Whether or not the creation of greater equality is a desirable aim for the welfare state depends on the theoretical perspective on welfare and the values which underlie it.

Activity 9 Social Inequalities

Item A

Percentage distribution of total original and post-tax income of households, adjusted for family size, divided into quintile groups (fifths), United Kingdom

Original Income	1979 %	1990 %
Quintile group		
Bottom	2.4	2
2nd	10	7
3rd	18	15
4th	27	25
Top	43	51
Post-tax income		
Quintile group		
Bottom	9.5	6.3
2nd	13	10
3rd	18	15
4th	23	23
Top	37	45

This table shows the distribution of household income. Two measures of income are used: *original income* (ie income before any taxes and benefits have been paid) and *post-tax income* (ie income after direct and indirect taxes and cash benefits). Both measures of income are adjusted for family size. Households are divided into fifths from poorest to richest. These are known as *quintile* groups.

Adapted from *Economic Trends*, January 1993

Item B

Distributional effects of tax and benefit changes 1979-92, by income decile (tenths)

Decile	Average gain/loss (£ per week)	% gaining	% losing
First (poorest)	−1	48	40
Second	2	66	24
Third	2	65	27
Fourth	4	69	24
Fifth	9	81	13
Sixth	13	84	10
Seventh	15	85	10
Eighth	21	89	7
Ninth	25	90	7
Tenth (richest)	87	92	6
All	18	77	17

From E. Davis et al *Alternative Proposals on Tax and Social Security*, Commentary No 29, Institute for Fiscal Studies, 1992

Item C *Tax cuts*

While the economy boomed in the mid-eighties and the rich got richer, the poor got poorer - not just because they failed to join in with the moneymakers, but also because the tax cuts introduced from 1986 onwards had a disproportionate effect on low income groups. While the average gain for all groups was about £7 per week, more than 70% of households gained £5 or less. Nearly a half of all the money spent on the tax and benefit system went to the richest 10% of the population.

Relaxing at the Henley Royal Regatta, an annual event in the calendar of the wealthy

The overall tax burden increased for those on low incomes during the eighties. In 1979, a married couple on 75% of average earnings paid just over 30% of their gross earnings in tax. By 1989 this had risen to nearly 34%. At the same time the richest 1% have seen their unearned income rise by 89% since the 1989 budget, and over the past ten years by 346%, as a result of tax cuts and salary increases.

Adapted from N. Fielding 'The Thatcher Audit' *New Statesman and Society*, 21/28 December 1990

Questions

1 Look at the distribution of income shown in Item A.
   a) How do taxes and benefits affect the different income groups?
   b) How has this changed since 1979?
2 Summarise the distributional effects of the tax and benefits changes shown in Item B.
3 Using data from Items A, B and C assess the view that the welfare state helps to reduce social inequality.

References

Abel-Smith, B. and Townsend, P. *The Poor and the Poorest* (Bell and Sons, London, 1965)

Allan, G. *Family Life* (Blackwell, Oxford, 1985)

Althusser, L. *For Marx* (Penguin, Harmondsworth, 1969)

Ashton, P. 'Poverty and its Beholders' *New Society*, 18.10.1984

Barrett, M. *Women's Oppression Today* (Verso, London, 1980)

Brown, C. *Black and White Britain: the Third PSI Survey* (Policy Studies Institute, London, 1984)

Bryson, L. *Welfare and the State* (Macmillan, Basingstoke, 1992)

Coates, K. and Silburn R. *Poverty: the Forgotten Englishmen* (Penguin, Harmondsworth, 1970)

Commission for Racial Equality *Hackney Housing Investigated: Summary of Formal Investigation Report* (CRE, London, 1984)

Davis, E. et al *Alternative Proposals on Tax and Social Security*, Commentary no 29, (Institute for Fiscal Studies, London, 1992)

Department of Health and Social Security *Income Related Benefits - Estimates of Take-up 1989* (Government Statistical Service, 1993)

Donnison, D. *The Politics of Poverty* (Martin Robertson, London, 1982)

Equal Opportunities Commission *The Experience of Caring for Elderly and Handicapped Dependents: Survey Report* (Equal Opportunities Commission, Manchester, 1980)

Equal Opportunities Commission *Who Cares for the Carers?* (Equal Opportunities Commission, Manchester, 1982)

Field, F. *Losing Out: the Emergence of Britain's Underclass* (Blackwell, Oxford, 1989)

Fielding, N. 'The Thatcher Audit', *New Statesman and Society*, 21/28.12.1990

Finch, J. 'Community Care: Developing Non-Sexist Alternatives' *Critical Social Policy*, Issue 9, 1984

Finch, J. and Groves, D. A. *Labour of Love: Women Work and Caring* (Routledge and Kegan Paul, London, 1983)

Forrest, R. and Murie, A. 'Fiscal Reorientation, Centralisation and the Privatisation of Council Housing' in L. McDowell, P. Sarre and C. Hamnet (eds) *Divided Nation: Social and Cultural Change in Britain* (Hodder and Stoughton/Open University, London, 1989)

Frayman, H. *Breadline Britain 1990s: the Findings of the Television Series* (London Weekend Television, London, 1991)

Friedman, M. and Friedman, R. *Free to Choose* (Penguin, Harmondsworth, 1980)

George, V. and Wilding, P. *Ideology and Social Welfare* (Routledge and Kegan Paul, London, 1985)

Ginsberg, N. *Class, Capital and Social Policy* (Macmillan, London, 1979)

Glendinning, C. and Millar, J. *Women and Poverty in the Twentieth Century* (Wheatsheaf, Brighton, 1987)

Goffman, E. *Asylums* (Penguin, Harmondsworth, 1968)

Goodman, A. and Webb, S. *For Richer for Poorer: the Changing Distribution of Income in the UK 1961-1991* (Institute for Fiscal Studies, London, 1994)

Green, D.G. and Lucas, D. 'Private Welfare in the 1980s' in N. Manning and R. Page (eds) *Social Policy Review 4* (Social Policy Association, Glasgow, 1992)

Halsey, A.H., Heath, A.F. and Ridge J.M. *Origins and Destinations: Family, Class and Education in Modern Britain*, (Clarendon Press, Oxford, 1980)

Harloe, M. and Paris, C. 'The Decollectivization of Consumption: Housing and Local Government Finance in England and Wales, 1979-1981' in L. McDowell, P. Sarre and C. Hamnet (eds) *Divided Nation: Social and Cultural Change in Britain* (Hodder and Stoughton/Open University, London, 1989)

Hayek, F.A. *The Road to Serfdom* (Routledge and Kegan Paul, London, 1976)

Holman, R. 'Another Model of Poverty' in E. Butterworth and R. Holman (eds) *Social Welfare in Modern Britain* (Fontana, Glasgow, 1975)

Jenkins, S.P. *Winners and Losers: A Portrait of the UK Income Distribution During the 1980s* (University College of Swansea, Swansea, 1994)

Johnson, N. *The Welfare State in Transition: The Theory and Practice of Welfare Pluralism* (Wheatsheaf, Brighton, 1987)

Joseph, K. *Stranded on Middle Ground*, (Centre for Policy Studies, London, 1976)

Kincaid, J.C. *Poverty and Equality in Britain: a Study of Social Security and Taxation* (Penguin, Harmondsworth, 1975)

Land, H. 'Sex Role Stereotyping in the Social Security and Income Tax Systems' in J. Chetwynd and O. Hartnett (eds) *The Sex Role System* (Routledge and Kegan Paul, London, 1978)

Le Grand, J. *The Strategy of Equality* (George Allen and Unwin, London, 1982)

Lewis, O. *La Vida* (Panther Books, London, 1968)

Low Pay Unit *Low Pay in Great Britain and the Regions* Low Pay Unit Parliamentary Briefing no 1, (Low Pay Unit, London, 1990)

Mack, J. and Lansley, S. *Poor Britain* (Allen and Unwin, London, 1985)

Mandel, E. *Marxist Economic Theory* (Merlin Press, London, 1968)

Mangin, W. 'Poverty and Politics in the Cities of Latin America' in W. Bloomberg and H.J. Schmandt (eds) *Urban Poverty: its Social and Political Dimensions* (Sage, Beverly Hills, 1968)

Marshall, T.H. *Sociology at the Crossroads* (Heinemann, London, 1963)

Marsland, D. 'Universal Welfare Provision Creates a Dependent Population' *Social Studies Review*, November 1989

McDowell, L. 'Gender Divisions' in C. Hamnet, L. McDowell and P. Sarre (eds) *The Changing Social Structure* (Sage/Open University, London, 1989)

Miliband, R. *The State in Capitalist Society* (Weidenfeld and Nicholson, London, 1969)

Murray, C. *The Emerging British Underclass* (Institute for Economic Affairs, London,1990)

Norris, D. 'Time to Abolish the Welfare State' *Daily Mail*, 28.2.1994

O'Connor, J. *The Fiscal Crisis of the State* (St. Martin's Press, New York, 1973)

Offe, C. 'Some Contradictions of the Modern Welfare State' *Critical Social Policy* vol 2 no 2, Autumn 1982

Oldfield, N. and Yu, A.C.S. *The Cost of a Child: Living Standards for the 1990s* (Child Poverty Action Group, London, 1993)

Oppenheim, C. *Poverty: The Facts* (Child Poverty Action Group, London, 1990 and 1993)

Oppenheim, C. *The Welfare State: Putting the Record Straight* (Child Poverty Action Group, London, 1994)

Ouseley, H. 'Resisting Institutional Change' in W. Ball and J. Solomos (eds) *Race and Local Politics* (Macmillan, Basingstoke, 1990)

Page, R.M. 'Social Policy' in M. Haralambos (ed) *Developments in Sociology* vol 9 (Causeway Press, Ormskirk, 1993)

Parker, G. *With Due Care and Attention* (Family Policy Studies Centre, London, 1985)

Pascall, G. *Social Policy: A Feminist Analysis* (Tavistock, London, 1986)

Piachaud, D. 'Peter Townsend and the Holy Grail' *New Society*, 10.9.1981

Piachaud, D. 'The Poor get Poorer' *New Society*, 5.6.1987

Pilkington, A. *Race Relations in Britain* (Unwin Hyman, London, 1984)

Rowntree, S. *Poverty: A Study of Town Life* (Macmillan, London, 1901)

Rowntree, S. *Poverty and Progress* (Longman, London, 1941)

Rowntree, S. and Lavers, G. *Poverty and the Welfare State* (Longman, London, 1951)

Rutter, M. and Madge, N. *Cycles of Disadvantage: a Review of*

Research (Heinemann, London, 1976)

Saunders, P. 'Beyond Housing Classes: the Sociological Significance of Private Property Rights in Means of Consumption' in L. McDowell, P. Sarre and C. Hamnett (eds) *Divided Nation: Social and Cultural Change in Britain* (Hodder and Stoughton/The Open University, London, 1989)

Saville, J. 'The Welfare State: An Historical Approach' in E. Butterworth and R. Holman (eds) *Social Welfare in Modern Britain* (Fontana, Glasgow, 1975)

Scull, A. *Decarceration: Community Treatment and the Deviant - a Radical View* (Polity Press, London, 1984)

Seabrook, J. 'Beveridge's Five Evils Return' *New Society* 28.2.1985

Segalman, R. and Marsland, D. *Cradle to Grave: Comparative Perspectives on the State of Welfare* (Macmillan in association with the Social Affairs Unit, London, 1989)

Sharkey, P. 'The Sociology of Welfare' in M. Haralambos (ed) *Developments in Sociology*, vol 3 (Causeway Press, Ormskirk, 1986)

Tawney, R. *Equality* (Allen and Unwin, London, 1931)

Taylor-Gooby, P. 'Citizenship and Welfare' in R. Jowell , S. Witherspoon and L. Brook (eds) *British Social Attitudes: The 7th Report* (Gower, Aldershot, 1990)

Timmins, N. 'Moore Says Poverty Levels are Exaggerated' *Independent*, 12.5.1989

Titmuss, R.M. *Essays on the Welfare State* (Allen and Unwin, London, 1963)

Titmuss, R.M. *Commitment to Welfare* (Allen and Unwin, London, 1968)

Townsend, P. *Poverty in the United Kingdom* (Penguin, Harmondsworth, 1979)

Townsend, P. with Corrigan, P. and Kowarzik, U. *Poverty and Labour in London* (Low Pay Unit, London, 1987)

Townsend, P. and Davidson N. *Inequalities in Health* (Penguin, Harmondsworth, 1982)

Westergaard, J. and Resler, H. *Class in a Capitalist Society* (Penguin, Harmondsworth, 1975)

6 Politics and Power

Introduction

For many people politics is an activity carried on by middle aged men - and a few women - at Westminster. It appears distant and removed from their everyday lives. Sociologists, however, see politics as an integral part of everyday life. When young people accept or reject the authority of teachers and parents, when a man puts a woman down for suggesting she is better informed than he, when a black person is refused a job because the employer is looking for a white person, these are all political acts. They all involve the exercise of power. Politics from this viewpoint covers any situation where an individual or a group has power over others.

Sociologists are interested in both the politics of everyday life and the broader structures of power in society as a whole. Their view of power is not limited to the activities of politicians. Decisions made at Westminster do affect our lives, but so for example do decisions taken by financiers and investors in the City which may result in significant changes in employment levels, mortgage rates and prices in the high street.

Power is an important dimension of social stratification. This chapter focuses on how power is distributed and exercised in British society. It forms a part of the wider discussion of stratification included in the chapters on class, gender and race.

Chapter summary

- Part 1 looks at the problems of **defining** and **measuring power**. It then considers the role of the **state** and the nature of **democracy**.
- Part 2 looks at **pluralism**, a theory which claims that Western societies such as Britain and the USA are democratic. It also examines the role of **political parties** and **pressure groups** in the democratic process.
- Part 3 looks at **elite theory** and **Marxism**, theories which see power concentrated in the hands of a small minority. It then examines the politics of **gender** and **race** and considers power on an **international** level.
- Part 4 looks at how people vote in British elections and considers a variety of social influences on **voting behaviour**.

1 Power and Political Systems

Key Issues

1 What are the problems of defining and measuring power?
2 How have modern nation states developed?
3 What are the problems in distinguishing between democratic and non-democratic political systems?

1.1 Defining and measuring power

Power is a 'contested concept' - in other words there is no agreed definition. The debate about how power should be defined and measured underlies many of the broader debates about how power is distributed in society (see Part 2).

Max Weber: power and authority

Max Weber's work is often taken as a starting point in the study of power. Weber defined power as 'the chance of a man or a number of men to realise their own will in a communal action even against the resistance of others'. Power is unequally distributed if some are more successful than others in achieving their aims.

Weber identified two types of power, *authority* and *coercion*. Authority is the exercise of power which is regarded as legitimate. Weber regards authority as the more effective form of power as it is based on the consent of those who are subject to it. Coercion is the exercise of power which is regarded as illegitimate. People are therefore forced to obey. Both forms of power are backed up by the threat of force though in practice this is more important for coercion than authority. Compare a demand for money from a tax inspector and an armed robber. The former is based on authority, the latter on coercion, the threat of force being more important to the robber for the successful exercise of power.

Weber identified three types of authority.

1 **Charismatic authority** This type of authority is based on the 'charisma' or personal qualities of the leader. Many religious and political leaders in history have attracted followers by the power of their personalities. Examples include Jesus Christ, Fidel Castro and Adolf Hitler. However, ordinary people may also exercise charismatic authority, for example one teacher may be able to control her pupils much more effectively than another because her personality inspires awe, admiration or affection.

2 **Traditional authority** This type of authority is based on established customs and traditions which dictate that certain individuals should hold power. In the Middle Ages the power of the king and the nobility was based on inherited positions. Tradition dictated that positions of power were passed on from father to son and that 'vassals' or subordinates owed certain obligations to their lords. The British monarchy and hereditary peerages in the House of Lords remain examples of this type of authority in modern Britain.

3 **Rational legal authority** This type of authority derives from impersonal rules which give the holders of certain positions or offices power over their subordinates. In armies a leader may be obeyed because his soldiers admire his courage and qualities of leadership (charismatic authority) or because members of his family have traditionally been military leaders (traditional authority). However, in a modern army an officer is obeyed primarily because rules and regulations stipulate who is able to give orders to whom.

Weber saw rational legal authority as the dominant form of authority in industrial societies. Not only armies but political, industrial, religious and educational organisations were based on rational legal authority. They were organised on bureaucratic lines with structures of authority determined by rational rules designed to ensure that the most competent individuals exercised power in order to achieve the goals of the organisation. (See pp358-361 for further discussion of rational legal organisations).

Weber's types of authority are 'ideal types'. Ideal does not mean best but pure. An ideal type is a model of the purest type. In reality ideal types do not exist. For example, traditional authority may contain aspects of charismatic and rational-legal authority. However, ideal types are useful for describing, classifying and comparing things in the real world.

Stephen Lukes: three faces of power

Stephen Lukes (1974) argues that power has three dimensions - the 'three faces of power'. An understanding of power requires an awareness of all three faces.

The first face of power: success in decision making
This approach has been adopted by pluralists such as Robert Dahl and Nelson Polsby. Pluralist theories argue that power can be seen from the outcome of a decision making process (see Section 2.1 for a discussion of pluralism). Dahl argues that 'A has power over B to the extent that he can get B to do something that B would not otherwise do' (1957). In order to study how power is distributed pluralists favour what is often termed the *issue method*. Polsby (1963), for example, argues that sociologists should study specific issues in order to determine who actually gets their own way in the decision making process. Those who are most frequently successful in getting the outcomes they want will have most power. For example, if Parliament passes a law on car emissions which is supported by the AA and the RAC but opposed by environmental organisations, then in this instance the car interest groups have more power than the environmental groups. In practice most studies based on this method suggest that no one group dominates decision making in Western democracies. Instead they paint a picture of many groups exercising some degree of political power.

The second face of power: managing the agenda
Critics of the pluralist view, such as Peter Bachrach and Morton Baratz (1962) argue that simply studying decision making ignores a second dimension of power: the ability to control the agenda for debate. In their view real power lies in the ability to prevent certain issues from being seriously considered. This means that those issues will never reach the point of decision making, they will remain 'non-decisions'. For example, a local council might be asked to vote on a number of alternative packages of cuts in expenditure. A pluralist would argue that the group supporting whichever set of cuts were actually decided would hold power in this situation. However, this ignores the question of who set the agenda, of who decided that the choice was between various cuts rather than other possibilities such as no cuts or even increases in expenditure. In this situation real power might lie in the hands of those who had succeeded in keeping the issue of whether cuts were necessary off the agenda.

The third face of power: manipulating the wishes of others Lukes argues that, although the second view of power represents a step forward, it still ignores a third dimension. This view sees power as the ability to shape the wishes and desires of others. Those others are persuaded that both they and the powerful share the same interests - what's good for the powerful is good for everybody. And this may allow the powerful to increase their wealth, prestige and privilege at the expense of others. Marxists take this view of power when they see a ruling class exploiting a subject class. Members of the subject class are unaware of this exploitation and unknowingly contribute to it by their acceptance of ruling class ideology. This imposed consensus about what is normal and reasonable may rule out a consideration of alternatives which might challenge the dominance of the powerful. (See Section 3.2 for Marxist views of power).

Lukes' own view of power shares certain aspects of this third face of power. In his view, 'A exercises power over B when A affects B in a manner contrary to B's interests', whether or not B knows that his or her interests are being harmed (1974, p27).

Further views of power

Zero sum approach The views discussed so far tend to see power as something which some hold to the extent it is not held by others. Thus if a powerful group holds 90% of the available power, this leaves only 10% for the rest of society. There is a fixed amount of power and the more one group holds, the less there is for others. This view is known as the zero sum approach to power.

Variable sum approach The American sociologist Talcott Parsons (1967) rejects the zero sum approach. He argues that power is something which resides in society as a whole and can increase or decrease according to how effectively the social system is able to achieve agreed social goals. For example, if improving living standards is a major goal, then society's power will increase to the degree that living standards improve. Or it can decrease, as in societies such as Bosnia in the 1990s, where central political authority broke down and civil war largely prevented the achievement of many social goals. In this sense power is not fixed or constant, it is variable - it can increase or decrease. As a result, this view is sometimes known as the variable sum approach to power.

This type of approach has received renewed interest from sociologists such as Anthony Giddens (1981, 1985) and Michael Mann (1986, 1993). Mann, for example, points out that modern institutions (such as states, armies and economic organisations) have much greater power than their equivalents in the past. This is because they have much greater *organisational effectiveness*. The modern state for example can intervene far more extensively in people's lives than those of the past because it has a large and powerful bureaucracy which can tax, supervise and police the conduct of the people it governs. In this respect societal power is variable - modern states are able to exercise a far greater amount of power than pre-modern states.

Activity 1 Faces of Authority

Item A *Adolf Hitler*

Item B *A judge*

Item C *A headteacher*

Item D *Henry VIII*

Questions

1 Match each Item with one of Weber's three types of authority (traditional, charismatic or rational legal). Give reasons for your choice.
2 Weber's types of authority are 'ideal types'. In practice authority may be a mixture of two or three types. Briefly explain this using the Items in this activity and other examples.

Activity 2 Faces of Power

Item A *Power and decision making*

Let us take the simplest possible situation to test for the existence of a ruling elite - that is a small powerful group that dominates society. Assume that there are a number of key political choices. The so-called ruling elite prefers one set of choices and its wishes are opposed by others. For a ruling elite to exist all or nearly all of its choices must be adopted. If they are not, then there is no justification for claiming that an elite rules. I do not see how anyone can suppose that they have established the dominance of a specific group in a community or a nation without basing their analysis on a careful examination of a series of concrete decisions.

Adapted from R. Dahl 'A Critique of the Ruling Elite Model' in J. Urry and J. Wakeford (eds) *Power in Britain*, 1973, p286

Item B *Power and non-decision making*

Matthew Crenson carried out a study in the United States to try to discover how and why air pollution became a political issue in some American cities much earlier than in others. Crenson showed that differences in the politics of air pollution were not simply attributable to differences in the actual level of pollution. He compared two neighbouring cities in Indiana, both equally polluted and both with similar populations. The first, East Chicago, took action to clear the air in 1949, while the other, Gary, did nothing until 1962.

For many years air pollution was not considered an important political issue.

Crenson argues that US Steel, which had built the town of Gary and was responsible for its prosperity, managed for many years to block the issue of air pollution from even being raised. When an air pollution ordinance was finally enacted, US Steel also managed to influence its content in its own favour. US Steel did all this without directly intervening in the political arena and was able to exert influence mainly by its reputation for power rather than by actual acts of power. Executives from the corporation took no clear stance on the air pollution issue and never directly opposed anti-pollution activists. Thus a study of the decision making process would find it very difficult to pin down what US Steel's involvement was in this issue. An examination of concrete decisions would tell us little or nothing about the company's power.

Based on M. Crenson *The Un-Politics of Air Pollution: A Study of Non-decision Making in the Cities*, 1971

Item C *Power and ideology*

In every social group there are systems of beliefs, more or less shared, about the nature and appropriate behaviour of women and men. People organise their actions in the light of their knowledge of 'how things are done'; of what they can expect of others; and of what others can expect of them. If there were no agreement social life would be impossible. Some of these common understandings are explicit, external 'rules' imposed from outside. However, a great many are simply common assumptions that people make about how things should be done. They may not feel like assumptions or beliefs at all. Rather they may feel like the 'facts of life' which do not change and are not questioned.

One of the many things that prevents women from seeing new possibilities is that many of the basic assumptions that people make about women's roles are not explicitly verbalised. Some are of course. For example, there is a much publicised debate as to whether mothers should work, and how old their children should be when they do. Some questions on the other hand are never asked, even by research workers. Where is the questionnaire which asks whether it is right for fathers of young children to work, or whether they should have shorter working hours to allow them to take half-shares in housework and childcare? The answers to questions about what women 'ought' to do, depend partly on assumptions which are not stated.

Adapted from F. Fransella and K. Frost *On Being a Woman*, 1977, pp13-15

Questions

1 Use Items B and C to criticise Dahl's argument in Item A that the study of power should focus on 'concrete decisions'.

2 Crenson (Item B) uses the idea of 'non-decision making'. What does he mean by this? How might this idea be useful?

3 a) Give examples of the kinds of assumptions about women's roles referred to in Item C.

   b) How might these assumptions help to keep women in a subordinate position in society?

1.2 The state and political systems

Most sociologists see the state as the basis for political authority in large scale industrial societies. Some simple societies can be described as 'stateless societies' since there is no central political apparatus or source of authority. While the fully developed modern nation state has only emerged in the last few centuries, other types of state have a long history, for example the ancient civilisations of Greece, Rome, Egypt, China and Central and South America. This section considers the role of the modern state and the differences between democratic and non-democratic states.

The rise of the modern state

Weber defined the state as 'a human community that successfully claims the monopoly of the legitimate use of physical force within a given territory'. This definition implies that the state has authority over those who live in a defined geographical area and that it can use force to back up this authority. Other groups, such as those defined as terrorists, may use force to achieve their aims, but this is not usually regarded as legitimate by the majority of the population.

Modern nation states in Europe emerged with the rise of capitalism and the decline of the feudal system. From the sixteenth century onwards European monarchs began to impose much more effective control over their kingdoms. Rule by local nobles was replaced by professional administrators who were loyal to the monarch. Customary laws were replaced by written codes of laws. This led to the kind of state suggested by Weber's definition where only the central authority of the state could legitimately use force, unlike the Middle Ages when powerful nobles often had their own private armies. The borders of states became more clearly defined which led to a sense of nationality.

For Weber the rise of bureaucratically organised states was part of the growing process of *rationalisation* which accompanied the rise of capitalism (see pp360;505;526). Life became increasingly governed by written rules and subject to bureaucratic authority. Power was increasingly centralised in the state and exercised by elected or appointed office holders rather than traditional leaders with inherited positions.

Not all social scientists accept Weber's definition of the state. Many Marxist writers have extended the concept of the state to include any institutions through which the dominance of the ruling class is perpetuated. For example, the mass media, the law and education have been described as ideological state apparatuses since they are seen to reproduce ruling class ideology (Althusser, 1969). For Marxists the development of modern nation states is linked to the development of capitalism. The state acts to ensure that political decisions are taken which allow capitalists to continue accumulating wealth.

The state and democracy

While the nation state is now recognised as the basic political unit in large scale modern societies, the form this state takes varies widely. Most modern states broadly correspond to Weber's definition with an agreed territory and a central authority exercising control over it. However, the extent to which democracy characterises different states varies widely.

The origins of democracy The concept of democracy has its origins in the political system of the ancient Greek city state of Athens. The word 'democracy' is in fact derived from the Greek words *demos* (people) and *kratos* (power). Thus democracy means power in the hands of the people. In Athens in the 5th century BC assemblies of all citizens were held to discuss important issues. This type of democracy, often referred to as *participatory democracy* or *direct democracy*, directly involves all citizens in decision making. In practice, however, it often excluded large numbers of people - in Athens women and slaves who made up over half the adult population.

Participatory democracy presents problems in a society on the scale of a modern nation state. As a result most liberal democracies have developed some system of *representative democracy* or *indirect democracy*, which involves citizens choosing representatives who exercise power on their behalf.

Democracy in its modern form developed in the last two hundred years. Liberal ideas influenced the French and American revolutions at the end of the eighteenth century and demands for extension of the franchise (voting rights) in England in the nineteenth century. Liberal thinkers argued that all people should have equal rights under the law. It is a short step to demand that all citizens should elect the lawmakers and therefore have some influence over how the law is made.

Modern liberal democracy The right of citizens to elect their own representatives in regular and fair elections is a basic component of liberal democracy. Many liberal theorists would also include rights such as freedom of speech, freedom to oppose the sitting government, and equal treatment under the law, including the right to a fair trial and freedom from arbitrary arrest and imprisonment.

The extent to which liberal democracies such as the United Kingdom do in fact allow ordinary citizens to exercise power is open to debate and is examined further in Parts 2 and 3 of this chapter. However, some critics would argue that even in terms of liberal definitions of democracy the UK has a number of undemocratic features. These include the continued existence of an unelected monarchy and House of Lords, an unelected judiciary which has considerable powers to interpret the application of the law and a civil service which carries out many of its activities in secret with limited public scrutiny.

Alternative views of democracy Those who support alternative views of democracy challenge the claim that countries such as the USA and UK are in fact democracies. They argue that democracy goes beyond such rights as freedom of speech and freedom of opposition. They support a more participatory system whereby citizens become more involved in their own government. Tom Bottomore (1993), for example, claims that Britain has a system of government which 'remains semi-feudal and exceptionally elitist'. He argues that much more radical devolution of power to regional and local authorities would be a step towards a more participatory democracy. Another goal might be extension of democracy into the process of production of both goods and services (including education, health and social welfare) allowing both workers and consumers some control over these areas.

Socialist theories of democracy argue that many of the rights embodied in the liberal concept of democracy are important but dispute the view that such rights alone give power to the people. Although socialist thinkers differ widely in how they view democracy (as do liberals) most agree that ordinary people cannot exercise real power while there are major economic inequalities in society.

Dictatorships

A high proportion of modern states claim to be democracies. In many cases this claim would be rejected by both liberal and socialist thinkers. In many other states there is little attempt to maintain even an illusion of democracy. Such states are often referred to as dictatorships or totalitarian systems of government. Under dictatorships those who govern make little or no reference to the people when taking decisions. Opposition to the government is usually suppressed by force and the civil rights of a democracy are often ignored. The *fascist* states of Germany and Italy in the 1930s under the dictators Hitler and Mussolini are well known examples of totalitarian states. Today there are military dictators in many parts of the world ruling by force and overthrowing many of the rights and institutions taken for granted in democracies.

Distinguishing types of political systems is not straightforward since there is no agreement on what constitutes a democracy or a totalitarian system. Many states claim to be democratic since democracy helps to legitimate the authority of those in power. However, the extent to which different types of states are democratic is open to debate.

Summary

1 Different theoretical perspectives define and use the concepts of power and democracy in different ways. They therefore reach different conclusions about how power is distributed and whether or not Western societies can be described as truly democratic.

2 Most sociologists see the state as the main legitimate source of power in industrial society. Analysis of the relationship between the state and society is therefore important for understanding the distribution of power.

3 Some see representative democracy as the only way in which the people can exercise power in large scale modern societies. Others, however, see the only truly democratic system as participatory democracy.

Activity 3 Views of Democracy

Item A *Direct democracy*

The Landesgemeinde or open air parliament of a group of Swiss cantons which takes place every April.

Item B *Indirect democracy*

Electors voting in a British general election

Item C *Western democracy*

During the French Revolution, the idea of exercising democracy through elected representatives and a legislature emerged. This form of indirect democracy, practiced in Britain, is frequently referred to as Western liberal democracy. Closely associated with it is an emphasis on individualism, competition, political rights, equality of opportunity and political opposition.

Item E *African democracy*

Two views of democracy have emerged in the African context. The first places emphasis on political cooperation where the interests and welfare of the group are seen as more important than those of the individual. Leaders discuss problems until solutions emerge rather than participating in adversarial party politics.

The second interpretation sees 'democracy' as an alternative to colonial or imperial rule. Democracy here is taken to mean self-government; that is rule by a government composed of people of that country.

Items C, D and E adapted from D. Roberts (ed) *Discovering Politics*, 1989

Item D *Soviet democracy*

At the time of Aristotle many took democracy to mean rule in the interests of the poor. This was used as a justification by Communists that their system is democratic. They argued that the government of the former Soviet Union was rule in the interests of the majority - the working class. In this case emphasis was placed on social and economic rights. Political participation existed but was strictly under the direction of the Communist Party.

Many argue that this constitutes dictatorship based on the rule of a single party. On the other hand, it could be argued that the Soviet system is closer to the original meaning of democracy as used by the ancient Greeks.

Questions

1 How do the pictures in Items A and B illustrate the difference between direct and indirect democracy.
2 Using data from Items C, D and E explain why it is difficult to reach an agreed definition of democracy.
3 a) Construct your own definition of democracy.
  b) How far does contemporary Britain fit your definition of a democracy?

2 Pluralism and Liberal Democracy

Key Issues

1 Does the state in liberal democracies represent the interests of the majority?
2 What role do political parties and pressure groups play in liberal democracies?
3 Can the interests of all groups be adequately represented in liberal democracies?

2.1 Pluralist theories of power

Pluralist theories of power have their origins in the work of Max Weber. While Marxists believed that socialism would lead to a true participatory democracy, Weber was sceptical about the possibility of direct democracy in large scale industrial societies. Instead Weber argued that multi-party representative democracy provided the best way of representing a range of interests. This must be combined with strong political leadership prepared to resist control by political bureaucrats, such as unelected civil servants.

Classical pluralism

Weber's theories were developed by American political scientists, such as Robert Dahl, into what has become known as *classical pluralism*. Classical pluralists accept that the majority of citizens in Western society have little direct involvement in political decision making. However, this does not mean that Western societies are undemocratic. They are seen as representative democracies. Pluralists see society as made up of many different groups pursuing different political interests. Such interest groups may combine into formal political organisations to promote their aims. Two types of organisation are important. Firstly political parties, which usually seek to gain political power by putting up candidates in elections with the aim of forming a government. Secondly pressure groups - groups which try to exert influence over those already in power to follow policies which they favour.

Pluralists see political parties and pressure groups as crucial for the democratic process since they are the means by which the views of sectional interests in society are articulated both inside and outside the legislature (Parliament in the UK, Congress in the USA). No one group in society is seen to dominate the decision making process. Power is therefore shared amongst a range of groups. Like Weber, pluralists reject the idea that democracy is possible in a one-party state, since there must be opposition parties (and indeed pressure groups) to represent the views of those who disagree with the governing party.

For pluralists the role of the state is to arbitrate between the various interest groups which seek to influence the decision making process. Pluralists see the involvement of groups representing all sections of society in decision making as essential. It enables the government to gauge the strength of support for different policies and to gain feedback from interested parties on proposals which may affect them. Democracy only works if these concerns are reflected in government decisions.

Pluralism and the study of decision making

Pluralists argue that the decision making process is the key to understanding the distribution of power in society. Robert Dahl believed that 'concrete decisions' must be examined to find out which groups achieve the outcomes they desire. Only then will it be possible to say who has power.

Dahl's approach is clearly illustrated in his classic study of the town of New Haven in Connecticut, *Who Governs?* (1961). He studied three major issues in the local politics of the town: urban renewal, political nominations and education. A number of groups with differing views were involved. However, few groups participated in making decisions on all three issues since groups only became involved when issues directly affected their own interests. From his analysis of the decision making process Dahl concluded that no single group dominated New Haven politics. Instead a variety of groups had some success in influencing outcomes and policies were often a compromise between the wishes of competing groups. In this study Dahl reflects the pluralists' preference for the study of specific issues and concrete decisions, Stephen Lukes' first face of power.

The role of political parties

Pluralists argue that participatory democracy is difficult, if not impossible, to achieve in large scale societies. There are simply too many people for direct participation. However, representative democracy can exist where the interests of different sections of the population are adequately represented. Competition between political parties is one of the main ways of ensuring this. It offers electors a chance to choose between different sets of policies. Parties are only likely to be elected if they put forward policies which find favour with the electorate.

Pluralists argue that political parties have a number of important functions in modern democratic systems.

These include:
1 Fighting election campaigns.
2 Developing policies which provide a choice for the electorate.
3 Providing the basis for the government and opposition in the legislature.
4 Articulating the interests of sections of society (eg social classes, religious and ethnic groups and regional interests).

Criticisms of classical pluralism

Classical pluralist theories have received considerable criticism.

1 **Non-decision making** Measuring power by examining decisions ignores non-decision making - managing the agenda so that certain issues never reach the point of decision making. This is Lukes' second face of power which most pluralists fail to examine.

2 **Manipulation of the wishes of others** There is a failure to consider the possibility that people might accept and even welcome decisions which are against their interests. This is Lukes' third face of power. Marxists for example argue that most people have been persuaded to accept the capitalist system even though it is against their real interests. Lack of opposition to decisions does not mean these decisions are in everyone's interests.

3 **The power of capital** Marxists argue that the pluralists' focus on the decisions taken by the local and national government ignores the possibility that the real centre of power is elsewhere. John Westergaard and Henrietta Resler (1976) point to the failure of Labour governments since 1945 to eradicate poverty and reduce inequalities of wealth and income. In their view such inequalities are created by the existence of private property and a capitalist economy and are not amenable to piecemeal reform even by left wing political parties.

4 **Unequal representation of interests** Even using the pluralists own method (focusing on decision making) it can be shown that some groups exercise more power than others. Economically powerful groups and groups containing a large proportion of middle class activists are usually more successful than those representing poorer and less educated groups.

5 **Non-representation of interests** Many interests may not be represented at all. It is only in the last ten years or so that women who are victims of domestic violence, children who are sexually abused by their parents, and schoolchildren who are systematically bullied have been brought to public notice and received any kind of representation. And the next ten years will bring a new set of unrepresented interests to public attention.

6 **The 'organising out' of outsiders** There are rules and conventions for influencing governments. Demands must be moderate and made in a moderate way - demands for revolutionary change backed by violent protest are unlikely to succeed. Groups such as peace campaigners, environmentalists, women's groups, anti-poll tax protestors and Irish Republicans, who step outside this 'consensus' about acceptable political methods, are likely to be branded as 'eccentric', 'extremist' or even 'subversive'. In this way 'outsiders' are kept on the outside, their demands dismissed as inconsequential and unrealistic, their interests unrepresented.

7 **The problem of overloaded government** New Right theorists argue that pluralism has put too much emphasis on the benefits of the government consulting widely with different interest groups and being responsive to the demands of the electorate. Writers such as Samuel Brittan (1983) claim that it is precisely this which has led to a problem of overloaded government. When this happens every issue becomes a concern of the government which then makes concessions (usually by spending more money) to a whole variety of interest groups in order to buy electoral popularity. New Right theorists argue that overloaded government leads to economic inefficiency and a failure to follow clear and consistent policies.

Elite pluralism

As a result of such criticisms many of the supporters of classical pluralism have changed or modified their positions. Robert Dahl (1982), for example, has accepted that the unequal distribution of wealth and income in the USA makes equal political influence impossible. David Marsh (1985) describes this modified position as *elite pluralism*.

Elite pluralists accept that many political interests, for example those of black people or the unemployed, are under-represented. However, since they constitute a significant number of voters the government will eventually be forced to take note of their interests. Elite pluralists accept the argument that some groups have greater access to government and the policy making process than others. However, they point out that governments and their departments must consult with a range of interest groups in order to minimise conflict. One way they accomplish this is by consulting with different policy communities. Each policy community is made up of a range of interest groups concerned with a particular set of issues. For example, there are policy communities on agriculture, health services and local government. Within each policy community the relevant government department will consult with 'insider groups' (pressure groups who have regular access to government departments) and may also receive representations from 'outsider groups' (who are consulted less frequently). (See Section 2.2 for types of pressure groups).

Evaluation Elite pluralism provides answers to some of the criticisms of classical pluralism. It acknowledges the existence of under-represented interests and accepts that power is to some degree concentrated in the hands of a few elites.

Some critics of elite pluralism argue that this in itself undermines the pluralist position that power is widely dispersed in capitalist societies.

Moreover, the assumption by elite pluralists that elites or leaders of interest groups act in the interests of their members is also open to question. In the USA corrupt union leaders have been accused of lining their pockets with the pension funds of those they are supposed to represent. Some British MPs have been seen as more concerned with securing lucrative directorships and consultancies than with the problems of their constituents.

Finally, elite pluralism, like classical pluralism, largely fails to take into account the third face of power - the ability to shape and manipulate the desires of others.

Activity 4 Pluralism and Power

Item A *The issue method*

Christopher Hewitt's study of the distribution of power in Britain was based on what he terms the 'issue method'. Hewitt's study covered the period 1944-1964. This included periods of both Labour and Conservative government. He analysed twenty four issues, six under each of four policy areas; these were foreign policy, economic policy, welfare policy and social policy.

The table below summarises his findings. It shows the issues, the policy outcome on each issue (ie the decision made by Parliament), the views of various interest groups and public opinion (based on public opinion polls). *Pro* indicates that the interest group supported the successful policy outcome, while *anti* indicates they were against. *Divided* indicates that there was no clear majority for or against a particular policy. A dash (-) indicates that no data was available for this group.

Issue	Successful policy outcome	Business	White Collar	Unions	Religious	Public Opinion
India	Independence for India	-	-	-	-	Pro
Russia	Hard-line policy to Russia	-	-	Pro	-	-
Abadan	Sanctions against Iran	Pro	-	-	-	-
Suez	Military intervention	-	-	Anti	Anti	Divided
Nuclear deterrent	Independent deterrent policy	Anti	-	Divided	Divided	-
Central Africa	Federation	-	-	-	Anti	-
US loan	Loan negotiated	-	-	-	-	-
Road haulage	Nationalisation	Anti	-	Pro	-	-
Steel	No effective nationalisation	Pro	-	Anti	-	-
Resale price maintenance	Abolition of RPM	Anti	-	-	-	Pro
Common Market	No entry	Anti	-	Pro	-	-
Railways	Beeching's rationalisation policy	Pro	-	Anti	-	Divided
Education Act	Education Act	Pro	Pro	Pro	Pro	Pro
National Health	National Health Service	-	Pro	-	-	Pro
National Insurance	National Insurance Act	Anti	-	Pro	Pro	Pro
Rent Act	Rent decontrol	Pro	Pro	Anti	-	-
Comprehensives	No support for comprehensives	-	Divided	-	-	-
Motorways	Motorway programme	Pro	Pro	Pro	-	Pro
Town and country	Town and Country Planning Act	Anti	Pro	Pro	_	Pro
Divorce	No change in divorce laws	-	Divided	-	Pro	-
Capital punishment	Abolition of capital punishment	-	Anti	-	Pro	Anti
Television	Commercial television	Divided	Divided	Anti	Anti	Divided
Immigration	Immigration control	-	-	-	Anti	Pro
Clean air	Clean Air Act	Divided	Pro	-	-	Pro

Adapted from C.J. Hewitt ' Elites and the Distribution of Power' in P. Stanworth and A. Giddens (eds) *Elites and Power in British Society*, 1974, p59

Item B *Non-issues*

The test of power is not who decides; but what is decided and what is not. The formula adopted by pluralist analysis for that test is quite inadequate. It is to examine disputes among rival groups on a number of 'key' issues; and to measure the respective power of those groups by the outcome of the disputes. The formula is inadequate - indeed irrelevant to the central questions of power - because it has nothing to say about those issues which do not come into dispute at all. They may be excluded through the capacity of one group or another to manipulate them off the agenda. That capacity is certainly power - the power of 'non-decision making', as this term has come to be used by critics of the pluralist school. But still more important is the power to exclude which involves no manipulation; no activity on or off stage by any individual or group; nothing more tangible than assumptions. For the most part these are unspoken assumptions. For example it is taken for granted that profit should be the normal yardstick of investment in most areas of activity; that the living standards of the propertyless majority should be set primarily by the terms on which they sell or once sold their labour; and so on.

Adapted from J. Westergaard and H. Resler *Class in a Capitalist Society*, 1976, pp 142-3 and 246-7

Questions

1 Study Item A. Explain how the evidence from this table might be used to support a pluralist view of the distribution of power in Britain.

2 Hewitt's study (Item A) used the 'issue method' in researching power.
   a) Explain what this method involves.
   b) Using data from Item B and elsewhere, examine the strengths and weaknesses of the issue method for measuring the distribution of power.

2.2 Pressure groups

Pressure groups are groups which attempt to influence policy making without actually seeking to form a government. Pluralists see them as a vital input into the decision-making process. Like political parties pressure groups put forward policies and seek support for them. However, they differ from political parties in two important ways. Firstly, they do not normally put up candidates in elections but seek to achieve their aims by putting pressure on those already in government. Secondly, they usually focus on a narrow range of issues while political parties cover a far broader range. It has been argued that pressure groups play a necessary role in democracy since they allow issues which may be ignored or overlooked by the main political parties to be publicised and debated.

Protective and promotional groups

Pressure groups differ widely in their aims, organisation, membership and methods of operation. A distinction is often made between *protective* groups and *promotional* groups. Protective groups - sometimes described as 'sectional groups' - primarily aim to protect their own interests. Many economic organisations come under this heading, for example trade unions, professional associations and employers' organisations. Other protective groups are brought together by other kinds of common interest - sharing the same leisure activity (Surfers Against Sewage), living in the same area (local residents associations), or experience of the same illness or disability (British Diabetic Association), are all reasons why people may join together in groups to influence government policy.

Promotional groups are often referred to as 'cause groups'. They are usually less concerned with their own sectional interests but instead seek to promote a cause which they see as neglected by government. The growth of groups concerned with environmental issues provides many examples, eg Greenpeace, Friends of the Earth, Royal Society for the Protection of Birds. Many promotional groups are concerned to promote their own particular moral views. For example, there are groups for and against abortion rights (National Abortion Campaign and LIFE), for and against smoking (FOREST and ASH), and for and against media censorship (National Viewers and Listeners Association and Campaign against Press and Broadcasting Censorship).

Insider and outsider groups

In practice the distinction between protective and promotional groups is not always helpful since many organisations share both sets of characteristics. Wyn Grant (1990) suggests an alternative classification - *insider* and *outsider* groups - based on how pressure groups are treated by the government. Insider groups are consulted by the government and invited to contribute their views during the policy making process. This is most common in the case of protective groups since they are more likely to have expertise in a particular field. The knowledge and experience of the British Medical Association of the health service, of the Road Hauliers Federation of road transport, or of the Confederation of British Industry of manufacturing industry, are useful to the government in developing policy in these areas. Such groups may thus become 'insiders'.

Promotional groups are more likely to be 'outsiders', according to Grant, with less access to government departments and ministers. Some outsiders may seek to become insiders by mounting well documented campaigns to convince government ministers that they are worth consulting. Grant suggests that the Ramblers Association and the British Association of Nature Conservationists are now potential insiders. However, not all promotional groups are outsiders. Some environmental groups have succeeded in gaining the government's confidence such as the CPRE (Council for the Protection of Rural England). The price to pay for such influence according to Grant is adherence to 'an unwritten code of moderate and responsible behaviour... insider groups usually "screen out" demands from their members which they know that government would regard as unreasonable or unacceptable' (1990, p108). Some interest groups which were insiders have become outsiders. Trade unions were closely involved in the 1974-79 Labour government's policy making. However, since 1979 they have been removed from positions of influence on many public bodies and have been less frequently consulted by the government.

Pressure groups and policy communities

Martin Smith (1993) points out that many pressure groups are now linked with other groups and government departments. Governments often need the support and advice of specific groups in order to implement their policies. Government departments thus maintain regular links with interested groups in what Smith calls *policy networks.*

Smith suggests that some policy networks have developed into what he calls a *policy community.* This is a much more closed network where one or more government departments maintain close contact with a limited number of pressure groups over a considerable period of time. Other groups may be excluded from consultation and thus the insider groups gain a considerable advantage in influencing policy making.

Smith uses agriculture as an example of this type of policy community in Britain. Governments wished to increase food production during and after the Second World War. Farmers were given subsidies to help boost production and were involved in annual consultations over levels of production and subsidies. The NFU (National Farmers Union) achieved a virtual monopoly in this process. Other groups with an interest in agriculture such as the Country Landowners Association and the Union of Agricultural and Allied Workers as well as groups representing consumers and environmentalists were largely excluded. Smith argues that between 1945 and 1970 the British government never really questioned whether subsidies to farmers were necessary. He sees this not simply as a result of the

power of the NFU but due to a combination of factors including government wishes and the way in which policy was made.

Smith argues that a pluralist interpretation of pressure group influence is questioned by such evidence since in certain circumstances insider groups can acquire disproportionate influence through membership of a policy community. However, he also points to the deficiencies of the elite model (see Section 3.1). In some policy areas a much wider variety of groups may exercise influence albeit in a limited way. Smith concludes that we cannot generalise about the degree of influence of pressure groups since this varies between different policy areas and over time.

Pressure group methods

Pressure groups use a wide variety of methods. To a large extent the strategies they employ depend on the nature of the group. Small insider groups may be able to exercise quite discreet influence especially if they are part of an established policy community. For example, traditionally there have been close links between the City of London financial institutions, the Bank of England and the Treasury. Thus financial leaders were able to communicate their views directly to the government through a variety of informal contacts. Outsider pressure groups, however, may have to mount much more high profile campaigns in order to gain public support and government attention. The following summarises some of the main methods used by pressure groups.

1 **Contacts with MPs and political parties** Some groups employ professional lobbyists to bring matters to the attention of MPs, others attempt to recruit MPs as members. Many Labour MPs are sponsored by trade unions, while it is common for Conservative MPs to hold company directorships and act as consultants for business organisations.

2 **Gaining public support** Pressure groups may use a variety of methods to gain public support such as using the mass media, advertising and organising local branches to recruit members and raise funds.

3 **Demonstrating levels of support** Public demonstrations, lobbying parliament and organising petitions are examples of such methods. They provide an indication of public support for pressure groups' policies.

4 **Providing evidence and information to decision makers** Many pressure groups are experts in their fields and can be useful to local and national government as sources of information. This may allow groups to influence the policy making process.

5 **Non-violent direct action** This involves action short of violence designed to prevent activities

which protestors are opposed to. Examples include disrupting fox hunts, lying in the path of trucks transporting nuclear missiles and using speed boats in an attempt to prevent dumping at sea.

6 **Violent protest and terrorism** Violent protests can be relatively disorganised - for example inner city riots such as those in Brixton in 1981 - or highly organised such as the terrorism of the IRA and other groups.

Pressure groups and democracy

Pluralists see pressure groups as essential for democracy. Without them a range of different interests might be unrepresented and unheard. As it is, pressure group activity means they are heard in both national and local politics. This ensures that power is not monopolised by a small minority with a single viewpoint since alternative views and a large number of groups are always represented. The veteran pressure group campaigner Des Wilson argues that pressure groups now provide the real

opposition to the government and are thus an essential part of the democratic process (quoted in M. Davies, 1985, p44).

Others are more critical of the role of pressure groups. 'New Right' thinkers have attacked pressure groups for being unrepresentative and raising unrealistic expectations. Samuel Brittan (1983) argues that the constant and vocal demands of pressure groups force governments to give in to them in order to gain electoral popularity. Since almost every group has a rival putting in a counter-claim, the government can never satisfy all the demands. But it spends more and more money in the vain hope of doing so. Pressure group politics thus weakens the government and drains the nation's income through excessive government spending.

Marxists have given little detailed consideration to pressure group activity. This is because they see such activity as largely inconsequential. Power is concentrated in the hands of the capitalist class. Pressure groups may win minor victories on behalf of the mass of the population but these have little effect on the basic structure of society.

Summary

1 Pluralist theories see power in liberal democracies as dispersed among many different interest groups. They base this view on studies of decision making - the first face of power.

2 Pluralists see both political parties and pressure groups as indispensable parts of democracy since they ensure that governments are responsive to the views of the people.

3 Critics of pluralism claim that it ignores the second and third faces of power - the power to manage the agenda and to manipulate the wishes of others.

Activity 5 Pressure Group Politics

Item A *The law and order policy network*

The government department most centrally involved in law and order issues is the Home Office. This department has overall responsibility for the police, prisons and the maintenance of public order. It also drafts new laws concerned with the administration of the legal system in England and Wales.

Professional organisations such as the Prison Officers' Association (POA), the Police Federation, the National Association of Probation Officers, and the British Association of Social Workers tend to be consulted about new legislation which will affect their areas of work. The Home Office needs the cooperation of such groups in order for changes to work effectively. However, sometimes this relationship breaks down. For example, in 1986 the POA threatened industrial action because it could not reach agreement with the Home Office over staff numbers on each shift.

The Home Office also has to deal with pressure

groups seeking reforms or protecting the rights of people who come into contact with the legal system. The National Council for Civil Liberties, for example, tries to defend civil and political rights such as freedom of speech and freedom of assembly. It organises campaigns to publicise cases of people's rights being threatened, tries to have some influence over the drafting of new legislation, and produces pamphlets designed to inform people about their rights.

The Howard League for Penal Reform enjoys close relationships with the Home Office and has representatives sitting on a great many policy making committees concerned with the running of the prison system. In the 1950s the Howard League supported the abolition of capital punishment but, for fear of damaging its relationship with the Home Office, it supported the separate National Campaign for the Abolition of Capital Punishment, rather than organising its own campaign.

Some pressure groups have the active support of the Home Office, The National Association for the Care and Resettlement of Offenders receives money from the government to aid its work. However, more radical pressure groups such as the Radical Alternatives to Prison (RAP) and the Preservation of the Rights of Prisoners (PROP) tend to have less influence. RAP is in favour of the abolition of prisons for all but the most serious offenders but is not consulted in the same way as the Howard League. PROP sees itself as a kind of prisoners' trade union but the Home Office does not even officially acknowledge its existence. Such organisations try to mobilise the mass media and public opinion in order to indirectly put pressure on the government.

Adapted from R. Stradling *The Politics of Law and Order*, 1988, pp12-16

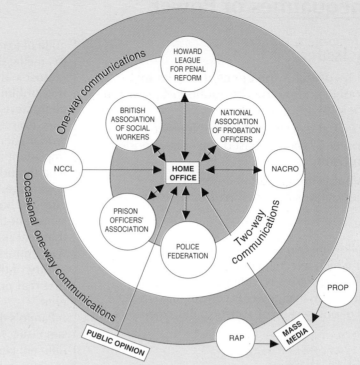

NCCL   National Council for Civil Liberties
NACRO   National Association for the Care and Resettlement of Offenders
PROP   Preservation of the Rights of Prisoners
RAP   Radical Alternatives to Prison

This diagram illustrates the relationship between law and order pressure groups and the government.

Item B *Pressure group activity*

Greenpeace demonstration

Miners protesting at pit closures at a rally in London, March 1993

Questions

1 Study Item A.
   a) Which pressure groups are 'insider groups' and which are 'outsider groups' in relation to the Home Office? How might the status of some groups change according to the issue under discussion?
   b) Using examples from the extract, discuss what advantages there are in being an insider pressure group. Are there any disadvantages associated with this status?

2 'Pressure groups are an essential component of a democratic society.' Discuss with reference to Item B and any other data.

3 Inequalities of Power

Key Issues

1 How useful is the concept of elite in understanding the distribution of power in society?

2 To what extent are there differences of power in society based on class, gender and ethnicity?

3 What is the significance of global inequalities between nation states?

The following two sections, examine theories of power which reject the pluralist view that power in liberal democracies is widely dispersed. These theories claim that power is concentrated in the hands of one section of society at the expense of others.

3.1 Elite theory

Elite theorists argue that power is concentrated in the hands of a small minority - an *elite*. Elite theory originally developed in response to Marxism which claimed that true democracy was only possible under socialism. The classical elite theorists asserted that rule by elites was inevitable in all societies, even socialist ones. However, not all versions of elite theory are so conservative. Many modern elite theorists argue that rule by elites results from the way societies are organised rather than being an inevitable and universal feature of human society.

Classical elite theory: Pareto and Mosca

Vilfredo Pareto (1848-1923) and Gaetano Mosca (1858-1911) rejected the idea that real democracy was possible either in liberal democracies or under socialism. Instead they argued that in all societies an elite, a small minority of individuals with superior personal qualities, would monopolise power.

For Pareto the psychological characteristics of elites separated them from the masses. He classified elites into two types: 'lions' who were distinguished by their ability to act forcefully to gain and retain power, for example military dictators; and 'foxes' who relied more on cunning and an ability to manipulate people, for example political leaders in Western democracies. Each type of elite eventually replaces the other, resulting in a 'circulation of elites'. Pareto claimed that 'History is the graveyard of aristocracies' - all elites are sooner or later replaced by others. Foxes lack the strength and decisiveness of lions and are eventually overthrown by a group of lions, as in a military coup. However, lions lack the subtlety and

guile of foxes. They are gradually infiltrated leading to an elite dominated by foxes.

Mosca also asserted that elite rule was inevitable but, unlike Pareto, he argued that the particular characteristics which give an elite its superiority vary from society to society. For example, in feudal societies ability as a soldier would be important for a leader, while in a capitalist society wealth and business connections would be an advantage. In his later work Mosca accepted that elites in liberal democracies might in some way represent the people. But he always maintained that real involvement by the majority in politics was impossible. Mosca was sceptical about the ability of the masses to govern themselves and felt that real power would always be exercised by an elite.

Pareto's theory has been criticised for being too simplistic. He makes little distinction between different types of political systems asserting that all societies are characterised by the same process of circulation of elites. But many elites have remained unchanged for hundreds of years, for example the ruling Brahmin caste in India and the *literati*, the educated ruling class of ancient China. Tom Bottomore (1993) suggests there is insufficient evidence to support Pareto's theory of circulation of elites.

Both Mosca and Pareto seem contemptuous of the of the mass of the population and of those who see the masses as capable of governing themselves. Mosca opposed the extension of the franchise to the working classes, seeing them as unfit to participate in the political process. He and Pareto dismiss the predictions of Marxism as nothing more than wishful thinking.

The power elite theory: C. Wright Mills

While Mosca and Pareto saw elite rule as inevitable, C. Wright Mills saw it as something which emerged in the USA less than 100 years before his book *The Power Elite* (1956) was written. Mills saw elite rule as a result of the structure of society which allowed a disproportionate amount of power to be held by a few individuals who occupied what he called the 'command posts' in key institutions.

Mills identified three key institutions as the centres of power: the federal government (which had increasingly taken power from the individual state governments as America became a world power); the major corporations (which have increasingly dominated the economy at the expense of small firms); and the military (which has become increasingly important in relation to foreign policy and government expenditure). Mills argued that the holders of the top positions in these three institutions constituted three important elites: the political, economic and military elites.

The three elites are closely connected. Firstly, because of similar social origins, education, kinship and other social ties. Secondly, because their interests are intertwined. For example, the economic elite prospers from the contracts for military equipment placed by the military and political elites. For these reasons Mills claimed that in reality the three elites are not separate but form a single *power elite*.

Mills claimed that key political decisions, such as dropping an atom bomb on Hiroshima in 1945, were taken by the power elite with little reference to the majority of citizens. The masses are hardly involved in politics and even elections fail to provide real choice since there is little difference between the two main parties, the Republicans and the Democrats. For Mills real democracy will only come about when the structure of society changes so that power is less centralised and is devolved to the people. This would involve a reduction in the power of the military and the large corporations and require politicians to become more responsive to the people.

Unlike the classical elite theorists Mills' theory was only intended to apply to the USA in the 1950s. Nevertheless critics of Mills, such as the pluralist Dahl, have argued that he has shown only that elites in the USA have the potential for control. He has failed to show they have actual control because he has not analysed a range of concrete decisions. In addition pluralists argue that there are many other elites such as pressure group leaders, church leaders, union leaders and so on, who provide a counterbalance to the more powerful elites. This means the elites identified by Mills cannot take decisions without opposition.

Marxists also reject the notion of a power elite arguing that real power in capitalist societies, such as the USA, derives not from positions in institutions but from ownership and control of the means of production.

The fragmented elite model

Some British elite theorists have modified and developed elite theory. One version, the fragmented elite model, put forward by Ian Budge and his colleagues (1983) suggests that there are a number of elites in Britain, all in competition with one another. Government ministers and their departments are included in the factions competing for power and influence. Unlike the power elite which Mills saw as cohesive, Budge argues that the various elites in Britain are often in conflict. Government policy frequently results from a trial of strength between different departments competing for funds or control, or between different elites competing to influence a particular aspect of policy. Budge argues that government policies are often neither rational nor consistent since they are shaped by the relative strength of prevailing elites.

This model shares many features with elite pluralism. It suggests that power is concentrated in a few hands but that rather than a single elite there are a number of competing groups. Like pluralism it tends to focus on decision making, the first face of power and gives little consideration to the second and third faces.

Elite recruitment in Britain

Much of the research into elites in Britain has been concerned with how members of elites are recruited and the social connections and relationships between different elite groups. There is considerable evidence that many elites in Britain are largely closed. In other words new members are mainly drawn from the same social groups as existing members. A number of studies have examined the educational backgrounds of elites and demonstrated that a high proportion of politicians, top civil servants, judges, military leaders, company directors and members of other elite groups are educated at fee-paying public schools which draw most of their pupils from wealthy families. Oxford and Cambridge Universities also appear to act as important recruiting grounds for elite positions.

For the economic elite in particular inherited wealth appears to be significant. A study by Harbury and McMahon (1974) based on data from the 1950s and 60s compared the estates left by wealthy men on their deaths with those of their fathers. Harbury and McMahon found that a high proportion of rich men had rich fathers and that the proportion had declined only slightly since the 1920s. Similarly a study of company chairmen by Philip Stanworth and Anthony Giddens (1974) found that only 1% came from working class backgrounds and 10% from middle class backgrounds, while 66% came from upper class backgrounds. Such studies suggest that mobility from humble origins into the most powerful elites is rare.

Elite integration in Britain

A further aspect of elites which has received considerable attention is the degree of integration between elite groups. Mills argued that the American power elite was united by its common outlook and social connections. In Britain a study by Tom Lupton and Shirley Wilson (1973) shows that many 'top decision makers' such as government ministers, top civil servants and financial leaders are related by kinship and marriage. A similar study by Richard Whitley (1974) reveals that many large firms are linked by overlapping directorships (having a director in common) or by kinship ties between directors. Such links help to create cohesion and unity between elites. Anthony Giddens notes that there is considerable movement between elites. Many civil servants and politicians (especially in the Conservative Party) come from business backgrounds, while it is common for an MP on retiring to be invited to become a company director.

The common origins and social connections of many elite members are seen by some elite theorists as evidence that some sort of 'power elite' exists in Britain. However, it is one thing to indentify these connections but quite another to prove that they result in a united, self-interested power elite. The fragmented elite model, for example, would suggest that, despite their common social origins, elite members do not work together but compete for power.

Activity 6 Elites in Britain

Item A *Business lobbyists*

Business interests have increasingly been brought together into highly organised pressure groups capable of engaging in propaganda on behalf of business and of lobbying the state to promote their preferred policies. Businesses use direct lobbying of the state at all levels, employing lobbyists, lawyers and others to act on their behalf, and they back this up through a network of formal and informal contacts, such as consultations, meetings and working lunches. The complex of informal connections range from the legal to the illegal - favours, gifts and bribes are not uncommon supports of the general 'give and take' of business relationships.

The major targets of lobbying are the regulatory agencies which affect the day-to-day operations and profit opportunities of enterprises, and the advisory bodies which shape the general conditions under which they act. The fact that the interests pursued are specific and sectional, and are therefore competing, has led many analysts to see the existence of lobbying as lending support to a pluralist view of power. It remains the case, nevertheless, that this competition is constrained within a framework of general business interests, and that non-business interests are far less likely to be successful in their lobbying.

The power of business interests is further enhanced through membership of advisory bodies. As 'experts', members of the inner circle of finance capitalists are co-opted by governments on to the numerous advisory and consultative bodies which play a key role in policy formulation. These bodies include permanent councils, authorities, and committees, as well as numerous temporary committees, inquiries and commissions.

Adapted from J. Scott *Who Rules Britain?*, 1991, pp145-147

Item B

Educational background of British elites 1982 numbers (percentages shown in brackets)

	Total	Public school *	Eton	Oxbridge +
Members of the Cabinet	22 (100)	17 (72)	3 (14)	19 (86)
Heads of Civil Service Departments	18 (100)	10 (55)	2 (11)	14 (78)
Directors of the Bank of England	18 (100)	16 (89)	4 (22)	16 (89)
Chairmen of major clearing banks	6 (100)	6 (100)	3 (50)	4 (67)
Chairmen of leading merchant banks	17 (100)	13 (76)	8 (47)	9 (53)
Chairmen of top life insurance companies	12 (100)	11 (92)	4 (33)	6 (50)
Law Lords	9 (100)	8 (89)	0 (0)	8 (89)

* Figures for public schools include Eton
+ Oxbridge = attended Oxford or Cambridge Universities

Adapted from A. Sampson *The Changing Anatomy of Britain*, 1982 (various pages)

Item C

The Athenaeum, a club frequented by the rich and powerful

Item D

Strolling at the Henley Royal Regatta

Item E

The educational background of MPs, 1992

Type of education	Con	Lab	Lib Dem
State School	19	34	2
State school + poly/college	28	61	2
State school + university	81	127	6
Public school	28	0	0
Public school + poly/college	16	2	1
Public school + university	164	38	9
Total	**336**	**271**	**20**
Oxford	83	28	4
Cambridge	68	16	2
Other universities	94	122	9
All universities	245	166	15
(% attending university)	(73%)	(61%)	(75%)
Eton	34	2	0
Harrow	7	0	0
Winchester	3	1	0
Other public schools	164	37	10
All public schools	208	40	10
(% attending public school)	(62%)	(14%)	(50%)

Adapted from D. Butler and D. Kavanagh *The British General Election of 1992*, 1992

Questions

1 To what extent does Item A support the fragmented elite model?
2 Study Items B and E.
   a) What do they show about recruitment patterns to elite positions?
   b) What do they suggest about the level of integration and cohesion of British elites?
   c) How useful is this kind of data for studying the nature of elites in British society?
3 Using Items C and D and any other evidence explain why sociologists might be interested in the leisure activities of elites in Britain.
4 Are the patterns of recruitment and the social connections of elites in Britain a cause for concern? Give reasons for your answer.

3.2 Marxist theories of power

For Marx the structure of any society is primarily determined by the way its economy is organised - its *mode of production*. Particular modes of production produce particular *relations of production*. For example under the capitalist mode, relations of production are based on private ownership and control. Capitalists invest their wealth in financing the production of commodities by workers who are paid wages for their labour. Capitalists are seen to dominate and exploit workers. This relationship produces the class system of capitalist society. For Marx and Engels, relations of class dominance and subordination characterise not only capitalist societies but societies throughout history (with the possible exception of 'primitive communism').

The state in capitalist society

Pluralists argue that in the later stages of capitalism universal suffrage and democratic rights gave power to every citizen. The state rather than acting as the agency of a privileged class now serves the interests of society as a whole. Marx and Engels rejected this argument. They agreed that 'bourgeois democracy' meant that the state relied less on coercion to enforce its power, since citizens were more likely to feel it was serving their interests. However, for Marx and Engels this was an illusion. In *The Communist Manifesto* they claimed, 'The executive of the modern state is but a committee for managing the common affairs of the whole bourgeoisie' (1977, p223). In their view, the operation of the political system is dependent on the economic structure of society. The political system is part of the *superstructure* and is thus shaped to meet the requirements of the economic system or *infrastructure*, the foundation of society.

The institutions, beliefs and values which make up the superstructure serve to maintain and reproduce the relations of production. As with other parts of the superstructure, for example the legal system and religious institutions, Marx and Engels saw the state as playing an ideological role. The state appears to be operating in the interests of society as a whole yet in reality it serves the interests of the capitalist class. Thus many Marxists point to the way in which the state identifies the 'national interest' with the need for businesses to make profits and compete internationally. From this perspective the state is acting to legitimate the existing economic arrangements and uphold the interests of the dominant class.

Marx argued that real democracy would only come about in a socialist society where private property was abolished. Members of society could only be politically equal when they were economically equal. Marx believed that the overthrow of capitalism was inevitable. Unlike the classical elite theorists he did not accept that the masses lacked the capacity to govern themselves. He believed that the working class had the potential to transform society in a revolutionary way.

Many modern Marxists argue that the relationship between the state and the ruling class is more complex than that outlined by Marx and Engels. The modern state is subjected to many pressures and influences and to see it as simply serving the interests of a unified ruling class is too simplistic. Modern Marxists have developed and modified Marx's ideas and this has led to considerable debate both within the Marxist tradition and with other perspectives.

Antonio Gramsci: hegemony and the state

One writer who has had considerable influence on Marxist theories of power and the state is the Italian Communist leader Antonio Gramsci (1891-1937). Gramsci rejected the determinism of many classical Marxists who saw the economic infrastructure as directly determining the superstructure. Gramsci argued that under certain circumstances the opposite might be true - ideas and beliefs may change the infrastructure. Much of his work explored ways in which the ideas and actions of individuals might change society economically and politically.

Gramsci emphasised the importance of the superstructure in shaping ideas and providing the means by which the ruling class could exercise power. He argued that the ruling class exercised power by a combination of force and consent. He saw the superstructure as divided into two main parts.

On the one hand *political society* consists of the institutions of rule by force, for example the army and police. On the other hand *civil society* consists of the institutions of rule by consent, for example the church, trade unions, political parties and the mass media. For Gramsci political and civil society make up the state. He defined the state as the 'entire complex of practical and theoretical activities with which the ruling class not only justifies and maintains its dominance, but manages to win the active consent of those over whom it rules' (1971, p244). Thus the state extends beyond what is conventionally regarded as 'political' into many areas of everyday life which help to sustain the ideology of the dominant class.

Hegemony A key concept in Gramsci's work is the notion of hegemony, which he defined as 'intellectual and moral leadership'. Gramsci argued that the bourgeoisie exercise hegemony in capitalist society because their ideas and values are dominant and that through them they are able to persuade other groups to consent to their rule. In this way Gramsci's work focuses on what Stephen Lukes calls the third face of power, the power to influence people through the dominant ideas in society. For Gramsci revolution is only possible in advanced capitalist societies if working class movements are able to challenge the hegemony of the ruling class by developing their own intellectual and moral leadership which would win over the hearts and minds of members of the subject class.

Gramsci recognised and emphasised the importance of divisions within the ruling class (for example between financiers, industrialists and landowners) and within the subject class (for example in Italy there was an important division between peasants and industrial workers). The ruling class could only maintain its hegemony by creating alliances or *power blocs* between different groups. Similarly the subject class could only challenge ruling class hegemony by forming similar alliances. In this way the subject class could occasionally force concessions from their rulers since the ruling class was not all powerful. They were occasionally prepared to make concessions to the subject class in order to maintain their consent to rule.

Gramsci's ideas have had a major influence on the development of neo-Marxist theories of power. However, not all Marxists accept his views uncritically. Some see him as placing too much emphasis on the role of hegemony in maintaining ruling class power and failing to give sufficient consideration to the economic structure as a source of power.

Ralph Miliband: an instrumentalist theory of the state

How does the state represent the interests of the

ruling class? What is the nature of the relationship between the state and the ruling class? These questions have received considerable attention from modern Marxist writers. One approach, often termed the *instrumentalist view*, is associated with the British sociologist Ralph Miliband (1974). He argues that the state (in the form of central and local government and its various agencies such as the police, military and judiciary) acts as the instrument of those who have economic power, the ruling class.

Miliband argues that the state is run by a number of elites including the business elite. Members of these elites are often related by kinship and marriage, they have similar social and educational backgrounds and share a common interest in maintaining the status quo. In practice this means defending private property and preserving the capitalist system. Because of this the state operates in the interests of the wider capitalist class.

Nicos Poulantzas: a structuralist view of the state

The work of the Greek sociologist, Nicos Poulantzas provides an alternative *structuralist* version of the Marxist approach. Poulantzas criticises Miliband for placing too much emphasis on the social background of members of elites. For Poulantzas (1975) the state operates in the interests of capital irrespective of the personnel who run it. This is because in a capitalist society the nature of economic relationships and the ideological dominance of the capitalist class constrain the choices available to those running the state. This means that in the long run they are forced to safeguard and promote capitalist interests. Thus even left wing governments must compromise with business and financial interests in order to ensure stability in capitalist societies.

Relative autonomy Like Gramsci, Poulantzas recognises the existence of divisions within the capitalist class. Different groups of capitalists may conflict over the policies they wish the state to pursue. Poulantzas sees the state acting as a partially independent representative of the interests of the capitalist class as a whole. He argues that the state must have what he terms *relative autonomy* from the ruling class. If the state has a degree of independence from sectional interests within the capitalist class it is better able to serve the long term interests of capital for the following reasons.

1   The state can arbitrate between the often competing interests of different groups of capitalists (for example, bankers may want high interest rates, which might be damaging to the interests of industrialists).
2   The state can make concessions to the working class (for example, better working conditions or

welfare services) which may be opposed by the ruling class but may serve the long term interests of capital by helping to reduce social tensions and conflicts.
3   The state can intervene directly in the economy (for example, by providing nationalised services such as transport, fuel and power which assist the process of capital accumulation) even when this is opposed to the short term interests of some capitalists.

Poulantzas' work has been criticised by Miliband and other sociologists. In particular Miliband argues that Poulantzas over-emphasises the degree to which capitalism acts as a structural determinant on the state. To suggest that every action taken by the state is determined by the infrastructure, is for Miliband, going too far. The concept of relative autonomy has been criticised by a number of sociologists for being too vague. As such it would appear impossible to prove or disprove its existence. Moreover, it is not clear under what circumstances the state is autonomous and when it is constrained by capital. Nevertheless, despite these criticisms the work of Poulantzas has had considerable influence on many neo-Marxists seeking to explore the complex relationship between society and the state.

Criticisms of ruling class theories

Orthodox Marxist theories of power argue that the capitalist class in societies such as the United Kingdom not only own and control the means of production but also act as a *ruling class* politically. A number objections have been raised to this argument.

1   In advanced industrial society there has been a separation of ownership and control. Control of businesses is passing increasingly from owners to salaried managers. If this is the case there may be little justification for seeing a ruling class both owning *and* controlling the means of production (see pp332-333).
2   Even in terms of ownership, existence of a ruling class is increasingly doubtful. Ownership of wealth has now spread from a small capitalist class to other groups in society. More and more ordinary citizens own shares and have a stake in capitalism. And more than half of all shares in private companies are now held by institutions such as pension funds and insurance companies rather than individuals. In this situation identifying a capitalist class becomes increasingly difficult.

David Coates: a neo-Marxist perspective

Some writers have modified and adapted Marxist theory in an attempt to apply it to modern Britain. David Coates (1984) for example, attempts to explain how a seemingly divided and competing series of interest groups can still be seen as comprising a ruling class. He argues that the British ruling class is not a unified social group but is made up of different fractions or interest groups. At different times in the historical development of British capitalism different *fractions* have become more or less dominant. Coates, following Gramsci, argues that ruling class power is exercised by 'power blocs' - alliances of important social forces, including the dominant fractions of the capitalist class. Coates sees the dominant power bloc in mid-nineteenth century Britain as an alliance between the increasingly powerful northern industrial capitalists and the old land-owning aristocracy. By the beginning of the twentieth century financial capitalists based in the City of London, such as merchants, bankers, shipowners, and stock and insurance brokers had become the dominant section of the capitalist class.

Coates argues that financial capital has remained the dominant group in the ruling class throughout this century, though it has been forced to continually forge alliances with other groups. For example, during the period 1945-1976 trade unions were increasingly brought into the government decision making process. Postwar governments were largely successful in maintaining an apparent consensus because of the long economic boom which lasted until the 1960s. In these circumstances capital was able to make concessions to the working class and trade union leaders became part of the power bloc on condition that they worked within the existing system.

Coates argues that the stability of liberal democratic governments can only be guaranteed if the state can mobilise sufficient support for a *national project* which represents ruling class interests but which also accommodates potentially threatening working class demands. Thus the postwar settlement involved extensive concessions to working class interests, such as the welfare state. By the 1970s British capitalism was in crisis because of a world oil crisis, high levels of inflation and the inability of trade union leaders to restrain rank and file militancy among their members. The success of Margaret Thatcher in the 1979 election marked the formation of a new power bloc from which the unions were excluded. Thatcher's success lay in her appeal not only to capitalist interests but also to the petty bourgeoisie and a more affluent section of the working class. Coates argues that Thatcherism represented an attempt to create an entirely new national project. The old project based on Keynsian state intervention in the economy was blamed for the crisis. The new project was based on a promise to improve Britain's competitiveness by cutting public spending and reducing government 'interference' in the economy.

This brief summary of Coates's work gives an indication of how a Marxist perspective can be applied to an historical period. It shows how it is possible to fit the details of shifting alliances and pressure group politics into the broader framework of Marxist theory.

Activity 7 Capitalism and Politics

Item A *One view of the future*

Statue of Lenin, founder of the Communist Party dismantled in Lithuania, 23 August 1991. Formerly part of the Soviet Union, Lithuania has now banned the Communist Party.

Item B *A second view of the future*

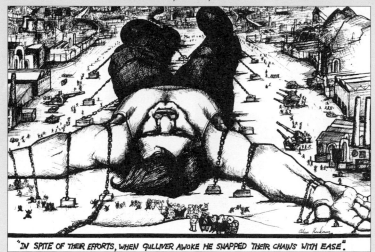

"IN SPITE OF THEIR EFFORTS, WHEN GULLIVER AWOKE HE SNAPPED THEIR CHAINS WITH EASE".

The working class as a sleeping giant

Item C *The welfare state*

State school

Item D *Lesbian and gay rights*

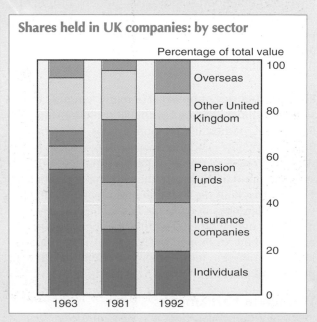

NHS hospital

Item E *Shareholding*

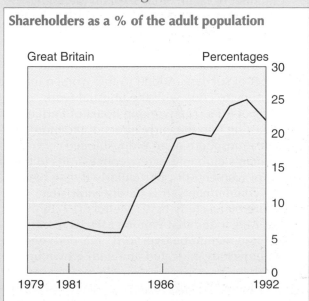

Shareholders as a % of the adult population

Great Britain — Percentages

Shares held in UK companies: by sector

Percentage of total value

Overseas

Other United Kingdom

Pension funds

Insurance companies

Individuals

1963   1981   1992

From *Social Trends*, 1993, p78

From *Social Trends*, 1993, p79

Item F *Public ownership*

Years of mismanagement and low investment had reduced the privately owned coal industry to near bankruptcy. It was brought into public ownership (nationalised) by the postwar Labour government. This picture shows Emmanuel Shinwell (left), Minister of Fuel, saluting the change of ownership at Merton Colliery in 1947.

Questions

1 Briefly discuss the possibility of the transition to communism using the pictures in Items A and B.

2 How might Item D be used to criticise the Marxist argument that all political conflicts are essentially manifestations of class struggles?

3 How might a Marxist interpret the pictures in Items C and F?

4 a) How might the data in Item E be used to criticise the Marxist argument that political power is held by a small but powerful capitalist class?

   b) How might Marxists respond to such criticisms?

3.3 Gender and power

Traditional sociological theories of power have given little consideration to gender differences in power relations. The growing influence of feminism in sociology has begun to change this. Feminists have insisted that one of the most obvious ways in which power is unequally distributed is between women and men. Feminists have also extended sociologists' understanding of differences in power to areas outside conventional politics by focusing on inequalities of power in areas such as sexual relationships, the family and the workplace.

Feminist theories of power For many feminists the study of politics starts not with the institutions of Parliament, parties and pressure groups, or even with the study of elites and the ownership of wealth, but with differences of power at the personal level. This is summed up in their slogan 'the personal is political'. This approach argues that the most obvious source of power differences in daily life lies in the power which men have over women. Feminist theories of gender and power are examined in Chapter 4. This chapter looks at women in terms of a more traditional view of power and politics.

Women in Parliament

Women hold few formal political positions in Britain. The number of women MPs in Westminster has increased slightly in recent years but women remain a small minority in both the House of Commons and in the House of Lords (see Activity 8). Margaret Thatcher became the first female Prime Minister in 1979 but during her period of office she appointed no women to her Cabinet. However, in John Major's 1994 Cabinet of 24 members, women doubled their presence to two.

A number of factors may explain the under-representation of women as MPs. Until recently women were unlikely to be accepted as parliamentary candidates by the main parties, apart from in seats where there was limited prospect of success. Added to this women may be less willing to cope with the unusual work patterns of MPs. The working hours of Parliament, often lasting into the early hours of the morning and its atmosphere of an old fashioned gentleman's club makes few concessions to the needs of women MPs, particularly if they have family commitments. It is hardly surprising therefore that a study by C. Mellors (1978) of British MPs found that women MPs were more likely than men to be over forty, married, middle class, university educated and with grown up children.

Vicky Randall (1982) suggests a number of reasons why women appear to be less active politically than men.

1 Women's lives tend to be dominated by the

private sphere of the family. This makes it difficult for women to participate in formal politics because of domestic commitments. It may also mean women prefer to exercise influence in more informal ways.

2 Because political institutions have traditionally been male dominated, male characteristics and behaviour patterns, for example aggressiveness, may be more valued, while feminine characteristics such as willingness to compromise may be under-valued. Women are therefore disadvantaged in competing for positions by male dominated selection criteria.

3 Political institutions are organised for the convenience of the men who established them. Thus timing of meetings and working hours may give little consideration to the needs of women members.

4 Political institutions may give little time to issues of concern to women, for example childcare provision or sexual harassment at work. Women may therefore feel that the agenda is set by men and their own concerns are regarded as marginal.

Women in other elites

Women are also under-represented in other positions within government and administration. Generally a much higher proportion of women gain seats on local government bodies than in Parliament, but they are still in the minority on most councils. In the Civil Service women form the vast majority of the clerical grades but only 6.6% of under-secretaries and above. Other elite positions in the state, such as ambassadors, university vice-chancellors and military leaders, also remain almost entirely male preserves.

Women are also under-represented in most other positions of power in society. In the economic sphere, for example, most company directors and senior managers are men - in 1991 only 28 of the main board appointments in the top 200 UK companies were held by women directors. Trade unions also tend to be male dominated - in 1991 only 20% of positions on union national executives were filled by women and a mere 2.7% of General Secretaries were female. Traditionally studies of elite recruitment have focused on the exclusion of working class men from elites. However, feminists have pointed to the even more marked absence of women.

Activity 8 Women and Politics

Item A Women in elites

	Number	Per cent
House of Commons (1992)	60	9
House of Lords (1988)	45	13
Government ministers (1988)	3	6
Ambassadors (1988)	4	3
Diplomatic service (1988)	735	24
Senior civil service (1988)	1,326	7
Officers in armed forces (1988)	2,381	6
Members of public bodies (1988)	8,529	19
Local councillors (1988)	-	25
Chief executives of local authorities (1991)	-	1.4
Circuit judges (1990)	19	5
House of Lords judges (1991)	0	0
BBC governors (1990)	3	25
Knighthoods (1988 Honours list)	0	0
Chief executives of companies (1991)	-	0.5

Adapted from various sources

Item B Women in Parliament

Whatever else it is remembered for, the 1987 election saw a significant increase in the representation of women in Parliament. The number of women MPs jumped from 28 to 41. Since 1945, there have usually been between 20 and 30 women MPs, with the exception of the Parliaments elected in 1951 (17) and 1979 (19). The 1983 Parliament started with only 23 women MPs, but gained a further five in by-elections over the next four years. If this by-election pattern had been repeated at the general election, there would have been over 200 women MPs elected.

The proportion of women in the 1987 House of Commons may have only been 6.3% but the 20 new women MPs amounted to 15.6% of all new members. Furthermore in the 77 seats in which a retiring MP was replaced by someone of his or her own party, one fifth of the new intake were women. The selection of women candidates in seats which parties expect to hold promises substantially higher female representation in the House of Commons in the future.

This prediction was not wholly borne out by the results of the 1992 General Election. 60 women won seats in the House of Commons (9% of the total). The number of female candidates increased from 327 in 1987 to 548 in 1992.

Adapted in part from A. Kennon 'Women in Parliament: Are Things Changing?' *Social Studies Review*, November 1987

Item C *Women and candidate selection*

The impediment to an expanded role for women in British politics tends to reside in local party candidate selection committees more than in the electorate. The key factor remains the widespread reluctance of selection committees - of whatever main party - to adopt women for desirable constituencies. As a result when a woman has managed to get elected to the Commons, it has usually been for a marginal seat where she has been vulnerable to defeat at the next election even though she has been as effective as a man in retaining support for her party. This is ironic since the evidence suggests that voters are just as likely to vote for a female candidate as a male.

In 1989 the Labour Party decided that half its MPs should be women by the year 2000. Candidates for a proportion of seats (including winnable seats) were to be drawn from all woman shortlists. Despite this, women in the Labour Party face an uphill task. In the 1992 General Election women were selected in only 10% of the safe Labour seats that became vacant. According to Labour Women's Network, the women only shortlists are unlikely to affect more than 55 seats.

Adapted from J. S. Rasumussen 'Women in Politics' in M. Burch and M. Moran (eds) *British Politics: A Reader*, 1987, p123 and D. Roberts (ed) *British Politics in Focus*, 1995

Item D

Demonstrating in favour of women priests, 1988

International Women's Day peace march

Questions

1 Of what significance, if any, is the information in Item A?
2 Read Items B and C.
   a) Should there be equal numbers of men and women in Parliament? Give reasons for your answer.
   b) What are the prospects for this?
3 Using Item D suggest why the study of women in politics should extend beyond their involvement in Parliament and various elites?

3.4 Ethnicity and power

Chapter 3 examines the position of ethnic minority groups in the UK and other Western societies. It presents evidence which indicates that many ethnic groups are excluded from any real political power. This section looks briefly at some of the responses of members of ethnic minorities to this situation.

Political participation

There is some evidence of an increase in the political participation of members of the Afro-Caribbean and Asian communities from the 1970s to the 1990s. This suggests that growing numbers feel that involvement in mainstream political institutions will offer some chance of redressing ethnic disadvantage.

1 **Voting behaviour** Surveys indicate that increasing numbers of ethnic minorities are voting in general elections (Layton-Henry, 1988, p21).

2 **Local government** There has been a growth in the number of local councillors from ethnic minority groups. However, their numbers are not large - 150 out of 25,000 in 1985 (Sewell, 1993, p14).

3 **National government** In 1987 four black MPs were elected to Parliament, the first since 1924. In 1992 they were re-elected along with two further black MPs. However, the number of Afro-Caribbean and Asian candidates for the main political parties is small - 18 in 1983, 27 in 1987 and 23 in 1992 (Sewell, 1993, p163).

4 **Ethnic organisations** There is a long history of community based self help and action groups in ethnic minority areas. There is some evidence that this approach is developing more into the mainstream. For example in 1986 the National Black Caucus was founded as an umbrella organisation to represent a range of black interests

and promote a specifically 'black' viewpoint. And there have been demands for 'black sections' within the Labour Party, again to directly represent ethnic minority interests. Such developments can be seen as ways of entering the political mainstream without losing ethnic identity.

Alternative forms of political action

Not all sociologists agree that ethnic minorities have made progress politically. Paul Gilroy in *There Ain't No Black in the Union Jack* (1987) argues that black people have felt increasingly powerless in British society and many have given up attempting to influence and participate in formal political institutions. As a result black political struggles have been expressed at local level in unorthodox forms, most spectacularly in riots in inner city areas from 1981 onwards. Gilroy (1983) also argues that movements such as Rastafarianism in the Afro-Caribbean community and even street crime in inner city areas are examples of political struggle by black people against white racism.

Gilroy's arguments have been strongly criticised, particularly his view that ethnic minority crime can be seen as a form of political struggle. For example,

John Lea and Jock Young (1984) point out that the victims of inner city crime are all too often other members of ethnic minority communities rather than 'white oppressors'. Nevertheless, some aspects of Gilroy's argument were echoed in Lord Scarman's report (1981) on the Brixton riots when he suggested that social conditions in Brixton had created 'a predisposition towards violent protest' among young black people. To Scarman the riots were not simply mindless or irrational but could be seen as a form of political protest.

Progress for ethnic minorities?

Some writers have argued that the influence of black people on the political process has already been felt in anti-discrimination legislation, in local authority initiatives on anti-racism in areas such as education, and in the growing involvement of black people in mainstream political organisations. However, there is considerable evidence that racial discrimination and racial disadvantage in the United Kingdom is extensive (see Chapter 4). It would seem that in a variety of ways black people are excluded from positions of power and influence in British society.

Activity 9   Race and Politics

Item A *The riots: a sociological view*

In 1980 police were virtually forced to withdraw from the St Paul's district of Bristol. A year later an even more violent confrontation between police and young blacks erupted in the Brixton riots. Throughout the summer of 1981 serious disturbances took place first in Liverpool and, then, in virtually every major British city. In 1985 there was another outbreak of major disturbances in Brixton, Tottenham, Toxteth (Liverpool) and in Handsworth (Birmingham).

In all of these disturbances conflicts with the police provided catalysts setting in motion the larger affairs. But black anger was not so much directed at police officers as at the system they personified. Black youths destroyed the houses in which they lived, the shops on which they depended for provisions, the environment in which they lived. They attacked the people whom they saw as their controllers. These didn't seem politically intelligible targets. But the rioting was directed at symbols: the properties and

Toxteth riots in 1981

institutions the youths attacked were the symbols of the system they saw exploiting them. So they burnt and looted the actual community in which they lived, a community which stood as testament to the impoverishment of their lives. They haven't destroyed property and wrought havoc because they wanted a new colour TV, ghetto-blaster or video, but because they have lost faith in the capacity and will of establishment institutions to take into account their interests

Adapted from E. Cashmore and B. Troyna *Introduction to Race Relations*, 1990, pp156-157 and E. Cashmore 'What Lay Behind Birmingham's Riots' *New Society*, 13.9.85

Item B *The riots: a government view*

'The sound which law abiding people in Handsworth heard on Monday night, the echoes of which I picked up on Tuesday, was not a cry for help but a cry for loot.'

Douglas Hurd, Home Secretary after the Handsworth riots, quoted in *Financial Times*, 13.9.85.

Questions

1 Briefly assess the view of the riots given in Item A.
2 Compare the views given in Items B and C. Why are they so different from each other?

Item C *The riots: a black poet's view*

You wonder why we uprise
Politically unstabilised
Economically destablised
People dehumanised
Youth criminalised
Mentally vandalised
Housing ghettoised
Politically unrecognised
And you wonder why we uprise.

Leroy Cooper, Liverpool 8 (Toxteth, the black area of Liverpool) quoted in Institute of Race Relations *The Fight Against Racism*, 1986, p45

3.5 Globalisation and politics

Traditionally the sociology of politics has focused on how power is distributed within nation states. Nation states are a relatively modern phenomenon. Many have only emerged in this century either from loose confederations of smaller states (eg Germany) or as a result of the break up of colonial empires (eg many African states). For some sociologists, such as Giddens (1990) the rise of the nation state is itself associated with modernity. Only the organisational power of modern bureaucracies enables the state to control a large geographical area. However, an analysis of power based on the nation state may be misguided. States increasingly operate within an international framework. There is a growing interdependence of world society, a process known as globalisation.

Globalisation

Globalisation refers to the fact that events in any one society are increasingly linked to events in other societies across the world. For example, the economies of nation states are now part of a global economic system. Transnational corporations (TNCs) have interests in many countries and can shift investment and production from one country to another wherever conditions are most favourable. Modern communications have meant that time and space have become compressed to the point that communication between countries is virtually instant. Western culture in the form of Coca Cola, McDonald's hamburgers and pop music can be found in the remotest corners of the world. Some sociologists have gone so far as to describe the world today as a 'global village'. Transnational corporations now sell their products to world markets - those who control such organisations exercise economic power on an international scale. Globalisation has also taken place in political terms.

Most nations are involved in some kind of international organisation such as the UN (United Nations) NATO (North Atlantic Treaty Organisation) or the IMF (International Monetary Fund). Sociologists are therefore paying more attention to politics at the international level. For example, the sociology of development examines the power relationships between the 'developed' and 'developing' world (see Chapter 16).

Nationalism

Globalisation would seem to suggest that movements such as nationalism will tend to disappear as larger and larger social units appear on the world stage. Yet it is possible to argue that just the opposite is happening. An increasing number of ethnic and linguistic groups within nation states are now identifying themselves as nations. Ethnic conflicts have broken out in former republics of the Soviet Union, in Yugoslavia and in many of the former colonial territories in Africa. In the Islamic world religious fundamentalism has been identified with new forms of nationalism, for example in the Iranian revolution and the civil war in Afghanistan. Even in the UK there has been a resurgence of Irish, Scots and Welsh nationalism in the last thirty years.

Some sociologists argue that the nation state is now challenged from both within by internal division and without by globalisation. Daniel Bell, for example, suggests that the nation state is 'too small for the big problems of life, and too big for the small problems of life' (1987, p14). Within its boundaries regional and nationalist movements threaten the unity of the nation state. Beyond its boundaries its sovereignty is undermined by international political organisations, for example intervention by the UN or European Union in national politics, or by international economic organisations, such as TNCs, which often have larger turnovers than the gross national product of many smaller countries.

New social movements: the end of class politics?

Traditionally the sociology of politics has focused on the relationship between economic inequalities and inequalities of power. Most political conflicts were seen to involve a struggle over the distribution of economic resources. Some writers suggest that more recent political conflicts are less concerned with material issues. R.Inglehart in *The Silent Revolution* (1977) argues that increasing affluence in Western societies has meant that non-economic issues such as the environment, consumer issues, women's rights and moral issues such as abortion and censorship have increasingly replaced concern about the distribution of resources reflected in traditional debates between parties of the left favouring greater equality and parties of the right arguing for the benefits of inequality. As more people have access to basic material resources such as decent food, clothing, housing and so on, other less material concerns have emerged as a focus for political debate.

Many sociologists are now interested in the growth of *new social movements* many of which reflect these concerns. Giddens defines a social movement as 'a collective attempt to further common interests through collaborative action outside the sphere of established institutions' (1989, pp629-30). Social movements often have little formal organisation and may involve very large numbers of people from different countries. They often include pressure groups and other types of formal political organisations. Examples of such movements are the environmental movement, the peace movement, the women's movement and many other movements concerned with civil rights and the interests of minorities such as disabled people, ethnic minorities and homosexuals. The growth of nationalism has created other forms of social movements based on ethnicity, language and religion.

Such movements have had enormous influence on politics at both national and international level. Feminism, for example has been one of the most influential social movements of the twentieth century. It has resulted in women gaining formal political equality in many countries. More recently feminists have campaigned for equal rights in work, education, sexual relationships and marriage as well as for access to contraception, abortion and childcare facilities.

Environmentalists have similarly influenced the agenda for political debate in North America and Western Europe. Few political parties can now ignore 'green' issues. While parties such as the British Green Party have had only limited success in elections, green pressure groups such as Greenpeace and the Council for the Protection of Rural England have achieved considerable success. The top eight environmental pressure groups in the UK had a combined membership of over 3 million in 1989, double their 1980 membership (J. McCormick, 1991).

Despite such developments, there is considerable evidence that class politics is not dead. The growth in poverty and unemployment, violent confrontations on picket lines in industrial disputes, such as the miners' strike of 1984-5 and protests against the poll tax in the late 1980s and early 90s can all be seen as evidence that class conflict remains significant. Moreover, most people have little direct involvement in new social movements such as the peace movement and the women's movement. Research suggests that the membership of such movements is overwhelmingly young, well educated and drawn from the 'new middle class' of professional and scientific-technical workers.

Modernity or postmodernity?

Some of the developments examined in this section have been seen as characteristics of postmodern society. Writers such as David Harvey (1989), argue that the modern world which emerged as a result of industrialisation and the rise of the nation state is being replaced by postmodern society. In the postmodern world economic relationships, mass communication and mass culture are increasingly globalised. And the same applies to our experience, our concerns and our fears. For example events like the Chernobyl nuclear disaster are given worldwide coverage by the media so heightening awareness of the possibility of global ecological catastrophe (Tester, 1995).

The postmodern world places increasing pressure on the nation state. The stronger the links between nations, the less power each individual nation has to influence the conduct or fate of its citizens. Thus the European Union passes laws which affect all member states; individuals take their governments to the European Court; countries such as Wales and Scotland bypass the British government and appeal directly to the European Commission. In this respect globalisation promises increasing unity on an international level and increasing fragmentation on a national level (Bonnett, 1994).

Postmodernism as a theory rejects the argument of many classical sociological theories that the development of societies is explicable in terms of underlying historical trends or economic forces. For example, modernisation theorists have emphasised a 'logic of industrialism' which states that all societies develop along a similar path, while Marxists tend to see the direction of capitalist societies as dictated by the requirements for capital accumulation. For postmodernists social life is the outcome of a multiplicity of factors which cannot be reduced to any simple underlying theme. For example political conflict cannot be reduced to an aspect of the class struggle as Marxists have claimed. Instead it results from a range of factors as the growth of new social movements indicates.

Whether the social changes examined in this section have led to a postmodern society is debatable. Anthony Giddens (1990), for example, accepts that globalisation is occurring but rejects the view that this reflects a change from the modern to the postmodern. For Giddens, we are witnessing a new higher stage of modernity. Just as modern technology and the power of bureaucratic organisations allowed for centralised control by the state, this has now been extended to international forms of global control.

Globalisation, power and democracy

Is the nation state threatened by globalisation? Can it still claim sovereignty, independence and self-determination? Or is power steadily moving to international organisations such as the European Union and the transnational corporation? Can the nation state deal with the challenges of the present and the future, challenges which are often transnational? For example, the environment knows no boundaries as global warming illustrates.

Many commentators believe that power is moving from national to international political organisations. And they see this move as essential to deal with global issues such as threats to the environment and global organisations such as TNCs.

But can democracy survive in a global context? David Held argues that transnational organisations such as the World Bank and the European Union must be made more accountable. In the case of the EU this might mean strengthening the powers of the European Parliament. Held believes that transnational organisations are essential to deal with transnational issues. Ultimately he looks forward to some form of world parliament which would become, 'an authoritative international centre for the consideration and examination of pressing global issues eg health and disease, food supply and distribution, the debt burden of the Third World, the instability of the hundreds of billions of dollars that circulates the globe daily, ozone depletion, and the reduction of the risks of nuclear war' (1993, p15).

Summary

1 Elite theory claims that power is concentrated in the hands of one or more elites. There is evidence that certain elites in British society exercise disproportionate power. Members of these elites often share a common social and educational background and similar political views.

2 Marxists argue that the state represents the interests of the ruling class, those who own and control the means of production.

3 Inequalities of power are related to gender and ethnicity as well as class. There is evidence that women and ethnic minorities are excluded from power in many areas of social life.

4 Globalisation has led some sociologists to question whether the nation state should be the focus for the sociology of politics. They argue that international organisations which transcend individual nations have challenged the centrality of the nation state as a political unit.

Activity 10 Politics in a Global Society

Item A *Kurdistan*

Distribution of the Kurdish people by country

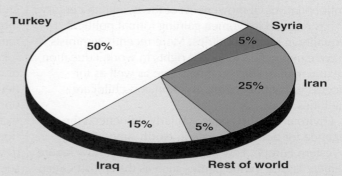

Turkey 50%

Syria 5%

Iran 25%

Rest of world 5%

Iraq 15%

The Kurdish flag. The wording reads 'Freedom for Kurdistan'. According to the Kurdish Organisation for Culture and Education, Kurdistan covers an area of 520,000 km² mainly in Turkey, Iran and Iraq and has a population of over 25 million Kurds.

Item B *Chernobyl*

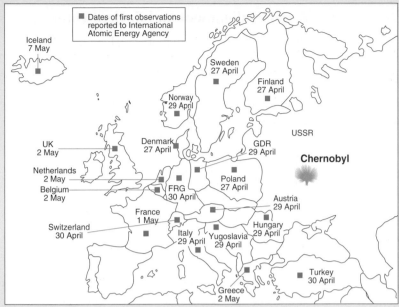

> ■ Dates of first observations reported to International Atomic Energy Agency

Iceland
7 May

Sweden
27 April

Finland
27 April

Norway
29 April

USSR

UK
2 May

Denmark
27 April

GDR
29 April

Chernobyl

Netherlands
2 May

Belgium
2 May

FRG
30 April

Poland
27 April

Austria
29 April

France
1 May

Switzerland
30 April

Italy
29 April

Yugoslavia
29 April

Hungary
29 April

Turkey
30 April

Greece
2 May

FRG = Federal Republic of Germany (the former West Germany)
GDR = German Democratic Republic (the former East Germany)

On 25 April 1986 the nuclear power station at Chernobyl in the Soviet Union exploded as a result of human error. 31 workers and firefighters died within days (of radiation burns) and 50,000 square kilometres of surrounding land was contaminated. The nuclear fallout reached 20 countries, including Britain. Scientists have estimated that between 280,000 and 500,000 deaths will result worldwide from this accident.

Greenpeace, *Nuclear Power*, 1992

Dates of first measurement of radiation fallout from Chernobyl in various countries, 27 April to 2 May 1986. Map based on information from the International Atomic Energy Agency.

Item C *The advent of a global society?*

Contemporary developments have suggested to many observers the transcendence of the traditional mentality and character of international statecraft. Advances in communications and transportation have unified the planet. New types of transnational and international actors more responsive to modern science, technology and economics have broken the monopoly of the state in the management and governance of international systems. Global ecological problems, as well as resource constraints and limits to growth, have placed on the world's agenda a set of pressing issues whose solutions are beyond the means of self-serving nation states.

Has there been a transformation in the human consciousness along with the advent of a global society? In actuality the political fragmentation of the world has increased in recent decades. The world now encompasses more than 150 separate sovereignties; nationalism has become the predominant religion of modern man. As has been the case in Europe, the continuing formation of nation states and the spread of nationalism have unleashed powerful and dangerous forces of destruction. The present era is witnessing the proliferation of the nation state, not its transcendence.

Adapted from R. Gilpin *War and Change in World Politics*, 1981, pp223-6

Item D *Global media and the revolutions of 1989*

The revolutions of 1989 in Eastern Europe all shared a common factor: they were significantly affected by the globalisation of information technology and have, in their turn, interactively shaped those media.For some time citizens of many Eastern European countries had been able to receive television and radio transmissions from Western countries. Video recorders had become a major vehicle for the dissemination of alternative information and ideology. Throughout the summer of 1989 first in Poland, then in Hungary and East Germany, a series of relatively sporadic changes began to occur. The key telecommunication connections were television, radio, telephone, print media and the complex and highly collaborative exchange of information, news, rumour and deep-seated fear in face-to-face settings.

It is not my intention to suggest that the media caused the revolutions. The political and economic crises in Eastern Europe have been years in the making. I have been concerned simply to highlight what I take to be a largely invisible yet new and significant aspect to these spontaneous events: the globalisation of communication.

Adapted from D. Boden 'Reinventing the Global Village: Communications and the Revolutions of 1989' in A. Giddens (ed) *Human Societies: A Reader*, 1992, pp327-31

Questions

1 Using Items A and B discuss the view that international organisations are essential to deal with the problems of a global society.

2 Why might globalisation go hand in hand with nationalist movements such as the movement for an independent Kurdistan (Item A).

3 Read Item C. Discuss the arguments for and against the claim that globalisation has undermined the importance of the nation state.

4 Read Item D. Suggest ways in which the development of global communications might assist the sort of revolutionary changes which occurred in Eastern Europe.

4 Voting Behaviour

Key Issues

1 What influence does social class have on voting patterns?
2 What influence do other social factors have on voting patterns?
3 How and why has voting behaviour changed in Britain since 1970?

This chapter has considered the role of parties and pressure groups in politics. However, the involvement of most citizens in such organisations is very limited. National elections are one of the few occasions on which most people are directly involved in politics (although even here around one quarter of the electorate does not vote). This part of the chapter examines social factors which influence the way people vote in United Kingdom general elections.

4.1 Changing patterns of voting behaviour and dealignment

Unlike other forms of political behaviour, for example pressure group activity, voting in elections is usually seen as an essentially individual and personal act. In most modern democracies voting takes place in secret. However, sociologists and pollsters have undertaken extensive research to find out how people actually vote. Sociologists have emphasised the extent to which voting follows social patterns, with people sharing common social characteristics tending to support the same party.

Political socialisation and voting behaviour

A good example of this approach is the work of Butler and Stokes (1974) who investigated the relationship between social factors and voting behaviour in a series of surveys between 1963 and 1970. Butler and Stokes argued that most voters acquire their political attitudes as a result of early *political socialisation*. The family in particular, but also local communities and workplaces, shape the political views of children and young adults. Children tended to follow the voting patterns of their parents. Class was an important influence with most people following the voting pattern of those in similar occupations. Most people therefore consistently aligned themselves with the party which traditionally represented their class, a process sociologists call *partisan alignment*. Thus most nonmanual workers (the middle class) were Conservative voters and most manual workers (the working class) were Labour voters.

Partisan alignment and deviant voters

Butler and Stokes' view that social class was the dominant influence on voting behaviour was shared by most researchers from 1945 to the 1960s. Indeed much of the research from this period focused on what were seen as a minority of *deviant voters*, those who apparently voted against their class interests. Working class Conservative voters were singled out for special attention.

One influential explanation of working class conservatism was developed by Robert McKenzie and Alan Silver (1968). They investigated the thesis put forward by Walter Bagehot in the nineteenth century that many of the working class defer to their social superiors and thus regard politicians drawn from the upper class (as many Conservative candidates are) as 'born to rule'. McKenzie and Silver found evidence of such *deferential voting* in about half the working class Tories they studied. However, they also identified what they termed *secular voters*. These were working class Conservatives who supported the party on the basis of its policies and a belief it would bring them direct benefits, for example higher living standards. Many recent studies argue that this type of secular voting has become more widespread since the 1970s.

Changing voting patterns and dealignment

By the 1970s many commentators were suggesting that traditional patterns of voting behaviour were breaking down. In particular it was argued that the alignment between class and voting behaviour which had been apparent in the postwar period was weakening. Some commentators saw the election of February 1974 as a watershed in British politics. This was the first election since 1945 in which the Liberal and Nationalist parties made a breakthrough. It also marks the beginning of the weakening of partisan alignment, with fewer people voting for the party traditionally associated with their social class. These trends continued into the 1980s and 90s.

Partisan dealignment

The political scientist Ivor Crewe argues that traditional theories, such as those of Butler and Stokes, fail to explain changes in voting behaviour. If political support was determined by parental socialisation it is difficult to explain how increasing numbers of voters have been deserting the party which they, and often their parents, had supported. Certainly increased social mobility meant that children's social class often differed from that of their parents, creating cross-cutting loyalties. However, Crewe argues that this is not sufficient to explain the general weakening of the link between class and party and the growing volatility of the electorate. Bo Sarvlik and Ivor Crewe (1983) argue that a process of *partisan dealignment* has occurred, whereby fewer voters are clearly aligned with one or other of the two main parties. This is apparent in two main trends.

Firstly, the decline in the share of the vote taken by the two main parties. In the elections between 1950 and 1970 an average of 92% of those who voted supported one of the two main parties, Conservative and Labour. Between 1974 and 1983 these two parties' share of the poll fell to 75%. This change has benefited the other parties, perhaps most significantly the centre parties, the Liberals and the Social Democratic Party now merged as the Liberal Democrats. Secondly, there has been a decline in political partisanship. Fewer voters now seem to strongly identify themselves as supporters of one party or another. Voters are more volatile, more likely to change their vote from one election to another. Partisan dealignment has been seen as a result of a more politically aware electorate. David Denver (1989) attributes this to both higher levels of education in the electorate and to more extensive coverage of politicians and political issues in the mass media. Both of these may have made the electorate better informed and less likely to resort to traditional partisan loyalties in deciding how to vote.

Issue voting

Some commentators, such as Himmelweit et al (1985), argue that a voter's stance on specific issues rather than their class loyalty is now the major influence on party choice. However, Ivor Crewe (1987) argues that the relationship between issues and voting is complex. In 1987 the issues that most concerned voters were unemployment, defence, the National Health Service and education. On all these except defence the majority of the electorate were in favour of Labour's policies yet the Conservatives won. Crewe claims that most voters attach more importance to their own prosperity than to issues which affect society as a whole. 55% of voters thought the Conservatives were more likely to produce prosperity, compared to only 27% for Labour. Crewe argues that voting behaviour cannot be explained simply in terms of issues and party policies. What matters is the relative importance voters give to the various issues.

Class dealignment

Writers like Crewe have argued that the process of partisan dealignment has been accompanied by a process of *class dealignment*. Class dealignment refers to the decline in the influence of social class on voting. Voters preferences are less likely to be aligned to the traditional party of their class. The relationship between class and voting, which dominated theories of voting up to 1970, seemed less and less strong.

This is most noticeable in the case of Labour whose share of manual workers' vote has been declining steadily since 1966. In that election Labour received 64% of manual votes; by 1979 this was down to 50%; and in 1983, Labour's worst showing since 1945, only 42%. The Conservative vote has always been less class based but they too experienced a decline in their traditional support from 64% of nonmanual workers in 1966 to only 51% in October 1974, although this increased slightly in subsequent elections. David Denver notes that in the 1960s around two-thirds of voters supported their 'natural' class party but in the 1980s less than half of voters did so. According to Ivor Crewe the decline in class voting is closely linked to the decline in political partisanship.

Changes in the class structure

Crewe relates class dealignment to broader changes which have occurred in the class structure which may have weakened voters' identification with their social class and strengthened other sources of social identity. Most notably there has been a decline in employment in the sectors where Labour support has traditionally been strongest, such as the heavy industries like coal, steel and shipbuilding many of which were state owned and highly unionised.

Partly as a result of these changes, Crewe suggests the working class has become socially and politically divided. A 'new working class' has emerged - manual workers who live in the South, are owner-occupiers, private sector employees and non-union members. They are more likely to vote Conservative. The 'traditional working class' - manual workers who live in the North and Scotland, are council tenants, union members and public sector employees - usually remain Labour supporters. Crewe acknowledges that not all voters fit neatly into one of these two categories. However, he points out that voters with new working class characteristics are steadily growing and this has undermined Labour's electoral base in the working class.

In an analysis of the 1987 election Crewe (1987) argues that similar divisions are starting to appear in the middle class. He points to a marked loss of support for the Conservatives amongst the university educated and public sector nonmanual workers. However, the non-university educated and private sector workers in the middle class tend to remain loyal to the Conservatives.

From the 1970s onwards theories of partisan and class dealignment became increasingly influential as an explanation for changes in voting patterns. Many sociologists and political scientists began to reject the traditional view that class was the basis of British politics. However, in the 1980s some sociologists began to question this argument. Their views are examined in the next section.

Activity 11   Dealignment in British Politics

Item A

'Class-voting': nonmanual and manual voting in selected elections, 1966-1992

Votes	1966		1970		1979		1983		1987		1992	
	NM %	M %	NM %	M %	NM %	M %	NM %	M %	NM %	M %	NM %	M %
Conservative	60	25	64	33	60	35	58	33	55	36	49	35
Liberal or minor party	14	6	11	9	17	15	26	29	27	22	25	20
Labour	26	69	25	58	23	50	17	38	18	42	26	45
Class index of Labour voting	43		33		27		21		24		19	
Nonmanual Conservative voters + manual Labour voters as % of all voters	66%		60%		55%		47%		48%		47%	

NM = Nonmanual workers   M = Manual workers

'Class index of Labour voting' is the percentage of manual workers voting Labour minus the percentage of nonmanual workers voting Labour.

Adapted from M. Haralambos and M. Holborn *Sociology: Themes and Perspectives, 1990*, p173; 1992 figures supplied courtesy of I. Crewe from Harris/ITN exit poll, 9 April 1992

Item B

Party choice of the 'old' and 'new' working class 1992 (per cent)

	Old Working Class			New Working Class		
	North/ Scotland	Council tenant	Union member	South	Owner-occupier	Non-union
Con	23	20	23	38	38	34
Lab	52	57	45	36	39	43
Lib Dem	13	12	16	22	18	16
Lab lead	+29	+37	+22	-2	+1	+9

Source A. King in *Daily Telegraph*, 14.4.92 (Gallup post-election poll)

Item C *Issue voting in the 1992 election*

At first sight it would appear that the argument that party choice in Britain has come to reflect more strongly voters' opinions about political issues cannot be sustained in the light of what we know about the 1992 campaign. On the dominant campaign issues - health, unemployment, education - Labour's policies were clearly preferred to those of the Conservatives. If the voters had voted on the issues Labour, it could be argued, would have won.

Three points can be made about this. Firstly, there were important issues on which the Conservatives were the most preferred party by a considerable margin - general ability to handle the economy and taxation policy - and the Harris exit poll found that 49% of voters cited taxation as the most important issue affecting their vote. Secondly, both the exit polls and the Gallup post-election survey found that there had been a significant shift to the Conservatives on the issues towards the end of the campaign. It seems likely, however, that this finding reflects a good deal of rationalisation after the event by voters. Thirdly, and most importantly, 'issue voting' should not be narrowly construed but should be widened to include

electors' judgements about party leaders and more general perceptions of the parties. It was in these respects that Labour suffered. Throughout the campaign Mr Kinnock (the Labour leader) lagged behind Mr Major (the Conservative leader) in opinion polls as the person likely to make the best Prime Minister.

Adapted from D. Denver 'The 1992 General Election: In Defence of Psephology' *Talking Politics*, 1992, p5

Item D *Why the Tories won in 1992*

Adapted from a cartoon by John Kent

Questions

1 Examine Item A. What evidence is there that class has become less important as an influence on voting behaviour?

2 a) What political divisions within the working class are suggested by Item B?
   b) What explanations would you give for the different political alignments of sectors within the working class?

3 Opinion polls carried out at the time of both the 1987 and 1992 elections suggested that on most of the main issues Labour commanded more support than the Conservatives. Using data from Items C and D and elsewhere explain why the Conservatives won these elections.

4.2 The continuing influence of class on voting behaviour

Not all sociologists have accepted the argument that the relationship between social class and voting behaviour has weakened. In *How Britain Votes* Anthony Heath, Roger Jowell and John Curtice (1985) question whether dealignment has taken place. Their study was based on research into the 1983 election as well as analysis of the British Election Surveys going back to 1963. Heath et al's approach differs methodologically from previous studies in a number of important respects. This helps to explain why they come to different conclusions about the importance of class in voting behaviour. These differences are summarised below.

Definitions of class

Traditionally psephologists - those who study voting behaviour - have used the social categories employed by market researchers (A, B, C1, C2, D and E) which are based on occupational status. These are often simplified into two classes, manual and nonmanual. Heath et al developed an alternative classification based on economic interests, which gave five social classes.

1 *The salariat* - managers, administrators, supervisors, professionals and semi-professionals.
2 *Routine nonmanual workers* - clerks, salesworkers, secretaries.
3 *The petty bourgeoisie* - farmers, small business owners, self-employed manual workers.
4 *Foremen and technicians* - manual workers with autonomy or in supervisory positions.
5 *The working class* - all other manual workers.

Heath et al's definition of the working class differs from conventional classifications since manual workers are spread across classes 3, 4 and 5. In addition, Heath et al do not classify women by their husband's occupation but by their own occupation when they are in paid employment.

Absolute and relative class voting

Heath et al argue that measures of *absolute* class voting (the percentage of the electorate who support the 'natural' party of their class) are misleading. This is because the share of votes the Labour Party has received in recent years has declined in the electorate as a whole, not just in the working class. Heath et al argue that dealignment would only be occurring if the working class were deserting the Labour Party in *relatively* larger numbers than other social classes. In reality support for the Labour Party fell by the same proportion in all social classes between 1974 and 1983. Thus Heath et al argue that what has happened is simply a general loss of support for Labour rather than class dealignment as such.

In order to measure the relative strength of the relationship between class and voting behaviour Heath et al use what they call the *odds ratio*. This is the odds of a member of the salariat voting Conservative divided by the odds of a working class person voting Labour. Heath et al argue that an examination of changes in the odds ratio since 1964 shows there is no discernible trend towards class dealignment. Instead there has been a 'trendless fluctuation' in the strength of class alignments which suggests that other commentators have read too much into short term changes in voting patterns.

Changes in the class structure

Heath et al see changes in the class structure as more important than class dealignment for the decline in support for the Labour Party. They argue that between 1964 and 1983, because of changes in the occupational structure, the working class contracted (from 47% to 34% of the electorate) and the salariat and routine nonmanual classes expanded (the salariat increased from 18% to 27%). This alone, in their view, accounts for nearly half the decline in Labour's vote, since its natural class support - the working class - is diminishing. However, Heath et al acknowledge that Labour's decline has been greater than that predicted on the basis of changes in the class structure and see the success of the centre parties (the Liberals and SDP) as an important factor.

Criticisms of Heath et al

How Britain Votes has been criticised by dealignment theorists, for example Crewe (1986) and Dunleavy (1987). Many of the criticisms are technical ones based on the methodology employed in the study. Four main issues have been raised.

1 Heath et al's definition of class results in a very small working class - only 34% of the electorate in 1983. This definition tends to exclude those manual workers most likely to vote Conservative. It therefore produces a distorted picture of relatively strong working class support for the Labour Party.
2 Crewe argues that the absolute decline in class voting *is* relevant since if fewer people are voting for their class party it must surely indicate a weakening of class alignment.
3 Dunleavy and Crewe are particularly critical of Heath et al's use of odds ratios to measure class voting. They argue these figures tend to exaggerate changes in class voting patterns. Also, by focusing on support for the two main parties it ignores the significance of support for the centre parties. The odds ratio only deals with the voting behaviour of the two extremes of social class - the working class and the salariat - only three-fifths of the electorate. Crewe argues that this ignores precisely those groups mostly likely to be undergoing dealignment such as routine nonmanual workers, foremen and technicians.
4 Crewe points out that even using Heath et al's own calculations, changes in the size of different classes account for only half of the changes in voting patterns. Crewe suggests that they have placed too much emphasis on this as a factor. He argues that changes in voting patterns *within*

classes have been more significant than changes in the relative size of classes.

Heath et al: further research

Heath and his colleagues (1991, 1994) carried out follow up studies based on the 1987 and 1992 elections. In response to criticism of the odds ratio they used a statistical method known as log-linear analysis to study the relationship between class and party choice. This allowed for the fact that the relative size of the classes had changed as well as for the fluctuations in support for different parties. In these studies Heath et al stand by the conclusions of their original study. They acknowledge that in *absolute* terms fewer people voted for the party traditionally associated with their class - for example, in 1987 the proportion of middle class people who voted Conservative plus working class people who voted Labour had fallen to 52% compared with 64% in 1964 (Heath et al 1991, p64).

Heath et al reiterate their view that it is relative class voting which is most relevant for assessing whether the relationship between class and voting has weakened. For example, if there had been a relative decline in class voting we would expect Labour's loss of support in the working class to be compensated by a corresponding increase in support in other social classes. Instead Labour has lost support relatively evenly in all social classes. For Heath et al Labour's lack of electoral success should not be equated with a process of class dealignment. Heath et al claim their analysis of relative class voting using log linear analysis reveals the same trends as their former use of odds ratios - what they describe as a 'trendless fluctuation' in the relative strength of class voting. They conclude that changes in voting patterns are attributable to the disappointing performance of Labour governments and the sharp increase in candidates from the centre parties which have attracted more votes from all social classes rather than to class dealignment.

David Denver (1993) suggests that the different conclusions reached by Heath et al and their critics are mainly due to different definitions of class dealignment. Class dealignment is understood by many writers, such as Crewe, to mean a decline in the propensity of members of a class to vote for a particular party - a decline in absolute, rather than relative, class voting. However, Heath et al maintain that only a measure of relative class voting can establish whether or not class dealignment is occurring. If we accept Crewe's definition and measurement - absolute class voting - then there is a clear trend indicating class dealignment. If we accept Heath et al's definitions and measurement - relative class voting - then there is no trend to class dealignment, simply 'trendless fluctuation'.

4.3 Other influences on voting behaviour

Gender While social class has been seen as the most powerful social influence on voting behaviour, sociologists have explored a number of other social factors which might be linked to voting patterns. In most elections up to 1974 women were slightly more likely than men to vote Conservative. This was traditionally attributed to women's isolation from the male world of paid employment, trade unions and industrial conflict which socialised male manual workers into attitudes sympathetic to Labour. Studies of elections since 1979, however, suggest that this difference has virtually disappeared (Norris, 1986; Walsh et al, 1991).

Ethnicity Afro-Caribbean and Asian voters were the most solidly Labour of any identified group of electors in 1983, with opinion polls suggesting that between 64% and 81% supported Labour (Fitzgerald, 1988). According to the Harris ITN poll 90% of Afro-Caribbean voters and 71% of Asians voted Labour in 1992.

This strong support for Labour has been explained in class terms - a disproportionate number of black voters are working class. And most Afro-Caribbeans and Asians say they vote Labour because of the party's support for the working class. However, nonmanual black voters are also more likely to vote Labour. This suggests that ethnicity is a factor in voting behaviour - Labour is seen as more sympathetic towards ethnic minorities (Sewell, 1993, pp82-86).

Region The most obvious geographical difference in party support is the so-called 'North-South divide'. The Labour Party has traditionally been stronger in the North of England, Wales and Scotland than in the South and this has become even more noticeable in recent years. In 1987 Labour held only 3 seats south of a line drawn from the Wash to the Bristol Channel. North of this line in England Labour held 153 seats to the Conservatives 357, while in both Wales and Scotland Labour held more seats than all the other parties put together. Ivor Crewe (1987) argues that as a result of Labour's loss of working class support in southern England, it has become 'a regional class party'. In 1987 only 28% of manual workers in the South voted Labour, while 57% of those in Scotland and the North did.

Three geographers, Johnston, Pattie and Allsopp (1988), argue that while class remains a significant factor in voting, there are important regional variations in the strength of support for different parties from each social class. The Labour Party for example tends to gain more votes from middle class voters in its industrial heartlands in Scotland, Wales

and the North, while the Conservatives have been most successful in attracting working class votes in southern England. Johnson et al argue that local influences need to be taken into account when explaining voting behaviour since it cannot be assumed that factors such as class have the same influence in all parts of the country.

The mass media Theories of dealignment and issue voting argue that voters' party loyalties are much weaker today than in the past. They suggest that a much higher proportion of the electorate is susceptible to persuasion to change their votes. In this context some social scientists have argued that the mass media is an increasingly important influence. Voters are likely to be swayed by any bias in the media and by the parties which are most successful in using the media to put across their messages.

Some commentators have asserted that a pro-Conservative bias in the media has helped the Conservatives to win recent elections. For example, after the Conservative victory in 1992 the pro-Tory *Sun* claimed 'It was the Sun wot won it'. However, some studies of this election campaign question the importance of media influence in the Conservative victory. John Curtice and Holly Semetko (1994) found that the predominantly Conservative press had a very limited influence on voters. Holly Semetko et al (1994) found little evidence of Conservative bias in their content analysis of the television coverage of the campaign (see pp537;548-550 for further discussion of the media and voting behaviour).

Opinion polls It has also been claimed that extensive media coverage of opinion polls can actually influence the results of elections since people may switch their vote because of opinion poll predictions. There is little clear cut evidence for this. However, Crewe (1992) suggests an element of tactical voting may have led to a Conservative victory in 1992. Some Liberal Democrat voters may have switched to the Conservatives at the last moment fearing predictions by opinion polls of a Labour victory.

The 1992 election

Prior to the 1992 election, the Conservative Party had won three consecutive election victories (in 1979, 1983 and 1987). However, many commentators felt that in 1992 the conditions were ideal for a Labour victory. Labour had transformed its public image and conducted an effective election campaign, while the Conservatives had presided over an economic recession and conducted a lacklustre campaign. Opinion polls, right up to polling day, predicted a Labour victory. However, despite improving on its 1987 performance, Labour failed to dislodge the Conservatives. Ivor Crewe (1992) suggests a number of reasons why Labour lost for the fourth time in a row.

1 **Party leaders** Neil Kinnock's rating as a potential Prime Minister was worse than John Major's. The replacement of Margaret Thatcher by John Major, a more popular Conservative leader, may have helped here.

2 **Issues** Labour was ahead of the Conservatives on many important issues such as health and education and had dropped its unpopular non-nuclear defence policy. Despite this, fears concerning possible tax increases under Labour and a feeling that the Conservatives were more competent in managing the economy may have been decisive issues swinging the important floating voters to the Conservatives.

3 **A last minute swing** Many voters may have changed their minds or made up their minds at the last minute. A Harris poll conducted just before the election suggested that there may have been a last minute surge to the Conservatives.

4 **The mass media** Most of the tabloids campaigned on behalf of the Conservatives. Lord McAlpine a senior Conservative paid tribute to their contribution after the election. But the influence of the press is not clear cut. The swing to the Conservatives was larger among readers of the pro-Labour *Daily Mirror* and the non-partisan *Independent* than among readers of some Tory papers.

5 **A squeeze on the Liberal Democrat vote** At the end of the election campaign a Labour-Liberal Democrat coalition government seemed a likely result. The Conservatives attacked the Liberal Democrats claiming that voting for them would allow a Labour victory. This seems to have worked. According to a MORI panel survey one in five potential Liberal Democrat voters defected to the Conservatives in the week before the election.

The Labour Party and the changing social structure

Many commentators now see Labour's chances of electoral success as slim. Heath et al (1991, 1994) while denying that there has been class dealignment point to the declining proportion of the electorate who are manual workers. This can make a real difference. Assuming that the class make-up of the electorate in 1992 was the same as in 1964 (when there was a large working class) then Labour might have got 5 percentage points more than in 1992 and the Conservatives 4 points less. Other social trends, however, may have the opposite effect. Ethnic minority groups

(traditionally strong Labour supporters) have gradually grown larger as have people with higher education (who are less likely to vote Conservative). However, these factors do not outweigh the reduction in the size of the working class. Partly as a result of these trends, Heath et al conclude that although Labour can make the main contribution to a Conservative defeat, it is very unlikely to win an election outright.

Although most long term social trends seem to be against Labour, few commentators would dismiss the party as a spent force. Most would agree with Ivor Crewe that 'Labour's task in trying to win elections is rather like climbing up a downward moving escalator - not impossible, but difficult' (quoted in Denver, 1993, p84).

Conclusion

A range of factors are linked to how people vote. Some are long term factors - such as upbringing and social background - others are short term - such as election issues and the performance of parties in the media and opinion polls. It is difficult to assess the relative importance of these influences. One way of drawing diverse influences together is offered by Richard Rose and Ian McAllister's (1990) *lifetime learning model*. They suggest that voters are influenced by a range of factors throughout life starting with early political socialisation in the family, and continuing with the socioeconomic concerns of adult life. These longer term factors remain an influence but may be reinforced or overridden by other immediate influences at the time of the election. Dealignment theorists claim that short term influences such as electoral issues and media campaigns are of growing influence. However, even they admit that long term influences such as class, ethnicity and region remain significant.

Summary

1 Political views and behaviour are likely to reflect the influence of a variety of social factors. Both short term influences such as party policies and media coverage of election campaigns and long term influences such as family background and social class identifications are likely to affect voting behaviour.

2 Social class has traditionally been seen as the dominant influence on voting behaviour. However, some commentators have identified a process of class dealignment. Others dispute this, arguing that voting is still patterned by social factors, in particular class.

Activity 12 Absolute and Relative Class Voting

Trends in class voting

	Absolute class voting %	Relative class voting log odds ratio
1964	64	2.2
1966	64	2.0
1970	60	1.4
Feb 1974	56	1.8
Oct 1974	57	1.9
1979	57	1.6
1983	52	1.9
1987	52	1.7
1992	56	1.7

Absolute class voting: the percentage of all voters who are middle class and vote Conservative plus the percentage who are working class and vote Labour.

Relative class voting: log odds ratio of the votes won by the Conservatives and Labour among members of the salariat and the working class.

Questions

1 How do the trends in the relationship between social class and voting behaviour differ depending on whether an absolute or relative measure of class voting is used?

2 Evaluate the usefulness of these two measures of class voting.

3 Does the phrase 'trendless fluctuation' adequately describe relative class voting from 1964 to 1992?

The long term trends in the relationship between social class and voting are shown in the table on the left. It is undoubtedly the case that the proportion of the electorate who vote for the party of their class (the proportion of the middle class who vote Conservative plus the proportion of the working class who vote Labour) did decline more or less continuously between 1964 and 1987. This we have called 'absolute' class voting.

We have also introduced the concept of relative class voting. Relative class voting refers to the relative strength of parties in the different social classes. It measures the relationship between class and party after controlling for any across-the-board movement between the parties. Thus if Labour's vote falls, or rises, across the board while at the same time remaining relatively stronger in its traditional base of the working class than in other social classes, then our measure of relative class voting would be unchanged. If on the other hand class were to lose its association with vote and the Labour Party were to become equally strong, or weak, in all classes alike, then the measure of relative class voting would decline. To illustrate this trend in relative class voting, we use the log odds ratio comparing the relative strength of the Conservative and Labour Parties in the salariat and working class. If social class had indeed been becoming irrelevant, what we should have seen is the log odds ratio declining to around zero. Instead there has been a 'trendless fluctuation' around a level in between that of 1964 and 1970.

Adapted from A. Heath, R. Jowell and J. Curtice 'Can Labour Win?' in A. Heath et al (eds) *Labour's Last Chance?*, 1994, pp282-283

References

Althusser, L. *For Marx* (Penguin, Harmondsworth, 1969)

Bachrach, P. and Baratz, M. 'The Two Faces of Power' *American Political Science Review*, 56, 1962

Baggott, R. 'Pressure Group Politics in Britain: Change or Decline?' *Talking Politics*, Autumn, 1988

Bell, D. 'The World and the United States in 2013' *Daedalus*, vol 116 no 3, 1987, pp1-32

Boden, D. 'Reinventing the Global Village: Communication and the Revolutions of 1989' in A. Giddens (ed) *Human Societies: A Reader* (Polity Press, Cambridge, 1992)

Bonnett, K. 'Power and Politics' in M. Haralambos (ed) *Developments in Sociology* vol 10 (Causeway Press, Ormskirk, 1994)

Bottomore, T. *Elites and Society* (Routledge, London, 1993)

Brittan, S. *The Role and Limits of Government* (Temple Smith, London, 1983)

Budge, I. et al *The New British Political System* (Longman, London, 1983)

Butler, D.E. and Kavanagh, D. *The British General Election of 1992* (Macmillan, London, 1992)

Butler, D.E. and Stokes, D. *Political Change in Britain* (Macmillan, London, 1974)

Cashmore, E. 'What lay behind Birmingham's Riots' *New Society*, 13.9.1985

Cashmore, E. and Troyna, B. *Introduction to Race Relations* (Falmer, London, 1990)

Coates, D. *The Context of British Politics* (Hutchinson, London, 1984)

Crenson, M. *The Unpolitics of Air Pollution: A Case Study in Non-Decision Making in the Cities* (The John Hopkins Press, London, 1971)

Crewe, I. 'On the Death and Resurrection of Class Voting: some Comments on how Britain Votes' *Political Studies*, vol 35 no 4, 1986

Crewe, I. 'Why Mrs Thatcher was Returned with a Landslide' *Social Studies Review*, September 1987

Crewe, I. 'Why did Labour Lose (yet again)?' *Politics Review*, September 1992

Curtice, J. and Semetko, H. 'Does it Matter what the Papers Say?' in A. Heath et al (eds) *Labour's Last Chance?: The 1992 Election and Beyond* (Dartmouth, Aldershot, 1994)

Dahl, R. 'The Concept of Power' *Behavioural Science*, 2, 1957

Dahl, R. *Who Governs? Democracy and Power in an American City* (Yale University Press, London, 1961)

Dahl, R. 'A Critique of the Ruling Elite Model' in J. Urry and J. Wakeford (eds) *Power in Britain* (Heinemann Educational, London, 1973)

Dahl, R. *Dilemmas of Pluralist Democracy* (Yale University Press, New Haven, 1982)

Davies, M. *Politics of Pressure* (BBC, London, 1985)

Denver, D. *Elections and Voting Behaviour in Britain* (Philip Allan, Hemel Hempstead, 1989)

Denver, D. 'The 1992 General Election: in Defence of Psephology' *Talking Politics* vol 5 no 1, March 1993

Denver, D. 'Elections and Voting Behaviour' in W. Wale (ed) *Developments in Politics* vol 4 (Causeway Press, Ormskirk, 1993)

Dunleavy, P. 'Class Dealignment Revisited' *Western European Politics*, vol 10 no 3, 1987

Fitzgerald, M. 'There is No Alternative...Black People and the Labour Party' *Social Studies Review*, September 1988

Fransella, F. and Frost, K. *On Being a Woman* (Tavistock, London, 1977)

Giddens, A. 'Elites in the British Class Structure' in P. Stanworth and A. Giddens (eds) *Elites and Power in British Society* (Cambridge University Press, Cambridge, 1974)

Giddens, A. *The Nation State and Violence* (Polity, Cambridge, 1985)

Giddens, A. *Sociology* (Polity, Cambridge, 1989)

Giddens, A. *The Consequences of Modernity* (Stanford University Press, Stanford, 1990)

Gilpin, R. *War and Change in World Politics* (Cambridge University Press, Cambridge, 1981)

Gilroy, P. 'Police and Thieves' in Centre for Contemporary Cultural Studies *The Empire Strikes Back* (Hutchinson, London, 1983)

Gilroy, P. *There Ain't no Black in the Union Jack* (Hutchinson, London, 1987)

Gramsci, A. *Selections from the Prison Notebooks of Antonio Gramsci* (Lawrence and Wishart, London, 1971)

Grant, W. *Pressure Group Politics and Democracy in Britain* (Philip Allan, London, 1989)

Grant, W. 'Insider and Outsider Pressure Groups' *Social Studies Review*, September 1985

Harbury, C.D. and McMahon, P.C. 'Intergenerational Wealth Transmission and the Characteristics of Top Wealth Leavers in Britain' in P. Stanworth and A. Giddens (eds) *Elites and Power in British Society* (Cambridge University Press, Cambridge, 1974)

Harrop, M. 'Press Coverage of Post-war British Elections' in I. Crewe and M. Harrop (eds) *Political Communications: The General Election Campaign of 1983* (Cambridge University Press, Cambridge, 1986)

Harvey, D. *The Condition of Postmodernity* (Blackwell, Oxford, 1989)

Heath, A. with Curtice, J., Jowell, R., Evans, G., Field, J. and Wotherspoon, S. *Understanding Political Change* (Pergamon Press, Oxford, 1991)

Heath, A., Jowell, R. and Curtice, J. *How Britain Votes* (Pergamon Press, Oxford, 1985)

Heath, A., Jowell, R. and Curtice, J. 'Trendless Fluctuation: a Reply to Crewe' *Political Studies*, 35, 1987

Heath, A., Jowell, R. and Curtice, J. 'Can Labour Win?' in A. Heath et al (eds) *Labour's Last Chance?: The 1992 Election and Beyond* (Dartmouth, Aldershot, 1994)

Held, D. *Democracy and the New International Order* (IPRR, London, 1993)

Hewitt, C. 'Elites and the Distribution of power in British Society' in P. Stanworth and A. Giddens (eds) *Elites and Power in British Society* (Cambridge University Press, Cambridge, 1974)

Himmelweit, H.T. et al *How Voters Decide* (Open University Press, Milton Keynes, 1985)

Inglehart, R. *Silent Revolution: Changing Values and Political Styles among Western Publics* (Princeton University Press, Princeton, 1977)

Institute of Race Relations *The Fight Against Racism* (The Institute of Race Relations, London, 1986)

Johnston, R.J., Pattie, C.J. and Allsopp, J.G. *A Nation Dividing* (1988)

Kennon, A. 'Women in Parliament: are things changing?' *Social Studies Review*, November 1987

Layton-Henry, Z. 'Black Participation in the General Election of 1987' *Talking Politics*, Autumn 1988

Lea, J. and Young, J. *What is to be done about Law and Order?* (Penguin, Harmondsworth, 1984)

Lindblom, C. *Politics and Markets* (Basic Books, New York, 1977)

Lukes, S. *Power: A Radical View* (Macmillan, London, 1974)

Lupton, T. and Wilson, S. 'The Social Background of Top Decision Makers' in J. Urry and J. Wakeford (eds) *Power in Britain* (Heinemann, London, 1973)

McCormick, J. *British Politics and the Environment* (Earthscan, London, 1991)

McKenzie, R.T. and Silver, A. *Angels in Marble* (Heinemann, London, 1968)

Mann, M. *The Sources of Social Power vol 1* (Cambridge University Press, Cambridge, 1986)

Mann, M. *The Sources of Social Power vol 2* (Cambridge University Press, Cambridge, 1993)

Marx, K. and Engels, F. 'The Communist Manifesto' in D. McLellan (ed) *Karl Marx, Selected Writings* (Oxford University Press, Oxford, 1977)

Marsh, D. 'Power and Politics' in M. Haralambos (ed) *Developments in Sociology vol 1* (Causeway Press, Ormskirk, 1985)

Mellors, C. *The British MP: A Socio-Economic Study of the House of Commons* (Saxon House, Farnborough, 1978)

Miliband, R. *The State in Capitalist Society* (Weidenfeld and Nicholson, London, 1974)

Mills, C.W. *The Power Elite* (Oxford University Press, New York, 1956)

Mosca, G. *The Ruling Class* (McGraw-Hill, New York, 1939)

Norris, P. 'Conservative Attitudes in Recent Elections: an Emerging Gender Gap?' *Political Studies*, March 1986

Pareto, V. *A Treatise on General Sociology* (Dover Publications, New York, 1963)

Parry, G. *Political Elites* (George Allen and Unwin, London, 1969)

Parsons, T. *Sociological Theory and Modern Society* (Collier-Macmillan, London, 1967)

Polsby, N. *Community Power and Political Theory* (Yale University Press, London, 1963)

Poulantzas, N. *Classes in Contemporary Capitalism* (New Left Books, London, 1975)

Randall, V. *Women and Politics* (Macmillan, Basingstoke, 1982)

Rasmussen, J.S. 'Women in Politics' in M. Burch and M. Moran (eds) *British Politics: A Reader* (Manchester University Press, Manchester, 1987)

Roberts, D. *Discovering Politics* (Causeway Press, Ormskirk, 1989)

Roberts, D. *British Politics in Focus* (Causeway Press, Ormskirk, 1995)

Rose, R. and McAllister, I. *The Loyalties of Voters: A Lifetime Learning Model* (Sage, London, 1990)

Sampson, A. *The Changing Anatomy of Britain* (Hodder and Stoughton, London, 1982)

Sarvlik, B. and Crewe, I. *A Decade of Dealignment* (Cambridge University Press, Cambridge, 1983)

Scarman, The Rt Hon Lord *The Brixton Disorders 10-12 April 1981* (HMSO, 1981)

Scott, J. *Corporations, Classes and Capitalism* (Hutchinson, London, 1985)

Scott, J. *Who Rules Britain?* (Polity, Cambridge, 1991)

Semetko, H., Scammell, M. and Nossiter, T. 'The Media's Coverage of the Campaign' in A. Heath et al (eds) *Labour's Last Chance?: The 1992 Election and Beyond* (Dartmouth, Aldershot, 1994)

Sewell, T. A. *Black Tribunes: Black Political Participation in Britain* (Lawrence and Wishart, London, 1993)

Smith, M. *Pressure, Power and Policy: State Autonomy and Policy Networks in Britain and the United States* (Harvester Wheatsheaf, Hemel Hempstead, 1993)

Stanworth, P. and Giddens, A. 'An Economic Elite: a Demographic

Profile of Company Chairmen' in P. Stanworth and A. Giddens (eds) *Elites and Power in British Society* (Cambridge University Press, Cambridge, 1974)

Stradling, R. *The Politics of Law and Order* (Longman, London, 1988)

Tester, K. 'Postmodernism' in M. Haralambos (ed) *Developments in Sociology* vol 11 (Causeway Press, Ormskirk, 1995)

Walsh, P., Oyekanmi, T. and Redknap, L. 'Gender and Voting' *Sociology Review*, November 1991

Weber, M. *Economy and Society: An Outline of Interpretive Sociology* (University of California Press, Berkeley, 1978)

Westergaard, J. and Resler, H. *Class in a Capitalist Society* (Penguin, Harmondsworth, 1976)

Whitley, R. 'The City and Industry' in P. Stanworth and A. Giddens (eds) *Elites and Power in British Society* (Cambridge University Press, Cambridge, 1974)

7 Families

Introduction

Most people in Britain today have been born into and brought up in families. And most will eventually have children and form families of their own. To most of us the family seems a normal, familiar and natural part of everyday life. This belief is reinforced by media images of the family - advertisements, soap operas and situation comedies often revolve around families. Sociologists try to examine the reality behind such everyday images. Sociological research reveals that our view of what a family should be may vary widely from that of other cultures, or even other groups within our own society. Moreover, families in Britain have undergone major changes historically and are still changing rapidly. Divorce rates have increased dramatically, many couples live together and have children outside marriage and the traditional division of roles between husbands and wives seems to be breaking down. It is difficult to assess the extent of such changes and their consequences without reliable evidence. This chapter examines some of the explanations sociologists give for why people live in families. It also considers evidence about the extent of changes in families in Britain and explanations for these changes.

Chapter summary

- Part 1 considers the claim that some form of family exists in all societies. It then looks at the **diversity** of family types.
- Part 2 examines the main **theoretical approaches** to the family.
- Part 3 looks at **changes in family life** in Britain from the industrial revolution to the present day.
- Part 4 focuses on three important aspects of family life - **gender roles, marriage** and **divorce**.

1 Families in Different Societies

Key Issues

1 Is the family a universal social institution?
2 How far does the organisation and role of the family vary between different societies?

1.1 The family as a universal institution

Many sociologists, anthropologists, and also zoologists have assumed that the family is a universal social institution. They claim that groups of kin living together as recognised social units - ie families - occur in all human societies. Other social scientists have criticised this universalist argument by showing that there are exceptions to virtually any definition of the family, except for those which are extremely broad. Such broad definitions are so general that they are arguably of little use.

Sociobiology and the family

Many zoologists see important similarities between animal and human behaviour. Both are seen as a response to biological drives which are the result of millions of years of evolution. This approach, often described as *sociobiology,* argues that social behaviour, such as living in families, is directed by biological drives, most importantly the drive to reproduce. Particular forms of social behaviour develop as a means of adapting to the environment and the most successful adaptations survive and flourish. The zoologist Desmond Morris argues that the nuclear family (one based on the unit of mother, father and children) has developed in the most successful human cultures, while exceptions to this 'typical' family are usually found in 'remote cultural backwaters so atypical and unsuccessful they are nearly extinct' (Morris, 1968, p9).

The family certainly fulfils important biological functions. However, most sociologists would reject the argument that the family is simply a result of biological necessity and would point to the important role which culture plays in influencing the organisation of families and kinship systems. Many sociologists and social anthropologists nevertheless agree that there is a fundamental need for a social unit called the family, but see the reasons for its existence more in social rather than biological terms.

George Peter Murdock: a functionalist perspective

The social anthropologist Murdock concluded from his study *Social Structure* (1949) that some form of family existed in every known human society. Murdock compared 250 societies and claimed that although there were wide variations in the kinship systems of these societies, they all corresponded to what he defined as a family. Murdock defined the family as follows:

'The family is a social group characterised by common residence, economic cooperation and reproduction. It includes adults of both sexes, at least two of whom maintain a socially approved sexual relationship, and one or more children, own or adopted, of the sexually cohabiting adults' (1949, p1).

Murdock, like Morris, sees the nuclear family as the basic unit around which all family systems are organised. However, he notes that in many societies the nuclear family may be part of a larger kinship group. Firstly, it may be part of a *polygamous family*, where individuals are permitted more than one wife (polygyny) or more than one husband (polyandry). Secondly, in many cultures the basic family unit is an *extended family*, a family including kin beyond a single nuclear family, for example three generations living together as a family unit.

Murdock argues that the reason why the nuclear family unit is universally present is that it performs four essential functions without which society could not continue. He calls these the sexual, reproductive, economic and educational functions. In other words, the family serves to regulate sexual behaviour; it produces the next generation of society; it acts as a basic economic unit, cooperating in tasks and sharing resources; and finally it socialises children into the culture of their society. Murdock sees the family as functional not only for society at large but also for its individual members. The family is, in his view, universal, since neither the individual nor society could survive without it.

Diversity in family systems

Felicity Edholm in *The Unnatural Family* (1982) suggests that many anthropologists have made sense of kinship groupings in other societies in terms of the culture of their own society and have thus tended to see universal similarities in family life. She goes on to say:

'When we look at the societies studied by anthropologists and at the variation in kinship systems, it is clear that the range of options is enormous, that the constraints on human behaviour do not produce uniformity, and that those assumptions we make about what is "natural" in respect of fundamental human kinship relations are profoundly challenged by the evidence from widely differing societies.'

Activity 1 provides some examples of the range of options alluded to by Edholm. What is clear is that different societies have very different arrangements for carrying out the important functions mentioned by Murdock. Certainly in many cultures the nuclear family seems to be the basic grouping, yet even here what seems to be natural in one society is viewed as deviant in another. Thus while Murdock may be correct in suggesting that the family is universal, this is only true in terms of a very general definition. When comparing human societies there is tremendous diversity in family and kinship arrangements.

There is evidence that organisations which are arguably not families are capable of performing the family's functions. Perhaps the best example of this is the Israeli *kibbutz*. A kibbutz is a settlement where members work together and share property. While men and women usually form couples and marry, their children are seen as the responsibility of the kibbutz as a whole. They are brought up by specially trained foster parents in a separate children's house, visiting their parents for only a short time each day. Some sociologists have argued that the family does not exist as a unit in the traditional kibbutz since some of its essential functions, for example economic cooperation and socialising children, are the responsibility of the whole community. The couple merely engage in sexual relations and reproduction but do not form a residential unit with their children.

Many sociologists now feel that the whole question of whether the family is universal is a non-issue. What is perhaps more important is to explore the diversity of families and the different meanings that the idea of a family has for different cultures and social groups. From this perspective the family is socially constructed, it is not simply a natural unit created by biological necessities. Rather, it is influenced by social factors, such as the cultural norms of society, the prevailing economic system, and even the particular stage an individual family has reached in its life cycle.

Activity 1 Family Diversity

Item A *The nuclear family*

The nuclear family is a universal social grouping. Either as the sole prevailing form of the family or as the basic unit from which more complex family forms are developed, it exists as a distinct and strongly functional unit in every known human society. Whatever larger family form may exist, and to whatever extent the greater unit may assume some of the burdens of the lesser, the nuclear family is always recognisable and always has its distinct and vital functions - sexual, economic, reproductive and educational. Without provision for the first and third society would become extinct; for the second life itself would cease; for the fourth, culture would come to an end. The immense social utility of the nuclear family thus begins to emerge in strong relief.

Adapted from G. P. Murdock *Social Structure*, 1949

Item B *Kinship in other societies*

The Lakker

The Lakker of Burma do not see children as having any blood relationship to their mother. The mother is only a container in which the child grows. Children of the same mother and different fathers are not considered to be related to each other and sexual relationships between them are not considered as incest.

Tahiti

In Tahiti, in the South Pacific, young women often give children to their own parents or other close kin for adoption if they do not consider themselves ready for settling down to a permanent relationship. Such girls are free to continue life as an adolescent and can involve themselves in bringing up their children as much or as little as they want. Adopted children come to see their adoptive parents as real parents and feel a strong sense of gratitude to them for bringing them up.

The Ashanti

The Ashanti of West Africa are a matrilineal society (descent is traced through the mother's line). While a child's father is important, he has no legal authority over his children. This rests with the wife's family, particularly her brother. It is from the mother's brother (the child's uncle) that children inherit, though the father is responsible for feeding, clothing and educating them. Many Ashanti men cannot afford to set up a household of their own when they first marry. Since men never live with their wife's brothers, and children are the property of the wife's family, this often means that couples live apart. Only about a third of married women actually live with their husbands.

Based on: R.M. Keesing *Cultural Anthropology: a Contemporary Perspective*, 1976; V. Carroll *Adoption in Eastern Oceania*, 1970; M. Fortes 'Kinship and Marriage among the Ashanti' in A.R. Radcliffe-Brown and D. Forde, *African Systems of Kinship and Marriage*, 1950

Item C

Polyandry among the Nyinba of Nepal. The 12 year old girl on the right is engaged to five brothers, three of whom are pictured here.

Children outside a communal dormitory in an Israeli Kibbutz. They are raised by child 'caretakers' or 'educators'.

Questions

1 How do families in Britain carry out the four essential functions of the family outlined by Murdock in Item A?
2 Do all families in Britain today fit Murdock's definition of the family given on page 233? If not, do the exceptions successfully carry out the family's 'essential functions'?
3 How do Items B and C suggest that culture is important in determining the way kinship is organised?
4 How far do the examples given in Items B and C fit Murdock's definition of a family? If you think any of them do not, explain why and discuss whether they should be defined as families.

Summary

1 Some sociologists claim that the family is universal. They believe that only the family is capable of performing certain essential functions required by society for its survival. In most human societies some form of social group based on parents and children does exist to perform these functions.

2 There are a number of exceptions which do not fit conventional definitions of the family, yet which carry out the functions performed by the family in most other societies. This suggests that functional alternatives to the family may be possible and that the family may not be universal.

3 The range of social organisations which might be described as families is extremely diverse. Thus the term 'family' covers a wide variety of social arrangements, many of them different from the family in our own society.

2 Theoretical Perspectives on the Family

Key Issues

1 Is the family a beneficial or an oppressive institution?
2 In what ways is the family important to individuals?
3 In what ways does the family serve the needs of society?

Traditionally the sociology of the family was dominated by functionalist theory which emphasised the universal and functional role that the family played in society and the benefits to the individual of being a family member. From the 1960s onwards, sociologists drawing on a number of perspectives, most notably Marxism and feminism, began to question these assumptions, arguing that the family served the interests of the capitalist economic system and/or the male sex. Such approaches stressed the disadvantages of the modern Western nuclear family. More recently there has been a reaction by the New Right to this perceived attack on the family. This has led to a reconsideration by many sociologists, including some Marxists and feminists, of the value of the traditional family. Other more recent approaches have drawn on interpretive perspectives to consider the meaning and importance of the family for individual members, and the ways in which family members interact with one another.

2.1 Functionalist approaches to the family

Functionalist theories of society are based on the assumption that society operates on the basis of consensus (agreement) and that there is a tendency towards equilibrium (balance) between the various parts of society so that they work together harmoniously. Functionalists tend to assume that if a social institution exists then it must have a function or purpose. The family is therefore often examined in terms of the functions it performs for the benefit of society and the individual. Murdock's analysis of the universal functions of the family is a good example of this approach, with its emphasis on the essential functions of the family in all societies.

Functionalists often see society as similar to a machine or an organism, with many different parts contributing to the smooth running of the whole. Functionalist theories therefore stress the interrelationship between the family and other social institutions. For example, the family prepares children to become adult workers and take on roles in the economy to support themselves and their dependents. In this way the family system and the economic system are linked.

Talcott Parsons: the family and functional differentiation The American sociologist Talcott Parsons (1955) saw industrial societies as becoming increasingly specialised, with a wider range of institutions carrying out more and more specialised functions. Parsons refers to this as the process of *functional differentiation*. Thus the family and the kinship system which were important in a whole range of areas in pre-industrial societies become increasingly specialised, concentrating on a few essential functions. For example, in many small scale societies the role of caring for elderly and sick people is the responsibility of their relatives; in industrial societies this is increasingly the responsibility of specialised agencies such as hospitals and social services. Parsons sees two functions of the family as being 'basic and irreducible'. In other words, however specialised the family becomes, it will always retain two functions. These are:
1 the primary socialisation of children;
2 the stabilisation of adult personalities.

In keeping with the consensus approach of functionalism, Parsons argues that every individual must internalise the norms and values of society. This means they must become part of the individual's personality and way of thinking. For Parsons it is the family which moulds the child's personality to fit the needs of society. This is the process of *primary socialisation* which takes place in the early years of childhood. In industrial societies much of the responsibility for secondary socialisation (preparation for adult roles) is taken over by specialist institutions, such as schools and occupational training agencies. However, in the primary phase of socialisation Parsons believes that the family is irreplaceable.

The second irreplaceable function is the *stabilisation of adult personalities.* By this Parsons means that adults need emotional security and a source of release from the stresses and strains of life in the wider society. The emotional support of partners in marriage, as well as the opportunity for parents to indulge in childish behaviour with their children, provides this security and release. It helps to prevent stress overwhelming the individual and threatening the stability of society.

For Parsons the nuclear family is the ideal institution to perform these essential functions in industrial society. Like other institutions, the family has become more specialised. It has lost many of its functions. Its ties with the wider kinship network have been weakened as it adapts to the needs of industrial society (see Section 3.1). However, it has not lost its two 'basic and irreducible' functions. The nuclear family in industrial society is no less important than it was, it is simply slimmed down and more specialised.

Criticisms of functionalist theories The functionalist approach has come under attack from a number of other sociological perspectives. Some of the main criticisms may be summarised as follows.

1 Functionalist theories tend to concentrate on the positive functions of the family and give little consideration to its disadvantages. Feminists, for example, emphasise the male dominated nature of traditional family relations. These arguments are examined in Part 2.

2 Functionalists assume that the family is of equal benefit to everyone. However, Marxists argue that society is shaped by the needs of the capitalist economy and that the family exists to service these needs rather than those of its members. It is the dominant class in capitalist societies who benefit most from the way families are organised rather than society as a whole.

3 Functionalists fail to consider the viability of alternatives to the family. For example, it has been argued that the Israeli kibbutz effectively carries out all the functions of a family but does not fit most definitions of the family.

4 Many functionalists, particularly Parsons, do not consider the diversity of family types. Even within one society, there are variations based on class, region, ethnicity, religion and so on (see Part 4).

5 Interpretive sociologists argue that functionalists concentrate too much on the importance of the family for society and ignore the meaning family life has for individuals - for example, the way individuals make sense of the world around them through other family members.

These criticisms are considered in more detail in later sections. However, as the functionalist writer Ronald Fletcher (1988b) points out, even those who criticise the family admit its social importance. While many seek to change the family, most admit that to abolish it would be impractical.

2.2 The New Right and the family

Like functionalist sociologists, New Right thinkers see the family as a cornerstone of society. They also tend to see a 'normal' family as the nuclear family unit. For example, John Redwood, a Conservative MP, stated in 1993 that 'the natural state should be the two-adult family caring for their children'. Such perspectives often reflect the sociobiological view that the family is a 'natural' institution based on biological requirements. For example, Ferdinand Mount author of *The Subversive Family* (1982) refers to the timeless 'duties of care prescribed by the biological ethic' in the 'natural' family.

In recent years, the view that the family is 'under threat' or 'in decline' has gained wide currency. This view has tended to be supported not so much by sociologists but by journalists, politicians and pressure groups. It has been particularly associated with New Right thinkers in the 1980s and 90s.

Such ideas challenge the functionalists' assumption that the modern family is performing its functions effectively and that in many respects the quality of family life is better than in the past. In recent years government ministers, newspaper editors and pressure groups such as the Moral Majority in the USA have suggested that the family unit has been undermined by social changes which have threatened traditional norms of marriage and family life.

Among the changes which have been blamed for this are greater sexual permissiveness, leading to couples living together outside marriage and to an increase in unmarried mothers; greater tolerance of homosexuality as an alternative to marriage; higher divorce rates, leading to more lone parent families; the financial support provided by the welfare state to lone parent families; and the influence of feminism, leading to more women working outside the home rather than devoting themselves to domesticity and childrearing. The New Right argues for a return to 'traditional family values' as a remedy for many of the problems of modern society, such as juvenile delinquency, educational underachievement and child poverty.

Criticisms of New Right theories Critics have suggested that New Right theories tend to lay the blame on victims for problems which are not of their own making. For example, single parent families have been criticised by government ministers for their inadequacy in raising children and their dependency on the welfare state. However, many of the problems of such families can be blamed on inadequate state benefits, lack of jobs and childcare facilities and other factors beyond the control of lone parents. Moreover, the model of the family to which New Right thinkers aspire is one which fits only a minority of households. A mere 15% of families now comprise a working father, a mother at home and dependent children. Even in Victorian England - often seen as a period when traditional family values were respected - single parenthood, working wives and sexual relations outside marriage were by no means uncommon. Marxists and feminists in particular have argued that alternatives to the traditional family are possible but, under contemporary capitalism, life is made difficult for those who fail to live up to what the majority sees as 'normal' family life.

Activity 2   Functions of the family

Item A *The nuclear family*
What has recently been happening to the American family constitutes part of a process of differentiation. This process has involved a further step in the reduction of importance in our society of kinship units other than the nuclear family. It has also resulted in the transfer of a variety of functions from the nuclear family to other structures of the society, notably the occupationally organised sectors of it. This means that the family has become a *more specialised agency than before*, probably more specialised than it has been in any previously known society. This represents a decline of certain features which have been traditionally associated with families; but whether it represents a 'decline of the family' in a more general sense is another matter; we think not. We think the evidence points to a *new* type of family structure in a new relation to a general social structure, one in which the family is more specialised than before, but not in any general sense less important, because the society is dependent *more* exclusively on it for the performance of *certain* of its vital functions.

Adapted from Talcott Parsons 'The American Family: its Relations to Personality and the Social Structure' in T. Parsons and R. F. Bales *Family, Socialisation and Interaction Process*, 1955, p192

Item B *The multi-functional family*
Ronald Fletcher argues that the family performs three essential functions together with six other non-essential functions. While other agencies have taken over much of the responsibility for non-essential functions, the family continues to have an important role in these areas. Fletcher disagrees with the view that the welfare state has undermined the role of the family. He sees the state as supporting the family in carrying out its responsibilities and argues that if the family is failing in this respect it is because of too little, rather than too much, state support.

Essential functions	Non-essential functions	
1 Stable satisfaction of sexual needs	1 Government	4 Health
2 Production and rearing of children	2 Economic	5 Religious
3 Provision of a home	3 Education	6 Recreation

It is quite untrue to say that the family in contemporary Britain has been 'stripped of its functions' and has, as a consequence, become less important as a social institution. On the contrary, the modern family fulfils more functions, and in a far more detailed and sophisticated manner, than did the family before or during the nineteenth century development of industrialisation.

Take, first of all, the 'essential' functions of the family - the satisfaction of sexual needs of the married couple, the careful upbringing of children, and the provision of a satisfactory home for its members. It is perfectly clear that the modern family - entailing the equal status of wife and husband and their mutual consideration in marriage; the high status of children; and the improved standards of income, housing, household equipment - aims at, and achieves, a far more satisfactory and refined provision of these needs. In the pre-industrial family, or the family of early industrial Britain, women were inferior and subjected, women and children were frequently exploited within and outside the family and conditions in the home were deplorably inadequate.

What is not commonly stressed, however, in stating this qualitative improvement in the 'essential' functions of the family is that the demands upon the members of the family for the satisfactory performance of them have become increasingly heavy. As the expected standards of fulfilment of the 'essential' functions of the family have improved, therefore, so have the demands for responsibility on the part of family members increased.

Adapted from R. Fletcher *The Family and Marriage in Britain*, 1966, pp44-45; 177-179

Item C *Typical Victorian images*

The family photograph

'The bottle'

'The abandoned mother'

Questions

1 'Specialisation does not mean a decline in the importance of the family.' Explain with reference to Item A.
2 a) How does Fletcher's view (Item B) of the functions of the family in modern society differ from that of Parsons?
   b) Why does Fletcher argue that the demands on the modern family have become increasingly heavy?
3 Examine Fletcher's six non-essential functions of the family and explain, using examples, how the family might still have an important role in these areas of social life.
4 Look at Item C. Those who see the family in decline sometimes argue that a return to 'Victorian values' will restore the family to its former glory. Critically assess this argument.

2.3 Conflict approaches to the family

Marxist theories

Marxists reject the functionalist view that society is based on value consensus and thus operates for the benefit of all. Instead they see the interests of powerful groups determining the way society is organised. The family is seen as part of the superstructure of society and is thus one of a number of institutions which serve the needs of and help to maintain the infrastructure or economic system. Marxists argue that it is the specific requirements of the *capitalist* mode of production which have shaped the development of the family in Western industrial societies, rather than industrialisation as such.

There is little detailed discussion of the family in the work of Marx. However, his collaborator Engels' book *The Origins of the Family, Private Property and the State* (1902) provides the basis for a Marxist analysis of the family. More recently this approach has been developed by feminist writers who have linked the idea that the family operates to maintain the capitalist system, with the idea that the family is the major obstacle to women's emancipation. Indeed many Marxist-feminist theories argue that the subordination of women within the family is a necessary part of the capitalist system.

Engels: the family and private property Like many nineteenth century writers, including Marx, Engels saw society (and with it marriage and the family) as evolving through a series of stages, from primitive communism, where there was little regulation of sexual behaviour, through to capitalism, where marriage is based on monogamy (marriage between one man and one woman). Engels argued that during this evolutionary process private property became more and more important as the basis for social organisation, culminating in the emergence of capitalism. He saw monogamy as the most efficient means of ensuring transmission of private property through the system of inheritance. With only one husband and one wife in a family questions about the paternity of children, or about which wife's children should inherit were unlikely to arise. A man could therefore be sure that he had legitimate children with a clear right of succession to inherit his wealth.

Engels saw the bourgeois nuclear family as an institution which oppressed women. Women were seen primarily as the producers of children. They were economically dependent on their husbands and expected to remain faithful to them. Yet at the same time adultery and the use of prostitutes were regarded as legitimate for men.

Although Engels was critical of the family, he did not wish see it abolished. In fact he condemned the way in which social conditions deprived working class people of any real family life. He believed that the central role of the family, as a source of legitimate heirs, would disappear with the abolition of private property. He argued for the 'socialisation' (taking over by society) of many of the family's functions in communist society - for example, socialised schemes of childcare to enable mothers to be economically independent. Engels approved of monogamy, but on the basis of love rather than economic motives. This would only come about if women were economically independent of men and divorce was freely available.

Much of Engels' evolutionary theory, based on the work of the anthropologist Lewis Henry Morgan, is simply inaccurate. Nevertheless his two essential points - that the family serves the requirements of the capitalist economy, and that the family prevents women from achieving equality both inside and outside the home - are still seen as central by many critics of the modern family.

Marxist-feminist theories Many feminist writers have been critical of both traditional Marxism - for failing to consider how women in particular are oppressed in capitalist societies - and of radical feminism (discussed below) which sees patriarchy (male domination) as the major problem but fails to relate this to the economic structure of society. Marxist-feminists therefore attempt to relate the unequal position of women in society to the roles they occupy within the capitalist system, an important part of this being women's place in the family. Like Engels, Marxist-feminists see the family as a major obstacle to female emancipation and as an institution which helps to maintain and service the capitalist system. Their main arguments are summarised below.

1 **The family is patriarchal.** Unlike functionalists who have tended to see male and female roles in the family as different but equal, Marxist-feminists argue that men dominate family relationships. The notion of 'symmetrical conjugal roles' (balanced and equal roles in marriage) is seen as a myth. (See Section 4.2 for further discussion of this issue).

2 **Domestic labour serves the needs of the capitalist economy.** Marxist-feminists, like Margaret Benston (1969), have analysed domestic labour (the unpaid work done within the household) in economic terms. They argue that part of the surplus value (profit) created by workers results from the labour of housewives whose work adds to the workers' labour power (ability to work). Thus by cooking, washing his clothes and even sleeping with her husband, a housewife makes him into a more productive worker. And by producing and rearing children - the workers of the future - at no cost to employers, housewives play a vital part in the reproduction of labour power.

3 **The family has an ideological role**. Marxist-feminist theories reject the functionalist view that socialisation in the family is beneficial for society as a whole. Peggy Morton (1980), for example, argues that modern capitalism relies less and less on direct coercion to control workers and more and more on their acceptance of hierarchical social relationships in capitalist societies. Thus the family acts as the first conditioning device, teaching children to accept an authoritarian and exploitive society. For example, by learning to accept the authority which parents, especially fathers, exercise over them, children learn to accept the authority of schools, employers and the capitalist state.

4 **The family is an obstacle to gender equality in employment.** Many sociologists have pointed out the disadvantages which women suffer in employment because of their domestic and childcare responsibilities (see Chapter 4). However, Marxist-feminists argue that such inequalities are built into the capitalist system. Women not only perform a valuable unpaid role as

domestic labourers, but also, according to Irene Bruegel (1979), they provide a 'reserve army of labour'. They are a source of cheap workers who can be brought into the paid labour force when needed, for example to do part time and temporary jobs, but who disappear into the family again when they are no longer required. Juliet Mitchell (1971) echoes Engels when she argues that women need to be freed from their domestic responsibilities by passing on the functions of the family to other agencies. This would free both women and men to live in whatever kind of relationships or domestic arrangements they chose. And it would remove a major obstacle to gender equality in the labour market.

Radical feminist theories

Radical feminists are critical of the family for many of the same reasons as Marxist-feminists. However, they emphasise the ways in which the family is a patriarchal institution, ie an institution which enables men to dominate, exploit and oppress women. The family is, therefore, not so much an institution which benefits a relatively small group - the capitalist class - but men in general. Writers like Kate Millett (1970) argue that the way society is organised enables men to dominate women. In its most extreme form this means violence. Studies of the extent of violence in the family, for example *Violence against Wives* by Russell and Rebecca Dobash (1980), indicate that for many women and children this is a real threat (see Activity 3).

Unlike Marxist-feminists, radical feminists do not see the solution as a socialist society, but argue that women must independently build an alternative society which challenges patriarchy and the polarisation of gender roles. Since it is part of the system of patriarchy the conventional family would have to be abolished or radically modified. (The extent to which the family remains a patriarchal institution is discussed further in Section 4.2).

In recent years, however, many feminists have concentrated not on replacing the family but on changing it for the better. They argue for more, rather than less, involvement by men in family life claiming it would take much of the strain off women. This would require changes in other areas such as employment - for example shorter working weeks, more job-share opportunities, longer paternity leave and better maternity rights.

Criticisms of Marxist and feminist theories

1 They see the nature of the family as determined by the needs of the economic system and/or patriarchy. In this sense, like functionalists, they see the family as performing predetermined functions. They also tend to see a specific form of the family as being necessitated by the social system. Thus like functionalists they tend to ignore the diversity of family forms both within and between capitalist societies.

2 They tend to focus on the negative aspects of family life and ignore the real satisfaction it gives to many individuals. This positive side is emphasised not only by functionalists but also by interpretive sociologists (see Section 2.4) who argue that positive perceptions of family life, for example women being satisfied with traditional roles, should be accepted as valid rather than dismissed as 'false consciousness'.

3 While the Western nuclear family has many disadvantages it is difficult to see a functional alternative to it. For example, the attempt to abolish the family in the Soviet Union was eventually abandoned as impractical. In many Israeli kibbutzim today parents spend more time with their children and even eat and sleep with them at weekends. According to Brigitte and Peter Berger (1983), despite its disadvantages, the nuclear family represents the best environment in which a child's individuality can develop. They suggest that collective childrearing systems (as in the kibbutz) create more conformist and less creative people than those raised in the nuclear family.

4 Black feminist writers such as Helen Carby (1982) have criticised white feminists for failing to consider the significance of racism alongside patriarchy as a form of domination. They agree that for many black women the family can be an oppressive institution. However, they also point out that black women (and men) are oppressed by racism and that the family often acts as a source of support and resistance to racial discrimination and harassment.

5 New Right defenders of the family have criticised radical sociologists for attacking the family and undermining it. Some politicians and journalists have argued that lack of respect for traditional family values is the reason for a variety of social problems including crime, youthful rebellion and educational underachievement. Few sociologists accept this. They see these problems as a part of much wider changes in society. Nevertheless, some like Ronald Fletcher (1988b) have argued that sociologists in recent years have spent too much time criticising the family and failed to consider how it can be strengthened and assisted in carrying out its role.

Despite the previous criticisms, Marxist and feminist theories have provided a useful balance to the somewhat uncritical views of many functionalists. In particular they have shown how features of family life, for example traditional gender roles, may be created or perpetuated by the requirements of powerful interests and not simply because they benefit the family and society as a whole. They have also begun to explore the concept of the family as an ideology, ie as a set of ideas about how things should be. From this perspective the family is not a 'natural' institution but is socially constructed around a set of ideas about what is normal. Thus the view of the nuclear family as the ideal is imposed by a powerful series of messages which state that there is no acceptable alternative. In contemporary Britain an increasing proportion of households do not conform to the nuclear family ideal (see Part 3). Critical theorists argue that many of the problems such alternative household units face are linked to their being seen as deviant from the 'normal' family, as failing to live up to accepted standards.

Activity 3 Critical Views of the Family

Item A *The nuclear family*

Shot from an Oxo commercial

An advert from the 1950s

Item B *Domestic violence*

Although it is not generally thought to be proper or masculine for a man to hit a woman, this constraint does not strictly apply to the treatment of one's wife. It is commonly believed that there are times when every woman needs to be taken in hand. On such occasions men will treat women with disdain and use either subtle or obvious means to degrade, isolate or ignore them. It is almost inconceivable that he would punch her in the jaw, unless of course, she happened to be his wife.

Although both partners feel that marriage allows them to make some demands upon the other, there is considerable difference in their abilities to achieve their own ends when there is disagreement. Even if a wife has a quite legitimate demand, request or complaint, she cannot go on too much about it as it is an affront to her husband's authority. She must plead, cajole and beguile and hope he will be convinced. She is almost never in a position to coerce him by physical means and has never learned the techniques of violence nor been taught to think in terms of physical control. The husband, on the other hand, feels he has the right to control his wife's behaviour and authority over most, if not all, areas of her life. It is these beliefs, coupled with his desire to maintain authority, that lead to his first assault. The more general taboo that it is not correct for a man to hit a woman is qualified - 'unless she is your wife' - as immediate demands for control supersede demands for propriety.

Types of assault occurring between family members

	Number	%
Wife assault	791	75.8
Husband assault	12	1.1
Child assault	112	10.7
Parent assault	73	7.0
Sibling assault	50	4.8
Mutual assault	6	0.6
Total	**1044**	**100.0**

These figures were compiled by Dobash and Dobash from statistics on domestic assaults reported to the police in all of Edinburgh and one district of Glasgow in 1974.

Adapted from R. E. and R. Dobash *Violence against Wives*, 1980, pp93-95

Questions

1 How might a Marxist-feminist interpret Item A?
2 a) How might feminists explain the attitudes and behaviour in Item B?
   b) What problems might there be with the accuracy of the statistics in Item B?

2.4 Interpretive approaches

Interpretive approaches see social life as a continuous attempt to make sense of and order the world. They argue that reality is socially constructed - we make our own reality within social groups. In daily life most of us, most of the time, strive to achieve a view of the world which corresponds with that of people around us.

Interpretive studies of the family seek to explore its role as one of the key groups within which we share our experience of the social world with others and construct a shared version of reality. In this sense interpretivists, like functionalists, see the family as performing a valuable social function, but their concern is with the meaning of the family for the individual rather than its relationship to the wider society. For example, they ask how individuals perceive their own and other's roles within the family. Such roles are seen as not merely given by society but negotiated and worked out among family members themselves.

Berger and Kellner: marriage and the construction of reality

Peter Berger and Hansfried Kellner (1964) were among the first sociologists to apply an interpretive approach to the family. They argue that individuals need to make sense of and create order in the world around them to avoid what Durkheim described as a sense of *anomie* or normlessness (see p663). Berger and Kellner see marriage as a crucial relationship for the construction of reality. In their daily interaction, particularly through conversation, husband and wife create a shared view of the world and their relationship to others.

Berger and Kellner argue that as the public sphere of life becomes increasingly impersonal, it is in the private sphere of marriage and the family that individuals find opportunities for self realisation. They suggest that when two people come together in marriage they must arrive at a common view of reality. They have come from two different families with different (although not necessarily dissimilar) definitions of the world. In marriage a couple socialise one another into a shared way of seeing the world. For example, both partners may have had different plans for the future, but together they work out a shared plan. When children join the family they too become part of this process and are socialised into the family's way of looking at the world.

K.C.Backett: becoming a parent

Much of Backett's (1980) work is concerned with the roles of parents in the family and how these roles are defined and developed. Like Berger and Kellner, she points out how family life is a socialisation process, not only for children but also for parents. Many parents she interviewed saw becoming a parent as a learning process involving trial and error.

Backett explores in some depth the images that parents have of their children and the ways in which they make sense of them. Again this draws on an interpretive approach with its emphasis on exploring individuals' meanings and seeing the world through their eyes. For example, many parents made sense of what they perceived as problems in their children's behaviour by reference to 'phases' or 'stages' in the child's development. They were able to cope with the uncertainty of how to respond as a parent by the reassurance that the child would 'grow out of it'.

David Clark: types of marriage

David Clark (1991) carried out a study of fifty couples in Aberdeen during the first few months of their marriages. Each couple was given two in-depth interviews. From their accounts Clark distinguishes four types of marriage.

1 **Drifting** These couple were unclear about the future and tended not to make long term plans but lived from day to day.
2 **Surfacing** All these couples included at least one partner who had been married before. They were recovering from previous marital breakups and continuing problems involving former spouses and children often intruded on their present marriages.
3 **Establishing** Unlike those who were drifting, establishing couples consciously planned their future together, often saving money to buy homes and other material comforts.
4 **Struggling** Most of these couples were suffering financial difficulties usually because of unemployment. This was often made worse by unplanned pregnancies, housing difficulties and problems with former partners. Unlike the 'establishing' couples, they were pessimistic about the future and often suffered strain in their personal relationships.

Clark's study explores the intimate world of marriage. He quotes extensively from the interviews with couples to illustrate their personal views. At the same time he emphasises how the private world of the family is linked to the public domain. For example, the opportunities available to individuals for well paid work were likely to a major factor in whether they were 'establishing' or 'struggling' at the beginning of their marriages.

Assessing interpretive approaches

Interpretive approaches represent a relatively new and promising direction for the sociology of the family. In particular they offer an understanding of family life as it is experienced rather than looking at the family as an abstract social institution. They emphasise the importance of individuals and their freedom to negotiate roles and meanings in the family. Similarly they show how socialisation is a two-way process, with parents learning from their children and from each other.

One of the main weaknesses of interpretive approaches is their tendency to ignore the wider social structure. Marxists and feminists, for example, argue that the way roles are constructed in the family is not merely a matter of individual negotiation, but a reflection of the way power is distributed in the wider society. However, more recent studies, such as Clark's quoted above, do explore the links between the private world of the family and the wider social structure.

Summary

1 From a functionalist perspective the family is a central institution in society. It performs essential social functions such as raising children. The family is seen as an important source of security and satisfaction for its members.

2 Conflict perspectives based on Marxism and feminism have highlighted the negative side of family life. They have also explored the issue of unequal power relations in families and how these may reflect inequalities in the wider society.

3 Interpretive approaches attempt to understand the family from the viewpoint of its members.

Activity 4 Interpretive Approaches

Item A *Negotiating parental roles*

One set of underlying assumptions which emerged from in-depth interviews with a sample of 22 couples was of *family life as a shared reality*. Respondents continually expressed their view that their behaviour was developed in the context of other family members. One example of this was that respondents' accounts were characterised by the assumption that individuals should be 'fairly' treated. This was frequently expressed in terms of marriage being a 'partnership of equals' which should be run on the basis of 'give and take'.

What was defined as 'fairness' varied between families since it was negotiated in terms of each family unit. For all families, however, it was often extremely problematical to sustain belief that a 'fair' situation existed. For example, respondents tended to perceive their sense of fairness as being contradicted by the fact that, after the arrival of children, the woman's everyday freedom of choice and action was more restricted than that of the man. Various *coping mechanisms* were implemented which could be seen as practical attempts to alleviate any disruption or dissatisfaction which might arise out of this contradiction. Two such mechanisms were the simple *verbal acknowledgement* of this problem, and *practical compensation*.

An illustration of verbal acknowledgement was given by one husband when he said about his wife's adaptation to parenthood:

'Well, I think the best way to put it, it's not so much adaptations but perhaps she has had to... has been more constrained in terms of, you know, what choices she can actually undertake. I mean, given the fact that we're committed to the children and want to bring them up basically ourselves, you know, there isn't much choice, one of us has got to be at home with them.'

In addition, it was seen as important that the husbands should facilitate the wife's freedom of action in practical ways. One of the wives who felt she was getting a 'fair deal' out of the marriage said:

'The main thing is that he's quite prepared to take charge and give me the freedom if I want to go; if there's anywhere special that I want to go I know he doesn't mind me going.'

Adapted from K.C. Backett 'Images of Parenthood' in M. Anderson *Sociology of the Family*, 1980, pp358-360

Item B *Interviews*

A formal structured interview

An informal unstructured interview

Item C *Researching family life*

Interpretive analysis is often concerned with the interaction between the observer and the observed and how these interactions are a central part of the process of doing research. Cornwell (1984), for example, in a study of East London families, makes a distinction between 'public' and 'private' accounts. 'Public' accounts are those more conventional or socially approved statements about family matters such as, 'He's always been a good husband to me!' These are the accounts which are most likely to be presented to a middle class researcher on a first interview. The private accounts are more complex, more individual, and more likely to be given when a considerable degree of rapport has been established between observer and observed.

Adapted from D.H.J. Morgan 'The Family' in M. Haralambos (ed) *Developments in Sociology* vol 7, 1991, p117

Questions

1 a) How did the couples in Backett's study (Item A) deal with the apparent contradiction between the ideal of fairness and the differences in their roles?
   b) Why might feminists question their notions of 'fairness'?
2 a) Read Item C. Why is it often difficult for sociologists to investigate personal interpretations of family life?
   b) What sociological methods would be suitable for this type of research? Refer to Item B in your answer.

3 Social Change and the Family

Key Issues

1 How did industrialisation change the structure and functions of the family?

2 How useful is the concept of 'privatisation' for understanding changes in family life in industrial societies?

3 What are the main characteristics of families in contemporary Britain?

4 To what extent have recent changes in British society led to a greater diversity of family types?

3.1 Industrialisation and the family

The period known as the industrial revolution began in Britain around the middle of the eighteenth century. Other countries have also undergone industrialisation, but have not necessarily followed the same path of development as Britain.

Industrialisation in Britain brought a number of important changes in society.

1 A large part of the workforce moved from agriculture and small cottage industries to industrial work, producing manufactured goods in factories.

2 Manufacturing industry was mechanised: powered machinery was used to mass produce goods. Small home-based family businesses could not compete with this.

3 There was a population explosion due to high fertility combined with falling death rates.

4 Towns and cities grew in size and the majority of the population was concentrated in large urban areas rather than small villages.

This section examines sociological debates about the impact of these changes on family life in Britain.

Talcott Parsons: industrialisation and the decline of kinship

The American functionalist sociologist, Talcott Parsons (1951) argued that such changes transformed the social system and the significance of kinship in society (see Section 2.1). The family became more specialised as other agencies took over functions it had previously carried out. For example, most families ceased to be production units. Production became organised on a large scale outside the home and family members became individual wage earners.

According to Parsons, this change in the *functions* of the family also involved a change in its *structure*. He argues that in pre-industrial societies an extended family system made it easier to carry out the wide range of functions required since a larger pool of kin was available. In industrial societies this extended family system is no longer needed and may, in fact, be a positive disadvantage. Parsons suggests three reasons for this.

1 The nuclear family unit contains the basic roles of mother, father and children needed to carry out the family's essential function. The functions of the wider kinship system have been taken over by specialised agencies, for example the welfare state.

2 The workforce in industrial societies needs to be geographically mobile. Nuclear families can move from place to place more easily in the search for jobs and are not so tied down by obligations to, and dependence on, kin.

3 Individuals increasingly achieve status through individual merit in industrial societies. The family is no longer required to ascribe status, for example by children following their parents' occupations. Instead young people need to be independent of their families of origin in order to find their own occupations and social positions.

Parsons argues that the *isolated nuclear family* is the typical family structure in industrial society. The family is no longer embedded in a wider kinship network. Although there are social relationships with relatives outside the nuclear family, these have become a matter of choice rather than obligation.

The classic extended family

Many traditional sociological theories echo Parsons' views, contrasting the isolated nuclear family of industrial society with the *classic extended family* seen as characteristic of peasant societies. Studies of peasant societies support the view that the classic extended family was typical of pre-industrial societies. For example, Arensberg and Kimball's famous study of rural Ireland in the 1930s, *Family and Community in Ireland* (1940), demonstrated the existence of a close knit community in which extended families and neighbours relied on one another for help and support (see Activity 5).

Peter Laslett: the family in pre-industrial England

More recent research into patterns of family life in England before the industrial revolution suggests that many traditional assumptions have to be questioned. The social historian, Peter Laslett (1965;1977), provides evidence which indicates that the large extended family household was relatively uncommon. He examined parish records which record births, marriages and deaths, and the names of people living together as households. From such data Laslett concludes that only about 10% of households in England from 1564 to 1821 included kin beyond the nuclear family.

Laslett suggests that the nuclear family household may have been characteristic of much of northwest Europe, though not of other parts of Europe. He argues that this may have been an important factor encouraging the process of industrialisation. The prior existence of nuclear families with a greater capacity for geographical mobility may have facilitated the movement of workers to urban areas, an important aspect of the industrial revolution.

Laslett's work has been criticised as inconclusive. The fact that most households were based on the nuclear family does not necessarily disprove the existence of a wider extended family network. It is not possible to discover from his data how much cooperation occurred between kin who were members of different households. In Arensberg and Kimball's study of Ireland, for example, relatives from other farms would often help a family to bring in their harvest and this favour would then be returned. Extended families may thus have been important while remaining residentially dispersed among several neighbouring households.

Michael Anderson: the extended family in industrial England

Michael Anderson (1971) carried out a study of the town of Preston, Lancashire based on a sample of 10% of the 1851 Census records. Anderson's research showed that 23% of households in Preston included kin beyond the nuclear family. He suggests that the process of industrialisation may, in fact, have strengthened the need for reliance on the extended family. Prior to the modern welfare state the family provided a home for parentless children, a means of sharing the cost of accommodation, a source of information about jobs and a means of financial support in sickness, unemployment and old age.

Anderson's research was mainly concerned with working class families for whom kin might well be a vital support in times of need. In Victorian England family life was sharply differentiated by class. However, it seems likely that for both the landed upper class and the rising industrial middle class ties of kinship remained important, both as a means of inheritance of property and as a source of social connections and influence.

The emergence of the modern family

Marxist and feminist historians have emphasised the way in which the ideology of family life of this rising middle class became increasingly dominant in Victorian England. Catherine Hall (1982), for example, shows how home and work became increasingly separated, with women's lives more and more centred on the domestic sphere. This middle class notion of the domestic ideal seems to have gradually extended to working class families, with the exclusion of married women from many areas of employment. Hilary Land (1976) suggests that this was further reinforced by a growing acceptance at the end of the nineteenth century of the idea of the 'family wage'. This was the claim by male workers to a wage which was sufficient to support a dependent wife and children.

Historical research calls into question any simple relationship between industrialisation and changes in the family. If Laslett is correct, the nuclear family was already the dominant household form before the industrial revolution. On the other hand, Anderson's research suggests that kinship ties may have been exploited by many families long after the industrial revolution. The nineteenth century was a period of important changes. The idea of family life, based on the private domestic sphere, supervised by a dependent wife supported by a husband working outside the home, came into existence for the first time.

Activity 5 Changing Family Structures

Item A *Families in rural Ireland*

The following extract describes some of the observations of the anthropologists Arensberg and Kimball who studied farming families in Ireland in the 1930s.

Between a man and his relatives there grows up an elaborate system of reciprocal cooperation. Men often lend one another tools and machinery. Women club together to make up a tub or firkin of butter or lend a girl when a family is shorthanded for the work of dairying. There is communal work at turf-cutting, the oat harvest and threshing - usually in the form of lending a boy (a farmer's son who was unmarried and still worked on his father's farm).

Arensberg observed the process most closely in the 1933 hay harvest at Lough. Only about half the farmers had horse-drawn mowing machines. They started early to bring in their hay working through the hours of daylight from dawn to dusk. At every stage in the process they had the assistance of boys from their neighbours who had no machines. The boys ate all their meals with the farmers they were helping. When the farmers with machines finished their own land they took the machines over to the meadows of the fathers of the boys who had helped them.

One farmer was helped by the sons of three others, his second cousins, and in due course he mowed their meadows. Another was helped by the son of his cousin and his nephew. In due course he took his mowing machine to do the fields of their fathers. There were however, five cases of farmers who although obviously short-handed had no help. Two of these were bachelors who could not reciprocate, and two 'strangers' who would not be expected to.

Adapted from R. Frankenberg *Communities in Britain*, 1966, pp36-37

Item B

A farming family from Lancashire

Harvesting in Berkshire

Item C *Families in pre-industrial England*

It is often assumed that families in the pre-industrial world were large and extended because the family was responsible for many functions and would therefore need to be large. But families were not large; at least the average family was relatively small. In fact the evidence we now have suggests that household size was remarkably constant in England at 4.75 persons per household at all times from the late sixteenth until the early twentieth century.

The general rule which governed the size and the constitution of the family went as follows: no two married couples or more went to make up a family group. When a son got married he left the family of his parents and started a family of his own. If he was not in a position to do this, then he could not get married, nor could his sister unless the man who was to take her for his bride was also in a position to start a new family.

Most young people therefore had to wait before they were permitted to marry. Our English ancestors had the same rules as we have, or would like to have, no two married couples in one family. As marriage was late and expectation of life was short, grandparents rarely lived long enough to see their grandchildren. Thus only two generations were typically alive at one time and the typical household was based on a nuclear family.

Adapted from P. Laslett *The World We Have Lost*, 1965

Item D

Households with kin beyond the nuclear family

England and Wales 1981*	9
England and Wales 1966 (approx.)	10
Swansea 1960 (approx.)	10-13
Preston 1851	23
Rural 1851	27
England (Laslett) 1564-1821	10

* Figure calculated from 1981 Census data.

Adapted from M. Anderson *Sociology of the Family*, 1971, p81 and OPCS 1981 Census data

Questions

1 a) Judging from Items A and B, why was kinship important for farming?
   b) Why is it less important today?
2 Read Item C. Outline the similarities and differences between families in pre-industrial England and families today?
3 Study Item D.
   a) Suggest reasons for the difference between the 1851 figures and those for earlier and later periods.
   b) What does the data suggest about the trend towards 'isolated nuclear families'?

3.2 Family and kinship in industrial society

Historical evidence suggests that industrialisation does not automatically lead to the development of kinship systems based on the independent nuclear family. However, many sociologists have argued that there is a long term trend in this direction. Talcott Parsons suggests that while the family may continue to carry out functions which involve kin beyond the nuclear family - such as care of elderly relatives and the provision of financial help - these have become non-essential or 'optional' functions.

William Goode (1963) reaches similar conclusions in his study of the impact of industrialisation on the family worldwide. He argues that the extended family has become a sort of optional extra. Individuals weigh up the costs and benefits of maintaining kinship ties and act accordingly. Goode argues that in developing countries the young in particular see fewer benefits and more costs in the obligations imposed by extended family networks. Many see the Western nuclear family, based on romantic love rather than arranged marriage, as offering greater personal freedom and as outweighing the practical benefits offered by traditional kinship relationships.

Young and Willmott: privatisation and the family

The British sociologists, Michael Young and Peter Willmott's research also suggests that there is a long term trend away from extended family networks towards what they term the *privatised nuclear family*.

In their first study *Family and Kinship in East London* (1962) Young and Willmott showed how the kind of extended family networks which Anderson suggests may have been widespread in early industrial England were still in existence in traditional working class communities in the 1950s. This study of Bethnal Green in the East End of London showed how a strong extended family network played an important role in mutual help and assistance for working class people. Mothers and daughters in particular had a very close relationship, with many daughters visiting their mothers several times a week for advice, help with their children and to keep in touch with with sisters and other female friends and relatives.

In the second part of their research Young and Willmott studied families from Bethnal Green who had been rehoused in Greenleigh, a new council estate in Essex some thirty miles from Bethnal Green. They show how this resulted in 'privatisation'. By this they meant that family life became more home-centred and based on the nuclear family. Wives lost regular contact with their mothers and became more dependent on husbands for companionship and support. Husbands were also cut off from social contacts in Bethnal Green, for example visiting the pub with workmates, and became more involved in domestic activities. Gardening, watching television and other home-centred leisure activities replaced the pub and visiting relatives and neighbours. For many women, however, privatisation was often experienced as isolation, as being confined to the home.

Young and Willmott's findings are reflected in subsequent studies such as John Goldthorpe and David Lockwood's (1969) research into affluent (highly paid) manual workers in Luton in the 1960s. Many had moved to Luton in search of better paid jobs. They led privatised, home-centered lives - the home and nuclear family were the centre of their leisure activities.

Young and Willmott: stages of family life

In a later study *The Symmetrical Family* (1975) Young and Willmott bring together their earlier research, historical evidence, and data from a survey they conducted in the London area in the early 1970s. They argue that the family in Britain has developed through three stages.

Stage 1 - The pre-industrial family The family at this stage was organised around its economic function as a production unit. Family members worked together in agriculture and in cottage industries. Home and work were not separated.

Stage 2 - The early industrial family The industrial revolution disrupted the unity of the family as its economic function was taken over by large scale industry. Men were increasingly drawn out of the home into industrial employment while the home became defined as the woman's sphere. Young and Willmott described the family as 'torn apart' by these changes. Women formed kinship networks to provide mutual support in working class communities like Bethnal Green.

Stage 3 - The privatised nuclear family This type of family emerged first in the middle class but gradually spread to much of the working class during the 20th century. It has three main characteristics:
a) it is home-centred and privatised;
b) the nuclear family is emphasised at the expense of the extended family;
c) it is symmetrical, the roles of husbands and wives are less segregated than in stage 2, husbands play a greater part in domestic life.

While family life in stage 1 revolved around production, in stage 3 consumption becomes more important. Joint leisure activities and spending money

on the home become the basis for the unity of the nuclear family.

Young and Willmott argue that the development of the stage 3 family has occurred through a process of *stratified diffusion*, whereby new ideas of family life were initiated by the higher social classes and gradually filtered down to the lower classes. As the working class has come to enjoy shorter working hours, more comfortable homes and a higher standard of living, family life has become increasingly privatised and nuclear. There is less need for the traditional mutual aid network of the extended family. There is more opportunity to devote time and money to home and children.

Young and Willmott hypothesise a possible fourth stage in family life. They argue that if stratified diffusion does occur then the upper class will be setting the trends for family life in the future. Their sample of managing directors' families suggests a trend away from the symmetrical family towards a more asymmetrical form. Husbands were highly involved in their work and domestic responsibilities devolved mainly onto the wives. Couples spent less time in joint activities than the typical privatised family.

Criticisms of Young and Willmott

1 Their theory suggests an historical 'march of progress' in which family life gets better and better. They have been criticised by conflict theorists for failing to address the negative aspects of changes in the modern family.

2 Many sociologists are unhappy about the concept of 'stratified diffusion', implying as it does that the working class automatically follows norms established by the middle class. Goldthorpe and Lockwood's study, while showing the prevalence of privatised lifestyles among affluent manual workers, showed that they still retained a distinctive working class outlook on life. It rejected the view that there was a convergence between middle and working class value systems.

3 Feminists have attacked Young and Willmott's concept of the symmetrical family. Ann Oakley (1974), for example, suggests that housework is still predominantly done by women with minimal assistance from their husbands (see Section 4.2).

4 The extended family may be more important than Young and Willmott's picture of the largely independent nuclear family implies.

Modified extended families

While Young and Willmott's work shows that the extended family survived well into the twentieth century, their thesis fits in with the broad thrust of functionalist theories about industrialisation and the family. In particular, they argue that while the short term consequence of industrialisation may have been the disruption of the family, in the long term it has created a new and stronger form of nuclear family. This family is nuclear, privatised, self-sufficient and self-centred.

However, this does not necessarily mean that the extended family has ceased to be important. Rosser and Harris (1965) in a study of Swansea found that while the nuclear family had become the focus of family life, the extended family continued to have a role, albeit in a modified form. They favour the use of the term *modified extended family* coined by the sociologist Eugene Litwak. This kind of extended family is often geographically dispersed, but continues to provide support for family members in times of need and comes together for important family events. Better communications, such as telephones and cars, mean that contacts between extended families over long distances are much easier than in the past.

Kinship in modern Britain

Peter Willmott (1986) himself has argued that sociologists have been too ready to underestimate the importance of kinship. His own research in North London in the 1980s found that most people had fairly regular contact with relatives and often relied on them for companionship and support.

Goldthorpe and Lockwood's argument that privatisation is increasingly characteristic of working class families is challenged in a study by Fiona Devine (1992). She replicated parts of Goldthorpe and Lockwood's research in her study of Vauxhall car workers and their families in Luton in 1986-87. Her findings suggest that the degree of privatisation of family life has been exaggerated. She found that most couples had regular contact with kin, especially with parents and to a lesser extent with grown-up siblings. Geographical mobility had not destroyed kinship networks as cars and telephones enabled relatives to keep in touch. Devine also points to the role of extended families in facilitating geographical mobility, showing that people continue to use kin as a source of information and contacts for finding jobs and housing.

A study by Janet Finch (1989) which draws together the findings of previous research indicates that there is still a strong sense of obligation to kin beyond the nuclear family. This is reinforced by state legislation, for example tax allowances for supporting dependent relatives, and by informal social norms which state that family members have a duty to help one another. Expectations about family obligations depend however on gender and closeness of relationship. Much more is expected of female relatives and the strongest sense of obligation, apart from that between spouses, is between parents and children.

A study of the Greater Manchester area by Janet Finch and Jennifer Mason (1993) largely confirms these conclusions. Over 90% of respondents had given or received financial help from relatives and almost 60% had shared a household with an adult relative (apart from their parents) at some time in their lives. In addition, many reported giving and receiving practical assistance, emotional support and help with children. While emphasising the way in which extended family relationships are based on a sense of obligation, Finch and Mason also found that help was negotiated and not necessarily given automatically.

The family and elderly people

A considerable body of research demonstrates the importance of kinship ties for the support of elderly relatives, especially parents. Women take on most of this responsibility. A study by Nissel and Bonnerjea (1982) calculated that husbands spend eight minutes a day compared to wives' two to three hours a day caring for an elderly dependent relative.

Janet Finch argues that the idea that in the past the family provided more care for elderly relatives is based on a myth of the 'golden age' of family life. In the nineteenth century far fewer people lived to an age where they became economically or physically dependent on kin. Finch concludes that 'people in late twentieth century Britain do not necessarily do less for their relatives than they have done for the past two centuries ... but they do have to work out the nature of their relationships and the patterns of support associated with them, in circumstances which are very different from the past' (1989, p84).

In recent years government policies on care for elderly people have emphasised the concept of 'care in the community'. This approach attempts to avoid the institutionalisation of the elderly in homes and hospitals. In fact only a small minority of elderly people live in institutions, while around a third live alone. It is clear that many elderly people benefit from contact with relatives, particularly from their children. However, as Graham Allan (1985) points out, it is unlikely that other relationships, such as those with neighbours, friends or kin other than children, will engender the same sense of obligation as that between parents and children. Given this, he argues, policies of community care which rely on the family will only be successful if families are given adequate support by agencies of the welfare state. Feminist critics of community care have argued that the resources provided are often insufficient and this creates an enormous burden of responsibility on carers, the majority of whom are women. (See pp159-160 for discussion of community care).

Activity 6 Mutual Aid in the Extended Family

Item A *Middle class families*

Mutual aid between members of an extended family flows in several directions depending upon stages in the family life cycle. Most of the families that I have been studying are in the first two stages of the family life cycle: that of 'home-making' and 'child-rearing'. These two stages are the time of greatest expenditure and because of the nature of middle class career patterns, the time of the lowest income.

The topics I concentrated on were careers, housing and children. In examining these subjects I found that over and over again where there had been aid from the extended family the important structural link was the father-in-law/father - son/son-in-law link.

One mechanism frequently utilised by the families I studied is the giving of aid on socially approved occasions: this is acceptable and can be received without any loss of independence. This begins at the wedding. I recorded one case of the house being given outright and two cases of a substantial deposit being put down on the house. In these cases naturally arrangements were made through the bank but it was the father or father-in-law that made them. This mechanism continues at Christmas and at birthdays - I noted a case of central heating being given as a Christmas present from the husband's parents.

Adapted from C. Bell *Middle Class Families*, 1968, pp88-94

Item B *Contacts with kin*

A number of recent surveys have shown that between about two-thirds and three-quarters of people - people of all ages, not just the elderly - still see at least one relative at least once a week. I recently completed a study of married people with young children in a North London suburb, a district where as many as a third of couples had moved in within the previous five years (Willmott, 1986). There, the proportion seeing relatives at least weekly was precisely two-thirds. Of those with parents alive, one in ten saw their mother or father or both every day, and nearly two-thirds of living parents and parents-in-law were seen at least once a month. Working class people saw rather more of their parents and other relatives than middle class people did, but the differences were not large.

The evidence from that and other recent studies also shows that relatives continue to be the main source of informal support and care, and that again the class differences were not marked. In my North London research, nearly two-thirds of people were helped by relatives, particularly mothers or mothers-in-law, when one of the children was ill; nearly three-quarters were helped with baby sitting, again mainly by mothers and mothers-in-law. Four-fifths looked to relatives, mainly parents or parents-in-law, when they needed to borrow money. Surveys of elderly people show that most of the informal help and care they receive comes from relatives, particularly children or children-in-law.

A small-scale but important study in the Greater London area compared the kinship patterns of people originating from mainly Victorian areas, who had stayed in the same district since before they got married, with people from similar areas who had moved out. Many of the second group turned out to have remained in close touch with their parents and siblings; they saw as much of them each week as those who had stayed put. This has come about because clusters of relatives - particularly parents and their married children - had moved out to suburban districts where they were within reasonable visiting distance of each other.

Adapted from P. Willmott 'Urban Kinship Past and Present' *Social Studies Review*, November 1988

Questions

1 a) In Item A, why is the type of help given by middle class parents likely to come from the father or father-in-law?

b) Why is this type of help likely to be more significant in middle class than in working class families?

c) How is the type of help given by mothers and mothers-in-law likely to differ? How would you explain this?

2 Bell (Item A) suggests that help flows in different directions at different stages in the family life cycle. At what stage is help likely to flow from children to parents and what form might it take?

3 What evidence does Peter Willmott (Item B) provide to show that greater geographical mobility has not necessarily destroyed extended family ties?

4 Look at Item C. Members of extended families finding it easier to maintain contact over long distances than in the past. Suggest reasons for this.

Item C

3.3 Changing life cycles and family diversity

A popular view of the family in Britain today is of a husband and wife with two or three children living in a nuclear family. This image - what Edmund Leach calls the 'cereal packet image' of the family - is fostered by advertisers who portray smiling families consuming their products. It is also upheld by politicians when they speak of the need to protect the family. And it is institutionalised in the assumptions made about dependent wives and children in the taxation and social security systems. For example, social security payments are normally made to the head of a family - usually male - with allowances for their dependent wife and children.

In many ways this picture of the typical family is a misleading one. In 1992 under 25% of households in Britain consisted of a married couple and one or more dependent children. Diana Gittins (1985) points out that the ideal of what a family should be acts as a powerful ideology, defining what is normal and desirable in family life and labelling alternatives as 'deviant' and less desirable. This ideology, however, obscures the reality. There is no such thing as *the* British family, but instead a diversity of family types, some of which are discussed below.

Family life cycles

Although only a minority of households are conventional nuclear families, most people will, for part of their lives, live as a member of such a family. Families are not static but pass through a life cycle. Any picture of family life in Britain is merely a snapshot of a constantly shifting scene. Thus a person might pass through several stages in their life cycle, some in a household containing family members, some not.

Possible stages in a person's family life cycle

1 Birth and childhood
2 Leaving home and single adulthood
3 Marriage, living with spouse but no children
4 Birth of children, family formation
5 Middle age, children leave home
6 Old age, possibly widow(er)hood

This life cycle is of course only one possibility. Individuals may not marry or have children and may divorce and remarry. The timing and duration of these stages are also affected by factors such as class, sex, ethnic group and region. Andrew Cherlin describes the following hypothetical life history.

'When Bill was ten his parents separated. He lived with his mother and saw his father every Saturday. Four years later, his mother remarried, and Bill added a stepfather to his family. At eighteen, Bill left home to attend college and after graduation he and his girlfriend moved in together. A year and a half later they married and soon afterwards they had a child. After several years, however, the marriage began to turn sour. Bill and his wife eventually separated, with Bill's wife retaining custody of the child. Three years later Bill married a woman who had a child from a previous marriage and together they had another child. Bill's second marriage lasted 35 years until his death (1981, p1).

In the example above Bill had lived in eight different households but only three of them were traditional nuclear families. The nuclear family is thus only one of a number of *household* types. Sociologists make a distinction between a household - a group of people who live together - and a *family* - a group of people who are kin. Not only is there a considerable diversity of families in the United Kingdom today, but there is also an increasing number of households which are not based on families. Several changes in British society have encouraged this diversity in recent years.

Increasing life expectancy A growing number of people survive into old age. An increasing proportion of households are composed of single persons or married couples only. Many of these households are composed of people whose children have grown up and left home. The fact that women live longer than men (there are about twice as many women as men over 65) means that a high proportion of lone person households are made up of elderly women.

Divorce and one parent families One parent, lone parent or single parent families are not something new. However, in the past most were created through the death of a parent. Today the majority are created through divorce. There were 1.3 million lone parent families in Britain in 1992, double the number of 20 years earlier. They accounted for about one in five of all families with dependent children. However, many children in one parent households have two parents alive, and may have regular contact with the parent outside the household. Thus the term one parent family may not always reflect the level of contact between parents and children. Another significant group of one parent families is headed by unmarried mothers. Again some of these children may have regular contact with their fathers.

Lone parent households are likely to share a number of characteristics.
1 The majority of lone parent households are headed by women.
2 The average age of children is generally older with fewer under-fives.
3 They are disproportionately concentrated in inner

city areas, particularly in inner London boroughs.

4 They are much more likely to live in poverty. In 1992 around 75% of lone parents were claiming Income Support.

5 Lone mothers are less likely to be employed than married mothers.

6 One parent families are more likely to live in poor housing, overcrowded conditions and are less likely to be home owners than other families. Over 50% live in council accommodation compared to less than 20% of two parent families .

The above points might seem to reinforce the widely held view that one parent families are in some way a 'problem'. In 1993 the MP John Redwood branded them as 'one of the biggest social problems of our day'. This is misleading - in many ways the problem is in how society deals with one parent families. The Finer Report (1974) recommended that more extensive benefits should be targeted to one parent families but most of its recommendations were ignored. Current government policy aims to encourage lone parents to support themselves through employment or to look for support from their former spouses. State childcare provision remains very limited making it difficult for lone parents to work outside the home and ex-spouses are often unwilling or unable to fulfil their maintenance obligations. It is not surprising therefore that one parent families often face problems. In 1993 the government launched the Child Support Agency with the aim of tracking down absent fathers whose ex-partners are dependent on state benefits and forcing them to provide financial support. How far this will be successful remains to be seen.

Apart from financial difficulties lone parents face other problems. One parent has to take on the roles and responsibilities of two parents. Moreover, lone parents neither fit the status of a couple nor the category of being single. This creates an ambiguous status. Despite the fact that divorce is now widespread, marriage is still the norm. Again the problem here may not be one parent families as such, but the way society treats them.

Remarriage and reconstituted families A high proportion of lone parents remarry and form new two parent families. According to the 1991 *General Household Survey* four-fifths of men and three-quarters of women who divorce before they are 35 remarry within ten years. Being a lone parent is a temporary status for many, though an increasingly common stage in the life cycle. In 1991 over a third of all marriages were remarriages in which one or both partners had been divorced. In many such marriages one or both partners already had children. And many couples who remarry also wish to have children in the new marriage. The *reconstituted family* - a family created from pieces of former families - is, therefore, another variety of family which is increasingly common in Britain. It is currently estimated that at least six million people live in such families, including some 10% of all children. Like one parent families, reconstituted families are nothing new. Peter Laslett (1965) reckoned that around one quarter of all marriages in seventeenth century England were remarriages. However, this was due to the death of a spouse rather than divorce.

Burgoyne and Clark's (1984) study of reconstituted families suggests that they experience a number of difficulties not faced by other families. For example, reconstituted families lack the boundaries which other families have. Children are still linked to natural parents and their families, and parents may have to negotiate with ex-spouses over holidays, access arrangements and so on. In this sense such families are not independent units in the same way as other families. As with one parent families, many of the problems of reconstituted families seem to be created by society. Reconstituted families do not fit into what is regarded by many people as a 'normal' family and may therefore experience difficulties in fitting into norms of behaviour designed for conventional nuclear families. Maybe because of such strains, the divorce rate among the already divorced is much higher than among those in their first marriage. It would seem that society has not yet adapted to the situation where divorce, lone parenthood and remarriage are seen as a normal part of the life cycle.

Activity 7 Family Types

Item A *The neo-conventional family*

Robert Chester argues that statistics such as those in Item B are misleading as they represent only a 'snapshot' of households at any one point in time. Most households which are not made up of nuclear families contain individuals who have been, or will be, members of nuclear family households. Moreover, while nuclear families constitute a minority of households, when expressed as a percentage of people over half the population live in nuclear family households at any one

point in time (see Item C). Thus, despite apparent diversity, the nuclear family remains the dominant family type.

It is clear that there have been many changes in family behaviour in Britain: later marriage, higher rates of divorce, a greater tendency for wives to work, and cohabitation as a temporary and childless phase in relationships between couples. But there is a very strong framework of continuity. The family, based on a married couple living with their children and committed to a permanent relationship, is still the norm. On the evidence, most people will continue not only to spend most of their lives in a family environment, but also to place a high value on it.

To say this is not to ignore the diversity of styles among families of conventional form, or the problematical aspects of family life. Still less is it to discount the existence of other domestic forms like the single parent family. It is important, nevertheless, to remember that these are minorities, which for various reasons excite attention disproportionate to their number.

Adapted from R. Chester 'The Rise of the Neo-Conventional Family' *New Society*, 9.5.85, pp 185-188

Item B

Households by type

Great Britain				Percentages
	1961	**1971**	**1981**	**1991**
One person				
Under pensionable age	4	6	8	11
Over pensionable age	7	12	14	16
Two or more unrelated adults	5	4	5	3
Married couple with				
No children	26	27	26	28
1-2 dependent children	30	26	25	20
3 or more dependent children	8	9	6	5
Non-dependent children only	10	8	8	8
Lone parent with				
Dependent children	2	3	5	6
Non-dependent children only	4	4	4	4
Two or more families	3	1	1	1
All households	100	100	100	100

Adapted from *Social Trends*, 1993, p 27

Item C

People in households: by type of household and family in which they live

Great Britain				Percentages
	1961	**1971**	**1981**	**1991**
Type of household				
Living alone	3.9	6.3	8.0	10.7
Married couple no children	17.8	19.3	19.5	23.0
Married couple with dependent children	52.2	51.7	47.4	41.1
Married couple with non-dependent children only	11.6	10.0	10.3	10.8
Lone parent with dependent children	2.5	3.5	5.8	10.0
Other households	12.0	9.2	9.0	4.3
All households	100	100	100	100

Adapted from *Social Trends*, 1993, p 28

Questions

1 Examine Item B.
  a) What trend is apparent in the proportion of households which could be described as nuclear families?
  b) Which types of households have increased as a proportion of all households?
  c) How would you explain these trends?
2 Explain why Robert Chester (Item A) argues that statistics such as those in Item B give a misleading picture of the social significance of the nuclear family.

3 Compare Items B and C.
  a) Why is there a difference between the percentages for the same categories?
  b) What effects might this have on an assessment of the significance of the nuclear family?
4 Using evidence from the data above and elsewhere discuss the arguments for and against the view that 'the nuclear family is in decline'.

Activity 8 Lone Parent Families

Item A *Starting out conventionally*

Most lone parents have been married or have previously had a stable relationship. Most start off by conforming to the conventional model of the two parent family. Subsequent arrangements, following disruption and breakdown, are necessary adjustments. Many have experienced violence, exploitation or harassment and 'chose' single parenthood as a means of protecting themselves and their children from harm.

Adapted from R. Smith 'Families 1994-style' *Poverty* Winter 1993, p 12

Item B *Hoping to end up conventionally*

Normally I hardly get any visitors at all. I get fed up. It does get lonely when Andrew [her child] is in bed. That's it, I'm on my own. It's just that sometimes I'd like to drop everything, you know, and go out and just let my hair down sort of thing. I'm young, you know, I'm 21, and I'm not going out and enjoying myself. I'll never meet anybody will I? Because one day I'd like to meet somebody and settle down. I'd like to, you know, meet Mr Right and maybe get married.

Lone parent quoted in R. Cohen et al *Hardship Britain*, 1992, p 79

Item C
Percentage of all families with dependent children headed by lone mothers and lone fathers

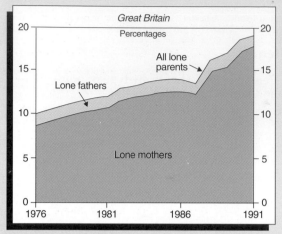

Great Britain
Percentages

All lone parents

Lone fathers

Lone mothers

1976   1981   1986   1991

Adapted from *Social Trends*, 1994, p36

Item E
Types of lone parent families

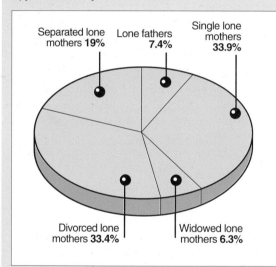

Separated lone mothers **19%**   Lone fathers **7.4%**   Single lone mothers **33.9%**

Divorced lone mothers **33.4%**   Widowed lone mothers **6.3%**

Adapted from *Guardian Education*, 11.1.94, p11

Item G   *Lone parent families as a problem*

'Lone parent families are one of the biggest social problems of our day.'

'The natural state should be the two adult family caring for their children.'

John Redwood, MP quoted in *Observer*, 4.7.93, p2; 11.7.93, p19

Item D
Attitudes to lone parent families (percentages)

'A single mother can bring up her child as well as a married couple.'

51   48   41
30

1987   1993

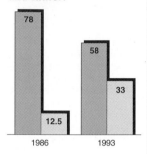

Key ▇ Agree ▢ Disagree

'To grow up happily, children need a home with both their mother and father.'

'People who want children ought to get married.'

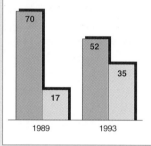

70   52   35   17

1989   1993

78   58   33   12.5

1986   1993

Adapted from *Guardian Education*, 11.1.94, p11

Item F   *Single lone mothers*

'I really wanted a child but I didn't want some guy around to drive me nuts.'

Michelle Pfeiffer quoted in Y. Roberts 'We are Becoming Divorced from Reality' *New Statesman and Society*, 24.9.93, p16

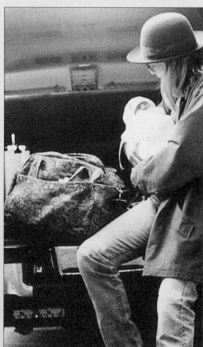

Michelle Pfeiffer with her baby

Despite there being an increase in the number of births outside marriage in England and Wales from 8% in 1971 to 31% in 1992, there is evidence that many more of such births were occurring within stable relationships. Three quarters of births outside marriage in 1992 were registered by both parents, compared with 45% in 1971.

Adapted from *Social Trends*, 1994, p40

Item H   *Do the children suffer?*

Are the children of lone parents disadvantaged compared to the children of two parent families? This is an area of claims and counter-claims where value judgements often cloud the issue. First it is difficult, if not impossible, to disentangle the effects of economic disadvantage - many lone parent families live in poverty - from other possible effects. A catalogue of 'disadvantages' has been drawn up by the critics of the lone parent family. These include lack of a father figure/male role model, the stigma of having a lone parent, the lack of effective socialisation and discipline, all of which are seen to result in relatively poor school performance and higher rates of juvenile delinquency.

In a survey of research, David H.J. Morgan states, 'The most cautious verdict would be that while it seems to be the case that children brought up in two parent families do tend to fare better than those who are brought up in single parent households, we still do not know enough about what causes these differences'. In the case of children whose parents are divorced and separated, the conflict which preceded the breakup may well have more effect on the children than living with a lone parent. And in many cases the breakup of the marriage may well benefit the children.

Adapted from D.H.J. Morgan 'The Family' in M.Haralambos (ed) *Developments in Sociology* vol 10, 1994

Questions

1 The increase in lone parents does not mean a rejection of the two parent family. Discuss using Items A, B and F.
2 How would you explain the difference in the proportion of lone fathers and lone mothers in Items C and E?
3 Suggest reasons for the changes in attitudes shown in Item D.
4 Use all relevant items to answer the following.
    a) Why have lone parent families become a matter for public concern and even alarm?
    b) Lone parent families are a problem because society has decided they are. Discuss.

3.4 Families and cultural diversity

The previous section discussed the ways in which longer and more diverse life cycles had contributed to a greater variety of household types in contemporary Britain. This is not the only source of diversity in families and households. Other variations are related to social differences based on class, ethnicity and locality.

Social class and families

As will be clear from Chapter 2, social class is important in many areas of life in Britain. Eversley and Bonnerjea (1982) point out a number of ways in which social class affects family life. For example, manual workers tend to marry and have children at an earlier age than nonmanual workers. Housing is closely related to class with professional workers constituting the highest proportion of home owners and unskilled workers the highest proportion of council tenants. This affects geographical mobility patterns as council tenants tend to stay in the same area as their parents where there is more chance of being housed. Young owner occupiers are more likely to to look for smaller cheaper properties away from their parents.

Social class position (as measured by the occupation of the male head of household) has an important influence on family life. In general, the lower a family's class position, the lower its income, the more likely its members are to live in overcrowded and substandard housing and the more likely the adults are to experience unemployment. And low income makes

the family holiday, the family car and the family outing less likely. The inequalities of social class may stay with the children for the rest of their lives. For example, the higher the class position of a child's family, the more likely she or he is to attain high educational qualifications and in turn a well paid, high status job. Despite an apparent convergence in the lifestyles of middle class and working class families, economic differences remain an important influence on the life chances of family members.

Locality and families

Eversley and Bonnerjea (1982) claim that there is a relationship between locality and family type. They identify six kinds of areas in England and Wales, each of which is associated with characteristic types of families and households.
1 **The 'sun belt'** This includes much of the more affluent southern and southeastern England, with an over-representation of the higher social classes, owner occupiers and two parent households.
2 **The 'geriatric wards'** These include many of the coastal areas of England and Wales. They are characterised by an increasing proportion of elderly, one and two person households, often living some distance from their nearest relatives.
3 **Older declining industrial areas** These are founded on industries such as coal, iron and steel, ship building and textiles. They tend to be characterised by older populations and stable family type households, with traditional patriarchal family structures and strong family and

neighbourhood loyalties. (For example, see discussion of Bethnal Green in Section 3.2).

4 **Newly declining industrial areas** These are found mainly in the Midlands, for example Coventry. Such areas were prosperous, with high rates of female employment, but now face high unemployment among older workers and migration by the young. As many people in such areas are recent arrivals, they often have little support from extended family networks.

5 **Truly rural areas** Few of these survive as in most rural areas commuters and others have moved in. In strongly agricultural areas family based farms and businesses remain important. There is a high proportion of two parent families and single old people, with few women in paid employment.

6 **The inner cities** These tend to be characterised by high measures of social deprivation and a high proportion of immigrants. They also have a high proportion of one parent and multi-adult households. Many people in these areas are isolated from extended families and social networks, for example, young single people, elderly people whose children have migrated, homeless people and discharged mental patients.

If one accepts Eversley and Bonnerjea's classification, then it can be seen that local influences affect the kind of families which prevail in different regions of the country. Their research points to the danger of generalising about the 'typical British family'.

Ethnicity and families

The patterns of family life among ethnic minorities are influenced by their own cultures and add further to the diversity of families in Britain. Again there is the danger of generalising about 'typical ethnic minority families'. Roger Ballard (1982), in his study of South Asian families, points out that there are important cultural differences within the Asian community between, for example, Sikh, Muslim and Hindu families. Many South Asian families have preserved aspects of the traditional family patterns of India, Pakistan and Bangladesh. This is particularly evident in the concern for the wider kinship network, an emphasis on loyalty to the family rather than concern for the individual, and in a sharp division in the roles and social worlds of men and women. Because the majority of South Asians have arrived in this country in the last 30 years, families tend to be youthful and household sizes tend to be larger with kin outside the nuclear family often living together.

Sallie Westwood and Parminder Bhachu (1988), however, point out that Asian families are as diverse as white families and warn against generalisations. They also point out that the changes which have affected families in general have also affected Asian households. Most Asian households are now based on the nuclear family. At the same time, concern for kinship ties remains strong and most young Asians have a high degree of respect for parents and family traditions.

West Indian families too tend to have their own characteristics, based in part on traditional family patterns in the Caribbean. In many parts of the Caribbean, whilst the nuclear family based on marriage is the norm, it is common for couples to live together outside marriage. In other cases women bring children up as lone parents, often helped by their mothers and other female relatives.

Geoffrey Driver (1982) suggests that these family patterns are also found amongst West Indians in Britain, with a significant proportion of *matrifocal* families, where the mother is the sole parent or the father plays a limited role in the family. Jocelyn Barrow (1982) argues that many of the problems faced by West Indian families arise from the fact that the support systems available to women in the Caribbean, for example female relatives and friends caring for children, are largely absent in Britain.

Like Westwood and Bhachu, Ann Phoenix (1988) warns against the danger of stereotyping ethnic minority families. She points out that there is no more a typical 'Afro-Caribbean family' than a typical 'white family'. Thus ethnic minority households are themselves characterised by diversity.

Apart from the ethnic groups discussed above there are also many other ethnic minorities, for example Italians, Cypriots, Irish, Jews and Eastern Europeans, all with their own family traditions, adding further to the diversity of families in Britain.

Summary

1 The industrial revolution changed the relationship between the family and the economic system, creating a sharper separation between the private world of the family and the public world of the workplace.

2 The nuclear family appears to be the most common family unit in industrial societies. However, there is considerable evidence to suggest that wider kinship networks continue to play an important part in the lives of many families.

3 Although most people experience life in a nuclear family, it represents only a stage in their life cycle. Social and demographic changes have meant that an increasing part of many people's lives is spent in households which are not based on conventional nuclear families.

4 Contemporary Britain is a culturally diverse society. It is a mistake to view any family form as typical or normal. Differences of class, ethnicity, locality, age and many other factors influence family life.

Activity 9 Ethnic Minority Families

Item A
Couples with dependent children as a percentage of all families: by ethnic group of family head, 1991

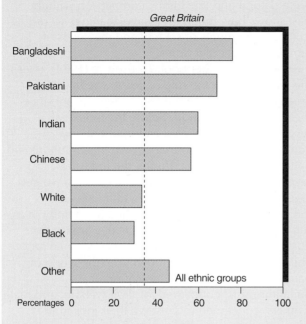

Great Britain

Bangladeshi
Pakistani
Indian
Chinese
White
Black
Other — All ethnic groups

Percentages 0 20 40 60 80 100

Adapted from *Social Trends*, 1994, p35

Item B
Lone mothers as a percentage of all mothers: by ethnic group, 1989-91

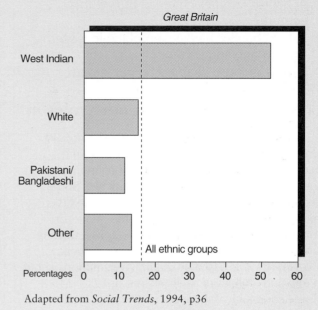

Great Britain

West Indian
White
Pakistani/ Bangladeshi
Other — All ethnic groups

Percentages 0 10 20 30 40 50 60

Adapted from *Social Trends*, 1994, p36

Item C *Asian families*

Generally, Asian households are larger, with 4.6 members, than 'white' or 'West Indian' households with 2.3 and 3.4 members respectively. 73% of Asian households include children (the figure is 31% for 'whites' and 57% for 'West Indians'). Extended families are most common among Sikhs and East African Asians based on households including more than one generation or where brothers and their wives live together. This sometimes means that adjoining houses are knocked together. Overall, the proportion of extended families living together is 21% - higher than among other groups but not the norm.

The trend, in fact, is towards nuclear families but this does not mean that the importance of extended family ties has diminished. On the contrary, economic and material assistance as well as emotional support are found in these enduring links. To say as many Asian people do, 'We are family people' expresses truth and a commitment to family life shown in the Sunday gatherings where food and news and the warmth and support of family members are shared across generations and households. People will travel miles to be together for family events, crammed into cars or minibuses for the journey.

Adapted from S. Westwood and P. Bhachu 'Images and Realities' *New Society*, 6.5.88

An extended family living in Wolverhampton. Karan Chand lived and worked in Britain for ten years before his wife and children could join him from the Punjab. His family life in India remains a benchmark for his family in Wolverhampton.

Questions

1 a) What differences between ethnic groups are indicated by Items A and B?
   b) What problems might there be in using these statistics to study long term trends in differences in family life?

2 Read Item C. Suggest reasons why:
   a) nuclear families might be increasingly the norm for Asian households;
   b) the extended family remains important in Asian communities.

4 Husbands and Wives

Key Issues

1 How have the roles of husbands and wives in British families changed during this century?
2 What changes have taken place in patterns of marriage and divorce?
3 How can these changes be explained?

4.1 Social change and gender roles in the family

In many societies family life is organised around gender roles - responsibilities within the family are allocated to members according to their sex. Some researchers have argued that there are certain tasks which are universally allocated to either males or females. They see this division of labour as reflecting biological differences between the sexes. Others, however, see it as based on cultural assumptions about the role and abilities of each sex (see pp121-124).

Some sociological theories have tended to see gender roles as natural and inevitable. Talcott Parsons, for example, suggested that within the modern nuclear family it was essential that one parent, the father, performed the *instrumental role* of leader and provider while the other, the mother, performed the *expressive role* of giving psychological support and taking responsibility for socialising children. This made sense because women give birth to and nurse children. Parsons was writing about America in the 1950s when this division of responsibilities may well have been the norm in most families.

Other sociologists have noted a gradual breakdown in the separation of roles of husbands and wives and point to the rise of what Young and Willmott (1975) describe as the *symmetrical family*. As more married women work outside the home and men spend more leisure time at home with their families, marital roles have become increasingly similar. This view has, however, been challenged by feminists, like Ann Oakley (1974). She argues that the sharing of responsibilities in most families is superficial. The family continues to be patriarchal, with the man as the main wage earner while the primary role of married women remains that of 'housewife'. The evidence concerning this debate is examined further in Section 4.2.

Industrialisation and the creation of the housewife role

One contribution which historians of the family have made is to show how far gender roles in the family are socially constructed - created by particular social and historical conditions. While the roles played by men and women at any one point in history may seem natural and inevitable, comparison with the past shows how much they have changed according to the requirements of society and the needs of families at particular times.

Ann Oakley, in her book *Housewife* (1974), traces the way in which the role of housewife has been created by changes in the family and society since the industrial revolution. Before the industrial revolution women played an important and complementary role to that of men in agriculture and cottage industries. Even during the industrial revolution men, women and children often worked together in factories and mines, although as individual wage earners rather than as a family in a self-contained economic unit. Oakley argues that during the period 1841-1914 married women and children were largely excluded from the world of paid employment by a combination of philanthropists, concerned for their welfare, and male workers, concerned to preserve their jobs from female competition. This process was also encouraged by Factory and Education Acts which made the employment of women and children increasingly difficult, and by a climate of opinion which saw a woman's place as in the home, looking after her husband and children. It was these changes which created the role of housewife as the primary role for married women in the twentieth century.

The feminist historian Catherine Hall (1980), however, points out that it was mainly middle class women who lived up to the Victorian ideal of domesticity. Working class women often had to work simply to make ends meet. However, this often involved activities which could be combined with running the home, for example taking in laundry, doing outwork or running a shop. Hall argues that while the dominant ideology stressed the desirability of domesticity, this was often contradicted in practice. For example, the middle class who espoused this ideal also needed women as domestic servants and employers needed them as factory workers and agricultural labourers.

Female dependency

These changes were accompanied by a growing economic dependence of women and children on men. Hilary Land (1976) argues that the development of the *family wage*, with the acceptance of the idea that a man's wage should be sufficient to support a wife and children, helped to create a situation where women and children became dependents, reinforcing the male's status as the head of the family.

Not all sociologists have seen such changes as disadvantageous. Functionalist writers, like Parsons, see a division of responsibilities as functional for everyone, ensuring the family is economically supported and that children are adequately cared for. Some Marxist-feminists also have suggested that the family wage system may serve the interests of women and working class people. Jane Humphries (1977) argues that the exclusion of married women from work actually helped to raise wages for working class men and thus improve living conditions for working class families.

Demographic changes and women's roles

During this century other changes have influenced gender roles in the family. Firstly, a number of important demographic changes have affected the family.

1 **Family size** The average size of families has declined in the last hundred years. In the 1860s average completed family size was around six or seven children. During the 1870s middle class couples began to limit their family size and this trend was followed by working class families after the First World War. Since the 1930s average completed family sizes have fluctuated between two and three children and by 1990 had fallen below two children.

2 **Marriage** Up to the early 1970s marriage became increasingly popular and couples were tending to marry at a younger age. This trend has, however, reversed in the last twenty years.

3 **Life expectancy** People are living longer which means that many women have a long period of life ahead of them after completing their families.

Most women therefore marry relatively young, have a small family and often return to paid employment in their middle years. Childbearing and childrearing now occupy a smaller portion of most women's lives. However, these activities still play a crucial part in their lives and have an important effect on ideas about their role in society.

Female employment and the family

A further important change, linked to family size, is the growth in paid employment of married women. In 1991, 67% of married women were employed outside the home, nearly half of them working part time (*General Household Survey*, 1993, p95). Women's earnings have remained on average around three-quarters of men's hourly rates since the mid 1970s. In many two income households women's work and earnings are seen as less important than men's. Yet married women's earnings make an important contribution to family income. Hilary Land (1975) cites a Department of Health and Social Security analysis of 1970 which indicated that the number of two parent families below the official poverty line would have *trebled* if it were not for the contribution made by the wife's earnings. While writers like Parsons may have dismissed female employment as insignificant in the 1950s, it is hard to do so today when women's work outside the home makes a significant contribution both to the national economy and to family income.

Conjugal roles

Previous sections have discussed the notion of privatisation in the family. Husbands appear to have become more home-centred in their leisure activities, encouraged by shorter working hours and improvements in the material comforts in the home. Greater geographical mobility has also meant that traditional extended family networks, often based on the support networks of women, have become weakened and wives rely more on their husbands for support.

Elizabeth Bott (1957), one of the first sociologists to study the effects of these changes on the roles of husbands and wives, identified two types of conjugal or marital roles.

1 **Segregated conjugal roles** These exist when husbands and wives lead largely separate social lives and have sharply differentiated roles within the family.

2 **Joint conjugal roles** These are characterised by more sharing of responsibilities, decision making and leisure activities. Husbands' and wives' roles are less sharply differentiated.

Bott investigated the factors which influenced the way couples organised their roles in marriage. She found no clear association between social class and conjugal roles. However, she did find that the kind of social networks couples were involved in was important. Couples who were part of a *close knit* social network (for example, in traditional working class communities) tended to have segregated conjugal roles. In these circumstances each partner would have their own network of relatives, friends and neighbours who they might have known all their lives. Most of the members of these networks would know each other well. The relationship between husband and wife was thus only one amongst many and husband and wife were therefore less socially dependent on each other.

Couples who had more *loose knit* social networks (for example, those who had moved to new areas because of work or rehousing) tended to have joint conjugal roles. Each spouse was less likely to have their own circle of friends and relatives outside the family. This type of couple tended to rely on each other more for support and leisure, spent more time together and shared domestic responsibilities. Writers like Young and Willmott (1975) have argued that the modern home-centred family is increasingly isolated from such social networks and conjugal roles have therefore become more joint. The extent to which this has actually occurred, and whether it is linked to a trend towards greater equality between husbands and wives, is discussed in the next section.

Activity 10 Changing Marital Roles

Item A *Women's lives 1901-1991*

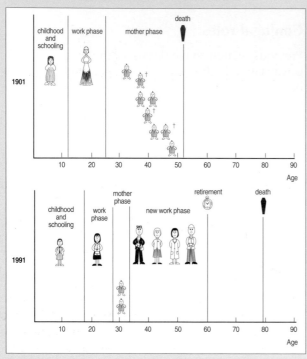

† In 1901 a high proportion of children could be expected to die before reaching adulthood. The crosses indicate children who would not survive.

Adapted from J. Thompson *Examining Sociology*, 1980, p202

Item C *Married women*

In Britain in 1900 one quarter of married women were in childbirth every year. Thirty years later it was down to one in eight. Between 1971 and 1992 the average number of children per woman fell from 2.3 to 1.8. At the start of the 20th century less than 10% of married women were in paid employment, by 1951 this had risen to 26%, in 1971 to 40% and in 1991 to 67%. A woman born in 1901 could expect to live 51.8 years, in 1931 62.5 years, in 1971 74.9 years and in 1994 79 years.

Adapted from various issues of *Social Trends*

Item B *Traditional workers and their wives*

In the early years of the 20th century manual workers tended to live in 'occupational communities' with many of the men sharing the same kind of work. Mining and dockland communities are typical examples. This extract describes the roles of husbands and wives in Featherstone, a coal mining community in Yorkshire, in the early 1950s.

In adolescence the young man starts work and the pattern of manliness which is so important in this community takes on its adult form. The strong interdependence of the men at work is reflected in their social relations outside work. If the woman's place is in the home, the man's place is definitely outside it. After work, the men go home for a wash and a meal and then go out again to meet their friends at the club, the pub or the sports ground. It is here than men experience most fully the emotional satisfactions which social life affords. It is with other men that they are at their most relaxed, at ease and emotionally expansive. A man's centre of activity is outside the home.

The wife's role is defined in terms of her husband's convenience, much as the husband's role of employee is defined in terms of management's convenience. The husband pays his wife an agreed weekly sum, called 'her wages'. She may not know how much he earns or what proportion of his earnings is given to her. With her wage, the woman rules her household and makes all expenditure decisions, except for big items, such as a new cooker, for which the husband will pay out a further share from his wages. Unlike the husbands, the wives spend little on themselves without the approval of their spouse. The husband will query expenditure on items outside the normal household budget. This budget includes little for her clothes, less for her leisure, nothing for her self improvement. In this way the wife's life is restricted to her family and her neighbours.

Adapted from J. Klein *Samples from English Culture*, vol 1, 1965, pp103-13

Item D *Affluent workers and their wives*

The following extract describes the family life of affluent manual workers in Luton in the 1960s. Many of these workers had moved to Luton from other parts of the country in search of high wages and secure jobs.

The men often made remarks which revealed that their home and family centred existence was something that in many ways they positively valued. Most notably, perhaps, was the frequency with which they emphasised the central place that 'wife and kids' held in their lives and their approval of this state of affairs. In comparison with what is known of the more traditional worker, the amount of time the men in our sample spent outside the home with 'mates' appeared to be very small. Also, within the home many men appear to take part in - or indeed to have taken over - activities usually seen as 'women's work'.

Most men's leisure activities were centered on the home. Only 16% of the activities reported by husbands were both outside the home and not involving other family members. Also, in naming their most frequent leisure companions apart from members of their family, 47% of affluent workers did not mention *any* friend whom they did not share with their wives. It is interesting to observe that while in the case of shopping and washing up some degree of segregation for conjugal roles is certainly in evidence, a majority of husbands who are fathers are likely to be involved in activities that are in some way concerned with children.

Adapted from J. Goldthorpe, D. Lockwood, F. Bechofer and J. Platt *The Affluent Worker in the Class Structure*, 1969, pp105-6

Questions

1 How might the changes described in Items A and C affect women's family lives and their relationships with husbands?
2 Read Items B and D.
   a) Briefly describe the difference between the roles of husbands and wives in 'traditional' and 'affluent' worker families.
   b) Suggest reasons for these differences
   c) Should we see either group as typical? Give reasons for your answer.

4.2 Gender roles in contemporary families

Families are made up of social relationships and social relationships involve power. Feminists in particular have examined power differentials within the family. They see families as *patriarchal* or male dominated. This contrasts sharply with the view that men and women are simply different but equal.

Measuring power is not easy (see pp192-194). Some sociologists measure power in terms of who makes decisions. However, some things may be taken for granted, never questioned or discussed and thus do not become an issue to be decided. Such non-decisions would not be apparent in an analysis which only focused on actual decisions. For example, it may be taken for granted that a wife looks after the home and sacrifices her own career to further that of her husband. In this case there is no decision to be taken.

Graham Allan (1985) outlines three main approaches that have been used to study power in the family. These will now be considered in turn.

Decision making

This approach examines who gets their way in family decisions. For example, Stephen Edgell in his study *Middle Class Couples* (1980) interviewed both husbands and wives from a sample of 38 professional couples. Previous studies using this approach did not relate decisions to how frequently they were made or their importance. Edgell tried to take these factors into account. He found that women controlled decision making in a number of areas, for example food purchases, children's clothing and household decoration. However, the couples did not see these decisions as important. Husbands had the main say in what were regarded as 'serious' decisions like moving house and buying expensive items such as cars (see Activity 11, Item C).

Edgell's study casts doubt on the views of writers like Young and Willmott who claim that middle class couples are in the forefront of changes towards more equality in marriage.

Jan Pahl's study *Money and Marriage* (1989) examines the control of finances in marriage. Pahl found a variety of patterns ranging from total control by the husband, to arrangements where finances were pooled, for example in a joint bank account which might be mainly the responsibility of husband or wife.

On the surface this suggests that in many families women have as much if not more control then men. In some households women did control the purse strings, particularly when families were dependent on state benefits. However, in this situation women tended to use their control for the benefit of husbands and children, often doing without food or new clothes for themselves. Pahl argues that while there are a variety of financial arrangements, in most cases men are the main beneficiaries.

Problems with the decision making approach

1 Critics argue that the decisions reached by husbands and wives cannot be viewed in isolation. Their roles are influenced by the wider society, by prevailing ideas about what is normal, and by the opportunities available to each partner. For example, decisions about where a family lives may be influenced by the career demands of the highest earner, in most cases the male partner. The fact that men usually have better career opportunities is structured by the wider society. It is not the result of decision making by individual couples.
2 Adding up who makes which decisions and assessing the importance of those decisions to husbands and wives says nothing about non-

decisions. Many issues never reach the point of decision making. Thus husbands may have power simply because their position as head of the household is never seriously questioned. From a feminist viewpoint this is because of patriarchal ideology which defines male dominance as normal and natural.

3   The decision making approach can be a blunt instrument. Kathy Davis (1991) suggests that in intimate relationships such as marriage, power can often be exercised in very subtle ways. These may not be amenable to analysis by simply asking couples who decides what in their relationship. Davis rejects a simple 'top down' view which sees women as passive victims of male power. She suggests that in many circumstances women either willingly choose to accept their situation or are able to undermine men's power quite skillfully.

The domestic division of labour

This approach involves looking at the division of day-to-day tasks in the family between husband and wife. This perhaps poses fewer methodological problems than the decision making approach but there are still difficulties. How, for example, can a researcher make the judgement that there is an equal division of labour when husbands and wives perform very different tasks?

A good example of this approach is Ann Oakley's study *The Sociology of Housework* (1974) based on a sample of forty housewives, six of whom were employed outside the home. She found that middle class husbands gave more help than working class husbands and that both gave more help with childcare than with housework. However, 'only a minority of husbands give the kind of help that modern assertions of equality in marriage imply' (Oakley, 1974, p138).

Although Oakley's sample was very small, her findings have been backed up by subsequent surveys. Martin and Roberts in their survey *Women and Employment* (1984), based on a sample of nearly 6,000 women aged 16 to 59, found that men were more likely to take an active role in housework and childcare if their wife had a paid job. Nevertheless 54% of women who worked full time and 77% who worked part time did all or most of the housework. In a smaller scale study of sixty-two women, Susan Yeandle (1984) found that most women still carried the double burden of paid work and household responsibilities.

Fiona Devine's (1992) study of car workers' families in Luton found that an increasing proportion of women work part time, often resulting in a greater involvement by men in childcare and to a lesser extent housework. However, she suggests that men's involvement was due to financial necessity rather than a desire for greater involvement in family responsibilities. She concludes that conjugal roles were, for the most part, segregated. 'Above all women remain responsible for child-care and housework and their husbands help them' (p131).

The above findings seem to contradict the optimistic view of Young and Willmott. However, their picture of the 'symmetrical family' in which husband and wife 'share their work' is based on responses to only one question: 'Do you/does your husband help at least once a week with any household jobs like washing up, making beds, helping with the children, ironing, cooking or cleaning?' (Young and Willmott, 1975, p95). It is hardly surprising that Young and Willmott find that 85% of husbands now help out around the home. This begs the question of how much help they actually give. Thus even a husband whose sole contribution was helping with the washing up once a week would be included in the 85%!

Perhaps surprisingly, even studies of families where the male wage earner is unemployed show that traditional roles persist and are even strengthened. A study by McKee and Bell (1986) suggested that men's masculine identity is threatened by losing a job and that wives are unwilling to threaten it further by insisting that husbands take on more domestic responsibilities. Ironically, unemployment puts further stress on wives since the burden of managing on a reduced budget falls largely on them. Wives also have to cope with husbands around the house, having a say in how the home should be run, so removing some of the wife's autonomy.

Problems with the domestic division of labour approach   Studies of the allocation of tasks in the home are open to a number of criticisms.

1   The tasks chosen can influence the picture given. For example, focusing on activities like cooking and cleaning tends to produce a picture that women do most of the work. On the other hand, an analysis of a broader range of household tasks, including, for example, fixing the car and mowing the lawn, not to mention paid employment, might reveal that men do more work. Young and Willmott, for example, added together the number of hours husbands and wives spent on both domestic work and paid employment and found that while men did less in the home their hours of paid work were longer. Overall, the difference in weekly working hours between husbands and wives was not that great.

2   Analysing contributions in terms of time can be

misleading. Wives are likely to be 'on call' for long periods even when not actually active, for example getting up for children in the night. Also women tend to have continuous responsibility for childcare, preparing meals and keeping the home clean. The kind of tasks done by men do not impose the same continuous pressure.

3 It can be argued that a simple analysis of who does what in the home ignores the satisfaction provided by different tasks and the value and status attached to them. On both counts the evidence suggests that female tasks come out worse, tending to be monotonous and repetitive and attracting little reward or recognition.

The structure of dependence

Both the approaches outlined above tend to study power by concentrating on what goes on *within* marriage. Critics argue that power relations in the family can only be understood by looking at the place of marriage in the broader structure of society. Most married women are in a position of at least partial economic dependence on men. While the proportion of married women in employment has increased dramatically, over 30% of married women under 60 are not employed outside the home. And being wholly dependent economically is still a stage in the life cycle of most women. Theories which look beyond the household focus on the way in which the broader economic structures of society reinforce women's dependence within marriage and the family.

Even where women are in paid employment their jobs are often seen as secondary to those of their husbands. This is partly because their earnings are generally lower and partly because the housewife role is still seen by many as the primary role for married women and still regarded as a low status occupation. Many women are also expected to actively support their husbands in their jobs although this does not usually work in reverse. Janet Finch in *Married to the Job* (1983) points out how wives often entertain clients and act as secretaries and messengers for husbands who are businessmen, clergymen and general practitioners. Furthermore, wives often sacrifice their own jobs, friends and social networks so that husbands can be geographically mobile in order to further their careers.

Graham Allan (1985) suggests that wives are not only dependent economically on husbands but also often socially dependent. Married women tend to be restricted to the domestic sphere and are therefore more reliant on their husbands for social contacts. Similarly, it is difficult for women to participate in many leisure activities outside the home without being accompanied by men. For example, women may feel reluctant to enter male dominated domains like pubs and sports clubs without a male partner, while men can move in these areas alone more freely.

The dependent status of women is also reinforced by a whole range of social assumptions about the roles of husbands and wives. For example, a man who participates in housework may be described as being 'henpecked' or 'under his wife's thumb'. Where children appear to be neglected, it is the mother who is criticised by neighbours or teachers rather than the father, since this is assumed to be her responsibility. Such assumptions are also built into the state's treatment of families. Hilary Land (1978) points out that the Social Security system is based on the notion of the male as the breadwinner. Thus most benefits are paid to the male head of the family with wife and children treated as dependents. Similarly, a woman who is deemed to be cohabiting with a man is expected to be economically dependent on him and cannot claim social security benefits in her own right.

Problems with measuring dependency

Operationalising a concept such as dependency, that is putting it into a form in which it can be measured, is extremely difficult. It is possible, for example to produce statistics to illustrate the extent to which women are financially dependent on male partners. Levels of employment and relative earnings can be measured reasonably accurately. However, others forms of dependence such as emotional dependence are harder to measure.

All three approaches discussed above suggest, in different ways, that within marriage husbands and wives play very different roles. For functionalists this is not a problem - a division of labour allows for specialisation of roles and ensures that the family carries out its functions efficiently. Marxist and feminist critics of this view, however, argue that it ignores the fact that these roles are not simply different, they are also unequal.

Activity 11 Conjugal Roles

Item A

Household division of labour by marital status in Great Britain, 1984 (percentages)

Allocation of tasks	Mainly husband	Mainly wife	Shared equally
Household tasks			
Washing and ironing	1	88	9
Preparation of evening meal	5	77	16
Household cleaning	3	72	23
Household shopping	6	54	39
Evening dishes	18	37	41
Organisation of household money and bills	32	38	28
Repairs of household equipment	83	6	8
Childrearing			
Looks after the children when they are sick	1	63	35
Teaches the children discipline	10	12	77

Adapted from *Social Trends*, 1986, p36

Item B

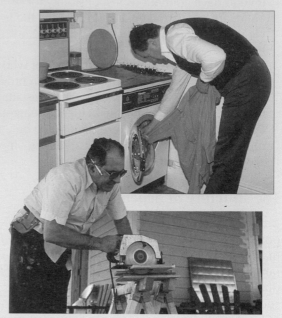

Item C

The importance, frequency and pattern of decision making in middle class family life

Decision area	Perceived importance	Frequency	Decision maker*
Moving	Very important	Infrequent	Husband
Finance	Very important	Infrequent	Husband
Car	Important	Infrequent	Husband
House	Very important	Infrequent	Husband and wife
Children's education	Very important	Infrequent	Husband and wife
Holidays	Important	Infrequent	Husband and Wife
Weekends	Not important	Frequent	Husband and wife
Other leisure activities	Not important	Frequent	Husband and wife
Furniture	Not important	Infrequent	Husband and wife
Interior decorations	Not important	Infrequent	Wife
Food and other domestic spending	Not important	Frequent	Wife
Children's clothes	Not important	Frequent	Wife

* This represents the partner who was the main decision maker according to the majority of the respondents in the survey

From S. Edgell *Middle Class Couples*, 1980, p 58

Questions

1 a) How far does the data in Item A support the argument of feminists like Oakley that the domestic division of labour between husbands and wives remains very unequal?

  b) What additional information might be useful for assessing the extent of gender inequalities in the domestic division of labour?

  c) Judging from Item B, which of the pictures is more typical? Is this what most people would expect?

Give reasons for your answer.

2 a) Look at Item C. Compare the frequency and importance of the decisions made by (i) wives and (ii) husbands. What differences are there in the types of decision taken by each partner?

  b) What grounds does Edgell have for arguing that 'decision-making among professional workers and their wives is not egalitarian but husband dominated'? (1980, p 59)

4.3 Marriage and alternatives to marriage

Until recently marriage was assumed by most people in Britain to be the basis of family life. However, in the last twenty years there are signs that this may be changing. An increasing number of couples may no longer see marriage as a necessary accompaniment to long term sexual relationships and producing children.

Patterns of marriage

For most of this century marriage has increased in popularity, reaching a peak in 1971. Since then there has been a significant decline in the number of marriages, from 459,000 in 1971 to 350,000 in 1991. This is due to a decline in 'first marriages' where neither partner has been married before. In 1991 the rate of first marriages was 37.2 per 1,000 single men compared to a rate of 82.3 in 1971.

From 1971 to 1991 the number of divorces more than doubled. This is reflected in the growing number of remarriages in which one or both partners have been divorced - 15% of all marriages in 1971, 34% in 1991 (figures from *Population Trends*, vol 70, 1992 and *Social Trends* 1994). However, this increase in remarriage had not halted the overall decline in the number of marriages.

Cohabition and births outside marriage

While marriage has declined, cohabitation - couples living together outside marriage - has increased. From 1979 to 1991 the proportion of non-married women in Britain who were cohabiting increased from 11% to 23% (*General Household Survey 1991*, 1993, p10). There has also been a steady increase in the number of marriages preceded by cohabitation, particularly second and subsequent marriages.

During the first sixty years of the 20th century there were around one in twenty live births outside marriage. By 1971 this has increased to 8% and by 1992 to 31%. (*Social Trends*, 1994, p40). What do these trends mean? Three-quarters of births outside marriage in 1992 were registered by both parents compared to 45% in 1971. This may indicate that a higher proportion of such births were occurring within stable relationships. In over 70% of the cases where both parents registered the birth, the parents gave the same address (*Social Trends*, 1994, p40). Many such relationships lead to marriage. As noted above, an increasing number of marriages are preceded by cohabitation.

For many couples cohabitation and childbearing may be seen as a normal prelude to marriage, for others as an alternative to marriage. Marriage for a significant minority may be seen as unnecessary for living together, having children, and 'legitimating' those children. And a growing number of women may not see a long lasting relationship with either the biological father or another partner as necessary for producing and rearing children.

A more pragmatic explanation for cohabitation and births outside marriage may simply be the cost of marriage - the average cost of a church wedding in 1992 having been estimated at £7,000. Some support is given to this argument by figures on regional variations in civil and church weddings. These show the biggest fall in marriage rates in areas hardest hit by the recession of the early 1990s.

Interpretations depend on values and outlooks. Feminist sociologists have tended to see the trends outlined above as a sign of the lack of satisfaction provided by traditional patriarchal marriage, with individuals seeking alternative types of relationships and living arrangements. New Right thinkers have seen these trends as a sign of the breakdown of the family and have argued for a return to 'traditional values'. On the other hand some supporters of the family, like Ronald Fletcher (1988a), have argued that cohabitation and births outside marriage often conceal what are in fact rather conventional nuclear families based on stable relationships, even if they are not legitimised by marriage. John Gillis (1985), in his historical study of British marriage, suggests that the custom of couples beginning sexual relations and even cohabiting once they were engaged was not uncommon in the past. Marriage often only took place once a child was conceived. He argues that the period 1850-1960 was historically exceptional, with a very high proportion of the population marrying and marriage taking place at a relatively young age.

Activity 12 Marriage and Cohabitation

Item A *Types of marriage*

United Kingdom	Thousands and percentages			
	1961	**1971**	**1981**	**1990**
Marriages (thousands)				
First marriage for both partners	340	369	263	241
First marriage for one partner only	36	54	74	75
Second (or later) marriage for both partners	21	36	61	60
Total marriages	397	459	398	375
Remarriages as a percentage of all marriages*	14	20	34	36
Remarriages of the divorced as a percentage of all marriages	9	15	31	34

* Includes remarriages following death of a spouse as well as divorce. Figures for remarriages refer to remarriages for one or both partners.

Adapted from *Social Trends*, 1994, p37

Item B

Live births outside marriage as a percentage of all births: by registration

Live births to parents who are not married are shown here according to whether only the mother registered the birth - *sole registration* - or whether both the mother and father's names appear on the birth certificate - *joint registration*. In recent years statistics have also been compiled on the proportion of joint registrations where the mother and father gave the same address.

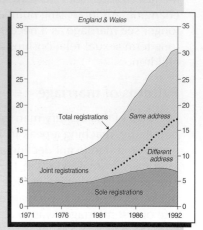

From *Social Trends*, 1994, p40

Item C

Men and women aged 16-59: percentage cohabiting by age: Great Britain, 1991

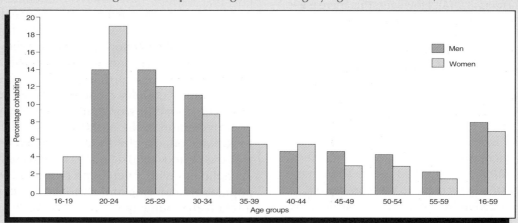

Adapted from *General Household Survey 1991*, 1993, p10

Item D

HAVING COHABITATED TOGETHER FOR NEARLY 20 YEARS WHAT ON EARTH INDUCED YOU TO SUDDENLY GET MARRIED?

WE NEEDED A NEW TEASMAID, TOASTER, DUVET, LINEN BASKET, AND ROLLING PIN!

Questions

1 Briefly summarise the trends shown in Items A and B.

2 Study Item C. How would you explain differences in cohabitation:
   a) between the age groups;
   b) between the sexes?

3 With reference to all four items, how it might be argued that:
   a) there has been a decline in traditional family values;
   b) that the two parent family still remains important.

4.4 Marital breakdown and divorce

One of the most dramatic changes in family life in Britain during this century has been the increase in divorce. In 1911, 859 petitions for divorce were filed in England and Wales of which about three-quarters were granted a decree absolute (final divorce); in 1987, 183,000 petitions were filed and 165,000 decrees absolute granted. This represents a more than two hundred fold increase in divorce during this century.

However, the simple number of divorces is not the best way of calculating how common divorce is, since if the number of marriages increases then divorce is also likely to increase. A better way of measuring divorce is some kind of *divorce rate*. This is usually expressed either as the number of divorces per thousand married people or as the number of divorces per thousand marriages in a year. In both cases the figures provide an estimate of the prevalence of divorce in relation to marriages.

Trends in divorce

While divorce has increased during this century, it has not increased at a steady rate. For example, there was a marked peak immediately after 1945. This was partly due to a backlog of divorces delayed by the Second World War and is also explainable in terms of the disruptive effects of war and separation on marriages. In contrast, the 1950s was a period of relative stability. However, in the 1960s the divorce rate began to climb and increased more rapidly after the Divorce Reform Act became effective in 1971. Since 1980 the number of divorces has not increased significantly. However, according to J. Haskey (1989) 32% of those marriages contracted in England and Wales in 1987 are likely to end in divorce during the first twenty years and nearly 40% before the thirty-third wedding anniversary.

Problems of interpreting divorce statistics

While official statistics are a reliable indicator of the extent of legal divorce, it cannot be assumed that there is a straightforward relationship between rates of divorce and rates of marital breakdown. Robert Chester (1984) points out that marital breakdown is very difficult measure, for example a marriage can break down when a couple remain in the same household. Nevertheless, Chester suggests that increasing divorce rates probably do reflect a growing level of marital breakdown, though by his own admission this cannot be proved.

William Goode (1971) suggests that divorce is only one mechanism adopted by societies for dealing with marital problems. In some countries, like the Republic of Ireland, divorce is not legally permitted. In such situations couples may resort to legal separations, anullments (a declaration that the marriage never legally took place) or staying together in so-called 'empty shell marriages'. A comparison of English and Irish divorce rates would therefore tell us nothing about the state of marriage in the two countries. Apart from the solutions mentioned above, Goode points to other alternatives to divorce. In polygynous cultures (where more than one wife is permitted) a man may marry again without divorcing. Similarly, in traditional China, wealthy husbands often took a concubine, a woman who lived with him alongside his wife. In nineteenth century Europe and America divorce was relatively rare - husbands and wives may simply have tolerated a good deal more marital dissatisfaction and discord than today. Goode argues that an explanation of the increase in divorce should focus on the factors which encourage individuals to see divorce as a more appropriate solution to marital breakdown than other options.

Explanations of changing divorce rates

Increases in divorce rates are a common feature of most industrial societies. They appear to be linked to more general changes in attitudes to marriage and the role of the family. A number of factors have been linked to higher levels of divorce.

The removal of legal and financial barriers   The fact that changes in divorce laws have generally made it easier and cheaper to get divorced is a major factor encouraging higher divorce rates. Before 1857 divorce was rare. It was expensive and was only obtainable by private Act of Parliament. The 1857 Matrimonial Causes Act simplified the procedure and set up courts specifically to deal with matrimonial cases. Grounds for divorce were based on 'matrimonial offences', in other words one partner had to prove that they had been wronged by the other. Men could get a divorce solely on the grounds of the wife's adultery but women had to prove other offences such as cruelty or desertion. This discriminatory anomaly was not removed until 1923.

Matrimonial offence remained the basis for divorce until 1971, though there had been a number of changes which made divorce easier. In 1937 grounds for divorce were extended to include insanity, desertion and cruelty. In 1949 the Legal Aid and Advice Act provided financial help to those involved in divorce cases who could not afford the legal costs. Before this the cost of divorce had often proved an insurmountable obstacle for many poorer people.

In the 1960s divorce rates were increasing and public opinion was beginning to favour a relaxation of the divorce laws. Many couples wished to divorce without having to prove matrimonial offences such as adultery. The Divorce Reform Act of 1969 (which became law in 1971) reflected this by replacing matrimonial offence with the 'irretrievable breakdown of marriage' as the basis for divorce.

This meant that in practice couples could divorce by mutual consent after two years separation, or after five years if one partner objected. Unreasonable behaviour, for example adultery, could still be cited as evidence of irretrievable breakdown.

In 1985 the 1984 Matrimonial and Family Proceedings Act became effective. This reduced the time limit for divorce from a minimum of three years of marriage to only one year. Following this Act the divorce rate rose again. According to Haskey (1986), this was largely attributable to couples who had been married for under three years now petitioning for divorce.

Whilst changes in legislation have normally resulted in increases in the number of divorces, they cannot be seen as the cause of higher divorce rates. Legal changes have tended to reflect other changes in society. Moreover, there have been noticeable increases in the divorce rate at times when the law has not changed significantly, for example in the 1960s. Legal changes allow more divorces to take place but do not explain why more individuals choose to take this option.

Changing expectations of marriage and family life
Writers like Ronald Fletcher (1966) see higher divorce rates as evidence of increased expectations and higher standards of marriage. Couples are no longer prepared to put up with unhappy 'empty shell' marriages and thus divorce is more common. At the same time most divorcees remarry, suggesting that they do not reject the institution of marriage but simply expect more from the relationship.

William Goode suggests that the Western style nuclear family is centred on the marriage relationship and thus a successful marriage is seen as essential to family life. In family systems where the wider kinship network is emphasised, loyalty to kin may be more important than personal fulfilment in marriage. Pressure from the extended family may keep a couple together. Marriage may be seen more in practical rather than in emotional terms, so lack of affection between spouses may not be seen as a problem. This tends to be less true in modern Western families. N. Dennis (1984) reflects this point when he suggests that modern marriages are relatively fragile and are only held together by emotional ties. If these turn sour there is little practical reason for a couple to remain together.

Changes in women's social position Today about three-quarters of divorce petitions are from women. For some sociologists like Fletcher this simply reflects the higher expectations women have of marriage due to greater equality and increased opportunities to escape from unhappy marriages. Better rights under divorce laws, more job opportunities and the provision of financial support by the state for divorced women have encouraged women unhappy with marriage to petition for divorce.

However, many feminist writers suggest that these statistics simply reflect the fact that women have less to gain from marriage than men (see Sections 2.3 and 4.2). It is also the case that fewer women remarry after divorce than men which may suggest a greater disillusionment with marriage. Nicky Hart (1976) in her study of divorce suggests that the growth of female employment may have increased the strain on wives by creating a conflict between women's new roles and traditional role obligations of domestic work and childcare. Higher divorce rates may, therefore, reflect both a desire by women for a better deal from marriage and a failure to find satisfaction from the traditional roles prevailing in most families.

Changing social values In the nineteenth century a good deal of stigma and shame was attached to divorce. In this century attitudes have slowly changed, divorce has become far more commonplace and socially acceptable. This in itself may make divorce a more attractive option than other solutions to marital breakdown. Some sociologists like Bryan Wilson (1966) have seen this change in attitudes as part of a process of *secularisation* (see pp521-531) whereby religious ideas of marriage have lost their influence. Less than half of marriage ceremonies are now religious ceremonies and, even among these, few couples are regular churchgoers. If Wilson is right then the Christian ideal of lifelong marriage is taken less seriously.

Ideas about divorce in relation to children have also changed. In the past couples often stayed together 'for the sake of the children'. Public opinion may have moved towards the view that the effects of a marriage based on conflict may be more damaging to children then divorce itself. This too would tend to make divorce a more socially acceptable alternative.

Demographic changes Social historians like Michael Anderson (1983) have pointed out that the lifelong marriages of the past often lasted a relatively short time. Marriage was often late and life expectancy short, so the average duration of marriages was not dissimilar to today. Remarriage due to the death of a spouse was common, sometimes several times over. Thus higher divorce rates today may partly reflect the longer potential duration of marriage due to people living longer. The growing number of divorces after more than ten years of marriage may give some support to this view.

The trend towards younger marriage in the 1960s and 70s has been seen as a contributory factor to the increase in divorce rates. According to *Population Trends* (1976), marriages where the bride is under 21 had twice the chance of ending in divorce compared to those who were 21 and over. In the 1980s more couples seem to have chosen to live together first and marry later and the average age at marriage increased. Some commentators have linked this to a levelling off in the number of divorces. However, according to the *General Household Survey* (1993), of couples who married for the first time in the early 1980s, those who lived together before their wedding were more, not less likely to divorce. 50% had divorced after five years of marriage and 60% after eight years of marriage. Such figures are difficult to interpret since couples who are prepared to live together may also have more liberal attitudes to divorce. And not all couples who stay together necessarily have successful marriages. Nevertheless, such figures do suggest that 'trial marriages' do not necessarily guarantee a more successful actual marriage.

Teenage marriages have often been blamed for higher divorce rates. However, a study by Ineichen (1977) of 179 marriages in Bristol suggested that teenage marriages are often linked to other factors associated with a higher risk of divorce, for example manual employment, poor housing and sharing accommodation with relatives. Teenage brides are also much more likely to be pregnant before marriage, another risk factor. Age at marriage thus needs to be seen in relation to a range of other factors in explaining divorce rates.

Conclusion Explaining divorce rates is difficult. Many factors are involved and their relationship changes. As David H.J. Morgan notes, 'We have no idea how many people would have availed themselves of divorce in the past had it been economically more accessible'. And, as he adds, 'Divorce, like foreign holidays, may simply be something that is now available to increasingly large numbers of the population rather than confined to an elite' (Morgan, 1994, p111).

Summary

1 The period after the industrial revolution saw a variety of social changes which encouraged the domesticity of married women. More recent changes have encouraged the wider employment of married women and this, combined with changing ideas about gender roles, may have led to a greater symmetry of roles within marriage.

2 There is considerable evidence that, despite such changes, roles in most marriages remain distinct and, according to feminists, based on a marked inequality in power between husbands and wives.

3 Marriage rates increased during the first 70 years of this century then declined during the following 25 years. In recent years more couples live together and have children outside marriage. Divorce rates have increased, particularly since the liberalisation of divorce legislation in 1971.

4 Changes in patterns of marriage and divorce may reflect changing views of the place of marriage in society. There seems to be a growing acceptance that marriage is no longer necessary for couples to produce children or to engage in long term relationships.

Activity 13 Divorce

Item A
Marriage and remarriage: by sex (Great Britain)

Between 1971 and 1991 marriages fell by almost 16% while divorces more than doubled. For every two marriages in Britain in 1991, there was one divorce.

From *Social Trends*, 1994, p37

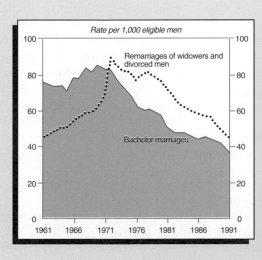

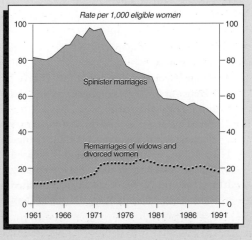

Item B   *The divorce rate*

Persons divorcing per thousand married people	1961	1971	1976	1981	1986	1988	1990
England and Wales	2.1	6.0	10.1	11.9	12.9	12.8	12.9

Adapted from *Social Trends*, 1993, p30

Item C

Divorce: decrees absolute in England and Wales 1901-1990

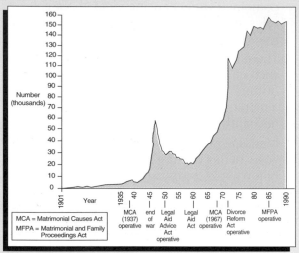

MCA = Matrimonial Causes Act

MFPA = Matrimonial and Family Proceedings Act

Adapted from A. Wilson *Family*, 1985 and *Social Trends*, 1993 and 1994

Questions

1 Look at Item A.
   a) What trends are apparent in the proportion of marriages which are remarriages between 1961 and 1990?
   b) How does the pattern of marriages for women differ from men?
   c) How would you explain these trends?
2 a) Compare the impressions of the rise in divorce given by Items B and C.
   b) What are are the merits of each measure?
3 Look at Item C.
   a) What effects do changes in the divorce laws and the extension of legal aid appear to have had on the number of divorces?
   b) What evidence is there that divorce may have increased for reasons other than changes in legislation?
4 How might the statistics in Item D be used to show:
   a) that social changes have given women greater freedom to escape from unhappy marriages;
   b) that women are increasingly dissatisfied with marriage?
5 a) Why does Robert Chester argue in Item E that divorce statistics are not a valid indicator of the extent of marital breakdown?
   b) Why might divorce statistics today be a better indicator of the extent of marital breakdown than past divorce statistics?

Item D

Petitions filed for divorce in England and Wales (thousands)

	1961	1971	1981	1987
By husband	14	44	47	50
By wife	18	67	123	133
Total	32	111	170	183

Adapted from *Social Trends*, 1989

Item E   *Marital breakdown*

Rising divorce figures are viewed with concern by many people because it is assumed that divorce provides an index of marriage breakdown. However, it is a very uncertain one, both because of the difficulty of defining marriage breakdown and the impossibility of measuring its components. Some would want to include in marriage breakdown those unions where the couple continue to cohabit, but only in deep disharmony and failure of emotional support. In practice we know nothing of the dimensions of this group of marriages, and we must measure breakdown only in terms of situations where there is deliberate absence of a spouse through divorce, annulment, separation or desertion. Marriages, that is, which have broken up as well as broken down.

Even here, however, accurate numbers of breakdowns cannot be given, because only some components are exactly known. Divorce and annulment figures are reliable, because marriages can be dissolved only be public processes. Figures for separated spouses, however, are currently a mystery. Some couples part purely informally, and the numbers and trends of these are completely unknown.

Adapted from R. Chester 'Divorce' in E. Butterworth and D. Weir (eds) *The New Sociology of Modern Britain*, 1984

References

Allan, G. *Family Life* (Basil Blackwell, Oxford, 1985)

Anderson, M. *Family Structure in Nineteenth Century Lancashire* (Cambridge University Press, Cambridge, 1971)

Anderson, M. (ed) *Sociology of the Family* (Penguin, Harmondsworth, 1971)

Anderson, M. 'How Much Has the Family Changed?' *New Society*, 27.10.1983

Arensberg, C. M. and Kimball, S. T. *Family and Community in Ireland* (Harvard University Press, Cambridge, Mass., 1940)

Backett, K. C. 'Images of Parenthood' in M. Anderson (ed) *Sociology of the Family* (Penguin, Harmondsworth, 1980)

Ballard, R. 'South Asian Families' in R. N. Rapoport , M. P. Fogerty and R. Rapoport (eds) *Families in Britain* (Routledge and Kegan Paul, London, 1982)

Barrow J. 'West Indian Families: an Insiders Perspective' in R.N. Rapoport , M.P. Fogerty and R. Rapoport (eds) *Families in Britain* (Routledge and Kegan Paul, London, 1982)

Bell, C. *Middle Class Families* (Routledge and Kegan Paul, London, 1968)

Benston, M. 'The Political Economy of Women's Liberation' in E. Mallos (ed) *The Politics of Housework* (Allison and Busby, London, 1980)

Berger, B. and Berger, P.L. *The War over the Family* (Hutchinson, London, 1983)

Berger, P. and Kellner, H. 'Marriage and the Construction of Reality' in M. Anderson (ed) *Sociology of the Family* (Penguin, Harmondsworth, 1980)

Bhavani, K.K. and Coulson, M. 'Transforming Socialist Feminism: The Challenge of Racism' *Feminist Review* no 23, June 1986

Bott, E. *Family and Social Network* (Tavistock, London, 1957)

Brown, A. and Kiernan, K. 'Cohabitation in Great Britain: Evidence from the General Household Survey', *Population Trends* 25: 4-10 (HMSO, London, 1981)

Bruegel, I. 'Women as a Reserve Army of Labour: A Note on Recent British Experience' *Feminist Review* no 3, 1979

Burgoyne, J. and Clark, D. *Making a Go if It: a Study of Step-families in Sheffield* (Routledge and Kegan Paul, London, 1984)

Carby, H. 'White Woman Listen! Black Feminism and the Boundaries of Sisterhood' in Centre for Contemporary Cultural Studies *The Empire Strikes Back* (Hutchinson, London, 1982)

Carroll, V. *Adoption in Eastern Oceania* (University of Hawaii Press, 1970)

Cherlin, A. *Marriage, Divorce and Remarriage* (Harvard University Press, Cambridge, Mass., 1981)

Chester, R. 'The One-Parent Family: Deviant or Variant?' in R. Chester and J. Peel (eds) *Equalities and Inequalities of Family Life* (Academic Press, London, 1977)

Chester, R. 'Divorce' in E. Butterworth and D. Weir (eds) *The New Sociology of Modern Britain* (Fontana, Glasgow, 1984)

Chester, R. 'The Rise of the Neo-Conventional Family', *New Society*, 9.5.1985

Clark, D. 'Constituting the Marital World: a Qualitative Perspective' in D. Clark (ed) *Marriage, Domestic Life and Social Change: Writings for Jacqueline Burgoyne (1944-88)* (Routledge, London, 1991)

Cohen, R. et al *Hardship Britain* (CPAG, London, 1992)

Collins, R. 'Horses for Courses' in P. Close and R. Collins (eds) *Family and Economy in Modern Britain* (Macmillan, London, 1985)

Cornwell, J. *Hard Earned Lives* (Tavistock, London, 1984)

Davis, K. 'Critical Sociology and Gender Relations' in K. Davis, M. Leijenaar and J. Oldersma (eds) *The Gender of Power* (Sage, London, 1991)

Dennis, N. 'Relationships' in E. Butterworth and D. Weir (eds) *The New Sociology of Modern Britain* (Fontana, Glasgow, 1984)

Devine, F. *Affluent Workers Revisited: Privatism and the Working Class* (Edinburgh University Press, Edinburgh, 1992)

Dobash, R. E. and Dobash, R. *Violence against Wives* (Open Books, London, 1980)

Driver, G. 'West Indian Families' in R.N. Rapoport, M. P. Fogerty and R. Rapoport (eds) *Families in Britain* (Routledge and Kegan Paul, London, 1982)

Edgell, S. *Middle Class Couples* (Allen and Unwin, London, 1980)

Edholm, F. 'The Unnatural Family' in E. Whitelegg et al (eds) *The Changing Experience of Women* (Martin Robertson in association with Open University Press, London, 1982)

Engels, F. *The Origins of the Family, Private Property and the State* (Chas. H. Kerr and Co., Chicago, 1902)

Eversley, D. and Bonnerjea, L. 'Social Change and Indicators of Diversity' in R. N. Rapoport , M. P. Fogerty and R. Rapoport (eds) *Families in Britain* (Routledge and Kegan Paul, London, 1982)

Finch, J. *Married to the Job: Wives Incorporation in Men's Work*, (George Allen and Unwin, London, 1983)

Finch, J. *Family Obligations and Social Change* (Polity Press, Cambridge, 1989)

Finch, J. and Mason, J. *Negotiating Family Responsibilities* (Routledge, London, 1993)

Finer, M. *One Parent Families, Report of the Committee* (HMSO, London, 1974)

Fletcher, R. *The Family and Marriage in Britain* (Penguin, Harmondsworth, 1966)

Fletcher, R. *The Shaking of the Foundations: Family and Society* (Routledge, London, 1988a)

Fletcher, R. *The Abolitionists: The Family and Marriage under Attack* (Routledge, London, 1988b)

Fortes, M. 'Kinship and Marriage among the Ashanti' in A.R. Radcliffe-Brown and D. Forde (eds) *African Systems of Kinship and Marriage* (Oxford University Press, London, 1950)

Frankenberg, R. *Communities in Britain* (Penguin, Harmondsworth, 1966)

General Household Survey (Office of Population Censuses and Surveys, London, 1991 and 1993)

Gillis, J. R. *For Better For Worse: British Marriages 1600 to the Present* (Oxford University Press, Oxford, 1985)

Gittins, D. *The Family in Question: Changing Households and Familiar Ideologies* (Macmillan, Basingstoke, 1985)

Goldthorpe, J. H., Lockwood, D., Bechofer, F. and Platt, J. *The Affluent Worker in the Class Structure* (Cambridge University Press, Cambridge, 1969)

Goode, W. J. *World Revolution and Family Patterns* (The Free Press, New York, 1963)

Goode, W. J. 'A Sociological Perspective on Marital Dissolution' in M. Anderson (ed) *Sociology of the Family* (Penguin, Harmondsworth, 1971)

Hall, C. 'The History of the Housewife' in E. Malos (ed) *The Politics of Housework* (Allison and Busby, London, 1980)

Hall C. 'The Butcher, the Baker, the Candlestick Maker: The Shop and the Family in the Industrial Revolution' in E. Whitelegg et al (eds) *The Changing Experience of Women*, (Martin Robertson in association with the Open University Press, London, 1982)

Hart, N. *When Marriage Ends: A Study in Status Passage*, (Tavistock, London, 1976)

Haskey J. 'Recent Trends in Divorce' *Population Trends*, 47: 34-42 (HMSO, London, 1986)

Haskey, J. 'Current Prospects for the Proportion of Marriages Ending in Divorce' *Population Trends*, 55:34-7 (HMSO, London, 1989)

Humphries, J. 'Class Struggle and the Persistence of the Working Class Family' *Cambridge Journal of Economics*, vol 1, 1977

Ineichen, B. 'Youthful Marriage in the Vortex of Disadvantage' in R. Chester and J. Peel (eds) *Equalities and Inequalities in Family Life* (Academic Press, London, 1977)

Keesing, R.M. *Cultural Anthropology, a Contemporary Perspective*, (Rinehart and Winston, New York, 1976)

Kiernan, K.E. and Estaugh, V. *Cohabitation: Extra Marital*

Childbearing and Social Policy (Family Policy Studies Centre, London, 1993)

Klein, J. *Samples from English Cultures vol 1* (Victor Gollancz, London, 1965)

Land, H. 'The Myth of the Male Breadwinner', *New Society*, October 1975

Land, H. 'Women: Supporters or Supported?' in D. Barker and S. Allen (eds) *Sexual Divisions in Society: Process and Change* (Tavistock, London, 1976)

Land, H. 'Who Cares for the Family?', *The Journal of Social Policy*, vol 7 no 3, 1978

Laslett, P.K. *The World We Have Lost* (Methuen, London, 1965)

Laslett, P.K. *Family Life and Illicit Love in Earlier Generations* (Methuen, London, 1977)

Leete, R. 'Changing Patterns of Marriage and Remarriage' in R. Chester and J. Peel (eds) *Equalities and Inequalities in Family Life* (Academic Press, London, 1977)

LePlay, F. *La Reforme Sociale* 7th edition, vol 1, pp. 380-519 (Tours, 1887), as interpreted and summarised by C. C. Zimmerman and M. E. Frampton *Family and Society* (Van Nostrand, Princeton, New Jersey, 1935)

Lukes, S. *Power: A Radical View* (Macmillan, London, 1974)

McKee, L. and Bell, C. 'His Unemployment, Her Problem: The Domestic and Marital Consequences of Male Unemployment' in S. Allen et al (eds) *The Experience of Unemployment* (Macmillan, Basingstoke, 1986)

Martin, J. and Roberts C. *Women and Employment: A Lifetime Perspective* (HMSO, London, 1984)

Millet, K. *Sexual Politics* (Doubleday, New York, 1970)

Mitchell, J. J. *Woman's Estate* (Penguin, Harmondsworth, 1971)

Morgan, D.H.J. 'The Family' in Haralambos M. (ed) *Developments in Sociology* vol 7 (Causeway Press, Ormskirk, 1990)

Morris, D. *The Naked Ape* (Corgi, London, 1968)

Morton, P. 'Women's Work is Never Done' in E. Mallos (ed) *The Politics of Housework* (Allison and Busby, London, 1980)

Mount, F. *The Subversive Family: an Alternative History of Love and Marriage* (Jonathan Cape, London, 1982)

Murdock, G. P. *Social Structure* (Macmillan, New York, 1949)

Nissel, M. and Bonnerjea, L. *Family Care of the Handicapped Elderly: Who Pays?* (Policy Studies Institute, London, 1982)

Oakley, A. *The Sociology of Housework* (Martin Robertson, London, 1974)

Oakley, A. *Housewife* (Penguin, Harmondsworth, 1976)

Pahl, J. *Money and Marriage* (Macmillan, London, 1989)

Parsons, T. *The Social System* (The Free Press, New York, 1951)

Parsons, T. and Bales R. F. *Family, Socialisation and Interaction Process* (The Free Press, New York, 1955)

Phoenix, A. 'The Afro-Caribbean Myth' *New Society*, 4.3.1988

Population Trends (HMSO, London, 1976 and 1992)

Roberts, Y. 'We are Becoming Divorced from Reality' *New Statesman and Society*, 24.9.1993

Rosser, R. and Harris C. *The Family and Social Change* (Routledge and Kegan Paul, London, 1965)

Smith, R. 'Families 1994-style' *Poverty*, Winter 1993

Thompson, J. *Examining Sociology* (Hutchinson, London, 1980)

Westwood, S. and Bhachu, P. 'Images and Realities' *New Society*, 6.5.1988

Willmott, P. *Social Networks, Informal Care and Public Policy*, (Policy Studies Institute, London, 1986)

Willmott, P. 'Urban Kinship Past and Present', *Social Studies Review*, November 1988

Wilson, A. *Family* (Tavistock, London, 1985)

Wilson, B. R. *Religion in a Secular Society* (C. A. Watts, London, 1966)

Yeandle, S. *Women's Working Lives: Patterns and Strategies* (Tavistock, London, 1984)

Young, M. and Willmott, P. *Family and Kinship in East London* (Penguin, Harmondsworth, 1962)

Young, M. and Willmott, P. *The Symmetrical Family* (Penguin, Harmondsworth, 1975)

8 Education

Introduction

Why do we spend the 'best years of our life' in school? Until recently most people have managed quite successfully without a formal education. They learned 'lessons for life', usually in a fairly informal way, from family, friends, peer groups and other members of the community.

This type of 'informal education' continues to be an important part of the socialisation process in modern industrial societies. What's new is formal education which is the subject of this chapter. It is a system through which the vast majority of young people pass. They are taught in specialised institutions - schools, colleges and universities - by professionals - teachers and lecturers - who are trained and paid to ensure that selected knowledge and skills are passed from one generation to the next.

Education is important. It takes up a significant proportion of people's lives - at least eleven years - and to some degree it affects the rest of their lives. And it's very expensive - in 1992 government expenditure on education in the UK was £32.3 billion, 12.7 % of all public expenditure (*Social Trends*, 1994).

Chapter summary

- Part 1 reviews the history of education. It examines the **tripartite** and **comprehensive** systems of secondary education, vocational education and the 1988 Education Reform Act.
- Part 2 looks at how the main **sociological**
theories see the role of education in modern industrial society.
- Parts 3, 4 and 5 examine the factors which affect educational attainment with particular reference to **class**, **gender** and **ethnicity**.

1 The History of Education in England and Wales

Key Issues

1 Why was formal education made compulsory in the 19th century?
2 What were the aims of the 1944 Education Act and to what extent were they met?
3 What factors have influenced the growth of vocational education?
4 What are the effects of the 1988 Education Reform Act?

1.1 The development of state education

The introduction of mass schooling

Education for everyone is a recent development. Before the 19th century formal education was confined to a small minority. Public schools and grammar schools educated the offspring of the rich and powerful. Church and charity schools provided a short and basic education for a minority of the 'lower orders'. But most people did without formal education. In the 19th century education was extended to everyone. Britain had become an industrial society and many believed that a literate and numerate workforce was required for continued economic growth. If education and training were ignored, Britain would fall behind its main rivals, Germany and the USA.

Not everybody supported universal education. On the one hand it was felt that basic standards of reading, writing and arithmetic were required to master the new techniques and practices needed for industrial expansion. In addition, a basic education might help to reduce 'unhealthy' political influences which could lead to political unrest. And it might help the masses to understand the essential justice of society and the social order. On the other hand, some saw dangers in a literate poor - they might read 'revolutionary' literature and acquire 'dangerous' ideas. This could lead them to question their station in life and cause social unrest. Some felt it unfair to educate the poor because they might expect a better life and be disappointed when these expectations were not realised. The concern and ambivalence about the spread of education are examined in Activity 1.

Activity 1 Educating the 'Lower Classes'

Item A *No education*

Giving education to the working classes would be bad for their morals and happiness. It would lead them to despise their lot in life instead of making them good servants in agriculture and other work to which their rank in society had destined them; instead of teaching them obedience it would make them difficult. It would enable them to read seditious pamphlets, vicious books, and publications against Christianity.

Davies Giddy MP, *House of Commons*, 1807

Item B *A little education*

I do not think it is any part of the duty of the Government to prescribe what people should learn, except in the case of the poor, where time is so limited that we must fix upon a few elementary subjects to get anything done at all. The lower classes ought to be educated to discharge the duties cast upon them. They should also be educated that they may appreciate and defer to a higher cultivation when they meet it, and the higher classes ought to be educated in a very different manner, in order that they may exhibit to the lower classes that higher education to which, if it were shown to them, they would bow down and defer.

Robert Lowe *Primary and Classical Education* 1867, quoted in S.J.Curtis *History of Education in Great Britain*, 1963, p256

Item C *The 1870 Education Act*

Upon the speedy provision of elementary education depends our industrial prosperity. Uneducated labourers are, for the most part, unskilled labourers, and if we leave our workfolk any longer unskilled they will become overmatched in the competition of the world.

W.E.Foster introducing his Education Bill, *Hansard*, 17.2.1870

Item D *Drill*

Boys doing arm exercises, 1906. Drills were the nearest many schoolchildren in the 19th and early 20th centuries got to physical education.

Questions

1 Education, or lack of it, in the 19th century was mainly concerned with protecting and furthering the interests of the rich and powerful. Discuss with reference to Items A, B and C.
2 Provide a brief sociological analysis of Item D.

The 19th and early 20th centuries

After 1870 state education was available to everyone. However the type of education people received depended on their class background. There were public schools and grammar schools for the upper and middle classes and elementary schools for the working classes. The aims of each were quite different.

Public schools aimed to develop social character and produce Christian gentlemen who would become the future leaders of society - they stressed leadership and character. Their pupils were fee payers and boarders, who stayed at school until 18 or 19. *Grammar schools*, for children of the better off middle classes, tended to be copies of public schools although they were not generally boarding schools.

Elementary schools were intended to cultivate personal qualities felt to be desirable and even necessary for the 'labouring' classes. There was an emphasis on punctuality, obedience and hard work. Pupils were expected to leave at the age of 10 or 11 after receiving a sound and cheap elementary instruction in reading, writing and arithmetic. Specialised knowledge would be learned at work rather than at school. This attitude is illustrated by James Fraser, Bishop of Manchester, speaking in 1858 about the working class child:

'We must make up our minds to see the last of him, as far as day school is concerned, at ten or eleven ... and I venture to maintain that it is quite possible to teach a child soundly and thoroughly, in a way that he shall not forget it, all that is necessary for him to possess in the shape of intellectual attainment, by the time that he is ten years old.'

The 1870 Education Act This Act provided a network of elementary schools to fill gaps in the provision from church and charity schools. It did not aim to change the class basis of education but rather to ensure that basic education was available to all children from the ages of 5 to 10. The writer H.G.Wells described it as 'an Act to educate the lower classes for employment on lower class lines, and with specially trained, inferior teachers'. However, the Act signified the first general acceptance of the principle that money raised by state taxation and local rates should be used to provide elementary education for all children. Thus it established the idea of state intervention in education. The 1870 Act explains why so many of today's primary schools are around 100 years old. Many schools were built in the years following the Act.

In 1880 elementary education to the age of 10 was made compulsory. The school leaving age was gradually raised to 12 in 1889 and 14 after the First World War. The curriculum was slowly widened, though the idea that only a limited education was suitable for the poorer sections of society continued until the Second World War. The type of school a child went to had little to do with ability, but depended primarily on his or her social class.

The first half of the twentieth century saw an expansion of grammar schools. At the turn of the century there was a shortage of qualified men to fill the growing number of white collar jobs resulting from Britain's expanding commercial and administrative concerns, both at home and abroad. In response to this shortage, the 1902 Education Act made secondary education, as well as elementary, a responsibility of local authorities. It encouraged the building of grammar schools to which children could transfer after elementary schooling. Fees had to be paid to attend grammar schools, although there were usually some free places for children who obtained scholarships.

In broad terms, up to the Second World War there were three types of school for children from different class backgrounds:
• elementary schools for the working classes
• grammar schools for the middle classes
• public schools for the upper classes.

1.2 The 1944 Education Act

During and after the Second World War there was widespread debate over the kind of society that should follow the war. The reconstruction of schooling was a central issue in this debate. It was widely felt that the nation was not making full use of the talents of its people and that changes in the education system were necessary to remedy this.

The basic aim of the 1944 Education Act was to give every pupil an equal chance to develop his or her talents and abilities to the full within a free system of state education. The structure of education in England and Wales was reorganised into three stages:
• Primary - up to the age of 11. This was subdivided into nursery, infant and junior stages.
• Secondary - from the age of 11 until 15 (from 1973, 16).
• Further/Higher - education beyond the school leaving age; education by choice.

The tripartite system

The major changes were in the secondary sector. The question was what sort of secondary education would provide equality of educational opportunity for all children from the age of 11.

The response owed much to the theories of psychologists and educationalists of the 1920s and 1930s. These theories were based on the idea that there were different 'types' of pupils, with differing 'aptitudes and abilities' and that a child's 'type' could be identified by intelligence testing. On the basis of this the 1944 Act introduced a national test for 11 year olds - the '11 plus' test - as a means of allocating children to one of three types of secondary school.

The three types of secondary school were grammar schools, technical schools and secondary modern schools. This became known as the *tripartite system* of secondary education.

Grammar schools were intended for pupils defined as 'bright' and 'academic' - those whose abilities lay in reasoning and solving logical problems. They were to study classics, mathematics, science and other 'difficult' subjects in preparation for GCE exams. Less than 20 % of the school population went to grammar schools. Technical schools were intended for children with an aptitude for technical subjects. These schools emphasised vocational training and technical skills and were attended by around 5% of the school population. Most children went to secondary modern schools. These children were seen as less academic and more practical. They were given a basic education with little opportunity to take external examinations until CSEs were introduced in the 1960s.

The tripartite system was intended to provide separate but equal types of schooling geared to the particular talents of the child. The Act stated that each school should have equal status, or 'parity of esteem',with buildings, equipment and staffing being of similar quality. However these ideals did not work in practice.

Not all children attended schools in the tripartite system. Firstly, the private sector of education was excluded from the scope of the Act. Independent schools continued to charge fees and attract the better off. Secondly, not all Local Education Authorities (LEAs) supported the tripartite system.

Some set up comprehensive schools. All the LEAs had to do was provide free, equal education and how they did this was left to individual authorities.

Criticisms of the tripartite system

1 **Intelligence tests** To what extent is intelligence testing, and the 11 plus test in particular, an adequate basis for dividing children according to their abilities? Activity 2 looks at this concern.
2 **Parity of esteem** Most parents wanted their children to go to grammar schools. Few technical schools were built and secondary modern schools were regarded as inferior by parents, pupils and employers. Looking back, it comes as no surprise that schools offering little or no provision for external examinations were seen as second class. Since there were few technical school places, the alternative for most children was either 'passing' the 11 plus and going to a grammar school, or 'failing' the 11 plus and going to a secondary modern school.
3 **Low self-esteem** Being selected for a low status school may affect children's picture of themselves. It might lead them to think they are not very clever and so not try very hard. The result will be low educational attainment. This process is known as a self-fulfilling prophecy (see pp299-300).
4 **Social Class** The tripartite system reflected the social divisions in society. In spite of the abolition of fees, working class children were much less likely than middle class children to go to grammar schools. The 1944 Act was based on the idea of equality of educational opportunity. Clearly this was not working when a disproportionate number of working class children were consigned to secondary moderns - schools which were seen as second rate and substandard. Unequal life chances were therefore reinforced by unequal education. This led many critics to ask: Why not have one type of secondary school for everyone?

As a result of these criticisms, comprehensive schooling was developed in England and Wales. Most LEAs now operate a secondary system of comprehensive schools, although not all have abolished grammar schools - a process of selection at 11 plus still operates in certain parts of the country. Some commentators are now arguing that the 1988 Education Reform Act, which allows schools to opt out of local authority control, may undermine the comprehensive system. And it may, in some schools, lead to the return of selection at the age of 11.

1.3 Comprehensive secondary education

The comprehensive system is based on the principle of one type of secondary school for everyone.

Children of all abilities and from all social backgrounds attend the same type of school. They are provided with the same opportunities to obtain qualifications and training. There is no entrance exam, no selection at age 11. Each school has a specific 'catchment area', a particular area or neighbourhood from which its pupils are drawn. Legislation during the 1980s provided parents and pupils with a greater choice of schools and enabled schools to recruit from outside their catchment areas. However the principle of local schools enrolling children of all abilities and providing them with the same opportunities remains. But this may be changing as a result of the 1988 Education Reform Act (see pp284-286).

The move from selective to comprehensive secondary schooling has been, and still is, a political issue. The Labour Party and the political left have, in general, favoured comprehensives. They saw a national system of comprehensive schools as the only way of providing equality of educational opportunity. This was based on the left's concern for social justice and equality. In contrast the Conservative Party and the right have been concerned with providing an 'appropriate' education for everyone. Since children are seen to have different abilities and talents, they require different types of education (and schools).

The politics of education can be seen from the stop-go introduction of the comprehensive system. In 1965 the Labour government asked Local Education Authorities to reorganise secondary education on comprehensive lines. By 1970, when Harold Wilson's Labour government was defeated, approximately one third of children in secondary education were attending comprehensive schools.

The trend to comprehensives slowed down after 1970, with the new Conservative government (under Edward Heath) issuing a circular allowing grammar schools to exist alongside comprehensives. This clearly undermined the comprehensive ideal - there is little point in calling a school comprehensive if the brightest pupils in its area attend a local grammar school.

The Labour government elected in 1974 introduced legislation requiring all LEAs to go comprehensive. By the end of its period of office (May 1979) over 80% of secondary school pupils attended comprehensive schools. The Conservative victory in 1979 (and again in 1983, 1987 and 1992) removed the pressure to go comprehensive from those LEAs which still had some form of selective system. Thus the pace of comprehensive reorganisation has largely depended on the party in power.

Activity 2 Intelligence Tests

Item A 'The Essential Intelligence Test'
OPPOSITES

Look at this: UP ... (high, sky, <u>down</u>, on)

The word Down is underlined because it is the ONLY ONE of the four words in the brackets which is OPPOSITE in meaning to the word Up. Now do these. Underline ONE word in each bracket which is OPPOSITE in meaning to the word in capital letters.

40.	OUT	...... (over, under, near, in)
41.	STRONG	...... (small, short, weak, thin)
42.	DAY	...... (light, night, moon, sun)
43.	SHORT	...... (thin, thick, wide, tall)
44.	SHALLOW	...... (deep, narrow, thick, wide)
45.	ENEMY	...... (evil, illness, friend, foe)
46.	DIFFICULT	...... (hard, soft, light, easy)
47.	TO FIND	...... (to keep, to lose, to get, to reward)
48.	TO EXTEND	...... (to lengthen, to shorten, to hope, to stretch)
49.	DEPARTURE	...... (station, time, arrival, travel)

FIND THREE ALIKE

Underline the three words which belong together or are alike in some way.

Like this: <u>fork</u>, cat, <u>spoon</u>, <u>knife</u>, red, poor.

Now do these. Underline JUST THREE words in each line which belong together or are alike in some way.

50. Mother, pen, father, children, hat, elephant.
51. Cat, train, mouse, cap, bus, battleship.
52. Carpenter, foreigner, hooter, shirt, baker, tailor.
53. Tumbler, chair, mirror, bottle, spade, smoke.

From *The Essential Intelligence Test, Form A, for pupils aged 8+ to 12+,* prepared by F.J.Schonell, 1940

Questions

1 Do the tests in Items A and B.

2 What are the problems of forecasting children's academic ability on the basis of intelligence tests?

3 Do the examples in Items A and B support the argument in Item C? Give reasons for your answer.

Item B *Examples from intelligence tests*

- Underline the odd-man-out:
  House Igloo Bungalow Office Hut

- Underline which of these is not a famous composer:
  ZOTRAM SATSURS REVID MALESO

- Insert the word missing from the brackets:
  Fee (Tip) End
  Dance (....) Sphere

- Underline the odd one out:

- Draw the next one in the sequence:

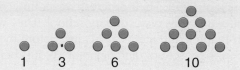

Item C *Ethnic minorities and intelligence tests*

In the United States, generations of black, Mexican-American, and other minority children have been measured by intelligence tests that seem to assume everyone grows up exposed to the same white middle class culture. Similarly, any written test in English discriminates against those for whom English is a second language, or against black children whose normal 'street English' differs markedly from that customarily used in middle class society, in schools, and in intelligence tests.

Adapted from B.Rice 'The Brave New World of Intelligence Testing', *New Society*, 11.10.79

Comprehensives: have they succeeded?

This is a difficult question to answer for a number of reasons. Firstly, what does success mean - better exam results, improved discipline, higher motivation, a more caring social environment? Secondly, success in comparison to what - the tripartite system, the independent sector ('private' schools), the ideals of comprehensive education? Thirdly, can a judgement be made when selection within the state education system still exists in some LEAs and around 8% of 11-15 year old secondary school pupils attend independent schools?

Examination results Critics of the comprehensive system claimed it would lower educational standards. They believed that the 'high academic standards' of the grammar schools would be diluted in the comprehensives. The following table suggests that they were wrong. Educational standards were higher in 1983, when less than 4% of secondary school pupils went to grammar schools, than in 1969, when 21% went to grammar schools.

Qualifications of school leavers

	1969 (%)	1983 (%)
One or more A-levels	12	14
5 or more O-levels (but no A-levels)	7	10
1,2,3 or 4 O-levels	18	28
O-level or A-level passes	37	52
No qualifications	50	10

Adapted from C.Townroe and G.Yates *Sociology for GCSE*, 1987, p 139

Higher ability children Supporters of the tripartite system believed that comprehensives would hold back more able pupils. They argued that special schools - grammar schools - were needed to develop their 'special' talents. This concern was examined in a study conducted by the National Children's Bureau. The research was based on a representative sample of 16,000 children, all born in the same week of 1958. Their progress was followed through different types of secondary school. They were tested on reading and maths at 11, just before they started secondary school, and again at 16, just before they left.

The results show that children of high ability (their scores were in the top 20% when they were tested at 11) made, on average, the same amount of progress in reading and maths over the five years of secondary education, regardless of whether they went to grammar or comprehensive school. Children of lower ability did slightly better if they went to comprehensives rather than to secondary modern schools.

This study indicates that bright children do just as well in comprehensives as in grammar schools. Despite such evidence, successive Conservative governments have questioned the ability of comprehensives to develop bright children.

'Creaming' In many areas comprehensives have coexisted with grammar and independent schools which have 'creamed' - drawn off - many of the brightest children. In 1991 3.6% of secondary school pupils aged 11-15 in England went to grammar schools and 7% (in Britain) to independent schools. The proportion of school pupils in independent schools increases dramatically with age - in 1991 20% of boys and 15% of girls aged 16 and over went to independent schools (*Social Trends,* 1993). Although the great majority of pupils go to comprehensives, a number of selective schools still exist. In 1993 there were 157 grammar schools in England and Wales. The existence of selective schools that 'cream' many of the brightest pupils places neighbouring comprehensives at a severe

disadvantage if they are judged in terms of exam results. A fully comprehensive system would have no selective schooling - no grammar schools and no independent schools.

Social class Educational attainment is linked to social class. In general the higher the class position of a pupil's parents, the higher the pupil's educational qualifications. Research on class and educational attainment is examined in detail on pp293-301.

Supporters of comprehensive education hoped that class differences in educational attainment would be reduced by the comprehensive system. In particular they hoped that the examination results of working class pupils would improve compared to those of middle class pupils. Although the educational qualifications of *all* school leavers have improved, class differences have remained largely unchanged. In other words examination results in general have got better but the gap between top and bottom has stayed more or less the same. The evidence for this claim is examined in Activity 3.

Some researchers have argued that it is unrealistic to expect schools, no matter how they are organised, to make up for the inequalities of the class system. From this point of view, as long as social class exists there cannot be equality of opportunity in education. Schools cannot compensate for society (see Activity 3).

Breaking down class barriers Many of those who supported the comprehensive system looked forward to schools attended by pupils from across the entire social class spectrum. They hoped that this social mix would help to break down class barriers. However most comprehensives recruit from a clearly defined local catchment area. Often these areas are largely middle class or working class. As a result many comprehensives are primarily 'single class', so tending to reinforce rather than break down existing class divisions.

Streaming and setting Many comprehensives divide pupils into groups based on their assumed ability. *Streaming* places pupils of similar ability in the same class. *Setting* does the same thing for particular subjects - eg a top, middle and bottom mathematics set.

Research has shown that a disproportionate number of middle class pupils are placed in the top streams and sets and a disproportionate number of working class pupils in the lower streams and sets - and that placement in lower streams and sets depresses educational attainment (see pp299-300).This has been seen as another form of selection, not unlike the tripartite system. And, like the tripartite system, the inequalities of social class are mirrored in the selection system.

Activity 3 Class in the Classroom

Item A *The evidence*

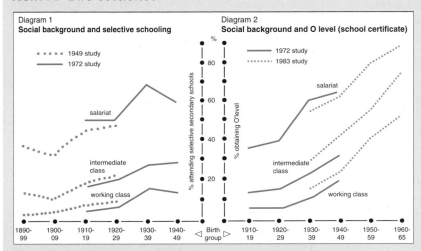

Diagram 1
Social background and selective schooling

• • • • • 1949 study
————— 1972 study

salariat

intermediate class

working class

1890-99 1900-09 1910-19 1920-29 1930-39 1940-49

◁ Birth group ▷

% attending selective secondary schools

% 80 60 40 20

Diagram 2
Social background and O level (school certificate)

————— 1972 study
• • • • • • 1983 study

salariat

intermediate class

working class

% obtaining O level

1910-19 1920-29 1930-39 1940-49 1950-59 1960-65

These diagrams show the results of a series of national surveys. The authors of the 1949 and 1972 studies were concerned with selection for secondary schools (see Diagram 1). To what extent did social class affect pupils' chances of gaining entry to grammar and private schools? The 1972 study shows the results of the 1944 Education Act which established the tripartite system. (The 1972 study covered only men. However, neither the 1949 nor the 1983 studies show any statistically significant class differences between men and women in access to selective schools).

Diagram 2 shows the history of class differences in gaining GCE O levels from the 1972 and 1983 studies. The 1940-49 birth group was educated in the tripartite system, the 1950-59 group was transitional (comprehensive reorganisation began in 1965 but it was not until the mid-1970s that most schools were comprehensive) and the 1960-65 group was largely educated in comprehensives.

Adapted from A. Heath 'Class in the Classroom', *New Society*, 17.7.87

Item B *The significance of class*

There has been constantly rising educational attainment (at least as measured by the acquisition of examination certificates - the only measure available to us) during the course of the 20th century, a silent revolution that has continued through both selective and comprehensive eras. But class inequalities first in access to selective secondary schools, then at O level, have shown no overall tendency to decline. Chameleon-like, they seem to reappear in a new guise but fundamentally unchanged as the educational environment changes around them.

In the face of this remarkable resilience of class inequalities, educational reforms seem powerless.

Adapted from A. Heath, *ibid*.

Questions

1 a) Judging from Diagram 1, what were the effects of the 1944 Education Act?
   b) Judging from Diagram 2, what were the effects of comprehensive reorganisation?

2 Judging from Item A, are Antony Heath's conclusions in Item B justified? Give reasons for your answer.

1.4 Independent schools

Independent schools are schools which charge fees for some or all pupils. They form the private sector of education as opposed to the state sector. The more famous independent schools, eg Eton, Harrow, Rugby, are known as public schools because traditionally they have prepared their pupils for important public offices. There are around 200 public schools out of a total of over 2,000 independent schools.

Independent schools, as their name suggests, are largely independent from the state sector. For example, they do not have to teach the National Curriculum which is a legal requirement for state schools. However, they do have to register with the Department for Education and have to conform to certain regulations - eg on hygiene and punishment. Independent schools are financed by the fees they charge and from gifts and endowments.

During the 1980s independent schooling became increasingly popular. However the growth in student numbers stopped in the early 1990s, possibly due to the recession. 7% of all pupils in Britain attended independent schools in 1991/92 and this percentage increases with age - 18% of boys and 15% of girls aged 16 or over attended these schools (*Social Trends*, 1994).

There is a strong link between independent schools, Oxbridge (the Universities of Oxford and Cambridge) and the top jobs in society. In particular, the proportion of people who attend public schools and reach top positions in politics, the civil service, the legal profession and the armed forces is very high. The composition of Prime Minister John Major's first cabinet in November 1990 demonstrates the influence of a public school and Oxbridge education. Of the 21 Cabinet Ministers, 17 had been to Oxford or Cambridge and 19 had attended independent schools.

Most of the pupils who attend independent schools are drawn from the upper classes. This is due partly to tradition and partly to the expense of tuition. Some critics claim that independent schools act as a mechanism to ensure that the rich and powerful maintain their privileged position. This view is examined in Activity 4.

Views on private education

The case for and against private education has been, and still is, hotly debated. Some would abolish it. They see it as perpetuating privilege, as class-ridden, as motivated by snobbery, as a means of giving some children a head start at the expense of others. Supporters of private education argue that in a free society parents should have the right to choose their children's education. They should have the freedom to spend their money as they see fit and if the result is a better education for their children, so be it. Parents who choose private education usually put 'academic reasons' at the top of their list and also include better discipline, superior facilities, smaller class sizes and better teachers. They see independent schools as giving their children a better start in life.

Part of the debate on private versus state education is summarised in the following table. At one extreme the 'collectivists' argue that only the state should provide education (column 1), at the other extreme the 'individualists' argue that there is no place for the state, that education should be provided only by independent institutions (column 4). Other views (columns 2 and 3) fall somewhere between these extremes.

	State vs private education		
Collectivist			**Individualist**
1	2	3	4
Policy for Education State system only. No opt out.	Education freely available. Individuals may opt out - using private schools at their own expense.	Mixed economy of education (combination of publicly and independently funded institutions).	No publicly funded education. Free market - independent institutions.
Possible role for independent sector None.	Competes with state sector.	Complements state sector.	Universal - all schools.
Extent of parental choice No parental choice.	Parental choice but full cost of independent education met by personal finance.	Parental choice with some state provision to help with costs of independent education.	Parental choice as full as possible - use of vouchers provided by state to pay for education.

Adapted from D.Johnson *Private Schools and State Schools: Two Systems or One?* 1987, p7

The Assisted Places Scheme

This scheme sponsors academically gifted children by helping to pay their fees for independent schooling. It was initiated by the 1980 Education Act and is operated by the Secretary of State for Education. Parents receive financial help with the cost of tuition fees at certain independent schools. In launching the scheme, Mark Carlisle, then Secretary of State for Education, said that the intention of the Assisted Places Scheme (APS) was:

'To widen the availability of the type of school to parents whose children are now being educated in the maintained (state) sector ... restoring to bright children of less affluent parents a high quality academic education ...the APS constitutes support for the parent and pupil rather than the school.'

By 1985 something like 17,500 were using the scheme and by 1990, 34,000; the cost of the scheme in 1988/89 was £50 million. In terms of overall spending on education the costs are small. The scheme does, however, reinforce the private sector of education while weakening the state sector. The Department for Education leaves it to the individual schools involved to select students and to set fees. This selection process often involves interviews with parents and children - a procedure that might disadvantage children from working class backgrounds. Indeed it would seem that many families who benefit from the APS may well have used the private sector anyway and are just receiving 'top up' help with the expense of doing so.

Whatever the pros and cons of the APS, it is clear

that the scheme has directed some state resources to the independent sector at a time when the state sector of education is short of funds. There is also an implicit assumption in the scheme that the schooling offered by independent schools is 'better' than that of the state system.

Activity 4   Private Education

Item A   *Views of private education*

Private schools have long been a major source of perpetuated division and the demarcation of privilege, status, esteem, power, opportunity and expectation that go with it. Private schools are not 'incidental' to the class system. They are the very cement in the wall that divides British society. The existence of private schooling with all its increments of status and complementary paraphernalia of quaint uniforms and traditions, language and accents is amongst the most effective means of perpetually imposing those divisions.

Neil Kinnock, 1981, quoted in G.Walford (ed) *British Public Schools:Policy and Practice* 1984, p1

Private schools, quite simply, are better than those of the state, if only because parents who pay will ensure they are getting value. It is absurd that, under the state, parents hand over their school fees, in the shape of taxes, to enable bureaucrats and teachers' unions to control the education of their children.

Terence Kealey 'Let Our Children Go', *The Spectator*, 18.5.91, p16

Item C   *Why parents choose private schools*

'I believe that the (independent) school will give my son a 5 % better chance, and he may just need that 5%.' (stockbroker, grammar school educated)

'The first thing an employer asks for is qualifications. The chances of getting these are improved by going to a public school.' (managing director, grammar school educated)

For most parents academic considerations were the most important in their choice of schooling - smaller classes, better teachers and better chance of exam passes were the most popular reasons. However the quality of education provided is not the only attraction of independent schools. About 30 % of the people who had used private education ticked 'better discipline' as a reason for paying fees while a similar proportion ticked 'better social environment'.

Adapted from 'Why Parents Choose Private Schools', *Sunday Times*, 28.3.82

Questions

1 Use Items A to D to support the view that independent schools help the rich and powerful to maintain their privileged position.

2 Discuss the view that private education is a necessary part of a free society.

Item B

The Conservative Cabinet's choice of schools

Minister	Children	Schools attended
John Major	2	State primary, private secondary
Kenneth Clarke	2	State primary, private secondary
Norman Lamont	2	Private
Douglas Hurd	3	Private
Tom King	2	Private
Kenneth Baker	2	Private
John Gummer	4	2 state primary, 1 private secondary 1 fee-paying choir school
Tony Newton	2	State
Michael Howard	2	Private
John MacGregor	3	Private
Michael Heseltine	3	Private
Lord Mackay	1	Private
Peter Brooke	3	Private
David Hunt	4	Private
Ian Lang	2	Private
Peter Lilley	0	
David Mellor	2	Private
Chris Patten	3	State primary, 1 private
Malcolm Rifkind	2	Private
John Wakeham	3	2 private
William Waldegrave	4	Private
David Waddington	5	Private

Guardian, 19.2.92

Item D

Eton - one of England's best known public schools.

1.5 Developments in vocational education

Over the last twenty years governments have emphasised the need to link educational provision more closely with the requirements of the economy and the world of work. There has been an attempt to provide a more 'vocationally relevant' education for young people. A number of factors influenced this development.

Unemployment

During the recession of the mid-1970s unemployment in Britain rose to around 3 to 4% of the workforce. This was seen as unacceptably high. By 1980 it had reached 7% and by 1982 12%. It remained at around that level - roughly three million people - until 1986. From a peak of 3.1 million in July 1986, unemployment fell sharply to 1.6 million in early 1990. It then rose rapidly to nearly 3 million in January 1993 then falling steadily to 2.66 million - 9.4% of the workforce - in May 1994. (*Social Trends* 1994, p61; *Employment Gazette* July 1994, pS2)

Unemployment is highest among the young, particularly the 16-19 year old economically active age group. In Spring 1993 22% of males and 16% of females in this group were unemployed. In the late 1970s there was growing concern about youth unemployment. Many blamed it on inadequate training. This diagnosis was a major factor behind the development of vocational initiatives such as the Youth Training Scheme (YTS), the Certificate of Pre-Vocational Education (CPVE - now known as the Diploma in Vocational Education, DVE) and the Technical and Vocational Education Initiative (TVEI).

Changes in government policy

During the 1950s and 1960s it was widely felt that education up to school leaving age should be general rather than specifically vocational in character. Vocational training was seen as the responsibility of employers rather than teachers. This view began to change with the rise in youth unemployment in the 1970s. Schools, it was argued, were producing young people who lacked the skills required by industry. And industry in turn was suffering from a skills shortage. This line of argument led to the 'new vocationalism', direct government involvement in youth training.

Much of this involvement came from the Department of Employment rather than the Department for Education. The Department of Employment manages initiatives such as TVEI and Employment Training (ET). It was given responsibility for the Manpower Services Commission (MSC) which became the key agency in developing youth training in the 1970s. Although the MSC was replaced by the Training Agency and then in 1990 by Training and Enterprise Councils (TECs), its influence has been considerable. It introduced the Youth Opportunities Programme (YOP) in 1978 - a six month programme that included elements of work experience and 'off the job' training, usually in colleges of further education. YOP was replaced by the Youth Training Scheme (YTS) in 1983 - initially a one year scheme (extended to two years in 1986) that aimed to provide broad based vocational training in a variety of occupational areas for school leavers. YTS became YT (Youth Training) in 1990.

The development of a range of vocational initiatives led to a proliferation of qualifications and awards. The NCVQ (National Council for Vocational Qualifications) was set up in1986 to try to bring some coherence to these qualifications by establishing a nationally recognised system of vocational qualifications. It established National Vocational Qualifications (NVQs) which are specific to particular occupations. These have been supplemented by GNVQs (General National Vocational Qualifications) which allow young people to keep their options open rather than specialise in a particular occupation. GNVQs assess skills, knowledge and understanding in broad occupational areas such as Art and Design, Business, Health and Social Care, Manufacturing and Leisure and Tourism.

Criticisms of the new vocationalism

1 Jobs not training are needed   There has been a rapid growth in the number of people continuing in education or training beyond the minimum school leaving age.

Staying on in education and training (percentage of all 16-18 year olds, UK)

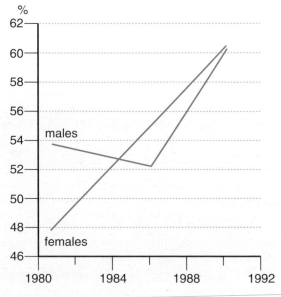

From *Sociology Update*, 1994, p35

Research has indicated that options such as YT would be 'deserted rapidly' by young people if jobs were available (Roberts et al 1989). And, according to some researchers, they would be right to do so. Youth unemployment is due not to an absence of skills but to an absence of jobs (D. Finn, 1987).

2 Blaming young people Phillip Cohen (1984) studied Youth Training Schemes in South London. He claims that youth unemployment is often presented as a failure of young people. The message behind much youth training is that if young people 'improve themselves' - increase their motivation, improve their presentation of self and learn appropriate social skills - then their chances of employment will be much better. According to Cohen, this deflects attention from the real cause of youth unemployment - the economy.

3 Quality and relevance of learning A number of researchers have criticised the quality of training provided by YT. Cohen found that many trainees spent a lot of time 'running errands' and generally 'being useful'. This was passed off as the learning of 'transferable skills' which would enable young people to work in a variety of occupations. According to Cohen few if any real occupational skills were taught. And even if such skills were taught, they might never be used. A survey found that only a small proportion of young people gained their full time jobs on the basis of skills acquired in their youth training (Raffe, 1990).

Youth training varies considerably and criticisms may not be generally applicable. Ainley (1990) points to the emergence of a hierarchy of youth training in terms of the access it provides to regular employment. At the top are schemes which guarantee employment in large companies, with the YT allowance often topped up by the employer. Next are schemes which offer training in occupational skills that are in demand in the labour market and so offer

trainees a fair chance of finding employment. Below this are schemes which tend to be used by smaller firms to screen potential workers and which offer trainees some chance of employment. At the bottom are schemes offering little chance of employment, which employers see either as a duty to 'disadvantaged youth', or as a source of cheap labour.

4 The academic-vocational divide Vocational education and training have been regarded as inferior to an 'academic' education. This has been reflected in the class differences of those entering these areas. 'Young people from better-off homes mostly avoid YT seeing it as being second best to staying on at school and college. YT has not overcome Britain's long history of social division between the "educated" and the "trained"' (Lee et al 1990, p189). Richard Pring suggests that a new form of tripartism has developed at the age of 16. 'Young people are forced into awkward choices at 16 between totally disconnected tracks - the academic single subject (and high status) track of A level, the more vocationally orientated but integrated educational experience of BTEC, and the narrowly focused training schemes of YT' (1990, p1). And it has been argued that YT is training for the less able which channels those who take this route into low status, low paid occupations. There is therefore a symmetry between class, training, occupation and pay.

The main political parties aim to remove the status divide between academic and vocational education. The advent of GNVQs might do this. It is now possible to take an Advanced GNVQ course which is the equivalent of a 3 A level course. If this equivalence is generally accepted, then vocational qualifications will carry the same weight as academic qualifications for entry into the job market and higher education. This is clearly the hope when the Department for Education refers to Advanced GNVQs as the 'vocational A levels' (DFE 1994, p19).

Activity 5 Youth Training

Item A *Experiences of training*
The experiences of trainees working in a number of different premises were very similar: 'There's nothing to do most of the time. The only decent time is when they go off and play golf on Wednesday and we've got the office to ourselves'. (clerical trainee in building firm)

The office supervisor stopped us having a cup of coffee in the morning and the atmosphere is awful'. (clerical trainee in office)

The chance of being kept on and offered regular work is a major control mechanism over trainees: 'I had high hopes of being kept on at the beginning. I was living in a dream world'. (retail trainee)

Adapted from C.Buswell 'Flexible Workers for Flexible Firms?' in A.Pollard, J.Purvis and G.Walford (eds) *Education, Training and the New Vocationalism*, 1988, pp166-169

Item B *'Keeps you off the streets'*
The only things round here for school leavers are schemes. One of my friends, who is eighteen, went on a transport training scheme but he can't find a job. Just because you're on a scheme doesn't mean you'll find a permanent job. I suppose they keep kids off the streets. If I wasn't doing this scheme, I'd be knocking round town looking for something to get up to. (Bruce Jackman, aged 16)

Adapted from R.White with R.Brockington *Tales Out Of School: Consumers' Views of British Education*, 1983, p98

Item C *Training at the bank*

Each year about 20 young people, many with no qualifications, are recruited from the inner city area to train under the Bank of England's clerical youth training scheme.

18 year old **Elton Thomas** is in his second year, and came in without any qualifications. However, he's working towards achieving an NVQ this summer.

'I use computers a lot at the moment. I spend a lot of time on the phone chasing statements and invoices. I've worked in four different offices and gained a variety of experience. It's great working here. I really like wearing a suit to work and looking sharp. I'm in the bank's football team. We play other banks and companies and win a few and lose a few!'

Marsha Wallace did work experience at a local bank when she was at school which whetted her appetite for working in a bank.

'You usually need good qualifications to get into a bank, and as I didn't get good grades, I didn't expect to get anywhere. I was delighted to get the chance to train here. It's very prestigious and must help when it comes to looking for a job elsewhere.'

Eastender **David Richards** is in his first year on the programme.

'I enjoy technical things so I like the opportunity to work with computers. Moving around the different offices gives you a lot of different experience. The work for the qualifications is going well at the moment, but I expect it to get harder next year. Lots of young people work in the Bank and I like the atmosphere here. There are social and sports clubs and a cafeteria for staff. It's a nice lively place to work.'

Adapted from Employment Department Group and BBC Radio One *Action Special 91*, 1991, p13

Trainees at the Bank of England

Item D *Screening potential employees*

Training schemes often have an important role to play for employers in allowing them to screen prospective employees for their 'suitability' and to socialise them at minimal cost. One study describes the whole process as one long interview, 'in which the group of trainees gradually shrinks as members are successfully "taken on". Anxieties about being taken on, in these circumstances, become particularly acute, inducing a willingness to acquire relevant "skills" and patterns of behaviour. Highly specific training is supplied in abundance. Thus YT becomes a most effective crucible for occupational socialisation, a narrowing tunnel in which the job represents the light at the end' (Bates 1989, p38).

Adapted from T. Jeffs and M. K. Smith 'Youth' in M.Haralambos (ed) *Developments in Sociology*, vol 8, 1992, pp73-74

Questions

1 Suggest reasons for the differences in the views expressed in Items A and C.
2 a) Provide a brief sociological analysis of the role of youth training given in Items B and D.
   b) Do you think this role is justified? Give reasons for your answer.

1.6 The Education Reform Act

The 1988 Education Reform Act is the most important and far reaching educational legislation since the 1944 Education Act. It established a national curriculum for all state schools in England and Wales and a national system of testing and assessment. It reduced the role of local educational authorities by giving greater control to individual schools and their governing bodies. It established city technology colleges and grant maintained schools, both independent of local authority control.

Competition and choice

The Education Reform Act reflects the Conservative Party's commitment to an education market place which involves competition, diversity and choice. Parental choice is a key element in this policy - where possible parents are able to choose the school they prefer for their children. And schools are required to provide information which will help them to make this choice. Each year schools must publish a prospectus which includes their examination and National Curriculum test results and information which allows comparison with both local and national results. And parental choice has important consequences. 'Your choice of school directly affects that school's budget; every extra pupil means extra money for the school' (Department for Education, 1994, p18). In theory the 'right to choose will encourage schools to aim for the highest possible standards'. Schools will compete with each other in order to attract pupils (and money) and in the process standards of education will rise.

This emphasis on competition and choice may have a number of negative consequences. Parents often look closely at examination results when assessing and choosing schools. But a simple league table which ranks schools in terms of results can be very misleading. There is evidence that some of the best schools in Britain do poorly on this kind of league table. These schools, often in run down inner city areas, are achieving extremely good results given the social background of their pupils. They may be doing a far better job than schools well above them in the league table. Yet they may be losing pupils (and money) to those schools. Parental choice may therefore have a detrimental effect if good schools in poor areas are losing pupils to less effective schools in better off areas. The losers will be the lower working class in the less desirable low income areas (see Activity 6).

Grant maintained schools

As part of the policy of diversity and choice, the Education Reform Act established grant maintained schools and city technology colleges (CTCs). There were 15 CTCs in 1994. They teach the National Curriculum with an additional emphasis on maths, science and technology. They are outside local authority control being funded partly by industry though mostly by the Department for Education.

Grant maintained (GM) schools are schools which have opted out of local authority control and are financed directly by central government. In July 1994, 592 out of 3,773 state secondary schools and 334 out of 18,828 state primary schools in England were grant maintained. These schools are self governing with governors and headteachers taking decisions about employment of staff, the curriculum, the provision of goods and services and the way pupils are selected for entry. The Conservative Party has supported the development of GM schools arguing that it frees schools to specialise, for example in particular subjects or particular types of pupils such as the 'more academically able'. In this way the choice for parents is widened.

Critics have seen this as a means of 'back door selection'. They see a return of the grammar school in the guise of the GM secondary school. And there will be no need for a selection process like the 11 plus. The government will have provided the evidence with its National Curriculum Tests at age 11. Some commentators foresee a return to the days of grammar and secondary modern schools. According to Simon Jenkins, 'There will be three categories of secondary education in Britain: private schools for the rich, "opted-out" government schools for the less rich but clever, and local council schools for the poor and rejected' (*Times,* 29.6.94). Time will tell whether these fears are realised.

The National Curriculum

For the first time in the history of state education the government has told teachers in England and Wales what to teach. From the age of 5-16 all pupils in state primary and secondary schools must study subjects prescribed by the National Curriculum - English, maths and science (the core subjects), technology, a foreign language in secondary schools, history, geography, art, music and PE. History, geography, art and music are not compulsory after the age of 14. Pupils are tested in the core subjects at the ages of 7, 11 and 14.

It has been claimed that a national curriculum for all pupils is an important step towards equality of educational opportunity. For example science has traditionally been a 'boys subject'. It is now compulsory for all pupils. In this respect it can be argued that a common curriculum is a move towards equal opportunity.

Critics of the National Curriculum have claimed that it may have the opposite effect. Key Stage 2 and 3 tests, taken by pupils at the ages of 11 and 14, are tiered in terms of difficulty. Teachers select and enter pupils for 'appropriate' tiers on the basis of their view of pupils ability. There is some evidence that National Curriculum testing has led to an increase in setting - ie the placement of pupils in different 'ability groups' (see Activity 6). Studies suggest that setting has a detrimental effect on the progress of those in lower sets and that a disproportionate number of pupils from working class backgrounds end up in lower sets. In this respect the National Curriculum may represent a backward step in terms of equality of educational opportunity.

Conclusion

It is too early to judge the Educational Reform Act. Will it lead to increasing diversity and choice and rising standards? Will it lead to increased selection both on entry to and within schools? Will the move to GM schools continue? Will the National Curriculum remain in its present form or continue to be revised as it was in 1994? Answers to these questions will take time and further research.

Summary

1 Changes in the educational system have reflected the different political and educational philosophies of the time.

2 State education was established in the late 19th century, partly as a means of protecting

and promoting British industry. This concern influenced the 'new vocationalism' of the 1980s and 90s.

3 Developments in education have also reflected a concern with equality of educational opportunity. To some extent this influenced, though in very different ways, the tripartite and the comprehensive systems of secondary education.

4 The Educational Reform Act aimed to raise educational standards by means of competition, diversity and choice. However the Act may have a number of negative consequences.

Activity 6 Educational Reform?

Item A *Measuring school performance*

The alternative school league
How valued-added ratings compare with official tables

1 Wirral	(31)	28 Bedford	(27)	55 Essex	(34)	82 Calderdale	(72)
2 Camden	(57)	29 Devon	(28)	56 Newcastle u T	(85)	83 Bexley	(58)
3 Barnet	(3)	30 Kens'ton & C	(71)	57 Ham'smith & F	(92)	84 St Helens	(79)
4 Kingston	(1)	31 Waltham Frst	(80)	58 Avon	(45)	85 Leics	(53)
5 Sutton	(9)	32 Shropshire	(21)	59 Walsall	(59)	86 Derbyshire	(48)
6 Bromley	(4)	33 Cambridge	(16)	60 Northu'land	(40)	87 Hereford	(36)
7 Liverpool	(98)	34 Sheffield	(63)	61 Cumbria	(44)	88 Tameside	(62)
8 Tower H'lets	(105)	35 N.Tyneside	(49)	62 Merton	(46)	89 Durham	(67)
9 Lambeth	(100)	36 Sutton	(50)	63 Doncaster	(75)	90 Wandsworth	(90)
10 Bucks	(5)	37 Oxford	(11)	64 Somerset	(24)	91 Notts	(76)
11 Bolton	(42)	38 Cornwall	(25)	65 Stockport	(35)	92 Lincs	(56)
12 Hackney	(102)	39 Suffolk	(15)	66 Coventry	(66)	93 Stafford	(60)
13 W.Sussex	(2)	40 Hampshire	(22)	67 Humberside	(64)	94 Trafford	(61)
14 E.Sussex	(17)	41 Newham	(99)	68 Dudley	(54)	95 Warwicks	(47)
15 Dorset	(12)	42 Croydon	(38)	69 Sunderland	(83)	96 Salford	(93)
16 Wigan	(30)	43 Lancs	(43)	70 Lewisham	(91)	97 Islington	(104)
17 Harrow	(7)	44 Hounslow	(33)	71 Wiltshire	(32)	98 Leeds	(78)
18 Cheshire	(18)	45 Brent	(68)	72 Kirkless	(70)	99 Oldham	(81)
19 Redbridge	(23)	46 Solihull	(37)	73 Hillingdon	(41)	100 Sandwell	(94)
20 Herts	(10)	47 Northants	(29)	74 Ealing	(77)	101 Bradford	(97)
21 Gateshead	(73)	48 Manchester	(103)	75 Rotherham	(74)	102 Westminster	(96)
22 Haringey	(86)	49 Bury	(26)	76 Enfield	(55)	103 Wakefield	(82)
23 Richmond	(8)	50 Berks	(19)	77 Knowsley	(106)	104 Rochdale	(88)
24 Gloucester	(13)	51 Havering	(20)	78 Wol'hmpton	(87)	105 Southwark	(107)
25 Birmingham	(84)	52 N.Yorkshire	(14)	79 Kent	(51)	106 Barnsley	(95)
26 Surrey	(6)	53 Isle of Wight	(39)	80 Norfolk	(52)	107 Barking	(101)
27 Cleveland	(69)	54 S.Tyneside	(65)	81 Greenwich	(89)		

Figures in brackets show positions in the official tables.

Some of the best schools in Britain have been accused of 'failing pupils' because they have done badly in government league tables of school examination results. For the past two years the Department for Education has published league tables based on raw exam results, outraging teachers and academics who claim it gives parents a misleading impression. Crude exam results reflect a school's catchment area.

Now statisticians working for Agency 26, a group of academics and researchers, have devised alternative league tables which take into account social factors.

The results show, although poverty is an important factor, schools can - and do - make an enormous difference. There are local authorities with a high proportion of very poor children who do badly in both tables. But the most significant finding is the number of inner city authorities, languishing in the lower regions of the Department for Education table, who do exceedingly well in the new table.

Adapted from *Observer*, 20.3.94

Item B *Setting*

The National Curriculum tests for 14 year olds are forcing schools to scrap mixed-ability teaching.

Setting - the practice of putting pupils into different ability groups for different subjects - fell out of favour with the introduction of the comprehensive school but there was clear evidence from the Office for Standards in Education (OFSTED) last week that it is on the increase.

An OFSTED report on science based on inspections of 98 primary, 15 middle, 227 secondary and 30 special schools says: 'The proportion of lessons taught to mixed-ability groups was much lower than in 1990-91. In that year, 85% of lessons in Year 7 and 8 were taught in mixed-ability groups. The figures for this year were 68% for Year 7, 48% for Year 8 and 41% for Year 9.'

Many teachers dislike setting. A headteacher in a North Humberside comprehensive states, 'As soon as you move into setting, disenchantment among pupils becomes a very serious problem'. A Head of English in a school in Watford calls the tiers in Key Stage 3 English tests 'divisive'. It's like 'driving a wedge through the classroom'.

Adapted from *Times Educational Supplement*, 19.3.93

Item C *Parental choice*

Promoting parental choice of schools is a retrograde step that does little to improve the quality of a child's education, according to a five year study in Scotland.

The Canadian Center for Educational Sociology's findings show that the principle effect of parents' right to choose, introduced in Scotland in 1980, has been to increase segregation between working class and middle class pupils. The impact on children's academic results was minimal.

It is middle rather than working class parents who choose schools for their children. They tend to pick schools with strong academic records which were likely to have benefited from their privileged intake rather than those which looked less impressive but might actually have greater impact on pupils' education.

But parental choice was probably having a detrimental effect on the school system. Good schools in poor areas may find themselves losing pupils, while less effective schools in better areas become more popular.

Adapted from *Times Educational Supplement*, 2.10.92

Questions

1 Read Item A. Do you think the 'alternative school league table' is justified? Explain your answer.
2 Read Item B. How can setting be 'divisive' and lead to 'disenchantment'?
3 'The problem with parental choice is that it is based on inadequate and misleading information.' Discuss using Items A and C.

2 Sociological Theories of Education

Key Issues

1 How do the main sociological theories see the role of education in modern industrial society?
2 What are the strengths and weaknesses of each approach?

2.1 Consensus theories: functionalist perspectives

The functionalist perspective was the dominant theoretical approach in the sociology of education until the 1960s. When considering education functionalists typically ask questions such as:

- What are the functions of education?
- What part does it play in maintaining society?
- What are the relationships between education and other elements of the social system?

A typical functionalist response to such questions sees education as transmitting society's norms and values and so promoting value consensus. For instance, through respecting the rules and standards of the school the child learns to respect the rules and standards of the wider society. Functionalists tend to see the various parts of society working together for the benefit of society as a whole. In this respect the educational and economic system are often seen as working hand in hand as schools develop the skills required for the world of work.

Emile Durkheim

Durkheim, one of the founding fathers of sociology, provided the basic framework for the functionalist view of education. He believed that for society to operate effectively individuals must develop a sense of belonging to something wider than their immediate situation. They must become 'social beings' with a loyalty and commitment to society as a whole. The education system plays an important part in this process. In particular, the teaching of history enables children to see the link between themselves and wider society. Thus today's National Curriculum, with its emphasis on British history, can be seen as a means of developing this link by showing young people that they are part of something larger than their immediate social group.

Talcott Parsons

The American sociologist Talcott Parsons developed Durkheim's ideas. Parsons argued that in modern industrial societies education performs an important socialising function. By transmitting the culture of society to new generations, education helps to ensure the continuity of norms and values. Parsons saw the school classroom as a 'microcosm of society'. This miniature society provides a training ground for the wider society and effects the transition from childhood to adulthood.

Parsons saw the school as a bridge between the family and the wider society. Within the family the child's status is ascribed - fixed at birth. But in wider society status is achieved. Adults achieve their status as bricklayers, doctors, clerks, hairdressers or teachers on the basis of ability and effort. It is a big jump from the ascribed status of the family to the achieved status of society as a whole. Schools help to bridge this gap.

Within the school young people are not judged in terms of their ascribed status as sons and daughters.

They are judged in terms of standards which are applied equally to all pupils - standards of conduct and academic success. In terms of these standards they achieve their status by effort and ability. In this way schools prepare young people to achieve their status in the adult world. At the same time schools promote the value of achievement. Young people are rewarded for academic achievement with good examination results. In this way the educational system reflects the wider society and socialises young people for their adult roles.

Parsons saw a further link between schools and the wider society. Schools help to select young people and allocate them to adult roles. Pupils are assessed and sorted in terms of their talents and abilities and this helps to allocate them to appropriate occupations. Thus the high achievers in the school system are likely to be selected for high status positions in the occupational system. Parsons' view of the selection and allocation function of schools is similar to the functionalist theory of stratification (see pages 37-38).

In summary functionalists see education as a crucial part of the socialisation process:

- transmitting and reinforcing society's norms and values
- preparing young people for adult roles
- selecting young people in terms of their abilities for occupational roles.

Functionalism: some critical comments

Functionalists have emphasised the importance of education as a means of transmitting society's values. However, they have paid little attention to the following possibilities. There may not be a single set of values to transmit. Society may consist of various groups with different or even conflicting interests, each group having its own set of values. If the educational system does transmit values, they may well be those of a ruling class or elite.

Functionalists tend to assume that the educational system is a meritocracy - pupils have an equal chance, they achieve on the basis of merit within a system that is basically fair. There is considerable evidence - examined later in the chapter - which indicates that this is not the case. In particular, working class and certain ethnic minority pupils underachieve in schools. The extent to which the educational system is able to develop and assess pupils' 'real' ability is questionable.

It can be argued that the educational system confirms people in their social positions rather than provides opportunities for advancement. Middle class pupils tend to get middle class jobs. In general they get higher qualifications than their working class counterparts. These qualifications can be seen as a 'rubber stamp' confirming their right to middle class

occupations. Their 'success' in school may result from the advantages of their class position rather than their ability. If this is the case then the functionalist claim that schools efficiently select and allocate pupils in terms of ability must be questioned.

Some functionalists claim that the demand in modern industrial societies for an increasingly skilled workforce is largely met by the educational system. Again this is questionable. It is difficult to see a direct link between many school subjects and the world of work.

2.2 Conflict theories: Marxist perspectives

In Marx's words the ruling class 'rule also as thinkers, as producers of ideas'. These ideas justify their position, conceal the true source of their power and disguise their exploitation of the subject class. In Marx's view this ruling class ideology is a far more effective means of domination than more obvious forms of coercion such as physical force. It is not difficult to see how education could play a crucial role in the transmission of ideology.

Education and ideology

Louis Althusser, a French Marxist philosopher, argues that no class can hold power for long simply by the use of force. Ideology provides a much more effective means of control - if people's hearts and minds are won over then force becomes unnecessary.

Althusser argues that in modern society the education system has largely replaced the church as the main agency for ideological control. In the past people tended to accept their station in life because they saw it as god's will. Today this acceptance comes in part from their experience in education. Firstly, schools transmit an ideology which states that capitalism is just and reasonable. Secondly, schools prepare pupils for their roles in the workforce. Most are trained as workers - they are taught to accept their future exploitation and provided with an education and qualifications to match their adult work roles. Some - the future managers, administrators and politicians - are trained to control the workforce. Their educational qualifications legitimate their position of power. They become the 'agents of exploitation and repression'.

Althusser argues that ideology in capitalist society is fundamental to social control. He sees the educational process as essentially ideological.

Correspondence theory

In *Schooling in Capitalist America* (1976) Samuel Bowles and Herbert Gintis claim that there is a close correspondence between the social relationships in the classroom and those in the workplace. This correspondence is essential for *social reproduction* - the reproduction of new generations of workers appropriately schooled to accept their roles in capitalist society.

School and workplace Schools like the wider society are based on hierarchies. Teachers give orders, pupils are expected to obey. Pupils have little control over their work, over the curriculum they follow. This corresponds to their later experience of lack of control in the workplace. Schools reward punctuality, obedience and hard work, they discourage creativity, independence and critical awareness. This is directly in line with the requirements of employers in capitalist society. Young people get little satisfaction from their education. They are motivated largely by external rewards such as educational qualifications. This is reflected in the workplace - work provides little intrinsic satisfaction, workers are motivated by external rewards such as pay. Bowles and Gintis argue that this correspondence between school and the workplace effectively reproduces labour power from one generation to the next.

Social inequality Capitalist society is unequal. If this inequality were seriously questioned it might threaten social stability. One way of avoiding this is to promote the belief that inequality is justified. According to Bowles and Gintis education legitimates social inequality by broadcasting the myth that it offers everybody an equal chance. It follows that those who achieve high qualifications deserve their success. And since high qualifications lead to top jobs people who get those jobs have earned them. In this way social inequality appears just and legitimate. However, Bowles and Gintis argue that rewards in education and occupation are based not on merit but on social background. The higher a person's class of origin, the more likely they are to attain high educational qualifications and a top job. The class system tends to reproduce itself from generation to generation and this process is legitimised by education. In Bowles and Gintis's words, 'Education reproduces inequality by justifying privilege and attributing poverty to personal failure' (1976, p114).

Criticisms Both Marxists and functionalists have been criticised for seeing people as mere creatures of the social system. Thus Bowles and Gintis see teachers as the agents of capital, pupils as its victims, their situations shaped by factors beyond their control. But many teachers are radicals who chose teaching to express their ideas. And not all pupils are passive recipients of a dominant ideology. If so how do we explain Bowles and Gintis's views?

Is the correspondence between the workplace and the classroom as close and as necessary as Bowles

and Ginits maintain? Capitalism managed quite well for many years without the help of compulsory state education. Although Bowles and Gintis present a well reasoned argument, their case is far from proven.

Social interaction and social structure

In a study entitled, *Learning to Labour: How Working Class Kids Get Working Class Jobs*, Paul Willis studied a group of 12 working class boys (the 'lads') during their last year and a half at school and their first few months at work. He observed the lads in a number of different situations. He then related this small scale interaction to the wider social structure.

Willis did not find a simple correspondence between school and work. Nor did he find that the lads were shaped by the educational system. Instead the lads rejected school and created their own counter school culture. But, paradoxically, this very rejection of school prepared them for the low skilled, low status jobs they were to take.

The lads rejected educational success as defined by the school. They saw the conformist behaviour of hardworking pupils - the 'ear 'oles' - as a matter for amusement and mockery. School was good for a laugh and not much else. Boredom was relieved by mucking around and breaking rules. The lads actively created a counter school culture based on a fierce opposition to authority (see Activity 7). In some respects this behaviour made sense. They were destined for low skilled jobs so why bother to work hard.

Willis found a number of similarities between the attitudes and behaviour developed by the lads in school and those of the shopfloor at work. Having a laugh was important in both situations as a means of dealing with monotony, boredom and authority. And at work, as at school, a bunch of mates to mess around with and support you in an 'us and them' situation remained important. So like Bowles and Gintis, Willis argues for a correspondence between school and work. But this is not produced by the school - the lads are not the docile, obedient pupils of Bowles and Gintis's study. They have produced the correspondence by their rejection of the school. And in doing so they have prepared themselves for their place in the workforce.

But the lads' culture is not entirely adapted to the requirements of the capitalist workforce. It contains an important, albeit largely hidden, criticism of the dominant ideology of individualism and equality of opportunity. There is an implicit recognition that individual effort does not necessarily bring success, that the meritocratic society does not exist and that collective action is needed to improve the position of the working class. However, this is a long way from recognising the true nature of capitalist exploitation and oppression.

Willis's study is based mainly on 12 boys - a small and unrepresentative sample. The 'lads' are only one of a variety of pupil subcultures found in schools. Despite these·drawbacks, Willis's research is important for its attempt to link structure and action, to link the wider society with the day to day activities of a small number of people.

Activity 7 Learning to Labour

Item A *Opposing authority*

The most basic, obvious and explicit dimension of counter school culture is entrenched, general and personalised opposition to 'authority'.

(In a group discussion on teachers)

Joey: ... they're able to punish us. They're bigger than us, they stand for a bigger establishment than we do, like, we're just little and they stand for bigger things, and you try to get your own back. It's, uh, resenting authority I suppose.

Eddie: The teachers think they're high and mighty 'cos they're teachers, but they're nobody really, they're just ordinary people ain't they?

Bill: Teachers think they're everybody. They are more, they're higher than us, but they think they're a lot higher and they're not.

This opposition involves an apparent inversion of the usual values held up by authority. It is lived out in countless small ways which are special to the school institution, instantly recognised by the teachers, and an almost ritualistic part of the daily fabric of life for the kids.

Adapted from P. Willis *Learning to Labour: How Working Class Kids Get Working Class Jobs*, 1977, pp11-12

Item B *Discrediting qualifications*

The lads reject the idea of qualifications. Since knowledge is opposed, so must qualifications be resisted and discredited. As in other things, the principal means of discrediting formal standards is to 'see behind' them to 'how things really work'. At a certain level, the lads really feel they know better. It is possible to get on without qualifications and school work because what really matters is 'knowing a bit about the world', 'having your head screwed on', and, 'pulling your finger out' when necessary.

Qualifications, to them, seem to be a deflection or displacement of direct activity. They feel that they can always demonstrate any necessary ability 'on the job', and that the doing of a thing is always easier than the account of it, or its representation in an exam, or its formal description seem to imply.

Adapted from P. Willis, ibid, p94

Item C

Questions

1 Look at Item A.
   a) Show how 'the usual values held up by authority' are inverted by a counter school culture.
   b) Suggest reasons for the development of a counter school culture.
2 Read Item B. Why is it important to the lads to reject the idea of qualifications?
3 Is there any evidence in Items A and B which a Marxist might use to suggest that the lads are not completely brainwashed by ruling class ideology? Explain your answer.
4 Explain why the actions in Item C might bring praise and encouragement from the lads.

2.3 Interpretive approaches

Willis's study looked at small scale interaction situations. It attempted to discover the meanings which the lads gave to their actions and to those of others. It tried to show how they constructed their own social reality. In these respects Willis used an interpretive approach.

Interpretive approaches usually focus on small scale interaction. They assume that people interpret the world in terms of meanings which are constructed in interaction situations. They are often critical of structural approaches such as Marxism and functionalism which tend to see behaviour as shaped by the social system.

In terms of education, interpretive approaches often focus on classroom interaction, on the meanings which direct that interaction and the relationships which develop.

Defining others

Symbolic interactionism, one of the main interpretive approaches, emphasises the importance of a socially constructed identity. This identity is shaped in part by people's perception of how others see them. It may become a self-fulfilling prophecy - there is a tendency for people to act in terms of the image of themselves which others project.

Social identities are often constructed rapidly and on the basis of very little evidence. John Beynon examined how boys classified and evaluated each other during their first three months of secondary school. Their classifications included *good kids* (who stood up to teachers), *TPs* (teachers' pets), *bullies*, *dippoes* or *weirds* and *snobs* or *toffees* (1985, pp84-86). On the basis of these and other categories the boys formed friendship groups. Social classifications are important as they define what a person is and what others think about and expect from them.

Labelling A label is the major identifying characteristic of a person. For example, if a pupil is labelled a *troublemaker* then it is likely that all their actions will be interpreted in terms of this label. Thus, even if they are seen to be behaving well, this will be judged as unusual, as out of character.

One of the first studies which tried to uncover the meanings which teachers use to classify pupils was made by the American sociologist Howard Becker (1977). He interviewed 60 Chicago teachers and found they tended to share a picture of the *ideal pupil*. This was used as a benchmark to judge the pupils they taught. The *ideal pupil* was highly motivated, intelligent and well behaved. Pupils judged to be closest to this ideal were likely to come from middle class backgrounds, those furthest from it from lower working class backgrounds. As a result the latter were often labelled as discipline problems, as unmotivated and as unlikely to succeed. These labels may well have a

significant effect on their educational careers. This point is examined in more detail in Part 3 (pp299-301).

Negotiation From an interpretive perspective, meanings and roles are not fixed and given, they are negotiated in interaction situations. David Hargreaves (1975) examined how teachers and pupils negotiate a 'working consensus' in the classroom. Each attempts to define and control classroom interaction. Teachers use a range of tactics to 'get their own way'. They might, for instance, make excessive demands and then compromise - perhaps setting a lengthy homework and agreeing to reduce it in response to their pupils' groans. They offer rewards and punishments - 'if you'll work hard now then I won't set any homework later'. They use cautionary tales of what happened to previous students as warnings to their current pupils. Teachers are in a more powerful position than pupils - they have formal authority which is backed up by sanctions. Nonetheless, pupils have ways of influencing the actions of teachers. For example, they can appeal to justice -'you let 3B off homework' - and try to set one teacher against another - 'Mr ... lets us do this'. Hargreaves argues that the order in classrooms is a negotiated order based on a consensus worked out between teachers and pupils.

Criticisms Interpretive approaches have provided valuable insights by focusing directly on interaction situations. However, it is this very focus which has been criticised. It has been seen as too narrow, looking at classroom interaction in isolation from the rest of society. What about, for example, the distribution of power in society as a whole? Won't this impinge on interaction situations and affect the construction of meanings and the outcome of negotiations?

Many sociologists argue that good sociology should combine a study of both interaction situations and the wider society. In this way it is possible to study both social structure and social action and to examine the relationship between the two.

Summary

1 Functionalist theories see education as playing a positive role in society. It performs valuable functions such as transmitting norms and values and preparing and selecting young people for occupational roles.
2 Marxist approaches see education in a negative light. It helps to support an oppressive system by legitimating the privileges of the rich and powerful and disguising the exploitation of the working classes.
3 Interpretive approaches tend to focus on small scale interaction. They examine the meanings which direct action and the consequences of those meanings for educational careers.

Activity 8   Be Realistic!

The following extract is taken from *The Autobiography of Malcolm X*. Malcolm, a black American, went to school in Lansing, Michigan in the 1940s. In the 1960s he became leader of the Black Muslims and a spokesperson for many black Americans. He was assassinated in 1965.

One day something happened which was to become the first major turning point of my life.

Somehow, I happened to be alone in the classroom with Mr Ostrowski, my English teacher. He was a tall, rather reddish white man and he had a thick mustache. I had gotten some of my best marks under him, and he had always made me feel that he liked me.

I know that he probably meant well in what he happened to advise me that day. I doubt that he meant any harm. It was just in his nature as an American white man. I was one of his top students, one of the school's top students - but all he could see for me was the kind of future ' in your place' that almost all white people see for black people.

He told me, 'Malcolm, you ought to be thinking about a career. Have you been giving it thought?'

Malcolm X

The truth is, I hadn't. I never have figured out why I told him, 'Well, yes, sir, I've been thinking I'd like to be a lawyer.' Lansing certainly had no black lawyers - or doctors either - in those days, to hold up an image I might have aspired to. All I really knew for certain was that a lawyer didn't wash dishes, as I was doing.

Mr Ostrowski looked surprised, I remember, and leaned back in his chair and clasped his hands behind his head. He kind of half smiled and said, 'Malcolm, one of life's first needs is for us to be realistic. Don't misunderstand me, now. We all of us here like you, you know that. But you've got to be realistic about being a nigger. You need to think about something you can be. You're good with your hands - making things. Everybody admires your carpentry shop work. Why don't you plan on carpentry? People like you as a person - you'd get all kinds of work.'

The more I thought afterwards about what he said, the more uneasy it made me. It just kept treading around in my mind.

What made it really begin to disturb me was Mr Ostrowski's advice to others in my class - all of them white. They all reported that Mr Ostrowski had encouraged what they had wanted. Yet nearly none of them had earned marks equal to mine.

It was then that I began to change - inside.

I drew away from white people. I came to class, and I answered when called upon. It became a physical strain simply to sit in Mr Ostrowski's class.

Adapted from *The Autobiography of Malcolm X* 1966, pp 35-37

Questions

1 What effects might Mr Ostrowski's advice have had on Malcolm's educational career?
2 How might a knowledge of the structure of American society add to our understanding of the interaction between Malcolm and Mr Ostrowski?

3 Education and Social Class

Key Issues

1 To what extent does social class affect educational attainment?
2 To what extent are class differences in educational attainment due to what happens inside the school rather than outside

3.1 Social class and educational attainment: the evidence

In Western industrial societies there is general agreement that education should be based on equality of opportunity. Everybody should have an equal chance to develop their talents and abilities to the full regardless of their class, ethnicity, gender and other social characteristics. However, the evidence shows clearly that in terms of educational qualifications people with certain social characteristics are likely to do better than others. This part looks at the relationship between social class and educational attainment.

Evidence from throughout the 20th century indicates that the higher a person's social class, the more likely they are to have a greater number and a higher level of educational qualifications. The following activity looks at some of this evidence.

Activity 9 Class and Qualifications

Item A

Social class and highest qualifications held, 1990-91

Great Britain   Percentages

	Professional	Employers and managers	Intermediate and junior nonmanual	Skilled manual	Semi-skilled manual	Unskilled manual	All
Degree	32	17	17	6	4	3	10
Higher education	19	15	18	10	7	5	11
GCE A level	15	13	12	8	6	4	9
GCSE, grades A-C	19	24	25	21	19	15	21
GCSE, grades D-G	4	9	7	12	12	10	10
Foreign	4	4	4	3	2	2	3
No qualifications	7	19	18	40	50	60	35

This table shows the highest qualification level of those aged 25-59 and not in full time education in terms of their class of origin, ie the social class of their father. GCE A levels and GCSEs include equivalents eg former qualifications such as O levels, Scottish qualifications etc.

Adapted from *Social Trends*, 1994, p52

Questions

1 Summarise the relationship between social class and educational attainment indicated by the above table.
2 What does this suggest about equality of opportunity in education?

General Household Survey Since 1971 the Office of Population Censuses and Surveys has conducted an annual survey of the population of Great Britain known as the General Household Survey. The 1991-92 survey, from which the table in Activity 9 is drawn, was based on interviews with 19,039 people aged 16 and over. The relationship shown in the table between social class and educational attainment reflects the results of General Household Surveys since they began in 1971. In the words of the 1991-92 survey, 'Throughout the period, however, men and women whose fathers belonged to non-manual socioeconomic groups have consistently formed a higher proportion of those gaining higher qualifications than would be expected from their representation in the sample, while those from a manual background were over-represented among the unqualified.' (*General Household Survey 1991*, 1994, p201)

Sociological surveys These findings are mirrored in a range of surveys conducted by sociologists. The results of the more important British surveys are summarised in Activity 3, p279. They show significant class differences in educational attainment (as measured by qualifications). They also show that despite constantly rising educational attainment for *all* social groups, class inequalities remain and have shown no tendency to decline. Reforms such as the move from the tripartite to comprehensive systems may have led to an increase in qualifications in general but they have had little effect on class differences. Given this Anthony Heath concludes, 'In the face of this remarkable resilience of class inequalities, educational reforms seem powerless' (Heath, 1987, p15).

Evidence from the 1990s indicates that the relationship between class and educational attainment remains strong. Jesson and Gray analysed the GCSE results of more than 2,000 pupils in Nottinghamshire in 1992. They found a close relationship between social class and GCSE grades. Children whose parents had professional jobs averaged 5.7 GCSEs with grades A-C, those from clerical backgrounds averaged 2.9 and those from manual backgrounds 1.2 (Denscombe, 1993, p14).

3.2 Explaining class differences

Intelligence and educational attainment

Those who do well in education tend to do well in intelligence tests - they have a high IQ (intelligence quotient). This has led many people to argue that intelligence is a major factor in determining educational attainment.

Heredity There is general agreement that intelligence results from the interaction of genetic and environmental factors. A person's intelligence is due in part to the genes they inherit from their parents, in part to their social environment. Some researchers such as Hans Eysenck (1971) argue that the genetic component (heredity) is the most important. In Eysenck's words, ' What children take out of schools is proportional to what they bring into the schools in terms of IQ'. From this viewpoint it has been argued that class differences in educational attainment largely result from class differences in genetically based IQ.

Environment While not denying the importance of heredity, most sociologists have emphasised environmental factors in explaining IQ differences. A person's score on an IQ test is seen to result mainly from their motivation, knowledge and skills, all of which are learned rather than genetically determined. Motivation, knowledge and skills may vary between social classes. If this is the case then class differences

in educational attainment may be due to differences in class backgrounds rather than class genes.

If there are cultural differences between social classes then this might explain why those in higher social classes tend to score more highly in IQ tests. The tests may be biased in their favour. For example the language used in IQ tests may be closer to middle rather than working class speech.

Many researchers have argued that this is indeed the case (see Activity 2, Item C, p277). Given this argument, comparisons of social groups in terms of IQ are invalid. And it is not therefore possible to explain class differences in educational attainment in terms of 'intelligence'.

Cause or consequence? How can the link between IQ and educational attainment be explained? One explanation states that IQ tests and education are biased in favour of the middle and upper classes, hence members of those classes will tend to do well in both. Intelligence, as such, is not the cause of educational success.

Another argument states that both qualifications and IQ are directly related to length of stay in the educational system. The longer people stay, the more qualifications they get and the more their IQ develops. And middle class students are more likely to stay longer in education than working class students.

Conclusion Most researchers would argue the following. IQ is a result of the interaction of heredity and environment. It is not possible to measure the contribution of each to a person's IQ. It is not possible to produce a 'fair', culture-free IQ test so we cannot compare the IQs of people from different social groups. If it were possible we would probably find that individuals would differ in intelligence but large social groups such as classes, ethnic and gender groups would not. The same range of intelligence would be present in each group. Given this, differences in educational attainment between social groups must be due to factors other than intelligence.

3.3 Material and cultural factors
Material factors

In general, educational attainment rises with family income. Children from well off families are likely to do better than children from low income families. Many researchers have seen material deprivation - a lack of money and the things that money can buy - as a major cause of inequality of educational opportunity.

The costs of education In *Origins and Destinations* (1980) Halsey, Heath and Ridge examined the educational careers of over 8,500 males born between 1913 and 1947. The data was drawn from the Oxford mobility study (see p48) which used three broad social class grouping - the service class, the intermediate class and the working class.

Over three-quarters of the working class left school at the minimum school leaving age while over three-quarters of the service class continued their education. A major reason for this difference was money - the cost to parents of supporting students between the ages of 16 and 18. This denied many working class people the chance of taking higher level courses. Halsey, Heath and Ridge see the lack of maintenance grants for 16-18 year olds as a major obstacle to equality of opportunity in education.

Living conditions Low income usually means a relatively low standard of living in terms of housing, food, clothing and a range of other factors. Living standards may have important effects on educational progress.

In *The Home and the School* (1964) J.W.B.Douglas traced the educational careers through primary school of 5,362 British children born in the first week of March,1946. He divided the sample into two groups - those from families which had sole use of hot water, bathroom and toilet and those which did not have these facilities, or shared them with others. The children living in 'unsatisfactory' conditions scored significantly lower in ability and reading tests than those living in 'satisfactory' conditions. And the differences between the two groups widened with time. Thus an impoverished home environment would seem to have a cumulative effect.

Many reasons have been suggested for the relationship between living standards and educational attainment. For example, poor housing conditions, overcrowding and inadequate diet can lead to ill health. This can lead to absence from school and tiredness and irritability when at school. This is hardly a recipe for educational success.

Cultural factors

Class differences in educational attainment have often been seen as a result of differences in class cultures. For example, a number of studies have argued that the values, attitudes and aspirations of parents have an important effect on their children's education. If these values and attitudes vary between social classes then this may account, at least in part, for class differences in educational attainment.

Parental interest In *The Home and the School* Douglas found that the degree of parents' interest in their children's education was the single most important factor affecting educational progress. His research suggested that in general middle class parents showed more interest than working class parents. They were more likely to visit the school and to encourage their children to continue education beyond the minimum school leaving age.

Douglas measured parental interest in terms of how often parents visited the school and how teachers viewed the parents. There are problems with this. Teachers will probably assess parental interest in terms of number of visits. And this may not be a valid measure of interest. For example, Douglas found the most striking difference was between fathers. Working class fathers seldom visited school to discuss their children's progress. However, this may have more to do with working practices than interest. Manual workers are more likely to work longer hours, shifts and to have more difficulty taking time off work. Also they are less likely to feel at ease in a middle class institution such as a school. Factors such as these, rather than lack of interest, may explain infrequent school visits.

Cultural deprivation theory Findings such as those of Douglas have been used to provide support for what came to be known as *cultural deprivation theory*. This theory states that those at the bottom of the class system are deprived of or deficient in certain values, attitudes and skills which are essential for educational success. These include lack of ambition - neither parents nor children place a sufficiently high value on education which means that children lack motivation and receive little encouragement from parents. Home life is seen to lack the kind of stimulation needed for high attainment - there is an absence of books and educational toys and family outings are unlikely to have an educational component such as visits to museums and art galleries. Those at the bottom of the class structure are sometimes seen as fatalistic - they accept the situation rather than work to improve it - and as less able to defer gratification - put off present pleasures for future rewards. Neither of these approaches will encourage the hard work and sacrifice needed for educational success.

In terms of cultural deprivation theory the child begins school deprived of many of the qualities needed to do well. The effect of this disadvantage is cumulative - it grows as the child moves through the educational system. As a result the attainment differences between the classes get wider.

Cultural deprivation theory has been strongly criticised. Does cultural deprivation actually exist? Are the values and attitudes of those at the bottom of the class system any different from those of the rest of society? Do working class students tend to leave school earlier simply because of lack of parental income rather than lack of parental encouragement? There is evidence that if class differences in culture exist, then they are slight and of little significance.

And they might not exist at all - see the criticisms of the culture of poverty theory, pp182-183.

Material vs cultural factors In *Origins and Destinations* Halsey, Heath and Ridge attempted to measure the effects of material and cultural factors on educational attainment. They found that both material (eg income) and cultural factors (eg parental values) influenced the type of secondary school - grammar or secondary modern - that a boy went to. However, once at secondary school, cultural factors appeared to have little effect on his attainment. Students from working class backgrounds who stayed on after 16 were almost as successful in examinations as those from service class backgrounds. The difference, as noted earlier, was the far higher proportion of service class boys who stayed on. And this was due primarily to *material* factors - service class parents could afford it.

Activity 10   The Odds Are Against Them

Item A

Inner city slums

Questions

1   a) Outline the disadvantages highlighted in Items A, B and C and place them under the headings of either material or cultural factors.

b) Which (material or cultural) do you consider most important? Give reasons for your answer.

2   How might the disadvantages be passed on from generation to generation?

Item B   *Against the odds*

Mandy Rogers (not her real name), 33, lives on a low income east London estate where she grew up in a family of five children. She is a single parent but her son, Carl, four, has contact with his father. A qualified nursery nurse, she is currently living on income support.

'My parents never put enough into our education. They were a loving mum and dad but they didn't see more for you than they had for themselves. My mum was a machinist and my dad a painter and decorator, when he worked. I don't remember having any books at home and I didn't know further education existed until after I left school. I did two O levels when I was 25, which was a big achievement for me, then got into a National Nursery Examination Board course.'

Adapted from *Times Educational Supplement*, 28.1.94, p3

Item C   *Homelessness*

In 1992 local authorities accepted responsibility for 167,000 homeless households, nearly two thirds with dependent children. A report on the effects of homelessness on schoolchildren by Her Majesty's Inspectorate for Schools makes the following points.

Their chances of doing well, say the inspectors, are slim. 'Sustainable achievement is often beyond their reach.' Cramped sleeping conditions leave the children tired, listless and unable to concentrate. In one London school a four year old boy spent a whole day sleeping outside a headteacher's office.

The inspectors found evidence of ill health caused by poor diet and stress from permanent insecurity. For some the crises which lead to homelessness produce social and emotional difficulties.

Weak reading, writing and verbal skills among primary school children are combined with a poor self-image. 'I can't read,' a seven year old girl told her teacher. 'Don't you know I'm simple?'

The report notes that many hostel rooms lack such basics as chairs and tables. As a result, children often find it hard to do homework. A fourth year GCSE pupil had to work on her bed and could only start when the sisters she shared the room with were asleep.

Adapted from *Social Trends*, 1994, p113 and *Times Educational Supplement*, 10.8.90, p5

3.4 The class structure and educational attainment

This section looks at the views of three sociologists on the relationship between social class and educational attainment. Each argues that the class structure systematically generates inequality of educational opportunity.

Raymond Boudon: positional theory

The French sociologist Raymond Boudon (1974) argues that inequality of educational opportunity is inevitable in a class based society. This is simply because people start their educational careers from different positions in the class system. Compare a student from an unskilled working class background, who aims to achieve the educational qualifications needed to become a clerical worker, with a student whose parents are professionals and who wants to become a dentist. The first student is aiming for social promotion and in this sense can be seen as more ambitious than the second student who is simply maintaining his or her position in the class system.

The costs and benefits of aiming for higher level qualifications are different depending on a person's starting point. Students from professional backgrounds are more likely to select higher level educational courses since lack of a university degree may lead to social demotion. But working class students taking a degree course may well move out of their class circumstances losing the security of friends, neighbourhood and a lifestyle they've grown up with. Given the costs and benefits involved, there is greater pressure on students from the higher levels of the class system to select higher level courses. And this, Boudon argues, results in inequality of educational opportunity.

Pierre Bourdieu: cultural capital

The French sociologist Pierre Bourdieu (1977) starts from the idea that there is a 'dominant culture' in society. The higher people's position in the class system, the greater the amount of dominant culture they are likely to have. This culture is generally regarded as superior because those at the top have the power to define it as such. In reality, however, it is no better or worse than any other culture. But because it is highly valued and sought after, it forms the basis of the educational system.

Children born into the middle and upper classes have a built in advantage. Their culture is closer to the culture of the school so they will be more likely to succeed. For example, their language is closer to that of teachers so they are more likely to understand what's being taught and to be rewarded for what they say and write.

According to Bourdieu, the dominant culture can be seen as 'cultural capital' since it can be converted into material reward - high qualifications, high status jobs, high salaries, high living standards.

Bourdieu concludes that the primary purpose of education is cultural and social reproduction. The education system reproduces the dominant culture and in doing so helps to reproduce the class system. And, by creating educational success and failure, it legitimates the positions of those at the top and those at the bottom.

Basil Bernstein: language and class

From 1954 to 1961 Basil Bernstein taught in the East End of London. During this time he became aware that the forms of communication his working class pupils felt most at home with were not those required by the school. Over the next 30 years he developed a wide ranging theory which relates social class, family relationships, forms of social control, speech patterns and educational experience. Only aspects of his work are examined here.

Speech codes   Bernstein identified two forms of speech pattern, the *restricted code* and the *elaborated code*. The restricted code is a kind of shorthand speech, usually found in conversations between people who have a lot in common eg friends and family members. It is often tied to a context eg it cannot be fully understood outside the family circle and its meanings tend to be particularistic, ie specific to the speaker and listener. Sentences are often short, simple and unfinished, detail is omitted, explanations not given and information taken for granted. This is because a considerable amount of shared knowledge between speaker and listener is assumed.

By comparison the elaborated code spells out what the restricted code takes for granted. Meanings are made explicit, explanations provided, details spelt out. As such the elaborated code tends to be context-free (not tied to a context such as a particular friendship group) and its meanings are universalistic (they can be understood by everybody).

Class and speech codes   According to Bernstein, most middle class children have been socialised in both the restricted and elaborated codes and are fluent in each, whereas many working class children are limited to the restricted code. Since teachers use the elaborated code, working class pupils are placed at a distinct disadvantage. They are less likely to understand what teachers say and are more likely to be misunderstood and criticised for what they themselves say.

Bernstein insists that working class speech patterns are not substandard or inadequate. However, he does imply that for certain operations the elaborated code is superior eg detailed descriptions of objects and events; the logical, step by step analysis of relationships between things.

Others have gone much further. Extreme versions of cultural deprivation theory see the speech patterns of those at the bottom of the class system as inferior and inadequate. They are seen as a major cause of educational failure.

Alternative views In a famous article entitled 'The Logic of Nonstandard English' the American linguist William Labov (1973) examined the speech patterns of black children from Harlem in New York. He claimed that their speech patterns were not inferior to standard English, they were simply different. He suggests that more often than not the so-called elaborated code is verbose and longwinded, distorting rather than clarifying. In his words, 'Many middle class speakers qualify and lose their argument in a mass of irrelevant detail ... The average middle class speaker is enmeshed in verbiage, the victim of sociolinguistic factors beyond his control' (1973, pp 34-35).

Activity 11 Talking in Harlem

Item A *Harlem, New York*

Item C *Three interviews*

Interview 1 An eight year old black boy from Harlem is interviewed by a 'friendly' white interviewer who presents him with a toy jet plane and asks him to describe it. The setting is formal. There are long silences followed by short two or three word answers, which hardly provide an adequate description of the plane.

Interview 2 Another black boy from Harlem is interviewed. Again the setting is formal but this time the interviewer is black and raised in Harlem. The boy responds in much the same way as the boy in the first interview.

Interview 3 The boy and the interviewer are the same as in the second interview. This time the interviewer sits on the floor, the boy is provided with a supply of potato crisps and his best friend is invited along. The change is dramatic. The boy's conversation is articulate and enthusiastic, and, in linguistic terms, rich and diverse.

Items B and C adapted from W. Labov '*The Logic of Nonstandard English*', 1973, pp26-33

Item B *It depends on the translation*

This is part of a statement made by Larry, a black American boy from a low income neighbourhood in Harlem. He is arguing that heaven does not exist.

'Cause, you see, doesn't nobody really know that it's a God, y'know, 'cause I mean I have seen black gods, pink gods, white gods, all colour gods, and don't nobody know it's really a God. An' when they be sayin' if you good, you goin' t'heaven, tha's bullshit, 'cause you ain't goin' to no heaven, 'cause it ain't no heaven for you to go to.'

William Labov translates this into standard English as follows.

1 Everyone has a different idea of what God is like.
2 Therefore nobody really knows that God exists.
3 If there is a heaven, it was made by God.
4 If God doesn't exist he couldn't have made heaven.
5 Therefore heaven does not exist.
6 You can't go to somewhere that doesn't exist.

Questions

1 a) Using information from Item B suggest why it has been claimed that black nonstandard English is inferior to standard English.
   b) Is it? Give reasons for your answer.
   c) Assuming no difference between the two forms of English, why is one seen as superior?
2 Read Item C. Explain the differences in the boys' behaviour.
3 How can Items B and C be used to explain class differences in educational attainment?

3.5 Class, educational attainment and schools

Type and quality of school

Do schools make a difference? Are there good schools and bad schools? To what extent are class differences in educational attainment due to what happens inside the school rather than outside? The evidence examined so far in this chapter suggests that the type and quality of school can make a difference to overall attainment levels but will be unlikely to reduce class differences in attainment.

Throughout the 20th century there has been a steady rise in educational attainment as measured by examination results. This has been accompanied by changes in the curriculum, the school leaving age, and types of school eg the move from the tripartite to comprehensive system of secondary education. But, as Anthony Heath's summary of the main surveys of social class and educational attainment shows, class inequalities 'seem to reappear in a new guise but fundamentally unchanged as the educational environment changes around them' (1987, p15; see Activity 3, p279). So although more people are doing better, the gap between the classes remains.

Part of this overall improvement may be due to schools. The 'alternative school league table' (see Activity 6, p286) suggests that they can make a real difference. It indicates that schools with similar social class intakes can vary considerably in terms of examination results.

What makes the difference? A research team led by Michael Rutter (1979) examined 12 inner London secondary schools. It found that schools only a few miles apart and taking children from similar social backgrounds produced very different results. Those with the best results were well organised with an emphasis on academic achievement. Teachers were dedicated and well prepared for lessons. Praise and encouragement were emphasised rather than criticism and punishment.

A four year survey of 2,000 children aged 7-11 in 50 London primary schools found that children of similar class, ethnicity and gender were more successful in some schools than others. 'Success' was measured in terms of reading and mathematics scores. The more successful schools had a number of factors in common. These included: purposeful leadership by the head; teachers having a major role in planning the school curriculum; consistency of teaching styles; challenging and stimulating teaching; a structured school day; a businesslike atmosphere in the classroom; an emphasis on praise and reward rather than criticism and punishment (Inner London Education Authority,1986).

The evidence suggests that schools can make a difference. They can improve the attainment levels of pupils in general. However even the best schools do not appear to remove class differences in attainment.

Classroom interaction

Part 2 looked at interpretive approaches which see education as directed by meanings and definitions which are negotiated in schools. From this perspective class differences in educational attainment are socially constructed in the classroom.

Labelling theory Pupils are constantly being assessed and classified. On the basis of this they are defined as able or less able, placed in particular sets or streams, entered for particular examinations and given or denied access to certain parts of the school curriculum. As Part 2 indicated, teachers are more likely to define middle rather than working class pupils as 'able', 'good students' and 'well behaved'. This may well disadvantage working class pupils.

A label is a major identifying characteristic. If, for example, a pupil is labelled as 'bright', others will respond to her and interpret her actions in terms of this label. There is a tendency for a self-fulfilling prophecy to result. The pupil will act in terms of the label and see herself as bright (so fulfilling the prophecy others have made).

Teacher expectations A famous study by Rosenthal and Jacobson (1968) examined the effects of teachers' definitions of pupils. They told teachers in an elementary school in California that they had identified a number of pupils - the 'spurters' - as likely to make rapid progress. Unknown to the teachers, these children had been selected at random. Yet, a year later, the spurters did indeed make greater progress than their classmates. Since there was no evidence that these pupils as a group were any different from others in the school, Rosenthal and Jacobson concluded that their progress was due to the way they were defined. In particular, teachers expected more from them, conveyed their expectation to them and they acted in terms of it. The result was a self-fulfilling prophecy.

Evaluation Rosenthal and Jacobson's study has been extremely influential. However their methodology has been questioned - for example the IQ tests they used have been dismissed as substandard and badly administered. Attempts to replicate (repeat) their research have produced mixed results with some suggesting that labelling was of little or no significance. However, many researchers argue that labelling is important, that the self-fulfilling prophecy is real, that it can help to explain class differences in educational attainment.

Later studies suggest that the picture is more

complicated than that provided by early research. David Hargreaves (1975) argues that whether or not a label 'sticks' - is accepted by the pupil - depends on a number of factors. These include: 1) how often the pupil is labelled 2) whether the pupil sees the teacher as someone whose opinion counts 3) the extent to which others support the label and 4) the context in which the labelling takes place, eg in public or private.

Research has also indicated that some types of label are more readily accepted than others. Bird (1980) found that pupils were more likely to accept 'academic labels' (referring to academic ability) than 'behavioural labels' (referring to conduct). She notes that consistent behavioural labelling is less likely in large secondary schools. In such schools a teacher may see up to three hundred pupils in one week and a pupil may be taught by up to fifteen teachers. The time for teachers to establish labels is limited as is the likelihood of them all applying the same labels. Different teachers have different interpretations of acceptable and unacceptable behaviour. Thus, a pupil who behaves consistently may be told off for misbehaving by one teacher but not another.

Setting and streaming

Most secondary schools have some system for placing pupils in teaching groups in terms of their perceived ability. These groups include *sets* in which pupils are placed in subject groups (they may be in set 1 for maths, set 3 for art) or *streams* in which they are placed into class groups (class 1,2,3) and taught at that level for all subjects.

A number of studies (eg Hargreaves 1967, Lacey 1970) have looked at the effects of ability grouping in secondary schools. In general they have found the following. There is a tendency for middle class pupils to be placed in the higher groups and for working class pupils to be placed in the lower groups. The 'ability gap' between these groups is likely to widen from year 7 to year 11. Most teachers prefer to teach higher ability groups. The conduct of pupils in higher groups is likely to be better than of those in lower groups. Those in lower groups will tend to develop an *anti-school subculture* in which breaking school rules is highly regarded by some pupils. Teachers spend more time controlling behaviour in these groups at the expense of teaching. They expect less from these pupils, deny them access to higher level knowledge and skills and place them in lower level examination tiers. The net result of setting and streaming is to advantage those in the higher groups and disadvantage those in the lower groups.

The summary in the previous paragraph contains broad generalisations. A study by Meyenn (1980) of girls' friendship groups warns against this. There were groups of girls who were quiet, well behaved, caused no trouble, said they were happy at school yet showed absolutely no interest in academic work and accepted their position in the lowest ability groups. On the other hand, some groups of girls who were much more successful academically were strongly opposed to certain school rules and enjoyed 'messing about' and 'causing trouble'.

Although research such as this indicates that the picture is more complicated than earlier studies suggest, most researchers would agree that the effect of ability grouping for those in the lowest groups is negative. In view of this, the apparent move away from 'mixed-ability' teaching is a cause for concern. As indicated in Activity 6 (p286) the advent of the National Curriculum appears to have led to an increase in setting.

Conclusion

This section has looked at social class and educational attainment in terms of what happens within the school. Some researchers, particularly those who take an interpretive approach, argue that class differences in attainment are socially constructed. They result simply from the sifting, sorting and assessment of pupils in terms of teachers' perceptions of social class, ability and conduct. Others argue that class differences in attainment are primarily due to what happens outside the school - to the social inequalities generated by the class structure. Schools from this point of view do little more than reflect and rubber stamp existing inequalities.

Other researchers see class differences in attainment resulting from a combination of what happens inside and outside the school. From this viewpoint the inequalities of the class system are reinforced by interaction in the classroom.

Summary

1 There are significant social class differences in educational attainment.
2 Despite an overall increase in educational attainment during the 20th century, class differences in attainment remain.
3 Some argue that equality of educational opportunity is not possible in a class structured society. There are two main views: 1) schools are powerless to reduce class differences in attainment given the social inequalities pupils bring into the classroom; 2) schools reflect the wider society, they are concerned with social and cultural reproduction so maintaining existing inequalities.
4 Some argue that class differences in attainment are socially constructed within schools. They result from the meanings which direct interaction in the classroom.

Activity 12 Class in the Classroom

Item A *Social class and streaming*

Stream	Nonmanual and skilled manual	Semi-skilled manual	Unskilled manual	No father or father unemployed	Not classified
A	62	17	16	4	1
C	53	13	22	10	2
E	48	13	12	22	5
All	53	17	19	9	2

Percentages

This table is taken from Hargeaves's study of a secondary modern boys school in a predominantly working class area. It shows the percentage of boys in years 1 to 4 from different class backgrounds in the top stream (A), middle stream (C) and bottom stream (E). Less than 6% of the boys' fathers had nonmanual occupations.

Adapted from D.H. Hargeaves *Social Relations in a Secondary School*, 1967, p 142

Item B *The 'ideal' pupil*

Teachers tend to use class differences in classifying their pupils and such differences lead to variations from the image of the 'ideal' pupil held by teachers. Children of the lowest group, from slum areas, are characterised as the most difficult to teach successfully, lacking in interest in school, learning ability and outside training. They are seen as not having the right kind of study habits or being able to apply themselves as well as other pupils.

In definite contrast are the terms used to describe children of the upper groups: 'In a neighbourhood like this there's something about the children, you just feel you're accomplishing so much more. The children know what you're talking about and they think about it.'

In the lower class school a major part of the teacher's time must be devoted to discipline. This emphasis on discipline detracts from the school's primary function of teaching, thus discriminating in terms of available educational opportunity, against the children of these schools.

Adapted from H. S. Becker 'Social Class Variations in the Teacher-Pupil Relationship', in B. R. Cosin et al *School and Society: A Reader*, 1977, pp108-110

Questions

1 a) Summarise the relationship between social class and streaming indicated by Item A.

   b) How might this lead to class differences in educational attainment?

2 a) Read Item B. Suggest how the teaching experienced by pupils in higher streams will differ from that experienced by those in lower streams.

   b) How might this lead to class differences in educational attainment?

3 How might the attitudes of teachers illustrated in Item B influence the educational attainment of children from different class backgrounds?

4 Gender and Education

Key Issues

1 Do males and females have equal opportunities in the educational system?

2 Do schools and colleges reinforce traditional views of gender?

Gender has always been an issue in education. Should both sexes take the same subjects, do they have the same aptitudes and abilities? Things have come a long way since the London examination board finally allowed women to sit examinations in the late 19th century. Despite this breakthrough, women had to be chaperoned in case the strain was too great and buckets of cold water were available if they fainted. Rumour has it that only one bucketful was ever used. Today the chaperones and buckets have gone but issues about gender and education are far from resolved.

Concerns have changed since the 19th century when a major priority was simply getting girls into schools. After the 1944 Education Act, with its commitment to free and equal education for all, concern focused on gender differences in the curriculum and in examination results. More recently there is a concern with what many see as discrimination against girls throughout the educational system. To feminists this is a reflection of the patriarchal nature of modern industrial society.

4.1 Educating women

The curriculum

The school curriculum for girls and boys has become increasingly similar. However, where choice is available, there is still a tendency for girls to choose some subjects and boys others.

State education, introduced in 1870 and made compulsory up to the age of 10 in 1880, provided the mass of the population with a basic education in reading, writing and arithmetic. However there were important gender differences in the curriculum with a strong emphasis on domestic subjects for girls. Writing in 1897 Christine Bremner states, 'the sight of small girls of eleven or even younger learning cookery, housewifery and laundry work is becoming common, as if little girls could not be too early pressed into a narrow mould' (quoted in Perkin, 1993, p49).

The development of secondary education usually meant single sex schools and gender specific subjects. The 1902 Education Act made domestic subjects such as cookery and needlework compulsory for girls but not for boys.

During the 20th century the school curriculum for boys and girls has become increasingly similar. The introduction of the National Curriculum in 1988 accelerated this process. For most of their time in primary and secondary schools pupils in the state system follow a common curriculum. The tradition of girls doing home economics and boys woodwork and metalwork has been largely replaced by technology for all pupils. Science, traditionally seen as a 'male' subject, is now taken by all pupils from age 5-16. However, where subject choice exists, eg at A level and degree level, there are still significant differences in the choices made by males and females.

Activity 13 Gender and the Curriculum

Item A *School rules*

Rules of the Haslingfield National School - Girls, 1880

The Mistress is required, in secular instruction, to teach the Girls Reading, Writing, Spelling, English Grammar, Tables, Arithmetic, General History and Geography, and such subjects of useful knowledge as may from time to time be directed by the Trustees; in Religious Instruction, Bible Reading and Bible History, Articles of the Church of England and general knowledge of the Liturgy.

The Mistress is required to teach the Girls every kind of plain Needlework, Marking, Stocking and Plain Knitting, Stocking Darning. The afternoon of each day is allowed for Needlework.

Quoted in R.G.Burgess *Education, Schools and Schooling*, 1985, pp14-15

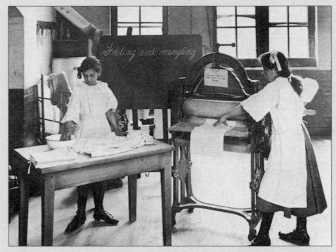

Girls at school learning to do the laundry, 1908. The girl on the right is using a mangle to get water out of the clothes.

A girl and boy in a technology class in the 1990s

Item B *The National Curriculum*

Your child will be taught the subjects he or she must study under the National Curriculum. These are English, maths, science, technology, a foreign language in secondary schools, history, geography, art, music and PE. History, geography, art and music are not compulsory after the age of 14. But your child must be given religious education unless you decide otherwise.

From Department for Education *Our Children's Future*, 1994, pp15-16

Item C

Students in Higher Education (thousands), 1990-91

Subject group	Male	Female
Medicine & Dentistry	16.2	13.8
Agriculture	6.3	4.7
Physical Science	34.3	15.4
Mathematical Science	47.0	17.7
Engineering & Technology	123.4	13.6
Social Sciences	53.1	61.1
Business & Financial	112.1	101.7
Languages	16.7	39.5
Creative arts	23.0	31.8
Education	20.6	49.7
All subjects	588.1	491.2

Adapted from *Annual Abstract of Statistics*, 1994, p95

Questions

1 a) Briefly outline the differences in terms of gender and the curriculum between Items A and B.
   b) Do you think this is a change for the better? Give reasons for your answer.
2 a) Summarise the main differences in subject choice between men and women shown in Item C.
   b) Do these differences matter? Give reasons for your answer.
   c) In view of Item B, do you think the differences will continue? Explain your answer.

Differential access and discrimination

There are many examples from the history of education of open and direct discrimination against female students. Women have been barred from educational courses, examinations and institutions.

Before 1877 no British university accepted female students and no examining body would grant a degree to women. Oxbridge (the universities of Oxford and Cambridge) held out until well into the 20th century. No woman had the right to attend lectures - it was left to the discretion of lecturers. Nor were they awarded full degrees - they were given 'certificates of degrees' and not allowed to put letters after their names. Not until 1920 (Oxford) and 1947 (Cambridge) were women admitted to full membership of these universities (Perkin, 1993, p43).

Less obvious - it was not made public - was the systematic discrimination against girls following the 1944 Education Act. Selection for secondary schools within the tripartite system was based on the 11 plus exam. On average girls achieved higher scores than boys which would result in them having more grammar school places. To 'rectify' this 'imbalance' girls' scores were 'weighted' to ensure that equal numbers of boys and girls went to grammar school. In this way boys got more places than they merited on the basis of 11 plus results (Skelton, 1993, p329).

Many of the more obvious forms of gender discrimination have disappeared from schools. However some researchers argue that girls still face widespread discrimination and this helps to explain their under-representation in higher education. These views will be examined shortly.

Differential attainment

The history of gender differences in educational attainment is of girls catching up and in many cases surpassing boys. If present trends continue then females will be the dominant gender in education. Their credentials will be higher at every level of the educational system.

Most of the research on gender differences in educational attainment has been concerned with explaining why males have traditionally done better than females at A level and degree level. If present trends continue then this concern will be reversed.

4.2 Explaining gender differences

Why have women been barred from certain areas of education? Why has there been a different curriculum for males and females? Why are there gender differences in attainment and choice of subjects and courses?

Biological explanations

Explanations based on biology have sometimes been used to explain supposed gender differences in aptitude and ability. For example, in the early 19th century it was (wrongly) claimed that women's brains were smaller than men's and as a result women were incapable of intellectual study.

More recently it has been claimed that because girls mature earlier than boys, they do better in the earlier years of education. This argument was used to explain why girls did better than boys in the 11 plus exam yet were later overtaken by boys at 16 plus. However it fails to explain why girls are now overtaking boys at 16-18 and rapidly catching them up at degree level.

Today there is little support for biological explanations.

Activity 14 Gender and Educational Attainment

Item A
Highest qualification attained by school leavers: by sex

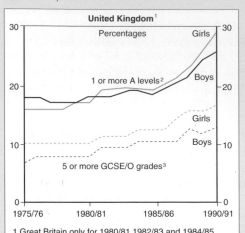

1 Great Britain only for 1980/81,1982/83 and 1984/85
2 Or 1 or more H grades
3 Includes GSCE/O grades A-C and CSE grade 1.

From *Social Trends*, 1994, p50

Item B
School leavers with no GCSE or equivalent qualifications

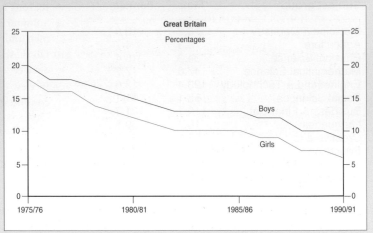

From *Social Trends*, 1994, p43

Item C

Full time students in higher education: by sex and type of establishment

United Kingdom   Thousands

	Males					Females				
	1970 /71	1975 /76	1980 /81	1985 /86	1991 /92	1970 /71	1975 /76	1980 /81	1985 /86	1991 /92
Universities										
Undergraduates	134	141	157	148	178	59	77	101	108	150
Postgraduates	33	37	34	37	46	10	13	15	17	28
Other[1]										
Undergraduates	107	123	120	146	207	114	123	95	129	211
Postgraduates	}		{ 7	7	11	}		{ 6	7	12
All full-time students	274	301	318	339	442	182	214	217	261	400

[1] Polytechnics and other Higher Education establishments

From *Social Trends*, 1994, p47

Questions

1 Briefly outline the trends shown in Items A, B and C.
2 How do you think men might respond if women overtook them at every level in the educational system?

Patriarchal ideology

Patriarchal ideology supports and justifies male dominance. More obviously in the 19th century and less obviously in the later years of the 20th century, patriarchal ideology has been an obstacle in the path of women's educational progress. It has used a range of rationalisations and justifications to limit women's opportunities. These include:

1 Women are inferior intellectually. This is due to genetic factors.
2 A woman's place is in the home. Education is therefore less important for women.
3 A woman's feminine nature is not suited to the 'evils of competition' which education involves. If women did compete they might lose their femininity.
4 The above arguments were often backed up by

reference to God and the Bible. In the words of Queen Victoria, 'Let a woman be what God intended, a helpmate for man but with totally different duties'.

From a feminist viewpoint, patriarchal ideology is a set of myths created by men to maintain power over women. Men wish to retain their dominance in the home and workplace. They see educated women as a threat to their jobs and the stability of their home life. This is based in part on the assumption that 'too much thinking interferes with the punctual discharge of household duties' (*The Englishwoman,* November 1919, quoted in Oakley, 1974, p84). Patriarchal ideology has kept many women out of universities, prevented many from continuing their education beyond the minimum school leaving age and steered many on to lower level courses, often with a domestic or 'caring' component. In this way women are prepared for their role as second class citizens, as housewives, and for their position in the lower levels of the labour force.

Attitudes and expectations

There is considerable evidence that girls' socialisation often does little to encourage educational progress. Sue Sharpe's study of working class girls in London (*Just Like a Girl,* 1976) showed that girls' priorities were marriage and family life rather than jobs and careers. She found that most girls held very traditional ideas about womanhood:

'They see many of their friends and relatives doing jobs from which they seem to gain minimal enjoyment. It therefore makes sense to make their priorities love, marriage, husbands, children, jobs and careers, more or less in that order...

Many girls' lives follow a similar pattern - boredom with school, early leaving into a local job that has marginal interest, finding a steady boyfriend, saving up to marry, settling down and having a family. Marriage and home-making appear as a meaningful distraction or welcome release for those with boring jobs or those who have no intention of making work a central part of their lives.' (1976, pp128-129)

The girls' attitudes to work reflected the general view of women's occupational roles. Office work was the most popular choice followed by a group of occupations which included teachers, nurses, bank clerks and shop assistants. Many of the chosen jobs did not require A levels. As a result many girls saw little point in continuing their education beyond the age of sixteen.

Following on from Sharpe's research, Sue Lees' study *Losing Out* (1986) examined girls' attitudes and expectations. Lees' research was carried out in three London comprehensive schools and involved interviews and group discussions with about a hundred 15-16 year old girls from various class and ethnic groups.

In spite of a greater emphasis on careers than indicated by Sharpe's earlier research, the girls still seemed to be reconciled to a life centred on domesticity, marriage and restricted job opportunities. Even those who hoped to enter professional occupations tended to see their future identities in terms of their relations to men. Many of the girls were already participating in their future roles of domestic labourers. They were helping their mothers with housework often to the detriment of school work:

'I don't mind 'cos my mum can't do it all herself. I've got my homework to do and half the time I can't do it. You wanna do your homework and you wanna help your mum, like you're sitting down doing your homework and your mum says, "Josie, can you do a job for me?"'(1986, p132).

Activity 15 Education for Girls

Item A *Don't go too far!*
In 1858 Dorothea Beale became principal of Cheltenham Ladies College. In 1895 she recalled some of the comments made to her during her career, 'Girls will be turned into boys if they attend the college.' 'I have not learned fractions, my governess told me they were not necessary for girls.'

'My dear lady, if my daughters were going to be bankers it would be very well to teach arithmetic as you do, but really there is no need.' 'It is all very well for my daughter to read Shakespeare, but don't you think it is more important for her to be able to sit down at a piano and amuse her friends?'

Quoted in P. Sauvain *British Economic and Social History,* 1987, p315

Item B
A step too far?

'A lady B.A. of London University' in 1885, a contemporary print by A.Hopkins

Item C *Social acceptability*

They (my parents) obviously could not see any great advantage in my staying at school, and they were having a struggle keeping my brother at the University. Had I been a boy any thought of my leaving school would have been discouraged immediately. I would have been told I must make a career for myself. I must get better qualifications. And I would have been easily persuaded.

This sort of thing is continually happening to girls. During their whole school career their parents and friends expect less of them. They do not expect them to plan for a great career. Education is something to make them a more socially acceptable person, and a career or job is something they pursue between leaving school and getting married.

Girls are encouraged to do 'suitable' subjects at school, socially acceptable subjects. Girls are encouraged to do lady-like subjects, suitable subjects like English, history and languages, but not the sciences or mathematics which are considered more difficult and more manly subjects.

Adapted from J.Nicholson *What Society Does to Girls*, 1977, p24

Questions

1 How can the comments in Item A be seen as aspects of patriarchal ideology?

2 Comment on the portrayal of the woman in Item B.

3 a) What expectations for a girl's future are given in Item C?

   b) What effect might they have on educational progress?

4.3 Gender in the classroom

A girl interviewed by Sue Lees complained, 'Girls get much less attention than boys 'cos boys make a fuss and make themselves noticed - they wanna be noticed so they make a racket' (1986, p129). This complaint finds support from a number of studies.

Dale Spender: invisible women

In *Invisible Women: The Schooling Scandal* (1983), Dale Spender argues that schools reinforce gender inequality in the wider society. Social relations in the classroom, the content of the curriculum, the attitudes and expectations of teachers, all prepare girls for male domination and control.

Spender tape recorded lessons given by herself and other teachers. Boys received over 60% of teachers' time - 62% in her case even though she tried to divide her time equally between boys and girls. Compared to boys, girls were 'invisible'. They tended to blend into the background, a strategy encouraged by the fact that boys often poked fun at their contributions to lessons. And teachers usually allowed boys to get away with insulting and abusive comments to girls.

There was evidence of double standards in the classroom. When boys questioned or challenged a teacher they were often met with respect and a serious response whereas girls tended to be rebuked or fobbed off. Spender found that boys' and girls' written work was judged by different standards. When she asked teachers to mark essays and projects, the same work got better marks when the teachers were told it was written by boys. This finding is supported by research by Goddard-Spear (1989). She gave science teachers some work to grade. Half the teachers believed that they were marking girls' work and the other half boys' work. When teachers believed they were marking boys' work they gave higher ratings for scientific accuracy and organisation of ideas than to identical work they believed was done by girls.

Spender concluded that in mixed education, the dice were loaded against girls. If they behaved as boisterously as boys they were considered 'unladylike', if they were docile and quiet they were usually ignored. She argues that mixed schools are essentially male schools which females have been allowed to enter and that discrimination is so deeply embedded that single-sex schools are the only answer.

Michelle Stanworth: classroom interaction

Stanworth's study (1983) is based on interviews with A level students and teachers of humanities subjects in a college of further education. She found that teachers gave more time and attention to boys and expected more from them. Teachers - both male and female - were more likely to know boys' names and expressed more concern and interest in boys. And it was boys rather than girls who were expected to do well in exams and the job market. Teachers' views were echoed by their pupils. Both boys and girls, when asked to rank their classes in order of ability, tended to upgrade boys and downgrade girls.

Stanworth concludes that girls' experience in the classroom places them at a disadvantage compared to boys. And it encourages them to accept their position as the second place gender in later life. In Stanworth's words, 'Girls may follow the same curriculum as boys - may sit side by side with boys in classes taught by the same teachers - and yet emerge from school with the implicit understanding that the world is a man's world, in which women take second place' (1983, p58).

Jane French: classroom and society

Some studies imply that if only teachers got rid of their sexist attitudes then everything would be alright.

Boys and girls would then be treated equally. But classroom interaction is a two-way process. It is not simply teacher led.

Jane French (1986) argues that pupils bring their own behaviour patterns to the classroom, patterns which differ for boys and girls. Basing her research on video recordings of children in infant schools, French found that boys were more mobile and active, they were more disruptive and demanded more attention. Although girls were eager and interested, they were more likely to obey rules eg raising their hands and waiting for permission to speak. Simply because their behaviour was more problematic, boys got more attention.

As children get older they become more aware of how to manipulate situations. In some top junior classes 4 or 5 boys tended to dominate lessons. And the same applies to secondary school. 'In a series of science lessons which I recorded and analysed, enthusiastic boys had to be quashed and girls almost forced to participate' (1986, p406).

French argues that although boys do get more attention from teachers, 'it is not simply *because* they are boys'. It is partly because of the way both boys and girls behave and this behaviour is shaped by the wider society. In French's view, 'the most determined action taken within the school cannot effectively counter the influence of peer group, magazines, television and family' (1986, p406).

Evaluation

Studies of classroom interaction have provided interesting and important insights. As with all research, however, there are problems of method. For example, Spender has been criticised for not spelling out her methods of data collection. This prevents replication of her study. Stanworth's research was based on interviews rather than direct observation of classroom interaction. What people say in interviews does not necessarily reflect what they do.

Despite these criticisms, the weight of evidence suggests that sexism is rife in the classroom. In view of this, there is a case for schools adopting rigorous anti-sexist policies.

Summary

1 The school curriculum has become increasingly similar for boys and girls.

2 Where students are allowed to choose subjects and courses, gender differences remain.

3 In terms of educational attainment women are rapidly catching up and in most cases surpassing men.

4 Despite changes, many girls' education is limited by traditional expectations of becoming a housewife and mother.

5 Classroom interaction reflects the sexist attitudes and male dominance of the wider society.

Activity 16 Sexism and Education

Item A *Chemistry*

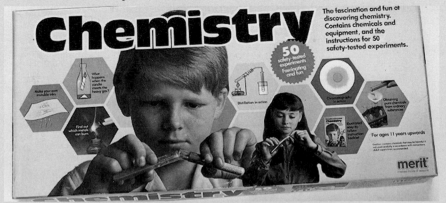

Item B *If you were boys...*

I had another teacher like that at my old school actually. It was really annoying. He kept saying things like - it was in Physics - and he said, 'Now if you were boys you would understand this'. God, ugh! It really annoys me.

A further education student quoted in M.Stanworth *Gender and Schooling*, 1983, p 41

Item C *It's a boys' subject*

A great many Physics and Chemistry textbooks (especially those intended for younger or less able students) refer to the student exclusively as 'he' and reinforce the masculinity of the subject through the pictures they use. For example one Chemistry textbook has a brightly coloured photograph on the front cover of a boy doing an experiment, and a girl standing behind him recording the results.

Adapted from R.G.Burgess *Education, Schools and Schooling*, 1985, pp 155-156

Item D An anti-sexist policy

The jumble of girls and boys playing together on the toy train in Hanover School playground reflects the general harmony between the sexes which deputy Christine Cosker believes has been achieved by a rigorous anti-sexism policy.

Her previous school in Wandsworth, south London, had a very different atmosphere, she said. There the boys were often more aggressive and were less likely to be encouraged to drift away from the Lego to play in the home area.

She admits her present school, in Islington, north London, has a better head start when it comes to introducing a non-sexism policy. Many of the children come from middle class homes where sexual stereotyping is less likely to be encouraged, the staff at Hanover are all committed to the policy and the head is a woman.

Christine Cosker says, 'When boys first come to school they have ideas based upon what they are taught at home, television advertising and other outside influences. But by having a school policy that gives both boys and girls positive role models, by giving children the opportunity to do a whole variety of tasks and games and by encouraging boys and girls to play together we create a positive relationship between the sexes.'

Adapted from *Times Educational Supplement*, 17.4. 92, p6

Questions

1 What do Items A, B and C 'say' about gender and science?

2 Read Item D. While applauding such policies, some people see them as wishful thinking.
   a) Why do they see them like this?
   b) Do you agree? Give reasons for your answer.

5 Ethnicity and Education

Key Issues

1 How reliable is the evidence for ethnic differences in educational attainment?

2 How useful are the theories claiming to explain ethnic differences in educational attainment?

5.1 Ethnicity and educational attainment

Department for Education statistics on examination results identify gender groups but not ethnic groups. For information on ethnicity and educational attainment we must rely on Labour Force Surveys, one-off government reports and surveys conducted by local education authorities, research organisations and individual researchers. These surveys are difficult to compare as they often differ in terms of time, place, sample size, ethnic classification and type and level of examination or qualification.

Activity 17 looks at two sets of statistics. The first (Item A) is taken from the Swann Report, the report of a committee appointed by the government to examine the education of ethnic minorities. The 1978/79 figures are for school leavers in the 6 local education authorities (LEAs) with the highest proportion of ethnic minority children (about half of all leavers were of Asian or Afro-Caribbean origin). The survey was repeated in 1981/82 for 5 of the original 6 LEAs. The second set of statistics (Item B) is from Labour Force Survey data. Instead of dealing with school leavers in the year they left school, it looks at age groups, in this case the 16-24 age group.

Activity 17 Statistics

Item A O level and CSE achievement (percentages)

	Asians		Afro-Caribbeans		All other leavers		Total school leavers from five LEAs		All maintained schools in England	
	1978/79	1981/82	1978/79	1981/82	1978/79	1981/82	1978/79	1981/82	1978/79	1981/82
No graded results (including those who took no exams)	20	19	17	19	22	19	21	19	14	11
At least 1 graded result but less than 5 higher graded results	63	64	80	75	62	62	64	63	66	66
5 or more higher graded results	17	17	3	6	16	19	15	18	21	23
Total leavers (nos)	466	571	718	653	5,012	4,718	6,196	5,942	693,840	706,690

Higher grades are grades A-C at O level and grade 1 at CSE. A grade 1 at CSE was seen as equivalent to a grade C at O level.

Adapted from Department of Education and Science, *Education for All*, 1985, p114

Item B

Highest qualification by ethnic group, 16-24 age group, 1988-90

(percentages)

	All Origins	White	Total ethnic minority	Afro-Caribbeans	African Asian	Indian	Pakistani	Banglad-eshi	Chinese	African	Other/Mixed
All persons (16-24)											
GCE A level/equivalent or higher	33	33	30	30	41	36	18	5	44	40	28
Of which: Degree/equivalent	4	4	5	1	13	6	2	2	12	5	7
Higher education below degree level	3	3	2	2	2	3	1	0	9	4	3
GCE A level/equivalent	26	26	22	26	26	27	15	3	24	30	18
Of which:											
BTEC (general)/ONC/OND	5	5	6	5	7	7	4	0	6	16	5
City & Guilds	10	10	7	12	7	8	4	0	4	7	4
GCE A level or equivalent	9	9	9	8	11	12	7	3	13	6	9
Trade apprenticeship	2	3	1	1	1	1	0	0	0	1	0
GCE O level/equivalent	30	30	25	28	20	25	18	16	31	30	31
CSE (not grade 1)	13	13	12	17	14	10	9	13	3	3	13
Other	3	3	5	3	7	5	5	10	5	8	6
None	21	20	27	21	18	22	48	54	15	7	20
(Never received any education)	0	0	2	0	1	0	8	5	0	2	0
Not stated/not known	1	1	2	2	0	2	3	1	2	2	2

Labour Force Surveys (Great Britain) 1988, 1989, 1990 in T. Jones *Britain's Ethnic Minorities* 1993, p49

Questions

1 a) Briefly summarise the relationship between ethnicity and educational attainment suggested by Items A and B.
   b) What other information would be useful in order to measure the strength of this relationship?
2 Why is direct comparison of Items A and B difficult?

Interpreting the evidence

The statistics presented in Activity 17 look at only two variables, ethnicity and educational attainment. It cannot be assumed that ethnicity is the cause of the variation in levels of educational attainment. Part or all of this variation may be due to other factors such as social class. The relationship between class, ethnicity and educational attainment will be examined in the following section.

It is not possible from the statistics in Activity 17 to discover whether members of certain ethnic groups have been barred from taking certain examinations because of their ethnicity. There is evidence to support this possibility. *Set to Fail* (Commission for Racial Equality, 1992), a study of a comprehensive school in northern England, found that Asian pupils of similar ability to whites were less likely to be entered for GCSEs.

Statistics on school leavers and their examination results are a snapshot at one point in time. As such they can be misleading. People may 'catch up' - improve and add to their qualifications after leaving school. There is evidence that ethnic minorities are more likely to do this. For example in 1988-90, 56% of ethnic minority 16-19 year olds were in full time education compared with 37% of whites (T. Jones, 1993, p44).

5.2 Class, ethnicity and educational attainment

The statistics in the Swann Report (Activity 17, Item A) are drawn from local authorities with a high ethnic concentration. The class position of Asians and Afro-Caribbeans living in these areas is likely to be lower than those living in largely white areas. Because of this we would expect the Swann Report to underestimate the educational attainment of both ethnic groups.

The Swann Committee was particularly concerned with the so-called 'underachievement' of Afro-Caribbean students. It estimated that when social class was taken into account the degree of 'underachievement' was reduced by 'around 50% and very possibly more'.

Class and ethnicity

In *The School Effect* (1989) David Smith and Sally Tomlinson followed the educational careers of over

2,400 children from the age of 11 to 16 in 18 multi-ethnic comprehensives. They found that ethnic group membership did not influence whether or not a pupil was entered for a non-examination course, a CSE course or an O level course. This depended mainly on attainment in school tests and to a lesser, but significant extent, on social class. Thus middle class children with a certain reading score were more likely to be placed on higher level courses than working class children with the same score. Ethnicity, as such, does not appear to influence set placement

and exam entry.

Children from ethnic minority groups do, however, tend to be allocated to lower level courses. However this is because on average their attainment in school tests was lower and they were more likely to belong to lower social classes. Smith and Tomlinson conclude that in terms of examination results the differences between ethnic groups 'are small'. By comparison, the differences between classes are large. The table in Activity 18 summarises some of their findings.

Activity 18   Class and Ethnicity

Item A

Number of higher grade passes at CSE and O level, by country of origin, sex and socioeconomic group (percentages and means)

	Base[2]	None	1-2	3-4	5 or more	Mean
Total	2,426	58	22	10	10	1.31
Country of origin [1]						
UK/Eire	1452	57	21	10	11	1.40
South Asian	664	59	23	8	10	1.18
West Indies	146	56	25	11	8	1.14
Mixed or other	136	59	24	9	9	1.23
Not known	28	64	21	4	11	0.89
Sex						
Male	992	59	21	9	11	1.30
Female	857	51	24	12	12	1.56
Family's socioeconomic group						
All of whom socio-economic group is known	1,467	53	24	11	12	1.47
No parent has worked	117	77	19	2	3	0.44
Unskilled manual	190	68	15	8	9	1.05
Semi-skilled manual	344	59	27	7	7	1.04
Skilled manual	387	52	23	12	12	1.53
White collar	328	40	27	16	17	2.03
Professional or managerial	101	24	30	17	30	2.99

[1] This classification by country of origin is based both on the survey of parents and on teachers' assessments.
[2] The base shown in the total line is all pupils present for some part of the first two terms of the fifth year. The base for the analysis by family's socioeconomic group is substantially smaller, as shown, because the information comes from the parental survey carried out in the second year.

From D.J. Smith and S. Tomlinson *The School Effect*, 1989, p253

Item B *Class and ethnicity*

From national surveys we know that the proportion in different socioeconomic groups varies between ethnic groups, and this pattern of variation is much the same among the study families. South Asians (except for African Asians) and West Indians tend to belong to lower socioeconomic groups than whites both among our study families and nationally. There are hardly any ethnic minority families belonging to the professional and managerial group in the study schools.

Adapted from D.J. Smith and S. Tomlinson *The School Effect* 1989, p43

Questions

1 Briefly summarise the relationship between examination results and
  a) ethnicity
  b) gender and
  c) social class shown in Item A.
2 Read Item B. In view of this, comment on the attainment of Asians and Afro-Caribbeans shown in Item A.

5.3 The school effect

How important an influence is the school a pupil attends on his or her examination results? This was one of the questions which Smith and Tomlinson tried to answer in *The School Effect*. They found that different secondary schools achieved very different results with children of similar background and

ability. Ability was measured by tests (in English, Maths and verbal reasoning) administered during the first two years of secondary school. The results indicated that schools have far more influence than ethnicity on examination results. Smith and Tomlinson conclude that 'differences in exam results attributable to ethnic groups are very much smaller than those attributable to the school. In other words, what school a child goes to makes far more difference than which ethnic group he or she belongs to' (1989, p281).

Evaluation Reviewing *The School Effect* David Gillborn and David Drew (1992) conclude that Smith and Tomlinson have produced new and important insights into multi-ethnic schools. 'Crucially the work reminds us that individual schools possess the power to influence the educational experiences, achievements and future life chances of their pupils' (1992, p562).

But they see two major problems. The first concerns methodology - in particular the size and nature of the sample. For example there were only 146 Afro-Caribbean pupils at 16 plus, too small a number on which to base conclusions. A second concern is Smith and Tomlinson's view that racism was not a significant factor in the education of ethnic minorities. The results of their questionnaire given to parents and teachers suggested that racism was not a problem in school. But there is a growing body of ethnographic research which suggests that racism is widespread in many schools. And it may well have a significant effect on educational attainment.

Activity 19 Racism at School

Item A *Racist graffiti*

Item B *Case studies*

Case 1
The parents of a nine year old Afro-Caribbean boy at a school in the West Country reported that he was continually being called racial names by other pupils, and that he was even called 'Nig-nog' by his teacher. The matter was investigated by the education committee, and at a meeting with the headteacher and local authority officers the parents were offered profound apologies.

Case 2
At a school in the Northeast a black girl was subjected to regular racial abuse and physically attacked once by an older girl. When she brought this to the headteacher's attention, he took no action, despite his instruction to her that she should report such incidents to him. It was only after she left the school that she brought the matter to the attention of her parents, saying that she had preferred to suffer in silence rather than get them involved.

Case 3
A young Sikh published his own account of the regular verbal and physical harassment that he had experienced in the seven years he had spent at schools in the South.

Much of that harassment was directed at his hair and turban, both regarded as sacred symbols. Sometimes teachers would join in or even initiate the jokes. The main effect, he said, was to erode his self-confidence and capacity to concentrate on learning.

Case 4
On a garage in a secondary school in the West Country, used daily by teachers, there were threatening and offensive racist graffiti: 'B.M. N.F. Coons out of school' and a Nazi swastika. They were allowed to remain there untouched for two years.

From Commission for Racial Equality *Learning in Terror*, 1988, p11

Questions

1 Read through the cases. Briefly comment on the teachers' responses.
2 What effect might such cases have on the children's educational progress?
3 Why might the results of questionnaires to teachers and parents significantly underestimate the extent of racism in schools?

5.4 Racism in schools

Racism doesn't have to be as open and direct as the examples given in Activity 19. People may be completely unaware that they are discriminating against others on the basis of ethnicity. And they are often shocked when this is revealed to them. This is the case with teachers at 'Jayleigh', a comprehensive school in northern England.

Racial discrimination and setting

In 1988, 41% of the pupils at 'Jayleigh' were of Asian origin. The table below shows GCSE results by ethnic origin for 1988. It gives no indication of discrimination against the Asian minority. Indeed Asian students have done marginally better than their white counterparts having a higher percentage of A-C grades. However, while white pupils got an average of 6 GCSE passes, the Asian average was 5. A study by the Commission for Racial Equality concluded that this difference had nothing to do with ability. Instead, 'here was a school which, however unintentionally, was using a setting system that appears to have set up barriers to a significant number of Asian pupils, and, in some instances, might have discriminated against them unlawfully' (1992, p44).

GCSE results, by ethnic origin, 1988

	Asian		White	
	No.	%	No.	%
Pass (A-C grades)	79	32	156	24
Pass (D-G grades)	155	63	451	69
Fail/Absent	12	5	43	7
Total	246	100	650	100

Commission for Racial Equality, 1992, p19

At 'Jayleigh' a greater proportion of white pupils (77%) were entered for GCSEs than Asian pupils (70%). On average white pupils were entered for more GCSEs (6.2) than Asian pupils (5.8). Whether or not pupils could take GCSEs depended largely on teachers' assessment of their attainment and potential.

Pupils at 'Jayleigh' were set in terms of ability. Asian pupils were more likely to be placed in lower sets even when they had the same assessment from the same primary school as white pupils. And to get in the top sets, Asians generally needed higher marks than whites. Pupils tended to remain in the same sets throughout secondary school. And set placement largely determined GCSE entry. As a result fewer Asians were entered for GCSEs and those that were took fewer GCSEs. This was due to discrimination on the basis of ethnicity. Since this study 'Jayleigh' has made fundamental changes to the way it operates.

It is impossible to estimate the extent of the 'Jayleigh situation'. However, similar examples of systematic discrimination on ethnic grounds have been found in other schools (see Activity 20). There is some evidence that since the Educational Reform Act of 1988 setting has become more widespread (see Activity 6, Item B, p286). This can be seen as a cause for concern not only because of the possibility of racial discrimination in allocation to sets but also because of the negative consequences for those in lower sets (see pp299-300). If setting is becoming more widespread, then David Gillborn (1995) fears that 'the first to suffer will be students of ethnic minority and/or working class background'.

Activity 20 looks at setting in a Midlands comprehensive school. It is based on a study carried out by Cecile Wright (1986).

Activity 20   Set to Fail?

Item A   Examination entries

	Asian	Afro-Caribbean	White
Number	92	36	55
	%	%	%
5 or more CSEs	65.2	78	57.6
1 or more O level	46.7	22.2	34.8
5 or more O levels	16.3	2.7	18.5

Item B   Setting and perceived behaviour

The deputy head admitted that setting was not based solely on exam results - 'It is the case that the school tends to put the dutiful children in O level groups'. Some teachers saw Afro-Caribbean students as 'less cooperative'. One English teacher described all her Afro-Caribbean students as 'a disruptive influence'. It appeared that at least some students were placed in lower sets on the basis of teachers' views of their behaviour rather than ability.

Items A, B, and C adapted from C.Wright 'School Processes - An Ethnographic Study' in J.Eggleston et al (eds) *Education for Some*, 1986, pp127-179

Item C *Setting*

Individual pupils and allocation to exam sets

Pupil		Third year exam results (marks out of 100)				Set placement (O = GCE O level)			
		English	maths	French	physics	English	maths	French	physics
Afro-Caribbean	A	73	44	58	-	CSE	CSE	CSE	-
	B	62	63	60	59	CSE	CSE	CSE	CSE
	C	64	45	56	72	CSE	CSE	-	CSE
	D	68	37	82	-	CSE	CSE	CSE	-
Asian	E	51	77	-	55	O	O	-	O
	F	60	56	58	-	O	O	O	-
	G	61	62	55.5	-	O	O	O	-
	H	54	55	-	40	O	O	-	O
White	I	61	62	-	62	O	O	-	O
	J	52	57	55	-	O	O	O	-
	K	75	82	77.5	72	O	O	O	O
	L	54	75	64	72	O	O	O	O

A CSE grade 1 is equivalent to an O level grade C.

Questions

1 What evidence does Item C provide to suggest that Afro-Caribbean students are allocated to lower examination courses than their ability merits?

2 Items A and C are from the same school. How might the evidence in Item C help to explain Item A?

3 In view of Item B, do you think that racial discrimination played a part in the setting of students? Explain your answer.

Classroom interaction

Primary schools The evidence examined so far suggests that ethnic minority students experience discrimination during their school careers. Studies of classroom interaction support this. Cecile Wright's research (1992) conducted in 1988/89 was based on classroom observation in 4 inner city primary schools. It found that teachers perceived and treated ethnic minority children differently from white children.

Asian children, especially the younger ones, were often seen as a problem, but as a problem that could be largely ignored. They received least attention, were often excluded from classroom discussions and rarely asked to answer questions. Teachers tended to assume that their command of English was insufficient for full classroom participation. Yet they saw Asian pupils as well disciplined and highly motivated.

Afro-Caribbean children - especially boys - were expected to behave badly. They received considerable attention - nearly all of it negative. Their behaviour was usually seen as aggressive, disobedient and disruptive. They were often singled out for criticism, even for actions which were ignored in other pupils. As a result they often felt picked on

and treated unfairly.

Wright concludes that although they were treated differently, both Asians and Afro-Caribbeans 'faced negative teacher interaction in the classroom' (1992, p39). And, given the importance of the early childhood years for a person's development, this is a cause for concern.

Secondary schools Research by David Gillborn (1990) largely reflects Wright's findings. He spent two years studying an inner city comprehensive school gathering a range of qualitative data from classroom observation, documentary analysis and interviews with teachers and students. He found that the vast majority of teachers tried to treat all students fairly. However, they perceived students differently and on this basis treated them differently. In particular, they often saw the actions of Afro-Caribbean students as a threat where no threat was intended. And they reacted accordingly with measures of control.

Despite the fact they rejected racism, 'the teachers' ethnocentric perceptions led to actions which were racist in their consequences: as a group, Afro-Caribbean pupils experienced more conflictual relationships with teachers; they were disproportionately subject to the school's reporting and detention systems; they were denied any legitimate voice of complaint' (Gillborn, 1990, p44).

Evaluation Wright and Gillborn's studies use an ethnographic approach. They are based on intensive first hand investigation of relatively small groups over a fairly long period of time. This kind of research does not lend itself to large samples so generalisations are not possible. However, this does not invalidate its findings. The insights it provides are unlikely to come from studies based on quantitative approaches such as questionnaires. For example, Smith and Tomlinson's questionnaire to parents revealed very little evidence of racism in schools. Ethnographic methods may well have given a very different picture.

Exclusion

Exclusion is one of the methods of social control which schools can use to deal with students they regard as troublesome. Exclusion can be permanent - the student is not allowed to return to that school - or temporary - the pupil is excluded from school for a fixed term. There are two more forms of exclusion, neither of which find their way into official statistics. The first, 'internal exclusion', refers to exclusion within the school eg a pupil being thrown out of a classroom or made to stand in the corridor. The second, 'informal exclusion', involves parents being invited to the school and encouraged to remove their child to another school.

The extent of exclusions is not known. A 1993 MORI poll estimates they might be twenty times higher than the figures provided by official statistics (Bourne et al, 1994, p 40). There is evidence to suggest that all forms of exclusion have risen rapidly in England and Wales during the late 1980s and early 90s. Since the Education Reform Act of 1988 school image has become a major priority with examination league tables and truancy tables being made public. There is a temptation to exclude students seen as disruptive and difficult to teach. One Sheffield school 'solved' its truancy problem by permanently excluding all its worst truants (Searle, 1994, pp17-18).

Afro-Caribbean exclusion Figures from the Department for Education (1992) indicate that Afro-Caribbeans form 8.1% of all permanent exclusion yet only 2% of the school population. This reflects similar figures from local education authorities throughout the 1970s, 80s and early 90s.

Why are so many Afro-Caribbean students excluded? There are two main explanations. The first sees the disproportionately high level as a result of racism. Afro-Caribbeans are perceived by many white teachers as aggressive and disruptive. According to Jenny Bourne, there is a tendency for even well

meaning white teachers to see 'black youth as undermining their authority and even threatening to them personally' (J. Bourne et al, 1994, p35). A second explanation argues that Afro-Caribbeans are more likely to experience the frustrations of racism and poverty and these frustrations will be expressed in their behaviour in the classroom.

A strong case can be made that Afro-Caribbeans are the very students who should not be excluded. According to A. Sivanandan, Director of the Institute of Race Relations, 'it is precisely because black children are already excluded, more than others, from most aspects of social life, that they need to be included, more than others, in the educational life of the school' (J. Bourne et al, 1994, pv).

5.5 Further explanations

This section briefly examines explanations of ethnicity and educational attainment which have been partly bypassed by more recent research.

Intelligence

The relationship between intelligence and educational attainment was examined earlier in the chapter (see p294). Today there is little support for the view that differences in educational attainment between social groups are due to differences in innate intelligence. Most researchers would totally reject the idea that differences in qualifications between males and females, young and old, working and middle classes or blacks and whites have anything to do with the genes of those groups.

The Swann Committee, appointed by the British government to examine the education of ethnic minorities, looked at the question of intelligence and educational attainment (DES, 1985). It found that when social and economic factors were taken into account, there were no significant differences in the IQ scores of different ethnic groups. As a result it ruled out IQ as a cause of ethnic differences in educational attainment.

Culture

A number of researchers, particularly during the 1960s and 70s, argued that ethnic differences in educational attainment could be explained in terms of culture. This was one of the conclusions of the Swann Committee - 'Wherever the truth may lie, the reasons for the very different school performance between Asians and West Indians seem likely to lie deep within their respective cultures' (DES, 1985, p87). However the Committee admitted that the evidence for this view was either lacking or at best 'sketchy'.

Explanations based on culture take two main forms.
1 Cultural deprivation theory which states that many

of the factors needed for high educational attainment are lacking in the culture of particular social groups.

2 Cultural difference theory which states that certain groups are placed at a disadvantage because of differences between their culture and the culture of the school.

Cultural deprivation Afro-Caribbean 'underachievement' has been explained in terms of cultural deprivation theory. For example, it has been claimed that Afro-Caribbean family life with its high proportion of lone mothers fails to provide the support and stability that children need for educational success. However, there is plenty of evidence to reject cultural deprivation theory. For example, many Afro-Caribbean parents are so concerned about their children's education that they have set up their own 'supplementary schools'. And Ken Pryce's study of the Afro-Caribbean community in Bristol found that, 'The majority of West Indian parents have great academic aspirations for their children' (1979, p120).

Cultural differences This view states that there is nothing 'deprived' about ethnic cultures. Instead they are simply different from the mainstream culture. And it is this difference which places members of ethnic groups at a disadvantage since schools operate in terms of mainstream culture. Thus Creole, a dialect spoken by some Afro-Caribbeans, is not a substandard form of standard English, it is simply different. Available evidence suggests that Creole speakers have little difficulty understanding standard English but some difficulty producing it because they are following the (different) rules of Creole. Constant correction by teachers may well reduce children's confidence, lower their motivation and slow their progress.

Evaluation In recent years there has been relatively little work on the relationship between ethnic minority cultures and educational attainment.
There are various reasons for this.
1 It is extremely difficult to discover:
   a) to what extent members of an ethnic minority group share the same norms and values
   b) to what extent these norms and values differ from those of other minority groups and
   c) to what extent these norms and values affect educational attainment.
2 Some of the descriptions of so-called ethnic cultures are little better than popular stereotypes. As such they have sometimes been seen as 'racist depictions' (Troyna and Carrington, 1990, p47).
3 The whole area is very sensitive as it can lead to negative pictures of certain groups. This has happened with some descriptions of Afro-

Caribbean culture. In fact part of the research into ethnic cultures initiated by the Swann Committee was abandoned due to strong objections from the Afro-Caribbean community.
4 There is the very real problem of the misuse of cultural research. For example, it can be used to justify what many would see as racist actions. In his introduction to *Outcast England : How Schools Exclude Black Children* A. Sivanandan writes, 'What our researches show, however, is not only that the number of black children excluded each month from schools in England and Wales is wildly out of proportion to their numbers on the rolls, but that the explanation sought for such exclusion tends to see black children as having particularly intractable behavioural problems by virtue of their culture, family structure or upbringing. The exclusion of the black child, in other words, is once again being regarded as another element in the social pathology of the black family, rather than as an indicator of a differentially structured racism that works against the poorest sections of the black community in particular.' (J. Bourne et al, 1994, pv)

Summary

1 An assortment of statistics over the past 20 years indicates ethnic differences in educational attainment.

2 Some researchers argue that quality of school and social class background are far more important than ethnicity in accounting for educational attainment.

3 Other researchers argue that this ignores the effects of racism. They claim that ethnic minorities are disadvantaged because of racism in the classroom, in the playground, in exclusion, in setting and in examination entry.

References

Ainley, P. *Vocational Education and Training* (Cassell, London, 1990)

Becker, H.S. 'Social Class Variations in the Teacher-Pupil Relationship' in B.R.Cosin et al (eds) *School and Society: A Reader* (Open University Press, Milton Keynes, 1977)

Benyon, J. *Initial Encounters in a Comprehensive School* (Falmer, London, 1985)

Bernstein, B. *The Structure of Pedagogic Discourse Vol.4: Class, Codes and Control* (Routledge, London, 1990)

Bird, C. 'Deviant Labelling in School: The Pupils' Perspective' in P.Woods (ed) *Pupil Strategies* (Croom Helm, London, 1980)

Boudon, R. *Education, Opportunity and Social Inequality* (John Wiley & Sons, New York, 1974)

Bourdieu, P. and Passeron, J. *Reproduction in Education, Society and Culture* (Sage, London, 1977)

Bourne, J., Bridges, L. and Searle, C. *Outcast England: How Schools Exclude Black Children* (Institute of Race Relations, London, 1994)

Bowles, S. and Gintis, H. *Schooling in Capitalist America* (RKP, London, 1976)

Burgess, R.G. *Education, Schools and Schooling* (Macmillan, London, 1985)

Buswell, C. 'Flexible Workers for Flexible Firms?' in A.Pollard, J.Purvis and G.Walford (eds) *Education, Training and the New Vocationalism* (Open University Press, Milton Keynes, 1988)

Cohen, P. 'Against the New Vocationalism' in I.Bates et al (eds) *Schooling for the Dole?* (Macmillan, London, 1984)

Commission for Racial Equality *Learning in Terror: A Survey of Racial Harassment in Schools and Colleges* (Commission for Racial Equality, London, 1988)

Commission for Racial Equality *Set to Fail? Setting and Banding in Secondary Schools* (Commission for Racial Equality, London,1992)

Curtis, S.J. *History of Education in Great Britain* (University Tutorial Press, London, 1963)

Denscombe, M. *Sociology Update 1994* (Olympus Books, Leicester, 1994)

Department of Education and Science *Education for All (The Swann Report)* (HMSO, London, 1985)

Department for Education *Technical and Vocational Education Initiative Review* (HMSO, London, 1990)

Department for Education *Exclusions* (HMSO, London, 1992)

Department for Education *Our Children's Education: The Updated Parent's Charter* (HMSO, London, 1994)

Douglas, J.W.B. *The Home and the School* (MacGibbon & Kee, London, 1964)

Eggleston, J., Dunn, D. and Anjali, M. *Education for Some: The Educational and Vocational Experiences of 15-18 year old Members of Ethnic Minority Groups* (Trentham, Stoke-on-Trent, 1986)

Finn, D. *Training Without Jobs* (Macmillan, London, 1987)

French, J. 'Gender and the Classroom' *New Society* , 7.3.1986

Gillborn, D. *Race, Ethnicity and Education: Teaching and Learning in Multi-Ethnic Schools* (Unwin Hyman, London, 1990)

Gillborn, D. *Racism and Antiracism in Real Schools* (Open University Press, Buckingham, 1995)

Gillborn, D. and Drew, D. '"Race", Class and School Effects' *New Community* vol 18 no 4, 1992

Goddard-Spear, M. 'Differences Between the Written Work of Boys and Girls' *British Educational Research Journal* vol 15 no 3, 1989

Halsey, A.H., Heath, A. and Ridge, J.M. *Origins and Destinations* (Clarendon Press, Oxford, 1980)

Hargreaves, D.H. *Social Relations in a Secondary School* (RKP, London, 1967)

Hargreaves, D .H. *Interpersonal Relations and Education* (RKP, London, 1975)

Heath, A. 'Class in the Classroom' *New Society*, 17.7.1987

Hugget, F.E. *Teachers: First Hand Views of the Classroom Crisis* (Weidenfeld & Nicolson, London, 1986)

Inner London Education Authority *The Junior School Project* (ILEA Research and Statistics Branch, London, 1986)

Johnson, D. *Private Schools and State Schools: Two Systems or One?* (Open University Press, Milton Keynes, 1987)

Jeffs, T. and Smith, M.K. 'Youth' in M.Haralambos (ed) *Developments in Sociology* vol 8 (Causeway Press, Ormskirk, 1992)

Jones, T. *Britain's Ethnic Minorities* (Policy Studies Institute, London, 1993)

Kealey, T. 'Let Our Children Go' *The Spectator,* 18.5.1991

Labov, W. 'The Logic of Nonstandard English' in N.Keddie (ed) *Tinker, Tailor...The Myth of Cultural Deprivation* (Penguin, Harmondsworth, 1973)

Lacey, C. *Hightown Grammar,* (Manchester University Press, Manchester, 1970)

Lee, D., Marsden, D., Rickman, P. and Dunscombe, J. *Scheming for Youth: A Study of YTS in the Enterprise Culture* (Open University Press, Milton Keynes, 1990)

Lees, S. *Losing Out: Sexuality and Adolescent Girls* (Hutchinson, London, 1986)

Malcolm X *The Autobiography of Malcolm X* (Grove Press, New York, 1966)

Meyenn, R.J. 'School Girls' Peer Groups' in P.Woods (ed) *Pupil Strategies* (Croom Helm, London, 1980)

Nicholson, J. *What Society Does to Girls* (Virago, London, 1977)

Oakley, A. *Housewife* (Allen Lane, London, 1974)

Perkin, J. *Victorian Women* (John Murray, London, 1993)

Pring, R. 'Spanning a Deep Cultural Chasm' *Guardian*, 13.2.1990

Pryce, K. *Endless Pressure: A Study of West Indian Life-styles in Bristol* (Penguin, Harmondsworth, 1979)

Raffe, D. 'The Transition from YTS to Work: Content, Context and the External Labour Market', in C.Wallace and M.Cross (eds) *Youth in Transition: Sociology of Youth and Youth Policy* (Falmer, Basingstoke, 1990)

Rice, B. 'The Brave New World of Intelligence Testing' *New Society*, 11.10.1979

Roberts, K., Siwek, M. and Parsell, G. *What are Britain's 16-19 Year Olds Learning?* (Social Statistics Research Unit, City University, London, 1989)

Rosenthal, R. and Jacobson, L. *Pygmalion in the Classroom* (Holt, Rinehart & Winston, New York, 1968)

Rutter, M., Maughan, B., Mortimore, P. and Ouston, J. *Fifteen Thousand Hours: Secondary Schools and their Effects on Children* (Open Books, London, 1979)

Sauvain, P. *British Economic and Social History: 1850 To The Present Day* (Stanley Thornes, Cheltenham, 1987)

Searle, C. 'The Culture of Exclusion' in J.Bourne et al, 1994

Schonnell, F.J. *The Essential Intelligence Test, Form A, for Pupils Ages 8+ to 12+* (Oliver & Boyd, Edinburgh, 1940)

Sharpe, S. *Just Like a Women: How Girls Learn to be Women* (Penguin, Harmondsworth, 1976)

Skelton, C. 'Women and Education' in D. Richardson and V. Robinson (eds) *Introducing Women's Studies* (Macmillan, London, 1993)

Smith, D. and Tomlinson, S. *The School Effect: A Study of Multi-Racial Comprehensives* (Policy Studies Institute, London, 1989)

Spender, D. *Invisible Women: The Schooling Scandal* (Women's Press, London, 1983)

Stanworth, M. *Gender and Schooling* (Hutchinson, London,1983)

Townroe, C. and Yates, G. *Sociology for GCSE* (Longman, Harlow, 1987)

Troyna, B. and Carrington, B. *Education, Racism and Reform* (Routledge, London, 1990)

Walford, G. (ed) *British Public Schools: Policy and Practice* (Falmer, London, 1984)

White, R. with Brockington, R. *Tales Out of School: Consumers' Views of British Education* (RKP, London, 1983)

Willis, P. *Learning to Labour: How Working Class Kids Get Working Class Jobs* (Saxon House, Farnborough, 1977)

Wright, C. 'School Processes - An Ethnographic Study' in J.Eggleston et al (eds) *Education for Some* (Trentham, Stoke-on-Trent, 1986)

Wright, C. 'Early Education: Multiracial Primary School Classrooms' in D.Gill, B.Mayor and M.Blair (eds) *Racism and Education* (Sage, London, 1992)

Introduction

'Living for the weekend' is a theme of many popular songs. It refers to the idea of work as an unfortunate necessity and leisure as a central life interest. This is how many people see work. For others work *is* a central life interest providing satisfaction and fulfilment. Why this is so is one of the traditional concerns of the sociology of work.

Work has a major influence on people's lives. It can affect their income, standing in the community, leisure activities and political views. Something of the importance of work can be seen from people's response to enforced non-work. Unemployment is regarded by many as a catastrophe.

This chapter looks at sociology's contribution to an understanding of work, leisure and unemployment.

Chapter summary

- Part 1 examines the problem of defining **work** and the **economy**. It goes on to consider some of the social factors which shape people's **attitudes to work.**
- Part 2 looks at ways in which **new technology** has affected how work is organised and the nature of the workforce.
- Part 3 considers **industrial conflict** and discusses recent changes in **industrial relations** in Britain.
- Part 4 looks at the relationship between **work** and **non-work**, in particular **unemployment** and **leisure**.

1 Work in Industrial Society

Key Issues

1 What is meant by work?
2 Is contemporary Britain best described as an industrial, capitalist or post-industrial society?
3 What is the significance of changing patterns of ownership and control of business organisations?
4 Are people's attitudes towards their work shaped more by factors inside or outside the workplace?

1.1 Defining work

Defining work is not straightforward. The sociology of work has traditionally focused on *wage labour* or paid employment. However, in recent years there has been a growing interest in work outside employment, in what sociologists call the *informal economy*. For example, Ray Pahl and Jonathan Gershuny (1980) suggest that there are three different economies in which people work in contemporary Britain.

1 **The formal economy** This is the official economy recognised by the government and based on paid employment. Such work is recorded in official statistics and subject to taxation and national insurance contributions.

2 **The informal economy** This economy - sometimes referred to as the 'black economy' - is not officially recorded. It includes people working 'off the books' to avoid tax and national insurance and those not declaring earnings because they are receiving state benefits. 'Fiddling' and pilfering at work might also be seen as part of the informal economy. It also includes work done for neighbours and friends which might be repaid in kind.

3 **The household economy** This involves the work done within households by their members to provide services for themselves -what feminist sociologists describe as *domestic labour*. Much of this work is done by women in the form of cooking, cleaning and caring for children and the sick - what is conventionally called 'housework'. It also includes 'do-it-yourself' and other self-service activities, for example home decorating, growing fruit and vegetables or building a home extension.

Ray Pahl's views on the informal economy have provoked a great deal of interest in work outside paid employment. In a later study *Divisions of Labour* (1984) he distinguishes a fourth type of economy, the *communal economy*. This involves unpaid work outside the household sphere, for example, voluntary work for a church or charity or unpaid work for a political party or trade union.

Because work includes many activities beyond paid employment, many sociologists argue that it cannot be defined precisely. It is important to understand the meaning that behaviour has for people -what is work for one person may be leisure for another. Moreover, not all non-work activities comprise leisure. Non-work time is filled by many work-like obligations - travelling to work, washing, household chores and shopping for food. For unemployed people their whole day may represent potential leisure time yet it is more likely to be perceived as empty time than as an opportunity for fulfilling leisure activities.

Activity 1 Work and Non-work

Item A

Item B

Item C

Item D

Item E *Women and the family economy*

According to Tilly and Scott (1978), a distinction can be made between three sorts of female activity: domestic (unpaid household labour), productive (wage earning labour) and reproductive (bearing and raising children). These activities have always been the major components of women's contribution to the family economy, although their meaning, value, location and nature have changed over time and the three forms have become increasingly distinct during industrialisation. Before industrialisation, activities such as keeping animals, making clothes, preparing food, growing vegetables had economic value since they were performed to satisfy household needs. During the 17th and 18th centuries the term 'work' encompassed all these activities. Today activities previously regarded as work are now excluded by a somewhat arbitrary definition of work concerned only with waged labour. The absurdity of this is underlined by an example: a housewife cooking a meal is not performing an economic activity, whereas she would be if hired to cook a similar meal in a restaurant.

Adapted from M. Maynard 'Houseworkers and Their Work' in R. Deem and G.Salaman (eds) *Work, Culture and Society*, 1985, p136

Questions

1 a) Write down what the terms 'work' and 'leisure' mean to you.
   b) Compare your response to that of someone else, if possible someone of a different age, sex and/or social background.
   c) What similarities and differences are there? How would you explain these?
   d) What problems did you have, if any, in trying to complete this exercise.
2 Examine the photographs in Items A to D.
   a) Which activities would you categorise as work and which as leisure?
   b) Are there any activities which you had difficulty in categorising? If so, why?
   c) What further information might help you to decide whether these activities should be defined as work or leisure?
3 With reference to Item E and any examples from you own experience discuss the claim that conventional definitions of work discriminate against women.

1.2 Theories of industrial society

Most sociologists agree that an understanding of work requires an understanding of the economic system within which work takes place. The nature of work in societies like Britain has been changed dramatically in the last two hundred and fifty years by the social and economic changes brought about by the industrial revolution. These changes have continued into this century as a result of technological innovations in production processes and worldwide changes in the nature of industrial organisations. Sociology as a discipline developed as an attempt to understand the enormous changes brought about by the process of industrialisation.

Emile Durkheim: industrial society and the division of labour

For Emile Durkheim the high degree of specialisation in work - the specialised *division of labour* was the most important characteristic of industrial societies. Pre-industrial societies are characterised by a limited division of labour - there is little specialisation in work roles. In this situation the unity of society is maintained by *mechanical solidarity*. This is based on the fact that as most people carry out similar work and have shared life experiences, so common norms, values and beliefs are appropriate to society as a whole. The things people have in common bind them together so creating the solidarity required to maintain society.

In industrial societies individuals have a much wider range of occupations and work becomes increasingly specialised. This threatens to undermine traditional norms and values and create a situation of *anomie* or uncertainty about social norms leading to social disorder and disunity. However, Durkheim argued that the division of labour could become the source of a new kind of social cohesion based on recognition of the interdependence of different specialist occupations. In this case the unity of society is based on *organic solidarity*.

Functional differentiation Durkheim's work influenced later functionalist theories of industrial society. For example, Talcott Parsons (1951) suggested that what characterises industrial societies is their high level of functional differentiation which means that a wide range of institutions come to specialise in particular functions. In simple societies kinship based organisations, such as extended families, meet virtually all economic needs. In industrial societies such needs are met by a wide range of specialist organisations, for example manufacturing industries, transport services, banks, restaurants and hairdressers. This means that the range of occupations and organisations in industrial societies is more diverse and specialised.

Karl Marx: capitalism and industrial society

For Marx, the economic system of any society is based on the *mode of production*. In pre-industrial Britain work was based on the feudal mode of production - agriculture was the most important sector of the economy and the most important form of wealth was land. Feudalism was gradually replaced by a new mode of production, *capitalism*. In capitalist societies the production of goods and services is financed by the owners of private capital who invest their wealth in businesses. Those without wealth are forced to sell their labour to the capitalists in order to live. Marxists argue that work in capitalist societies is organised by a small number of wealth owners in order to create profits for themselves at the expense of their workers. Labour becomes a commodity to be bought and sold rather than an activity fulfilling human needs.

According to Marx, the change in the mode of production from feudalism to capitalism transformed the nature of work. Under feudalism most workers were serfs tied to working for a lord by a range of feudal obligations. However, serfs had their own land, animals and agricultural equipment and in this respect they owned their own means of production. The rise of capitalism transformed most of the workforce into wage labourers who were legally free to sell their services to any employer. However, as most workers no longer owned land or machinery - the means of production - they were compelled by economic necessity to sell their labour to those who did - the minority of capitalists.

Marxists claim that the way in which work is organised is based on the need to extract maximum effort and profitability from labour at minimum cost. This creates a sense of *alienation* or lack of fulfilment in workers. Work becomes a site of conflict with workers organising themselves in a variety of ways to resist attempts at control by employers.

Max Weber: industrialisation and rationalisation

For Max Weber the key characteristic of industrial society was the development of a *rational* approach to organising work and indeed social life in general. Rational behaviour involves actions designed to achieve a planned goal as opposed to behaviour influenced by tradition or personal emotion (see pp665-666). Weber traced the origins of this rational approach to life to the Protestant Reformation of the 16th century (see pp504-505). However, he suggests rationality has now lost its religious motivation and has become part of the secular 'spirit of capitalism'.

As a result work is organised according to rational rules with a strict demarcation of responsibility and a hierarchy of authority. Factories based on assembly line production with a highly specialised division of labour and many ranks of supervisors and managers are examples of work organisations based on this rational approach.

The end of industrial society?

Some sociologists believe that industrialism is giving way to a new form of economic system. For example Daniel Bell (1973) argues that advanced industrial societies are developing into what he calls *post-industrial societies*. In such societies the kind of unskilled work typically found in many manufacturing industries is being taken over by machines. As a result the workforce is increasingly made up of highly skilled professionals in the service sector. These changes are discussed in Section 2.2. However, many sociologists dispute Bell's claims arguing that there are important continuities between past industrial societies and those of today.

Capitalist, industrial or post-industrial society?

The debates about terminology discussed in this section are important in that the choice of terms carries assumptions about industrial societies. Those who use the term industrial society wish to emphasise the way in which industrial technology imposes certain requirements on *all* industrial societies. On the other hand those who use the term capitalism wish to emphasise what is *distinctive* about this particular form of industrial economy, for example the primacy of market forces. Post-industrial theories suggest industrial society has been superseded by a further stage of economic development. Such differences underlie many of the debates about the changing nature of work discussed later in this chapter.

Activity 2 Capitalism and Industry

Item A *Cottage industry*

Spinning in a cottage in the early 1700s

Around 1720, Daniel Defoe (author of *Robinson Crusoe*) journeyed to Halifax in the West Riding of Yorkshire. This is what he saw.

People made cloth in practically every house in Halifax. They keep a cow or two and sow corn to feed their chickens. The houses were full of lusty fellows, some at the dye-vat; some at the loom, others dressing the cloths; the women and children carding, or spinning; all employed from the youngest to the oldest. The finished cloth was taken to the market to be sold.

Adapted from P. Sauvain *British Economic and Social History 1700-1870*, 1987, pp46-47

Item B *The factory system*

Richard Arkwright was a highly successful businessman. His cotton mills made him a fortune. In 1780 he introduced steam power into his factories putting his workers on 12 hour shifts in order to operate the machinery 24 hours a day. By 1782 he was employing over 5,000 workers in his mills.

Adapted from P. Sauvain *British Economic and Social History 1700-1870*, 1987, p76

Item C *The factory bell*

O happy man, O happy thou
While toiling at thy spade and plough
While thou amidst thy pleasures roll
All at thy labour uncontrolled
Here at the mills in pressing crowds
The high built chimneys puff black clouds
And all around the slaves do dwell
Who're called to labour by a bell.

From the first half of the 19th century

Item D

Computers at the Stock Exchange

Item E

Electricity generating plant

Item F

Robot at Nissan car factory

Questions

1 Capitalism and technology went hand in hand to change the nature of work. Discuss with reference to Items A, B and C.

2 Look at Items D, E and F. Suggest similarities and differences between work and capitalism in the 19th and late 20th centuries.

1.3 Ownership and control

Whether Britain is best described as a capitalist, industrial or post-industrial society can partly be answered by examining debates about patterns of ownership and control of industry. Marxists have pointed to the increasing dominance of large transnational corporations in the economies of capitalist societies. This has been interpreted as part of the inherent tendency towards monopolisation of ownership identified by Marx in the 19th century. This would support the argument that such societies are still essentially capitalist, albeit in a later stage in their development. However, other sociologists argue that control of the economy has increasingly passed from capitalist owners into the hands of salaried managers, professionals and other technical experts. They also argue that private industry is no longer typically owned by an individual or family. Instead ownership is increasingly divided between more and more shareholders. In these respects both control and ownership in capitalist society have been transformed.

The rise of monopoly capitalism

Marx, writing in the 19th century, argued that work in capitalist societies is shaped by the need of those who own the means of production - capitalist investors - to make profits. At that time most business enterprises in Britain were owned by individual entrepreneurs or families who also ran their own firms. However, Marx recognised the significance of the development of joint stock companies. These are companies where ownership is in the hands of a number of shareholders. Often such shareholders leave decisions about the day to day running of the company to salaried managers. As the scale of capitalist businesses has grown, so joint stock companies have become more and more important as a means of raising the capital required for large scale enterprises.

Many modern Marxists have argued that the growth of large corporations has led to *monopolisation*, a process predicted by Marx. This means that the ownership of the means of production is increasingly concentrated in fewer companies. This process is encouraged by takeovers, mergers and interlocking directorships and shareholdings which help to link different companies together. Marxists have seen such developments as a higher stage in the development of capitalist society rather than representing any fundamental change in the principles of private property and profit.

The separation of ownership and control

This view has been challenged by theories which emphasise the notion of industrial rather than capitalist society. Perhaps the most famous example of this is the work of Adolf Berle and Gardiner Means (1932). They argued that the rise of large corporations in the USA led to a separation of ownership and control. Ownership was in the hands of an increasingly large and diverse group of shareholders whose main interest was in realising a profit on their investments. At the same time, the actual control over decision making was passing into the hands of non-owning professional managers whose main concern was the growth and long term stability of the firm rather than profits as such. Evidence to support the view that ownership is becoming increasingly diverse and separated from control is provided by the growth of institutional shareholding. An increasing proportion of shares is owned not by private individuals but by other firms or by commercial organisations such as banks, insurance companies, building societies, pension funds, unit trusts and even trade unions. It can be argued that there is no longer an identifiable capitalist class which owns and controls businesses.

This approach fits with a pluralist view (see pp199-200) which sees society as characterised by a large number of competing interest groups rather than dominated by a capitalist ruling class. Ralf Dahrendorf's work (1959) is a good example of this approach. He argues that the capitalist class has become 'decomposed' into owners (shareholders) and controllers (managers) with potential for conflict between the two groups over how businesses should be run. Theories of post-industrial society also see the separation of ownership and control as a factor which distinguishes the newly emerging form of industrial society. For example, John Kenneth Galbraith (1967) argues that increasingly power in society is exercised not by capitalists but by industrial bureaucrats. He sees the growing complexity of research and development, planning and decision making as taking economic power out of the hands of wealth owners and into the control of technical experts.

Criticisms The thesis of the separation of ownership and control has not gone unchallenged. Many writers, especially those influenced by Marxism, have argued that the interests of owners and controllers of business organisations largely coincide. Michael Useem (1984) points out that in most large firms many senior managers are themselves shareholders, often encouraged by discount share ownership schemes. Moreover, top executives' salaries are often linked to the company's performance, with high profits meaning bigger bonuses. All this means that those who control big business may have very similar financial interests to shareholders. This argument is supported by an intensive study of the directors of nineteen British companies by Ray Pahl and Jack Winkler (1974). They found that professional managers were as committed to the value of profit seeking as traditional entrepreneurs.

While a director or group of directors of a firm may hold only a minority of its shares, this may be sufficient to control the firm. A group with as little as 5% of the shares may be able to control a firm if it faces no concerted opposition from other shareholders. John Scott (1985) points out that even where one individual or small group does not control a firm it may be controlled by what he calls a constellation of interests - a number of shareholders with similar interests. Such constellations of interests are reinforced by the fact that many firms have *mutual shareholdings* (own shares in each other) and *interlocking directorships* (one or more directors in common). This calls into question the view that ownership and control are largely separate in Western industrial capitalism.

Concentration of ownership and control

Recent studies of the economies of Britain and the USA show that an increasing proportion of both manufacturing and service industry is owned by fewer and fewer large corporations. Many such corporations have large assets both in their country of origin and worldwide. ICI with an annual turnover of approximately £5,000 million has plants scattered throughout every continent. Modern capitalist societies are increasingly corporate economies where a wide diversity of products is produced by a limited number of large corporations. A number of factors have contributed to this.

1   **Takeovers, mergers and conglomerates** One reason why fewer firms control the market for particular products is that small firms have been taken over by large ones. As a result economic activity is increasingly controlled by large conglomerates - corporations controlling a number of subsidiary companies. They often hold near monopoly positions in certain sectors, having replaced many smaller independent firms which were formerly in competition.

2   **The increasing concentration ratio** This is normally expressed as the share of total sales or output of a given number of top firms in a particular industry. Most evidence seems to point towards an increasing degree of concentration. Leslie Hannah (1976), for example, estimates that the top 100 manufacturing firms in Britain shared only 15% of net output in 1909 but by 1970 this had increased to 45%.

3   **Interlocking shareholdings and directorships** According to John Scott (1985) there are important links between firms in the form of overlapping ownership, whereby one firm has a shareholding in another. This will normally entitle a firm to nominate one of its own directors as a director of the company in which it has a shareholding. This results in networks of interlocking directorships with many large firms linked by common directors. This can have advantages for the firms involved - for example, industrial and financial companies can cooperate for their mutual benefit since one requires capital and the other requires a good return on its investment.

4   **Transnational ownership** The process of concentration and merger increasingly occurs on an international scale. Most large corporations have interests in a number of countries and are thus described as transnational corporations. Since the 1970s there has developed a *new international division of labour*. Third World countries provide a pool of cheap labour. They often have less stringent laws in areas such as pollution control and the protection of workers. As a result production is often moved there. Research, finance and corporate planning usually remain in wealthy countries where the skills required are more plentiful. One consequence has been job losses in countries like Britain as labour intensive operations in industries such as textiles and electronics are shifted to developing countries such as Malaysia, Korea and Taiwan.

Changing patterns of ownership and control

Much of the evidence points to a growth in the scale of capitalist enterprises due to takeovers and mergers and the growth of large conglomerates and transnationals. Marxists see this as evidence of an increasing concentration of ownership and control. Other sociologists counter that large corporations have no single owner and offer the possibility of many small investors becoming part owners either directly through shareholding, or indirectly through investments such as unit trusts and pension funds. Moreover, they see the power of capitalist owners counterbalanced by the separation of ownership and control with control passing increasingly to managers and technical experts.

Activity 3 Patterns, Ownership and Control

Item A

Shareholders as a percentage of the adult population

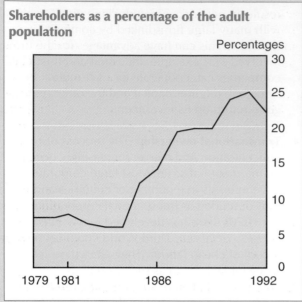

From *Social Trends*, 1993, p78

Item B

Shares held in United Kingdom companies: by sector

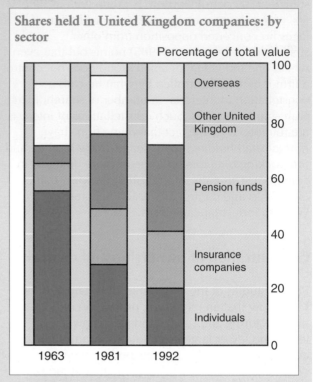

From *Social Trends*, 1993, p79

Item C *Concentration ratios*

Percentage share of 5 largest enterprises of total net output in manufacturing industry

Iron and steel	95.6
Wines, cider and perry	95.2
Manmade fibres	94.8
Motor vehicles & engines	87.3
Railway & tramway vehicles	75.7
Agricultural machinery & tractors	60.5
Office machinery & data processing equipment	57.8
Water supply	53.5
Pharmaceuticals	48.3
Brewing and malting	37.3
Building products (concrete, cement, plaster)	32.3
Metal doors, windows etc	29.6
Foundries	18.7
Bolts, nuts, springs, non-precision chains, metal instruments	13.4
Hand tools and finished metal goods	9.9

Source *Business Monitor*, PA 1002

The table on the left shows the five firm concentration ratio for selected manufacturing industries (ie the share of the five largest firms in the total market for a particular product as measured by total net output). For instance, in the iron and steel industry one firm dominates output - British Steel. This is because steel making requires large plants and considerable amounts of capital. At the other end of the scale, in hand tools and finished metal goods, the five largest companies only account for 9.9% of the total net output. Here capital costs are low. A hand tool company can be started with one small machine in a garden shed.

Adapted from A. Anderton *The Economy in Focus* 1992/3, p14

Questions

1 Summarise the trends shown in Items A and B.
2 Use data from Items A and B to evaluate the following views.
   a) Ownership of private industry is concentrated in the hands of a few rich people.
   b) There has been a separation of ownership and control.
3 Using evidence from Item C, evaluate the view that Britain's economy is dominated by a few large corporations.
4 What are the problems of drawing conclusions about changes in ownership and control from the data in this activity?

1.4 Attitudes to work

People's attitudes to work are shaped by a variety of factors. For some sociologists it is the experience of work itself which determines how workers feel. Other sociologists place more emphasis on influences from outside the workplace. This section examines these debates.

Karl Marx: capitalism and alienation

For Karl Marx work was an essential activity - it was the key to human happiness and fulfilment. Marx believed that human beings were creative and constructive by nature. However, in most societies no more than a few individuals have been allowed to develop this human potential and express themselves in their work. This leads to a feeling of *alienation* - work becomes something alien to the worker rather than an expression of their inner needs. Work becomes a means to an end - for example, a means of earning money - rather than an end in itself.

Marx believed that the capitalist mode of production was even more alienating than previous economic systems since private property and profit seeking are central to the whole system. Under capitalism the labour process is controlled by capitalists who own the means of production and therefore control how work is organised and the nature of the finished product. Workers are simply paid a wage for their labour. Work is something they do to stay alive rather than something which satisfies their creative needs.

For Marx alienation is the main evil of capitalism. The solution lies not in redesigning work, for example by introducing new technology, but in changing the entire relations of production that exist between capital and labour. As long as the primary object of work is to generate profit, as long as work is organised and controlled by the capitalist class, as long as that class owns the products of work, then workers will remain alienated wage slaves. They will be cut off from their work, from their fellow workers and from the products of their labour. And this is the case even if they think their work is interesting and fulfilling. Even workers in apparently satisfying jobs are objectively alienated. For Marx alienation was not a subjective state experienced by the worker but an objective situation created by the relationship of the worker to the means of production.

The solution for Marx was a communist society where workers themselves own and control the means of production. They will work for themselves and everyone else at one and the same time. They will share the fruits of their labour. And in this way they will express and fulfil their needs as workers and as human beings.

Robert Blauner: technology and alienation

Marx's concept of alienation has been criticised as being too vague to measure with any precision. Robert Blauner's (1964) work is an example of an attempt to operationalise and measure the concept of alienation. However, he uses the idea of alienation in a very different sense than Marx. While Marx saw alienation as a creation of capitalist relations of production, Blauner sees it as a result of specific forms of *work technology*. Moreover, while Blauner's focus is on workers' subjective feelings of satisfaction, Marx argued that even workers who express satisfaction with their jobs are objectively alienated.

Blauner argued that alienation had four dimensions - *powerlessness*, *meaninglessness*, *isolation*, and *self-estrangement*. He believed that these dimensions could be measured by questionnaire data about workers' attitudes and behaviour.

Blauner looked at workers in four industries in the USA. Each industry was an example of a different type of production technology. They were:

1 **Printing** An example of *craft technology*, typical of work before industrialisation and mechanisation.
2 **The textile industry** An example of *machine technology* introduced by the industrial revolution where workers become subservient to machines which mass produce standardised commodities.
3 **The automobile industry** An example of *assembly line technology*, in which work is broken down into small, simple, repetitive tasks comprising different stages in the assembly process as the product moves along an assembly line.
4 **The chemical industry** An example of *continuous process technology* based on automation. Machines actually process the product with workers monitoring and controlling the machines.

Blauner analysed questionnaire data on attitudes to work in these four industries and found considerable variation in the degree of workers' satisfaction and involvement. He claimed that the kind of technology employed in the workplace was the key factor explaining variations in levels of alienation.

Blauner concluded that production technology is related to alienation in a ∩ curve (an inverted letter U). The lowest levels of alienation are found in pre-industrial technology. Historically alienation has increased as technology has advanced, first with mechanisation and then with assembly line technology. However, this trend is reversed by automation - for example, with the continuous process technology of the chemical industry - which restores control and meaning to workers as they now supervise rather than serve machines. Blauner claimed that this results in an increase in job satisfaction and a reduction in industrial conflict. Management and workers would work together as a team and the class conflicts, which Marx saw as endemic to the system, would disappear as the working class became integrated into the capitalist system.

Criticisms

1 Blauner's methodolgy has been criticised. His work relies heavily on data from questionnaires administered over 15 years before his own study.

2 Other studies of production technology have produced very different findings. Huw Beynon and Theo Nichols (1977) studied a chemical plant in southern England employing the continuous process technology which Blauner claimed reduces alienation. They found little evidence to support his view. Most workers were still involved in heavy and monotonous manual labour, for example filling and carrying sacks of fertiliser. Even the technicians who operated the plant were usually bored - they often worked alone, spending hours watching dials on a control panel.

3 Blauner's work places too much emphasis on technology. There is evidence that other factors from both inside and outside the workplace have an important influence on workers' attitudes and behaviour.

Technology and exploitation

Marxists reject the view that changes in technology can reduce alienation. Such changes cannot alter the fundamentally exploitive nature of economic relationships under capitalism. Marxists go further - they reject the idea that technology is somehow neutral. Instead it is seen as a means of controlling workers and extracting maximum profits.

Huw Beynon's study *Working for Ford* (1973) is a good example of this approach. Beynon worked at the Ford plant at Halewood on Merseyside and his study combines participant observation with interviews with management and workers. Managers attempt to use production technology to get more and more work out of the workers so reducing labour costs, improving productivity and increasing profits. For example, they tried to increase the speed of the assembly line. Workers sometimes resisted by pulling out the safety wire to stop the line. Beynon sees work in the car plant as a constant struggle between managers concerned to maximise production figures and workers resisting this process of exploitation and fighting to make a demanding job as bearable and financially rewarding as possible. In the hands of management, technology becomes a tool for exploitation. However, to Beynon it is a secondary source of alienation. The primary source is the basic economic relationships of capitalism,

Critics argue that there is a tendency for Marxists to see class conflict and revolutionary potential where none exists. For example Goldthorpe and Lockwood (1968) claim that conflicts at work are based on limited economic goals with few workers actually questioning the basic legitimacy of the capitalist system.

Work orientations

From a social action perspective individuals define and give meaning to their situation. The experience of work will therefore result, at least in part, from the way they define work, from their *work orientation*.

Goldthorpe, Lockwood, Bechofer and Platt's (1968) study of 'affluent workers' (well paid manual workers) in Luton provides an example of this approach. They compared workers from three firms with a range of production technologies including assembly line and continuous process production. They found some support for Blauner's claims - for example, assembly line workers seemed least satisfied with their actual tasks. However, in terms of the workers' general view of their work - their work orientation - production technology appeared to make no difference.

The affluent workers were home and family centred. Their main priorities in terms of work were high wages and job security. They had an *instrumental orientation* to work, defining it as a means to an end, in particular as a means of improving the living standards of themselves and their families. It was this orientation which largely determined their attitudes towards work and their behaviour at work. As a result they did not expect or look for satisfaction or fulfilment at work. Goldthorpe et al explain workers' attitudes in terms of prior orientations which they bring to work from outside the factory. These orientations are largely unrelated to production technology and little changed by workers' experience of the work process.

Goldthorpe et al reject Marxist interpretations which see affluent workers as blinded by the false consciousness of materialism. Instead they see the affluent workers response as rational. Workers appreciate the real material advantages to be gained from accepting, albeit grudgingly, the demands of the capitalist system.

Criticisms Most of the workers in Goldthope et al's sample were married men with dependent children. As such they would be more likely to define work in instrumental terms and be particularly concerned with money and job security. However, these concerns cannot be simply explained in terms of their domestic situation. But, apart from vague references to changes in working class life, Goldthorpe et al fail to explain where these instrumental attitudes come from in the first place. The affluent workers are pictured as striking a rational and reasonable bargain with their employers resulting in harmonious industrial relations. This harmony was shattered by a bitter strike at Vauxhall Motors (one of the firms in the study) not long after the research was completed. Despite these criticisms, the Luton study is important for pointing out the significance of work orientation which had been largely overlooked in previous research.

International comparisons

Support for Goldthorpe et al's views comes from Duncan Gallie's (1978) study which compared oil refinery workers in Britain and France. Gallie found very different attitudes and industrial relations in the British and French oil industry despite the fact that they both use virtually identical continuous process technology. This suggests that attitudes are shaped by non-technological factors. While the French industry was characterised by a high degree of industrial conflict and militancy, there was little evidence of this amongst the British workers. Gallie suggests that this shows how factors outside the workplace affect work itself - in this case the different history, culture and union organisation of French and British workers. Within the workplace non-technological factors were also influential, for example British workers were more likely to be consulted and involved in decisions while French management was more autocratic, thus tending to provoke conflict.

Women's work orientations

Feminist writers argue that a problem with many studies of workers' orientations is researchers' neglect of women who now make up an increasing proportion of the workforce. Anna Pollert (1981) suggests that while working class boys readily embrace manual employment (though they may come to regret this later) girls from similar backgrounds are usually groomed for marriage and childrearing by their socialisation. Because of this

Pollert suggests that the women she studied in a tobacco factory were 'immediately painfully aware of the futility, the dehumanisation, the mind-destroying emptiness of their jobs' (1981, p98). In this case women's instrumental attitudes to work may be seen as a reflection of their definition of work as a temporary phase before escape into marriage and the family. For those who were already married with children paid work and housework usually represented a double burden which few male workers have to cope with.

Summary

1 There are many forms of economic activity which could be described as work. Not all take place within the paid economy.
2 Marxists argue that the nature of ownership and control in industrial society largely determines the nature of work. Other sociologists see the organisation and technology of production as more important.
3 There is evidence that ownership of private industry is becoming increasingly dispersed and that there is a growing separation of ownership and control. There is also evidence of a concentration of production and power in giant transnational corporations.
4 Workers' experience of and attitudes towards work have been seen to result from the nature of capitalist society, from production technology, from work orientations and from the history and culture of the society in which they live.

Activity 4 The Experience of Work

Item A *Assembly line work*

Robert Linhart a French intellectual describes his experiences of working on the Citroen car assembly line.

The crash of a new car arriving every three or four minutes marks out the rhythm of the work.

As soon as the car has been fitted into the assembly line it begins its half circle, passing each successive position for soldering or another complementary operation, such as filing, grinding, hammering. It's a continuous movement and it looks slow. When you first see it the line almost seems to be standing still, and you've got to concentrate on one actual car in order to realise that car is moving, gliding progressively from one position to the next. Since nothing stops, the workers also have to move in order to stay with the car for the time it takes to carry out their work. In this way each man has a well defined area for the operations he has to make, although the boundaries are invisible. As soon as a car enters a man's territory, he takes down his blowtorch, grabs his soldering iron, takes his hammer or his file, and gets to work. A few knocks, a few sparks, then the soldering's done and the car's already on its way out of the three or four yards of his position. And the next car's already coming into the work area. And the worker starts again. Sometimes, if he's been working fast, he has a few seconds respite before a new car arrives. Short-lived happiness: the next car's already there.

Adapted from R. Linhart 'The Assembly Line' in C. Littler et al (eds) *The Experience of Work*, 1985, pp118-119

Item B *Women's work*

The daily routine of most women began around 5.30 to 6 am to 'do a bit of work'. They then had to catch the bus and often wait for half an hour in case they missed it. Work started at 7.30 am prompt. Work 'finished' at 4.30 pm, but of course started again. They shopped, caught the bus, got home, had a quick cup of tea, cooked the tea and did more housework. It was quite normal to have less then an hour's 'free time', perhaps to watch the television, before going to bed ready to get up the next day - and start again, the same old pattern.

Home was something they brought into the factory. It was always with them. After all, it was something more useful to care for people and children than pack tobacco to go up in smoke. But they not only talked about it: they lived out their family lives at work, sometimes expressed silently in distant far-away looks, but sometimes aloud in detailed sagas.

Adapted from A.Pollert *Girls, Wives, Factory Lives*, 1981, pp112-113

Questions

1 How might (i) a Marxist, (ii) a social action theorist and (iii) a sociologist who gives priority to production technology begin to explain the experience of the work described in Item A?

2 What are the advantages and disadvantages of studying assembly line work as a participant observer, like Linhart in Item A?

3 Women's attitudes and behaviour at work can only be understood in relation to their domestic and family roles. Discuss with reference to Item B.

2 Technological Change and Work

Key Issues

1 Has new technology been used by employers and management to deskill workers?

2 What is the significance of changes in the nature of work and the composition of the workforce in advanced capitalist societies?

3 To what extent have 'flexible' work practices been adopted in British industry. What are the implications of such changes?

2.1 New technology and deskilling

Marx saw production technology in capitalist society as a means of controlling workers and raising profits. Labour costs could be reduced by replacing skilled workers with machines. Workers would lose control over their work as they became little more than machine minders, mere appendages of production technology. The working class would become increasingly homogeneous, its members more and more similar as they were deskilled to the level of unskilled workers.

To many sociologists just the opposite has happened in the 20th century. The workforce, rather than becoming more homogeneous is becoming more diverse, with a growth of white collar, managerial and professional occupations. Writers such as Blauner believed that new technologies promise to eliminate alienating work and industrial conflict.

Harry Braverman: the degradation of work

This view was strongly challenged by Harry

Braverman (1974). Braverman believes that far from an increase in skills in the 20th century, there has been a progressive degradation or *deskilling* of work. He claims that the principles of *scientific management* have been used by employers and management to take control of the labour process and to remove skills from workers. The idea of scientific management was developed by the American management theorist Frederick Winslow Taylor at the turn of the century. Taylor (1947) recommended that managers should remove all decision making from workers. Jobs should be designed using 'work study' techniques so that each worker had only to carry out a series of simple tasks designed and coordinated by managers. The assembly line system of making cars pioneered by Henry Ford was strongly influenced by Taylor's ideas. In this case each worker carried out a single task - for example, tightening a wheelnut - the cars being moved from worker to worker along an assembly line.

Braverman argues that the innovations of Taylor, Ford and others led to more and more jobs being deskilled. The planning and thought required from workers is increasingly taken over by managers or programmed into machines. Skilled workers can threaten the ability of management to control the labour process since their skills are often required to organise their work. This can make it difficult for managers to supervise or regulate them. Braverman claims that deskilling workers has become a strategy used by managers for taking control of the labour process. This occurs as follows.

1 Following Taylor, management studies the skills required and uses this knowledge to redesign jobs.

2 In the next stage, 'the separation of conception from execution', management takes responsibility for the conception - planning the methods, procedures, tools and so on for jobs - leaving the workers nothing but the execution - the performance of pre-planned simple and repetitive tasks.
3 This extends management control over workers. Workers are deskilled since jobs are broken up into small simple tasks. This reduces their bargaining power since unskilled workers are easier to replace.

Braverman rejects the argument that the growth of white collar occupations means that the intermediate strata in the class structure are growing and the working class is shrinking. He claims that many of the new white collar and service sector occupations are proletarian in character. While many jobs have titles implying they are skilled, these titles are often meaningless.

One aspect of Braverman's theory which has been widely researched is his claim that new technologies based on microelectronics and computers have been employed to deskill workers and increase managerial control. Operations are programmed into computers by small numbers of highly skilled workers leaving the majority to carry out simple routine tasks (see Activity 5).

Evaluation of the deskilling thesis

As a result of the wave of research prompted by Braverman's views, there have been many modifications and criticisms of the deskilling thesis. While accepting Braverman's basic argument that there is a tendency towards deskilling, many researchers argue that reality is far more complex than his theory suggests.

The universality of deskilling Braverman seems to imply that there was a golden age in the 19th century when most workers were highly skilled while today the workforce is almost entirely deskilled. His critics claim that only a tiny minority of workers in the 19th century were skilled artisans, while most were unskilled or semi-skilled. Furthermore, while some jobs have been deskilled by new technology, new skilled jobs have been created (eg computer programmers) and some existing jobs have been *reskilled* (eg typists moving to wordprocessors).

Workers' resistance Critics have argued that Braverman places too much emphasis on the ability of employers to assert control through deskilling, and too little on the ability of workers to resist this process. Andy Friedman (1977) shows how car workers in Coventry were able to exercise considerable control over the labour process through trade union negotiations in the 1940s and 1950s. Such control was strengthened by the rise of the shop stewards movement whereby ordinary workers negotiated pay rates and conditions with management on behalf of their colleagues within each department of a firm.

Studies have also pointed out the limits of resistance by workers. After all the machinery and plant is owned by the employers and workers have to develop strategies of resistance in a system already established by capital. In the long run such resistance may not be successful. Friedman notes that workers were relatively successful in resisting managerial control during the postwar boom years. Increased unemployment in the 1970s and 80s severely weakened trade unions and allowed employers to abandon agreements and impose new working practices.

Management strategies Critics argue that Braverman sees Taylorism as the only method used by management to control workers. As Stephen Wood puts it 'he takes the logic of Taylorism to be the logic of capitalism' (1982, p15). In recent years a number of sociologists have explored the variety of strategies used by management to control workers. Such studies suggest that the method advocated by Taylor, now described as *technical control* (for example, using assembly lines to control the speed and methods of work) is only one strategy, and not necessarily the most effective.

Friedman describes what he calls *responsible autonomy* whereby workers are allowed limited freedom to control their own methods and pace of work. An example of this was an experiment at Volkswagen in the 1970s where some workers were allowed to work in small teams organising their own work patterns, rather than on assembly lines. In such instances workers are often required to exercise greater skill and initiative than suggested by Braverman. However, some Marxists argue responsible autonomy is simply a more sophisticated and insidious mode of control.

A third method of management control is what Richard Edwards (1979) calls *bureaucratic control*. This involves using a complex hierarchy to control workers. For example, at Polaroid the workforce was divided into hundreds of grades with different statuses and rates of pay. Workers were encouraged to compete for promotion, allowing management to divide and rule the workforce, with each grade exercising control over those beneath them.

Gender and deskilling Feminist writers such as Veronica Beechey (1982) argue more attention needs to be paid to the significance of gender differences when examining deskilling. Women are particularly vulnerable to deskilling because they are less likely to be organised into trade unions. Employers have exploited gender divisions in the workforce to deskill jobs, for example using less skilled female workers on lower rates of pay to replace skilled male workers.

Beechey claims that notions of skill are socially constructed. Often jobs performed by women require considerable skill but are categorised as unskilled or semi-skilled simply because the skills required are readily available among female workers - for example, cooking and cleaning skills. Male workers are often better organised in trade unions and so may be able to protect the so called skilled status of their jobs through strategies of resistance and of exclusion. This means that women are often excluded from certain types of 'skilled' work reserved for men.

Activity 5 New Technology and Deskilling

Item A *Numerical control systems*

Braverman shows how metal cutting using machine tools has become virtually automatic. Numerical control tapes direct the movement of the tool, relieving workers of the need to be in close control of the machine. Work tasks can be more easily fragmented between operators, who are required to know less. Conceptual knowledge is placed in the hands of programmers.

Supportive evidence exists in the research of Noble (1979). Visits to twenty-four plants using numerical control (NC) established that 'in nearly every case management had attempted to transfer skill from the shopfloor to the programming office, to tighten up the lines of authority, and to extend control over all aspects of production'. One of the interesting things he shows is that there were other ways of automating machine tools that retained operator skills and control, but he also shows that competitive pressures and deliberate managerial choice of the most effective means of control excluded this possibility. This strengthens Braverman's point that although conventional engineering approaches treat machinery as neutral, different conceptions of machinery embody alternative designs and uses.

The new generation of direct numerical control (DNC) and similar systems can further erode the discretion of workers. Because the machine tool is linked to a central computer that guides and monitors the machine operation, it allows greater control of the machinist's activity. There is no inevitability in this. The systems embody the possibility of greater creative input from the operator through the powerful mini-computers that allow the part program to be altered at the machine.

Indeed recent research at Manchester University has shown that programming at the machine by skilled workers can be more efficient. However, this course of action can be blocked by a key on the control panel that locks it against unauthorised operator use. Shaiken (1979) quotes the chairman of an industrial development division as noting that it would be 'very undesirable to have the operator do any programming. This would take away control of the production environment.'

Adapted from P. Thompson *The Nature of Work*, 1983, pp79-80 and 113-114

Item B *The impact of automation on clerical work*

According to the Department of Employment's Classification of Occupations and Directory of Occupational Titles (CODOT) insurance clerks carry out a wide range of tasks in their work. In reality, insurance clerks at Lifeco hardly ever carried out a combination of tasks; the extent of functional specialisation within the organisation meant that each of the tasks identified in the CODOT description would be carried out by a separate individual. Task fragmentation meant that many clerks had little conception of the nature of the insurance business, or how their work related to the organisation (or even department) as a whole.

Extreme task specialisation is clearly facilitated by computerisation. At Southbank all branch business is fed into the terminal as it occurs. Cheque clearing is carried out overnight, and each branch has available, by the following morning, a complete record of the previous day's transactions. The terminal may be instantly accessed for any information that is needed -

National Westminster Bank

for example, statements. Entering data into the terminal is the lowest graded job in the branch - grade 1. Depending on the size of the branch, machine operators also carried out a number of other tasks including cheque printing, dealing with the post, answering the telephone or staffing the enquiry desk. Cashiering - the most 'visible' aspect of branch banking - is a grade 2 job, the highest level that most women working in the bank will achieve. More complex work such as foreign and safe custody, is carried out by grade 3 clerks, and at the grade 4 level are securities clerks and managers' clerks. Grade 4 clerks work closely with the management and, in the case of managers' clerks, will normally have delegated responsibilities (up to a limit) for lending. Within each branch therefore, the level of functional specialisation is high, in sharp contrast, according to our older informants, with the pre-mechanisation situation. Before job-evaluation, clerical grades were relatively undifferentiated; each clerk had been expected to undertake a range of tasks depending on age and experience.

In summary, therefore, our case study evidence indicates that as far as clerical work is concerned, computerisation 'deskills' tasks, enhances the functional specialisation, and centralises control within the organisation. The clerical workforce, therefore, is increasingly stratified. In the bank, for example, there has been a clear and recognised trend towards an occupational structure comprising on the one hand, routine clerks (largely grades 1 and 2) who input and process data according to tightly specified procedures, and on the other, a much smaller proportion of higher level staff who actually use the information in the course of their work.

Adapted from R. Crompton and G. Jones *White Collar Proletariat: Deskilling and Gender in Clerical Work*, 1984, pp50-53

Questions

1 According to Item A:
  a) How has new technology made possible the separation of conception and execution in the labour process?
  b) Why might management wish to prevent workers from programming their own machines?
  c) How might new technology lead to reskilling?
2 According to Item B:
  a) How has new technology deskilled clerical workers?
  b) What evidence is there that the deskilling of office work is more likely to affect female, rather than male, workers?
  c) How might new technology make clerical work more like manual work? What implications might this have for the class situation of clerical workers?

2.2 The changing workforce

In the last thirty years the nature of work in advanced industrial societies has changed dramatically. This has had a major impact on the nature of the workforce. The world of work is often still seen in terms of the full time male worker, usually working from the end of formal education until official retirement age. In many respects this image of work and workers is no longer accurate.

Part time work

The employment of part time workers has increased rapidly in recent years. Over a million part time jobs were created in the 1970s alone and this trend has continued through the 80s and into the 90s. In 1994 part timers accounted for some 25% of the workforce. Part time workers offer employers many advantages. They are usually cheaper to employ than full timers, less likely to belong to trade unions and not protected by many areas of employment legislation (making it easier for employers to dismiss them). Writers such as Atkinson (1985) have described this as a move to greater *flexibility* in the deployment of workers (see Section 2.3). For example, in a shop or restaurant more staff may be required at peak periods - this is when part timers are particularly useful. Veronica Beechey (1987) found part timers were used in manufacturing industry to maintain continuous production by filling gaps and coping with the overflow of work from full time workers.

Part time workers are predominantly female. In 1994 there were over 5 million female part time workers but also less than a million males. Women with dependent children are particularly likely to work part time. Part time work offers flexibility not only to employers but also to women who usually have the major responsibility for housework and childcare, albeit at the expense of equal pay and career prospects with full time males. The growth of part time work also reflects the expansion of the service sector of the economy. A high proportion of lower paid jobs in areas such as cleaning, clerical work, hairdressing, waitressing, shopwork, health, education and social services is part time.

Women workers

The number of women in the workforce has grown steadily since the 1950s. However, the number of male workers peaked in 1966 at 14.7 million and has since declined - to 12.9 million in 1994. In 1994 women comprised 45% of the workforce, with 46% of them working on a part time basis.

Some writers have seen the increase in part time work as evidence of a growing divide in the workforce. Christine Hakim (1987) argues that there is a permanent full time workforce on the one hand and a 'flexible' part time and temporary workforce on the other. A high proportion of women workers are found in the second category.

The growth of the service sector

One of the main changes in the economy of Britain and other advanced industrial societies has been the growth of the *tertiary* or *service* sector of the economy. Services are often defined as anything outside the *primary* or extractive sector (agriculture, fishing, forestry and mining) and the *secondary* or manufacturing sector. The service sector is very diverse and includes industries with little in common - transport, finance, health, education, research, leisure, personal services and public administration.

Deindustrialisation

Changes in patterns of work in Britain are often seen as part of a broader process of deindustrialisation. This is the term used to describe the decline of the manufacturing sector. This decline has been apparent in Britain throughout the 20th century and particularly during the 1980s.

Deindustrialisation has been defined and measured in a number of ways. They include:

1   A relative decline in the proportion of total employment in manufacturing.
2   An absolute decline in employment in manufacturing.
3   A decline in the share of manufacturing in total output, ie in the value of all goods and services produced.
4   An increase in the consumption of imported as compared to home produced manufactured goods.

In terms of all these measures there has been a trend to deindustrialisation in 20th century Britain.

Daniel Bell: a post-industrial society

Writers such as Daniel Bell (1973) have argued that the growth of the service sector is transforming countries like the USA and Britain into *post-industrial societies*. Bell argues that as people's material needs are increasingly satisfied, more and more emphasis will be placed on the satisfaction of other needs. This will move the emphasis from the provision of food and manufactured goods to services. In industrial society most people were concerned with getting adequate food, clothing and housing in order to stay alive. These basic needs have now been met for the majority. People now spend more and more of their income (either directly or through tax contributions) on services such as leisure activities, health care and education. This creates more and more employment for workers employed in such service sector industries.

Just as industrialisation involved the displacement of agricultural work by manufacturing industries as the leading sector of the economy, so the development of post-industrial society entails a shift from manufacturing to services as the lead sector. Bell is optimistic that the decline of manufacturing will be more than compensated by the growth of new forms of employment in services.

For Bell, these changes will mean the nature of work itself is transformed. White collar jobs become the norm as machines take over more and more manual tasks. Bell sees professional, technical and scientific occupations as particularly significant in post-industrial society. As a result, this society is increasingly a *knowledge society* where a growing proportion of the population uses theoretical knowledge and technical expertise in their work. The revolution in information technology and computers while giving more control over many areas of life requires greater knowledge and technical understanding. Bell claims that in this new society technical experts will take the lead in decision making. Those in control will achieve their positions through their demonstrated abilities and professional expertise rather than as a result of ownership of wealth.

Bell has been criticised for exaggerating the extent of changes in capitalist society and ignoring important continuities. Marxists like Braverman (1974) reject the argument that work is increasingly skilled and suggest that many in the growing white collar and professional workforce are in fact carrying out routine and low skilled functions. Jobs are often professional in name only, for example plumbers become 'sanitary engineers' and insurance salespeople 'financial consultants'. The growth of the service sector may simply represent a new stage in the development of capitalism, rather than the emergence of a radically new form of society. Bell's optimism about post-industrial society is also tempered by the increase in unemployment in many advanced capitalist societies.

Jonathan Gershuny: a self service economy

Gershuny (1978) disagrees with Bell. He argues that while consumption needs have risen they are not necessarily met by increased personal service provision and a growth of personal service occupations. Instead they may also be met by individuals providing services for themselves. Thus as public transport costs rise more people will buy cars and drive themselves around. Similarly, products like washing machines, vacuum cleaners and videos replace laundries, domestic servants and cinemas. Gershuny argues there is a trend towards a *self service economy* in which the emphasis will be away from the consumption of services provided by others towards the provision of goods which consumers can use to service themselves. He claims that much of the growth of service occupations is linked to the fact that many such jobs provide services for the self service products provided by the manufacturing sector. For example, the consumption of more cars, televisions and washing machines creates more jobs for repair and maintenance workers in the service sector.

Gershuny argues that the self service economy will create new demands for manufactured goods. Critics of his argument note that there appears to be a long term decline in manufacturing jobs in Britain and it is optimistic to assume that this will be reversed.

Ernest Mandel: the continuity of capitalism

Most Marxists have rejected both Bell's and Gershuny's interpretations of the growth of the service sector. Ernest Mandel (1975) argues that capitalism is based on the accumulation of capital and the search for profitable investments. The growth of the service sector does not change this. Capitalists have simply found services a more profitable area for investment than manufacturing. There is evidence that many large transnational companies have diversified from manufacturing into services when their profits have been threatened. British American Tobacco (BAT), for example, now has a financial arm which includes Eagle Star Insurance and Allied Dunbar (formerly Hambro Life); a retail arm, in the Argos catalogue showrooms; and a paper arm, in the Wiggins Teape group. The priorities of capitalism remain the same in both manufacturing and service sectors.

Activity 6   Changing Work Patterns

Item A *Manufacturing output*

The share of manufacturing in total UK output (percentage of value)

1960	1970	1979	1986	1992
32.1	28.1	24.9	21.8	19.9

Adapted from S. Bazen and T. Thirwall *Deindustrialisation*, 1989, p5 and G.B.J. Atkinson *Economics: Themes and Perspectives*, 1994, p130

Item C

Full and part time employment: by gender

United Kingdom   Thousands

	Males		**Females**	
	Full time	Part time	Full time	Part time
1984	13,240	570	5,422	4,343
1985	13,336	575	5,503	4,457
1986	13,430	647	5,662	4,566
1987	13,472	750	5,795	4,696
1988	13,881	801	6,069	4,808
1989	14,071	734	6,336	4,907
1990	14,109	789	6,479	4,928
1991	13,686	799	6,350	4,933
1992	13,141	885	6,244	5,081
1993	12,769	886	6,165	5,045
1994	12,875	998	6,131	5,257

From *Social Trends*, 1995, p69

Item B

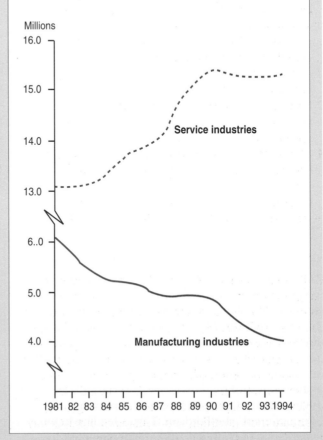

Employment in service and manufacturing industries in millions: Great Britain 1981-94 (seasonally adjusted)

Adapted from *Employment Gazette*, March 1995, p57

Item D *Part time work*

The way in which employers in a variety of industries make use of part time workers is shown by their hours of work, occupations and pay. In food manufacturing establishments, where from 33 to 87 per cent of the female labour force in manual occupations work part time, production is maintained over 15-16 hour days by employing full time day workers and separate shifts of morning, afternoon and evening workers on production and packing jobs. The timing of work schedules eliminates loss of output due to meal breaks, thus maximising the use of capital equipment by adding approximately 1 to 2 hours to daily production time without incurring extra costs from higher rates of pay for overtime or the rotating shifts worked by full timers. Elsewhere part time hours have been altered to maintain output over an unchanged working day at plants where the length of the full time working week was reduced from 40 to 37 hours.

The patterns of employers' labour requirements are the main reason for the employment of part time labour. Part time jobs exist in their own right. Part time workers are not engaged as substitutes for full time employees in short supply. In organisations with significant levels of part time employment managers have waiting lists of women seeking full time jobs and of part time employees wishing to transfer to full time work.

Adapted from O. Robinson 'The Changing Labour Market: the Phenomenon of Part Time Work in Britain' *National Westminster Bank Quarterly Review*, November 1985

Item E *Flexible work at McDonald's*

'We take the business of making hamburgers more seriously than anyone else', claims McDonald's. Since the unveiling of the first

McDonald's

British store in Woolwich in 1974, the company has revolutionised fast food. McDonald's secret for success comes not from the Big Mac sauce but from the new production process, using a combination of the Fordist conveyor belt with the Japanese emphasis on flexibility. Each store is a factory where workers skills

have been kept to a bare minimum. No chefs, no apprentices wanted on this burgerline. Everyone has been levelled down to the uniform 'crew member' rushing between stations to perform tasks learnt in a day. Computerised machines do the cooking for you and regulate your movements to the second. The stated aim is to take the guesswork out of cooking. From Oxford Street to Manila, McDonald's workers follow identical steps to produce identical burgers.

Adapted from H. Lamb and S. Percy 'Big Mac is Watching You' *New Society*, 9.10.87

Questions

1 What evidence do Items A and B provide to support the view that deindustrialisation is occurring in Britain?
2 a) Summarise the evidence is Item C.
   b) Suggest reasons for the gender differences.
3 Judging from Item D, who are the main beneficiaries of part time work. Explain your answer.
4 Using data from Item E and elsewhere, evaluate the view that the growth of the service sector will lead to a greater number of skilled jobs.

2.3 Flexibility and post-Fordism

Writers like Braverman claimed that work in the 20th century was becoming increasingly 'degraded' as a result of the minute division of labour advocated by scientific management theorists and put into practice by manufacturers like Henry Ford. Post-Fordist theorists, however, reject this view arguing that a radical shift is occurring in the way work is organised in industrial societies. They claim the inflexible technology and rigid division of labour of 'Fordism' is giving way to the more flexible methods of production of post-Fordism. This is leading to the re-emergence of craftwork and a widening of skills.

Alan Warde (1989) argues that flexibility can be identified in four aspects of industrial production.

1 **Technology** Developments in areas such as computer aided design and computer aided manufacture (CAD/CAM) allow small batch production. In the Fordist assembly line system technology was 'dedicated' to producing large quantities of virtually identical products which could be sold cheaply. For example, the assembly line developed by Henry Ford enabled large numbers of virtually identical cars, washing machines, televisions and so on to be produced cheaply for a mass market. New machinery is more flexible and can be adapted to the requirements of rapidly changing products and designs.

2 **Products** Products are produced in smaller quantities for more specialised markets with

regular changes to meet the demands of customers. The Benetton chain which produces clothes for a rapidly changing fashion market is a good example of this. Benetton produces jumpers from undyed wool and then dyes small batches in the colours required for the latest fashions. Under post-Fordism consumers are seen as more affluent and more discriminating. They seek exclusive products which have been specially designed for a particular group or lifestyle rather than a mass produced product which is identical to thousands of others.

3 **Jobs** The extreme division of labour characterised by Fordism is being replaced by 'functional flexibility' whereby workers are expected to perform a range of tasks and be prepared to change jobs during their time with an employer. Japanese firms in particular have adopted this approach removing demarcation lines between jobs and expecting workers to acquire new skills. The management theorist, John Atkinson (1985), suggests that British firms are increasingly adopting Japanese flexibility and expecting their *core* (mostly full time permanent) workers to exercise a wider range of skills so breaking down the specialised division of labour characteristic of Fordism.

4 **Contracts** Under Fordism firms employed a large, mostly full time permanent workforce. Under post-Fordism the *core workforce* of full time workers is supplemented by a large number of temporary, part time, casual or subcontracted workers, providing a *peripheral workforce* which can be used as and when needed. Atkinson argues that such workers provide numerical flexibility in the form of additional workers who are needed only for short periods. It may also be cheaper for firms to buy in services such as catering or cleaning on a subcontract basis rather than employing their own full time permanent workers. (Item C in Activity 7 illustrates Atkinson's view of the flexible firm).

Post-Fordism: a new economic order?

While many commentators have identified a trend towards post-Fordism, the consequences of these trends are disputed. Some writers are optimistic. For Michael Piore and Charles Sabel (1984) small scale work organisations, based on flexible production techniques and aimed at specialist markets, represent a welcome alternative to the large scale mass production of capitalist transnational corporations. New technology has assisted in the growth of flexibility. Small firms are able to use computer controlled machinery to rapidly reprogramme for new products. This often calls for a good deal of skill from craftworkers who need to both operate and

programme machines and in many cases even design products. For Piore and Sabel such small scale, flexible enterprises based on craftwork and specialist production techniques offer the possibility of workers developing new skills and gaining greater control over their work.

Not all post-Fordist theorists are as optimistic. For example, Atkinson, although clearly a supporter of flexibility, acknowledges that there will be winners and losers. For the core workers the rewards of flexibility will be security of employment (provided they are willing and capable of retraining), better promotion prospects and career development and improved pay and conditions. For other workers, particularly those in the peripheral group, conditions of employment are likely to deteriorate, with less job security, fewer fringe benefits such as paid holidays and pensions, and a lack of protection from trade unions.

Regulationist theories and neo-Fordism

Some writers influenced by Marxism prefer the term neo-Fordism rather than post-Fordism. For *regulationist theorists* like Michael Aglietta (1979) we are witnessing a new phase of capitalism rather than its transformation. For Aglietta capitalism has been characterised by a series of phases each dominated by a different combination of *regime of accumulation* (means of organising work to make profits) and *mode of regulation* (means of organising society to ensure economic efficiency). Under Fordism capitalism was dependent on mass production for a mass market to make profits and the system was regulated by state intervention in both the economy and in welfare provision. Aglietta claims this system has become increasingly inflexible and inefficient and is being replaced at the end of the 20th century by neo-Fordism.

Neo-Fordism is based on a move away from mass production to small scale batch production. This means that production is more flexible. There is also a move towards competitive individualism away from collectivism with a consequent weakening of trade unions and collective welfare provision. Standardised mass produced products are replaced by more individualised products produced in small numbers for specific groups of consumers.

In this respect Aglietta echoes some of the arguments of Piore and Sabel. However, unlike Piore and Sabel, who see a choice on offer about the way in which work will be organised in future, the regulationists do not. They argue that there are general laws which determine or 'regulate' the development of the economic system. Aglietta is also much less optimistic about the possibility of workers gaining new skills and greater control. Like Braverman, he sees an inherent tendency to deskilling and managerial control within capitalism.

Criticisms of theories of post-Fordism and flexibility

Critics argue that while there are certain trends towards more flexible methods of organising work, these are not as coherent or as universal as the term post-Fordism implies.

Small scale and mass production The first problem is that small scale flexible production has a long history. It has always existed in Britain for specialist products (Pollert, 1988). On the other hand mass production continues to be very important in many industries, for example food processing. It might not seem so in the West because some of the routinised and deskilled mass production has been exported to the Third World where labour costs are cheaper (Warde, 1989).

Skill levels Critics have questioned the suggestion of some post-Fordists that flexible working will increase skill levels. Flexibility may instead lead to deskilling or simply continuing dependence on traditional skills. Where it leads may depend on a whole range of factors, for example how workers and management see the situation, their relative strengths and so on. Thus Maryellen Kelley (1989) in her study of programmable automation in the American engineering industry found examples of both 'Taylorist' and 'worker centred' types of control. This suggests that neither deskilling nor worker centred control necessarily result from the introduction of new technology.

Gender and flexibility A number of feminist writers have criticised theories of flexibility for failing to address the issue of gender and work. Sylvia Walby (1989) argues that Atkinson's distinction between 'core' and 'peripheral' workers fails to consider the gendered nature of the workforce. This is not to say that men simply constitute the core and women the peripheral workers. 57% of women workers are full time and, in areas like clerical work, they constitute a significant part of the core workforce. However, Walby argues that the growth of part time female employment does represent a strategy by employers for exploiting workers more effectively as well as providing the numerical flexibility discussed by Atkinson. As trade unions and legislation have given full time workers more protection, so employers have seen greater advantages in making use of part timers.

The peripheral workforce Writers like Atkinson see the growth of the peripheral workforce - for example, part time temporary and self-employed workers - as evidence of greater flexibility in employment. There is little doubt that these categories of workers have increased but the implications of this are open to debate. Anna Pollert (1988) argues that such workers have always existed and the changes represent fluctuations rather than major increases in the use of peripheral workers.

Post-Fordism as the cause of changes Clearly a large number of important changes are taking place in the nature of work in advanced capitalist societies. However, critics of post-Fordism argue that it is a mistake to see all these changes as part of a unified transformation. As Stephen Wood puts it 'flexible specialisation theory runs the risk of over-packing a whole set of elements which are all assumed to be marching to the same drummer - technology, scale of production, labour skills, job flexibility, market strategies, internalisation and product differentiation - and also of neglecting the multi-dimensionality of these' (1989, p42).

Summary

1 According to Marxists like Braverman, new technology's most important effect is to deskill the workforce. Some post-Fordist theorists have pointed to the capacity of new technology to reskill workers, break down the specialised division of labour and enable the development of new 'flexible' forms of work.

2 There is evidence that new technologies can have the effects described by both these perspectives.

3 Changes in the organisation of work result in changes in the nature of work and the workforce. These include a growth in the employment of women, increases in the employment of part time and other 'peripheral' groups in the workforce, and an expansion of the service sector at the expense of manufacturing.

Activity 7 Flexible Production Systems

Item A *Flexible production in textiles*

The textile industry in the town of Prato in northern Italy provides an example of the development of flexible specification production techniques. From the late 19th century to the 1930s large factories produced woollen fabrics in Prato. In the 1950s the Pratese were forced to become more flexible and develop new fabrics in order to compete with Japan and Eastern Europe. They experimented with incorporating different coloured threads to create 'fantasy fabrics' (*tessuti fantasia*). They also began to use artificial fibres and faster, more sophisticated looms. Through such experimentation the Pratese were able to produce garments with the appearance of luxury from relatively cheap materials.

Another development in Prato from the 1930s onwards was the break up of large integrated firms using factory based production systems into many small workshops. Firms found it less risky to contract work out, often to former employees. These small workshops were linked together in networks coordinated by an *impannatore*. The *impannatore* purchased raw materials, organised the network of small workshops to produce cloth to buyers specifications, and brought the product to market or sold it to a merchant. From the 1950s onwards such networks of small businesses almost completely took over textile production from the larger integrated firms.

The introduction of automatic looms in the 1970s enabled further technical innovation as the Pratese modified new machines to perform unsuspected tricks. By the late 1970s numerically controlled machines were introduced. The technological flexibility that resulted from these machines meant that firms which were unsuccessful in marketing their own designs could act as subcontractors to a competitor who had an overflow of orders. The flexibility of the new machines meant that production could be quickly switched from the firm's own designs to those of another firm. Next year these roles might well be reversed.

Adapted from M. J. Piore and C. Sabel *The Second Industrial Divide: Possibilities for Prosperity*, 1984

Item B *Numerical control systems*

1 **Numerical control** Manually controlled machines are replaced by numerically controlled machines. Each machine still requires a human operative though the machining is controlled by a microcomputer.

2 **Direct numerical control** A single computer is able to control a number of individual machines. Each machine has a variety of tools which can be selected for specified jobs. This system enables one operator to control several machines from a central computer. Workers are still needed to load machines with the material to be manufactured and take away finished products.

3 **Flexible manufacturing system** In this system the computer not only controls machines but also a transportation system (eg a conveyor belt) which transports parts around the system according to the computer's instructions. Not only can each machine carry out a wide range of functions but parts can be sent to different machines in any sequence according to the manufacturing specifications which are programmed into the system.

Based on P. Marsh *The Robot Age*, 1982, pp100-104

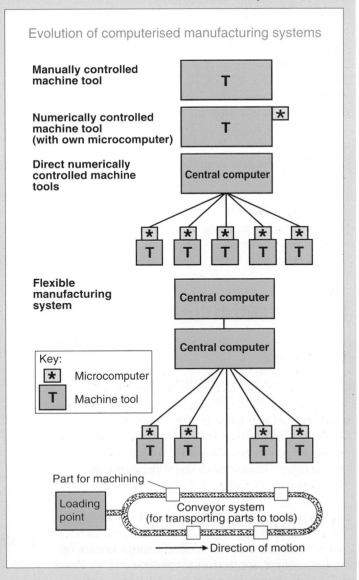

Evolution of computerised manufacturing systems

Manually controlled machine tool — T

Numerically controlled machine tool (with own microcomputer) — T *

Direct numerically controlled machine tools — Central computer

Flexible manufacturing system — Central computer / Central computer

Key:
* Microcomputer
T Machine tool

Part for machining

Loading point

Conveyor system (for transporting parts to tools)

Direction of motion

Item C *The flexible firm*

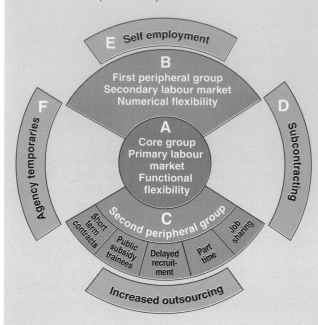

From J. Atkinson 'The Changing Corporation' in D. Clutterbuck (ed) *New Patterns of Work*, 1985, p19

Item D *Flexible production in Benetton*

A well known example of flexible production based on a network of small firms is the fashion clothing chain Benetton. It is often quoted in order to exemplify a major firm continually adapting its stocks and products to an assumed highly volatile fashion market.

But the Benetton case does not match up to the image of a network of firms all flexibly specialised and employing highly committed, skilled workforces. At the centre is in fact a large firm which grants retail franchises to smaller firms. On the production side much of the skilled work is done in-house by the main company, and the small firms in the network, often employing a large percentage of women, are left the less skilled tasks such as weaving and making up. Much of the supposedly skilled and creative aspect of the work is thus highly standardised. Basic products are produced in a standardised form, for example jumpers are made undyed so they can be dyed immediately to respond to market demands. Benetton is also a huge international network with shops as far apart as Scotland and Sao Paolo selling basically the same products.

Adapted from S. Wood *The Transformation of Work*? 1989, pp24-25

Questions

1 What evidence of flexibility is shown in Item A in:
   a) the relationship between different firms;
   b) the way they used new technology?
2 How does the automated flexible manufacturing system illustrated in Item B differ from the traditional Fordist assembly line?
3 a) In Item C, how does the role of the core group of workers differ from the roles of the peripheral groups?
   b) How are workers in the peripheral groups likely to differ from the core group in terms of factors such as sex, age, levels of pay and conditions of work?
4 Piore and Sabel suggest that networks of small firms like Benetton represent a real and welcome alternative to the mass production model of international capitalist corporations. How is this questioned by Item D?

3 Industrial Relations

Key Issues

1 To what extent is conflict a normal part of industrial relations?
2 How can strikes and other expressions of industrial conflict be explained?
3 How have broader political and economic changes affected industrial relations in Britain?

3.1 Industrial conflict

Conflict in the workplace is often treated as a social problem. Strikes are frequently portrayed in the mass media as undermining economic efficiency and disrupting the provision of services to consumers (see pp553-554). Some theories see management and workers sharing the same basic interests. Given this, conflict is an abnormal and temporary feature of industrial relations. Other theories see conflict as a normal feature of work in capitalist societies. It is in employers' interests to control workers in order to maximise productivity and profits. It is in workers interests to seek higher wages and greater control over their work. From this viewpoint, the existence of industrial conflict is not surprising.

Institutionalisation of industrial conflict

Industrial conflict can be expressed in a number of ways. Strikes are the most obvious and publicised expression but are a relatively rare occurrence. A survey by Daniel and Millward (1983) of around 2,000 establishments showed that only a quarter had experienced any industrial action (including strikes and other forms of organised protest) from mid-1979 to mid-1980. And this was a period that experienced the highest number of working days lost through strikes since the 1920s.

Trade unions are generally as anxious as employers to avoid strikes. Most disputes between employers and employees are dealt with through the process of collective bargaining. Representatives of workers belonging to a trade union or group of unions negotiate with representatives of the employers. Some sociologists (Dahrendorf, 1959) claim that class conflict in the workplace has not disappeared but has become *institutionalised*. Trade unions act as interest groups both in the workplace and in the wider society, articulating the interests of workers to the government of the day. From this perspective the working class has become integrated into capitalist society and is able to influence industrial and political decision making. Marxists, on the other hand, have argued that such structures merely create an illusion of power. Industrial conflict is simply channelled into safe institutionalised forms which do not threaten the capitalist system (Hyman, 1989).

Types of industrial conflict

Even where workers take organised industrial action strikes are often regarded as a last resort. Other organised forms of action include overtime bans, refusal to carry out certain duties and working to rule. Such actions can create considerable disruption in the workplace.

Not all industrial conflict is organised. Employees may express their dissatisfaction with work in a variety of ways such as absenteeism, resignation, industrial sabotage (see Activity 9) and even theft. Even industrial accidents have been seen as a manifestation of industrial conflict - accident rates may go up when conditions make it difficult to express discontents through striking. A study by Handy (1968) of the British coal mining industry showed that absenteeism, high labour turnover and industrial accidents were all expressions of conflict which increased when strikes were seen as inappropriate.

As Richard Hyman (1984) notes, employers can instigate conflict. Plant closure, sackings, victimisation of workers, speeding up production lines, safety hazards and arbitrary discipline are all actions or inactions of management which may provoke conflict.

Since the 1970s governments of both main parties have seen strikes as a major economic problem and have attempted to reduce their incidence, both through cooperation with the unions and more

recently through attempts to curb union power. Such attempts to reduce industrial conflict may, however, be in vain. A decline in strikes may simply be reflected in an increase in other expressions of conflict. And even the absence of any open conflict may conceal suppressed conflict which may influence employees' morale and productivity.

Measuring strikes

It is not easy to define strikes. In general they involve an organised stoppage of work by a group of employees. One problem is that official statistics on strikes, collected by the Employment Department, include only certain categories of strikes (those which either last a full day, or involve at least ten workers or lead to a loss of 100 working days or more). Also only 'industrial' disputes are included - strikes which are defined as 'political' are not counted. A further problem is that not all strikes are reported to the Department of Employment which relies mainly on reports from employers and newspapers to compile its statistics.

The significance of strikes can be measured in various ways. The two most common are the *number of strikes* and the *number of working days* lost through strikes. Both can be misleading - there might be a large number of very short lived strikes each involving few workers or a small number of long strikes involving large numbers of workers, for example the 1984/85 miners' strike. For this reason it is useful to consider the average number of workers involved in each strike and the average duration of each strike.

Explaining strikes

Some explanations of strikes have tended to see them as a social problem to be cured by legislation or better management. Strikes are sometimes seen as the fault of 'agitators', such as shop stewards. However, this does not explain why supposed agitators are much more successful in some situations than others. The Human Relations School of management emphasises bad communications as a cause of disputes seeing strikes as a problem to be dealt with by better face-to-face relationships between individual managers and workers. But this does not explain why whole industries have high strike records.

Most sociological explanations see strikes as a normal part of industrial relations in capitalist societies. Some have focused on differences in strike rates between different industries or regions. This approach uses the comparative method to identify variables which affect strike rates. Other explanations look for the basic causes of strikes.

Community integration Clark Kerr and Abraham Siegel (1954) analysed the international strike records of a number of industries. They found that certain occupational groups, such as miners, lumbermen, dockers and seamen, had a higher than average strike record. They argue that the factor such industries have in common is the relative isolation of their occupational communities from the wider society. This gives rise to a strong sense of working class solidarity favourable to trade unionism and collective action.

However, as Hyman (1984) points out this does not explain the variations in strike rates for the majority of workers who do not live in such integrated communities. Nor does it explain how workers in the same industry, for example steel making, from different countries have very different strike rates.

Workplace characteristics A survey of industrial relations in Britain by Daniel and Millward (1983) investigated the relationship between workplace characteristics and strike rates. They found that higher strike rates were associated with the following:
1 agreed negotiating procedures between management and unions;
2 a high proportion of manual workers;
3 large establishments;
4 a high proportion of male workers;
5 a high proportion of union members;
6 a high proportion of full time workers;
7 most bargaining between unions and management taking place in the workplace rather than elsewhere (for example at national level).

The changes in the workforce discussed in Sections 2.2 and 2.3 mean that fewer workplaces have these characteristics.

Workers' definitions Little has been said so far about how workers themselves see strikes. From a social action viewpoint it is necessary to discuss workers' definitions of situations in order to explain their actions. The evidence indicates that workers see wage disputes as the main reason for strike action. This would make sense in terms of Goldthorpe et al's finding that affluent workers defined their work as a means of earning money to improve their living standards (see p326).

Richard Hyman (1984) argues that workers'

definitions of the situation should form part of an explanation, but researchers should look further. For example, in *Wildcat Strike* Alvin Gouldner (1955) describes how workers went on strike over a wage claim. However, an equally if not more important reason for the strike was a new manager who imposed what the workers saw as very strict and rigid supervision. Dissatisfaction grew but the workers felt they could not legitimately challenge management's right to manage. However, a pay dispute provided a legitimate reason to express this discontent in the form of strike action.

Strikes are often about control as this example indicates. And often, this is how workers see the situation. Beynon's (1973) analysis of a strike at Fords at Halewood found that a dispute over control, in particular management's attempt to impose a 'good behaviour clause' on the workers, was seen as the main reason for the strike.

Class inequality Industrial conflict takes place within an unequal society with wide variations in income and wealth. Given this, as Hyman (1984) notes, disputes over the distribution of these scarce resources are bound to occur. And the workplace is where most people, for a large part of their lives, obtain their income.

Industrial societies are also characterised by inequalities of power. Again the workplace is a site where most people experience supervision and control. Given that it is a scarce and valued resource, disputes over power are bound to occur in the workplace.

Marxists see industrial conflict as a natural outcome of an economic system founded on the principle of controlling and exploiting the workforce in order to maximise profits. Given this, industrial conflict whether it finds expression or not is built into the social system.

Explanations of strikes and industrial conflict which look to structural inequality and class conflict are very general. They do not, for example, fully explain variations in industrial conflict between different groups of workers. However, combined with other approaches, they provide a broader picture.

Activity 8 Industrial Conflict

Item A *Variations in industrial conflict*

Edwards and Scullion studied industrial conflict in seven British factories.

In two clothing factories the main expressions of conflict were high labour turnover - leaving the job - and absenteeism - taking time off. Most of the workers were women who were not in trade unions. Most found their jobs boring and their managers overbearing.

In a large metals factory there was less labour turnover and relatively little absenteeism. Workers exercised considerable control over their work. Shop stewards organised them to meet quotas agreed with management. This meant that workers could often finish early or take unofficial days off if they had completed their quotas. When the company was having financial problems, management made periodic attempts to reassert control. Workers (who were mostly skilled and hard to replace) resisted these attempts with some success by short strikes and withdrawal of cooperation which disrupted production.

In a process factory, which required round the clock shifts, management avoided open conflict by using a system of 'sophisticated control'. Employees were selected carefully and guaranteed an annual salary. They were given a certain amount of independence and were regularly consulted by managers. Those who stepped out of line were issued with warnings. There was a certain amount of absenteeism but absences were recorded and regular absentees were disciplined. By using sophisticated control techniques management were able to minimise, although not entirely eliminate, conflict.

Based on P. K. Edwards and H. Scullion *The Social Organisation of Industrial Conflict: Control and Resistance in the Workplace*, 1982

Item B *Industrial sabotage*

They had to throw away half a mile of Blackpool rock last year, for, instead of the customary motif running through its length it carried the terse injunction 'Fuck Off'. A worker dismissed by a sweet factory had effectively demonstrated his annoyance by sabotaging the product of his labour. In the Christmas rush in a Knightsbridge store, the machine which shuttled change backwards and forwards suddenly ground to a halt. A frustrated salesman had demobilised it by ramming a cream bun down its gullet. In our researches we have been told by Woolworth's sales girls how they clank half a dozen buttons on the till simultaneously to win a few minutes rest from 'ringing up'. Railwaymen have described how they block lines with trucks to delay shunting operations for a few hours. Materials are hidden in factories, conveyor belts jammed with sticks, cogs stopped with wires and ropes, lorries 'accidentally' backed into ditches. Electricians labour to put in weak fuses, textile workers 'knife' through carpets and farmworkers cooperate to choke agricultural machinery with tree branches.

Adapted from L. Taylor and P. Walton 'Industrial Sabotage Motives and Meanings' in S. Cohen (ed) *Images of Deviance*, 1971, p219

Item C *Strikes*

Pickets outside News International's printing works at Wapping, 1986

Questions

1 Explain the differences in the way industrial conflict was expressed in the workplaces in Item A?
2 Read Item B. Suggest reasons why workers might express their discontent with work through industrial sabotage rather than other actions.
3 Strikes are often seen as a 'social problem'. Discuss with some reference to Item C.

3.2 The changing face of industrial relations in Britain

According to many commentators the 1980s and 90s have witnessed a decline in the power of trade unions and in the importance of collective bargaining in industrial relations. This contrasts with the 1970s when trade unions were widely recognised by employers and were regularly consulted by government.

The Social Contract

The Labour government of 1974-79 established the 'Social Contract'. This was an attempt to persuade the trade unions to accept pay restraint in return for the repeal of the unpopular 1971 Industrial Relations Act and a promise of greater consultation between the government and the TUC (the Trades Union Congress which represents most of the main trade unions). During this period a number of bodies were set up which brought together representatives of the government, trade unions and employers for consultative purposes. For example, the National Enterprise Board was set up in 1975 to develop policies for firms receiving state aid. This era has been seen as the height of trade union power. However, Richard Hyman (1989) suggests that the unions' position was symbolic - they exercised little genuine political power.

By 1977 many groups of workers were increasingly disillusioned with the policy of pay restraint. Low paid workers, such as those in the health service, felt that little was being done to improve their position and the number of days lost through strikes increased markedly in 1977. This culminated in the so-called 'winter of discontent' of 1978-79 when a number of public service unions took strike action.

Thatcherism and the trade unions

In the general election of 1979 a Conservative government under Margaret Thatcher took office. It was firmly committed to reducing the power of trade unions. Many commentators argue that a combination of government policies and changes in the economy in the 1980s severely weakened the trade unions. Several factors have been important.

1 **Union representation on public bodies** Many of the public bodies on which unions were represented have been abolished or reduced in function. Where new bodies have been created the government has often excluded trade union nominees from participation.

2 **Industrial relations legislation** A series of Acts have restricted the ability of trade unions to take effective industrial action. Trade unions which are deemed to have infringed the law are now liable to have their funds sequestrated (taken away for a period of time). The law increasingly controls how trade unions run their internal affairs, for example voting on industrial action and the election of senior officers. The ability of unions to discipline their own members, an important means of enforcing collective decisions, has been largely removed. Legislation has also outlawed secondary industrial action. This means workers are not allowed to act in support of a dispute which is not at their own place of work, thus weakening more general worker solidarity.

3 **The recession and restructuring of the workforce** High levels of unemployment and redundancies have weakened many of the strongest trade unions. Heavy industries, such as coal, engineering and shipbuilding which were the backbone of the union movement have experienced the greatest decline in employment. New jobs are increasingly part time, white collar, female and in the service sector. These are workers who traditionally have been poorly organised by trade unions. Unemployment also reduces workers' bargaining power by creating a 'reserve army of labour' ready to take over their jobs.

4 **New attitudes from employers** Many employers are now bypassing trade unions and established collective bargaining procedures. They are moving towards individual bargaining - negotiating pay and conditions with individual workers rather than trade unions - with flexible rates of pay rather than a fixed rate for the job.

Some firms have experimented with worker representation on company boards which may bypass union representation. In other cases unions in a mood of so-called 'new realism' have signed no strike deals and agreed to more flexible working practices in return for union recognition and guaranteed pay increases.

Theories of post-Fordism see this as part of the movement away from collectivism to individualism and part of the new 'flexibility' in the workforce. Marxists like Hyman, however, argue that the 1980s was an era of 'coercive pacification' in which employers, aided by legislation from the government, attempted to suppress industrial conflict by weakening trade unions and the institutions of collective bargaining.

Changes within trade unions

During the 1970s trade unions underwent a period of considerable growth, reaching a peak in 1979 when over 58% of the workforce was unionised. Union density (the proportion of the workforce in trade unions) has fallen sharply since then, though if the unemployed are excluded from the total workforce the fall is much less dramatic. In general the fall in membership has been most severe in unions with a large proportion of members in manual jobs, for example the TGWU (Transport and General Workers Union), (see Activity 9).

These changes are partly explained by the fact that the biggest job losses have been in manufacturing industries with high union densities. Employment in the service sector has grown but most occupations there are poorly unionised. Thus the sectoral shift in employment, combined with high levels of unemployment has brought about a decline in union membership. Many unions have responded by merging - increasingly small unions are finding it difficult to survive and are being absorbed into larger 'general' unions.

The 1984 Workplace Industrial Relations Survey (Millward and Stevens, 1986) found that union membership densities were generally lower in workplaces employing less than 50 workers and in those with higher proportions of female and part time workers. Such groups have been associated with the growth of the 'peripheral workforce'. Unions have generally been slow to organise such workers. This is partly due to the difficulties of union organisation in small service sector workplaces often with a high turnover of workers and large numbers of temporary and part time staff. For example, McDonald's fast food chain is said to have a turnover of labour in London of 200-250% each year. Moreover, unions have traditionally been male dominated with the vast majority of positions of power, such as National Executive seats, filled by men. Some unions are beginning to change in this respect - TGWU, GMB and USDAW (the shop workers' union) have made active attempts to recruit part time and women workers. Some unions have now introduced reserved seats for women on decision making bodies in order to encourage female participation.

The future of trade unions

The extent to which the changes discussed above have seriously weakened trade unions is open to debate. Ken Coates and Tony Topham (1986, p20) argue that unions at shop floor level have been 'shorn of power and function'. At national level they go on to suggest that, 'Their behaviour in the face of government and employers is thus likely to seem increasingly irrelevant and sometimes, indeed, it may be seen as mere posturing'. However, John Kelley (1988) suggests that British trade unions have done well in view of the severe recession in the early 1980s. He notes that while some large and powerful unions like the TGWU and the NUM have experienced large falls in membership others have seen little decline (unlike the USA where union membership has fallen from 23% to 15% of the workforce in a decade).

Some commentators now believe that unions will only survive and grow if they can successfully recruit more members in areas which have traditionally been poorly unionised. Cynthia Cockburn suggests that 'a change in attitude towards women is needed if they are to survive into the twenty first century' (1987, p7).

However, if writers like Braverman are correct, changes in white collar work may blur the distinctions between manual and nonmanual work and encourage white collar union membership.

Since 1979 the *number* of recorded strikes has declined - one possible indicator of the reluctance or lack of ability of unions to take action. The *number of days lost* through strikes has also declined, but has been particularly high in certain years. While unions have come under attack from both government and employers, groups of workers have continued to show their willingness to use industrial action to defend their interests.

Summary

1 Conflict is seen by most sociologists as a normal part of industrial relations. It can be expressed in a variety of ways of which strikes represent only one example.

2 Strikes have been explained in a number of ways, including the propensity of particular groups of workers to take strike action, the motives of particular groups of strikers, and the tendency of the capitalist economic system to generate conflict.

3 Government policies and economic changes since 1979 have reduced collective bargaining and weakened trade unions in Britain.

Activity 9   Changing Industrial Relations

Item A

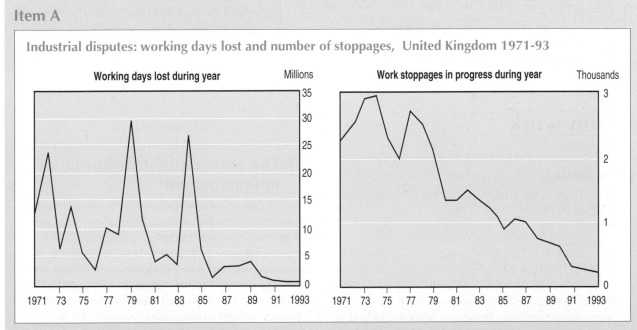

Industrial disputes: working days lost and number of stoppages, United Kingdom 1971-93

Adapted from *Social Trends*, 1993, p59; 1995, p73

Item B *Collective bargaining in the 1990s*

In 1990 the third Workplace Industrial Relations Survey (WIRS) (Millward et al 1992) was carried out. It collected evidence from over 2,000 workplaces based on questionnaires distributed to 2,550 management representatives and 1,466 worker representatives. The 1990 study confirms the trend noted in two earlier surveys (in 1980 and 1984) that the proportion of workers covered by collective bargaining arrangements is declining. Collective bargaining arrangements exist where one or more unions are recognised by the employer as having the right to negotiate on behalf of the workforce. In 1984, 71% of workplaces had collective bargaining arrangements, by 1990 this had fallen to 54% and 36% of workplaces contained not a single union member. The lowest levels of union recognition were in firms in the private services sector.

The WIRS found a clear relationship between trade union membership and pay levels. The more employees that were covered by union recognition the lower the proportion of workers on low wages in an industry. The WIRS also found that firms with high proportions of women workers and part time workers had higher levels of low pay. In non-union workplaces differentials between low paid and high paid workers tended to be relatively wide. Such establishments also made more use of freelance and temporary contracts, and forced redundancies and other forms of dismissal were much more common than in the union sector.

Based on N. Millward et al *Workplace Industrial Relations in Transition*, 1992

Item C

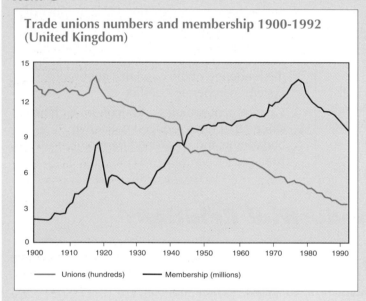

Trade unions numbers and membership 1900-1992 (United Kingdom)

From *Employment Gazette*, June 1994, p190

Questions

1 Study Item A.
  a) What trends are indicated in the table showing working days lost? How would you explain the particularly high figures for 1979 and 1984?
  b) How does the picture of industrial disputes indicated by the second graph differ? How would you explain this difference?
2 a) Using data from Item B discuss the advantages to workers of being represented by a trade union.
  b) Suggest reasons for the decline in collective bargaining arrangements.
3 a) Summarise the trends shown in Item C.
  b) How would you explain these trends?
4 What effects might the changes revealed by Items B and C have on industrial relations in Britain?

4 Non-work

Key Issues

1 Why has unemployment risen since the end of the 1970s?
2 Which social groups suffer most from unemployment?
3 What are the consequences of unemployment for the unemployed and for society generally.
4 To what extent are people's leisure activities patterned by social factors?

4.1 The extent and distribution of unemployment

A small degree of unemployment is inevitable in any economy. There will always be workers who are in the process of changing jobs - *frictional unemployment* - and those who choose not to work - *voluntary unemployment*. However, the high levels of unemployment in the 1980s and 90s cannot be explained in this way. In 1983, for example, over 3 million people were officially registered as unemployed, comprising 12.6% of the working population.

Explaining unemployment

Keynsian theory The length and severity of world recession of the 1930s led the the economist John Maynard Keynes (1936) to question the classical economic view that recessions would correct themselves if left to market forces. He argued that unemployment was caused by the underutilisation of productive resources, both human and financial. Unemployment meant that workers had less money to spend which reduced demand for goods thus reducing profits and leading to further job losses - a vicious spiral. Keynes claimed that this process could only be reversed by state intervention in the form of economic investment. This would help to create jobs, increase spending power and boost demand for goods.

Market liberal theories Market liberal theories became increasingly influential in the 1970s when countries like Britain suffered from recession despite attempts by the state to intervene in the economy and maintain full employment. In terms of market liberal theory it is precisely this state intervention which is the problem since it interferes with the freedom of the market for goods and services, including labour.

Market liberals argue that several problems result from what they see as excessive state intervention. Firstly, unions become too powerful leading to high wage demands and inflation. Secondly, high rates of taxation and government spending take away incentives for the rich to invest, while over generous welfare benefits remove incentives for the poor to work. Thirdly, by trying to maintain full employment the state props up 'lame duck' industries which means that labour and capital are misdirected, instead of being channelled by market forces into more worthwhile enterprises. In this way state intervention restricts the freedom of investors to maximise profits. This leads to a decline in businesses and a rise in unemployment. Milton Friedman (1977) advocated *monetarist* policies to counter these tendencies and restore a free market. He claimed that the government's failure to control the money supply by spending too much led to inflation and ultimately to unemployment.

Marxist theories Marx saw periodic recessions accompanied by unemployment as an inevitable feature of capitalism. In boom periods there is full employment but this leads to a falling rate of profit since employers have to pay higher wages to attract workers and keep them. Lack of profitability leads to a decline in investment and the failure of less successful businesses, creating an increase in unemployment. This, in turn, tends to reduce the level of wages, restoring profitability which encourages investment and results in a further upturn in employment.

Marx argued that these periodic crises would become progressively worse. Capitalists will introduce new machinery in order to boost productivity and reduce labour costs but this is expensive and requires increased exploitation of workers to fund. Eventually the contradictions of capitalism will become plain for all to see and a worker's revolution will lead to socialism.

Economic historians, both Marxist and non-Marxist, trace Britain's economic decline to the last century. Eric Hobsbawn (1969) argued that Britain suffered from being the first country to industrialise. This meant that competitors who industrialised later had the benefit of more modern machinery and equipment. In addition Britain had an empire which provided a protected market for its goods so British industry was not forced to face real competition. There was therefore less incentive to modernise.

Andrew Glyn and John Harrison (1980) agree but argue that economic decline resulted not only from lack of investment in new plant but also from the strength of Britain's labour movement. This meant wages rose faster than profits and further discouraged investment in British industry.

From a Marxist perspective the introduction of monetarism and government attacks on the trade union movement represent an attempt to weaken the working class and restore the profitability of capitalism. And increasing unemployment is one of the ways of doing this.

New technology and unemployment Both Keynsian and market liberal theories see unemployment as something which can be avoided if labour is used correctly. However, many writers are less optimistic about the prospects for avoiding large scale unemployment. The process of deindustrialisation and the impact of new technology may mean that Britain's workforce will become steadily smaller.

This is the view of Clive Jenkins and Barrie Sherman (1979) who claimed that new technology would lead to the 'collapse of work' by the end of the 20th century. Firms introducing machinery controlled by microprocessors would be able to reduce their workforces dramatically. Jenkins and Sherman suggest that the only alternative to permanent mass unemployment is a society geared to leisure. The limited amount of work would be shared and leisure pursuits would become a major life interest for the majority. Not all forecasts have gone so far. However, it seems likely that many less skilled jobs will disappear, including many service sector occupations (for example many clerical jobs) which have created jobs for women in recent years.

The extent of unemployment

Measuring unemployment is notoriously problematic. There is no satisfactory definition. Even the official definition has changed many times in recent years. This makes the analysis of unemployment trends from official statistics very difficult (see Activity 10 and p626).

Those on the left argue that official statistics on unemployment grossly underestimate its true extent since only those registered as unemployed and receiving benefits are counted. This excludes groups such as those on training schemes and married women seeking work but not eligible for benefits. Many would argue that they should be counted as unemployed. The government figure estimated that 2.5 million people - 8.9% of the working population - were unemployed in January 1995. For the same month the Unemployment Unit, an independent research organisation, estimated that the number of people who want jobs but cannot get them is 3.4 million - 12.2% of the workforce (*Labour Research*, March 1995, p32).

On the other hand, those on the right have argued that many claiming to be unemployed are either not seriously looking for work or are working without declaring it. From this viewpoint official statistics on unemployment are an overestimate of its real level. However, according to Ray Pahl (1984) the involvement of the unemployed in the informal economy has been exaggerated. The majority of those who work in the 'black economy' appear to be those who have full time jobs already.

Stocks and flows in unemployment David Ashton (1985) points out that the unemployed are not a static group. He likens the stock of unemployed (the total number of people unemployed at any one time) to a bath which is being filled by those entering unemployment and emptied by those finding jobs. He shows that the big increase in unemployment in 1980-81 occurred because of a substantial increase in the inflow to the unemployment stock with little change in the outflow. Ashton suggests that high unemployment is as much due to a failure to create new jobs as it is a result of high rates of job losses.

The idea of stocks and flows in unemployment helps to explain why rates of unemployment vary between different groups. Those with the highest rates (for example, the young, lower working class and ethnic minorities) tend to be those who are most likely to become unemployed. However, these groups are also those who are likely to find it hardest to get new jobs and thus tend to remain in the unemployed stock longest. Adrian Sinfield (1981) notes that in times of high unemployment employers have a greater choice of workers and thus tend to narrow their definition of an 'acceptable worker'.

Groups seen as less desirable workers such as those with few skills, ethnic minorities, and those with a record of previous unemployment are likely to find it hardest to get jobs.

The social distribution of unemployment

Although official statistics on unemployment need to be treated with caution, they do give some indication of the extent of unemployment in different social groups. Since October 1982 official statistics have been based on those actually claiming benefit - *claimant unemployment*. More recently the Employment Department has also produced statistics based on the International Labour Organisation (ILO) definition of unemployment which includes all people who are actively seeking and available to start work whether or not they are claiming benefit. Figures for the 1990s in this chapter refer to *ILO unemployment* unless otherwise stated.

Social class and unemployment The risk of unemployment is strongly related to occupational class. The highest levels of unemployment are amongst the least skilled categories of workers. David Ashton (1986) found that in 1982 while semi-skilled, unskilled and personal service workers constituted only 18% of the working population they comprised 41% of the unemployed. In Spring 1993 unemployment rates for those who previously held manual occupations were 13.0% compared with 5.6% for nonmanual. The rate was lowest for those with professional experience (*Employment Gazette*, July 1994, p255).

Ethnicity A person's ethnic origin affects their chances of unemployment. In Spring 1994 the unemployment rate for whites was 9.1% compared with 10.4% of those of Indian and 27.9% of those of Pakistani/Bangladeshi origin (*Social Trends*, 1995, pp77-78; see Item C in Activity 10). Moreover, as unemployment has increased it has disproportionately affected black workers. Research by the Runnymede Trust (1983) found that while total registered unemployment increased by 309% between 1973 and 1982, among black people it rose by 515%.

Youth Unemployment statistics indicate that unemployment disproportionately affects young people. In 1994 the unemployment rate for males aged 16-19 was 31% compared to 11.4% for all males aged 16 and over. The comparable rates for females were 16.1% and 7.2%. David Ashton (1986) notes that when the business cycle is in a downward phase with decreasing demand for labour, those coming into the labour market for the first time will be hardest hit. Employers tend to respond by first stopping recruitment and then by making their most recent employees redundant. Thus young people's rates of unemployment rise fastest in a recession. In a boom period, when the demand for labour is increasing, the opposite is true and rates of youth unemployment fall quicker than unemployment generally.

Gender Official statistics suggest that the high levels of unemployment from the 1980s affected men far more than women. In 1988 the annual average rate of unemployment for men was 9.8% compared to 5.8% for women, in 1994 11.4% compared to 7.2% (*Social Trends*, 1995, p76). The industries and occupations which have seen the largest decline in employment have been those which traditionally employed large numbers of men, for example skilled manual workers in heavy manufacturing industries. The growth of the service sector and part time work has created greater opportunities in the types of jobs traditionally taken by women.

However, official statistics on female unemployment are, if anything, more unreliable than those for males. Since October 1982 unemployment has been measured on the basis of those actually claiming benefit. However, according to the 1983 Labour Force Survey, over half of the married women who are seeking work do not claim benefit. The figures for the 1990s given in the above paragraph are based on the ILO definition of unemployment. There is likely to be considerable under-recording whichever measure is used. Statistics for the number of women in work are probably also an under-estimate - large numbers

of women who engage in homework, casual or seasonal work never appear in official statistics.

Regional differences There are wide variations in the rate of unemployment between different parts of the country. These can be seen in the official figures compiled by the Employment Department based on the standard regions of the UK. The ranking of regions in terms of unemployment levels has not changed much since the 1950s. Northern Ireland, Scotland, Wales and Northern regions of England have had consistently higher rates than Southern regions. In the early 1980s the situation in the North West and the formerly prosperous West Midlands deteriorated faster than other regions, while in the early 90s unemployment increased significantly in Southern England and the North-South divide narrowed somewhat.

There are also significant variations within regions which are concealed by regional averages. Brian Showler and Adrian Sinfield (1981) note that in 1980 northern parts of central Liverpool had unemployment rates of around 40% compared to 13% for the city as a whole and 8% for the North West region as a whole. This reflects a general pattern of higher unemployment rates in inner cities.

Regional rates of unemployment reflect the varying fortunes of different sectors of British industry. Areas which are largely dependent on declining industries, for example traditional heavy manufacturing industries like shipbuilding and steelmaking, have suffered most.

Activity 10 Measuring Unemployment

Item A *Alternative definitions of unemployment*

Claimant unemployment

The current official unemployment count is based on the number of people who actually claim unemployment related benefits. It is an administrative measure of unemployment. As critics are quick to point out, this excludes 16-17 year olds because they are technically guaranteed a place on a training scheme. It excludes anyone who is not eligible to claim unemployment related benefits. This means that a large number of women are effectively missed from the count. For example, women whose partners are working and are therefore unlikely to get income support are not included. Nor are single mothers who usually get single parent benefits rather than unemployment benefits. And new rules mean that claimants must be able to prove that they are 'actively seeking work'.

ILO Unemployment

The International Labour Organisation (ILO) definition of unemployment refers to people without a paid job, who are available to start work within the next two weeks and who had either looked for work in the four weeks prior to interview or were waiting to start a job they had obtained. Unemployment based on the ILO definition includes all those people who are actively seeking and available to start work whether of not they are claiming benefit. The ILO rate is the percentage of economically active people who are ILO unemployed

A comparison

Around a million people in each measure of unemployment are not included in the other. For example, in 1993 there were 510,000 women classified as ILO unemployed but who were not claiming benefit. Because of this they would not appear as claimant unemployed. Despite such differences both measures show broadly the same levels and trends.

Adapted from M. Denscombe *Sociology Update*, 1994, p42; *Employment Gazette*, October 1993 and July 1994; *Social Trends*, 1995, p75

Questions

1 With reference to both Items discuss some of the problems of measuring unemployment.
2 Why is the validity of different measures of unemployment hotly debated by politicians as well as sociologists?

Item B

Comparison of alternative measures of unemployment

From *Social Trends*, 1995, p75

Activity 11   Patterns of Unemployment

Figures for unemployment in this Activity are based on ILO definition except for Item A.

Item A

Claimant unemployment and job centre vacancies

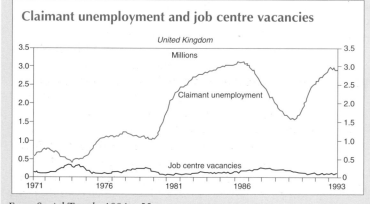

From *Social Trends*, 1994, p55

Item B

Unemployment rates: by gender and age, United Kingdom, 1994

Percentages

Males		Females	
16-19	21.0	16-19	16.1
20-29	14.8	20-29	9.3
30-39	10.2	30-39	7.0
40-49	7.6	40-49	4.7
50-64	11.0	50-59	3.0
All males aged 16 and over	11.4	All females aged 16 and over	7.2

From *Social Trends*, 1995, p76

Item C

Unemployment rates: by region, United Kingdom, 1994

Percentages

North	11.7
North West	10.2
West Midlands	9.9
Yorkshire & Humberside	9.8
South East	9.6
East Midlands	8.3
South West	7.5
East Anglia	7.4
Wales	9.4
Scotland	9.9
Northern Ireland	11.5

Adapted from *Social Trends*, 1995, p77

Item D

Unemployment rates: by ethnic group, Spring 1994, Great Britain

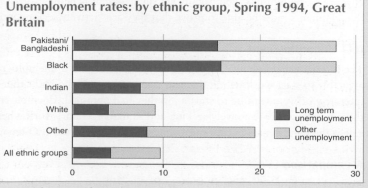

Adapted from *Social Trends*, 1995, p78

Item E

The unemployed: by gender and previous occupation group, 1993, United Kingdom

Percentages and thousands

	Males	Females	All
Percentage of the unemployed in each occupational group			
Managers and administrators	5.2	4.4	4.9
Professional occupations	4.1	2.7	3.5
Associate professional and technical	6.5	3.4	5.0
Clerical and secretarial	12.2	5.5	7.2
Craft and related	14.6	10.3	14.1
Personal and protective services	11.3	5.9	7.8
Sales	11.3	7.7	9.0
Plant and machine operatives	13.2	13.5	13.3
Other occupations	20.1	7.6	14.1
All nonmanual	6.2	5.0	5.6
All manual	15.3	8.3	13.0
Total unemployment (rate)	12.3	7.4	10.2
Total unemployed (thousands)	1,904	900	2,804

Adapted from *Employment Gazette*, July 1994, p255

Questions

1 Unemployment is due to the unwillingness of the unemployed to find work. Comment on this with reference to Item A.
2 Study Items B and E.
a) What relationships are indicated between unemployment and:
i) age; ii) gender;
iii) social class?
b) How would you account for these relationships?
3 a) Summarise the regional differences shown in Item C.
b) Suggest reasons for these differences.
4 a) Briefly summarise the data in Item D.
b) Suggest reasons for the differences in unemployment between ethnic groups?

4.2 The social consequences of unemployment

There is considerable evidence that unemployment has a variety of negative social and psychological consequences. Unemployment not only affects those who are unemployed but also the wider society. For example, higher crime rates, a widening gap between rich and poor and disillusionment of young people with society may all be related to high levels of unemployment.

There are, however, problems in assessing the impact of unemployment.
1 It is difficult to disentangle the effects of unemployment from the effects of other factors associated with unemployment. For example, higher rates of illness amongst the unemployed may be a consequence of the poverty which often accompanies unemployment, rather than a result of the actual experience of not having a job.
2 Different people experience unemployment in different ways. It is therfore difficult to make generalisations about the effects of unemployment.

Bearing these points in mind, a large body of research indicates the following consequences of unemployment.

Poverty Since the early 1980s the unemployed have grown steadily poorer. The Joseph Rowntree *Inquiry into Income and Wealth* found that throughout the 1980s and early 1990s the income gap between those dependent on benefits and those in employment widened. This has been due in part to the government linking benefit levels to prices rather than average earnings - average earnings have risen faster than prices (1995, pp6-7).

Psychological effects An early study of unemployment by Jahoda, Lazarfield and Zeisel (1933) claimed that it produced negative psychological effects and these were due to work deprivation. They argued that work was crucial to psychological wellbeing - without it people experienced apathy and depression.

A number of studies have identified stages which individuals pass through during unemployment. For example, a study of unemployed men in London by Leonard Fagin and Martin Little (1984) identified four stages.
1 **Shock** (experienced by only a minority of those studied). Disbelief and inability to come to terms with job loss.
2 **Denial and optimism** Enthusiastic work seeking combined with a sense of being on holiday, sometimes using time to catch up on household jobs.
3 **Anxiety and distress** As unemployment lengthens concern about the future increases.
4 **Resignation and adjustment** After a time most accepted their situation and became apathetic.

There is a problem in generalising. Different groups appear to experience unemployment in different ways. For example, a study by Jean Hartley (1980) of unemployed managers suggested that their self esteem was not generally affected by unemployment.

Leisure For those in work there is often a sharp contrast between work and leisure - work structures leisure time into set periods. However, for the unemployed leisure is not a precious commodity to be looked forward to but empty space with little to fill it. Fagin and Little note how unemployed people find it hard to structure their time in order to occupy themselves purposefully.

Unemployed people also suffer from lack of social contacts. This is particularly so for older people whose social world had previously revolved around work. Lack of money further reduces the range of leisure activities available. Ray Pahl's (1984) study of the Isle of Sheppey showed that the unemployed were least able to take advantage of their leisure time in order to provide services for themselves. It was households with members in work who had the surplus income to invest in tools, equipment and materials to save money on activities such as decorating, car maintenance and growing their own produce.

Family life The poverty and psychological stresses of unemployment affect family life. Thornes and Collard (1979) found that the average duration of unemployment amongst divorcing couples was twice that of stable marriages.

Lorna McKee and Colin Bell in their study of Kidderminster (1986) claim that wives suffer as much as their unemployed husbands. They found little change in husbands' involvement in housework and childcare. Men explained this in terms of their need to be free to search for work. Many wives accepted the continued responsibility for domestic work,

feeling that anyway they were more competent. Wives also resented the constant presence of husbands in the home and this created further strains in their relationships.

Health A number of studies suggest that unemployed people are likely to suffer higher rates of both physical and mental illness. Given the stressful nature of job loss and unemployment this would seem to make sense. An analysis of mortality statistics for 1971 in England and Wales by Brenner (1979) found that differences in the unemployment rate were the only factor significantly associated with differences in the standard mortality rates between different areas. Brenner argues that the stress of unemployment affects not only the unemployed but also workers in intermittent employment and those in insecure jobs.

Such studies are however only suggestive and Stern (1981) argues that higher death rates may be due to poverty rather than unemployment as such. Also a high proportion of the unemployed come from social classes IV and V which have higher mortality rates anyway. Moreover, while job loss leads to stress and possible illness, it can also remove an individual from the hazards of work which are themselves a cause of premature death.

The wider society While it is difficult to prove that unemployment has specific effects on individuals, assessing its impact on the wider society is even more problematic. Nevertheless, many sociologists along with other commentators have seen a link between unemployment and and a variety of 'social problems' including crime and delinquency, racial discrimination and social unrest. However, these links are far from proven.

Activity 12 Unemployment and Social Order

Item A *Experiencing unemployment*

Andrew and Christine Downing, aged 31 and 29, have three small children aged 8, 6 and 2 years and a baby aged 15 months. The family have been on benefit for 10 years. Despite attending various government training schemes, Andrew has found it hard to get a job. He believes this to be the result of his (minor) criminal record. Christine and two of the children suffer from asthma; the youngest daughter has a heart defect and the baby boy has a milk allergy. The family's council house has damp in nearly all the rooms and is hard to heat because of defective windows.

Not being able to afford the things that most families take for granted has consequences for family relationships and for the Downing's self-esteem as parents. The strain is made worse by limitations imposed on parent's activities:

'We don't go out, we don't go anywhere, we can't even afford to go to the pictures once a month.'

Mr Downing sums it all up:

'Imagine spending a year where the best thing you can look forward to is running a Hoover around the living room and washing up. You go mad, your grey cells start turning purple. The kids are running around screaming their heads off, you tend to get ratty, the more often you lose your temper it has an effect on you. I think it does have an effect on your health both physically and psychologically. It depresses you looking at what other people have and what you can't have.

Adapted from R. Cohen et al *Hardship Britain: Being Poor in the 1990s*, 1992, pp15-18

Item B *Unemployment and parasuicide*

Stephen Platt carried out a study of the relationship between parasuicide and unemployment in Edinburgh between 1968 and 1982. He defines parasuicide as 'a non-fatal act in which an individual causes self-injury'. This includes overdoses resulting from habitual misuse of drugs, but excludes intoxication with alcohol alone. He based his analysis on official statistics on unemployment and hospital admissions categorised as parasuicides.

Platt found an association between areas of the city with high levels of unemployment and high parasuicide rates. He also found a higher parasuicide rate among the unemployed than among the employed. He found the highest risk was among the long term unemployed and among those who had recently lost their jobs.

Sleeping rough

Platt's findings may support the argument that unemployment is a cause of parasuicide. However, he recognises the complex interaction of many other factors. Many male parasuicides lead a marginal existence. Their lives are characterised by petty crime, excessive alcohol consumption and loneliness. Being unemployed may be a consequence rather than a cause of this marginality. The marginality may come first with the resulting unemployment reinforcing it.

Based on S. Platt 'Recent Trends in Parasuicide ("attempted suicide") among Men in Edinburgh' in S. Allen et al (eds) *The Experience of Unemployment*, 1986, pp165-166

Item C *Unemployment and crime*

Crime is the only booming industry in Merseyside. For example, vandalism is not just a matter of smashed lamp-posts and graffiti, but of the systematic destruction of housing and other social facilities by young people. Juvenile crime figures are alarming. Something like a quarter of all prosecutions by the Merseyside police involve children under 16 and another quarter of young people between 16 and 21. Though prosecutions run high they are only the tip of the iceberg as only a small proportion of offenders are ever caught.

Crime cannot be directly attributed to unemployment. The crime rate, though gradually increasing, was high before the present high levels of unemployment and many of the offenders are still of school age in any case. But under 16 crime is particularly high in those districts where unemployment is also high and the latter is inseparable from the environment of social malaise in which crime becomes a normal way of life. In the words of one 19 year old: 'People can't get jobs and the dole money is useless and so people take to robbing; it's as simple as that'. It isn't as simple as that, but enforced idleness is doubtless a factor, as is the feeling of exclusion from work.

Adapted from F. F. Ridley 'View from a Disaster Area: Unemployed Youth in Merseyside' in B. Crick (ed) *Unemployment*, 1981, p25

Item D *Living on the outside*

You feel poor because you are poor, you don't feel part of the system. You feel like you've been shoved in the corner, you're just like an extra statistic because I'm not contributing nothing. You feel like you're having to beg from the system to get something out of the government to survive. If the system was different, where you could work and we could afford to work, contribute to our children, live happy, pay our way, I think everyone would have a different attitude. The worst thing about being on social security is that it takes away your pride, people treat you different, they don't treat you as a person.

Melanie Baker quoted in R. Cohen et al *Hardship Britain: Being Poor in the 1990s*, 1992

Item E

Unemployment has been seen as a major cause of urban riots.

Questions

1 Briefly summarise the effects of unemployment indicated by Item A.
2 Read Items B and C. Why is it difficult to pinpoint the relationship between unemployment and other social factors?
3 With some reference to all the Items discuss the possible relationships between unemployment, social exclusion and social unrest.

4.3 Leisure

Leisure can be defined as time in which individuals are free from other social obligations. However, as Section 1.1 indicates, distinguishing work from leisure is not straightforward. Many activities outside paid work can be described as forms of work in the informal economy. Stanley Parker (1971) points out that work and leisure are only two categories of 'life space' with a number of intermediate activities - for example eating and sleeping - which are neither clearly work nor leisure.

Factors influencing leisure

Industrialisation According to E. P. Thompson (1967), work and leisure only came to be sharply differentiated with the development of capitalist industrial society. Time came to be bought and sold by employers and workers so work time came to be clearly demarcated from free time or leisure.

For the German sociologist Norbert Elias (1978) changes in leisure are part of a longer term *civilising process* which has been going on since the end of the Middle Ages. This has involved higher standards of self control in personal behaviour. For example, belching at meals, eating with fingers from a common bowl and sharing beds with guests which were tolerated in the past would shock many people nowadays. This has affected leisure activities and meant that leisure too has become increasingly civilised and rule governed. For example, football, which was once a violent game with no formal rules, has developed into the rule governed games of rugby and soccer controlled by bureaucratic organisations.

However, leisure also provides a forum in which excitement and aggression can still be expressed, in contrast to the regularity, steadiness and emotional control increasingly required in other areas of life. Leisure is seen by Elias as fulfilling a *mimetic* function - it allows the release of intense emotions in a controlled form. This occurs in activities like sport, watching films, concerts and even competitive games like chess or cards.

Work Many sociologists have seen work as a major influence on leisure. For example, Stanley Parker (1971) distinguished an *extension pattern* where work spills over into leisure time (characteristic of

professional occupations); a *neutrality pattern* where leisure is a major source of life interests in contrast to unfulfilling work (characteristic of routine white collar and manual jobs); and an *opposition pattern* where leisure compensates for the hazards and physical demands of dangerous jobs (characteristic of jobs like deep sea fishing and coalmining).

Age Other sociologists have explored how age and social situation influence leisure. Rhona and Robert Rapoport (1975) suggest that choice of leisure activities is largely shaped by the stage people have reached in the life cycle. For example, many people's leisure activities change dramatically when they move from being a young single adult to having a partner and family responsibilities.

Big business In the 1980s sociologists influenced by Marxism began to criticise traditional approaches to leisure. John Clarke and Chas Critcher (1985) point out that leisure is increasingly dominated by commercial interests. They argue that consumers are just as exploited by big business interests in leisure time as they are as producers in work time. Package holidays, theme parks, pop concerts, cinemas, hotels and restaurants are all part of a multi-million pound leisure industry heavily promoted by advertising. For Clarke and Critcher leisure patterns, far from representing freedom of choice, are heavily influenced by commercial interests intent on making profits from consumers.

Gender Feminists too have criticised traditional perspectives on leisure. Susan McIntosh (1987), for example, claims that theories such as Parker's are riddled with sexist assumptions. For most male workers it may be true that once paid work and physiological needs (such as eating and sleeping) are completed there is plenty of time for leisure. However, for many women most of this time is occupied with domestic obligations. For women their gender role rather than their paid job is the main influence on life outside paid employment.

Rosemary Deem (1986) notes how women often combine leisure with other obligations - watching television may be combined with ironing, reading with listening out for the baby. Women also often engage in leisure activities for the sake of husbands, boyfriends or children rather than for their own pleasure. Green, Hebron and Woodward (1987) in a study of Sheffield found that women were often constrained in their leisure activities, either because their partners objected to them going out alone or because of fear of sexual attack or harassment.

Postmodernity and leisure

Many of the theories of leisure discussed so far emphasise the way in which leisure time is structured by a person's position in society, for example their occupation, age, gender and so on. While leisure is perceived by most people as the area of life in which they exercise maximum personal choice, sociologists have pointed out how this choice is subtly influenced, or in some cases strongly constrained, by social factors.

In recent years sociologists influenced by postmodernism have questioned this approach. Individual's identities are no longer seen to be determined by groupings such as class, gender and ethnicity. Instead postmodern society offers a multiplicity of identities from which individuals can choose. Accompanying this has been an increasing interest in the sphere of consumption. Classical sociology (see Section 1.2) was concerned with the sphere of production and the division of labour - the world of work. Postmodern sociologists are increasingly concerned with the sphere of consumption - including leisure.

Lifestyle and personal identity In postmodern society individuals increasingly construct their own lifestyles and express their individuality in leisure (Veal, 1993). For many people the furniture and decor of their homes, the style of clothes they wear, the music they listen to and even the kind of food they eat are all part of a 'lifestyle'. Individuals build their own lifestyle around their own personal identity. Thus a person may eat vegetarian food, keep fit, grow their own vegetables and play the guitar because these activities are seen to be part of a lifestyle which in turn is the expression of their identity.

Not all sociologists agree that such concerns are a sign of a postmodern society. Anthony Giddens (1991) agrees that for many individuals their leisure activities represent an attempt to construct a lifestyle which gives a sense of identity. However, for Giddens this sense of self - of the significance of the individual - is characteristic of *modern* societies. Current developments simply represent a higher stage in the development of modernity rather than an entirely new kind of society as implied by the term postmodern.

Tourism and leisure Developments in tourism have been seen as a further sign of postmodern trends in leisure. John Urry (1990) points out that many leisure activities involve travelling to new destinations to seek new activities, sensations and stimulations. This involves a particular way of looking at people and places which Urry describes as the *tourist gaze*. This gaze is framed and re-collected by repeat visits, holiday pictures and postcards and video recordings. Urry suggests that this tourist gaze represents a new approach to travel and leisure - a further sign of postmodernity.

To some sociologists tourism increasingly involves an element of 'virtual reality' and 'hyperreality'. A classic example of this is Disney theme parks. In the Epcott Centre, Florida, for example, there is a series of pavilions representing different countries. These pavilions provide simulations of Mexico, Morocco, Norway and so on. Museums are following this trend presenting ever more realistic images of the past. The Beamish Museum, for example, presents a reconstruction of life in the industrial Northeast of England at the end of the last century. The Jorvik Centre even provides the appropriate smells to accompany your trip through York in Viking times.

Class, gender and ethnicity The postmodernist view of leisure suggests that previous sociological approaches may be increasingly irrelevant. For example, people are no longer seen to be constrained by conventional gender identities. Traditional 'macho' male identities now compete with the image of the caring 'new man', gay lifestyles and other alternative masculine identities. Women are no longer trapped in the role of housewives but are offered alternative identities as career women and opportunities in traditional male leisure activities like sport.

Critics of postmodernism, however, claim that the constraints of class, gender and ethnicity are still present in leisure as in other areas of life. Sheila Scraton and Peter Braham (1995) point out that for all the strides women have made towards equality, 'for many women leisure remains influenced by little disposable income and jobs with unsocial hours making access to formal leisure difficult if not impossible'.

Class too remains a relevant factor. Access to the pleasures offered by 'postmodern' leisure activities is conditional on relatively high income. For the unemployed and those in low paid work there may be little opportunity to experiment with different lifestyles and little choice of personal identities.

Ethnicity also remains relevant. Postmodernists point to the way in which the postmodern celebrates ethnic diversity. For example musical styles from around the world are increasingly influencing popular music and 'ethnic' styles of dress have provided the inspiration for both mainstream fashion and subcultural styles. However, Braham and Spink (1990) point to the ways in which high unemployment and the decline of inner city areas have disproportionately affected ethnic minorities. Ethnic minorities have certainly developed their own lifestyles, often as a form of resistance to the dominant white culture. However, this does not necessarily represent a freely chosen personal identity, as implied by postmodernism, but rather a response to the constraints resulting from racism and ethnic disadvantage.

Summary

1 High levels of unemployment in Britain in the 1980s and 90s appear to be related to deindustrialisation and the impact of new technology on the workforce.

2 There is no one definition and measure of unemployment.

3 Unemployment is uneven in its impact. Some parts of the country and some social groups are more affected than others.

4 Unemployment appears to have a variety of negative social, psychological and physical consequences. However, different groups and individuals are affected in different ways.

5 Modern society offers increasing choice and diversity in leisure activities. Sociologists have indicated that a wide variety of social influences - including work, gender, ethnicity, class and age - may influence leisure.

Activity 13 Patterns of Leisure

Item A *Postmodern leisure?*

With new technologies of broadcasting, fibre optics, satellite and cable, the individual has a multiplicity of available choices. Data processing information systems now extend over time and space to provide domestic and commercial information, education, entertainment on a global scale. One can buy or rent video programmes and games whatever one's taste. One obvious consequence is that leisure experiences no longer need to be tied to a particular time or place. One can

Pizza delivery

watch programmes as suits one's personal timetable, thus disengaging the individual from collective or mass timetables. Individuals can map out and plan their distinctive pathways through time and space. Eating out

in fastfood restaurants, for example, permits individuals to choose to have meals at any time. There need be no rigid meal times or tea breaks collectively shared at work, or at home for the whole family to eat together. Meals can be brought into the home, or ordered over the telephone, paid by Visa, delivered by 'Pizza Express' with the individual specifying precisely the particular flavour or ingredients desired, whether vegetarian, non-vegetarian, spicy, bland and so on.

vegetarian, spicy, bland and so on.

Adapted from S. Scraton and P. Braham 'Leisure and Postmodernity' in M. Haralambos (ed) *Developments in Sociology*, vol 11, 1995, p19

Item B

Free time in a typical week: by gender and employment status, 1992-93

From *Social Trends*, 1994, p129

Item C *Big business and leisure*

Since the middle of the 1950s, the brewing industry has undergone a major transformation, involving the creation of a national market almost completely dominated by six major companies, in place of the many small breweries serving a local regional market before the war.

This concentration of ownership resulted in 'rationalisation' of the brewing and distribution of beer in three main ways: the closing of many 'surplus' small breweries; the closing of many public houses and replacement of tenants by salaried managers; and thirdly nationally marketed 'keg' beers replacing locally produced varieties. The breweries also set out to change the character of the pub itself, in line with what they perceived as the changing character and tastes of their clientele. The decor and interior were modernised; facilities for traditional games, such as darts and cards were withdrawn since they were held to be less profitable than fruit machines and video games; and music was made compulsory with the introduction of jukeboxes. It is no coincidence that each of these innovations developed by the breweries was designed to yield additional profits, both from the new entertainments provided and from the increased drink sales which the new customers would provide.

This reduction of choice about what to drink, and about the context in which to drink it, produced one of the few collective consumer revolts in the leisure market in the form of the Campaign for Real Ale. The campaign ran a concerted attack against the 'gassy' beers being supplied by the major breweries, contrasting them unfavourably with the traditional products of the independent breweries. This reaction has led to the big breweries rethinking their market strategy, and introducing 'real' as opposed to pasteurised beers to compete with the independents.

Adapted from J. Clarke and C. Critcher *The Devil Makes Work: Leisure in Capitalist Britain*, 1985, pp103-105

Item D

Participation in selected leisure activities away from home: by social class, 1993-94

Great Britain   Percentages

| | Social class | | | | |
	AB	C1	C2	DE	All persons
Visit a public house	67	70	65	59	65
Meal in a restaurant (not fast food)	81	74	56	44	61
Drive for pleasure	50	53	45	39	46
Meal in a fast food restaurant	48	49	39	37	42
Library	57	46	32	31	39
Cinema	46	39	29	24	33
Short break holiday	41	34	28	19	29
Disco or night club	21	25	25	28	25
Historic building	41	29	19	12	23
Spectator sports event	25	24	23	18	22
Theatre	33	24	16	10	19
Museum or art gallery	34	23	14	10	19
Fun fair	12	13	15	16	14
Exhibition	24	17	10	8	14
Theme park	12	10	12	9	11
Bingo	3	6	11	17	10
Visit a betting shop	5	8	13	11	10
Camping or caravaning	9	9	10	7	9
Pop or rock concert	8	9	8	6	8
Classical concert or the opera	15	9	3	3	7
Attend an evening class	11	6	4	4	6
Circus	1	1	3	4	2

Class A: Higher managerial, administrative and professional
Class B: Intermediate managerial, administrative and professional
Class C1: Supervisory or clerical, and junior managerial, administrative, or professional
Class C2: Skilled manual workers
Class D: Semi and unskilled manual workers
Class E: State pensioners or widows (no other earners), casual or lowest grade workers, or long term unemployed

From *Social Trends*, 1994, p129

Questions

1 Postmodernists claim that leisure is increasingly privatised, individualised and based on personal choice. Use examples from Item A and elsewhere to illustrate this.

2 Using Item C and any other examples assess the view that patterns of leisure are increasingly dominated by big business interests rather than consumer choice?

3 Using data from Item B, explain how:
   a) gender;
   b) employment status;
   may influence the amount of leisure time available to an individual.

4 Using data from Item D assess the view that social class is still a significant influence on leisure activities.

References

Aglietta, M. *A Theory of Capitalist Regulation: The US Experience* (New Left Books,London, 1979)

Ashton, D. 'Unemployment: Why Pick on Youth?' *Social Studies Review*, September 1985

Ashton, D. *Unemployment under Capitalism* (Wheatsheaf, London, 1986)

Atkinson, G.B.J. *Economics: Themes and Perspectives* (Causeway Press, Ormskirk, 1994)

Atkinson, J. 'The Changing Corporation' in D. Clutterbuck (ed) *New Patterns of Work* (Gower, Aldershot, 1985)

Bazen, S. and Thirwall T. *Deindustrialisation* (Heinemann, Oxford,1989)

Beechey, V. 'The Sexual Division of Labour and the Labour Process: a Critical Assessment of Braverman' in S. Wood (ed) *The Degradation of Work? Skill, Deskilling and the Labour Process* (Hutchinson, London, 1982)

Beechey, V. *Unequal Work* (Verso, London, 1987)

Bell, D. *The Coming of Post-Industrial Society* (Heinemann, London, 1973)

Berle, A. A. and Means, G. C. *The Modern Corporation and Private Property* (Macmillan, New York, 1932)

Beynon, H. *Working for Ford* (Allen Lane, London, 1973)

Blauner, R. *Alienation and Freedom* (University of Chicago Press, Chicago, 1964)

Braham, P. and Spink, J. 'Leisure and the Postmodern City' in Henry I.P. (ed) *Leisure: Modernity, Postmodernity and Lifestyles* (Leisure Studies Association, 1994)

Braverman, H. *Labour and Monopoly Capital: The Degradation of Work in the Twentieth Century* (Monthly Review Press, New York, 1974)

Brenner, M.H. 'Health Costs and Benefits of Economic Policy' *International Journal of Health Services* vol 7 no 4, 1979

Clarke, J. and Critcher, C. *The Devil Makes Work: Leisure in Capitalist Britain* (Macmillan, Basingstoke, 1985)

Coates, K. and Topham, T. *Trade Unions and Politics* (Blackwell, Oxford, 1986)

Cohen, R. et al *Hardship Britain: Being Poor in the 1990s* (CPAG, London, 1992)

Cockburn, C. *Women, Trade Unions and Political Parties* (Fabian Research Series 349, London, 1987)

Crompton, R. and Jones, G. *White Collar Proletariat: Deskilling and Gender in Clerical Work* (Macmillan, Basingstoke, 1984)

Dahrendorf, R. *Class and Class Conflict in an Industrial Society* (Routledge and Kegan Paul, London, 1959)

Daniel, W.W. and Millward, N. *Workplace Industrial Relations in Britain: the DE/PSI/SSRC survey* (Heinemann, London, 1983)

Deem, R. *All Work and No Play: The Sociology of Women and Leisure* (Open University Press, Milton Keynes, 1986)

Denscombe, M. *Sociology Update* (Olympus Books, Leicester,1994)

Durkheim, E. *The Division of Labour in Society* (The Free Press, New York, 1947)

Edwards, P.K. and Scullion, H. *The Social Organisation of Industrial Conflict: Control and Resistance in the Workplace* (Blackwell, Oxford, 1982)

Edwards, R. *Contested Terrain: The Transformation of the Workplace in the Twentieth Century* (Heinemann, London, 1979)

Elias, N. *The Civilising Process Vol 1: The History of Manners* trans E. Jephcott (Basil Blackwell, Oxford, 1978)

Fagin, L. and Little, M. *The Forsaken Families* (Penguin, Harmondsworth, 1984)

Friedman, A. *Industry and Labour: Class Struggle at Work and Monopoly Capitalism* (Macmillan, London, 1977)

Friedman, M. *Inflation and Unemployment: The New Dimensions of Politics* (Institute of Economic Affairs, London, 1977)

Galbraith, J. K. *The New Industrial State* (Hamish Hamilton, London, 1967)

Gallie, D. *In Search of the New Working Class: Automation and Social Integration within the Capitalist Enterprise* (Cambridge University Press, Cambridge, 1978)

Gershuny, J. I. *After Industrial Society? Emerging Self Service Economy* (Macmillan, Basingstoke, 1978)

Giddens, A. *Self-Identity and Modernity* (Polity, Cambridge, 1991)

Glyn, A. and Harrison, J. *The British Economic Disaster* (Pluto Press, London, 1980)

Goldthorpe, J., Lockwood, D., Bechofer, F. and Platt, J. *The Affluent Worker: Industrial Attitudes and Behaviour* (Cambridge University Press, Cambridge, 1968)

Gouldner, A. *Wildcat Strike* (Routledge and Kegan Paul, London, 1955)

Green, E., Hebron, S. and Woodward, D. *Gender and Leisure: A Study of Sheffield Women's Experiences of Leisure* ESRC/Sports Council Report (Sports Council, 1987)

Hakim, C. 'Trends in the Flexible Workforce' *Employment Gazette* vol 95 no 11, 1987

Handy, L.J. 'Absenteeism and Attendance in the British Coal Mining Industry' *British Journal of Industrial Relations*, vol vi no 1, 1968

Hannah, L. *The Rise of the Corporate Economy* (Methuen, London, 1976 and 1983)

Hartley, J.F. 'The Impact of Unemployment on the Self-esteem of Managers' *Journal of Occupational Psychology*, 53, 1980

Hobsbawm, E.S. *Industry and Empire* (Penguin, Harmondsworth, 1969)

Hyman, R. *Strikes* (Fontana, London, 1984)

Hyman, R. 'What's Happening to the Unions?' *Social Studies Review*, March 1989

Jahoda, M., Lazarfield, P.F. and Zeisel, H. *Marienthal: the Sociography of an Unemployed Community* (Tavistock, London, 1933)

Jenkins, C. and Sherman, B. *The Collapse of Work* (Eyre Methuen, London, 1979)

Joseph Rowntree Foundation *Inquiry into Income and Wealth* vol 1 (York, 1995)

Kelley, M. R. 'Alternative Forms of Work Organisation under Programmable Automation' in S. Wood. (ed) *The Transformation of Work?* (Unwin Hyman, London, 1989)

Kelly, J. *Trade Unions and Socialist Politics* (Verso, London, 1988)

Kerr, C. and Siegel, A. 'The Interindustry Propensity to Strike' in A.Kornhauser, R. Dubin and A.M. Ross (eds) *Industrial Conflict* (McGraw Hill, New York, 1954)

Keynes, J.M. *The General Theory of Employment, Interest and Money* (Macmillan, London, 1936)

Lamb, H. and Percy, S. 'Big Mac is Watching You' *New Society*, 9.10.1987

Linhart, R. 'The Assembly Line' in C. Littler (ed) *The Experience of Work* (Gower in association with the Open University, Aldershot, 1985)

McIntosh. S. 'A Feminist Critique of Stanley Parker's Theory of Work and Leisure' in M. O'Donnell (ed) *New Introductory Reader in Sociology* (Nelson, Walton-on-Thames, 1987)

McKee, L. and Bell, C. 'His Unemployment, Her Problem: the Domestic and Marital Consequences of Male Unemployment' in S. Allen et al (eds) *The Experience of Unemployment* (Macmillan, Basingstoke, 1986)

Mandel, E. *Late Capitalism* (New Left Books, London, 1975)

Marsh, P. *The Robot Age* (Abacus Books, London, 1982)

Marx, K. 'Alienated Labour' in T.B. Bottomore (ed) *Karl Marx: Early Writings* (Penguin, Harmondsworth, 1963)

Marx, K. *Capital, Volume One* (Penguin, Harmondsworth, 1976)

Maynard, M. 'Housewives and their Work' in R. Deem and G. Salaman (eds) *Work, Culture and Society* (Open University Press, Milton Keynes, 1985)

Millward, N. and Stevens, M. *British Workplace Industrial Relations 1980-84* (Gower, Aldershot, 1986)

Millward, N., Stevens, M., Smart, D. and Hawes, W. *Workplace Industrial Relations in Transition: The ED/ESRC/PSI/ACAS Surveys* (Dartford, Aldershot, 1992)

Nichols, T. and Beynon, H. *Living with Capitalism: Class Relations and the Modern Factory* (Routledge and Kegan Paul, London, 1977) .

Noble, D. F. 'Social Choice in Machine Design: The Case of Automatically Controlled Machine Tools' in A. Zimbalist (ed) *Case Studies in the Labour Process* (Monthly Review Press, New York, 1979)

Pahl, R. E. *Divisions of Labour* (Basil Blackwell, Oxford, 1984)

Pahl, R. E. and Gershuny, J.I. 'Britain in the Decade of Three Economies' *New Society*, 3.1.1980

Pahl, R. E. and Winkler, J. 'The Economic Elite: Theory and Practice' in P. Stanworth and A. Giddens (eds) *Elites and Power in British Society* (Cambridge University Press, Cambridge, 1974)

Parker, S. *The Future of Work and Leisure* (MacGibbon and Kee, London, 1971)

Parsons, T. *The Social System* (The Free Press, New York, 1951)

Piore, M. J. and Sabel, C. F. *The Second Industrial Divide: Prospects for Prosperity* (Basic Books, New York, 1984)

Platt, S. 'Recent Trends in Parasuicide ("attempted suicide") and Unemployment among Men in Edinburgh' in S. Allen et al (eds) *The Experience of Unemployment* (Macmillan, Basingstoke, 1986)

Pollert, A. *Girls, Wives, Factory Lives* (Macmillan, Basingstoke, 1981)

Pollert, A. 'Dismantling Flexibility' *Capital and Class*, no 34, 1988

Rapoport, R. and Rapoport, R.N. *Leisure and the Family Life Cycle* (Routledge, London, 1975)

Ridley, F.F. 'View from a Disaster Area: Unemployed Youth in Merseyside' in B. Crick (ed) *Unemployment* (Methuen, London, 1981)

Robinson, O. 'The Changing Labour Market: the Phenomenon of Part-time Work in Britain' *National Westminster Bank Quarterly Review*, November 1985

Runnymede Trust *Bulletin*, September 1983

Sauvain, P. *British Social and Economic History 1700-1870* (Stanley Thornes, Cheltenham, 1987)

Scott, J. *Corporations, Classes and Capitalism* (Hutchinson, London, 1985)

Scraton, S. and Braham, P. 'Leisure and Postmodernity' in M. Haralambos (ed) *Developments in Sociology* vol 11, (Causeway Press, Ormskirk, 1995)

Shaiken, H. 'Numerical Control of Work: Workers and Automation in the Computer Age' *Radical America*, vol 1 no 6, 1979

Showler, B. 'Political Economy and Unemployment' in B. Showler and A.Sinfield (eds) *The Workless State* (Martin Robertson, Oxford, 1981)

Sinfield, A. 'Unemployment in an Unequal Society' in B. Showler and A. Sinfield (eds) *The Workless State* (Martin Robertson, Oxford, 1981)

Stern, J. *Unemployment and its Impact on Morbidity and Mortality*, LSE Discussion Paper no 93 (Centre for Labour Economics, London, 1981)

Taylor, F. W. *Scientific Management* (Harper Row, New York, 1947)

Taylor, L. and Walton, P. 'Industrial Sabotage Motives and Meanings' in S. Cohen (ed) *Images of Deviance* (Penguin, Harmondsworth, 1971)

Thompson, E.P. 'Time, Work-Discipline and Industrial Capitalism' *Past and Present, a Journal of Historical Studies*, 38, December 1967

Thompson, P. *The Nature of Work: An Introduction to Debates on the Labour Process* (Macmillan, Basingstoke, 1983)

Thornes, B. and Collard, J. *Who Divorces?* (Routledge and Kegan Paul, London, 1979)

Urry, J. *The Tourist Gaze* (Sage, London, 1990)

Useem, M. *The Inner Circle: Large Corporations and the Rise of Business Political Activity in the United States and the United Kingdom* (Oxford University Press, Oxford, 1984)

Veal, A.J. 'The Concept of Lifestyle: a Review' *Leisure Studies*, vol 12, 1993

Warde, A. 'The Future of Work' *Social Studies Review*, September 1989

Walby, S. 'Flexibility and the Changing Sexual Division of Labour' in S. Wood (ed) *The Transformation of Work* (Unwin Hyman, London, 1989)

Weber, M. *The Protestant Ethic and the Spirit of Capitalism* (Allen and Unwin, London, 1952)

Weber, M. *Economy and Society* (University of California Press, Berkley, 1968)

Wood, S. (ed) *The Degradation of Work? Skill, Deskilling and the Labour Process* (Hutchinson, London, 1982)

Wood, S. (ed) *The Transformation of Work* (Unwin Hyman, London, 1989)

10 Organisations

Introduction

Organisations are important. We are educated in them, we work in them and we rely on them for a thousand and one goods and services. Yet we don't appear to like them. And our main dislike is directed at a particular form of organisation - the bureaucracy.

There is a stereotype of a bureaucratic organisation. It is covered in red tape - there are rules for practically every activity and forms to be filled in before any action can be taken. Jobs are highly specialised and precisely defined. Picture clients attempting to obtain state benefits being passed from one bureaucrat to the next until the correct official is found. And then it may take several officials to complete the process. To the client the buck is being passed and it's more than the official's job is worth to bend the rules.

In terms of the stereotype, working in a bureaucratic organisation is just as bad. Innovation and creativity are crushed as employees follow rules mechanically. Officials in a rigid hierarchy control the actions of those below them and bow and scrape to those above them, fearful of harming their promotion prospects. Life in the organisation continues on its predictable path until it's time for those who have become faceless bureaucrats to draw their pensions.

Some of the concerns underlying this stereotype have informed sociological research. Do organisations stifle creativity? Can they be democratic? Is work in organisations rigidly controlled? Should it be in the interests of efficiency? These are some of the questions examined in this chapter.

Chapter summary

- Part 1 looks at the main **sociological theories** of organisations.
- These theories are assessed in terms of **case studies** of organisations.
- The next section considers the relationship between **bureaucracy** and **democracy**.
- Part 2 looks at the **managerial tradition** in organisation theory and the **radical theories** which oppose it.
- Future trends are considered with the possible emergence of **postmodern organisations**.
- The chapter closes with a discussion of **social control** organisations.

1 Bureaucracy and Organisations: the Debate with Weber

Key Issues

1 Is bureaucracy an inevitable feature of organisations in industrial societies?
2 What are the advantages and disadvantages of bureaucratic forms of organisation?
3 Is bureaucracy compatible with democracy?

The work of the German sociologist Max Weber is taken by many sociologists as a starting point in the study of organisations. Writing at the beginning of the twentieth century, Weber (1948) saw bureaucratic organisations as having an increasing and dominant influence on social life in industrial societies. He pointed to the increasing bureaucratisation of the civil service, the armed forces, educational institutions, manufacturing companies and even churches. This part of the chapter examines Weber's work on bureaucracy and goes on to consider debates inspired by his work.

1.1 Weber and bureaucracy

Weber acknowledged that the extent of bureaucratisation varied between different types of organisations and indeed between different industrial societies. However, he believed bureaucratic organisations were essential for the operation of industrial society. For Weber, the growth of bureaucracy was a result of the development of new forms of *power* in industrial society. In all societies some individuals exercise power over others. For Weber, this meant the ability to get others to comply with one's wishes whether they agree with them or not. Power becomes *authority* when it is seen as legitimate. Thus a person or organisation is obeyed because they are seen as having a right to command obedience (see pp192-193 for further discussion of Weber's views on power and authority).

Rational legal authority and bureaucracy

Weber argues that organisations in pre-industrial societies were based mainly on either *traditional authority*, where the power of leaders is upheld by longstanding customs and traditions (for example, feudal monarchies) or *charismatic authority*, where the exceptional personal qualities of leaders (for example, Jesus or Hitler) cause people to follow and obey them.

According to Weber *rational legal authority* is increasingly prevalent in industrial society. Here authority is based on legal rules rather than tradition or personal charisma. Thus tax inspectors, police officers and council officials are obeyed because the law upholds their right to tell people what to do under certain circumstances. This authority is not only legal but also rational. By this Weber meant that the rules on which authority is based are specifically made to attain particular goals. Thus the rules which govern the actions of a tax inspector are designed to collect taxes in a specific way for a specific purpose. The organisational structure which derives from rational legal authority is bureaucracy. Weber defined bureaucracy as 'a hierarchical organisation designed rationally to coordinate the work of many individuals in the pursuit of large scale administrative tasks and organisational goals'.

Bureaucracy as an ideal type

Many of the concepts elaborated by Weber, including that of bureaucracy, represent what he called *ideal types*. By ideal Weber did not mean best but pure. An ideal type is a model of the purest type. In reality ideal types do not exist, for example even within bureaucracies elements of traditional and charismatic authority tend to persist. However, ideal types represent useful models against which things in the real world can be compared to help in describing and classifying them.

Weber's description of bureaucracy is an ideal type. He did not claim that bureaucratic organisations in Western societies necessarily had all the elements of his ideal type, rather they approximated to it and were increasingly coming to resemble it. Weber also acknowledged that some organisations in pre-industrial societies displayed many of the traits of bureaucracies, for example the governments of the New Empire of ancient Egypt and the Chinese empire.

The characteristics of bureaucracy

Weber's ideal type bureaucracy contains the following elements.

1 **Specialisation** Official tasks and positions are clearly demarcated, each covering a distinct and separate area of competence. For example, bureaucratic organisations are often divided into departments with specific responsibilities and each official has a specified role within a department.
2 **Hierarchy** There is a series of ranks or levels of authority, each official is accountable to and supervised by one above.
3 **Rules** There are clearly established rules which govern the management of the organisation. In taking decisions personnel have to refer to rules and procedures, they cannot simply follow their personal inclinations.
4 **Impersonality** Everyone within the organisation is subject to formal equality of treatment since the same rules apply to all.
5 **Officials** are:
   a) selected and appointed on the basis of technical qualifications (on some clearly recognisable criteria);
   b) full time appointments, in that the particular post is the sole or main occupation of the individual;
   c) subject to formal career structure with a system of promotion according to either seniority or merit or both (in other words there are objective criteria for promotion).
6 **Public private division** There is a clear separation between official activity and private life, for example money handled by an official at work is kept clearly separate from his or her private income.

The advantages of bureaucracy

Weber saw bureaucracy based on this ideal type as having many advantages. He laid particular emphasis on the importance of impersonal rules. Rules reduce tension between people, they allow people to feel they are following a rule rather than the whims of a particular individual. For example, a social security official can point out that they are refusing a person's request for a benefit because of the rules rather than because of personal dislike. Similarly, the money which the official hands over to clients is clearly separate from his or her own income.

Weber sums this up by stating that 'the decisive reason for the advance of bureaucratic organisations has always been its purely technical superiority over any other form of organisation. The fully developed bureaucratic mechanism compares with other organisations exactly as does the machine with non-mechanical modes of production' (1948, p214).

The threat posed by bureaucracy

While Weber recognised the efficiency of bureaucratic organisations and saw them as essential to modern society, he viewed them with foreboding. His overriding fear towards the end of his life was the rise of a deadening and dictatorial bureaucracy. He feared that bureaucrats would become 'specialists without spirit', little men clinging to their jobs frightened to show any initiative, preoccupied with order and 'nervous and cowardly if for one moment this order wavers'. Weber was worried that bureaucrats might become accountable to no one but other bureaucrats. He feared that bureaucratic power might be usurped by sectional interests such as the capitalist class. He therefore believed it essential that elected politicians, accountable to the public, should control state bureaucracies.

Weber saw the development of bureaucratic organisations as an expression of the wider process of *rationalisation* in Western society (see p526). Rational and scientific thought was replacing traditional values, emotion, spirituality, indeed everything which gave depth, meaning and purpose to life. The result in Weber's words was the 'disenchantment of the world'. The cold, calculating impersonal machine-like bureaucratic organisation contributed to this disenchantment.

Rationality and bureaucracy

Did Weber see bureaucracy as the most efficient form of administration? Many sociologists, like Peter Blau (1963), argue that Weber equated technical superiority and rationality with efficiency. Others reject this view. Martin Albrow (1970) argues that Weber simply saw rational bureaucratic procedures as the most effective way of *measuring* efficiency, not necessarily of ensuring it. Bureaucracies permit the amount of time, money and effort expended in achieving objectives to be precisely calculated. Bureaucracies thus provide a means of measuring how efficient organisations are in achieving their goals. But this does not necessarily mean they are effective in reaching those goals.

Certainly Weber seems to imply that bureaucracy is an efficient form of administration with his references to its technical superiority. It is this view which has provoked considerable criticism from other sociologists. Their views are examined in the next section.

Activity 1 The McDonaldisation of Society

George Ritzer (1993) uses the McDonald's restaurant chain as a metaphor for describing some of the harmful effects of bureaucratisation. The success of McDonald's has spawned countless other fast food chains: Kentucky Fried Chicken, Taco Bell, Domino's Pizza and so on. McDonald's fast food formula has also influenced other types of business both in the USA and in Britain. Examples include Toys 'R' Us, Halfords car accessories and W H Smith which all provide a standard range of goods and services which are more or less the same across the country. Decisions about what products are sold, how they are presented and the procedures adopted by staff are taken at head office. Most workers require a limited range of skills, as jobs are broken down into simple tasks which can be quickly learned.

According to Ritzer, McDonald's has been so successful primarily because it's organised along the lines of Weber's model of the classic bureaucracy. It has a clear division of labour and a uniform system of rules that make it highly efficient and predictable. No matter where you are, you know what to expect when you go into a Mcdonald's. The filet-o-fish sandwich in Manchester tastes the same as the one in Moscow. If you've ever watched the workers behind the counter, each has specialised tasks that are narrowly defined.

McDonald's in Moscow

McDonald's in London

By combining 20th century computer technology with 19th century time-and-motion studies, the McDonald's corporation has broken the jobs of griddleman, waitress, cashier and even manager down into small, simple steps. The corporation has systematically extracted the decision making elements from filling french fry boxes or scheduling staff. They relentlessly weed out all variables that might make it necessary to make a decision at the store level, whether on pickles or on cleaning procedures.

McDonaldisation will continue for several reasons. First it is impelled by economic interests. Other organisations have copied McDonald's bureaucratic model because it leads to higher profits and lower costs.

Secondly, McDonaldisation has become such a culturally desirable process that many enterprises pursue it as an end in its own right. We live in a culture that treasures efficiency, speed, predictability and control, and we seek these things, whether or not economic gains are involved. Our desire for these values often blinds us to the fact that fast foods, as well as their domestic equivalent, microwave foods, actually cost more than if we had prepared the meals ourselves.

While the efficiency, speed and predictability of McDonaldised systems may be appealing and comforting to some, the system as a whole has made social life more homogeneous, more rigid and less personal. The 'fast food' model has robbed us of our spontaneity. Our creativity and desire for uniqueness have been reduced, trapping us in Weber's 'iron cage' - a bureaucratic culture that requires little thought and leaves virtually nothing to chance.

Adapted from D. M. Newman *Sociology: Exploring the Architecture of Everyday Life*, 1995, pp274-275 and G. Ritzer *The McDonaldisation of Society*, 1993

Questions

1 What aspects of Weber's ideal type of bureaucracy are apparent in the organisation of McDonald's fast food restaurants?
2 Using McDonald's and other examples outline possible advantages and disadvantages of bureaucratic organisations.

1.2 The dysfunctions of bureaucracy

Much of the later work on bureaucracy has been a response to Weber. It sought to answer many of the questions he raised. Are bureaucracies the most efficient form of organisation? Do they threaten individual freedom? Are there alternatives to bureaucratic organisations in industrial society?

Robert Merton: bureaucratic personality

Weber saw the machine-like efficiency of bureaucracy as the main reason for its spread in advanced industrial society. However, this quality can develop into the common stereotype of the faceless impersonal bureaucratic organisation. Weber appreciated this danger - a concern developed by the American sociologist Robert Merton (1949). He looked at the *dysfunctions* - harmful consequences - of bureaucracy. He pointed to the danger of the 'virtues' of discipline and efficiency being exaggerated to the point where officials became obsessed with rules and procedures. They may become so enmeshed in their rules and in 'doing things by the book' that they are unable to help their clients speedily or effectively. Merton describes this as *goal displacement* - the objectives of the organisation become replaced by the goal of 'playing safe' and adhering rigidly to the rules.

Merton argues that bureaucracies tend to create a *bureaucratic personality*. This sort of personality stresses conformity. Initiative and innovation are stifled and replaced with inflexibility and timidity. This makes it difficult for bureaucrats to respond to new and unforeseen situations where existing rules and procedures may be inappropriate.

There can also be a conflict between those who use bureaucracies (the clients) and officials. The peculiarities of individual cases tend to be ignored by bureaucrats. The client will be convinced of the uniqueness of his or her own case and will object to being treated as one of many. The bureaucrat usually has little choice but to treat people in terms of general rules, but this often leads to bureaucrats being seen as arrogant or off-hand. This can lead to conflict. The client wants individual, special consideration while the official provides formal, impersonal treatment.

While accepting that Weber's ideal type of bureaucracy might further organisational efficiency, Merton attempts to show that in specific instances these same characteristics may have dysfunctional consequences. In particular, the nature of bureaucracy encourages a particular type of personality in officials, which can undermine the goals of the organisation.

Alvin Gouldner: industrial bureaucracy

Weber saw bureaucracy as the dominant from of organisation in industrial society. He gave little consideration to organisations where bureaucracy is less developed or to situations where bureaucratic forms of organisation might be inappropriate. These themes were explored in detail by Alvin Gouldner (1955) in a famous case study of a gypsum plant.

The plant had two main parts - a mine from which gypsum, a light pink coloured rock, was extracted and a factory where the gypsum was turned into plaster and used in the manufacture of wallboard. Under the old manager the plant had been run on what Gouldner calls an 'indulgency pattern' - there were few formal rules and these were rarely strictly enforced. The arrival of a new manager concerned with increasing productivity led to the bureaucratisation of the plant with much stricter discipline and supervision of workers. This created considerable resentment and resistance among the workers who had become accustomed to the 'give and take' of the indulgency pattern.

The new management found most difficulty in imposing bureaucratic regulations and procedures in the mine. In the factory the production of wallboard was a relatively routine and predictable process and the new manager was able to tighten supervision and increase productivity, albeit at the expense of a considerable loss of goodwill. However, the miners had always enjoyed a high degree of independence and tended to use their own initiative in taking decisions. In the mine there had to be flexibility and trust to cope with the unpredictable and often dangerous work. In this context Gouldner found that strict supervision and the rigid enforcement of rules were often dysfunctional. The result was a reduction rather than an increase in productivity. The miners resisted the imposition of bureaucratic regulations and were eventually successful.

Two important conclusions can be drawn from Gouldner's study:

1 Bureaucracy is better suited to routine predictable work situations - as in the wallboard factory. In situations which are non-routine, where discretion or innovation may be required - as in the mine - bureaucratic procedures can be dysfunctional.
2 The advance of bureaucracy is not inevitable but can be resisted.

Peter Blau: informal structures

According to the American sociologist Peter Blau, Weber's view of bureaucracy implies that any deviation from the rules, procedures and structure of the organisation will reduce efficiency. Blau maintains that in some circumstances the opposite may be true. His research indicates that in many situations organisations function more efficiently when workers disregard, adapt or even break official rules.

The necessity of 'bending the rules' can be seen when workers engaged in industrial disputes 'work to

rule'. They follow the rules of the job to the letter, for example by insisting on carrying out lengthy and time consuming safety checks which are normally overlooked, or by refusing to carry out duties which are not strictly part of their job description. While workers cannot be disciplined in this situation - they are actually following the rules - such tactics are extremely disruptive and often make normal working almost impossible.

Blau argues that Weber's analysis ignores the *informal structure* of organisations. Workers often form informal groups which are not officially recognised within the organisation. These groups not only operate alongside the formal structure, they may be essential for the efficiency of the organisation.

Blau's arguments can be illustrated by his study of federal agents in Washington DC (1963). Their job was to find out whether employment laws had been broken. Agents had their own cases which were strictly confidential - they were not allowed to discuss them with other agents. This official rule was regularly broken, agents discussed their cases with each other seeking advice, guidance and reassurance. Blau claimed that efficiency was greatly improved by these unofficial practices. The employment laws were complex and difficult to interpret. Working together the agents saved time, solved problems more efficiently and in the process formed a cohesive and mutually supportive informal group.

Blau argues that a bureaucratic structure is too inflexible to maximise efficiency. No set of rules can anticipate all the problems that will occur and often such problems are best handled informally. Blau concluded that a 'real' bureaucracy functions very differently from the model of bureaucracy portrayed in Weber's ideal type.

Burns and Stalker: mechanistic and organic systems

In recent years many organisation theorists have recognised that the classic bureaucratic structure identified by Weber is not necessarily suited to all organisational contexts. One of the first studies to argue this was Tom Burns and G.M. Stalker's *The Management of Innovation* (1966). Burns and Stalker outlined two ideal types of organisation.

Mechanistic systems This type of organisation is similar to Weber's model of bureaucracy with a clear chain of command, specialisation of departments and posts and fixed rules and procedures for carrying out tasks. The term mechanistic is used to point to similarities with a machine.

Organic systems This type of organisation moves away from the rigid form of bureaucracy and is more like an organism which is constantly changing and adapting to its environment - hence the term organic. Important decisions are no longer taken solely by management - any employee can be involved. Communication travels in any direction rather than simply from the top down. Rigid hierarchies and strict divisions of labour are replaced by a more fluid and flexible system. Employees are encouraged to solve problems, to cooperate and adapt in order to further organisational goals rather than simply following rules.

Burns and Stalker examined the organisational structure of the electronics industry in Scotland. They found that mechanistic systems were unsuited to this industry. A more fluid organisation was needed in which people were not constrained by rules and fixed job descriptions. The electronics industry must adapt to rapid technological change. Those companies that stuck to traditional bureaucratic structures had difficulty in adapting and innovating. The inflexible character of the mechanistic system was not suited to rapidly changing situations. In such firms higher management were afraid of losing their seniority to new, junior scientists who often had more up-to-date knowledge. There was a tendency for them to exclude well qualified juniors from decision making processes and, by doing so, to harm their firms' competitiveness.

In firms which had adopted a more organic structure there was a move away from the strict chain of command to a system of shared decision making. The structure was far more flexible and new staff were not excluded from decision making. Team work rather than a strict division of labour was encouraged and groups of workers exchanged information and ideas. They were concerned with solving problems and furthering organisational goals rather than sticking rigidly to strict job descriptions. Companies which adopted this type of structure appeared to adapt better to technological change.

Burns and Stalker put forward these two types of organisational structures as ideal types - in reality many firms do not fit precisely into one type or the other. They do not suggest that either form is necessarily more efficient or inefficient. Instead the degree of efficiency depends on the nature of the environment in which a particular company operates. A mechanistic structure would be more appropriate for an organisation which uses an essentially unchanging technology and has a relatively stable market. An organic structure would be more suitable for a company which has to cope with rapid change - with new tasks, new technology and new markets. Like Gouldner, Burns and Stalker emphasise the importance of the organisation being adapted to its environment and point out that Weber's ideal type may be ill-suited to some circumstances.

Activity 2 Formal and Informal Structures

Item A *Red tape in the French Civil Service*

Mr Ford Madox Ford related his adventures in trying to trace a postal order gone astray. When this occurs, the usual course is to take the matter up through official channels, give the postman a big tip, or put the case into the hands of 'an adviser of public companies'. On this occasion, however, Mr. Ford decided to go directly to the head office of the postal service on the Boulevard Montparnasse in Paris. At two o'clock he was ushered into the Director's office by a smiling charwoman. After half an hour the Director returned from lunch and scrutinised the documents with great care. Following further consultation with an official in blue uniform, the Director announced that Ford should betake himself to the 'Chief Sub-Office for the Recovery of Money Orders' on the other side of Paris. There he was directed to Room V on the sixth floor. While he conversed with an attractive young woman on the value of face powders and the like, her chief examined the papers and asked questions about Ford's war record and family, finally instructing him to return to the Boulevard Montparnasse, this time to Room XVI on the third floor. From there he was sent back to Room XI in

Item B *A French cartoonist's view*

I'VE QUICKLY UNDERSTOOD THAT, IN A BUREAUCRACY, THE ESSENTIAL THING IS ALWAYS TO KEEP YOURSELF COVERED

the Chief Sub-Office; thence to Room IV, Boulevard Montparnasse; next to Room III, Chief Sub-Office; and finally to the 'open sesame' - Room XIII on Montparnasse. Although assured there that he would receive his money by the first delivery the following day, it actually arrived seven weeks later, only after a generous tip had been showered on the postman.

Adapted from W. Sharp *The French Civil Service*, 1931, quoted in P. Blau and R. Meyer *Bureaucracy in Modern Society*, 1971

Item C *Informal bureaucracy in the navy*

The US Navy had established an air base on an unpopulated island. Because of its isolation the informal structures within the organisation of the base had gradually become accepted as the formal procedures by which personnel operated. One visiting officer described this as a 'breakdown' of the organisation. This was clearly not the case, as shown by the high morale and the effective accomplishment of missions. What had 'broken down' was a large part of the formal structure, or rather it had been submerged as the informal structure rose into overt recognition and use. Fortunately the 'skipper' as well as several other officers and petty officers were 'natural leaders', their status and role definitions were the same in both the formal and informal structures. However, unmistakable indications of greater importance of the informal included the replacement of the social isolation of the commanding officer by his keen participation in all activities of the unit and the emergence of natural leaders to what amounted to official recognition (from amongst those who formally had a low official rank), the abandonment of most of the officially governing protocol (except in the treatment of visitors) for example saluting and deferring to higher ranks, and the accomplishment of the day-to-day and long-run tasks with efficiency, zeal and spontaneous initiative not characteristic of official bureaucratic machinery.

Adapted from C. H. Page 'Bureaucracy's Other Face', *Social Forces* 25, 1946.

Item D *Bureaucracy as comedy*

The cast of MASH

The television series MASH was based on a fictitious Mobile Army Surgical Hospital in the Korean War. The heroes of the programme were two young surgeons who had little respect for authority, army discipline or bureaucratic rules. They were more concerned with the overriding goals of treating wounded soldiers and saving lives. The series made fun of attempts by both an officious but incompetent second-in-command and by various outside agencies to impose military discipline and regulations on the unit.

Questions

1 In what ways might Items A and B be used to illustrate Merton's arguments about the dysfunctions of bureaucracy?
2 How do Items C and D illustrate the idea that informal structures in organisations are just as important, and in some cases more important, than formal bureaucratic structures?

1.3 Interpretive approaches

Writers such as David Silverman (1970) argue that organisation theorists have paid too much attention to the formal features of organisations - the way organisations are supposed to operate according to 'the book'. They have given insufficient attention to how members of organisations actually create and sustain rules and procedures through their interaction. Such approaches are referred to as *interactionist* or *interpretive* perspectives, since they focus on the meanings and interpretations which social actors give to their own actions and those of others.

Silverman argues that roles within organisations are not simply fixed and 'given' by the organisation. Instead members of organisations develop expectations about each others' roles through their interaction. In order to understand their actions it is necessary to understand the meanings they give to their situation. Silverman points to Gouldner's study to illustrate this, noting how the gypsum miners had developed their own definitions of the situation,

their own informal rules which came into conflict with the official rules when the new manager attempted to break the 'indulgency pattern'.

Organisations as negotiated order

One of the most famous studies using an interactionist approach was carried out by Anselm Strauss and his colleagues. *The Hospital and its Negotiated Order* (1963) is based on research in two psychiatric hospitals. Strauss found there were no clear cut rules defining how staff and patients should behave. Moreover, the goals of the organisations were not clearly defined but open to considerable interpretation and negotiation. Staff shared the goal of improving patients' mental health and returning them to the community, but there was considerable disagreement over how this should be achieved. Many different professions with different approaches worked together and even within a single profession such as psychiatry there was no agreement - for example, over the best forms of treatment for particular disorders.

Strauss argues that staff are engaged in a constant process of negotiation. For example, nursing staff and unqualified aides may feel they are closer to patients because they deal with them on a day to day basis. This may lead them to disagree with a psychiatrist's diagnosis or the treatment prescribed. Patients may also engage in negotiation with staff, for example for more privileges or for different treatment.

In a psychiatric hospital patients are not dealt with by fixed and routinised procedures. Their careers as patients are the outcome of a complex set of negotiations between many actors. A psychiatrist may advocate a particular treatment but may be forced to change this decision because of pressure from nursing staff, resulting in a very different outcome for the patient.

Strauss et al conclude that their concept of the hospital as a 'negotiated order' may be applied to other types of organisations such as universities, business corporations and government agencies. However, critics have argued that psychiatric hospitals may have special features which make them different from other organisations. For example, the goals of psychiatric hospitals and the means of achieving them are less clearly defined than those of the other organisations that Strauss mentions.

Ethnomethodology and organisations

By the 1970s many writers working from an interactionist perspective were influenced by ethnomethodology, in particular the work of the American sociologist Harold Garfinkel (1967) (see pp685-687). Ethnomethodologists reject the idea that organisations have an objective reality. Organisations are simply ideas in the minds of members of society. They only continue to have this subjective reality because members work hard in daily life to sustain a belief in their existence. Thus a school only continues to be a school because pupils attend it, teachers continue to teach and its members work together to sustain a shared understanding of the meaning of activities taking place within the institution. If pupils and teachers no longer accepted 'commonsense' ideas of what should go on in school, then school would cease to exist.

Ethnomethodologists have explored the ways in which the rules of social life are continually constructed and reconstructed in daily social activities. Weber emphasised that bureaucratic organisations are above all rule governed. Ethnomethodolgists take a very different view as the following example illustrates.

Organisational rules and commonsense

Don Zimmerman's *The Practicalities of Rule Use* (1971) is a study of the work of a Bureau of Public Assistance in the USA, an organisation concerned with financial assistance for those in need. The nearest British equivalent would be an office of the Department of Social Security. In order for their needs to be assessed, applicants were interviewed by a caseworker. On arrival the applicant would see a receptionist who would ask them to fill in a form and allocate them to a caseworker. The official rule governing this allocation was to assign applicants to each caseworker in turn. The main priority for receptionists was to keep clients moving through the system.

Most of the time things worked well. Sometimes, however, a caseworker would take longer than normal to deal with a client. In such instances receptionists often 'switched' clients to another caseworker so they would be dealt with more speedily. On the surface this would seem to be a violation of the official procedure for dealing with clients. However, Zimmerman suggests that rules are interpreted according to what commonsense says they are intended to achieve. Receptionists saw it as reasonable to suspend the allocation rule in order to achieve what they saw as its original aim - to keep clients moving through the system.

Ethnomethodologists argue that members of society are constantly trying to make social life appear orderly and sensible. To this end they construct rules - which do not create order but rather give the appearance of order. And, just like the receptionists, they even make sense of breaking rules by convincing themselves they are following rules.

Criticisms of interpretive perspectives

Interactionism and ethnomethodolgy have produced some fascinating studies of the day to day activities of members of organisations, (see the examples in Activity 3). However, critics argue that such perspectives fail to consider the influence of the wider structures of society on the interaction of individuals. Mike Reed (1985) accuses them of an obsessive concern with the minutiae of everyday life. Marxists argue that their focus on small scale interaction largely prevents a consideration of the development of organisations in capitalist society and of the question of whose interests these organisations serve.

Activity 3 Interpreting Rules

Item A *Rule bargaining*

In this extract from a study of an exclusive private school for girls, Sara Delamont describes how a geography test was marked in Mrs Hill's class. The girls, swapped papers and marked their neighbours' scripts.

Mrs Hill announces a strict marking schedule and says there are to be no arguments about it. She then starts asking round the class to get the answers.

Mrs Hill: Right, now what do you call the area of fertile farmland that includes Perthshire?
Jackie: The golden girdle.
Karen bursts out laughing, and Mrs Hill asks her what is funny.
Karen: Angela has got 'golden griddle', not 'girdle'.
Mrs Hill laughs and the whole class dissolves into laughter.
Mrs Hill: She can have half a mark for ingenuity.
A chorus of protests about half marks - for the schedule had stated 'no half marks'.
Mrs Hill ignores protests. They go on. Another question asked for 'the industries of Glasgow after the American War of Independence'. After the right answers have been given, Karen raises her hand and is asked what she wants.
Karen: I had 'the slave trade'. Does that count?
Mrs Hill: That's not an industry.
Karen: Well, for modern Scotland we've got 'tourism' as an industry - if tourists are an industry surely slaves are too?
Mrs Hill gives in and lets her have half a mark too. Another chorus of 'Not fair' breaks out and is silenced.

Adapted from S. Delamont *Interaction in the Classroom*, 1983, pp106-7

Item B *Bending the rules*

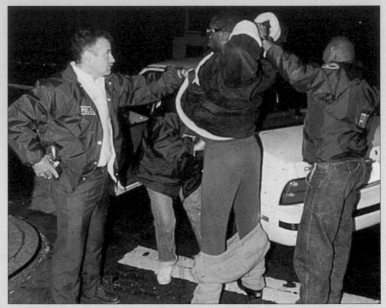

Making an arrest

In a study entitled 'The Police on Skid Row' Egon Bittner explains how police patrolmen go about their work in a squalid American inner city area inhabited by drunks, vagrants and petty criminals. The patrolmen have a rich body of knowledge about the area and its people, knowing many of the inhabitants by name. Officers see their main task as keeping the peace. This sometimes means that people get arrested not because they are guilty of a crime but because their arrest is seen by officers as helping to solve a problem which might lead to serious disorder. And sometimes officers don't seem particularly concerned with discovering the guilty party.

Bittner gives the example of an argument over a stolen pair of trousers. The officer involved was less concerned with investigating who had stolen the trousers than with preventing a fight from developing. He argued that in this area 'no one could tell what "belongs" to whom' and took the case no further once the participants dispersed, exhausted from their argument.

Bittner argues that 'patrolmen do not really enforce the law, even when they do invoke it, but merely use it as a resource to solve certain practical peace keeping problems'.

Adapted from Egon Bittner 'The Police on Skid Row: a Study of Peace Keeping' *American Sociological Review* 32, no 5, October 1967

Questions

1 Give examples from Item A which illustrate the idea that rules in organisations are often negotiable.
2 How might the patrolmen in Item B justify the fact that they did not follow the letter of the law with the people on Skid Row?

1.4 Marxism and bureaucracy

Marx had little to say about bureaucracy. He saw state bureaucracy as an instrument of class oppression which maintained the dominance of the bourgeoisie. He assumed that after the proletarian revolution administrators would be elected and truly responsible to the people. Bureaucracy was simply a class instrument and would cease to exist in a classless society.

Lenin and bureaucracy under communism

Lenin, the leader of the Bolshevik Party following the Russian revolution, developed many of Marx's ideas. He saw the state going through a transitional phase - the 'dictatorship of the proletariat' - in which some members of the proletariat would govern on behalf of everybody. Once communism proper was established, this 'dictatorship' would be unnecessary and disappear. Lenin believed that administrators should be elected and accountable to the people with no distinctions of wages and status between them and other workers.

He also believed that administrative tasks could be simplified to the point where anyone with basic literacy and numeracy could do them. Once communism was established the state would wither away. Some form of administration would still be required but this would be run by ordinary workers with everyone taking turns to fill official posts.

This did not happen for a number of reasons. Firstly, there was still a need for skilled specialists in many bureaucratic positions and these jobs could not be done by ordinary workers. Lenin seems to have underestimated the complexity of a modern state. Secondly, in order to supervise the activities of bureaucrats in both government and the economy the Communist Party itself became a huge and centralised bureaucracy. For practically every official there was a party member to ensure he or she was following party orders. Finally, the rise to power of Stalin after Lenin's death led to further centralisation of power in the hands of the party leader and a consequent spread of bureaucracy. These developments led many Marxists to ask what had gone wrong.

Trotsky and Djilas: criticisms of bureaucracy under communism

Leon Trotsky was a leading Communist at the time of the Russian revolution. In *The Revolution Betrayed* (1937) Trotsky argued that while private ownership of the means of production had been abolished and replaced by state ownership, a socialist political order had not developed. Instead the Soviet Union was governed by a bureaucratic elite. Trotsky saw this as a temporary phase caused by the backwardness of the Soviet economy. Once the economy developed the Soviet Union would complete its transition from a bourgeois to a socialist system.

Another influential critic of bureaucracy under communism was Milovan Djilas, the former Vice-President of Yugoslavia. In his book *The New Class* (1957), Djilas argued that the Communist Party bureaucracy in the Soviet Union, and indeed in other communist states such as Yugoslavia, had become a new class. This bureaucratic elite made all the important decisions with little or no reference to the mass of the population. Members of the new class directed the economy to serve their own interests. They controlled the distribution of wealth and privilege and feathered their own nests at the expense of the masses. Exploitation by the bourgeoisie was replaced with exploitation by the new class of political bureaucrats. Unlike Trotsky, Djilas saw this situation as permanent rather than transitional, as an integral part of communist society.

This section has looked briefly at Marxist views of bureaucracy in communist societies. Section 2.2 looks at Marxist views of organisations under capitalism.

Activity 4 Communism and Bureaucracy

Item A *Bureaucratic revolution*

When Communists said they did not want a bureaucracy, they meant that they did not want an administrative structure that would not or could not respond to revolutionary commands. They wanted an administrative structure whose officials were willing to accept orders from the revolution's leaders and were eager to carry out policies of radical social change. This was the revolutionary function that the party bureaucracy should perform and most Communists instinctively recognised the need for a bureaucratic apparatus.

Most Communists also believed that the 'proletarian dictatorship' ought to be proletarian, meaning that former workers should hold responsible administrative jobs. In the 1920s a 'party maximum' kept most Communist officials' salaries from rising above the average wages of a skilled worker. In the 1930s, however, a higher standard of living became a normal and almost obligatory privilege of elite status, and the 'party maximum' disappeared. The party bureaucrats were set apart from the masses by high salaries, by privileged access to goods and services and by a variety of material and honorific rewards.

Members of the elite could use shops that were not open to the public, buy goods that were not available to other consumers and take their vacations in special resorts and well appointed dachas (country houses). They often lived in special apartments and went to work in chauffeur driven cars.

Adapted from S. Fitzpatrick *The Russian Revolution 1917-1932*, 1982, pp96 and 151-152

Questions

1 In Item A why does Fitzpatrick suggest that while the Communists disliked the idea of bureaucracy they recognised the need for some kind of administrative structure?

2 What evidence is there for the claim by Djilas that under Soviet Communism party officials had become a new ruling class?

Item B

Leaders of the former Soviet Union take the salute in Moscow to mark the anniversary of the revolution.

1.5 Bureaucracy and democracy

Marx and Lenin hoped that the arrival of socialism would lead to the subordination of bureaucracy to the interests of the working class. Some reformist socialist thinkers have also argued that while capitalist organisations are inevitably anti-democratic the organisations of the working class could be run on democratic lines so allowing ordinary working people a say in trade unions and socialist political parties. Sidney and Beatrice Webb (1920), for example, held up the organisation of the Amalgamated Association of Operative Cotton Spinners as an example of a truly democratic trade union. Weber was less optimistic arguing that bureaucracy did not lend itself to democratic controls whether in a socialist or capitalist society. He did, however, admit that democratically elected representatives might prevent unelected bureaucrats from becoming too powerful. A far more pessimistic view is offered by Weber's student, the Italian sociologist Roberto Michels.

Michels: the iron law of oligarchy

In his study *Political Parties* first published in 1911, Michels maintains that in large scale societies organisations such as political parties and trade unions are essential to achieve democratic objectives. Individuals with common beliefs and interests must join together to have any chance of achieving their aims. Working class people, in particular, are unlikely to exert much influence in either workplaces or in the political system unless they join together in organisations.

For Michels this results in a contradiction. While democracy demands that people form themselves into organisations, the creation of an organisation sounds the death knell of democracy. So-called democratic organisations are based on 'representative democracy' whereby representatives are elected to carry out the wishes of rank and file members. But, there is a tendency for leaders to take decisions with little reference to ordinary members. This is reinforced by the technical complexity of much decision making - many members do not have the knowledge and understanding of issues to make decisions for themselves. In this way an *oligarchy* or small elite comes to dominate decision making. The elected representatives are full time officials, paid to perform administrative tasks. This leads to the creation of a bureaucracy which by its very nature is undemocratic. Democratic ideals are replaced by a specialised division of labour, a rigid hierarchy and control from the top. This is what Michels terms the 'iron law of oligarchy', a process he saw as inevitable.

Michels' study is based largely on his observations of the German Socialist Party (SPD). The party was established with democratic socialist ideals to represent the interests of the working class and replace capitalism with socialism. Michels claimed that the leaders of the party lost touch with their working class supporters and became increasingly concerned with maintaining their own power even when this meant compromising party ideals. The gulf was widened as leaders enjoyed higher status, income and privileges than ordinary working class members and became more like members of the middle class in their outlook and lifestyle.

Michels claimed that similar tendencies were discernible in German trade unions. He points out that if democracy is not attainable in organisations which are supposedly committed to radical and democratic political aims there is little chance of democracy in society as a whole. The state too is taken over by an oligarchy which perpetuates its own interests at the expense of the citizens it purports to serve. In this respect Michels ideas echo those of classical elite theorists (see p206).

The ITU: a case study of union democracy

One of the most famous studies responding to Michels' work was carried out by Lipset, Trow and Coleman (1956). They examined the American printers' union, the International Typographical Union (ITU) as an example of a trade union which appeared to contradict the iron law of oligarchy. Lipset et al claim that a unique combination of factors in the organisation of the ITU allowed ordinary members to play a genuine role in determining union policy and controlling the leadership.

The elements which promoted democracy included the following.

- The frequent use of referenda to determine policy.
- Leaders had a similar level of income to ordinary members. Loss of office did not mean a drastic reduction in their income.
- Twice yearly elections of both national and local officials by the membership.
- A two party system which meant there were alternative policies and candidates to those offered by the existing leadership.

Lipset et al argued that certain historical and cultural factors promoted democracy in the ITU. For example, printers had a strong craft identity and tended to participate in social clubs and leisure activities linked to their occupational group. This encouraged greater involvement in the union.

Despite these findings Lipset, Trow and Coleman do not disagree with Michels' basic argument. They argue that the ITU is, in many respects, the exception which proves the rule. Democracy only survived in the ITU because of its unique characteristics. They point out that these factors are rarely found in other trade unions and that oligarchic leadership is the general rule. Despite this pessimism, the ITU study does demonstrate that union democracy is possible under certain conditions.

Democracy in British trade unions

A number of studies of British trade unions support Michels' thesis. For example a study of the Transport and General Workers Union by Goldstein (1952) found that few members exercised their right to vote in elections or attended branch meetings. In practice decisions at both local and national level were taken by a small minority of active members. Michael Jackson (1988) notes that later studies have found similar tendencies in other British unions.

However, not all unions appear so oligarchic. A study by Clegg (1954) of the General and Municipal Workers Union found that it was not unknown for ordinary members of the union's congress to defeat a motion proposed by the executive, or for a district secretary to be dismissed by his district council. Roderick Martin (1968) carried out a detailed study of the National Union of Railwaymen (NUR) and the Amalgamated Engineering Union (AEU). He argued that as long as a faction providing opposition to the current leadership was able to survive, democracy could prevail. Martin identifies a range of factors which help to encourage opposition factions. In the AEU, for example, a strong tradition of local autonomy and involvement by ordinary members meant the leadership was frequently faced by challenges. The NUR by contrast was a larger and more centralised union where most decisions were taken by a central executive remote from the members. Such studies suggest that there is at least the potential for democracy in trade unions.

Summary

1 Weber saw bureaucracy as the most rational means of administration. He saw it as the dominant form of organisation in industrial society. He feared its power as a threat to democracy.

2 Case studies have indicated that bureaucracy is neither inevitable nor necessarily the most efficient form of organisation.

3 A number of studies have suggested that most if not all organisations have a tendency to oligarchy. However, examples of organisations which operate on democratic principles have been found.

Activity 5   Democracy and the Labour Party

The debate over Clause 4

In April 1995 the leadership of the Labour Party called a special conference to vote on proposals to rewrite Clause 4 of the party's constitution. Clause 4 committed the party to secure public ownership of the means of production. The reform of Clause 4 would end this commitment.

In 1992 the Labour Party established the principle of one member one vote. This meant that each party member was allowed to vote on a range of important issues such as the election of leader. In 1995 the membership stood at 330,000, an increase of 100,000 in a single year. The leadership hoped that this increase would result in party members becoming more representative of Labour supporters generally.

One member one vote reduces the power of local party activists. In December 1994 the Tribune produced a long list of local parties whose activists had voted to retain Clause 4. Yet in almost every case their memberships voted for change. The result of the special conference vote shows that 90% of party members supported the new Clause 4.

Trade unions affiliated to the Labour Party have always had an important say in the party's affairs. For example, the union vote counts for 70% of the vote at the party's annual conference. Two of the largest trade unions, the Transport and General Workers Union led by Bill Morris and Unison the public sector union, announced their intention to vote against the revision of Clause 4. However, a MORI poll of TGWU members published in *Today* showed a 2-1 support for reform.

Neither the TGWU nor Unison held ballots of their members. The TGWU said a ballot would cost £500,000 and there was not enough time to consult its nearly one million members. Both unions voted against change. In the case of the TGWU this was 14% of the total vote. Despite this the overall vote was 65% in favour of changing Clause 4, 35% against. Tony Blair, leader of the Labour Party, attacked certain trade union leaders for being 'so badly out of tune' with their ordinary members.

Adapted from various issues of the *Times* and *Guardian*, 27.4.95 to 2.5.95

Labour leader Tony Blair launching the 'New Labour, New Britain' tour in which he travelled round the country to convince party members that Clause 4 must be rewritten.

Questions

1 Judging from the above, to what extent can
   (i) the Labour Party;
   (ii) the TGWU be seen as democratic?
2 Assess the relevance of Michels' iron law of oligarchy to the above evidence.

2 Organisation Theory: Beyond the Debate with Weber

Key Issues

1 How can organisations be designed to achieve their goals effectively? Who benefits from this?

2 Do new forms of work organisation represent the end of bureaucracy?

3 Are new forms of organisation simply a more sophisticated means of social control?

Debates over Weber's theories of bureaucracy have dominated the sociology of organisations for much of this century. However, other traditions have also contributed. Some of these ideas are examined in this part of the chapter.

2.1 The managerial tradition

Much of the sociology of organisations has been concerned with theoretical issues concerning the role of bureaucracy in society. By contrast other approaches have been more concerned with practical issues, for example how to achieve maximum efficiency within organisations. Such approaches have often been influenced by management science, industrial psychology and business studies. This section introduces examples of managerial approaches.

Scientific management

Frederick Taylor's book *The Principles of Scientific*

Management was first published in the USA in 1911. Regarded as the father of modern management theory, Taylor claimed that firms rarely utilised the full productive capacity of their workers. He argued this could only be achieved if management took control of the work process from the workers. Inefficient traditional work practices could then be replaced with rational planned methods. This would boost productivity.

The job of management was to discover the 'one best way' of performing every work task. Work study engineers would study employees at work to find out the minimum time required for each task and the most efficient procedures to be followed. A task design would then be formalised and workers selected and trained to follow it to the letter. Those who complied would be paid incentives, those who did not would not be employed. Taylor recognised that this would require higher wages and the employment of additional supervisors and managers to ensure that workers followed instructions. However, this would be more than repaid by greater efficiency and productivity.

The kind of work organisation advocated by Taylor includes many of the elements of Weber's ideal type of bureaucracy. Work roles are rationally planned, there is a specialised division of labour and a hierarchy of positions with orders passed down from management to subordinates. Taylor's ideas had a considerable influence on industrialists like Henry Ford and were widely adopted in the 1920s and 1930s.

The Hawthorne studies

Taylor believed that workers were motivated solely by financial incentives and recommended that managers offer bonuses to those who cooperated in implementing scientific management techniques. However, other management theorists became increasingly aware that workers were motivated by factors other than financial rewards. This can be seen from a famous series of studies carried out at the Hawthorne electrical plant in Chicago in the 1920s and 1930s (Roethlisberger and Dickson, 1939).

Initially the studies focused on factors which, according to scientific management, would affect workers' performance. In one experiment the researchers tried changing the lighting to see how this affected productivity. They found that output increased under all types of lighting, even semi-darkness. Moreover, the control group whose lighting was not changed also increased its output. The researchers realised that workers' productivity was affected, not by the lighting, but by the experiment itself. Workers felt for the first time that the management was concerned about them and interested in their work. A strong team spirit developed which helped to improve performance.

Human relations

Research such as the Hawthorne studies led management theorists such as Elton Mayo (1946) to develop the *human relations* approach. Mayo described the ideas of writers like Taylor as 'the rabble hypothesis' since they assumed that workers were a disorganised bunch of individuals who could only be coordinated by management and motivated by money. Mayo pointed out that workers formed cohesive groups, often with powerful group norms. For example in the Bank Wiring Room study (see Activity 6, Item C) workers restricted output because it was the group norm, even though this meant a loss of bonuses.

Like many sociologists, human relations theorists recognised the existence of informal groups which might have norms and goals which differ from those of the organisation. Rather than forcing them to toe the line, Mayo argued that management should work out ways of encouraging them to support organisational goals. This would require better communication between management and workers, the discovery of grievances in the workforce and measures to resolve those grievances.

Criticisms of human relations theories

The human relations school has had considerable influence on management theories and industrial psychology. Many employers now recognise the need to treat workers as human beings and motivate them not just by financial rewards but by creating a sense of loyalty to the organisation. Nevertheless, many critics see little difference between the human relations approach and scientific management. Marxists, in particular, argue that both are simply methods by which management can more effectively exploit workers and increase profits.

Theo Nichols and Huw Beynon (1977) studied a British chemical plant in which management had introduced a human relations style approach. They found that this made little difference to how workers experienced work. For most work remained a monotonous, unrewarding and (for some) physically exhausting activity which was motivated primarily by the need to earn a living. Few workers felt much loyalty to their firm and most stayed on only because of a lack of other employment opportunities (see Activity 7, Item B).

Organisational design and types of bureaucracy

Weber's ideal type of bureaucracy was not intended to correspond precisely to organisations in the real world. Nevertheless, Weber believed that organisations based on the key elements of his ideal type represented the dominant tendency in industrial societies. However, by the 1960s many organisation theorists had come to recognise that organisations could not be described by reference to a single ideal type. They were also recognising that different tasks, products, services and markets required different types of organisational structures.

According to Hall (1973) bureaucracy should be seen as one part of a continuum. At one end of the scale are jobs which lend themselves to a highly bureaucratic system, for example workers on an assembly line or in a routine clerical job where tasks are standardised with little room for autonomy or decision making. At the other end of the scale are areas of work - as in some professional occupations - where it is difficult to organise work according to set rules. Professionals may have to use considerable discretion in making decisions and often have more expert knowledge than their superiors. In these circumstances following rules and obeying instructions from above may not be the most effective form of organisational design.

In response to this type of argument, some organisation theorists suggested that different forms of organisation may be suited to different contexts. This view was based on studies of a range of organisations. Many of these studies used a comparative approach and relied heavily on quantitative data. They were concerned with identifying key differences between types of organisations and establishing statistical links between the structure of organisations and other features of the organisation or its environment. This was in marked contrast to the case study approach adopted by sociologists such as Gouldner and Blau (see Section 1.2) which tended to focus on one organisation with an emphasis on qualitative data. Such studies provided a rich source of information about the workings of particular organisations but it was difficult to know how far their findings could be generalised to other organisations.

The Aston Group: the organisation and its environment

A sophisticated example of the comparative approach can be seen from the Aston studies of Derek Pugh and his colleagues carried out in the 1970s (Pugh et al, 1987). The researchers developed a procedure for classifying and comparing organisations. They identified four main factors which distinguished various types of organisation.
1 **Structuring of activities** eg how far activities of workers were standardised and involved following formalised procedures.
2 **Concentration of authority** eg how far authority was centralised, how far the workgroups were autonomous from the larger organisation.
3 **Line** eg was communication direct or indirect,

personal or impersonal.
4 **Relative size of supportive component** eg percentage of clerks and other support staff to workflow personnel (those directly producing goods or providing services).

Each factor was measured and a profile produced of each organisation. Based on this, Pugh and Hickson concluded 'that bureaucracy is not unitary... organisations may be bureaucratic in any one of a number of ways... The concept of bureaucratic type is no longer useful' (1976, pp60-61). Thus while the Aston Group use Weber as a starting point, they argue that few organisations correspond to his ideal type.

In fact they found four main types of bureaucracy based on their measurements for the first two dimensions (the degree to which activities were structured and the degree to which authority was concentrated).

Types of bureaucracy

	High concentration of authority	Low concentration of authority
High structuring of activities	**Full bureaucracy**	**Workflow bureaucracy**
Low structuring of activities	**Personnel bureaucracy**	**Implicitly structured organisation**

Based on Pugh and Hickson, 1976, Chapter 6

1 **Full bureaucracies** These approximated Weber's ideal type but did not really exist in pure form outside central government.
2 **Workflow bureaucracies** These were likely to be found in large manufacturing concerns where production was tightly structured but authority was more decentralised.
3 **Personnel bureaucracies** These tended to be found in smaller branch plants and parts of local government organisations. Here employment relationships tended to be bureaucratised but activities were less structured.
4 **Implicitly structured organisations** These were mostly small factories with operational control in the hands of the owners. They were less bureaucratic in both respects than the other types.

The Aston Group concluded that different types of organisational structures were suited to different situations. It was the organisation's environment that was critical. If the structure of the organisation did not 'fit' its environment, then it could not be effective. This message echoes the work of Burns and Stalker who argued that mechanistic systems are only suited to routine predictable work and market environments and that companies operating in environments requiring innovation and change are more likely to be successful if they adopt an organic system (see Section 1.2).

Mintzberg: differing organisational configurations

The type of approach developed by Burns and Stalker and the Aston Group is known as *contingency theory*. It states there are many contingencies (or circumstances) which need to be taken into account when deciding the best structure for a particular organisation. One of the most sophisticated versions of contingency theory is provided by the American organisation theorist Henry Mintzberg (1983).

Mintzberg observes that as organisations grow in size and complexity, their structure becomes increasingly differentiated - different parts of the organisation come to have increasingly specialised functions. He identifies five elements in modern organisations each of which carries out specialist functions.

Operating core The majority of employees who carry out basic production and service functions. For example, assembly line workers in a factory or teachers in a school.

Strategic apex The senior management who are responsible for overall planning and decision making at the top of the organisation.

Middle management They act as a link between the strategic apex and the operating core and other sections.

Technostructure Areas such as design, planning, personnel and training which provide support for and control over other areas of the organisation. Includes staff such as work study engineers and accountants.

Support staff In many large complex organisations specialist sections provide services which support those who are engaged in the main activity of the business, for example printing or catering services.

Mintzberg argues that in different types of organisations each of these components can assume the dominant role in coordinating the rest of the organisation. He suggests that these elements can be combined into five basic *configurations*.

1 **Simple structure** Workers in the operating core are directly supervised by the strategic apex. For example, in a small and newly formed business the owner may directly supervise a small group of employees. This allows for a good deal of informal communication but cannot be sustained when the organisation grows too big to be coordinated by one person.

2 **Machine bureaucracy** Work is standardised by the technostructure. This comes closest to Weber's ideal type bureaucracy. The tasks of ordinary workers are highly standardised and specialised and governed by rules designed by experts, for example work study engineers. This configuration is most frequently found in mature organisations where work is relatively routine and predictable. Mintzberg notes that many of the disadvantages of bureaucracy already discussed in this chapter are associated with this configuration.

3 **Professional bureaucracy** The standardisation of skills is based on the operating core. This is most common where workers are highly trained professionals, for example in hospitals, schools or social work departments. Standardisation of work is achieved by ensuring that professional workers are trained to a high standard before being employed. For example, a team of surgeons and nurses performing an operation will not need to communicate much because each knows from their training what to do and when. Professional bureaucracies are relatively democratic because professional workers tend to enjoy a high degree of autonomy, and control from management is weak. However, this can also be a disadvantage in that coordination of activities and innovation of new ideas are difficult to achieve.

4 **Divisional form** The standardisation of outputs is based on the middle line, for example each middle manager is responsible to senior management for work in his or her department. This is characteristic of large organisations such as major corporations which have a number of subsidiaries or local divisions. Middle managers in charge of divisions may be given a certain degree of freedom to run their own part of the organisation but are ultimately accountable to the strategic apex in head office, for example for achieving specified production targets. This system offers many advantages for large organisations operating in a number of markets or geographical areas. Problems occur where the performance of divisions is difficult to measure in quantitative terms, for example an education or social services organisation.

5 **Adhocracy** This rests on mutual adjustment and informal communication. Support staff play a key role here. Staff communicate not only with their manager but may call on specialists for advice and support. Adhocracies share many of the characteristics of Burns and Stalker's organic organisations. There is a loose division of labour, structures are flexible so that the organisation is constantly changing and adapting in order to innovate and adapt to new circumstances. Mintzberg suggests that power in an adhocracy is shared between all five elements, since the expertise of all groups of workers is required to achieve success. Mintzberg argues that adhocracies are best suited to a dynamic and unpredictable organisational environment, for example a film production company. They also offer the possibility of greater democracy and the chance for creativity for workers. However, adhocracy may not be suited to stable and predictable environments. Also people who enjoy order, stability and well defined relationships may have problems in coping with the fluidity of adhocracy.

Debates over contingency theory

Contingency theories have had considerable influence on the design of organisations. In particular they have often led to the replacement of traditional bureaucratic structures by less hierarchical systems (see Section 2.3). Contingency theories demonstrate that no one type of organisation is ideal. Organisational structures must vary in accordance with varying environments.

Both the methodology and the values which are seen to underlie contingency theory have been criticised. For example, the Aston studies have been accused of ignoring anything that cannot be quantified and measured statistically. Moreover, much of their data was collected from management sources and thus may reflect how organisations are officially supposed to work rather than the informal procedures followed in practice.

Radical critics argue that contingency theory derives from the managerial tradition. As such it is simply concerned with maximising efficiency on behalf of employers and lacks any critical perspective on the role of organisations under capitalism. They also point out that particular organisational forms may be the outcome of conflicts within the organisation rather than adaptation to the external environment. For example, pressure from trade unions may lead an organisation to allow workers more control over their work. These criticisms are discussed further in the next section.

In reply Lex Donaldson (1985) has defended the managerial tradition arguing that there is nothing wrong with using scientific methods to study organisational efficiency. If detailed prescriptions for organisation help managers to be more effective, then organisation theory has nothing to be ashamed of.

Activity 6 Motivation in Work Organisations

Item A *Scientific management*
In this extract Frederick Taylor gives an example of an imaginary conversation between himself and a worker called Schmidt. He shows how he would get the man to load 47 tons of pig iron a day instead of the usual 12½ tons.

'Schmidt, are you a high priced man?'
'Vell, I don't know vat you mean.'
'What I want to find out is whether you are a high priced man or one of these cheap fellows here. What I want to find out is whether you want to earn $1.85 a day or whether you are satisfied with $1.15 a day, just the same as all those cheap fellows are getting.'
'Did I vant $1.85 a day. Vas dot a high priced man? Vell yes, I vas a high priced man.'
'Well, if you are a high priced man you will load that pig iron on the car tomorrow for $1.85. Now do wake up and answer my question. Tell me whether you are a high priced man or not.'
'Vell - do I get $1.85 for loading dot pig iron on dot car tomorrow?'
'Certainly you do - certainly you do.'
'Vell den, I vas a high priced man.'
'Well, if you are a high priced man, you will do exactly as this man tells you from morning till night. When he tells you to pick up a pig and walk, you pick it up and walk, when he tells you to sit down and rest, you sit down. You do that right straight through the day. And what's more, no back talk. Now you come on to work here tomorrow morning and I'll know before night whether you really are a high priced man or not.'

Adapted from F. W. Taylor *The Principles of Scientific Management*, 1947

Item B *'Scientific control'*

Item C *Informal work organisation*

Fourteen men regularly worked in the Observation Room of the Western Electrical Company in Chicago. Nine were wiremen, three were soldermen and two were inspectors. The men made parts of switches for office telephone equipment. Wiremen would take banks of terminals and connect them with wires. This would be followed by a solderman fixing in place the connections and finally an inspector would test and check the work they had done.

Although there was no formal rule in the company that one man should not help another, in practice helping was forbidden. Nevertheless men often helped each other when they had fallen behind in their work, usually by doing some of their wiring for them. The wiremen said it made them feel good to be helped and everyone took part in it.

Men also participated in all sorts of games in the lunch hour. Most involved some form of betting and ranged from card games to betting on the serial numbers of weekly pay checks. Participation in games occurred in two groups and nearly all the friendships in the factory were based on these two groups. Each group had its own games and activities which were noticeably different from those of the other group.

Apart from these leisure activities each group also had strict informal norms about how much work a man should do. Men who worked too fast were described as 'chisellers' and might receive subtle threats from their workmates. The amount of work produced by each man had little to do with individual intelligence or manual dexterity but was clearly related to which group he belonged to. Although individual men might have increased their earnings by increasing their daily output this rarely happened - most men conformed to the norm of their group as to what was a reasonable day's work. As a result one group had a higher output than the other. This could only be accounted for by the different group norms governing a reasonable output.

Based on F.J. Roethlisberger and W.J. Dickson *Management and the Worker*, 1939

Questions

1 a) Read Item A. How does Taylor intend to make Schmidt more productive?
   b) What does this extract suggest about Taylor's opinion of manual workers?
2 How can the cartoons in Item B be used to criticise scientific management?
3 Find three examples in Item C of workers' behaviour which was directed by informal group norms rather than formal organisational rules.
4 How does Item C suggest that Taylor's method of motivating workers may not always be successful?
5 Should sociologists make recommendations to managers about organisations?

2.2 Conflict perspectives

The management oriented theories outlined in the previous section have come under considerable criticism from radical sociologists. Such critics have drawn on the ideas of Weber and more especially Marx about the role of organisations under capitalism. Many managerial theories, for example the human relations school, seem to be based on the assumption that a harmonious relationship between management and workers is the norm and that conflict is dysfunctional and abnormal. However, many sociologists argue that conflict in the workplace is normal (see pp338-340) and that the nature of organisations can only be understood as the outcome of struggles between competing groups.

Under capitalism many organisations are concerned with maximising profits. Managerial perspectives tend to take this for granted and fail to question whether capitalism and the type of organisations that it entails are rational and desirable. Thus they see activities such as strikes which disrupt the smooth running of organisations and inhibit productivity as 'irrational'. However, such activities become reasonable if conflict is accepted as normal and capitalist organisations are seen as neither inevitable nor operating in everyone's interests.

Harry Braverman: organisations and control

The American writer Braverman (1973) provides one of the most influential Marxist theories of work organisations. Braverman suggests that the key to understanding work organisations under capitalism lies in the drive by capitalist employers and their managers to control workers in order to exploit their labour more effectively. Braverman argues that methods such as scientific management have been used to *deskill* workers. With management taking control of the labour process there has been a 'separation of conception from execution'. Jobs are designed and planned by managers leaving workers to carry out pre-planned tasks requiring minimal skill or initiative.

Braverman rejects the view that human relations theories represent a more human approach to work. He sees them as a device used by management to conceal their control by making it appear they are concerned with workers as human beings.

Braverman's ideas have been extensively debated and criticised. Critics have focused on evidence that management does not always successfully deskill - workers may resist this process. Moreover, new forms of organisation seem to be moving away from simple top down control by management, with workers increasingly involved in decision making and expected to exercise a considerable range of skills. (See pp328-331 for further discussion of the debates over Braverman's thesis).

Craig Littler: alternative systems of control

A number of radical theorists have sympathised with Braverman's general argument that work organisations can only be understood in the context of capital's need to control labour. However, such writers have criticised Braverman for ignoring alternative control strategies within work organisations. Craig Littler (1982), in a study of employment practices in nineteenth century Britain and the USA, argues that a variety of forms of control existed. These included subcontracting work which left direct control of workers to the subcontractor, and the employment of skilled workers who then managed or even employed less skilled workers to assist them.

Littler acknowledges that the period he studied witnessed a bureaucratisation of the employment system and a tightening of managerial control as employers replaced indirect control through subcontractors with more direct employment and more direct control systems. Littler's argument differs in two important respects from Braverman.

1 He rejects the view that these changes can be explained simply as a process of deskilling. Skilled workers lost control over unskilled and semi-skilled workers but did not necessarily become deskilled. Old craft skills survived and new industries created demands for new skills.
2 Management strategies were not necessarily based on a rational and coherent approach such as Taylorism. Instead they were often a pragmatic accommodation to immediate problems. For example, employers often had to cope with conflicts between different groups of workers, such as skilled and unskilled grades, as well as resistance from workers to management control.

Andrew Friedman: responsible autonomy

Other critics of Braverman point to the emergence of new forms of control which appear on the face of it to give workers more responsibility. Andrew Friedman (1977), for example, points to the strategy of *responsible autonomy* whereby workers are allowed a certain degree of discretion and control over their work. In such systems workers are often encouraged to identify with the company and with the goals of senior management. Friedman sees strategies such as responsible autonomy as simply a more sophisticated method of controlling workers. Granting some autonomy helps to overcome the resistance created by crude attempts to deskill workers and establish top-down controls. Instead workers largely control themselves, a much more effective system than more obvious and coercive measures.

Conflict theories have provided a useful counterbalance to the managerial approaches examined in the previous section. In particular, they have raised the question of who benefits from organisations. They have also considered how particular organisational forms result from and give rise to conflicts between social groups. However, they provide few practical prescriptions as to how organisations might operate for the benefit of all their members. For example, the Marxist argument that this is only possible in a socialist system has been dismissed as wishful thinking, particularly after the collapse of communism in Eastern Europe and the former Soviet Union.

Activity 7 Capitalism and the Organisation of Work

Item A *'Human relations' and capitalist exploitation*

In the early 1970s Theo Nichols and Huw Beynon carried out a study of a chemical plant called Riverside, part of a firm they called Chemco. Following a report which revealed that British firms used more workers to produce the same level of production as their American and Continental counterparts, the firm had introduced a new productivity deal and management structure which was called the New Working Arrangements (NWA). In return for a reduction in the workforce and greater flexibility in work, workers were offered big pay increases. The agreement also included clauses about the need to 'enrich' work and to 'involve' people. Managers were encouraged to adopt the ideas of the human relations school concerning job enrichment and treating workers as human beings.

Nichols and Beynon point out 'The aim of NWA was to rationalise the system of wage payment and the "use of labour" (between 1970 and 1973, for example, the manning levels in the packing areas at Riverside, the most labour intensive, dropped by a sixth). At the same time NWA aimed to promote the identification of the workers with their jobs and the company. This was the tension within the package - a tension which points to the central contradiction of capitalist production; the recognition that production is essentially social while at the same time it is organised for profit. The trick and the problem which faced ChemCo was to socialise production the capitalist way to bring about a capitalist socialisation. Workers were to be invited to get more "involved" in their work, to "self-actualise" and actually to be more exploited.'

Adapted from T. Nichols and H. Beynon *Living with Capitalism: Class Relations and the Modern Factory*, 1977, pp7-10

Questions

1 a) What does Item A see as the contradiction in the requirements of capitalist work organisations?
   b) How did the New Working Arrangements at ChemCo attempt to resolve this contradiction?
   c) Why are the authors critical of the human relations approach?
2 a) What does Item B suggest is the main priority of capitalism?
   b) How might this cause conflict?

Item B *'Capital'*

A 1919 poster from the Soviet Union

2.3 Postmodern organisations: the end of bureaucracy?

In recent years many writers on organisations have identified a trend towards the dissolution of bureaucracy. Mintzberg (1983), for example, sees *adhocracy* as 'tomorrow's organisation'. The sharp division of labour, rigid hierarchies, highly formalised tasks and centralised control of bureaucracy is, in terms of this view, being replaced with more flexible and democratic systems.

Post-Fordism and organisations

British Telecom has been given as an example of this new organisational trend (Clutterbuck, 1985). BT developed a corporate structure in which each division operated as a an autonomous profit centre. In this way responsibility for decision making and profitability is passed down to lower levels of the organisation. Another instance of the move away from centralised bureaucratic control, cited by Charles Handy (1984), is *intrapreneurship*. Intrapreneurs are key employees who bid to provide functions and services in an internal market within the firm. Again this means responsibility and decision making are passed down to smaller semi-

autonomous units within the organisation.

Murray's (1983) study of the Italian clothing firm Benetton provides a further example of a 'new' form of organisation. Benetton gradually shed most of its directly employed labour, reducing its workforce to only 1,500 in small plants of 50-60 workers. However, up to 10,000 other workers were employed by a network of subcontractors undertaking work for Benetton. In much the same way Benetton shops are not owned by the firm but are franchises sold to independent retailers who Benetton then supply.

Murray sees this type of decentralised, flexible production as characteristic of *post-Fordism*. Post-Fordist organisations contrast sharply with the highly bureaucratic character of Fordist organisations. Fordist organisations are geared to mass production with centralised and hierarchical structures and a highly specialised division of labour.

Murray believes that post-Fordist developments challenge the views of both Marx and Weber. Marx saw a growing concentration of ownership and control in ever larger corporations as an inevitable feature of capitalism. Weber saw bureaucracy becoming the dominant organisational form in industrial society. To Murray the trend to post-Fordist organisational structures casts doubt on both these scenarios.

Other writers, such as Stewart Clegg (1992), have used the term *postmodern* to refer to these new types of organisation. Whether the term post-Fordist or postmodern is used the implications are similar. Bureaucratic organisations are being superseded by new types of organisations exhibiting key differences from their modernist/Fordist predecessors.

Flexibility in organisations

A key concept in post-Fordist managerial writings is the idea of flexible work organisations. (See, for example, discussion of Atkinson's work, pp335;338). This involves the use of *numerical flexibility* - for example, bringing in temporary or subcontracted workers to supplement a permanent core workforce, and *functional flexibility* - breaking down the rigid specialisation of workers characteristic of traditional 'Fordist' bureaucracies, encouraging workers to develop a range of skills and breaking down boundaries between areas of work.

This type of flexibility has been taken furthest by certain Japanese firms. For example, Nissan's new Sunderland plant has only two categories of manual workers - manufacturing staff and technicians.

Some firms have taken the ideas of the human relations school a stage further by organising workers into teams or groups and involving them in low level decision making and problem solving. The Japanese *quality circle* is a well known example of this - small groups of workers meet regularly to discuss ways of improving quality and efficiency in their work. This again moves away from Taylorist and Fordist organisational structures where decision making is the responsibility of management and workers are simply expected to follow orders.

The way workers are rewarded is also changing. In many firms the 'rate for the job' for each trade negotiated by trade unions is being replaced by a single pay scale for all workers. At the same time workers doing the same job may receive different rates of pay based on an annual appraisal of the quality of their work.

Characteristics of modern and postmodern organisations

Modern organisations	Postmodern organisations
Rigid	Flexible
Mechanistic	Organic
Mass production & consumption	Production for specialised 'niches'
Production methods dictated by technology	New technology used to enable flexibility and choice
High division of labour	Overlap between areas of work
Specialisation and demarcation of jobs	Breakdown of demarcations, multi-skilled workers, greater use of subcontracting and networking

Based on S. Clegg, 1992

Japanese firms as postmodern organisations

Japanese organisations have been seen as a model for the future of organisations in the industrial world. Stewart Clegg (1992) argues that Japanese industrial firms are closest to his model of the postmodern organisation. Their characteristics include:

1   **Lifetime employment** In many Japanese firms workers spend their whole career with one firm and are virtually guaranteed a job for life. Firms provide internal education and training. In return workers are expected to show a high degree of loyalty and commitment to the company.

2   **Enterprise unionism** Most Japanese workers belong to unions which are closely linked to the company. Apart from bargaining for pay awards, unions make little attempt to challenge managerial control. Management consults workers about important decisions and attempts to achieve changes through consensus rather than coercion.

3   **Payment systems** Workers' pay levels usually increase throughout a person's career. Bonuses may be given for performance, but these are normally given to teams rather than individuals and competition between workers is discouraged.

4   **Networks and subcontracting** The Japanese economy is dominated by a small number of large firms. Each subcontracts a considerable amount of work, for example the supply of parts and materials by numerous smaller firms. This reduces risks for big companies and means that it is smaller firms who usually have to shed workers in a recession.

5   **Just in time system** Most Japanese manufacturing firms employ the 'just-in-time' (JIT) production system. Rather than stocking large amounts of materials and spare parts, these are delivered just in time for when they are needed. This saves the considerable expense of capital tied up in materials in warehouses. However, Japanese firms need to ensure that halts or blockages in production are quickly dealt with to ensure the system works smoothly.

6   **Flexible work practices** The flexibility often said to be characteristic of post-Fordism is especially apparent in Japanese firms. Workers are expected to work wherever they are assigned and to develop a range of skills. Even managers are much less specialised than in the West and are frequently moved between different areas of work to gain experience.

7   **Quality control** Japanese firms have a high reputation for quality control. This is partly

because of a philosophy which sees this as the responsibility of every worker. Features such as quality circles mean that groups of workers are constantly encouraged to improve quality and efficiency in their areas of work.

8 **Government support** The Japanese government through its Ministry of International Trade and Industry gives a great deal of support to businesses. It coordinates business strategy, helps to fund research and development and encourages companies to switch from declining markets to new and more profitable products.

Clegg points out that these organisational characteristics apply primarily to the core workforce in large firms. They are less likely to apply to small firms and to peripheral workers. Women are particularly disadvantaged since they tend to be restricted to the peripheral sector where pay is lower and there is little job security. In fact two-thirds of Japanese workers work in this sector which includes most of the smaller firms which are subcontracted by the large firms.

The influence of Japanese organisations

Clegg believes that Japanese style organisations are likely to become widespread in other parts of the world. However, a consequence of this may be a widening of social inequalities. As in Japan a core of highly skilled workers may benefit from new forms of organisation. However, the majority of workers, especially women, ethnic minorities and the less skilled are likely to comprise a low paid and insecure peripheral workforce without access to the secure labour markets of the core workforce.

Although aspects of Japanese organisations have been copied in other parts of the world, Glenn Morgan (1990) thinks it unlikely that they will be transplanted on a large scale. Such organisations are rooted in the culture and history of Japanese society. They also rely on a high degree of government support in directing research and strategic planning which is rare in other countries. As Paul Thompson and David McHugh (1990) point out, Japanese work practices have been drawn on selectively by British managers but few have attempted to adopt them wholesale. For example, British firms are unlikely to concede the lifetime job security offered to many Japanese workers in return for the loyalty and flexibility demanded by their employers.

Power and control in postmodern organisations

Paul Thompson (1989) questions whether the new organisational forms represent changes for the better.

He is particularly concerned about the way in which computerised information technology systems offer greater control to management. While decentralisation and changes such as intrapreneurship appear to pass decision making down to lower levels, these decisions can be closely monitored by senior managers who have access to computerised information. The efficiency of individual workers or work units can be monitored by collecting information on work output, sales, stock flows and so on. Local autonomy and decentralised decision making exists but only within tight and centralised controls.

Thompson criticises writers such as Mintzberg who see increasing democracy and worker autonomy as characterising advanced forms of organisation. Thompson argues that what we are seeing is the development of *parallel* structures. Many organisations are becoming more *decentralised* and flexible on one level. However, on another level power remains *centralised* in the hands of top decision makers.

A further change observed my many writers is a move away from *task based rules*. These are the very basis of Weber's model of bureaucracy. Thompson acknowledges that many workers now are less likely to follow rule based procedures and are indeed expected to be flexible. However, he points to the emergence of a new form of bureaucratic regulation based on *behavioural rules*. This means that workers are expected to exhibit qualities such as cooperativeness, adaptability and self-discipline. Recruitment and selection procedures, even for routine workers, aim to 'screen out' those with 'undesirable' attitudes. Training procedures aim to socialise those considered suitable into attitudes consistent with company objectives. Peer group pressure may also be important here. Japanese style quality circles, for example, may put pressure on members who are seen as 'not pulling their weight' or 'having the wrong attitude'.

Do postmodern/post-Fordist organisations herald an end to bureaucracy? Are we witnessing, as some management theorists believe, the death of bureaucracy? The answer, according to Thompson, is a resounding No! Simply because many organisations lack some of the characteristics of Weber's ideal type does not mean bureaucracy is dead. From Weber's point of view bureaucracy is an instrument of power of the first order. And this is how Thompson and others see many organisations today. In crucial respects control from above has increased. In Thompson's words 'the new division of labour requires more sophisticated central coordination and a strengthened control of strategic resources and decisions' (1989, p68). This is bureaucracy changing and adapting rather than bureaucracy dying.

Activity 8 Working for Japan

Item A Diamond Star Mitsubishi

The joint venture between Mitsubishi and Chrysler looks incongruous set in the rich black earth of McLean County in central Illinois. The plant is one of the most highly automated and robotised in the world. 90% of welding is done robotically, releasing the associates (as the workers are called) from dangerous and tedious operations. Almost half a billion dollars worth of investment has gone into the 636 acre site. This has produced just under 3,000 jobs.

It turns out that Japanese management can be seen as simply a matter of commonsense. 'Kaizen', or continuous improvement, is at the heart of the Mitsubishi philosophy, and who could quarrel with that? As an employee of DSM (Diamond Star Mitsubishi), your advice and suggestions are sought for the enhancement of safety and efficiency. All suggestions are considered. If they are not implemented, you are given an explanation.

The training manual applies to all 3,000 associates. There is a common programme of work discipline. All wear the grey and maroon DSM uniform which removes the last traces of any 'them and us' attitude. All are part of the Diamond Star family.

The team concept pervades the plant. There are teams of 10-15 people, who all work together under a team leader. Each team has 20-30 job responsibilities. People are trained in all of these, and work rotated on a two hourly basis, so that the working day remains varied. It also means that there is flexibility - if an employee is absent, someone else can cover. It is the antithesis of the monotony of the assembly line, where people have always been given one simple, repetitive function. Naturally the strong sense of belonging means there are many collective social activities. On the Friday I was there, I was told, 'tomorrow some people are going to the ball game in Peoria, there is a golf outing to Chicago, some women are shopping in Chicago, and there is a trip to the home of Abraham Lincoln in Springfield'.

While the robots take care of the work that is monotonous and dangerous, the associates become responsible only for what is most creative. There are three key words in Japanese: 'Muri' means unreasonable; 'Mura' means uneven; 'Muda' means unnecessary. The approach is to remove all these from the workplace experience. This gains workers' loyalty.

Adapted from J. Seabrook 'House of the Rising Sun' *New Statesman and Society*, 23.3.90

Item B

Japanese workers at the start of a working day

Questions

1 In what ways can DSM be seen as a post-Fordist/postmodern organisation?

2 a) DSM did not offer high wages. It did not want to disrupt the local economy by attracting workers from other companies. Given this, what motivated workers to join DSM and how was this motivation maintained?

b) How does this compare with the arguments of scientific management theory concerning motivation?

3 Would you like to work for a Japanese style organisation? Explain your answer.

2.4 Social control organisations

This section looks at organisations such as psychiatric hospitals and prisons which are concerned with controlling or reforming the behaviour of their inmates. Some sociologists see the development of such institutions of social control as part of a more general process of the bureaucratisation of social life.

Erving Goffman: total institutions

These organisations are examples of what Erving Goffman (1968) called *total institutions*. He defines a total institution as 'a place of residence and work where a large number of like-situated individuals, cut off from the wider society for an appreciable period of time, together lead an enforced, formally administered, round of life'. Total institutions include boarding schools, monasteries, homes for the elderly, army barracks and merchant ships.

For most people everyday life - for example work, leisure, sleep and so on - involves different groups of people and relationships. In total institutions these aspects of everyday life are conducted in the same place, under the same authority, according to a strict schedule, with one activity leading to the next at a prearranged time. All activities are part of an overall plan which is designed to fulfil the official aims of the establishment. Thus in total institutions practically every detail of daily life, even activities such as eating, washing and sleeping, is likely to be subject to bureaucratic regulation.

Goffman developed his ideas from observations of a psychiatric hospital in which he worked as a member of staff. He notes a number of features of total institutions.

Division between staff and inmates Particularly in institutions concerned with social control, there is a basic division between a large managed group (the inmates) and a small supervisory group (the staff). Each group will tend to see the other in terms of narrow and often hostile stereotypes. Staff may conceal important information from inmates. Thus patients in hospitals or prisoners in gaols may feel their 'fate' is being decided by others.

Institutionalisation While inmates enter institutions with their own culture, a long stay may result in 'disculturisation' whereby inmates lose the ability to deal with life on the outside simply through lack of practice. The regulation of every aspect of behaviour and limited contact with friends and family reinforce this process and can lead to inmates becoming 'institutionalised'.

Mortification of self In many total institutions individuals are 'mortified' - their sense of self is denied and systematically stripped away. This can be seen from admission procedures. Clothes and personal property may be removed, new inmates may be showered and disinfected, their hair may be cut and they may be provided with an institutional uniform. In certain cases they are given a number - as in some armed forces - or a new name - as in some religious orders.

Rules and procedures in many total institutions can be seen as an attack on an inmates self image. Things in which a person invests their sense of self are often stripped away - their privacy, their control over their own lives, their dignity. Sometimes they are subjected to physical indignities - they may be beaten or have their heads shaved. They may be humiliated by having to bow and scrape to those in authority. They may be treated like children, for example inmates in some mental hospitals have to eat only with a spoon. Often activities which are taken for granted on the outside such as going to the toilet or posting a letter require permission. And this permission may be witheld, especially if inmates have not behaved themselves. This is part of the 'privilege system' found in many total institutions. A small number of rewards are given in exchange for 'good behaviour' and withdrawn for 'bad behaviour'. In these and many other ways a person's dignity and sense of self are threatened.

Not everyone responds in the same way to life in a total institution. Goffman identifies five main types of responses or 'adaptations'.

1 **Withdrawal** Inmates take as little part as possible in the life of the institution, not involving themselves in any voluntary activities.
2 **Intransigence** Inmates challenge the institution and refuse to cooperate. This tends to be a temporary phase, often at the start of an inmate's stay.
3 **Colonisation** Inmates prefer life in the institution to life on the outside. Staff may become embarrassed or suspicious about this and feel the institution is being misused.
4 **Conversion** Inmates take on the official view of themselves (eg as mentally ill or criminal) and try to reform by becoming 'perfect inmates'.
5 **Playing it cool** This is the strategy adopted by the majority of inmates. It involves doing enough to get by and avoid trouble. Goffman sees this as the adaptation most likely to maximise an inmate's chances of getting out physically and psychologically undamaged.

As Goffman points out there are important differences between total institutions. For example, in a religious institution, where people volunteer in response to a calling, life may be very different from a prison, where inmates are sent involuntarily as a punishment. The status of inmates may also vary on leaving an institution. Compare, for example, public schoolboys going on to universities and elite positions in society with mental patients returning to the community.

While bureaucracy infringes on many parts of our lives, most of us retain a private sphere, an arena of autonomy which provides a degree of personal freedom. For inmates in total institutions this autonomy has been either forcibly or voluntarily given up and their lives subjected to bureaucratic controls in even the most intimate areas. Goffman's work, however, makes little attempt to consider the historical or social reasons for the emergence of total institutions as one of the dominant means of social control in the last two hundred years. One writer whose work is closely concerned with this question is the French philosopher Michel Foucault.

Michel Foucault: carceral institutions

In his book *Discipline and Punish* (1977) Foucault traces the birth and development of the modern prison system from the late 18th century onwards. Before this time, Foucault argues, rulers exercised power over their subjects by *sovereign rule*. Power was centred in the person of the king or queen. Those who went against the ruler's wishes were punished, often in public, by methods which involved physical assault on the body, such as whipping, torture and execution. Such spectacles served to reinforce the sovereign's right to rule.

Foucault shows how in Western Europe this 'gloomy festival of punishment' was dying out by the end of the 18th century. Physical punishments, including public executions, were steadily replaced by imprisonment as the most common penalty for crime.

Although punishment still involved the body, this was only as a means to an end. The goal of punishment was to instill discipline rather than demonstrating to others the dreadful consequences of breaking laws made by the sovereign. Early prison reformers experimented with regimes where the body was manipulated, for example by rationing food and regulating daily activities such as sleeping patterns. The intention was to mould and transform the body in such a manner that it ensured that all prisoners functioned in a uniform way with their minds and bodies contributing to the smooth functioning of the prison system.

Disciplinary power Foucault argues that the development of modern prisons coincided with a new social movement which sought to understand and control the human body. This movement gave birth to 'new sciences' such as criminology, psychiatry and modern medicine. The knowledge and technologies which derive from these new sciences form the basis of disciplinary power.

For Foucault the development of prisons resulted from the replacement of sovereign power - power centred in the person of the ruler - with disciplinary power - power based on knowledge and control of the human body. Disciplinary power is applied by a whole range of authorities, for example judges, prison officers, probation officers and psychiatrists. They assess the individual's crime in relation to his or her mind and circumstances, in order to devise the most efficient and effective methods of punishment and reform.

Normalisation This assessment is based on examining people - a key aspect of disciplinary power. Individuals are observed, analysed, classified and documented in official records. The aim is to discover the extent to which they deviate from the norm - from a 'normal' person. This information is then used to select appropriate methods to correct their behaviour and return them to conformity. Foucault refers to this process as *normalisation*.

Like Weber, Foucault sees bureaucracy, with its emphasis on expert knowledge, records and files and hierarchical control, as a new and enormously potent method of exercising power. The development of the modern prison system involved a bureaucratisation of punishment. The system was informed and justified by the 'new sciences' of criminology, psychiatry and modern medicine.

Surveillance Foucault suggests that the development of prisons - and by implication other similar institutions of social control such as psychiatric hospitals, workhouses and reform schools - was the logical result of these new forms of disciplinary power. He sees this reflected in the 19th century philosopher Jeremy Bentham's idea of the 'panopticon'. This was a building constructed in circular form around a central axis. Inmates would be housed in cells around the building in such a way that guards posted at the centre could observe any inmate at any time. However, since the guards would be screened from view, no inmate would know exactly when they were being observed (see Activity 9, Item B). Bentham's ideas were reflected in the design of the new prisons, such as Pentonville, which were built in Britain from the 1830s onwards. Foucault argues surveillance is apparent not only in the development of prisons but in other bureaucratic organisations - for example, public health services which conduct surveys and collect statistics about disease.

The issue of surveillance has become even more relevant today because of modern technology. Shoppers and football fans are monitored on video screens by security staff and police; government agencies use complex computer systems to keep records on citizens and check whether they have paid taxes or claimed benefits; employers now use computerised systems to check the hours worked by staff and to record and calculate sales and productivity. In the USA there have been experiments in which 'electronic tags' have been attached to criminals so their whereabouts can be monitored without the need for imprisonment. For Foucault, the type of surveillance symbolised by the panopticon not only emerged within prisons but developed as a new means of control throughout society. Hospitals, schools and asylums are all part of the panoptican world. The extension of surveillance and the diffusion of disciplinary mechanisms throughout society led to the formation of the 'disciplined society'.

The change from savage and painful methods of punishment to imprisonment and a concern for normalisation might appear to be inspired by humanitarian motives. However, Foucault rejects this arguing that the development of disciplinary power has in fact tightened the restrictions on individual freedom and resulted in more subtle and pervasive methods of social control.

Evaluation

Foucault's ideas have had considerable influence on sociology. They have attracted both criticism and praise. Marxists argue that he fails to appreciate the link between power and economic relations. For example Andrew Scull (1977) argues that the growth of social control organisations is directly linked to the need to control those who might disrupt the process of capital accumulation.

David Garland (1990) points out that the development of the prison system and similar forms of disciplinary organisations does not necessarily enhance control as Foucault seems to assume. There is considerable evidence that prisons have failed as a means of social control - most of those imprisoned are likely to re-offend. The popularity of imprisonment as a punishment may simply reflect the public's desire for retribution, or the state's failure to create a better system. This echoes Goffman's pessimism about mental hospitals. He sees them as simply 'dumping grounds' for those who cannot be dealt with elsewhere in society.

Despite these reservations, many sociologists have found Foucault's ideas stimulating and useful. Stanley Cohen (1985), for example, points out how new forms of disciplinary control have been greatly extended in this century. Imprisonment has been supplemented by a whole range of control methods many of them involving 'treatment in the community' rather than in total institutions. For Cohen such developments represent a further extension of discipline. He describes it as 'a widening of the net and a narrowing of the mesh'. New categories of deviants are constantly being created, for example, growing concern by formal agencies of control about the behaviour of children and young people leads to increasing numbers being defined as deviant. Deviant activities which would have been considered too petty to be formally dealt with are now seen as the responsibility of the police, courts, social workers and other formal agents of social control.

If writers like Foucault and Cohen are correct, then sociologists studying organisations will need to give more attention to the parallels between forms of bureaucratic control in work organisations and the forms of control concerned with deviant behaviour in the wider society. Gibson Burrell suggests that we are all incarcerated within an organisational world and that the disciplinary society is so pervasive that we are imprisoned even as we sit alone at our desks (1988, p228). This echoes Weber's fears. For him the 'great question' is 'what can we oppose to this machinery in order to keep a portion of mankind free from this parceling-out of the soul, from this supreme mastery of the bureaucratic way of life' (quoted in Nisbet, 1967, p299).

Summary

1 Scientific management sees high productivity resulting from financial incentives and the rational planning of work tasks by management.

2 Human relations theories argue that workers develop their own work norms. These have an important effect on productivity.

3 Contingency theories argue that different organisational structures are suited to different environments.

4 Managerial theories usually judge the effectiveness of an organisational structure in terms of productivity and profit.

5 From a Marxist perspective organisational structure reflects the needs of capital to control and exploit workers in order to maximise profits.

6 Some observers have seen the emergence of post-Fordist and postmodern organisations which represent a decisive break with traditional bureaucracy. Others see these organisations as bureaucratic power in a new guise.

7 Studies of social control organisations reveal the pervasiveness of bureaucracy as a means of social control. Bureaucratic organisations increasingly control and monitor the lives of every citizen.

Activity 9 Social Control Organisations

Item A *The punishment of the body*

Up until the end of the eighteenth century many punishments involved the infliction of pain upon the victim.

If he is judged to be a vagabond, he is to be whipped and a hole burnt in the lobe of his ear with a hot iron. If he is found guilty again his other ear will be burnt and he will be made a servant. If he is found guilty a third time he will be condemned to death.

William Harrison *The Description of England*, 1586

Item B *The panopticon*

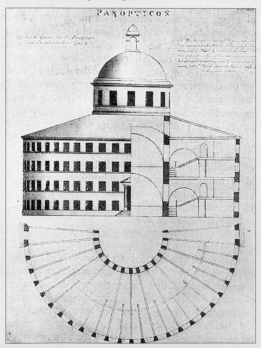

The panopticon designed by Jeremy Bentham allowed guards to observe every prisoner without being observed themselves. It was the basis for the design of many of the new prisons in the nineteenth century.

Item C *Electronic surveillance*

New technology has made possible the invention of new forms of surveillance and social control. This remote control camera is used to monitor Tiananmen Square in Beijing.

Questions

1 Using data from Items A, B and C and elsewhere discuss how far methods of social control have become bureaucratised in the last two hundred years.

2 How do you regard the spread of surveillance?

References

Albrow, M. *Bureaucracy* (Pall Mall Press, London, 1970)

Bittner, E. 'The Police on Skid Row: a Study of Peace Keeping' *American Sociological Review*, 32, no5, 1967

Blau, P. M. *The Dynamics of Bureaucracy* (University of Chicago Press, Chicago 1963)

Blau, P. M. and Meyer, M. W. *Bureaucracy in Modern Society* (Random House, New York, 1971)

Braverman, H. *Labour and Monopoly Capital: The Degradation of Work in the Twentieth Century* (Monthly Review Press, New York, 1973)

Burns, T. and Stalker, G. M. *The Management of Innovation* (Tavistock, London 1966)

Burrell, G. 'Modernism, Postmodernism and Organisational Analysis 2: The Contribution of Michel Foucault', *Organizational Studies*, 9 (2) 1988

Clegg, H. A. *General Union* (Blackwell, Oxford 1954)

Clegg, S. 'Modern and Postmodern Organisations', *Sociology Review*, April, 1992

Clutterbuck, D. *New Patterns of Work* (Gower, Aldershot 1985)

Cohen, S. *Visions of Social Control* (Polity Press, Cambridge 1985)

Delamont, S. *Interaction in the Classroom* (Methuen, London 1983)

Djilas, M. *The New Class* (Thames and Hudson. London 1957)

Donaldson, L. *In Defence of Organisation Theory* (Cambridge University Press, Cambridge 1985)

Fitzpatrick, S. *The Russian Revolution 1917-1932* (Oxford University Press, Oxford 1982)

Foucault, M. *Discipline and Punish* (Penguin, Harmondsworth 1977)

Friedman, A. *Industry and Labour: Class Struggle and Work and Monopoly Capitalism* (Macmillan, London 1977)

Garfinkel, H. *Studies in Ethnomethodology* (Prentice-Hall, Englewood Cliffs, 1967)

Garland, D. 'Frameworks of Inquiry in the Sociology of Punishment' *British Journal of Sociology*, March, 1990

Garson, B. *The Electronic Sweatshop* (Penguin, New York, 1992)

Goffman, E. *Asylums* (Penguin, Harmondsworth, 1968)

Goldstein, J. *The Government of a British Trade Union* (The Free Press, Glencoe, 1952)

Gouldner, A.W. *Patterns of Industrial Bureaucracy* (Routledge and Kegan Paul, London, 1955)

Hall, R. H. 'Professionalisation and Bureaucratisation' in G. Salaman and K. Thompson (eds) *People and Organisations* (Longman, London, 1973)

Handy, C. *The Future of Work* (Basil Blackwell, London, 1984)

Jackson, M. *Trade Unions* (Longman, London, 1988)

Lenin, V. I. *Selected Works* (Lawrence and Wishart, London, 1969)

Lipset, S. M., Trow, M. and Coleman, J. *Union Democracy* (The Free Press, Glencoe 1956)

Littler, C. *The Development of the Labour Process in Capitalist Societies* (Heinemann, London, 1982)

Martin, R. 'Union Democracy: an Explanatory Framework' *Sociology*, vol 2, 1978

Marx, K. 'The Spirit of Bureaucracy and beyond Bureaucracy: the Paris Commune' in F. Fischer and C. Sirriani (eds) *Critical Studies in Organisation and Bureaucracy* (Temple University Press, Philadelphia, 1984)

Mayo, E. *Human Problems of an Industrial Civilization* (Macmillan, New York, 1946)

Merton, R. K. *Social Theory and Social Structure* (Free Press, Chicago, 1949)

Michels, R. *Political Parties* (The Free Press, Glencoe, 1949)

Mintzberg, H. *Structure in Fives: Designing Effective Organizations* (Prentice-Hall, Englewood Cliffs, 1983)

Morgan, G. *Organisations in Society* (Mamillan, London, 1990)

Murray, F. 'The Decentralisation of Production and the Decline of the Collective Worker', *Capital and Class*, 19, 1983

Newman, D. M. *Sociology: Exploring the Architecture of Everyday Life* (Pine Forge, Thousand Oaks, California)

Nichols, T. and Beynon, H. *Living with Capitalism: Class Relations and the Modern Factory* (Routledge and Kegan Paul, London, 1977)

Nisbet, R. A. *The Sociological Tradition* (Heinemann, London, 1967)

Page, C.H. 'Bureaucracy's other Face', *Social Forces*, 25, 1946

Reed, M. *Redirections in Organisational Analysis* (Tavistock, London, 1985)

Roethlisberger, F.G. and Dickson, W. J. *Management and the Worker* (Harvard University Press, Cambridge, Mass., 1939)

Pugh, D. and Hickson, D. (eds) *Organisational Structure: The Aston Studies, vol I* (Saxon House, Farnborough, 1976)

Pugh, D. et al *Writers on Organisations* (Penguin, Harmondsworth, 1987)

Ritzer, G. *The McDonaldisation of Society* (Pine Forge Press, Thousand Oaks, California, 1993)

Scull, A. *Decarceration* (Basil Blackwell, Oxford, 1977)

Seabrook, J. 'House of the Rising Sun' *New Statesman and Society*, 23.3.1990

Silverman, D. *The Theory of Organisations* (Heinemann, London, 1970)

Strauss, A. et al 'The Hospital and its Negotiated Order' in E. Friedson (ed) *The Hospital in Modern Society* (Macmillan, New York 1963)

Taylor, F.W. *Scientific Management* (Harper and Row, New York, 1947)

Thompson, P. 'The End of Bureaucracy: New Developments in Work and Organisation' in M. Haralambos (ed) *Developments in Sociology*, vol 5, 1989

Thompson, P. and McHugh, D. *Work Organisations: A Critical Introduction* (Macmillan, London, 1990)

Trotsky, L. *The Revolution Betrayed* (1937)

Webb, S. and Webb, B. *Industrial Democracy* (Longman, Green and Co, London, 1920)

Weber, M. *From Max Weber: Essays in Sociology*, H. H. Gerth and C. Wright Mills (Routledge and Kegan Paul, London, 1948)

Zimmerman, D. 'The Practicalities of Rule Use' in J. Douglas (ed) *Understanding Everyday Life* (Routledge and Kegan Paul, London, 1971)

11 Community

Introduction

On a spring day in 1993 a man set out on a walking tour of the United States. He was convinced that the country was full of good people and he wished to meet them. Within the first mile he was attacked by two robbers who threw him into a river which carried him downstream and washed him up on an island. He was found two days later suffering from broken ribs, a fractured skull and multiple cuts and bruises. Afterwards, while recovering in hospital, he told reporters that he intended to continue his walk because his faith in people remained undimmed.

This man has a great deal in common with certain sociologists. These sociologists search for good people in things called 'communities'. Fortunately, this search is seldom dangerous (there is only a slight risk to ribs, skull and wallet). Unfortunately, sociologists soon realise that communities are rather difficult to find. Or, if they do happen to stumble across one, it is not quite the utopia they imagined. But just like the man in the story they continue their search. This persistence is useful, for the investigation of communities tells us a great deal about the kind of society we live in. It tells us about the way people relate to one another, the things that divide them and the things that bring them together. These themes are explored in this chapter.

Chapter summary

- The chapter starts by defining **community** and then proceeds to an exploration of **community studies**.
- The middle parts deal with **class**, **gender**, **race** and **age** dimensions of community.
- Finally the chapter ends with an examination of the role of **space** in social life.

1 What is Community?

Key Issues

1 What is the meaning of community?
2 How does community differ from society?
3 Is community still relevant in modern society?

1.1 The meaning of community

Everyday meanings The term 'community' crops up in many ways in everyday life. It is applied to things like places (the Little Puddington community), social groups (the student community), politics (the European Community, or European Union), welfare (community care), ethnicity (the Muslim community) and sexual orientation (the gay community). These examples show that it has a wide range of meanings. For instance, the European Community is not as intimate as Little Puddington where people are on first name terms with neighbours, shopkeepers and the milkman. Some communities (eg anglers) are concerned with a specific pursuit while others (eg Sikhs) have a much broader range of social and cultural interests. To add to the confusion, the term is not even a reliable guide to the strength of social relationships. Normally we expect the members of a community to be united by strong bonds of friendship and goodwill. But 'community policing' is often found in places where there is a glaring *absence* of neighbourly spirit!

Sociological definitions We might expect sociologists to attach a more precise meaning to community, especially since Nisbet (1970) describes it as the most fundamental of sociology's 'unit ideas'. Yet sociological discussion of community has been marked by a great deal of uncertainty and confusion. This comes across in an investigation by Hillery (1955) who surveyed the way sociologists use the term. He discovered 94 different definitions and the only thing they agreed upon was that community has something to do with people! Even among sociologists, then, community has no single, fixed meaning. But Hillery's survey probably exaggerates the lack of consensus. Sociologists might argue over fine details but they usually agree on the broad outlines of community. According to Newby (1980) sociologists define it in three main ways.

1 as a *social system* (a set of social relationships).
2 as a *fixed locality* (a geographical area).
3 as a *quality of relationship* (the spirit of community, or what Newby calls 'communion').

Some sociologists regard these three aspects of community as interlinked but Newby insists they are distinct (ie the presence of one does not guarantee the presence of the others). For example, we cannot assume that living in the same locality automatically promotes a warm spirit of community.

Images of community

Another way to clarify the meaning of community is to think of the images normally associated with it. These images represent the various ways that writers have visualised community. Some of these overlapping images are described below.

Community as a set of social relationships The most basic image of community is a group of people who are related in some socially significant way. The Central African BaMbuti tribe and inner city Liverpudlians do not belong to the same community except in the relatively trivial sense that they inhabit the same planet. In contrast, members of an active community are connected by such things as shared values, institutional ties and regular social interaction.

Territorial community Most people think of a community as a particular place. When people live close together they are more likely to form social and emotional ties. Indeed, some sociologists feel the term 'community' should be restricted to small scale localities (eg streets, villages) where people know each other really well. On the other hand, cities, regions and nations also possess some of the features of community. Sometimes a city gives its citizens a common sense of identity (eg stereotypes of the chirpy Cockney, the dour Aberdonian).

Subcultural community Sometimes community means much the same thing as subculture. Each subculture shares some of the values of the wider society but it also possesses its own cultural identity. It has a recognisable way of life which is based on its particular values and behaviour patterns. In some communities this cultural distinctiveness is not very marked but in others (eg Gypsies or 'travellers') there is a sharper contrast with the rest of society. Some subcultural communities are territorial but others (eg Catholics) are 'interest groups' whose members are scattered throughout society.

Imagined community Anderson (1983) notes that it is highly unusual for all the members of a community to really know one another. In that sense every community is a product of imagination - people imagine their common attachments and bonds. This is especially true of the national community: 'the members of even the smallest nation will never know most of their fellow members, meet them, or even hear of them, yet in the minds of each lives the image of their communion' (Anderson, 1983, p15). This imagined community can inspire a strong sense of commitment. As Anderson observes, people are usually more willing to die for their nation than for their immediate locality!

Symbolic community Cohen (1985) suggests that community is best understood in terms of symbols, meanings and identities. People construct these meanings as they try to make sense of the community's past, present and future. In this view community is something that goes on mainly inside people's heads. For example, each individual creates a 'mental map' of the community's membership and core values. So a settler who has lived in a village for many years might feel part of the community but still be regarded as a 'newcomer' by people born there.

Spirit of community This is probably the dominant image of community. It portrays community in terms of a distinctive *spirit* or *quality* of human relationship. Thus, Nisbet (1970) contrasts the warm personal qualities of community with the anonymity and impersonality of large scale society. Community indicates commitment, solidarity, emotional bonds and sentimental attachments. That is why it is such a potent source of identity. It is where we belong, where we feel most at home.

Exclusive community 'Every social community...is exclusive in the sense that not everybody can take part' (Eriksen, 1993, p62). So community always involves a relationship between 'insiders' and 'outsiders'. For example, Beattie (1993) describes how the Belfast communities of the Shankhill (Protestant) and the Falls (Catholic) treat each other as enemies. This has violent consequences but it helps to maintain the internal solidarity of these communities.

Activity 1 Communities

Item A *The tartan army*

Item B *A rave*

Item C *Hippies*

Item D *A street party*

Item E

Communities are best viewed as if they were Chinese nesting boxes in which small communities (families, neighbourhoods) are nestled within larger ones (local villages and towns) which in turn are situated within still more encompassing communities, the national and cross-national ones (eg the European Union).

Adapted from A.Etzioni, *The Spirit of Community*, 1994, p32

Questions

1   Look at Items A-D. State, giving reasons, whether you think these are communities.
2   Look at Item E. Do you agree that the term 'community' can be applied to large units? Give reasons for your answer.

1.2 Gemeinschaft-gesellschaft

We can form a clearer idea of what community is by contrasting it with what it is not. Hence the important distinction between *gemeinschaft* (community) and *gesellschaft* (society). This distinction, coined by the German sociologist Tonnies (1855-1936), has its origins in the social turmoil of the nineteenth century.

The great transformation Community was a key concept for social thinkers as they tried to understand the dramatic social changes of the nineteenth century. Western European societies were being transformed by urbanisation, industrialisation and political change. The direction of change was away from the familiar forms of community towards a much more impersonal social order ('society'). This prompted sociologists to construct *typologies* which highlighted the key differences between the old and the new. Thus, Max Weber (1864-1920) drew a distinction between traditional and rational society while Emile Durkheim (1858-1917) contrasted mechanical solidarity and organic solidarity. Of course, sociologists sometimes disagreed over the precise characteristics of the two types and the reasons for the transition. Nevertheless, the areas of agreement are perhaps more striking. Nisbet (1970) argues that, regardless of their individual political views, the reaction of sociologists at that time was basically a conservative one. Almost without exception they rediscovered the attractive qualities of community. Consequently they called for the restoration of community or, failing that, the creation of new forms of moral and social community. Karl Marx (1818-93) may have mocked the 'idiocy of rural life' and welcomed the Industrial Revolution but he also looked forward to the formation of genuine (communist) communities.

Ideal types Gemeinschaft and gesellschaft are examples of *ideal types*, a concept developed by Weber. He realised that it is futile for sociologists to try to capture social life in all its complexity and detail. So, instead of attempting to produce exact and exhaustive empirical descriptions, sociologists should set up broad models (ideal types) which select the most *significant* features of whatever is being studied (eg social groups, organisations, social systems). In each case the ideal type deliberately highlights and exaggerates its most distinctive features. The ideal type reflects the basic 'idea' or essence of what is being described (so 'ideal' does not necessarily mean that it is desirable or good).

Sociologists use empirical evidence to construct and to modify ideal types. But the gemeinschaft-gesellschaft models are not intended to be faithful descriptions of any particular community or society and so it is not really appropriate to judge them true or false. Rather, they are analytical tools which are helpful (or misleading!) in drawing attention to important features and relationships. The types simply provide the sociologist with preliminary ideas which guide research into real communities. Saunders (1986) notes that the typologies also play a useful role in comparative studies. They are used for comparisons over time (eg assessing the extent to which a given community has changed) and for spatial comparisons (eg contrasting rural and urban areas at the same point in time). The contrasts between gemeinschaft and gesellschaft are sometimes expressed in terms of *polar opposites* (ie either/or) and sometimes in the form of a *continuum* (where differences are a matter of degree). This can be illustrated by looking at some examples of these ideal types.

Ferdinand Tonnies: gemeinschaft and gesellschaft

Gemeinschaft Tonnies (1887) treated gemeinschaft and gesellschaft as contrasting types of social bond. In traditional villages people are bound together by the intimate ties of gemeinschaft. These bonds are based on blood (kinship), mind (sense of being a distinct people) and land (enduring ties with a particular place). Traditional community is close knit and culturally homogeneous and it is regulated by the moral laws laid down by church and family. There is little social or geographical mobility. Tonnies admired the way gemeinschaft maintains social cohesion and so he was alarmed by its long term decline. Nevertheless, he saw this decline as a necessary precondition for the emergence of industrialism and capitalism. In other words, he reversed the common argument that industrialisation led to the loss of community; for Tonnies, it was the prior loss of community which allowed industrialism and urbanism to develop.

Gesellschaft Tonnies recognised the social benefits of the expansion of trade and the growth of urban centres. The metropolis, for example, encourages the development of culture and science. But he was less impressed by the gesellschaft relationships which prevail in modern society. Instead of being guided by traditional norms, people increasingly follow their own selfish interests. They adopt a 'contractual' attitude, becoming more deliberate, rational and calculating in their social transactions. As social and geographical mobility increase, so the intimate ties of gemeinschaft are replaced by social relationships which are impersonal, superficial and fleeting. Yet, in a more complex turn in Tonnies' argument, he states that gemeinschaft can also be found *alongside* gesellschaft, even in cities. But gesellschaft principles play a dominant role in modern society.

Robert Redfield: folk and urban society

Redfield (1947) was less concerned with historical changes than with comparisons between different types of settlement in contemporary times. He drew a broad distinction between folk societies and more industrialised urban societies. This distinction closely resembles the other gemeinschaft-gesellschaft models (see Activity 2).

Continuum Redfield pictured folk and urban society as resting on a continuum. There is a line stretching from 'rural' at one end to 'urban' at the opposite extreme and every community can be located somewhere along this line. Redfield derived this idea from his anthropological field work in Mexico where he studied four different kinds of settlement: a tribal settlement, a peasant village, a town and a city. He claimed that these represented successive positions on the continuum (with the tribal group nearest the 'folk' end). The larger settlements had a greater likelihood of cultural disorganisation, secularism and individualism.

Activity 2 Ideal Types

Item A *Redfield*

Folk	Urban
small	large
sacred	secular
spontaneous	restrained
intimate	impersonal
ascribed status	achieved status
traditional	rational
family centred	'mass society'
cohesive	individualistic
homogeneous	heterogeneous
low mobility	high mobility

Adapted from R.Redfield, *The Folk Society*, 1947

Item B *Notting Hill carnival*

Questions

1 Read Item A. State (giving reasons) whether the residential area you live in is nearer the folk or urban end of the continuum.
2 Tonnies wrote that 'Gemeinschaft exists within the Gesellschaft, and Gesellschaft within the Gemeinschaft'. In what way does Item B illustrate Tonnies' statement?

1.3 After community

Some sociologists scoff at the idea that real communities still exist in Britain. They refer to the 'eclipse' or 'loss' of community and suggest that the close knit communities of the past have largely disappeared. If this is so, it means that concepts other than 'community' might be needed to describe social relations in modern society. This issue can be illustrated by looking again at the three main meanings of community.

Community as a set of social relationships

The myth of community studies Stacey (1969) opened an important debate when she claimed that community studies were based on a myth, the myth that it is sensible for sociologists to fix attention on something called 'community'. According to Stacey most so called communities are too large for detailed empirical study. For example, it would be very difficult to examine all the face to face relationships on a council estate. In another sense, however, community is too *small* a unit for sociological analysis. Local communities are never completely isolated and self governing. Many of the important decisions which affect them are taken by outsiders (eg transnational corporations, the central state). So it is necessary for sociologists to explore the links between the community and external institutions.

Locality social system Stacey's solution to these problems was to abandon the concept of community and replace it with the 'locality social system'. When we move beyond the immediate family circle we do not encounter something called 'community'. Rather, we come into contact with particular social institutions (eg school, church, police, peer groups). And it is these institutions which play a large part in deciding the quality of neighbourliness. Woolly terms like 'community' or 'community spirit' only distract sociologists from their proper task. What is required is a detailed study of the relationships between institutions in a locality (always remembering the need to identify external links as well).

Community as shared territory

Mobility Nowadays social relationships are no longer neatly contained within distinct territories. People drive miles to see friends (rather than neighbours), they drink in distant pubs (rather than the local) and they use supermarkets (rather than the corner shop). The immediate locality becomes less important as people exercise greater choice over who they mix with and where they go. It seems there has been a shift from 'community of place' to 'community of interest'. People seek out those with similar interests wherever they happen to live.

Social networks In recognition of these changes some sociologists propose replacing the concept of community with 'social network' (Bott, 1957). A social network can be represented by dots (people) and lines (relationships). We can then plot the pattern of relationships in a social network by drawing lines to connect the dots. So there may be a line between friends A and B and between friends B and C but not between A and C. The 'density' of a network is measured by the percentage of possible links which are active. Networks can also be analysed in terms of the size, duration and frequency of contacts. This kind of analysis reveals people's 'real' social relationships: 'the network of actual social relationships they maintain, regardless of whether these are confined to the local area or run beyond its boundaries' (Bott, 1957, p99).

The spirit of community

Community is a sentimental term which conjures up soothing images of compassion, warmth and friendship. It is difficult to imagine that anybody could ever be against community. But this means it is difficult for sociologists to remain objective when they are researching communities. There is a special danger that sociologists might assume a 'spirit of community' when it is not really justified. Indeed, critics allege that claims about community spirit are often exaggerated or downright false. This can be demonstrated by two examples.

The small town myth The small town occupies a special place in American folklore. It sums up the homely virtues of 'middle America': neighbourliness, concern for others, family values and common decency. These qualities are regularly celebrated in the media (eg Garrison Keillor's Lake Wobegon stories). But is this an accurate description of small town life? Not according to Vidich and Bensman (1958) who studied Springdale, a small town in New York state. Springdale saw itself as neighbourly, egalitarian and democratic. But the investigators found it was bitterly divided by class and racial divisions, people were judged according to their wealth, and local politics were tightly controlled by a small clique. Vidich and Bensman concluded that the small town image was a phoney myth which concealed the harsh realities of life in Springdale.

The myth of socialism East German socialists once claimed that they lived in an authentic community, one quite different in tone from the selfish, capitalist West. However, there were some unpleasant surprises after Germany was reunited and the secret files of the Stasi (East German security police) were made public in 1991. These files contained details on over one million people, mostly compiled from a network of 100,000 part time informants. Citizens had been paid to spy on their friends, colleagues and even members of their own family. Predictably, the naming of these spies created a public storm. Reputations were destroyed, marriages wrecked and old friendships broken. Above all, the revelations succeeded in exposing the high levels of fear, deceit and suspicion which existed within this 'ideal' community.

In defence of community

Day and Murdoch (1993) point out that the concept of community gradually fell from favour in sociology precisely because of the kinds of criticisms mentioned above. Nevertheless, there are a number of reasons why community remains a relevant and useful concept.
1   Communities have not completely disappeared. The empirical evidence shows that the 'loss of community' argument is oversimplified (see Section 2.4).
2   The rival frameworks have not lived up to their early promise. For example, Bulmer (1987) notes that social network analysis is exceptionally complex and time consuming and this perhaps explains why it has not become more popular with sociologists.
3   The competing concepts (community, locality, social network) are not necessarily mutually exclusive. Sociologists often use these terms interchangeably.
4   Newby (1980) argues that community provides a convenient focus for considering major social

Activity 3 Networking

Item A *Virtual communities*

Dave Winder: 'For me, the computer is like an extension of the pub. I get home from the pub and I log on to the computer. I go from chatting to a guy in the pub to chatting to a guy in cyberspace. The same things go on in cyberspace as in the real world.'

Dave Winder is a member of one of the 'virtual communities' currently flourishing on computer networks around the world. With cyberspace (the electronic 'information superhighway') you can netsurf around the world without leaving your room. Inside one virtual community, Cix, people from all over Britain post up their thoughts on sport, politics, sex, drugs and rock'n'roll. Other Cix users read them and respond to them. The result is a kind of drifting conversation which rolls out over days or weeks. People communicate with an honesty and intimacy that's rare in RL (real life). The on screen community provokes real feelings, real bonds and strong loyalties to particular networks.

Some people argue that virtual communities contribute to the decline of real communities. They keep people indoors and off the streets, encourage them to hide from real life and spend their time goofing off in cyberspace. But defenders insist that there is something democratic and empowering about virtual communities, about the way they allow people to circulate information, to associate, organise and come together without interference from the media or the government.

Adapted from J. McLellan 'Netsurfers', *Observer*, 13.2.94

Questions

1 Read Item A.
   a) Identify the differences and similarities between the virtual community and real life communities.
   b) In what sense is the virtual community a 'social network'?
2 Look at Item B. What are the main differences between close knit and loose knit social networks?

Item B *Social networks*

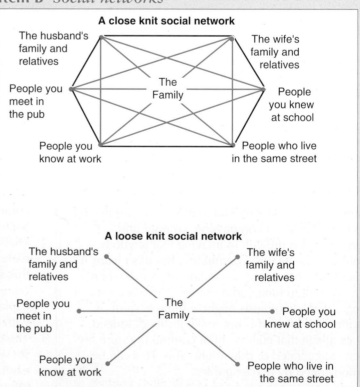

Adapted from P. J. North *Understanding Evidence*, 1984, p140

issues. It draws attention to the direction of social change and the impact this change has on particular localities. It also reminds us of the gap between social ideals (communion with others, harmony etc) and everyday realities.

5   The spirit of community is not yet extinct. Indeed, the longing for community keeps surfacing in every generation.

The spirit of community   Etzioni (1994) makes a persuasive case for the importance of community. He argues that over the past few decades the United States has placed excessive emphasis on individual rights ('me-ism') and neglected the legitimate claims of community. As a result, social life is characterised by materialism, irresponsibility, rising crime rates and widespread family breakdown. In response, Etzioni has established a social movement (communitarianism) which aims to shore up moral values and strengthen democratic community institutions. Although his description is based on the United States, there are clear parallels with Britain.

When Mrs Thatcher declared 'there is no such thing as society' she implied that individualism is a paramount value. Her term of office as Prime Minister saw the elevation of free market principles at the expense of the values of cooperation and community. In the opinion of some critics (eg Kingdom, 1992) this has resulted in a more selfish, greedy and dispirited nation. Consequently, both the Liberal Democrats and the Labour Party have promised to restore 'community' values to Britain.

Summary

1   Community refers to a set of social relationships, a shared territory and human communion.

2   The gemeinschaft-gesellschaft distinction highlights important contrasts in social life.

3   The concept of community helps sociologists to explore important social issues.

2 Studying Community

Key Issues

1   What are the aims and limitations of community studies?
2   What has happened to the traditional working class?
3   Has community been lost?

2.1 Community studies

There is a long tradition of community studies in sociology. These studies are usually based on particular localities and their main aim is to describe the values, relationships and lifestyles of the people living there. They are especially useful for capturing the totality or 'wholeness' of social experience. Even when the study is primarily interested in one sphere (eg housing or family) it usually tries to set this within the wider round of life in the surrounding locality.

The heyday of British community studies was the 1950s and 1960s. But after that period they dwindled in popularity because of the growing conviction that communities had more or less disappeared. Nevertheless, the tradition of community studies did not die out entirely. For instance, researchers began to investigate Britain's ethnic communities in greater depth. Also, research on subcultures (eg youth groups) became very popular and these investigations shared many of the features of community studies. Finally, community studies enjoyed a revival in the 1980s when sociologists realised that locality was still

an important feature in social relationships. Another reason for the revival of community studies was the recognition that sociological theories had outstripped the available empirical evidence. Sociologists were making sweeping generalisations about broad social trends (eg deindustrialisation) but there was little firm evidence about how this was affecting people. There was an urgent need for field studies to provide the necessary information and so community studies once again became fashionable.

Limitations   Community studies are subject to certain limitations.

1   **Time**   Communities change over time and so it cannot be assumed that what was true of Chipping Sodbury in 1965 applies equally in 1995. But this does not mean that studies soon become outdated and irrelevant. For example, early studies can be compared with later studies in order to identify major social trends. Moreover, the 'old' ways of life tend to live on in the folk memories of people today. Cornwell (1984) shows how contemporary East Enders still draw on the old myths of East End life (eg they see themselves as warm hearted people smiling in the face of adversity).

2   **Place**   Communities differ from one another and so it cannot be assumed that research findings for, say, Oswaldtwistle apply to Auchtermuchty as well. Indeed, one of the fascinations of community studies is the way they reveal local differences. Nevertheless, sociologists hope that

some generalisations are possible, based on a wise choice of sample communities. Otherwise a separate study would have to be conducted for every community in Britain!

3 **Methodology** Some community studies are more convincing and authoritative than others. Some studies (eg Roberts, 1973) are barely disguised autobiographies while others (eg Parker, 1983) are journalistic in style. The classical British studies of the 1950s and 1960s (eg Young and Willmott, 1957) usually observed the rigorous conventions of sociological research methods (eg random sampling, interviewing, questionnaires). More recently, computers have made it easier to collect statistical data on communities. But the most valuable community studies still try to move beyond mere statistics to reveal the deeper meanings and intimate experiences of community life.

2.2 Traditional working class

Most sociologists date the traditional working class from around the end of the nineteenth century until the 1950s or 1960s. Community researchers have probably devoted more attention to this group than to any other, and this research can be used to construct an ideal type. But it is important to remember that there were many local variations in working class communities. Also, ideal types gloss over the wide differences in interpretations of traditional culture. For example, Seabrook (1978) tends to romanticise this culture while Campbell (1984) condemns it as a prime example of patriarchal exploitation! These limitations should be borne in mind when reading the following sketch.

An ideal type

1 **Work** Men usually worked in heavy industries such as mining, steel, shipbuilding and the docks. The physically exacting nature of this skilled manual work placed a high value on rugged masculinity and male camaraderie (Dennis et al, 1956). Women were normally expected to become full time housewives after marriage but financial hardship sometimes forced them to do part time work (eg cleaning jobs).

2 **Class consciousness** Traditional workers had a strong sense of class solidarity. The traditional working class was 'us' and the enemy was 'them' (bosses, nonmanual groups, anyone in authority). They adopted 'proletarian' views and mostly gave their loyalties to trade unions and the Labour Party.

3 **Respectability** There was an important divide within the working class between 'roughs' and 'respectables'. The traditional working class held

respectable values (eg honesty, the work ethic). They tried to maintain strict moral standards in order to distance themselves from the discredited roughs with their disgraceful behaviour (eg sexual promiscuity, drunkenness, crime).

4 **Home** The home was a haven from the outside world of work and authority. Many commentators describe the typical home as noisy and bustling (although neighbours were usually kept at the doorstep). It was also based on a sexual division of labour. Housework was a woman's province and she was expected to make the home a warm, comfortable place and have a meal ready on the table for the male breadwinner.

5 **Family** Family life was deeply valued. The respectable working class believed in marriage and disapproved of divorce. People were sentimental and affectionate towards children but they also taught them to respect their elders. Most people lived near their relatives and so there was frequent and spontaneous visiting between members of the extended family.

6 **Community** The traditional working class lived in close knit communities ('urban villages'). People had long connections with their locality and they built up large circles of friends and acquaintances. The kin network was the main source of social support and mutual aid but friends and neighbours also provided help (eg looking after children or sick people). Of course, people sometimes quarrelled with neighbours and occasionally there were bitter feuds and conflicts. But at least people were not 'anonymous'. They felt part of an all encompassing community.

7 **Leisure** The sexual division of labour within the home and workplace carried over into leisure pursuits. 'Men in these communities tend to spend their leisure time in pubs and clubs drinking with their workmates' (Saunders, 1990, p108). Men also played and watched sports, gambled and followed interests such as pigeon racing and brass bands. Women, in contrast, led more home based lives and they had fewer 'hobbies'. Much of their leisure time was spent in all female networks (mainly consisting of kin) which provided them with companionship and social support.

Classical studies

Certain studies stand as major landmarks in the exploration of traditional working class community. Two of these studies are summarised below.

Uses of Literacy Hoggart's (1957) portrait is based largely on his home area of Hunslett in Leeds, with its nonconformist chapels, small corner shops, back to back houses and cobble stoned roads. It is a community where people chat frequently and take a keen interest in local affairs and personal relationships. Hoggart skilfully identifies their central values and themes. These include a 'healthy scepticism' about figures of authority, a strong emphasis on 'self respect', a 'tolerant' attitude to life (live and let live), and a 'stoical' outlook (they simply get on with life). They are not regular churchgoers but they have a deep sense of right and wrong. This does not prevent them from indulging in mild hedonism (what Hoggart calls 'enjoy y'self while y'can'). The weekend binge or the family party provide opportunities to escape from the drabness of everyday life.

In the second part of his book Hoggart expressed alarm at what was happening to working class culture in the postwar period. He argued that the emerging 'mass culture' was less enriching than the traditional culture it was replacing. 'Candy floss' entertainments were corrupting the solid values of the older culture. For example, mild hedonism was being transformed into selfish materialism; cheerful debunking was being converted into crude cynicism. He warned that superficial media values might undermine the sense of purpose and dignity of traditional cultures.

Bethnal Green Young and Willmott's (1957) research in Bethnal Green in East London in the early 1950s is probably the single most influential British community study. Where Hoggart's book was a 'cultural reading', the Bethnal Green study was a more conventional sociological investigation. It used a variety of research methods (eg questionnaires, interviews) to collect data from a large random sample (just under 1,000 men and women). Young and Willmott fully expected to confirm the prevailing view at that time, namely that postwar social change had resulted in the breakdown of communities and the decline of the extended family. To their surprise they found a vigorous and tightly knit community. 'There is a sense of community, that is a feeling of solidarity between people who occupy the common territory, which springs from the fact that people and their families have lived there a long time' (1957, p112). Other residents were familiar figures rather than strangers. 'Bethnal Greeners are not lonely people: whenever they go for a walk in the street, for a drink in the pub, or for a row on the lake in Victoria Park, they know the faces in the crowd' (1957, p116).

Kin were even more important than friends and neighbours. The extended family gave emotional and material support to its members and linked them with the wider community. Kin visited regularly and helped each other in tangible ways (eg shopping, running errands, babysitting and 'speaking for kin' in order to get them a job or a rented house). There was an especially strong bond between mothers and their married daughters and this expressed itself in a matrilocal pattern (ie a young married couple usually set up house near, or even lived with, the wife's mother). The extended family network was an important prop for women in an area with the familiar 'traditional' pattern of sexual segregation (eg full time housewives, all male leisure groups). (See pp247-248 for further discussion of the extended family in Bethnal Green).

Greenleigh Young and Willmott were less impressed by what they found in their subsidiary study of 47 young married couples who moved to Greenleigh, a new council housing estate some 20 miles from Bethnal Green. Newcomers to Greenleigh appreciated the fresh air, the pleasant surroundings and a home of their own (there was an acute housing shortage in Bethnal Green). But the atmosphere in Greenleigh was quite different from Bethnal Green. People were reasonably polite to each other but there was little warmth or friendship. Young and Willmott attributed the lack of community to the low density of housing, the lack of social meeting places and the diverse origins of many of the people on the estate. Lacking a supportive community, families became much more materialistic and home centred. 'Their relationships are window to window, not face to face' (1957, p135). There was a general problem of isolation and loneliness although this was partly alleviated by a closer relationship between husband and wife. According to Bott (1957) close knit communities such as Bethnal Green tend to have 'segregated' conjugal relationships (ie husband and wife have separate roles and spend leisure time with their respective circles of friends and kin). Loose knit networks like Greenleigh mean that husband and wife rely much more on each other for company and so their relationship tends to be 'joint' (ie they share work and leisure activities). (See pp259-260 for further discussion of joint and segregated conjugal roles).

2.3 The new working class

In the 1950s and 1960s sociologists rushed to record the features of traditional working class communities before they finally disappeared. Researchers sensed that traditional community was being rapidly undermined by major social changes. A 'new' working class was emerging, one which shared many of the values and lifestyles of Greenleigh or the mass culture which Hoggart criticised.

A privatised society

As far as community issues are concerned the most important feature of the new working class is their apparent preference for a home centred lifestyle. Sociologists describe this as *privatism* (a lifestyle mostly restricted to the home and nuclear family) or *privatisation* (the process of moving towards this pattern). One of the baffling things about privatisation is the dispute about when it began. Pahl (1984)

Activity 4   Traditions

Item A   *Gossip*

From early morning to late at night little groups formed and faded, trading with goodwill, candour or cattishness the detailed gossip of a closed society. Over a period the health, honesty, conduct, history and connections of everyone in the neighbourhood would be examined. Each would be criticised, praised, censured openly or by hint and finally allocated by tacit consent a position on the social scale.

Adapted from R. Roberts, *The Classic Slum*, 1973, p42

Item B   *Skivvies*

Traditional housework involved a great deal of drudgery and hardship but it is condescending to portray the traditional housewife as purely a victim and skivvy. She had many skills (sewing, cooking, gardening etc) which her modern counterpart lacks. She enjoyed the support of a real community. And her 'sacrifices' for her husband were based on love as much as duty.

Adapted from J. Seabrook, *Landscapes of Poverty*, 1985, p111

Questions

1   Read Item A. Using this item, identify the social functions of gossip.
2   Read Item B. Do you agree with Seabrook? Give reasons for your answer.

---

claims that a home centred lifestyle was the norm in the pre-industrial era while Marshall et al (1989) date its origins in the late nineteenth century. But most sociologists agree that privatisation was boosted by the rise in absolute living standards in the recent postwar period.

The affluent worker   The trend to privatised lifestyles was highlighted by the 'affluent worker' studies in Luton (Goldthorpe et al, 1969). The Luton researchers described a pattern of working class sociability which was quite different from the traditional kind. First, there was little sense of a wider community. The leisure time of the affluent workers and their families was largely centred on the home or on 'private' pursuits (eg the family car ride). Admittedly, community participation was hampered by the working pattern of shifts and overtime but it seems that most people preferred a privatised lifestyle anyway. Secondly, the Luton families saw their relatives much less frequently (partly because their kin often lived far away). On the other hand, they were slightly more likely to socialise with neighbours and to belong to associations. In these respects the lifestyles of the Luton workers differed from the traditional working class. But they were not exactly middle class either. First, there was very little social or residential mixing between the classes in Luton. Secondly, middle class people were more skilled at cultivating new friends and they were more likely than the affluent manual workers to socialise with work colleagues.

Types of privatisation   The Luton research popularised the idea that modern British society was becoming more home centred. But later researchers pointed out that privatisation was actually quite a complex affair. Marshall et al (1989) identify three different senses of the term. *Structural privatisation* refers to the way different spheres of life (eg work, leisure, family, locality) have increasingly separated out. For example, nowadays people are less likely to socialise with workmates. *Cultural privatisation* refers to the decline of 'class consciousness' and the trend for central life interests to be based on the home rather than work or community. Lastly, *privatised politics* indicates a preference for voting according to individual rather than 'class' interests. However, Marshall and his colleagues found very little evidence to support these three trends. For example, they argue that work and workmates are still quite important in people's lives. Also, they insist that there is no wholesale 'retreat' into the home as an escape from wider social activities. Procter (1990), too, argues that it is misleading to draw a sharp distinction between the traditional and the new working class. 'Communal sociability' and 'privatism' are recurring features of working class life rather than mutually exclusive categories. It is quite possible to take a strong interest in the home *and* to participate actively in the community.

Affluent workers revisited   Devine (1994) returned to Luton in the 1980s to interview 62 residents (Vauxhall workers and their wives). She found that people who moved to Luton from other parts of the British Isles were often followed by kin, neighbours and friends. This allowed them to continue their 'old' networks to some extent. And most of her sample had reasonably active social lives outside the home and family. Men visited pubs and participated in sports; full time housewives maintained cordial contacts with neighbours; and male and female workers socialised with their colleagues outside the workplace. Overall, then, Devine concluded that 'traditional' working class lifestyles had not changed as much as the earlier Luton study predicted.

Traditional working class	New working class
community centred	home centred (privatism)
close knit social networks	loose knit networks
extended family	nuclear family
segregated conjugal roles	joint conjugal roles
poverty	consumer affluence
traditional occupations	social mobility
heavy industry	flexible workforce
full time housewives	employment of women
centrality of work	leisure interests
homogeneous	multicultural/multiracial
religious	secular
authority of old	cult of youth

2.4 Loss of community?

The arguments over privatisation are part of a wider debate about the loss of community. Many people maintain that communities in the past were warmer, friendlier and more supportive than present day communities. The whole gemeinschaft-gesellschaft tradition seems to support this view. But is it really true that community has been lost? Sociologists have drawn conflicting conclusions from the empirical evidence. Wellman (1979) identifies three different interpretations: community lost, community saved and community liberated.

Community lost Most sociologists think that the large cohesive communities of the past have been disrupted and fragmented into weaker social networks. For example, Holme (1985) conducted an updated study of Bethnal Green and found that the area had become much more home centred. Thrift (1989) interprets the fate of traditional working class community in terms of a distinction between 'dominant', 'residual' and 'emerging' cultures. He believes the traditional culture has declined since its 'dominance' in the 1950s and 1960s. It is still 'residually' strong in most industrial cities but it is being progressively eroded and replaced by an 'emerging' consumer culture.

Community saved This view states that modern localities retain many of the features of traditional communities. This argument comes in three versions. One version suggests that the 'anonymity' of new

areas like Greenleigh is merely a temporary affair. Over time these areas settle down and acquire the trappings of a traditional community. In a later edition of their classic study Young and Willmott (1986) speculated that Greenleigh after 30 years had probably developed local networks fuller and more supportive than they originally believed possible. A second version argues that Britain's ethnic communities (see Section 4) bear a close resemblance to traditional communities. A third version simply insists that traditional values still persist to some degree. For example, Widgery (1991) argues that modern Cockneys still possess a coherent set of East End values: 'that you shouldn't jump the queue, that you are not just in it for yourself, that it's right to help people in trouble and that loyalties matter more than cash' (Widgery, 1991, p74).

Community liberated This view argues that the old close knit communities have broken up but this is not such a great misfortune. Bulmer and Abrams (1986) point out that traditional communities usually arose from common deprivation (eg poverty and economic insecurity). Williams (1973) calls this the 'mutuality of the oppressed' (ie poor and powerless people were forced to rely on each other for survival). Few people would want to return to the social conditions of those times. Moreover, the general rise in living standards has freed people from the constraints of the old communities. Now people can choose new and more satisfying forms of community life (eg flexible, non-territorial social networks based on a select number of contacts). This pattern allows people to balance their desire for privacy and independence with a need for wider social contacts.

A sense of loss

Many people in Britain have a strong sense that community has been lost. Often this is based on their feelings and emotions rather than on hard empirical evidence.

The romanticised past In a speech on St.George's Day 1993, the Prime Minister, John Major, fondly recalled the England of his childhood: 'the long shadows falling across the county ground, the warm beer, the invincible green suburbs, dog lovers and pools fillers...old maids bicycling to Holy Communion through the morning mist'. This nostalgic view is widely shared. Many older people remember the collective spirit of wartime Britain and the halcyon days of the 1950s when the working class (allegedly) never locked their doors and always helped their neighbours. Yet one of the striking things about collective folk memory is its highly selective nature. People choose to sentimentalise the warmth and comradeship and forget the harsher realities such as poverty and disease. Yet there is plenty of evidence that past communities had their full share of hardships, misery and cruelty. There is little room for nostalgia in the following description of a Gorbals tenement in Glasgow in the 1930s: 'The Victorian building was in decay...Rats and mice moved about freely...On the common staircases, six or eight flats shared two lavatories...Going to the lavatory we had to remember to carry a supply of newspaper, not only for use as toilet paper but also to clean the soles of our boots of excrement and urine before going back into the flat' (Glasser, 1987, p7).

Explanations The myth of the golden past seems to surface in every historical period. Each generation thinks that it faces unique problems and that the past was so much better. Yet if we turn the clock back to the supposed golden age we find people were voicing exactly the same sentiments! For example, the Victorian public was just as anxious as modern commentators about the problems of unruly youth (Pearson, 1983). So why do people persist in regarding the past as a golden age? The obvious explanation is that the past *was* better, at least as far as social relationships are concerned. Communities may well have deteriorated in recent decades. For example, Beattie (1993) relates the damaging effects of 1970s redevelopment on the Shankhill community of Belfast: 'Redevelopment took away the band halls, the boxing clubs, the shops. It attacked the very fabric of the community on the Shankhill by destroying the support systems which allowed the people to live through poverty...The people of the Shankhill were rehoused...They were shunted away to a life where there was no social structure. There were better houses in these far away places, but there was no life. Or no life that they would recognise' (Beattie, 1993, p158).

A more complicated explanation is offered by Williams (1973) who suggests we conjure up a golden age myth in order to express our dissatisfaction with the present. The development of capitalism has created a deep sense of alienation and so we use the imagery of a golden past (especially our childhood days) to express our unmet needs and our longing for a more fulfilling life. According to Williams the myth is not merely an exercise in nostalgia, it is also a form of resistance against the dehumanising features of modern society.

Summary

1 Community studies are informative but they are limited by time, place and methodology.

2 Most sociologists agree about the 'decline' of the traditional working class but they disagree about the extent of 'privatisation' and its implications for community.

3 Nostalgia romanticises the past but it is also a way of expressing dissatisfaction with contemporary society.

Activity 5 The Good Old Days

Item A *Tattooed jungle*
The old working class were the salt of the earth but the new working class are more like the scum of the earth. They might have gained cars, VCRs, a satellite dish on every roof, the shell suits they all wear, but they have lost their souls. They hardly cut a stylish dash - men with beer bellies and pit bull terriers, a tattooed 'white trash', women obsessed with greed and selfish enjoyment. They are models of avarice, gluttony and spiritual sloth.

Older people are the first to recognise this spiritual decline. The old (or 'real') working class were decent, hard working and neighbourly. But the cultural values of the working class have become warped.

Adapted from Tony Parsons 'Double-Barrelled Condescension', *Spectator*, 24.10.92, p24

Item B *Eastenders*
Ethel: We might have had a few fleas in the old days but at least we knew our neighbours.
Den: The old days are gone for good, thank God. You don't see kids running around with snotty noses, rickets or ringworms.
Ethel: Not them old days. Not the bad old days. They're coming back. I'm talking about the good old days when everyone cared for each other. They're not coming back.
Den: They're both the same. Now is where we are.

A scene from the TV series 'EastEnders', cited in C.Geraghty *Women and Soap Operas*, 1991, p95

Questions
1 Read Item A. Do you think Parsons exaggerates? Give reasons for your answer.
2 Contrast the views of Ethel and Den (Item B). Give your own views on this.

3 Models of Community

Key Issues

1 What is the relevance of class to community?
2 In what sense is Britain a pluralist society?
3 Has Britain turned into a mass society?

Sociologists who study communities always approach them with certain assumptions based on their theoretical models. These models are important because they influence the questions community researchers ask, the evidence they collect and the conclusions they reach. There are a number of possible models but Roberts (1978) identifies three leading ones: class, pluralism and mass society.

3.1 Class

For radical class theorists, class remains the most significant force in modern society. So they insist that any discussion of community must be placed within its wider class context. Capitalist society, they say, is based on massive class *inequalities* and sharp class *conflict.* Classes struggle with each other for a larger share of resources and power, and this struggle takes place not just in the workplace or factory but also in the community. Cockburn (1977), for example, suggests that the class war is waged over community issues such as housing, transport, child care facilities and recreational amenities.

Many class theorists are highly critical of conventional community studies. Clarke et al (1979) claim that the classical community studies of the 1950s and 1960s concentrated too much on fragmented slices of community life (eg family patterns) and lost sight of the overarching factor of class. Even when the classical studies turned their attention to class issues they seldom ventured beyond documenting class *differences* in community lifestyles. They ignored the sharp class *conflicts* that spring from deep inequalities in the distribution of material resources and political power. The studies were more interested in cultural issues (eg values and lifestyles) than in structural and political matters. Furthermore, class theorists tend to be sceptical about the 'spirit of community'. They sometimes see this as an ideology which is used by powerful groups to control the working class. For example, Dennis (1968) speculates that powerful groups in society fear the masses and so they try to control them by diverting them into 'safe' activities in the community. If people are happily engaged in local dances and recreational clubs they will not be plotting revolution!

The inner city

The plight of the inner city shows clearly that Britain is not yet a 'classless' society. While some sections of society enjoy comfortable living standards, the 'inner city' has become a catchphrase for material and social deprivation and loss of hope. It conjures up harrowing images of urban neglect, dilapidated housing, graffiti, vandalism and an 'abandoned' population. In geographical terms it is the area which verges on the central business districts of most cities. However, some sociologists broaden the definition of inner city to include *all* deprived areas, including 'outer' estates. In the slum clearance programmes of the 1950s and 1960s new council estates were built on the edges of cities. Broadbent (1985) claims that many of these outer estates are now the 'forgotten' areas of deprivation. Their living standards and unemployment problems are just as bad as those of the inner estates and they also suffer from isolation and poor transport systems.

Not all people within the inner city are poor. Indeed, some inner city areas have witnessed a process of *gentrification* (eg affluent young professionals buying and restoring property which is conveniently near the city's commercial centre). Nevertheless, the older inner city areas are deeply troubled by a wide range of social problems. The *Faith in the City* report (1985) identified three main afflictions: *economic decline* (with unemployment rates as high as 50-80%), *physical decay* (of both the Victorian terraced housing and the modern high rise flats) and *social disintegration* (eg family breakdown, crime).

Inside the inner city A good illustration of these problems is provided by Harrison's (1983) study of Hackney in London. According to Harrison, Hackney was a serious contender for the title of the 'Most Awful Place in Britain' because of its high ranking on indices of social and economic deprivation (eg low incomes, single parent families, children in care, low educational attainment). The local economy relied on outmoded labour intensive industries (eg clothing) which were no longer competitive. In spite of population loss the area still suffered from overcrowding and poor housing (eg the high rise flats built in the 1960s were badly designed and poorly ventilated). Moreover, Harrison takes issue with those sociologists who argue that deprivation leads to social solidarity (the 'mutuality of the oppressed'). For Harrison, Hackney demonstrated the 'divisiveness of deprivation'. The fragmented population turned on one another and there was a great deal of conflict and fear.

Docklands development Successive governments have tried various measures to regenerate derelict inner city areas. The Thatcher governments largely relied on a free market approach which involved a partnership between private enterprise and specially created 'public' bodies. Planning power was progressively stripped away from elected local authorities and invested in DCs (development corporations). These DCs are intended to encourage industry and commerce, create a pleasant environment and promote housing and social facilities. This policy has proved highly controversial, especially in the case of LDDC (London Docklands Development Corporation) which in the 1980s piloted the huge Canary Wharf development in the Isle of Dogs in London. Commercial interests have taken priority over social considerations in this project (Lawless, 1989). Developers and speculators have erected huge office blocks and upmarket housing for affluent 'outsiders', while locals have been provided with few amenities or social housing (they cannot afford the new private houses). Many people have been compulsorily rehoused elsewhere in order to make way for a motorway link. Moreover, very little extra employment has been created by the scheme and most of the 'new' jobs have gone to outsiders.

Class and the inner city The inner city illustrates the relevance of class to community issues. Harrison's study reveals how the 'community' in Hackney is undermined by severe material deprivation. The Docklands case exposes the lack of power of the local community to resist or control large scale developments which threaten it. Powerful groups have effectively disrupted the local community on the Isle of Dogs. In their anger and frustration, some people in the area have turned to racist politics which further splits the community. (For further information on this, see pp90-91).

Activity 6 Conflicts

Item A *Hackney*

In Hackney there are many conflicts: young against old; rentpayers against squatters; taxpayers against claimants; dog owners against non-owners; black against white; not to mention political, moral, religious, sexual or class cleavages. The collapse of social control is seen in the high crime rates. There is precious little 'community' to start with but crime dissolves it even further.

Adapted from P. Harrison, *Inside the Inner City*, 1983, pp236, 345

Item B *Apartheid*

Social apartheid is emerging on the Isle of Dogs. Islanders feel the London Docklands Development Corporation is taking away their communities. It buys up their homes and cafes, closes down local businesses and builds imposing office buildings and motorways. Islanders are excluded from these new sites. The new housing developments for affluent yuppies have fences, barriers and security patrols to keep the working class out. Proletarian-free zones have been created in order to let the yuppies live invisibly behind their safety barriers.

Adapted from D. Widgery, *Some Lives!*, 1991, p219

Canary Wharf Tower in Docklands

Questions

1 Read Item A.
   a) In what ways might crime 'dissolve' the community?
   b) Suggest reasons why the people in Hackney turn against each other rather than against more powerful social groups.
2 Read Item B. Identify the reasons why the locals and the middle class yuppies are in conflict.

3.2 Pluralism

The pluralist model recognises that society is now more dynamic and mobile and as a result the old communities have been eroded and fragmented. Nevertheless, it takes a generally optimistic view of these trends, arguing that community has been 'liberated' rather than 'lost'. After all, the old locality based communities were sometimes a bit claustrophobic and stifling. Nowadays, in contrast, rising living standards have released people from the old class norms. People's identities and lifestyles are no longer narrowly restricted by social class. They have much greater *choice* of lifestyles and this is expressed in the emergence of diverse *interest groups* (or subcultural communities). One sign of this is the vast range of magazines, covering almost every conceivable hobby, leisure pursuit or interest, which are stocked in High Street shops.

A pluralist interpretation is adopted by Young and Willmott (1973) in their 'symmetrical family' study. This survey of some 3,000 families in the London area revealed that most young couples had lifestyles which were largely privatised and home centred. They were not surrounded by a close knit community and they had little time to cultivate friendships. Nevertheless, most couples seemed happy with this existence which allowed them to pursue a wide range of leisure interests within and outside the home. Young and Willmott conclude that prosperity enlarges people's choices and enhances their cultural experiences. Another example of the pluralist model is Pahl's (1984) study of the Isle of Sheppey. Pahl found that the majority ('middle mass') of people were 'individualists' who followed their own particular pursuits and interests rather than any collective tradition. Far from regretting this, Pahl praises their plural lifestyles, which he describes as refreshingly brisk and energetic.

Postmodernism

Postmodernism is a more recent model than pluralism but it resembles it in many ways. At its simplest, it suggests that a new cultural mood has emerged in the postmodern age. Strinati (1992) identifies some key features of this new culture.

1 People's lifestyles and identities are no longer based solidly on the enduring realities of work, home and locality. Instead, their sense of reality is increasingly based on signs, symbols and images. For example, advertising images help people to define themselves and the world around them.
2 Style is more important than substance or content. People shift from one cultural lifestyle to another without any great sense of commitment.
3 The distinction between 'high art' and popular culture breaks down. People raid all kinds of cultural traditions and mix them in an ironic and playful fashion.
4 Time and space no longer impose such severe constraints on patterns of behaviour. (See Section 5.3.)
5 There is little sense of any absolute 'truth' or paramount 'reality'. One point of view or one lifestyle seem just as valid as any other.

Postmodernism resembles pluralism in its celebration of diversity, consumerism and choice. Moreover, it shares the view that people do not have stable personal or collective identities in a fast changing world. Nevertheless, it remains a very controversial concept and not everyone is convinced that Britain has truly entered a postmodern age.

3.3 Mass Society

Mass society theorists agree with pluralists about the general direction of social trends (eg the rise in living standards, the increase in geographical and social mobility). But they take a much more pessimistic view of these trends (ie they take the 'community lost' view). Above all, mass society theory is concerned with the deteriorating *quality* of life. The central image is one of a mass of 'atomised' individuals who lack connectedness with others and are therefore relatively defenceless against moral and aesthetic corruption. People can be easily manipulated by unscrupulous advertisers who encourage them to see themselves mainly as 'consumers'. People no longer participate actively in the community and so they feel alienated and estranged from one another. But they refuse to confront the shallowness of their lives and prefer to bury themselves in short term distractions such as television.

Jeremy Seabrook (1978, 1990) shares many of the sympathies of mass society theory. Seabrook argues that capitalism once impoverished the working classes in material terms but in the postwar period their living standards have improved considerably. Ironically, this has not brought them contentment or fulfilment. The reason for this is that capitalism now impoverishes them spiritually. The traditional values and culture of the working class have been corrupted and people have become much more materialistic and selfish.

Second hand community

Some mass society theorists argue that the closest many people come to experiencing community is through television soaps. Soap viewers are often invited to enter a fictional world which has a firm sense of place and continuity. British soaps (eg *Coronation Street, EastEnders, Emmerdale Farm*) usually project the image of a local 'community' and they play on regional characteristics (eg Northern earthiness, Cockney wit). Viewers feel they are interacting with a well defined, almost 'real' community. Horton and Wohl (1956) use the term 'para-social interaction' to describe this relationship. Unlike normal social interaction there is little feedback, and this reduces the prospects for mutual development. Nevertheless, Horton and Wohl concede that soaps have sociable features and they allow viewers to 'participate' (from a distance) in community life of a sort. Many viewers become deeply attached to the characters in the series and they follow plot developments with avid interest. Rosen (1986) suggests that lonely and alienated viewers are especially likely to seek consolation in the familiar communities represented on television.

Geraghty (1991) suggests that soaps manage to reflect the precarious nature of community. Within the plots the fictional community is threatened by outsiders (eg developers) and by troublesome insiders (eg the 'gossip', the 'bastard' and the 'tart'). *Brookside* conveys a healthy scepticism about the reality of community spirit in the 1980s and 1990s. However, Geraghty believes that 'one of the most important and hard-fought functions of British soaps in the eighties has been to keep the ideal of the community as a utopian possibility at a time when the tide in political

thought was firmly running the other way' (Geraghty, 1991, p122).

Summary

1 Class inequalities and class conflicts have a marked effect on Britain's inner cities.

2 Modern Britain has some features of a 'pluralist' or 'mass' society but sociologists disagree about the extent and influence of these features.

Activity 7 Diverse Pleasures

Item A *Leisure pursuits*

Percentages in each group participating in each activity in the 4 weeks before interview

	Socioeconomic group		
	professional	skilled manual	unskilled manual
A)			
Plays/musicals	13	8	5
Ballet	1	1	1
Operas	2	1	1
Classical music	6	1	1
Art galleries/museums	15	6	4
Stately homes/castles	14	6	4
B)			
Golf	13	5	1
Swimming	8	4	2
Walking	51	40	31
Cycling	13	9	8

A) 1987 figures, adapted from *Social Trends*, 1991
B) 1990 figures, adapted from *Social Trends*, 1993

Item B *Soaps*

Top television ratings, week ending 22.8.94

BBC 1	ITV
1. EastEnders (Tues)	1. Coronation St.(Mon)
2. EastEnders (Thurs)	2. Coronation St.(Wed)
3. Neighbours (Wed)	3. Coronation St.(Fri)
4. Neighbours (Tues)	4. Emmerdale (Tues)
5 .Neighbours (Mon)	5. The Bill (Tues)
6. EastEnders (Mon)	6. The Bill (Fri)
7. Neighbours (Thurs)	7. Home and Away (Mon)
8. Neighbours (Fri)	8. Home and Away (Tues)
9. Chandler and Co	9. Home and Away (Wed)
10. Raw Deal	10. Home and Away (Thurs)

Adapted from *Guardian*, 22.8.94

Questions

1 Look at Item A. Suggest ways in which class, pluralist and mass society theorists might interpret this data.

2 Look at Item B. Explain why soaps are the most popular programmes on television.

4 Gender, Race and Age

Key Issues

1 What does community mean for women?

2 What are the main community patterns and problems among racial and ethnic minorities?

3 Are there age differences in community lifestyles?

4.1 Gender

Women have been relatively invisible in some community studies. For example, male community researchers have sometimes preferred to focus on the 'male' worlds of work and leisure. The study of the Yorkshire mining village of 'Ashton' (Dennis et al, 1956) is one example of this neglect of women. Nevertheless, women have not been ignored entirely. After all, the famous studies by Hoggart (1957) and Young and Willmott (1957) are very 'woman' and 'home' centred. In recent years, however, feminist researchers have investigated women's community roles in greater detail and they have paid far more attention to the conflicts of interests between men and women.

Women in the community

From the studies conducted so far, it is possible to draw a rough (and tentative) sketch of the position of women in the community.

1 **Separate spheres** The experience of community is different for men and women. The classical studies described a high degree of sexual segregation among the traditional working class. Young and Willmott (1973) detected signs that the family was becoming more 'symmetrical' but they also found that, in terms of social contacts, there was still a women's world and a men's world. More recently, Green et al (1990) conducted research in Sheffield and found that it was still common for men and women to engage in independent leisure pursuits outside the home.

2 **Community isolation** Full time housewives spend a great deal of their time in the home and the locality and so they suffer if community breaks down. For example, Gavron (1966) described the bleak life of 'captive wives' in London tower blocks. The absence of a 'woman's world' and a related street life created problems of isolation and loneliness for the young working class mothers she studied.

3 **Community contacts** Generally, however, women seem to be more active than men in community life. Cornwell (1984) argues that nowadays many men derive their sense of community mainly from the local pub. But women occupy a far wider range of communal spaces (eg shops, the street, the school) and they have a much wider variety of contacts. It is usually women who hold the informal community networks together.

4 **Community action** It is women 'who are at the front line of negotiations over nurseries, schools, housing, health and other welfare agencies. Not surprisingly, then, women have also been central in community based actions to organise, defend or protest about such services' (Bornat et al, 1993, p383). Women also played a major part in setting up community support groups during the miners' strike of 1984-5.

5 **Conflicts** Community has contradictory meanings for women. It gives them a 'space' where they can decide their own needs and lifestyles. It is 'their' domain to some extent. On the other hand, it sometimes confines them to a routine of stereotypical 'women's tasks' (Bornat et al, 1993). For example, Campbell (1984) argues that mining communities may be cohesive and supportive but they also force women to sacrifice themselves to domestic duties and the housewife role.

6 **Leisure** Women have less leisure time than men and this is mainly because of their greater responsibility for housework and childcare. Also, their freedom of movement in public places at night is curtailed by the fear of attack or sexual harassment (Green et al, 1990). However, Deem (1990) notes that when women get jobs they are more likely to insist on their rights to leisure time. Also, Roberts et al (1990) argue that young females have as much leisure time as young males and they have an even wider range of leisure interests.

Community care

Women are usually expected to take on the main burdens of community care. So they have been affected by the 1990 NHS and Community Care Act which introduced a bold new policy of community care in Britain. The basic aim was outlined in an earlier consultative document: 'Most people who need long term care can and should be looked after in the community. This is what most of them want for themselves and what those responsible for their care believe to be best' (*Care in the Community*, 1981, p1). But community care can take a number of different forms. Sometimes it refers to institutional care on a 'human' scale (eg replacing large and remote mental hospitals with small hostels which help residents to integrate with the local community). Alternatively, community care may refer to support systems (eg meals on wheels) to maintain frail or elderly people in their own homes. Another important distinction is between care *in* the community (where the state provides financial support) and care *by* the community (where the financial burden falls mainly on kin). Finally, community care can be provided by a variety of agents: *informal* carers (eg kin, friends, neighbours), *statutory* services (eg social services departments), *voluntary* organisations (eg self help groups) and *private* firms (eg commercial outfits providing nursing homes on a profit basis).

Criticisms The new policy after the 1990 Act soon attracted fierce criticism (eg Walker, 1993). Local authorities were given a key planning role as 'care managers' but they seemed unprepared and underfinanced for their new role. Hospitals were accused of hastily discharging psychiatric patients on to the streets where they were a danger to themselves and others. Often the community seems unwilling to accept community hostels (this is called the problem of NIMBY - not in my backyard!). In many cases the physical, emotional and financial burden seems to have fallen on family members rather than the wider community.

Women carers The *General Household Survey* (1988) estimated there are about 6 million carers in Britain. Many of these, of course, are just 'good neighbours' who help on a casual basis. But one quarter give over 20 hours a week of their time caring for others (usually a relative). Moreover, the majority of these carers are women. This is why feminists have complained that 'in practice community care equals care by the family, and in practice care by the family equals care by women' (Finch and Groves, 1980, p494). So it is fraudulent to talk about 'community' care when the main burden usually falls on female relatives. Women are expected to look after kin (husbands, partners, ageing parents) even although this is highly demanding work which is either unpaid or inadequately supported by state benefits. It usually entails sacrifices in a woman's career because the caring role restricts employment opportunities. Consequently, some feminists conclude that the best solution is high quality residential care for dependent people.

But this feminist orthodoxy has been challenged in recent years. Graham (1993) summarises the main arguments against the orthodoxy. Basically, it ignores

the interests of too many groups. For example, it ignores care receivers (who often prefer to remain at home) and paid domestic helpers (who earn a living from providing services for people in their homes). Moreover, the orthodoxy neglects men, the 'forgotten carers'. Although there are certainly more female than male carers, men constitute 1 in 3 of those caring for at least 20 hours per week (Graham, 1993). And Parker (1990) suggests that 'spouse carers', the single most important category of carers, are made up of equal numbers of men and women. In recent years, then, feminists have started to reconsider their views on community care. They are now more willing to recognise the positive aspects of care in the home. Some of them point out that they are not opposed to the general principle of community care. Rather, they are unhappy with the unfair conditions (eg sexual inequality, inadequate financial support) under which it is delivered. (For further discussion of community care, see pp159-160; 162).

Activity 8 A Woman's World

Item A Differences
Mick Chalmers: I think the world has changed since I was a kid. All the street doors would be open and there'd be chairs out in the streets, and you'd walk along and talk to neighbours. You can walk down here in the daytime and you don't even see a soul. I mean I don't know who lives two doors away from me.
Sarah Chalmers: See, it's different with me, I can walk round to the shops. It only takes me five minutes to walk there and back but I'll be about half an hour, three quarters of an hour. Because I bump into people that I know and talk and everything else.

Adapted from J. Cornwell, Hard Earned Lives, 1984, pp49-50

Item B Community Care
To the politician community care is a useful piece of rhetoric; to the sociologist it is a stick to beat institutional care with; to the civil servant it is a cheap alternative to institutional care; to the visionary it is a

One view of community care

dream of the new society in which people really do care; to social services departments it is a nightmare of heightened public expectations and inadequate resources to meet them.

Adapted from K. Jones, cited in 'The Crisis in Community Care', New Society, 18.9.87, p1

Questions
1 Read Item A. Why might men and women have different views on the existence of community?
2 Suggest how feminists might respond to the viewpoints expressed in Item B.

4.2 Race and ethnicity

Britain's racial and ethnic minorities tend to be concentrated in certain regions (eg the South East), conurbations (eg Greater Manchester, West Yorkshire) and inner city neighbourhoods. It might be an exaggeration to describe these locations as ghettos but 'it is hard to dismiss altogether the evidence that in some urban areas Britain's black population is sufficiently segregated to develop the basis of a

relatively separate community life' (Smith, 1989, p38). This section contains some descriptions of the values and lifestyles of these communities. It also includes a discussion of 'urban riots' and the 'Rushdie affair' to show how ethnic communities sometimes come into conflict with the wider society.

Afro-Caribbeans

Pryce's (1979) ethnography of St Paul's in Bristol is

one of the most detailed studies of an Afro-Caribbean community. He describes this area as an 'internal colony' where poor and powerless black people suffer 'endless pressure'. Two main features emerge from Pryce's work. First, he questions whether St Paul's is a community in any meaningful sense. 'Beneath the romantic's illusion of a tight knit, friendly, organic, warm, harmonious community, the divisions are deep. There is much suspicion between groups' (p30). Pryce believes that 'West Indians lack a group identity and a tight, communal form of group life based on a sense of collective interdependence and mutual obligation among kinsmen' (p119). Secondly, he describes the range of different lifestyles in St Paul's. The 'stable law abiding' group consists of *Saints* (Pentecostalist churchgoers with a rather puritanical outlook), *proletarian respectables* (regular wage earners with an individualistic outlook) and *mainliners* (the black middle class, mainly teachers and community workers). The 'expressive-disreputable' group is divided into *hustlers* (mainly males in their 20s who earn money illegally through drugs or pimping) and *teenyboppers* (a high risk group of young, unemployed and often homeless males). Pryce also identifies an intermediate group, the 'in-betweeners' (a career minded group with an interest in black culture). Pryce's work was highly controversial, especially his stress on the weakness of Afro-Caribbean community and family life and his attention to 'deviant' lifestyles. Nevertheless, it was valuable in demonstrating the diversity of lifestyles within one locality.

Black consciousness A more positive view of Afro-Caribbean communities is provided by Hall et al (1978). Although they share many of Pryce's observations on 'internal colonialism' they detect more visible signs of cultural cohesion and solidarity. Basically they argue that Britain's black ghetto populations are starting to develop an alternative lifestyle based on a revival of black consciousness. They note with approval 'the colonisation of certain streets, neighbourhoods, cafes and pubs, the growth of the revivalist churches, hymn singing and mass baptisms in the local swimming baths, the spilling out of Caribbean fruit and vegetables from the Indian shops, the shebeen and the Saturday night blues party, the construction of the sound systems, the black record shops selling blues, ska and soul - the birth of the "native quarter" at the heart of the English city' (Hall et al, 1978, p351).

Gilroy (1987), too, has stressed the importance of community to Britain's Afro-Caribbean population. Gilroy believes that the historical experience of slavery and the African diaspora (forcible scattering of the black population around the globe) provides an important reference point for most black people in the present day. This common background creates strong cultural links between black communities in Britain, the United States, Africa and the Caribbean. Nevertheless, Gilroy cautions that there is no single black culture or black identity and he states that Britain's black population 'is too small, too diverse and too fragmented to be conceptualised as a single cohesive nation' (Gilroy, 1987, p66). To a large extent the black population has been fragmented into local communities which vary according to their social class and ethnic composition, their political traditions and their employment and housing profiles. Gilroy speculates that the local community is now an important influence in shaping what it means to be black. It is also an important focus for anti-racism struggles. For example, certain Afro-Caribbean communities played a prominent role in the urban riots of the 1980s.

Urban riots

The civil disturbances which broke out in British cities in the 1980s (see Table below) presented a vivid and frightening spectacle. Newspaper headlines spoke of 'mob rule' and 'rampaging looters' while television carried pictures of torched buildings, overturned cars and police hiding behind riot shields as petrol bombs and bricks hurtled towards them. The riots resulted in major destruction of property, serious injuries and some deaths. Some commentators claimed that the disturbances were not really *race* riots since a significant number of white youths were involved (eg the majority of those arrested in Toxteth in 1981 were white). These experts suggested that the riots were simply a reflection of the general problems of deprived areas, regardless of their racial and ethnic composition. Nevertheless, the most prolonged and violent outbreaks occurred in areas with a high concentration of Afro-Caribbeans (one exception was Southall, where many of the rioters were of Asian origin). By the time of the 1985 riots, it was widely accepted that the riots were in large part an expression of the frustrations and grievances of Afro-Caribbean communities (Solomos, 1993).

Explanations Jewson (1990) maintains that each riot is rooted in a particular locality with its own history of grievances and its own pattern of local concerns. But it is still possible to identify some general causes, and these are usually broken down into 'preconditions' and 'precipitants' (Taylor, 1981). Preconditions are the long term background problems such as unemployment, poverty, political marginalisation and racism, many of which were documented in the famous Scarman (1981) report on the Brixton disorders. These sorts of problems create a pool of frustration but this will spill over into a riot only if there is some precipitant or 'trigger'. The most common trigger in the 1980s riots was a highly charged incident between police and black people. In the 1981 Brixton riot it was insensitive saturation policing ('Operation Swamp') of the area. In the case of Broadwater Farm in 1985 it was the unfortunate death of a black woman, Mrs Cynthia Jarrett, during a police raid (another hapless victim, PC Blakelock, was brutally hacked to death during the ensuing riots).

However, any explanation of riots is highly controversial. Conservatives stress the lawbreaking aspects of riots rather than the social injustices which led to them. They usually place the blame for riots on 'riff-raff' (eg criminals, political agitators and mindless copycats who get carried away by the excitement of the mob). Liberals and radicals, on the other hand, are attracted to 'pressure cooker' explanations. They stress that riots occur in disadvantaged areas which suffer great structural strains and problems.

The 1980s riots

1980	St Paul's, Bristol
1981	Brixton, London
	Southall, London
	Toxteth, Liverpool
	Moss Side, Manchester
1985	Handsworth, Birmingham
	Brixton, London
	Broadwater Farm, Tottenham
	Toxteth, Liverpool

Activity 9 Riots

Item A *Terms*

The outbreaks of collective violence in the 1980s were described by a variety of terms: disturbances, disorders, riots, uprisings, revolutionary actions, terrorist attacks, criminal enterprises, mindless violence.

Adapted from N.Jewson, 'Inner City Riots', 1990

St Paul's, 1980

Brixton, 1981

Item B *Media*

'Hand picked death squad trained in Moscow and Libya' (*Daily Express*, 8.10.85).

'Masked figures on motor cycles' (*Daily Mail*, 7.7.81).

'He walks with a chilling swagger, a petrol bomb in his hand and hate burning in his heart...' (*Daily Express*, 11.9.85).

'A spree of naked greed' (Mrs Thatcher, *Times*, 9.7.81).

'Black War on the Police' (*Daily Mail*, 6.7.81).

Questions

1 Read Item A.
   a) Identify the assumptions which lie behind these terms.
   b) Who would you expect to use each of these terms and why?
2 Read Item B. Identify the assumptions which lie behind these phrases and headlines.

Asians

Britain's Asian communities resemble the traditional working class in certain ways (eg emphasis on extended family, close knit networks and 'respectable' values). Of course, there are also striking differences in social customs (eg arranged marriages). Moreover, there are many variations within Asian communities. They vary in terms of country of origin, language and culture and they also contain deep internal divisions (eg sexual, class, caste). The most obvious division is the religious one between Hindus, Sikhs and Muslims.

Sikhs Bhachu (1985) provides a rich ethnographic description of East African Sikhs in Britain. This group migrated earlier this century from the Punjab to certain East African countries (eg Kenya, Uganda) but was later forced to migrate to Britain when these countries introduced 'Africanisation' policies in the late 1960s and early 1970s. Bhachu points out that they are an unusual Asian community in the sense that they came to Britain with a great deal of 'cultural capital' (eg fluent English, good educational qualifications and occupational skills). Also, they do not cling to any 'myth of return' (ie they do not express any intention of eventually returning to an Asian 'homeland'). The myth of return is normally interpreted by sociologists as a device to motivate younger Asians to learn the language and culture of their parents. But the Ramgarhia (artisan) Sikhs in Bhachu's study managed to sustain their unique cultural traditions without this kind of motivation.

Bhachu describes a cohesive community which is deeply attached to its cultural values and has little wish to assimilate into mainstream British culture (although they show a 'progressive' attitude to work and education). Sikhism is a monotheistic faith which places stress on a correct way of life and active involvement in the world. This cultural tradition is transmitted through the strong networks which link the Sikh communities in places as far afield as Southall, Wolverhampton, Leeds and Cardiff. Bhachu suggests that in some ways migration to Britain has increased their cultural conservatism. Contact with whites and with other Sikh 'castes' has made them more acutely aware of their minority position. They have reacted to this by asserting their distinctiveness, reflected in their separate temples (gurdwara), unique turbans and practice of caste endogamy (choosing marital partners from the same caste group). On the other hand, some of their customs are slowly changing. For example, dowries are now more frequently seen as the property of the bride rather than the groom's kin. Also, arranged marriages now give greater weight to individual preferences.

The Rushdie affair

Britain's large Muslim population consists of a number of different communities. The main division is between the (majority) Sunni tradition and the (minority) Shi'ah tradition, but these are further broken down into various sects (eg Ismaili) and territorial and language groupings (eg Mirpuri). However, their shared faith and identity as one nation (ummah) creates a certain bond between these communities. At the same time, Muslim belief systems and codes of conduct (eg on dress, diet, behaviour) single out these communities as different from their non-Muslim neighbours.

Building up mutual understanding and respect between Muslim and non-Muslim communities has been a slow and sometimes uneasy process, but the relationship suffered severe strain when Salman Rushdie's *Satanic Verses* was published in 1988.

Muslim groups argued that this work of 'fiction' was actually a thinly disguised and offensive portrait of the Prophet Muhammad. Their protests were initially peaceful (eg calls for the book to be pulped) but soon escalated towards violence (eg firebomb attacks on bookshops). Anti-Rushdie demonstrations were organised in Britain and overseas, and the Iranian religious leader, Ayatollah Khomeini, imposed a *fatwa* (order of death) on Rushdie who was forced to go into hiding. Since 1989 a number of publishers and translators have been killed or injured because of their contacts with Rushdie.

Issues

The Rushdie controversy raises a number of complex social, moral and cultural dilemmas.

1 **Censorship vs freedom of speech** Should the government have banned the *Satanic Verses?* In any civilised society some consideration has to be given to the feelings and sensitivities of minority groups (eg Britain has laws against the incitement of racial violence or hatred). On the other hand, censorship might prevent the legitimate discussion of controversial ideas. And who decides what is socially 'acceptable'?

2 **Religious fundamentalism vs secular liberalism** Some commentators suggested that Britain's blasphemy laws should be extended to protect non-Christian faiths from insults. On the other hand, many liberals were alarmed at the prospect of intolerant and dogmatic 'fundamentalist' religions trying to dictate what the public can think or say. This issue was complicated by disagreements over whether Islam was really a fundamentalist religion.

3 **'One nation' vs cultural pluralism** British society has been culturally enriched by the presence of racial and ethnic minorities. Nevertheless, the Rushdie affair provoked some writers (eg Weldon, 1989) to argue that Britain had cultivated cultural diversity and pluralism at the expense of cultural unity. Social harmony was now threatened by Muslim groups who were pressing for equal consideration for their 'separate' cultural traditions. How far should the state go in meeting these claims?

Rushdie and Muslim communities The Rushdie affair had a dramatic impact on Britain's Muslim communities. Members of these communities were shocked into re-examining what it means to be a Muslim in Britain. Should they side with Western 'liberal' and 'secular' values? Should their loyalties lie with Islam? Is there some way of reconciling these conflicts? At one level the affair has brought the different Muslim communities closer together. At another level, however, it has created deeper internal splits. It has sharpened the conflict between those Muslims who interpret Islam as a tolerant and flexible religion and those who take a more fundamentalist line (eg the Barelvi sect in Bradford). One Muslim group (Women Against Fundamentalism) staged a demonstration in support of Rushdie in order to express their opposition to sexism and fundamentalism within their communities.

The Rushdie affair has also widened the rift between Muslim communities and the wider society. For example, it has fanned a great deal of racist resentment against Muslims (some racists now shout 'Rushdie!' in order to taunt Muslims). According to some commentators, Britain's Muslims have 'retreated' back into their own communities in order to protect their religious values.

Activity 10   Rushdie

Item A   *Anti-Rushdie*

Slough, 1989

Item B   *Bradford*

When I visited Bradford I expected to see a Muslim community in a bell jar, sealed off from the rest of British society. Instead I found a community that is deeply British, even down to the Yorkshire accent. But I also found that the Rushdie affair has been a trauma for them, leading them to draw back from us, to defend a heritage they feel we don't understand.

Adapted from M. Ignatieff, *Guardian*, 9.5.89

Item C   *Cultures*

The Rushdie conflict has raised the issue of ethnic cultural incompatibility in a way that cannot be avoided. The stark possibility is that certain cultural assumptions of Muslims may contradict those of the majority of Britons. We have long been aware of racism but the possibility of severe cultural conflict between ethnic groups appears to have come as a shock.

Adapted from M.O'Donnell 'Culture and Identity in Multi-Ethnic Britain', *Social Studies Review*, January 1990

Questions

1 Look at Items A and B. Use these items to identify the motives and feelings of Muslims on the Rushdie affair.
2 Read Item C.
   a) What are the incompatible values in the case of the Rushdie affair?
   b) Suggest, giving your reasons, ways in which the *Satanic Verses* conflict might be resolved satisfactorily.

4.3 Age

Our lives seem to be mapped out in 'decades' which are associated with certain traits. For example, people are expected to be restless and moody in their teens, mature and confident in their forties but 'slow' and fixed in their ways in their sixties. These differences are commonly attributed to the 'biological clock' (ie ageing is seen as a biological process which brings about inevitable changes in outlook and behaviour). But sociologists point out that age is also socially constructed (ie it is shaped by cultural norms and social factors). Striking examples of this are found in those pre-industrial societies which choose to stratify

people into 'age grades' with clearly defined rights and responsibilities. Modern societies, by contrast, adopt a slightly more flexible attitude to age and ageing. People in these societies often try to resist rigid age-linked expectations. In spite of this, values and lifestyles often run along age lines and people tend to mix with others of the same age. So age groups can be regarded as yet another form of community.

Youth

Youth is defined not only by biological age but also in terms of social roles, responsibilities and expectations. Aries (1973) argues that adolescence is actually a social 'invention' of the past few centuries (previously there was no transitional stage between childhood and adulthood). In recent times youth has been 'extended' in length because of the need for prolonged education and training. So the British Youth Council (1992) defines youth as the 16-25 age group, which includes about 8.7m (15.2%) of the United Kingdom population.

Youth subcultures Sociological interest in youth was largely sparked by the postwar emergence of youth subcultures. As young people became more affluent they started to develop their own styles of dress, music and behaviour. It seemed to some British commentators that youth were becoming an increasingly distinctive community. This community was 'exclusive' in the sense that a wide gulf was opening up between young people and their elders. For example, Leech (1976) spoke of a 'youthquake' which was creating a huge generation gap. The community was also 'subcultural' and 'symbolic' in the sense that it possessed its own unique cultural values. In fact, the emerging lifestyles seemed not only different but downright oppositional or 'counter-cultural' (ie they posed a radical challenge to conventional values). So it is little wonder that sociologists rushed to make sense of these subcultures.

Frith (1985) suggests that sociological approaches to youth subcultures fall into two broad camps, *functionalist* interpretations and the study of *meanings*.

1 **Functionalism** This approach concentrates on the functions that youth culture performs for its members and for the wider society. Eisenstadt (1956) argues that an extended period of 'youth' is required in order to socialise young people into the increasingly complex values and skills of modern society. Therefore society segregates young people and allocates them a marginal, transitional status. But this can lead to confusion and identity problems for those young people. However, Eisenstadt argues that youth culture provides them with a community solution to these problems. It helps them to work out their identities and it provides them with necessary support and companionship during a difficult phase of their growth.

The main criticism of the functionalist approach is that it is too general. The problems of 'growing up' are likely to vary immensely according to social class, race and gender. Also, it exaggerates the self-contained and 'separate' nature of youth culture (sometimes even treating youth as a separate 'class'). This underestimates the overlap between the values of youth and adults.

2 **Meanings** British sociologists have explored the deeper meanings of youth subcultures such as the Teddy Boys of the 1950s and their successors of the 1960s (mods and rockers, hippies, skinheads) and 1970s (punks, rastas). The stress in these studies has been on the collective values, lifestyles and symbols of these groups. One line of argument (Centre for Contemporary Cultural Studies, 1975) saw subcultural rituals as a form of resistance to subordination. They allowed youths to generate subversive meanings and stake out their own cultural space. For example, skinhead culture was seen as a desperate (and largely symbolic) attempt to reassert declining 'traditional' working class values (eg masculinity) and to reclaim lost 'community' (Cohen, 1972).

These subcultural studies have been criticised for concentrating on exotic groups and ignoring the blander lifestyles of majority 'conformist' youth. And perhaps they read too much into the apparently rebellious stance of these groups (many of whose members soon settled for conventional lifestyles!). How many of the participants would have recognised the motives attributed to them by the subcultural theorists? Moreover, with a few exceptions (eg McRobbie and Garber, 1975), these studies tended to ignore middle class youth, ethnic minorities and females.

The 'new' sociology of youth

Studies of exotic youth subcultures now seem rather dated. Of course, this does not mean that these subcultures have entirely disappeared (eg skinheads and punks are still around, and the 1980s and 1990s have seen the emergence of groups such as metallers and ravers). It is just that attention to the *leisure* styles of youth seems far less relevant in the harsh economic climate of recent years. For example, a British Youth Council Report (1992) mocks the idea that youth is still the 'time of your life'. It documents mounting problems of unemployment, low income, homelessness, dependence on parents and social marginalisation. Consequently, sociologists of youth have turned their attention to labour markets and education and training policies. Maguire (1993) notes that the decline in labour intensive industries, the introduction of new technology and the general rise in unemployment have created severe problems for youth (eg cuts in the number of apprenticeships).

Earlier in this chapter (Section 3.1) it was shown that social class has important effects on community life. This is true also of youth communities. Although middle class youth have been harmed by the economic recession of recent years, it is early school leavers (mainly working class) who have suffered most. This may account for the apparent increase in drugtaking and crime and a rising sense of despair. In 1991 'youth riots' broke out in a number of working class housing estates (eg Ely in Cardiff, Meadowell in Tyneside). Most of the riot areas had suffered a general decline in economic conditions (eg Scotswood in Newcastle had a male unemployment rate of 80%). In addition, some commentators (eg Campbell, 1993) interpreted the riots as an expression of the collapse of community, expressed most visibly in the lack of community facilities and the numerous boarded-up shops.

Old age

During the last century the age profile of Britain has changed dramatically. There are more old people and they form a larger proportion of the total population. People aged 65 and over have increased from 1.7m (4.7%) in 1901 to 8.8m (15.8%) in 1991. It is estimated that they will comprise one fifth of the entire population by the year 2031 (Family Policy Studies Centre, 1991). Clearly this growth has many implications for community care policies (see Section 4.1). However, one of the striking features of old age is the apparent lack of involvement in wider community life. Older people may belong to a 'subcultural community' insofar as they share many values, experiences and memories. But stereotypes of old age depict them as 'withdrawn' and 'disengaged' rather than active participants in the wider community.

Disengagement The disengagement theory of Cumming and Henry (1961) suggests that ageing has certain fixed effects. *Physically* it involves a gradual deterioration (eg older people have less energy and coordination). *Psychologically* it entails a narrowing range of interests and diminished powers of concentration. And *socially* it is accompanied by a disengagement from 'normal' social roles (eg they withdraw from the community and retreat into the safe and undemanding world of home and family). Disengagement theory regards this social withdrawal as natural and functional because old age is a time to prepare for eventual death. So society imposes fewer demands on older people and they in turn surrender some of their community roles.

There is no denying that advancing age carries a higher risk of health problems and disability. Also, people's leisure styles become more home centred when they retire from work. But some critics (eg Johnson, 1978) have exposed the flaws in the disengagement model.

1   Disengagement is not found to the same extent in pre-industrial societies. Rather than being 'natural', it seems to depend on cultural values and the way society is organised. In Britain, for example, the inactivity of old age is partly created

by the policy of compulsory retirement.

2   The elderly population is not uniform. The lifestyles and living standards of elderly people vary according to social class, ethnicity and gender. Even after retirement middle class people are able to enjoy higher living standards because of their private pensions and accumulated savings (Oppenheim, 1993). Also, elderly people are individuals and there are great differences in their lifestyles and attitudes (Abrams, 1982).

3   Disengagement theory rests on a value judgement that withdrawal is sensible and desirable. But an alternative view is that older people should be encouraged to participate fully in the community rather than settle for a 'safe' existence. A more active life might help to delay the more degenerative aspects of ageing.

Ageism Some experts deny that social withdrawal is due to a 'natural' ageing process. Rather, old people are forced to withdraw because they are the victims of *ageism* (insensitive attitudes and assumptions which treat them as if they were somehow less important or capable than 'normal' citizens). They do not suffer from old age so much as from discriminatory attitudes and treatment. For example, Norman (1987) notes that younger people often use derogatory terms such as 'senile', 'crumbly', 'wrinklie' and 'geriatric' to describe elderly people. Fortunately, older people are now starting to challenge ageism and the 'cult of youth'. They are using 'Grey Power' (eg their spending and voting power) to persuade politicians, retailers and organisations to recognise their special needs and interests. Also, Featherstone and Hepworth (1989) speculate that many people are throwing off the 'mask of old age' to reveal their 'personal' selves. They are increasingly rejecting stereotypes of elderly people and refusing to be pushed into narrow roles. These people lend support to the view that 'youthfulness' is not simply a matter of chronological age. It is also about personal qualities (eg impulsiveness, spontaneity, energy, curiosity, playfulness) and these qualities do not necessarily diminish with age.

Elderly lifestyles

It would be misleading, then, to assume that all elderly people are isolated from community activities. A Eurobarometer survey (Centre for Policy on Ageing, 1993) of elderly people in the European Union found that two thirds of the sample led reasonably active lives. The most common pastime was watching television but this was closely followed by seeing or looking after relatives and friends. 70% of the sample liked shopping, 40% enjoyed gardening or DIY, and 50% took a regular walk or exercise. As for clubs and organisations, 33% attended church and 10% were involved in voluntary work. But Jerrome (1986) notes that clubs specially designed for elderly people are not always popular (they are often reluctant to participate in activities organised on their behalf). Instead, they often prefer private or kin networks or voluntary organisations where they can construct their own patterns of activities and interests. Sometimes, too, they prefer to mix with other age groups rather than confine themselves to the company of their peers.

Summary

1 Men and women have different but overlapping patterns of community involvement.
2 Afro-Caribbean communities face severe socioecomonic pressures.
3 The Rushdie affair created major tensions between Muslim communities and the wider society.
4 Young people are facing increasing socioeconomic problems, but elderly people are starting to resist ageism.

Activity 11 Passing the Time

Item A *Street corners*

Locality is an important focus for working class youth. It constitutes their 'social space', the territory where they act together. The streets and alleyways are public and less tightly regulated than other areas (home, school, youth club etc). It also allows them to develop a cultural identity. It is here that they learn the oral tradition of their local working class community.

Adapted from J. Clarke et al, *Working Class Culture*, 1979, p251

Item B *Clubs*

At about half past one on a normal weekday afternoon there occurs a shift in the elderly population. On foot, by bus or taxi, or car of a kind daughter or friend, the sociable and able bodied go in search of company and occupation. Their destination is probably a club, or one of their clubs, for people who go to the clubs at all tend to belong to several. Club going is a way of life.

Adapted from D. Jerrome, 'Me Darby, You Joan!', 1986, p350

Questions

1 Read Item A. State, giving reasons, whether you think localities fulfil similar functions for middle class youths.
2 Read Item B. Using this item, suggest the social functions of clubs for elderly people.

5 Spaces and places

Key Issues

1 How do sociological theories deal with space?
2 Are there differences between rural and urban lifestyles?
3 Has globalisation eroded local and national differences?

Each episode of *Star Trek* begins with a voice announcing 'Space - the final frontier'. Clearly this is a reference to unexplored planets and the mysterious edges of the universe. But in some ways space is just as big a mystery on Earth itself. Sociologists are still struggling to make sense of the role that space and place play in social life. Does where we live determine how we live? What effect does physical location have on the patterns of community life? This section explores these kinds of questions.

5.1 Theories of space

The rural-urban framework

Sociological analysis of community was dominated for a long time by the rural-urban framework. This approach emerged from the gemeinschaft-gesellschaft tradition and it is perhaps most clearly represented by Robert Redfield's typology. Its main assumption is that social relationships vary according to physical setting. City life, therefore, is seen as quite distinct from rural life.

Urbanism as a way of life In a highly influential work Simmel (1903) argued that the metropolis imposes new forms of 'mental life' on people. Its sheer size intimidates individuals (who are constantly bombarded with stimuli); its advanced division of labour fragments social life; and its money economy breeds a calculating approach to other people. Cities certainly enlarge personal freedoms (eg individuals are more 'anonymous' and shielded from constant scrutiny). But they also create a deep sense of alienation. Life in the city is depersonalised and regimented, and punctuality is more highly prized than individuality. Simmel's arguments were developed further by Wirth (1938) who claimed that there is an urban 'way of life'. Wirth recognised the attractions and dynamism of city life but his description of urbanism is largely a bleak one. Social relationships are superficial since people respond to each other in terms of their formal roles rather than as 'whole persons'. There is very little spontaneity or warmth and the city dweller is lonely and insecure, possessing large circles of acquaintances but few real friends.

Criticisms In the 1960s the rural-urban framework was severely criticised by sociologists.
1 The ideal types are oversimplified and misleading. Empirical research indicates that real communities are far more complex and diverse than the model suggests.
2 Far from being uniform, most communities contain both rural (gemeinschaft) and urban (gesellschaft) features. Even Wirth recognised the existence of gemeinschaft-like 'urban villages' (eg ethnic enclaves) in the heart of the city.
3 Rural lifestyles in Britain have been progressively eroded by the spread of urban culture (Newby, 1987). Urbanism has invaded the countryside to such a degree that rural-urban contrasts now seem rather pointless.
4 The framework takes an unbalanced view of urbanism by identifying the city with unavoidable problems (disorganisation, alienation etc). But not all cities are alike and even the bleakest city usually has a number of redeeming features.
5 Is there a close link between localities and lifestyles? According to Pahl (1975) it is foolish to expect a neat match between places and social relationships. Even when the inhabitants of an area share common lifestyles this is usually because they belong to the same social class or age group (Gans, 1967). It has little to do with the effects of locality as such.

New directions in urban sociology

Increasing disenchantment with the rural-urban framework created something of a crisis for urban sociologists. If rural-urban differences are insignificant, is there anything left for urban sociologists to study? If *all* of society is more or less urban then it becomes difficult to distinguish urban sociology from sociology in general. It seemed to many observers that urban sociology would vanish as a specialised field unless it found some topics or problems to claim as its own. Responding to this challenge, urban sociologists branched out in new directions. Saunders (1987) identifies three main stages in this development: urban managerialism, political economy and the 'rediscovery' of space.

Urban managerialism This approach focuses on the way 'urban managers' exercise power within the city. It is best understood as a reaction to the Chicago School, an influential group of urban sociologists in the interwar years. The Chicago theorists drew an analogy between the city and ecological systems (eg plant or animal habitats where all the species adjust to each other and to their environment so that the system maintains its delicate balance). Just like plants and animals, city dwellers compete for space and 'invade' adjoining territories. The Chicago School described these and other urban processes as largely 'natural' and unplanned but this is what the new approach contested. Pahl (1975) argued that, far from being 'natural', urban processes are the result of conscious decisions by powerful urban managers. These managers (or 'gatekeepers') regulate the city's spatial development and they determine the allocation of urban resources. For example, town planners and private developers decide the sites of new housing estates; councillors and housing officers control access to council housing. Pahl believed the power of urban managers was growing and he was especially keen to identify the values and ideologies which guided their decisions.
Critics accused the managerialist approach of exaggerating the autonomy and power of urban gatekeepers. These managers only occupy the middle levels of power and they are hardly a ruling elite. They may seem to act freely but their decisions are ultimately dictated by the 'logic' of capitalism and by the interests of powerful capitalists. Consequently, the critics called for a more rigorous political economy approach.

Political economy Marxist sociologists and geographers (eg Harvey, 1973; Castells, 1977) shifted attention away from urban managers towards the political and economic structure within which they operate. These theorists claimed that urbanism can only be understood in terms of the broader processes and constraints of capitalism. Castells looked in particular at the way capitalism tries to ensure its own *reproduction*. It needs a healthy, educated workforce and a population prosperous enough to buy the goods it produces. So it cannot let levels of *collective consumption* drop too low. It must ensure that most people can afford food and shelter and have access to education and healthcare. However, capitalists do not wish to pay for all this since it would cut too deeply into their profits. In the postwar period, then, the solution was for the state to use general taxation to fund the provision of schools, hospitals, parks etc. But in the 1970s the state ran into a 'fiscal crisis' when it found it increasingly difficult to finance the growing welfare state. So it introduced cuts and restructuring. But these measures created public discontent and weakened the legitimacy of the state and the capitalist system. For Castells, the city was

the territory within which this struggle over consumption issues was conducted. Urban resources were already distributed very unevenly and the cuts further fuelled the burning sense of injustice felt by many people. Castells predicted that the emerging urban social movements (eg tenants' groups, ethnic organisations) would pose a radical socialist challenge to capitalism.

Castells' arguments were pitched at a very abstract level, dealing mainly with 'structures' rather than the actions and motives of people. Critics soon pointed out that his confident generalisations were insufficiently supported by empirical evidence. Later research revealed some of the flaws in the arguments and even Castells (1983) eventually admitted that urban protest movements are not very visible (at least in Britain). Where they do exist they are typically 'defensive' rather than radical.

Activity 12 Community Destruction

Item A *Factory closure*

The closure of the factory in Hackney was a tragedy. It illustrates how Britain allows companies (whose centres of control often lie far away, even in other countries) the unquestioned right to destroy old factories, marginalise and deskill their workers, destabilise their families and devastate their communities. No democratic accountability limits this power: no requirement to consult the workers, to consider their alternative plans, to consult the local authority or the central government. Only owners and shareholders are considered, only private profit is accounted, not the massive bill in social costs picked up by the taxpayer and above all by the victims.

Adapted from P. Harrison, *Inside the Inner City*, 1983, p91

Item B *Pit closure*

Demonstration against pit closures

A study of two mining villages in Yorkshire reveals the effects of the recent closure of local pits. It is not an exaggeration to say that the two communities were devastated. The closures resulted in continuing high unemployment, personal trauma and stress and a more competitive attitude between ex-miners as they vainly searched for jobs. Men felt the loss of their status as principal breadwinner while women bore the brunt of family poverty and male despair. The physical fabric of the villages was eroded by economic decline and there was a rise in youth crime and drugtaking. Moreover, families could not sell their houses in order to move off elsewhere in search of a new life.

Adapted from C. Critcher et al, 'Portrait of Despair', *New Statesman and Society*, 23.10.92

Questions

1 Read Item A. Suggest ways in which the factory closure undermined the community in Hackney.
2 Read Item B. State (giving reasons) whether you think the consequences of closure are the same in the Yorkshire villages as they are in Hackney.
3 How would a 'political economy' approach explain the events described in Items A and B?

The rediscovery of space

Social scientists have 'rediscovered' space in recent years. Indeed, 'one of the most notable developments in social science during the 1980s was a return to the study of place and a renewed insistence on the importance of spatial variation in social processes' (Day and Murdoch, 1993, p85). This revived interest can be illustrated by the work of Giddens (1984).

Time-space paths Giddens argues that sociological analysis must take full account of space and time. This goes beyond simply recognising that social behaviour is always situated in a particular place at a particular time. Rather, it involves a detailed study of the way place and time enter deeply into everyday life, giving it meaning and structuring its activities. For example, people tend to develop particular routines around time and place. They compile their own personal timetables (eg 'I always get up early, walk the dog in the park, go to work at 8.30...' etc). Giddens calls these routines 'time-space paths' and he explores the way they frame and organise people's lives. One aspect of this is the way our lives are zoned. A house, for example, consists of a number of specialised zones such as bathroom, kitchen and bedroom. Each zone (or 'locale') is associated with a particular type of appropriate behaviour (eg sleeping in the bedroom, cooking in the kitchen). But even within any zone our behaviour depends on the time of day (eg a hurried wash in the basin in the morning, a more leisurely bath in the evening).

Does space matter? After the 'demise' of the rural-urban framework many urban sociologists concluded that space is not a significant factor in social life. The city was seen as little more than the setting where most social action happens to take place. The city simply *reflects* wider social forces (class etc) rather than having distinctive features of its own. So space has no real explanatory value since it is not a 'cause' of anything. However, the 'rediscovery' of space challenged this view. The new urban theorists (eg Massey, 1984) insisted that spatial setting is not just a backdrop since it actually *influences* social action in significant ways. But this is an issue which still divides sociologists.

Saunders (1987) accepts that space is always a *feature* of social relationships but he is not convinced that space has *causal* power. He argues that 'space as such is not important. What is important is the way in which different things come together in different places and thereby produce different effects' (Saunders, 1987, p102). For example, class and gender interact in different ways in different geographical locations. The single mother in the inner city usually has better access to amenities than her counterpart who is stranded in an isolated

housing estate, even although they both belong to the same social class. Moreover, Saunders maintains that 'working class' is not the same thing in Liverpool as it is in Eastbourne. Apart from their different employment prospects, the two areas differ in history, culture and typical lifestyles. So, although space is not the 'cause' of anything, sociologists must pay attention to the important variations of place and location.

5.2 Town and country

The theoretical disputes about space are sometimes quite difficult to follow. But community studies are often pitched at a simpler, more descriptive level. This section deals with some descriptions of life in rural and urban areas.

Country life

Many British people state a preference for rural life. They believe it is cleaner, quieter, safer, more fulfilling and 'natural' than urban life. There are two problems with this kind of argument. First of all, it assumes that rural life is uniform and unchanging. And secondly, it overlooks the drawbacks of country life.

The changing countryside Romantic myths about rural life have a curiously timeless quality as if the countryside has remained undisturbed through the centuries. But Newby (1987) observes that country life has changed and evolved in line with agricultural developments. Take the mid-Victorian village, an occupational community whose fortunes were largely bound up in farming. Many people think of this as the 'traditional' village but it was quite novel at the time (previously, villages usually had some small scale manufacture and domestic handicrafts). Important changes have also taken place in the rural class system. In Victorian times there was a tripartite class structure consisting of landowner, tenant farmer and landless labourer. As absentee landowners became less common this gradually turned into a bipartite division between owner-occupying farmers and farm workers. More recently, in the postwar period, small farmers have become increasingly marginalised with the emergence of 'agribusiness' which is based on large holdings and intensive monoculture. Increased mechanisation has resulted in a huge reduction in the numbers of farm labourers. Consequently, many rural dwellers now work in small industries and services rather than in agriculture.

Perhaps the most controversial development in recent years is the population movement from towns and cities to the villages. By the end of the 1960s the motorway network linked up many 'commuter' villages to the major conurbations. Urban dwellers started buying rural homes to use either as a weekend retreat or as a base from which to commute to the city. These commuter villages might be largely deserted during the week while people work in the city.

Rural bliss? Cohen (1982) maintains that Britain's rural communities differ significantly from one another (eg they include Highland crofts, Welsh hill farms and Home Counties commuter belts). Therefore it is dangerous to generalise too freely about country life. Nevertheless, there is mounting evidence that rural areas face severe problems. The *Faith in the Countryside* report (1990) declares that the tranquil exterior of the countryside masks sharp conflicts and unsuspected poverty. This report paints a gloomy picture of the impact of economic, environmental and social change on rural communities. Village employment has declined, affordable housing is scarce, village shops and post offices are under threat, local transport is almost non-existent in many areas and public services are poor. Although the absolute living standards of farm workers have risen in the postwar period they still lag well behind urban workers. Moreover, many country dwellers feel they have suffered a 'loss' of community (Newby, 1987).

Activity 13   Rural Conflicts

Item A   *Welsh nationalism*

Thirteen English families are nearing a deadline issued by the shadowy nationalist group Meibion Glyndwr to leave Wales for good. The stencilled letters said 'You are an English colonist. You are racist and anti-Welsh. You are on Meibion Glyndwr's blacklist. You must leave Wales by March 31 or we will take revenge'.

Meibion Glyndwr first struck in 1979 with a string of firebombings of rural homes throughout Wales. During that time more than 200 English owned properties have been burnt. Police maintain it is lucky no one has been killed. Detectives have run into a conspiracy of silence in the tight knit communities of the mainly Welsh speaking Lleyn peninsula where there is widespread sympathy for the bombers, particularly among young people.

Adapted from *Guardian*, 27.2.93

Welsh nationalists in paramilitary uniform march in Clywd.

Item B   *Commuters*

The commuters brought with them an urban middle class lifestyle which was alien to the local village population. The locals, resentful of the invasion of 'their' community by outsiders, retreated in upon themselves by forming a community within a community. From the late 1960s commentators spoke of the 'decline of the village' and questioned whether the village was still a real 'community'. There were fierce conflicts over housing and the environment (eg commuters often wished to preserve the rural idyll while locals were keen to 'develop' the village). But it is certainly the case that some villages might have declined even further if the newcomers had not arrived.

Adapted from H. Newby *Country Life*, 1987, pp221-222

Questions

1 Read Item A.
   a) Give reasons why the 'rural homes' issue is an especially controversial issue in Wales.
   b) State (giving reasons) whether you approve of the attitudes and actions of Meibion Glyndwr.

2 Read Item B. In what ways might the newcomers have helped prevent the further decline of the village?

Urban society

Cities have a long history stretching back to Mesopotamia in 3000 BC (Sherlock, 1991). Cities of the past were established mainly as trading and market centres or as centres of great empires and civilisations. In pre-capitalist times, however, the great majority of the population lived in small settlements and rural dwellings. In the Middle Ages urban settlements seldom exceeded a population of around 40,000. Even at the beginning of the sixteenth century London contained only about 2% of the English population. But a number of developments pushed Britain on the road to a predominantly urban society. The agricultural revolution (16th to 18th centuries) forced peasants off the land but at the same time it created a food surplus which could sustain the growing urban population. Another boost to urban growth was the Industrial Revolution (18th and 19th centuries). The early industrial machinery was based on water power and so the mills were located in rural areas near rivers and canals. But the development of steam power led to the construction of factories in the towns and cities. The growth of cities was boosted also by the transport revolution which provided improved means (canals, roads, railways) of moving workers and goods around. As a result of all these developments, Britain was transformed into an urban society. In 1801 one-fifth of the population of England and Wales lived in towns but by 1911 this had increased to four-fifths.

The changing city The shape and function of British cities has changed dramatically over the last two hundred years. Jewson (1991) charts the movement from the grim 'industrial city' of the Victorian era through to the growth of the dominant 'metropolis' (or conurbation) and then, more recently, the gradual emergence of the 'megalopolis' (a sprawling, decentralised urban complex which is linked by fast roads and high-tech electronic communications). The new emphasis on flexibility and decentralisation means that cities have become more 'open' and 'polycentric' (with no obvious focal point). The single, dominant metropolis is being replaced by a lattice work of small or medium sized settlements. Examples include Los Angeles and, in this country, the motorway corridors from London to East Anglia or Bristol.

Town centres One of the most visible expressions of urban change is the transformation of town centres. Historically the town centre has performed a number of important social functions: a focus for civic identity, a meeting place, tourist site, leisure area and a major centre for public facilities and services. However, Worpole (1992) warns that the town centre is losing its pivotal position in social, political and cultural life. It is being reduced to a shopping and commercial centre by day and a ghost town at night. There seem to be fewer places where people can simply meet, chat and watch the world go by. Fast food outlets have replaced the more leisurely cafes, tea rooms and coffee houses of the past. Worpole identifies some of the forces which have changed town centres over the last two decades.
1 **Domination by the motor car** This has had a disastrous effect on town centres. It surrounds them with ring roads (which create a psychological barrier to walking in and out of the centres) and it fills them with barren multistorey car parks.
2 **The retail revolution** Many town centres are devoted almost exclusively to covered shopping centres. There are now very few houses in or near town centres, and public buildings (eg libraries) have become increasingly marginalised. Even more recently, the development of large out-of-

town shopping complexes has threatened the continued existence of shops in town centres. Quite possibly the town centre of the future will consist almost entirely of commercial and financial activities (eg offices, banks, building societies).
3 **The privatisation (or domestication) of leisure** Many people prefer to spend their leisure time either at home or at suburban leisure sites. They are sometimes frightened of venturing into the town centre at night because it is associated with rowdy teenagers and drunks.

Living in cities

Soft city Wirth (1938) popularised the idea that cities dictate the lifestyles and attitudes of their inhabitants. But Gans (1967) rejects the notion of a uniform urban (or suburban) way of life. Instead, he argues that the city offers a great deal of *choice* over lifestyles (even if this choice is influenced by social class and by age factors). This view is developed further by Raban (1975) who suggests it is misleading to regard the city as something totally 'fixed' or 'hard'. The city sometimes appears to closely regulate the actions and thoughts of its inhabitants. But at other times it becomes a 'soft city' which offers rich opportunities for people to impose their own meanings on it. Raban claims that cities are much more 'plastic' (flexible) by nature than villages or small towns. The city is a huge screen on to which we can project our own illusions, aspirations and nightmares. It encourages our imagination, creativity and playfulness as we mould it in our own image.

A similar view of the city is taken by Worpole (1992) who reports that people carry around 'mental maps' of their town centre. 'Space is an attitude of mind as much as a piece of geographical territory' (Worpole, 1992, p35). Every street, building, alley, department store or park has particular associations for people. For example, Worpole and his researchers discovered that women in Woolwich have their own personal lists of 'secure' and 'unsafe' places in the town centre. They can name individual bus stops, empty shop premises, even certain bushes or blind corners as places that cause them anxiety.

Suburbia Thorns (1972) defines the suburb as a residential area which is on the edge of the city but depends on it as a source of goods, services and work. The term conjures up rows of identical semi-detached houses filled with regimented people. In the words of a folk song by Pete Seeger, they all live in little boxes which are all made out of ticky-tacky and they all look just the same. Thorns notes that most social commentators take a disdainful view of the suburb. It is regarded as 'the centre of the middle-brow, conformist, respectable uninspiring members of society who are quite content to potter around in their own rather limited world' (Thorns, 1972, p149).

But is this an accurate view of suburbia? Gans (1967) argues there is considerable diversity within and between suburbs in the United States. Also, the suburbs may not be perfect examples of *gemeinschaft* but most suburbanites manage to maintain 'quasi-primary' social relationships (ie a more selective and less all-embracing form of community life). As for Britain, Sudjic (1994) contends that the stereotypes of suburbia are divorced from reality. Suburbs are anything but uniform and many of them are dynamic 'test beds' for new ways of life rather than simply places where people go home to sleep and wash the car. Moreover, most people still aspire to suburban life and they continue to enjoy it despite the sneers of cynics.

Destructive gemeinschaft A much more gloomy view of city life is taken by Sennett (1973, 1976). He argues that the modern search for community is motivated largely by fear of the city and the 'stranger'. Faced with the dangers of the city, people retreat into safe forms of intimacy. Town planners respond to this need by designing homogeneous 'communities' where people can be with their 'own' kind (eg ethnic communities, middle class suburbs). However, Sennett insists that this is fundamentally misguided. He believes that the attraction of cities lies precisely in their diversity, complexity and disorder. 'Real' communities do not screen themselves off from these attractions. Cities should be places where we take risks, where we mix freely with people from all walks of life. Public spaces should be designed to encourage flexible forms of sociability. But the creation of enclosed pseudo-communities (what Sennett calls 'destructive gemeinschaft') prevents people from discovering the exciting pleasures of city life. As a result, most city dwellers find the urban experience disturbing and unpleasant.

Activity 14 City Life

Item A *Urban myths*

We've all heard stories about alligators in the sewers and psychopathic babysitters. These are examples of urban myths. Urban myths are saucy, implausible, bizarre and scary but also strangely moral. We want to believe them, no matter how far-fetched or ridiculous.

Urban myths share a common formula. Nearly all are testaments to people's vanity and stupidity. They deal with our irrational fears, especially concerning life's rituals like getting married, getting drunk, working, courting, going to parties, eating out, driving, dying, DIY-ing, and, most perilous of all, going to the toilet. They are a safety valve for our deep-seated fears and prejudices.

Adapted from P. Healey and R. Glanvill *Urban Myths*, 1992, pxi

Item B *Cars*

The motor car is useful and liberating but it has been a mixed blessing.

It causes atmospheric pollution and serious damage to the physical environment.

It encourages people to live further from their work. We now waste more time than ever on travelling.

It encourages retailers to concentrate on a few large outlets far away from where people live.

It allows planners to site hospitals, county offices etc remote from the members of the public who need to visit them.

Hamburg, Germany

Adapted from H. Sherlock *Cities Are Good For Us*, 1991, p16

Questions

1 Read Item A. Explain what is meant by saying that urban myths are a sort of 'safety valve'.

2 Read Item B. Suggest ways in which the damaging effects of cars can be reduced or eliminated.

5.3 Globalisation

The global village

The world is shrinking. Not physically, of course, but socially, culturally and economically. The nations of the world are coming closer together in terms of cultural contacts and economic transactions.

'Globalisation' is the general term used to describe this trend. McGrew (1992) defines globalisation as the process by which events, decisions and activities in one part of the world come to have significant consequences for people in quite distant parts of the globe. Globalisation theorists argue that these links have become more pronounced in recent decades. Globalisation has been assisted by the growth of international trading and manufacturing systems, the rising prominence of transnational corporations and the spread of global communications networks. As a result, 'Nowadays goods, capital, people, knowledge, images, communications, crime, culture, pollutants, drugs, fashions and beliefs all readily flow across territorial boundaries' (McGrew, 1992, p65).

Global fears A number of critics have voiced fears about the possible effects of globalisation.

1 **Standardisation of consumption patterns** Local producers find it difficult to compete with the advertising and marketing power of the transnationals. So local goods are squeezed out and international brand names (eg Coca Cola, McDonald's) start to dominate in all countries. Wherever people travel they will encounter the same narrow range of products.

2 **Erosion of local cultures** The global media networks transmit their programmes across many countries and regions. There is a risk that these networks might impose their own cultural values on the worldwide audience. Some critics talk about the 'Hollywoodisation' of local cultures. When EuroDisney was built near Paris many French people complained that this would undermine the distinctiveness of French cultural life.

3 **Insecurity** Giddens (1984) describes the 'compression' of time and place. Improvements in transport mean that time and distance have 'shrunk' (eg it once took 4 months to travel from the east to the west coast of the United States by stagecoach; now it takes two hours by jet). Increasingly, social activities are freed from the constraints of time and space. For example, we often find it easier to phone a distant relative than to contact a neighbour face to face. Giddens argues that this has eroded people's sense of place. They no longer feel they really 'belong' to their immediate locality and this increases their sense of rootlessness and insecurity.

Making sense of globalisation

Most commentators accept that there is a broad trend towards globalisation in the modern world. But it is difficult to measure its extent or specify its detailed effects with any degree of confidence. There is still very little solid empirical research to fall back on. Indeed, globalisation is a very difficult area to research. First, it is an extremely complex matter which involves social, cultural, economic and political processes. Secondly, globalisation is not a uniform process and it has an uneven impact on nations, communities and social groups (Smart, 1993). Thirdly, Giddens (1990) maintains that globalisation consists of mutually opposed tendencies (eg it encourages centralisation *and* decentralisation, fragmentation *and* integration, homogenisation *and* differentiation). Therefore any generalisations about globalisation need to be treated with caution.

Certain critics have challenged the speculations of globalisation theorists. For example, Massey (1991) questions whether time-space compression really creates widespread feelings of personal insecurity. Another critic, Morley (1992), challenges the vision of an 'emerging placelessness'. He argues that it is quite possible that 'new' sensibilities have not *replaced* older ones but have simply been *added* to them (eg people may have a strong sense of locality *and* a 'global' outlook). The computer games promoted by giant transnationals may seem to 'detach' people from their local community but they also *strengthen* it (eg computer fans meet to swap or play games). To take another example, national media may encourage a 'cosmopolitan' outlook but they also help to develop a keener sense of locality through soap operas which have a firm geographical base (eg *Brookside*, *EastEnders*).

Summary

1 Sociologists have 'rediscovered' the importance of space but its exact role in social life remains a controversial issue.

2 Rural and urban areas have changed over the years and so have their characteristic lifestyles.

3 Globalisation is a complex process. Some sociologists believe it has undermined people's firm sense of place.

Activity 15 The Shrinking World

Item A *Ethnic foods*

It is hard to think of 'Indian cooking' as something distinctive of the ethnic traditions of the Asian subcontinent when there is an Indian restaurant in the centre of every city and town in Britain.

Adapted from S.Hall 'The Question of Cultural Identity', 1992, p302

Item B *Third World*

People in small, apparently remote villages in poor Third World countries can receive the messages and images of the rich consumer cultures of the West. Their TV sets and radios bind them into the global village.

Adapted from S.Hall 'The Question of Cultural Identity', 1992, p302

Item C *Worldwide vacations*

Questions

1   Read Item A. Give three other examples of the way globalisation has reduced the 'strangeness' of other cultures.
2   Read Item B. What do you think are the effects of globalisation on the Third World villages described by Hall?
3   How might the activities pictured in Item C affect the perceptions of time and place of
    a) the tourist and b) those they visit?

References

Abrams, M. 'Lifestyles of the Elderly' in J. Lishman and G.Horobin (eds) *Developing Services for the Elderly* (University of Aberdeen, 1982)

Anderson,B. *Imagined Communities* (Verso, London, 1983)

Aries,P. *Centuries of Childhood* (Peregrine, London, 1973)

Beattie,G. *We Are the People* (Mandarin, London, 1993)

Bhachu,P. *Twice Migrants* (Tavistock, London, 1985)

Bornat,J., Pereira,C., Pilgrim,D. and Williams,F. *Community Care* (Macmillan, Basingstoke, 1993)

Bott,C. *Family and Social Network* (Tavistock, London, 1957)

British Youth Council *The Time of Your Life?* (report, 1992)

Broadbent,P. 'Estates of an Outer Realm', *New Society* 14.6.1985

Bulmer,M. and Abrams,P. *Neighbours* (Cambridge University Press, 1986)

Bulmer, M. *The Social Basis of Community Care* (Allen & Unwin, London, 1987)

Campbell,B. *Wigan Pier Revisited* (Virago, London, 1984)

Campbell,B. *Goliath* (Methuen, London, 1993)

Care in the Community, HMSO, 1981

Castells,M. *The Urban Question* (Edward Arnold, London, 1977)

Castells,M. *The City and the Grassroots* (Edward Arnold, London, 1983)

Centre for Contemporary Cultural Studies *Resistance Through Rituals* (University of Birmingham, 1975)

Centre for Policy on Ageing *Older People in the European Community* (London, 1993)

Clarke,J., Critcher,C. and Johnson,R. (eds) *Working Class Culture* (Hutchinson, London, 1979)

Cockburn,C. *The Local State* (Pluto, London, 1977)

Cohen,A. (ed) *Belonging* (Manchester University Press, 1982)

Cohen,A. T*he Symbolic Construction of Community* (Ellis Harwood, Chichester, 1985)

Cohen,P. 'Subcultural Conflict and Working Class Community', in Centre for Contemporary Cultural Studies *Working Papers in Cultural Studies 2* (Spring, 1972)

Cornwell,J. *Hard Earned Lives* (Tavistock, London, 1984)

Critcher,C., Dicks,B. and Waddington,D. 'Portrait of Despair', *New Statesman and Society* 23.10.1992

Cumming,E. and Henry,W. *Growing Old* (Basic Books, New York, 1961)

Day,G. and Murdoch,J. 'Locality and Community', *Sociological Review*, vol 41 no 1, 1993

Deem,R. 'Women and Leisure', *Social Studies Review* vol 5 no 5, March 1990

Dennis,N., Henriques,F. and Slaughter,C. *Coal is Our Life* (Tavistock, London, 1956)

Dennis,N. 'The Popularity of the Neighbourhood Community Idea', in R.Pahl (ed) *Readings in Urban Sociology* (Pergamon, Oxford, 1968)

Devine,F. 'Affluent Workers Revisited', *Sociology Review* vol 3 no 3, 1994

Eisenstadt,S. *From Generation to Generation* (Free Press, Chicago, 1956)

Eriksen,T. *Ethnicity and Nationalism* (Pluto, London, 1993)

Etzioni,A. *The Spirit of Community* (Touchstone, New York, 1994)

Faith in the City Archbishop of Canterbury's Commission on Urban Priority Areas (Church House Publishing, London, 1985)

Faith in the Countryside Report of the Archbishops' Commission on Rural Areas (Churchman Publishing, Worthing, 1990)

Family Policy Studies Centre *An Ageing Population* (London, 1991)

Featherstone,M. and Hepworth,M. 'Ageing and Old Age' in B.Bytheway et al (eds) *Becoming and Being Old* (Sage, London, 1989)

Finch,J. and Groves,D. 'Community Care and the Family', *Journal* of Social Policy vol 9, 1980

Frith,S. The Sociology of Youth (Causeway, Ormskirk, 1985)

Gans,H. The Levittowners (Allen Lane, London, 1967)

Gavron,H. The Captive Wife (Routledge, London, 1966)

Geraghty,C. Women and Soap Operas (Polity Press, Cambridge, 1991)

Giddens,A. The Constitution of Society (Polity Press, Oxford, 1984)

Giddens,A. The Consequences of Modernity (Polity Press, Cambridge, 1990)

Gilroy,P. There Ain't No Black in the Union Jack (Hutchinson, London, 1987)

Glasser,R. Growing Up in the Gorbals (Pan, London, 1987)

Goldthorpe,J.,Lockwood,D., Bechhofer,F. and Platt,J. The Affluent Worker in the Class Structure (Cambridge University Press, 1969)

Graham,H. 'Feminist Perspectives on Caring', in J.Bornat et al (eds) Community Care (Macmillan, Basingstoke, 1993)

Green,E., Hebron,S. & Woodward,D. Women's Leisure, What Leisure? (Macmillan, London, 1990)

Hall,S., Critcher,C., Jefferson,T. and Clarke,J. Policing the Crisis (Macmillan, London, 1978)

Hall,S. 'The Question of Cultural Identity', in S.Hall, D.Held and T.McGrew (eds) Modernity and its Futures (Polity Press, Cambridge, 1992)

Harvey,D. Social Justice and the City (Edward Arnold, London, 1973)

Harrison,P. Inside the Inner City (Penguin, Harmondsworth, 1983)

Healey,P. and Glanvill,R. Urban Myths (Virgin Books, London, 1992)

Hillery,G. 'Definitions of community', Rural Sociology, vol 20 no 2, 1955

Hoggart,R. Uses of Literacy (Chatto & Windus, London, 1957)

Holme,A. 'Family and Homes in East London', New Society 12.7.1985

Horton,D. and Wohl,R. 'Mass Communication and Para-Social Interaction', Psychiatry vol 19, 1956

Jerrome,D. 'Me Darby, You Joan!' in C.Phillipson et al (eds) Dependency and Interdependency in Old Age (Croom Helm, London, 1986)

Jewson,N. 'Inner City Riots', Social Studies Review vol 5 no 5, 1990

Jewson,N. 'The Development of Cities in Capitalist Societies', Sociology Review vol 1 no 2, 1991

Johnson,M. 'That Was Your Life' in V.Carver and P.Liddiard (eds) An Ageing Population (Hodder & Stoughton, London, 1978)

Jones,K., cited in 'The Crisis in Community Care', New Society 18.9.1987

Kingdom,J. No Such Thing as Society? (Open University Press, Milton Keynes, 1992)

Lawless,P. Britain's Inner Cities (Paul Chapman, London, 1989)

Leech,K. Youthquake (Abacus, London, 1976)

Maguire,S. 'Training for a Living?', Sociology Review vol 1 no 1, 1993

Marshall,G., Rose,D., Newby,H. and Vogler,C. Social Class in Modern Britain (Unwin Hyman, London, 1989)

Massey,D. Spatial Divisions of Labour (Macmillan, London, 1984)

Massey,D. 'A Global Sense of Place', Marxism Today June 1991

McGrew,A. 'A Global Society?', in S.Hall et al (eds) Modernity and its Futures (Polity Press, Cambridge, 1992)

McRobbie,A. and Garber,J. 'Girls and Subcultures' in S.Hall & T.Jefferson (eds) Resistance Through Rituals (Hutchinson, London, 1975)

Morley,D. Television, Audiences and Cultural Studies (Routledge, London, 1992)

Newby,H. Community (Open University Press, Milton Keynes, 1980)

Newby,H. Country Life (Sphere, London, 1987)

Nisbet,R. The Sociological Tradition (Heinemann, London, 1970)

Norman,A. 'Overcoming an Old Prejudice', Community Care 29.1.1987

Oppenheim,C. Poverty (Child Poverty Action Group, London, 1993)

Pahl,R. Whose City? (Penguin, Harmondsworth, 1975)

Pahl,R. Divisions of Labour (Basil Blackwell, Oxford, 1984)

Parker,T. People of Providence (Penguin, Harmondsworth, 1983)

Parker,G. A Typology of Caring (Social Policy Research Unit, University of York, 1990)

Parsons,T. 'Double-Barrelled Condescension', Spectator 24.10.92

Pearson,G. Hooligan (Macmillan, Basingstoke, 1983)

Procter,I. 'The Privatisation of Working-class Life', British Journal of Sociology vol 41 no 2 June, 1990

Pryce,K. Endless Pressure (Penguin, Harmondsworth, 1979)

Raban,J. Soft City (Fontana, London, 1975)

Redfield,R. 'The Folk Society', American Journal of Sociology, vol 52 no 3, 1947

Roberts,K. Contemporary Society and the Growth of Leisure (Longman, London, 1978)

Roberts,K., Campbell,R. and Furlong,A. 'Class and Gender Divisions', in C.Wallace and M.Cross (eds) Youth in Transition (Falmer Press, London, 1990)

Roberts,R. The Classic Slum (Penguin, Harmondsworth, 1973)

Rosen,R. 'Search for Yesterday', in T.Gitlin (ed) Watching Television (Pantheon Books, New York, 1986)

Saunders,P Social Theory and the Urban Question (Hutchinson, London, 1986)

Saunders,P. 'Urban Sociology' in M.Haralambos (ed) Developments in Sociology vol 3 (Causeway Press, Ormskirk, 1987)

Saunders,P. Social Class and Stratification (Routledge, London, 1990)

Scarman,Lord The Brixton Disorders (HMSO, London, 1981)

Seabrook,J. What Went Wrong? (Gollancz, London, 1978)

Seabrook,J. Landscapes of Poverty (Basil Blackwell, Oxford, 1985)

Seabrook,J. The Myth of the Market (Green Books, Devon, 1990)

Sennett,R. The Uses of Disorder (Penguin, Harmondsworth, 1973)

Sennett,R. The Fall of Public Man (Cambridge University Press, 1976)

Sherlock,H. Cities are Good for Us (Paladin, London, 1991)

Simmel,G. 'The Metropolis and Mental Life', in K.Wolff (ed) The Sociology of Georg Simmel (Free Press, Glencoe, 1950, originally pub. 1903)

Smart,B. Postmodernity (Routledge, London, 1993)

Smith,S. The Politics of Race and Residence (Polity Press, Cambridge, 1989)

Solomos,J. Race and Racism in Britain (Macmillan, Basingstoke, 1993)

Stacey,M. 'The Myth of Community Studies', British Journal of Sociology, vol 20 no 2, 1969

Strinati,D. 'Postmodernism and Popular Culture', Sociology Review vol 1 no 4, 1992

Sudjic,D. 'Nightmare on Acacia Avenue', Guardian 14.4.1994

Taylor,S. 'Riots: Some Explanations', New Community vol 9 no 2, 1981

Thorns,D. Suburbia (Paladin, St. Albans, 1972)

Thrift,N. 'Images of Social Change' in C.Hamnett et al The Changing Social Structure (Sage, London, 1989)

Tonnies,F. Community and Society (Harper & Row, New York, 1957, originally pub.1887)

Vidich,A. and Bensman,J. Small Town in Mass Society (Princeton University Press, 1958)

Walker,A. 'Community Care Policy' in J.Bornat et al (eds) Community Care (Macmillan, Basingstoke, 1993)

Weldon,F. Sacred Cows (Chatto & Windus, London, 1989)

Wellman,B. 'The Community Question' American Journal of Sociology vol 84 no 5, 1979

Widgery,D. Some Lives! (Sinclair Stevenson, London, 1991)

Williams,R. The Country and the City (Chatto & Windus, London, 1973)

Wirth,L. 'Urbanism as a Way of Life', American Journal of Sociology vol 44, no 1, 1938

Worpole,K. Towns for People (Open University Press, Buckingham, 1992)

Young,M. and Willmott,P. Family and Kinship in East London (Penguin, Harmondsworth, 1957)

Young,M. and Willmott,P. The Symmetrical Family (Penguin, Harmondsworth, 1973)

12 Health and Medicine

Introduction

Health and medicine are among the fastest growing areas of sociology. And in this respect, sociology mirrors popular culture, for the popularity of health and medicine is evident in TV programmes, magazines and newspapers, in sports and fitness centres, health farms and health food shops and in government programmes to improve the health of the nation.

Chapter summary

- This chapter starts with the idea that health and illness are **social constructions** and therefore relative concepts.
- It then looks at disease in the context of **human history** and assesses **medicine's contribution** to the decline of infectious diseases.
- The next part considers the ways in which different peoples **perceive disease** and its treatments.

- The growth in status and power of the **medical profession** is then discussed.
- This is followed by a consideration of the relationships between **doctors and patients**.
- Finally, evidence of and explanations for **inequalities in health**, related to social class, gender and ethnicity, are outlined and evaluated.

1 The Social Construction of Health and Illness

Key Issues

1 What is meant by the idea that health and disease are social constructions and relative concepts?

2 How do 'explanatory medical models' differ between societies?

1.1 Defining terms

Defining terms is always a problem in the social sciences, particularly in the field of health. There is a raft of popular terms concerning health and ill-health. For instance, people talk about being healthy, fit, poorly, 'one degree under', low, below par, diseased, even 'sick as a parrot'. Amazingly, we often seem to know what we are each talking about! Additionally, health professionals may use some of the same terms in a different way from lay people. To try to minimise confusion, this section begins by suggesting definitions that can be agreed on for working purposes.

1.2 Health as a relative concept

According to the World Health Organisation (WHO), health is 'a state of complete physical, mental and social wellbeing and not merely the absence of disease and infirmity.' In this view then, we are suffering from ill-health when we fall short of

'complete wellbeing'. Given the probability that large proportions of any population are unlikely to feel complete wellbeing at all times, it is little wonder that René Dubos and Maya Pines describe the WHO definition of health as 'utopian' (how things might be in an ideal world).

Though the WHO appears to view health in absolute terms, it makes more sociological sense to see health as a relative concept and acknowledge that people understand different things by it. The same is true of associated words like unhealthy, sick and fit.

In general, ordinary people also see health in relative terms. When people say, 'You're alright as long as you've got your health', they don't necessarily mean that you're entirely without aches or pains. They recognise health is relative. And a person is seen as fortunate if their health is no worse than expected at, or is 'appropriate' to, their particular age.

Social scientists such as Dubos and Pines extend the notion that health is a relative concept by claiming that its meaning will also vary according to other statuses, in addition to age. 'Good health may mean different things to an astronaut and to a fashion model, to a lumberjack and to a member of the Stock Exchange. Their ways of life require different levels of physical activity; their food requirements and stresses vary, and they are not equally vulnerable to all diseases' (Dubos and Pines, 1980). In this view, health is most usefully defined as 'the ability to function effectively within a given environment'.

For Ivan Illich, however, good health and wellbeing imply functioning effectively in many environments. According to Illich we can only function effectively and experience relative wellbeing if we can come to terms with and accept our various aches and pains and less than perfect physical and mental condition. So, given that for much of the time most of us do feel 'below par' or 'one degree under', we must make the best of this, whatever our circumstances. As Illich notes: 'Mankind is the one living species whose members are aware of being frail, partly broken, and headed for total breakdown. Our wellbeing increases with our ability to assume personal responsibility for pain and impairment, and in our attitude to death' (Illich, 1976). Wellbeing, in this view, depends upon an ability to come maturely to terms with our own pains and sicknesses, and, not least, the inevitability of our own death, without despairing resignation but with acceptance.

As health is a relative concept, what it means and how it is recognised varies both between and within societies. Thus, within any one society individuals differ in their thresholds of discomfort and their tolerance of pain, in their readiness to define certain symptoms as indicative of sickness, in their sense of what feels healthy and what doesn't, and in their ideas about the 'appropriate' responses to particular sickness.

The same applies cross-culturally. Societies differ in the levels of discomfort and pain which are accepted as normal, or which are seen to signify ill-health. And different societies may interpret similar symptoms very differently. In some West African societies, for instance, rolls of body fat on females are regarded as both healthy and desirable, and young women do their best to acquire them. And, while in one society the person who hears voices may be accorded the status of a shaman or priest, in another they may be shut away as a schizophrenic.

1.3 Disease, illness and feeling ill, and sickness

Disease The term disease is used in two main senses. It can refer, as a general concept, to any pathological (unhealthy) condition, bodily or mental, whether caused through illness, accident or injury. This is the main way in which the term is used in this chapter. In a more limited sense, a disease refers to a specific, medically diagnosed condition, such as scarlet fever or mumps, with its distinctive, recognisable and predictable symptoms.

Illness or feeling ill Illness or feeling ill is the subjective experience of disease or ill-health. You may feel ill without having a specific disease. Conversely, if you have a disease, you may or may not feel ill. For instance, you may have schizophrenia or hypertension (high blood pressure) without feeling ill.

Sickness and being 'officially sick' Sickness is a social state; a social role with appropriate rights and obligations. In Western societies, for instance, the sick person is exempted from many other social roles but is expected to seek the advice of a health authority - typically a doctor - and cooperate with the advice given.

1.4 Measuring health and ill-health

Although it seems impossible to construct a universally applicable definition of health, and therefore to measure health with much validity or reliability, practical demands ensure that attempts are made. In practice, we usually try to measure health levels by using two indicators: *morbidity* (sickness) and *mortality* (death). Since morbidities are difficult to measure and quantify because of the heavily subjective element in identifying them, mortality is more commonly used in studies of health differences within and between societies.

Activity 1 The Relativity of Health

Item A Ill-health

'In fact, a universal definition or measure of ill-health is probably impossible to achieve.'

From Doyal, *Demystifying Social Statistics*, quoted in AEB 'A' level Sociology exam, paper 2, November 1984

Item B 'Normal' injuries

One of the questions which the prison doctor asks prisoners when they enter prison is whether they have ever had any serious injuries. The answer to this question is almost always no. Three questions later, the prisoners are asked whether they have ever been in hospital. The answer to this question is almost always yes.

'What for?' asks the doctor. The most usual reasons given are a car crash or an assault. 'And what happened to you?' 'I had a fractured skull, two broken ankles and a punctured lung.' Injuries are usually seen as a normal hazard of life. To accept them as such is part of the prisoners' subculture.

Adapted from T. Dalrymple 'If Symptoms Persist', *The Spectator*, 13.3.93

Item C *Harmful to health?*

Lighting a cigarette

Rastafarian lighting a marijuana pipe

Questions

1 In Item A, why is 'a universal definition of ill-health probably impossible to achieve'?
2 Read Item B.
   a) Why do some people have this view of injuries?
   b) Are social class and gender likely to affect their views. If so, how and why?
3 Look at the pictures in Item C. How do they illustrate the point that views of healthy/unhealthy behaviour are relative?

1.5 How do people make sense of health and illness?

What makes people healthy? Why do they get ill? What are the diseases which can attack them? What symptoms can they expect? What course will a sickness take? How will it affect them? What are the treatments? Why do they recover?

Questions posed about health and disease are often similar in different societies. However, although the questions are similar, the answers differ widely because different societies have very different ideas about health and disease.

A people's ideas about health and illness are related to and reflect their theories of biology, of disease - including their notions of the roles of hygiene, pollution, perhaps even evil in inducing sickness - and their theories of treatment. Ideas about health and illness vary because they are created, passed on and modified as part of the process of living together in societies. As such, they are social constructions. And it is because they are social constructions that the concepts of health and illness are relative.

However, to say that health and illness are social constructions is not to deny that health and illness are 'real'. It doesn't imply that diseases are mere imaginings and that different peoples in different geographical locations and at different points of history are not struck by the same diseases. They may be.

It is, however, to recognise that whether a person feels healthy or ill is determined within a cultural context, and that health and ill-health are perceived and identified differently by different individuals and by different cultures.

Different cultures provide different interpretations of health and illness partly because they have different ideas about the structure and functioning of the human body, ie different ideas about how the body is constituted and how it 'works'. Chinese acupuncturists, for instance, see the body as having a system of energy channels unknown to Western science. And among Hindu practitioners of yoga, the body is believed to house a number of *chakras* or energy centres, similarly unrecognised by Western science.

Additionally, different cultures also construct different explanations of why people become ill, and have their own proposals about how to treat the sick. That is, they have different theories of disease and treatment as well as different models of anatomy and biology. All of these interpretations are included when we talk of health and illness being social constructions.

Sociologists are interested, then, in cultural interpretations of health and illness, and in the different explanatory medical models used by people of different cultures. But they are also interested, of course, in structuralist issues about who it is in a given society who creates and shapes these diverse ideas about the body, health and illness.

1.6 The social construction of the body, its structure and functions

Societies do not, of course, literally construct their members' bodies. However, because societies differ markedly in their ideas about the optimal size, shape, and appearance of the body, they do almost literally 'shape' their members. Artificially elongated necks, tightly bound feet or waists, extended lower lips, scarred faces, fat-free torsos and metal-bearing earlobes are all regarded as attractive in some societies, and bodies there are shaped and fashioned accordingly.

Societies, and subcultures within societies, also differ in their conception of the inner structure (ie the composition and constituents) of the body, and of how it functions. In one study of low-income women in Michigan, USA, for instance, many were found to believe that the womb remained tightly closed between periods, while slowly filling with blood which escaped when the womb opened during the period. They reasoned, therefore, that they could only become pregnant just before, during or just after their periods, when their wombs were open - during their least fertile time in fact.

Summary

1 'Health' and 'illness' are social constructions and therefore relative concepts. What constitutes health varies between and within societies.

2 Attempts to compare the health of groups usually rely on two indicators, mortality (death) and morbidity (illness), although the latter has an important subjective component which may undermine the validity of any comparisons.

3 Different cultures provide different explanatory medical models, which include that culture's conceptions of the structure and functioning of the body and its theories of disease and treatment.

Activity 2 The Social Construction of Health and Ill-health

Item A English colds and chills
A study of English beliefs about 'chills', 'colds' and 'fevers' found that most people believed that certain areas of skin - the top of the head, the back of the neck and the feet - were more vulnerable than other parts to penetration by environmental cold, damp or draughts. One 'caught cold' if one 'went out into the rain without a hat on, or after a haircut', or 'stepped in a puddle' or 'on a cold floor'.

Adapted from C.G. Helman, *Culture, Health and Illness*, 1990, p14

Item B Menstruation and disease
Zulu women of South Africa are believed to 'pollute' humans, animals and crops if they have contact with them during menstruation. Men's virility may be weakened, crops ruined and cattle fall ill. And women in the Michigan study believed that they were most vulnerable to illness during menstruation because the uterus was then open, thus allowing cold air, water, 'germs' or witchcraft to enter.

Adapted from C.G. Helman, *Culture, Health and Illness*, 1990, p27

Coughs and sneezes spread diseases

Trap the germs by using your handkerchief

Help to keep the Nation Fighting Fit

A World War II poster

Item C *The beauty of fat*

In parts of West Africa, wealthy men frequently sent their daughters to 'fatting houses' where they were fed on fatty foods, with minimal exercise, to make them plump, a culturally defined shape believed to indicate both wealth and fertility. In the Western world, however, 'obesity' is seen as a major health problem, and also carries with it a significant social stigma.

Adapted from C.G. Helman, *Culture, Health and Illness*, 1990, p13

Question

1 Explanations for disease are culturally defined. Discuss using Items A, B and C.

2 The History of Disease

Key Issues

1 How has the importance of humanity-threatening diseases changed over time?
2 What role has medicine played in suppressing infectious diseases, and in extending life?

2.1 The epochs of disease

In humanity's long social evolution, as some diseases have assumed a greater role, so others have become less important. Historians of disease suggest that human disease history falls into three main periods: 1) the pre-agricultural, 2) the agricultural, and 3) the modern industrial periods. Each period is characterised by different ways of life and different disease problems.

1 Pre-agricultural society For the greater part of humanity's past, before the invention of agriculture, societies survived on hunting, fishing and gathering food. During those many thousands of years, life is thought to have been short but generally healthy. Adult death was probably often linked to the search for food supplies and competition over them. Relatively common causes of death, therefore, are thought to include homicide, tribal wars, hunting accidents, death by exposure and malnutrition. Early humanity is thought unlikely to have commonly suffered infectious diseases.

2 Agricultural society Some 10,000 years ago, humanity began the cultivation and domestication of plants and animals. This led to settled communities capable of supporting larger groupings, and so created the conditions required for the spread of infectious diseases (ie the diseases caused by micro-organisms - 'germs' - and spread via air, water, touch or a carrier such as insects). In general, there was a link between disease levels and food supplies. When food supplies and levels of nutrition improved,

disease diminished; when they deteriorated, infectious disease advanced. In Europe a major infectious killer for centuries was the plague, spread by the fleas carried by black rats. In the particularly virulent phase of the disease, during the so-called Black Death of the late 1340s, it is thought to have killed somewhere between one third and one half of the population of England and Western Europe. Other fatal infectious diseases in Europe were tuberculosis, bronchitis, pneumonia, influenza and cholera. Malaria, carried by the mosquito, was always largely limited to tropical countries.

3 Modern industrial society The modern industrial phase has been characterised by a decline in mortality from infectious diseases. Especially important has been the decline (though not necessarily the elimination) of former killers such as tuberculosis (T.B., called 'consumption' in the 19th century), measles, scarlet fever, pneumonia and whooping cough. Interestingly, these important advances, which began in the West in the 18th century and continued throughout the 19th, owed little to modern medicine.

By about the mid-twentieth century, infectious diseases had been overtaken as a cause of death by the types of diseases which are now characteristic of all modern Western societies. The main killers now are cancers, heart disease and strokes. And like other diseases of modern industrial societies, such as diabetes or osteoarthritis, they tend to be non-communicable, chronic (long lasting) and progressive. They are also believed to be due to a number of risk factors, rather than a single one like a germ, and to be significantly linked to lifestyle. They are therefore substantially avoidable but cannot generally be 'cured', ie returning the person to an earlier state of health.

It may be that such diseases now appear commonly in Western societies because previously they were seldom seen as people died prematurely from other causes. However, it is more likely that they are mainly new diseases, caused by conditions of life associated with industrialisation. In support of this view is the finding that, in the Third World, those closest to Western lifestyle are most likely to suffer Western diseases. According to the medical historian Thomas McKeown, the main factors contributing to this include changes in diet - especially a reduction in fibre and increase of fat, sugar and salt, increased use of alcohol, tobacco and illicit drugs, and a reduction of physical exercise (McKeown, 1988, p154). These behaviours often increase, he argues, as Third World populations grow and become more densely distributed and people move from a rural to urban environment.

Recognising that degenerative diseases are now the major killers, it is often argued that health policy should focus on combating the risk factors associated with chronic illnesses, such as tobacco smoking, excessive alcohol intake, insufficient exercise and a high fat diet. If such a policy were successful, it is claimed, vigorous good health could be extended until well into old age and serious illness and decline confined to a short period before death.

2.2 The role of medicine in the decline of infectious diseases

However health is measured, there is no doubt that people living in the West today are much healthier than a few centuries - and even just a few decades - ago. Why this is so is widely misunderstood.

If asked why health has improved in the West, many people would see the advance of science and medicine as the main cause. As science came increasingly to understand the body, (so the reasoning would go), it developed more effective medicines, immunisations and anaesthetics. It would also be assumed that science produced better doctors and better surgeons, and led to the construction of more and better hospitals. All these improvements, it would be argued, have led to the decline in the death rate.

However, this view finds little support among medical historians. According to McKeown, the fall in the death rate, which began in the 18th century, was largely due to three non-medical factors : improvements in nutrition, in public hygiene and birth limitation.

Nutrition The earliest and most important factor in McKeown's view, was the improvement in people's diets which came from advances in agriculture spreading across Europe from about the end of the 17th century onwards. The introduction of new crops such as potatoes and maize, and of improved techniques such as new forms of crop rotation and manuring, increased the availability of food and raised the population's nutritional levels. Further strides in agricultural productivity were made in the

second half of the 19th century with the introduction of mechanisation, which again raised nutritional levels, increased people's resistance to infectious diseases and reduced death by starvation.

Public hygiene A second crucial factor, progressively effective from about 1870 in England and Wales, and somewhat later in other countries, was improvements in public hygiene, such as a cleaner, piped water supply and better sewage disposal. These public health measures significantly reduced risks of exposure to disease, particularly to water-borne diseases such as typhoid and cholera. And, from about 1900, improvements in food hygiene and in milk supply - with the introduction of sterilisation and bottling - were also important.

Birth limitation A third reason for the transformation in health, according to McKeown, was the fall in the birth rate and in family size, beginning among the middle class in the 1870s. If the birth rate had not fallen, McKeown calculates, the present population for England and Wales would now be some 140 million rather than 50 million! Without this limitation on population, he thinks, the other advances would soon have been reversed. Also, he believes, the avoidance of unwanted pregnancies directly affected mortality by virtually eliminating infanticide, probably a significant cause of death up to then.

Medicine Importantly, however, and contrary to popular belief, McKeown doubts that either medical care or specifically immunisation had any significant effect on mortality before the 20th century. Indeed, he concludes that 'they contributed little to the reduction of deaths from infectious disease before 1935, after which the first powerful chemotherapeutic agents, and later antibiotics, came into use' (McKeown, 1979, p77). In other words, although, in the latter part of the 20th century, immunisation, surgery and medical treatment have had a very welcome impact upon suffering, morbidity and mortality, their impact has been relatively late. The most significant improvements in mortality had a lot to do with preventive medicine (in the form of public hygiene measures) and only relatively little (and then only recently) with the modern medical profession and curative intervention. And McKeown claims that his comparative studies of Sweden, France, Ireland and Hungary show a similar pattern, and that comparable conclusions have been drawn in the USA.

In McKeown's conclusion then, while some forms of medical intervention (such as routine treatments like the repair of fractures) have clearly proven successful, it is mistaken to assume that the undoubted improvements in the morbidity and mortality rates of the last three centuries have been mainly due to advances in medical knowledge and in its application. Medicine's role in contemporary health has thus been significantly overestimated, by lay people and medics alike.

So it is that critics of the medical profession, such as Nicki Hart, question its claims. Nevertheless, it has successfully persuaded public and politicians alike that it is the profession's high standards and achievements of medical care, (rather than for instance public hygiene), which have ushered in longer, healthier lives, and on which our personal health continues to depend (N. Hart, 1985, p1). Hence, the profession has been able to achieve a largely uncritical acceptance of the view that the high-technology hospitals, surgeries and clinics characteristic of modern medicine are essential for a high level of health in a population. Critics disagree. And they claim that, even now, we remain largely unaware of what value any clinical treatment has because little treatment has ever been carefully evaluated. Because outcomes of treatments in the NHS have not been systematically documented and analysed, the limited data means that we often cannot be sure which techniques and interventions have been successful and which have not. Thus, we cannot be at all sure of medicine's contribution to the nation's health even today.

Summary

1 The importance of diseases which have threatened humanity has changed over time. Infectious diseases, which spread with the concentration of people in settled communities and low levels of nutrition, have declined and been largely superceded by chronic, degenerative diseases associated with lifestyle factors such as diet, smoking and insufficient exercise.

2 Contrary to popular assumptions, increased life expectancy and improvements in health seem to owe little to advances in science and medicine but reflect improvements beginning in the 18th and 19th centuries in nutrition, public hygiene and birth limitation.

Activity 3 Changing Patterns of Disease

Item A *19th century England*

As time went on, house building could not keep pace with the influx into the towns. Taking in lodgers and sub-letting became the rule. Few families occupied more than a single room, and a two-roomed house might contain as many as twenty people. Cleanliness, privacy, decency, proper sanitation and water supply were all impossible in conditions such as these. The uncleaned privies, in daily use by dozens of people, overflowed and filled the courts with a morass of excrement. This soaked through the ground to contaminate the shallow wells from which the inhabitants drew a scanty supply of water.

Adapted from F. F. Cartwright *A Social History of Medicine*, 1977, pp94-95

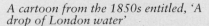

A cartoon from the 1850s entitled, 'A drop of London water'

A cartoon, published in 1852, called 'A Court for King Cholera'.

Sewers being built, 1862

Item B *Changing patterns of disease and death*

Despite a significant fall in cigarette consumption, 32% of the population still smoke cigarettes. This is despite the clear evidence - and public awareness - that cigarette smoking causes about 30% of all cancer deaths (some 29,000 deaths a year through lung cancer alone) and is a significant contributor to coronary heart disease, chronic respiratory disease and other diseases.

Despite considerable health education activity, the 1980s saw virtually no change in the average contribution made by fat to energy derived from food - about 42% compared to the maximum intake of 35% recommended. Between 1980 and 1987 the proportion of adults aged 16-64 in Britain who were overweight or obese increased from 39% to 45% of men and from 32% to 36% of women.

Alcohol consumption has risen with affordability as have deaths from chronic liver disease. Alcohol is also a major cause of accidents in Britain: about 20% of drivers and riders killed in road traffic accidents have blood alcohol levels over the legal limit.

Adapted from *The Health of the Nation*, 1991, pp11; 14

Questions

1 Significant improvements in health and life expectancy began in the 18th century and continued through the 19th. With reference to Item A and other sources, how have historians and sociologists explained these improvements?

2 Read Item B.
   a) What are the main characteristics of the so-called 'new' killer diseases, and how do they differ from the former major killer diseases?
   b) How might health policy to combat the 'new' diseases differ from earlier policy?

3 Theories of Disease

Key Issues

1 How do belief systems about health and disease differ?
2 What are the bases and criticisms of biomedicine?

3.1 'Civilised' vs 'primitive' explanatory medical systems

Closely linked to people's ideas about the structure and functioning of the body are their ideas about why and how people become sick and why and how they recover or don't - ie their theories of disease and treatment, their medical explanatory systems or models.

For perhaps thousands of years, some societies have characterised others as either 'civilised' or 'primitive'. Though the distinction makes a number of contentious assumptions, it remains in popular use and was commonplace even in Western social sciences until about the 1950s. Consequently, it was commonplace, too, to assume that 'civilised' and 'primitive' medical systems clearly differed. The former were assumed to be based on objective and rational science and the latter on ideas of religion, magic and superstition.

Yet, from about the 1950s, social scientists at least have grown cautious about making claims for the superiority of Western thought. For, although many non-Western medical systems are undeniably based on magical or religious beliefs, no clear distinction between 'primitive' and 'civilised' societies is now believed to exist. For instance, many so-called 'primitive' practices - such as prescribing herbal remedies for certain ailments - are now recognised as efficacious (they work) and not at all magico-religious. Whatever else the differences between Western medicine and those practised elsewhere, they are not simply ones of 'rationality' versus 'magic' (Stainton Rogers, 1991, p17) .

3.2 The classification of explanatory medical systems

A number of attempts have been made to classify the range of medical systems which anthropologists have discovered to exist in the world.

1 Dunn, for instance, distinguishes between systems on the basis of the geographical extent of their influence. Thus, *local medical systems*, such as those of the !Kung people of the Kalahari desert, are limited to a small geographical area; *regional systems*, such as Ayurvedic medicine, found throughout the Indian subcontinent, have a wider influence, and *cosmopolitan* medical systems, such as Western medicine (biomedicine), homeopathy and traditional Chinese medicine involving acupuncture, are exported and adopted worldwide.
2 Other classifications focus on the nature of the belief systems. Foster, for instance, distinguishes between what he calls *personalistic* and *naturalistic* systems. Personalistic systems (such as voodoo in Haiti) interpret sickness supernaturally. The sick person is being punished either by an

offended supernatural being (eg a witch or a god) or by an individual practising black magic.

In naturalistic systems, such as in traditional Greek, Indian or Chinese medicine, health and ill-health are explained in terms of a balance or imbalance in what are regarded as the basic elements of the body. In the ancient Greece of Hippocrates (5th century BC), for instance, the human body was believed to comprise four 'humours': blood, phlegm, yellow bile and black bile. Health resulted from the four humours being in correct proportion, and disease from an imbalance or one humour not being adequately mixed with the others. And in traditional Chinese medicine, health reflects an equilibrium of *yin* (representing such negative elements as cold, dampness and darkness) and *yang* (representing the sun, heat, fire and light). An excess of *yin* is believed to cause chills, while excessive *yang* causes fevers.

Whereas personalistic systems require a priest or shaman with magical powers, naturalistic cures require a physician or herbalist who knows which treatments will restore the body's balance. The revived interest in the West in herbalism and the popularity of acupuncture and yoga as forms of therapy reflect the renewed appeal of naturalistic theories and systems in the latter part of this century.

3 One of the most comprehensive classificatory systems is provided by Leslie, who distinguishes between what he calls *mechanistic theories*, such as 'Western medicine', in which the human body is seen as machine-like, and illness seen as a breakdown; *equilibrium theories*, much as the naturalistic theories described above, in which health is seen as a consequence of balance or harmony and illness as their absence; and *ethical theories*, in which health is seen as a consequence of 'right living' and illness as a punishment.

Activity 4 The Causes and Treatment of Disease

Item A *Curative rites among the Ndembu of Zambia*

For the Ndembu, all serious illness is ascribed to causes such as the secret ill-will of sorcerers or witches, or punishment by the spirits of ancestors. These spirits cause sickness in an individual if his family and kin are not 'living well together', and are involved in grudges or quarrelling. Divination (diagnosis) takes place publicly. The Ndembu ritual specialist, the *chimbuki* (shaman), conducts a divinatory seance attended by the victim, his kin and neighbours. The diviner is already familiar with the social position of the patient, who his relatives are, the conflicts that surround him, and other information gained from the gossip and opinions of the patient's neighbours and relatives. By questioning these people and by shrewd observation he builds up a picture of the patient's 'social field' and its various tensions.

Actual divination takes place by peering into medicated water in an old meal mortar, in which he claims to see the 'shadow soul' of the afflicting ancestral spirit. Or he may detect witches or sorcerers who have caused the illness among the spectators. The diviner calls all the relatives of the patient before a sacred shrine to the ancestors, and induces them to confess any grudges and hard feelings they may nourish against the patient.

The patient too must publicly acknowledge his own grudges against his fellow villagers if he is to be free of his affliction.

Treatment involves rituals of exorcism, to withdraw evil influences from the patient's body. It also includes the use of certain herbal and other medicines, manipulation and the application of certain substances to the skin. These remedies are accompanied by dances and songs, the aim of which is the purification of both the victim and the group.

Adapted from C.G. Helman, *Culture, Health and Illness*, 1990, pp210-11

Item B *A shaman*

A shaman from Eastern Russia

Item C 'Colds' and 'chills' in a London suburb

The concepts of 'colds' and 'chills' can be found throughout much of the English speaking world. In a 1978 study of popular explanations in a London suburb, C.G. Helman found that both colds and chills are widely believed to be caused by the penetration of cold or damp across the boundary of the skin and into the body. In general, damp or rain (cold-wet environments) are thought to cause cold-wet conditions in the body, such as a 'runny nose' or a 'cold in the head', while cold winds or draughts (cold-dry environments) cause cold-dry conditions, such as shivering and muscular aches. Once they enter the body, these cold forces can move from place to place - from a 'head cold' for example, down to a 'chest cold'.

Chills occur mainly below the belt ('a bladder chill', 'a chill on the kidneys', 'a stomach chill'), and colds above it ('a head cold', 'a cold in the sinuses', 'a cold on the chest'). These conditions are caused by careless behaviour, by putting oneself in a position of risk vis-à-vis the natural environment : for example, 'by walking barefoot on a cold floor', 'washing your hair when you don't feel well' or 'sitting in a draught after a hot bath'. 'Catching cold' is believed especially likely when temperatures change from hot to cold, going outdoors after a hot bath or when summer gives way to autumn.

Because colds and chills are thought to have been brought about primarily by one's own behaviour, they provoke little sympathy among others. Individuals are often expected to treat themselves by rest in a warm bed, eating warm food and drinking a hot drink.

Adapted from C.G.Helman, *Culture, Health and Illness*, 1990, pp112-13

Questions

1 Read Item A. What are the social functions of Ndembu curative rites?

2 In many societies the shaman combines the roles of a doctor and priest (Items A and B). What does this tell us about views of the causes and treatment of illness in these societies?

3 Ideas about illness in small scale societies are sometimes seen as irrational and 'primitive' by people in the West. Assess this view with reference to Items A and C.

3.3 The bases of biomedicine: the Cartesian revolution, germ theory and the doctrine of specific aetiology

Until well into the 19th century, medicine in Europe comprised a diversity of beliefs and practices, and theories of disease abounded. In the first half of the 19th century, for example, many doctors believed that disease was caused by a miasma. This was believed to be an air-borne poisonous gas, probably coming from sewers and cesspits, which infected open wounds or the lungs. But, as the 19th century proceeded, the diversity of medical belief was gradually contained by the growing acceptance of a developing scientific model. In particular, developments in research introduced new ways of thinking about disease and the body. The medical system of explanation and treatment which resulted is referred to as *biomedicine* or the *biomedical model*, or sometimes as 'Western medicine' because it is the dominant form throughout the West.

Modern biomedicine rests upon two major developments, both of which remain influential. First, the so-called Cartesian revolution (after the 17th century French philosopher René Descartes) encouraged the idea that the body and mind are independent, or at least not closely interrelated. In this mechanistic view, the body is perceived to function like a machine, with its individual parts individually treatable.

The second conceptual shift which transformed medical thinking was Louis Pasteur's development, from the 1850s, of 'germ theory' and Robert Koch's elaboration of it. Germ theory claimed that, in certain (ie infectious) diseases, tiny micro-organisms invisible to the naked eye - 'germs that float in the air', Pasteur called them - are always present. And in the 1870s Pasteur was able to demonstrate that germs were the cause rather than the product of disease. By the 1880s, Robert Koch had elaborated Pasteur's germ theory into the 'doctrine of specific aetiology' which claimed that each disease is always caused by a particular micro-organism (or germ). In each case of a disease, that organism is present.

3.4 Stress and the aetiology of disease

There have been many developments in 20th century medical thinking which have taken medicine beyond germ theory and the Cartesian body-mind dichotomy. One has been the growing acceptance in medical circles of the probable significance of stress in disease aetiology (aetiology means cause).

Biomedicine traditionally concentrated on what disease does organically in the human body. In more recent stress-illness models of disease the actual contraction of a disease is seen as the tail end of a process of becoming ill which begins some time previously. In this view, the 'prior causes' of disease exist in our everyday experience of life. Put simply, personal crises encourage disease by provoking stress - by which is meant actual changes in the body which are either directly harmful to the body or which lower the body's resistance to disease.

The concept of stress was first analysed by Hans Selye in 1936. Stress, for Selye, is a body's physiological response to a *stressor*, that is, a potentially threatening stimulus from outside the body. Faced with a stressor, the body automatically prepares itself for action by making a wide range of physical changes. These changes include increased blood pressure, excessive secretion of adrenalin, the release of a potentially dangerous volume of corticosteroids and a temporary fall in the body's level of immunity. At a moderate level, stress can benefit the individual by better preparing him or her for defence or other adaptation. At higher levels it exhausts the organism and can kill.

In this view, then, the contraction of disease follows a sequence of stages. One model is provided by Hart (1985, p83):

1 potential stressor(s)
2 perception of stressor(s) as threatening
3 stress - the bodily response
4 increased susceptibility, partly through damage to lymphatic system
5 exposure to virus or bacterium or other noxious agent
6 little resistance because of weakened immune system
7 physical symptoms.

Stressors Common stressors include a range of personal crises, such as bereavement, migration, marital conflicts and breakdown, persecution, unemployment, excessive exposure to heat, cold, damp or noise, retirement, and so on.

Stressors may therefore include what Gerhardt called 'long-term difficulties', such as chronic economic insecurity, or more acute 'loss events', which deprive the individual of a valued person, an important social relationship or of a significant social role. And there is now considerable evidence that loss events can lead to disease. For instance, as a number of studies confirm, mortality rates of recently bereaved widowers or of the recently retired are significantly higher than those of men the same age. So too are those for the recently separated and recently divorced.

The idea that anxiety, unhappiness and misery arising from personal crises can lead to illness or even death is not new or uncommon, either in other cultures or even in our own. Among the Nuer of Sudan, for instance, illness is often explained by such events as sexual infidelity. We suggest a link between social relationships and illness when we talk about someone as a 'pain in the neck' or say they'll 'be the death of me yet'. And in the West, the notion of dying of a broken heart is long established in popular culture.

Problems with the stress-illness model

However, there are important problems with models focusing on stress. Firstly, even with a reasonable knowledge of the stressors facing individuals, it is difficult to predict confidently the likelihood of stress - much less of disease - in any particular individual. Different people may or may not perceive the same event as a stressor (ie as a threat). Indeed, even experiences which are culturally valued, such as the birth of a child or promotion, will be perceived by some as threatening. Secondly, people's susceptibility to disease will also be influenced by their differing coping abilities and behaviour. Thirdly, the same stressors can provoke different and unpredictable disease responses. One cannot, for instance, anticipate accurately which organ will be attacked.

3.5 'Alternative' or 'complementary' medicines

In the West, although biomedicine is the dominant explanatory medical system, there have always been alternative or additional systems and practices. But rather than replacing each other they often coexist and even compete over time. In the West, such practices have enjoyed a revival of popularity since the 1960s, in part relating to the growth of interest in new religious movements with which many are ideologically compatible.

Those who base their approach on different explanatory medical systems are known in the West as practitioners of 'alternative' medicines. Many prefer the term 'complementary' medicines to emphasise that they do not necessarily claim to treat all disorders and that they can accept a legitimate role for biomedicine and other medicines. In general, these therapies are based upon naturalistic theories of health and disease, which are claimed to be holistic - by which is meant that the individual is seen as a whole entity in which body, mind and (in some therapies) spirit or soul are closely inter related.

Two of the most institutionalised alternative/ complementary medicines are osteopathy and chiropractic. Osteopathy was developed by an American Civil War army surgeon and focuses attention on the mechanics of the body, on the body's musculoskeletal system. It involves physical manipulation of the body rather than the prescription of medicines or surgery. In practice, however, in the USA particularly, osteopathy has moved very close to conventional medicine in those respects. Chiropractic too focuses on the musculoskeletal system but claims that illness results from lack of normal nerve functions and treats by body manipulation and heat, especially of the spinal column. Although there are signs that chiropractic has gained some respectability among some doctors, and has a growing number of patients, it continues to bear a controversial status in health care.

In addition to these relatively institutionalised practices, with their limited focus on the structural and mechanical problems of the body, are a range of others, such as reflexology, homeopathy, aromatherapy, an imported orthodoxy such as acupuncture, folk healing and faith healing and many more.

The popularity of alternative medicines

In Britain, there has been a growth in popularity of alternative and complementary therapies and a recognition of a certain public disenchantment with orthodox medicine, both to some extent given expression in public pronouncements by the Prince of Wales. This led the British Medical Association to set up, in 1983, a scientific committee to 'consider the feasibility and possible methods of assessing the value of alternative therapies, whether used alone or to complement other treatments' (quoted in Pietroni, 1991).

The committee concluded that the effectiveness of the therapies themselves was impossible to prove scientifically. However, there were so many reports of positive effects from using acupuncture for pain relief and chiropractic or osteopathy for back problems that these therapies should have a place in orthodox treatment. They also endorsed the use of hypnotherapy, biofeedback and some special diets for a number of other conditions. Additionally, the committee concluded that modern conventional medicine was failing to give patients what they wanted and listed a number of the likely appeals of the alternative therapies.

First, patients of alternative therapists liked the quality of care received. Alternative practitioners were felt to be generally able to offer patients more time, were more prepared to listen than busy doctors who could not stop to discuss problems in detail. They seemed therefore more compassionate.

People also liked the 'holistic' approach of alternative therapies which sought to provide care for the whole person rather than simply treating an illness. This suggests that medicine is still widely perceived as being unduly - and detrimentally -

influenced by a Cartesian dichotomy of mind and body.

Patients also liked the use of touch as a means of healing in therapies such as massage, acupressure, osteopathy, chiropractic, reflexology and faith healing - something often perceived to be lacking in orthodox medicine, where it was felt that the technology could come between doctor and patient.

Finally, the very familiarity and relative demystification of orthodox medicine was felt to be counting against it. The BMA committee noted a tendency among some patients to seek therapists who had 'magical' qualities, and whose strange words and unfamiliar practices conveyed to the patients the feeling of benefiting from a powerful healing force (Pietroni, 1991, pp6-7).

Summary

1 A number of classifications of medical explanatory systems have been proposed. One focuses on the geographical extent of a system's influence. Others distinguish between systems which explain disease as a punishment, or as reflecting bodily imbalance or disharmony, or as the breakdown of a machine.

2 The dominant system in Western medicine is biomedicine. It traditionally draws upon Descartes' mechanistic view of the separation of body and mind, Pasteur's germ theory and Koch's doctrine of specific aetiology.

3 Twentieth century developments in biomedicine have included an awareness of the probable role of stress in facilitating disease.

4 There has been a rise of alternative and complementary therapies throughout the West. Their appeal includes an explicitly holistic approach, an apparently more attentive and personalised experience of care, the use of touch in healing and, in some cases, the employment of exotically unfamiliar words and practices.

Activity 5 Competing or Complementary Systems?

Item A *The physico-chemical model of disease*

When I began medical training just before the Second World War, some observant practitioners were already aware that cancer of the lung was becoming a common disease. 'Doctors must become cancer-of-the-lung-conscious,' we were told. The condition was being discovered too late for surgery to be effective and earlier diagnosis was needed. So far as I can recall, there was little discussion of why the disease was increasing, or the possibility that the disease could be due to influences which could be modified or removed.

Today, the importance of smoking, exercise and diet would be given due attention. Nevertheless in medicine as a whole the traditional mechanistic approach remains essentially unchanged and will remain so as long as the concept of disease is based on a physico-chemical model.

Adapted from T. McKeown, *The Role of Medicine*, 1979, pp12-13

Bill Clinton, US President, jogging

Item B *Health and disease as evidence of spirituality*

(In the following extract, the reviewer is comparing a new (1989) edition of the feminist book, *Our Bodies, Ourselves*, with the original edition published in 1978 and noting with misgivings the ideological changes).

I have particular reservations about the way in which illness and health are nowadays being saturated with religious associations. We are told by some complementary therapists that 'wholeness' and 'harmony' will bring total health which can resist any illness. Conflict and imbalance, on the contrary, will lead to 'disease' - a psycho-spiritual, rather than a viral, condition.

It's utterly unimaginable that in 1978 a feminist self-help manual would have included ideas on a par with 'If you believe in God you might get better'. But in 1989 no one seems to blink an eyelid on hearing that 'most spiritual healers see chronic ill health, including devastating diseases like cancer or multiple sclerosis, as having an emotional or spiritual root'.

Adapted from R. Coward 'Body Language: the New *Our Bodies, Ourselves*', *New Statesman and Society*, 8.12.89

Questions

1 a) In Item A, what is meant by the idea that in biomedicine 'the concept of disease is based on a physico-chemical model'?
   b) What are some of the implications of such a model for the treatment of disease?
   c) How might emphasis on factors such as 'smoking, exercise and diet' affect views on the causes and treatment of disease?
2 How does the view of health and illness outlined in Item B differ from the biomedical model?

4 Medicine's Rise to Preeminence

Key Issues

1 What is the source of medicine's (ie the medical profession's) power?
2 How has medicine achieved its current preeminence?
3 What are the threats to medicine's preeminence?

4.1 The source of medical power

What is the basis of medicine's power and influence in society? There are three main types of explanation which differ according to the theoretical preference of those who support them. For neo-Marxists, medicine operates as an institution of the superstructure. In a number of ways, medicine functions to protect the interests of the capitalist class. By conceptualising disease as a merely individual phenomenon and divorcing it from its social structural context, medicine serves to disguise the true nature and aetiology of disease. Medicine - with its massive reliance on drugs and expensive technologies and facilities - also forms part of the profit making commodity production process of capitalism. And, by maintaining the health of the workforce and minimising malingering, medicine improves industrial productivity and profit. The high rewards of medicine reflect the profession's usefulness to the capitalist class in maintaining the status quo.

For functionalists such as Talcott Parsons, however, the prestige and power of medicine derives from practitioners' possession of scarce knowledge and skills which are essential to the community. Their rewards reflect the crucial and effective nature of their knowledge and skills to the community. By implication, a grateful society gives physicians high rewards because of their demonstrated ability to promote good health and longer life.

Those more influenced by Weber, however, see professional power - not least that of the medics - as a consequence of their successful organisation, propagandising and political activity. In a view articulated by Freidson (1970), far from medics being the grateful but passive recipients of high rewards following their impressive demonstration of competence, their power and privilege is a consequence of success in power struggles with competing groups. This success resulted in the state granting medicine two exclusive and crucial rights: to determine both who can legitimately perform the work and how it should be done. Medicine's success in gaining recognition and legitimacy in competition with rival groups of healers had little to do, Freidson believes, with its possessing essential or even particularly valid knowledge. Indeed, it gained its success at a time when its methods were of limited value and in some cases positively dangerous. It achieved success in having its definitions of health, illness and treatment accepted as the only legitimate ones, thereby gaining autonomy and monopoly, centrally important characteristics of a profession. And, concludes Freidson, it is primarily because nurse education and training is seen to lack autonomy - that what nurses learn in their training is believed to be ultimately determined by doctors - that nursing is often excluded from professional status.

4.2 The professionalisation of medicine

Historical studies lend clear support to the view that medical 'success' in gaining power and influence came primarily as a result of organisation and campaigning. A major step towards achieving a monopoly of medical practice came with the Medical Registration Act of 1858. Prior to the Act, 'orthodox' medical practice had consisted in the main of three rival groups, each with their own occupational body which controlled training and entry to the occupation. The physicians and surgeons had high status and treated the well-to-do middle class, while the apothecaries (or apothecary-surgeons) had low status, little training and had lower status patients. Although both physicians and apothecaries tended to use the same practices and drugs, the main difference between them was merely that physicians wrote out their prescriptions (in Latin, demonstrating their superior education) but left the dispensing of the drugs to others, while apothecaries supplied the drugs themselves.

Professional monopoly Medical practitioners had long campaigned for legal measures to ensure their monopoly but many MPs were unsure about whether they could safely entrust it to them. However, as Hart

observed : 'The key to their political success was to join together into a single profession which could be clearly identified and which claimed to offer a uniformly high standard of competence and ethical conduct. By sheltering under the reputation of their profession, doctors appear as a standard product, equally skillful and equally trustworthy' (1985, p115). Finally, the Act was passed and although it did not directly give doctors the legal monopoly for which they had campaigned - because it did not directly outlaw such 'unqualified' practices as homeopathy - it effectively did so indirectly. The newly-established General Medical Council (GMC) was authorised to keep a register of 'suitably qualified' practitioners, from which the likes of homeopaths were excluded. Increasingly, therefore, those wishing to employ medical practitioners, such as voluntary organisations, local governments and the growing middle class, limited their selection to those registered. The Act further squeezed medicine's rival therapeutic groups by preventing 'unqualified' practitioners charging lower fees than those on the GMC's list of the approved.

A second major step towards the establishment of professional monopoly came with the increasing control doctors gained in their dealings with organised working class patients. By the end of the 19th century, voluntary Friendly Societies, consisting mainly of working class men, already offered insurance protection against sickness and death to some 4 million members. Each Society employed one doctor - only doctors registered with the GMC were used - and by the turn of the century some 50% of all general practitioners were employed by them either full time or part time.

Although the Societies provided welcome employment, the doctors greatly disliked the fact that they were supervised by the Society's elected committee to whom a dissatisfied member could complain. Following an intense campaign by doctors and the British Medical Association, the Health Insurance Act of 1911 transferred most of the functions of the Societies, including responsibility for the supervision of the doctors, to local health committees, on which doctors were strongly represented. In addition to freeing general practitioners from patient control and increasing doctors' autonomy, the 1911 Act substantially increased doctors' incomes, encouraged a significant increase in their numbers, brought large numbers of working class people into contact with doctors for the first time and encouraged the concept of the family doctor. And, as Scrambler points out, these changes, and medicine's other political 'successes', were achieved through the active attempts of doctors to influence the state, but before doctors were able to affect significantly the course of most diseases.

The third major piece of legislation which

consolidated and legitimised the position of doctors, though this time particularly hospital doctors, was the 1946 National Health Service Act, which established the NHS. However, although it strengthened the position of the whole profession, the division and gap in status between hospital doctors and general practitioners has remained.

Challenges to medical autonomy

Despite the present position of power of doctors, the profession's autonomy may be under threat from a number of developments. Morgan (1985, pp120-123) identifies four major threats. First, the shift in morbidity from infectious to degenerative diseases, and consequently the probable declining contribution of curative medicine may be undermining the belief of both public and health workers in the legitimacy of the dominance of physicians. A greater emphasis on preventive medicine - if it occurs - is likely to mean a loss of resources for those involved in curative medicine, and a transfer of responsibility and power from doctors to patients and to other health workers.

Secondly, the increasing professionalisation of paramedical occupations, such as physiotherapists and occupational therapists, which has included a growth in degree-level training courses, has been accompanied by a growing independence from doctors.

The third challenge comes from within the medical profession itself. From the early 1970s, junior hospital doctors, dissatisfied with their long hours, poor conditions of work and limited promotional opportunities, began to negotiate independently of their professional superiors whom they felt had not been adequately representing them. The new

contracts they succeeded in negotiating have reduced the advantages of promotion to consultant and reduced junior doctors dependence upon consultants.

And fourthly, the NHS reforms introduced in 1991 brought many more managers and administrators into the health service, and they seem to have limited to some extent the decision making powers of the medical profession.

Summary

1 The power of the medical profession is explained by Marxists as a consequence of its acting in the interests of the ruling class, and by functionalists as a reward for its practice of scarce skills vital to the community.

2 Weberians, however, claim that medicine's power and prestige are a consequence of its successful historical struggles against competing groups thereby gaining the rights of monopoly and autonomy. The 1858 Medical Registration Act, the 1911 Health Insurance Act and the 1946 National Health Act were key successes in this long campaign.

3 Possible threats to medical autonomy come from the possibly declining role of curative medicine; the professionalisation of paramedical occupations; dissatisfied junior doctors; and the 1991 government reforms to the NHS which may have reduced medical influence.

Activity 6   Questioning Professionalism

Item A *St Thomas' Hospital*

In 1871 I entered as a first year student at the newly erected St Thomas' Hospital in London. The ways of the operating surgeon, looking back on them, seem almost incredible. I remember the house surgeon in the theatre with his threaded needles dangling from the front flap of his outworn old coat, the silken threads sweeping the well-worn cloth which had grown old in the presence of sepsis (germs). He always changed into it for an operation. An operation was a dirty job and an outworn coat was a suitable garment! I see it now, faded with age, stained with blood and spotted with pus.

Operation in Bellevue Hospital in the 1870s

And the 'ward sponge' appeared at all dressings. It was simply wrung out in warm water and passed from case to case. It was the fashion then to 'clean up ulcers', and nothing did the work so well as the sponge. An old sister who had spent her life in the service of the hospital once sadly said to me: 'I really do not think the physicians do much good, and as for the surgeons, I think they do as much harm as they do good'.

Adapted from Schools Council History 13-16 Project *Medicine Through Time* Book Three, 1976, pp46-47

Item B *The bases of professionalism*

Given the many forms of treatment which are not properly evaluated, either before being introduced or even after they have been in use for a long time, there seems a problem with Parsons' explanation of the power of medicine. One would expect that in granting a legal monopoly the state would expect the profession to demonstrate a high degree of occupational competence and effectiveness in practice. Yet over a century ago when the profession obtained its legal privileges from the state there would have been even less to go on in terms of effective therapy.

Adapted from N. Hart *The Sociology of Health and Medicine*, 1985, p116

Questions

1 Comment on Nicky Hart's view (Item B) in the light of Item A.
2 Do you think her views are applicable to the medical profession today? Give reasons for your answer.

5 Doctors and Patients

Key Issues

1 How may medicine function as an agency of social control?
2 What are the characteristics of the sick role and how is it created?
3 How do doctors and patients interrelate?

In contemporary Western societies, when people feel ill they are most likely to turn to a doctor. That is particularly the case if we feel the need to be absent from work. We do so because the medical profession has established itself in a strategic position in society. As *the* recognised authority on illness, it has established a monopoly on the official identification of sickness. It has also established a monopoly on the legitimate practice of healing. And having gained the monopolistic power to pronounce individuals either well or ill, the profession has also played a part in shaping ideas and expectations of how those pronounced sick may behave.

5.1 The nature of the sick role

In a pioneering analysis, Talcott Parsons developed the argument that 'being sick' is not simply 'a state of fact' or 'condition' but a specifically patterned social role. And in Western society, the sick role implies four major expectations; two rights and two duties (1951, pp436-37).

Rights

- The sick person is temporarily exempt from 'normal' social roles. The more severe the sickness, the greater the exemption.
- The sick person is not generally held responsible for their condition and so is not usually blamed. A person's illness is usually considered to be beyond their control and not curable simply by will power

or motivation. Moreover, it is accepted that the sick person needs taking care of.

Obligations

- The sick person is expected to see being sick as undesirable. They are under an obligation to try to get well. To encourage that view, the exemption from normal responsibilities is seen as only temporary and conditional upon wanting to get better.
- Given the above, after a certain time the sick person is required to seek technically competent help, usually from a doctor, and to cooperate with the doctor in the process of trying to recover.

The rights and duties depend upon each other. If the sick person does not seek medical advice when 'appropriate', and demonstrate their wish to recover and resume normal responsibilities, their immunity from blame will not hold.

5.2 The sick role as vulnerable and deviant

According to Parsons, the specific rights and duties of the sick role reflect two underlying value themes or characteristics: those occupying it are seen as both vulnerable and deviant.

1 Vulnerability The sick are perceived as vulnerable, first because of threatening symptoms, but also because they are seen as particularly open to exploitation by others. This reflects a particular view of the sick: that they are passive, trusting and prepared to wait for medical help. That they are, in a word, patient.

In this view of sickness, the sick must be looked after. The sufferers are not responsible for their illnesses. Disease is something that happens to people and not something that is within their control. Getting better therefore cannot be achieved by individuals of their own accord. It is up to others to care for and cure them.

That, however, makes people vulnerable to exploitation. First, because the patient must submit his or her body to inspection. And the doctor's healing techniques are often physically invasive, breaching many social taboos, and carry a high potential for intimacy. Secondly, because the relationship is very unequal and requires of the patient a high degree of trust. Social regulation is therefore needed to protect the vulnerability of the patient.

2 Deviance In contrast, however, sick people are also a social threat. They are deviant because they are relieved of their normal social obligations and roles. And they are socially threatening because being allowed to shed normal responsibilities has its attractions, and the more people who feel that, the greater the threat to the social system.

So a second theme - of fear that sickness will be used more or less consciously to evade responsibilities - is ever present. This second theme, then, stresses the difficulty of identifying genuine sickness, the fear of society being exploited and the need for experts to distinguish between the sick and the fake. And the medical profession acts as society's gatekeeper against this form of deviance, seeking to determine who are the genuinely sick, the malingerers and the hypochondriacs. They provide, indeed, a form of social regulation to protect society.

5.3 The sick role and self identity: interactionist approaches

Parsons' ground breaking work, in identifying sickness as a social role shaped by the expectations of others, has been developed by interactionists concerned to explore how the sense of identity of individuals defined sick or disabled is shaped and constructed. Health tends to be associated with moral virtues such as strength, beauty, goodness and competence. Becoming sick or disabled, on the other hand, is to move into a stigmatised status, in which the individual is denied full social acceptance. Thus the sick and disabled tend to be defined and related to - both by health care professionals and lay people - in terms of their condition and according to existing stereotypes associated with it. Negative labels tend to attach to all diseases or impairments, though to some much more than to others.

Any hospital patient, including delivering mothers, may find themselves being treated as if they were children. But the experience of chronic conditions such as epilepsy or AIDS or blindness, for example, is very significantly shaped by societal reaction. Thus, people with physical impairments may find themselves being ignored or spoken to as if they were mentally impaired.

5.4 Critique of Parsons' conception of the sick role

Although Parsons' analysis is valuable, it has been criticised on a number of counts.

Rejecting the sick role First, Parsons' model assumes that, due to prior socialisation, once sick the individual voluntarily adopts the sick role. However, though the sick person may be officially released from normal social obligations, they do not always comply voluntarily with the expectations of the sick role. For instance, some resist the sick role, even when they feel ill - because they resist the dependency required, or have an aversion to medical treatment or simply cannot afford not to continue working. Some avoid the public sick role because their particular disease is stigmatised. Indeed, as discussed in more detail below, although doctors may try to control the interaction in a consultation, the patient is often far from passive. Rather than both parties merely playing out preordained roles, what often happens between doctor and patient, according to interactionist research, is more a process of negotiation.

Blaming the sick Secondly, the sick person's 'right' to be absolved of blame and provided with care does not always apply, and people are sometimes held responsible for their disease. While acute illnesses such as measles are seldom considered the sick person's fault, with a number of chronic conditions, such as heart disease, lung cancer and high blood pressure, the sufferer's lifestyle - and therefore the sufferer - is commonly held responsible. In a study of social workers' attitudes to alcoholics, for instance, Chalfont and Kurtz (1971) found that alcoholics were not generally accepted as legitimate incumbents of the sick role because they were seen as able to avoid their disorder if they chose to.

Indeed, in stigmatised diseases generally the sufferer is often not accepted as legitimately sick. Inevitably, the experience of suffering a stigmatised disease is very different. He or she is often blamed for their condition and not accorded the usual rights to care or even compassion. Epilepsy, leprosy, syphilis and AIDS, for instance, have all been associated with evil at different times in the West, and those afflicted denied care or even persecuted.

Chronic illness Thirdly, Parsons' model fits acute illness better than chronic. Getting well is not an expectation in chronic conditions such as diabetes or blindness. And in chronic cases, acting the sick role is often less appropriate and less functional, for both the individual and the social system. Whereas the acutely sick person is relieved of their normal responsibilities and encouraged into dependency, a more appropriate response to the chronically sick or impaired often is to encourage them to continue their social role as far as they are able.

Activity 7 The Sick Role

Item A *Withholding the sick role*

Mr Brown received a severe electric shock at work. He appeared to recover completely. Several months later he went to see his doctor complaining about chest pains which he believed were caused by the shock. A thorough examination revealed no organic damage. Mr Brown's GP then referred him to a specialist. Again there appeared to be nothing wrong. Mr Brown rejected this conclusion. The pains were getting worse. He said, 'They seem to think I'm imagining things - I know what I've got'. This disagreement changed the relationship between Mr Brown and his GP from warmth and trust to hostility and suspicion.

Adapted from M. Balint 'The Patient's Offers and the Doctor's Responses' in D. Tuckett and J. M. Kaufert (eds) *Basic Readings in Medical Sociology*, 1978, pp135-138

Item B *Self identity and the social role of blindness*

According to psychological theory, blindness encourages certain personality characteristics, such as passivity and compliance. However, Scott's classic (1969) study of blindness, in which he studied the interactions of health care professionals and blind clients in the United States, suggests a different explanation. He argues that the 'blind personality' is the product of a socialisation process, in which the experts emphasise the likely psychological problems of the client adjusting to loss of sight. 'Blindness' then is a learned social role, whereby people come to accept (particularly) the expert's view of who they are. In Sweden, where blindness is viewed less as a loss and more as a technical handicap, blind people are more integrated and the blind personality is less common.

Adapted from S. Taylor 'Beyond the Medical Model', *Sociology Review*, September 1994, p6

Item C *Reactions to stigmatised diseases*

In the Middle Ages, epidemic diseases such as plague were often the metaphors for the breakdown of social, religious and moral order. This century, cancer - and more recently AIDS - have been used as contemporary metaphors for evil. Crime, drug abuse, strikes, immigration and even political dissent have all been described as 'a cancer', a demonic force gradually destroying the very fabric of society.

These metaphors of ill health can seriously affect how the sufferers perceive their own condition, and how other people behave towards them. In her study of 100 women with breast cancer, Peters-Golden described how the stigma associated with breast cancer can cause other people to avoid the sick person and withdraw their social support from her. After diagnosis, 52% found they were 'avoided' or 'feared', 14% felt they were pitied and only 3% thought people were nicer to them than previously.

Adapted from C.G. Helman *Culture, Health and Illness*, 1990, pp99-100

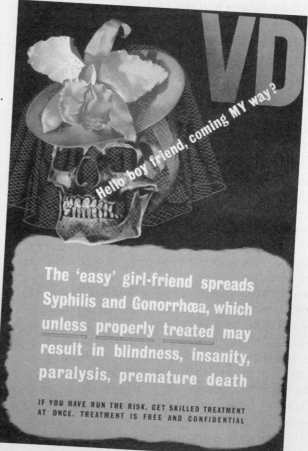

A poster about VD (venereal disease) issued during World War II

Questions

1 With some reference to Parsons' idea of the sick role, explain Mr Brown's reactions to the doctors in Item A.

2 Illness or disability can be viewed in many different ways. With reference to Items B and C, discuss the implications of this for patients' wellbeing.

5.5 Doctor-patient relationships

Parsons' sick role model is best seen as an ideal type (see p389 for an explanation of ideal types). In reality the doctor-patient relationship shows significant variations. It is often distant from Parsons' image of harmony and cooperation, with the patient as compliant, cooperative and submissive. Both doctors and patients complain about the other. For instance, Cartwright (1967) found that 56% of the general practitioners she surveyed complained that their patients lacked sufficient humility and that more than a quarter complained that over half of their patients consulted them for trivial reasons. This and other empirical research, which shows a range of doctor-patient interaction, has prompted the development of a number of classificatory schemes to try to conceptualise the variations.

Degrees of control Parsons himself acknowledged that doctor-patient relationships could take different forms. He constructed a model which allows for different degrees of control between doctor and patient. The terms in brackets characterise the relationship.

1 High physician control, low patient control (paternalism).
2 Both have knowledge and are on relatively equal footing (mutuality).
3 Patient control high, doctor control low (consumerist).
4 Doctor reduces control of consultation but patient continues to adopt passive role (default).

Another way of looking at the relationship, developed by Byrne and Long (1976), concentrates on the communication between doctor and patient. They found that consultation styles ranged from *doctor-centred* (making very substantial use of the doctor's knowledge and experience) to *patient-centred* (making use of the patient's knowledge and experience), although, significantly, doctor-centred interaction was by far the most prevalent. One doctor explains : 'The doctor's primary task is to manage his time. If he allows patients to rabbit on about their conditions, then the doctor will lose control of time and will spend all day in his surgery listening to irrelevant rubbish. Efficient doctoring is characterised by a quick clean job' (quoted in Hart, 1985, p104).

Controlling information While control can be exercised by the doctor attempting to direct the conversation and limit the patient's contributions to those the doctor is interested in, it can also be exercised by the doctor restricting the information given to the patient. And there is considerable evidence of this, so providing a major source of dissatisfaction among patients. This control of information may be interpreted in part as a professional strategy to protect the social distance between doctor and patient by reinforcing the perception by the patient of a 'competency gap'. According to a number of writers, a major source of a profession's power is its ability to develop social distance between its practitioners and its 'customers'. This, according to Johnson (1972), is primarily determined by the perception of a so-called 'competence gap'. The greater the perceived gap between the professional's and the customer's knowledge and skills in that particular area, the greater the professional's dominance and the customer's uncertainty and dependence.

There are also some specific benefits for doctors of the limitation of information to patients. It may cover up their own uncertainties about diagnosis or the likely success of treatment, or minimise the ability of patients to evaluate the doctor's performance and to detect mistakes if they occur. Thus, restricting information perpetuates patients' uncertainty and limits their role in decision making while maintaining the doctor's control and the prestige of the profession.

Class and gender Doctor-patient interaction, including the degree of relative control and the extent to which it is doctor or patient-centred, is significantly influenced by the class and sex of the patient and, according to some American research, by the class origins of the doctor. Middle class patients have longer consultations, and ask for and get more information. The social distance and 'competence gap' between doctors and their working class patients is wider than between doctors and their middle class patients. It is made even wider because doctors are less willing to divulge information to working class patients. Similarly, women are generally less happy with doctor-patient interaction, particularly when the doctor is male.

Severity of diseases Whereas other analyses have focused on power and control as a key to doctor-patient relationships, Szasz and Hollender (1956) claim that the main factor influencing the relationship is the severity of the disease. They identify three types of relationship.

1 **The activity-passivity model** (doctor active, patient passive) applies where the patient is seriously ill and helpless because of serious injury, as in a medical emergency. Typically, the situation is desperate, with decision making and power all on the side of the doctor and the patient contributing little or nothing.
2 **The guidance-cooperation model** (doctor guiding, patient cooperating) is most likely when the patient has an infectious disease such as flu or chickenpox. The patient feels they know what is happening and can cooperate with the doctor by

following his or her guidance but the doctor makes the decisions.

3 **The mutual participation model** (doctor and patient fairly equal) applies to the management of chronic illnesses which involve a lot of self care. Here, patient and doctor work together to control disease in a relationship of relative equality.

In the activity-passivity and guidance-cooperation models, the doctor can be seen to be capable of performing the social control function Parsons described. However, where the relationship is egalitarian rather than asymmetrical, medicine's social control function is absent. This reinforces the point above, that it is chronic illness which Parsons' sick role model deals with least satisfactorily. As Hart points out, 'by the fact of its persistence, chronic illness has proved resistant to treatment and, by exposing the limitations of medicine, it undermines the technical superiority of the doctor (1985, p102). This can help transform the therapeutic relationship. First, the patient may well come to be more of an expert on his or her own condition than the doctor. Secondly, as no cure is available the doctor may be able to offer little other than a signature on an invalidity certificate. In other words, the doctor can merely legitimise the deviance and give formal long term permission for role avoidance.

Context Finally, many writers note that the doctor-patient relationship is also significantly affected by the context in which it takes place. Doctor-patient interaction differs in the consulting room, in the patient's home and in the hospital.

5.6 The hospital and the mortification of the self

It is in the hospital that the pressure to adopt Parsons' passive sick role is greatest. In this setting, doctors possess much more power to achieve conformity. And patients find that their condition as sick becomes a master status which dominates their identity. As a result their ability to influence events is minimised.

This shift in the balance of power is well illustrated by Erving Goffman's analysis of 'total institutions' (1961). Total institutions are organisations in which people sleep, work and take leisure and include prisons, monasteries, residential homes for the elderly and boarding schools. They are relatively 'cut off' from the world outside and 'inmates'' activity is regulated from above according to a plan or timetable which suits the organisation. Total institutions typically aim to effect significant change in their residents and often begin this process with rituals of admission which Goffman described as involving 'a mortification of the self'.

Mortification of self The procedures involved in admission to hospital are in effect a *rite de passage* which signify that a person is moving from one status to another. The old identity is stripped away and a new one allocated. The patient is delivered and passed over by kin to an unknown person impersonally identified by a uniform as staff. Personal clothing and possessions are removed and loss of control may be reinforced by cleansing procedures such as shaving, bathing or enemas being imposed by people in white, who hereafter clearly have a right to manipulate and act on the patient's body. Symbolising this new identity is an identity bracelet, signifying the patient's anonymity and lack of allies, and a dossier of personal notes on the patient which staff may consult but which the patient may not. This asymmetry of power is further symbolised by the uniforms and insignia of office of medical and nursing staff and the patient's state of semi-undress.

And the process of social and psychological stripping of identity continues after admission since daily personal routines which preserve identity outside cannot be maintained and clearly count for nothing. Being perpetually dressed for bed highlights the irrelevance of time. Attempts to restore a sense of personal identity by drawing on past experience - sharing reminiscences or photos - are ineffectual given the shortage of staff time. And the lack of personal power is further highlighted by the unpredictability and brevity of visits from the consultant physician whose decisions are of central importance but whose comings and goings are little influenced by the patient. And when a consultation does occur, often only a flimsy screen and a few feet of space may prevent the patient's neighbours from hearing of his or her most intimate concerns. Thus to the fears and anxieties of threatening symptoms is added an equally threatening transformation of self which strips away a person's social and psychological props and undermines their self-esteem. (For further discussion of Goffman's views on total institutions, see pp380-381).

5.7 The medicalisation of deviance

In Parsons' view, medicine is an institution of social control. It formally defines a person's condition as deviant, then functions to control the deviant's behaviour in ways which minimise risks to society.

However, medicine's social control function has grown as it has been given responsibility for an ever greater proportion of deviant behaviours. In a process sometimes called the 'medicalisation of deviance', undesirable and deviant behaviour - previously typically adjudged by religion (as sinful) or the law (as criminal) - has increasingly been redefined by the medical profession as sickness. And its containment is therefore seen in medical terms. Deviant behaviours relatively recently defined as sickness or evidence of sickness by doctors, especially psychiatrists, include alcoholism, drug addiction, homosexuality, arson, promiscuity, suicide, overeating, child abuse, civil disobedience and even participation in a religious cult. In an extreme form of the tendency, in the former Soviet Union, people were defined as sick and locked away in psychiatric hospitals for unacceptable political views.

However, just as medicine can be seen as an instrument of control of deviant behaviour, so claiming the sick role can be people's method of dissent. It can become their act of refusal or strategy of passive resistance, in which they express dissent from other social roles. For instance, the epidemic of hysteria among middle and upper class Victorian women can be seen as an expression of dissent against their limiting social roles. Or high absenteeism from work may be an indication of worker dissatisfaction. However, although such a tactic may win temporary relief, it typically fails to address the social arrangements which are the underlying causes of tension and is thus usually only a short term escape.

Summary

1 Medicine's monopolies include a monopoly on officially pronouncing people either well or ill. Once diagnosed as officially sick, people are assigned to what Parsons identified as a socially prescribed sick role, in which individuals are absolved from blame and accorded support on condition that they demonstrate their wish to recover.

2 The sick are seen as both vulnerable and deviant. Because sickness can be used to evade social responsibilities, doctors act as society's gatekeepers - as agents of social control - to prevent abuse of the system.

3 However, Parsons is criticised for overlooking those who actively resist the sick role, and those diseases for which the individual is blamed or even punished. The sick role model also seems less appropriate for chronic conditions.

4 Interactionists develop Parsons' insights by identifying the stigma often attached to the sick role and the consequences of this for people's identity.

5 Different analyses of doctor-patient interaction focus on the relative power and control exercised by each, the doctor or patient-centredness of the communication, the severity of the patient's disease, and the location in which contact occurs.

6 Parsons' passive sick role is most likely to be adopted in hospitals, where the power difference between doctor and patient is greatest. This is facilitated by hospital procedures which can effect the 'mortification' of the patient's self.

7 There is evidence of a growing 'medicalisation of deviance' whereby deviant behaviour is defined as sickness requiring medical treatment.

Activity 8 The Power of Medicine

Item A Doctors and patients

Four out of five family doctors would lie to a dying patient, according to a survey by *New You* magazine. Doctors said that they would keep the truth from a patient they felt could not cope, but many just did not know how to break the bad news, the Gallup poll found. The survey said that 94% of adults questioned wanted to be told if they were dying.

The survey also found that 44% of the 1,050 patients questioned felt their doctors did not properly explain their illness and treatment. Two thirds claimed they had been 'fobbed off' with hastily written prescriptions, and most appealed for more openness from doctors.

Adapted from 'GPs "Would Lie to Dying Patients"', *Independent*, 5.3.90

Item B Doctor-patient negotiation

As well as having to interpret and explain his symptoms to himself and the doctor, the patient is also 'figuring out' the doctor. Both parties are 'sizing each other up'. The patient may not agree with the doctor's interpretation of the symptoms. One young woman, consulting the doctor about her young child whose problem the doctor had interpreted as unimportant and 'nothing to worry about', persistently reiterated that the symptoms in her child were both unusual and worrying, 'Yes, but it's most unusual for him to keep vomiting up his food like this. And as I say, he's never been like this before.' In cases such as this, the patient may make further and more obvious attempts to persuade the doctor to acknowledge her own perspective: 'I said, "Well, what about those dizzy spells I've been having, doctor?" And he just sat back and stared at me blankly...so to help him I said, "Could it be anything to do with my age?"'

Adapted from G. Stimson and B. Webb 'The Face-to-Face Interaction and After the Consultation', in D. Tuckett and J. M. Kaufert (eds) *Basic Readings in Medical Sociology*, 1978, p147

Item C *Informing patients*

In a report today by the Audit Commission, recommendations are made for far reaching changes in the way patients are given crucial information about hospital operations, the likely complications and the chances of success.

The report is critical of the small amount of time doctors spend discussing patients' options for major treatment. Patients with solid breast lumps, for example, will have about ten minutes to discuss the diagnosis and options for treatment. In the majority of urology clinics, men with a prostate problem are put on a surgical waiting list after a consultation that on average lasts seven minutes. In that time the patient is examined and hears everything he is going to hear about his condition, treatment, surgical procedure, risks and outcomes before he is admitted as an in-patient. The study found that half of urologists and surgeons in out-patient clinics do not mention the risks and complications associated with

Doctor and patient - a typical image from a West End play

prostate surgery unless the patient asks. Patients treated in hospital after a stroke are often sent home without fully understanding what has happened to them or what their treatment involves, says the report.

Adapted from D. Fletcher 'Give Hospital Patients back their Dignity, says Watchdog', *Daily Telegraph*, 24.11.93

Item D *The medicalisation of deviance*

At first slowly, such things as hysteria, hypochondriasis, obsessive-compulsive neuroses and depression were added to the category of illness. Then, with increasing zeal, physicians and especially psychiatrists began to call 'illness' anything and everything in which they could detect any sign of malfunctioning which deviates from the norm. Hence agoraphobia is illness because one should not be afraid of open spaces. Homosexuality is illness because heterosexuality is the social norm. Divorce is illness because it signals failure in marriage.

Adapted from T. Szasz *The Myth of Mental Illness*, 1974, p45

Questions

1 Give a sociological explanation for the behaviour of the doctors in Items A and C.
2 The roles of doctor and patient are not simply acted out, they are negotiated. Comment on this statement with reference to Item B.
3 Medicine is a very effective form of social control. Comment on this view with some reference to Item D.

6 The Social Patterning of Health and Disease

Key Issues

1 How do different social classes, gender and ethnic groups differ in their mortality and morbidity rates?
2 How do sociologists account for the differences?

Mortality (death) and morbidity (sickness) rates vary significantly between societies and between groups within societies. In this part, the focus is on differences related to social class, gender and ethnic groups in Britain. (For a discussion of health in the Third World, see pp601-606).

6.1 Health and social class

The most comprehensive information on class-related health in Britain in the last twenty years comes from two sources: the *Report of the Working Party* on *Inequalities in Health*, known as the *Black Report* after its Chairman Sir Douglas Black and published in 1980, and *The Health Divide*, first published in 1988 but updated and republished in 1992. In essence their conclusions are the same.

'Despite more than thirty years of a National Health Service expressly committed to offering equal care for all', and despite rising standards of health in the general population since World War Two, Black found: (i) that there remained 'a marked class gradient' in health'; (ii) that such class differences were more marked in Britain than in many comparable countries; and (iii) that in certain respects these class differences were increasing (Townsend and Davidson, 1982, p15). Research conducted throughout the following decade and collated in *The Health Divide* (1992) confirmed that despite a continuing improvement in the nation's health the gap between the classes had continued to widen through the 1980s.

Class and mortality

At every stage of life, from birth to old age, mortality and survival rates show similar patterns: whether newly born or elderly, the higher the occupational class the better the chance of survival.

With regards to the causes of death, the lower classes are more vulnerable to almost all the killer diseases, whether the 'major' contemporary killer diseases - coronary heart disease, stroke and lung cancer - or the 'minor' ones. In one analysis by Townsend, mortality rates for lower class males were higher in 65 out of 78 disease categories and for lower class females in 62 out of 82. The only exception to this trend for both males and females was in malignant melanoma (skin cancer caused by over-exposure to the sun) and for females three other forms of cancer, including cancer of the brain and of the breast (the remainder showed no clear pattern). Accidental death, whether by violence or injury, is also more common in the lower classes. Moreover, the gap has increased during the 1980s as death rates have declined faster among the higher classes than among the lower, particularly from lung cancer and heart disease.

Class and morbidity

As well as being more likely to die at any age, the available evidence suggests that the lower socioeconomic groups experience more sickness and ill-health throughout their lives. Disadvantage begins early. Lower class children are more likely to begin life with a low birth weight, and as children are more likely to suffer a range of health disadvantages including obesity, cerebral palsy, hearing and visual impairment, accidents and a higher incidence of decaying and missing teeth.

Social class differences in childhood increase significantly in adulthood. Although the working class are more likely to suffer acute (short term) diseases, the gap between classes is greatest for a whole range of chronic (long term) conditions, including bronchitis, arthritis and rheumatism, obesity, hypertension (high blood pressure), haemorrhoids ('piles'), angina, varicose veins, persistent coughs, back trouble, headaches, heart palpitations, alcohol-related diseases, anxiety states and psychotic disorders. Not surprisingly, working class people are also more likely to perceive their health as poor.

6.2 Health and gender

Throughout the industrial world, and in almost all other countries, males live shorter lives and are more likely to die at any age than females. However, despite higher male death rates, it is females who are most likely to experience ill health.

Gender and mortality

Over the last 100 years, in all contemporary advanced industrial societies, life expectancy has increased for both males and females but remains higher for females. In the UK in 1994, average female life expectancy was approximately 78 years and 72 for males.

While British males are particularly prone to die of heart disease, lung cancer, bronchitis, and accidents and other violent deaths, for women, cancers of the breast, cervix and uterus are major causes of mortality. However, contrary to popular misconceptions of its being overwhelmingly a 'man's disease', coronary heart disease is *the* major female killer, though female rates are lower than male.

Gender and morbidity

Paradoxically, although women live longer than men, at almost any age more women claim to be suffering from physical and mental disorders. In particular, women report a higher incidence of chronic diseases, including strokes, rheumatoid arthritis, diabetes and varicose veins, which are sufficiently severe to limit their activity. The higher risks of chronic disease, and women's longer life expectancy, help explain why females also constitute two thirds of those with disability. Females are also more likely to have been hospitalised, including in mental hospitals, where they are a majority of those diagnosed as suffering from a neurotic, psychotic, depressive or dementia disorder. Not surprisingly, perhaps, women in or out of hospital also seem to be more at risk of iatrogenic disease (disease caused by medical treatment), especially cardiovascular disease associated with the contraceptive pill and disorders following a hysterectomy or after post-menopausal oestrogen administration.

6.3 Health and ethnicity

Comparing the health levels of different ethnic groups is difficult because the data is seriously inadequate. Before the 1991 Census which asked for the ethnic group of respondents, researchers had to rely mainly on documents such as birth and death certificates, which merely record an individual's country of birth, in order to identify members of ethnic groups. So, when comparing mortality rates, for instance, the ethnic origin of people born in this country will not be evident on death certificates which merely identify their place of birth. And conversely, for people of European origin born in the Caribbean, Africa or Asia, their ethnic group may also not be evident. Consequently, apart from comparisons of mortality rates between people born in Britain and people born abroad, very little is still known about the health and morbidity of British born ethnic minorities.

However, insofar as the ethnic minority population have been identified as having a background in Africa, the Indian subcontinent (including India, Pakistan, Bangladesh and Sri Lanka) or the Caribbean, research suggests some differences in the patterns of mortality and morbidity between ethnic groups and between them and the white population. However, the data remains limited and must be viewed cautiously.

Ethnicity, mortality and morbidity

Despite the methodological difficulties, a number of studies have now provided generally consistent data on causes of mortality among different ethnic groups. These analyses of the causes of mortality also suggest some likely patterns of morbidity among ethnic minorities. Provisional findings suggest that those groups originally from India, Pakistan, Bangladesh, Africa and the Caribbean are more likely than the white population to die from heart disease (excepting Africans and Afro-Caribbeans), stroke (especially Africans and Afro-Caribbeans, who also suffer very high rates of

hypertension - high blood pressure), liver cancer, tuberculosis, diabetes and maternal mortality. And Caribbean and Asian communities seem to suffer disproportionately from deaths due to accidents, poisonings and violence. However, mortality (and probably morbidity) rates are low for obstructive lung infections such as bronchitis and many types of cancer, notably lung cancer.

All these ethnic minorities also tend to have higher rates of stillbirths (born dead), perinatal mortalities (dead within one week or stillborn) and neonatal mortalities (dead within the first month). However, only Afro-Caribbeans and Pakistanis continue to show 'excess mortality throughout infancy' (Whitehead, 1992, p260).

Additionally, a small number of relatively rare diseases seem to attack a particular group disproportionately, though this is uncommon: most suffer and die from the same diseases as the white majority. However, children from Asian families seem to have an above average risk of developing rickets, people from the Caribbean of contracting sickle-cell anaemia and a number of immigrant groups have a relatively high risk of contracting tuberculosis.

The Afro-Caribbean population also appear more likely than whites to be admitted to mental hospital, and more likely to be committed on a compulsory admission. Once there, they are more likely to receive relatively harsh forms of treatment such as electro-convulsive therapy, ie electric shock treatment.

Activity 9 Inequalities in Health

Item A *Chronic and acute sickness by sex and socioeconomic group, 1984*

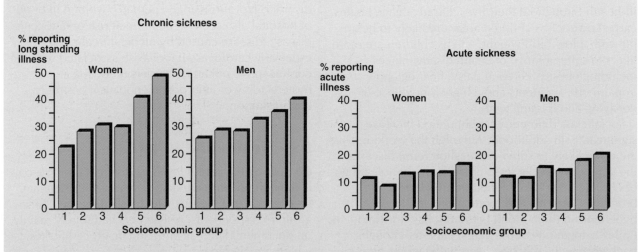

Adapted from General Household Survey 1984 in H. Graham 'Women, Health and Illness', *Social Studies Review*, September 1987, p17

Item B *Social class differentials*

The *Health and Lifestyle Survey* of 1986 found a remarkably regular and in some cases steep social class gradient with a variety of measures of morbidity and fitness. For example, with self-perceived health the percentage of men believing their own health was only fair or poor increased from 12% of Class I to 36% of Class V. Likewise, when the experience of illness was assessed using a list of twenty-four common symptoms, the gradient appeared for a wide range of conditions from persistent cough and back trouble in men to headaches, palpitations, deafness and anxiety in women. Physiological measures of fitness, like weight, blood pressure and lung function showed the same trend. The author of the study concluded that there was strong evidence of a high degree of inequality in health, not just in a particularly disadvantaged subgroup, but throughout the social scale.

Adapted from M. Whitehead, *The Health Divide*, 1992, p234

Item C *Perinatal and infant mortality by mother's country of birth*

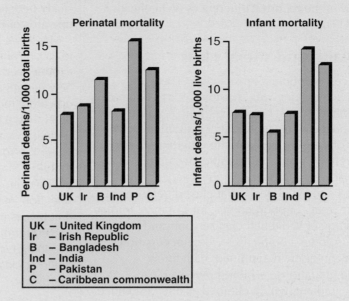

Adapted from P. Townsend et al *Inequalities in Health*, 1992, p261

Questions

1 Summarise the relationship between health and social class indicated by Items A and B.
2 Compare the incidence of perinatal and infant mortality in the groups identified in Item C.

6.4 Sociological explanations of health inequalities

Sociological explanations of differences in health between different groups can be classified into four main theoretical approaches, (i) social constructionist approaches, (ii) theories of natural or social selection, (iii) materialist or structuralist explanations and (iv) cultural and behavioural explanations.

1 **Social constructionist** explanations claim that, for a variety of reasons, the evidence on which analyses are based is largely invalid. It may be because of methodological inadequacies or to do with the socially constructed (and changing) nature of key concepts. One social constructionist approach is the labelling perspective. This approach challenges the validity of the statistics by stressing that illness is a social construction and that disease labels are applied differentially to different groups, either class, gender or ethnic. Thus, doctors are believed to apply specific disease labels more readily to some groups than others. So different morbidity rates are primarily a product of differential labelling rather than a reflection of objective 'reality'.

2 **Natural and social selection** approaches assume that the evidence is essentially valid. Natural selection interpretations are applied particularly to gender and ethnic groups and seek to explain their health differences in terms of alleged genetic, biological or physiological differences between groups. Social selection analyses suggest that rather than seeing ill-health as a consequence of low social class position, it is instead a major cause of class position. Thus one reason for people being in a high social class is their relatively good health.

3 **Materialist-structuralist** analyses seek to explain the rates of mortality and morbidity of different classes, gender and ethnic groups by focusing on their different location in the social structure and the different material circumstances and experiences which result from this.

4 **Cultural-behavioural** analyses also assume the general validity of the evidence and attribute group differences to members' allegedly different norms, values, knowledge and behaviours.

There is widespread agreement among sociologists with Black's and Whitehead's conclusions that structural and cultural factors are the main contributors to health differentials between classes, that in reality these factors are intertwined, and that constructionist and selectionist explanations play some part in the reported differences (Whitehead, 1992, p311).

6.5 Health and social class

1 Social constructionist approaches There are difficulties in making valid comparisons of different occupational groups' health over time because occupational classes are social constructions which change; jobs are reclassified into different classes; and the relative status and significance of jobs change. However, most researchers accept, with Townsend and Whitehead, that class differences in health are 'real'. Support comes, for instance, from a famous study of Whitehall civil servants and another of British soldiers - both cases where occupational status was precisely determined, with finely demarked gradations - which showed a clear mortality gradient, which climbed as one descended the ranks.

From the labelling perspective however, different social classes are vulnerable to being differentially labelled. This argument has been applied particularly to mental illness - for instance by Scheff (1975), who argued that those possessing least power and fewest resources are most likely to be labelled mentally ill. Hence the lower classes appear most in the statistics of the officially designated mentally disordered because doctors are particularly ready to interpret their behaviour as symptomatic of mental illness.

In a perhaps rare, non-psychiatric, example of labelling, Marmot, Booth and Beral (1981) argue that coronary heart disease gradually came to be perceived by doctors between the 1930s and 1960s less as a 'disease of affluence' but as one associated with the lower classes. As a result doctors came to diagnose an increasing proportion of fatal heart conditions in the working class as coronary heart disease, rather than as other types of heart ailment as they had done previously.

2 Social selection In this interpretation, relatively poor working class health is seen primarily, not as a consequence of social class membership, but as a cause. The concentration of ill health in the lower social classes is said to reflect processes of *social selection*. It is ill health which results in the disproportionate concentration of sickly people in the lower strata, not the circumstances of working class life. People's health largely determines their class position, for the sickly either sink or fail to rise and the healthiest and most energetic are likely to be upwardly mobile and successful.

From an early stage, in the 'sifting and sorting' processes of school, ill health means poor

performance and so the sickly are less likely to be allocated positions - and later, jobs - involving pressure and responsibility. Once into the job market, sickly people find themselves either unable to move upwards or unable to avoid drifting downwards.

Meadows (1961), for instance, found that compared to a control group, chronic bronchitis sufferers experienced downward occupational mobility between 45 and 64 years of age. Illsley (1980) found upwardly mobile females in Aberdeen were healthier, taller, had a better physique and had a lower perinatal death rate in their first pregnancies than either the socially non-mobile or the downwardly mobile.

However, although differential labelling and social selection analyses contribute to explanations of class differences in health, theories which stress structural and cultural factors - the material circumstances, occupations, lifestyles, behaviours and beliefs of different classes - are generally regarded as more significant.

3 Cultural-behavioural explanations These approaches interpret differences in health primarily as reflecting the different lifestyles and behaviours of social classes and the knowledge, attitudes and values of people in different social positions. As MacIntyre reports, 'epidemiological studies have shown that smoking and drinking, and a range of other behaviours such as taking recreational physical exercise, diet, engaging in high risk activities and so forth are associated with health and risk of ill-health or death, and are differentially engaged in by different social groups' (1986, p408). Often implicit in such an approach - and common in health promotional literature - is the view that such apparently health damaging behaviours are essentially 'voluntary'. Hence, improvements to health will be effected primarily by improving individuals' knowledge and reforming individuals' attitudes and behaviours. By contrast structuralist analyses, which locate the key factors in the social and physical environment, imply intervention at the social level. Hence the two approaches are often seen as competing.

Behavioural explanations tend to focus on allegedly health damaging habits and lower socioeconomic groups' alleged underuse of health services. Four 'voluntary' behavioural habits are most commonly associated with health and ill health: tobacco smoking, alcohol consumption, diet and exercise. Of the four, cigarette smoking has been most clearly demonstrated to be a major cause of premature death, ill-health and disability. The practice is also highly class related. In 1982, 20% of men and 21% of women in professional jobs smoked cigarettes, compared with 49% and 41% of men and women in unskilled manual occupations (quoted in MacIntyre, 1986, p407), though with significant area variations (Blaxter, 1990, p117).

'Heavy' drinking too seems to be associated with class, though not in a wholly straightforward way. For instance, although one estimate claims that, in 1982, 8% of men in professional occupations were 'heavy' drinkers compared to 33% of men in unskilled manual occupations (MacIntyre, 1986, p407), Blaxter notes that geographical differences can reverse this commonly assumed relationship between alcohol consumption and social class. In London and in owner-occupied, non-industrial, middle class 'high status' areas elsewhere, her research found 'non-manual men to be the more frequent heavy drinkers' (Blaxter, 1990, p119). And both moderate to high consumption and abstinence have been found to be associated with poor health (Marmot et al, 1981b).

A number of studies have also found that diet is associated with social class, with 'better' diets found in higher social classes. (Blaxter found that the most effective indicator of a nutritionally approved diet combined seven specific food habits : (i) eating predominantly wholemeal/brown bread, (ii) low fat or polyunsaturated spreads, (iii) regular fresh fruit in summer and (iv) salads or raw vegetables in winter, and limiting (v) chips and (vi) fried foods to twice a week and (vii) avoiding daily sweets and biscuits; 1990, p123).

And exercise also appears related to socioeconomic group, (as well as to age, geographical location and sex) though again not entirely straightforwardly. Blaxter (1990, p122) found that a higher proportion of nonmanual females than manual had high levels of exercise, whatever their age group (18-39 or 40-59) or geographical location. Among males, except for middle aged males from traditional industrial areas where the pattern was slightly reversed, more nonmanual males had high levels of exercise than manual males.

Whether, and to what extent, lower socioeconomic groups 'underuse' health services is debatable. According to MacIntyre, in Britain, 'there is evidence that the use of most types of health care, whether general practitioner or hospital based, and preventive or curative, varies systematically' with socioeconomic and other social positions. She adds, however, that 'there is much less evidence than there is about smoking and drinking that use of health services actually contributes much to patterns or morbidity and mortality' (1986, p408).

There are two serious objections to explanations which focus exclusively on lifestyle and behaviours (and most sociologists would probably acknowledge that *exclusive* attachment to any one interpretation is both unnecessary and theoretically impoverishing). First is that some studies have shown that, even when such health-related factors as smoking, heavy drinking, lack of physical exercise, poor diet and obesity are controlled for, differences in the mortality rates of the different social classes remain. For

instance, in Marmot's study of Whitehall civil servants (1978), though he found that cigarette smoking declined and taking physically active leisure increased the higher the employment grade, these behaviours and other risk factors explained only a small part of the variance in mortality between grades. So, for example, lower grade smokers were more likely to die from either coronary heart diseases or lung cancer than higher grade smokers. As MacIntyre puts it, 'a working class smoker is more likely than a middle class smoker to be adversely affected by smoking' (1985, p408). And Marmot also found that lower grade *non-smokers* were also more likely to die than higher grade non-smokers from a range of diseases, some linked to smoking and others which are not (Wilkinson, 1986, p28). Similarly, a study in Alameda County in the USA which controlled for behavioural factors such as smoking, alcohol consumption, sleeping patterns, obesity and exercise found, nevertheless, that the poorest groups had death rates 1.5 times those of the richest (Berkman and Breslow, 1983).

A second objection to explanations which focus on behavioural/cultural factors is that behaviour cannot be divorced from its social context. In other words, adverse living and working conditions can significantly influence people's ability to choose a healthy lifestyle. Some health damaging behaviour, such as poor diet, may be due not to health damaging subcultural norms, or ignorance of the value of fibre or the dangers of cholesterol, but more to do with 'the accessibility, opening hours and buying policies of food shops in the locality; the division of domestic labour in the home; the time and money available for food shopping and preparation; or whether his/her employer supplies a canteen and what it supplies' (MacIntyre, 1986, p410).

4 Materialist-structuralist analyses These explanations emphasise the 'real differences in living conditions and personal circumstances between social groups that may contribute to differences in their health experiences' (MacIntyre, 1986, p405); differences such as housing, work and income, access to amenities, and physical and social threats from their environment. They are sometimes called 'life circumstances', and include both material and social circumstances.

A number of studies comparing different geographical areas, by political ward or postcode, have found strong and positive correlations between a range of indices of material deprivation on the one hand and poor health and high mortality on the other.

At a neighbourhood level, damper, poorer housing, overcrowding and air pollution are all worse in working class residential areas and contribute to higher rates of disease, particularly respiratory infections. A poor general environment makes accidents more likely. Low income is associated with maternal undernutrition during pregnancy and a generally inadequate diet in childhood and adult life. It also makes accessing health services more difficult. The higher unemployment rates traditionally suffered by the working class are also linked to a less nutritious diet and stress and stress-related behaviours such as smoking, alcohol abuse and suicide. In general, according to the *Black Report*, low social class and ill health are associated with a sense of lack of personal control over one's life, low self esteem and less ability to deal with stress in a healthy way.

Although occupations classified as the same social class can have very different accident, injury and mortality rates, those of the lower socioeconomic groups tend to be higher. Certain - typically working class - occupations carry higher noise levels, greater risk of accidents, and exposure to toxic substances, such as coal dust, lead and asbestos, which may be inadvertently brought home, thereby increasing the health risks for workers' families.

Social circumstances, including factors such as social support, integration and isolation, have also been found to be significant in health and associated with socioeconomic group. In the Alameda County study (Berkman and Breslow, 1983), for example, relatively high levels of social contacts and relatively low mortality rates were found among the higher socioeconomic groups.

In addition to evidence about the association between individuals' current material and social circumstances and their health, there has been growing support for the so-called 'delayed effects' thesis. This claims that poor conditions in early life are associated with later adult morbidity and premature mortality. Thus, Barker (1994), has suggested, for instance, that cardiovascular disease in adulthood is associated with undernutrition in the womb and in infancy. And in a Norwegian study, poverty at birth and in infancy was found to be a better predictor of coronary heart disease in adult life than was adult poverty (Forsdahl, 1977).

Activity 10   Health and Social Class

Item A   *The poor are dying younger*

Life expectancy for some groups in Britain has worsened for the first time in 50 years, research published today in the *British Medical Journal* (BMJ) shows. The research, by Dr Peter Phillimore of Newcastle University, Alastair Beattie of North Tyneside Health Care and Professor Peter Townsend of Bristol University is the first to examine the impact of the social upheavals of the 1980s on a particular region; in this case on Cleveland, Cumbria, Durham, Northumberland and Tyne and Wear.

The study shows that mortality rates in the most deprived areas in the North are now as bad for some age groups as in the 1940s, and are four times higher than in the most affluent areas. In the poorest areas, mortality rates have risen in absolute terms in men under 45 and women aged 65 to 75, reversing previous improvements.

In his BMJ editorial, Dr Richard Wilkinson of the

University of Sussex says the widening of income differences and growth of poverty during the 1980s have been unprecedented. 'If risks as great as these resulted from exposure to toxic materials, then offices would be closed down and populations evacuated from contaminated areas.'

Dr Phillimore said the research into health inequalities showed the poorest people had 'come adrift' from the rest. The gap could not be explained by differences in behaviour, he said. 'Inequalities have been widening since at least the 1960s. What is new is that the widening has been quite dramatic.' Health promotion campaigns, he argues, are a diversion. 'The economic circumstances of inequality must be taken seriously.'

Adapted from L. Jury 'Study Shows Poor are Dying Younger', *Guardian*, 29.4.94

Item B   *Loss of work and early death*

A study of the impact of unemployment on death rates by Dr Derek Cook of St George's Medical School, London found an increased risk of mortality among middle aged men who lost their jobs after stable employment. The increase could not be explained by previous ill-health.

The survey of 6,191 men across Britain showed that those who became unemployed or took early retirement were twice as likely to die during the following 5^1/2 years as those who stayed in work.

Adapted from L. Jury 'Study Shows Poor are Dying Younger', *Guardian*, 29.4.94

Item C 'Chips with everything!'

Mrs Edwina Currie, the flamboyant health minister, yesterday threatened to raise the collective blood pressure of the North by telling northerners that their relatively poor health was due in part to their own ignorance, compared with the more enlightened South. Speaking at Newcastle upon Tyne, she rejected any direct link between ill-health and poverty.

Mrs Currie argued that personal health was taken more seriously in 'advanced societies', including the South of England. 'We have problems here of high smoking and alcoholism,' she said. 'These are things we can tackle by impressing on people the need to look after themselves better. That is something which is taken more seriously down South.'

The Cherryfield Social Club, Kirkby, Merseyside

'I honestly don't think the problem has anything to do with poverty. The problem very often for people is, I think, just ignorance and failing to realise that they do have some control over their lives.'

Adapted from M. Wainwright 'Currie tells North to Heal Itself', *Observer*, 24.9.86

Item D *The cost of healthy food*

The government has banned publication of a report commissioned by the Health Education Authority showing that people living on low incomes cannot afford to eat healthily. The study, by an NHS dietician, contradicts the government view that it is lack of knowledge, not money, that results in poor people eating unhealthy food.

The banned report suggests that the cost of a healthy diet in 1986 was £14 a week for an adult in a family of four, but that the average adult on a low income had only £9.82 to spend a week on food. The report shows that the cost of healthy food, such as leafy green vegetables, fish, wholemeal bread and citrus fruit, has risen faster in recent years than the cost of less healthy items.

Poor people spend about half as much on food a week as wealthy people but the expenditure represented about a quarter of their income, compared to about a sixth of a wealthy person's income. The rich spend about four times as much on alcohol as the poor.

'People with low incomes buy food relatively efficiently within their scarce resources. They get more value for money in terms of quantities of food and also most nutrients. Vitamin C is a notable exception to this. However, they also get more fat, saturated fat and sugar; relatively cheap sources of calories,' the report says. 'People on income support may need to spend 40 to 50% of their disposable income on food if they are to eat healthy diets.'

Reviewing the impact of food poverty on health, it concludes: 'Of all the many nutritional factors associated with ill health, the strongest inverse relationship between death rates and food consumption in the UK and other developed countries is the amount of vegetables and fruit eaten.'

Adapted from A. Ferriman 'Poor's Unhealthy Diet Findings Blocked', *Observer*, 15.10.89

Questions

1 In Item A, explain the thinking behind the controversial assertion by one of the researchers that health promotion campaigns may be 'a diversion.'
2 How would you explain the findings reported in Item B?
3 With reference to Items C and D, explain the difference of emphasis between materialist-structuralist and cultural-behavioural interpretations of health inequalities.

6.6 Health and gender

1 Social constructionist analyses Social constructionist approaches stress that definitions and therefore statistics concerning health and illness are social constructions. Although proponents of this position would not necessarily claim that gender differences in disease do not exist, they are likely to claim that the statistics which are said to demonstrate them are not valid or, at least in morbidity, are greatly exaggerated.

First, for a variety of reasons, female illness is

more likely to be recorded than male illness. A major source of information on morbidity rates comes from general practitioners' reports of consultations with patients. Because women do consult their GP more, (on average six times a year compared to men's four times), and because, once there, women report a higher rate of both acute and chronic health problems, this translates into a higher official morbidity rate. However, it could alternatively be interpreted as reflecting differential gender socialisation. Thus, males consult doctors less and report less illness because of their greater need to appear self-reliant and tolerant - even contemptuous - of pain. For females, it is argued, admitting discomfort and dependence on others is more acceptable. So women are better able to acknowledge illness and seek medical help.

Secondly, women may be more likely to visit a doctor and report their own sickness or disease because they are more sensitive to the symptoms of illness because of their generally greater involvement in family health. Also, it is suggested, their more flexible role makes access to health care facilities easier than for their (generally full time, employed) partner.

A labelling analysis suggests that women may appear to suffer higher morbidity rates because doctors are readier to apply a sick label to them. This may be particularly the case in certain psychiatric diagnoses. Even in drug advertisements which feature in professional journals, (predominantly male) doctors are exposed to a stereotypical representation of women as more emotional and as more likely to suffer from psychiatric symptoms and disorders than supposedly rational and stoic males.

Moreover, though females are typically claimed to suffer higher rates of psychiatric disorder, the figures vary significantly depending on which categories of mental illness are used. Reported neuroses and psychoses may be higher among females, but if personality disorders - which are higher in men - are included as mental illnesses, the impression is very different.

2 **Natural selection** The natural selection or genetic explanation suggests that the lower mortality rate and higher life expectancy rate for females is biologically based. However, with the important exception that female hormones are believed to offer some protection against heart disease, there is little evidence that physiological sex differences make more than a small contribution to the higher male mortality rates. Female foetuses do have better survival rates than male foetuses. And one of the few other examples is that, at birth, males are more vulnerable to injury and asphyxia because they are slightly larger. Also males suffer more malformations and genetically transmitted disorders. However, as female life expectancy is actually lower in some Third World countries (eg on the Indian subcontinent), and as morbidity differentials between the sexes vary, sometimes substantially, within a single country, it would seem that the differential can be significantly modified by social and cultural factors.

3 **Cultural-behavioural analyses** In cultural-behavioural analyses, evidence of gender differentials in mortality and morbidity is accepted as largely valid. It is explained in terms of alleged differences in the attitudes, norms and behaviours of males and females. Thus, higher male rates of mortality are interpreted in part as resulting from males 'choosing' to pursue more dangerous leisure time activities. They drink and smoke more, they drive faster and suffer more accidents. They are also more likely to commit suicide and murder. In support of this sort of interpretation is evidence that, although the gap between male and female mortality rates remains, since 1970 it has not been increasing. Men have stopped smoking more than women (between 1972 and 1982 a 14% compared to an 8% drop). And women are drinking more than they used to. Between 1978 and 1987, women's weekly alcohol consumption increased by 14%, while that of men fell by 4%. Women are also driving more and may be doing so more recklessly.

It has also been suggested that higher female morbidity reflects a greater inability among females to deal with stress in a way which avoids illness. According to Seligman (1975), for instance, females have traditionally been socialised into being less able to cope with stress than males and are thus more at risk of depressive (and other stress-related) illness. He argues that gender role socialisation teaches females to 'learn helplessness': that females become ill partly because they are encouraged to regard passivity, helplessness and dependence as appropriate feminine virtues. Against such an interpretation, however, is the claim that females may periodically employ 'helplessness' as a health protecting coping mechanism not available to males, and that they are also culturally better prepared to diffuse stress by sharing concerns with friends and significant others.

4 **Materialist-structuralist analyses** In structuralist analyses, differential mortality and morbidity rates for males and females are interpreted as due mainly to differences in their positions in, and experiences of, the social structure. In particular, men's location in the occupational structure, ie the jobs many males do, is frequently cited as significant. Thus, more males work in physically

hazardous occupations - such as in the construction industry, mining (including in the oil industry), deep sea fishing, diving, lumberjacking, in action in the military, in factories using heavy machinery, and so on. The loss of work also appears to be highly significant in male mortality. Both unemployed and early retirers die earlier than those who remain in work, indicating the centrality of work for males' self-image and sense of purpose. Women's increasing participation in the labour market (46% of all UK employees in 1994) may lead to their mortality patterns becoming more like those of men.

The higher incidence of female morbidity has been interpreted in terms of their main roles in the social structure. Some research shows that women doing clerical work are particularly prone to coronary heart disease. Structural theorists have suggested that this may be because they are likely to suffer, both at work and at home, from certain specifically gender-related difficulties. At work they suffer the stresses and frustrations of relatively low status work with its expectations of traditional female behaviour - pliable, submissive and suppressing their anger. Meanwhile, at home they continue to take on the bulk of the domestic burdens, which are still seen as both low status and primarily their responsibility.

Some have also pointed to that key female role of housewife as encouraging disease, perhaps particularly psychiatric illnesses. The problem is felt to lie with the role itself, which is widely perceived to carry little prestige and to be underappreciated. The role is unstructured; expectations of the role - including its hours - are unclear and more work can always be done. If the housewife also takes paid employment she is placed under greater strain because she is still primarily responsible for household chores and childcare. Moreover women tend to be the buffer and absorber of stresses of the other members of the family. Hence, according to a 1988 report of the government's advisory Women's National Commission, women are said to be twice as likely to suffer severe stress as men. And, unlike men, many women have no major alternative source of gratification to the family.

A higher incidence of some female mental disorders may also partly reflect the central significance, for many women's sense of achievement and status, of reproduction. Females in Western societies are particularly prone to suffer depressive illness at certain life stages, such as following childbirth or at menopause. Natural selection explanations would emphasise the significance of hormonal changes at such times. However, although depressive illness following childbirth or at menopause may be significantly related to hormonal change, the depressive response to such changes may also be partly socially determined. If the main avenue for achievement and status for many women is through reproduction, any major event pertaining to reproduction is likely to produce emotional reactions. Thus, Brown and Harris (1979) claim that the higher rates of post-natal and menopausal depression among working class women suggest their greater dependence on wife and mother roles for a sense of achievement.

6.7 Health and ethnicity

There are four main types of explanation for ethnic differences in mortality and morbidity. First, natural selection based on supposed genetic differences between groups. Second, cultural and behavioural explanations based on the allegedly health damaging behaviours of different ethnic groups. Third, structural explanations which focus on the social class position of ethnic minorities. Fourth, racism, which is seen to compound other disadvantages. However, as mentioned above (pp443-444), detailed and valid data in this area is seriously limited.

1 Natural selection Although genetic factors may influence the propensity of African and Afro-Caribbean groups to high blood pressure and strokes, social and economic factors are thought to be more important. A few disorders do appear to be genetically associated with ethnicity, however. Haemophilia, an inability of the blood to clot, is largely limited to North Europeans. On the other hand, sickle cell anaemia, a highly painful and potentially fatal blood disorder, mainly affects people of Afro-Caribbean descent.

2 Cultural-behavioural analyses Some ill health is said to be linked to health damaging behaviours engaged in by some ethnic groups. For instance, the high perinatal mortality rate of Asian mothers is said to be linked to their low attendance at ante-natal classes. Relatively high rates of coronary heart disease among Asians are blamed on the use of traditional cooking fats, and high rates of diabetes on high carbohydrate foods which encourage obesity. Set against such explanations, however, is evidence that, among equivalent groups in the Indian subcontinent, heart disease rates are lower. In any event, it is argued, many Asian diets - especially vegetarian ones - may well be closer to the advice given by Western health educators than are many of the traditional British diets.

3 Materialist-structuralist analyses More significant in explaining different rates of morbidity and mortality in the view of many sociologists are structuralist explanations which focus on the position of ethnic minorities in the class structure. Most male employees with origins in the Asian subcontinent or Caribbean, are concentrated in low paid manual occupations and particularly in industries which are hazardous to health, such as textiles and clothing, and/or have been badly hit by recession and competition, such as textiles and footwear. Many Asian women are employed as 'outworkers', working at home on very low piece-work rates of pay. Among such groups, poorer health is linked to low pay and limited fringe benefits, often excessive shift work, job insecurity and high unemployment.

4 Racism The likely contribution of racism to ill health is complex and various. In general, the poor material conditions associated with low social class appear to be compounded by racism. Indeed, racism is probably a more effective explanation than low social class of certain health damaging experiences of ethnic minorities such as their relatively high rates of unemployment and redundancy, excessive shiftwork, compulsory overtime, unsocial working hours and poor housing. Even in the NHS, a major employer of ethnic minorities, black people are disproportionately concentrated in low paid ancillary work such as cleaning and catering. In nursing and medicine they tend to occupy the lower ranks and work in the less prestigious specialisms such as geriatrics and mental health. They are significantly under-represented in technical, clerical and administrative posts and the ambulance service has been described by one researcher as a virtual 'no-go' area for black people (Butler, 1992).

The quality of housing for ethnic minorities is generally inferior. Of those in privately rented accommodation, that occupied by the more recently arrived ethnic minorities such as Bangladeshis and Pakistanis is more likely to be of poor quality. Of those in council property, blacks are more likely to occupy high rise flats rather than houses with gardens, and their homes are likely to include fewer amenities, such as an indoor toilet or central heating.

Racism is also a factor in shaping ethnic minorities' experience of health care. Despite often praiseworthy attempts to rectify the situation, health professionals are still often inadequately trained in the religious, cultural and dietary requirements of various ethnic groups. Consequently, health services often take little or no account of these factors and may therefore appear as offensive, threatening or irrelevant. And despite attempts in this direction, information in appropriate languages is often lacking.

Summary

1 At any age and for either sex, the likelihood of either death or disease increases the lower the social class. However, while females have lower mortality rates than males, they seem to suffer higher rates of non-life-threatening illnesses. Data on ethnic differences in health is limited. However, people of African, Afro-Caribbean and Asian origin appear to have relatively high mortality rates from strokes, liver cancer, tuberculosis, diabetes, perinatal, neonatal and maternal mortalities, accidents and violence; and low mortality rates for bronchitis and certain cancers.

2 Health inequalities between groups are explained by a combination of analyses stressing social construction, natural or social selection, materialist-structuralist and cultural-behavioural factors. For class and gender differentials, the last two approaches are regarded as the most significant. Racism is seen as an important factor in explaining the higher morbidity rates among ethnic minorities.

Activity 11   Health and Gender

Item A Women and the 'man's disease'

Women are almost as prone to heart disease as men, at least in their menopausal years, and probably always have been. According to the Director of the National Forum for Coronary Heart Prevention, Imogen Sharp, 'Despite the fact that coronary heart disease is the leading single cause of death among women, it is typically seen as a male disease. As a result, GPs and other health professionals may not initially diagnose symptoms as heart disease.'

Ellen McEwen, 54, a maths teacher was told by her GP that the severe chest pains she had suffered the previous night were symptoms of the menopause. Later an angiogram revealed she had suffered a serious heart attack. 'I am pretty sure that if I had been a man and described those symptoms I would have been sent straight to hospital.' Instead she was sent home with no medication or advice and 12 hours later was rushed to hospital where tests revealed a severely diseased heart. 'Like most women, I thought of heart disease as a male condition and it just never occurred to me I could have a heart attack,' she recalled.

Doctors are generally slower to diagnose heart disease symptoms in women, are less likely to refer a woman for tests and are less likely to recommend medical or surgical treatment. Thus, women are referred later in their illness than men and take longer to recover.

Adapted from S. Clark 'Heartbreaking Truth about Women and the "Man's Disease"', *Sunday Times*, 27.11.94

Item B *A matter of lifestyle*

But women will have to do something about their lifestyles. And according to Brian Pentencost, a cardiologist, 'There is a great deal they can do: stop smoking, improve their diet and take up more physical activity. It is vital we get this message across.'

In these areas women of all ages are scoring increasingly badly. High blood pressure, a fatty diet and smoking are the three main causes of heart disease, and of these three smoking is the biggest villain. Today 29% of adult men and 28% of adult women are smokers, but women are less likely to give up the habit and younger women smoke more than men.

Adapted from S. Clark 'Heartbreaking Truth about Women and the "Man's Disease"', *Sunday Times*, 27.11.94

Item C *The ideal body*

In the view of Deanne Jade, a psychologist and founder of the National Centre for Eating Disorders, the problem of eating disorders among teenage girls has now reached an unprecedented level. She estimates that one in every 100 girls will become anorexic - refusing to eat out of fear of becoming fat - and even more will suffer from bulimia - a condition where sufferers binge and then make themselves vomit.

From Jade's regular school visits to talk to pupils about the dangers, she believes teenage girls still do not understand the link between dieting and eating disorders. 'There isn't a single girl who doesn't know about eating disorders. But there's something contagious about the problem because when one girl starts dieting it affects all her female classmates, making them feel insecure.'

According to the National Centre for Eating Disorders, 70% of 15 year old girls - and one-third of nine year olds - have dieted. 'Girls regard their bodies as objects,' says Jade. 'They think they will be valued only for their looks, and that to be attractive and therefore loved they must be as slim as the images of thin women they are bombarded with by the media.'

Many have learned to diet from their mothers. 'When I give talks in schools where parents are invited too, I often have more problems with the mothers, who also think they have to diet and be thin to be loved. The insidious message they have passed on to their daughters is that to be a woman is to play around with food to change your body shape.'

Adapted from S. Clark 'Disorder in Class', *Sunday Times*, 4.12.94

Item D *Women's 'double life'*

Another explanation for the rising rates of coronary heart disease in younger women is that many more women lead a double life, keeping full time demanding jobs going while taking the main responsibility for children and running a home.

Recent research showed that women in stressful jobs who had frequent arguments with their husbands were almost twice as likely to have heart attacks than women in less high-powered jobs.

Adapted from C. Doyle 'Women Have Hearts Too', *Daily Telegraph*, 22.11.94

'Supermodels' setting the standard for the ideal figure

Questions

1 Read Item A. Why do you think doctors are less likely to diagnose heart disease symptoms in women?
2 Changes in the position of women in society may lead to a worsening of their health. Discuss this view with some reference to Items B and D.
3 Read Item C. Suggest reasons for the actual or apparent increase in eating disorders among teenage girls.

References

Barker, D. J. P. *Mothers, Babies and Disease in Later Life* (British Medical Association, London, 1994)

Berkman, L. and Breslow, L. *Health and Ways of Living: the Alameda County Study* (Oxford University Press, Oxford, 1983)

Blaxter, M. 'Equity and Consultation Rates in General Practice' *British Medical Journal* no 6345, 1984

Blaxter, M. *Health and Lifestyles* (Routledge, London, 1990)

Brown, G.W. and Harris, T. *The Social Origins of Depression* (Tavistock, London, 1979)

Butler, G.A. 'Racism in Employment Practice within the NHS' *Journal of Advances in Health and Nursing*, vol 2 no1, September 1992

Byrne, P.S. and Long, B.E. *Doctors Talking to Patients* (HMSO, London, 1976)

Cartwright, A. *Patients and their Doctors* (Routledge and Kegan Paul, London, 1967)

Cartwright, A. and O'Brien, M. 'Social Class Variations in Health Care' *The Sociology of the NHS*, Sociological Review (Monograph), 1976

Cartwright, F. F. *A Social History of Medicine* (Longman, London, 1977)

Chalfont, H. P. and Kurtz, R. A. 'Alcoholics and the Sick Role' *Journal of Health and Social Behaviour*, vol 12, 1971

Clark, S. 'Heartbreaking Truth about Women and the "Man's Disease"' *Sunday Times*, 27.11.1994

Clark, S. 'Disorder in Class' *Sunday Times*, 4.12.1994

Coward, R. 'Body Language: the new Our Bodies Ourselves' *New Statesman and Society*, 8.12.1989

Culley, L. and Dyson, S. '"Race", Inequality and Health' *Sociology Review*, September 1993

Dalrymple, T. 'If Symptoms Persist' *The Spectator*, 13.3.1993

Doyle, C. 'Women have Hearts too' *Daily Telegraph*, 22.11.1994

Dubos, R. and Pines, M. *Health and Disease* (Time-Life Books, Alexandra, VA, 1980)

Ferriman, A. 'Poor's Unhealthy Diet Findings Blocked' *Observer*, 15.10.1989

Fletcher, D. 'Give Patients back their Dignity, says Watchdog' *Daily Telegraph*, 24.11.1993

Forsdahl, A. 'Are Poor Living Conditions in Childhood and Adolescence an Important Risk Factor for Arteriosclerotic Heart Disease?' *British Journal of Preventive and Social Medicine*, vol 31, 1977

Freidson, E. *The Profession of Medicine* (Dodd Mead, New York, 1970)

General Household Survey, 1987 (HMSO, London, 1989)

Goffman, E. *Asylums* (Penguin Books, Harmondsworth, 1961)

Goldberg, E. and Morrison, S. 'Schizophrenia and Social Class' *British Journal of Psychiatry*, vol 22, 1963

Graham, H. 'Women, Health and Illness' *Social Studies Review*, September 1987

Hart, N. *The Sociology of Health and Medicine* (Causeway Press, Ormskirk 1985)

Helman, C. G. Culture, *Health and Illness* (Butterworth, London, 1990)

Illich, I. *Limits to Medicine: Medical Nemesis* (Boyars, London, 1976)

Illsley, R. *Professional or Public Health?* (Nuffield Provincial Hospitals Trust, London, 1980)

Johnson, T. *Professions and Power* (Macmillan, London, 1972)

Jong, E. 'Women and the Way of all Flesh' *Sunday Times*, 13.2.1994

Jury, L. 'Study shows Poor are Dying Younger' *Guardian*, 29.4.1994

Kleiner, K. 'A Sackful of Money helps the Medicine go down' *New Scientist*, 12.3.1994

MacIntyre, S. 'The Patterning of Health by Social Position in Contemporary Britain: Directions for Sociological Research' *Social Science and Medicine*, vol 23, 1986

Marmot, M. G. 'Social Inequalities in Mortality: the Social Environment' in R. G. Wilkinson (ed) *Class and Health* (Tavistock, London, 1986)

Marmot, M., Booth, M. and Beral, V. 'Changes in Heart Disease Mortality in England and Wales' *Health Trends*, vol 13, 1981a

Marmot, M. G., Rose, G. A., Shipley, M. J., and Thomas, B. J. 'Alcohol and Mortality: a U-shaped curve' *Lancet*, 1, 580, 1981b

Marmot, M. G., Rose, G. A., Shipley, M. J., and Hamilton, P. J. S. 'Employment Grade and Coronary Heart Disease in British Civil Servants' *Journal of Epidemiology and Community Health*, vol 32, 1978

McKeown T. *The Role of Medicine: Dream, Mirage of Nemesis?* (Basil Blackwell, Oxford, 1979)

McKeown T. *The Origins of Human Disease*, (Basil Blackwell, Oxford, 1988)

Meadows, S. 'Social Class Migration and Chronic Bronchitis' *British Journal of Preventive and Social Medicine*, vol 15, 1961

Morgan, M., Calnan, M. and Manning, N. *Sociological Approaches to Health and Medicine* (Croom Helm, Beckenham, 1985)

Parsons. T. *The Social System* (The Free Press, Glencoe, 1951)

Pietroni, P. *Reader's Digest Family Guide to Alternative Medicine* (Reader's Digest Association, London, 1991)

Scheff, T. *Labelling Madness* (Prentice Hall, New Jersey, 1975)

Schools Council History 13-16 Project *Medicine Through Time*, Book Three (Holmes McDougal, Edinburgh, 1976)

Seligman, M. *Helplessness: On Depression, Development and Death* (W. H. Freeman, San Fransisco, 1975)

Stainton Rogers, W. *Explaining Health and Illness* (Harvester Wheatsheaf, Hemel Hempstead, 1991)

Szasz, T. *The Myth of Mental Illness* (Harper & Row, New York, 1974)

Szasz, T. and Hollender, M. H. 'A Contribution to the Philosophy of Medicine' *AMA Archives of Internal Medicine*, vol 97, 1956

Taylor, S. 'Beyond the Medical Model' *Sociology Review*, September 1994

The Health of the Nation (HMSO, London, 1991)

Townsend, P. and Davidson, N. 'The Black Report' in P. Townsend, N. Davidson and M. Whitehead (eds) *Inequalities in Health* (Penguin Books, Harmondsworth, 1992)

Tuckett, D. and Kaufert, J. M. (eds) *Basic Readings in Medical Sociology* (Tavistock, London, 1978)

Wainwright, M. 'Currie tells North to Heal Itself' *Observer*, 24.9.1986

Whitehead, M. 'The Health Divide' in P. Townsend, N. Davidson and M. Whitehead (eds) *Inequalities in Health* (Penguin Books, Harmondsworth, 1982)

Young, A. 'The Discourse on Stress and the Reproduction of Conventional Knowledge' *Social Science and Medicine*, 14b, 1980

Introduction

We are both fascinated and disturbed by crime and deviance. Our fascination is evident from the fact that they are essential ingredients in the mass media and popular culture. Crime and deviance intrigue us because they comprise activities which are seemingly out of the ordinary. We are also often disturbed by crime and deviance. This is evident in our fear of crime and the embarrassment we feel when taken for granted norms are broken. Our anxiety is aroused because such activities disrupt our sense of social order.

Chapter summary

- This chapter starts by asking 'What is **crime** and **deviance**?' It then moves on to examine **media representations** of crime and deviance.
- Evidence on the **extent** of crime, trends in

the **crime rates** and the **identity of offenders** is explored.
- Finally a range of very different **explanations** of crime and deviance is investigated.

1 The Nature of Crime and Deviance

Key Issues

1. What is crime and deviance?
2. What is distinctive about the sociological approach to crime and deviance?

1.1 Defining crime and deviance

Human social life is governed by norms and rules. Much sociological work is concerned with the question of how society's norms and rules are maintained. However, as Giddens has remarked, there is another side to the story which sociology also has to address and that is how and why do rules and norms get broken (Giddens, 1989). In other words how and why does deviance occur.

Deviance

There is no simple definition of deviance in sociology although Downes and Rock perhaps come closest to an acceptable one when they suggest 'deviance may be considered as banned or controlled behaviour which is likely to attract punishment or disapproval' (1988, p28). Such behaviour would include exceptional forms of deviance such as murder and rape which are explicitly banned in most cultures and are subject to severe state-organised punishment. At the other end of the scale, Downes and Rock's definition would comprise trivial misdemeanours such as burping and farting which attract at most informal social controls such as mild disapproval but no legal

sanction - unless perhaps in front of a judge in court when they may be construed as contempt of court!

Crime

Crime seems a more straightforward category compared to the elastic definition of deviance offered by Downes and Rock. Some commentators simply define crime as the infraction of criminal law. From this perspective, Pease presents a useful working definition.

'Crime comprises those actions which are deemed so damaging to the interests of the community that the state determines that it must take a direct role in identifying and acting against the criminal' (1994, p659).

However some sociologists find this definition somewhat limiting. Heidensohn (1989), for example, makes the point that the infraction of the criminal law covers a vast array of incidents from the trivial to serious, impersonal to highly personal, violent to non-violent, and lucrative to petty in terms of profit. This leads some sociologists to avoid talk of crime in the singular given the very different events encompassed by the term. In other words there's 'crime and crime'.

1.2 The contexts and diversity of deviance

Deviance, as with conformity, may take varied forms within human societies. For example, we can distinguish secret and private deviance as against

Activity 1 Defining Vandalism

Item A

Item B

Item C

Item D

Item E

Item F

Questions

1 Look at the pictures. Which (if any) would you see as examples of vandalism? Give reasons for your answer.
2 Using examples from this activity, briefly discuss the problem of defining crime and deviance.

open and public deviance and individual as against collective deviance.

Deviance is often concealed and therefore devious in character, not least due to the heavy personal costs of unwanted exposure to the public gaze. It is often undercover and may be found, hidden, in normal settings such as the home or the workplace. Take the example of the recently deceased Gloucester 'serial killer' Frederick West. This person by all accounts appeared to be a fairly normal family man keen on 'adoption' as well as being a self-employed builder. Yet he indulged privately in murders of two members of his family as well as a number of vulnerable young women. Furthermore, he was able to use his 'normal' skills as a builder to hide the dead bodies in his house under the guise of being a DIY enthusiast.

On the other hand, deviance may also be a public and collective experience which involves conforming to a clearly identified outsider group's norms and rules. Take the example of the so-called 'New Age Travellers' in contemporary Britain. This deviant group is viewed with distaste and hostility by some sections of the public. Yet, being a member of the 'New Age Travellers', with its shared dress code and lifestyle, may be a source of *collective* pride for the participants in this *public* group.

1.3 The relativity of crime and deviance

Time and again sociological research illustrates how a particular form of behaviour may in one situation be classified as deviant yet, given different circumstances, may be viewed as perfectly normal.

Plummer (1979) captures this point in his distinction between 'societal' and 'situational' deviance. *Societal deviance* refers to those categories of behaviour which are either 'commonly sensed' by most members of society to be deviant or are defined as such by the dominant beliefs and institutional practices such as the law. There exists a high degree of consensus within the population over the identification of societal deviance, for example armed robbery. *Situational deviance* on the other hand concerns the actual manner in which people go about the task of creating rules and interpreting rule violations as 'deviance' in contexts such as their own worlds of friends, colleagues and acquaintances. Plummer accepts that situational deviance is affected by society's dominant beliefs but argues that in certain situations people are free to either neutralise or reject the societal version of deviance and to construct rules at odds with those of 'society'. Using Plummer's example, it is possible to acknowledge that homosexuality is societally deviant in contemporary Britain, but it will not always be situationally deviant. In certain contexts such as gay bars and parties people may create rules which normalise homosexuality. Furthermore, homosexuals may create categories of deviance within their own ranks, such as being too camp or too promiscuous or too politically correct.

Summary

1 The range and scope of behaviour encompassed by the terms crime and deviance are extremely diverse.

2 Sociological analysis suggests that crime and deviance need to be understood in relation to both the general and specific social contexts in which they are found.

Activity 2 Deviance is Relative

Item A *Consenting adults only!*

A couple of weeks ago New York's anti-smoking laws came into full force. Smoking is forbidden in nearly all shared public places. In offices and work premises, smokers have to huddle together in designated smoking areas which, it is said, tend to be grotty, fuggy places littered with cigarette ends. Restaurants above a certain size must offer non-smoking sections to their customers; in theatres and cinemas, smoking is permitted only in segregated areas of the lobby. Confronted with these laws, many establishments have simply banned smoking altogether. Smoking is illegal in taxis and, theoretically, on the concourse of Grand Central Station.

According to Stanley Michels, the New York City councilman who sponsored the anti-smoking legislation: 'This is one of the most fantastic social changes we've seen in our lifetime. Smoking is now considered anti-social behaviour.'

In Washington I lunched with an old friend, a defiant two-pack-a-day man. He started smoking a cigarette with his cocktail but put it out when the people at the next table got sniffy. 'We've lost,' he said. 'There's no smoking in government buildings in this town except in the designated smoking recesses and your own private office, if you have one. Now they've put smoke detectors in the johns so that alarm bells ring and they can rush in and shoot you in the kneecaps.'

However, all is not lost for smokers. According to Athena Mueller of the non-smokers' rights lobby, 'We're not opposed to smoking between consenting adults in private.'

Adapted from P. Jenkins 'Only for Consenting Adults in Private', *Independent*, 28.7.88

Item B

The late American film star John Wayne advertising Camel cigarettes

Questions

1 Use information from Items A and B to illustrate the point that deviance is relative to time and place.
2 Look at Item B. Why would it be unlikely for a film star today to endorse cigarettes?

1.4 The normality of crime and deviance

Social rules and their violation are an intrinsic feature of any social organisation and arguably a part of the human condition. As David Garland observes: 'The discourse about crime and criminals - or sin, villainy, roguery, deviance, whatever the local idiom - is thus as old as human civilisation itself' (1994, p28).

According to Garland every society generates its own deviants and, in turn, its own propositions to explain and understand them. In former systems of knowledge, such as the Christian tradition of thought, we have seen the hand of God or the Devil used to account for and explain both conformity and deviance.

What then distinguishes the sociological perspective from competing modes of knowledge, both past and present? First, there is its emphasis on the social context and an emphasis on deviance and crime as rational and understandable behaviour rather than a sick or pathological condition. Unlike John Major's famous sound bite of 1993 that 'we should understand (the criminal) less and condemn more', the sociologist is driven by the goal of understanding more and more about the causes and consequences of crime and deviance.

However, this is not a sufficient definition of the sociological approach to deviance. Some everyday ideas also emphasise the importance of social factors. This can be seen from statements such as 'he was led astray by those bad boys from the other estate' or 'he fell among thieves' which suggest social causes for deviance. Apart from the emphasis on social context, the second and crucial distinction between sociological knowledge and commonsense is the sociologist's commitment to a scientific approach. Unlike commonsense, sociology begins and ends by questioning the nature of the evidence, how it has been gathered and analysed, and the logic and coherence of theories used to explain the evidence. Put briefly, sociology is a systematic study using concepts, theories and data to test ideas. This is the crucial difference between sociological and everyday views of crime and deviance.

2 Representations of Crime and Deviance

Key Issue

How important are media representations in structuring popular perceptions of crime and deviance in contemporary society?

2.1 Public concern over crime and deviance

Crime and deviance are a major source of public concern. There is no end to discussions, images and dramatic representations of crime in politics, in households and of course in the press, film and television. Indeed one might argue that there is a boom industry associated with crime and deviance of which sociology itself may be a small part (Christie, 1993). Witness the fashion for 'factual' reconstructions of crimes such as *Crime Stalker* on British TV whose appeal seems to have more to do with titillation than public information. But this is nothing new. In Victorian times our contemporary reconstructions of crime were matched by the popular *Penny Dreadful*, cheap sensational accounts of recent murders which whetted the Victorian appetite for both blood and indignation in a tantalising cocktail. Indeed concern over and explanations of crime are age old as evidenced in the lessons of the Bible and the Koran and in the cautionary tales handed down to children in such fairy stories as *Little Red Riding Hood.*

2.2 Media representations and public perceptions

Popular images of the criminal and the deviant are built around an array of stereotypes such as the mugger, child molester, robber, burglar, rapist, joy rider, terrorist and serial killer. Given the size, complexity and anonymity of contemporary society, few people are likely to have direct experience of a wide range of criminal and deviant behaviour. Most people's awareness of crime and deviance is therefore based mainly on secondary sources.

Some sociologists claim that the mass media plays a major role in structuring public perceptions of crime and deviance. It does this by (a) defining certain behaviour as criminal and deviant; (b) defining certain activities as newsworthy; (c) defining certain activities as suitable for fictional presentation in novels, movies and television programmes. In this way the media projects society-wide images of conformity and deviance, of 'crime waves', 'unnatural behaviour' and 'anti-social behaviour'. In doing so it creates a shared experience and constructs public perceptions.

If these claims are correct, then it is important to examine media coverage of crime and deviance. Here are some of the findings of research based on content analysis of newspapers and television over the past 20 years in Britain.

1 At both national and local levels, the media is a major source of information about crime and deviance. Smith's study of crime news in Birmingham showed that 52% of her sample saw newspapers as their main source of information about crime, whilst only 3.2% drew primarily on their own experiences (Smith quoted in Muncie, 1986). More recently Schlesinger and Tumber's study of TV coverage of crime news has revealed the massive popularity of programmes such as *Crimewatch UK* which are based on reconstructions of murder, armed robbery and sexual crimes. By the late 1980s *Crimewatch UK* had become more popular than the national news. In order to achieve high viewing figures, however, *Crimewatch UK* has focused on atypical and violent crimes (Schlesinger and Tumber, 1993).

2 Newspapers offer a staple diet of crime news at both national and local levels. There is evidence that, like *Crimewatch UK,* they focus on violent and sexual crime stories so distorting the public's view of 'the crime problem'. Research by Williams and Dickinson (1993) found that personal violent crime made up 64.5% of the space allocated to crime news in British newspapers but constituted only 6% of the official total of all reported crime. As Young argues in the context of his analysis of the drugs problem in the 1970s in Britain, 'newspapers select events which are *atypical*, present them in a *stereotypical* fashion and contrast them against a backcloth of normality which is *overtypical*' (1974, p241). News stories are shaped according to certain news values and present a selective and often sensationalised picture of crime and deviance for public consumption.

3 We must not assume, however, that *all* types of media and *all* newspapers present a similar picture of crime and deviance. The media is not a totally unified set of institutions all preaching the same message. For example, research by Williams and Dickinson (1993) reveals significant differences in the amount of news space devoted to crime in major UK newspapers. Popular 'tabloids' such as the *Sun, Star* and *Mirror* devote over a quarter of their news space to crime whereas the less popular 'broadsheet' papers such as the *Guardian* and *Independent* may devote as little as 5% to crime stories. Such differences between newspapers may well affect their readers' perception of the crime problem.

Summary

1 It is often claimed that media representations are crucial in structuring the public's perceptions of crime and deviance in contemporary society.

2 The picture painted by the media is selective. It emphasises the more sensational and violent forms of crime and deviance.

Activity 3 Reporting Crime

Item A *The Times 28.9.94*

Crime figures show overall fall but violence increases

A political row erupted last night as new crime figures for England and Wales showed the largest drop since 1954. Reported crime fell by 5.5 per cent overall, but violent and sexual offences rose sharply, according to Home Office figures.

Police recorded 5,365,400 crimes in the year to June 1994 - 311,500 fewer than the year before. The Government heralded the figures as 'encouraging', but Labour called the rise in violence 'frightening'.

David Maclean, the Home Office minister, said the overall drop showed crime

was 'not bound irredeemably and irrevocably to rise. By targeting and crime prevention campaigns, we can make a difference. The message has to be that the fear of crime must now reduce. The fear of crime in many people is worse than the problem itself.'

Burglaries were down 107,000 to 1.3 million - their largest fall for five years - while thefts were down 8 per cent to 2.6 million, and vehicle crime fell by 136,000 (9 per cent) to 1.4 million, the first decrease since 1989. Property crime, accounting for 93 per cent overall, fell

by 6 per cent, from 5.3 million to 5 million.

However, these successes were tempered by the unyielding rise of violent offences. There was a 12 per cent increase in sexual offences and a 5 per cent rise in violent crimes. For the

first time in four years there was an increase in sex attacks on men - 5,847 attacks (up 19 per cent). Robberies, mainly muggings, accounted for 19 per cent of violent crime - up by 5 per cent to 59,000, the smallest rise since 1988.

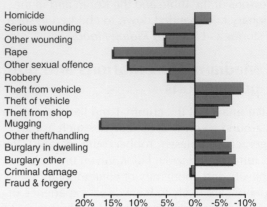

RISE AND FALL OF CRIME IN BRITAIN
England and Wales July 1993 to June 1994

- Homicide
- Serious wounding
- Other wounding
- Rape
- Other sexual offence
- Robbery
- Theft from vehicle
- Theft of vehicle
- Theft from shop
- Mugging
- Other theft/handling
- Burglary in dwelling
- Burglary other
- Criminal damage
- Fraud & forgery

20% 15% 10% 5% 0% -5% -10%

Item B *Today 28.9.94*

The terrifying violence that shames Britain

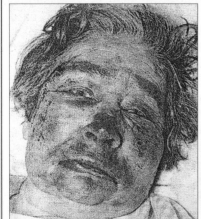

Mugged... Louisa La Rouche was savagely attacked.

Threatened... Customers cower under a shotgun-wielding raider in a Leeds building society.

Bike thefts down - violence soars

Home Office Minister David Maclean stunned battered, burgled Britain yesterday by claiming crime was on the RETREAT.

'We have turned the corner', he crowed in London. 'We haven't won the war yet, but we have got the enemy in the clear.'
And we have got it in retreat.

Mr Maclean was speaking as official figures showed that the police recorded 5,365,000

offences last year - a drop of 5.5 per cent.

Hollow

But a closer reading of the statistics revealed that violent crime was up 6.1 per cent, with rapes soaring by 15 per cent.

And Mr Maclean's hollow boast came as details of two more sickening crimes shocked Britain.

Two thugs snatched a 32-year-old married woman's pet dog before brutally

raping her in Birmingham.

While at the Old Bailey a teenager was branded 'dangerously evil' after stamping an 88-year-old woman to death.

Much of the drop in the official statistics results from a decrease in burglaries.

There have also been fewer thefts from cars.

And the number of stolen bicycles has plummeted by a massive 17 per cent.

Questions

1 Compare the style and content of Items A and B.
2 What effect might each story have on the reader?
3 Suggest why the reports are so different.

3 Crime Statistics

Key Issues

1 How extensive is crime in contemporary Britain?
2 Are we currently living through a 'crime wave'?
3 How distinctive are offenders?

3.1 Measuring crime

Crime is a social construct, consisting, as we have seen, of a highly varied set of activities which have in common the fact they are forbidden by the criminal law. Each year estimates produced by the police give an official account of the volume of crime and trends in crime, while statistics compiled from court and police cautioning records tell us about those officially responsible for criminal offences, ie the 'criminals'. Together these give us a picture of the 'crime problem' - a picture which, interpreted for us by politicians, is transmitted to us through the mass media.

3.2 The volume of crime

According to the official statistics compiled by the police there were 5,365,400 recorded offences in the year to June 1994, of which property crimes constituted 93%. These do not of course comprise the total volume of crime. For it has long been recognised by sociologists that there is a 'dark figure' of unrecorded crime, something which is now more widely acknowledged.

There are various reasons why official statistics present an incomplete picture of crime and may indeed convey a systematically biased portrait.

1 Official statistics do not even comprise a complete record of those criminal offences known to the authorities. They don't for example cover 'summary offences' (ie those triable in magistrates' as opposed to Crown Courts) and offences dealt with administratively by organisations such as the Inland Revenue and Customs and Excise. It might be thought that official statistics at least deal with the more serious offences. However, it's highly questionable whether theft from an automobile or criminal damage, which often involve small amounts of loss or damage are more serious than common assault (tried in a magistrates' court) or income tax fraud (often dealt with by negotiation with the Inland Revenue).

2 The number of recorded offences depends on certain counting rules whereby if several offences are committed in one incident, generally only the most serious is counted (Maguire, 1994). Alternative rules would result in a different record. As it is, the current rules underplay the incidence of domestic violence and fraud. For domestic violence usually takes place over a prolonged period and fraud often consists of a series of transactions.

3 Over 80% of all recorded crime results from reports by the public (Bottomley and Coleman, 1981). But there are plenty of occasions when crime will not be reported to the police. There may be a lack of awareness that a crime has taken place (eg fraud); the victim may be relatively powerless (eg child abuse); the offence may seem too trivial (eg vandalism); there may appear to be no victim (eg prostitution); the victim may feel that the offence won't be taken seriously (eg rape).

4 Only about 40% of offences reported to the police are recorded by the police (Mayhew and Maung, 1992). While the police have a statutory obligation to record crimes, they also have some discretion as to whether or not a particular offence is serious enough to warrant their attention. The reason Nottinghamshire appeared in 1981 to be the most criminal area in the country was primarily because of 'differences in police recording practices' with crimes involving £10 or less being much more likely to be recorded there than comparable counties like Leicestershire and Staffordshire (Holdaway, 1988).

5 The number of offences of a particular kind discovered by the police themselves in the course of their operations will fluctuate in the light of their priorities of the day (priorities which of course will be influenced by other agencies). Since an urgent priority for the police at the moment is to improve their clear up rate, police resources will be targeted at those offences which

are more likely to fulfil that objective. As the retired officer in charge of the Obscene Publications Squad puts it: 'If you don't catch a burglar, he will go out and he will commit a lot of crime which will then be reported and it will damage your detection rate. But if there's a paedophile out there, the chances are that the children he is abusing will not report him. You can't blame the child for that. We all know what they go through, the pressure they're under. So we may have a whole load of intelligence on a paedophile but if we don't catch him and he carries on committing his offence, the chances are that it won't be reported and so it won't damage the detection rate.

If it is not reported crime, it is not what we call "black ink" crime - written down in the book, to be detected. If you look at crimes against property - burglary, car crime, mugging - then that's crime that is reported. So the commissioner has said this year that he'll give top priority to burglary, armed robbery, firearms. That's very laudable. But where do kids come into this? They will say, "Oh, we have Child Protection Teams, we are fully committed to this area". I beg to differ. The Child Protection Teams are doing a great job dealing with offences if they are reported. But that is not enough. We need a proactive national squad to go out and gather information and to target these people, like they do for burglars and robbers.' (Davies, 1994 pp2-3)

6 Finally, numbers aren't everything. Offences against the person and fraud may constitute a relatively small proportion of recorded offences but there are other criteria than quantity to measure significance. Violent and sexual offences often have a traumatic effect upon victims and their seriousness is evident from the number and length of prison sentences they warrant (over 40% of prisoners are serving sentences for violent or sexual offences). 'If one measures the importance of property offences in terms of the value of goods stolen, rather than the quantity of incidents, fraud comes out as of enormously greater significance than other categories' (Maguire, 1994, p252). If we take any *one* of the major cases of alleged fraud recently investigated by the Serious Fraud Office - Barlow Clowes, Guinness, Maxwell, BCCI, Polly Peck - we find that by itself it exceeded the total amount stolen in thefts and burglaries recorded by the police (Levi, 1993).

It is clear that the official statistics provide an incomplete picture of the volume of crime and that they may indeed be systematically biased in underestimating the extent, let alone significance, of crimes such as domestic violence and fraud. 'The hard figures presented to us by the police and media as the state of play regarding crime in the country

have to be interpreted with extreme caution. It is not that they are meaningless; they do reflect public, police and court definitions of crime, the disposal of limited resources and the extent of infractions thus defined; but what they do not do is tell about an independent entity called "crime"' (Lea and Young, 1984, p15). Or as another writer puts it, 'Official statistics of crime are not so much the facts about crime, as the end product of a complex series of decisions. An incident occurs and someone decides that it is a crime. A decision is made to telephone a police officer and the police officer receiving the call decides to regard the incident as a crime. Another officer attends the scene and, hearing the various accounts of the incident, makes a further decision about its being a crime, and so on. The official statistics are socially constructed; they are the end product of a range of decisions' (Holdaway, 1988, p24).

3.3 Trends in crime

The official statistics since 1876 indicate little change in the crime rate until the 1930s. Then there is a gradual rise to the mid 1950s and a sharp and sustained increase since, except for the occasional slight fall as in 1993-4. Every decade since the mid 1950s has witnessed a doubling of the crime rate, a phenomenon paralleled in most other Western societies over the same period.

Crimes recorded by the police 1876-1994

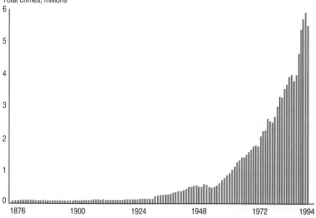

Adapted from Maguire, 1994, p258

If there are problems with the official statistics in any one year, these are in many ways compounded when we examine them over a long time period. At least two additional problems are evident.

Firstly, more crime may be reported. This may be due in part to increased telephone ownership which makes reporting easier. The increase between 1981 and 1993 of burglary and auto theft may be a function of an increase in valuable goods in the home - TVs, videos, etc - wider car ownership, and more insurance policies covering house contents and cars

(Mayhew et al, 1994). The increase in violent crime may be due to reduced levels of tolerance to it. And increases in other crimes may be a function of the break up of traditional communities, with people more willing to bring in the police to deal with incidents which would have previously been dealt with informally.

Secondly, changes in legislation and law enforcement may result in more crimes being recorded. The decision in 1977 to include offences of criminal damage of £20 or less - which had previously not been counted - 'immediately raised the "total volume of crime" by about 7 per cent' (Maguire, 1994, p248). Similarly the greater use of formal cautions for young people in the 1970s did not simply divert 'work away from the courts - as was its intention - but added substantially to the volume of recorded crime and recorded police activity. Among boys under 14 years of age, the increased use of the formal caution is enough to account for the whole increase in recorded crime for this age group during the 1970s' (Pearson, 1983, p217). More recently, the increase in the numbers involved in law enforcement (for example a 50% increase in the number of police officers in the last 15 years) coupled with more sophisticated technology may have resulted in more crimes being recorded.

Crime waves

In the light of the above, it's not surprising that some scepticism has been expressed towards the notion that we are currently living through a crime wave and that crime is soaring inexorably upwards. Surveying over 400 years of British history, one writer has noted a perennial refrain - how each period harkens back to a golden age 'twenty years ago' when crime, violence and disorder were rare, discipline was firm, and the national character was not corrupted. 'The crystallising focus for this immovable preoccupation with the erosion of social discipline and the corruption of the national character is the awesome spectre of crime and violence, perpetually spiralling upwards. The fact that young people are over-represented in the criminal statistics is repeatedly rediscovered in each successive wave of concern as a particularly "new" and shocking feature of the problem. While at the heart of the matter stands the "un-British" crime of violence, its supposedly alien presence asserts itself time and time again in "new" and unparalleled forms: the lawless tribes of "street Arabs" of the 1840s; the ungentlemanly garotters of the 1860s; the degenerated "un-British" Hooligan of the 1890s; the Hollywood-inspired motor-bandits and bag snatchers of the 1930s; the new streak of violence shown by the "Americanised" Teds; the foreign importation of street crime by the black muggers' (Pearson, 1983, p209). Such an analysis is

useful in reminding us that nostalgia is highly selective and that crime, violence and disorder are by no means novel features in British society. To accept this is not, however, to admit that nothing has changed and indeed by the 1990s scepticism of increasing crime is less prevalent. The reason for a more widespread acceptance of the view that crime is indeed rising results at least in part from the advent of the victim survey.

The British Crime Survey

Although national crime surveys have been undertaken in the United States since 1973, it was not until 1982 that Britain witnessed its first national survey. Such surveys, which have been repeated in 1984, 1988, 1992 and 1994, seek to find out from a representative sample of the population whether they have been the victim of particular crimes in the previous year. The British Crime Survey (BCS) does not purport to provide a complete count of crime. Many crimes, such as drug offences, fraud and crimes against business, cannot be covered in a household survey. Nonetheless, 'for the offences it covers, it provides a more complete picture of the extent of crime than police figures. It can also give a better measure of trends in crime should readiness to report crimes to the police vary over time, or police recording practices change'. (Mayhew et al, 1994, p1).

What then is the picture of crime which British Crime Surveys give us?
1 Firstly, there is a lot more crime evident than in comparable police figures, though much of it is

Recorded and unrecorded crime, 1993

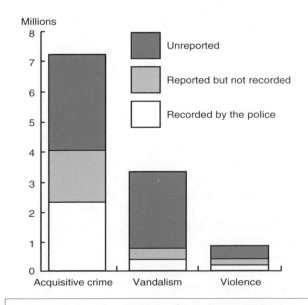

Acquisitive crime	Burglary; all vehicle and bicycle theft from the person.
Vandalism	Against household property and vehicles.
Violence	Wounding and robbery.

Adapted from Mayhew et al, 1994, p 2

petty. In 1993, the BCS estimated a total of 18 million crimes. 'For BCS crimes which can be compared with police statistics, incomplete reporting and recording mean that only just over a quarter are estimated to end up in police records' (Mayhew et al, 1994, p1).

2 The BCS suggests, like most surveys in the USA, that the overall increase in crime has been less steep than police figures suggest. 'Between 1981 and 1993, for those crime types that can be compared, the number of crimes recorded by the police increased by 111%; the BCS showed a lower rise of 77%. The divergence in the figures is due to a smaller increase in vandalism and violence according to the BCS. Acquisitive crime has risen by much the same extent on both measures. Recorded crime shows a larger rise than the BCS mainly because a greater proportion of crimes are now reported to the police than 1981. In the case of vandalism and violence, more reported crime may also have been recorded by the police' (Mayhew et al, 1994, p1).

3 The picture of crime which the BCS conveys is not dissimilar in its broad shape to that of the police with low levels of violent offences relative to property offences.

4 'The BCS, perhaps even more so than the police figures, promotes a picture dominated by the types of crime that are generally committed by strangers, as it were "out of the blue"' (Maguire, 1994, p265). Most of us do not have a high risk of being the victim of a serious crime. Indeed it is young men, who have less fear of crime than women and the elderly, who are most at risk of being the victim of a crime of violence.

Two problems have been highlighted in relation to the BCS's picture of crime. Firstly, there are certain inner city areas where the risks of being the victim of a serious crime are high. 'For example, the first Islington survey [a local victim survey] indicated that a third of all households had been touched by burglary, robbery or sexual assault within the previous twelve months (a situation light years away from that of the notional, 'statistically average' person referred to in the BCS)' (Maguire, 1994, p267). Secondly, there are some crimes which are underestimated by the BCS because of people's reluctance (for obvious reasons) to tell the truth. This applies particularly to sexual offences which local surveys, such as the Islington surveys, and special surveys of women, indicate are much higher than the BCS suggests.

Despite any reservations we may have about the BCS, it is noteworthy that it points to an upward trend in crime and is in that sense congruent with the official statistics compiled by the police. 'In conclusion it seems that we cannot accept without question the dramatic increase in recorded crime as corresponding to a real increase of the same proportions. But it would be wishful thinking to explain away all, or even most, of the increase as an artifact of recording changes. We can plausibly infer that crime has been increasing in the last two to three decades' (Reiner, 1991, p52).

Activity 4 The 1994 British Crime Survey

Item A

Comparison of British Crime Survey and notifiable offences recorded by the police

Figures in thousands	1993 Police	1993 BCS	% reported to police	% recorded of number reported BCS	% recorded of all crimes
Vehicle vandalism		1,787	22		
Vandalism to other property		1,591	32		
Burglary	727	1,754	69	60	41
Attempts and no loss	185	948	53	37	20
Burglary with loss	542	806	87	77	67
All vehicle thefts	1,424	4,312	53	63	33
Theft from motor vehicles	785	2,546	50	61	31
Theft of motor vehicles	497	541	97	95	92
Attempted thefts of and from vehicles	143	1,225	40	29	12
Bicycle theft	208	595	72	49	35
Wounding	169	692	54	45	24
Robbery and theft from person	102	835	32	38	12

Item B

The 1994 BCS has a nationally representative 'core' sample of 14,500 people aged 16 or more. Face to face interviews were carried out mainly between February and April 1994 by the Office of Population Censuses and Surveys. The sample was drawn from the Postcode Address File - a listing of all postal delivery points. The response rate in the 1994 survey was 77%.

Items A and B adapted from P. Mayhew, et al *Trends in Crime : Findings from the 1994 British Crime Survey* 1994, p 6

Questions

1 Examine Item A.
   a) Briefly summarise the differences between the police and BCS figures.
   b) Why are some crimes more likely to be reported to the police than others?
   c) Why are some crimes reported to the police more likely to be recorded than others?
2 Read Item B. Evaluate the methodology of the 1994 BCS.

3.4 Offenders: how different are they?

If statistics compiled by the police produce an official account of the volume of crime and trends in crime, statistics compiled from court and police cautioning records produce a picture of those held officially responsible for crimes. 'Taken overall, these data clearly illustrate that the social characteristics of people who are arrested and processed by the criminal justice system - and particularly of offenders who are eventually sent to prison - present a very different pattern from that found in the general population. There are many more males, young people, black people, poor people, poorly educated people and people with disturbed childhoods than one would find in a random sample' (Maguire, 1994, p272). There are obvious problems here - not more than 1 in 10 offences recorded by the police results in a caution or conviction and 'only about 1 in 50 of the comparable crimes identified by the BCS results in a conviction'. The question obviously arises as to whether 'if only 2% of known crimes end in a conviction ... the other 98% are likely to have been committed by a similarly skewed section of the population' (Maguire, 1994, p272). This is where self report studies come in.

Self report studies

Here a sample of the population are asked whether they have ever committed one or more of a series of offences. Despite the evident problem involved in generating truthful responses, the results do suggest that most of us have at some stage in our lives committed one or more crimes. That said, self report studies, which have mainly been conducted on young men, also indicate that 'convicted offenders tend to admit to both more serious and more frequent offending behaviour than people who have not been convicted' (Maguire, 1994, p272). We must be careful, however, not to conclude too readily that this means that the most serious crimes do indeed tend to be committed by a specific section of society - young working class males. For respondents are usually asked in self report studies about a limited range of offences, mainly street offences, and not about, say, domestic violence or fraud. 'It may be that intra-family violence and abuse are much more evenly distributed throughout the population ... And without doubt, the social class distribution of people involved in business fraud is skewed in a different direction from that of burglary and street robbery.' (Maguire, 1994, p276)

While self report studies do confirm that street offences are most likely to be committed by young working class males, we can't say the same for crime as a whole. For, as a number of sociologists have indicated, the statistics may simply reflect the fact that 'most police resources are devoted to uniformed patrol of public space' (Reiner, 1994, p726) where young working class males are more likely to spend their social lives. As one writer puts it, 'persons are arrested, tried and sentenced who can offer the fewest rewards for non-enforcement of the laws and who can be processed without creating any undue strain for the organisations which comprise the legal system ...The lower class person is (i) more likely to be scrutinised and therefore to be observed in any violation of the law (ii) more likely to be arrested if discovered under suspicious circumstances (iii) more likely to spend the time between arrest and trial in jail (iv) more likely to come to trial (v) more likely to be found guilty and (vi) if found guilty more likely to receive harsh punishment than his middle or upper class counterparts' (Chambliss quoted in Muncie, 1986, p34).

Summary

1 At first sight official statistics appear to give us a picture of the volume of crime, trends in crime and the identity of those responsible for crime. But the statistics are clearly incomplete and may well be systematically biased, underplaying both white collar and domestic crime.

2 The British Crime Survey supports the view that there has indeed been a rise in crime in the last three decades.

3 Self report studies suggest that street crimes are committed mainly by young working class men.

Activity 5 Your Self Report

Incident	Offence	Maximum Penalty
1. Have you ever bought goods knowing or believing they may have been stolen?	Handling stolen property	£5,000 and/or 6 months imprisonment
2. Have you taken stationery or anything else from your office/work?	Theft	£5,000 and/or 6 months imprisonment
3. Have you ever used the firm's telephone for personal calls?	Dishonestly abstracting electricity	£5,000 and/or 6 months imprisonment
4. Have you ever kept money if you received too much change?	Theft	£5,000 and/or 6 months imprisonment
5. Have you kept money found in the street?	Theft	£5,000 and/or 6 months imprisonment
6. Have you taken 'souvenirs' from a pub/hotel?	Theft	£5,000 and/or 6 months imprisonment
7. Have you tried to evade customs duty on a small item bought on holiday?	Intending to defraud	Three times value of goods or £5,000 fine, whichever is greater and/or 3 years imprisonment
8. Have you used a TV without buying a licence?	Using a TV without a licence	£400 fine
9. Have you ever fiddled your expenses?	Theft	£5,000 and/or 6 months imprisonment
10. Have you ever driven a car knowing you are 'over the limit'?	Driving with excess alcohol	£5,000 and/or 6 months imprisonment

Adapted from *Daily Mail*, 31.5.72 and updated 1994

Questions

1 a) How many of these offences have you committed?
  b) Add up the maximum penalties which you could have received.
  c) Compare your answers to a) and b) with those of other students.
2 Now you have completed Question 1 what does this suggest about a) the accuracy of official statistics and b) the picture of the 'typical criminal' drawn from official statistics?

4 Explaining Crime and Deviance

Key Issues

1 What is distinctive about the sociological approach to crime and deviance?
2 What are the main sociological explanations of crime and deviance?
3 What are the strengths and weaknesses of different sociological explanations?

4.1 Normalising the deviant

Sociology is not the only subject concerned with crime and deviance. Indeed Lombroso, the first writer to seek to explain crime scientifically 'based on the premise that criminals can somehow be scientifically differentiated from noncriminals', drew upon biology (Garland, 1994, p18). Many others have drawn upon psychology. What these approaches have in common is a picture of the deviant as somehow different from the rest of us. For some writers, the distinctiveness of the deviant is a product primarily of heredity; for others, the difference arises primarily from experiences in childhood. In both cases the deviant is seen as abnormal.

Sociologists tend to be highly sceptical of this view and insist that a satisfactory explanation of crime and deviance must take into account the social context. In previous sections we've stressed that crime and deviance are socially constructed. What constitutes crime and deviance depends upon the social context; the picture we have of crime and deviance is influenced by social institutions such as the mass media; and even the statistics on crime are the product of countless decisions taken by social actors. Sociologists look to the social situation for explanations of why people commit deviant or criminal acts or are defined as deviants or criminals. There is no suggestion of abnormal genes or abnormal personalities. From a sociological viewpoint, the criminal is as 'normal' as the rest of us.

Activity 6 Deviants are Different

Item A *Throwbacks*

Cesare Lombroso is credited with being the founding father of criminology, a new discipline which sought to explain crime scientifically. From his studies of convicted criminals he claimed to have discovered biological characteristics which were the outward signs of an inborn criminal nature. These included 'enormous jaws, high cheek bones, prominent superciliary arches [eyebrow ridges], solitary lines on the palms, extreme size of the orbits, handle shaped or sessile ears found in criminals, savages and apes, insensibility to pain, extremely acute sight, tattooing, excessive idleness, love of orgies and the irresistable craving for evil for its own sake'. Lombroso believed that criminals were a throwback to an earlier and more primitive form of human being.

Adapted from C. Lombroso *L'Uomo Delinquente* first published in 1876

Item B *Criminal types*

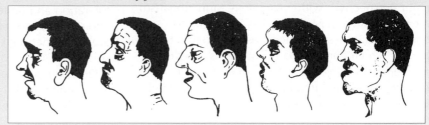

Typical 'criminal types' identified by the Victorian criminologist Havelock Ellis.

Item C *Cartoon from 'Punch' 1881*

CIVILISATION OF THE ROUGH
Professors of Dancing and Deportment giving Lessons to the Convicts

Item D *Crime and personality*

Criminality is obviously a characteristic in the same way as intelligence, or height, or weight. It would, however, be grossly oversimplified to say that every person either is or is not a criminal. Criminals vary among themselves, from those who only commit one crime to those who spend most of their lives in prison. Clearly the latter have far more 'criminality' in their make-up than the former.

Criminals are not completely different from the rest of the population. They simply represent the extreme end of a continuous distribution, very much as a mental defective represents the extreme end of a continuous distribution of intelligence, ranging upward through the average to the very high IQ of the student or even the genius.

What is the case is that heredity is a very strong predisposing factor as far as committing crimes is concerned. But the actual way in which the crime is carried out is subject to the uncertainties of everyday life. While recognising the tremendous power of heredity we would by no means wish to suggest that environmental influences cannot also be very powerful and important indeed.

Adapted from H. J. Eysenck *Crime and Personality*, 1977, pp78-79

Questions

1 The criminal types identified by Victorian criminologists are little different from popular stereotypes. Discuss with reference to Items A, B and C.

2 What similarities and differences are evident in Lombroso's and Eysenck's views of criminal behaviour? (Items A and D)

4.2 Functionalism, anomie and subcultural theory

Sociological theories of crime and deviance are diverse, they are often competing, but they share one thing in common - they offer *social* rather than biological or psychological explanations.

We begin by grouping these theories under three major perspectives within sociology - functionalism, interactionism and Marxism. It is important to recognise that these perspectives are broad schools of thought which contain many variations and that a number of sociological theories of crime and deviance straddle different perspectives. Nonetheless, this approach does enable us to provide a chronological overview which shows how new theories developed from a critique of earlier work.

Functions of crime and deviance

In view of the importance they attach to shared values and norms as the basis of social order, it is not surprising that functionalists consider crime and deviance (beyond a certain level) to be dysfunctional, ie a threat to order and thus the survival of the social system. What is perhaps surprising is the view that a certain amount of crime and deviance is not only 'normal' but also 'an integral part of all healthy societies' (Durkheim, 1964). A crime-free or a deviance-free society is a contradiction in terms. As Durkheim put it, 'Imagine a society of saints, a perfect cloister of exemplary individuals. Crimes, properly so called, will there be unknown; but faults which appear venial [trivial] to the layman will create there the same scandal that the ordinary offence does in ordinary consciousness.' While too much crime or deviance constitutes a threat to social order, too little crime or deviance is unhealthy because it indicates that the values and norms are so strong and stultifying that they prevent the innovation and change necessary for a healthy society.

How then is a certain amount of crime and deviance functional? For Durkheim, it is functional because of the response such activities elicit from society. Through such 'degradation ceremonies' as criminal trials we are reminded of our shared norms and values. By publically condemning those who have broken significant rules, not only are norms and values reaffirmed but also we learn the limits of toleration and unite against the condemned. Crime and deviance (or at least the public response to them) are thus functional because they serve to integrate society.

Do crime and deviance serve any other functions? Some functionalists believe they do. One writer for example has argued that crime and deviance can act as a 'safety valve'. There is, it is argued, a conflict between man's instinctual need for sexual satisfaction and society's need to restrict the legitimate expression of sex to within the family. Prostitution in this context is functional because it provides sexual satisfaction without threatening the family as an institution (Davis, 1961). Another writer has identified a 'warning function' of crime and deviance. They 'may serve as a signal or warning that there is some defect in the social organisation' which may 'lead to changes that enhance efficiency and morale' (Clinard, 1974, p31). For example, truancy from school may indicate unsuspected causes of discontent and the need for changes in the education system.

Suggesting functions for crime and deviance, however, is not the same as finding an explanation for them. To argue that crime and deviance have certain social consequences does not explain their presence in the first place. 'It is one thing to assert that crime can be made to serve some social end or other once it has occurred, eg to heighten solidarity by uniting against the offender. It is another step altogether to explain crime as promoted in advance by society to bring about that end' (Downes and Rock,1988, p106).

Activity 7   Functions

Item A *Prostitutes*

Times Square, New York

Item B *Riots*

Los Angeles, 1992

Item C *Public execution*

Hogarth's engraving of a public execution at Tyburn

Question

Suggest how the activities shown in Items A, B and C can be seen as functional for society.

Suicide: a case study

Emile Durkheim's *Suicide: A Study in Sociology*, published in 1897, is the first major study of deviance from a functionalist perspective. Keen to establish the value of a sociological approach, Durkheim chose suicide, a highly personal act, which seemed more suited to a psychological rather than a sociological explanation. If he could show that suicide was linked to society rather than simply to individual psychology then the value of sociology would be established.

Durkheim's chief concern was with the suicide rate, the rate of suicide per million inhabitants, in different European countries. The statistics revealed a number of patterns. First, suicide rates varied between different countries. For example, they were generally higher in Protestant countries than Catholic countries. Second, the differences between countries remained even when suicide rates across Europe rose and fell. Third, the rise and fall appeared to be related to social factors. For example, suicide rates rose during periods of economic depression and, more surprisingly, during periods of economic prosperity; they fell at times of war and political upheaval. Fourth, there were consistent variations in the suicide rate between different groups within the same country, with Protestants, the unmarried and childless having higher rates than Catholics, the married and those with children.

These patterns could not in Durkheim's view be explained in terms of the psychology of individuals. Instead the answer lay in the relationship between individuals and society and, in particular, the degree to which they were integrated into social groups and the degree to which they were regulated by society. On this basis Durkheim distinguished four types of suicide.

Types of suicide		
	Integration	Regulation
Too strong	Altruistic	Fatalistic
Too weak	Egoistic	Anomic

Types of suicide

Altruistic and fatalistic suicides are found mainly in pre-industrial societies where the individual is powerfully constrained by society. Altruistic suicides occur when individuals are so strongly integrated into society that out of duty they take their own life and, in doing so, exhibit their commitment to the shared beliefs and values of the society. An example would be the traditional practice of Hindu widows throwing themselves on their husband's funeral pyre. Fatalistic suicides occur when individuals are excessively regulated by society. Although this type of suicide is, in Durkheim's words, of 'very little contemporary importance', oppressive discipline in the past did lead, for example, to a high suicide rate among slaves.

Of more significance in modern societies are the two other types of suicide. Egoistic and anomic suicides are characteristic of societies which, in the transition to modernity, are temporarily unable to constrain individuals sufficiently. Egoistic suicide is an offshoot of individualism. As individualism develops so does the tendency for people to think primarily of themselves and be less concerned with their duties and obligations to others and with the opinions of others. Unless this tendency is tempered through membership of a strongly integrated group, the individual will be more likely to commit suicide since moral pressure from others against this act will be weaker. The reason that the suicide rate falls during times of war and political upheaval is, Durkheim argued, because the level of integration into society increases as people draw together in their focus on a common goal. Similarly the reason for the higher suicide rate of Protestants, the unmarried and childless compared to Catholics, the married and those with children arises from the fact that the latter belong to more integrated groups.

Anomic suicide, like egoistic suicide, is mainly found in modern industrial societies. Such societies are characterised by rapid social change which disrupts the norms governing social behaviour. The result is a situation of *anomie* or 'normlessness', a moral vacuum. This does not bring freedom to individuals but makes them prisoners of their own inexhaustible desires. Without norms governing what people can reasonably expect from life, desires are uncontrolled and can never be satisfied. This can occur during a 'boom', a time of rapid economic growth. According to Durkheim, when consensus is threatened or breaks down the pressure for anomic suicide is increased. (For further discussion of Durkheim's study of suicide, see pp636-637).

Evaluation

Durkheim's study is generally considered to be a sociological classic. Nonetheless, his reliance on official statistics has been severely criticised. Suicide statistics, like any other statistics, are socially constructed. Whether a sudden death is classified as a suicide is ultimately the decision of a coroner who will be influenced by other people such as the family and friends of the deceased. A person who is well integrated into a group is much less likely to have their death classified as a suicide than a person who is poorly integrated for the following reasons.

First, family and friends are likely to be reluctant to admit the possibility of suicide and will, if necessary, seek to cover it up (Douglas, 1967). Second, coroners have their own theories about why people commit suicide which influence their judgement. Inasmuch as they consider lack of family ties and lack of friends as a cause of suicide, a person who is well integrated into such groups is less likely to have their sudden death classified as a suicide (Atkinson,1971). For both these reasons the link which Durkheim saw between the degree of integration and the suicide rate has been rejected.

The reason for the correlation it is argued is because the degree of integration influences the chances of sudden death being recorded as suicide. For example, coroners are more likely to see the sudden death of a lonely old man with no family or friends as suicide than they would the sudden death of a middle aged man surrounded by friends and in the bosom of his family. Thus sociologists looking for the causes of suicide may simply be uncovering the reasons used by coroners for defining deaths as suicide.

An interpretive view This possibility has led some researchers to argue that suicide is simply that which is defined as such. For example, J. Maxwell Atkinson (1971) claims that official statistics are not 'wrong' or 'inaccurate'. Suicide is a social construction and so therefore are suicide statistics and suicide rates. The job of the sociologist is not to 'discover' the 'causes' of suicide. Rather, in Atkinson's words, it is to interpret how 'deaths get categorised as suicide'.

Atkinson's research suggests that the following characteristics of the deceased and their situation influence definitions of suicide. Whether or not suicide notes are left or threats of suicide made; whether the death indicates suicide - hanging, gassing and drug overdose are seen as 'typical suicide deaths'; whether the deceased has a 'typical suicide biography' - a history of depression, a recent divorce, personal bankruptcy and problems at work are seen as possible causes of suicide. (For further discussion of Atkinson's study of suicide, see pp642-643).

Merton's theory of anomie

The concept of anomie has been influential in the sociology of crime and deviance. Initially used by Durkheim to refer to an exceptional situation in which individuals are no longer controlled by a moral code, it was taken up in the 1930s by Robert Merton to account for deviance among the lower strata of American society. What for Durkheim was a temporary condition characteristic of societies as they make the transition to modernity, for Merton was an integral feature of American society. The source of anomie did not stem from a temporary lack of social regulation but rather from the recurring contrast between the American dream and persistent economic inequality. While the culture of American society encouraged people to seek 'money success', the social structure was unable to provide unlimited opportunities for all. Merton argued that this resulted in a 'strain to anomie' which led to four types of deviance. These types of deviance are distinguished by 'their combination of either acceptance or rejection of the goal and the means for realising the goal'.

	Culturally prescribed goal	Institutionally available means
Conformity	acceptance	acceptance
Deviant adaptations:		
Innovation	acceptance	rejection
Ritualism	rejection	acceptance
Retreatism	rejection	rejection
Rebellion	replacement	replacement

Adapted from Downes and Rock, 1988, p122

Despite the 'strain to anomie' evident to American society, Merton recognised that most people used legitimate means such as career advancement in order to achieve 'money success'. For those unable to do this, four 'deviant adaptations' were available. The first 'innovation' involved the adoption of illegitimate means such as crime in order to attain the cultural goal, 'money success'. The second, its mirror image, 'ritualism' entailed the abandonment of the cultural goal and a rigid attachment to legitimate means, an adaptation characteristic of people who obsessively stick to the rules. The third, 'retreatism' involved the rejection of both the culturally prescribed goals and institutionally available means, an adaptation evident in people who drop out. The fourth, 'rebellion' was the rarest deviant adaptation involving as it did the search to replace existing goals and means with alternatives, the deviance of the revolutionary (Merton, 1968).

Merton's first deviant adaptation, innovation, has become one of the standard structural explanations for working class crime. It argues that those at the bottom of the class system have fewer opportunities to achieve success in monetary terms. They are less likely to attain high educational qualifications or to have contacts in high status occupational groups. Given that mainstream routes to success are largely blocked, there is pressure to find alternative routes. Innovation in the form of crime is an obvious alternative.

Anomie theory, as formulated by Merton, has been very influential within the sociology of deviance, not least because it constituted an early attempt to explain working class deviance in terms of the nature of society rather than as a result of individual pathologies. Nonetheless, it does raise a number of

questions. Firstly, why do some people adopt one form of deviance while others adopt another form? Secondly, how can the fact that deviance is not simply an act of an individual but often a collective activity be explained? Thirdly, how can we account for deviance, such as vandalism, which does not seem to be motivated by a search for 'money success'? In seeking to answer these questions subcultural theory was born.

Subcultural theory

Albert Cohen The first writer to use subcultural theory to explain working class deviance was Albert Cohen (1955). For Cohen, gang delinquency constituted a way of life in certain inner city areas. It took various forms but was often characterised not so much by a concern for 'money success' as a concern for immediate gratification. The destructiveness evident in the behaviour of gangs - to which members exhibited great loyalty - indicated rejection of the norms and values of the wider society.

Cohen's explanation for the seemingly irrational nature of such delinquency drew on anomie theory. He agreed with Merton that adherence to dominant values creates problems for working class male adolescents in inner city areas. For as they experience failure in school they begin to recognise that they can't make it by legitimate means. In this context, they 'evolve the delinquent gang solution as a means both to acquire status in a more accessible form, and to hit back at the system that has branded them as failures' (Downes and Rock, 1988, p143).

Frustrated by their low status, working class male adolescents don't adopt illegitimate means such as crime in order to attain the cultural goal 'money success', as Merton thought. Faced by a common 'problem of adjustment' occasioned by failure in school, they develop instead a distinct subculture, characterised by norms and values which are markedly different from those held by other members of society. In Cohen's words 'the delinquent subculture takes its norms from the larger culture but turns them upside down'. Activities such as stealing and vandalism which are condemned in the wider society are valued within the subculture. In the process the gang is not only able to take its revenge on a society which has branded people failures, but is also able to provide its members with opportunities to acquire status and thus be successful. Cheeking the teacher is deviant in terms of the norms of the wider culture but is esteemed by members of a delinquent subculture and therefore offers an individual status in the eyes of his fellow delinquents.

Cloward and Ohlin In stressing that juvenile delinquency is collective deviance and in seeking to understand its seemingly irrational character, Cohen's subcultural theory provided answers to the second and third questions we identified earlier. Cloward and Ohlin (1961) in contrast were more concerned with the first question - to explain the different forms that deviance takes. Although sympathetic to Cohen's theory, they 'argued that he had seriously underrated the degree of specialisation that existed, and overrated the role of the school as the crucible of delinquency' (Downes and Rock, 1988, p143). Cloward and Ohlin distinguished three types of delinquent subculture and argued that each emerged in different areas. 'Criminal subcultures', in which adolescents used crime in order to attain 'money success', tended to emerge in areas where there was an organised pattern of adult crime and where therefore young men were able to learn the tricks of the trade. 'Conflict subcultures', in which adolescents belonged to fighting gangs, tended to emerge in areas where such an 'illegitimate opportunity structure' was absent. Without access to either legitimate or illegitimate opportunity structures they felt frustrated, often responding to their situation by resorting to gang violence. 'Retreatist subcultures', centred on illegal drug-using and hustling, were characteristically found among adolescents who were 'double failures'. Unable to succeed legitimately and unable to be successful members of either a criminal or conflict subculture they retreated. 'The root cause of the original emergence of delinquent subcultures was not so much the school - largely an irrelevance to the downtown street corner youth - as the economic pursuit of 'money success' earlier emphasised by Merton in his anomie theory, and reinstated by Cloward and Ohlin as the prime source of embittered frustration in the metropolitan slums' (Downes and Rock, 1988, pp143-144).

Activity 8 Latino Gangs

Item A *Latino gangs in LA*

Los Angeles has 570 Latino gangs and 315 black gangs.

The Latino gangs are split into two groups. The chicanos, Mexican-Americans born in the US, often don't speak any Spanish. Their rivals are those Latino gangs whose members are recent immigrants from Mexico and other Spanish speaking countries and which have evolved a language of their own called *calo*. Older members (*veteranos*) are held in great respect by their 'home boys', having defended the honour of their *barrio* for over a decade or more of fierce urban warfare.

Each gang has its own initiation ceremony. For example, to become a Playboy, a prospective member has to get 'jumped in' - beaten up - by a minimum of three gang members and has only limited means to defend him or herself. While the beating takes place, others look on and count up to 13 slowly.

Once initiated, members take on nicknames and adopt the dress codes of their comrades.

Adapted from *Observer*, 6.2.94

Item B *An LA Latino Gang*

Item C *Latinos in the USA*

Latinos groups are increasing their numbers in the USA as a result of high rates of immigration and fertility. Their average income in the USA is two-thirds that of whites and they are roughly twice as likely to be poor.

Adapted from H. Winant, 'Racial Formation and Identity' in A. Rattansi and S. Westwood (eds) *Racism, Modernity and Identity*, 1994, p287

Item D *Hand signals and tattoos*

Hand signals and tattoos are important signifiers of gang loyalties. Tattoos are usually done by *carnals* (fellow gang members) often using home-made instruments. They cannot be removed by the authorities and are thus a symbol of defiance.

Adapted from *Observer*, 6.2.94.

Question

Examine Items A to D. Explain the behaviour of the Latino gangs in terms of (i) Merton's theory of anomie (ii) Cohen's subcultural theory and (iii) Cloward and Ohlin's theory.

Consensus or conflict?

The theorists we've looked at so far share a common picture of society. The social system is presented in consensual terms with individuals, at least in America, all initially committed to the ideal of 'money success'. In this context, subcultures are seen as reactions by male working class adolescents to their inability to attain this goal. Other theorists who utilise the subculture concept do not share such functionalist assumptions. Rather, they portray society as consisting of different social classes, each with its distinct set of values. We shall briefly examine two very different subcultural approaches which picture society in this way.

Lower class subculture The first approach can be found in the work of the American sociologist Walter B. Miller (1958) who sees delinquency arising from the attempt by male adolescents, brought up in a particular kind of household, to conform to the values of lower class culture. According to Miller, lower class (ie unskilled working class) culture in the USA is distinguished by its adherence to a distinct set of values which include a search for excitement, a stress on a macho form of masculinity and a fatalistic attitude towards life. Brought up frequently in female based households where little reliance is placed on the stability and earning power of men, male adolescents seek to demonstrate their masculinity in street corner gangs. For Miller, the attempt to live up to the values of the lower class culture in this context tends to involve lower class adolescents in breaking the law, a law which after all reflects middle class values.

Stress on lower class culture constituting 'a long established, distinctively patterned tradition with an integrity of its own' means that Miller pays relatively little attention to structural factors which sustain the culture. By emphasising how a distinct subculture is passed on from generation to generation, Miller tends to underplay the way intermittent and boring work underpins the search for excitement. The same cannot be said of the second approach to be explored, which is associated with the Centre for Contemporary Cultural Studies. Here a Marxist approach is employed to explain the rise and fall of various youth subcultures in postwar Britain.

Resistance through rituals Capitalist societies since the Second World War have witnessed a series of economic changes. These have included the break up of traditional working class communities centred on manufacturing and the emergence of markets targeted at teenage consumers. Such changes have proved particularly unsettling to working class youngsters, who have continued to experience a disadvantaged economic situation and have thus been less able than other groups to enjoy the fruits of consumer society. A recurring problem for them has been to make sense of and deal with their marginal situation. What has made this problem so acute is that the advice which they have been given by parents, schools and the media has been contradictory - 'traditional working class emphasis on the importance of workplace solidarity, community and family life, middle class emphasis on educational opportunity and individual ambition, media emphasis on consumption and fun' (Frith, 1984, p44). One solution has been to steer a path through such competing value systems and develop a distinctive subculture.

Teddy boys in the 1950s, Mods in the 1960s, Skinheads in the 1970s and Punks in the 1980s adopted this solution. These different subcultural styles did not merely reflect traditional working class values, as Miller might argue; nor did they just provide opportunities for youngsters failing in school to gain status among their peers, as Cohen might suggest. Rather, they represented a continuing tradition of working class resistance to domination. As one writer who stresses the subversive character of subcultural styles puts it: 'These "humble objects" (bikes, clothes, make-up) can be magically appropriated: "stolen" by subordinate groups and made to carry "secret" meanings which express, in code, a form of resistance to the order which guarantees their continued subordination' (Hebdidge, 1979, p18). Thus the Teddy boy's adoption of a form of clothing originally designed by Saville Row tailors for wealthy young men represented a parody of the upper classes and the Mod's choice of the motor scooter transformed a formerly respectable means of transport 'into a menacing symbol of group solidarity'.

In reality, subcultures do not provide sustainable solutions to the problems faced by working class youth because these problems arise from inherent features of a capitalist society which are not confronted. Nothing can be done about the fact that the work available is humdrum and insecure. In the words of Clarke et al (1976), subcultures '"solve", but in an imaginary way, problems which at the concrete material level remain unsolved'. This is illustrated by looking at Skinheads. Their appearance - a combination of cropped hair, braces and Doc Marten 'bovver boots' - celebrates a form of toughness which is increasingly being devalued as the demand for unskilled manual labour falls; while their collective presence in the streets and on football terraces represents a desire to recreate a form of community which is fast disappearing. Even their most notorious 'feats' - 'Paki-bashing' and 'queer-bashing' - are not what they seem. The first expresses a yearning for a mythical past when working class communities were culturally homogeneous and the second seeks to solve a crisis of masculinity by turning the clock back

(Muncie, 1984). While it is recognised that Skinheads and other subcultural groups do not consciously challenge dominant values, it is agreed that they use their free time 'to make a gesture against their lot' and in this way 'symbolise a refusal to accept dominant accounts of their position' (Frith, 1984, p47).

In many ways, what has been labelled 'new subcultural theory' entails an imaginative decoding of subcultural styles but it does raise in graphic form a problem common to subcultural theory - 'how to establish whether or not the distinctive meaning systems of the various subcultures are in reality those imputed to them' (Downes and Rock, 1988, p161). How do we know, for example that 'Teddy Boys attacking Cypriot café owners, Mods and Rockers attacking each other, Skinheads beating up Pakistanis and gays, or football hooligans smashing up trains, are all really (though they might not know it) reacting to different things, for example, threats to community homogeneity or traditional stereotypes of masculinity' (Cohen, 1987, p xi). Isn't it as plausible to interpret the behaviour of Skinheads as conformist or indeed over conformist to dominant norms in their racial and sexual attitudes rather than as resistant to dominant values?

Structure or action?

Functionalist sociologists sometimes imply that criminal and deviant behaviour are the result of forces beyond the individual's control. For example, from Robert Merton's theory of anomie it almost appears as though people at the bottom of the class system who have few legitimate opportunities for success are forced to turn to crime. Similarly, Albert Cohen's theory implies that young working class males have little choice other than to act out a deviant subculture. To an extent such theories picture people as prisoners of the social structure, acting out predetermined roles with little or no say in the matter.

David Matza The work of David Matza (1964) provides a critique of and an alternative to this view of human behaviour. As he points out, the assumption that deviant behaviour is determined by social forces raises three problems - first, it tends to make the deviant more distinctive than he or she really is; second, it 'over predicts' delinquency, ie accounts for far more of it than exists; and third it denies the deviant freedom of choice. Matza's own work on delinquency tried to correct these weaknesses by stressing that delinquent acts are chosen and that such activity is not a way of life but casual and intermittent behaviour which most young people have no problem giving up as they approach adulthood. Delinquents are therefore similar to other young people. They are not committed to a distinctive set of values but generally adhere to

dominant values. What distinguishes them is that they place greater emphasis on 'subterranean values' which are widely held by other members of society: the search for excitement, disdain for routine and a macho concept of masculinity. These values are usually expressed in non-criminal ways in leisure activities such as sport. However, during adolescence males may 'drift' into delinquency in their search for thrills, a process made possible by the employment of justifications for deviance. Matza calls these 'techniques of neutralisation'. The techniques are: 1) denial of responsibility - deviant acts are an accident; 2) denial of injury - no one got hurt; 3) denial of the victim - he deserved it; 4) condemnation of the condemners - the police/judges, etc are just as bad; 5) appeal to higher loyalties - I did it for my mate (Heidensohn, 1989, p48).

Downes and Rock argue that Matza's theory is particularly applicable to the British context, where studies of delinquency and youth subcultures have typically demonstrated that male adolescents 'were not members of structured delinquent gangs, with a marked sense of territory, leadership, hierarchy, and membership. Delinquency was a *fact* of life, not a *way* of life. The most frequent of the reasons quoted by the boys themselves for their delinquency was boredom . In this context, delinquency is a repertoire of possibilities for the display of toughness, daring and panache' (1988, p148). Although Matza's emphasis upon the process of drift helps to account for the episodic and generally 'mundane' character of delinquency, his theory is not without its critics. In particular, questions can be raised about whether in the process of seeking to remedy theories which 'over predict' delinquency he doesn't under predict its scale. It is noteworthy for example that 'of all British men born in a single month in 1953, one in three had a criminal record by the time he was 30' (*Observer*, 17.2.1991).

Blue collar or white collar crime?

The starting point for most of the sociological studies of crime and deviance we've looked at so far is the social pattern indicated by the official statistics, that the most serious and frequent offenders are young working class males. As we saw earlier, however, there may be a systematic bias to the statistics with the result that white collar crime is understated.

Sutherland (1949), who first coined the term 'white collar crime' and pioneered its study, challenged the assumption that crime is a predominantly working class phenomenon. Unfortunately his own definition is not very helpful. 'The basic ambiguity in Sutherland's definition of white collar crime as a crime committed by a person of high status in the course of his or her occupation is that it does not distinguish crimes committed *for* an organisation or business from those carried out *at its expense'* (Nelken, 1994, p361). Later writers have therefore tended to distinguish *corporate crime* (carried out on behalf of the organisation such as non-payment of VAT) from *occupational crime* (carried out at the expense of the organisation such as defrauding the company of money). Sutherland's empirical studies in the 1930s and 1940s focused on corporate crime which he demonstrated was extensive, with senior executives of the seventy largest industrial corporations in America having consistently violated the law with regard to misrepresentation in advertising, trade restraint, infringement of patent rights and unfair labour practices (Sutherland, 1949). Such activities have not only economic but also social costs. Well known examples include the deliberate fabrication of test data on the fertility drug thalidomide in the 1970s which resulted in thousands of deformed babies being born, and more recently the flouting of safety regulations on cross channel ferries and the North Sea oil industry, with the consequent loss of hundreds of lives. What's more, the state is not exempt from involvement in criminal activities. Examples include the 'Watergate Affair' in the USA and reported links between Italian politicians and the Mafia.

Occupational crime covers a range of offences from employee theft to fraud. Although such offences may be committed by lower level employees as well as senior executives, the opportunities to offend and make large sums of money tend to be higher at the top end of the occupational hierarchy. Crime committed in the course of legitimate employment differs in a number of respects from other crime. There are no obvious signs of breaking and entering so that it is less visible; it often involves expert technical or financial knowledge and therefore is more complex; and because the offender and victim rarely confront each other, victimisation is more indirect. What's more there is a fine dividing line between what is considered acceptable or unacceptable practice - 'perks' vs theft; 'borrowing' vs fraud. The result is that we tend to be less fearful of occupational crime so that 'many offences are described using "soft" words like "fiddles", "cons" and "rip offs" rather than "hard" words such as "theft" or "fraud" (Croal, 1993).

Whether corporate, or more generally white collar, crime is widespread is a matter of debate. It is certainly relatively invisible and thus less likely than many other crimes to be reported to, or detected by, legal authorities. Even when white collar crimes are detected, few cases are taken to court and these 'almost always result in comparatively mild punishment - 30 days in jail, 60 days, even more often a fine and no jail or prison sentence at all' (Goode and Ben-Yehuda, 1994, p83). There may, in short, be a systematic bias in the criminal justice system whereby the crimes of the powerful are not targeted and censured as much as the crimes of the less powerful - a bias which is reflected not only in media representations and official statistics but also, as Sutherland indicated, in much sociological work.

4.3 Interactionism and labelling theory

To move from functionalism to interactionism is to move to a radically different theoretical perspective. Interactionism, or more specifically symbolic interactionism, is - as Blumer (1969) indicates - characterised by three central beliefs. Firstly, 'human beings act towards things on the basis of the meanings that things have for them'. Human behaviour is not determined by social forces. Rather, people are self conscious beings who choose what to do on the basis of their subjective perceptions. Secondly, 'the meaning of things is derived from, or arises out of, the social interaction that one has with one's fellows'. Meanings are not fixed but are continually modified as people negotiate with each other. Thirdly, 'group action takes the form of a fitting together of individual lines of action'. Society is not so much a determinant of human action as a product of human activity. Social order is therefore inherently fragile, being dependent on shared meanings.

Although symbolic interactionism first emerged in the 1930s, it did not grow to prominence until the 1960s. That decade witnessed the growth of a range of social movements which challenged the dominant social order and made the picture of a consensual social system less plausible. Within the sociology of crime and deviance in particular, symbolic interactionism gained many converts as it not only challenged functionalism but also changed the focus of inquiry.

Functionalism was challenged on three grounds. Firstly, the assumption that there was agreement about what forms of behaviour constituted crime or deviance. What intrigued interactionists was why the same behaviour is defined as criminal or deviant in some contexts but not others. Secondly, the claim that deviants were somehow distinctive, comprising a specific group of the population. We are asked instead to look at the process of interaction and question why certain groups are more likely to be defined as deviant. Thirdly, the search for the causes of deviance is seen to be fruitless. We all commit acts which break rules. What is more interesting is the way agencies of control respond to different individuals and the effects of that response on their future actions.

Labelling theory

The new approach which interactionism initiated is generally called *labelling theory*. The classic formulation of this theory is that of Howard Becker (1963): 'the central fact about deviance [is that] it is created by society. I do not mean this in the way it is ordinarily understood, in which the causes of deviance are located in the social situation of the deviant or in "social factors" which prompt his action. I mean, rather, that social groups create deviance by making the rules whose infraction constitutes deviance and by applying those rules to particular people and labelling them as outsiders. From this point of view, deviance is not a quality of the act the person commits but rather a consequence of the application by others of rules and sanctions to an "offender". The deviant is one to whom that label has successfully been applied; deviant behaviour is behaviour that people so label' (1963, pp8-9).

Becker's words have been frequently quoted because they represent a shift within the sociology of crime and deviance in the focus of enquiry - away from a concern with the deviant and the causes of deviant behaviour and towards a concern with agencies of social control and the process by which they label certain behaviours as deviant and the consequences of such labelling. In view of this, how is deviance created?

Defining deviance Society creates the rules, the infraction of which constitutes deviance. Deviant behaviour is not a distinctive form of behaviour but behaviour which contravenes certain rules. Becker (1963) illustrates this point well. 'The act of injecting heroin into a vein is not inherently deviant. If a nurse gives a patient drugs under a doctor's orders, it is perfectly proper. It is when it is done in a way that is not publicly defined as proper that it becomes deviant.' What applies to the use of drugs also applies to other forms of behaviour. Even the act of taking someone else's life is in some contexts considered appropriate. Indeed in a war it is the refusal to kill which is often seen to be deviant.

Labelling Agencies of social control do not however, have unlimited resources and therefore are necessarily selective in their enforcement of these rules. Labelling theorists go further and argue that the police and other agencies not only shift their priorities over time but also use their discretion to target specific groups. Studies of policing have indicated that 'those who are stopped and searched or questioned in the street, arrested, detailed in the police station, charged, and prosecuted are disproportionately young men who are unemployed or casually employed, and from generally discriminated against ethnic minorities' (Reiner, 1994, p726). For labelling theorists such groups are targeted not so much because they are involved in a higher rate of offending but rather because of stereotypical perceptions held by the police and other

agencies. Cicourel's study of the way juvenile justice operated in two Californian cities illustrates how the stereotypes which are held may result in systematic bias. Both the police and probation officers held a picture of the 'typical delinquent' as 'coming from broken homes, exhibiting "bad attitudes" towards authority, poor school performance, ethnic group membership, low income families and the like' (Cicourel, 1976, p67). The result was that youth who fitted this picture tended to be arrested and charged while those who did not were, if arrested, typically 'counselled, cautioned and released'.

Primary and secondary deviance

Society may in the process of creating and enforcing rules inadvertently generate further deviance. To clarify the way in which *societal reactions* to deviance may generate further deviance, it is helpful to distinguish primary and secondary deviance (Lemert, 1972). *Primary deviance* encompasses deviant acts which have not been publicly labelled. Most of us have engaged in such acts at one time or another and for all sorts of reasons. Generally speaking such acts have little effect on our identity or our status in society. *Secondary deviance* by contrast refers to deviant acts which result from being publicly labelled deviant. Such acts may well have dramatic implications for the individual's identity and status in society.

Societal reaction How then does societal reaction to primary deviance generate secondary deviance? Although labelling theorists recognise that people do label themselves, particular importance is placed on public labelling. The labelling of people as deviant will tend to mark them out. The label may indeed become a 'master status' which overrides all other statuses so that the individual is no longer seen as a parent or a friend or a worker but only as a criminal or mentally ill or a homosexual. Rejected by conventional society, they may embark on a 'deviant career', engage in further deviant acts and ultimately join 'an organised deviant group'. Public labelling may in short result in a self-fulfilling prophecy whereby the person labelled deviant not only commits further deviant acts but also eventually accepts the label. Young's study of hippie marijuana users in Notting Hill during the 1960s illustrates this process well. The police targeting of a group, whose bohemian lifestyle included smoking marijuana, served to accentuate the differences between the hippies and conventional society. In the process drug taking, which initially had been 'essentially a peripheral activity' became 'of greater value to the group as a symbol of their difference and of their defiance against perceived injustices' (Young, 1971, p191). In this context a deviant subculture, characterised by distinct values and norms, grew and individuals labelled outsiders began to recognise that they were indeed different from non-drug takers, all of which made it difficult for hippies to re-enter the wider society.

While labelling theorists highlight the way that societal reactions to primary deviance lead to secondary deviance, they do not see this process as inevitable. This is borne out by Goffman's study of *total institutions*, organisations such as prisons and mental hospitals where 'like minded individuals, cut off from the wider society for an appreciable period of time, together lead an enforced, formally administered round of life' (Goffman, 1968, p11). From his observation of a mental hospital in Washington DC in the late 1950s, Goffman argues that such organisations 'seem to function merely as storage dumps for inmates'. On entry, people are stripped of their clothes and possessions and issued with a new 'identity kit' and in the process deprived of their

individuality. And throughout their stay they are rewarded for obedience and given little opportunity to be autonomous. The upshot of such treatment is to remind the individual that they are indeed deviant. As Goffman puts it in relation to mental hospitals, 'the setting and the house rules press home to the patient that he is, after all, a mental case who has suffered from some kind of social collapse on the outside, having failed in some overall way, and that here he is of little social weight, being hardly capable of acting like a fully-fledged person at all' (1968, p139). Despite this, he argues that the effect of total institutions upon the self images of most inmates is short lived. While it is true inmates find difficulty shrugging off the labels of 'ex-mental patient' or 'ex-convict', some are actually successful in resisting these labels and are able to re-enter conventional society. (For further discussion of total institutions, see pp380-381).

Activity 9 Labelling Theory

Item A *Defining deviance*

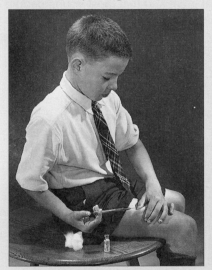
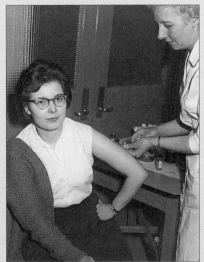

Item B *Labelling deviance*

Item C *Secondary deviance*

Questions

1 Use Item A to show how deviance is socially constructed.
2 Research indicates that if there was crowd trouble at a soccer match then the police would be more likely to single out and question the person pictured on the left in Item B than those on the right. Use labelling theory to explain this.
3 How might the police activity in Item C lead to secondary deviance?

Amplification

So far we have focused upon the effects of societal reaction upon individuals. Social reaction may, however, have a wider social impact. This is apparent from a study of the 'mods and rockers' phenomenon of the mid 1960s (Cohen, 1987). What concerned Cohen was not so much the emergence of mods and rockers, which he explained in subcultural terms, as the social reaction to the disturbances which took place in Clacton over the Easter bank holiday in 1964. The mass media represented the disturbances as a confrontation between rival gangs 'hell bent on destruction'. On inspection, however, Cohen

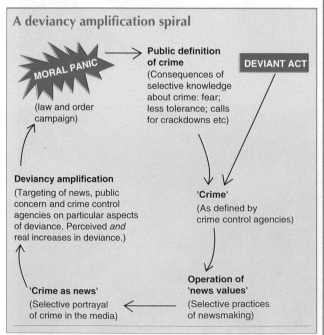

A deviancy amplification spiral

MORAL PANIC
(law and order campaign)

Public definition of crime
(Consequences of selective knowledge about crime: fear; less tolerance; calls for crackdowns etc)

DEVIANT ACT

Deviancy amplification
(Targeting of news, public concern and crime control agencies on particular aspects of deviance. Perceived *and* real increases in deviance.)

'Crime'
(As defined by crime control agencies)

'Crime as news'
(Selective portrayal of crime in the media)

Operation of 'news values'
(Selective practices of newsmaking)

Adapted from Muncie, 1987, p42

discovered that the amount of serious violence and vandalism was not great and that most young people who'd gone to the seaside that weekend did not identify with either the mods or the rockers. The mass media in short produced a distorted picture of what went on. Nonetheless, the coverage initiated a wider public concern with the 'mods and rockers' phenomenon and in the process set in motion a 'deviancy amplification spiral'. Sensitised to the phenomenon, the police made more arrests; the media reported more deviance; and young people more readily identified with mods or rockers. Further disturbances followed on subsequent bank holidays, attracting increased police activity, continuing media attention and a greater propensity for young people to identify with the labels given to them. The social reaction to the initial deviance over the Easter bank holiday in 1964 thus not only resulted in there appearing to be more deviance but also generated an increase in deviance.

Moral panic Cohen, however, went further and argued that the reaction of the media generated a *moral panic*. The latter can be said to exist when 'a condition, episode, person or group of persons emerges to become defined as a threat to societal values and interests' (Cohen, 1987, p9). In this particular case, mods and rockers were singled out as 'folk devils' whose behaviour constituted a threat to the social order. During a decade of significant social change, in which cherished norms were challenged, the mods and rockers served as symbols of what was wrong with society. In subsequent decades, young people have continued to be the focus of moral panics. Thus the 1970s witnessed the moral panic of mugging, a phenomenon which attracted the attention of Marxist theorists as we shall see in the next section (Hall et al, 1978), and the 1980s witnessed the moral panic of football hooliganism. While it is true that the behaviour of young people has always proved consternating to an older generation, the media's reach is now more extensive and moral panics have therefore become more widely diffused. The result is that the media's reaction to primary deviance may not only lead to a deviancy amplification spiral but also more authoritarian forms of control.

Activity 10 Hooliganism

Item A *Moral panics and social control*

```
┌─────────────────────────────────────────────┐
│   ┌─────────────────────────────────────┐   │
│   │   IDENTIFICATION OF A PROBLEM       │   │
│   └─────────────────────────────────────┘   │
│            (eg football hooliganism)         │
│                      ↓                        │
│      Identification of a subversive minority  │
│   (eg the 'few who spoil the enjoyment of     │
│   millions': identification by styles -       │
│   skinheads, casuals etc)                     │
│                      ↓                        │
│            Simplification of cause            │
│   (eg decline in moral standards, lack of     │
│   discipline etc)                             │
│                      ↓                        │
│         Stigmatisation of those involved      │
│   (Media use of emotive and disparaging       │
│   significations eg 'morons'; 'animals';      │
│   'savages' etc)                              │
│                      ↓                        │
│          Stirring of public indignation       │
│   (eg media campaigns calling for 'action':   │
│   criticism of 'soft' sentences; evocation    │
│   of the 'national image', etc)               │
│                      ↓                        │
│              Stamping down hard               │
│   (eg government responds to 'public demand'  │
│   as presented by the media. Stiffer          │
│   sentences; more 'anti-hooligan'             │
│   legislation; bans on spectators etc)        │
│                      ↓                        │
│   ┌─────────────────────────────────────┐   │
│   │  MORE AUTHORITARIAN FORMS OF CONTROL │   │
│   └─────────────────────────────────────┘   │
└─────────────────────────────────────────────┘
```

Adapted from *Muncie*, 1987, p44

Item B *Hooligans abroad*

Although reference to football hooliganism can be found in the press much earlier, it was in the mid 1960s that concern about it began to reach present proportions. At first it was spectator misbehaviour at domestic matches that was the source of this concern. Since the mid 1970s, however, it is the behaviour of British - especially English - fans abroad that has come increasingly to form the principal focus of anxiety.

Adapted from J. Williams et al *Hooligans Abroad*, 1989, p xv

Switzerland 2, England 1. World Cup qualifier at Basle, 1981.

Item C *Newspaper headlines 1988*

Before the European Championship
Sun Euro hoolies league
Daily Mirror Plague of the Euro yob : Dutch go top of the Thug's Table
During the European Championship
Sun World War III
Star Yobs Plot War

Item E *The police response*

In the last twenty years increasing attempts by police to control football hooliganism have included separating rival groups at matches in pens surrounded by spiked fences; closed circuit television crowd surveillance techniques; the use of identity card schemes; soccer hooligan group infiltration through police undercover operations and the formation of a National Football Intelligence Unit with computerised data banks on known soccer hooligans.

Adapted from J. Kerr *Understanding Soccer Hooliganism*, 1994, p73

Item D *Reaction in Parliament*

'We must really eradicate this blot on our reputation ... We want those guilty of it caught and convicted, and given a severe sentence as an example to others.'

Mrs Thatcher 1988 after rowdiness by English fans at the European championships

Item F *The hooligan's view*

We just don't have the time we used to have. The moment a fight starts we're immediately surrounded by dogs and horses. That's why everyone has started using knives. I suppose it might sound stupid but because the policing has got so good we've got to the point where we have to inflict the greatest possible damage in the least amount of time, and the knife is the most efficient instrument for a quick injury. In fact the knifings - because there is so little time - have been quite symbolic. When someone gets knifed, it amounts to an important victory to the side that has done the knifing. If the policing was not so good, I'm sure the knifings would stop.

Quoted in J. Kerr *Understanding Soccer Hooliganism*, 1994, p74

Labelling theory assessed

There are a number of questions which later theorists feel that labelling theory fails to adequately answer. They relate to each of the three ways in which society is said to create deviance. Firstly, although labelling theorists emphasise that deviance presupposes the existence of rules, they do not really address the question of who makes the rules. There is a tendency to focus upon lower level agents of social control such as the police and not the role of the state. Secondly, while labelling theorists point to the way agents of control draw upon stereotypes in their selective enforcement of the rules, they do not examine the origin of these stereotypes. Thirdly, the concern with the effects of societal reaction to primary deviance results in labelling theorists neglecting to examine the origins of primary deviance. While it may be true that the search for what prompts much deviance is unilluminating, the origins of deviance do merit examination.

4.4 Marxism and radical criminology

From a Marxist perspective crime and deviance in Western society can only be understood in terms of capitalism and the class struggle. Coercion and conflict are seen as the key features of capitalist society in contrast to functionalism's emphasis on consensus and integration. However, like functionalism, Marxism sees the structures and institutions of society as largely determining how people behave.

Causes of crime From a Marxist viewpoint crime is systematically generated by the structure of capitalist society. Capitalism is an economic system based on the private ownership of the means of production and the maximisation of profit. As such it emphasises individual gain rather than collective wellbeing. Capitalism is a competitive system which encourages aggression and emphasises the importance of winning. It is also an exploitive system in which some gain at the expense of others.

Given these priorities it is a short step to seeing the end as justifying the means - to be so obsessed with personal gain and coming out on top that breaking the law seems a minor barrier to success. Pressures to break the law will affect people across the social spectrum from wealthy business people to the poverty stricken unemployed. In this respect fiddling business expenses and fiddling the dole have similar causes.

From a Marxist perspective capitalism encourages greed and self-interest, it generates frustration and aggression. Breaking the law can be seen as a rational step in order to satisfy these desires and express these feelings. Crimes motivated by financial gain can be seen as a logical outcome of the priorities of profit. Crimes with no apparent financial motive can be seen as an expression of the frustration, aggression and hostility which the system produces.

The law Laws in capitalist society are seen to reflect the interests of the dominant capitalist class. Thus the many laws protecting private property which have appeared on the statute books over the past 200 years reflect the growth of industry and the expansion of trade and commerce. In this respect private property, the essence of capitalism, is protected.

Laws which appear to protect the interests of workers can be seen as concessions to the working class to maintain if not its loyalty, then its acceptance of the system. For example, health and safety laws protecting workers can be seen in this light - and they have the additional benefit to capitalism of helping to provide a fit and healthy workforce.

Law enforcement 'There is one law for the rich and another for the poor.' This piece of folk wisdom summarises how many Marxists characterise law enforcement in capitalist society. The law is enforced selectively - there is a systematic bias in favour of those at the top. The crimes of the powerful such as corporation crime - for example, failing to pay business taxes and breaking trading laws - if discovered are rarely prosecuted. By comparison, those at the bottom of the class system who are caught breaking the law are regularly prosecuted. Yet in monetary terms their crimes are a drop in the ocean compared to the vast sums involved in the criminal activities of those at the top. Some of the evidence for this claim can be seen from the following activity.

Activity 11   Scrounging

Item A

'I got the loot, Charlie, but after bank costs, services and handling charges,
we owe them £6.25p.'

Item B *'The real scroungers'*

Cost of dole fraud .. .. £500 million	Cost of tax fraud .. .. £5,000 million
Number of prosecutions 14,000	Number of prosecutions 20

In the eyes of the law all people may be equal but the government's treatment of tax and social security offenders suggests there is one law for the rich and another for the poor. For every individual who is pursued through the courts for tax fraud, about 700 are prosecuted for welfare offences. This disparity cannot be accounted for by arguing that benefit fiddling is a more serious social menace than tax fraud. Official estimates indicate that losses from benefit abuses are dwarfed by losses from tax evasion. The Inland Revenue sees prosecution as a last resort and seeks to secure 'a reasonable settlement by agreement'. As one tax accountant put it, 'You have to be very unlucky, very stupid and very crooked to be done by the Revenue'.

Adapted from *Observer*, 23.10.88

Questions

1 Using a Marxist perspective briefly comment on the cartoons in Item A.
2 Read Item B. Suggest reasons for the different treatment of tax fraud and welfare fraud.

Radical criminology

Radical criminology represents the most influential attempt to apply a Marxist perspective to the study of crime and deviance. It emerged in Britain in the 1970s out of a dissatisfaction with existing theories (including Marxism) of crime and deviance. What these theories failed, in varying degrees, to grasp were two central points. First, that deviance represents a normal assertion of 'human diversity', namely the capacity for human beings to think and act differently from each other. Second, that people are not forced by economic or other circumstances into crime but choose whether or not to break the

law, frequently resorting to crime to hit back at a society which treats them unjustly.

We are urged to abandon the fruitless search for an explanation of why people become criminals and focus instead on the process by which the state defines certain activities as criminal and thereby criminalises certain groups, particularly the oppressed and disadvantaged. This stress on the process of criminalisation is reminiscent of labelling theory. Where radical criminology diverges from labelling theory is in emphasising that we need to move beyond a concern with the interaction between lower level agents of control and deviants. We need to examine the process of criminalisation within a wider context and in particular pay attention to the role of the state as it seeks to manage a capitalist system in crisis. With a radical transformation of society and the advent of socialism, radical criminology looks forward to a crime free society in which there will no longer be a need to criminalise deviance.

A 'fully social theory of deviance'

The ambition of radical criminology is evident in the final chapter of *The New Criminology*, (Taylor et al, 1973) when the authors outline their model of what they term a 'fully social theory of deviance'. The model has seven dimensions:

1 'The wider origins of the deviant act'
  The radical criminologist needs to locate the deviant act within the wider social system - capitalism with its attendant class divisions.

2 'Immediate origins of the deviant act'
  He or she then needs to look at the immediate social context within which an individual chooses to commit an act of deviance.

3 'The actual act'
  Attention needs to be given to what the deviant act means to the individual concerned.

4 'The immediate origins of social reaction'
  He or she then needs to look at the immediate response of other people, such as members of the deviant's family and the police, to the discovery of deviance.

5 'Wider origins of deviant reaction'
  The immediate reaction needs to be located within the wider social system, with particular attention being paid to the question of who has the power to define certain activities as deviant.

6 'The outcomes of social reaction on the deviant's further action'
  While most deviants recognise that there will be a reaction against them, it is important to examine the effects of the labelling process on the deviant.

7 'The nature of the deviant process as a whole'
  Finally these six aspects of the deviant process need to be connected together for there to be a 'fully social theory of deviance'.

The closest approximation to a fully social theory of deviance is *Policing the Crisis* (Hall et al, 1978), a study of the moral panic which took place in the early 1970s over 'mugging'. In the following summary, particular attention will be given to the way this study illustrates what Taylor et al call a 'fully social theory of deviance'.

Policing the Crisis: a fully social theory of mugging?

1 **The wider origins of mugging** Mugging is a term imported from America which refers to the street crime of robbery or theft involving the threat or actual use of violence. The authors argue that a full understanding of this phenomenon demands that it is located within the context of the wider society - capitalism with its attendant class divisions. For the most disadvantaged members of the working class, whose employment is insecure and who suffer unemployment during an economic crisis, street crime has traditionally been one 'survival strategy'. In the postwar period, racism has resulted in people of Afro-Caribbean origin being the most disadvantaged members of the working class. Rejected by white society, the first generation of Afro-Caribbeans turned to each other and created a space for themselves in particular areas where they could feel at home. In other words, they created a 'colony' within white society. The birth of this colony not only made possible 'an alternative black social life' but also enabled 'a new range of survival strategies' to emerge. While 'the majority survived by going out from the colony every day to work, ... others survived by taking up permanent residence inside the ghetto' and in some cases taking up 'that range of informal dealing, semi-legal practices, rackets and small time crime known ... as hustling' (Hall et al, 1978, p351). Brought up in this colony, 'black youth has had to survive and make a life by choosing among the range of strategies pioneered by the first immigrant wave' (Hall et al, 1978, p353).

2 **The immediate origins of mugging** Acutely aware of the racism of British society, black youth are less willing than their parents to put up with a stigmatised position. This 'refusal' sometimes gives rise to conflict between the generations with the result that the youth leave home, take to the streets and drift into petty crime. It is in this context, the authors argue, that some black youngsters take up the 'mugging solution'.

3 **The actual act of mugging** The authors provide a brief outline of a mugging committed by 3 youths of mixed ethnic origin in Handsworth, Birmingham in August 1972. However, they explicitly avoid any analysis of the actual act of mugging and the possible motives of the offenders. In the course of discussing crime more generally, Hall et al express more hesitancy than Taylor et al in seeing crime as a political act, given that victims are usually in a similar class position. While they argue that 'few young blacks consciously *choose* crime as a form of political revenge against white society,' (Hall et al, 1978, p359) they acknowledge that mugging may 'express' opposition to white society.

4 **The immediate origins of the social reaction to mugging** Hall et al clearly plot the immediate origins of the social reaction to mugging in the weeks and months surrounding the Handsworth case in August. The study explores in great detail

the role played by an array of institutions (the police, the courts, the government and the media) in the construction of a moral panic over mugging. The media were central in 'orchestrating public opinion' against the black mugger. The term, 'mugging' was first used by the press to describe a specific crime in England during this period. The term had served to symbolise the crisis of law and order in American cities so that when it was transferred to Britain it meant more than a particular kind of street robbery. It evoked images of black youth mindlessly creating havoc in the inner city. The authors point out that the police, the courts, the government and the media did not conspire together to create a moral panic. The media followed their normal news values and turned to 'accredited sources' to define the main issues. The result was that the media tended to define the problem of mugging in a similar way to their sources and give the misleading impression that the problem was both new and growing at an alarming rate.

5 **The wider origins of the social reaction to mugging** In view of the fact that mugging was not a new phenomenon, and that it was growing more slowly than it had done in the previous decade, the authors argue that the moral panic can only be properly understood in the context of the problems that British capitalism was experiencing in the early 1970s.

For most of the postwar period open class conflict was exceptional. Rather, there was an 'inter-class truce', as the state took more responsibility for managing the economy. Full employment, rising living standards and the growth of welfare services resulted in the working class accepting the authority of the state. As the economic crisis, however, deepened in the early 1970s - bringing with it rising unemployment and a slowing down of the rise in people's living standards and a halt to the expansion of welfare services - the authority of the state came under challenge from various groups, especially trade unions. The state, in short, faced not only an economic crisis but also a crisis of authority. The response of the state to the challenge to its authority was to present this as an issue of 'law and order'. Mugging in this context served to symbolise a threat to the stability of society resulting from increasing lawlessness. In the process, attention was diverted away from the real causes of the problems that British capitalism was experiencing and deflected on to the black mugger. The result was to divide the working class on 'racial' grounds and, given the need to stamp out mugging as quickly as possible, to justify the state increasing its powers.

6 **The outcome of social reactions on the muggers' further action** Given the perceived threat posed by mugging, the police targeted this crime and set up special squads to deal with it. Black youth were particularly subject to suspicion. Being stopped, searched and questioned randomly in the street, they sometimes responded by reacting in self defence - which then led to their arrest and thus seeming confirmation that they were indeed especially prone to crimes of violence. The authors in short detect a process of deviancy amplification, whereby the labelling of black youth as deviant led to more arrests, which in turn justified even stronger police measures against the black mugger.

7 **The mugging process as a whole** The originality of *Policing the Crisis* arises from its attempt to link the Marxist emphasis on the crisis faced by British capitalism with the interactionist emphasis on the process by which labelling leads to moral panics. The state's response to the crisis, the authors argue, was to mount a law and order campaign. This led to a moral panic over mugging with the result that black youth became increasingly criminalised and the state was able to justify increasing its powers.

Radical criminology assessed

Despite its influence throughout the field, radical criminology has been subject to severe criticism.

1 The Marxist stress on the 'total interconnectedness' (Taylor et al, 1973, p278) of crime and capitalism is challenged by Rock (1979). Many laws, for example those governing traffic speeds, cannot be seen merely as an expression of capitalist class interests. Such laws will be necessary in any future socialist society and, since inevitably these will be broken by some people, the notion of a future crime free society is hopelessly idealistic.

2 According to Lea and Young (1984) the interactionist emphasis on the social reaction to crime tends to underplay the reality of crime. While there are indeed moral panics, nonetheless crime has risen and the victims are usually working class, for whom crime is a very serious problem.

3 The most sophisticated attempt to integrate Marxism and interactionism and apply radical criminology to a specific crime is *Policing the Crisis*. According to Downes and Rock (1988) this attempt was not successful. For to demonstrate that the moral panic over mugging was caused by a crisis of British capitalism involves at the very least the need to point to a correlation historically between economic crises and moral panics, and this is not done.

4.5 Current developments in the sociology of crime and deviance

New approaches to crime and deviance are partly a reaction to the shortcomings of previous approaches, partly a reflection of changing academic and political priorities, partly a response to changing fashions. Previous approaches have neglected certain social categories. In the cases of gender and ethnicity this neglect has now ended and research in these areas will be reviewed shortly.

In the 1980s and 90s there was increased concern about law and order in Britain. This was accompanied by a growing awareness of vast levels of unreported victimisation, especially amongst the most vulnerable sections of the population. These concerns were reflected in two new approaches to the study of crime - right realism and left realism. Both see crime as a major problem in society especially for its victims, both claim to take crime seriously and to put forward practical proposals to combat it.

'Realist' approaches can be seen as a reaction to both labelling theory and radical criminology. Neither of these perspectives appeared to show much concern for the victims of crime. Indeed labelling theory implied that in many cases the 'victim' was the person labelled as 'criminal'. And the problem of crime often seemed to be the labellers who created and amplified deviance. Radical criminology tended to see the 'system' as the guilty party rather than the offender. Blame was directed towards the structure of society rather than to those who committed the offence.

The rest of this chapter examines recent developments in the sociology of crime and deviance. We begin with feminist perspectives.

Feminism, gender and crime

'Gender is on the agenda.' So wrote Frances Heidensohn (1989), herself one of the most influential feminist sociologists of crime. Yet only in the last twenty years has the simultaneous neglect of women and distorted analysis of the female offender been challenged. In the 'prehistory' of gender and crime, before the emergence of the feminist perspective, women were largely invisible in sociological research. When they were considered, the analysis tended to see female crime as a special case which resulted from characteristics linked to sexuality and biology. Although biological explanations of the male offender had lost credibility in sociological circles by the mid 20th century, such non-sociological theories still held sway in much analysis of the female offender. This neglect and distortion of female crime may of course themselves be sociologically explained. Not least has been the male character of the discipline and the undoubted influence of the ideology of gender on the

academic world. In the past much of the research on crime and deviance has been a case of college boys hanging out with street corner boys!

Feminist sociologists have begun to change this. The major findings of their research into crime may be summarised as follows.

1 The world of the female offender and criminal has been opened up by ethnographic studies of such groups as gang members (Campbell, 1981) and ex-prisoners (Carlen, 1985). This research has shown that women gang members are still under the control of 'their' men and female offenders who are incarcerated are faced by the oppression of institutions run on sexist lines whereby the female criminal is doubly deviant as both 'criminal' as opposed to 'law-abiding', and 'unnatural' as opposed to 'natural' ie 'mothering' woman (Worrall, 1990).

2 There is a growing body of research on the processing of women throughout the criminal justice system (Heidensohn,1985). Such research has raised serious questions regarding the supposed leniency and chivalry shown towards female offenders by the police, courts and the like. According to researchers such as Mary Eaton (1986), certain female offenders may in fact receive tougher treatment and sentencing should they be viewed as failing in the primary role of homemaker. Prostitutes are an example as they are often seen as doubly deviant. And we should not assume that all males are treated severely. Consider the leniency traditionally shown in cases of domestic crime and corporate crime whose perpetrators are usually male.

3 Official statistics indicate that in every age group males are much more likely to commit crimes than females and are twenty times more likely to be sentenced to prison (*Social Trends*, 1995, pp161 and 166). Official statistics also suggest that there are gender differences in types of crime with women less likely to be involved in violent crime. Shoplifting, handling stolen goods and prostitution appear as typical female offences. There is some evidence from victim studies to support the official view of gender and crime. This lends support to Frances Heidensohn's view that, 'sex is therefore a crucial variable, indeed the crucial variable in predicting crime' (1989, p88).

New theories are emerging to explain the differences in male/female offending. For example, with men dominant in the public sphere and freer to move around this sphere, the high level of male offending relative to that of women may be understandable. For men have more opportunities to commit offences. Feminist research has also shown that the private domain of the home is 'even more male-dominated than public street crime' (Heidensohn, 1989, p88). This may be due to the crucial significance of the private domain to men's sense of dominance.

Domestic crimes such as spouse and child abuse

are now recognised as real crimes and as more widespread than were once thought. The concept of gender plays a pivotal role in explaining them. For 'the overwhelming majority of such cases involve men, usually fathers and husbands injuring or abusing their wives and children' (Heidensohn, 1989, p87).

Victimology, while it does not owe its origins to feminism, is a growing subfield of sociology which increasingly relies on the insights of feminism in its analysis of the distress caused by victimisation, the problem of the fear of crime and the measures taken to avoid victimisation (Zedner, 1994). Thus studies of the victims of domestic violence have alerted us to the fact that victimisation is often not a one-off incident but a habitual and prolonged affair. And an appreciation that women may have good reasons to be more fearful of crime than men has sensitised us to the traumatic effects some crimes have on vulnerable groups. Such fear may lead them to be reluctant to go out, especially after dark. These insights have been applied, for example, to racial harassment whose cumulative effect is far greater than an account of one incident would suggest. The consequent anxiety can in turn lead to families living like prisoners in their own homes or being forced to move.

Feminist research is broadening the debate. As Frances Heidensohn (1994) has argued, the understanding of the low levels of female offending relative to that of men requires us to ask questions first and foremost about conformity and the socialisation of women as against that of men. Maybe the big question awaiting the sociology of crime is not what makes women's crime rates so low but why are men's so high.

Activity 12 Gender and Crime

Item A

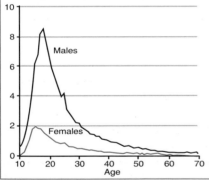

Known offenders [1] as a percentage of the population: by age and gender, 1993

England & Wales
Percentages

[1] Persons found guilty or cautioned for indictable offences.

From *Social Trends*, 1995, p161

Item B

Home Office statistics show that serious offences by women have risen by 250% since 1973, with large increases in the numbers of robberies and drugs offences. The government recorded 101,000 serious crimes by women in 1993, an increase of 12% over the past five years - four times the rate of increase for men.

Actress and model Elizabeth Hurley, accompanied by minders, arrives at Southwark Crown Court to give evidence against four teenage girls accused of robbing her.

Item C *Girl gangs*

It is 8pm on Friday and the girls from Busch Corner are ready for a night on the town. Dressed in miniskirts, low-cut tops and platform shoes, they know what they want and they know how to get it. Boyfriends, though, are the last thing on their minds.

As they stand at the bus stop whispering and giggling, the girls are discussing neither pop music nor sex. They are talking tactics for taking money and jewellery from wealthy and vulnerable women.

These are teenagers, some as young as 14, who can hold a stare with insolent defiance as they sit opposite you on a bus. Worse, they can usually fulfil the threat they promise, especially if you are a woman travelling alone. The Busch Corner girls, who claim to be the roughest female gang in west London, are based on a depressed council estate in Brentford, known only for the blot its tower blocks leave on the landscape.

The girls drink high strength wine to steel their nerve to fight and rob. Of the 10-strong gang, formed four years ago in school, only one has a job. Those who should be in school often play truant. After all, easy pickings are only half an hour away.

They take the bus into the West End, armed with bottles and scissors, looking for victims. Between them, they already have convictions for assault, grievous bodily harm, criminal damage and being drunk and disorderly. Their targets are invariably young businesswomen returning home from an evening out. At Waterloo station last month, some of the gang cornered two young women in the Tube station and forced them to hand over money and jewellery.

On estates in Britain's inner cities police have observed gangs of young girls, some armed with machetes and army knives, competing with men for a share of the drugs trade. Colin Cripps, of the Newham Drugs Advice Project in east London, said: 'Their violence is not just drug-related. Fights break out over boys, money or just for the assertion of power.'

Items B and C adapted from *Sunday Times*, 27.11.94

Questions

1 Briefly summarise and suggest reasons for the differences shown in Item A.
2 Suggest reasons for the trends indicated in Item B.
3 Read Item C. How convinced are you that girl gangs are menacing the streets? Explain your answers.

Ethnicity and Crime

Ethnicity, like gender, is a fairly recent concern of sociologists of crime in Britain. What first prompted interest was the postwar migration of people from the New Commonwealth and Pakistan. In the early phase of migration, according to a major investigation into police-immigrant relations in 1972, 'black people were more law-abiding than the general population' and 'there were few public manifestations of violence towards black immigrants' (Layton-Henry, 1992, pp125, 138). During the following ten years, however, relations between the police and the black community deteriorated and evidence mounted of increasing racial attacks.

Two reports published in November 1981 signalled official concerns. The Scarman Report into the Brixton disorders emphasised how the riots earlier in the year were essentially an outburst of anger and resentment by young Afro-Caribbeans against the police (see pp95;405-406) and the Home Office report into racial attacks revealed that South Asians were 50 times, and Afro-Caribbeans 36 times more likely to be the victims of racially motivated attacks, than whites (see pp81-2). Evidence 'documenting the differential involvement of black people with the criminal justice system, whether as suspects, victims or general customers (is now) undeniable' (Reiner, 1993, p2).

Criminalisation and racism The issue which has attracted most attention from sociologists concerns the criminalisation of black people, especially those of Afro-Caribbean origin. At the end of the criminal justice process, Afro-Caribbeans - who comprise more than 10% of the male prison population and about a quarter of the female prison population - are about seven times as likely to be in prison as white people, or indeed South Asians (Smith, 1994). Two broad explanations have been put forward for this. The first sees the criminal justice system as racist and

discriminating against black people of Afro-Caribbean origin. The second sees black people of Afro-Caribbean origin as disproportionately criminal. Although the debate between these two positions is extremely contentious, some analysts have tried to move beyond the either/or of racist criminal justice vs black criminality (Reiner, 1993, p3) The authors of *Policing the Crisis*, for example, argue on the one hand that Afro-Caribbean young men - because of racism in the wider society and their subsequent vulnerability to unemployment - are likely to turn to crime as a survival strategy and, on the other hand, that it is because of racism at various stages in the criminal justice system that they are more likely to be defined as criminal and thus become criminalised. A recent assessment of the limited evidence reaches the same conclusion. There is 'substantial bias' against Afro-Caribbeans at various stages in the criminal justice process: in the use of stop and search powers by the police; in the decision to prosecute juvenile offenders; and in sentencing by the Crown Court. At the same time, 'in large part the difference in rate of arrest and imprisonment' between Afro-Caribbean and white people 'arises from a difference in the rate of offending' (Smith, 1994, pp1089-1090). In view of this, many analysts such as Hudson (1993) argue that both racism in the criminal justice system and the greater involvement of Afro-Caribbean young men in street crime contribute to the criminalisation of black people. 'And furthermore the criminal justice system, prejudice and discrimination on the one hand, and black crime on the other, reinforce and feed off one another in a vicious circle of amplification' (Reiner, 1993, p14).

Realist criminologies

Recent years have seen the development of competing academic approaches in America and Britain to the problem of crime and law and order. These approaches have been called 'realist' due to their shared emphasis on treating crime as a real and serious problem which requires practical solutions. Furthermore realist criminologists take it as their duty to engage in pragmatic, policy-orientated research which stands in sharp relief to the revolutionary and, in realist terms, 'idealist' position of radical criminology (Young, 1994). Two competing perspectives have come to the fore in realist criminology, namely 'right realism' particularly associated with the work of J.Q. Wilson (1975) and 'left realism' pioneered by Jock Young (1994).

The political events of the 1980s in the USA and the UK are crucial to the emergence and rise to prominence of both right and left realism. This decade saw a heightened concern over crime in the media and political circles together with a rise in recorded crime and public disorders. Conservative politicians in both countries were quick to explain this as the outcome of a general decline in moral values as a result of the permissive 1960s. Such an explanation continues to this day in the 'back to basics' anthem of the Major government in Britain. The 'law and order' debate became a central electoral issue in the 1980s with both President Reagan's and Mrs Thatcher's rise to power built on the appeal to 'social authoritarianism' involving increased state coercive powers (Hall, 1980).

Right realism

The importance of such developments for the sociology of crime should not be underestimated. As Young has noted, the debate on law and order was effectively hijacked by the political right and evacuated by the left. As early as the mid 1970s in the United States Wilson claimed that crime resulted from selfish and wicked people who were undeterred by the criminal justice system which had gone 'soft' on criminals. The remedy offered by Wilson, later Reagan's adviser on crime, was, among other things, the strengthening of penal sanctions. This led to the United States by the 1990s having the highest rate of imprisonment in the world.

The right realists are a difficult group of theorists to describe. Much of their analysis feeds off common sense yet also draws on liberal views on freedom and choice together with functionalist ideas regarding communities and social order. Criminologists such as Wilson in the USA and sociologists such as Dennis and Waddington in the UK (Dennis and Erdos, 1992; Waddington, 1991) do make some telling criticisms of the predominant liberal and left analyses of law and order which have prevailed in sociology. What then are the central features of the right realist analysis of crime?

1 Poverty and crime First and foremost these writers question the thesis that poverty causes crime. Indeed Wilson in the following passage makes a telling critique of this thesis by arguing that affluence and prosperity

may go hand in hand with rising crime.
'If in 1960 one had been asked what steps society might take to prevent a sharp increase in the crime rate, one might well have answered that crime could best be curtailed by reducing poverty, increasing educational attainment, eliminating dilapidated housing, encouraging community organisation, and providing troubled or delinquent youth with counselling services.

Early in the decade of the 1960s, this country began the longest sustained period of prosperity since World War II. A great array of programmes aimed at the young, the poor and the deprived were mounted. Though these efforts were not made primarily out of a desire to reduce crime, they were wholly consistent with - indeed, in their aggregate money levels, wildly exceeded - the policy prescription that a thoughtful citizen worried about crime would have offered at the beginning of the decade.

Crime soared. It did not just increase a little; it rose at a faster rate and to higher levels than at any time since the 1930s and, in some categories, to higher levels than any experienced in this century.

It all began in about 1963. That was the year, to overdramatise a bit, that a decade began to fall apart' (Wilson, 1975, pp3-4).

2 Cultural explanations Having argued that crime is not in any direct sense caused by poverty and inequality, the right realist sociologists then suggest other factors which may be at work. Amongst these they cite the decline in 'civility' and respect for authority in communities which are characterised by anomie and cultural disorganisation. In particular, they point to the rise of the 'fatherless family' and its detrimental effects on young men who are denied an appropriate role model and authority figure.

Right realists claim that there is no direct relationship between economic factors, such as poverty and unemployment, and crime rates. According to Dennis and Erdos, 'High unemployment was associated with low criminality in the 1930s. Low unemployment was associated with growing criminality in the 1960s. Unemployment between these extremes was associated with high and rapidly increasing crime in the mid-1980s. In the early 1990s there was high unemployment and high crime rates' (1992, p97).

Given this apparent lack of correlation between unemployment and crime, such writers turn to a cultural explanation. They see a decline in 'family values', in particular a lack of sufficient discipline both inside and outside the home as the crucial social and psychological factors explaining rising rates of crime.

Other writers like Murray (1990) blame the welfare state for sapping moral fibre, eroding Christian ethics and threatening family values. They picture a 'nanny state' creating an over dependency on welfare which results in a weakening of the work ethic. The upshot of all this is a social sickness which reduces the strength of those moral values and mechanisms of social control so essential for preventing criminal behaviour.

3 Opportunity and choice It would however be inaccurate to suggest that the right realist writers place exclusive blame on cultural factors outside the individual's control (a position often termed 'cultural determinism'). Given their allegiance to New Right thinking with its commitment to choice and freedom of action, these sociologists also wish to argue that there is an important element of choice in becoming deviant.

A similar emphasis on choice is apparent in the work of researchers such as Clarke and Mayhew (1980) at the Home Office in Britain. They have been concerned with practical answers to the problems of controlling crime, chiefly by means of situational crime prevention measures. According to *control theory*, the traditional criminological question of why do people commit

crime is turned on its head by asking 'why do we not commit crime' and their answer is because of social controls and deterrents. Two factors in particular make it less likely for people to choose to break the law - 'target hardening' and 'surveillance'. The first, which includes such measures as property marking, makes crime more difficult while the second, which involves designing the built environment so that people feel responsible for what is happening about them, encourages people to exert informal controls over outsiders. Although it would be incorrect to locate this Home Office research within the ranks of right realism, its approach does lend some support to the latter's emphasis on choice and opportunity.

Right realism has had considerable influence on policy making in contemporary Britain. Often it has led to what some see as a negative preoccupation with retribution and punishment, eg the rising prison population. More positively it has fuelled debate and controversy which is the life and soul of sociology. Indeed the next theoretical development to be discussed offers a sustained critique of right realism.

Activity 13 Beggars

Item A

How to sweep these beggars from our streets by David Marsland

In all of our major cities and larger towns beggars have multiplied over recent years like fungus spreading in a damp cellar. Their aggressive hassling of men, women, and children is an intolerable blot on the complex but orderly copy-book of a modern civilised society.

Their arrogant contempt for the values of most decent, ordinary people - honesty, hard work, and civility foremost among them - is intolerable. Their possessive occupation - like locusts swarming on the harvest - of the most celebrated and attractive streets and squares they can find, is contemptible.

Analysis of historical and international evidence serves to disprove most fashionable explanations of begging. Neither

'capitalism' nor poverty is the cause. Begging on any scale is unheard of in some of the richest countries in the world - such as Switzerland - and some of the poorest - such as Malaysia.

Nor is it unemployment which causes begging. The current scale of begging was unheard of in the Britain of the 1930s, when unemployment was at much higher levels and much crueller in its impact.

Victorian experience provides the clue to the real explanation. Faced with a problem very like today's, politicians, businessmen and community leaders carefully analysed cause and effect, and rapidly set up a practical system which solved the problem in short order.

The Poor Laws and the workhouses were modernised and

toughened up.

Help without a return of effort was outlawed. The values of hard work, self reliance and respectability were reinforced and unapologetically defended by a powerful consensus of public opinion in the schools, the churches, the media and Parliament. Begging was shamed out of existence.

What is causing the escalation in modern begging is:

- The hand-out culture of the decaying welfare state.
- The cultivation of tolerance for 'doing nothing' and 'doing your own thing' by teachers, intellectuals and political leaders.
- The impact on established British values of the sloppy, alien thinking of the Sixties.

Adapted from *Daily Mail*, 1994

Item B *Orderly begging*

Given the growth in poverty and the exclusion of many young people from work, housing and mainstream society, the question is not why are there so many crimes committed in inner-city areas; it is, rather, why aren't there more? It says something extraordinary about the English character that these armies of young people sit peacefully to beg. They similarly make extraordinary attempts to keep clean. They queue quietly in supermarkets to get their sliced white bread and margarine and then walk peacefully away. Some drink. It is amazing that they don't all want to stay drunk all the time. It is equally amazing that most of us shuffle past them in embarrassment.

Adapted from F. Field *An Agenda for Britain*, 1993, p72

Questions

1 Read Item A. To what extent does Marsland's analysis fit the right realist approach?
2 How does Field's view in Item B differ from the right realist approach?

Left realism

Left realism emerged in the early 1980s in Britain as a reaction to 'law and order' politics and to the perceived vacuum in radical left thinking on crime and crime control. Its rallying call to sociologists has been 'to take crime seriously'. Much of the publicity about this perspective has been generated by its chief advocate, Jock Young (1988, 1994).

A realistic alternative Left realism aims to avoid what it sees as the worst excesses of both the 'right realist' and 'left idealist' approaches to the problem of crime in modern society. The right is accused of both over-dramatising and distorting the nature of the problem with its talk of sick societies, moral decay and crime rates out of control. The left is accused of not taking the issue of crime seriously, of reducing it to a form of ideological distortion on behalf of the capitalist state, seeing for example 'mugging' as little more than a moral panic induced by the problems of British capitalism (Young, 1994). By contrast, left realism claims to take crime seriously, particularly street crime, but without the moral hysteria of the right . Throughout its analysis, crime committed by working class people against other working class people is viewed by left realists as a problem of the first order due to its real, symbolic and growing impact on society in general and working class communities in particular. And what should not be underestimated is the untold suffering and heartbreak that such crime can bring to its victims.

A real problem Like right realism, left realism sees crime as a real problem and much of the public's fear of crime as rational and justified. This assessment is based on the following evidence. Their own local victim studies (Jones et al 1986; Crawford et al 1990) generally of high risk areas, appear to offer a more accurate and disturbing picture of the nature and extent of crime than that provided by official statistics and national victim surveys. Local surveys indicate that people see crime as a major problem and regard as serious crimes which others may see as minor or

trivial, eg so-called petty theft. In this way left realism attempts to bring the victim on to the centre stage of criminological study.

A losing battle Such surveys also provide support for left realist claims that the police are losing the 'fight against crime', especially in the inner cities. While seeing structured inequality and perceptions of injustice as the major causes of crime, left realism seems at times to suggest that better policing is a crucial means of reducing crime. Low clear up rates and in turn loss of public confidence all lead to the alienation of both the police and the community and the growth of discriminatory, military policing (Lea and Young, 1984). True to its manifesto of addressing what is to be done about law and order, left realism calls for greater democratic control of the police. It also argues that a genuinely accountable police force will be more efficient since the flow of information from the public, on which the police rely heavily, will be restored.

Explaining crime Left realism accepts the picture presented by official statistics that there has been a growth in working class crime. It explains this growth with reference to changes in the class structure, in particular the marginalisation of a section of the working class.

It argues that increasing numbers of the working class are now being expelled from the process of production with the unskilled young working class particularly vulnerable to such marginalisation. Lea and Young (1984) point to a 'growing army of young unemployed' for whom collective violence and the temporary control over their territory through riot is a substitute for organised politics. Thus for left realism, the growing unrest and criminality of sections of working class youth has to be located in the context of wider structural processes associated with capitalist industrialisation. Here the link with the earlier perspective of radical criminology is apparent.

However, like right realism, the left realists do not see unemployment and poverty as sufficient conditions for a growth in crime. Lea and Young suggest that culture and subjective meanings also need to be analysed. In order to explore this dimension, left realism draws on American subcultural theory and the concept of relative deprivation.

Subcultural explanations Subcultures are seen as creative adaptations to changing material and historical circumstances. One adaptation to marginalisation and the feeling of relative rather than absolute deprivation is the emergence of a criminal subculture. Left realism characterises the criminal adaptation as 'part of a series of individualistic adaptations which promote the notion of the hard individual' (Lea and Young, 1984). We are invited to see the values of the criminal as being the same as the dominant values of the capitalist social order: aggressive, acquisitive and selfish. Subcultures of crime in the marginalised working class represent a response to capitalist dehumanisation and a further contribution to that dehumanisation.

Relative deprivation Lea and Young reject any direct causal link between absolute deprivation, injustice and crime. At this point left realism draws on the concept of relative deprivation to further its argument. From this viewpoint it is not the existence of deprivation and injustice that counts but how they are perceived. In this sense deprivation is relative - people can see it anywhere on a spectrum from perfectly acceptable to completely unacceptable. And how they respond to deprivation will depend on how they see it.

Left realists believe that young Afro-Caribbean men are the group most at risk from being criminalised in the 1980s and 1990s. Part of the explanation for this lies in relative deprivation. There is a lack of fit between what they feel they should reasonably expect in terms of jobs and material rewards and what they experience - high levels of unemployment and low paid jobs which are seen to result from blocked opportunities and racial discrimination. This is part of the explanation for what left realists see as the growth in street crime and public disorder among young, working class inner city Afro-Caribbean men - the most relatively deprived section of the working class.

Evaluation The emergence of left realism has been greeted by two opposed responses within sociology. On the one hand, many in mainstream sociology and criminology have been favourably impressed by Young et al's 'realistic' and policy-oriented concerns with the problems of street crime, victimisation and policing (see Downes and Rock, 1988; Reiner, 1992). On the other hand, 'radical' criminology, made up of Young's former disciples and fellow-travellers, has reacted with outright condemnation and moral indignation over what has been alleged to be the

anti-working class and even racist tendencies of the left realist agenda (Scraton ed, 1987). To some then, using biblical metaphors, Young appears to be a latter-day Paul on the road to Damascus, a Marxist who has seen the light; but to others, he has the dubious status of a Judas who has betrayed the faith.

Radical criminologists reject what they see as left realism's naive hope that social injustice can be solved within the framework of liberal democracies. From their point of view criminology should expose 'criminal justice systems "which protect, and often brutally enforce, the exploitation of international capital, the power of established elites, bureaucratic and political corruption, male chauvinism (and dominance) and widespread racism" (Summer, 1990, p4). Always dressed in the clothes of rationality, justice, fairness and due process, their appearance of consent disguises the reality of coercion - a monopoly on legitimate violence - which underwrites the ultimate authority of the democratic state' (Scraton, 1990, p104).

Summary

1 Functionalism was the dominant perspective from the late 1930s to the late 1950s. Its central concern was with the *causes* of crime and it is within this tradition that anomie theory and subcultural theory first emerged.

2 Interactionism which became very popular in the 1960s, challenged the notion that criminals are essentially different from noncriminals and shifted the focus of attention to the way *agencies of control* like the police label some activities as deviant. It is within this tradition that labelling theory first emerged.

3 Although sympathetic in some ways to labelling theory, Marxism gained adherents in the 1970s by emphasising the wider social context within which interaction between agents of control and deviants operates. For radical criminology, the wider context is capitalism and the focus of attention is shifted in particular to the role of the *state*, which among things manufactures a crime problem in order to justify strengthening its capacity to control a rebellious populace.

4 The apparent rise in the crime rate at the same time as a rise in the standard of living has created problems for these three perspectives.

5 New theories have emerged from different sides of the political spectrum which have shifted the focus of attention to *victims* and the traditional concern with class has been supplemented by a greater attention to gender and 'race'.

Activity 14   The Politics of Despair

A left realist view

Two youths stole a police BMW motorbike in Hartcliffe, Bristol, on Thursday night; in the subsequent police chase they crashed, and were killed. Trouble ensued: crowds of young people, white and black, set fire to the local library and community centre, and looted shops. The following night, there were more riots. It is a familiar pattern, repeating what has occurred in depressed estates from Teeside to Salford.

Riots are the politics of despair, the collective bargaining of the dispossessed. Whether in Brixton or Los Angeles, whenever a part of the community is economically marginalised and feels politically impotent, riots occur.

But history never repeats itself, and the causes of riots today are specific to the modern recessions. First, there is a notion of consumer citizenship. With political and social rights, the affluent societies of the West have fostered new expectations. Advertising and the rules of an economy based on mass consumption teach us that if we are truly to belong to our society we must possess its glittering prizes. Hunger no longer propels the riots: in its place is the video-recorder the BMW and the mountain bike. Kids may be robbed, not for their pocket money, but for their trainer shoes or designer clothes.

Second, although black, youths were certainly to the forefront in the riots in Britain of the early 1980s, this was simply because they were the first to face the cutting edge of the recession. It is class, not race, which unites rioters today. The distinction was clear in Los Angeles, where the targets were not only whites and Asian business people, but also better-off blacks.

Much play has been made of the word 'underclass', which, in the work of the neo-conservative Charles Murray, has the resonance of a group which has lost all motivation and, shored up by welfare, is unwilling to help itself. But there is another definition of underclass, which does not contrive to blame the poor for their own misfortunes: those young people who face a lifetime on the dole, whose welfare benefits are being cut, who regard the police as persecutors, who are impotent to make any change in their lives and who, perhaps most pressingly, are chronically and endlessly bored.

It is riots and crime which have confronted the 'haves' with the despair and hopelessness of the 'have nots'. No society can permanently exclude so many people from the rewards and prospects which the majority takes for granted, without bearing these consequences.

Adapted from J. Young 'Riotous Rage of the Have-nots' *Observer*, 19.7.92

'Big Sale'

Tyne and Wear riots, 1991

Questions

1   How is the concept of relative deprivation used to explain riots?

2   In what ways can Young's view of the riots be seen as a structural explanation?

References

Atkinson, J. M. 'Societal Reactions to Suicide: The Role of Coroner's Definitions' in S. Cohen (ed) *Images of Deviance* (Penguin, Harmondsworth, 1971)

Becker, H. *Outsiders: Studies in the Sociology of Deviance* (Macmillan, London, 1963)

Blumer, H. *Symbolic Interactionism - Perspective on Method* (Prentice Hall, Englewood Cliffs, 1969)

Bottomley, A.K. and Coleman, C.A. *Understanding Crime Rates* (Saxon House, Farnborough, 1981)

Box, S. *Deviance, Reality and Society* 2nd edition (Holt, Reinhart and Winston, New York, 1981)

Campbell, N. *Delinquent Girls* (Blackwell, Oxford, 1981)

Carlen, P. *Criminal Women* (Polity, Cambridge, 1985)

Chibnall S. *Law and Order News* (Tavistock, London, 1977)

Christie, N. *Crime Control as Industry* (Routledge, London, 1993)

Cicourel, A.V. *The Social Organisation of Juvenile Justice* (Heinemann, London, 1976)

Clarke, J. et al 'Subcultures, Cultures and Class: A Theoretical Overview' in S. Hall and T. Jefferson (eds) *Resistance Through Rituals; Youth Subcultures in Post-War Britain* (Macmillan, London, 1976)

Clarke, R. and Mayhew, P. *Designing out Crime* (HMSO, London, 1980)

Clinard, M. *Sociology and Deviant Behaviour* 4th edition (Holt, Rinehart and Winston, New York, 1974)

Cohen, A. *Delinquent Boys* (The Free Press, Glencoe, 1955)

Cohen, S. *Folk, Devils and Moral Panics* 2nd edition (Blackwell, Oxford, 1987)

Croal, H. 'White Collar Crime: Scams, Cons and Rip Offs', *Sociology Review* vol 3 no 2, 1993

Cloward, R. and Ohlin, L. *Delinquency and Opportunity* (The Free Press, Glencoe, 1961)

Crawford, A. et al *The Second Islington Crime Survey* (Middlesex Polytechnic Centre for Criminology, 1990)

Davies, N. 'Dirty Business : Red Light for Blue Squad' *Guardian*, 29.11.1994

Davis, K. 'Prostitution' in R. Merton and R. Nisbet (eds) *Contemporary Social Problems* (The Free Press, New York, 1961)

Dennis, N. and Erdos, J. *Families Without Fathers*. (I.E.A., London, 1992)

Douglas, J. D. *The Social Meanings of Suicide* (Princeton, New York, 1967)

Downes, D. and Rock, P. *Understanding Deviance* 2nd edition (Clarendon Press, Oxford, 1988)

Durkheim, E. *The Rules of Sociological Method* (The Free Press, New York, 1964)

Durkheim, E. *Suicide; A Study in Sociology* (Routledge and Kegan Paul London, 1952)

Eaton, M. *Justice for Women* (OUP, Milton Keynes, 1986)

Field, F. *An Agenda for Britain* (Harper Collins, London, 1993)

Frith, S. *The Sociology of Youth* (Causeway Press, Ormskirk, 1984)

Garland, D. 'Of Crimes and Criminals: The Development of British Criminology' in M. Maguire et al (eds) *The Oxford Handbook of Criminology* (Clarendon Press, Oxford, 1994)

Giddens, A. *Sociology* (Polity, Cambridge, 1989)

Goffman, E. *Asylums* (Penguin, Harmondsworth, 1968)

Goode, E. and Ben-Yehuda, N. *Moral Panics* (Blackwell, Oxford, 1994)

Hall, S. et al *Policing the Crisis* (Macmillan, London, 1978)

Hall, S. *Drifting into a Law and Order Society* (Cobden Trust, London, 1980)

Hebdidge, D. *Subculture : The Meaning of Style* (Methuen, London, 1979)

Heidensohn, F. *Women and Crime* (Macmillan, London, 1985)

Heidensohn, F. *Crime and Society* (Macmillan, London, 1989)

Heidensohn, F 'Gender and Crime' in M. Maguire et al (eds) *The Oxford Handbook of Criminology* (Clarendon Press, Oxford, 1994)

Holdaway, S. *Crime and Deviance* (Macmillan, London, 1988)

Hudson, B. 'Racism and Criminology: Concepts and Controversies' in D. Cook and B. Hudson (eds) *Racism and Criminology* (Sage, London, 1993)

Jones, T. et al *The Islington Crime Survey*, (Gower, Aldershot, 1986)

Kerr, J. *Understanding Football Hooliganism* (Open University, Milton Keynes, 1994)

Layton-Henry, Z. *The Politics of Immigration* (Blackwell, Oxford, 1992)

Lea, J. and Young, J. *What is to be done about Law and Order?* (Penguin, Harmondsworth, 1984)

Lemert, E.M. *Human Deviance, Social Problems and Social Control* 2nd edition (Prentice Hall, Englewood Cliffs, 1972)

Levi, M. *The Investigation, Prosecution and Trial of Serious Fraud*, Research Study no 14, (Royal Commission on Criminal Justice, London, 1993)

Maguire, M. 'Criminal Statistics' in M.Maguire et al (eds) *The Oxford Handbook of Criminology* (Clarendon Press, Oxford, 1994)

Matza, D. *Delinquency and Drift* (Wiley, London, 1964)

Matza, D. *Becoming Deviant* (Prentice Hall, Englewood Cliffs, 1969)

Mayhew, P. and Maung, N.A. 'Surveying Crime : Findings from the 1992 British Crime Survey' *Home Office Research and Statistics Department Research Findings* no 2 (HMSO, London, 1992)

Mayhew, P. et al 'Trends in Crime : Findings from the 1994 British Crime Survey' *Home Office Research and Statistics Department Research Findings* no 18 (HMSO, London, 1994)

Merton, R.K. 'Social Structure and Anomie' in R. Merton *Social Theory and Social Structure* (The Free Press, New York, 1968)

Miller, W. 'Lower Class Culture as a Generating Mileu of Gang Delinquency' *Journal of Social Issues* vol 14, 1958

Muncie, J. *'The Trouble with Kids Today'* (Hutchinson, London, 1984)

Muncie, J. 'Issues in the Study of Crime' in The Open University, *Crime, Justice and Society* (Open University, Milton Keynes, 1986)

Muncie, J. 'Much Ado about Nothing? The Sociology of Moral Panics' *Social Studies Review*, November 1987

Murray, C. *The Emerging British Underclass* (Institute of Economic Affairs, London, 1990)

Nelken, D. 'White-Collar Crime' in M. Maguire et al (eds) *The Oxford Handbook of Criminology* (Clarendon Press, Oxford, 1994)

Pease, K. 'Crime Prevention' in M. Maguire et al (eds) *The Oxford Handbook of Criminology* (Clarendon Press, Oxford, 1994)

Pearson, G. *Hooligan : A History of Respectable Fears* (Macmillan. London, 1983)

Plummer, K. 'Misunderstanding Labelling Perspectives' in D. Downes, and P. Rock (eds) *Deviant Interpretations* (M. Robertson, Oxford, 1979)

Polsky, N. *Hustlers, Beats and Others* (Penguin, Harmondsworth, 1971)

Reiner, R. 'Race, Crime and Justice: Models of Interpretation' in L. Gelsthorpe (ed) *Minority Ethnic Groups in the Criminal Justice System* (Institute of Criminology, Cambridge, 1993)

Reiner, R. *Politics of the Police*, (Harvester Wheatsheaf, Brighton, 1992)

Reiner, R. 'Crime and Policing' in S. MacGregor and B. Pimlott (eds) *Tackling the Inner Cities* (Clarendon Press, Oxford, 1991)

Reiner, R. 'Policing and the Police' in M. Maguire et al (eds) *The Oxford Handbook of Criminology* (Clarendon Press, Oxford, 1994)

Rock, P.'Sociology of Crime' in D. Downes and P. Rock (eds) *Deviant Interpretations* (M. Robertson, Oxford, 1979)

Schlesinger, P. and Tumber, H. 'Fighting the War Against Crime : Television, Police and Audience' *British Journal of Criminology* vol 33 no1, 1993

Scraton, P. et al (eds) *Law, Order and the Authoritarian State* (OUP, Milton Keynes, 1987)

Scraton, P. 'Crime and Deviance' in M. Haralambos (ed) *Developments in Sociology* vol 7 (Causeway Press, Ormskirk, 1990)

Smith, D. 'Race, Crime and Criminal Justice' in M. Maguire et al (eds) *The Oxford Handbook of Criminology* (Clarendon Press, Oxford, 1994)

Sutherland, E. *White Collar Crime* (Holt, Rinehart and Winston, New York, 1949)

Taylor, I. et al *The New Criminology* (Routledge, London, 1973)

Waddington, P. *Strong Arm of the Law*, (Clarendon, Oxford, 1991)

Williams, J. et al *Hooligans Abroad*, 2nd edition (Routledge, London, 1989)

Williams, P. and Dickinson, J. 'Fear of Crime : Read All About It?' *British Journal of Criminology* vol 33 no1, 1993

Wilson, J.Q.*Thinking about Crime* (Basic Books, New York, 1975)

Worrall, A. *Offending Women* (Routledge, London, 1990)

Young, J. *The Drugtakers* (Paladin, London, 1971)

Young, J. 'Mass Media, Drugs and Deviance' in P. Rock and M. McKintosh (eds) *Deviance and Social Control* (Tavistock, London, 1974)

Young, J. 'Radical Criminology in Britain : The Emergence of a Competing Paradigm', *British Journal of Criminology*, vol 28, 1988

Young, J. 'Ten Points of Realism' in J. Young and R. Matthews (eds) *Confronting Crime* (Sage, London, 1992)

Young, J. 'Incessant Chatter: Recent Paradigms in Criminology' in M. Maguire et al (eds) *The Oxford Handbook of Criminology*, (Clarendon Press, Oxford, 1994)

Zedner, L. 'Victims' in M. Maguire et al (eds) *The Oxford Handbook of Criminology* (Clarendon Press, Oxford, 1994)

14 Religion

Introduction

Something recognisable as religion can be found in every known human society. Yet, despite this apparent universality, religion's decline and eventual disappearance have been predicted by some of history's greatest thinkers. But, as we approach the end of the second millenium after Christ, many of the world's major religions, such as Christianity and Islam, appear remarkably vigorous.

Even among the unbelieving, sometimes especially among them, other people's religious beliefs and practices are a source of fascination. And sometimes, when one or other little known religious group implodes in a mass suicide or other ghastly flurry of violence, the world's attention is grabbed in a fascination which is gruesome.

Chapter summary

- This chapter begins with the question: **What is religion?**
- It goes on to consider the **roles** and **functions** of religion in societies.
- It then considers the **variety of religious organisations, beliefs** and **practices** which occur within Christianity, and the major non-Christian **religious movements** now established in the West.
- Finally, it examines the **current position** and **significance** of religion in the West.

1 The Nature and Interpretation of Religion

Key Issues

1. What is religion? How may it be defined?
2. How has religion been interpreted by the major sociological thinkers?

1.1 Defining religion

What is religion? How may we define it? Clearly, it would help if sociologists had an agreed definition of religion when they discuss such central concerns as whether religion is a declining or growing force in the modern world. But this agreement is lacking - sociologists do not have a common definition of religion.

As a starting point, most sociologists would probably agree that religions typically involve at least three characteristics: 1) an *organised collectivity* of individuals, with 2) a *shared system of beliefs* and 3) a set of *approved activities and practices*.

However, even this apparently straightforward statement is not as simple as it seems. For example, to what extent do members of a given religion share the same beliefs and practices? Each of the so-called 'world religions' - Judaism, Christianity, Islam, Hinduism and Buddhism - is split into (often rival) groupings, whose members do not accept certain of the beliefs and practices of the others. Indeed, conflict between groups *within* the same religion - Catholic and Protestant Christians, Sunni and Shi'ite Muslims, orthodox and liberal Jews - is a recurring feature of world religions.

A second difficulty in defining religion is to identify the essential difference between the religious and the non-religious. The commonsense answer is that religion involves a belief in the *supernatural* - a belief in a being or force, such as a god, with powers above and beyond those of the natural world and beyond scientific or everyday explanation. Many sociologists adopt such a definition. Others, such as Emile Durkheim, regard it as too restrictive.

Durkheim: the sacred and profane

For Durkheim, beliefs and practices can be regarded as religious insofar as they relate to things which a society's members perceive as *sacred*. He argued that in all societies people divide the world about them into things which are regarded as *sacred* and those which are considered *profane* (ie non-sacred or secular). In practice, a supernatural being (such as a god) is likely to be regarded as sacred. However, sacred things do not have to be supernatural. Anything could be regarded as sacred - the Black Hills of South Dakota to Sioux Indians, the bones of a saint to medieval Christians - however ordinary and mundane it might appear to outsiders. Among group members, however, those objects which are regarded as sacred - and the people, places, rituals, ideas and beliefs associated with them - are sharply distinguished from profane objects and are 'elevated' above them. Moreover, things which are regarded as sacred evoke strong emotions of awe, respect and deference. Thus, group members feel both distanced from and drawn towards those things considered sacred.

By showing that such belief systems share with supernatural beliefs a sense of sacredness, and that they too can inspire intense devotion and encourage

group solidarity, Durkheim's approach has been highly influential.

However, his identification of religion with sacred things, rather than simply with supernatural beings or forces, has been criticised. By denying that belief in the supernatural is the distinguishing characteristic of religion, Durkheim is accused of including as religious many belief systems - such as communism, humanism and nationalism - which are at odds with religion as most understand it, or, as in the case of Marxist beliefs, even hostile to it.

Activity 1 Religion and the Sacred

Item A *Born again Elvis*

Elvis Presley has now been dead 18 years. Each year, on the anniversary of his death in August, thousands of fans gather by his grave at his American home, Graceland. They sing, they pray and hold a candlelight vigil in his memory. One close friend has claimed that Elvis experienced a vision of God and also had the power of healing. Some say that Elvis is alive and frequently sighted in America. Really dedicated followers do charitable works in the name of Elvis, their King. And a network of fans holds meetings and rallies at which the presence of Elvis is still felt.

Some fans tell of how mysterious things have happened to them. For instance, pictures fall off the wall when someone connected with Elvis dies. One British fan, awaiting the birth of his child in hospital, reports that 'I felt someone touch my shoulder and experienced this lovely warm feeling as though someone was telling me, "Don't worry, everything will be all right." And I knew straight away it was Elvis.'

Adapted from T. Harrison 'Born Again Elvis' *The Listener*, 6.12.90, pp26-27

Elvis Presley (1935-1977), the 'king of rock 'n' roll'

Item B *Creating sacred things*

In the present day just as much as in the past, we see society constantly creating sacred things out of ordinary ones.

If society happens to fall in love with a man and it thinks it has found in him the principal aspirations that move it, as well as the means of satisfying them, this man will be raised above the others and, as it were, deified (treated as a god). Opinion will invest him with a majesty similar to that of the gods.

The simple deference inspired by men invested with high social functions is not different in nature from religious respect. It is expressed by the same movements: a man keeps at a distance from a high personage; he approaches him only with precautions; in conversing with him, he uses other gestures and language than those used with ordinary mortals.

Adapted from E. Durkheim *The Elementary Forms of the Religious Life*, 1968, pp212-213

Item C *Sacred things and social values*

Remembrance Day service at the Cenotaph led by the Queen in memory of the members of the armed services killed in the two World Wars.

Questions

1 Consider the view that the 'Elvis movement' (Item A) is a religion.

2 a) Look at Items B and C. Durkheim argued that if a person or thing is considered 'sacred', this will affect people's behaviour towards them. First, select some examples of sacralised (made, or regarded as, sacred) people or things from Western society. Is Durkheim right in his suggestions about how people respond to them?

   b) Durkheim also suggested that people and things which are sacralised embody some of a society's most cherished values. Which values are embodied in the examples you have given?

1.2 Functionalist interpretations of religion

Emile Durkheim: religion and the collective consciousness

Durkheim's analysis of religion begins with the claim that all societies divide the world into sacred things and profane things. Even apparently ordinary objects can provoke powerful emotions of awe, deference and respect. It seems, therefore, that their significance is as symbols - they must represent something. And what they represent, Durkheim concluded, is the *collective consciousness* - the basic set of shared beliefs, values, traditions and norms - which make social life possible.

Religion and collective consciousness Without a collective consciousness, a society can not endure. And for Durkheim, collective worship and ritual have a crucial social significance, both in reinforcing the collective consciousness and in unifying the group. Put simply, in worshipping a society's 'sacred symbols', Durkheim concluded, its members are worshipping the society.

Hence, when members of a society are worshipping the group's sacred symbols, they are unconsciously expressing their sense of the supreme importance of the collectivity and of their own relative insignificance and dependence on it. They are also unknowingly re-pledging their support for the basic values and beliefs of the collective conscience, the cultural 'cement' which binds and legitimises the group.

Durkheim's conclusion was largely drawn from studies of the religion of Australian aborigines, which he called totemism. Aboriginal society was divided into clans, whose members shared various duties and obligations towards each other. Each clan had a totem - a symbol, usually either an animal or plant - by which it distinguished itself from other clans. The totem was regarded as sacred and was carved on the bullroarer, the most sacred of aboriginal objects. According to Durkheim, the totem was both the symbol of the aborigines' god and of the clan. And this was the case, he argued, because the god and the society are one. Though the aborigines consciously worshipped their god, the society was the real object of their veneration. And, Durkheim surmised, 'Primitive man comes to view society as something sacred because he is utterly dependent on it'.

Religion and social solidarity The worship of sacred things also functions to bind together a society's members so promoting social solidarity or social unity. Whether celebrating the group's myths or history in commemorative rites, or coming together in mourning rituals, society's members are thereby renewing their sense of membership and unity. The very act of communal worship and the practice of rituals raises people's awareness of their common situation and strengthens the bonds between society's members.

Thus, Durkheim suggested, a religion could be seen as 'a unified system of beliefs and practices relative to sacred things, that is to say, things set apart and forbidden...which unite into one single moral community...all those who adhere to them'.

Religion and the individual Though he attached primary importance to the social functions of religion, Durkheim was not blind to its importance for individuals. Hence, he recognised that religious belief and practice can provide a sense of renewed strength, confidence, serenity and enthusiasm, helping an individual 'either to endure the trials of existence, or to conquer them' (Durkheim, 1968, p595).

In Durkheim's view, therefore, all religions fulfil certain functions for the individual and for society. For the individual, religion provides continuing motivation to face up to life, and social support based upon a sense of belonging. From a societal point of view, religion unifies members around the shared values, norms, meanings and traditions of the collective consciousness and thereby encourages social integration and social solidarity. The symbols which members of the group 'worship' may or may not be regarded as 'supernatural'. But, to committed 'believers', they inspire the love and awe appropriate to sacred things.

Durkheim and the 'cult of man' Durkheim's views of the functions of religion were largely based on an analysis of small pre-industrial societies. His views have often been criticised as inappropriate to complex, modern societies. However, Durkheim did offer some interesting ideas about how religion in modern societies might develop.

In Durkheim's view, as the division of labour in modern society becomes more complex and specialised, so the collective consciousness becomes weaker and less able to direct individuals' behaviour. Increasingly, he believed, individuals would decide their actions with less reference to the collective. And increasingly, they would cease to regard society as

supreme. In short, people's attitudes *to society* would cease to be religious.

However, rather than seeing society as sacred, people in modern industrial societies might come to see the *individual* as sacred. Thus, Durkheim anticipated that the religion of the future might be one in which individuals are bound together, not through their adherence to society, but by their common commitment to the 'divine' within each person and to individual dignity. This form of religion, which he believed might bind modern societies together, he called 'the cult of man'.

Activity 2 The Coronation of Elizabeth II

Item A *An act of national communion*

According to our interpretation of the Coronation of Queen Elizabeth in 1953, it was a ceremonial occasion for the affirmation of the moral values by which the society lives. It was an act of national communion. Like Independence Day, Thanksgiving Day, May Day, or any other great communal ritual, the Coronation is exactly this kind of ceremonial in which the society reaffirms the moral values which constitute it as a society, and renews its devotion to those values by an act of communion.

The key to the Coronation Service is the Queen's promise to abide by the moral standards of society. In her assurance that she will observe the principles of mercy, charity, justice and protective affection, she symbolically proclaims her community with her subjects who, in the ritual - and in the wider audience outside Westminster Abbey - commit themselves to obedience within the society constituted by the moral rules which she has agreed to uphold.

Just as the Coronation Service in the Abbey was a religious ceremony in the conventional sense, so then the popular participation in the service throughout the country had many of the properties of the enactment of a religious ritual. The Coronation was, throughout, a collective not an individual experience. The fact that the experience was communal means that one of society's values, the virtue of social unity or solidarity, was acknowledged and strengthened in the very act of communion

The Coronation, like any other great occasion which in some manner touches the sense of the sacred, was a time for drawing closer the bonds of the family, for re-asserting its solidarity and for re-emphasising the values of the family - generosity, loyalty, love - which are *at the*

Item B *The Queen is crowned*

Queen Elizabeth II crowned by the Archbishop of Canterbury in Westminster Abbey, 1953.

same time the fundamental values necessary for the well being of the larger society.

A society is held together by its internal agreement about the sacredness of certain fundamental moral standards. The Coronation provided at one time and for practically the entire society such an intensive contact with the sacred that we believe we are justified in interpreting it as we have done, as a great act of national communion.

Adapted from E. Shils and M. Young 'The Meaning of the Coronation', 1953, pp63 - 81

Questions

1 Look at Items A and B. Do you agree with Shils and Young's interpretation of the Coronation? Give reasons for your answer.

2 Referring to Shils and Young's analysis in your answer, how would you explain the police report that on Coronation Day , 'contrary to expectations, the pickpockets were entirely inactive'?

Bronislaw Malinowski: religion and situations of emotional stress

Malinowski was one of the first anthropologists to live for a long period in a small scale society. His interpretation of religion placed more emphasis on its psychological functions for the individual. He accepted that religion played a central role in promoting social solidarity, but argued that it had developed, not as Durkheim had claimed as a celebration of society or human sociality, but as a response to the psychological needs of individuals in specific situations of emotional stress. Situations which provoke anxiety, uncertainty and tension threaten social life and it is with such potentially disruptive situations that religion is typically concerned. In particular, Malinowski identified two types of event with which religion is characteristically involved.

In all societies - but perhaps most acutely in small scale societies with few members - 'life crises' such as birth, puberty, marriage and death are potentially disruptive and typically involve religious ritual. In particular, religion minimises the potential disruption of death by creating 'valuable mental attitudes' towards it. Religion's forceful assertion of immortality comforts the bereaved, and the religious rituals of the funeral ceremony bind together the survivors and counteract the sense of meaninglessness which might otherwise undermine social life.

The second type of event which Malinowski identified as creating anxiety and involving religion includes activities whose outcome is important but uncertain and uncontrollable. In his study of the Trobriand Islanders, Malinowski noted that when they fished in the calm waters of the lagoon, where they used the safe and reliable method of poisoning the fish, they felt no need for religious ritual. When they fished beyond the barrier reef, in the open sea, however, where success and even survival were much less certain, fishing was preceded by rituals. Again, Malinowski suggested, the use of ritual increases people's sense of control, diminishes anxiety and unifies the group.

Talcott Parsons: religion and 'problems of meaning'

Another influential interpretation of religion in the functionalist tradition - reflecting Durkheim's and Malinowski's contributions but also the influence of Weber - was developed by Talcott Parsons. In his view, religion is the primary source of meaning for members of a society. It also provides and legitimises the 'core values' of a culture and thereby promotes social solidarity and stability.

Religion provides meaning by furnishing answers to the 'eternal' questions about humanity and the world such as those concerning suffering, justice and death. Why do people suffer? Why do villains prosper? Often there appears no natural justice in such happenings and they threaten to undermine people's sense that life has meaning. Yet religion offers answers. Suffering tests a person's faith, punishes them for their sins and gives dignity to those who struggle in the face of adversity; villains receive their come-uppance in the afterlife, and so on. By providing explanations of events, particularly those which threaten our sense of meaning, religion makes sense of the apparently meaningless, helps people adjust to their situation and promotes social stability.

Religion also provides core values and norms, which it sacralises and legitimises. Following Weber (see pp504-506), Parsons argues that values derived from, and sacralised by, Protestantism in the United States include individualism, democracy, self-discipline and upward mobility. Religion also sacralises and supports the web of norms which are derived from such values - norms such as universal access to legal rights and life chances and the formal separation of the state and religion. Hence, by establishing and legitimising values and social norms, religion further promotes the social consensus which Parsons argues is a prerequisite for order and stability in society.

Activity 3 The Functions of Religion

Item A *The problem of meaning*

Buddhism
'Bad human beings think it is to their advantage to prevail over their fellow men...to use any method which seems expedient, no matter how cruel, in order to achieve this advantage. The advantage will not last; the methods used only create more problems, more suffering, more mistrust, more resentment, more division. The result is not good for anyone.'

'Better it were to swallow a ball of iron, red-hot and flaming, than to lead a wicked and unrestrained life eating the food of the people!'

Christianity
'You who oppress the poor and crush the destitute...the Lord has sworn by his holiness that your time is coming.'

Judaism
'The righteous suffer for the sins of their generation.'

Hinduism
'Great souls who have become one with Me have reached the highest goal. They do not undergo re-birth, a condition which is impermanent and full of pain and suffering.'

Islam

'Or do you think that you shall enter the Garden (paradise) without such trials as came to those who passed away before you?'

'For those nearest to God will come rest and satisfaction and a garden of delights, and...peace; but

if you are one of those who have...gone wrong, then your entertainment will be boiling water and hellfire. Truly, this is the absolute truth and certain.'

Adapted from W.O. Cole (ed) *Moral Issues in Six Religions*, 1991

Item B *Individual and social stress*

British soldiers praying during the Gulf War, 1992

A Christian funeral

Questions

1 According to Talcott Parsons there are situations which can make life appear meaningless. Using Item A:
   a) give examples of these situations;
   b) show how religion addresses them;
   c) suggest how, in doing so, religion contributes to the wellbeing of the individual and society.
2 Malinowski argued that certain situations threaten psychological and social stability and integration. Using the examples in Item B, show how religion might function to reduce this threat.

Robert Bellah: civil religion

Durkheim's interpretation of religion's traditional function - to bind together members of a society by encouraging awareness of their common membership of an entity greater than themselves - was largely based on an analysis of small scale, pre-industrial societies. However, it still provides for many a powerful insight into the collective rituals of people in modern societies.

The concept of 'civil religion' was popularised in sociology by the American Robert Bellah, who drew upon the ideas of both Durkheim and Parsons. Parsons had argued that Americans were unified by values and orientations derived from Protestantism, such as individualism and self-discipline. Durkheim's insights led Bellah to conclude that, despite their apparent differences, what largely

unified Americans - whether Catholic, Protestant or Jew - was an overarching 'civil' religion which was distinct from each: *a faith in Americanism*. Unlike Catholicism, Protestantism and Judaism, which are unable to claim the allegiance of all Americans, civil religion generates widespread loyalty to the nation state. And, though a nation's civil religion does not necessarily involve supernatural beliefs, in American civil religion, Bellah argues, it does.

God and Americanism appear to walk hand in hand. American coins tell the world 'In God We Trust', American Presidents swear an oath of allegiance before God and the phrase 'God Bless America' ends speeches given by dignatories across the USA. This is not the particular God of Catholics, Protestants or Jews; it has a more general application as 'America's God'. In this respect, the faith in Americanism helps to unite the American people.

Activity 4 Civil Religion in America

Item A *Symbols of Americanism*

A wagon train heading West

In the 19th century there was a vast migration to new lands in the West. Many migrants travelled in wagon trains, pushing back the American frontier and opening up new land to white settlement. These 'heroic treks' are pictured in books, paintings and on postage stamps, featured in films and commemorated in statues. Sometimes the 'virgin territory' of the West is pictured as the 'promised land' and the settlers as the 'chosen people'.

The Lincoln Memorial

Every American knows the story of Abraham Lincoln who was born in a log cabin and rose from these humble origins to live in the White House as President of the United States before dying from an assassin's bullet in 1865. Pictured on coins and sculpted in marble in the Lincoln Memorial, he has become an almost mythical figure.

Item B *America's national faith*

While some have argued that Christianity is America's national faith, few have realised that there actually exists alongside the churches and synagogues an elaborate and well-institutionalised civil religion in America: a collection of beliefs, symbols and rituals with respect to sacred things which are an established part of American society. This religion - there seems no other word for it - while not opposed to, and indeed sharing much in common with, Christianity, is not in any specific sense Christian.

   Behind this civil religion at every point lie Biblical models: the Exodus, Chosen People, Promised Land and New Jerusalem, Death and Rebirth. But it is also genuinely American and genuinely new. It has its own prophets and its own martyrs, its own sacred events and sacred places, its own solemn rituals and symbols.

Adapted from R. O'Toole *Religion: Classic Sociological Approaches*, 1984, pp198-200

Item C *Shrines, saints and ceremonies*

Many American civil ceremonies have a marked religious quality. Memorial Day, which remembers Americans killed in war, the Fourth of July, which commemorates the American's Declaration of Independence from Britain, and the anniversary of presidential inaugurations, all celebrate national values and national unity. There are national shrines such as the Lincoln Memorial in Washington DC, the birthplaces of key presidents, war memorials and other 'special' places. It is not their age or even historical significance that inspires awe and reverence, but their ability to symbolise the nation as a 'people'.

   Likewise there are sacred objects of the civil religion - especially the flag. The extent to which these ceremonies, shrines and objects are set apart as sacred can be seen in the intensity of outrage at inappropriate behaviour or 'desecration'. Some people were arrested during the 1960s for wearing or displaying a copy of the American flag improperly (eg on the seat of their pants).

   American civil religion also has its myths and saints. Lincoln is an historical figure who particularly symbolises the civil religion, and his life, from humble birth to martyrdom, typifies its values. Other 'saints' include key presidents such as Washington and Kennedy, folk heroes such as Davy Crockett, who died in 1836 fighting for Texan independence from Mexico, and military heroes such as Eisenhower, commander-in-chief of Allied Armies in World War Two, who defended democracy and freedom against the fascist governments of Germany and Italy. Similarly there are stories that enshrine American values such as individual achievement and upward social mobility. Lincoln's story of rising from log cabin to White House is one. So is Davy Crockett's when, after years of hunting bears and fighting Indians on the frontier, he was elected to Congress where he was known as the 'Coonskin Congressman'. Socially important myths include America as the land of plenty, unlimited social mobility, economic consumption and achievement.

While these shrines, saints and ceremonies are not religious in the same sense as, for example, Greek Orthodox shrines, saints and ceremonies, they are still set apart as special and not to be profaned.

Adapted from M.B. McGuire *Religion: The Social Context*, 1981, pp151-152

Questions

1 Read Items A, B and C.
   a) How are the symbols of Americanism linked to Biblical models? Why might this make them more effective?
   b) Why have the wagon train and Abraham Lincoln become symbols of Americanism?
2 How can the symbols of Americanism in Item C be seen as 'religious'?
3 What are the social functions of civic religion in America?
4 Give examples of Britain's civil religion under the headings: 'ceremonies', 'shrines', 'saints' and 'myths'. Briefly explain your choices.

1.3 Marxist interpretations of religion

Karl Marx and Friedrich Engels

In contrast to Durkheim and Weber, Marx and Engels wrote relatively little about religion. For Marx, people's religious beliefs reflect their alienation. In pre-socialist societies, people are in alienated relationships with their work, with the products of their work and with each other. Religious beliefs and practices thus arise in response to, and as a protest against, people's lack of control of their destiny and their dehumanisation and oppression. In a much quoted passage, Marx argues that religion is both 'the expression of real distress and the protest against real distress. (It) is the sigh of the oppressed creature, the heart of a heartless world, just as it is the spirit of a spiritless situation. It is the opium of the people.'

In Marx's view, 'Man makes religion, religion does not make man. In other words, religion is the self-consciousness and self-feeling of man who has either not yet found himself or has already lost himself again. 'Truly liberated individuals have no need of religion. Thus, if the alienation and exploitation associated with classes are eradicated, and people are freed to develop their human potential and 'find themselves' as in a truly socialist society, religion will no longer be needed and will cease to exist.

Religion and ideology However, although religion represents a protest against a dehumanising social world and human alienation, it also leads people in a false direction and the hopes and 'solutions' it promises are illusory. Religion, for Marx and Engels, is part of ideology, a systematised pattern of beliefs which obscures and distorts the true nature of reality in ways which benefit the ruling class. 'The ideas of the ruling class are in every epoch the ruling ideas.' Insofar as members of subject classes accept religious ideas, they suffer false consciousness. Thus, although religious ideas appear to express social consensus, those ideas are essentially tools in the domination of one class by another.

Religion and social control The argument that religion functions to maintain ruling class domination may be developed in a number of ways. First, religion distorts reality by encouraging the belief that people are dependent upon supernatural beings or sacred powers. For example, the belief that events are controlled by supernatural powers means there is little people can do apart from trying to influence the supernatural powers by prayer, sacrifice or some other means. In this way, religion obscures the human authorship of, and responsibility for, social inequality and thereby discourages the realisation that working for social change may be possible and desirable.

Secondly, religion often appears to lend sacred support to the current social order, and in so doing reinforces prohibitions against actions which would challenge those in power. Thus, in his letter to the Christians in Rome, St Paul wrote:

'Let every soul be subject unto the higher powers. For there is no power but of God: the powers that be are ordained of God. Whosoever therefore resisteth the power, resisteth the ordinance of God: and they that resist shall receive to themselves damnation' (*Romans* Ch 13, vs 1-2).

Likewise, in medieval Europe, for example, the Church taught that the various unequal 'estates of the realm' - monarch, barons and bishops, knights, freemen and serfs - were God's creation. This meant that attempts to change the social order would have been not merely acts of treason against the monarch but also a blasphemous rejection of God's plan, punishable by eternal damnation.

In modern capitalist societies, however, in which change, innovation and high rates of social mobility are required for the success of capitalist enterprises, such religious teachings have been largely abandoned.

Nevertheless, it can still be argued that mainstream religion continues to legitimise privilege and inequality - by giving its blessing to rituals involving royalty, such as the Coronation, and by the continuing presence in the House of Lords of the Archbishops and Bishops of the Church of England. Indeed, the relationship between the supernatural, inequality and national wellbeing may be said to be neatly summarised in the phrase 'God, Queen and Country'.

Just as religion typically supports and legitimises the ruling class, that class is prepared to employ religion to defend its perceived interests. According to Engels, in the years following the eruption of working class insurrections across Europe in 1848, the British bourgeoisie spent large sums of money in supporting mainstream Christian organisations and in backing a variety of evangelising groups such as the Salvation Army. Some religious groups were even encouraged to come from the USA, in a more or less conscious effort by the capitalist class to pacify and contain the proletariat by setting up missions among them.

Religion as compensation While religion operates primarily as a means of social control for the exploiters, for the exploited it has psychological functions as a source of solace and compensation for the misery of their alienation. So, whereas Durkheim sees religion as an expression and celebration of people's sociality, Marx sees it as a consolation for experience which lacks the genuine sociality of which people are capable.

Which specific compensations religion offers varies according to the different teachings and practices of different religions. In Christianity, Judaism and Islam, for example, religion offers the fantasy escape of heavenly rewards - and, in Christianity, the intriguing promise that the poor would have less difficulty gaining access to heaven than the wealthy. In Hinduism and Buddhism, followers are taught that life may be better in later incarnations.

Many religions offer their followers hope by promising supernatural intervention into human affairs. In the religious history of the Jews, for instance, God is believed to have intervened many times to assist or protect his chosen people, as in parting the Red Sea to allow the Jews to escape their Egyptian pursuers.

According to Marx, religion promises happiness, but the happiness it promises is an illusion. True happiness and fulfilment are possible only when the exploited shake off the chains of their oppression and seize and practice their freedom.

Activity 5 Monarchy and God

Item A *The divine right of monarchy*
Kings are called Gods by the prophet David because they sit on God's throne on earth. Kings exercise divine power on earth. They have the power of life and death, they are judges over all their subjects and yet are accountable to no one but God only.

James I, King of England from 1603-1625

Henry IV at his coronation in 1399 receiving a blessing from archbishops. Medieval monarchs ruled by divine right - they were seen to have a God-given right to rule. Although modern British monarchs no longer claim divine right, Elizabeth II's coronation in 1953 was in many ways similar to that of Henry IV. She too was crowned and blessed by archbishops.

Item B *The Coronation - an alternative view*
Shils and Young's analysis of the Coronation of Elizabeth II (see Activity 2, p496) assumes that there is a moral consensus in society. Our evidence shows that societies like our own are arenas for conflicts of belief and moral standards unmatched in history.

When Shils and Young try to show that a single scheme of values unites different components of the social structure, they are not very convincing. And, where there may be unspoken agreement about moral standards, it may well be a sort of enforced agreement, the result of some form of psychological manipulation. At times they write as if conflict, and especially class conflict, were unknown in Great Britain.

Another argument might run this way. The very absence of shared values in Great Britain accounts for some of the attention paid to the Coronation. The Coronation provided, for some sections of the populace, some measure of respite and relief from that condition of conflict which is more or less permanent for complex societies of a capitalist type.

From this viewpoint, the role of the press in stirring up popular enthusiasm for the Coronation is understandable. In response to the class interests it generally represents, the press continually seeks to minimise awareness of the real conflicts characteristic of British society. In this context, the personality of the Queen and her family functioned as the object of various fantasies and identifications in a way not much more 'sacred' than the cult of adulation built up around certain film stars. But the tawdry baubles of the Coronation celebration constitute no adequate substitute for the lost faith of millions.

Adapted from N. Birnbaum 'Monarchs and Sociologists' *Sociological Review*, July 1955, pp7-20

Questions

1 Analyse the information in Item A from a Marxist view.
2 Why does Birnbaum (Item B) argue that it could be 'the very absence of shared values in Great Britain' which accounted for the attention paid to the Coronation?
3 How and why, in Birnbaum's view, did the press encourage false class consciousness through their coverage of the Coronation?

1.4 Neo-Marxist interpretations of religion

Until fairly recently Marxist sociologists have generally shown little interest in religion. After all, for Marx religion was merely a reflection or symptom of something more basic - the contradictions in the economic infrastructure. Moreover, it has no future beyond the socialist revolution. In the last few decades, however, there are signs of increasing interest in religion among Marxists.

One significant departure from orthodox Marxist thinking which has encouraged this renewed interest among neo-Marxists has been the modification of Marx's view that the superstructure, and specifically ideology, merely reflects society's economic base. Many modern Marxists have moved away from the view that religious ideas merely reflect the interests of the ruling class and are always a form of false class consciousness for the oppressed. This view is not entirely new. For instance, although Engels regarded religion as part of ideology and therefore primarily important as a protector of ruling class interests, even he recognised that, periodically throughout history, it has also served rebellious elements in society, even if only as a short-term rallying cry. This shift from orthodox Marxism has led many neo-Marxists to consider whether and in what ways religion can be an authentic expression and tool of resistance against class based oppression.

Antonio Gramsci

One of the most influential figures in this neo-Marxist reassessment of religion has been the Italian, Antonio Gramsci. He was particularly influential in rejecting the traditional Marxist view that the cultural superstructure merely reflected society's material base or infrastructure. In his view, the superstructure is more autonomous and independent than Marx acknowledged, and beliefs are no less 'real' or less important than economic forces.

For Gramsci, if the socialist age were to come it would require proletarian action, but this action must be guided by theoretical ideas. And, just as intellectuals of the Roman Catholic Church had shaped the minds of its followers over centuries, so must the industrial working class produce its own intellectuals who can articulate working class experience in intelligible language and so help shape working class consciousness.

As an Italian, Gramsci was well aware of the control over consciousness which the Catholic Church had traditionally exercised over its members. This control he referred to as *hegemony*. He was also highly critical of what he regarded as the church's characteristic subservience to the state and ruling class interests. Nevertheless, he did not assume that religion must inevitably play such a role. He argued that, at different historical times, popular forms of religion had emerged which expressed and supported the interests of oppressed classes. Thus, he accepted the possibility that religious beliefs and practices could develop and be popularised, particularly by working class intellectuals, to challenge the dominant ruling class ideology and support working class consciousness and liberation.

Otto Maduro

The possibility that religion may play a progressive role in the political struggles of oppressed classes, noted by Gramsci and, before him, by Engels, has been taken up by a number of modern Marxists, including Maduro. Writing of developing countries, Maduro argues that, in societies in which religion remains a dominant, and conservative, institution, social liberation can only be achieved if significant change occurs within the churches. This could occur if the oppressed, finding that all possible forms of protest are blocked by the central power, take their discontent to the churches - as in certain Latin

American societies, in South Africa, and in Poland before the abandonment of communism. In this situation, Maduro argues, the anguish and aspirations of the oppressed may be reflected and voiced by members of the clergy. Thus, the clergy may then fulfil the functions of Gramsci's proletarian intellectuals, by expressing the discontents of the oppressed, by shaping their consciousness of the situation, and by working with them to devise strategies of action.

Activity 6   Liberation Theology

Item A   *Liberating the poor*

Liberation theology is a religious justification for the liberation of oppressed peoples. It developed in Latin America in the 1950s and 60s as an alternative to the standard view of the First World's duties towards the Third World. It criticised the view that the First World could end the poverty of the Third by transferring economic resources from one to the other. The theology of liberation said that, far from being the passive objects of aid, it was essential that the poor themselves should be the principal agents of their own disimpoverishment.

That meant understanding their own condition and the reason for it, and responding accordingly. In liberation theology's purest form, the sort the Vatican was most worried about, those conditions and the reasons for them are analysed in Marxist terms, and so is the remedy.

What the theology of liberation has to say is that the only escape from poverty which does justice to human dignity is that engineered and struggled for by the poor themselves.

Adapted from C. Longley 'Robin Hood and Liberation Theology', *Times*, 27.1.86

Item C   *Archbishop Romero*

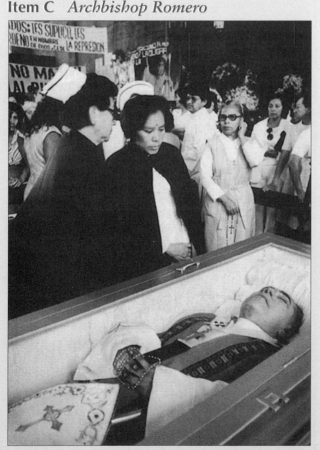

Item B   *Father Camilo Torres*

Father Camilo Torres was a Roman Catholic priest in Colombia in South America. The vast majority of the Colombian people are desperately poor. Sixty-five per cent of the land is owned by a handful of powerful families. Father Torres believed this was unjust - his solution was a Christian revolution. In his words: 'Revolution is necessary to feed the hungry, give drink to the thirsty, clothe the naked and procure a life of wellbeing for the needy majority of our people. I believe that the revolutionary struggle is appropriate for the Christian and the priest. Only by revolution, by changing the concrete conditions of our country, can we enable men to practise love for each other.'

The Catholic Church did not support Torres. Believing that the government would crush peaceful protest, he joined a guerrilla movement. Torres was killed fighting government forces in 1966. The peasants saw him as a martyr and in 1968 many priests followed his example and pledged their support for revolutionary struggle against the state.

Adapted from J. Jenkins *Contemporary Moral Issues*, 1987, p 148

Mourners in El Salvador gather round the corpse of Archbishop Romero. He was shot dead in his cathedral in 1980 by four gunmen, allegedly members of a right wing death squad. Archbishop Romero was a champion of social and economic reforms to improve the lot of the poor.

Questions

1 'Liberation theology sounds like a Christian version of Marxism.' Comment on this statement.
2 Use the information in this activity to assess the differing views of Marx and Maduro on the role of religion in society. Does the information disprove Marx's view?

1.5 Weber's approach to religion

While functionalist and Marxist approaches can be comfortably identified as structuralist, rather than social action or interpretive perspectives, Weber is much less easy to categorise. Indeed, he spans both approaches. His insistence that social enquiry must begin with the individual, and attempt to understand the motives and ideas which influence social actors' behaviour, makes Weber an important early model for interpretive sociology. And his 'macro' approach and structural analyses show him also as a structuralist.

Marx paid little attention to the specific religious beliefs of different groups and cultures. Durkheim based his general statements about religion on a small number of examples. Weber's studies, however, involved an ambitious series of detailed analyses of major religions: Confucianism and Taoism (in China), Hinduism and Buddhism (in India) and ancient Judaism (in Palestine). Additionally, in his most famous work, *The Protestant Ethic and the Spirit of Capitalism*, he analysed the influential Calvinist tradition within Christianity.

Although Weber accepted that religion often functioned to justify social inequality, as Marx had argued, he was also concerned to show that religion did not inevitably function in this conservative manner. Religion existed, he believed, because people everywhere needed a system of basic beliefs to make sense of their existence and have a sense of their identity. Religion provided people with 'meaning'. However, Weber's major argument was that societies developed differently in part because the religious beliefs and ideas about ethical conduct of their members were different. In other words, religious beliefs and religious movements *can* help shape social change.

Calvinism and the 'spirit of capitalism'

The major question which Weber addressed in much of his writing about religion was why the capitalism which had developed in some Western countries had not also emerged in the East. He concluded that the eastern religions (eg Hinduism, Buddhism) embodied certain key teachings and values which had discouraged the development of capitalism, while Judaism and Christianity, and especially the Calvinist and Puritan varieties of Christianity, had facilitated it.

Protestanism and capitalism Although individual greed and the pursuit of gain may be found in all societies, Weber argued, only in the West did entire societies develop, and come to accept, rational capitalism: a system which encouraged the methodical pursuit of profit by legal means, involving calculation, book-keeping and long term planning, and which relied on the creation of free markets and a formally free labour force. In Weber's view, modern capitalism had been able to develop in the West, and particularly in predominantly Protestant areas, because it was compatible with the Calvinist teachings which guided many of the early Protestant movements such as the Puritans, Presbyterians, Baptists and Quakers. And it was among these movements, he argued, that capitalism flourished. It was much less compatible with religions such as Hinduism which taught that, if believers accept their lot in this life and act in accordance with tradition, they will gain the reward of a higher caste position in the next. Such beliefs discourage rational calculation and innovation and therefore the development of capitalism.

A question of salvation The most significant teaching of John Calvin (1509-64) was that of 'predestination'. According to this doctrine, even before their birth, God has selected some for salvation and others for eternal damnation. Neither the saved nor the damned could influence the decision, either by the strength of their faith or by their earthly actions. And moreover, no one could be sure whether he or she had been preselected for heaven or for hell.

Such terrifying beliefs could well have driven followers into an attitude of helpless fatalism, resignation and inactivity. Instead, Weber argued, the 'salvation anxiety' with which they were plagued provoked the opposite response. Despite Calvin's teaching that people's behaviour could not influence God's decision, some followers developed doctrines which held out a measure of hope that individuals could discover reassuring 'signs' that they were among those chosen for salvation.

Work as a 'calling' While none could be sure of their salvation, all were required to pursue an intensely active life of labour. Work was a 'calling', and God was most effectively worshipped through a rigorously disciplined life of work and denial of indulgence. Any activity which unnecessarily detracted from work was evil. Mere socialising, sleeping longer than strictly necessary, or even religious contemplation if it interfered with a person's daily labours, were regarded as sins, for they detracted from the active performance of God's will. But if a person's work was rewarded with material success, this may be a sign of God's grace and indicate that they were among the elect, that they had been chosen by God for salvation.

Thus, to cope with the chronic anxiety of damnation, Calvinists threw themselves energetically into highly disciplined economic activity and a lifetime of 'good works'. Those in business pursued profit and wealth, not as ends in themselves, but as Christian obligations to make the best use of their God given gifts and talents and as indications of God's favour. And, because they were limited in how they could spend their wealth - they could not 'waste' it on expensive 'luxuries' - they tended to save and reinvest in their businesses.

According to Weber, the Calvinist idea of the calling affected not just the employer but also the worker. For capitalism to take root, drastic changes were needed in the attitudes of workers who traditionally were concerned merely to earn the wage necessary to meet their modest expectations and otherwise to spend their time in leisure. The Calvinist notion of the calling transformed the traditional, easy-going, undisciplined workforce into 'sober, conscientious, and unusually industrious workmen, who clung to their work as to a life purpose willed by God' (Weber, 1958, p177). Thus, the Protestant ethic encouraged not merely the 'spirit of capitalism' but a new 'spirit of labour' as well, and the former could not have succeeded without the latter.

Religion and rationality In these ways, Weber concluded, Calvin's influential religious teachings, popularised and interpreted by generations of Puritan successors, had significant, though unintended, consequences for the economic system of capitalism. For, alone among the teachings of the world's major religions, they encouraged among believers a rational, calculating, efficient and highly committed approach to work which provided capitalism with a fertile and compatible soil in which to take root. And it is the growth of rationality which provides a key, perhaps *the* key, to understanding the nature of modern societies.

In developing his argument about the significance of Calvinist teachings for the development of capitalism, Weber believed that he had successfully challenged Marx's somewhat deterministic thesis that religious and other ideas merely reflect a society's economic base. Weber was careful to make clear that he was not claiming that Calvinism was the sole 'cause' of capitalism: he acknowledged that, even in countries with a significant Calvinist population - such as Scotland or Switzerland - capitalism would not develop if economic conditions were not right (eg if there was a shortage of skilled labour or investment capital, as was the case in Scotland). Nevertheless, he could reasonably claim to have demonstrated that religious beliefs can have a significant role in influencing a society's economic system and development.

Criticisms of Weber's thesis

There are, however, a number of challenges to Weber's thesis. The most central is perhaps the challenge to Weber's claim that Calvinism chronologically preceded capitalism. Eisenstadt, for instance, argues that the first great upsurges of capitalism occurred in Catholic Europe - in Italy, Belgium and Germany - before the Protestant Reformation and were much more 'developed' than those occurring later in the first Protestant or Calvinist countries.

The historian Tawney also challenges Weber's interpretation that Calvinism preceded capitalism. He claims that society had already changed radically, in a capitalist direction, before the advent of Calvinism. New technologies had been invented and introduced, a capitalist class had emerged and new ways of viewing society had developed. In this view, as Calvinism emerged, it was adopted by the rising bourgeoisie and, with some changes in emphasis, provided a religious justification for a rational capitalism which was already established and developing.

Another important criticism, voiced by some writers on Hinduism and Islam, is that Weber misunderstood those religions and failed to recognise the many elements in them which could have been (and could still be) supportive of rational economic action. At least as significant is Weber's apparent underestimation of the capitalist spirit of the Jews. Because they were openly interested in profit, would trade in anything, would compete and try to undercut the competition, and would lend money at interest (all of which were typically regarded as shocking by Christians, even by many early Calvinists), Jews proved formidable business competitors, and surely more capitalist than Weber acknowledged.

Doubt has also been cast on Weber's interpretation of the attitudes of influential Calvinists to wealth and the pursuit of gain. As Weber himself recognised, many Calvinist preachers taught that wealth was a great danger, providing unending temptations, and that its acquisition was morally suspect. Moreover, it is not clear why Calvinists should come to regard economic success as the major criterion which God might use to indicate his favour. Nor is it clear why Calvinists would necessarily have had to reinvest the profits they accumulated. Could they could not alternatively have been given away to the poor (for which practice there seems some scriptural support) or used to boost employees' wages?

There is also the puzzling question of why and how Calvinism was able to attract converts - or, even more baffling, succeed as a major religious movement. As depicted by Weber, Calvinism had little to offer its followers. It did not promise them salvation. And it made it disconcertingly clear that membership made not the slightest difference to their prospects either in this life or the next.

Activity 7 The Protestant Ethic

Item A *A pre-capitalist view*

It is much sweeter to spend money than to earn it. I think that I have done more by having spent money well than by having earned it. Spending gave me a deeper satisfaction, especially the money I spent on my house in Florence.

An example, from a medieval Florentine, of a pre-capitalist attitude towards money

Item B *The Protestant ethic*

The Godly and hardworking man shall have prosperity, but he that follows pleasures shall have much sorrow. Don't be too concerned about being popular and sociable - it can waste a lot of valuable time.

John Browne, a 16th century Protestant merchant

Even if you are called to the poorest labouring job, do not complain because it is wearisome, nor imagine that God thinks any the less of you. But cheerfully follow it, and make it your pleasure and joy that you are still in your heavenly master's services, though it be the lowest thing.

Richard Baxter, a prominent 17th century English Puritan

Items A and B quoted in M. J. Kitch *Capitalism and the Reformation*, 1967, pp164, 82-3, 157-8

Religion must necessarily produce hard work and discourage the wasting of money. We must encourage all Christians to gain what they can and to save all they can - that is, in effect to grow rich.

John Wesley (1703-1791) English Methodist leader, quoted in M. Weber *The Protestant Ethic and the Spirit of Capitalism*, 1958, p175.

From a pamphlet published in 1653. Father Christmas is driven out of town by a Puritan.

A Puritan family meal in the early 17th century. Their dress is simple and their food is plain. The children are standing at the table to eat. This was considered good discipline by Puritan parents.

Questions

1 Read Item A. How does this view differ from Calvinist attitudes?
2 What attitudes, identified by Weber as characteristic of Calvinism, are expressed in Item B?
3 Using Weber's argument, show how these attitudes could encourage the growth of capitalism.

1.6 An interpretive view of religion

Peter Berger: religion, rationalisation and 'the problem of modernity'

Weber's analysis of Calvinist Protestantism forms an important part of a broader argument. Weber believed that the modern world was characterised by a process of 'rationalisation'. This involved 'the methodical attainment of a definitely given and practical end by...a precise calculation of means'. This can be seen in the rise of capitalism which emphasised rational calculation in business activity and rationally organised work practices in order to maximise efficiency and profit. In particular, it can be seen in the spread of bureaucracy, the characteristic institution of modern society. Bureaucratic institutions are rational - they systematically and efficiently organise people in order to attain particular goals.

Weber believed that rationalisation has its costs. Reason replaces faith and the support which faith provides disappears. This leads to disillusionment, to 'disenchantment'. The world is 'demystified', its richness, mystery and magic taken away. It now appears cold. And social relationships, particularly in bureaucratic settings, become increasingly impersonal (see pp358-360 for Weber's views on rationalisation and bureaucracy).

These themes have been taken up since the 1960s by the Austrian-born American sociologist Peter Berger. Berger's main concern has been with what he calls 'modernity': in particular, with questions of how changes in social structure and social interaction in modern society are experienced by individuals, and how they strive to create a meaningful reality. He takes an interpretive approach, seeking to discover the meanings which people impose upon the world in order to make sense of it.

Berger begins by elaborating on Weber's argument that Protestantism has played a unique role in rationalising attitudes and social structures, particularly in the spread of bureaucracy. And, like Weber, he believes that the process of rationalisation, encouraged by Protestantism, has tended to 'demystify' the modern world and has led to modern people's 'disenchantment of the world'.

The spread of rationalisation - and associated disenchantment - he argues, has been accompanied by other changes in the conditions and experiences of people in modern societies. Significantly, the high levels of social and geographical mobility, combined with widespread exposure to the electronic media, have given people an unprecedented awareness of alternative social worlds, lifestyles and belief systems. As a result, each person's life-world has become pluralised. It is no longer a single, unified and integrated world. Instead it is fragmented and diverse.

In this situation, traditional religion is plunged into a crisis of credibility as individuals are faced with any number of competing belief systems and ways of living. In today's pluralistic and multicultural societies, each religion becomes one among many. It becomes increasingly difficult to maintain that *any* religion has a monopoly of truth. And all religions have to compete with a rapidly growing diversity of secular belief systems. This undermines traditional religious teachings, it erodes past certainties about morality and people's identity, it encourages a sense of meaninglessness. The result is *anomie* or normlessness, whereby people lack direction and guides to action. Using Berger's term, people are 'homeless', cut off from traditional supports and comforts and sense of self, all of which made them feel 'at home'. And religion - whose main function, Berger believes, has been as a shield against anomie - has been rendered largely impotent. It no longer has the power to give meaning to life.

Summary

1 For some sociologists, beliefs and practices are religious only if they acknowledge a supernatural being or force. For Durkheim and others, they are religious if they 'relate to sacred things' which may or may not be supernatural.

2 Functionalists see religion as performing positive functions for society - reinforcing social solidarity and promoting social stability.

3 For Marx and Engels, religion reflects the exploitation and alienation of class based society. When socialism removes exploitive social relations, religion will disappear.

4 For Weber, religion is a source of cultural meanings, through which people construct their identities and give order and meaning to their existence. Weber saw the trends to rationality in modern society, unintentionally encouraged by Protestantism, as leading to a growing sense of 'disenchantment with the world'.

Activity 8 Problems of Modernity

Item A *Social diversity*

A Muslim mosque in Preston, Lancashire. Preston was one of the traditional northern cotton towns of the industrial revolution.

A multi-ethnic crowd in a market in the East End of London

Item B *Homelessness*

Many of the discontents of modern society stem from the pluralisation of social life-worlds. These discontents can be characterised as 'homelessness'. The pluralistic structures of modern society have made the life of more and more individuals migratory, ever-changing, mobile. Not only are an increasing number of individuals in a modern society uprooted from their original social settings, but, in addition, no succeeding milieu succeeds in becoming truly 'home' either. A world in which everything is in constant motion is a world in which certainties of any kind are hard to come by. The age-old function of religion - to provide ultimate certainty - has been severely shaken.

The problem becomes most clearly apparent when one looks at that ancient religious function which Weber called 'theodicy'. This means any explanation of human events that gives meaning to the experiences of suffering and evil. Modern society has threatened the plausibility

of religious theodicies, but it has not removed the experiences that call for them. Human beings continue to be stricken by sickness and death. They continue to experience social injustice and deprivation. What modernity has accomplished is to seriously weaken those definitions of reality that previously made the human condition easier to bear. This has produced an anguish all its own.

Adapted from P Berger, B. Berger and H. Kellner *The Homeless Mind*, 1974, pp165-166

Questions

1 With reference to Items A and B, explain what you understand by the 'pluralisation of social life-worlds'. What sort of 'discontents' may pluralisation encourage?
2 How may the pluralisation of social life-worlds have undermined religion?

2 The Variety of Religious Organisations

Key Issues

1 How do religious organisations and movements differ?
2 Under what conditions do new religious movements begin and change?
3 Do all religions and religious movements play similar political roles? Are religions necessarily conservative?

2.1 Types of religious organisations and movements

Can Britain today be called a Christian country? Christianity remains the dominant religion. Yet within Christianity there is a range of organisations and movements which differ in their practices, beliefs and organisational structures.

It was Weber, and then his friend Ernst Troeltsch, who first focused attention, in the early part of this century, on the different types of religious organisation which exist within Christianity. However, interest in developing typologies (classificatory systems) of religious organisations and movements only really 'took off' in the 1970s, as sociologists became aware of the dramatic mushrooming of new religious movements throughout the West.

Church and sect

Although Weber introduced the distinction between *church* and *sect*, it was Troeltsch who more fully developed the idea. Troeltsch saw churches and sects

as almost polar opposites. However, they are similar in one respect: both claim that only their teachings offer the truth and both are seen by their members to be the only legitimate religion.

Church In their most fully developed or 'purest' form, churches aim to be *inclusive* - to include everyone - in their membership. They aim to be 'spiritual home' to all within a society or within an ethnic group, and membership is easily obtained and open to all. The Roman Catholic Church of the Middle Ages or the Greek Orthodox Church today are churches which come close to this model. Typically, they have a complex, formal hierarchy, largely comprising a professional clergy. Worship is restrained and makes much use of ritual. Churches mainly accept and compromise with the wider society and its values and institutions. Indeed, in medieval England the Church was centrally involved with the State and the Archbishop of Canterbury was often a very important political figure. In general, churches have close relationships with social elites but they are also broadly accepted by the wider society.

Sect Sects, on the other hand, are *exclusive* - they erect strong barriers between themselves and the world outside and exclude people considered 'unworthy'. There is therefore a clear distinction between members and non-members. Jehovah's Witnesses, Seventh Day Adventists, Moonies, Hare Krishnas and the Amish of the United States are examples today, as were the Methodists earlier in their history. Membership of sects is not a right but has to be gained by personal merit. This might be indicated by a knowledge of doctrine, a conversion experience or the recommendation of existing members. Sects demand high standards of behaviour from their members and high levels of commitment. Much of the members' spare time is spent in sectarian activities - in Bible study, trying to gain converts or socialising with sect members. Contact with non-members is generally discouraged except during an attempt to convert them. However, if members fail to meet the sect's high standards, they may be punished and perhaps expelled, a powerful sanction when members' lives have been built around the group.

Sects appeal partly because they map out an alternative way of life. They draw people out of a wider, largely impersonal society and into a warm and supportive group. Not surprisingly, therefore, given what they offer, sects have traditionally tended to recruit from the lonely, the deprived and the marginal, that is from those least integrated into society, such as the poor, ethnic minorities, the homeless, alcoholics, and so on.

Sects are supportive of the individual but generally critical of the wider society and members must stand apart from it. Sects are also critical of the mainstream religious bodies, whom they regard as too worldly, and also distance themselves from other religious groupings, even other sects. Members are encouraged to think of themselves as an elite who possess special enlightenment or spiritual insight and salvation is generally claimed to be reserved for them alone.

Organisationally, sects generally lack a professional clergy and a complex hierarchy. Instead, they depend for leadership upon the special, God-given talents of members. And in Christian sects at least, worship makes little use of ritual and is typically emotional, expressive and, ideally, spontaneous. Hence, in Christian sects members often cry out phrases such as 'Halleluja' and 'Praise the Lord', supposedly spontaneously.

Troeltsch's distinction between church and sect remains interesting and influential. It was developed solely from his study of Christianity and its applicability probably remains largely limited to that religion. Although the church and sect typology may offer interesting insights into some other religious traditions - perhaps Judaism and Islam - it is doubtful if it can greatly illuminate others such as Hinduism and Buddhism.

Activity 9 Sects

Item A *Jehovah's Witnesses*

'Government by God', *The Watchtower*, Watchtower Bible and Tract Society of Pennsylvania, undated, p3

Item B *The Bob Jones University*

The Bob Jones University (BJU) in Greenville, South Carolina considers itself to be the most extreme fundamentalist Christian university in America, a military-style training camp which turns out the Lord's toughest, most loyal soldiers. Like many other fundamentalist organisations, the university believes that the only way to achieve spiritual purity in these 'satanic' times is by withdrawing from the world at large and harking back to an aggressively wholesome vision of American life - a world where young men and women are well-scrubbed, model Christian citizens who keep their well-scrubbed, model Christian hands off each other until entering into holy matrimony. However, at BJU the matrimonial state is not necessarily easy to attain. Male and female students are not allowed to associate freely outside of class although a large lounge above the student union functions as a 'dating parlour' to which students can come on weekend nights, though the parlour is always chaperoned.

'The idea behind these rules,' explained Wilbur, a crew-cut guy in his early twenties with a smile with enough kilowatt power to light up Alaska, 'is to make your relationship with girls spiritual, mental and social. That's why holding hands is forbidden. It's not like we think that holding hands is the Devil incarnate. It's just...where do you draw the line?'

At BJU the line between good Christian behaviour and bad Christian behaviour was clear. Good Christians adhered to the dress code which stipulated that skirts should not expose regions above the knee and that men should be seen in jackets and ties at all times. Good Christians didn't go to movies shown outside the university. Good Christians didn't complain about the fact that no newspapers or periodicals were sold in the college bookstore. Good Christians attended the compulsory chapel service every morning at ten. And good Christians were in their rooms at 10 pm every night for group prayers led by a 'prayer captain' before lights out at 11 pm.

Adapted from D. Kennedy *In God's Country: Travels in the Bible Belt, USA,* 1989, pp175-178

Item C *The March for Jesus*

The 'March for Jesus' offers good songs, energetic affirmations of faith and a no-nonsense message. It is a powerful religious cocktail that galvanises the congregation, and its emotional simplicity appeals particularly to the young.

'I love Jesus and he loves me and we have a good relationship going,' said 15 year old Peter Jones from Basingstoke. 'Churches don't have to mean wooden pews any more. God wants you to have fun, and that's what we're doing. We're having fun with God.'

The congregation believe the Bible is true in every respect: that the world was created by God in six literal days, that animals of all species really went aboard Noah's ark, that the theory of evolution is a fraud, and that people who do not share their faith are damned for eternity.

Adapted from B. Deer 'Actress and the Bishop Upstaged', *Sunday Times*, 17.9.89

Questions

1 How do the sect-type groups described in Items A to C differ from a church?

2 What aspects of 'church-type' religion are sect members likely to reject?

3 Sect-type movements have traditionally recruited heavily from 'marginal' social groups: the poor, migrants, ethnic minorities, 'drug abusers', etc. Explain the appeal of sects for 'marginal' social groups.

Denomination and cult

Unlike churches and sects, denominations and cults do not claim an exclusive monopoly of the truth and so are less dogmatic and less demanding of their members. Because they acknowledge that there are other 'paths' to salvation, they will more readily cooperate with other religious organisations. However, they differ from each other in much the same way that churches differ from sects: denominations are widely accepted as conventional, respectable, mainstream; cults on the other, hand are generally regarded as unconventional, deviant and marginal.

Denomination The concept of denomination was introduced to sociology by the American Richard Niebuhr in 1925. In Niebuhr's view, all present-day denominations began as sects and did not develop into denominations until the 19th century. While churches tend to be closely associated with the state, denominations are explicitly separate from the state but, unlike sects, do not reject it or the wider society. Hence, in Britain, clergy of such denominations as the United Reformed and the Methodists appear at national occasions, such as the 'Poppy Day' commemoration of this century's war-dead, alongside Church of England clergy, who usually officiate as representatives of the 'national church'.

Although denominations have a professional clergy, their hierarchy is less complex and elaborate than that of a church, but more developed than that of a sect. Lay people play a more substantial role than in a church but less than in a sect, which is likely to have at most a semi-professional clergy. Although membership is open to all, and without a sect-like test of merit, denominations tend to be disproportionately middle class. Worship is relatively formal and both ritual and spontaneity are limited. Most sociologists would agree that in the USA the so-called 'churches' are closer to denominations.

Cult Although the media often use sect and cult interchangeably, Roy Wallis proposed that the term cult should refer to those movements which, like sects, are widely regarded as deviant but which, unlike sects, do not claim to have a monopoly of the truth. Therefore, unlike sects, cults are relatively tolerant of their members' involvement with other groups.

Whereas in churches and sects God is primarily seen as 'outside' of human beings, cults often emphasise the 'inner divinity' or 'inner power' of individuals and aim to help people to experience this divine spark within. However, cults generally make no demand on individuals to accept the teachings on offer; they simply ask 'seekers' to be 'open' to spiritual experiences, believing that if someone has such an experience in the cult they will then wish to learn about the teachings in order to understand and interpret the experience. Thus, cults demand only relatively low levels of commitment from 'members' (indeed, there may be no concept of 'membership' at all) and have minimal organisational structure. As a result they are prone to break up and are often short-lived.

Activity 10 Cults

Item A *The Company of Avallon Society*

The Company of Avallon Society (COAS) was formed in 1985 by student researchers of esoteric philosophy, occult science, and Earth Mystery phenomena. The COAS publicly revealed its existence in 1989 so as to expand and advance its aims, work and contact with others of like mind and interest.

The Society takes its name from the group of spiritual entities who supplied archeological data to Frederick Bligh Bond during his work at Glastonbury Abbey from 1907 to 1922. Glastonbury folklore and legends are of especial interest to the COAS, particularly those concerning the origins of Celtic Christianity and its links with Druidism. Study is focused mainly on the Western Mystery Traditions, and to 'areas of linkage' between these and other Mystery Traditions, especially those of Ancient Egypt.

COAS overall aims include:

- Rational understanding, development, plus beneficial use of those extraordinary faculties and functions of the human psyche ('soul-powers'), that result in telepathy, telekinesis (movement of objects using the power of the mind), precognition, intuition and the like.

- To establish and develop contact and rational communication with:

    (a) those 'organising intelligences' at work in the Kingdom of Nature and known as Devas, Nature Spirits, Angels, etc.

    (b) intelligent entities and 'souls' existent in alternative, complementary and/or parallel dimensions of consciousness or reality that are empathetic and supportive to the wellbeing, evolution and needs of the human race and its environment.

Adapted from introductory circular letter to enquirers, undated

Item B *'Is there anybody out there?'*

The Raelians were founded in 1973 after a young Frenchman, out walking in wild countryside, came upon a flying saucer from which emerged a benign, four-foot tall, humanoid alien. Over a few afternoons, the extraterrestial (ET), who could speak any human language, dictated his messages to Rael, messages which provide humanity with a revolutionary account of its origins, and offer guidance and hope for our future. In a nutshell, long ago a group of ETs had settled Earth and perfected their ability to create life in forms like their own. We Earthlings were the result. Thereafter they withdrew, but kept a kindly eye on us and sent periodic messengers, such as Buddha, Christ and Joseph Smith of the Mormons, to inform us of our origins and - with limited success - to try to guide us. Although they created us, we mistook them for gods.

However, suddenly aware of the scale of our ability for destruction at Hiroshima (where the first atomic bomb was dropped), they became very alarmed and felt an urgent, and perhaps final, need to help before we ran out of time. Unsurprisingly, however, they are not entirely confident of their likely reception by the Earthlings. Our reactions to Rael and the messages he conveys are the litmus test. Rael is the messenger for this 'Age of Revelation'. But he also comes bearing a set of meditative techniques taught him by his ET contact which can remove the root causes of most of our earthly ills. It's called 'Sensual Meditation' and proposes to 'awaken the mind by awakening the body'.

Though humanity is not perhaps inevitably doomed to self-destruct without their guidance, Rael's task is to persuade us to ponder our unexpected origins, practice the meditative techniques they taught him, and demonstrate that we are capable of wisdom and benevolence by building the aliens a home, an embassy, which is theirs, in which to welcome them. Then they will return.

Worldwide, the Raelians claim between 15,000 and 25,000 followers. In Britain there are about 300 names on the mailing list but only a dozen or so whom the British Representative regards as really committed. Enquiries are welcome and no commitment is required.

Adapted from A. Yeo, 'Is There Anybody Out There?', *Midweek*, 28.7.88, pp8-13

New Religious Movements

Sociological interest in nonconventional religious movements increased dramatically throughout the West in the 1960s and 1970s as sociologists belatedly became aware of the rapid growth in their numbers, size and variety. As more and more groups emerged, sociologists increasingly found the terms 'sect' and 'cult' inadequate to describe, categorise and analyse the new movements. For instance, although some, such as the meditative, Hindu-based Siddha Yoga movement, appeared to be cult-type religions (emphasising inner experience and the divine within, and remaining undogmatic and tolerant), they quickly developed complex organisational structures quite untypical of cults. Gradually, the use of 'sect' and 'cult' gave way to the broader and more general concept of *New Religious Movements* (NRMs).

One influential attempt to identify types of NRM was made by Roy Wallis. Wallis noted that they mainly drew upon either Christian traditions (such as the Jesus People), on non-Western religions (usually Hindu, Buddhist or Muslim), or ideas and techniques drawn from Western psychology and psychotherapy, as in the various 'human potential' or 'self-development' movements such as Scientology.

His main point, however, was that NRMs also differed significantly in how they are 'orientated to the world'. He proposed that NRMs are either primarily *world-affirming, world-rejecting* or *world accommodating.*

World-affirming NRMs broadly accept the world. Many do not appear conventionally 'religious' at all and their language may be more akin to business. What they offer their members or 'clients' are techniques or other help to enable them to live more satisfactorily or successfully in the world. In Transcendental Meditation, for instance, each person is assured that they will relax and cope better with life if they meditate on a secret *mantra*, or sacred word, given to them personally during initiation.

World-accommodating NRMs encourage their members to remain within the wider society. Though they are dissatisfied with and critical of the secular nature of society, they try to help their followers cultivate an awareness of their 'inner power' or inner

divinity. However, like the denomination, they claim to be merely one of a variety of paths to the truth or salvation. In Siddha Yoga, for instance, meditation and chanting are practiced regularly, not primarily to help people cope with or 'succeed in life', but as a spiritual experience in which people come into contact with their own spiritual core or 'inner self'. The churches and denominations are seen not as corrupt, but as not helping people to have such spiritual experiences.

World-rejecting NRMs are sect-like organisations, often founded by a charismatic leader. They are critical of or even hostile to the secular world, they keep their distance from it and often from other religious organisations. Like sects, they are seen by their members as *uniquely legitimate* - as the sole means of access to truth or salvation. They therefore draw clear boundaries between members and non-members, set strict conditions for entry and continuing membership and require a high level of commitment. For instance, Jehovah's Witnesses will not join trade unions, political parties or other secular organisations in order to keep their involvement in the wider society to a minimum. A high proportion of their non-work time is devoted to Bible study, door to door conversion attempts and other sect-related activities. 'Immoral behaviour' could result in expulsion.

Although an NRM may have a predominant orientation to the world, we cannot assume that this applies to all its members. Different individuals may have a quite different relationship to the same movement. Some may be totally committed to it, for instance, and accept its orientation to the world. Others may be using it for a limited purpose. They may, for instance, be trying to improve their ability to relax, or to gain confidence by taking one of the courses the movement offers. Also, the same movement may have a different character at different organisational levels or facing different publics. Thus, a movement's elite may be living largely world-rejecting lives in a sect-like refuge while others may be living world-accommodating or even world-affirming lives in the community. We cannot therefore assume that each movement has only one distinctive, identifying stance to the world.

A further note of caution will be raised here and

developed later. Sociologists have tended to regard such movements as new. Yet many of them spring from well-established traditions. Most so-called NRMs are either groups which derive from a religious tradition which was long-established in a foreign culture (eg the Hare Krishna movement), or come from a 'homegrown' subcultural tradition which preceded them and which offers broad sympathetic support (eg various occult and pagan groups).

Activity 11 New Religious Movements

Item A *Scientology and Transcendental Meditation*

Psychologically based movements such as Scientology typically place little emphasis on collective ritual or worship but focus instead on the problems of individuals. They market themselves as a service which individuals can purchase and consume at their convenience. Their practices are directed more to reducing the problems of this life than to achieving salvation in the next. Such movements often draw upon ideas from the fringes of modern psychology or Eastern thought. Even some of the new religions which draw more directly from an existing religious tradition, such as Transcendental Meditation, also seem to be oriented to enabling people to achieve the conventional goals of this life such as better jobs, a higher IQ or greater success in personal relationships. These movements seem to form a type, sharing the common characteristics of accepting most of the goals and values of the wider society but providing new means to achieve them. Their organisational form is also distinct from traditional religion. Rather than organising as churches or chapels, they typically organise themselves in the form of multinational business corporations and employ the techniques of modern marketing and advertising.

ISKCON members

Item B *Neo-Pentecostalism and Charismatic Renewal*

A service

Some religious movements neither fully accept the norms and values of the surrounding society, nor entirely reject them by cutting themselves off completely in communities of the like-minded. Rather, they feel that the secular world and even many religious bodies have slipped away from God's design for human life. However, individuals can overcome this problem in their own lives without separating entirely from the secular world. Believers will normally continue in conventional jobs and family life, their religious practice reinvigorating and re-equipping them to face a degenerating secular world. This group includes such movements as Neo-Pentecostalism and the Charismatic Renewal. Both claim that the Holy Spirit is still alive in the world and can be experienced through various divine 'gifts', notably through the gift of 'speaking in tongues'.

Such groups are essentially a protest against the loss of vitality in existing religious institutions and their abandonment of a living spirituality. The new movement restores this spirituality and returns to traditional certainties in a world where religious institutions have become colder, more bureaucratic and less certain of their role and even of their fundamental beliefs.

Item C *ISKCON and the Children of God*

Some religious movements reject the world around them, seeing it as utterly corrupt. The world has to be abandoned or totally transformed. Such movements separate themselves from the wider society in communities of the faithful. Some look forward to a spiritual revolution. Members of the International Society for Krishna Consciousness (ISKCON) spend much of their lives in ritual prayers and chants, seeking spiritual truth to escape the illusion and corruption of the outside world.

Other movements look forward to a supernatural intervention. For example, the Children of God live in a state of high expectation, awaiting the imminent return of Christ who will transform the world around them.

Items A-C adapted from R. Wallis 'The Sociology of the New Religions' *Social Studies Review*, September 1985, pp3-7

Questions

1 Each of the items provides an example of one of Wallis' types of NRM - world-accommodating, world-rejecting, world-affirming. Match each item to one of these 'orientations to the world'. Give reasons for your choices.
2 Each type of NRM holds out a promise to its members. In each case identify the promise and suggest its appeal to followers of the movement.

2.2 Religions and politics

Most functionalists and Marxists would argue that religions generally play a conservative role in society. They mainly act to support the *status quo* - the way things are - and so discourage political change. Hinduism or the medieval Roman Catholic Church are often cited as examples which legitimise and support social inequality. However, there are different groupings in all major religions and they span a range of political attitudes and sympathies.

Churches and politics Within Christianity, the churches are generally accommodating to, and supportive of, the secular authorities. And that broadly seems to be the stance taken traditionally by most Muslim clerics within Islam. In many Muslim countries, notably Egypt, *ulama* (Muslim clerics) are employed by state institutions and are sometimes called upon to bestow approval on government policies, which they generally do.

The neo-Marxist Maduro argues that churches are encouraged to play a conservative role in order to attract a mass membership. This membership is drawn from a highly diverse and stratified public - a public which is divided by internal conflicts. In their attempt to gain a wide following, churches tend to gloss over such division and conflict and appeal to all as members of God's family. This message is socially and politically unifying. They thereby almost inevitably perform a conservative function. By concealing or minimising the conflicts of class society, they encourage social stability and thereby support the continued dominance of the ruling classes.

During periods of stability the common interest of the church in preserving its public and of the dominant classes in preserving the social order tends to remain hidden. But there are times when the dominant classes lose the people's consent to their rule, and social movements develop against them. Then the conservative function of a church may suddenly become visible as it throws its weight against those who threaten authority. This became apparent during the Russian revolution of 1917 which overthrew Tsar Nicolas II. Chosen by God as the 'little father of the people', Tsar Nicolas was supported by the Russian Orthodox Church.

While churches may generally support secular

authority, Maduro accepts that the same church can fulfil very different functions in different countries and at different times. During the 1980s in Britain, the Church of England repeatedly criticised Mrs Thatcher's Conservative government for presiding over a decline in community. And, contrary to government ideology, it explicitly linked apathy, depression and anger in the cities with poverty and the widening gap between rich and poor. Yet, though they may criticise specific policies, the churches appear very cautious about criticising the capitalist system as such. However, even that may not apply to clergy at all levels of the church hierarchy or to clergy working with particular groups or classes. Parish priests working with impoverished peasants in South America, for instance, have been highly critical of national elites and some have openly advocated political revolution (see Activity 6, p503). Hence, as Maduro argues, the same church may be performing very different functions simultaneously.

Sects and politics Sects, on the other hand, stand generally in opposition to society's secular authorities. Some play an active political role while others stay uninvolved with politics - unless forced to make an oppositional response by the state, as when pacifist Jehovah's Witnesses are subjected to military call-up.

According to Bryan Wilson, sects which remain distanced from political involvement are likely to be those which are hostile to the wider society and are more concerned with preparing for the Second Coming of Christ than with gaining recruits. If God is about to transform the world, there's no need to get involved with politics. Such movements encourage self-imposed isolation from the world by providing members with status within the movement and a sense of their own good fortune.

Wilson argues that sects whose main concern is to convert people are more likely to become involved with politics. These sects do not keep themselves apart from the world but try to save people's souls by such means as evangelistic revival meetings. Early Methodism provides an example. And, as Wilson argues, like Methodism, 'conversionist' sects are the ones most likely to evolve into denominations.

Not all sects which involve themselves in politics are right wing. Again, Methodism provides an example. It has been said that the Labour Party owes more to Methodism than to Marxism. Whether or not that is the case, Methodism does have strong historical links with socialism in some areas at least, as for instance in South Wales.

As well as conversionist sects, there are some cult-like groups sympathetic to oppositional politics. Followers of paganism, witchcraft and other New Age movements, for instance, are likely to support animal rights and Green politics and have liberal or left wing sympathies. In the United States in the 1980s such groups became heavily involved in both the environmental movement and the Democratic Party.

Moreover, religious movements involved in oppositional politics are not confined to Christianity. Perhaps unexpectedly for Westerners, the rise of militant Islam has also spawned movements influenced by socialist and reformist ideas. For instance, the left wing Islamic People's Mojahidin, drawing heavily on neo-Marxism, played an important role in the Iranian revolution of 1979. Its supporters saw the revolution as a war to end US imperialism and the dictatorship of the Shah (Emperor).

Rastafarianism provides another example of a religion which actively opposes the secular authorities. In Jamaica, Rastafarianism challenges secular authority by its emphasis on the need for blacks to migrate to Africa, by its sharp criticism that despite independence from Britain the black masses remain oppressed, and by its confident claim that 'Babylon' - the corrupt and evil society of the dominant brown middle classes - will one day be overthrown.

In the main, however, Christian sects which engage in political affairs tend to be right wing, conservative or even reactionary. Often they wish not to conserve, not to keep things as they are, but to regain what they imagine to be a lost past. Reflecting their desire for an imagined lost past, members of conservative sects demand a 'return' to law and order and the sanctity of the family and a crackdown on homosexuality, abortion, pornography and so on.

Some of the most striking examples of the right wing political involvement of religious movements come from the American religious broadcasters - the so-called 'televangelists'. Religious broadcasters have pursued a conservative political agenda since the radio days of the 1930s. From the mid-1970s they became increasingly active in politics. And in 1980, Presidential candidate Ronald Reagan gained many votes from conservative Christians following his public endorsement of the political agenda of the televangelist-led New Christian Right movement. Following Reagan's presidency, the Reverend Pat Robertson challenged George Bush for the Republican Party nomination in 1988. Despite his failure he was again addressing the Republican National Convention in prime TV time in the 1992 presidential campaign.

Activity 12 *Religion and Politics*

Item A *Jehovah's Witnesses*

Jehovah's Witnesses believe that, to start with, man was under divine government. But in the Garden of Eden, our first parents turned their backs on that. They chose to be independent of God, wanting to rule themselves. Really, though, man was not created to rule himself. Jehovah (God) has generously allowed thousands of years for man to try every conceivable form of government. With what result? It has become evident that no human government can remove oppression, inequity, or other causes of unhappiness.

Today, millions of individuals have become united in their desire to obey God and serve his heavenly government. They do not share in the divisive politics of this world, although they subject themselves to human governments as long as God patiently allows these to function. Instead they patiently await the Day of Judgment and the unfolding of God's Plan for men on Earth.

Adapted from 'How Long Will God's Patience Last?' *The Watchtower* 1 October 1991, p6

Item B *The Reverend Pat Robertson*

'When the Christian majority takes over this country,' proclaimed TV evangelist and former US presidential candidate Pat Robertson, 'there will be no satanic churches, no more free distribution of pornography, no more abortion on demand, and no more talk of rights for homosexuals. After the Christian majority takes control, pluralism will be seen as immoral and evil and the state will not permit anybody to practice it.'

Pat Robertson

Adapted from 'Fundamentalism: Reaching for Certainty', *New Internationalist*, August 1990, p5

Item C *Islam and revolution*

Many of the Islamic groups behind the Iranian Revolution were motivated by ideas very different from those of the Ayatollah Khomeini and the Muslim clergy who formed the new government. The main such group was the Islamic People's Mojahidin.

The Mojahidin believed that God had created a world rooted in a class conflict between the oppressors and the oppressed that went all the way back to Cain and Abel. The Prophet of Islam, Muhammad, was sent to champion the oppressed and to abolish slavery and exploitation. After Muhammad's death, Islam was taken over by ruling classes aided by clerics and twisted to serve their interests. For the Mojahidin it was up to the revolutionary intelligentsia to reveal the true religion to the masses and to lead them in the struggle to overthrow their oppressors.

This revolutionary socialism was the leading Islamic ideology of the Revolution. Khomeini and the militant clerics were in a position to hijack the Revolution because they were the only group with organisation, practical strategy and money. The Mojahidin were among their early victims.

Adapted from S. Zubeida 'Hijacked by Khomeini', *New Internationalist*, August 1990, p8

Questions

1 Read Item A.
   a) What is the attitude of Jehovah's Witnesses towards politics?
   b) Suggest reasons for their lack of involvement in politics.
2 A religious movement may be right wing and conservative yet still turn to politics in order to change society. Support this statement using examples from Item B.
3 The Mojahidin have been described as left wing and radical. Support this statement with evidence from Item C.

2.3 The emergence of new religious movements

New religious movements can appear at any time. However, they seem most likely to emerge during periods of particular uncertainty or of especially rapid and unsettling change. Such circumstances can lead to social dislocation, to a feeling of being uprooted and to anomie - a sense of normlessness. Anthropological and historical research suggests that the normative breakdown and insecurity which encourages such movements can result from a variety of collective experiences.

First, the experience of disasters, whether natural or man-made, may spawn new movements. As Norman Cohn's studies of medieval Europe illustrate, such movements may be precipitated by outbreaks of plague, devastating fires, long droughts, serious economic slumps or calamitous wars, any of which may lead to a deep sense of doom and a fervent desire for salvation (N. Cohn, 1957).

It can come from unsettling contact with a powerful alien culture, especially if accompanied by the experience of being occupied and colonised. For example, the colonisation of Palestine by the Romans saw the birth of Christianity and the emergence of many competing religious and/or political movements among the Jews. In such contact between cultures, traditional norms, values and institutions may be shaken and undermined. And the contact often demoralises those who find themselves confronted by a more powerful and apparently superior culture. In extreme cases, the actual survival of the group may appear under threat. This fear triggered the so-called 'Ghost Dance' movement among North American Plains Indians in the 19th century. They mistakenly believed the claims of an Indian 'prophet' that they would be invincible against the white man's bullets.

People who feel that their way of life is threatened or has collapsed experience a sense of disorientation, frustration, deep anxiety and even rage. They will be predisposed to follow a messianic leader who clearly identifies the enemy, preaches a doctrine of the final struggle and promises the coming of a new age.

In advanced industrial societies, such collective society-wide experiences are much less likely. However, people still experience anomie, insecurity and a sense of impending doom and this may encourage new movements. For instance, fears of military, urban or ecological disaster have gripped some people. They have gathered like-minded persons into a movement and retreated to secluded places such as mountain tops in the hope of avoiding the predicted disaster.

A number of sociologists have argued that the social changes involved in the process of industrialisation and modernisation have encouraged the emergence of new religious movements. These changes lead to a crisis of meaning and identity. People are less able to make sense of the world, they are increasingly unsure about who they are. Among the changes most commonly identified are: rationalisation and bureaucratisation; the decline of social support groups such as the extended family and the community; the multiplication of lifestyles and belief systems; the failure of science, capitalism *and* mainstream religion to offer satisfactory normative guidance and a sufficient sense of meaning. For some, NRMs can provide certainty in the face of uncertainty, social support within a close knit group despite the breakdown of community support and a strong sense of who they are in the face of a society which threatens their identity.

There is evidence to support the view that NRMs emerge during periods of social dislocation and unrest. However, a study by Gordon Melton suggests that this does not apply to the origin of all NRMs. He analysed the founding dates of 836 nonconventional religious groups in the USA this century. He found

that a rapid growth in numbers occurred in the 1950s, a period of social stability. This rapid growth preceded the social unrest and counter-cultural movements of the 1960s and early 1970s - the student riots, black riots, the Vietnam War, the hippy movement, the search for a new consciousness which often involved drugs as a route to awareness. Although the number of NRMs grew during the1960s, it grew even further during the 70s and 80s. And the 1980s are seen as a period of stability compared to the 60s. Thus Melton finds no relation between social unrest and the emergence of new religious groups.

Activity 13 The Origins of NRMs

Item A *The Ghost Dance religion*

By 1890 the traditional way of life of the Sioux Indians had ended. They had been defeated by the US army, rounded up and confined to reservations. The buffalo, their main source of food, had all but disappeared, slaughtered by professional white hunters such as Buffalo Bill.

The US government was determined to stamp out the Sioux way of life. Traditional customs such as the Sun Dance, an important religious ceremony, were banned. The reservation authorities tried to force the Sioux to become farmers - an occupation despised by Sioux warriors.

The frozen body of Chief Big Foot, leader of the ghost dancers at Wounded Knee

Farming was doomed to failure. The land was unsuitable, there was a drought and the cattle became diseased. Undernourished, the Sioux had little resistance to the measles and whooping cough which swept through the reservations in 1890. On one reservation, the death rate rose to 45 a month in a population of 5,550.

In 1890 the Sioux received news of a messiah, a Paiute Indian called Wovoka. He had been visited by Christ and founded a new religion - the Ghost Dance. This was his message.

In the beginning God made the earth and then sent the Christ to earth to teach the people. But white men treated him badly, leaving scars on his body, and so he went back

to heaven. Now he has returned to earth as an Indian, and he will renew everything as it used to be and make it better.

In the next springtime, when the grass is knee-high, the earth will be covered with new soil which will bury all the white men. The new land will be covered with sweet grass and running water and trees. Great herds of buffalo and wild horses will come back. The Indians who dance the Ghost Dance will be taken up in the air and suspended there while a wave of new earth is passing, and then they will be set down among the ghosts of their ancestors on the new earth. There they will follow their traditional way of life, forever free from death, disease and misery. Only Indians will live on this regenerated earth - the white race will disappear.

About half the Sioux nation believed in the new religion. They danced the ghost dance and wore 'ghost shirts' which they believed made them invulnerable to white men's bullets. Fearing trouble, the authorities called in the army. Troops surrounded a group of ghost dancers at Wounded Knee Creek. Fighting broke out and 150 Indians, including 60 women and children, were massacred. The Ghost Dance was over.

Adapted from R.M. Utley *The Last Days of the Sioux Nation*, 1963 and D. Brown *Bury My Heart At Wounded Knee*, 1975, pp341-2

Item B *The Rastafarian Movement*

The Rastafarian religion originated in the West Indies and was based on the ideas of Marcus Garvey, who preached that the only way for black people to escape their poverty and oppression was to return to Africa. When Haile Selassie was crowned emperor of the North African country of Ethiopia in 1930, and took the title 'Lion of Judah' (Ras Tafari), this was seen as a fulfilment of prophecy and followers claimed him as the Messiah, the incarnation of God. Rastafarians see themselves as the ancient lost tribe of Israel, enslaved and transported from Africa by whites. They will remain forever oppressed and suffering, even in Jamaica, until they return to Africa. In Jamaica, its appeal has been greatest among the most disadvantaged sections of the Jamaican populace - the urban underclass. Some key beliefs are included in the 'Charter of the Rastafarians' below.

From the Rastafarian Charter

1 Members of the Rastafarian Movement are an inseparable part of the Black people of Jamaica.

3 The Rastafarian Movement consists of the most advanced, determined and uncompromising fighters against discrimination, ostracism and oppression of the Black people of Jamaica.

4 The Rastafarian Movement stands for freedom in its fullest sense and for the recovery, dignity, self-respect and sovereignty of the Black people of Jamaica.

11 The Rastafarian Movement has as its chief aim the complete destruction of all vestiges of white supremacy in Jamaica, thereby putting an end to economic exploitation and the social degradation of the Black people.

12 The Rastafarian Movement stands for Repatriation (to Africa) and power and for the fullest cooperation between the Governments and people of Africa and a free and independent people of Jamaica.

20 All men...are free irrespective of colour to join this political crusade. The only condition is that they must abandon evil.

Adapted from 'Charter of the Rastafarians' quoted in K. M. Williams *The Rastafarians*, 1981, pp58-60

Questions

1 Read Item A. Give a sociological explanation for the Ghost Dance religion.

2 Read Item B.

a) Give a sociological explanation for the origins of Rastafarianism.

b) Why do you think many Afro-Caribbean people in Britain have become Rastafarians?

2.4 The evolution of religious movements

New religious movements appear in a variety of forms. In the history of the West, some have been born as cults, some as sects, and others as denominations. And in the last few decades, movements have emerged which don't seem to fit any of these classifications - hence the more general term, new religious movements.

From cult to sect What happens to NRMs? Some are short lived. From Melton's sample of 836 NRMs in the USA from 1900 to 1985, 125 had disappeared by 1990. According to Roy Wallis, some of the groups which begin life as cults (or as world-affirming or world-accommodating NRMs) do appear able to maintain this form. However, because little or no commitment is required of followers, who are free to sample other 'paths', cults are precarious movements. And it is to try to counteract their precariousness, according to Wallis, that some cults become more sect-like. A body of distinctive teachings and doctrine is elaborated, a hierarchy developed, and authority becomes more centralised in the leader and his or her 'lieutenants'. At the same time, more commitment is required of followers (who are now members) and a greater control exercised over them. Members increasingly think of themselves as a chosen group, an elect. The movement's boundaries become more sharply drawn and the group puts a greater distance between itself and the world. Scientology (previously the cult-like Dianetics), and the Orange People or Rajneeshies (followers of the late Bhagwan Shree Rajneesh, whose attempt to build their 'City of God' in

rural Oregon ended in literally murderous exchanges between themselves and their township neighbours) are examples of such an evolution. According to Stark and Roberts, one explanation of why cult founders often encourage a sect-type 'turning inwards' is that the cult founders lose hope. This is because, despite considerable effort, the actual number of recruits attracted during the first generation remains discouragingly small.

While some sects begin life as cults, others originate as sects. Some sects begin as a movement of dissatisfied individuals within a church who feel betrayed by its corruption, worldliness or spiritual 'falling away'. These sects emerge then from division or schism, as the members of the emerging sect are expelled or break away. Methodism, for instance, was a schismatic breakaway sect of the Church of England. On the other hand, sects such as the Elim Four Square Gospel Church were never part of another organisation but developed independently from organised revivalist campaigns.

From sect to denomination According to Niebuhr, all sects must evolve into a denomination or face extinction. However, he was wrong to suggest that these are the only alternatives. For those sects which do evolve into denominations, Niebuhr's explanation is that sectarians would lead frugal and ascetic (strict, self-denying) lives, and that this would unintentionally but inevitably result in their rising social status. As they increasingly come into contact with, and are accepted by, 'conventional' society, they compromise and the distinctive character of their theology, their ethics and their religious organisations is progressively undermined and weakened. In addition, the second generation, who were not converted into the faith but merely born into it, are unlikely to show the same degree of motivation, enthusiasm, commitment and asceticism as their parents. Consequently, Niebuhr argued, they increasingly make the compromises with society which lead to their becoming a denomination, by for instance limiting their criticism of the secular authorities.

Niebuhr's account may well cast light on the history of the Methodists, English Presbyterians and certain other denominations which began as sects. However, not all sects do evolve into denominations. Some become what Yinger called 'established sects'. They often do so by creating powerful boundaries between themselves and the outside world and, as in the case of the Amish, by largely withdrawing physically from society. Some, such as the Exclusive Brethren, succeed in insulating their members very effectively from the outside world by substantially limiting contact with non-members, forbidding exposure to the mass media and other measures.

The path to salvation According to Bryan Wilson, however, the crucial factor which determines whether a sect is likely to develop into a denomination or remain a sect is the way the sect answers the question, 'What shall we do to be saved?' Only one type, the 'conversionist sect', is likely to develop into a denomination. Conversionist sects, such as the early Salvation Army, aim (as Wilson's term for them suggests) to convert as many people as they are able. They often use large-meeting revivalist techniques to generate conversions, which are the only test of admission. They can become a denomination without necessarily compromising their position. They can still save souls.

The other types of sect cannot maintain their basic position in a denominational form. 'Adventist sects', for instance, such as the Jehovah's Witnesses, Seventh Day Adventists or Christadelphians, are less concerned with conversions and much more concerned with preparing themselves for what they believe will be growing world chaos and the Day of Judgment. Because adventist sects are highly critical of - even hostile to - the wider society, and look forward to its being overthrown by God, their members are not likely to welcome the sect becoming more adjusted to society. And because they are careful about who they admit, and often demand that new members have a knowledge of their teachings, adventist sects are more likely to resist becoming a denomination. Therefore, Wilson concludes, whether or not a sect becomes a denomination is largely determined by its prescription for salvation.

Summary

1 Sociologists have tended to see churches and sects at opposite ends of the religious spectrum. Churches are seen as open to all members of society, as broadly accepting of the state and the political and economic systems, and as hierarchical, with a professional clergy. Limited demands are made on members and worship is ritualised and restrained. Both churches and sects are likely to claim a monopoly of the truth. Sects, however, maintain distinct boundaries between themselves and the wider society.

2 Denominations and cults are similar in that both acknowledge alternative 'paths' to salvation and are therefore less dogmatic and demanding of members. Denominations are separate from the state. They have a professional clergy but a less elaborate and complex hierarchy (with greater involvement of laity) than the church. Worship is less ritualised than a church but less spontaneous than a sect.

3 Cults, like sects, are widely regarded as deviant by the wider society. Unlike sects however, they claim no monopoly of the truth and are therefore less demanding of their members and more tolerant of other paths. Many emphasise an 'inner divinity' or 'power within', and try to help seekers to experience or develop it. Because they make few demands on followers, organisation may be minimal and cults tend to be short-lived.

4 With the emergence in the West of large numbers of new movements which did not fit existing classifications, the term New Religious Movement (NRM) was coined. Wallis distinguished between world-rejecting, world-accommodating and world-affirming NRMs.

5 Churches are generally accommodating to the secular authorities and tend to play a mainly conservative, integrative role. Sects are more likely to oppose the secular authorities and the values of the wider society. Some, including adventist sects, shun all political and social involvement. Others, including conversionist sects, may be politically committed. Although some denominations and cults are sympathetic to green and left wing or liberal politics, most sects are politically right wing.

6 New religious movements seem most likely to emerge during periods of particular uncertainty, change and anomie. Many new movements begin as sects, either from splits within a church or developing from revivalist campaigns. Other movements start as cults. Many of these become sects, and demand higher levels of commitment from members.

7 Adventist sects are less likely to evolve into denominations than conversionist sects. A few denominations seem to be born already fully-formed.

Activity 14   The Evolution of NRMs

Item A *Conversionist sects*

It is 3.15 pm on a nice spring day at Funcoast World, Butlin's megacamp by the sea at Skegness. And at the Evangelical Alliance's seminar on the occult, part of the EA's 1990 'Spring Harvest' meeting, things are coming to a head. Round the back of the chalets 250 people are shoehorned into a marquee - the occult is one of the notable pullers among the programme's 400-odd seminars - and the emotional temperature is rising by the minute.

'I pray, Lord, that you will forgive me my interest in the occult', says Faith Forster, one of the two coordinators of the session. 'I ask, Lord, that you will cleanse me from all the effects of that occult activity. Deliver me from the Evil One now, in Jesus' name. Amen!' Now strident, suddenly: 'And now, Lord, we come against all these things!' More strident still: 'We break the power of witchcraft, freemasonry and every evil practice!' Really bellowing now: 'Evil Spirits, your power is broken! In the name of Jesus - koram sige ne suma king, kaime narasamwi! Orea, tigmar wah oguna, tigmar weho, oyuma otignmo...!' Shrieks! Applause! Yells of 'Alleluia!' and 'Thank you, Jesus!' and suddenly everyone is singing and the 25 year old beside me, eyes shining, declares that, yes, it is so, yes indeed: Faith Forster has truly been 'talking in tongues'.

Evangelical Christians

When this coming together of evangelically minded Christians started in 1978 there were 2,700 participants. This year (1990) there were 70,000 and 90,000 are expected in 1991. They are spontaneous, passionate and noisy and highly conservative in doctrine. That housewife cheering the miracle of 'tongues' will almost certainly be anti-abortion, anti-adultery and have a literal belief in the Devil and all the Biblical miracles. The attraction is plain. The world may be becoming more relativist every year, yet for true believers a rock remains - the moral absolutes.

Adapted from I. Cotton 'Share it, Brother', *Sunday Times Magazine*, 16.12.90, pp49,51

Item B *Established sects: the Old Order Amish*

The Amish are the American descendants of a group which broke away from the Swiss Anabaptists in the late 17th century. Their distinctive dress - black for the males, with broad brimmed hats, and simple and plain for the females - symbolises their separatism. They practice adult baptism and refuse to bear arms, swear oaths, or take public office. They don't use cars or electricity or petrol driven farm implements. Among themselves they speak Pennsylvania Dutch, a type of German, and with non-Amish they speak English.

Their beliefs are associated with a total way of life: religion to the Amish is not a separate activity. The Amish are however willing to accept other people the way they are, but have no interest in converting them to the Amish way of life. This is entirely compatible with the value they place on separation. To actively try to convert would put them into a position of deeper contact with outsiders.

The Old Order Amish have a doctrine of separation which means physical isolation from non-Amish, making a living from the soil and

Amish women at a Saturday market

keeping the rules of the past unchanged where possible. In the New Order Amish, the doctrine is modified and adapted to their changing relationships with the wider society. Geographical isolation is now much more difficult to maintain because of the growth of the road system and the tourist crowds who come to see the Amish. Also, making a living from the land has become more difficult as land has become scarcer and more expensive. Lack of land has forced many to work in the wider community. The New Order interpret separation from the world to mean spiritual rather than physical isolation. They meet in churches rather than in people's houses and have modified their distinctive dress.

Adapted from A. Sim 'Did you see "Witness"?', *Sociology Review*, February 1994, pp12-15

3 The Decline of Religion?

Key Issues

1 What is secularisation?
2 What is the evidence for and against secularisation?
3 Are New Religious Movements evidence of a religious revival?
4 Is the USA a religious or a secular society?

3.1 Secularisation

The word secular means 'worldly, not sacred, temporal, profane' (*Concise Oxford Dictionary*). Secularisation is 'the process whereby religious thinking, practice and institutions lose social significance' (Bryan Wilson, 1966). Accepting this as a convenient definition, three types of question are raised. Compared to past ages:

1 What power, prestige and influence do *religious institutions* have?
2 What influence does religion now have on people's *thinking, attitudes and consciousness*?
3 To what extent are *religious practices* (including private prayer and collective worship) observed?

   Those who support the secularisation thesis claim that religion has lost social significance in all three respects.

   There are, of course, important definitional and methodological problems thrown up by these questions. As Bryan Wilson has acknowledged, statistically based surveys are not very useful for measuring the influence of religion on either public opinion or government, nor for measuring the strength of individuals' religious commitment or their motivation or reasons for church-going. Even participant observation studies cannot overcome these problems, though they can help in some. In any event, to assess an historical process requires comparison with the past, and it is difficult to obtain reliable and valid information from past ages.

   The evidence for and against secularisation is not conclusive. First, the evidence that secularisation has occurred and is occurring will be examined.

3.2 Evidence of the decline of religion

The power of the Church With regard to the question of the power and influence of the churches historically and today in Western Europe there can be little doubt. As a social institution, the Roman Catholic Church in medieval Western Christendom had power to rival that of kings. At its probable peak in the 12th and 13th centuries, the Roman Catholic church was central to the political life of Western societies and to the lives of the people, from king to serf. The Church was the major employer, with its own courts, judges and lawyers and its own physicians. In its heyday it has been estimated that throughout Western Europe one out of every thirty adult males was in the service of the Church.

   And it could shape and dominate the imagination. It provided one of the very few opportunities for literacy. And 'at a time when not one man in a thousand could read, the Church taught its story in stone, painting, glass and embroidery, in buildings which, in an age when most people lived in huts little bigger or cleaner than pigsties, towered above the landscape and blazed within with colour and wealth' (A. Bryant, 1953, p205). Today, in Britain and Western Europe, the power, prestige and the influence of religious bodies have long since shrunk. Church buildings can be seen in ruins or put to secular use, fewer people present themselves for ordination as priests and ministers, the clergy are paid a pittance and churches have long since been eclipsed by the media as providers of information and guidance.

Religious beliefs Secondly, supporters of the secularisation thesis claim that people's thinking and attitudes are no longer based on religious beliefs. They are not suggesting that in the past everybody's outlook was dominated by religion. For example, Wilson accepts that superstitious and magical beliefs, indifference and unbelief were common in the Middle Ages. He does not assume a mythical 'golden age' of universal religious belief and practice.

However, to accept that secularisation has occurred, Wilson argues, 'All that needs to be assumed is that society was much more preoccupied with supernatural beliefs and practices, and accorded them more significance, than it does now' (quoted in R. Wallis and S. Bruce, 1989, p495).

Critics of the secularisation thesis nevertheless claim that Wilson understates 'the volume of apathy, heterodoxy (officially unapproved beliefs) and agnosticism which existed long before the onset of industrialism' and thus exaggerates today's lack of religiosity (Keith Thomas quoted in D. McLellan, 1987, p169). And David Martin points to the frequency of complaints throughout the Middle Ages about the laxity in both religious observance and individual morality of many of the medieval clergy.

Wilson's response is to stress that however widespread the scepticism and heterodox beliefs and practices, those concerned were nevertheless 'believers'. The heterodox and the sceptical shared with the orthodox a belief in the 'reality' of the supernatural even if they did draw on traditions of magic, mysticism or occultism which were opposed by the established church. Thus, their beliefs were not 'secular' in any modern sense.

Religious practices Thirdly, with regard to the mainstream churches and denominations in Western Europe, there is general agreement that religious practices have declined. The evangelical revivals of 18th and 19th century Britain (Methodism, Salvation Army, and others) led to gains in membership until perhaps the 1930s. Thereafter most Protestant organisations declined. Thus, church membership, church attendance, church marriage, church funerals, christenings, Sunday School and Bible reading are all down. According to Steve Bruce, 'The high point for the British churches was between 1860 and 1910 when around 28% of the adult population were active members. The corresponding figure now would be about 12%. The 1851 census showed that about 40% of the population went to church; now about 10% go to church "at least once a month"' (1992, p11). For many people, churches offer little more than rituals for rites of passage - birth, marriage and death. Even Roman Catholics, whose numbers grew until the early 1960s through immigration from Ireland and relatively high fertility, appear to be part of this general decline in religious practice.

Bryan Wilson believes that secularisation has reached into every aspect of modern life. And his view of its consequences is profoundly pessimistic. In the family, it reflects in a decline in the importance attached to the socialisation of children into appropriate moral attitudes. Rather than being educated to control their emotions and inner impulses, children are encouraged to 'express themselves' freely. This allows hedonism (pleasure-seeking) to replace asceticism (strict self-denial). This process is accelerated as TV and advertising, with their emphasis on material goods as a means to happiness and fulfilment, replace the church and the school as the main source of social values. Morality becomes an increasingly private matter, no longer shaped and enforced by the religious organisations. And work, which no longer has any religious justification and requires no moral commitment, becomes impersonal, demoralising and diminished to a mere 'job'.

Activity 15 Evidence for Secularisation

Item A *From God to Rock FM*

A church in Preston converted into a radio station

Item B *A medieval painting*

Part of a medieval painting called the Great Doom. It shows some of the horrors of hell - a miser is being roasted and cheating traders are suspended over the fire on a bridge of spikes.

Item C *Medieval beliefs*

The God in whom medieval man believed was an intensely personal God, forever appearing in acts of nature, visions and apparitions, plagues and cures, storms, fires and miracles. And not only God, but the whole hierarchy of Heaven, angels and saints, apostles and martyrs, lay on the frontiers of the visible, tangible world, ready at any moment to reveal themselves.

So too did the Devil and the fiends, witches and ministers of evil. A flight of crows seemed a swarm of demons, the howling of the wind was the cry of some wicked lord, borne through the middle air to Hell. At a time when men knew little of the laws of nature or the world outside their village homes, they accepted such

ideas with no more question than their twentieth century descendants the latest scientific marvels.

Beyond all this superstition lay a conception shared by rich and poor alike, educated and ignorant. It was that the universe, from its greatest to its minutest part, was governed by divine law. Everything that happened in the world - everything that had happened, was happening and was going to happen - was a part of God's plan, only partly intelligible to man's puny intellect. The Church existed to help explain the plan, to help men obey it and, through Christ's love and sacrifice, to obtain forgiveness for them when they broke God's law.

Adapted from A. Bryant *The Story of England*, 1953, p204

Item D *Religion today*

Except for the occasional ancient ceremony, such as the coronation, the Church has ceased to preside over our national life. A Prime Minister's correspondence 80 years ago dealt seriously with the opinions of Archbishops. Today, we have even seen the occasion when the Prime Minister was 'too busy' to see the Archbishop of Canterbury.

The mass media have virtually eclipsed the pulpit as a source of information and guidance. Armies of specialists now fulfil the educational, counselling, rehabilitative, and pastoral functions that were once the virtual monopoly of the clergy. Religion itself is no longer news, except when a clergyman commits a moral misdemeanour, or when exorcism or the occult is involved.

The content of the message that the churches seek to promote, and the attitudes and values that they try to encourage, no longer inform much of our national life. The workplace is perhaps the environment most alien to religious values, and this has become more and more the case as work activities have become increasingly more technological. In schools religious instruction is often religious in name only - many teachers use the periods for current affairs.

And the decline in the numbers of parents sending children to Sunday schools means that a much lower proportion of children are exposed to even the rudiments of Christian ideas - ideas that are not so readily learned later on.

Adapted from B. Wilson 'How Religious Are We?', *New Society*, 27.10.77, pp176-177

Item E

Marriages: religious and civil ceremonies, 1971 and 1990

	1971	1990		
	All marriages	First marriages (*)	Second or subsequent (**)	All marriages
Manner of solemnisation (thousands)				
Religious ceremony				
Church of England/ Church in Wales	160	107	3	116
Church of Scotland	20	10	3	13
Roman Catholic	48	24	1	26
Other Christian	37	17	7	37
Jews and other non-Christian	2	1	-	37
Civil ceremonies	180	72	53	171
Civil marriages as a percentage of all marriages				
England & Wales	41	31	82	47
Scotland	31	30	68	43
Great Britain	40	31	79	47

* First marriage for both partners; ** Remarriage for both partners

Adapted from *Social Trends*, 1993, p154

Item F *Christmas*

Question
What is the thinking behind the choice of Items A to F as evidence of secularisation? Comment briefly on each item saying whether or not you regard it as evidence of secularisation.

3.3 NRMs as evidence of secularisation

During the last few decades there has been a marked increase in religious activity outside mainstream church and denominational religion. Supporters of the secularisation thesis do not deny this. But they do not accept that this 'resistance' to secularisation is as powerful a force as secularisation itself. Indeed, Bryan Wilson regards the rapid growth of NRMs, and even the rise of vigorous, sectarian Christianity, as yet further evidence of secularisation rather than of religious revival.

From this view, the development of NRMs is regarded as 'only superficially religious. Fundamentally it manifests many of the characteristic commercial, self-centred and manipulationist concerns of a post-industrial society. It is the secular masquerading as religion, and does not constitute evidence of religious revival' (C. Campbell undated, p4). The organisational weaknesses and precariousness of NRMs, their volatility, their reaching for the alien and exotic and their concern with 'self' at the expense of 'self-control', all ensure, in the view of Wilson and others, that their contributions will prove minor and short-lived. If anything their emergence will speed the processes of secularisation by trivialising religion and making religious choice like shopping at a spiritual supermarket.

To his critics, however, Wilson's denial of the significance of recent developments in Western religion (both within and outside the churches) is mistaken. Moreover, he seems to argue, they say, that magical and heterodox beliefs held in the Middle Ages are evidence of religiosity but that similarly magical and heterodox beliefs held in the late twentieth century are evidence of secularisation. As John Eldridge complains, Wilson seems to reject 'any and every (new religious) alternative as a self-indulgent attempt to achieve personal fulfilment - whether through pleasure or discipline, withdrawal or radical action'. And he concludes: 'To dismiss all contemporary movements as irrelevant, both in practical terms, and as providing clues for an understanding of social consciousness, is an astonishing thing to do' (Eldridge, 1980, p138).

Activity 16   NRMs and Secularisation

Item A   Members and followers (1)
There always have been, and there remain, very few full time members dedicated to NRMs. The Unification Church (Moonies) has never had as many as a thousand British members. Although Bhagwan Rajneesh and Transcendental Meditation can claim several thousand followers, each has only around a couple of hundred full time members. There are fewer than 500 full time British Hare Krishna members and the same applies to the Children of God.

Adapted from E. Barker, 'New Religious Movements in Britain, 1983, p42

Item C   Members and followers (3)

Membership of Anglican and Jehovah's Witnesses' Churches, United Kingdom (thousands)

	1975	1980	1985	1992
Church of England	2,272	2,166	2,058	1,810
Jehovah's Witnesses	80	84	92	130

Adapted from *Social Trends*, 1988, p175 and 1994, p145

Item B   Members and followers (2)
The link between NRMs and their followers is often loose. Thus, the local Krishna temple in Montreal includes 66 adult members, but some 250 people regularly attend their Sunday open houses. Most Yoga and therapy groups provide courses for hundreds of students, who take classes but never accept the invitation to become more closely involved. While some Charismatics belong to specific prayer groups, many simply attend periodic retreats, luncheon meetings, or occasional prayer services established by a core of committed members. Thousands of people who have been initiated into Transcendental Meditation or have had their palms read make no attempts to pursue a closer connection with these groups. In the recent census of nine New Religious Movements in Montreal, 95 per cent of the 29,000 persons participating in the groups would be classed as affiliates rather than members. The drop out rate is also extremely high. According to the Montreal survey, 75.5 per cent of all those who had ever participated in these movements were no longer participants.

Adapted from F. Bird and B. Reimer, 'Participation Rates in New Religious and Para-Religious Movements', 1982, pp4-5

Item D *The birth and death of NRMs*

NRMs reported as defunct as of 1990 (USA)

Date formed	Number formed	Number defunct
Before 1940	169	38
1940s	35	7
1950s	88	8
1960s	175	29
1970s	216	30
1980 - 85	103	2
Unknown	50	11
Total	**836**	**125**

J. G. Melton 'Another Look at New Religions', 1993, p103

Item F *In the beginning*

In the beginning all religions are tiny, deviant movements. And if new faiths are being born, they will be found among such obscure movements. Thus, to assess the future of religion, close attention must always be paid to the movements on the fringes. It is foolish to look only at sunsets and never observe the dawn.

Adapted from R. Stark and W. S. Bainbridge *The Future of Religion*, 1985, pp2-3

Item E *New faiths have to start somewhere*

Jesus, leader of a small messianic sect. This statue is in Rio de Janeiro, Brazil.

Questions

1 Supporters of the secularisation thesis often claim that NRMs do little or nothing to halt the tide of secularisation. Assess this view with reference to Items A to D.
2 'It is foolish to look only at sunsets and never observe the dawn' (Item F). What do Stark and Bainbridge mean by this? Make reference to the origins of Christianity in your answer.

3.4 Explanations of secularisation

Social theorists of the 19th and early 20th centuries generally agreed that religion was a declining force in Western societies. Modern societies were becoming increasingly complex and were perhaps fragmenting. Social institutions and occupations were becoming more specialised. Classes and status groups were moving further and further apart. Given the trends to individualism and fragmentation, could capitalist industrial societies survive? Could religion survive?

Marx For Marx, secularisation was to be expected because religion was inevitably dying as socialism approached. Religion would die, with the overthrow of capitalism, when the need for it had gone.

However, of Marx, Durkheim and Weber, only Marx regarded the death of religion as inevitable.

Durkheim For Durkheim, secularisation - the weakening of religion - reflects a weakening of people's sense of the sacredness and the greatness of society. Durkheim was concerned that the ethos of individualism and the processes of social differentiation would continue to undermine the collective consciousness. Individualism and social fragmentation were encouraged by industrialisation and urbanisation, which led people to live in separate social spheres and be divided by different life experiences. Also, the rapid changes associated with industrialisation and urbanisation - including geographical and social mobility - led to feelings of anomie and lessened people's confidence in society's traditional beliefs and practices. Instead of binding society, Durkheim feared that religion would be relegated to a corner of life - a privatised matter no longer capable of overarching society and unifying its members.

On the other hand, Durkheim did believe that secularisation was not an irreversible trend. At a certain point in religion's decline it will always reassert itself, because all societies must have sacred symbols and communal ritual if they are to survive.

Weber Weber was concerned with the spread of rationalisation through society's institutions - institutions increasingly organised and operated according to rational principles which he believed stripped the world of its mystery. Calvinism had played an important part in this process, demystifying the world and unintentionally fostering our disenchantment with it. According to Bryan Wilson the process of rationalisation was also encouraged by later Protestant groupings such as the Methodists, Congregationalists, Quakers and Unitarians who continued to limit the use of ritual in worship. And gradually, rationalisation - unintentionally encouraged by Protestant Christianity - has also undermined religion by diminishing religion's ability to provide meaning for people. Not surprisingly, according to this interpretation, it is precisely the most 'rationalised' strands of Christianity - the liberal Protestant denominations, which are seen to have accommodated most to secular opinion on issues such as premarital sex, divorce and abortion - which have experienced the greatest decline in both Europe and the USA. The sects on the other hand, which are more set apart from the values and norms of the surrounding secular culture and less affected by rationalisation, have more often been experiencing growth, not decline.

Berger For Peter Berger, writing in the late 20th century, industrialisation and urbanisation have fostered secularisation by encouraging an unprecedented range of alternative belief systems. Particularly for those living in cities, people have been increasingly exposed to a variety of often unfamiliar religions because of their greater geographical and social mobility and through media coverage. However, faced with so many rival religions and movements, it has become increasingly difficult to accept the teachings of any one as unchanging truths. So the plurality of belief systems has undermined each one. They can't all be true so each appears to be teaching only relative truths. And because religion no longer seems capable of providing unquestionable truths, people's religious beliefs and practices have come to be seen as a private matter. Even discussing religion has come to be seen as inappropriate and even risky except within a group of like minded people. In short, religion has become privatised.

3.5 Challenges to the secularisation thesis

In this section, the secularisation thesis is challenged, first by evidence from Britain and Western Europe. The controversial case of the USA is also considered, as are possible global trends.

1 Britain and Western Europe

Bryan Wilson may well be right that, in Western Europe at least, there has been a decline in supernatural beliefs and practices. Nevertheless, there is evidence that such countries are far from secular. Attendance at services and Sunday schools has declined and specific religious beliefs and a religious world view are now less common than a century ago. Yet, in a number of respects, religion remains important to many people and to their perception of themselves. For instance, a 1987 Church of Scotland survey found 58% of Scots regarding themselves as definitely Christian, with only 18% saying emphatically that they were not and 24% uncertain. Over half claimed to pray to God and 41% believed that Christ rose from the dead.

Also, David Hay and colleagues claim that almost half Britain's adult population have had what they identify as 'a religious or transcendental experience'. Almost a fifth of the population claim to have been aware of the presence of the dead - often a recently deceased close relative - and 12% reported having been aware of an evil presence. Such evidence does not indicate a secular society. And compared to the United Kingdom - as measured by active church membership - many continental European countries are relatively religious.

Although the mainstream Christian churches and denominations have declined in Britain and Western Europe throughout this century, cultic and sectarian movements have generally grown. For example, conservative and non-Trinitarian Christian bodies such as the Mormons and Jehovah's Witnesses have grown. So have the evangelical Charismatic movements in the Anglican and Roman Catholic churches. So has the house-church movement. And so too have so-called 'New Age' groups such as magick, pagan and UFO cults and the quasi-religions of the human potential movement such as Scientology.

In addition to the growth of Christian sects (some of which is due to immigration) and New Age movements, immigration from Third World countries has added significantly to the membership of other world religions in Britain and Western Europe. In the UK between 1975 and 1990, for instance, while membership of the mainstream Christian bodies fell by 17%, that of other world religions more than doubled. Muslims now outnumber Methodists in Britain by 2 to 1.

Despite these examples of growth, however, the

numbers gained by all these religions do not yet compensate, in most Western countries, for the numbers lost by the mainstream churches and denominations. However, they are at least growing at a faster *rate* than the churches and denominations are declining. And it should also be remembered that millions now tune in regularly to the religious services broadcast on radio or television, many of whom may never appear in any other statistics on religious observance. In the last few decades there has been a substantial increase in the numbers practising a privatised form of religion which the growth of religious broadcasting has made possible.

Given this evidence of continuing, even reviving, religious activity in Britain and Western Europe, how have sociologists responded? For some, such as David Martin, it suggests that secularisation in Britain and Western Europe has probably reached its limits and that the process is about to reverse. Martin notes that secularisation seems to be associated with a number of factors which may now be waning. Secularisation seems to be especially associated with large urban concentrations, especially if that area is dominated by heavy industry and has a homogeneous working class population. Western economies have been moving towards service industries, with fewer concentrations of workers in factories and with a possible trend towards home-based work. This may halt or even reverse the trend to secularisation.

Similarly, as people vacate the inner cities, abandoning them to the single, the poor, and members of ethnic minorities, urban populations have become increasingly diverse. Inner city deprivation, an emerging underclass and a differentiated urban population provide fertile ground for sects. And those who leave for the towns, villages or suburbs are likely to cultivate a sense of community in their new area. The local church could well provide a focal point for this 'new community'.

For the American sociologists Stark and Bainbridge - following Durkheim - secularisation is, in any event, a self-limiting process because it always generates religious revival. On the one hand, as the established religious organisations come to be seen as too worldly, there is an impetus for vigorous sectarian groups to emerge within them and break away. On the other hand, new faiths are formed or imported. In their view, those who argue that religion is in decline typically focus their attention too narrowly on the decline of *conventional* religious organisations and ignore the equally constant cycle of birth and growth of *new movements*.

Activity 17 Religious Revival in the UK?

Item A *Church membership, United Kingdom*

	Adult members (millions)	
	1975	**1992**
Trinitarian Churches		
Anglican	2.27	1.81
Presbyterian	1.65	1.24
Methodist	0.61	0.46
Baptist	0.27	0.23
Other Protestant Churches	0.53	0.66
Roman Catholic	2.53	2.04
Orthodox	0.20	0.28
Total	8.06	6.72
Non-Trinitarian Churches		
Mormons	0.10	0.15
Jehovah's Witnesses	0.08	0.13
Spiritualists	0.06	0.04
Other Non-Trinitarian	0.09	0.14
Total	0.33	0.46
Other Religions		
Muslims	0.40	0.52
Sikhs	0.12	0.27
Hindus	0.10	0.14
Jews	0.11	0.11
Others	0.08	0.08
Total	0.81	1.12

Adapted from *Social Trends*, 1994, p145

Item B *Religious beliefs in the British Isles*

Percentages	Great Britain	Irish Republic	Northern Ireland
Believe in God	69	95	95
Believe God is personally concerned	37	77	80
Believe the Bible is the 'actual' or 'inspired Word of God'	44	78	81
% believing in:			
Life after death	55	80	78
Heaven	54	80	78
Hell	28	53	74
The Devil	28	49	69
Religious miracles	45	73	77

Adapted from R. Jowell et al (ed) *British Social Attitudes*, 1992

Item C *Religious broadcasting*

Religious programmes are listened to or watched by nearly 60% of the population. Every week between 7 and 8 million people tune into the BBC's *Songs of Praise*, which in 1990 will celebrate 28 years on the screen - and research suggests that they are not the same 8 million who are to be found at a place of religious worship every week. The popularity of the mixture of familiar hymns and interviews with ordinary people about their faith may partly be explained as a sentimental escape into a lost world of simple values. But the programme's appeal also suggests the existence of a powerful folk culture, unmistakably religious and, indeed, unmistakably Christian.

Adapted from I. Bradley 'Religious Revival', *New Society*, 6.11.87, p17

Item D *Anglican revival*

Every Sunday morning St Michael-le-Belfrey, an Anglican church in the shadow of York Minster, is overflowing with children, flowers and many of the town's well-heeled doctors, university staff and Queen's Counsellors.

Yet barely twenty years ago, St Michael's was a redundant church with few attenders. Fittingly, perhaps, it was on the verge of being converted into a museum for York Minster. But its young pastor, David Watson, was determined to save the church from that fate and fill its aisles once more. He did so by 'prayer and fasting' and by using the gifts of prophecy, healing and 'wondrous signs'.

The audience participation and enjoyment of the service is undeniable. The children welcome people at the doors, do readings, lead prayers and take up the offertory. The church has a lively drama group, and a choir which is making its fifth record. Perhaps for these reasons, St Michael's is packed every week.

Adapted from J. Picardie and D. Wade 'New-born Christianity', *New Society*, 5.12.86, p16

Questions

1 a) Summarise the trends shown in Items A and B.
   b) What do they imply for the secularisation thesis?
2 a) Explain the popularity of religious broadcasts (Item C).
   b) What does this imply for the secularisation thesis?
3 Suggest reasons for the 'religious revival' at St Michael's (Item D).
4 Read Item E. Do you regard the apparent growth of witchcraft as evidence for or against the secularisation thesis? Explain your answer.

Item E *Witchcraft and paganism*

Earth magic

In 1980, there were thought to be some 60,000 witches in Britain; in 1985 the number was estimated to have grown to 80,000. So who are the new recruits, and why? 'People who are taking up witchcraft and paganism are the type who are interested in ecology' says Chris Bray, owner of Britain's largest occult suppliers. 'They tend to be slightly left-wing, anti-nuclear, nature lovers, into saving animals.'

He rejects the black magic, sex-thrills image of witchcraft. 'There are nutcases who use witchcraft as a front for their indulgences, but behind this there is a genuine pagan religion. Witches put themselves in touch with the psychic forces which run through our planet. Being in tune with your environment makes you more in tune with your life. You expand yourself through the creative power of nature. To do that, you observe the seasonal rites and witches' coven meetings link up with these.'

Adapted from J. Melville 'Spell Bound', *Guardian*, 6.3.85

The USA

For well over a century, church attendance and religious belief in the USA have been much higher than in Western Europe. Not surprisingly, therefore, American religious enthusiasm has often been used to attack the secularisation thesis. If secularisation is encouraged by conditions of individualism and rationalisation, as is argued for Western Europe, secularisation should be most advanced in the USA, with its emphasis on the individual and on rational action.

According to a variety of criteria, the USA remains a highly religious society and any falling off has been slight. Indeed, the proportion of Americans saying they were in church last Sunday when asked in the 1940s was around 40% but in a 1989 study had actually edged up to 43%. The proportion saying they believe in God has remained around 95% since 1944. Those believing Jesus Christ to be God or the

Son of God has held relatively steady at between 75 and 84%. And between 1973 and 1989 reported church membership fell - but not greatly - from 73% to 69%.

However, as in Europe and Latin America, some Christian movements have done much better than others, particularly conservative and evangelical groups. For instance, from about 1960 conservative denominations and sects such as the Southern Baptist Convention and the Seventh Day Adventists have continued growing, while more liberal denominations such as the Presbyterians, Methodists and the United Church of Christ have lost members. In the Roman Catholic Church membership is still increasing, though attendance at mass and financial contributions have both declined quite sharply in the last two decades or so. Membership of other world religions and non-Christian cults has been growing and looks set to continue, with the growth of quotas of Asian and Middle Eastern immigrants from 1990.

'New Age' groups, including pagan, witchcraft and personal growth groups, have grown as in Western Europe in the last few decades.

A manifestation of the growth of conservative, evangelical Christianity, which is particularly American, is the rise of the TV evangelist or 'televangelist'. From the late 1960s to the early 1980s, there was considerable growth in religious television: in the number of viewers, programmes made, local stations airing them and in the number of televangelists. Although the 1980s saw a decline, many survived and some are showing signs of growing strength.

Despite this evidence of apparent religious vigour in the USA, however, there remains considerable controversy over the nature of American religion. The American case is considered further in the final section of this chapter.

Religion worldwide

If the American experience seems to cast doubt on the secularisation thesis, the global picture seems to make it look even less plausible. Gathering accurate global statistics presents major problems, of course, and they are inevitably rough estimates. However, a 1991 estimate calculated about 1,400 million Christians worldwide, with about 800 million Muslims and 550 million Hindus. Estimates of Buddhists range from 200 million to 400 million.

Despite significant regional variations, almost all the so-called 'world religions' seem to have increased their followings worldwide. In part, as Gordon Melton argues, this reflects Christianity's continuing spread into previously non-Christian countries, as well as its growth in countries where it is already established. However, that mobility is now matched by other religions, such as Islam, Buddhism, Jainism and Sikhism, through the migration of believers and the activities of missionaries.

At a global level, the religious trend most readily discernible has been the rise of 'religious fundamentalism'. In Christianity the term refers to the belief that the Bible is literally true. Muslims often object to the term being applied to their faith on the grounds that all Muslims accept the Qu'ran (Holy Book) as the literal word of God. Nevertheless, the term has come into popular usage in the West as a convenient description of those of any faith who profess passionate certainty of the teachings of their religion, deny any other group's truths, generally want to return to an imagined less corrupt age and are prepared to try to impose their beliefs and norms of behaviour on others, sometimes by force. Seen in a global context, the growth of Christian fundamentalism in the USA seems typical of world trends rather than exceptional.

3.6 The USA: the secularisation of mainstream religion?

Sociologists are divided on how to interpret the high levels of membership and attendance at mainstream denominations and the apparent general religious vitality of the USA. On the face of it, they present a problem to those who propose that secularisation is a worldwide process. Why, when only 20% of the UK population say they attend a church of some sort at least once a month, is the figure in the United States 54%? *(British Social Attitudes Special International Report:1989)* How has religious enthusiasm been maintained in the world's richest and most technologically advanced society more than a century after it began large-scale industrialisation?

There is another question, at least as confusing. In all sorts of other respects, the USA is a notably secular society: 'a country in which instrumental values, rational procedures and technical methods have gone furthest, and the country in which the sense of the sacred, the sense of the sanctity of life, and deep religiosity are most conspicuously absent' (B. Wilson, 1966, p109). In other words, why high church attendance in a markedly secular society?

Answers to these questions have been proposed in a famous thesis by the American theologian, Will Herberg. Herberg suggested that to be an American, to demonstrate one's American identity, required public commitment to religious beliefs within a religious organisation. It didn't much matter which - either Protestant, Catholic or Jewish faiths were regarded as acceptable evidence of an American identity. Over time these three religious traditions became increasingly similar in their teachings and in their function of supporting the nation. This abandonment of distinctiveness was in response to second and third generation immigrant Americans who wanted to abandon those churches which reminded them of their diverse and non-American pasts. They wished instead to express their unified sense of American nationality. Commitment to a religious organisation (either Protestant, Catholic or Jewish), and to religious beliefs (it doesn't greatly matter what) are the acceptable ways of expressing American identity and evidence of being a complete American. In Bryan Wilson's words, '"The American way of life" thus embraced "going to church" as one of its facets, without much concern about which church anyone went to. Religion became privatised, and different preferences became as significant as different brands of cigarette or different family names - at least in the case of the major denominations. Belonging to a faith in America thus becomes unconnected with distinctive belief to an extent quite unparalleled in Europe' (Wilson, 1966, pp109-122).

Herberg explains American religious enthusiasm in terms of the unique experience of a nation which had to weld together the world's richest mix of people. In doing this American religion has itself become secular. To a large extent 'religion' has gone out of religion. Thus, Herberg's argument provides support for those who see secularisation as a worldwide process. In this view, the USA is part of this process even though it has taken a different route.

3.7 The rise of the 'televangelist'

Although Herberg's argument has been influential, those who challenge the idea of global secularisation may note that it is precisely those mainstream organisations which Herberg identifies as compromised and secularised which now seem to be experiencing the greatest difficulties.

Secondly, the period since Herberg developed his thesis has also seen the highly visible rise of the fundamentalist televangelists. As satellite and cable television spread throughout the world, exposure to American-inspired televangelists may prove typical rather than exceptional in the future.

Fundamentalist preachers began to dominate the religious airwaves in the USA from the late 1960s. This occurred partly because the mainstream denominations were uneasy about religious broadcasting. But the main reason was their unwillingness to solicit funds on the air and they couldn't afford it otherwise.

They began to decline in the early 1980s, almost a decade *before* a series of scandals embroiled some of the biggest names in religious broadcasting. The decline was partly due to market saturation - eventually there were too many broadcasters, too many programmes and too many stations for a market which refused to keep on growing. Interestingly, several televangelists lost further support as they moved into politics. The apparent success of televangelists in mobilising mass support for Ronald Reagan's presidential candidacy did not increase their viewers and lost them some of their former support. The Reverend Pat Robertson was the most openly ambitious politically, with aspirations for the Presidency himself, but his audience ratings began to slip when his political ambitions became common knowledge. Televangelism declined further in the late 1980s when some of its leading figures were involved in highly publicised sex and money scandals.

However, there are indications that televangelism and its fundamentalist and conservative message are making a comeback in the 1990s. Pat Robertson in particular has not abandoned his political ambitions and remains a powerful force. By the end of 1991 his Family Channel could reach 92% of all cable TV households in the USA and 52% of all households. And at the 1992 Republican National Convention he again addressed the delegates in prime time. As long as televangelists can raise the finance, they can be expected to remain highly visible in the mass media and in politics.

However, it is doubtful if televangelism is successful at converting those not already predisposed. About 25% of the American population are already fundamentalists or evangelicals and they provide the bulk of the audience. In other words, televangelism largely preaches to the converted. Nevertheless, that 25% of the population of the USA is conservative Christian is itself impressive and politically significant. It is also significant that many have the urge to take their message abroad.

Via the mass media and politics, right wing fundamentalist Christians have a high profile in the USA. However, there are opposing religious views. Liberal Christians are worried about the influence of fundamentalism. And New Age groups, whose outlook tends to be left wing, liberal and green have also made a political impact in some parts of the USA.

Summary

1 The secularisation thesis proposes that religion has been losing social significance - religious institutions are less powerful and influential, religion has less influence on people's consciousness and beliefs, religious practices have declined.
2 In the Middle Ages, the Roman Catholic Church had considerably more political power than today, and exercised a much greater hold over people's experience and imaginations. In Britain and Western Europe, church-related activities appear to have declined in the 20th century.
3 Although critics of the secularisation thesis point to the growth of new religious movements, Wilson argues that this merely confirms the secularisation of society. He sees such movements as only superficially religious, as short-lived and making little contribution to society.
4 Secularisation in Western Europe seems to have been encouraged by industrialisation and urbanisation which brought anomie and a plurality of belief systems. However, secularisation may now have reached its limits with the decline of heavy industry and the growing diversity of urban populations.
5 Despite probable long term decline in Britain and Western Europe, levels of belief and 'religious' experience remain at significant levels. Church decline has been accompanied by growth in non-Trinitarian and evangelical groups and in various cults. In the USA religious affiliation remains high. Worldwide, almost all the world religions are gaining adherents.
6 Herberg sees American religion as merely a way of demonstrating Americanness and as evidence of secularisation. However, the strength of fundamentalism in the USA suggests an anti-secular movement typical of current global trends.

Activity 18 Fundamentalism and New Age

Item A *Fundamentalism*

Of the 60 million born-again Christians in the USA, about half describe themselves as fundamentalists. From here they have spread the message to Latin America, the Philippines and parts of the Caribbean and Africa. Every hour 400 Latin Americans convert to fundamentalism or evangelical churches such as the Pentecostals.

Christian fundamentalists see God and the Devil as active forces in everyday life and ascribe the most mundane decisions and events to divine intervention. Most of them believe society is not far from the final judgment where God will descend to earth and take the side of the righteous against a plethora of enemies - secular humanists, homosexuals, supporters of abortion, communists, false Christians and so on.

A main fundamentalist goal is to protect the Christian family from moral decay, and the national state against the forces of atheism, be they communist or secular humanist. Their level of activity ranges from passive support for right-wing causes to direct action against abortion clinics (including 34 bombings and 47 arson attacks between 1977 and 1989 in the USA). In Central America and the Philippines the fundamentalist right is implicated in paramilitary campaigns.

Adapted from 'Fundamentalism, the Facts', *New Internationalist*, August 1990, p16

An old time tent service

Item B *Day of Judgment*

There are many fundamentalist versions of the Day of Judgment. Race wars, nuclear holocaust, total environmental collapse, an AIDS plague, economic collapse under a mountain of debt and cultural decadence and decay are all held up as possible scenarios for the undoing of the wickedness of this world.

Adapted from 'The Fundamentals', *New Internationalist*, August 1990, p22

Item C *New Age*

High in the pine covered Rocky Mountain foothills above Boulder, Colorado, live the thousands of entrepreneurs, teachers, spiritualists, holistic medical practitioners and psychic astrologists who have helped transform Colorado - and Boulder in particular - into a magnet for what has become known as the New Age. It is an extraordinarily broad 'church', encompassing everything from Eastern mysticism to Jungian psychology, from the Hebrew Chabbalah and Jin Shin Jyutsu healing to Chrystals ('enhance vibrational qualities and harmonise the body, mind and spirit'), and the Celtic rune.

'"New Age" is a cult conglomerate with the ideology of the political left and the counter-culture of the 1960s,' argues Professor Carl Raschke, director of the Institute for the Humanities at the University of Denver. The professor, an historian of New Age, believes the movement cannot be lightly dismissed.

Scratch away the flaky facade and you are left with a powerful political network which is gaining control of the environmental movement, has infiltrated the educational system, increasingly dominates the Democratic Party and only blew its chance of capturing the White House when local Presidential candidate Gary Hart went off on a love jaunt.

Adapted from A. Brummer 'New Age Tentacles Dig Deep into Colorado', *Guardian*, 3.6.88

Question

1 Read Items A and B.
  a) What do you understand by the term 'fundamentalist'?
  b) How would you explain the present popularity of Christian fundamentalism in the West?
2 Read Item C. What are the main similarities and differences between fundamentalist Christianity and New Age in the USA?
3 Some sociologists have seen the American religious experience as 'the shape of things to come'. Comment on this view.

References

Barker, E. 'New Religious Movements in Britain' Social Compass, vol 30 no I, 1983

Berger, P., Berger, B. and Kellner, H. The Homeless Mind (Penguin, Harmondsworth, 1974)

Bird, F. and Reimer, B. 'Participation Rates in New Religious and Para-Religious Movements' Journal for the Scientific Study of Religion vol 21 no 1, 1982

Birnbaum, N. 'Monarchs and Sociologists: a Reply to Professor Shils and Mr Young' Sociological Review, July 1955

Boyes, R. 'Thousands Mourn Solidarity Priest' Times, 28.1.1986

Bradley, I. 'Religious Revival' New Society, 6.11.1987

British Social Attitudes Special International Report: 1989 quoted in Guardian, 15.11.1989

Brown, D. Bury my Heart at Wounded Knee (Pan Books, London, 1975)

Bruce, S. 'The Twilight of the Gods', Sociology Review, November 1992

Brummer, A. 'New Age Tentacles Dig Deep into Colorado' Guardian, 3.6.1988

Bryant, A. The Story of England: Makers of the Realm (Collins, London, 1953)

Campbell, C. The Secularisation Debate and the New Religions (unpublished, undated article)

Chaney, D. 'A Symbolic Mirror of Ourselves: Civic Ritual in Mass Society' in R. Bocock and K. Thompson (eds) Religion and Ideology (Manchester University Press, Manchester, 1985)

Cohn, N. The Pursuit of the Millenium (Secker and Warburg, London, 1957)

Cole, W.O. (ed) Moral Issues in Six Religions (Heinemann, Oxford, 1991)

Concise Oxford Dictionary (Clarendon, Oxford, 1976)

Cotton, I. 'Share it, Brother' Sunday Times Magazine, 16.12.1990

Deer, B. 'Actress and the Bishop Upstaged' Sunday Times, 17.9.1989

Durkheim, E. The Elementary Forms of the Religious Life (George Allen and Unwin, London, 1968)

Eisenstadt, S.N. 'The Protestant Ethic Thesis in Analytical and Comparative Context' Diogenes vol 59, 1967

Eldridge, J. 'Religion: Where the Action Isn't' in Recent British Sociology (Macmillan, London, 1980)

'Fundamentalism, the Facts' New Internationalist, no 210, August 1990

'Fundamentalism: Reaching for Certainty' New Internationalist, no 210, August 1990

'Government by God' The Watchtower, undated

Harrison, J.F.C. The Early Victorians, 1832-1851 (Weidenfeld & Nicolson, London, 1971)

Harrison, T. 'Born Again Elvis' The Listener, 6.12.1990

Hay, D. and Heald, G. 'Religion is Good for You' New Society, 17.4.1987

Heelas, P. 'Californian Self-religions and Socialising the Subjective' in E. Barker (ed) New Religious Movements: a Perspective for Understanding Society (Edwin Mellen Press, New York, 1982)

'How Long will God's Patience Last?' The Watchtower, 1.10.1991

Jenkins, J. Contemporary Moral Issues (Heinemann Educational, Oxford, 1987)

Kennedy, D. In God's Country: Travels in the Bible Belt, USA (Unwin Hyman, New York, 1989

Kitch, M.J. Capitalism and the Reformation (Longman, Harlow, 1967)

Longley, C. 'Robin Hood and Liberation Theology' Times, 27.1.1986

Maduro, O. Religion and Social Conflicts (Orbis, New York, 1982)

Martin, D. A. General Theory of Secularisation (Blackwell, Oxford, 1978)

Martin, D. Tongues of Fire (Blackwell, Oxford, 1990)

McGuire, M.B. Religion: The Social Context (Wadsworth Publishing Co., California, 1981)

Meditate (SYDA Foundation, Oakland, 1982)

Melton, J.G. 'Another Look at New Religions' The Annals of the American Academy of Political and Social Science vol 527, May 1993

Melville, J. 'Spell Bound' Guardian, 6.3.1985

Morley, P. 'Wear a Red Nose for England' New Statesman and Society, 10.3.1989

Muktananda, Swami, Light on the Path (SYDA Foundation, Oakland, 1972)

O'Toole, R. Religion: Classic Sociological Approaches (McGraw-Hill, Toronto, 1984)

Parekh, B. 'Between Holy Text and Moral Void' New Statesman and Society, 21.3.1989

Picardie, J. and Wade, D. 'New-born Christianity' New Society, 5.12.1986

Shils, E. and Young, M. 'The Meaning of the Coronation' The Sociological Review, vol 1 no 2, 1953

Sim, A. 'Did you see "Witness"?' Sociology Review, February 1994

Stark, R. and Bainbridge, W.S. The Future of Religion: Secularisation, Revival and Cult Formation (University of California Press, Berkeley, 1985)

Stone, D. 'New Religious Consciousness and Personal Religious Experience' Sociological Analysis vol 39 no 2, 1978

Thomas, K. quoted in D. McLellan, Marxism and Religion (Macmillan, London, 1987)

Thomas, L. Company of Avallon circular letter to author (Horfield, Bristol)

Thompson, K. 'The Secularisation Debate' in P. Gee and J. Fulton (eds) Religion and Power: Decline and Growth (BSA Sociology of Religion Study Group, 1991)

Tiryakian, E.A. 'American Religious Exceptionalism: a Reconsideration' The Annals of the American Academy of Political and Social Science vol 527, May 1993

Utley, R.M. The Last Days of the Sioux Nation (Yale University Press, New Haven, 1963)

Wallis, R. 'The Sociology of the New Religions' Social Studies Review, September 1985

Wallis, R. and Bruce, S. 'Religion: the British Contribution' British Journal of Sociology, vol 40 no 3, September 1989

Weber, M. The Protestant Ethic and the Spirit of Capitalism (Charles Scribner's Sons, New York, 1958)

Williams, J. 'In Focus: "Keeping the Faith", Sociological Review, September 1992

Williams, K. M. 'Charter of the Rastafarians' quoted in The Rastafarians, (Ward Lock Educational, London, 1981)

Wilson, B. R. Religion and Secular Society (C. A. Watts, London, 1966)

Wilson, B. R. 'How Religious are We?' New Society, 27.10.1977

Yeo, A. 'Is There Anybody Out There?' Midweek, 28.7.88

S. Zubeida, 'Hijacked by Khomeini' New Internationalist, No 210, August 1990

Introduction

The British are well and truly plugged in to the mass media. Almost all households (99%) have a TV and by 1993, 73% had video recorders. Nearly 10% of homes have three or more colour TVs - more than twice the European figure. People in the UK watched an average of 25.41 hours of television a week in 1993 and listened to the radio for 16.27 hours a week. As these figures might suggest, the most popular weekly magazines are *Radio Times* and *TV Times*.

Television and radio don't seem to have diminished our appetite for other forms of media. Seven out of ten people visited the cinema at least once in 1993, up from four out of ten in 1984. Over half of us read a newspaper every day and over two thirds of us read a Sunday newspaper (figures from *Social Trends*, 1993; 1995).

The focus of the chapter is the extent to which this widespread use of the mass media influences our attitudes and behaviour. Do we believe everything we read in the newspapers? Do news programmes on television influence our political views? Who owns newspapers and TV stations? Are the views of owners reflected in media output? And, if so, are we influenced by the views of a small minority?

Chapter summary

- Part 1 looks at the structure of the mass media, in particular aspects of **ownership** and **control**.
- A brief review of **theoretical approaches** to the mass media is provided in Part 2.
- In Parts 3 and 4 the issues of **impartiality** and **bias** provide the focus for an analysis of the **content** of the mass media. Four areas are examined - in Part 3 the media treatment of **politics** and **news** and in Part 4 the portrayal of **women** and **ethnic minorities**.
- Part 5 reviews the debate about the influence of the mass media on **violent behaviour.**

1 The Structure of the Mass Media

Key Issues

1 How do different forms of mass media operate and what constraints do they work within?
2 Who owns the mass media?
3 What is the link between ownership and control and the content of the mass media?

1.1 What is the mass media?

The mass media is so called because it involves large numbers of people in the process of communication. The mass media includes all forms of communication to mass audiences. The most obvious, and probably most important, are television, newspapers and radio, but the mass media also includes the cinema, magazines and books.

In general, the audiences for the various forms of mass media are very large while the numbers involved in 'sending out' the communications are comparatively small. Furthermore, the communication is almost entirely one way - the audience (those who receive the communication) have little opportunity to respond to and communicate with the mass media. Having said that, there are ways in which the audience can be heard. It is possible to write to newspapers and magazines and there are occasional phone-in programmes on television and radio. These responses, however, nearly always pass through some form of editing system before being printed or aired. Thus, the audience has very limited access to those who produce and disseminate mass communications. This lack of access puts those who own and/or control the mass media in a very powerful position (see Section 1.2). However, the audience can have a powerful negative influence - it can decide not to watch a TV programme, not to buy a particular newspaper. TV stations are very sensitive to viewing figures and newspapers can and do go out of business if they don't sell enough copies.

The mass media has expanded enormously in scope and influence in recent years. It occupies a large, and often the largest, part of most people's leisure time, to the extent that entertainment and social life in general is sometimes organised around the mass media, and television in particular. The table below shows the average viewing times per week for different social class groups. It shows that the lower a person's class position, the more time they are likely to spend watching TV. In terms of age, the 65+ group is the greatest consumer of television. In 1987, the average weekly viewing time for this group was 37 hours and 41 minutes, well above the overall average of 26 hours. Given that few people in the 65+ age group would have had access to television during the first half of their lives, this represents a significant change in lifestyle.

Television viewing by social class (United Kingdom, hours:mins per week)

Social class	1986	1988	1990	1992
AB	19:50	18:39	17:52	19:56
C1	23:05	23:41	23:12	25:08
C2	26:00	26:23	26:17	27:30
DE	33:35	32:20	31:51	31:54
All persons	26:32	26:08	25:33	26:44

Adapted from *Social Trends* 1993, p 142; *Social Trends* 1994, p130

Social class categories are based on head of household's occupation as follows:

Class A	Higher managerial, administrative or professional
Class B	Intermediate managerial, administrative or professional
Class C1	Supervisory or clerical, and junior managerial, administrative or professional
Class C2	Skilled manual workers
Class D	Semi and unskilled manual workers
Class E	State pensioners or widows (no other earners), casual or lowest grade workers, or long term unemployed

In terms of time spent per week, television is the predominant mass media institution in the UK. However, the spread of television in the last two or three decades has not made major inroads into newspaper readership. Circulations have dropped since the late 1940s, but the British remain avid newspaper readers. Over 60 per cent of adults read a morning national paper. The *Sun,* with over 3.7 million sales a day (July - December 1993) and an estimated readership of almost 10 million, is the most popular daily. In addition to the national press, there are also local and free papers which reach large numbers of people in their particular areas.

The mass media is a major source of information. Most people's picture of the world is to some extent provided by the media. We don't directly experience what is happening in other parts of the world or of Britain and rely to a large extent on the mass media to keep us informed. Twenty million people in the UK watch TV news each day. This gives some indication of the importance of the media.

1.2 The structure of the mass media: ownership and control

Much of this chapter will discuss the mass media in general terms. However, there are important differences between various areas of the media which affect both the content and style of what is communicated, as well as the influence and power of the particular media agency. The press and television are generally regarded as the most influential media. A crucial difference between them is that the press has considerable freedom to print whatever it wants, within the laws of libel and the requirements of official secrecy. Television, however, is bound by law to be impartial, with clear guidelines governing content. That is the case with both BBC and Independent Television, although the organisation of each is different - BBC being financed by government grants based on revenue from license fees, whereas Independent Television's costs are met almost entirely from advertising revenue. The question of television's impartiality will be discussed in Part 3 as part of a general examination of the issue of impartiality in the mass media.

Concentration of ownership

Perhaps the most important aspect of the structure of the mass media is the *concentration of ownership*. With regard to the press, the tradition in Britain has been for newspapers to be owned by wealthy individuals and families. These old style 'press barons' exerted considerable influence on the content and style of their papers. For example, Lord Beaverbrook (*Daily Express*) and Lords Northcliffe and Rothermere (*Daily Mail*) ensured that 'their papers' put over a strong Conservative and nationalistic line. Beaverbrook's comment to the Royal Commission on the Press in 1949, that 'I run the *Daily Express* purely for the purpose of making propaganda, and with no other motive', clearly illustrates his approach. The personal and political views of these press barons were reflected in their papers. Rothermere's support for the British Union of Fascists in the 1930s was clear from the *Daily Mail's* headlines, 'Give the Blackshirts a Helping Hand' and 'Hurrah for the Blackshirts'. This support thrust a relatively obscure political organisation into the limelight, even though Rothermere's backing was only short-lived.

More recently, because of the increasing number of mergers, much of the press, and indeed commercial broadcasting, is owned by transnational companies. These transnationals have developed out of the family groups which established many of the national newspapers in the early twentieth century. The transnationals are led by strong willed individuals who have become our present day 'barons' - men like Rupert Murdoch and the late Robert Maxwell.

Activity 1 Who Owns Our Newspapers?

Item A *Concentration of ownership*

Newspapers in Britain are in private ownership. During the period since the Second World War these newspapers have diminished in number and their ownership has become more concentrated. The era of the famous press barons (Beaverbrook, Rothermere, Northcliffe, Kemsley, etc) has given way, it is said, to the age of the conglomerates: large transnational corporations with extensive holdings both within, and beyond, the media field.

For example, *The Times*, *Sunday Times*, *Sun* (Britain's most popular daily newspaper) and the *News of the World* (the most popular Sunday) are all owned by News International, the massive corporation built up by Rupert Murdoch, which also has extensive media interests in Australia and the USA. The *Daily Mirror*, *Sunday Mirror* and *Sunday People* were absorbed into the business empire of the entrepreneur Robert Maxwell, while the shipping company Trafalgar House sold the *Daily Star*, *Daily Express* and *Sunday Express* to United Newspapers in 1986. (United Newspapers already owned many local papers, particularly in the Yorkshire area). Both the *Daily Mail* and the *Mail on Sunday*, along with 32 local papers, are owned by Viscount Rothermere. Both the *Daily* and *Sunday Telegraph* now belong to Conrad Black, a Canadian construction and shipping magnate. By 1990, of the major British

Rupert Murdoch

newspapers, only the *Guardian* and the *Independent* are not part of huge corporations. However, since the death of Robert Maxwell in November 1991, his controlling share in Mirror Group Newspapers has been taken over by a consortium of banks and financial institutions led by the Nat West.

Adapted from S. Wagg 'Mass Communications: The Debate about Ownership and Control', *Social Studies Review*, March 1987 and S. Peak (ed) *The Media Guide 1994*, 1993, p15

Item B *Newspaper ownership - main national newspapers*

Ownership	Titles	Percentage share of market
News International plc	*The Times, Sun, Today* *News of the World, Sunday Times*	34.2
Mirror Group Newspapers Ltd	*Daily Mirror, Daily Record* *People* and *Sunday Mirror*	27.1
United Newspapers plc	*Daily Express, Daily Star* *Sunday Express*	13.3
Daily Mail and General Trust plc (which owns Associated Newspapers Ltd)	*Daily Mail, Mail on Sunday*	12.7
The Hollinger Group	*Daily Telegraph,* *Sunday Telegraph*	5.3
The Guardian and Manchester Evening News plc	*Guardian, Observer*	3.1
Newspaper Publishing plc	*Independent* *Independent on Sunday*	2.4

Adapted from S. Peak (ed) *The Media Guide 1994*, 1993, p14

Item C *Owners and editors*

It is the owners, more than the editors, who determine the general content of the papers. As Victor Matthews put it when he took over the Trafalgar Group in 1977, 'By and large the editors will have complete freedom - as long as they agree with the policy I have laid down'. If they do not, they are apparently as expendable as football managers. The *Daily Express*, for example, has had ten editors in the last twenty years.

Adapted from M.Grant *The British Media*, 1984, pp 4-5

Item D *Safeguarding media pluralism*

In December 1992 The European Commission produced a discussion document entitled 'Pluralism and Media Concentration in the Internal Market'. It expressed concern about the concentration of ownership not just of newspapers but within the media generally. For example, Rupert Murdoch's New International plc not only has the largest share of the British newspaper market but also controls the largest British satellite broadcasting company B Sky B. The commission noted that, 'The UK is alone in the EC in not having a written constitution from which an obligation to safeguard media pluralism could be deduced'.

Adapted from S. Peak (ed) *The Media Guide 1994*, 1993, pp14-15

Questions

1 What do Items A and B indicate about the ownership of newspapers?
2 Read Items C and D
   a) What effects might the concentration of ownership and the attitudes held by the owners have on the content of newspapers?
   b) What factors might limit the influence that owners have over the content of newspapers?

Ownership of the British press is highly concentrated. One reason for this is the large amount of money it costs to launch and then sustain a national newspaper. Stephen Wagg (1989) points out that Eddy Shah spent £22.5 million in the first 10 weeks of his paper *Today* before running out of funds and selling it to Rupert Murdoch's News International.

Concentration of ownership is not new. Seymour-Ure (1991) notes that Northcliffe had a bigger share of newspaper circulation in 1910 (39%) than Murdoch had in 1989 (35%). Concentration of ownership is not confined to the press. Transnational companies tend to have interests in various areas of the mass media. The expansion of new forms of media, such as the growth of cable and satellite TV, CDs, audio tapes, videos, has provided increasing scope for concentration of ownership across media boundaries. In the 1990s, the largest organisations are operating on international levels, are involved in a range of different media, and are diversifying into areas outside the media.

The Virgin Group provides an example. It began with a national magazine called *Student* published by Richard Branson. Branson then set up a chain of record shops and started the Virgin record label. He then launched Virgin Vision to distribute videos and films and diversified into property development, hotels, Virgin Atlantic Airways and Virgin Cola. Although Virgin Records has now been sold, the Virgin Group still has a range of media holdings in television, radio, book publishing and computer games. Virgin has 120 operating companies in 23 countries.

In much the same way non-media companies are diversifying into media ownership. A good example of a company moving into newspaper ownership is provided by Trafalgar House. From a property and building firm, Trafalgar House grew under the chairmanship of Sir Nigel Broackes to incorporate shipping (it owned Cunard and the QE2), aviation, hotels (the Ritz, for example) and investment concerns. It took over Express Newspapers in 1977 and launched the first new national newspaper for decades, the *Daily Star*. As indicated in Activity 1, it sold its newspaper holdings in 1986 to United Newspapers.

Should we be concerned about the growth of the transnational media industry? Does it matter that the ownership of the British press is concentrated? Does it matter that this ownership is private and that owners may, to some degree, influence the content of their papers and in turn the views of their readers? Answers to these questions will be examined throughout the chapter. Here we will look briefly at the politics of the press.

It is generally accepted that newspapers can and do support particular political viewpoints and parties. It could be argued that this would not matter if the newspapers were spread fairly evenly across the political spectrum. However, the great majority of papers are pro-Conservative, as can be seen from the advice on voting they give to their readers at elections. Of the major national newspapers, the *Guardian* and the *Independent* aim to maintain a politically neutral position (though the *Guardian* is historically identified with the Liberal Party), while the *Daily Mirror* is the only pro-Labour paper. The following activity explores the political bias of the British press.

Summary

1 The mass media has developed and expanded rapidly in recent years.

2 It is now a major source, and may well be the major source of information for most people.

3 Television viewing is the main leisure activity for many people.

4 Ownership of the mass media is increasingly concentrated in the hands of transnational companies. This concentration may narrow the range of political views broadcast by the media. Media output may reflect the views of the owners.

Activity 2 Politics and the Press

Item A

The 'Sun' claiming credit for the Conservative victory in the 1992 election

Item D Party support

Readers' view of the *Sun*'s party support

Con	Lab	Lib/Dem	None/Don't Know
63%	12%	7%	18%

Party support of the *Sun*'s readers

Con	Lab	Lib/Dem	Other
41%	31%	19%	9%

Adapted from J.Benyon 'General Election 1987' *Social Studies Review*, November 1987, pp60-62 and I. Crewe 'Why did Labour Lose (yet again)?' *Politics Review*, September 1992, p11

Voting by *Sun* readers in the 1992 election

Con	Lab
45%	36%

Item B *The Tory press*

Surely the Tory tabloids clinched the Conservative election victory in 1992? Lord McAlpine, former Conservative Treasurer, described Tory newspaper editors as 'heroes' and said, 'Never in the past nine elections have they come out so strongly in favour of the Conservatives'. Obviously the media makes some difference - it is mostly through media that we experience the campaign. Obviously, too, *Sun* readers are not the unthinking instruments of *Sun* journalists. But even if it could be shown that the Tory tabloids did sway more voters in more critical seats than did the Labour campaigning *Daily Mirror*, the question remains whether there should be limits on papers' opportunity to try, or on the methods they use.

Adapted from C. Seymour-Ure 'The Media Under Major' *Politics Review*, February 1993, pp13-16

Item C *Democracy and the press*

Democracy can only function properly if citizens are well informed and educated about political matters. In the modern world this means that the mass media must provide the population with a full and fair account of the news, and with a wide and varied range of political views and opinions. Some people hold strongly to the belief that the press should be in private hands because any form of public control or ownership lends itself to danger of state censorship or propaganda. The theory claims that if the ownership and control of the press is left to free market competition, then newspapers will have to cater for a wide range of demands for political news and opinion. In short, the free market will produce a competitive and pluralist press, in which a wide diversity of political positions will find expression. And so the truth will out. Instead of showing the competitive features of a free market demanded by the liberal theory of democracy, the privately owned media seem to be in the hands of an oligopoly, to be concentrated in fewer and fewer hands. Moreover, three-quarters of the national dailies in circulation give strong support to the Conservative Party, about one-fifth to the Labour Party, and none at all to the Liberal/Democrats or political Centre. This suggests rather little of the political pluralism which the free market is supposed to produce.

Adapted from K.Newton 'Making News: the Mass Media in Britain' *Social Studies Review*, September 1990, pp12-15

2 Theoretical Approaches to the Mass Media

Key Issues

1 What are the major theoretical approaches to the media?

2 How do these approaches relate to different sociological perspectives?

3 What part does the mass media play in postmodern society?

2.1 Classifying theories of the mass media

Theories of the mass media are not confined to sociology. There is a large body of psychological work on the mass media and its effects. This section looks briefly at psychological approaches and introduces sociological theories.

Hypodermic syringe model

The early theories of the mass media were essentially psychological. Research from the turn of the century up to the 1930s argued that the mass media had a direct effect on behaviour - an immediate and dramatic effect. The argument is mirrored by the name given to this approach - the *hypodermic syringe model*. The effect of the media was seen as similar to that of the injection of a drug into a vein. The notion that the media had a direct effect on its audience encouraged the development of laboratory experiments to measure this effect, on the assumption that the laboratory and 'real life' were interchangeable. Implicit in this sort of approach is the belief that the mass of the population could be manipulated and controlled by the media.

Two-step flow model

The hypodermic syringe model largely ignored the fact that people are social beings, that they have families, friends and work colleagues. Katz and Lazarsfeld's influential *two-step flow model* (1955) emphasised the importance of social relationships in determining people's response to the media. They argued that opinions are formed in a social context. Within this context certain people - 'opinion leaders' - are influential in shaping the views of others. These individuals are more likely to be exposed to the media, for example to read more newspapers and magazines. As a result they are more likely to be influenced by the media and, as opinion leaders, to transmit media messages to others. Hence the idea of a two-step flow - attitudes and ideas 'flow *from* radio and print *to* opinion leaders and *from them* to the less active sections of the population' (Katz and Lazarsfeld, 1955, p32).

The two-step flow model was largely based on research into short term changes in attitudes and opinions. For example, media presentations of election campaigns were examined in order to discover to what extent they changed people's voting intentions. Often such studies showed that the media had little effect on people's opinions. However, this ignores the possible long term effects of the media.

Cultural effects theory

This theory assumes that the media does have important effects on its audience. These effects are not as immediate and dramatic as those indicated by the hypodermic syringe model. Nor are they relatively insignificant as suggested by the two-step flow model. Rather they can be seen as a slow, steady, long term buildup of ideas and attitudes.

Cultural effects theory assumes that if similar images, ideas and interpretations are broadcast over periods of time, then they may well affect the way we see and understand the world. Thus if television and radio broadcasts, newspapers and magazines all present, for example, a certain image of women, then slowly but surely this will filter into the public consciousness.

Like the two-step flow model, cultural effects theory recognises the importance of social relationships. It argues that media effects will depend on the social position of members of the audience, for example their age, gender, class and ethnicity. Thus black working class teenagers may well interpret a news broadcast very differently from white middle class business people.

Researchers who attempt to examine the 'effects' and influence of the mass media on attitudes and behaviour have a basic problem to solve. How can these effects be measured? How can they be separated from the range of other factors which influence people's attitudes and behaviour? Some of these problems are examined in the following activity. It is taken from an article by Greg Philo (1993), a member of the Glasgow University Media Group (an important centre for research into the British media). Philo's study examined audience response to television news' coverage of the miners' strike of 1984/5.

Activity 3   Measuring Media Effects

Item A

Pickets and police at Orgreave Coke Works

Pickets and police at Bolsover Colliery

Item B *The method*

169 people were interviewed. Some were selected because they had specific knowledge of the strike - miners and police. Others were selected to provide a range of social backgrounds and locations. For example, two groups who worked in solicitors' offices were chosen, one in Glasgow and one in southeast England. The study took place one year after the strike ended.

Everyone answered questions on their own beliefs and memories. In addition they were divided into small groups and given a set of photographs of the strike taken from TV news programmes. They were then asked to write their own news stories based on these photographs. This would show what they thought the content of the news was. It would then be possible to compare this with what they believed really happened and to examine why they accepted or rejected media accounts.

Item D *Understanding the results*

The way people interpret TV news is complex. Some members of the sample trusted the BBC and ITV. They felt their news broadcasts were fair and impartial. The main reason for rejecting TV accounts is a result of direct or indirect personal experience which relates to the content of the broadcasts. Both acceptance and rejection are influenced by previously held beliefs and attitudes in terms of which media output is interpreted.

Items B, C and D adapted from G. Philo 'Getting the Message: Audience Research in the Glasgow University Media Group' in J. Eldridge (ed) *Getting the Message: News, Truth and Power*, 1993, pp 253-270

Item C *The results*

The 'news programmes' written by the interviewees showed amazing similarities with TV news. People could clearly recall key themes and even key phrases such as 'escalating violence' and the 'drift back to work'. 98% believed that most picketing they had seen on TV was violent and 54% believed that, in reality, picketing was mostly violent. But none of those who had direct knowledge of the strike - miners and police - believed that picketing was mostly violent. They rejected TV images as being typical. According to them, strikers and police spent most of their time sitting round and doing nothing. Others in the sample who believed that picketing was mostly peaceful based this view on their experience of knowing or having met police officers and/or miners.

Questions

1   Look at Item A.
   a) Which picture do you think a news programme would use? Why?
   b) What problems might result from this selection?
2   Read Item B. Briefly comment on the selection of the sample.
3   Using Items B and C, discuss the advantages and disadvantages of asking people to write news programmes based on pictures from TV news.
4   Based on Items C and D, why did people respond to TV news in different ways?

2.2 Pluralist theories

This title provides one way of categorising some of the theoretical work on the media. Other names sometimes given to these theories are 'market theories' or 'liberal theories'. The basic pluralist argument is that the mass media reflects what the public, or a section of it, wants. It simply responds to market demand. The media does have an influence and may well be biased in certain ways - it may, for instance, be pro-Conservative. However, its influence is seen as reflecting and reinforcing generally held attitudes and beliefs. The views it broadcasts are those that most people sympathise with and want to hear. It is argued that those who want to see or hear or read about other, non-mainstream viewpoints or subjects will be catered for by specific media output. For example, the growing interest in computer games is reflected in specialist TV programmes and a range of computer games magazines.

Those who own and control the media argue that they are serving the market. Television and the press have to remain financially viable - they must therefore provide what the public wants.

The pluralist theory of power in society is that no one group or elite dominates the rest of society - power is shared by a range of interest groups (see pp199-200). The mass media from the pluralist perspective is seen to reflect this diversity of interests. A wide range of views and interests are presented by the various forms of the mass media, allowing the audience freedom to 'pick and mix'.

As a consequence of this 'free choice', pluralists argue that there is little direct media influence and what influence there is tends to reinforce already existing beliefs and attitudes. As a result, most pluralists do not see the influence of the media as a cause for concern. This is very different from the Marxist perspective which sees media influence as more direct and much more worrying.

2.3 Marxist theories

The 'influence' of the media has been referred to a number of times in the preceding discussion. There is a difference between influence and control. While the pluralist approach acknowledges some media influence, a Marxist approach stresses the power of the media to control people in society. Few people would deny the media's power to influence; whether it 'controls' is, however, far more controversial.

The Marxist approach emphasises the way in which the media transmits a conservative, conformist view and promotes established attitudes and values. Furthermore, given that it is through the media that most information is filtered to the mass of the population, the media's power is seen as self-

evident. The media works against change and, therefore, against the interests of the majority. It supports the interests of the rich and powerful who control the media and who have a vested interest in portraying capitalist society in a positive light. It promotes a false consciousness, preventing people from seeing the reality of their situation.

Ideology Ralph Miliband's study, *The State in Capitalist Society* (1973), provides an example of a Marxist approach. Miliband rejects the pluralist view that in a democracy power is widely distributed throughout society. He argues that the state (consisting of government, police, judiciary, military) exercises power in the interests of the ruling classes - it maintains the dominance of those who have economic power.

In examining how the state is able to exercise power in favour of the ruling classes, Miliband emphasises the central importance of ideology - it is the most effective means of social control. It is the mechanism by which people are persuaded to accept and not to question the gross inequalities which are present in modern society. How is the mass of the population persuaded that a system which gives one person far more money for the same or less effort than someone else is fair? According to Miliband this sort of question can be answered by pointing to the power of the dominant classes to control the ideas and knowledge available to the general population, a control that is exercised through the mass media, as well as through other institutions, such as education and the law.

With regard to the mass media, the notion of pluralist diversity is seen by Miliband as superficial and misleading. As he puts it, 'Most newspapers in the capitalist world have one crucial characteristic in common, namely their strong, often their passionate hostility to anything further to the Left than the milder forms of social-democracy, and quite commonly to these milder forms as well' (Miliband, 1973, p198). The mass media may give some degree of impartiality, but this is only within the limited sphere of what is seen as 'acceptable'. There is a steady stream of propaganda against any views that fall outside what is seen as the general consensus. The choice of alternative opinions and ideas presented by the media is very limited, with the content of the media reflecting the viewpoint of the dominant group in society - specifically, a white, male and middle class viewpoint. It is not just political programmes and reporting that support the system, the content of entertainment programmes is also seen as supporting the status quo, portraying the present social system in a generally favourable light.

In a similar vein to Miliband, Marcuse suggests that programmes which simply entertain, together with the promise of consumer satisfaction that advertisements and game shows provide, help to remove any doubt the mass of the population may have about the social order. Thus programmes such as *Neighbours* and *Coronation Street* divert attention from and distort our view of the social system, give the impression that nothing is radically wrong with the world we live in, and provide enjoyment and a sense of wellbeing for millions.

Indoctrination Miliband argues that the media conditions us against dissent, acting as an 'agency of conservative indoctrination'. He describes the media as the new 'opium of the people', paraphrasing Marx's famous phrase, 'religion is the opium of the people'. As such, the media keeps the working classes quiet and supportive of a system which, in reality, works against their interests. Of course, the media cannot ensure complete conformity but, according to Miliband, it can and does contribute to

the 'fostering of a climate of conformity, not by the total suppression of dissent, but by the presentation of views which fall outside the consensus as curious heresies, or even more effectively by treating them as irrelevant eccentricities which serious and reasonable people may dismiss as of no consequence' (Miliband, 1973, p213).

Finally, Miliband argues, we must not lose sight of the fact that most of the media is privately owned. The mass media is big business and, naturally, those who own and control it are overwhelmingly people whose 'ideological dispositions run from soundly conservative to utterly reactionary'.

In summary, Marxists see the media as part of the system of ideological domination which supports the position of the ruling class. The role of the media is to socialise the mass of the population to a life of subordination. The media's message is simple - accept the way things are.

Activity 4   The Audience Shapes the Media

Item A   *Readers in control*

It is readers who determine the character of newspapers. The *Sun* illustrates the point in its simplest and saddest form. Until 1964 the *Daily Herald*, and between 1964 and 1969 the *Sun*, had struggled to interest working class people principally through their intellect. The paper had declined steadily. Murdoch gave up the attempt and went for baser instincts. Sales soared. By May 1978, selling just under 4 million copies, the *Sun* was reckoned to have overtaken the *Mirror* - which had held the lead, since winning it from the *Express* in 1949, as the biggest selling national daily paper. At the *Express* the message was received. The year before it had been bought by Trafalgar House, a shipping and property concern. The new chairman was Victor Mathews and in November 1978 he launched the *Daily Star* which extended the *Sun* formula even further downmarket. These were owners' decisions, but they would have meant nothing without the support of readers.

The press is predominantly conservative in tone because its readers are. If a substantial number of people seriously wanted the structure of society rebuilt from the bottom, the *Morning Star* (a communist newspaper) would sell more copies than it does. The reason why national newspapers fall tidily into two bundles - popular and posh, with the popular ones selling five times as many copies - is that British life remains similarly and obstinately divided. Certainly there are people who read both a posh and a popular paper, just as there are gradations between the popular papers: both the *Mirror* and the *Sun* aim at readers who are more squarely working class than the *Express* and *Mail* do. This shows the complexity of the class pattern, without denying its general lines. The broad shape and nature of the press is ultimately determined by no one but its readers.

Adapted from J. Whale *The Politics of the Media*, 1977, pp84-5

Item B
Magazines

Questions

1 a) Which theory of the media does Item A support?

   b) What are the 'key' sentences or phrases which demonstrate this?

2 What points in the extract would Marxists take issue with, and how might they criticise them?

3 Suggest how the magazines shown in Item B can be used to support a) a pluralist and b) a Marxist perspective on the mass media.

2.4 Postmodernism and the mass media

Some observers believe that we are living in a postmodern society, a society that comes after and is different from modern society. This section looks at some of their views on the nature and influence of the mass media in postmodern society. The section is largely based on a summary of postmodernism and the media by Dominic Strinati (1992).

Media realities

We live in a media saturated society. The media bombards us with a multitude of images which increasingly dominate the way we define ourselves and the world around us. Media images, it is argued, do not reflect or even distort social reality. They are realities in and of themselves. Our consciousness is invaded by the multiple realities provided by news, documentaries, pop music, advertisements, soaps and movies set in the past, present and future, on this world and on other worlds.

Style and images

Postmodern society is characterised by style and images. We increasingly consume these images for their own sake. Style itself has become a commodity. This can be seen in the priority given to designer clothes and their identifying designer labels. And the media plays a central part in this process. Adverts sell images and style rather than content or substance. Jeans are not marketed as hard wearing and value for money but rather as style in the context of rock and blues music. In the same way drinks such as Budweiser and Guinness are sold on style and image rather than taste and quality. The priority of style can be seen from movies and TV series such as *Miami Vice* - the designer clothes of its main characters, the rock music of the soundtrack and the carefully chosen settings of Miami are in many ways more important than the quality of acting and story line.

Time and space

In the cinema we can go *Back to the Future* or forward to the future with films like *Blade Runner*. Watching TV news we can go round the world in 30 minutes from Bosnia to Northern Ireland, from Israel to Angola, from Russia to the USA.

The media allows us to cross and criss-cross time and space. Television splices together pictures and information from different times and places into a collage of images. Adverts use rock and blues music from the 1960s to sell beer and jeans in the 1990s. Rap music in the 1990s samples soul music by James Brown from the 1960s and 70s. James Brown records from the same era are used in TV commercials to sell Lucozade and Clariol hair products. Movies take images from different times and places and combine them in new ways. *Who Framed Roger Rabbit?* is a combination of an early Hollywood detective movie and old style cartoon characters, a hybrid of the past that makes something new.

What does all this do to our sense of time and place? It is argued that it leads to 'increasing confusions and incoherence in our sense of space and time, in our maps of the places where we live, and our ideas about the "times" in terms of which we organise our lives. Time and space become less stable and comprehensible, more confused, more incoherent, more disunified' (Strinati, 1992, p3).

A media culture

The mass media increasingly dominates our definition and sense of reality. To a large extent our world now consists of images from TV broadcasts, advertisements, computer games, videos, CD players and personal stereos. This collage of disjointed and disconnected images spanning time and space presents multiple truths and multiple realities. Certainty and fixed standards have been replaced by uncertainty and scepticism. For many this is a very worrying trend. Media images 'encourage superficiality rather than substance, cynicism rather than belief, the thirst for constant change rather than the security of stable traditions, the desires of the moment rather than the truths of history' (Strinati, 1992, p7).

Summary

1 Early theories of the mass media were primarily psychological and based largely on laboratory experiments.

2 The two-step flow model emphasises the importance of social relationships in determining response to the media.

3 Cultural effects theory sees media effects as a slow, long term buildup of ideas and attitudes.

4 Pluralist theories see the mass media responding to public demand. Media output reflects both general and specific concerns. It gives people what they want.

5 Marxist theories see the media as an instrument of domination. It reflects the interests of the powerful and indoctrinates and subordinates the mass of the population.

6 The media in postmodern society is seen by some observers as a major source of our reality.

Activity 5 Television, Time and Place

Item A *BBC News*

BBC 9 o'clock News, 9.12.93

Items covered in this broadcast

Iraq - release of jailed Britons and their
    return to Hertfordshire

Sunday shopping in England and Wales

Health Service

Storms - Devon, Sussex, Yorkshire,
    Wales and Northern Ireland

Russia - Boris Yeltsin

Brussels summit - EU leaders

Redundancies at Ferranti

GATT - world trade meeting - Geneva

BBC licence fees

NASA space walks - film of moon walks

Westminster

Death of Danny Blanchflower

Item B *'Back to the Future'*

He's the only kid ever to get into trouble before he was born.

STEVEN SPIELBERG Presents

BACK TO THE FUTURE PG

A ROBERT ZEMECKIS Film

"BACK TO THE FUTURE" starring MICHAEL J. FOX
CHRISTOPHER LLOYD · LEA THOMPSON · CRISPIN GLOVER
Written by ROBERT ZEMECKIS & BOB GALE
Music by ALAN SILVESTRI
Produced by BOB GALE and NEIL CANTON
Executive Producers STEVEN SPIELBERG
KATHLEEN KENNEDY
FRANK MARSHALL
Directed by ROBERT ZEMECKIS

Distributed by UIP A UNIVERSAL Picture

In 'Back to the Future' Michael J. Fox plays a teenager who travels back to the time when his mother and father were teenagers. In the sequels, he moves back and forward in time through the lives of his family and community - re-writing their histories and their futures.

Item C *An evening's viewing*

Summary of television programmes on 8 December, 1993, broadcast between 6pm and 12am

BBC 1	BBC 2	ITV	Channel 4
News	USA - Star Trek	Australian soap	Game show
USA film	Def II - Chile	News	News
UK sitcom	Open Space - tattoos	Game show	UK soap
News	Documentary -	UK soap	Travelog -
Documentary -	Algerian journalist	Entertainment	Japan
Lebanon	Salman Rushdie -	Crime story -	Documentary
Sport -	ethnic cleansing	Yugoslavia	USA sitcom
USA boxing	USA sitcom	News	UK comedy
Italy football	Drama -Australia	USA film	1920s film -
USA detective	Documentary -	Football -	Berlin
	Paloma Picasso	Spain, Belgium	
	News		
	Australian film		

Item D

John Lee Hooker, a blues singer in his 70s singing 'Boom Boom', a song he recorded in the 1960s, advertising jeans in the 1990s

Questions

1 How might Items A to D affect our sense of time and place?
2 In the light of Items A to D, comment on Strinati's view that media images 'encourage superficiality rather than substance, cynicism rather than belief, the thirst for constant change rather than the security of stable traditions, the desires of the moment rather than the truths of history' (Strinati, 1992, p7).

3 The Content of the Mass Media: Impartiality, Politics and News

Key Issues

1 What do we mean by the term 'impartiality' with regard to the mass media?
2 How impartial is the media treatment of politics and news?
3 To what extent does government control media output?

3.1 The mass media and the notion of impartiality

In the UK around 20 million people watch at least one television news presentation every day. Is the information they receive accurate and unbiased?

Spokespersons for the media often claim that the mass media offers a wide variety of independent, objective sources of information which provide an essentially balanced presentation. The media is said to serve the public - to inform, to educate, to entertain and to perform these functions in a neutral way.

Is complete objectivity possible? Can the media present a balanced and impartial output? The answer is no. To take an example, selecting items for a news bulletin involves a range of judgements about what's important and significant. Why cover one civil war and not others? Why focus on one industrial dispute rather than others? These choices involve judgements which are based on values. Given this, complete objectivity and impartiality are not possible. It has therefore been argued that the mass media has to

adopt a stance of 'due impartiality'. Due impartiality means that there can only be 'objectivity' and 'impartiality' within the boundaries of what is generally agreed and accepted by the particular society. In Britain, for instance, there is a widespread condemnation of certain activities such as terrorist murders and trafficking in drugs. It is generally felt that the media should reflect this consensus and should be openly critical of such activities - it should be anti-terrorist and opposed to drug trafficking. It should therefore call the IRA 'terrorists' rather than 'freedom fighters' and refer to deaths caused by the IRA as 'murders'. However, in terms of due impartiality, the media should report the actual activities of the IRA as accurately as possible. If it fabricated these activities in order to portray the IRA in a bad light then due impartiality would simply become propaganda. The notion of due impartiality raises the question of whether minority interests and viewpoints are given adequate recognition and coverage by the media and whether there is a case for having such views presented without prejudice.

In addition to the difficulties with due impartiality, it is also inevitable that there will be some national and cultural bias in the mass media. The British media focuses on British news, British sport, the British economy and so on. Few people complain about this - we want 'our' news. However, as with due impartiality, cultural bias in the media can work against objectivity. Activity 6 examines the coverage of the Falklands War of 1983 by the British media and highlights some of the problems the media faced. This war involved a dispute over 'ownership' of the Falklands Islands between Britain and Argentina.

Argentinian forces invaded the islands and were eventually defeated by a British task force. It is interesting that the government criticised the Argentinian media for being biased (and there was, no doubt, some truth in this), yet did not want impartiality in the British reporting of the war. As the extracts in Activity 6 illustrate, the government exerted strong pressure on programmes such as *Newsnight* to present the war as the government wanted it presented. Politicians can, of course, argue that they are acting in the best interests of the nation in putting pressure on the mass media. And it is difficult to counter such claims without access to all the information.

If the media operates in terms of due impartiality, it must not consistently present a single viewpoint to the exclusion of others. Instead it must present a range of views, a variety of opinions. It can be argued that a mixture of 'biases' will at least allow the audience some choice. And variety can be seen as the next best thing to no bias whatsoever. Without this variety, one consistent portrayal and interpretation of reality may well become accepted as correct and authoritative by an audience which has no alternative sources of information on which to base its understanding. A number of academics and politicians claim that this variety is lacking. As a result the mass media is biased in a way that restricts our information, distorts our knowledge of the world and constrains our freedom of choice.

Activity 6 Bias and War Reporting

Item A *The other battle for the Falklands*

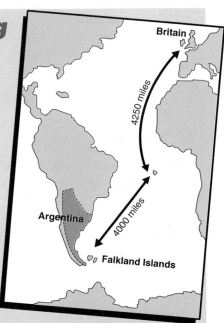

Strains between broadcasters and politicians are inevitable. Broadcasters depend upon politicians for their licence to operate. Politicians depend upon broadcasters to put over their ideas and personalities to the electorate. Broadcasters always want more freedom. Politicians always want more control.

The Falklands War highlighted this conflict. The British authorities were helped by the fact that the Falklands are so remote. Without their permission and help no TV crew could get to the islands or, once there, send their pictures back. The authorities were less than eager to help. One result was that by the time the first pictures were shown in Britain, the war was very nearly over. In the islands themselves, all reporters had to submit to strict censorship. And the authorities were not above telling them lies in the hope that they would be broadcast and so confuse the Argentines.

One incident, involving the BBC, highlighted the conflict between the broadcasters' desire for more freedom and the politicians' desire to handle news to their own advantage.

Newsnight tried to piece together what was happening in the South Atlantic using reports, not just from British sources, but from the United States and Argentina too.

Mrs Thatcher (then Prime Minister) was highly critical of *Newsnight*. She told the House of Commons, 'Many people are very concerned indeed that the case for our British forces is not being put over fully and effectively. There are times when it seems that we and the Argentines are being treated almost as equals and almost on a neutral basis. I can only say that if this is so it gives offence and causes great emotion among many people.'

This statement struck at the heart of television tradition. The BBC is, after all, bound by Parliament to be neutral in news coverage. Yet here was the most powerful figure in Parliament attacking the BBC for being neutral.

Adapted from 'Society Today: Television', in *New Society*, 1.12.83

Item B *The bombing of Port Stanley*

The conflict in the South Atlantic became a major shooting war on 1 May 1982. British aircraft launched a full-scale attack on the airfield at Port Stanley in the early hours of that morning. The purpose was to put the runway out of action and render the airfield unusable for Argentine aircraft. According to the Ministry of Defence, the attack was completely successful. The BBC accepted and broadcast this statement

The Argentine military announced that afternoon that the 'attack by the English seaborne airforce resulted in damage only to buildings surrounding the Malvinas (Argentinian name for Falklands) military airbase. The runway remains undamaged.'

Argentine TV films of the first raids on Port Stanley began to arrive in London during the second week of May. The *Daily Telegraph* of 11 May carried a report of an eight minute film, shown on Argentine TV on 9 May. The film included footage of the 1 May raids and the condition of the airstrip following the raids. The article reported that 'film of the Port Stanley airstrip showed several ruts but as the camera passed along its length it seemed serviceable'. These shots would have been hard to fake because they included bomb damage to the buildings.

Television news had some difficulty in admitting that the runway could still be operable. It appeared as if some broadcasters had difficulty in saying that the Argentines could be telling the truth and the Ministry could be misinforming them.

The bombings of the runway at Port Stanley airfield illustrates how television news overestimated the ease with which a military operation could be conducted to re-take the Falklands. The portrayal of the military option as relatively unproblematic was a central factor in legitimising the decision to fight in the South Atlantic.

British troops coming ashore in the Falklands

Adapted from Glasgow University Media Group *War and Peace News*, 1985, pp70-92

Questions

1 Read Items A and B.
   What case could be made for government control of the media's coverage of the Falklands War?
2 How do Items A and B show the difficulties of translating the idea of due impartiality into practice?

3.2 Politics and the media

This section looks at a number of related questions.

1 To what extent is media output controlled by government?
2 To what extent do politicians use the media for their own purposes?
3 Is media output politically biased?
4 Does the media influence people's political behaviour?

Government control

In every modern society governments, to a greater or lesser degree, try to control the media. The greater government control, the less chance the media has of presenting a balanced and impartial view of the political process.

Bob Franklin claims that in recent years the UK government has 'tried to influence and regulate the flow of political information and messages via the mass media to an unprecedented degree' (Franklin, 1993, p2). This has been done in two ways. Firstly, by attempting to restrain political communication from the media which opposes government policy. Secondly, by attempting to manipulate the media by promoting government policy. First, some of the restraints on the media.

Restraints on investigative journalism As their name suggests, investigative journalists conduct their own investigations rather than relying on information produced by government departments and other official bodies. Government attempts to inhibit investigative journalism led to a number of well publicised clashes with broadcasters. In 1985, Leon Brittan, then Home Secretary, persuaded the BBC to postpone and then edit the documentary *Real Lives* about the Irish Republican leader Martin McGuinness. Persuasion was replaced by direct action in the case of the Zircon affair. The journalist Duncan Campbell had been commissioned in 1985 to make a series of six programmes called *Secret Society*. One of the programmes concerned a spy satellite project, code named Zircon. Campbell argued that information on Zircon had been deliberately kept secret from Parliament. The screening of the programme was delayed and then banned after a meeting between the Assistant Director-General of the BBC, Alan Protheroe, and the head of Government Communication Headquarters. The *New Statesman* magazine, which Campbell worked for, went ahead and published the Zircon story. Both the BBC and the *New Statesman* were raided by the Special Branch, as were the homes of Duncan Campbell and two other journalists. The raid on the BBC in Glasgow led to the seizure of all six

Secret Society programmes on the grounds of a possible breach of the Official Secrets Act.

In 1988 the government tried to prevent the broadcast of Thames Television's *Death on the Rock*. This programme investigated the shooting of three members of the IRA in Gibraltar and challenged the official version of events. Although the programme was shown, the criticism it received from the government cannot have helped Thames Television in its unsuccessful attempt to renew its franchise to broadcast in 1991. Franklin argues that the effect of these battles between broadcasters and politicians has been to encourage 'self censorship' among programme makers in anticipation of opposition from politicians. The result has been to undermine investigative journalism.

Controlling the BBC The BBC is a public broadcasting corporation financed by licence fees which are set by government. Governments have used their power to try to influence BBC policy. It was used by the Conservative government during the Suez crisis in the 1950s, and in the 1960s and 70s by Labour governments displeased with coverage of their administration. In 1978, James Callaghan, then Prime Minister, threatened that 'hell will freeze over before you get a licence increase unless we get a better deal out of you' (quoted in Franklin, 1993, p10).

BBC policy is set by a board of governors whose members are appointed by the government. During the 1980s a number of Conservative Party supporters (eg William Rees-Mogg) were appointed. There have been criticisms that the board has been 'packed' with political appointees in order to bring the BBC into line with government policy.

Censorship In every society governments have certain powers to censor the media. In the UK the D-notice (defence notice) system was set up in 1912 to prevent newspapers from publishing sensitive military information. Editors are advised to contact the Secretary of the Services Press and Broadcasting Committee and seek advice before publishing or broadcasting information covering areas such as defence, the intelligence service and nuclear weapons.

The Official Secrets Act (re-enacted 1989) specifies certain categories of information about which nothing can be published - information obtained in confidence from a foreign government or international organisation, interception of communications, disclosure by former agents about the security services and certain disclosures by journalists about the security services. Franklin argues that these categories are so wide ranging that it is difficult for editors and journalists to decide whether or not a story falls into a prohibited category (Franklin, 1993, p9).

Assessing government control Stephen Hunt (1992) summarises the arguments for and against state secrecy and government control of the media. A certain amount of official secrecy and government control of information has been seen as essential for and compatible with a democratic society. It is necessary to counter foreign powers and groups within a society which are hostile to a democratic state. It is also required to protect government information which could lead to financial gain, such as advance knowledge of the budget.

Those who support 'open' government and an end to official secrecy claim that all citizens have a basic right to freedom of speech and information. These freedoms provide controls on government. Governments will be unable to hide inefficiency, blunders and broken promises. They will be unable to deceive the public. Citizens will be able to judge whether governments are acting in their interests. They will be able to participate more fully in the democratic process if they know what government is doing. Governments will be made more accountable and more sensitive to people's concerns and interests.

Activity 7 Political Control of Information

Item A *Northern Ireland*

In 1989 the Home Secretary announced that television and radio were banned from broadcasting any words spoken by members of eleven political and paramilitary groups in Northern Island, including the legal political party Sinn Fein. However, their words could be spoken by an actor or screened as subtitles. The overall effect of the censorship of these groups was to deny them a voice in the British media and the broader political debate. The ban was lifted in 1994.

Adapted from B. Franklin 'Packaging Politics: Politicians and the Media' in M. Haralambos (ed) *Developments in Sociology* vol 9, 1993, p9

A Sinn Fein election mural, Belfast 1989

Item B *Secrecy*

'Secrecy, being an instrument of conspiracy, ought never to be the system of regular government.' *Jeremy Bentham*, 1843

'Knowledge is power. It is important to recognise that the issue of open government is about power, political power, a shift in power, its redistribution.' *Lord Franks*, 1979

'With confidence and competence so much lower than they should be, it is not surprising that Whitehall fiercely defends its traditions of secrecy. The Official Secrets Act and the Thirty Year Rule, by hiding peacetime fiascos as though they were military disasters, protect ministers and officials from embarrassment. They also ensure

there is no learning curve.' *Sir John Hoskyns*, 1983

'The greatest restraint on government is that people know.' *Professor Bernard Crick*

Quotations from S. Hunt 'State Secrecy in the UK' *Politics Review*, April 1992, pp2-6

Questions

1 Give the case for and against the ban outlined in Item A.
2 Read Item B.
   a) Why are governments so concerned about secrecy?
   b) Is government control of the mass media compatible with democracy?

Politicians and the media

To what extent do politicians and governments attempt to use and even manipulate the media to promote themselves and their policies? Lord Young, when Minister at the Department of Trade and Industry, stated that government 'policies are like cornflakes, if they are not marketed they will not sell' (quoted in Franklin, 1993, p2).

Throughout the 1980s UK government expenditure on advertising increased over threefold - publicity for privatisation of electricity alone cost £76 million in September 1989. Whether such advertising can be seen as 'political' is a matter of opinion. Part of it can be seen as simply informative, such as publicity for government training schemes and public health campaigns about AIDS. However, there is a thin line between providing information and promoting government policies. For example, privatisation is a political issue about which the major parties strongly disagree.

The so-called lobby system provides government with opportunities to manage the media. The Prime Minister's press secretary has daily meetings with the 220 senior political journalists who make up the Parliamentary Lobby. They are briefed on the government's views on important issues. According to Franklin, such briefings 'help to structure and inform' political news on television, radio and in the newspapers (Franklin, 1993, p3).

Political parties are increasingly concerned with using the media, particularly during election campaigns. They have even commissioned the talents of film directors like Hugh Hudson and John Schlesinger to direct their party election broadcasts. Quite what effects such glossy productions have is unclear. Neil Kinnock, former leader of the Labour Party, was generally judged to have won the 1992 media election campaign, but he lost the actual

general election.

Something of the degree to which political parties attempt to manipulate the media can be seen from Bob Franklin's study of local parties' media strategies in the 1992 general election. Their press releases were designed to present their candidates and policies in the best possible light. And in some cases they were successful. In one constituency 28 out of 29 of the local Labour Party press releases produced a story in the local newspaper. In many cases these 'stories' were little different from the press release. As one Labour Party agent stated, 'We actually write the press releases and so all they've got to do is re-type it or just edit it into the paper' (quoted in Franklin, 1993, p21).

Political bias

Politicians from all parties have claimed that the media is politically biased. The BBC has been accused by the Conservatives as being left wing, by Labour as being right wing and by the Liberal Democrats of ignoring them. During the run up to the 1992 election the Conservatives criticised the BBC for allegedly giving Labour more favourable coverage. And Labour accused the largely Conservative tabloid press of misrepresenting its policies. However, the major problem with identifying bias is that one person's bias is another person's objectivity.

Most newspapers freely admit their political stance. As noted earlier, the problem has been seen not as one of bias but of imbalance - the preponderance of papers supporting the political right (see p536). What of the 'due impartiality' of television? The fact that political broadcasts from the BBC and ITV have been criticised by both left and right has been seen as a possible indication of due impartiality. However, looked at from a more radical view, television and the media in general are a long way from even due impartiality.

The journalist John Pilger takes a broader view of political bias. He sees the media in capitalist societies as 'propaganda that shapes what is called news and fixes the limits of public scrutiny' (Pilger, 1993, p14). This goes far beyond accusing the media of supporting one or other political party. Pilger is pointing to the lack of fundamental criticism of government and society, the failure to present real political alternatives. This is similar to the Marxist view which sees the media as an instrument of social control that promotes the ideology of the powerful and supports established power structures.

Political effects of the media

Neil Kinnock blamed the largely Conservative tabloid press for Labour's defeat in the 1992 general election. And the *Sun*, with its famous headline, 'It's The *Sun* Wot Won It', agreed with him.

Whether there is any justification for these views is difficult to say (see Activity 2 p537 and Activity 8 below). It is not possible to disentangle the effects of the media from the range of other influences on political behaviour. Although those who study the media accept that elections are not won or lost on television or in the press, most agree that the media has some effect. For example, Colin Seymour-Ure states, 'Obviously the media makes some difference to how citizens in aggregate vote: it is mostly through the media that we experience the campaign' (1993, p16). But exactly what this 'some difference' is has yet to be discovered.

Activity 8   The Media and the 1992 Election

Item A   *The late swing*

There was a late swing to the Conservatives just before election day - 9 April 1992. Without this they would have lost. Opinion polls suggest that the main reason for this late swing was that voters placed more trust in the Conservatives on economic issues - the economy, taxation and inflation.

Adapted from I.Crewe 'Why did Labour Lose (yet again)?' *Politics Review*, September 1992, p10

Conservative Party poster for the 1992 general election campaign

Item B   *The press*

The day before the election, under the front page headline 'A Question of Trust', the *Sun* asked 'When you're in trouble, who do you go to for help: the big mouth or the bank manager?'('big mouth' refers to Neil Kinnock, then leader of the Labour Party). The following day the *Sun* claimed to have won the election for the Conservatives. But did it? As shown in the table, according to one estimate *Sun* readers swung by a massive 7.5% to the Conservatives in the last days of the campaign. Moreover, the *Sun* is particularly popular among the working class in the South - a large and key group of

The impact of the press on the late swing to the Conservatives (%)

Newspaper	Vote intention 7-8 April		Actual Vote		Swing to Conservative
	Con	Lab	Con	Lab	
Daily Telegraph	76	9	72	11	-3.0
Times	62	13	64	15	0.0
Independent	18	44	25	37	+7.0
Guardian	10	57	15	55	+3.5
Daily Express	64	16	68	15	+2.5
Daily Mail	61	18	65	14	+4.0
Today	33	33	43	31	+6.0
Sun	36	42	45	36	+7.5
Daily Star	32	58	32	53	+2.5
Daily Mirror	14	68	20	63	+5.5
None	34	34	41	34	+3.5
All voters	37	39	43	35	+5.0

relatively non-partisan voters. But one should avoid hasty conclusions. By the same estimate there were about average swings to the Conservatives among readers of the non-partisan *Independent* (7%) and of the stridently Labour *Daily Mirror* (5.5%) whereas the swing was below average among readers of the *Daily Express* (2.5%), *Daily Mail* (4%) and the *Times* (0%) - all solidly Conservative newspapers. The most one can infer is that some Tory tabloids, like the *Sun* and *Today*, gave an extra push to a Conservative bandwagon that was already rolling. An analysis of constituencies with large *Sun* readerships suggests that, at most, the *Sun* may have saved six highly marginal seats for the Conservatives.

Adapted from I.Crewe 'Why did Labour Lose (yet again)?' *Politics Review*, September 1992, pp10-11

Item C   *Financial News*

By the end of the 1980s, financial news had become a regular part of news reports. Good news was seen as shares rising and a healthy stock market. The political preferences of the City were made clear on TV news programmes. When Labour took the lead in opinion polls prior to the 1992 election, ITN news stated, 'Billions of pounds were wiped off the values of shares this morning as the City, which traditionally prefers Conservative government, took fright at the clear Labour lead in opinion polls' (ITN, 1 April 1992). Such coverage must help the Conservatives.

Adapted from G.Philo 'There is No Alternative' *New Statesman and Society*, 13.11.92, pp12-14

Questions

1   Using Items A and B, assess the impact of the media on the late swing to the Conservatives.
2   Read Item C. What influence if any did financial news have on the late swing to the Conservatives?

3.3 The media and news reporting

Is the reporting of news on television, radio and in newspapers impartial? Or is it biased and if so, how biased? A great deal of sociological research has attempted to answer these questions. The results of some of this research will be examined in this section.

Agenda-setting A widely used concept for analysing news coverage is *agenda-setting*. Essentially, this refers to how journalists and broadcasters select news, how they prioritise what to include in news programmes. Journalists (the term refers to TV and press reporters and editors) choose to include some items in news coverage and not others. While they might argue that the content of the news is outside their control and depends on what is happening in the world, it is important to bear in mind that *news is news because journalists make it news*. Clearly, some events merit inclusion in practically anyone's definition of what is news - they are obviously of major public interest. However, there are other considerations that affect what is included in the news and what is not. There are various 'organisational factors' such as deadlines - when does an event happen, does it meet our deadline?; space available in a particular programme or newspaper; the number of 'competing events' at any particular time (a major disaster, for instance, reduces the amount of space for other news items); location of the news 'event' and availability of photographs or film. (Some of these points on agenda-setting are explored in Activity 9).

News does not just happen and then appear on our televisions and in our newspapers. It is a socially manufactured product and news gathering is a selective process. This is not to say that journalists routinely invent the news, although there are cases where they do, but they do make choices about what to cover and how to cover it. Journalists would no doubt say that they select the most 'significant' and 'newsworthy' items and events. These concepts of significance and newsworthiness are, however, by no means straightforward, they depend on particular views and interpretations of reality. The term *gatekeeper* has been used to refer to people who determine what material will be communicated to the public via the media. Editors are the main gatekeepers. As Dutton (1986) puts it, 'Editors fulfil what is essentially a filtering role - selecting or "opening the gate" for some stories, whilst "closing the gate" for others, since there is usually an excess of material available to fill limited newspaper or broadcasting space' (p32).

News agencies An additional organisational constraint on news reporting is the reliance on news agencies for material. Many newspapers, in particular local newspapers, have a relatively small number of reporters and often have to rely on outside sources for their information and stories. The main agency for British news is the Press Association, while for foreign news Reuters, United Press International and Associated Press are particularly influential agencies. These international agencies control a vast amount of information, and make large profits out of it. Very few newspapers can afford to keep reporters spread across the world. A glance at the sources of much of the international news in newspapers illustrates the importance of the international news agencies.

Activity 9   The Editor as Gatekeeper

Item A   *Front pages*

Item B   *What is newsworthy?*

Past example is an important guide to the selection and interpretation of story, angle and detail. In this sense there is nothing new about 'news'; the same topics, angles and clichés recur with comforting regularity. When one rape case hits the headlines, others - for a time - promptly become topical and 'newsworthy', and are therefore also extensively covered, until the viewer or reader could be forgiven for thinking that a plague of rapists was sweeping the country . As quickly as a topic becomes the 'issue of the moment', it may disappear without trace - and often without conclusion - when some alternative item or angle is defined as more newsworthy.

Adapted from M. Grant *The British Media*, 1984, p 22

Item C   *Space and time*

Space Policies affecting the layout of a newspaper predetermine what can be reported about the world. They map out the rough system of priorities, decide the proportions that those reports will occupy in the total presentation and limit the entire volume of events. Newspapers do not vary substantially in size from day to day; neither do they vary in their composition. The inclusion of photographs, advertising and standardised matter such as cartoons and stock-exchange reports further defines what is recordable. Although policies differ between newspaper organisations, each one imposes a firm grid on the distribution of events that will be recognised. Such a grid enhances the probability that consistent amounts of crime, sport, foreign conflict and so on will occur. After all, it is this layout policy which supports the journalistic division of labour. Crime reporters, sports commentators and foreign correspondents are occupationally committed to producing a relatively constant output of knowledge about their particular worlds.

Time The timetable of newspaper production imposes itself upon what can be recorded. Developments which unfold very gradually tend to be unreportable by the daily press unless some distinctive stage is reached. Things which do not change appreciably have a lesser chance of being recorded unless they are expected to develop. There is thus a constant strain within the reporting enterprise to adapt the world of events to the timetable of the newspaper.

Adapted from P. Rock 'News as Eternal Recurrence' in S.Cohen and J. Young (eds) *The Manufacture of News*, 1981, pp75-6

Item D

'And tonight as Iran declares war on China, and unemployment reaches seven million, we ask, what about that royal divorce?'

'And to ensure a balanced and impartial discussion of the latest government measures, I have with me a government spokesman and a wild-eyed militant from the lunatic fringe.'

Adapted from Glasgow University Media Group *Really Bad News*, 1982, pp2 and 81

Questions

1 Describe the editorial policy of the *Sun* and the *Times* (Item A) to the 'news' of July 24, 1995.
2 Read Item B.
   a) How might newspapers' preoccupation with 'issues of the moment' prevent 'balanced' news coverage?
   b) Why do some newspapers focus on 'issues of the moment'?
3 'News is created to fit the requirements of newspapers.' Discuss using Item C.
4 Are the cartoons in Item D making valid points?

Journalistic assumptions

The commonsense view of news reporting is that the news merely reflects what is going on in society; newsrooms are run by professionals who know their job and work under pressure in a fast moving world. Journalists, however, have their own assumptions about what makes a good story and about what their audiences like. They also have their own beliefs and values and their own prejudices. These are often taken for granted - journalists are largely unaware of them. If and when their own views and prejudices are expressed in their reporting - in the selection and interpretation of news items, for example - then there may well be a cause for concern.

This issue is examined in the detailed studies carried out by the Glasgow University Media Group. Their first study, *Bad News* (1976), was followed by *More Bad News* (1980), *Really Bad News* (1982), *War and Peace News* (1985) and *Getting the Message - News, Truth and Power* (1993). These studies were based on content analyses of TV news. They reject broadcasters' claims to impartiality.

The essence of the Glasgow group's argument is captured in the following quote from *More Bad News*. 'In the period of our study, the news was organised and produced substantially around the views of the dominant political group in our society. We have shown how the views of those who disagree fundamentally with this position, or who offered alternative approaches, were downgraded and under-represented in the news coverage' (1980 p111).

With regard to agenda-setting in the news, the Glasgow University Media Group argue that journalists' and broadcasters' claims that certain items have 'news value' assume that everyone sees and interprets the world in the same way. It assumes that news is an objective, 'real' phenomenon. In *Getting the Message*, Eldridge(1993) points out that journalists have to organise a coherent picture of the news from a mass of information and opinions. Once an item has been defined as 'newsworthy', it is processed. The story is interpreted and edited. Certain viewpoints are emphasised to the exclusion of others. Particular aspects are defined as more important than others.

To illustrate these points the Glasgow group quote from one of the BBC's own pamphlets on the news: 'The news value of a story is something immediately recognisable, intuitively sensed by a journalist ... (who) learns to spot the significant news point, the relevant detail, the interesting human touch which distinguishes the newsworthy story' (1980 p113).

This quote raises important questions - 'What is the significant news point, the relevant detail and the interesting human touch?' These are recognised in terms of the world view of the journalist. Thus, what is presented as news is based on the inherited 'wisdom' of journalistic assumptions about the society that is being reported on and the audience they hope to reach. It is these assumptions which allow the journalists to recognise the newsworthiness of particular items as against others. To use the Glasgow group's own words: 'Against this background, the assertion of impartiality as a regular professional achievement is little more than the unsupported claim to a unique understanding of events. This serves only to obfuscate [obscure] what is in fact the reproduction of the dominant assumptions about our society - the assumptions of the powerful about what is important, necessary and possible within it' (1980, p115).

Power and News

The Glasgow group's view that news reflects the interests and assumptions of the powerful is illustrated by their study of industrial disputes. They found, for example, that in the reporting of strikes management received a far better press than striking workers. These findings were supported by the Annan Committee's Report on the Future of Broadcasting, 1977: 'Difficult as the reporting of industrial stories may be, the broadcasters have not fully thought it through. They too often forget that to represent management at their desks, apparently the calm and collected representatives of order, and to represent shop stewards and picket lines stopping production, apparently the agents of disruption, gives a false picture of what strikes are about' (quoted in *New Society*, 25.1.1979).

The Glasgow group found that in the reporting of strikes little coverage was given to the background of the dispute. The emphasis was invariably on its effects on the public. News coverage of a Glasgow refuse collectors' strike concentrated on the health hazard rather than the grievances of the workers. In terms of access to the media, management and the 'experts' receive far more coverage than trade unionists. In the refuse strike, for instance, not one of the twenty-one interviews broadcast nationally was with a striker. Furthermore, and in line with the Annan Committee's findings, the treatment of management and trade unionists was quite different; the former were usually allowed to make their points quietly and at length, the latter often had to shout over the noises around them or were interrupted by reporters.

In a review of bias in news reporting, Michael Meacher (1982) summarises the work of the Glasgow group on industrial affairs coverage. This summary highlights the group's argument. 'In industrial coverage, one view is given dominance over all others; namely, that inflation is caused by excessive wage increases and that the economic malaise of Britain is predominantly caused by strikes. Trade unionists are typically asked: "What are you doing to end the strike?" Management is typically asked: "How much production or exports have been lost?" The subtle innuendo is thus conveyed that trade unions cause strikes, even though disputes may well be forced by management errors. Aggressive interviewing of shop stewards, and accusations of "acting irresponsibly", "destroying the company", "cutting their own throats", all serve the same purpose, ignoring the complexity of industrial breakdowns. The Glasgow Media Group found that over a long period of systematic monitoring, wage demands were reported on TV news programmes eight times more as the cause of inflation than any other factor. Other factors, such as money supply expansion, a big hike in profits, a big increase in government tax take, or higher unit costs in a slump, were thus wholly played down. The case against TV news presentation is not that strikes or excessive wage demands are not a problem - of course they are. It is that this explanation of Britain's troubles is not presented neutrally as one among others, but adopted as the authoritative one' (Meacher, 1982, pp17-18).

One particular case of industrial affairs reporting that the Glasgow group looked at was a dispute at British Leyland that received extensive media coverage over a five week period from January 1975. A short account of this case study illustrates the content analysis research method used by the Glasgow group. The intention of the study was to determine the extent to which the conventional view that 'unions cause industrial problems' underpinned television news coverage.

At the time of the research, there were other explanations for problems in the car industry; in particular, bad management and low investment. On January 3, Harold Wilson, then Prime Minister, made a speech which referred to government investment and criticised the record of car production using the words 'manifestly avoidable stoppages of production'. The speech was reported on BBC News that evening:

'The Prime Minister, in a major speech tonight on the economy, appealed to *management and unions* in the car industry to cut down on what he called "manifestly avoidable stoppages"' (BBC Early Evening News 3.1.75, quoted in *Really Bad News*, 1982, p22). In the BBC News later that evening, there had been some subtle changes to the way in which this speech was reported. It is introduced as a speech about strikes with an appeal to workers alone:

'The Prime Minister has appealed to *workers* in the

car industry to cut down on avoidable stoppages. He said that the industry had a record of strikes out of proportion to its size, and he singled out, for particular blame, British Leyland's Austin-Morris division' (BBC Late News 3.1.75, quoted in *Really Bad News*, 1982, p24).

This change in emphasis is important, particularly as Harold Wilson's speech was referred to on a large number of occasions in the coverage of the dispute at Leyland. The ITN coverage made no reference to the criticism of management made by Wilson. Again this example suggests that television news tends to favour the interests of the powerful.

In summary, the work of the Glasgow University Media Group rejects the pluralist or market model of the media (based on the essential neutrality of the media which reporters themselves tend to support). News broadcasts are seen as leading rather than following opinion, they structure people's attitudes and 'set the agenda'. The Glasgow group's intention was to 'prove' bias in the news by careful content analysis, thereby avoiding allegations that they were themselves politically biased (Glasgow group members do not hide their individual socialist leanings). Of course, one of the problems with investigating media bias is the tendency for all sides to argue that the media takes the opposite view from their own. However, the Glasgow group have produced considerable evidence to suggest that television news coverage is biased in favour of the interests of the powerful.

More recently the Glasgow Media Group has broadened its focus to examine the way Western audiences are informed about the Third World. Again there is evidence that 'news' reflects power relationships. Third World countries are relatively powerless compared to Western countries. Third World issues are therefore defined as relatively unimportant and not particularly newsworthy by the Western media. Activity 10 is based on Greg Philo's (1993) study of British TV news coverage of the catastrophic Ethiopian famine in 1984.

Summary

1 There is a large body of evidence which indicates that the media is not impartial.

2 There is evidence that government control of media output in the UK has increased.

3 Complete media impartiality is not possible. Some argue it is not even desirable as the media should reflect the core values of society. Others argue that in a pluralistic society there are different and sometimes conflicting values. The media should reflect this range of values. Research suggests it does not. For example, the Glasgow University Media Group claims that the media is strongly biased in favour of the values and interests of the dominant groups in society.

4 There is evidence to suggest that the media restricts access to information and therefore limits freedom of choice. For example, agenda-setting defines a large amount of information as 'non-news'.

Activity 10 TV News and the Ethiopian Famine

Item A *The famine*

Starving children in Ethiopia. It is estimated that between 600,000 and one million people died in Ethiopia in 1984.

Item D *A plea for help*

We have been asking for help since early 1983. It seems you have to have thousands of corpses before people will sit up and take notice.

UNICEF representative in Ethiopia, November 1984

Item B *Reporting the famine*

Despite warnings from aid agencies from 1982 onwards about the impending famine, the first TV coverage was a documentary in July 1984. There were a few items after July on BBC and ITN News, but not until 23 October 1984 did the BBC treat the disaster as a major news story.

Item C *News priorities*

Why did the Ethiopian famine take so long to appear on TV screens? To justify spending money on an overseas story, the story must be 'big' with dramatic pictures and mass appeal. For much of 1984 the famine apparently did not fit this description. In early 1984 an ITN reporter visited Ethiopia and apologised for doing nothing. As there were no *acute* cases of starvation to film, the famine wasn't news. In terms of media priorities, Third World issues are secondary to UK news. Only when the famine reached catastrophic proportions did the BBC decide to treat it as a major issue to headline the *Six O'Clock News* on 23 October 1984. That was a slack news day and even then there was a discussion on whether to use other lead stories.

Item E *News or not news?*

Item E *News or not news?*

A BBC team filming a famine in Sudan in June 1985 was asked, 'What happens if what you find isn't worse than Ethiopia?' 'There's no story', they replied.

Items B to E quoted and adapted from G. Philo 'From Buerk to Band Aid: the Media and the 1984 Ethiopian Famine' in J. Eldridge (ed) *Getting the Message: News, Truth and Power*, 1993, pp104-125

Questions

1 Look at Item A. Would you describe the Ethiopian famine as a major news story? Give reasons for your answer.
2 Read Items B, C and D. Why did it take so long for the famine to make headline news?
3 'News doesn't make itself. It is made by media organisations.' What evidence in the activity supports this statement?
4 How can the concept of power help us to understand the reporting of Third World issues in the West?
5 Read Item E. Explain the reply given by the BBC team.

4 Media Representations of Women and Ethnic Minorities

Key Issues
1 How are women and ethnic minorities represented by the media?
2 To what extent are these representations based on stereotypes?

4.1 Media portrayal of women

Is the role of women influenced by their portrayal in the mass media? If so, how important is the media's influence compared to that of other institutions such as the family, education and religion? It is difficult, if not impossible, to separate, measure and prioritise these various influences. However, one thing is clear, the media is able to present a very graphic and immediate picture of the position of women in society.

Despite these qualifications, an examination of the portrayal of women helps to demonstrate the media's potential to reflect and reinforce conformist views and to foster cultural uniformity. Women are often represented in the media, and especially in advertising, in the form of stereotypes. They tend to be shown as household consumers or as exuding the kind of glamour and appeal that attracts men. In advertising, women are usually portrayed as either sex objects or domestic servants. It is important to emphasise adverts - they aim to get a message over quickly and effectively. Stereotypes make an immediate impact - women in adverts for washing up liquid and washing powder, men drinking lager and buying cars.

Feminists argue that media presentation of women reinforces men's continuing domination. It is not just in advertising that women are portrayed as wives, mothers and sex objects. The same sort of messages are provided, perhaps in a less obvious manner, by the general media presentation of women. Bourne (1980) quotes a study by Mary Gallagher: 'Although in reality almost half the labour force in both the USA and Canada is female, studies show percentages of working women in television portrayals which vary

from 30% to as low as 12%. Even in the Soviet Union, where 93% of women work, one study of youth magazines found that men were five times more likely to be associated with their occupation than were women' (p108).

Furthermore, the women who are shown in paid employment on television programmes often have unstable or unsatisfactory relationships with male partners. Married women with jobs, particularly more demanding, higher status jobs, are much more likely than full time housewives to be portrayed as being unhappily married in television drama and comedy programmes (as Item A in Activity 11 illustrates).

Women as a minority group The media tends to treat women as a minority group, in spite of the fact that they make up over half of the world's population. Many newspapers, both national and local, have designated 'Women's Pages' (the *Guardian* and *Daily Mail*, for example); and there is a 'Woman's Hour' on Radio 4. It is also apparent, from the 'throw away' lines of television presenters and newspaper reporters, that women are still widely perceived as a minority group whose interests should be treated as minority interests. The following comments, taken from the 'Naked Ape' page of the *Guardian* and quoted in Grant (1984), illustrate this type of treatment:

'You may have noticed we had two women in our team this week. Next week we will be back to normal.'
(David Jacobs, *Any Questions*)

'Who will watch breakfast television when the BBC launches it next year? Some wives will watch it, of course, particularly if soap operas and feminine programmes are shown. The result will be many burnt offerings in the cooker, and holes scorched in shirts as the iron is forgotten during some dramatic screen moment.'
(Bristol Evening Post)

The following quotation from Tunstall (1983) provides a summary of the main findings of research into gender presentation in the media. 'The presentation of women in the media is biased, because it emphasises women's domestic, sexual, consumer and marital activities to the exclusion of all else. Women are depicted as busy housewives, as contented mothers, as eager consumers and as sex objects. This does indeed indicate bias because, although similar numbers of men are fathers and husbands the media has much less to say about these male roles; men are seldom presented nude, nor is their marital or family status continually quoted in irrelevant contexts. Just as men's domestic and marital roles are ignored, the media also ignore that well over half of British adult women go out to paid employment, and that many of both their interests and problems are employment-related' (Tunstall, 1983, p148).

Activity 11   Men, Women and the Media

Item A   *Television*

Over the last ten years or so, a growing body of research has confirmed that the roles allocated to the sexes on television are often highly distorted. Males tend to be assertive, tough and dynamic; females tend to be soft, deferential and, whenever possible, physically attractive. Even to viewers who are conscious of some bias, the raw figures may still be striking. Have you ever noticed, for example, that in commercials it often tends to be a woman showing how to use the latest vacuum cleaner, or carrot peeler, while on the sound track a resonant male voice is assuring you of the scientifically tested quality of the product? This tendency turns out to account for the vast majority of ads: up to 97 per cent of voice-overs are performed by males, with women nearly always being shown using the product, especially if it is a household article. If the product is aimed at men, then women in the ads tend to serve as sex objects, unbuttoning shirts, stroking closely shaven chins, or wriggling around petrol pumps. Women are the main stars of about 14 per cent of mid-evening programmes. Most women shown on television are under 30, and their occupational activities tend to fall into the range of housewife, secretary and nurse. Women in television programmes rarely combine a successful career with a family life: one American study found that if a female is shown as married and working, then she is ten times more likely to be depicted as unsuccessful in the marriage than a woman whose sole occupation is that of housewife.

Adapted from K. Durkin and P. Akhtar 'Television, Sex Roles and Children', *New Society*, 7.4.83

Item B   *Patriarchal ideology*

Patriarchal ideology works to represent gender roles as 'natural' and inevitable, rather than a product of male power. Such an ideology supports the interests of men and so helps to maintain the subordination of women. Various studies have shown that a patriarchal ideology runs through the media, whether in children's comics, adverts or the cinema. Women's and girls' magazines are particularly crucial in defining a 'woman's world'. They exist for all stages of life - from child to adolescent to young single adult to married woman. In contrast, men's magazines exist solely for the leisure interests of male groups of different ages - an indicator of the difference (and greater freedom) of their role. *Jackie*, as a teen magazine, is especially important as it is popular with girls who are beginning to lose the restrictions on their leisure lives. In common with other popular women's magazines, the emphasis is on the female as someone who is looked at rather than who does things and on romance as being the most important aspect of her life.

Adapted from B. Dutton *The Media*, 1986, pp40-41

Item C

Advertising beer

Questions

1 Read Items A and B
   a) Is the portrayal of women by the media an accurate reflection of their position in society?
   b) Why are women presented in this way?
2 Judging from Item C what are women's main attributes?
3 'Women deserve what they get from the media.' Discuss from:
   a) a feminist perspective;
   b) a pluralist or market perspective.

Effects on children A major concern of those critical of the media's stereotyping of women is the possible effect on young children. Again, it is difficult to separate out the influence of the media from other social factors. There have been studies that attempt to measure the correlation between television viewing and children's beliefs about sex roles. One such study (reported by Durkin and Akhtar, 1983) examined the effects on young children of 'counter-stereotype' television, with males and females shown in non-traditional roles and activities. An episode of the programme *Rainbow* which focused on the theme of role reversal was shown to a group of 5 to 7 year old children. The programme starts with the story of a conventional family, beginning the day with Mum serving breakfast, Dad going to work, Mum clearing up, taking the children to school and doing the shopping. During the story Dad loses his job at the factory and the programme's stars (the puppets) have to find a solution to this problem. They come up with the idea of Mum working and Dad staying at home and taking over the domestic responsibilities and the story continues by illustrating this role reversal. The message seemed to reach the children. Those who watched the 'role reversal' programme responded in a much more liberal manner to questions on sex roles (for example, 'Who should look after the children?' 'Who should go to work?') than did a control group of children who watched a 'neutral' programme.

Durkin and Akhtar admit that a one-off experiment like this might 'work' simply because it is novel and presents a new idea to children. But it is difficult to find out how enduring any changes in attitude might be. However, studies like this do suggest that television, and the mass media generally, might have the potential to change social attitudes. Obviously television cannot by itself shape children into new sex roles, but children may consider a wider range of male and female possibilities if they are presented with them. At present, children tend to get a conventional and stereotypical picture of sex roles from the media.

Patriarchal ideology Gender in the media reflects ideas and practices prevalent in other areas of social life. It fits the feminist critique of modern society as patriarchal - characterised by male domination. The failure to rebel against this oppression is partly explained by patriarchal ideology that represents conventional gender roles as being both natural and inevitable.

Various studies have examined the role of the media in promoting and reinforcing patriarchal ideology. Angela McRobbie's review of the teenage girl's magazine *Jackie* provides an example. In common with other popular women's magazines, *Jackie* stories revolve around romance as the be all and end all of life:

'Female solidarity, or more simply the idea of girls together - in *Jackie* terms - is an unambiguous sign of failure. To achieve self respect the girl has to escape the "bitchy", "catty" atmosphere of female company and find a boyfriend as fast as possible. But in doing this she has not only to be individualistic in outlook - she has to be prepared to fight ruthlessly - by plotting, intrigue and cunning, to "trap her man". Not surprisingly, this independent-mindedness is short-lived. As soon as she finds a "steady", she must renounce it altogether and capitulate to his demands, acknowledging his domination and resigning herself to her own subordination' (A. McRobbie, '*Jackie*, an Ideology of Adolescent Femininity', quoted in B. Dutton, 1986, p 41).

The message is that female independence is simply a means to an end - female dependence. And it is this picture of female dependence which, according to most researchers, dominates media presentation of women.

4.2 Media portrayal of ethnic minorities

Numerous studies have catalogued the disadvantages faced by ethnic minorities in employment, education and housing (see Chapter 3). Clearly the mass media cannot be wholly blamed for these disadvantages. However, this is not to say it is free from blame. The media's influence is perhaps most potent in the way it colours perceptions of ethnic minority groups. As with other areas of media coverage, it may be that the media plays a part in reinforcing attitudes, in this instance, racist attitudes. As with media portrayal of women, it is difficult to separate the influence of the mass media from the wider aspects of social life that shape people's attitudes and, therefore, their prejudices.

Ethnic minorities as a problem Research into the media treatment of 'race' has emphasised the way in which ethnic minorities are almost invariably presented as a 'problem'. They tend to be reported as the cause of social disorder such as street crime or riots. The 1981 riots in Toxteth and elsewhere were described as 'black' or 'race' riots. While black youths were involved, so were large numbers of white youths. Similarly, when the 'new' crime of mugging hit the headlines it was widely reported as a 'black' crime. According to Hall et al (1979) the media focus on the street crime of mugging encouraged the development of a stricter style of policing in areas with large ethnic minority populations. This style of policing included aggressive 'stop and search' operations. In 1981, for example, during the police operation known as 'Swamp 81' in Brixton, over 1,000 people were stopped and searched yet less than 100 were charged with any offence. It can be argued that many of these offences were caused by the police operation itself - offences of obstruction, for example, may only have occurred because of the heavy police presence. The media, fed by police reports, placed the blame for mugging on black youths. Headlines in the national press suggested that it had reached epidemic proportions. However, mugging, which police statistics do not even recognise as a separate category of crime to robbery in general, constitutes less than one per cent of all recorded crime in London. (See pp482-483 for a discussion of the media and mugging).

Racial attacks Media coverage of 'racial' attacks clearly demonstrates differential treatment of whites and non-whites. Two inter-racial murders in 1981 illustrate this. On April 10th a seventeen year old black youth was murdered in Swindon. While the local press reported this as a racially motivated murder the national press ignored it altogether. The following month, a white man, was murdered in Thornton Heath, London, by a group of black youths. This time the killing got massive and detailed coverage, with headlines such as 'Race Murder in Suburbia' (*Daily Mail*); 'Innocent Victim of Race Hate' (*Daily Express*). Although this killing was a particularly horrible affair, no killing of a black person has received equal coverage. Home Office figures show that blacks and Asians are much more likely than whites to be the victims of street attacks. Many of these attacks are racially motivated. They get little publicity.

Media effects What effects might media portrayal of ethnic minorities have? Hartmann and Husband (1974) suggest that if a person is living in a multi-racial community the media may help to create and/or increase social divisions. If the person already has a negative perception of blacks, he or she will find plenty of material in the media to confirm and strengthen those attitudes. On the other hand, people who live in essentially 'all-white' communities and areas (Wales, Devon and Cornwall, for example) are likely to rely on the media for information about ethnic minorities. And the picture they get will be pretty negative.

The essence of Hartmann and Husband's argument is that the media operates within a British culture that has tended to see foreigners, and especially blacks, as inferior. The media helps to perpetuate this tradition by using images and stereotypes based on Britain's colonial past. From their analysis of the media treatment of ethnic minorities, Hartmann and Husband discovered a strong emphasis on racial conflict. They then attempted to measure the extent to which this type of coverage actually influences people's attitudes. Although based only on a small sample of school children, their research indicated

that those children who relied on the media for their information about ethnic minorities were much more likely to think about race relations in terms of conflict than were those who had regular contact with ethnic minorities.

Racism and the press

In a detailed examination of racism and the press, Van Dijk (1991) focuses on the reporting of ethnic affairs in the 1980s. His study aims to explain how racism is perpetuated by the press. It is based on the reporting of ethnic issues in a sample of British newspapers (*The Times, Guardian, Daily Telegraph, Daily Mail* and *Sun*) during the second half of 1985 and the first six months of 1989 (when the *Independent* was added to the newspapers studied).

One particular issue Van Dijk examined was the 1985 'riots' in Handsworth, Brixton and Tottenham. He noted a clear tendency for newspaper editorials to support a 'criminal' explanation for the riots and to attack 'social' explanations. Although a number of editorials mentioned the social deprivation of inner cities and black communities there was a strong tendency to argue that a crime is a crime and social explanations do not provide any excuse. The right wing popular press were most blatant in taking this line. The *Sun*, for instance, attacked 'sociological' explanations: 'In no time, the sociologists will be picking among the debris of Handsworth for evidence of social protest. They will be eager to find signs of resentment over deprivation and unemployment' (*Sun*, 11.9.85).

Van Dijk's research is based on a discourse analysis of press coverage of ethnic affairs. In studying the press, discourse analysis involves an examination of the meaning, style and ideology found in particular newspaper reports. This can be illustrated by Van Dijk's interpretation of the following editorial on immigration from the *Daily Mail:*

'We have to be more brisk in saying no, and showing the door to those who are not British citizens and would abuse our hospitality and tolerance. To do this is not to give way to prejudice, but to lessen the provocation on which it feeds' (*Daily Mail*, 28.11.85).

This passage uses meanings and ideologies that are frequently found in right wing discourse on ethnic affairs. It presupposes that the British are hospitable and tolerant. Van Dijk points out that presuppositions are less easy to challenge than straightforward assertions - they often express an underlying ideology, in this case about the characteristics of the (white) British. This positive self-presentation is followed by a comment which implies that prejudice is due to immigrants abusing British tolerance - and the verb abuse can be seen as portraying ethnic minorities in a negative manner. Van Dijk suggests that words and phrases like 'brisk', 'show the door' and 'prejudice' could well be read as euphemisms for 'harsh', 'throwing out' and 'racism'.

This example illustrates Van Dijk's approach and reflects his main finding - a positive presentation of white British citizens and a negative presentation of non-white British and potential British citizens.
Van Dijk shows that the voice of the British press is overwhelmingly 'white'. Minority group members are quoted less often and less fully than majority group members - even when the topics directly concern them and even when minority 'experts' are available for comment. White authorities - especially the police and politicians - are the major speakers defining the ethnic situation. As a result, the press tend to marginalise ethnic minorities. Although the coverage of ethnic affairs has gradually become less blatantly racist, the definitions of minorities as a 'problem' or even a 'threat' continues - especially in the popular press. And the press helps to set the agenda for public discussion, an agenda that can limit how people think about ethnic affairs.

The problem in assessing the influence of the media portrayal of ethnic minorities on attitudes and behaviour is that people do not respond in a simple and straightforward way to what they see, hear or read. While recognising this difficulty, Howitt (1982) identifies two possible consequences of the generally unfavourable presentation of ethnic minorities in the media: 'The first is that the whites accept this negative view. The second is that the blacks accept it'. Thus media portrayal of ethnic minorities may both reinforce white prejudices and encourage blacks to accept those prejudices.

Much of the media portrayal of ethnic minorities is based on narrow and often unflattering stereotypes. While this sort of treatment does not necessarily increase racist attitudes, it does nothing to reduce them. And the possibility remains that it might reinforce existing racism and even create racist attitudes. (For further discussion of ethnicity and the media, see pp79-80).

Summary

1 Research indicates that media portrayal of women and ethnic minorities is based largely on negative stereotypes.

2 This portrayal probably reinforces these stereotypes.

Activity 12   Ethnicity and the Media

Item A   *The Sun*

The *Sun*, perhaps more than any other element of the mass media in this country, deals in simple, 'no nonsense' stereotypes. This approach is illustrated in the way it portrays ethnic minorities.

The *Sun's* position toward black people and its promotion of racism can be seen in its attitude to Africa and Africans. In its cartoons, Africans are typically shown holding spears, standing outside mud huts. African political leaders are shown with the whites of their eyes gleaming as they mingle with Western politicians.

To say that the *Sun* treats the culture of Asian and Islamic peoples with contempt would be putting the truth mildly. The 'Liars' was a huge headline on the front page of the *Sun* on 16 October 1986, on the occasion of the arrival of prospective immigrants from Bangladesh seeking to gain entry to join their families before the introduction of further immigration restrictions. The so-called '1001 lies' and 'whoppers' allegedly told to *Sun* journalists by the new arrivals were spread across the page, along with the use of words like 'flood', 'hordes' and 'swamped'.

A photograph of the Rastafarian poet, Benjamin Zephaniah, appeared illustrating a leader article in the *Sun* on 27 April 1987 alongside the headline: 'Would you let this man near your daughter?', recalling the ultimate question common in British racist folklore: 'Would you let a black man marry your daughter?' The editorial concerned the invitation by Trinity College Cambridge for Zephaniah to take up a fellowship there, and indignantly quotes some lines of his poetry unflattering to the Royal Family. 'Is this really the kind of man parents would wish to have teaching their sons and daughters?' asks the *Sun*, and continues, insulting his dreadlocks: 'from his picture Mr Zephaniah could do with a good shampoo and set'.

Adapted from C. Searle 'Your Daily Dose: Racism and the *Sun*' *Race and Class* 29:1, 1987, pp57-64

Item B   *Newspaper images*

'The number of migrants from stranger cultures must be controlled if the heritage is to be preserved, however difficult it might be'

In black and white, time for the truth

Item C   TV *news and current affairs*

Most worrying of all is news and current affairs. I watched, astonished, something called *Sixty Glorious Years* on ITV. It was a fairly feeble account of the Queen's career and achievements. But what angered and surprised me was its treatment of black Britons. This community was dismissed in a few derogatory sentences, which referred to racial tension, and the pictures used concentrated on shots of street riots. There was no evidence of the contribution made to this country by people working in transport, in the health service, the motor or textile industries. No mention was made of the majority of British blacks who live conventional lives, many with an old-fashioned devotion to Christian values and beliefs. And who would guess from the news, I wonder, that there are black nurses in the hospitals, black and Asian workers in the car factories, teachers, lawyers, technicians, business people and students within all the ethnic minority communities?

Adapted from B. Anderson 'How Television Depicts Blacks', *New Society*, 11.3.88, pp20-22

A black professional - an image rarely seen on the media

Questions

1 What sort of picture of ethnic minorities is provided by the examples in Item A?
2 What stereotypes and fears does Item B reflect?
3 Read Item C. Why are ethnic minorities portrayed in this way?

5 The Mass Media and Violence

Key Issues

1 Is there a link between media presentation of violence and violent behaviour?
2 What are the problems with research evidence on this question?

5.1 The mass media and violent behaviour

Does watching a lot of violence on television or in films or reading about violence in newspapers, magazines and books lead people to commit violent acts? The notion that there is a strong and clear link between popular entertainment and delinquency and violence has a history stretching back well into the last century. Comics, films, radio and, more recently, television and video have all been accused of being responsible for an increase in crime and violence, as well as being blamed for a host of other social problems.

 Before considering the arguments and research on this issue, one or two general comments are appropriate. Firstly, the world of today is probably no more violent than it was in the past - violence has been a constant theme in human history. However, it is through the mass media, and particularly television, that the horrors of violence and war can enter our homes soon after they happen and in very graphic forms. Secondly, there are difficulties in defining violence - the term can cover a wide range of different actions. Often it is the intensity or seriousness of a person's behaviour, the extent to which such behaviour is considered excessive or unrestrained, that is used as the basis for defining violence. Furthermore, behaviour defined as violent may be seen either as undesirable or as acceptable and even praiseworthy. In his analysis of television violence, Barrie Gunter makes the following points: 'Destructive and injurious behaviours such as murder for financial gain, school vandalism, juvenile gang assaults and football hooliganism, are generally disapproved in the strongest terms by most of society. Other pain-inducing behaviours though may be approved under particular circumstances or when used within certain degrees only, eg fighting and even killing in self-defence, physical violence in a prize-fight ring, a parent spanking a child for misbehaviour, or police using physical force to capture dangerous criminals or to control a riot. Thus, various kinds of injurious or "aggressive" behaviours differ in their severity, not simply in terms of the amount of pain and suffering they cause, but also in terms of what they are intended to achieve and in their legal and moral justification' (Gunter, 1985, p3).

Thus the first problem with researching the possible effects of media violence is the definition of violence. Once defined, the next problem is to operationalise the definition, ie put it into a form which can be measured. These problems can be seen from the following examples. Should sports such as boxing and wrestling be defined as violent? Should cartoons such as *Tom and Jerry* and *Roadrunner* be seen as violent? And how should the intensity of violence be measured? For example, how should the degree of violence of a murder in *The Bill* be compared with news footage of killings in the civil war in Bosnia?

5.2 Research evidence on the media's influence

There is no doubt that the media portrays a considerable amount of violence. For example, research indicates that the average American child will have witnessed 11,000 murders on television by the time he or she is fourteen. It has been argued that so much violence is bound to have some effect, even if it only produces a blasé attitude - 'nothing shocks us anymore'. However, this remains a supposition - research to date is inconclusive, it does not show a direct link between violence in the media and violent behaviour.

Laboratory experiments There have been many experiments, mainly laboratory based, that have focused on the extent to which people (especially children) copy or are influenced by the media. One well documented early experiment was Albert Bandura's 'Bobo doll study'. This involved children being shown one of three TV sequences. Each sequence involved an inflatable doll being subjected to violent attacks. In one, the person attacking the doll was rewarded, in another punished and in the third neither rewarded nor punished. After seeing one of the film clips the children were allowed to play with the doll. Bandura found that the children who had seen the attacker punished tended not to copy the TV sequence, whereas the other two groups of children tended to imitate the violence they had seen.

Another experiment in a similar vein conducted by Liebert and Baron is described in the following extract. 'This involved 136 boys and girls aged from five to nine. Half watched a violent TV sequence. The other half watched an exciting sports sequence. Then each child was taken to a room where there was a box with buttons marked HELP and HURT. They were told that in another room a child was

playing a game involving turning a wheel. Each time the game started, a light would come on. At that point the subject would either aid the other child by pressing the HELP button (which made the wheel easier to turn), or hinder him by pressing the HURT button (which made the wheel hot). In fact there was no child playing, and the HELP/HURT button had no effect. But the subjects did not know this. The results showed that the children who watched the violent TV sequence were significantly more likely to hurt another child than were those who watched the sports sequence' (*New Society,* 1.12.1983).

Many other studies have produced broadly similar results. Such experiments have, however, been criticised for being too artificial to be generalised to real life situations (the extracts in Activity 13 also highlight the artificiality of the experimental method).

Types of media violence A number of studies have emphasised the importance of distinguishing between different types of violence presented by the media. Gunter (1985), for example, attempted to assess how television viewers perceive and evaluate different kinds of violent portrayals. The type of programme was critical. In particular, as the fictional setting of violent episodes approached closer to everyday reality the violence was seen as more serious. Violence in fantasy settings, such as cartoons and science fiction, was perceived as essentially non-threatening and non-disturbing. However, perceiving some programmes as more violent than others does not necessarily mean that watching such programmes causes violent behaviour.

William Belson In a detailed study that has attracted a good deal of attention and criticism, William Belson (1978) attempted to measure the effects of long term exposure to television violence on adolescent boys in London. First he tried to eliminate other possible causes of violent behaviour by matching the boys in his sample with a wide variety of factors which might lead to an increase in violent behaviour. He then compared groups that were alike apart from one single factor or characteristic. In order to check his findings he obtained information from the boys at different times and under different conditions - for example, they were interviewed both at home with their parents and individually away from their homes. Belson's overall finding was that high exposure to television violence increases the degree to which boys engage in serious violence. In particular, he found that certain types of violence appear to be more powerful in releasing violent behaviour from adolescent boys. These 'types of violence' included plays or films in which violence occurred in the context of close personal relations; programmes in which violence was not necessary to the plot but 'thrown in for the sake of it'; and programmes where violence was seen to be in a 'good cause', such as police programmes. By contrast, Belson found little evidence that the following had any effect - violence in sporting programmes, violent cartoons, science fiction violence and slapstick comedy involving violence or verbal abuse.

Belson's study and findings have been strongly criticised. There are inconsistencies in his results which are not explained. As well as showing that there is a link between violent acts and watching a lot of television violence, his findings show a correlation between violent acts and television viewing in general. Also, the relationship between watching violence on television and behaving violently reaches a peak and then declines - it is those who watch a moderate amount of violence on TV who were found to be most violent in their behaviour. Such a finding suggests that the more violence that is watched the less likely is violent behaviour! Belson's research methods have also been questioned. The boys were asked how many times they remembered seeing particular

programmes over a number of years - such questioning relies heavily on memory and, in this case, on recalling events when the boys were only a few years old. Similarly, the data on the violent acts committed by the boys was based on self-reporting - again raising the problem of bad memory and also the possibility of exaggeration.

Research on the influence of the mass media on violent behaviour indicates that we know relatively little about the social effects of the media. Despite this uncertainty, many 'experts' claim that violence on TV does lead to an increase in aggressive behaviour by children and adolescents who watch such programmes. Obviously, there are many other, and probably greater influences on behaviour. However, the media, and TV and video in particular, have a visibility which is easier to 'blame' than less visible factors such as lack of parental affection. To some extent, the media provides a convenient scapegoat for social problems. It can be blamed for screening violence in the home and for translating that violence into behaviour. This can be seen from Activity 14.

Activity 13 Inconclusive Evidence

Item A

'Victor' comic, 14.3.87

Item B   *Copycat violence*

There are difficulties in dealing judicially with the 'copycat' syndrome, ie the acting-out in real life of a crime seen on stage or screen. An example is Ronnie Zamorra, a 15 year old TV addict whose parents are suing all three major US networks for $12,500,000. Ronnie, who is serving a life sentence for shooting and killing a neighbour, is claimed by his lawyer to be unable to tell real life from the TV programmes to which he is devoted. Legal actions over 'copycat' crimes have not yet occurred in England, but they may. The difficulty is, of course, in proving that a particular film or TV show produced a particular effect in a particular person. It is not enough to show that there is general evidence for a causal connection between TV violence and acting-out of violence in viewers.

Adapted from H. J. Eysenck and D. K. B. Nias *Sex, Violence and the Media*, 1980, p36

Item C   *Lack of agreement*

There may be little doubt in Fleet Street or among senior clerics as to the social effects of viewing violent films, but the most obvious feature which strikes anyone examining the available social scientific evidence is that there is precious little agreement among the experts.

Dr Barry Gunter of the IBA had this to say, 'My own feeling is that much of the research, although it points in one direction, should not be taken at face value, simply because many of the experiments that have been carried out are so artificial in the way they've measured aggression and in the way they've measured viewing that I think one cannot generalise from those experiments. They have all used the same kind of procedures and they've all been flawed in the same way.' And the fact that something happens in a laboratory does not mean it will happen outside its doors.

Professor Tom Cook felt that the relationship between exposure to TV violence and aggressive behaviour was small. He added, 'The fact is that television violence by itself is not going to make any child aggressive'. He went on to list a number of other influences - parental rejection of the child, low intellectual ability, lower socio-economic status, and so on.

Any researcher worth his salt knows that there are many other, probably more profound, influences than television causing violent and aggressive behaviour. Television and video, however, have a visibility and attract research funds. A vacuum of love, or social deprivation or whatever, remains invisible or inconvenient to consider and therefore does not attract research grants.

Adapted from M. Tracey 'Television Affects Everything We Do, Everything We Think', *The Listener*, 19.1.84, pp2-4

Questions

1 Look at Item A. Are such presentations likely to encourage violent behaviour in young people? Give reasons for your answer.
2 Read Item B. Do you think the boy's parents were justified in suing the TV companies? Explain your answer.
3 Read Item C.
   a) Why are laboratory experiments often described as 'artificial'?
   b) Why is so much attention given to violence on television and video compared to other media?

Summary

1 There is no conclusive evidence that the presentation of violence in the mass media directly causes violent behaviour. Any effect the media has is likely to be indirect and to work in conjunction with other influences on behaviour such as the family, the school and friends.

2 Laboratory experiments into the media's effects have indicated a relationship between watching violent film sequences and behaving aggressively and violently. Such experiments have, however, been criticised for artificiality - they are a long way from the 'real world'.

3 It is easy to blame the media for violence in society. Maybe, as James Halloran suggests, 'We must get away from thinking in terms of what TV does to people and substitute for it the idea of what people do with TV' (1964,p20).

Activity 14 Moral Panic

Item A   *'Child's Play'*

In November 1993, two 11 year old boys from Merseyside were found guilty of murdering a two year old child. The 'horror' video, *Child's Play 3* had been rented by the father of one of the boys shortly before the murder. There were certain similarities between scenes in the video and the killing of the child. But there was no evidence that either boy had seen the video. Despite this the judge at the trial stated, 'I suspect that exposure to violent video films may in part be an explanation'.

Adapted from *Guardian*, 26.11.93

Item B *The police view*

Merseyside police detectives who had interviewed the boys for several weeks before the trial rejected any suggestions that 'horror' videos had influenced the boys' behaviour. One detective said, 'I don't know where the judge got that idea from. I couldn't believe it when I heard him. We went through something like 200 titles rented by the family. There were some you or I wouldn't want to see, but nothing - no scene, or plot, or dialogue - where you could put your finger on the freeze button and say that influenced a boy to go out and commit murder.'

Quoted in *Independent*, 26.11.93, p1

Item C *Reaction in Parliament*

In the Commons, the Conservative MP Sir Ivan Lawrence QC called for action to curb 'the constant diet of violence and depravity' fed to youngsters through television, videos and computer pornography. Sir Ivan, chairman of the Home Affairs Select Committee, said it was becoming 'daily more obvious' that this was a major reason for the rise in juvenile crime.

Quoted in *Independent*, 26.11.93, p1

Item D *Burning videos*

Azad Video, Scotland's largest video renting chain, burned its *Child's Play* videos including 300 copies of *Child's Play 3*. Xtra-Vision, the Irish Republic's biggest video chain withdrew *Child's Play* from its shelves.

Adapted from *Sun*, 26.11.93, pp1 and 11

Item F *Press editorials,*
26.11.93

The uncanny resemblance between the film *Child's Play 3* and the murder must be of concern. A link between the film and the crime would not prove that the former caused the latter. Yet it seems quite possible that exposure to images of brutality could turn an already disturbed child towards violence.

(Independent)

More and more children are growing up in a moral vacuum, which for so many is being filled with fetid junk from the lower depths of our popular culture - video nasties, crude comics and violent television.

(Daily Express)

Instead of urging legislation to ban violent films, it would surely be more to the point if we took it upon ourselves as adults to ensure their prohibition in our own homes.

(Daily Telegraph)

Item E *The 'Sun's' reaction*

Sun, 26.11.93, p1

Item G *Moral panics*

At the turn of the century, there was great concern about violent images in Penny Dreadful comics. In the 1950s, panic that horror comics would lead to children copying the things they saw, led to the Children and Young Persons (Harmful Publications) Act 1959. Ten years ago, there was the huge panic about films such as *Drillerkiller*, which also led to a new law. There's been a recurrent moral panic about violent images which looks to a mythical golden age of tranquil behaviour.

T. Newburn, Policy Studies Institute, quoted in *Guardian*, 26.11.93

Questions

1 Read Items A, B and C. What justification is there for the views of the judge and Ivan Lawrence? Why do you think they reacted in this way?

2 Read Items D to G. Do you think the reactions in Items A, C, D, E and F can be described as a moral panic? Give reasons for your answer.

References

Anderson, B. 'How Television Depicts Blacks' *New Society*, 11.3.1988

Belson, W. A. *Television Violence and the Adolescent Boy* (Saxon House, Farnborough, 1978)

Benyon, J. 'General Election 1987' *Social Studies Review*, November 1987

Bourne, R. 'Why the Media are Conservative' *New Society*, 16.10.1980

Crewe, I. 'Why Did Labour Lose (Yet Again)?' *Politics Review*, September 1992

Curran, J. and Seaton, J. *Power Without Responsibility: The Press and Broadcasting in Britain* (Fontana, London, 1981)

Durkin, K. and Akhtar, P. 'Television, Sex Roles and Children' *New Society*, 7.4.1983

Dutton, B. *The Media* (Longman, London, 1986)

Eldridge, J. 'News, Truth and Power' in J. Eldridge (ed) *Getting the Message: News, Truth and Power* (Routledge, London, 1993)

Eysenck, H. J. and Nias, D.K.B. *Sex, Violence and the Media* (Paladin, London, 1980)

Franklin, B. 'Packaging Politics: Politicians and the Media' in M.Haralambos (ed) *Developments in Sociology* vol 9 (Causeway Press, Ormskirk, 1993)

Glasgow University Media Group *Bad News* (Routledge & Kegan Paul, London, 1976)

Glasgow University Media Group *More Bad News* (Routledge & Kegan Paul, London, 1980)

Glasgow University Media Group *Really Bad News* (Writers & Readers, London, 1982)

Glasgow University Media Group *War and Peace News* (Open University Press, Milton Keynes, 1985)

Glover, D. *The Sociology of the Mass Media* (Causeway Press, Ormskirk, 1984)

Gunter, B. *Dimensions of Television Violence* (Gower, Aldershot, 1985)

Grant, M. *The British Media* (Comedia, London, 1984)

Hall, S., Critcher, C., Jefferson, T., Clarke, J. and Roberts, B. *Policing the Crisis* (Macmillan, London, 1979)

Halloran, J. D. *The Effects of Mass Communication* (Leicester University Press, Leicester, 1964)

Hartmann, P. and Husband, C. *Racism and the Mass Media* (Davis Poynter, London, 1974)

Howitt, D. *The Mass Media and Social Problems* (Pergamon, Oxford, 1982)

Hunt, S. 'State Secrecy in the UK' *Politics Review* vol 1 no 4, April 1992

Katz, E. and Lazarsfeld, P. *Personal Influence* (The Free Press, New York, 1955)

Meacher, M. 'Jenkins, Heath and Healey are the Good Guys' *Listener*, 19.7.1982

Miliband, R. *The State in Capitalist Society* (Penguin Books, Harmondsworth, 1973)

Newton, K. 'Making News: The Mass Media in Britain' *Social Studies Review*, September 1990

Peak, S. (ed) *The Media Guide 1994* (Fourth Estate, London, 1993)

Philo, G. 'There is no Alternative' *New Statesman and Society*, 13.11.1992

Philo, G. 'Getting the Message: Audience Research in the Glasgow University Media Group' in J.Eldridge (ed) *Getting the Message: News, Truth and Power* (Routledge, London, 1993)

Philo, G. 'From Buerk to Band Aid: The Media and the 1984 Ethiopian Famine' in J.Eldridge (ed) *Getting the Message: News, Truth and Power* (Routledge, London, 1993)

Pilger, J. 'The Brave New Media World' *New Statesman and Society*, 11.6.1993

Rock, P. 'News as Eternal Recurrence' in S.Cohen and J.Young (eds) *The Manufacture of News: Social Problems, Deviance and the Mass Media* (Constable, London, 1981)

Schlessinger, P. *Putting 'Reality' Together* 2nd edition (Methuen, London, 1987)

Searle, C. 'Your Daily Dose: Racism and the Sun' *Race and Class* vol 29 no 1, 1987

Seymour-Ure, C. *The British Press and Broadcasting Since 1945* (Blackwell, Oxford,1991)

Seymour-Ure, C. 'The Media Under Major' *Politics Review*, February 1993

Strinati, D. 'Postmodernism and Popular Culture' *Sociology Review*, April 1992

Tracey, M. 'Television Affects Everything We Do, Everything We Think' *Listener*, 19.1.1984

Tunstall, J. *The Media in Britain* (Constable, London, 1983)

Van Dijk, T. *Racism and the Press* (Routledge, London, 1991)

Wagg, S. 'Mass Communications: The Debate About Ownership and Control' *Social Studies Review*, March 1987

Wagg, S. 'Politics and the Popular Press' *Social Studies Review*, September 1989

Whale, J. *The Politics of the Media* (Fontana, London, 1977)

16 Development

Introduction

The sociology of development is concerned with the countries of the so-called 'Third World', that is, with most of the countries of Africa, Asia and Latin America. Because these countries are part of a wider world, the sociology of development is also concerned with the relationships between this Third World and the First and Second Worlds. (The 'First World' refers to the capitalist or mixed-economy countries of the West. In practice, the term 'Second World' has seldom been used, but refers to the countries of Central and Eastern Europe which, until the late 1980s/early 90s, were officially communist or socialist). Development is unlike any other area in sociology. Its scope is massive, for it sets out to be nothing less than 'the sociology of most of the world' (A. Foster-Carter, 1993, p29).

Chapter summary

- This chapter starts by considering what is meant by terms such as **Third World** and **development**.
- It then looks at the connections between '**developed**' and '**underdeveloped**' societies and the **theories** claiming to explain the different levels of development of different societies.

- The next sections consider the causes and consequences of **demographic changes**, in both developed and underdeveloped societies, and the processes of **urbanisation** and **industrialisation** in relation to development.
- Finally, **health** is examined in the context of development.

1 One World, Divided

Key Issues

1 How do rich and poor countries differ?
2 What is meant by the term 'development'?
3 How may the world's richer and poorer countries be described?

1.1 Rich and poor countries

Although there is no simple, satisfactory definition of 'rich' and 'poor', the differences in wealth and income between countries are often dramatic. Approximately 75% of the current world population live in the world's poorer countries. Yet these countries together have only about 17% of the world's wealth. They own less than 10% of its manufacturing industry, and control less than 20% of world trade and investment.

In general, they share certain characteristics. They are likely, for instance, to suffer relatively high rates of mortality and illiteracy and have low levels of full time, paid employment. They are also likely to be heavily dependent on producing a few primary commodities (eg foods, raw materials), which makes them very vulnerable to falls in the price paid for those commodities.

However, a very important caution should be emphasised from the outset. Although poor countries are often bracketed together, (in terms such as 'Third World'), and discussed as if they were homogeneous, they are of course highly diverse. And even within any one country, there is often considerable cultural and ethnic diversity. So any generalisation about the 'Third World' must be treated with extreme caution. Indeed, many now feel that any term, such as Third World, which brackets the world's poorer nations, has outlived any usefulness it may once have had.

1.2 The controversial notion of 'development'

Although the term 'development' gained popularity in the 1940s, its use has become increasingly controversial as people wonder whether it is any longer appropriate or valid (if it ever was) as a description of what has been happening to Third World societies.

The most common use of development identifies it with economic growth, usually measured in terms of per capita (per head) Gross National Product (GNP). There are, however, a number of objections to such a narrow usage.

Perhaps most importantly, talking of development in terms of economic growth looks increasingly problematical because in many parts of the world it just isn't happening. Indeed, even in the world's richest countries, the early 1990s witnessed widespread 'negative growth'. And many poor countries are getting poorer.

However, if development is used more broadly to mean social and political development, it often implies that development is a positive process, a good thing. And there are also problems with this.

Firstly, even where economic growth has occurred it may not lead to social development. Increases in a country's wealth do not inevitably lead to better health, more employment, greater literacy, democracy and a greater ability to take control of one's life. Indeed, according to Foster-Carter, the

problem goes deeper. 'In the real world of development, where desired goals are many but resources all too few', gains or improvements in one respect - economic, or social, political or cultural - must sometimes lead to losses in another (1993, p38). There must be 'trade-offs'. Gains brought by industrialisation, for instance, such as increased life expectancy and broader personal horizons, are likely to be accompanied by various social, psychological or environmental losses such as pollution or the decline of gemeinschaft and the growth of alienation and anomie. How people evaluate the trade-offs will differ. But the positive sounding word 'development' seems too simple to reflect the complexity of gains and losses that such changes involve.

Secondly - a point made forcibly by the Greens - even assuming future economic growth, there are serious doubts that it is desirable or sustainable.

And thirdly, just as wealth does not necessarily equal wellbeing, being poor is not necessarily being miserable.

Activity 1   Poor Countries and Development

Item A *Gross National Product (GNP)*

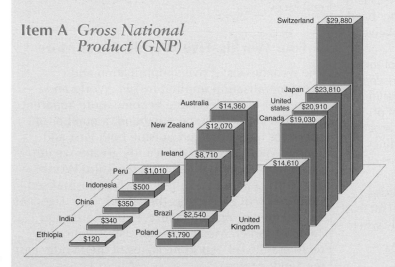

Adapted from *New Internationalist*, June 1992, p18

Item B *Views of poverty*

There's poverty and poverty. The West's stereotyped talk of 'poverty' fails to distinguish between frugality and scarcity. Frugality (implying carefulness) is a mark of cultures free from the frenzy of accumulation. To our eyes, people have rather meagre possessions, with money playing only a marginal role. Yet everyone usually has access to fields, rivers and woods, while kinship and community duties guarantee services which elsewhere must be paid for in cash. Along with community ties, land, forest and water are the most important prerequisites for subsistence without money. Nobody goes hungry. Here is a way of life which recognises and cultivates a state of sufficiency.

Scarcity derives from modernised poverty. It affects mostly urban groups caught up in the money economy as workers and consumers whose spending power is so low that they fall by the wayside. Their capacity to achieve through their own efforts gradually fades, while at the same time their desires, fuelled by glimpses of high society, spiral towards infinity.

Adapted from W. Sachs 'Development: a Guide to the Ruins', *New Internationalist*, June 1992, p9

Item C *Child mortality*

Under five mortality rate per 1,000 live births in 1990
(Selected countries ranging from the best through to the worst in the world)

Country	Rate
Japan	6
Canada	9
UK	9
Australia	10
United States	11
Aotearoa/NZ	12
Cuba	14
China	42
Brazil	83
Indonesia	97
India	142
Angola	292
Afghanistan	292
Mozambique	297

Adapted from *New Internationalist*, June 1992, p19

Questions

1 a) Compare the relative positions of China and India in Items A and C. How would you explain the difference?

   b) How might this be used to argue that child mortality may be a better indicator of quality of life than GNP?

2 Read Item B. Why may it be misleading to apply Western notions of poverty to Third World countries?

1.3 How many 'Worlds'?: problems of terminology

1 North and South

There is a broad pattern to the geographical distribution of the world's richer and poorer nations. In general, countries in the North are richer than those in the South. Strictly speaking, all of Central America, two thirds of Africa and almost all of Asia lie north of the Equator. However, if you think of the North as the more northerly countries, the 'rich' North and the 'poor' South divide works quite well.

Even so, Australia and New Zealand are, of course, notable exceptions: both are wealthy countries located geographically in the South, but, because of their wealth (and European-type cultures), are usually referred to as if part of the North. On the other hand, the supposedly rich North includes such a relatively poor country as Albania.

Despite these inconsistencies, the authors of the so-called 'Brandt Report' (1980), which popularised the terms North and South, regarded them as a justifiable shorthand. Not only is the global distribution of wealth, poverty and decision-making power broadly patterned geographically along North-South lines, but, as the Report acknowledges: 'The nations of the South see themselves as sharing a common predicament' (pp 31-2). Many of these countries shared the experience of colonialism and feel (at least sometimes) a conscious solidarity, particularly when participating in global negotiations.

2 First World, Second and Third

Since the 1980s, the terms North-South have become widely used for their convenience. Prior to that, however, many people preferred to acknowledge the North's division from the end of World War Two into two mutually hostile 'power blocks', and referred instead to three 'worlds'. In this usage, the so-called 'First World' referred to the capitalist, market economy nations of Western Europe, North America, Australasia and Japan, and the 'Second World' to the centrally-directed economies of the socialist/communist nations of Eastern Europe. The 'Third World' was then a residual term to refer to the world's poorer countries.

This Three World model not only had the virtue of distinguishing between economic and political systems in the North whose rivalries led to the massive armaments expenditures and security risks of the 'Cold War'. But also, as the Brandt Report pointed out, East Europeans did not share the West's responsibility for colonising the South. Consequently, they did not wish to be 'lumped together' with the West.

The collapse of communism throughout Eastern and Central Europe from 1989 and the attempts to introduce free market economies, have raised large doubts about whether it is any longer useful to distinguish between a First and Second World and if so how they now differ. Nevertheless, the term Third World remains in use (as it is throughout this chapter) despite the enormous diversity of countries it embraces.

3 Four Worlds, Five Worlds, Six or More

The weaknesses of oversimplification and overgeneralisation implicit in Two World and Three World models have become more apparent since the 1970s. On the one hand, a number of countries have emerged outside both First and Second Worlds with significantly greater wealth than normally associated with the Third World. These include the so-called Newly Industrialised Countries (NICs), such as the famed 'Four Tigers of Asia' (Hong Kong, Singapore, South Korea and Taiwan), Israel, Mexico and Brazil. Additionally, there are the oil exporting states of the Middle East (eg Saudi Arabia).

On the other hand, among the world's poor countries, a distinction can be made between the relatively poor (eg many Latin American countries) and the very poor (eg Ethiopia, Sudan, Bangladesh), whose plight continues to deteriorate alarmingly. And the Asian giants, China and India, do not easily fit into any global categorisation.

In practice, however, most writers - including myself - continue to use convenient, if seriously simplistic, Two World or Three World models. That such diverse nations are still grouped together reflects both their often shared histories of colonialism and their continuing sense of dependence upon - and political, economic and military inequality with - the richer countries.

Activity 2 Worlds Apart

Item A *The world's major 'poverty belts'*

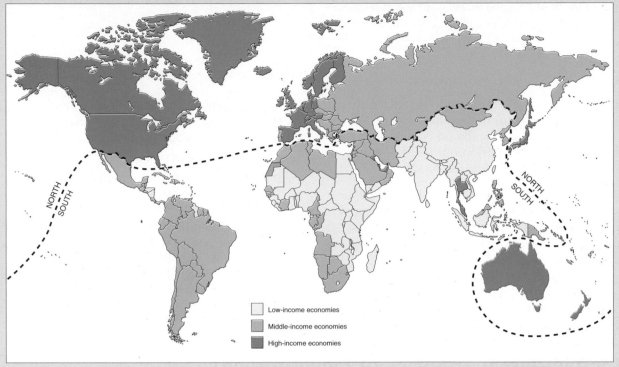

Based on a map in The World Bank *World Development Report 1994*, pp158-159

Item B *What we eat*

Lowest calorie intake per day, 1983			
	Country	Calorie intake (per head per day)	% of requirement
1.	Ghana	1,573	68
2.	Chad	1,620	68
3.	Mali	1,731	74
4.	Kampuchea	1,792	81
5.	Uganda	1,807	78
6.	Mozambique	1,844	79
7.	Burkina Faso	1,879	79
8.	Haiti	1,903	84
9.	Bangladesh	1,922	83
10.	Guinea	1,987	86
11.	Laos	1,992	90
12.	Vietnam	2,017	93
13.	Nepal	2,018	86
14.	Angola	2,041	87
15.	India	2,047	93
16.	Sierra Leone	2,049	85
17.	Zambia	2,054	89
18.	Kenya	2,056	88
19.	El Salvador	2,060	90
20.	Ecuador	2,072	91
30.	Ethiopia	2,162	93
39.	Sudan	2,250	96
60.	China	2,562	109

Highest calorie intake per day, 1983			
	Country	Calorie intake (per head per day)	% of requirement
1.	Ireland	4,054	162
2.	Denmark	4,023	150
3.	East Germany	3,787	145
4.	Belgium	3,743	142
5.	Bulgaria	3,711	148
6.	Yugoslavia	3,642	143
7.	USA	3,616	137
8.	Czechoslovakia	3,613	146
9.	UA Emirates	3,591	n.a.
10.	Libya	3,581	152
11.	France	3,572	142
12.	Holland	3,563	133
13.	Greece	3,554	142
14.	New Zealand	3,549	134
15.	Austria	3,524	134
16.	Italy	3,520	140
17.	Hungary	3,520	134
18.	Switzerland	3,451	128
19.	Canada	3,428	129
20.	Kuwait	3,423	n.a.
27.	UK	3,232	128
30.	Australia	3,189	120

Adapted from The World Bank, *World Development Report 1985* in *New Internationalist*, September 1985, pp10-11

Questions

1 With reference to Items A and B, try to justify using the following terms to classify countries:
   a) North-South and
   b) First World, Second World and Third World.
2 What are the problems with these classifications?

Summary

1 Despite a general increase in manufacturing, many poorer countries remain heavily dependent economically on commodity sales. Compared to wealthy countries, they suffer lower levels of literacy and health.

2 The concept of 'development' is problematic because it suggests economic, technological and even social 'progress'. But a) in many parts of the world, this just isn't happening; indeed, many countries have been getting poorer; b) economic growth may not translate into social development. Indeed, gains in one area may result in losses in another; c) given that economic growth carries social and environmental costs, there are doubts whether growth is desirable or sustainable.

3 The world's countries are often categorised according to models which identify Two, Three, Four, Five (or more) Worlds. All such models inevitably involve oversimplification and overgeneralisation of similarities and differences between unique countries. Nevertheless, the term 'Third World' is still commonly used, despite the collapse of communism in Eastern and Central Europe from the late 1980s.

2 Sociological Theories of Development

Key Issues

1 Why are some societies more 'developed' than others?
2 Is development occurring in the Third World? Can all countries develop?
3 Why do some advocate 'alternative technologies' to those pioneered by the West?

2.1 Optimists, pessimists and sceptics

The various theories discussed in this part are grouped into two broad categories. Dividing them this way increases the risk of oversimplification. However, it should allow an early indication of the main issues of the debate.

Broadly, the first group regard 'development' positively and are optimistic that it is occurring worldwide (though more evidently in some countries than in others). *Modernisation theory* is of this type.

Against this view are those who argue that, while some countries (eg the West) have clearly become more technologically advanced and wealthier, such development has been at the expense of other countries. Consequently, while some continue to develop, the position and prospects of many others continue to worsen. *Underdevelopment theory* exemplifies this perspective.

Many are sceptical of development as conventionally defined (ie primarily in economic terms) and question whether it can ever become a universal phenomenon, particularly in view of its apparent costs for the environment. *Neo-populists* and the politically Green raise such challenges to the optimism of modernisation theory.

2.2 Modernisation theory

In many respects, modernisation theory is an updating of 19th century social evolutionism, whose proponents, such as Comte, Spencer, Tonnies and Durkheim, believed that human societies evolve in the same direction over time through a sequence of stages. Though they differed in how they conceived of the stages, they shared the belief that the more 'advanced' societies had evolved from simpler societal types and that the latter would evolve along similar lines.

Modernisation theory emerged in the United States in the late 1940s and early 1950s. Despite acute American concerns about the threats posed by the newly enlarged communist block in the East, optimism and a confidence in internationalism were flourishing. International cooperation had already resulted in the founding of the United Nations and had achieved considerable success (through the UN Relief and Rehabilitation Association, and the Marshall Plan which offered large US grants) in reconstructing postwar Europe.

Like 19th century evolutionists, modernisation theorists regarded Western societies as further along a recognisable route which others, in time, would also follow. To achieve their goal, Third World countries would have to industrialise and modernise. Industrialisation was seen as an essentially liberalising and progressive force, giving individuals and societies political and economic power and freedom of choice. Such benefits more than compensate, they believed, for the conflicts and pains which are inevitably experienced by societies as they shift from being mainly agrarian (agricultural) to industrial. And the wealth thus created would ultimately 'trickle down' to the benefit of all.

In general, modernisation theorists have assumed that technological innovations will be developed in modern, industrial societies and then introduced into Third World societies. Developed countries (DCs) invent and then export them. Unlike their social evolutionary predecessors, therefore, they acknowledge that important changes may originate abroad.

Nevertheless, their focus of attention remained, and remains, primarily on factors which are internal to specific societies. What is it, they ask, about the cultures and social structures of undeveloped or less developed societies which has discouraged progress? And what is it about the West which has encouraged it? What, in short, needs changing in Third World societies?

W.W. Rostow: industrialisation and modernisation

In the main, modernisation theorists identified the need for both economic, and cultural and political changes; the twin goals of industrialisation and 'modernisation'. Culturally, Third World populations need to acquire key 'modern' values, attitudes and practices of the sort that Calvinism encouraged in the West. Indeed, the best known modernisation theorist, the American economic historian W.W. Rostow, proposed that a formerly traditional society could only achieve the critical stage of economic 'take-off' - at which level of industrialisation and economic development it is able to sustain economic growth - after many years of cultural change, in which the necessary cultural preconditions are gradually met.

For economic take-off to be achieved, an education system must have been developed to educate and train the workforce. The population must have largely accepted the idea of economic and other

progress, and the discipline of paid employment: the need for punctuality, regular hours and attendance. They must have learnt to value achievement, individual enterprise and profit. They must have learnt to save money and invest it in businesses. Banks must have been established, as must some modern manufacturing enterprises. Many of the people must also have come to accept high levels of geographical and social mobility and have become more urban. Very importantly, a modern nation state must have emerged, buttressed by sufficient nationalistic sentiments to bind together the inevitably diverse elements of the population. No less interesting are Rostow's conclusions about the final, most advanced stage of development (to date) - 'the age of high mass-consumption' - a stage supposedly achieved in Western Europe and Japan in the 1950s and in the USA somewhat earlier. Rostow sees it as characterised by high levels of consumption of consumer durables (the most significant of which has probably been the cheap mass automobile), but also of comprehensive welfare and health state services (reflecting the wealth of the society and its members' concern for their health and security). The population are highly urban and increasingly employed in skilled manual or service occupations. As his critics have pointed out, when Rostow was writing this the most obvious example of a society in 'the age of high mass consumption' was the USA. And his model of the desirable society at which Third World countries should aim was a barely disguised version of his own country. Like the 19th century social evolutionists, he appears ethnocentric, equating his own society with unquestioned superiority.

2.3 The New Right

During the 1980s, liberal, free market economics gained influence with politicians and governments throughout much of the western world. Indeed, propounded by Mrs Thatcher in Britain and President Reagan in the USA, New Right economics even spread in the late 1980s to Second World countries, such as Poland and the Baltic States, who found themselves suddenly trying to shake off a 'communism' which had been the dominating ideology since the Second World War.

Not surprisingly, in the 1980s, New Right analyses of development were also highly prominent. In many respects, such analyses represented a radical version of modernisation theory. Like modernisation theorists, the New Right claimed that countries fail to develop largely as a result of internal factors, though the New Right blame government interference rather than cultural factors such as the population's traditional and conservative attitudes. In this view, any country can make progress by opening up to the world economy and leaving everything to market forces.

Like Margaret Thatcher and Ronald Reagan, New Right theorists claimed that governments invariably seek to play too large a role in economic and social affairs. In much of Africa, they argued, government intervention had often proved disastrous. And the 1989 revolutions in Eastern Europe demonstrated, they said, the inevitable failures of state-planned economic development.

Governments should not 'interfere' beyond the necessary minimum in economic and social affairs - beyond perhaps providing some infrastructure and ensuring the safeguarding of individual contracts. Otherwise, as wide a range of activities as possible should be opened up to market forces (and hence as far as possible subsidies should be abolished). These steps would then encourage innovation, entrepreneurship and internal and international investment - and would ultimately deliver growth.

Also, for many of the New Right, such as Peter Berger, Third World acceptance of the ideology of free markets and political non-intervention would also foster political pluralism; a crucial precondition, they believed, of political democracy. Political pluralism and democracy would emerge as a consequence of the ideology of individualism which capitalism necessarily entails.

2.4 Classical Marxism: Marxist modernisation theories

Although many Marxist writers have been highly critical of modernisation theory, by the 1980s some Marxists had already published analyses which appeared strikingly similar to - and were at least consistent with - much of modernisation theory. In general, these Marxists differed from evolutionary modernisation theorists in emphasising the often sharp and revolutionary nature of change. And they stressed that, in the Third World, sudden change had often been imposed from outside, under various types of colonialism. Nevertheless, they typically regarded the development of capitalism in Third World societies as 'progress' (albeit towards socialism) and were inclined to argue that what most Third World countries needed was more capitalist development, not less.

In all these respects Marxist theorists have a lot in common with evolutionists such as Rostow. And they can point to Marx's famous quote, with which any evolutionist could have agreed: 'the country that is more developed industrially only shows, to the less developed, the image of its own future' (1954, p19).

Bill Warren

Among those claiming to follow Marx in viewing

capitalism as essentially dynamic and preferable to what it replaced, Bill Warren has been prominent in arguing that capitalism's influence on Third World countries has been largely beneficial. In his view, capitalism destroys the structures and ideas which otherwise prevent societies from developing. Moreover, it does not merely benefit the capitalist West, for it has allowed many Third World countries to develop their own 'indigenous ("home grown") capitalisms'. While these indigenous capitalisms were largely made possible by the transfer of capital and technology from the West, Warren maintains that they do allow less developed countries a growing independence from the capitalist centres. For they can take advantage of the periodic structural crises of the centres by 'playing them off' against each other. Over time, Warren argues, the domination and control of the capitalist centres over their peripheries is gradually withering away and Western capitalist imperialism declines.

Nigel Harris

Another Marxist theorist claiming a positive role for capitalism in the Third World is Nigel Harris. Harris believes that the spread of manufacturing capacity in Third World countries is a beneficial and encouraging development, both for those countries and for the world. However, not all the world's countries can participate in the global accumulation of wealth which is occurring, and the poorer countries - many in Africa and heavily dependent on agriculture - are the most vulnerable. These, he argues, will continue to need considerable help from abroad. Otherwise, however, he is encouraged by the trends he perceives: the globalisation of manufacturing and trade and the growing interdependence of nations hold out real prospects of hope for many countries of the Third World.

2.5 Underdevelopment theory

From about the early 1950s - at much the same time as modernisation theory was beginning to emerge in the United States - the first stirrings of a rival perspective were being heard from Latin America and elsewhere. Underdevelopment theory, known in its early version as dependency theory, broke with both the modernisation and classical Marxist theorists. And it did so using a neo-Marxist perspective.

Underdevelopment theory's key claim is that, from the West's early contacts with today's poorer countries in the 16th century, the West has actively exploited and underdeveloped them. Though they were often economically wealthy and culturally complex when they first had contact with the West, for centuries they have been pushed back, exploited, distorted, damaged, perhaps ruined. And Western

Activity 3 Modernisation

Item A A disciplined workforce

Factory workers in the Philippines

A poster from India

Item B Tradition

Custom, religious attitudes and lack of education often limit the farmer's horizon and make him reluctant to change established methods. Thus, attempts to improve livestock kept by the Masai in East Africa have foundered because they and many other African pastoralists keep cattle for the prestige which accrues to sheer numbers; any improvement must adjust cattle numbers to the grazing resources available. The Masai are reluctant to cull their animals so the overgrazing, soil erosion and further reduction of grazing resources continue.

Adapted from D. Grigg 'The Rural Revolution' in
A. B. Mountjoy (ed) 1971, pp57,58,60

Item C The Four Little Tigers

It was the accidental good fortune of the Four Little Tigers of East and South East Asia to stumble upon an alternative development strategy. Hong Kong, Singapore, South Korea and Taiwan expanded by exporting, not raw materials, but manufactured goods, precisely the goods where the rich countries were supposedly at their strongest.

Now, contrary to the conventional wisdom, over half the exports of the Third World are manufactured goods, not raw materials, and the share is expanding swiftly. Nor are these just cheap, labour-intensive goods. South Korea has come from nowhere to become the second largest shipbuilder in the world and is now set to become a major exporter of cars. Malaysia exported its first 10,000 Proton cars to Europe last year. Brazil exports aircraft, China satellites and India computer software.

Adapted from N. Harris 'Halfway to Liberation', *New Internationalist*, February 1990, pp18-19

Questions

1 With reference to Items A and B, explain the role of values and attitudes in encouraging or discouraging modernisation.

2 Read Item C.
   a) What was the 'alternative development strategy' which seems to have allowed the 'Four Tigers' to establish indigenous capitalisms?
   b) How could a Marxist use the developments described here to support a Marxist analysis?

imperial powers were able to finance their industrial revolutions and build their ascendancy by impoverishing and underdeveloping their colonies - the countries of today's Third World.

From this view the 'success' or 'failure' of societies to develop cannot be explained in terms of intrinsic factors - such as the alleged attitudes and psychology of their inhabitants. Societies are not isolated, self contained systems, and understanding the historical links between First and Third World societies is crucial to understanding why some societies seem to have been so much more successful than others.

Underdevelopment theory therefore challenged the central assumption of modernisation theory and classical Marxism: that societies everywhere are engaged in a more or less inevitable process of capitalist modernisation and economic and social progress. In the view of underdevelopment theorists, it is wrong to see less developed societies as simply behind the more developed but along the same road, for that road no longer exists. Third World countries cannot follow the same path to development as the West, for the world in which they find themselves is very different. Most importantly, they cannot duplicate First World history and accumulate wealth through colonialism, as did the West. Instead, they are the weaker side of a relationship with extremely powerful Western societies. In one reading of this view, the changing historical relationship between First and Third World countries has unfolded in three more or less distinct phases: a merchant capitalist stage, a colonial stage and a neo-colonial stage.

Phases of underdevelopment

1 **Mercantile capitalism** In the merchant-capitalist stage, which began about 1500 AD and was ushered in by the pioneering voyages of seafarers such as Columbus (to the Americas) and da Gama (to India), European merchants established trading outposts in Africa, Asia and the Americas. According to underdevelopment theorists, for those societies affected, these contacts largely resulted in an economic, demographic and political decline from which they have never recovered.

Well before their exploitation, and in some cases ruination by Europeans, many of today's Third World countries had achieved impressive levels of cultural and economic development. And when Europeans embarked on their voyages of discovery, conquest and plunder towards the end of their 'Middle Ages', many African, Asian and Latin American societies had levels of civilisation at least rivalling those of medieval Europe. Crucially, however, they were less developed in military technology, and highly vulnerable to European diseases. Nevertheless, contrary to the assumptions of most modernisation theorists, many were emphatically not 'undeveloped' prior to their contact with the West.

Economic decline came as the superior military technology backing these enterprises - in particular the gunned ships - allowed these European seafarers to impose terms of trade which in many cases were virtually indistinguishable from plunder. And in Latin America in particular, much wealth was acquired by undisguised looting.

The transfer of enormous wealth from the continents of Asia, Africa and Latin America to Europe was accompanied in many places by a similarly debilitating loss of population. In Africa, millions were lost to slavery; throughout Latin America between 1500 and 1650, the population is estimated to have declined, through slaughter, forced labour, malnutrition, disease, and so on, from about 40 million to 12 million; in Asia, the introduction of European diseases decimated indigenous peoples. And on each continent - in India, China, Ethiopia, Zimbabwe, Java, Sumatra, South America and elsewhere - states which were already centralised and politically developed, with social and economic structures as advanced and complex as those of pre-Renaissance Europe, mostly eroded and crumbled in the face of sustained contact with Western commerce, firepower and, in many cases, disease.

2 **Colonialism** In the stage which followed merchant capitalism, European nation states (rather than private companies) actually acquired overseas territories as colonies, mainly through conquest, which they occupied, administered and adapted primarily to suit the requirements of the 'mother country'. This stage lasted until the colonies gained their formal political independence. For most Latin American countries, this happened early in the 19th century. For most in Africa and Asia, national independence came after the Second World War.

The colonists introduced tax systems, encouraged the setting up of capitalist industries from the mother country and used their colonies as protected market outlets which were closed to rivals. In many cases they undermined and exterminated indigenous industries. Very importantly, the European colonists moved their colonies firmly towards monoculturism in agriculture. More and more arable land was brought under the cultivation of one or two 'cash crops' (crops to be sold for cash on world markets, such as coffee, rubber, sugar) with less and less being available for the indigenous populations on which to grow their staple foods. As these commodities tend to be sensitive to fluctuations in world demand, colonies often developed 'boom and bust' economies. This dependence upon one or two primary products has been described as 'the single most important and enduring colonial heritage' (Hoogvelt, 1976, p73), and still haunts former colonies from Cuba to Kenya to Sri Lanka.

Yet, as most underdevelopment theorists now acknowledge, the impact of the Western imperial powers was not completely negative. They did not merely extract and underdevelop. To change their colonies in ways which benefited themselves, the various mother countries transferred capital, technology, their methods of production and forms of social organisation, their political and legal structures, their cultural and religious ideas. As Marx noted of the British in India, the role of the imperial power was both to destroy and to build. And New Right theorists, of course, go much further in identifying the advantages which, they claim, Third World countries derived from their colonial experiences: their parliamentary democracies, their bureaucracies modelled upon the West, their 'more developed' legal, educational and communication systems, and so on.

3 **Neo-colonialism and the global economy** Since 1945 and the end of World War Two, most previously colonised countries have gained formal political independence. In Latin America, political independence had arrived earlier, in the 19th century. Yet, while modernisation theorists refer to this current phase as post-colonialism, the allegedly continuing exploitation of Third World countries by

the West leads underdevelopment theorists to describe post-World War Two relationships as a new form of colonialism: *neo-colonialism*.

For theorists in the underdevelopment tradition such as André Gunder Frank and Immanuel Wallerstein, such neo-colonial relationships are nowadays played out in the context of a global capitalist economic system. It is a worldwide system, dominated by the West, from which no single country can now stand apart.

Frank described his view of the global system in a famous metaphor, as a whole chain of 'metropolis-satellite' relations. Each metropolis dominates, exploits and draws wealth from its satellite or satellites. At the top of the global hierarchy, perhaps, is the USA, a metropolis which is no one's satellite. Below it are metropolises which have their own satellites but are also themselves satellites to a metropolis. Latin American cities, for instance, may be simultaneously satellites of the USA, while dominating and exploiting their own hinterlands. The ultimate satellite, at the receiving end of a chain of domination and exploitation, is the powerless Third World individual who has no one to exploit.

For Wallerstein, the worldwide capitalist system is more complex than Frank's model allows. In his view, as more and more countries have been drawn into the developing capitalist world economy, an international division of labour has developed in which different countries or regions find themselves in one of three positions: *core*, *semi-periphery* or *periphery*. Over time, countries may drop out of the core, and those in the semi-periphery may advance to core status or drop back to the periphery.

The core in this capitalist world economy is made up of the most industrialised countries (eg the USA, Western Europe). With a disproportionate share of the wealth and trade and a virtual monopoly on the production of certain items, they occupy the most advantageous positions. The countries which make up the semi-periphery are states which are closely linked to core countries in various dependent trading relationships. Economically, they are often moving either up or down. However, they are usually politically and economically stronger than the countries on the periphery. Typically, their economies are seriously distorted and dependent, with their low cost labour producing cheap commodities or manufactures needed by the core, and providing a market for core countries' more expensive (and more profitable) manufactures.

While Frank implied that the gains in international relations have all gone one way, to what Wallerstein would call core countries, Wallerstein claimed that countries of the semi-periphery could make gains and 'progress', despite their vulnerability. While they are typically exploited by the core countries and largely limited to exploiting countries of the periphery, they do have some freedom to choose with which competing core countries they wish to trade. Especially during one of the capitalist system's periodic crises, they may be able to play capitalist core countries off against each other.

Ultimately, Wallerstein hoped Marx may yet be proved correct and capitalism be replaced internationally by socialism, though he expected the process to take at least another century. The collapse of Second World communism appears to make this less likely. And the disappearance of the Soviet Union as the world's second 'superpower' may already have weakened the bargaining position of countries of the semi-periphery.

Also, like other underdevelopment theorists, Wallerstein has been accused of underestimating the importance of internal factors in the underdevelopment of Third World countries. For instance, his critics claim that he largely ignores the significance of the massive corruption of many Third World leaders and their monumentally wasteful spending on armaments or fruitless prestige projects, all of which also play a role in underdevelopment.

Activity 4 Development or Underdevelopment?

Item A

The remains of the Aztec city of Teotihuacán in modern Mexico

Item B *Scenes from an inferno*

It's the same everywhere you look in the Third World. Millions upon millions have their backs pressed to the wall. From this posture they face a First World whose soothsayers have recently been pronouncing 'victory' for capitalism. But round the Third World 'victory' is not a word that slips easily off the tongue. Almost everywhere you look outside the upper middle class citadels of the capitalist heartland in the United States, Western Europe and Japan, the news is awful.

In Argentina, Venezuela and Peru per capita income is now (1989) lower than it was in 1970. In Mexico, workers are earning 40% less than they did in 1980. In Brazil, home of the 'economic miracle', the purchasing power of the minimum salary has halved in the past 50 years. In the nightmare of Peru, between 1972 and 1983 the number of malnourished children in the poorer neighbourhoods of the capital, Lima, increased from 24 to 36%. Between 1972 and 1979 the average daily calorie intake of the poor dropped from 1,900 to 1,500 calories, the latter being a starvation level rate.

Economically the African continent is in a state of virtual collapse. From the early to mid-1980s, 20 African nations had economies that remained stagnant or declined. In Zaire, with great natural resources, 80% live in absolute poverty and real wages are a tenth of what they were at independence. Nigeria's per capita income more than halved, from $800 to $380, between 1985 and 1987. In Kenya, the minimum wage declined by 42% between 1975 and 1984. A government health survey in 1982 found that 28% of the children were stunted as a result of poor nutrition, up by 4% from 1977.

Adapted from A. Cockburn 'Scenes from an Inferno' *New Statesman and Society*, 12.5.89, pp14-15

Item C *Cush*

The oldest civilisation in black Africa has been discovered by archeologists. The kingdom of Cush in what is now Sudan was established nearly 5,000 years ago, long before the civilisations of Ethiopia (2,600 years old), northern Nigeria (2,400) and Zimbabwe (1,000).

The heart of the kingdom was a large city, covering at least 60 acres. A spectacular temple and the remnants of a 1.5 mile long city wall, 40 ft thick and partly made of fire-baked red bricks, have also been discovered. This is the earliest known systematic use of fired bricks in the world. It is estimated that the city had a population of between 2,000 and 3,000. Some buildings were thought to be several storeys high, perhaps reaching heights of more than 70ft.

Adapted from D. Keys 'Ancient African Kingdom Discovered in Sudan' *Independent on Sunday*

Item D *Winners and losers in the 1980s*

The world divides clearly between countries that have got richer during the 1980s and those that have got poorer (measured by increases or falls in GDP). A total of 48 countries have been getting poorer during the 1980s - almost as many as those that have got richer.

	Number of countries with rising GDP per capita 1980-7	% of primary commodities to total exports 1987	Country Examples
High-income countries	22	28	US, EEC, Singapore
Upper-income countries	9	50	S. Korea, Brazil
Lower-income countries	14	50	Mauritius, Malaysia,
Low-income countries	9	52	Chine, India, Pakistan
Total	**54**	**42**	
... and falling GDP			
High-income countries	3	87	Saudi Arabia, Kuwait
Upper-income countries	5	76	Trinidad, Argentina
Lower-income countries	18	55	Guatemala, Chile
Low-income countries	22	86	Zaire, Mozambique
Total	**48**	**74**	

Adapted from *New Internationalist*, February 1990, p17

Questions

What are the implications for modernisation theory of:
1 Items A and C, and
2 Items B and D?

2.6 Populism and alternative technologies

Populism rejects modernisation theory at a very fundamental level, for it flatly denies that the goal of modernity, as attained by the industrially most advanced nations, is either desirable or sustainable. Whereas 'conventional' underdevelopment and modernisation theorists may well agree on the desirability of modern living standards and lifestyles, achieved by high technologies - merely differing on how these desired ends may be attained by more of

the world's population - populists challenge some of the argument's basic premises.

Populism is an economic and social theory dating back to the early days of industrialisation. Like the 18th and 19th century 'romantic' movements in art and literature, it arose in shocked response to the suffering and dehumanisation associated with industrialisation and rapid urbanisation.

Populists do not necessarily reject material progress. Instead, they argue that an increase in material prosperity can occur - indeed should occur -

without large scale industrialisation and urbanisation. Because these processes prove so costly and damaging in so many ways, they should be actively avoided. The populist aim, then, is to achieve material progress by preserving small scale agricultural producers (peasants) and non-agricultural producers (artisans) as a large majority in society.

Neo-populism In its modern form of neo-populism, it generally rejects large scale capital-intensive industrialisation on the grounds that it is inappropriate for the Third World (which is not short of people). It accepts some large enterprises if they are labour intensive but generally favours industrial de-concentration. It argues in favour of small-scale agricultural, manufacturing and servicing enterprises - what E. F. Schumacher called 'intermediate technologies' - claiming that they can be more productive as well as less dehumanising and

environmentally damaging than large scale ones. Consequently, neo-populists argue that peasant agriculture and small scale artisan and construction services should be supported and modernised, not obliterated by larger concerns. Similarly, they argue against the build up of large cities, which are seen as destructive of the peasantry and agriculture and dehumanising and alienating for their residents.

Among the better known advocates of neo-populist approaches in recent years are President Nyerere of Tanzania, E. F. Schumacher (the title of whose popular book *Small is Beautiful* suggests a guiding principle of Green politics), and the International Labour Office (ILO), based in Geneva. Often populism is seen as a route to the establishment of a form of socialism; often, too, it is tied into nationalism. Both Tanzania and Nicaragua are frequently cited as examples of countries which have applied populist policies in the last few decades.

Activity 5 Intermediate Technologies

Item A *Intermediate technology*

Today, we suffer from an almost universal devotion to giantism. It is therefore necessary to insist on the virtues of smallness.

As Gandhi said, the poor of the world cannot be helped by mass production, only by production by the masses. The system of mass production pre-supposes that you are already rich, for a great deal of capital is needed to establish one single workplace. The system of production by the masses mobilises resources which are possessed by all human beings, their clever brains and skilful hands, and supports them with first-class tools.

The technology of mass production is inherently violent, ecologically damaging, self-defeating in terms of non-renewable resources, and stultifying for the human person. The technology of production by the masses is conducive to decentralisation, compatible with the laws of ecology, gentle in its use of scarce resources, and designed to serve the human person instead of making him or her the servant of machines. I have named it intermediate technology. To go for giantism is to go for self destruction.

Adapted from E. F. Schumacher *Small is Beautiful: Economics as if People Mattered*, 1974, pp66, 153-4, 159

Item B

A sugar-cane mill, India, an example of intermediate technology

Item C *Improvements rather than replacements*

The ILO favours technologies which are labour enhancing rather than labour displacing, ie forms of modernisation of peasant agriculture which allow the same number of people to work the land but to increase the productivity both of their land and labour. Hence, extensions or improvement of simple irrigation systems, new seeds and plant varieties, more and better fertiliser applications, improved hoes, wheelbarrows and simple spraying equipment, rather than large tractors, mechanised harvesting or threshing equipment and highly mechanised irrigation or storage systems.

Adapted from G.N. Kitching *Development and Underdevelopment in Historical Perspective: Populism, Nationalism and Industrialisation*, 1982, pp72-73

Item D *Traditional technology*

Western technology destroys traditional ways of doing things which can be better. The ox-plough is cheaper and less likely to go wrong than a tractor. Bulldozers rust before spare parts arrive. Africa is littered with useless equipment imported from the West and development projects abandoned because they did not meet local needs.

Adapted from 'Simply...African Ecology', *New Internationalist*, June 1990, p20

Question

Why might intermediate technologies be particularly suitable for Third World countries?

2.7 Postmodernism: globalisation and pessimism

1 Pessimism Whereas both modernisation and underdevelopment theory emerged in a postwar context of optimism and internationalism, discussion of development issues in the early 1990s is likely to take place against a background of relative pessimism, even serious alarm. As large tracts of the world, most particularly much of Africa, sink deeper into poverty, as communism collapses and Third World elites continue to pursue ill-judged, often corrupt and violent policies, and as environmentally damaging programmes continue to be vigorously pursued by governments of all political hues and at all stages of development, modernisation theorists, underdevelopment theorists and neo-populists find little support or encouragement for their views. Instead, the 1990s look like encouraging a perspective which can be called postmodern pessimism.

Writing in 1993, Foster-Carter finds much cause for pessimism. He fears that internationalism is under threat as people sense few international successes, but many failures and dangers. The list includes an unceasing string of wars and conflicts throughout the world, (from which, as civil wars in Northern Ireland and the former Yugoslavia remind us, the West is not exempted); widespread ethnic tension; recurring famines, particularly in northern Africa; fears of further national fragmentation, as throughout the former USSR; massive international migration (encouraging further ethnic tension); the international debt crisis; and a global recession.

Paradoxically, even the demise of communism in Central and Eastern Europe, which briefly offered hope, now fuels concern. It allows the USA a monopolistic superpower role, either to intervene abroad at will, as in the case of Iraq, or to leave poorer, strategically less important countries 'to fester or stew' (Foster-Carter, 1993, p42). The collapse of communism may also have weakened the position of Third World countries in a second way. First and Second World rivalry at least allowed Third World countries some bargaining power (as Wallerstein argued of the semi-periphery), which they have now lost. And, very importantly, the sudden emergence of many politically independent, but economically backward, states from the former Second World has significantly increased the competition for whatever financial assistance the West makes available.

Faced with so discouraging a panorama, Foster-Carter finds the insights of postmodernism helpful (though hardly cheering). Postmodernism rejects the idea of 'grand metanarratives', of 'Big Stories' which claim to offer macro-level accounts of, for instance, world history. Although there may well be trends which are broadly worldwide, such as 'globalisation' (discussed below), within that broad context will be many counter-developments or local or regional variations, many little stories. Foster-Carter is sceptical of relatively deterministic models of world history as in modernisation or underdevelopment theories, stressing instead the likelihood of local and regional variablity and diversity. 'In development, there is no magic cure, no built-in deliverance, certainly no short cut or easy option, no single answer. There may even be no deliverance at all' (1993, p39). Nevertheless, despite this, he believes that it is crucial that social scientists aim for a global overview. 'The big picture comes first, otherwise the detail won't make sense. But insisting on starting with the big picture emphatically does not involve any claim that the big picture contains just one or any Big Story. Sociologists will find many stories being told' (1993, p53).

2 Globalisation Though postmodernists doubt the validity of a meta narrative claiming to describe a universal pattern of societal change, many do claim to see evidence of a process, or processes, which they and others have termed 'globalisation'. Despite much of sociology's continuing focus on the nation state, globalisation acknowledges that 'an increasing number of social processes and phenomena are largely and inherently international' (Foster-Carter, 1993, p51).

Globalisation refers, first, to the increased economic interdependence of countries. As Wallerstein argued, all countries are now part of a global economic system, though postmodernists reject his tripartite classification of core, semi-periphery and periphery as simplistic and over-rigid. Economic interdependence reflects, to an important extent, the now considerable significance of transnational corporations (TNCs) (see pp580-581). TNCs plan, produce and market on a global scale, fragmenting their functions and allocating bits to countries and regions where the returns are greatest. And much of the trade between states now is really between different parts of the same company. Their products are marketed globally; the same brands of jeans, hamburgers, chocolate bars can be found the world over, though their names may change to suit local markets.

Tendencies towards globalisation can also be seen at a cultural level, accelerated by continuing advances in communications technology, such as satellite TV and fax machines. TV channels, like the USA's CNN, film companies and certain newspapers are known worldwide. The same cultural referents exist around the world. Madonna, Michael Jackson, McDonald's hamburgers, Princess Di, Pavarotti, even computer game characters, are known on all continents. Also, as Foster-Carter points out, social problems increasingly have a global dimension. AIDS, drugs, refugees,

migration and a range of environmental problems, all need a global perspective to be understood.

However, apparently global processes may be resisted. On every continent are political movements determined to achieve the break up of an existing state into smaller political units, very often along ethnic lines. Czechoslovakia achieved it peacefully; Ethiopia and Yugoslavia with appalling violence.

More internationally, militant Islam opposes many economic and cultural changes which it identifies with the modernised West - and with the USA, the 'Great Satan', in particular. This may be interpreted in a number of ways: for instance, as a more or less atypical regional backlash or as a conflict between competing global tendencies, between a materialistic West and a resurgent Islam.

Summary

1 Modernisation theory tends to see development as occurring from within societies rather than being imposed or imported from 'outside'. It emphasises that traditional attitudes can hold back development.

2 In the 1980s, modernisation theory formed the basis for New Right analyses which argued that development is most likely where government plays a minimal role, where central planning is avoided and changes occur as far as possible in response to market forces.

3 Some Marxists, such as Warren and Harris, claim that capitalist development in the Third World represents progress and is predominantly beneficial to Third World countries. Ultimately, however, the capitalist stage will be superceded by socialism.

4 Underdevelopment theory argues that some countries are significantly less developed than

the West because they have been exploited by the West and forced into a state of underdevelopment. Underdevelopment theories tend to ignore internal factors which may contribute to underdevelopment, in particular widespread corruption, and wasteful and excessive spending on armaments and prestige projects.

5 Neo-populists deny that material progress should be pursued by continuing the large scale industrialising and urbanising paths of the First and Second Worlds. They claim that many small scale technologies and enterprises can be more efficient than large scale ones, as well as less damaging to people and the environment.

6 Postmodernism rejects the 'grand theories' of modernisation and underdevelopment. However, it recognises the general pattern of globalisation.

Activity 6 Globalisation

Item A *Global culture*

China

Philippines

Item B *Breaking up and joining up*

The Union of Socialist Soviet Republics

KEY
1 Estonia
2 Latvia
3 Lituania
4 Belrussia
5 Moldavia
6 Georgia
7 Armenia
8 Azerbaijan
9 Turkmenistan
10 Uzbekistan
11 Tajikistan
12 Kirghizia

In 1991 the USSR broke up and each of the 15 republics became an independent country.

The European Economic Community, 1957

The European Union, 1995

Questions

1 Look at Item A. Many globally recognised 'cultural referents' are from the USA. Should we not just refer to the process as Americanisation? Try to provide further evidence to justify your answer.
2 How could Item B be used to support postmodernism's rejection of 'grand metanarratives'?

3 Relationships of Developed and Less Developed Societies

Key Issues

What are the consequences to the Third World of:

1 transnational companies
2 world trade
3 Western aid, loans and debt?

Introduction This part considers three controversial aspects of First and Third World inter-relationships: transnational companies, trade and aid. Some see the consequences of all three as mainly beneficial.

For others, they maintain global inequalities, inequalities which are further buttressed by the West's dominance of international institutions (eg the UN, World Bank and International Monetary Fund) and, ultimately, by its overwhelming military might.

3.1 The growth and spread of transnational companies

A major development in the world economic system this century, and particularly since World War Two, has been the massive growth and spread of transnational companies (TNCs). TNCs are companies with subsidiaries (offices, plants or both) in two or more countries, and are currently owned almost entirely by the West.

The wealth of some of these companies is formidable. In 1980, of the hundred largest economic powers in the world, 53 were countries and 47 were TNCs. Among these were companies such as Coca Cola, with plants and sales in more than 100 countries, Nestlé in 60 and Rio Tinto Zinc in 23. Of the world's top 50 companies in 1980, 21 were based in the US, 8 in West Germany, 6 in Japan, 6 in Britain and the Netherlands, and 5 in France. Most of their foreign investment is in other industrialised countries. However, about 25% of their investment is in the Third World. Many of the TNCs have large investments in agriculture, often owning large acreages or, increasingly commonly, individually contracting peasants and agricultural labourers to produce what the TNCs require. They are, therefore, major players in what has come to be called agribusiness.

In the 1970s, over half their Third World investment was in Latin America. Since then, investment has swung towards the newly industrialised countries (NICs) of Asia such as South Korea, Singapore and Hong Kong, and in the 1990s appears to be increasing in East Europe (very possibly at the expense of the Third World). Because TNCs look for certain conditions before investing in a country - including political stability, a certain level of industrialisation and of infrastructure - they tend to avoid the poorest countries.

Sociologists differ about the consequences of the growth in TNCs. Broadly, modernisation theorists emphasise the alleged benefits which TNC subsidiaries can have in Third World countries - the introduction of foreign capital and advanced technologies, the training of local workers, the boost to local markets of more disposable income, the access to world markets. They also note their role in helping integrate the nation states of the world in a general process of globalisation.

Underdevelopment theorists, on the other hand, argue that any benefits are outweighed by disadvantages, that TNCs primarily enrich themselves and perpetuate the distorted, dependent role of most of the Third World. They point out that the 'industrialisation' which TNCs introduce into Third World countries is typically only a specialised part of a whole industrial process, different parts of which are spread internationally, each of which is vulnerable to the strategic planning decisions of the parent company. Moreover, many companies draw substantially more money from the Third World than they put into it by the widespread practice of 'transfer pricing'. This practice allows TNCs to repatriate (transfer back to the parent company) much of their profits, but in such a way as to minimise the taxes payable to the 'host' country, or indeed to their own.

3.2 The disadvantageous terms of world trade

Although this point is hotly disputed, many analysts claim that, over time, the international terms of trade operate to the disadvantage of most poorer countries. Put simply: over time, poorer countries have received relatively less for their exports while having to pay more for their imports. This largely reflects the continuing dependence of many Third World countries on the production and export of just one or two primary (unmanufactured) products.

For primary products, demand tends to grow only slowly, if at all. Manufactured goods, disproportionately produced in the North, have a much greater potential growth in demand. Consequently, the North sells more and more to the South but not vice-versa. Because of this imbalance in demand, the prices for primary products or commodities decline over the long term (and often also short term) compared to the prices of manufactured goods. So Third World countries receive fewer and fewer revenues for similar quantities supplied to the North.

Short term improvements in the conditions of trade for non-Northern countries can periodically occur. In 1973 this was dramatically confirmed, with OPEC's quadrupling of oil prices and the near doubling of almost all other commodity prices in the world economy. Yet even when countries of the South have been able to raise prices for their commodities - for instance by organising successful cartels (manufacturers' organisations to maintain profits) - they have seldom gained longer term. What profits they make are often eroded by price rises for imported Western manufactures. And in any event, it is other Third World countries who have found those higher prices (eg for oil) most devastating. They are much less able to find and afford alternatives than is the West.

Other periodic 'booms' in world commodity prices occur and may briefly benefit some Third World countries. These are, however, invariably followed by 'busts', as core countries undergo slow-down, recession or slump. Unable to invest sufficiently in the booms to expand productive capacity and ensure benefits which will assist in the slump, Third World countries are particularly vulnerable to slow-downs and recessions in the world economy.

Activity 7 Manufactures and Commodities

Item A *Percentage shares of world manufacturing trade 1973 and 1987*

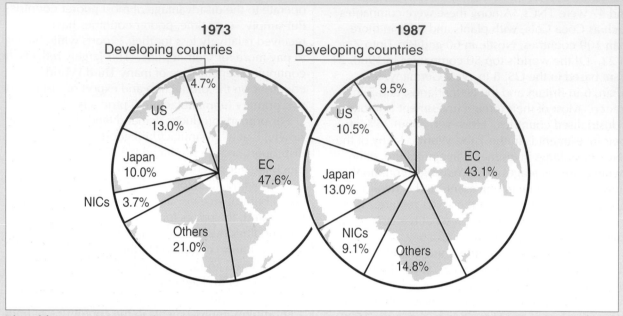

Adapted from *New Internationalist*, February 1990, p16

Item B *Comparison of prices for primary commodities (excluding fuels) and manufactures: 1900-90*

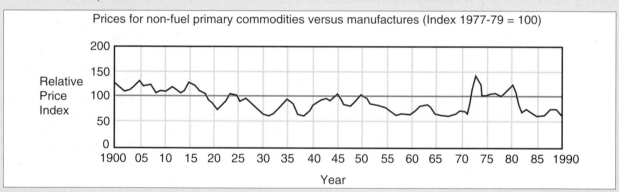

Note: The graph sets the 1977-79 price ratio of primary commodities (excluding fuel) to manufactures at 100. If the number goes above 100 this shows a rise in (non-fuel) primary commodities' prices compared to those of manufactures, if it goes below 100 then commodity prices fall relative to manufactured goods. The Third World depends most on selling commodities.

Adapted from 'Number Crunching the World', *New Internationalist*, June 1992, p18

Item C *The decline of commodity prices*

In the 1980s world production of cocoa soared and world cocoa prices fell by half. Yet the chocolate bars we buy in the West never go down in price. Their prices are raised 'in line with inflation', but never cut.

Adapted from John Tanner 'Cocoa Addicts', *New Internationalist*, February 1990, p14

Farmers in the EC have received massive subsidies to grow sugar beet. Instead of importing most of our sugar, as we used to, we now produce too much - and dump it on the world market.

Adapted from *One World: Time for Action*, Oxfam, 1990, p4

Questions

1 Summarise the experience of developing countries as indicated by Items A and B.

2 What are likely to be the consequences of the actions described in the extracts in Item C?

3.3 Aid, loans and debt

1 Aid

The word 'aid' means help. For many, it suggests charity. Yet, as Paul Harrison points out, for the rich world to take so much from the poor (see below), and then call the small proportion it returns 'aid', is 'the crowning irony' of the international economic order (1979, p359).

What is generally regarded as aid consists of official government grants and loans, and assistance (in cash or kind) from the charitable agencies such as Oxfam, Christian Aid or Charity Projects (the charity behind Red Nose Day and Comic Relief). In all Western countries, government aid dwarfs the amounts given through the voluntary agencies. In 1991, for instance, the British government gave about £1,500 million (about 35-40p a week on behalf of each person in Britain); approximately five times the amount raised by the top 400 British charities for overseas aid. (Incidentally, this combined annual total is a little short of the £2,000 million Britain is estimated to have spent on the 1991 Gulf War).

The UN recommends that governments give a minimum of 0.7% of their GNP as aid but very few countries attain even the minimum. Most fall far short. Moreover, during the 1980s, Western countries cut their aid (as a proportion of GNP) even further. Between 1978 and 1988, for example, the UK's aid contribution as a percentage of GNP fell from 0.48% to 0.28%.

Advantages of aid to the West Government aid is controversial in the West among both public and politicians, and criticised from both left and right. Most Western general publics are unaware that their own economies often benefit because much government aid, known as 'tied aid', is given on condition that the recipient country buys specified goods or services from the donor country. In 1984-85, for example, two-thirds of Britain's direct aid to India was tied to the purchase of British goods and services.

Western donor countries find other ways too of using aid to benefit their own industries. In Britain, part of the money in the aid budget provides subsidies to British companies to help them secure Third World contracts. In this way, subsidies not merely help First World companies secure work and sales; they can also undercut potential Third World competitors and stunt the prospects of indigenous industries.

Western governments also use aid to protect their geo-political interests. For instance, the US gives massive aid to Israel for 'security' reasons. Critics claim that, over the past few decades, much Western government aid has gone to Third World regimes because their foreign policy stance was anti-communist, eg to the Philippines under President Marcos and to Chile under General Pinochet, even though they were undemocratic, unpopular and authoritarian - often downright repressive - at home.

Disadvantages of aid to the Third World Official aid has also been much criticised as suffering from what Schumacher called the worship of 'giantism'. Large amounts of money are spent on employing Western 'experts' - in 1991 there were some 100,000 in Africa, costing about $5 billion a year - to design and implement large scale, expensive projects. (Many agencies will not even consider projects costing less than $50,000). Most of the remaining official aid goes to support the mechanisation of industry and agriculture. This often means that the poor lose land which is given over to industry which, being capital-intensive, yields few extra jobs.   All too often, so the critics say, projects are devised without adequate knowledge of local conditions, customs or preferences and without adequate consultation of, and advice from, local people. Consequently, a number of major projects have been funded which now appear to have been economically disadvantageous for many of those they were intended to help and sometimes also seriously damaging ecologically.

Ecological damage occurs because Third World governments' desperation for industry often means that they allow Western firms and governments to keep costs low by permitting much lower safety and environmental standards than would be allowed in the West. Hence, pollution and injury are generally much worse in the countries receiving aid.

However, Western governments are now more aware of the dangers of 'giantist' approaches to development and, as in Britain, are now channelling much more money through non-governmental organisations (NGOs) such as the Western-based charities and indigenous Third World groups. Most NGOs concentrate on long term, small scale, 'appropriate technology' developments, whose aim is to give people the means to help themselves.

2 Loans and debt

In the past 20 or so years, Africa's debts have mushroomed, from $6 billion in 1968 to $134 billion in 1988. That amount is roughly equal to the total value of the goods and services its 450 million people produce (and is about the same as the GNP of Belgium, which has a population of only 10 million).

Since 1973, in particular, the growth of Third World debts - and the struggle of Third World governments to service them - has played an important role in keeping hundreds of millions of people throughout the Third World in abject poverty. Between 1980 and 1986, the external debt of 109 developing countries nearly doubled, from $500 billion to $1,000 billion. Four years later it had increased by another $300 billion. Third World debts are now so large, and interest rates so high that, for every year since 1983, the Third World has paid out more money to the North just to service its debt (ie pay interest charges and repayments) than it has received from the North in new investment and loans: in 1989 $52 billion more.

In 1973, when world oil prices quadrupled, Western banks, awash with massive deposits from governments of the oil rich countries, encouraged many developing countries to take low-interest loans with which to buy oil and industrialise. In the late 1970s and early 1980s, however, interest rates rose sharply. Consequently, in order to keep pace with rising debt service payments, many countries were obliged to increase their production of cash crops, such as cotton, jute and groundnuts, often taking over land previously used for the production of food.

For many Third World countries, the servicing of these debts consumes between a third and a half of all their export earnings. This is quite crippling enough. Additionally, however, if a country needs to apply for a further loan, it must satisfy the demands of the International Monetary Fund (IMF) that it implement a Structural Adjustment Programme (SAP). Such a programme typically involves drastic cuts in public spending - for instance on health, education, public transport, food subsidies - and, although the IMF argues that such policies are necessary for economic health, they are damaging for the poor and appear to have had very little success in encouraging growth.

Summary

1 While modernisation theorists claim that transnational companies (TNCs) benefit developing countries (introducing capital, technology, training, etc), underdevelopment theorists emphasise the specialised nature and precariousness of the industry located by TNCs in the Third World, and their repatriation of profits and avoidance of tax.

2 Though disputed, it is claimed that many Third World countries' continuing overdependence on a few primary products means they suffer disadvantageous terms of trade. Commodity prices generally decline against prices for manufactured goods. Any short term improvements are often followed by slumps.

3 Most Western aid is governmental. Very few countries in the world (including Britain) give the UN's recommended minimum.

4 Much government aid is 'tied' to the recipient government buying goods or services from the donor country. Some money from the aid budget goes directly to Western companies to help them win Third World orders. This can impede Third World businesses by undercutting them.

5 Given that, annually since 1983, more money has gone from the world's poorer countries in loan repayments than the West has invested and 'given' in aid, perhaps the word 'aid' is (to say the least) inappropriate.

6 Third World governments' attempts to service their debts help keep their people impoverished.

Activity 8   Giving and Taking

Item A *Wheat aid and wheat prices*

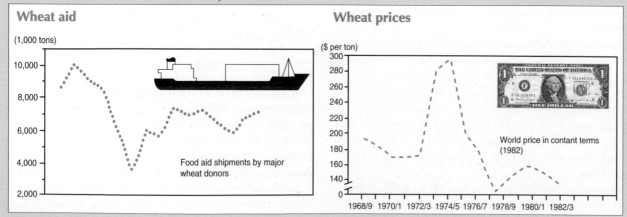

Wheat aid

(1,000 tons)

Food aid shipments by major wheat donors

Wheat prices

($ per ton)

World price in contant terms (1982)

1968/9 1970/1 1972/3 1974/5 1976/7 1978/9 1980/1 1982/3

Adapted from *New Internationalist*, September 1985, p10

Item B

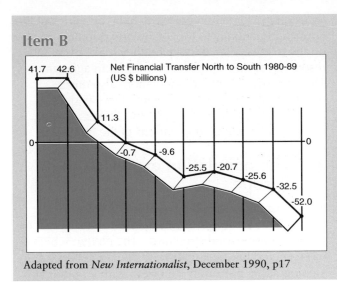

Net Financial Transfer North to South 1980-89
(US $ billions)

41.7 42.6

11.3

0

-0.7 -9.6

-25.5 -20.7

-25.6

-32.5

-52.0

0

Adapted from *New Internationalist*, December 1990, p17

Questions

1 Describe and explain the apparent relationship between the two charts in Item A.
2 In Item B, explain what the chart shows was happening before and after 1983.
3 Suggest possible consequences for Third World countries of the trends shown in Items A and B.

4 The Demography of First and Third World Countries

Key Issues

1 What are the demographic changes which have occurred throughout the world, particularly since the West's industrial revolution?
2 What are their causes?
3 What are their consequences?

4.1 The reasons for demographic change

All changes in the size and structure of populations occur because of change in one or more of three variables: birth rate, death rate and net migration. Birth rate is usually defined as the number of live births, in any one year, per 1,000 of the population. Death rate is the number of deaths in any given year, per 1,000 population. Net migration is the difference in the numbers emigrating from, and immigrating to, a specified area (usually a particular country) in a given year. If we use these three variables, we can compare population changes of different countries, or changes in the same country over time.

Population growth If we assume, in a hypothetical example, that net migration for a particular year is insignificant, (and we are therefore left with just two main variables), we can say that the population will increase whenever the birth rate is higher than the death rate. Population growth which is simply due to birth rate being higher than death rate (and not, for instance, to migration) is called 'natural increase'.

Population structure Changes in any of these three variables (birth rate, death rate or migration) affect not just the size of populations but can also affect their structure - their age, sex and ethnic composition.

4.2 World population growth and population distribution

In 1994 the world's population stood at about 5.7 billion (5,700,000,000). According to current projections, by 2050 AD it will be 10 billion. However, on the very optimistic assumption of less developed countries moving towards zero population growth, world population would be expected to stabilise around 2100 AD at about 11 billion - nearly double its 1994 figure. Sceptics expect closer to 15 billion by the end of the 21st century.

Currently, about three-quarters of humanity live in the Third World, including about 94% of the world's newly born. By 2020 AD 84% of the world's people are expected to live there. Third World population is growing about 2% annually. That implies a doubling every 35 years. It is little wonder, perhaps, that even otherwise sober sociologists and demographers will use the emotive term 'population explosion' to describe the sharp rates of population increase in many Third World societies.

Although over 90% of global population growth is in the Third World, there are significant regional differences in demographic trends. In Asia as a whole, population growth has now declined to below 2% a year, and in China is expected to proceed at around 1.2% in the 1990s. In most of Latin America, also, rates of population growth are declining and expected to be about 1.9% in the 1990s. In most of Africa, however, the trend is still upwards, with rates of over 3% a year forecast for the 1990s in sub-Saharan Africa.

4.3 The controversial concept of world overpopulation

World population growth is a topic which raises many emotive issues and on which widely different opinions are often fiercely held. For many people, the world is already unable to accommodate and adequately provide for its population. The urgent need to stop world population growth - and preferably to reverse it - is, for them, the single most important issue of our time. On it depends not just the survival of millions of the world's poor but perhaps the very survival of our planet. Programmes encouraging much wider access to, and use of, contraceptives are a priority.

For others, however, the continuing high rates of population growth and the alleged 'overpopulation' of the planet are not the central problem. They are symptoms of a deeper problem, namely the enormous inequality of wealth and poverty which afflicts the world. Poverty, they argue, encourages people to have large families. Unless Third World poverty can be relieved, the problem of overpopulation will not be solved. If such societies were to become more affluent, their rapid population growth would slow down - just as it did when the First World industrialised - and the 'problem' would resolve itself. In this view, Third World countries will only opt for significant family limitation when they feel it suits their situation.

Some go further and deny outright that the world is overpopulated. Even now, they claim, there is the space, the wealth, the resources and the productive capacity on this earth to provide a decent standard of living for all, if we seriously wish to do so. Whether a given country or area is regarded as 'overpopulated' depends less upon simple numbers of people than on whether there exists an infrastructure which provides adequate food, housing, jobs, and so on. It is the distribution of resources and power which primarily determines 'overpopulation'. In this view, the question is whether the nations of the world will ever agree to cooperate in developing the world's assets and in ensuring that the world's wealth is distributed fairly.

Because so much of the growth in world population comes from countries in the South, it is they which are usually seen in the West as the major concern. However, population growth also raises questions about the using up of the world's finite resources. Individuals from the rich West consume the world's resources at a much higher per capita rate than do those of the Third World. According to one estimate, each individual born into a Western society will consume on average approximately 40 times as much energy and eat three times as much food as someone born into a Third World society. Concern about the size of the world's population should not then simply focus on the large numbers which the countries of the South add annually to the total world population, but on the relatively small demand they make on world resources, serious though that may be in aggregate. The controversy of 'overpopulation' also raises questions about how much more of the world's resources will be consumed by the slower growing, but very demanding, populations of the North.

4.4 The population explosion in Europe

In the past 200 years, the countries of Western Europe have undergone considerable changes in their population sizes and structures. The pattern which has emerged has been called by demographers a 'demographic transition'. It began with a population which was relatively stable in size and structure, moved into a period of significant change and finally returned to a relatively stable state, though one which is quite different from the original. This pattern of changes began first in Britain and was then repeated in most West European and North American countries.

In the first phase, prior to the agricultural and industrial revolutions (which began in Britain in the 18th century), both birth rate and death rate were relatively high. Population growth was therefore slow. And, because children were particularly vulnerable to disease and death, parents needed to produce many children to ensure the survival into adulthood of at least some.

The intermediary, transitional phase began as death rates started to fall, while birth rates remained high. This growing gap between birth and death rates led to a spurt in population growth: a population 'explosion'.

The third and current stage began when birth rates started to fall near to the level of death rates. In Britain, birth rates began to fall from about the 1870s and continued downward until the 1930s. In the third stage, then, population growth is again low and relatively stable. In fact, in many developed countries including the UK, birth and death rates are now again so close that population size is static or even declining.

4.5 Reasons for the fall of birth and death rates in Europe

Europe's transitional phase was ushered in with a sustained fall in the death rate. This decline was largely the result of three sets of factors. First, and perhaps most significantly, the quality and quantity of food available improved due to a combination of agricultural advances and improvements in the food distribution system. Secondly, public health measures were adopted (such as the introduction of piped water and effective sewage disposal systems) which significantly diminished the incidence and effects of hitherto common diseases. Thirdly, and most recently, advances in medical science and the extension of medical facilities to a larger proportion of the population have also played an important role.

In Britain, the third phase - of birth rates falling towards death rates - began among the middle classes from about the 1870s, and among the working class from about the turn of the century. It is generally argued that birth rates fell, indirectly, because the continuing industrialisation of Western societies was producing a growing affluence which allowed a number of changes.

Reductions in child mortality meant that parents need produce fewer children to try to ensure support in old age. Indeed, in Britain, state assistance to the elderly in the form of pensions, later supplemented with health care and residential homes, made people less dependent on any children to support them into old age.

Also, from the latter part of the 19th century, children became a more expensive 'investment'. In the middle class especially there was a growing need for qualifications and hence for longer (and expensive) schooling. And children's ability to earn was especially squeezed with the introduction of compulsory education (in 1880 to 10 years old in England and Wales). Moreover, though artificial contraceptives became more effective, more publicised and more widely available in the latter part of the 19th century, there is controversy about how influential a factor they were, perhaps especially among the working class, until well into the 20th century. For many, it seems withdrawal and abortion remained the main choices.

4.6 Comparison of the population explosions of the First and Third Worlds

The population explosion of the Third World is largely due to their having entered stage two, in which death rates have fallen but birth rates remain high. The crucial question is, of course, whether they will imitate the pattern of the West and move on to stage three. There are, however, a number of crucial differences between the situation of the Third World today and the West during the same stage, which make the South's population explosion much more traumatic.

First, the population explosion in the Third World has been compressed into a much shorter space of time and growth rates have been steeper and more dramatic. The West's more gradual population explosion was due to a declining death rate caused by factors such as new techniques in food production

and advances in public hygiene and medicine's ability to control diseases, changes which came relatively slowly. However, having produced these developments, the West now exports them wholesale to the Third World where their impact is much greater. In the UK, for instance, a fall in the death rate of 1% per annum took 70 years. In Sri Lanka, a similar fall took just seven years with the wiping out of malaria. For these and other reasons, the rapid growth in population in Third World countries may so inhibit the ability to develop their economies, that stage three - the stage at which people can feel secure to limit family size - may never come.

Secondly, unlike most Third World countries today, the developed countries were in many ways relatively wealthy before they began to industrialise. Additionally, the First World's population explosion was accompanied by increases in agricultural output, a continuing influx of relatively cheap items from the colonies, and foreign markets for export. That of the Third World is accompanied by a decline in the availability of food and wealth and disadvantageous terms of trade.

Thirdly, Western countries had more opportunities for their additional populations. As happened in the West, the population explosion in the Third World has been accompanied by a large-scale migration of people from rural to urban areas. However, the early industries of the West were more labour intensive than much industrial development in the Third World today and so could better absorb rural migrants. Additionally, migration abroad (for instance, to their colonies) was less restricted than for Third World citizens today.

4.7 Why do Third World birth rates remain high?

As we have seen, population growth - both in 18th century industrialising Europe and the Third World today - has occurred, not because of a 'baby boom', but because the death rate falls while the birth rate remains high. Some of the reasons for the fall in Third World death rates have already been mentioned (eg the import of Western medicines). The question remains, however: why do people in poorer countries not immediately reduce their birth rates?

Economic insecurity If the experience of the West is an indicator, birth rates in Third World countries are only likely to fall when people feel more secure economically. In general, people in the Third World who have large families do so as a response to poverty, for the economic and social benefits which large families bring, not because of ignorance.

Economically, children are labour power. From a young age, all are expected to work: to help with household chores, work in the fields, tend the

Activity 9 The Weight of Humanity

Item A *The demographic transition*

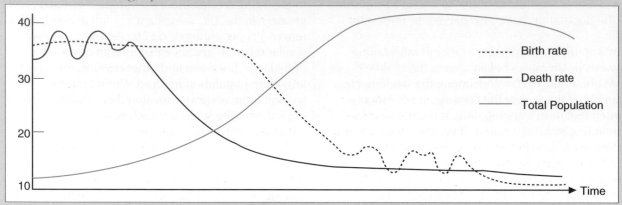

This graph is based on evidence from the early 19th century onwards in Western Europe. It shows falling death rates followed by falling birth rates. Eventually the population stabilises and may even decrease - shown as a projection on the graph - with birth rates falling below death rates.

Item B *Food and energy consumption*

CERTAINLY HUNGER IS A PRODUCT OF OVER-POPULATION.... THERE JUST ISN'T THE FOOD TO GO ROUND.

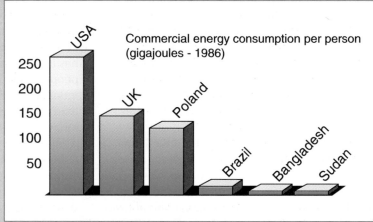

Commercial energy consumption per person (gigajoules - 1986)

Adapted from Oxfam *Time for Action*, undated

Questions

1 Do you think that Third World countries will follow the demographic transition shown in Item A? Give reasons for your answer.
2 With reference to Item B, why might people in the Third World be critical of First World pleas to slow or reverse their population growth?

livestock. In the towns, they may beg or sell. Also, in the absence of a welfare state, children are depended upon to provide security and support in old age.

One type of measure which some advocate to help reduce birth rates, though highly controversial, is land reform. Land reform programmes usually involve the redistribution of land from a few large landowners to a number of peasant farmer families. Although often politically difficult for Third World governments to introduce successfully, evidence suggests that land reform can improve family income

and, by encouraging the use of appropriate technology, lessen the need to have large families to labour on the land. Similarly, the introduction of forms of economic security such as pensions and sick pay reduces the need to 'over-reproduce'. The problem, of course, is that Third World countries do not have the money to put into such things and would need massive injections of overseas aid to be able to do so.

Without a greater sense of economic security, therefore, birth control policies alone are unlikely to achieve a falling birth rate. In short, (apart from programmes imposed quite ruthlessly) they will only succeed if people feel economically and socially secure enough to want them.

Status of women Social factors are also important in discouraging smaller families. In many Third World societies, the low status of women and the role of religion both operate to keep birth rates high. The low status of women in much of the Third World means that they have limited opportunities to work outside the home and earn an independent income. Hence, mothering many children - preferably sons - provides women with one of their few routes to status and security. In Latin America, especially, men also gain status by producing large families. For the macho male, many children are proof of virility.

The preference for sons both reflects the inferior status of females and reinforces it. Sons can earn more than daughters and, in Asia, sons often attract dowries. They can generally provide better for their parents in old age. So many parents keep on trying until they have produced at least one son - and preferably at least two in case one doesn't survive.

Hence improved educational and occupational opportunities for women tend to diminish the birth rate. First, because improved opportunities provide women with alternative sources of satisfaction and status beyond childbearing. Secondly, because educated women, and women with their own income and assets, tend to marry later. This encourages couples to delay having children and thus reduces women's child-bearing span. (Educated women are also generally better able to use contraceptives).

Religion Finally, in many areas religion also functions to discourage smaller families. Islam and Roman Catholicism are often particularly potent in maintaining high levels of fertility. And, indeed, the decline in birth rates has been particularly slow in the belt of Muslim countries which stretches from North Africa to Pakistan and Bangladesh (though not in Indonesia), and in Roman Catholic Latin America.

4.8 Consequences of the Third World's population explosion

One vital consequence of population growth appears to be that it is, to an important extent, self-generating (it keeps itself going). The combination of reduced infant and child mortality rates and a still high birth rate means that many Third World countries have a disproportionately youthful age structure. Thus, the next generation of parents is already growing up and a significant decline in the number of births is unlikely for at least a generation.

A second consequence of the population explosion in Third World countries is that it makes economic growth more difficult to achieve. The faster the

population grows, the more difficult it becomes to find the large savings needed to invest and raise output in agriculture and industry. Just to keep pace with population growth, a significant proportion of national income must be spent on producing food and developing the infrastructure: the transportation network, energy production and education system. In a survey of 21 underdeveloped countries, the International Labour Office economist Felix Paukert calculated that population growth drained off 70% of the increase in their national incomes, leaving little for income-improving investment.

Thirdly, although the number of jobs available may increase, they are typically unable to keep up with rapid population growth. Even when new jobs are created, they often absorb relatively few potential workers because, compared with 19th century Europe, contemporary Third World industrialisation is largely capital-intensive rather than labour-intensive. Capital-intensive industry is often encouraged both by First World TNCs and First World governments, whose tied aid frequently requires the purchase of machinery needing relatively little labour to operate it.

Fourthly, while the deterioration of environments in Third World countries can reflect many factors - climatic change, the production of 'inappropriate' cash crops and so on - Third World population increases also play a role. In many areas, population growth - and associated problems such as overgrazing, the depletion of timber supplies and desertification - have led to land shortages and often to the fragmentation of land holdings. The repeated division of a family's or community's holdings to try to provide land for members of the next generation often results in a drop in output and insufficient food being produced. That may mean that families have to abandon their holdings and seek employment on the larger farms, or join the growing numbers of unemployed seeking work in the cities.

When costs outweigh benefits

Throughout the Third World, then, mass poverty - whatever its causes - encourages a downward spiral of vulnerable, multi-pregnancy families, continuing population growth and further economic and environmental regression. Yet there are now clear signs from a number of Third World countries that, when poverty and overpopulation become extreme, family limitation may ultimately occur. In several poor countries such as India, Thailand, Indonesia and Egypt, it seems that parents have reluctantly been forced to opt for smaller families because the costs of additional children have clearly come to outweigh the expected benefits. Eventually, for those with any land, its division each generation means that each holding becomes so small that children are not needed to work them. And for the landless, the labour surplus becomes such that wages are driven down so low that they cannot compensate for the costs of child rearing. When people reach such rock-bottom, as in Bangladesh, if a vigorous birth control programme is in place, they may be sufficiently desperate to avail themselves of it. But dependence upon such suffering and desperation hardly seems a satisfactory basis for optimism about world population growth. The outlook for most in the Third World remains grim, as they attempt to provide for continuing significant population growth.

Summary

1 About three-quarters of humanity live in the Third World and 90% of population growth is occurring there, though growth is slowing in Asia and Latin America.

2 While many see population as the most important issue of our time, some argue that the root problem is poverty. Only with increased financial security is substantial family limitation likely.

3 It is poorer countries which are likely to be regarded as overpopulated. The rich countries of the North do not generally see themselves as overpopulated, though they are much more of a drain on the world's resources.

4 The population explosion in the Third World is largely due to a reduction in death rates without a corresponding reduction in birth rates. However, the Third World's population explosion is more sudden than that of the industrialising 18th and 19th century West. It has happened much more quickly, with rapid improvements in hygiene and the introduction of Western medicine. Also, the Third World has not experienced a similar growth in food supply and job opportunities (its industrialisation is less labour-intensive), and lacks the colonies to absorb its surplus populations.

Activity 10   Population - Costs and Benefits

Item A *Parents and children*

If I don't have children, life will be very, very boring, nothing else changes very much, but children change, and they love you. I want to have friends and companions and helpers and people who love me.

What else can a woman be in life except a mother and a home-worker? I never had an education and a job or a career.

They say it makes you old and ill very quickly if you have too many children too close together, and anyway perhaps I would be able to look after my children better if I only have two or three, but it is not really my choice. My husband will decide.

Of course, I don't mind what our next child is, but I hope it is a boy.

I don't like my wife to talk about birth control. It's not right. Anyway, she is my wife and it is her duty to be my companion in my bed and to bear my children.

Each child I have will be able to earn half as much as I can by the time they are 10 - harvesting and tilling in the landlord's fields, and children cost hardly anthing extra - they sleep in the same room and wear cast off clothes and eat very little food. So I'm obviously going to have more money and be better off if I have lots of children, and they will also be able to help me work my own bit of land and I certainly can't afford to pay anyone to help.

If I don't have children, who will look after me when I am ill or old - nobody else will help me.

Nearly half the children around here die before they are grown up; I am going to have several children so that even if some die, I will still be left with some.

If I have children one or two of them might go to school and get a good education or go off to the town and get a good job. Then they will be able to send money back to us like Mr Radhid's children do.

Adapted from *New Internationalist*, June 1977

Item B *Small landowners*

The customs of inheritance in Asia (as in most of the Third World) call for a shareout of property among a dead man's heirs. This usually means that farms are constantly being fragmented into smaller and smaller holdings. In the Punjab, small landowners were aware of the problem of land fragmentation through inheritance but their chief concern was surviving in the present.

At harvest time many of them needed extra labour, and feeding an extra son at home worked out at one quarter of the cost of hiring outside workers. They also hoped that if their sons worked hard, or got paying jobs in the nearby town, they could save up enough money to buy extra land. This would get their heads above the dangerously close waters of total ruin - and overcome the fragmentation problem.

Adapted from P. Harrison, *Inside the Third World: an Anatomy of Poverty*, 1979, pp81, 225

Item C *Age structures*

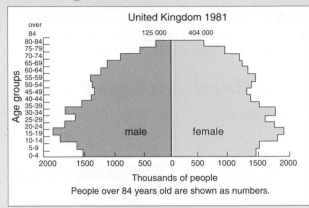

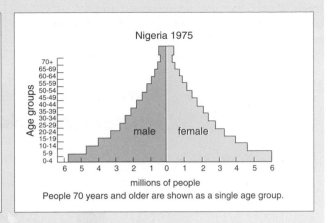

Adapted from S. M. Wood *Population*, 1990, pp 4 and 5

Questions

1 In Item A are some comments which might be made by people living in the materially poorer parts·of the world. Which ones are still sometimes made in the wealthier parts?
2 With reference to Items A and B, what are some of the main reasons why parents in the Third World are reluctant to have fewer children? What changes would be required to encourage parents in the Third World to have fewer children?
3 Explain the charts in Item C. What are some of the consequences for Third World countries of this?

5 Industrialisation and Development

Key Issues

1 What is industrialisation and why is it important?
2 What have been the main obstacles to industrialisation?
3 What have been the main strategies for industrialisation?
4 What are the 'costs' of industrialisation?

5.1 The importance of industrialisation

Since sociology's earliest days, industry and industrialisation have been topics of central concern. For modernisation theorists, industrialisation is, after all, the key feature which distinguishes 'modern' Western societies from all others.

In development studies, industrialisation remains a central issue, though theorists are divided on the role it should play. Modernisation and underdevelopment theorists agree that large scale industrialisation is the route to rapid and long term economic growth. Neo-populists on the other hand argue that Third World countries should favour agriculture and small scale production, because industrialisation is not conducive to social, physical or psychological wellbeing.

5.2 Escaping the traditional role?

From the 16th century beginnings of European mercantile capitalism, Third World countries have been suppliers of primary produce to the First World. (Primary produce is whatever is produced through extractive industry before processing: the raw produce of agriculture, of mining, of the forests and of the seas).

Such international specialisation has long since been justified in the West by neo-classical economics and the so-called 'doctrine of comparative advantage'. The doctrine of comparative advantage argues that countries should specialise in those branches of production in which they have 'natural' abundance. At present, so the argument goes, the Third World is suited to the production of primary produce, such as minerals or cash crops. Hence, this is what they should specialise in.

However, from the 1940s onwards, many in the Third World concluded that they must escape this traditional role. National salvation would depend upon political independence accompanied by a programme of industrialisation. Merely continuing to export a limited range of primary products would never allow them to accumulate sufficient capital to industrialise. They needed to industrialise to generate higher living standards, and to modernise by eroding the power of traditional, conservative elites, enfranchise the peasantry and working class and establish democracy. Additionally, industrialisation might absorb the rural unemployed and underemployed and ultimately lead to a fall in birth rate.

In the 20 or so years following the Second World War, many countries in Africa, Asia and the Caribbean joined Latin American countries as independent nation states and decided to make the painful move away from dependence on primary produce. In all cases, though, they faced serious obstacles, both from within and without.

Activity 11 Trade between Underdeveloped and Developed Societies

Item A *World trade, 1986*

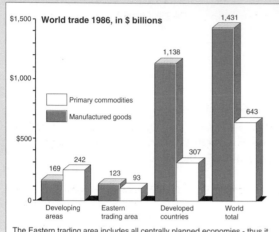

The Eastern trading area includes all centrally planned economies - thus it includes countries like China and Vietnam which are more normally grouped with developing countries.

New Internationalist, February 1990, p17

Item B

A poster from India

Questions

1 Give some examples of a) primary commodities and b) manufactures.
2 Compare and comment on the figures in Item A for developing and developed countries.
3 Look at Item B. Why do you think posters such as this are often seen in the Third World?

5.3 Obstacles to industrialisation

'Internal' obstacles are those existing within the Third World country itself. 'External' obstacles come from beyond their boundaries and are often beyond their control or influence.

1 Internal obstacles The economies inherited by the newly independent, former colonies in the post-Second World War period were usually weak and distorted. In many countries of Africa and Asia, colonial policy had deliberately discouraged industrial development (which might have competed with home producers), and encouraged instead the export of cheap primary produce to the 'mother country'.

Such newly independent countries typically faced a barrage of problems. Their savings and foreign exchange supplies were insufficient so they couldn't afford the machinery and equipment to begin industrialising. The money spent on education and training had been seriously inadequate. Consequently, on independence, in most parts of Africa and in many countries of Asia, literacy levels were only around 20% and the pool of skilled labour and management expertise was quite insufficient.

In Africa, especially, the economic infrastructure was rudimentary: in some areas power supplies, transport networks and communications were virtually non-existent. Necessary raw materials were often needed for export and couldn't be diverted. Without an adequate supply of all of these, any factories established were doomed to work below capacity. They also needed adequate markets to provide additional demand, but home markets were often small, and the country's potential consumers lacked adequate disposable wealth for home markets to develop.

Many of these difficulties still remain serious obstacles to industrialisation. Indeed, in many Third

World countries, the chronic shortages of capital have worsened as political leaders have diverted foreign loans to their personal accounts abroad and spent large amounts on wasteful and inappropriate 'prestige projects' and on building up military might. In the late 1980s, total Third World spending on the military was estimated as almost 70% more than on education.

2 External obstacles As discussed above, as commodity prices fall further behind those of manufactures, Third World countries are increasingly unable to buy the machinery they need to industrialise without taking out further loans.

Moreover, the tendency for commodity prices to fluctuate significantly in the short and medium term has made planning an industrial policy, calculating borrowing requirements, and much else, very difficult.

In addition, the West demands payment for goods - which Third World countries need to industrialise - in the 'hard' currencies of the West. To earn that hard currency they must then spend any surplus investment funds on boosting exports rather than on industrialisation. But it is difficult to boost exports because developed countries impose trade barriers to protect their own industries - such as textiles - which are vulnerable to Third World competition.

Activity 12 Difficulties of Industrialising

Item A *Industries in the colonies*

A British Minister in 1935: 'The suggestion that the colonies should actively promote industrialisation requires special consideration. It is obvious that manufacturing countries like ours could not afford to provide free or assured markets for manufactured goods in direct competition with our own. All questions of starting new industries in the colonies must be examined with regard to the welfare of the colony as a whole and as a primary producer.'

Quoted in E. A. Brett, *Colonialism and Underdevelopment in East Africa: the Politics of Economic Change*, 1973, p273

Item B *Defence and social welfare*

Spending on defence and various social welfare services in selected Third World Countries, 1972-87 (percentage of total government expenditure)

	Defence		Housing, amenities, social services and welfare	
	1972	1987	1972	1987
Malawi	3.1	6.6	5.8	2.3
Tanzania	11.9	15.8	2.1	1.7
Uganda	23.1	26.3	7.3	2.9
Kenya	6.0	9.1	3.9	1.7
Liberia	5.3	8.9	3.5	1.9

Adapted from *New Internationalist*, June 1990, p17

Item C *How it hurts: changes in commodity prices and terms of trade 1970-87*

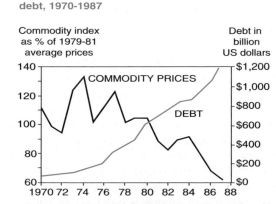

Commodity price index and total Third World debt, 1970-1987

Commodity index as % of 1979-81 average prices / Debt in billion US dollars

Commodity prices fell throughout most of the 1980s. The fall was particularly severe for agricultural (as opposed to mineral) products. This played a big part in the 'Debt Crisis', as poor countries had to borrow to make up the difference. It also forced them to compete with each other - which sent the price of their commodity exports down still further.

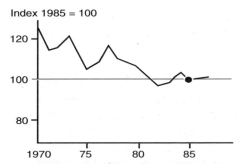

Terms of trade for non-oil developing countries, 1970-1987

Index 1985 = 100

Nothing makes it clearer that developing countries have been losing out than 'the terms of trade' - how much you get paid for what you export compared with what you have to pay for imports. Because Third World countries export primary commodities (which have been falling in price) and import manufactured goods (which have not) they have become poorer.

Adapted from New Internationalist, February 1990, pp16-17

Questions

1 Referring to Items A and C, explain some of the problems experienced by many former colonies in modernising and industrialising.
2 With reference to Item B:
   a) describe the trends shown;
   b) suggest why Third World governments may spend relatively heavily on the military;
   c) suggest some of the possible consequences.

5.4 The nature of Third World industrialisation

In practice, progress towards industrialisation and economic growth since World War Two has been extremely diverse and uneven. However, contradicting the more extreme versions of underdevelopment theory, some significant industrialisation has taken place, showing it is possible in at least some non-Western countries. Clear examples are the famous 'Four Tigers of Asia': Singapore, South Korea, Hong Kong and Taiwan. But others, such as Brazil, Nigeria, India, China and North Korea, also expanded manufacturing faster than population growth. The last two have also challenged an assumption of most modernisation theorists, by achieving substantial industrialisation by a non-capitalist, command economy route.

Also, South Korea and Taiwan illustrate that modernisation theory can underestimate how important foreign intervention can be: massive US aid in the 1950s (to help contain the spread of communism) gave both countries a considerable springboard for industrialisation in the late 1960s.

Observers remain deeply divided, however, on whether these few former Third World countries can be other than exceptions in the world economy. Looking at the industrialising strategies which Third World countries have tried to adopt illustrates some of the difficulties.

1 Industrialisation through import-substitution

Most early Third World attempts to industrialise began with import substitution industrialisation (ISI). This strategy, developed in the 1940s, aimed to produce goods locally for an anticipated expanding home market and thereby reduce imports. This would save scarce foreign exchange and allow further investment. They were mainly light industries. The production of heavy manufactures and goods for export would come later.

Because agriculture remained the major productive and employment sector, many began by producing consumer goods which were most closely related to the land, such as processed food and drinks, agricultural tools and machinery, and fertilisers.

Some household items and textiles were also commonly produced.

But as Barnett points out (1988, p89), import substitution ran into a number of difficulties. Believing that their infant industries needed protection from established foreign competition, Third World leaders had intervened to create tariff barriers, import quotas, subsidies, and so on. However, this divorced those in charge of industries from market forces, and made it impossible to take 'rational' decisions about investment levels, and what and how much to produce.

Secondly, to establish new industries required machinery and technical know-how. Importing these needed 'hard' foreign currency. To earn this meant increasing exports of primary products. And although the TNCs could provide machinery and know-how, they would only invest if they could sell in the local market and this undermined the indigenous 'infant industries'.

Thirdly, in many cases the home market was inadequate to allow for indigenous industries to be set up. Too few people could afford to buy the manufactures, especially those such as cars, televisions and other luxury goods.

Overall, many concluded, Third World dependence on the West had not lessened. Indeed, with the expanding role of the TNCs, it had probably increased. And, far from delivering stable, integrated, modern democracies, authoritarian governments, social division and cultural alienation were widespread. Consequently, many felt that further growth based on the home market and import-substitution was no longer possible. The solution proposed was export-oriented industrialisation.

2 Export-oriented industrialisation

Export-oriented industrialisation (EOI) strategies were developed to produce manufactured goods for export. Since their emergence in the late 1960s, these strategies can claim some startling successes, including the much quoted 'Four Tigers of Asia' as well as countries such as Brazil. Initially, they concentrated on light industrial products, such as clothing, textiles and electronic goods, suitable both for home consumption and export. But the longer term plan was to diversify into heavy, export-oriented industries, such as steel, shipbuilding and chemicals, where they have long since become formidable competitors to industries in the West.

These successes encouraged other Third World countries to devise their own export-oriented strategies. Many consciously sought to attract foreign investment, particularly from the TNCs. One common device was to establish export processing zones (EPZs): special areas set aside for the production or finishing of (mainly) light industrial goods for export. 'Host' countries typically provided the infrastructure free, waived import duties, often banned trade unions, guaranteed the full remission of profits and so on in an attempt to make EPZs particularly attractive to the investors.

Despite the apparent signs of success of EOI in countries such as Brazil, Argentina and Mexico, however, critics argue that most NICs have only succeeded because their typically authoritarian political regimes have kept wages low by suppressing trade unions and democracy. They also wonder how many Third World countries can afford the long term, costly process of creating the skilled workforce and trained management necessary to produce for export.

Critics also question how many Third World countries can emulate the successes of the NICs. Many 'took off' during the international boom years of the 1960s, but only following massive inputs of foreign aid, which few other countries can ever realistically hope for, and state aid, which few others could afford. In the 1990s, with former Second World countries more serious competitors for international aid and trade, there may be little space left for new NICs, at least from the Third World.

Despite the substantial interference with market forces of the NICs (who, like most Western industrialising countries in the 19th century, protected, promoted and helped finance many of their 'infant' industries), their successes seem clearly to have disproven Frank's extreme dependency view that no Third World country can make further progress under capitalism. Yet, while the NICs might appear to offer a beacon of hope to other Third World countries, their achievements have been gained under particular circumstances that may offer little comfort to those who would wish to emulate them.

Activity 13 Third World Industrialisation

Item A *The sequence of industrial growth*

The first industries to develop are usually those processing locally produced, perishable materials, especially food: baking, food processing, canning, soft drinks, beer. Next come industries using bulky, locally available materials, where high transport costs make foreign goods too expensive: cement, bricks, sanitary ware, furniture. The first steps into consumer durables come with the assembly business: local workers assemble kits of components, for cars, fridges, cookers, shipped in from industrialised countries. Gradually the locally made content of these products is increased, creating jobs in component making, tool and die and mould making. Finally, a capital goods industry making machinery might develop.

Adapted from P. Harrison *Inside the Third World: an Anatomy of Poverty*, 1979, p182

Questions

1 In Item A, what term would be used to describe such a process?
2 What are the alleged benefits of such a process?
3 What are the main dangers or weaknesses of such developments for Third World countries?
4 How would you explain the data in Item B?

Item B *Shares of world manufacturing trade, 1987*

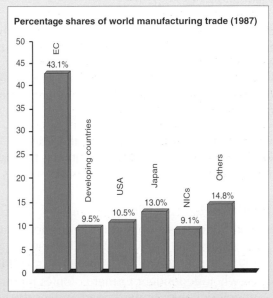

Adapted from *New Internationalist*, February 1990, p16

5.5 The 'costs' of industrialisation

In the West, industrialisation has made possible the development of societies whose members enjoy standards of living, political democracy and cultural breadth which are historically unprecedented. Around the Third World, leaders are trying to devise ways of making many of the same gains. Yet, as has been increasingly recognised, industrialisation has also had its 'costs'. For present purposes, the costs of industrialisation can be divided into economic, social and cultural, and ecological ones. The economic and sociocultural costs of industrialisation are usually borne by the people of the industrialising society themselves. The ecological costs are increasingly shared with all other societies. In this context the ultimate question becomes: can the world bear the costs of continuing industrialisation?

1 Economic costs Economically, industrialisation involves shifting the balance in a society from consumption to investment, postponing rewards today for hoped-for rewards tomorrow. In every case, industrialisation has been pursued by the nation's leaders as a conscious strategy, in which it is recognised that some will gain at the expense of others. Present generations suffer in order to improve the lot of successive generations. And within the present generations, some groups are more vulnerable than others: the rural poor, the elderly, children, women. Any economic belt-tightening is likely to be felt particularly keenly by them. Everywhere it has occurred it has been a painful and drawn out process, and the Third World is proving no exception.

2 Social and cultural costs Industrialisation also has its social and cultural costs. As Foster-Carter puts it: 'Old ways are shattered or eroded. Small scale activities become uneconomic and disappear. A brash new smoky squalid urban industrial society thrusts its way onto centre stage, while the old rural world is pushed to the margins. The impersonal replaces the personal, community is superseded by organisation' (1985, p39).

No doubt there is also much in 'undeveloped' societies which is repressive, squalid, impoverished and constricting. However, there is no denying the common experience of anguish, of mounting alienation and anomie, as traditional cultures seek to adapt to the bewildering changes introduced from societies a world away.

3 Ecological costs Third, there are the growing ecological costs. In the West, pollution is perhaps the most sharply felt concern. On issues such as the depletion and holing of the ozone layer, global warming, acid rain, industrial toxic wastes and the proliferation of garbage, media publicity has both reflected and amplified a profound anxiety which transcends barriers of class and nation. There is widespread concern that the world and its atmosphere are approaching a point of irreversible and catastrophic damage. If the industrialised nations are already rapidly destroying the world's life-support systems through pollution, surely further industrialisation elsewhere along similar lines is unsustainable?

There is concern, too, about the depletion of non-renewable energy supplies such as oil and coal. Globally, coal reserves are still substantial: it has been estimated that less than 2% of available coal has so far been extracted. However, coal is a serious pollutant, producing global-warming carbon dioxide and implicated in bronchial illnesses. Further work to try to make its use safer is sorely needed. Even resources which are potentially renewable - such as land, forests and clean water - are under threat from industrialisation.

One major pressure is the industrialised countries' methods of food production. In the West, food production has been increased in large part through the 'industrialisation' of agriculture. Bigger fields, bigger land holdings and mechanisation of production have allowed economies of scale. But agricultural industrialisation has also entailed the destruction of hedgerows and woodland, the widespread use of oil-based fertiliser and of often toxic herbicides and pesticides. A system of agricultural production which rests on non-renewable resources which pollute seems ultimately self-defeating and no model for the Third World. Again, the conclusion seems to be that continuing industrialisation in the North, and further movement towards manufacturing and agro-industrialisation in the South, must, in future, be more sustainable.

Summary

1 Both modernisation and underdevelopment theorists believe that large scale industrialisation is the necessary route to Third World economic growth. But neo-populists argue for smaller scale industry, claiming that the alternative is self-destructive.

2 Newly independent former colonies inherited many obstacles to industrialisation. Internally, an undereducated, undertrained and insufficiently literate population, a rudimentary economic infrastructure, insufficient savings and foreign exchange to buy necessary machinery and a military which was high spending and corrupt. External factors, such as low and fluctuating commodity prices and First World trade barriers, compounded the difficulties.

3 Early attempts to industrialise, by way of import-substitution industrialisation (ISI), aimed to produce goods locally for an expanding home market and thereby reduce imports. However, in trying to protect their infant industries, Third World governments made it difficult for managers to make informed decisions about production and investment. Also, home markets often proved too small.

4 The later strategy of export-oriented industrialisation (EOI) aims to develop larger scale capital intensive industries. Despite the successes of the 'Four Tigers of Asia' and others, critics claim that

few can emulate them because they succeeded only after considerable foreign aid and during an international 'boom'.

5 The prospect of continuing industrialisation is prompting growing concern about its 'costs'. Everywhere, it seems to be initially economically and socially painful, especially for the most vulnerable. The main concerns, however, reflect the mounting ecological costs, which affect the whole planet.

6 Urbanisation and Development

Key Issues

1 How rapid and extensive is urban growth and urbanisation in the First and Third Worlds?
2 How does Third World urbanisation differ from that which has occurred in the West?

6.1 Urban growth and urbanisation

Of the many alarming issues facing Third World countries today, urban growth and urbanisation are among the most critical. Throughout the Third World, urban authorities have declared that their towns and cities are in crisis. Third World city growth has been dramatically rapid and usually haphazard. As the expanding urban areas continue to sprawl, their inhabitants face inadequacies in housing, job opportunities, water, sewage and transportation. Roads are choked, power and sewage systems overloaded, and land and secure tenure so scarce that many must find whatever space and shelter they can, wherever they can. For most, however, even this is preferred to rural living.

It is useful, at the beginning, to distinguish between two concepts. The term *urban growth* refers to increases in the size of towns and cities. Urban growth may occur whether the rural population is rising, falling or remaining stable. *Urbanisation*, however, refers to an increase in the proportion of the population who are living in cities and towns: in other words, urbanisation occurs when the urban population is growing faster than the rural population.

6.2 Urban growth and urbanisation in historical context

In 1900, less than 14% of the world's population is believed to have lived in urban areas. By the year 2000, it will be an estimated 50% or more. The growing concentration of the world's population in urban areas has been remarkably rapid.

Although cities - even relatively large ones - could be found in ancient times (Rome in 150 AD had about a million inhabitants), they were set within societies which were primarily agrarian. In Europe, for centuries following the decline of the Roman Empire, a number of Mediterranean European cities - Venice, Genoa, Florence - remained and grew as important centres of population and trade. Throughout the medieval period, European cities were centres of important economic activity. At the same time, substantial cities also existed in many other parts of the world. Here, too, however, city dwellers were a minority of the population.

Urbanisation began in the West - in Britain - with the beginnings of the Industrial Revolution in the 18th century. By 1851 a majority of England's population was urbanised. The pace accelerated throughout the 19th century with industrialisation in the USA, Japan, Germany and elsewhere in Europe, but by 1900 England remained the world's only predominantly urban nation.

In the twentieth century, however, and particularly since the Second World War, the advance of urbanisation has been breathtaking. As recently as 1960 only 20% of the world's population lived in cities; by 1980 it was over 40%. And urban growth and urbanisation are fastest in the South, though, as in other respects, there are significant differences between continents and regions.

6.3 Changing patterns of urban growth and urbanisation

Although the statistics must be regarded cautiously, some patterns of change are clear.

First, a quickly growing proportion of the world's city dwellers live in the Third World. Until the mid-1970s most of the world's urban population lived in the North. By the year 2000, the South will account for three times as many urban dwellers as the North.

Secondly, the actual number of large cities in the South has increased rapidly. In 1950, for instance, only seven cities worldwide had more than five million inhabitants, just two of which - Shanghai in China and Buenos Aires in Argentina - were in the Third World. Twenty-five years later cities of five million or more had jumped from seven to 34. According to UN projections, by 2025 there will be 93, of which 80 will be in the Third World.

Thirdly, it is not merely that the major cities of the Third World are growing in size. The countries are urbanising. In other words, the population in the cities is growing faster - and usually much faster - than that of the rural areas. In the last fifty years total Third World population is estimated to have increased two and a half times. The population increase of Third World cities has been eight-fold. By the year 2015, most people in Third World countries are expected to live in an urban environment.

Third World urbanisation is highest in Latin America, which in 1986 was approximately 65% urbanised. In Asia as a whole, urbanisation is around 30% of the population, with significant regional variations. In Africa, too, urbanisation is around 30% although here is where the fastest urban growth is occurring. In many countries in the First World, by contrast, urbanisation is actually declining (although this is largely because suburban growth is regarded as distinct).

6.4 First and Third World urbanisation

Urbanisation is a result of migration (mainly internal) and natural increase (an excess of births over deaths). Before considering the role of these factors in Third World urbanisation, a comparison between First and Third World urbanisation will be made. With the First World now approximately 75% urbanised, how has the process differed?

1 First, as will be discussed below, a larger proportion of Third World urban growth comes from high rates of natural increase within the cities than was the case with First World urbanisation. In the First World, the expanding towns and cities grew mainly by attracting migrants from the countryside. In the Third World, however, less than 50% of the growth is from rural migrants, although there is considerable regional variation.
2 This reflects a second major difference. In the West, urbanisation occurred because of the growth of industry - large and small - which needed and attracted workers on a growing scale. There were shortages of labour for the new factories, mines and shipyards of the towns. In the cities of the South, however, urban growth has not been accompanied by a similar expansion of industries and work opportunities.
3 Also, Third World industrialisation is generally much more capital intensive and makes little demand of local labour. Relatively few work in large scale factories. Instead, millions earn a precarious living by working in the bloated 'informal' sector of the economy. With the development of very substantial informal sectors, Third World cities are said to be characterised by

dual sector economies.
4 The growth of industrial cities in the First World was preceded by advances in agriculture which produced a food surplus. To this were added cheap imports from the colonies. In most Third World countries today, food is scarce.
5 Cities in the South are fewer and bigger than those in the North and have grown faster. A common feature of Southern urbanisation is the so-called 'primate city', a city which dominates the country and reduces any other urban areas to the status of satellites. Mexico City, Baghdad and Cairo provide examples.
6 Given the speed at which Southern cities are growing and the context of relative national poverty, the authorities are less able to plan and implement the provision of services for their rising urban populations than was the case in the West. And the infrastructural developments, on which many Third World governments spend substantial sums to attract foreign industrial investment, are often limited to export processing zones and are of little benefit to the indigenous population (see p595).

6.5 Natural increase and internal migration

As mentioned above, natural increase has played a much more important role in stoking Third World urbanisation than it did in the West. These high rates of natural increase occur largely because those most likely to move to the cities are young adults. Hence, urban populations are disproportionately young and disproportionately reproductive.

Although contributing a lower proportion to the urban total than in the West's urbanisation, internal migration is, nevertheless, very important. In a number of Third World countries, rural migration has accounted for over 50% of city population growth. And in absolute terms, the numbers of rural migrants to cities in the Third World has been considerable. For almost all Third World countries, rural migration to the towns and cities is a significant, and usually deeply worrying, phenomenon.

Why do so many people in the Third World move from their rural homes to the city? Why, given the relative lack of industrial growth and demand for labour, and the need to compete for the limited available work with a high proportion of locally born people? For many, migration to the city is a mark of desperation.

Analyses of migration usually distinguish between so-called 'push factors' (reasons for leaving) and 'pull factors' (perceived attractions of the destination). Explanations are, then, a combination of the two.

Push factors Throughout the Third World, the loss of land provides a major push factor. Usually this is through subdivision and debt. In many countries the division of land between sons means that each has insufficient to subsist on. For a range of reasons, including natural disasters and crop failure, the need to borrow puts many subsistence farmers in debt. In the absence of proper credit facilities, this often results in their loss of land and the moneylenders - frequently wealthy local landowners - accumulating landholdings.

For many others, a variety of changes which have been detrimental to rural living have provided further push factors. In many cases, ironically, it has been rural 'development' projects themselves which have ushered in such changes. In many Third World countries, for instance, agribusiness and large landowners have been the main beneficiaries of government help (and often of foreign aid) to modernise farming methods. The resultant mechanisation of agriculture has frequently led to less wealthy, independent farmers being undercut and forced out of business, and tenant farmers, being rendered unnecessary by the introduction of machinery, dispossessed of the land they have worked and of their livelihoods.

Landless labourers, who in many Third World countries make up a substantial proportion of the population, have also often suffered as a consequence of rural 'development'. These are the very poor, with no regular means of sustaining themselves. In Latin America they account for over half the rural population. Again, mechanisation reduces the work available and, with a growing concentration of land in the hands of large owners, mechanisation allows economies of scale and has become increasingly viable.

Craft workers, such as potters, weavers, builders, roofers, metal workers, cobblers and tailors, have also found themselves under growing pressure to leave rural areas. Increasingly, the more prosperous farmers prefer factory made goods and have no use of their services. The progressively impoverished, on the other hand, can no longer afford them. With the dispossession of small landowners, the decline of available work, increasing poverty and the deskilling or disappearance of craft workers, rural life breaks down, and people have no option but to try the towns or cities.

Pull factors Though for many the reality of city life is grim, the hope (and often the reality) is of something better than what was left. Industrial and public sector jobs are concentrated in the cities and they in turn spawn other work opportunities in both the formal and informal sectors. If work can be found, urban incomes are higher than in rural areas: on average about three times in the Third World. Hospitals and doctors tend to be concentrated in the cities, and other services, such as education, electricity and water tend to be more accessible. In African cities, some 36% have access to a safe water supply compared to 21% of rural people; in Latin America, 67% to 30%, in Asia 47% to 19%.

6.6 Dual sector economies

Whereas in the West, urbanisation was accompanied by industrialisation and a substantial growth in occupational opportunities, in much of the Third World industry is scarce. It is, in any event, largely capital intensive, and full time employment opportunities are relatively few. Yet, although poverty in Third World cities is undeniably widespread, millions nevertheless manage to survive. And they survive because of the existence of the so-called informal sector, which exists, distinct though interrelated, alongside the relatively secure and well paid formal sector of the economy.

The formal sector To oversimplify, the formal sector consists of 'modern', Western-derived industries and occupations, bureaucratically organised and usually capital-intensive. It also includes state sponsored, bureaucratic occupations such as education, administration and law and the larger businesses with officially registered payrolls.

The formal sector usually involves large scale activity, provides relatively permanent employment and offers set wages and hours of work and pensions. It requires formal qualifications of its employees. If it is a business or industry, its scope of operations is often international, typically importing machinery and often even labour, and its market is global. However, it constitutes a relatively small part of most Third World countries' economies.

The informal sector By contrast, the informal sector is swollen and precarious. Throughout Third World cities, millions struggle to eke out a living in jobs whose income and hours are variable and undependable. If people are unable to work, for instance because of illness, they receive no income. Much of the work is self-employed or in small businesses and often involves whole families rather than an individual. It is usually based on a locality and can include almost every imaginable service. It is labour-intensive and the level of technology used is relatively low.

The interrelationships of the formal and informal sectors have long been debated. It was once thought that the two sectors had almost no contact and that those in the informal sector mainly made a living by selling to one another. However, it is now clear that the two sectors interrelate in a number of ways.

First, the informal sector supplies the formal sector and any other customers with a range of cheap goods and services: pots and pans, soft drinks, snacks, shoe-shines, prostitution. In return, the formal sector sells the informal sector consumer goods, such as electrical items.

Second, it has become clear that, in many Third World cities, some groups of workers in the informal sector are being 'employed' and organised by highly capitalised organisations in the formal sector. Usually this is done through 'middle-men' who, by keeping them off the official payroll, avoid the need for the companies to pay minimum wages, social security contributions or a share in the profits. There is evidence of such organised 'out-working' systems in trades such as carpetmaking, tailoring, carpentry and shoemaking in Africa, Asia and Latin America.

Summary

1 Urban growth is fastest in the Third World. So too is urbanisation: ie Third World city populations are growing faster than rural populations. Rural migrants to the towns are disproportionately young: hence the growth of Third World cities is particularly fuelled by natural increase (ie more births than deaths).

2 Compared to the First World, Third World urbanisation is less likely to be accompanied by labour intensive industrialisation (which would have provided jobs) and adequate food supplies.

3 Rural migration results from a combination of push and pull factors. A major push factor is land loss as a consequence of debt and the subdivision of land between offspring. The pull factors of city life include somewhat better prospects of work, education, health care and safe water.

4 The scarcity of labour-intensive industry in cities has encouraged the development of a large informal sector. Work is self-employed, variable, undependable, local, and often involves other family members.

Activity 14 Urbanisation

Item A

Urban population as a percentage of total population, by level of economy, 1965 and 1990

	1965	1990
Low income economies (excl. China & India)	16	27
Middle income economies	42	60
High income economies	72	77

Adapted from *Development and the Environment: World Development Report*, 1992, pp278-279

Item B

Population in capital city 1990

	% of urban population living in capital city	% of total population living in capital city
Low income economies (excl. China & India)	26	7
Middle income economies	25	14
High income economies	12	9

Adapted from *Development and the Environment: World Development Report*, 1992, pp278-279

Item C *Making ends meet*

Rajil, a 25 year old with one child, owns half a hectare but you need about a hectare and a half in this area to be self-sufficient. Four times a year he goes to the regional capital of Jogjakarta for two or three weeks at a time. There he joins the throng of cycle rickshaw drivers who line every street. Competition is so stiff that he is lucky if he earns 500 rupiahs (60p) in a day. He spends his night sleeping on the metre-long seat, legs up; it saves money and protects the rickshaw against thieves.

Adapted from P. Harrison, *Inside the Third World: an Anotomy of Poverty*, 1979

A rickshaw in Jogjakarta

Questions

1 With reference to Item A, in which category of economy is urbanisation proceeding most rapidly? Justify your answer.

2 Explain the idea of 'primate cities' with reference to Item B.

3 a) With reference to Item C and other sources, what are the usual characteristics of the informal sector?

b) In what ways does a city's informal sector typically depend upon the formal sector?

7 Health as an Aspect of Development

Key Issues

1 What are the major health problems of Third World countries?

2 What has been the impact of the West on Third World health and health care?

3 What are the requirements for improved health in the Third World?

7.1 Measuring health

Measuring the health of a country's population is a subjective and problematic business, even in a highly educated, numerate society, blessed with the most sophisticated statistical systems. But making valid comparisons between the world's diverse countries is vastly more difficult. Often, crucial data are lacking and what exists may be of doubtful validity. As ever, higher recorded rates in one country (of births, deaths, disease, etc) may reflect its better recording systems rather than real differences. Despite the difficulties, however, comparisons are often made by referring to a few key indicators. Death rates, including infant mortality rates, and life expectancy levels, are the most commonly used.

In broad terms, what the evidence suggests is that, from about the 1950s or 1960s, there has been steady global progress: death rates, including infant mortality rates, have been falling and life expectancy rising. However, in all these respects, there are significant variations, both between North and South and between regions.

7.2 National wealth and national health

Given these continuing variations, to what extent do health standards simply reflect a population's economic status? As one might expect, there is a broad correlation between a country's per capita GNP and its levels of health, as measured by its life expectancy, and infant mortality and death rates. So, broadly speaking, the lowest levels of health are reported in African countries, middle levels in Asia, and relatively high levels - much closer to those of the developed world - are found in the generally richer countries of Latin America. However, there are many significant health level differences between countries in the same GNP bands. And lowest income countries are not always the least healthy.

Nevertheless, in broad terms it remains true that disease thrives in an environment of poverty. As Harrison notes: 'Chronic disease proneness causes poverty, while poverty provides the ideal breeding ground for disease' (1979, p287). Throughout the Third World, hundreds of millions live in a downward spiral of poverty, proneness to disease and ill-health, redundancy and unemployment, and further poverty. Poverty drains energy, and saps the capacity to learn, to produce, to earn and to provide.

7.3 Third World patterns of health and ill-health

1 Increased life expectancy In the Third World, as elsewhere, life expectancy continues to rise. Over the last few decades, throughout much of the South, the gains in life expectancy have been proportionately bigger than in the North. However, in absolute terms life expectancy generally remains substantially lower; in many African countries by about 30 years. Between 1975 and 1987, for example, Japanese life expectancy rose by 7%, from 73 to 78. In Mali (Africa), it rose by 18%, from 38 to 45.

In 19th century Europe and the USA, lower mortality rates and increased life expectancy were primarily a response to general improvements in socio-economic living standards: better sewerage and sanitation systems, cleaner water, less overcrowding, better education and standards of personal hygiene. Medical advances, in drugs and technology, didn't give a particularly significant boost to further increases in life expectancy until the mid-1930s.

In the South, however, particularly from the 1950s, the rapid fall in mortality rates and rise in life expectancy were largely effected by the growing availablility of Western drugs and medical techniques and technology. The improvements in socioeconomic conditions - better sanitation and hygiene, etc - which 'kick-started' the process in the West, have been, and still are, largely missing in the South. Not surprisingly perhaps, the fall of mortality rates and the rise in life expectancy have slowed more recently. Indeed, as discussed below, further substantial progress looks unlikely without the sort of socioeconomic improvements which led the attack on disease in the 19th century West.

2 Patterns of disease In the North, the major causes of death are diseases of affluence. Cancers and heart disease, along with road accidents, reflect the relative old age, and rich diet and consumption patterns, of their populations. In the South, such diseases are spreading. But the biggest killers remain communicable diseases, which, when combined with malnutrition as they often are, are particularly lethal for children. For instance, more than half of all Third

World child fatalities are accounted for by diarrhoeal diseases (eg dysentery) and respiratory infections (eg tuberculosis), aided as always by malnutrition. The most common diseases are carried in human faeces, or in water, or by insects.

Where such diseases can be successfully fought by immunisation, there have been significant successes. Smallpox was eradicated in the late 1970s and polio is likely to be wiped out by 2000 AD. And 80% of the developing world's children were estimated to have been immunised against such common diseases as measles, tetanus, whooping cough and polio by the end of 1990. The World Health Organisation's new target is 90%.

However, the diseases killing most Third World children cannot be prevented either by immunisation or by attacking insect carriers with chemicals. Instead, as in the 19th century industrialising West, improvements are required in water quality, the

sanitary disposal of human waste, hygiene and diet.

3 Incidence of disease: the vulnerable groups Some categories of people are, of course, more prone to disease than others. Children are the most vulnerable and are the largest disease-affected group in the South. In the South as a whole about 17% of children die before their fifth birthday and in the poorest countries the figure rises to about one third. Women also suffer disproportionately. Their often inferior diet compounds the hazards of frequent pregnancy and inadequate care. The rural populations of the South are also more at risk than the urban. They are less likely to have access to clean water and adequate sanitation and they are much further from doctors, health centres and hospitals. And, of course, the poor, whether urban or rural, are much more likely to suffer disease than their richer compatriots.

Activity 15 Health and Wealth

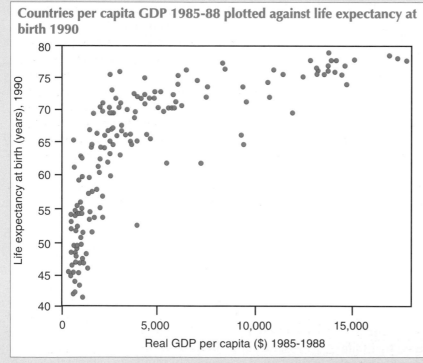

Countries per capita GDP 1985-88 plotted against life expectancy at birth 1990

Adapted from World Health Organisation *Our Planet, Our Health*, 1992, p9

Questions

1 a) What is the relationship between life expectancy and GDP suggested by the graph?
   b) Give a brief explanation for this relationship.
2 a) Using the graph, show exceptions to this relationship.
   b) Suggest reasons for such exceptions.

7.4 Third World health and the West

For imperialist countries such as Britain and France, colonial expansion brought cheap imported commodities (including food), increased wealth, and improved life expectancy.

On the other hand, to millions in Africa, Asia, Australasia and the Americas, European merchant capitalism and colonialism brought disease and death. For numbers unknown, the loss of land and

destruction of culture provoked disorientation and anomie, alcoholism, neurosis and suicide.

Secondly, Third World countries (and often including those not formerly colonised) suffered an almost certain deterioration in the nutritional level of diets with the replacement of a variety of locally produced and consumed subsistence food crops by cash crops for export. The consequent monoculture has also led to continuing, chronic food crises.

Thirdly, in the last few decades, politically independent Third World countries have found themselves being used by Western-based transnational corporations (TNCs) as markets for products regarded as undesirable or dangerous in the West, often with Western governmental approval. Drugs, pesticides and herbicides have all been tested in Third World countries before being marketed in the West. Many such items are prohibited in the West but nevertheless sold widely to Third World populations, whose governments have on occasions been pressured into compliance by threats of withdrawal of Western government aid. For many TNCs, the inability of many Third World countries to demand similar safety and anti-pollution standards to those in the West makes factory location and operation there cheaper and is part of their attraction.

Similarly, expensive but relatively unnutritious foods and drinks - such as baby milk powder, refined sugar derivatives (eg chocolates), white flour products (eg crackers) and soft drinks (eg colas) - have been widely promoted by mass advertising campaigns. In the notorious campaign to sell baby milk, cases have been unearthed in which health centre staff were bribed and sales women dressed as nurses to promote the product, and paid on a commission basis. Western tobacco companies, with prospects in the West more gloomy, have worked hard to sell their products - especially the more profitable, high tar cigarettes - in the Third World. At the same time, the United States' government has pursued a military and political campaign to eliminate the drug exports of some of its neighbours in Latin America.

Fourthly, health care in many Third World countries has imitated the health industries of the West. The model of health services introduced under colonialism and inherited by the newly independent countries established a pattern which remains influential in the post-colonial Third World. Such health care was (and is) overwhelmingly based on hospitals and in urban areas, and is often inaccessible to the mainly rural population who lack even clinics. It was (and is) also heavily dependent upon expensive, usually imported, high technology and the relatively few, highly and expensively trained doctors that the country can afford to train. Many are trained in Western countries and many don't return.

The inherited Western model also emphasised curative rather than preventative medicine and today makes much use of manufactured pharmaceuticals. Traditional medicines were devalued and rejected. In many countries this Western model has retained prestige and the support of those urban elites who most benefit from it. Despite this, in many Third World countries, the political elites have opted for increased arms spending while cutting expenditure on health and education.

Today, trained doctors and nurses remain scarce in most Third World countries. While the richer countries of the North have approximately one doctor for every 520 people, the poorest countries have one per 17,000. And their concentration in urban areas means that about three-quarters of the doctors serve only one-quarter of the population. Yet, on average, urban hospitals in Third World countries consumed in 1987 some 75% of central government resources available for health (*New Internationalist*, March 1990, p28).

Activity 16 Western Influence

Item A *Babyfood*

A poster from South Africa

Item B *Western medical technology*

Most of the medical technology in underdeveloped countries comes from the developed world. For example, it has been estimated that 80% of Latin American medical equipment is imported, mostly from the USA. So in Bogota, Colombia, a city of over two million, where nutritional and communicable diseases predominate, the annual running costs of its three open-heart surgery units could provide a quarter of the city's children with a half litre of milk daily for a year!

Adapted from D. Sanders and R. Carver *The Struggle for Health*,1985, p148

Item C

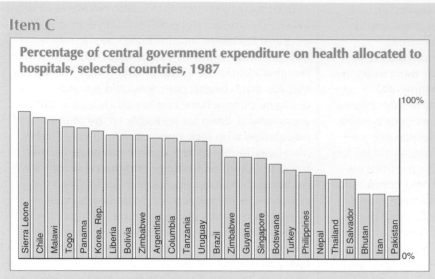

Percentage of central government expenditure on health allocated to hospitals, selected countries, 1987

Sierra Leone, Chile, Malawi, Togo, Panama, Korea. Rep., Liberia, Bolivia, Zimbabwe, Argentina, Columbia, Tanzania, Uruguay, Brazil, Zimbabwe, Guyana, Singapore, Botswana, Turkey, Philippines, Nepal, Thailand, El Salvador, Bhutan, Iran, Pakistan

Adapted from UNICEF *The State of the World's Children*, 1990, quoted in *New Internationalist*, March 1990, p28

Questions

1 a) With reference to Item A, why might Third World mothers have been persuaded to abandon breast feeding in favour of milk powder?
    b) Why might this cause problems?

2 a) With reference to Items B and C, suggest ways in which the Western medical model may be inappropriate for Third World countries.
    b) Why do so many Third World countries nevertheless follow it?

7.5 Requirements for improved Third World health

Although immunisation policies in the South have had major successes against certain diseases such as smallpox and polio, other diseases (including diarrhoea and various respiratory infections, which remain major killers) are unlikely to be eradicated without improvements in the socio-physical environment. In particular, there need to be improvements in people's access to clean water, in the sanitary disposal of human waste and in attacking malnutrition. In order for these goals to be understood by the population, acted upon and achieved, two further goals are also necessary, at the very least highly desirable: the development of a literate population and greater sexual equality. Additionally, health care provision must be more available for the rural population.

1 Water and sanitation According to a 1988 World Health Organisation Report, real progress has been made in the last few decades in increasing the proportion of Third World populations with access to safe drinking water and adequate sanitary systems of waste disposal. The Report claimed that access to safe water in Third World rural areas had trebled between 1970 and 1985 (from 13% to 43%) and was now 77% in urban areas. Although access to adequate sanitation was limited to 16% of rural populations, it had almost doubled for those in urban areas (from 30% to 58%).

Nevertheless, despite such welcome progress, it is clear that, particularly in rural areas where most still live, access to safe drinking water and adequate sanitary systems remains disturbingly low. Hundreds of millions have access to neither and remain vulnerable to the major killer diseases.

2 Nourishment In the early 1980s, UN agencies calculated that, quite apart from major famines which claim tens of thousands of lives each year, the number of chronically malnourished people in the Third World was approximately 450 million, with almost half of them children under five. Some 10,000 people a day were believed to die from not having enough to eat. According to the Food and Agricultural Organisation (FAO), about half the young children in the Third World are probably inadequately fed. In many areas the numbers are growing. According to Alexander Cockburn, in Lima, capital of Peru, the number of malnourished children in the poorer neighbourhoods increased from 24% in 1972 to 36% in 1983. In Kenya, a 1982 government health survey found that 28% of the children were stunted as a result of poor nutrition, up by 4% from five years earlier.

The problem of malnutrition in the South is not one of world food shortage. On the whole, the world produces more food than its individual citizens need for health. In the 1980s, for instance, the world surplus of cereals led to farmers in the European Community actually being paid to keep cereal-producing acreage out of production. And there is little doubt that worldwide output could rise significantly. A study in the 1970s by the University of Wageningen in the Netherlands, based on UNESCO soil maps of the world, concluded that the earth could sustain the production of 25 times the amount of grain which was then being produced annually!

The 'failure' of the South to 'feed itself' is multicausal. The production of cash crops, inherited from colonial days, occupies much good - but scarce - agricultural land in the South. And the need to service foreign debts or gain hard currency or both often leads countries to export foodstuffs while their people go hungry.

Much land is unusable for production of local foods because it is given over to producing foodstuffs to give to animals which the rich North will then eat. In one grotesque example, Ethiopia in 1984, at the height of a desperate famine, with thousands dying daily, was transporting shiploads of food crops to Europe to be eaten by animals in Western factory farms. Gold calculates that: 'An area of the Third World the size of the UK, France, New Zealand and Italy combined is being devoted solely to the production of animal feeds for European livestock' (1991, p9). Animal feeds are grown on some of the best Third World land - land that could have been used for growing food for the hungry local population.

3 Literacy and sexual equality If high standards of sanitation and personal hygiene are to become widespread in the South, those goals must be understood and acted upon by as large a proportion of the population as possible. In the view of many, this requires widespread literacy. (How sufficient a role audio-visual media may play in this is not yet clear). As women are particularly responsible for the socialisation of children, female literacy is especially important.

Many studies have shown that, irrespective of family income, the more educated the mothers, the less likely to die are their children. High levels of female literacy, and correspondingly low infant mortality rates, strongly suggest that literate mothers are more aware of, and willing to try, recommended health, hygiene and nutritional practices.

Female literacy rates vary significantly by region, with Latin America being trailed by Asia and especially Africa. Nevertheless, of the world's estimated 800 million illiterates, 3 in 5 are women, mostly rural dwellers. In all but a handful of Third World countries (eg Philippines, Mexico, Cuba), female literacy rates are inferior to those of males. Most worryingly, although global literacy rates are improving, in absolute terms global illiteracy is growing and especially among females (ie the proportion of illiterates is falling but the actual numbers are increasing). During the 1970s, for instance, male illiteracy is estimated to have grown by about 2 million per annum; for females annual growth was estimated at 5 million.

4 Primary health care To try to overcome some of the limitations of a Western-derived, urban, hospital-based system, the World Health Organisation (WHO) has endorsed a strategy of 'Health for all by the year 2000'. That is, by 2000 AD everyone everywhere should have the opportunity of a level of health which will allow them to lead socially and economically productive lives. A key part of the

strategy to achieve this goal puts emphasis on what is called primary health care.

Fully trained doctors and nurses are expensive to train and pay and are therefore scarce and inaccessible. In the Third World, primary health care relies heavily on cheaply trained Community Health Workers (CHWs) who, it is hoped, will be locally accessible to rural dwellers and will be able to help prevent and treat most common illnesses. The 10% or so of cases the CHWs cannot diagnose and treat will be referred to more fully trained personnel elsewhere. Much of the work of the CHWs is preventative. They encourage family planning, educate people about nutrition and hygiene, organise immunisation and mass treatment programmes as well as monitoring epidemics, water quality and sanitation.

However, as noted above, despite more than twenty years of the WHO's 'Health for All' strategy, a 1990 UNICEF Report found primary health care in the South largely starved of funds, with central governments' health budgets still consuming some 75% of the total.

Summary

1 Although non-infectious, degenerative diseases associated with the North (eg cancers, heart disease) are spreading, most Third World diseases (eg malaria, dysentery) are of the communicable variety, spread via human waste, impure water and insects. Children are particularly at risk and vulnerability for all is greatly increased by malnutrition.

2 Throughout the Third World, early contact with the West brought disease and death on a massive scale. The colonial introduction of cash crops and monoculture has probably resulted in a deterioration in the nutritional quality of diets and in chronic food crises. Third World countries have largely retained their colonial inheritance of high technology, hospital-orientated, urban-based health services. Primary health care, utilising personnel with less training than doctors, has been seriously underfunded.

3 Further significant improvements in health will require greater access to safe water and sanitary disposal of wastes, especially in rural areas, improvements in the distribution of food to allow adequate diets and the success of primary health care policies. Such goals are unlikely to be achieved without higher levels of literacy, especially among females, which require, in turn, greater sexual equality.

Activity 17 Improving Health?

Item A *Safer water*

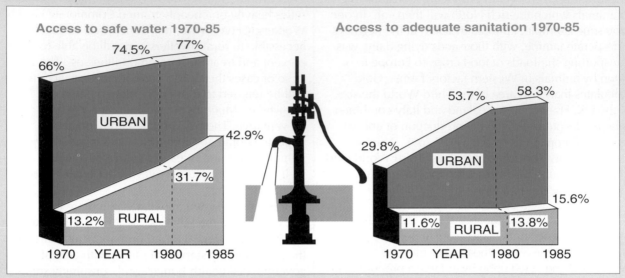

Adapted from *New Internationalist*, October 1989, p17

Item B *The ideal part time health worker*

Class background From the peasantry, known for years by those he serves. May have grown up with them.

How chosen By the community, for interest, compassion, knowledge of community, ability for hard work. Already a respected person.

Preparation Mainly from experience. Limited key training appropriate to serve all the people in a given community; management and treatment of important diseases; prevention; community health; teaching skills; health care in terms of economic and social realities, and of needs (felt and long-term) both of individuals and of the community; humanisation (conscientisation) and group dynamics.

Qualifications More qualified than the doctor to deal effectively with the important sicknesses of most of the people. Non-academic qualifications are intimate knowledge of the community, language, customs, attitudes towards sickness and healing, willingness to work and earn at a level of the community where the needs are greatest. Not qualified to diagnose and treat certain difficult and unusual problems: knows those conditions he or she must refer.

Adapted from D. Sanders and R. Carver, *The Struggle for Health: Medicine and the Politics of Underdevelopment*, 1985, p186

Questions

1 With reference to Item A:
   a) compare the gains made between 1970 and 1985 with regards to access to safe water and adequate sanitation;
   b) what are likely to be some of the consequences of these gains?

2 Judging from Item B, what are the strengths and weaknesses of community health workers?

References

Barnett, A. *Sociology and Development* (Hutchinson, London, 1988)

Brandt, W. *North-South: a Programme for Survival* (Pan, London, 1980)

Brett, E. A. *Colonialism and Underdevelopment in East Africa: the Politics of Economic Change* (Heinemann, London, 1973)

Cockburn, A. 'Scenes from an Inferno' *New Statesman and Society*, 12.5.1989

Foster-Carter, A. *The Sociology of Development* (Causeway Press, Ormskirk, 1985)

Foster-Carter, A. 'Development' in M. Haralambos (ed) *Developments in Sociology*, vol 6 (Causeway Press, Ormskirk, 1990)

Foster-Carter, A. 'Development' in M. Haralambos (ed) *Developments in Sociology*, vol 9 (Causeway Press, Ormskirk, 1993)

Gold, M. 'On the Meat-hook', *New Internationalist*, January 1991

Grigg, D. 'The Rural Revolution' in A. B. Mountjoy (ed) *Developing the Undeveloped Countries* (Macmillan, London, 1971)

Harris, N. 'Halfway to Liberation', *New Internationalist*, February 1990

Harrison, D. *The Sociology of Modernisation and Development* (Unwin Hyman, London, 1988)

Harrison, P. *Inside the Third World: an Anatomy of Poverty* (Penguin, Harmondsworth, 1979)

Hoogvelt, A. *The Sociology of Developing Societies* (Macmillan, London, 1976)

Kitching, G. N. *Development and Underdevelopment in Historical Perspective: Populism, Nationalism and Industrialisation* (Methuen, London, 1982)

Marx, K. *Capital* vol 1 (Lawrence & Wishart, London, 1954)

One World: Time for Action (Oxfam, 1990)

Our Planet, Our Health (World Health Organisation, 1992)

Sachs, W. 'Development: a Guide to the Ruins' *New Internationalist*, June 1992

Sanders, D. and Carver, R. *The Struggle for Health: Medicine and the Politics of Underdevelopment* (Macmillan, Basingstoke, 1985)

Schumacher, E. F. *Small is Beautiful: Economics as if People Mattered* (Sphere, London, 1974)

Tanner, J. 'Cocoa Addicts' *New Internationalist*, February 1990

World Bank, *World Development Report 1985* in *New Internationalist*, September 1985

World Bank *World Development Report 1994* (Oxford University Press, New York, 1994)

17 Methodology

Introduction

Methodology means the study of methods. At its simplest, it refers to the study of research methods used to collect data - methods such as interviews and questionnaires. What are their strengths and weaknesses, how good is the data they produce? At the other extreme, methodology deals with philosophical questions such as the nature of knowledge. How can we say that one statement is true and another false? How can we 'know' anything? This chapter examines some of the attempts to answer such questions.

Chapter summary

- Parts 1 and 2 examine **research methods** and **sources of data**.
- This is followed by an assessment of the **reliability** of different research methods and the **validity** of the data they produce.
- Various views of **science** and the scientific method are then examined in relation to sociology.
- This is followed by a comparison of a number of **interpretive methodologies**.
- Finally, the question of **value freedom** in terms of research methods and sociology as a whole is considered.

1 Primary Sources

Key Issues

1 What are the main methods for collecting primary data?
2 What are the strengths and weaknesses of each method?

Primary sources refer to information which was not present before the research began. It is generated by the researcher during the actual process of research. It includes data produced by questionnaires, interviews and observations.

Secondary sources refer to data which already exists. It includes historical records, official statistics, government reports, diaries, autobiographies, novels, newspapers, films, recorded music and data already produced by sociologists from other research projects.

Part 1 of this chapter looks at research methods used to collect primary data. It begins with experiments, a method rarely used in sociological research.

1.1 Experiments

For most people the word experiment conjures up a picture of white coated researchers in a laboratory using scientific equipment to prove or disprove something. This is quite a good starting point for understanding the experimental method.

Laboratory experiments

The main aspects of the experimental method can be illustrated by the following example. This experiment was conducted to test the *hypothesis* or supposition that, 'The speed of a boat depends on the shape of its hull'.

Controlling variables In order to discover the effect of hull shape on speed it is necessary to identify and control all the variables or factors which might affect speed. This is difficult to do outside a laboratory since variables such as wind strength and temperature cannot be controlled. In a laboratory it is possible to control such variables and keep them constant so that hull shape is the only factor which varies - from oval, to triangular, to rectangular, etc. In this way it is possible to find out how hull shape affects speed.

Quantifying results The results of experiments are usually quantified - presented in the form of numbers. Thus the speed of a model boat in the laboratory can be measured in centimetres per second using a metre rule and a stopwatch. Using a standard objective system of measurement is important as it reduces reliance on the judgement of the investigator and is therefore more likely to produce reliable data. And, it allows other researchers to *replicate* or repeat experiments and directly compare the results.

Correlation and causation If changes in one variable (eg the shape of the hull) are matched by changes in another variable (eg the speed of the boat) then there is a *correlation* between the two variables. But this does not mean that one causes the other. However, being able to control variables in a laboratory does help us to judge whether the correlation is causative rather than coincidental. In the case of the boat, the only apparent change is hull shape so any change in speed is likely to result from this.

Laboratory experiments and people Laboratory experiments have been very successful in the natural sciences such as physics and chemistry. However, many sociologists have serious doubts about their application to human beings. This is partly because people act in terms of their definitions of situations. They are likely to define laboratories as artificial situations and act accordingly. As a result, their actions may be very different from their behaviour in the 'real' world. An attempt to get round this is the 'field experiment', an experiment which takes place in people's everyday situations.

Field experiments

Field experiments are conducted in normal social situations such as the classroom, the factory and the street corner. The following example was devised to test the effect of social class on interaction between strangers. An actor stood outside Paddington Station in London and asked people for directions. The actor, place and request were kept the same but the actor's dress varied from a businessman to a labourer. The experiment indicated that people were more helpful to the 'businessman'. It could therefore be argued that people were responding to what they perceived as the actor's social class. However, there are other possibilities. For example, the actor may behave more confidently in his role as businessman and people might respond to his level of confidence rather than level of class.

Experiments involving people are always going to be inexact and 'messy'. It is impossible to identify and control all the variables which might affect the results. In the above example, different people are responding to the actor in each case. Ideally the same person should interact with both the

'businessman' and the 'labourer' in the same place at roughly the same time. But this would probably 'blow' the experiment.

The Hawthorne effect Whether in the laboratory or in more normal social contexts, people are often aware they are the subject of an experiment. And this in itself is likely to affect their behaviour. This 'experimental effect' is often known as the 'Hawthorne effect' since it was first observed during a study at Hawthorne works of the Western Electricity Company in Chicago in the late 1920s. The researchers conducted an experiment to discover whether there was a relationship between productivity and variables such as levels of lighting and heating and the frequency of rest periods. The researchers were puzzled as the results appeared to make little or no sense. For example, productivity increased whether the temperature in the workplace was turned up *or* down. The only factor which appeared to explain the increase in productivity was the workers' awareness that they were part of an experiment - hence the terms experimental effect and Hawthorne effect.

Experimenter bias People act in terms of how they perceive others. They will tend to respond differently if the experimenter is young or old, male or female, black or white and so on. People also tend to act in terms of how they think others expect them to act. This might explain the results in the experiment involving the actor dressed as a businessman and a labourer. He might be conveying two different expectations and this may affect the responses to his request for directions. The unintended effect of the experimenter on those being studied is known as experimenter bias.

Ethical questions Is it right to experiment on human beings? This depends partly on the nature of the experiment. Nearly everybody would reject the medical experiments performed on inmates against their will in Nazi concentration camps. However, few people would object to the actor asking directions outside Paddington Station. Should people be told they are the subject of an experiment? Yes, according to the British Psychological Society, unless it's absolutely necessary to deceive them, and then they must be told immediately afterwards (Gross, 1987, pp43-44). However, there are many instances where the issues are far from clear-cut as the following activity illustrates.

Activity 1 Experiments

Item A *Imitative aggression*

A group of nursery school children watched an adult mistreating a bobo doll - a large inflatable rubber doll - by punching it, kicking it and hitting it with a mallet. The experimenter, Albert Bandura, then exposed this group (the experimental group) and another group who had not watched the violence (the control group) to a 'frustrating experience'. They were shown a room full of exciting toys and given the impression they could play with them. They were then told they could not and taken individually to a room of unattractive toys which included a bobo doll and a mallet. As Bandura had predicted, those who had earlier watched the mistreatment of the bobo doll were more likely to imitate this behaviour and show aggression towards the doll.

Adapted from R.D.Gross *Psychology*, 1987, pp534-535

Item C *Labelling in the classroom*

In the 1960s Robert Rosenthal and Leonora Jacobson conducted a now famous experiment in an elementary school in California. They investigated the effect of teachers' expectations on pupils' academic performance. For ethical reasons they decided not to test the proposition that low expectations led to low performance.

20% of the children were defined as 'spurters' - those who would make rapid progress. Their teachers were informed of this prediction believing it to be based on intelligence (IQ) tests. In fact the researchers made the selection from a table of random numbers. After a year 47% of the 'spurters' had gained 20+ IQ points compared to only 19% of the other children - the control group. Rosenthal and Jacobson argued that this difference was due to 'expectation advantage' - teachers expected and so got more from the 'spurters'.

A number of attempts to replicate this study have failed. Other research suggests that there is a relationship between expectations and performance but it is fairly limited.

Adapted from M.D.Shipman *The Limitations of Social Research*, 1981, pp57-58

Item B *The real world*

Can the results of laboratory experiments be applied to the real world? For example, does the bobo doll experiment suggest a causal link between violence in films and violence in real life? Unlike people, bobo dolls are designed to be knocked around, they invite violent behaviour. As such they are hardly suitable subjects for an investigation into imitative aggression. Critics of experiments argue that the many differences between the laboratory situation and real life undermine any attempts to apply research findings to the claim that films promote aggressive or violent behaviour by imitation.

B. Williams *Obscenity and Film Censorship*, 1981, p68

Described as 'sickeningly violent, appallingly funny and arrestingly accomplished', 'Reservoir Dogs' became a cult movie in the mid 1990s. ('Chronicle of the Cinema', 1995, p828)

Questions

1 Read Items A and C.
   a) What hypotheses are being tested in these experiments?
   b) Why were control groups used?
   c) Briefly discuss the ethical questions raised by these experiments.

2 Do you agree with the views outlined in Item B? Give reasons for your answer.

1.2 Social surveys

The General Household Survey tells us that in 1992 33% of British households had a CD player. National Readership Surveys Ltd reports that *Reader's Digest* was the most widely read magazine in 1992. And Cinema and Video Industry Audience Research found that 89% of the 15-24 age group attended a cinema at least once in 1992. (All figures are for Great Britain and taken from *Social Trends*, 1994).

The above information comes from social surveys. A social survey involves the systematic collection of the same type of data from a fairly large number of people. Social surveys are usually designed to gather information on the same variables - eg age and cinema attendance - from those in the survey. This often means asking everybody the same set of questions.

Nearly all social surveys are based on a sample of the population to be investigated. 'Population' is the term given to everybody in the group to be studied. The population might be adult males, female pensioners, manual workers, 16-19 year old students, parents with dependent children and so on. A sample is a selection of part of the population. Samples are necessary because researchers rarely have the time and money to study everybody in the population. For example, if their research was based on women aged 16 and over in the UK, it would cover over 23 million people.

Most researchers try to select a sample which is representative of the population. This means that the sample should have the same characteristics as the population as a whole. Thus if a researcher is studying the attitudes of British women, the sample should not consist of 1000 nuns, 1000 women over eighty or 1000 divorced women since such groups are hardly representative of British women. With a representative sample generalisations are more likely to be true; findings from the sample are more likely to be applicable to the population as a whole.

Sample design and composition

Who should be included in a sample? In many cases it is fairly easy to define a *sampling unit* ie a member of the population to be studied. Dentists, males between 30 and 40 years of age, females who own their own businesses, people with one or more GCE A level, can be defined without too many problems. However, other groups are not so easy - how would you define a semi-skilled manual worker or a person living in poverty? Who would you include in a population of 'criminals'? Do you limit the population to those convicted of a crime? Or do you include everybody who has ever broken the law in which case you would include nearly every adult in the UK?

Once the research population has been defined, the sample is selected from a *sampling frame* - a list of members of the population to be studied. In some cases an appropriate sampling frame is readily available, eg the Electoral Register for a study of voting behaviour. In other cases researchers may have to rely on listings such as the Postcode Address File and telephone directories which may or may not be suitable for their purposes. And all listings have drawbacks - not everyone is included, they are often out of date, certain groups are likely to be over or under-represented, eg the poor are less likely to appear in telephone directories. Sometimes those who have data needed for a sampling frame are unwilling to release it. This happened to Howard Newby (1977) when the Ministry of Agriculture refused to supply information for his study of Suffolk farmworkers. Newby had to use the *Yellow Pages* for his first sampling frame. Many farmworkers were absent from this directory and those included were probably unrepresentative of the group.

The design and composition of the sample will partly depend on the type of sample used. Some of the more common types will now be outlined.

Types of sample

Random samples A random sample gives every member of the sampling frame an equal chance of being selected. Every name is given a number and then a list of random numbers is used to select the sample. This avoids bias in selection. If researchers choose who to include and who to leave out, they may select a sample which supports their hypothesis.

Systematic samples This form of sampling systematically selects people from the sampling frame by choosing every 5th, 10th, 20th or whatever, sampling unit. This method was used by Willmott and Young in their first study of Bethnal Green (see p247). They selected every 10th name from the borough's electoral register.

Neither random nor systematic samples necessarily produce representative samples. Few sampling frames cover everybody in the research population. For example, on electoral registers certain groups are unrepresented (those not old enough to vote) or under-represented (the unemployed). Even if the sampling frame covers the entire research population, a representative sample is not guaranteed. Simply because it *is* random, a random sample may select, for example, a disproportionate number of Labour voters from an electoral register. However, the larger the sample the less likely this will be. Systematic sampling can lead to an unrepresentative sample if the sampling frame is organised systematically. For example, a list of married couples in which husband follows wife would lead to an all male sample if every 10th person was selected.

Stratified samples Stratified samples offer a solution to the problem of representativeness. The population is divided into separate strata in terms of one or more characteristics, eg age, gender, ethnicity, class. A sample is then drawn which reflects those characteristics. Thus if the aim is to reflect gender divisions in the UK, 51% of the sample will be randomly selected from the female stratum and 49% from the male stratum. In terms of gender the sample will be representative of the population as a whole.

A stratified sample can only be selected if researchers have sufficient information. In some cases this is fairly easy to obtain. For example, the distribution of age in the UK population can be obtained from census data and this can then be mirrored in the sampling frame. In other cases the necessary information is difficult or impossible to obtain. Religion provides an example. How do we get accurate information on the distribution of atheists, agnostics, Catholics, Protestants, Muslims, Hindus and so on in the population as a whole? And even if we can discover this, available sampling frames such as electoral registers may be no use at all since they provide no information about religious belief and practice.

Quota samples A market researcher stands on a street corner looking for likely 'victims'. She has to find twenty women between the ages of 30-45 to answer a questionnaire on magazine readership. She fills her quota with the first twenty women passing by who a) fit the required age group and b) agree to answer her questions. The sample selection is not random; it is not randomly selected from a sampling frame. The researcher simply fills her quota from the first available bodies. This method is known as *quota sampling*. It is 'a method of stratified sampling in which the selection within strata is non-random' (Moser and Kalton, 1971, p127).

Quota sampling is often used for opinion polls and market research. It has its advantages - it is simpler, quicker and cheaper than stratified random sampling. However, it is less likely to produce a sample which is representative of the research population. For example, where and when a quota is filled can make significant differences to the sample. Stopping people on the street during weekday working hours would exclude many people in paid employment. And the fact that researchers can choose who they interview can bias the sample still further. Faced with two young men one 'smart' and 'pleasant' looking, the other just the opposite, researchers would probably choose the former. In quota sampling people in the same strata do not have an equal chance of being selected.

Multistage cluster samples A random sample covering the entire country can be very expensive and time consuming. For example, it would be costly to pay researchers to interview people dotted across the United Kingdom. Multistage cluster sampling provides a cheaper and quicker alternative.

There are various stages in the sampling procedure hence the term multistage. And at each stage the sampling units or 'clusters' are subdivided into areas which are then subdivided into districts. A number of districts are then randomly selected and from them the final sample is drawn. As this sample is grouped into clusters, it is cheaper and easier to manage than a sample spread evenly across the country.

However, multistage cluster sampling can increase error as the following example given by O'Connell Davidson and Layder illustrates (1994, p93). If three retirement resorts (eg Bournemouth) in the south of England were selected as clusters, then wealthy, elderly and white people would probably be over represented in the final sample. Since class, age and ethnicity are not evenly distributed across the country, it is advisable to select as many clusters as possible. And, even better, the final sample can be stratified to represent the research population as closely as possible.

Snowball and volunteer samples Sometimes researchers have great difficulty obtaining people for their samples. First, lists for a sampling frame might not be available. Second, the research population might be so small that normal sampling methods would not supply the numbers needed. Third, members of the research population might not wish to be identified. Think of the problems in locating the following: burglars, heroin users, collectors of ancient Greek coins, gay men, members of a Masonic Lodge. One possibility is to use a network of like-minded or like-situated individuals. This is the basis of *snowball sampling*, so-called because of its similarity to rolling a snowball.

Snowballing works like this. The researcher finds someone who fits the bill. They are asked to find another person who fits and so on. In this way a network of members of the research population is built up and this forms the basis for the sample.

Snowballing has the obvious advantage of creating a sampling frame where other methods may fail. However, it is unlikely to provide a representative sample since it is not random and relies on personal recommendation.

Volunteer samples provide an alternative to snowballing. Advertisements, leaflets, posters, radio or TV broadcasts, newspaper or magazine articles announce the research and request volunteers for the sample. This method has been used in studies of prostitutes in the USA. Volunteer sampling has much the same advantages and disadvantages as snowballing. In addition volunteer samples are self-selected which may systematically bias the sample in a particular direction.

Response rates It's one thing creating a representative sample, it's quite another getting everybody in the sample to participate in the survey. The *response rate* - the percentage of the sample that participates - varies widely. For example, Shere Hite's *The Hite Report on the Family* (1994) based on questionnaires in magazines had a mere 3% response rate, whereas everybody Ann Oakley (1974) asked to take part in her research on housework agreed to do so.

There are many reasons for non-response. They include:

1 Failure to make contact because people have moved, are on holiday, in prison, working away from home or simply out when the researcher calls.
2 Contact is made but the interview cannot be conducted because the person is ill, deaf, experiencing some personal tragedy or can't speak English.
3 The person refuses to participate. Reasons may include no time, no interest, sees no point in the research, is suspicious of, dislikes, or is embarrassed by the researcher.

Problems of non-response Does non-response make the sample unrepresentative? Does it bias the sample and produce systematic error? Often the answer is we don't know since little or nothing is known about those who do not participate. Sometimes information on non-participants does become available. This happened in the surveys attempting to predict the 1992 general election result. Opinion polls underestimated the Conservative vote by 8.5%. Over half of this underestimate was due to those who refused to participate - they were much more likely to vote Conservative. This produced an unrepresentative sample and in large part accounted for the failure to predict the election result (*Horizon*, BBC TV, 1994).

Evidence such as this suggests that non-response can be a serious problem.

Activity 2 Sampling

Item A *A stratified random sample*

We wish to study the career plans of university students and have sufficient funds to interview 125. Before selecting the sample, the sampling frame is stratified into departments, eg Physics and Chemistry, and years, eg students in their first year of study. There are 5,000 students in the university and the sample of 125 is one fortieth of this total. The example on the right shows the numbers of students randomly selected from years 1, 2 and 3 in the Physics department.

Adapted from S.Arber '*Designing Samples*' in N.Gilbert (ed) 1993, pp87-88

Stratification by department and year

Department	Year	Number in year	Number in sample
Physics	1	120	3
	2	100	3
	3	100	2
Total		**320**	**8**

Item B *Official statistics*

How do you find a sampling frame to study marital breakdown? Official statistics provide information on divorce - the legal termination of marriage - but separated couples are not included in these figures. Faced with this problem, Nicky Hart in her study of marital breakdown drew her sample from a club for the divorced and separated.

Adapted in part from N. Hart *When Marriage Ends*, 1976, p232

Item C *A self-selected sample*

The report on family life in three Western industrial countries carried out by Shere Hite in 1994 received a great deal of publicity in the British press. Its claims about the 'dark side' of family life made for fascinating reading. However, many commentators were unhappy about its methodology, in particular, its approach to sampling.

The figures are certainly dramatic. More than one in four women 'have no memory of affection by their father'. Four out of ten fathers frighten their sons with their violent tempers. Most shocking of all, fully 31% of girls and young women 'report sexual harassment or abuse by a male family member'.

Such findings are scattered through *The Hite Report on the Family* (1994). I should love to commend Hite's book as a model of social research. Sadly, I cannot. Her figures are drivel. She bases her findings on 3,208 completed questionnaires: 'a far larger sample than is typical of most psychological studies', as the *Daily Telegraph* proclaimed last week. Oh dear, the *Telegraph* has succumbed to one of the most basic fallacies of sampling theory: the belief that big samples are invariably more reliable than small ones.

In fact, sample sizes matter far less than sampling methods. Few methods are more suspect than those that involve self-selection - Hite's technique. She distributed 100,000 questionnaires via such outlets as *Penthouse* magazine in America, *Women Against Fundamentalism* in Britain and *Nouvelles Questions Feminists* in France. Her statistics come from the 3% who responded. She claims that self-selected samples are acceptable as long as the study is large enough.

History, and not just theory, says otherwise. In 1936, an American magazine, *Literary Digest,* conducted the biggest election survey ever. Two million out of a possible 10 million people responded to a mailshot asking them how they would vote in that autumn's presidential election. Their replies pointed to a heavy defeat for Franklin Roosevelt. He won by a landslide. Soon afterwards, *Literary Digest* went bust.

Adapted from P.Kellner, 'The Figures are Shere Nonsense', *Sunday Times*, 27.2.94

Questions

1 Read Item A. Why was the sample stratified?
2 a) Using Item B and other examples, briefly discuss the problems of basing a sample on official statistics.
   b) Evaluate Hart's 'solution' to the problem.
3 Read Item C. What are the problems of using a self-selected sample?

Will the readership of 'Penthouse' provide a representative sample?

1.3 Questionnaires

Questionnaires are lists of questions. They are the main method for gathering data in social surveys. They are sometimes handed to or posted to the respondent - the person answering the questions - and he/she is asked to fill them in. This is known as a *self-completion questionnaire.* They are sometimes read out by an interviewer who records the answers. This is known as an *interview questionnaire* or a *structured interview.*

Comparable data In theory questionnaires produce data which can be compared. Everybody is answering exactly the same questions and are therefore responding to the same thing. Any differences in the answers will therefore reflect real differences between the respondents.

This is fine in theory. However it's easier said than done. As we shall see, the same questions worded in exactly the same way can mean different things to different people. And in the case of the structured interview there is the problem of *interviewer bias* - the effect an interviewer may have on respondents' answers. Imagine how the age, gender and personality of an interviewer might affect your

answers on a sensitive subject such as sexual behaviour.

Quantifiable data Questionnaires are usually designed to generate data which can be easily quantified - put into numbers. Here is an example from *British Social Attitudes: the 11th Report* (Jowell et al, 1994, p124). It shows the percentage of respondents who chose each option. Constructing questions in this way makes it easy to quantify the results.

How often do you ...	
make a special effort to sort glass or tins or plastic or newspapers and so on for recycling?	%
Always	19
Often	23
Sometimes	30
Never	21
Not available where I live	6

Numerical data lends itself to statistical techniques. It makes it possible to discover whether or not there is a correlation - a statistical link - between two or more variables. For example, survey after survey has shown

Highest qualification held: by socioeconomic group, 1992-1993

Great Britain   Percentages

	Professional	Employers and managers	Intermediate nonmanual	Junior nonmanual	Skilled manual and own account non-professional	Semi-skilled manual and personal service	Unskilled manual	All persons
Degree	61	19	21	3	2	1	-	12
Higher education	16	19	29	6	9	4	2	13
GCE A level	7	16	12	13	14	7	3	12
GCSE, grades A-C	7	21	20	35	23	21	12	22
GCSE, grades D-G	1	7	5	16	15	12	10	10
Foreign	4	3	3	3	2	4	3	3
No qualifications	3	15	10	24	36	51	70	28

Adapted from *Social Trends*, 1995, p57

a correlation between social class and educational attainment. This is shown in the above table based on data from the General Household Survey.

Operationalising concepts Questionnaires are designed to measure things. And to do this, those 'things' must be operationalised, ie put in a form which allows them to be measured. How, for example, do you measure the strength of religious belief. Here is an example from the 1991 British Social Attitudes Survey. It is an attempt to measure people's belief in God. Respondents were asked to choose the statement which best fits their beliefs.

Belief in God, Britain, 1991 (%)

I don't believe in God.	10
I don't know whether there is a God and I don't believe there is any way to find out.	14
I don't believe in a personal God but I do believe in a Higher Power of some kind.	13
I find myself believing in God some of the time but not at others.	13
While I have doubts, I feel that I do believe in God.	26
I know God really exists and I have no doubts about it.	23
Don't know and no answer.	2

Quoted in Bruce, 1995, p4

Operationalising concepts is difficult, especially when sociologists themselves cannot agree on their meaning. In this respect, how do we operationalise concepts such as poverty and social class? Often concepts are operationalised in different ways in different studies which means the results are difficult, if not impossible, to compare. And the problem of comparability becomes even greater when we attempt to discover what respondents really mean when they answer questions. This problem will be looked at shortly.

Types of questions There are two main types of questions used in questionnaires - closed and open. In *closed questions*, the range of responses is fixed by the researcher. The respondent usually has to select one answer from two or more given alternatives. The questions above on recycling and belief in God are examples of closed questions. Here is a different example in which the respondent is asked to rank the alternatives provided.

Which do you feel are the most important factors in choosing a university? Please rank the following in order of importance to you. Number them from 1= most important, to 7= least important.

Closeness to a town or city.
Good academic reputation.
Good chance of getting a job after graduation.
Attractive campus.
Good social facilities.
Good accommodation.
Availability of real ale.

From Newell, 1993, p103

Closed questions are relatively easy, quick and cheap to classify and quantify. They are pre-coded in the sense that the categories are set and the respondent simply has to choose one or rank some. However, the researcher has chosen the available responses and in this respect is imposing his or her choice of alternatives on the respondent. Look at the question above on choosing a university. Can you think of any 'important factors' not given? There is a way round this problem by adding 'other, please specify' which asks the respondent to add, in this case, any other reasons for choosing a university.

An open question asks the respondent to answer a question in their own words. Open questions give the respondent more freedom but coding the responses can be difficult and time consuming. Imagine classifying answers to a question on belief in God under the 7 categories used in the questionnaire on belief in God quoted earlier. In many cases it might be difficult to fit responses into a particular category.

Most researchers see closed questions as suitable for simple, factual data such as age, gender and income level. Open questions are usually seen as more suitable for data on attitudes and values where respondents are required to express how they feel. An open question allows them to say things in their own way.

Types of questionnaires *Self-completion questionnaires* can be left with respondents either to be picked up later or posted back to the researcher. *Postal questionnaires* as their name suggests, are mailed to respondents with a request to mail them back to the researcher. Usually most of the questions in self-completion questionnaires are closed and pre-coded.

Self-completion questionnaires have the following advantages and disadvantages.

Advantages

- Inexpensive - no interviewers to pay, cheap to classify results.
- As a result, often possible to survey a large sample.
- Fast and efficient analysis possible with pre-coded closed questions. Answers can be easily quantified and entered straight on to computers.
- Postal questionnaires allow a geographically dispersed sample to be contacted easily and cheaply.
- No interviewer bias - the interviewer does not influence the respondent's answers.

Disadvantages

- A relatively low response rate - often well below 50% for postal questionnaires. This may destroy the representativeness of the sample.
- Respondents may not understand the questions or follow the instructions.
- Answers may be incomplete, illegible or incomprehensible when respondents complete questionnaires themselves.
- Closed questions may seriously limit what respondents want to say.

Structured interviews In a structured interview the interviewer reads out the questions and records the responses in writing, on audio-tape or on a portable computer.

Advantages

- Response rate usually much higher than for postal questionnaires.
- Interviewers can explain the purpose of the research, clarify questions and ask for further details. This can result in more information.
- Respondents who cannot read and write can be included in the survey.

Disadvantages

- More expensive - interviewers are usually paid.
- Cost increases if sample spread over a wide area.
- Interviewer bias.

Questions and answers

Constructing a questionnaire is not easy. The researcher must make sure that questions are clear and unambiguous. Where possible words and phrases should be simple and straightforward. Leading questions, eg 'Don't you agree that ...' should be avoided as they direct the respondent to a particular answer. Questions should be meaningful and relevant - there's not much point in asking people if they've enjoyed their holiday abroad if they've never been out of the country. And, most importantly, the questions must mean the same thing to all respondents. If they mean different things respondents are, for all intents and purposes, answering different questions. And this means that their answers cannot be directly compared.

Researchers sometimes use a *pilot study* to iron out problems with questionnaires. They test the questions on a relatively small number of people who share the characteristics of the main sample. A pilot study can be invaluable for removing ambiguity and misunderstanding. Yet all the preparation in the world cannot completely remove the basic problems of questions and answers .

What do answers mean? Are respondents telling the truth? Yes and no. Are they giving the answers they think the researcher wants? Sometimes. Do all respondents understand the questions? Not always. Do the questions mean the same thing to all respondents? Probably not. Given all this, what appears to be a precise, reliable and efficient research method - the social survey - may be nothing of the sort.

Creating an impression Everybody plays the game of 'impression management'. They try to manage the impression of themselves which others form. This can shape their responses to a questionnaire and more particularly to a structured interview. Consider the following example.

Survey after survey has shown a high level of church attendance in the USA, far higher than for any comparable Western industrial society. Yet figures produced by the churches tell a somewhat different story. For example, surveys conducted by Gallup suggested that 35% of Episcopalians in the USA had been to church in the last 7 days, yet figures from the churches indicated that only 16% actually did so. Why the discrepancy? It appears that many respondents were concerned with giving the 'right' answer to the interviewer - they wished to appear upright, decent and respectable and regular church attendance was to many, a way of giving this impression (Bruce, 1995, pp2-3).

Examples such as this suggest that researchers must know as much as possible about what questions and answers mean to respondents. Only then can they write appropriate questions and be in a position to interpret the answers.

Words and meanings For a questionnaire to do its job, questions have to have the same meaning for all respondents. The following example illustrates how easy it is for a question to be interpreted differently. A survey of reading habits produced the unexpected result that working class respondents read more books than middle class respondents. This result was largely due to the interpretation placed on the word 'book'. Unlike most middle class respondents, those from the working class included magazines in their definition of books.

Again this illustrates that the more researchers know about those they study, the better the questions they ask and the better their interpretation of the answers.

Activity 3 Asking Questions

Item A *On the toilet*

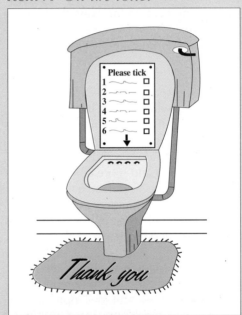

A study based in Bristol asked nearly 2,000 people to fill out a questionnaire on how many times they went to the toilet during the week and the shape, size, consistency and texture of their faeces. They were required to tick whether it was 'like a sausage or snake but with cracks on its surface' or 'fluffy with ragged edges' and so on.

Adapted from J. O'Connell Davidson and D. Layder *Methods, Sex and Madness*, 1994, p106

Questions

1 Read Item A. Comment on the accuracy of the data which this questionnaire might produce.

2 Briefly discuss the strengths and weaknesses of the questions in Item B.

Item B *Domestic violence*

The following questions are taken from a structured interview on domestic violence.

84. I am going to read a list of things that couples do not always agree on. First, I would like you to tell me if this has ever been a problem, and then rank order those items that have been a problem, giving 1 to the problem that has been of most concern, etc, until you get to 3.

	Ever a problem (yes/no)	Rank
a. arguments over money		
b. husband jealous of wife's involvements		
c. wife jealous of husband's involvements		
d. husband's use of alcohol or other drugs		
e. things about the children.		

92. At the immediate time that it happened, were you
1. not at all upset
2. slightly upset
3. quite upset
4. very upset.

104. What happened immediately after the incident?
a. partner left the house
b. respondent left the house
c. partner asked forgiveness
d. respondent asked forgiveness
e. partner became more violent
f. respondent became more violent
g. police called.

127. If someone's help was sought after this incident, tell me what happened - that is, whom did you ask for help, and what did he/she do about the problem?

Adapted from J. Giles-Sim *Wife-battering*, 1983

1.4 Interviews

Structured and unstructured At one end of the continuum, interviews are simply questionnaires which are read out by the interviewer who then writes down the respondent's answer. This is the structured or standardised interview discussed in the previous section. The same questions are read out in the same order to all respondents. At the other extreme is the unstructured or non-standardised interview which will be examined in this section.

Compared to structured interviews, unstructured interviews are more like an everyday conversation. They are more informal, open ended, flexible and free flowing. Questions are unlikely to be preset though researchers usually have certain topics they wish to cover which gives the interview some structure and direction.

Why use one or other type of interview? Many researchers see structured interviews as particularly suitable for simple, straightforward, 'factual' information such as a respondent's age, gender, educational qualifications and occupation. Structured interviews are seen as more likely to produce comparable data - since all respondents answer the same questions this should allow researchers to directly compare their responses and identify similarities and differences. Quantifiable data is more likely since questions can be structured to provide yes/no answers or choices between given alternatives. And, as structured interviews are more formal, there may be less chance of interviewer bias.

Advantages of unstructured interviews

Unstructured interviews are often seen to have the following advantages.

Sensitive groups Some groups are less likely than others to provide information for researchers. They might be suspicious of outsiders, hostile towards them, afraid of them or simply uncomfortable in their presence. An unstructured interview can allay these feelings as it provides an opportunity for rapport and trust to develop between interviewer and interviewee. This can be seen from the following example. Postal surveys were used in London to find out why people did not apply for welfare benefits to which they were entitled. The response rate was very low, due partly to fear and suspicion, a reaction often found amongst the frail and the elderly. Research indicated that a one to one interview was the most effective way of gaining information, in large part because interviewers were able to put respondents' minds at rest (Fielding, 1993, p137).

Sensitive subjects Unstructured interviews are also seen as particularly suitable for sensitive subjects.

Respondents may be more likely to discuss sensitive and painful experiences if they feel that the interviewer is sympathetic and understanding. Unstructured interviews provide the opportunity for developing this kind of relationship. Dobash and Dobash's (1980) study of marital violence produced detailed and in-depth information using unstructured interviews.

Respondent's viewpoint Structured interviews give respondents few opportunities to develop their answers and direct the interview into areas which interest them. The researcher has constructed the questions and, in the case of closed questions, the range of possible answers. In these respects the researcher has decided what's important.

An unstructured interview offers greater opportunity for respondents to take control, to define priorities and to direct the interview into areas which they see as interesting and significant. In this way, they have a greater chance to express their own viewpoints. And this can lead to new and important insights for the researcher.

Validity and depth If respondents feel at ease in an interview situation they will be more likely to open up and say what they really mean. Unstructured interviews can provide this opportunity. They are therefore more likely to produce valid data and to produce richer, more vivid and more colourful data. They also allow interviewers to pursue a topic, to probe with further questions, to ask respondents to qualify and develop their answers. In this respect the resulting data has more depth.

Meanings and attitudes Many researchers see unstructured interviews as particularly suited to discovering meanings, values, attitudes, opinions and beliefs. People often take these for granted and find it difficult to spell them out. For example, what exactly are people's religious beliefs; what does music really mean to them; what do they really think about the welfare state? Unstructured interviews can explore such areas. For example, Haralambos (1994), in his study of the meaning of blues and soul music to black Americans, found unstructured interviews particularly useful (see Activity 9).

Meanings and opinions are not simple and clear-cut. There are shades of meaning. Opinions are not cut and dried, they are hedged with qualification. A skilled interviewer can encourage and enable people to spell out this complexity. Structured interviews with preset questions are unlikely to capture this range of meaning. However, not everybody agrees with this view. The British Social Attitudes Survey uses a very detailed interview questionnaire and a self-completion questionnaire to discover attitudes on a range of issues (see Jowell et al 1994, pp177-233 for a copy of these questionnaires).

Problems with unstructured interviews

Interviewer bias Interviewer bias or interviewer effect is unavoidable. To some extent the interviewer will affect the responses of the interviewee.

Interviewers are people with social characteristics - they have a nationality, ethnicity, gender, social class, age group and so on. They also have particular personalities - they may be introverted or extroverted, caring or uncaring, aggressive or unaggressive. These social and psychological characteristics will be perceived in certain ways by interviewees and will have some effect on their responses. In some cases this may systematically bias the results.

A number of American studies have examined the effect of the social characteristics of interviewers and respondents. J. Allan Williams Jr (1971) claims that the greater the status difference between interviewer and respondent, the less likely respondents are to express their true feelings. He found that black Americans in the 1960s were more likely to say they approved of civil rights demonstrations if the interviewer was black rather than white.

Social desirability In general people like to present themselves in a favourable light. This can result in respondents emphasising socially desirable aspects of their behaviour and attitudes in the presence of interviewers. As the section on structured interviews shows, Episcopalians in the USA tend to exaggerate the frequency of their attendance at church in order to appear upright and respectable (see pp616-617). Respondents tend to be open about and even exaggerate aspects of their behaviour which they see as socially desirable and to conceal or minimise aspects seen as undesirable.

Validity Do respondents tell the truth? Is their memory hazy or faulty? Is what they say in interviews different from what they have done or will do? In some cases the answer is yes to all these questions. An instance has been given above in the case of church attendance. Voting intention is a case where people's intentions expressed in interviews and their actions at a later date are sometimes different. And there is evidence that some people tell downright lies, for example when recounting their sexual activity to an interviewer (O'Connell Davidson and Layder, 1994, p131).

Comparability Interviews, particularly those at the unstructured end of the continuum, can develop in all sorts of directions. As a result, data from one interview to the next can vary considerably. This makes comparisons between data from different interviews difficult. It also means that generalisations should be treated with caution.

The interview process

Books on research methods are full of advice on how to conduct effective interviews and avoid pitfalls and problems.

Non-directive interviewing The standard advice is to be non-directive, to avoid leading respondents and to allow them to express themselves in their own way. The idea is to minimise interviewer bias. It is important to establish rapport - a friendly and understanding relationship - while at the same time appearing sensible and businesslike. Interviewers should not be too familiar, they must maintain a certain distance or respondents will be unduly influenced. Probing is allowed, in order to get respondents to clarify or develop their answers, but it must be used with care as it can easily lead to bias (Fielding, 1993, p141).

Active approaches Non-directive interviewing can result in an artificial situation which makes respondents feel uneasy. Some sociologists have found that non-directive approaches can be frustrating for both parties. Platt (1976) notes that respondents 'would have liked guidance on what I regarded as relevant, but I was anxious not to mould the data to my preconceptions by giving them any. This produced a few tortured interviews in which an unhappy respondent spoke at length on aspects of the research which it was probably clear were not of interest to me.'

There is some evidence that more direct and aggressive interviewing techniques can produce more information. Howard Becker (1971) used this approach with some success in his interviews with Chicago schoolteachers. He found that many of the teachers were prejudiced against working class and ethnic minority pupils, information they would not normally volunteer. However, by adopting an aggressive approach Becker states, 'I coerced many interviewees into being considerably more frank than they had originally intended'.

Activity 4 Violence Against Wives

The following items are taken from 'Violence Against Wives' by R. E. Dobash and and R. Dobash (1980). The study was based on in-depth interviews with 109 women who had experienced battering. During each interview a number of specific questions were asked which provided data which could be quantified (see Item B).

Item A

He punched me, he kicked me, he pulled me by the hair. My face hit a step. He had his bare feet, you know, with being in bed, and he just jumped up and he pulled on his trousers and he was kicking me. If he had his shoes on, God knows what kind of face I would have had. As it was I had a cracked cheek-bone, two teeth knocked out, cracked ribs, broken nose, two beautiful black eyes - it wasn't even a black eye, my whole cheek was just purple from one eye to the other. And he had got me by the neck and, you know, he was trying, in fact, practically succeeded in strangling me. I was choking, I was actually at the blacking-out stage. I was trying to pull his fingers away, with me trying to pull his fingers away, I scratched myself, you know, trying to get his fingers off. He hit me and I felt my head, you know, hitting the back of the lock of the door. I started to scream and I felt as if I'd been screaming for ages. When I came to he was pulling me up the stairs by the hair, I mean, I think it was the pain of him pulling me up the stairs by the hair that brought me round again.

Item B

Types of injuries resulting from the first, worst, and last violent episode*

Injuries	Violent episode					
	First		Worst		Last	
	Number	%	Number	%	Number	%
Bruises to face and/or body	101	74	182	64	148	70
Abrasions	0	0	2	1	3	1
Burns	0	0	4	1	5	3
Cuts	18	13	48	17	27	13
Hair torn out	5	3	13	5	10	5
Fractured bones or broken teeth	6	5	11	4	9	4
Internal injuries, miscarriages	4	3	8	3	2	1
Knocked unconscious	2	1	14	5	7	3
Total	**136**	**100**	**282**	**100**	**211**	**100**

* We recorded up to five *different* types of physical injuries in any single violent episode. These figures reflect only the *different* types of injuries, and not the number of times a particular type of injury was received.

Questions

1 What does Item A suggest about the strengths of in-depth interviewing as a research method?
2 Why is it useful to combine the data in Item B with the type of account found in Item A?

1.5 Participant observation

How do we really find out about the way of life of a group of people? One way is to join them - to participate in their daily activities and observe what they say and do. This research method is known as *participant observation*.

It was used by John Howard Griffin (1960) a white journalist who dyed his skin black in order to discover what it was like to live as a black man in the southern states of America in the late 1950s. It was used by the anthropologist Bronislaw Malinowski who spent many years studying the Trobriand Islanders of New Guinea. He observed the most intimate details of their lives as he peered into grass huts gathering data for *Sex and Repression in Savage Society* (1927). And it was used by the sociologist Erving Goffman when he adopted the role of assistant to the athletics director in order to study the experience of patients in a mental hospital in Washington DC.

Ethnography Participant observation is one of the main research methods used in *ethnography*. Ethnography is the study of the way of life of a group of people - their culture and the structure of their society. Often researchers attempt to 'walk a mile in their shoes' - to see the world from their perspective, discover their meanings and appreciate their experiences. Many argue that participant observation is the most effective method for doing this.

Participant observation gives researchers the opportunity to observe people in their natural setting as opposed to the more artificial contexts of the laboratory or the interview. It allows researchers to see what people do as opposed to what they say they do.

Participant observation has produced a number of classic ethnographies - Elliot Liebow's (1967) study of black 'streetcorner' men in Washington DC; William F. Whyte's (1955) account of an Italian American gang in Boston; a range of anthropological studies of small scale non-Western societies from the Yanomamo Indians of Amazonia (Chagnon, 1968) to the Mbuti pygmies of Zaire (Turnbull, 1961).

Gaining entry Participant observation cannot work unless the researcher gains entry into the group and some degree of acceptance from its members. This can be difficult. Many groups don't want to be studied, especially those whose activities are seen as deviant or criminal by the wider society. However, as the following examples indicate, it is often possible to enter even closed groups.

For his research into casual sex between men in public toilets - the 'tearoom trade'- Humphreys (1970) acted as a lookout. By performing this useful and accepted role he gained the trust of those he observed without having to join their sexual activities. On other occasions researchers have to participate more directly in order to gain entry. Festinger (1964) found that the only way to observe a small religious sect was to feign membership and become a member.

The above examples are of *covert* research where the identity and purpose of the researcher are kept hidden. *Overt* research, where those being studied are aware of the researcher's role and purpose, has its own problems of access and acceptance. People often reject what they see as nosy, interfering outsiders, unless they are sponsored by a trusted member of the group who grants the researcher entry. This happened in Judith Okely's (1983) study of traveller-gypsies. Entry was a long and difficult process until she gained the friendship and trust of a family who had recently suffered a tragic death. The sympathetic and understanding relationship she developed with members of this family provided entry to the rest of the group.

Conducting research Participant observation involves looking and listening. The general rule is to 'go with the flow' rather than forcing the pace and influencing people's behaviour. Since the aim is to observe people in their normal setting, the researcher must not disturb that setting. Blending into the background is usually recommended, though this is not always possible. For example, a participant observer in a classroom can stand out like a sore thumb. This can result in an 'artificial' lesson. However, it's surprising how soon he or she becomes invisible and taken for granted.

Watching and listening are not always adequate for the researcher's purposes. Sometimes a participant observer must take a more active role in order to obtain information. This usually involves asking questions. In such cases the dividing line between participant observation and unstructured interviews is blurred. For example, William Whyte (1955) discussed his observations with his sponsor Doc to the point where Doc became 'a collaborator in the research'.

A good deal of participant observation is informal, unplanned and unstructured - it consists of 'hanging around'. In his study of pilferage from the docks in St Johns, Newfoundland, Mars (1982) wandered round the wharves and sheds chatting to the dockers, and hung round bars drinking with them in the evening.

Recording the findings of participant observation can be a problem, especially when the research is covert. Researchers usually write up the day's findings each evening whilst events are still fresh in their mind. In some cases the toilet has proved a useful place to make brief notes to be written up in a more detailed form later (Festinger, 1964; Ditton, 1977). However, a lot relies on the researcher's memory which is inevitably selective.

Participant observation can be a long process with a year or more being spent 'in the field'. It can require dedication, stamina and courage. Researchers are often cut off from the normal supports of family and friends, sometimes living a double life in an alien setting. And participant observation can be dangerous. For example, Haralambos (1994) was threatened with guns on more than one occasion during his research on the south side of Chicago.

Many of the advantages and disadvantages of participant observation have been mentioned already. Some of the more important will now be summarised.

Advantages of participant observation

Validity What people say and what they do are sometimes very different, as indicated earlier in the sections on questionnaires and interviews. Participant observation offers the chance to discover what people actually do, the chance to obtain valid data. For example, Haralambos (1994) observed black Americans who a few hours earlier had said they disliked blues, singing and dancing to blues music and quite obviously enjoying themselves.

Insight Looking back on his observation of a streetcorner gang in Boston, William Whyte noted, 'As I sat and listened, I learned the answers to questions that I would not have had the sense to ask if I had been getting my information solely on an interviewing basis' (1955, p305). This comment has been echoed by many participant observers.

Other research methods rely to a greater extent on prior knowledge. For example, to ask relevant questions in an interview you must already know something about the group under investigation. Participant observation can provide the kind of insight, fresh information and new directions for research which are less likely to come from other methods.

Insider's view Many supporters of participant observation argue that it offers the best opportunity to discover how people see the world in which they live. Other research methods are more likely to reflect the priorities of the researcher to the exclusion of those of the researched. For example, the designer of a questionnaire has decided what is relevant and significant and this may bear little relationship to the lives of those being studied.

By watching and listening a participant observer has the chance to discover the priorities and concerns, the meanings and definitions of people in their everyday situations. There may therefore be less likelihood of distorting people's social construction of reality.

Practicality Sometimes participant observation may be the only method with any chance of success. Some groups are closed to outsiders - their members reject requests for information. Such groups may include those involved in criminal activity, those whose behaviour is regarded as deviant by the wider society (eg certain religious sects) and those who are hostile to the wider society (eg some members of ethnic minority groups). Under these circumstances joining the group, participating in its members' activities, obtaining their cooperation and even their trust, may be the only way of obtaining information.

Disadvantages of participant observation

Time, money and personal cost As already noted participant observation can involve personal cost - stress and even danger. And costs in terms of time and money can be considerable - some researchers spend years in the field. However, given the quality of information that participant observation can produce, many would see these costs as reasonable.

Loss of objectivity The personal involvement which participant observation demands can reduce objectivity. An observer can identify so strongly with a group that the behaviour of its members is invariably seen in a positive light. In rare cases this identification is carried to its extreme - observers 'go native', join the group and never return to their former lives.

Conversely, researchers can view their subjects in a negative light. Something of this can be seen from the Policy Studies Institute study of policing in London. At times researchers had to walk away from situations when they found the behaviour of the police racist and offensive. This does not necessarily result in a biased view but it does little to encourage objectivity.

Changing behaviour Would you change your behaviour if a participant observer joined your social circle? The answer is yes, even if you weren't aware you were being observed. This is how 'Doc', William Whyte's sponsor and main informant in the streetcorner gang, saw the effect of participant

observation on his own behaviour. In Doc's words, 'You've slowed me up plenty since you've been down here. Now, when I do something, I have to think what Bill Whyte would want to know about it and how I can explain it. Before, I used to do things by instinct' (1955).

Given the importance of observing everyday life in its normal setting, do comments like this invalidate the findings of participant observation? While recognising the problem, many researchers would say no. After a while most people get used to an observer and carry on more or less as normal. This is how David Hargreaves (1967) saw his effect as a participant observer in a boys' secondary school. 'Initially my presence caused changes in the boys' behaviour though once they became accustomed to me, they behaved normally.'

Replication Participant observation studies are difficult if not impossible to replicate - repeat under the same or very similar conditions. There are various reasons for this. Participant observation is often unsystematic - there are no fixed procedures; things happen and the observer tags along.

Participant observation relies heavily on the personal qualities of the researcher. To some degree these qualities will affect how well they get on with their subjects, what they see and how they interpret it. And this reduces the chance of replication as the following example suggests. In the late 1920s, Robert Redfield (1930) studied the village of Tepoztlan in Mexico. He found a close knit society characterised by cooperation and a strong sense of belonging. Seventeen years later Oscar Lewis (1951) studied the same village. He pictured a society divided by fear, envy and distrust. Maybe the differences were due to changes during the intervening years but more probably they reflect differences between the two observers.

Generalisation Sample sizes in participant observation studies are small. The researcher can't be everywhere observing large numbers of people. In view of the small numbers it is not possible to generalise from the findings of participant observation. However, these findings can be used to refute or support generalisations from larger studies. Or they can produce fresh insights which can then be investigated on a larger scale.

Ethical questions All research involves ethical issues - questions of right and wrong. Participant observation, particularly when it is covert (hidden), brings these issues centre stage. According to the British Sociological Association, sociologists should explain the purposes of their research to those they study. However, these are guidelines rather than hard and fast rules (Hornsby-Smith, 1993, pp63-65). Many sociologists would justify covert research under particular circumstances. For example, Nigel Fielding justified his 'limited' use of covert observation of the National Front 'on the basis that this racist group was particularly hostile to sociology' (1993, p158).

Activity 5 Participant Observation

Item A

The following extracts describe Ken Pryce's fieldwork among Afro-Caribbeans in the St Paul's district of Bristol.

Having gained entry into the St Paul's area, the second major problem was to work out a focus for the research. This was a difficulty inasmuch as I did not enter the field with any preconceived idea of what I would find. I only knew that I wanted to study lifestyles and that I would go about it in a way that would make full use of my identity as a West Indian. I had no worked out theory or hypothesis I was going to develop, no blueprint for action.

St Paul's Bristol

Part of Pryce's research involved participant observation in a pentecostalist church.

There was no way in which I could take notes on the spot without giving rise to anxiety and suspicion from the congregation. I found I needed to take notes most in my first encounters when I was getting to know them, yet this was the time when I was most closely watched by sect members. In addition to these strains, I found the services - which were generally whole day affairs - too wearisome and physically exhausting. Each service always left me groggy and, temporarily, somewhat mentally incapacitated, and this further interfered with my note-taking.

Adapted from K. Pryce *Endless Pressure*, 1979

Item B

Erving Goffman made the following comments about his participant observation in a mental hospital in Washington DC.

I want to warn that my view is probably too much that of a middle class male; perhaps I suffered vicariously about conditions that lower class patients handled with little pain. Also, unlike some patients, I came to the hospital with no great respect for the discipline of psychiatry nor for agencies content with its current practice.

E.Goffman, 'Preface', *Asylums*, 1968

Item C

When Judith Okely began her research among traveller-gypsies there were all sorts of rumours about her identity.

I was a journalist, a police collaborator, a footloose heiress, a girl friend of the warden, a drug addict and hippy or someone on the run from the police. I discouraged all of these images except the last. The journalist rumour had been inflated by a warden, a classic 'gatekeeper' possessive of 'his' travellers and apparently threatened by 'academics', especially female ones. The day before my visit to his site, he told the travellers that I would be writing about their sex lives for the local newspapers.

In the long run, the warden's description of me did not fit what the travellers saw. They judged me by observed behaviour and the personal interaction with them which never involved a barrage of questions. Any mention of 'writing' produced a defensive reaction among all travellers. Taking the advice of those long acquainted with travellers, I did not emphasise this aspect.

Adapted from J. Okely, *The Traveller-Gypsies*, 1983, pp40-41

Questions

1 What does Item A suggest about the advantages and disadvantages of participant observation?
2 The findings of participant observation can say as much about the observer as the observed. Comment with some reference to Item B.
3 a) Suggest reasons for the behaviour of those mentioned in Item C.
   b) Do you think Judith Okely's fieldwork was successful? Explain your answer.

1.6 Life histories

As their name suggests, life histories are accounts of people's lives which they recount to researchers.

Something of the flavour and significance of life histories can be obtained from a brief discussion of *Cheyenne Memories*, the life history of John Stands In Timber (1884-1967) as told to the anthropologist Margot Liberty. He was a member of the last generation who experienced the traditional way of life of the Cheyenne Indians and knew those who participated in the major events of Cheyenne history during the 19th century.

The Cheyenne were a non-literate society so oral accounts are particularly important. Stands In Timber's account of his life and the history and culture of his people is given from the Cheyenne point of view. In Margot Liberty's words, 'John has given us the history of the Cheyennes as they themselves recall and interpret it' (1967, p8). Much of the material is new, that which isn't confirms, complements and amplifies 19th century ethnographic accounts.

Life histories have illuminated many areas of social life. For example, *The Polish Peasant in Europe and America*, a five volume work first published from 1918 to 1920, included an extensive life history of a Polish peasant which provided many valuable insights into the experience of migration from Poland to the USA (Thomas and Znaniecki, 1958). *The Jack Roller* (Shaw, 1930) is a story, written in his own words and from his own point of view, of a young American 'jack roller', the 1930s equivalent of today's 'mugger'. It is this first hand account of people's experience of their life as they see it which many researchers regard as the main value of the life history. It can provide insights and information which are not obtainable from any other source as Stands In Timber's life history shows. It can give a picture of the process and development of social life over time. It can also serve as a basis for confirming or questioning other interpretations and accounts. And it can direct researchers into new areas and encourage them to ask new questions.

However, as the title *Cheyenne Memories* suggests, the life history is heavily dependent on people's memory which is inevitably patchy and selective. To some extent it will also reflect their attitudes and opinions. Some would see this as a serious criticism of the life history. For example, Stands In Timber has been criticised by other members of his tribe for being too pro-Crow - the Crow are traditional enemies of the Cheyenne.

A further criticism concerns the researcher. There is a temptation for researchers to lead as life histories are recounted, particularly when areas of interest to them are touched upon. For example, Margot Liberty writes, 'My tendency was at first to press him for stories. I soon found it far better to trust his own instinct. Where he did not volunteer material freely he usually had little to say' (1967, p7). While accepting many of the criticisms of life histories, supporters argue that they are far outweighed by the valuable information that a good life history can provide.

1.7 Case studies

A case study is an examination of one particular case or instance of something. The life history is an example of a case study. It is an examination of the life of a single individual. Using examples from the previous section, it is the study of one Cheyenne Indian or one Polish peasant.

Case studies have a number of advantages.

1 They can disprove or qualify a general statement. For example, Michels' 'iron law of oligarchy' states that no organisation can be democratic - be it a political party, trade union, school or factory. However, a case study of the International Typographical Union, an American trade union, showed that this was not necessarily so (see pp368-369).

2 Case studies can produce new insights. Paul Willis studied a small group of boys in a secondary school (see pp289-290). This one case produced a number of new and interesting ideas which could then be examined on a wider canvas. For example, Willis found evidence that the boys' anti-school attitudes and behaviour actually prepared them to accept low status, low paid manual work. Rebelling at school prepared them for work after school.

3 Case studies are sometimes used in the early stages of a research project. They may generate ideas which can be examined later using a larger sample. Or they may help to make a questionnaire or interview relevant and meaningful for respondents. In these respects a case study is used as a *pilot study* - as a way of generating ideas and trying things out before the main study.

4 In one sense every social act, every event, every historical development is unique. If we wish to examine this uniqueness - which may be very important - then the case study is essential. Max Weber's study of the relationship between Protestantism and the rise of capitalism shows the value of this approach (see pp504-505). The rise of capitalism is in many respects a unique process. And it clearly has global significance.

Case studies have sometimes been criticised as limited and unrepresentative. As such they cannot be used as a basis for generalisation. However, this is their strength. If for no other reason they are valuable as a warning to rash and sweeping generalisations.

1.8 Longitudinal studies

How can you show what a person looks like? One way is to produce a photograph. This is similar to most sociological research which consists of a snapshot, a one-off investigation of an aspect of social life. Another way of showing what a person looks like is to produce a series of photographs taken at different points in their lifetime. This shows how their appearance changes and develops. The equivalent in sociology is the longitudinal study which examines the same group of people over a fairly long period of time.

As the following example shows, longitudinal studies can provide important insights. In 1947 the Population Investigation Committee carried out a survey of every mother who had a child in Britain between 3 and 5 March 1946. This was followed up by an examination of the children which focused on their health. Using the same sample, a team led by J.W.B. Douglas (see p295) studied their educational careers from primary through secondary school until they left in 1962. Two of the findings of this study indicate the importance of a longitudinal perspective. Douglas (1964) found that parental encouragement became increasingly important for educational attainment as the children grew older. He also found that performance in the early years of primary school is often reflected throughout the secondary school.

As these findings suggest, the strength of the longitudinal study is its ability to examine developments over time. By studying the same group, ie by keeping the same sample, the researcher can be sure that any changes in attitudes and behaviour are not simply due to changes in the makeup of the sample.

But keeping the same group is one of the main difficulties with longitudinal studies. Douglas's sample began with 5,362 children and ended with 4,720. Similarly the National Child Development Study began with 17,000 children born in England, Scotland and Wales between 3 and 9 March 1958. By the close of the study in 1981, researchers were able to contact only 12,500 members of the original sample. Reasons for this 'sample attrition' included death, emigration, refusal to participate and failure to trace. The result is not just a smaller sample but, in all probability, a less representative one.

Researchers are aware of this and attempt to minimise the problem of sample attrition. This can be seen from the lengths that some go in order to trace members of an original sample. They contact relatives, visit previous addresses and former workplaces, send letters and make telephone calls, search electoral registers and telephone directories, as well as contacting local housing departments and the Criminal Record Office. As this suggests, longitudinal studies can cost a great deal of time and money. Few organisations have the resources to fund an investigation which continues for twenty years or more.

Summary

1 Sociologists use a variety of research methods.

2 Each method has its strengths and weaknesses.

3 In view of this researchers sometimes use a combination of methods.

4 Each method produces particular types of data.

5 Sociologists select methods in terms of their suitability for particular research projects.

2 Secondary Sources

Key Issues

1. What are the main secondary sources of data?
2. What are the advantages and disadvantages of using secondary sources?

2.1 Official statistics

Official statistics are numerical data produced by national and local government bodies. They may be a by-product of the normal workings of a government department - for example, the claimant count measure of unemployment is a by-product of administering the benefit system. Or they may result from research designed to produce them - for example, the Labour Force Survey collects information on unemployment from a quarterly survey of 60,000 households.

Official statistics cover a wide range of social behaviour including births, deaths, marriage and divorce, the distribution of income and wealth, crime and sentencing and work and leisure. The following are among the main sources of official statistics.

1 Government departments Departments such as Education and Employment and the Home Office regularly request information from organisations such as local tax offices and social services departments, job centres and police stations. This information is then processed and much of it published. For example, the Department for Education and Employment publishes the monthly *Employment*

Gazette which includes a statistical supplement with details of earnings, prices, employment, unemployment, vacancies, industrial disputes and training and enterprise programmes.

2 Surveys Every ten years the Office of Population Censuses and Surveys carries out the Census of the Population which covers every household in the UK. Each head of household must, by law, complete a questionnaire that deals with family composition, housing, occupation, transport and leisure. The response rate for the 1991 census was 98% (*Social Trends*, 1995, p230). Other large scale surveys include the annual General Household Survey based on a detailed questionnaire given to a sample of nearly 12,000 people and the New Earnings Survey based on a 1% sample of employees drawn from Inland Revenue PAYE records.

Using official statistics

Advantages Sociologists often make use of official statistics. They have the following advantages.
- Published statistics are readily available and cost little or nothing to use.
- Sample sizes are often large which may increase the likelihood of the sample being representative. Surveys as large as the General Household Survey are usually outside sociologists' research budgets.
- Many government surveys are well planned and organised with detailed interview schedules. As such they meet the standards of sociological research.
- Surveys are often conducted regularly, for example on a fortnightly, monthly, annual or ten yearly basis. This can allow for comparisons over time and the identification of trends.
- Sometimes official statistics are the only major source of information on a particular topic.

Disadvantages Care is needed in using official statistics. Reasons for this include the following.
- Do official statistics really measure what they claim to measure? For example, do the annual crime statistics produced by the Home Office provide an accurate measurement of crime? Even the Home Office now agrees the answer is no (see pp461-465). Similar criticisms can be made for a range of official statistics from unemployment (pp346-348) and suicide (p470) to the distribution of income and wealth (pp39-42).
- Official statistics are often presented in a form which is not particularly useful to sociologists. For example, the Registrar General's classification of social class is used in government surveys. Many sociologists are critical of this classification. For

instance, it fails to identify a capitalist class and is based on occupational status rather than market situation.
- Official statistics are government statistics. As such they may be politically biased in favour of the government of the day. For example, according to the Labour Party, Conservative governments have changed the method used to count unemployment over 30 times since 1982. And in practically every case these changes have resulted in a drop in the official level of unemployment (M. Denscombe, 1994, p42). At best, some would argue, this is politically convenient, at worst it is outright fiddling to present the government in a better light.

An interpretive view From an interpretive view official statistics do not represent some objective reality 'out there'. Take crime statistics. The question is not whether they are accurate or inaccurate. To ask this misunderstands the nature of crime. There is no crime out there to be counted. It has no reality other than the meanings and interpretations constructed by social actors. Thus in Cicourel's words, 'rates of deviant behaviour are produced by the actions taken by persons in the social system which define, classify and record certain behaviours as deviant' (1963, p135). In other words deviance *is* the definitions and classifications - they constitute deviance.

Official statistics from this point of view are essentially no different from any other aspect of social reality. They are meanings and the job of the sociologist is to understand their construction.

A Marxist view From a Marxist viewpoint official statistics are part of the ideological state apparatus. Generated by government departments and agencies they derive from questions asked by, information processed by and results either suppressed or made public by a state which represents the interests of the capitalist class. As such they provide information which helps to maintain and justify the power of capital and disguise the reality of exploitation and oppression.

Activity 6 Official Statistics

Item A *Democracy and statistics*

Muriel Nissel was the first editor of *Social Trends*, an annual publication produced by the Central Statistical Office. She was asked to write the introductory article for the 25th edition in 1995. The article was turned down for publication. The following extract was written after this happened.

From time to time, there has been great pressure on directors of statistics in departments to withhold or modify statistics, particularly in relation to employment and health, and professional integrity has forced some to threaten resignation. Most recently, a major introductory article by myself, reviewing the development of the publication and of social statistics over the past 25 years, was turned down at senior level on 'political' grounds shortly before it was due to go to press, despite its having been written in consultation with all the editors concerned.

Genuine democracy must be based on sound and reliable information free from government interference. It is above all important that the Government Statistical Service should be independent. Maybe the time has come to review the organisation and its present place within the Civil Service.

Adapted from M. Nissel 'Vital Statistics', *New Statesman and Society*, 27.1.95

Item B *The social construction of crime statistics*

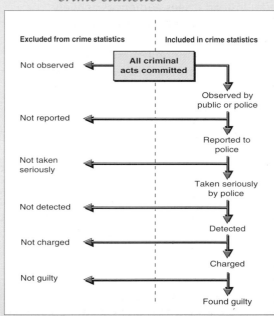

Item C *The 'real criminals'*

'The real criminals in this society are not all the people who populate the prisons across the state, but those who have stolen the wealth of the world from the people.'

Angela Davis, former leader of the Black Panthers, a militant black American organisation quoted in Taylor, Walton and Young, 1973, p27.

Angela Davis

Questions

1 Read Item A. Comment on the problems it raises for (i) sociologists (ii) democracy.
2 Look at Item B.
   a) Why does it suggest that crime statistics must be treated with caution?
   b) Item B assumes that there are such things as 'criminal acts' which are either included in or excluded from official statistics. Criticise this view.
3 Read Item C.
   a) What does this 'say' about official statistics?
   b) Is there a case for producing 'alternative' official statistics?

2.2   Documents

The term documents covers a wide range of written and recorded material. It includes letters, diaries, memoirs, autobiographies, novels, newspapers, advertisements, posters, photographs and radio and television broadcasts.

This section looks at some of the ways sociologists have analysed documents. Ray Pawson (1995) distinguishes three main types of analysis, 1) formal content analysis 2) thematic analysis 3) textual analysis.

Formal content analysis This method attempts to classify and quantify the content of a document in an objective manner. Say you were interested in the portrayal of gender roles in children's fiction published during the last five years. You could take a sample of the books and analyse each in terms of the same preset categories. For example, which activities are shared by girls and boys and which are limited to one or the other. The results are then quantified and interpreted (see Item A, Activity 7). If, for example, preparing food and taking care of younger brothers and sisters is limited to girls, then it could be argued that gender roles remain distinct.

Critics accept that formal content analysis can often effectively measure simple straightforward aspects of content. However, they argue that it says little about the meaning of a document either in terms of its meaning to the audience or the meaning the producer intends to communicate.

Thematic analysis This approach looks for the motives and ideologies which are seen to underlie documents. For example, a news broadcast may reflect the interests of powerful groups in society. The job of the researcher is to uncover this underlying ideology. The Glasgow University Media Group combined content and thematic analysis in their analysis of news broadcasts. They made a strong case that there is a pro-management, anti-union bias in the reporting of industrial disputes (see pp553-554).

However, there are a number of problems with thematic analysis. Who is to say that the sociologist's interpretation of the underlying ideology is correct? And if it is correct, does the existence of such ideology matter? Readers of the *Sun*, for instance, may see through or ignore or be unaware of its right wing views which may well explain why a significant minority of *Sun* readers regularly vote Labour (see p537).

Textual analysis Rather than looking for underlying ideologies, this method involves a close examination of the 'text' of a document to see how it encourages a particular reading. Ray Pawson (1995, p121) gives the following example from a newspaper headline, GIRL GUIDE, 14, RAPED AT HELLS ANGELS CONVENTION. This is an example of the 'innocent victim'/'wicked perpetrator' pair which creates the impression of two extremes, one good, the other evil. It is one of the many tricks of the trade used to convey particular messages.

As with thematic analysis, the problem with textual analysis is reading things into the text which may have little or nothing to do with the intentions of the producers or the interpretations of the audience.

Audience research Some researchers argue that the focus of document research should be the audience. From this viewpoint the audience is not made up of passive consumers who are brainwashed by underlying ideologies or swayed by textual tricks of the trade. Instead it sees audiences actively negotiating the meaning of messages with the outcome of negotiation ranging from acceptance to indifference to opposition (Pawson, 1995, p124).

But finding out how audiences respond is far from easy. Jenny Kitzinger's use of the 'news game' provides a novel and interesting alternative to the methods examined so far. Small 'audience groups' averaging three people from different social backgrounds were given a set of 13 photographs taken from TV news items and documentaries about AIDS. The groups were asked to select pictures and use them to write a news report on AIDS. Kitzinger concluded from this exercise that, 'Audiences selectively highlight, oppose or reconstruct statements and they are able to deconstruct dominant themes and to construct alternative accounts drawing on personal experience, political belief or a general critique of media or government sources' (1993, p300). This gives some indication of the variety and complexity of audience responses.

The 'news game' was first used by Greg Philo to study audience response to the media and the miners' strike of 1984/85 (see p539). It represents an important change of direction - from the document to the document in relation to the audience.

Activity 7 Analysing Documents

Item A *Content analysis*

Frequencies with which the main genres of factual programmes occurred and the numbers containing reference to or depiction of disability

Genre	Number of programmes	Percentage of total programmes	Number with disability	Percentage of total with disability
News	221	27	54	42
Current affairs	28	4	0	0
Documentary	155	19	21	16
Magazine	70	9	20	16
Informational	59	7	4	3
Debate	15	2	2	2
Religious	9	1	2	2
Quiz	24	3	3	2
Music/dance	38	5	0	0
Educational	5	0.6	2	2
Game show	44	5	0	0
Chat show	24	3	4	3
Sport	36	4	1	1
Special broadcast	46	6	12	9
Special interest programme	3	0.4	3	2
Other	27	3	0	0
Total	**804**	**99**	**128**	**100**

From G. Cumberbatch and R. Negrine *Images of Disability on Television*, 1992

Item B *Newspaper headlines*

These headlines refer to men and women infected through blood transfusions and mother to child transmission in the womb.

From J. Kitzinger 'Understanding AIDS', 1993, p277

Item C *First World War posters*

Questions

1 a) What does Item A tell us?
   b) What further information might be useful?
2 Analyse the headlines in Item B using thematic and textual analysis.
3 What use might sociologists make of the posters in Item C?

Historical documents

For studying the past documents are often the major and sometimes the only source of information. Max Weber's classic study *The Protestant Ethic and the Spirit of Capitalism* (see pp504-505) could not have been written without a range of historical documents. For example, he illustrates the spirit of capitalism with quotes from two books by Benjamin Franklin, *Necessary Hints to Those that would be Rich* (1736) and *Advice to a Young Tradesman* (1748). Weber builds a strong case for the religious basis of the capitalist work ethic by quoting from the speeches and writings of ministers such as John Calvin (1509-64).

   Geoffrey Pearson's *Hooligan: A History of Respectable Fears* (1983) provides a more recent example of the use of historical documents. Pearson looks back to Victorian England and forward to today to show that 'for generations Britain has been plagued by the same fears and problems' (p ix). He looks at 'hooliganism' - street crime and violence - the moral panics it generates and its 'discovery' time and time again as something new, in stark contrast to the 'good old days'. Pearson builds up a substantial case for this argument with a range of historical documents which include newspapers, magazines such as *Punch* and *The Teacher's World*, contemporary novels and government reports.

Using historical documents Historical documents are often a long way from the objectivity which sociologists strive for. They are usually biased, prejudiced, one-sided and concerned with putting over a particular point of view. However, as long as researchers take them for what they are, historical documents provide a rich and valuable source of data. Thus Lord Ashley's announcement in the House of Commons in 1843 that, 'the morals of the children are tenfold worse than formerly' (quoted in Pearson, 1983, p119) cannot be seen as a balanced assessment of juvenile morality. However, for Pearson's study of 'respectable fears' it is a very useful piece of data since it exemplifies a fear that has recurred throughout the past two centuries.

   Historical documents bring their own problems of interpretation because they are from a different era, a different culture and those who produced them are often dead. Add to this the fact that interpretation relies heavily on the researcher's viewpoint and background and it is clear that there is plenty of room for disagreement. For example, J. Berger argued that a number of paintings from the 17th and 18th centuries showed how art patrons at the time were very concerned with material possessions. He saw this concern as linked to the rise of capitalism. However, as Berger himself notes, this interpretation was hotly disputed by an art critic (discussed in Macdonald and Tipton, 1993, pp193-4).

Assessing historical documents John Scott (1990) provides four 'quality control criteria' for assessing documents which are particularly applicable to historical documents.

Authenticity The first refers to authenticity. Is the document genuine or a forgery? As the famous 60 volume *Hitler Diaries* which surfaced in 1983 showed, forgeries can fool even top historians. Is the document an original or a copy? For example, the writings of Roman historians have been copied and recopied by hand. How true to the originals are the copies?

Credibility Is the author of the document 'sincere' or does he or she distort the evidence in order to mislead the reader? There are plenty of examples of distortion, deceit and outright lies in documents. Former US President Nixon denied all knowledge of the illegal break-in at the Democratic Party's headquarters which became known as the Watergate Affair. This lie appeared in TV and radio broadcasts by Nixon and his officials and in White House press releases.

Representativeness To what extent is the document representative? For example, is a newspaper article typical of the articles which appear in that particular newspaper? The question of representativeness is particularly important in the case of historical documents as many have been lost or destroyed. Those that remain may be untypical. For example, a study of witchcraft in 17th century New England was based on court records relating to 114 suspects. The researcher believes that these surviving records are only the 'tip of the iceberg', a 'tip' which may well be unrepresentative (discussed in O'Connell Davidson and Layder 1994, pp192-3).

Meaning What does a document mean? This ranges from the literal meaning of the text - can the researcher 'literally' understand it, eg can the researcher read a text in Anglo Saxon English - to higher level interpretations of meaning and significance. As the previous section on analysing documents has indicated, questions of meaning will never be settled.

Summary

1 Despite the many problems involved with using secondary sources, they are invaluable for many types of research.

2 Historical documents are particularly valuable since they are often the major source of data for studying the past.

Activity 8 Historical Documents

Item A *The Diaries of a Cabinet Minister*

Richard Crossman was an MP and Cabinet Minister in the Labour government of 1964-1970. His political diaries were published after his death in 1975.

Memory is a terrible improver - even with a diary to check the tendency. And it is this which makes a politician's autobiography so wildly unreliable. But if I could publish a diary of my years as a minister without any editorial improvements, as a true record of how one minister thought and felt, I would have done something towards lighting up the secret places of British politics and enabling any intelligent elector to have a picture of what went on behind the scenes between 1964 and 1970.

Of course the picture which this diary provides is neither objective nor fair - although as a lifelong political scientist I have tried to discipline myself to objectivity. In particular I have tried to avoid self-deception, especially about my own motives; the tendency to attribute to others my own worst failings; and the temptation to omit what might make me look silly in print. I have been urged by many to remove all the wounding passages about colleagues or officials. I have not done so because it would make the book untrue, and I hope that when some of them find me intolerably unfair, they will recall the follies and illusions I faithfully record about myself. A day-by-day account of a Government at work, as seen by one participant, is bound to be one-sided and immensely partisan. If it isn't, it too would fail to be true to life.

Adapted from R.Crossman *The Diaries of a Cabinet Minister*, 1975, pp12-13

Item B

The crest of Sir William Hawkins, an English sea captain who made a fortune from the slave trade in the 16th century.

TO BE SOLD, on board the Ship *Bance-Yland*, on tuesday the 6th of *May* next, at *Afbley-Ferry*; a choice cargo of about 250 fine healthy

NEGROES,

juft arrived from the Windward & Rice Coaft. —The utmoft care has already been taken, and fhall be continued, to keep them free from the leaft danger of being infected with the SMALL-POX, no boat having been on board, and all other communication with people from *Charles-Town* prevented.

Aufin, Laurens, & Appleby.

N. B. Full one Half of the above Negroes have had the SMALL-POX in their own Country.

A bill of sale

This advert for Pears soap was actually painted on a rock in the Sudan by invading British forces.

Questions

1 With some reference to Item A suggest why diaries might be preferable to autobiographies as a source of information.

2 a) Provide a sociological interpretation of the pictures in Item B.

   b) Critically assess your interpretation.

3 Assessing Research Methods

Key Issues

1 How can the reliability of research methods and the validity of data be assessed?
2 To what extent do researchers affect the data they collect?
3 What are the advantages of combining various research methods and types of data?

Parts 1 and 2 outlined and evaluated various research methods and forms of data. This part takes a more general view. It begins with a comparison of quantitative and qualitative methods and data.

3.1 Quantitative and qualitative methods and data

Quantitative data is data in a numerical form - in the form of numbers. Official statistics are an obvious example. Questionnaires and structured interviews are the usual research methods used to obtain quantitative data. Their responses can often be fairly easily transposed into numbers.

Some researchers argue that unless human behaviour is expressed in numerical terms, it cannot be accurately measured. Without accurate measurement conclusions will be based on impressions and as such will be little more than unsubstantiated opinion.

Qualitative data covers a range of material from the descriptions of social life provided by participant observation and unstructured interviews to information from written sources such as diaries, autobiographies and novels. Some researchers argue that qualitative data provides greater depth, a richer and more detailed picture of social life. It is more likely to capture the subtleties, nuances and shades of meaning than the numerical data provided by quantitative methods.

Use of the contrast quantitative/qualitative implies either/or and better/worse - that researchers use and favour either one or other type of data. In practice most researchers use both kinds of data recognising their strengths and weaknesses and seeing them as suited to different purposes. For example, the findings of a small scale participant observation study can form the basis for a questionnaire used in a large scale social survey. And, as we shall see shortly, quantitative and qualitative data can be used together as 1) a means of checking the other and 2) building up a more complete picture of social life.

3.2 Validity and reliability

Validity refers to the truth and accuracy of a description or measurement. Data is valid if it gives a true picture of a way of life or an accurate measurement of something. For example, Willis's ethnography of 'the lads' in a secondary school (see pp289-290) is valid if it is a true portrayal of their lifestyle. Official statistics on crime are valid if they provide an accurate measurement of the extent of crime.

Some researchers argue that qualitative data with its depth and richness is more likely than quantitative data to provide a valid picture of social life. However, as noted earlier, methods such as participant observation rely heavily on the interpretive skills of the researcher. It is therefore difficult to assess the validity of the data they produce. Possible ways of doing this will be examined shortly.

Reliability Research methods and data are reliable when different researchers using the same methods obtain similar results. For example, if the same questionnaire and the same sampling procedure produce similar results when used by different researchers, then the methods and the data are reliable. A reliable method allows studies to be replicated, ie repeated.

3.3 Triangulation

Triangulation is a term used to describe various ways of assessing the validity and reliability of research methods and data (Denzin, 1970). It looks at the topic under investigation from different angles and vantage points. Triangulation can take various forms. These include:

1 **Investigator triangulation** This involves the use of different researchers, eg different observers and interviewers. The aim is to check for observer and interviewer bias by, for example, using interviewers from different social backgrounds.
2 **Data triangulation** This involves collecting data at different times from different people in different places. It can also involve combining primary and secondary data. Data triangulation serves as a cross-check for validity. It can also serve as a means of assessing researchers' interpretations and conclusions.
3 **Methodological triangulation** This takes two forms. 'Within-method' triangulation uses a variety of techniques within the same method, for example open and closed questions within a questionnaire. Asking similar questions in a

variety of ways can check on the validity of the answers and the reliability of the method. 'Between-method' triangulation refers to the combination of a number of research methods, for example questionnaires, unstructured interviews and participant observation. The data produced by each method can be checked by comparing it with the data produced by the other methods.

The idea of triangulation is illustrated by the following quotation from *Belfast in the 30s: an Oral History* (quoted in Macdonald and Tipton, 1993, p199).

'In the first place we carried out ... "investigator triangulation". That is, each transcript was checked by two or three researchers to ensure that it said what people had meant to say. In the second place, we systematically did a cross-method triangulation, in that every piece of oral evidence that could be, was checked against a range of written sources: newspapers, parliamentary reports, documents etc. Finally, there was a considerable amount of data triangulation possible within the oral sources themselves' (Munck and Rolston, 1987, p12).

3.4 Reflexivity

A white male middle class researcher - and most of them are - will tend to see the social world he studies through white male middle class eyes. And to some extent he will be seen by those he studies in terms of his social identity which will influence the way they respond to him. In these respects social research is *reflexive* - it reflects and is shaped by the researcher.

As a researcher our findings will be coloured by our social background, our experiences and our culture. What we see and how we interpret it will be influenced by the fact we are social beings. Social research involves social relationships. To some extent those being studied will be influenced by the presence of the researcher.

The idea of reflexivity also refers to a recognition, an awareness of the fact that research is reflexive. This awareness means that as researchers we should be critical of ourselves, our research and our findings. We should examine ourselves in order to discover to what extent our findings reflect our own beliefs and values. We should question whether our presence affects the actions of those we study. This critical awareness will help us get nearer to our goal - a valid picture of social reality.

Assessing validity Some of the ways of assessing research findings have been discussed under the heading of triangulation. Some others will now be examined.

Asking the researched In his study of an Italian American gang in Boston, William Whyte (1955) discussed his findings with Doc, the leader of the gang. Doc assessed Whyte's interpretation of the gang's behaviour from an insider's viewpoint.

Playing the part Aaron Cicourel (1976) spent four years studying probation officers in California. Part of this time was spent as an unpaid probation officer. His aim was to discover the meanings used by probation officers to define young people as delinquent. Cicourel claimed that by learning to play the part of a probation officer, he was able to identify the same young people as delinquents as his full time colleagues. This provided support for his interpretation of the meanings they used to define delinquency.

Presenting the data In *The Social Organisation of Juvenile Justice*, the published report of his findings, Cicourel presents lengthy extracts from conversations between probation officers and juveniles along with detailed descriptions of their interaction. Although this presentation is selective - it represents only a small part of his field notes - it gives others some opportunity to assess Cicourel's interpretation of the data.

Comparing results Researchers often compare their findings with those of others who have conducted similar research. This comparison encourages them to question their results and to assess to what extent their findings reflect their research methods and their own beliefs and values.

Critical self-awareness None of the above methods is foolproof but they do encourage a critical self-awareness which can only assist the quest for validity. Recognising the reflexive nature of social research is an important step forward. (The final part of the chapter develops this point).

3.5 Methodological pluralism

Methodological pluralism is similar to triangulation and can serve a similar purpose. However, its aim is not so much as a means of checking validity and reliability but rather to build up a fuller picture of social life by combining different research methods and different types of data. It recognises that each method and type of data has its particular strengths and weaknesses. Combined they are seen to produce a more comprehensive and rounder picture of social reality. And their combination can also provide new insights and new directions for research.

Some of the strengths of methodological pluralism can be seen from Eileen Barker's (1984) study of the Moonies - the Unification Church. She conducted in-depth interviews, each lasting 6-8 hours, with a number of Moonies. The interviews dealt with their background, why they became a Moonie, their life in the church and the meaning of religion as they saw it. Barker also lived as a participant observer in several centres with the Moonies at various times during the six years of her research. This enabled her to gain the trust of many members of the church resulting in information which would not have been given to an outsider. Two years after the start of her research she constructed a large (41 page) questionnaire based on her findings from interviews and observation. This provided information from a larger sample and was intended to reveal 'social patterns, trends and tendencies and gain a more reliable understanding of regularities between variables - of "what goes with what"'.

Barker claims that combining different methods of investigation gave her a much fuller picture than any one method or data source could have provided.

Summary

1 Triangulation is a means of assessing the reliability and validity of research methods and the data they produce.

2 Reflexivity refers to the influence of the researcher on his or her research findings. It also refers to an awareness that research is reflexive.

3 Methodological pluralism refers to the use of various research methods and types of data in order to produce a more comprehensive picture of social life.

Activity 9 Methodological Pluralism and Triangulation

Item A *Participant observation*

Poster advertising a blues show at the Regal Theatre on the south side of Chicago. The audience, except for the researcher, was made up of black Americans.

Observations from the Regal Theatre, Chicago

Introducing *Five Long Years*, Junior Parker says, 'Alright, we're gonna put you there. Everybody got the blues tonight. We're gonna take you straight back to Jackson, Mississippi'. Later he shouts, 'Everybody from Tennessee, Arkansas and Mississippi say yeah!' and is greeted with an affirmative roar. 'I've been down so long' sings Albert King, and shouts of 'yeah' and 'me to' greet the first line of *Down Don't Bother Me*. He gets a similar response as he sings 'If it wasn't for bad luck I wouldn't have no luck at all' from *Born Under a Bad Sign*.

Item B *Quantitative data*

States of birth of blues singers

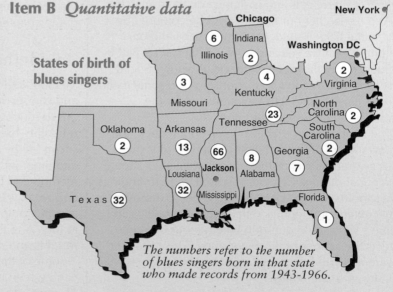

The numbers refer to the number of blues singers born in that state who made records from 1943-1966.

Item C *Official statistics*

The Mississippi Delta region has the highest percentage of poor rural people in the United States. 79% of the black households and 84% of the black population are poor compared to 28% and 31% for whites (*Agricultural Economic Report Number 170*, 1970, pviii).

In 1966 the median income for black households in the Mississippi Delta was $1,373. This compares with the 1968 median for black households in the South of $4,278 and the national black average of $5,359 (*Bureau of Labor Statistics Report Number 375*, 1970, p15).

Item D *Secondary source*

John Howard Griffin, a white man, dyed his skin black and travelled through the Deep South as a black man. He describes a bus journey in 1959 from New Orleans into Mississippi.

The blacks were in their place sat at the back of the bus. A man called Bill turned to Griffin and said, 'Mississippi is the worst place in the world. If you're not used to things here you'll have to watch yourself till you catch on.'

As we drove more deeply into Mississippi, I noted that the blacks comforted and sought comfort from each other. We felt strongly the need to establish friendship as a buffer against the invisible threat.

As we neared Poplarville agitation swept through the bus. Everyone's mind was on the black youth who had been lynched there by whites. An all-white jury had refused to consider evidence against them.

Bill pointed out places in a quiet expressionless voice. 'That's the courthouse where they made that decision. That's where they as much as told the whites, "You go ahead and lynch those niggers, we'll see you don't get in any trouble."'

Adapted from J.H.Griffin, *Black Like Me*, 1960, pp 59, 60, 63, 64

Item E *Documentary evidence with interview data*

Memphis Slim In his autobiographical song *Boogying and Bluesing*, blues singer Memphis Slim sings of being born in Memphis, Tennessee, moving to East St Louis, then to Chicago, but when he went to Harlem in New York:

‘Finally I made Harlem and was I confused,
My people there didn't dig no blues.’

Enoch Gregory is a disc jockey who worked at WBEE a black radio station in Chicago. During the first half of the 20th century, millions of black Americans migrated from the southern states to the north west, north central and west coast regions of the USA. Enoch Gregory looks at the relationship between blues and migration patterns. His observations are confirmed by statistical data.

Chicago's a funny place. I lived there for a year and a half when I worked at WBEE. The blues in later years have remained a musical entity more in the states of Mississippi, Alabama and some parts of Louisiana and Arkansas, rather than in North Carolina, Virginia, South Carolina, Georgia and Florida. The migration pattern has a good deal to do with it. The people in Mississippi and Alabama and those states go up to Chicago. The people in the coastal states come to Baltimore, Washington DC, and primarily New York. So you find a deep appreciation for blues in Chicago, and in spite of attempted revivals by programme directors and show promoters here in New York, it does not exist in New York.

Item F *Interview with B B King*

Where I lived, a little place between Itta Bena and Indianola in Mississippi, the people are practically the same way today, they live practically the same way, and that is under the fear of the boss in a manner of speaking. Because so many blacks down there have been killed many, many different types of ways if you said the wrong thing at the wrong time. Very few were able to get away with speaking up with what they thought was right or what was wrong. So when they use the word frustration, I don't think that really tells the whole story because a guy get to feeling a lot of times he's afraid, he's actually afraid. They use the word brainwash, because if you live under that system for so long, then it don't bother you openly, but mentally, way back in your mind it bugs you. Later on you sometime will think about all of this and you wonder why, so that's where your blues comes in, you really bluesy then, y'see,

B B King

because you are hurt deep down, believe me, I've lived through it, I know. I'm still trying to say what the blues is to me. So I sing about it. The next thing, which is relatively minor compared to living like I have, is your woman. Y'see your woman is the next thing that can make a man pretty blue too y'know.

Apart from Item D, the data in this activity is from M. Haralambos, *Right On: From Blues to Soul in Black America*, 1994

Questions

1 Using all the items provide a sociological explanation for blues which includes a) an interpretation of its meaning for black Americans and b) its relationship to black American society.
2 Discuss the advantages of methodological pluralism and triangulation in terms of the data in this activity.

4 Sociology and Science

Key Issues

1 What is science? What are scientific methods?
2 Are the methods and assumptions of the natural sciences appropriate to the study of human behaviour?

Sociology is often referred to as a social science. Whether or not it can be seen as a scientific discipline is one of the major debates within the subject. The founding fathers of the subject in the 19th century were, however, in no doubt. By following the rules and logic of the scientific method sociology could discover the laws underlying the development of human society. And in this respect it was a science just like the natural sciences of physics and chemistry which seek to discover the laws underlying the behaviour of matter.

4.1 Auguste Comte: positivism

Auguste Comte (1798-1857) is credited with inventing the term sociology. He argued that sociology should be based on the methodology of the natural sciences. This would result in a 'positive science of society' which would reveal the 'invariable laws' which governed the evolution of human society. Comte's approach is known as *positivism*.

Comte insisted that only directly observable 'facts' were acceptable as evidence in his science of society. Anything that couldn't be directly measured, such as subjective meanings and purposes, was ruled out. The facts of society must be objectively measured and quantified, ie put into a numerical form. It would then be possible to identify cause and effect relationships and discover the laws underlying social evolution.

Positivism has often been used as a general catch-all term to describe a range of approaches in sociology which are seen to reflect the methods and assumptions of the natural sciences. However, since its application has become so general and its meaning so vague, its use will be largely avoided in this chapter.

4.2 Emile Durkheim: the rules of sociological method

Social facts In *The Rules of Sociological Method*, first published in 1895, Durkheim outlined the logic and methods to be followed for sociology to become a science of society. The starting point, 'the first and most fundamental rule is: Consider social facts as things'. Social facts are the institutions, beliefs and values of society. As things, social facts can be treated in the same way as the objects, events and processes of the natural world. They can be objectively measured, quantified and subjected to statistical analysis. Correlations can be drawn between social facts, cause and effect relationships established and theories developed to explain those relationships. In this way 'real laws are discoverable' in the social world as in the natural world.

But how can social facts be treated as things? Aren't beliefs, for example, part of human consciousness? And aren't human beings, because they have consciousness, fundamentally different from the inanimate objects which make up the natural world? In view of this is natural science methodology appropriate for the study of human behaviour?

Durkheim accepted that social facts form part of our consciousness - they have to for society to exist. Without shared norms and values, for example, society could not operate. But, although they are a part of us, social facts also exist outside of us. In Durkheim's words, 'collective ways of acting and thinking have a reality outside the individuals'. Members of society do not simply act in terms of their particular psychology and personal beliefs. Instead they are directed to act by social facts, by values and beliefs which are over and above the individual and part of the wider society. In this respect social facts 'have a reality outside the individuals' and can therefore be studied 'objectively as external things'.

Thus just as matter is constrained to act by natural forces, so human beings are constrained to act by social forces. Given this, social facts can be studied using the methodology of the natural sciences.

The social facts of suicide Durkheim's *Suicide: A Study in Sociology* was published in 1897. This study exemplified his rules of sociological method. Durkheim argued that the causes of suicide rates (the number of suicides per million of the population) are to be found in society, *not* in the psychology of individuals. Suicide rates are social facts. They are also a product of social facts, of 'real, living, active forces which, because of the way they determine the individual, prove their independence from him'.

Statistical evidence Durkheim examined official statistics on suicide from a number of European countries (see Item A, Activity 10, p640). He found that 1) suicide rates within each country were fairly constant over a number of years and 2) there were significant differences in the rates both between societies and between social groups within the same society.

Correlation and analysis Durkheim correlated suicide rates with a wide range of social facts. For example, he found statistical relationships between suicide rates and religion, location, age and family situation. Some of these are illustrated in the following diagram. In each of the pairs the group on the left had a higher suicide rate than the group on the right.

Protestants	-	Catholics
City dwellers	-	Rural dwellers
Older adults	-	Younger adults
Unmarried	-	Married
Married without children	-	Married with children

Causation Having established correlations between social facts, Durkheim's next task was to see if he could discover causal connections. He argued that variations in suicide rates were caused by variations in levels of social integration. In the case of the examples given above, the groups on the left have lower levels of social integration than the groups on the right. For example, older adults are less socially integrated than younger adults because their children have grown up and left home, many of their friends and relatives have died and if they have retired from work they may well have lost touch with their workmates. Using examples such as this, Durkheim claimed that 'suicide varies inversely with the degree of integration of the social groups of which the individual forms a part'.

Theory and explanation Durkheim's final task was to explain why suicide rates vary with levels of social integration. Part of his explanation runs as follows. As members of society, people are social beings - they have been socialised to play a part in society. The greater their social isolation the less they can participate in society. Their lives lack meaning and purpose unless they are shared with others. In Durkheim's words, 'The individual alone is not a sufficient end for his activity. He is too little'. In a situation of social isolation 'the individual yields to the slightest shock of circumstance because the state of society has made him ready prey to suicide'.

Durkheim doesn't claim to explain all aspects of suicide. For example, he does not explain why only a small minority of socially isolated individuals commit suicide. He sees this as the job of the psychologist because it concerns individual behaviour rather than social facts.

Durkheim believed that his research on suicide proved that scientific methodology was appropriate for the study of society because it had shown that 'real laws are discoverable'. (For further discussion of Durkheim's study of suicide see pp469-470. For a broader discussion of Durkheim's view of society, see pp661-664).

4.3 Karl Popper: deduction and falsification

Induction vs deduction Durkheim argued that theories should come from evidence, from gathering data, from describing, classifying and analysing social facts. It is from this process that theories are generated. This is known as an *inductive* approach.

A *deductive* approach reverses this process. It begins with a theory and uses data to test that theory. This is the approach advocated by Karl Popper. From his viewpoint it is the only way science can proceed.

Falsification According to Popper rather than looking for evidence to confirm their theories, scientists should do their best to disprove or falsify them. This is the distinguishing characteristic of science - the development of theories which can be tested against evidence and be capable of *falsification*.

This means that theories must be constructed in such a way that falsification is possible. Popper argues that Marx's theory of history fails in this respect - it cannot be falsified and is therefore non-scientific. In particular it fails to specify precisely what has to happen before the proletarian revolution occurs in capitalist society. And when the revolution does not happen Marxists simply push its coming further and further into the future, thus preventing the possibility of falsification.

Popper rejects the search for laws governing the evolution of human society which he sees as a 'unique historical process' (1961, p108). However, he sees no reason why the methodology of the natural sciences can not be applied to the social sciences. Theories of human behaviour which are open to the possibility of falsification can be developed.

Theories that survive falsification tests however, are not necessarily true. They have simply not been falsified. The following oft quoted example illustrates this point. 'All swans are white' is a scientific statement because it can be falsified. However many times it is confirmed by observation, it cannot be accepted as true because the very next swan might be black, red, blue or yellow. In this respect there are no absolute truths in science.

Sociology and falsification Despite Popper's claim to the contrary, there are real problems in applying his model of scientific methodology to the study of human society. In the closed system of the laboratory where variables such as matter, temperature and pressure can be limited and controlled, it may be possible to falsify a theory. However, human societies are open systems which means it is impossible to limit and control variables. Because of this it is difficult to see how a theory can be falsified.

4.4 Thomas Kuhn: normal science

For Durkheim science consists of accumulating evidence and developing theories from that evidence. For Popper science consists of creating testable theories and attempting to falsify them. For Thomas Kuhn 'normal science', the vast majority of work which is called science, differs from both these views. Kuhn's *The Structure of Scientific Revolutions* (1962), argues that the way science has developed bears little relationship to conventional views of the scientific method.

Paradigms According to Kuhn most of the time scientists are busily preoccupied with 'normal science'. Normal science operates within a *paradigm*. A paradigm is a framework of concepts and theories which states how the natural world operates. It identifies appropriate methods for studying that world and specifies what questions to ask and how to answer them. A paradigm is shared by members of the scientific community. It shapes the way they see the world they study.

In some respects paradigms are like blinkers - they place limits on inquiry, they erect barriers to alternative views, they restrict the scientific imagination. This is because normal science operates within the confines of a paradigm, albeit developing and refining it but *not* challenging it. For example, until the 16th century Western astronomy was based on the theory of terracentricity - the idea that planets and the sun move round the earth. It is perfectly possible to confirm this idea with observations and measurements. And it is also possible to ignore or explain away contradictory evidence which might challenge it. So committed are scientists to the existing paradigm that they operate within it rather than attempting to falsify it.

Scientific revolutions Kuhn rejects the conventional view which sees science as a progressive accumulation of knowledge based on the testing and proving and disproving of hypotheses. Change does occur, but only when one paradigm is replaced by another. Kuhn calls this process a *scientific revolution* - it is sudden and revolutionary as a whole way of thinking about the world is swept away within a relatively short period of time. An example is the replacement of Newton's paradigm in physics with Einstein's. Once a new paradigm is established normal science resumes and any real change has to wait until the next scientific revolution.

Scientific revolutions occur when evidence accumulates which cannot be explained in terms of the existing paradigm. This evidence accumulates to the point where it cannot be ignored, dismissed as an anomaly or as the result of incorrect observation and measurement. This happened with the Copernican

revolution in astronomy in the 16th century. Copernicus stated that the sun, not the earth was the centre of the universe and that the planets orbited the sun. This view of the universe appeared to make sense of observations that could not be explained in terms of the previous paradigm.

Kuhn's view of paradigms and scientific revolutions has been criticised as a distortion of the history of science. For example, Lakatos (1970) rejects the view that normal science is dominated by a single paradigm. Instead he sees the development of science as a history of constantly competing paradigms.

Sociology and paradigms In terms of Kuhn's view of science it has been argued that sociology is in a pre-paradigmatic and therefore pre-scientific situation. There is a range of competing sociological perspectives and there is little indication that this variety will develop into a single paradigm which will be acceptable to the sociological community. However, in terms of Lakatos's view, this does not disqualify sociology from being a science. In fact, sociology's history of competing perspectives largely accords with his view of the history of science.

4.5 The realist approach to science

The realist view of science while accepting that there are basic differences between the social and natural worlds, maintains that a social *science* is possible. It argues that events in both the social and natural worlds are produced by underlying structures and mechanisms. According to Roy Bhaskar the essential task of *realism* is to uncover and explain these structures and mechanisms (Bhaskar, 1978, p4).

Open and closed systems Andrew Sayer (1992) distinguishes between open and closed systems as arenas of study. The laboratory is the prime example of a closed system. Sciences like physics and chemistry have the advantage of being able to create closed systems in which conditions can be fixed and variables controlled. This allows them to reveal 'more clearly the operation of mechanisms' (1992, p123).

However, a large body of scientific research takes place within open systems where it is not possible to control variables. Meteorology is an example of a natural science where closed systems are rare. As a result it is unable to predict the weather with any degree of accuracy as daily weather forecasts indicate. However, it is able to offer an explanation of the weather after the event in terms of underlying mechanisms. In much the same way geology is able to provide explanations for the occurrence of oil deposits. However, geologists' attempts to predict its presence have only limited success as the billions of dollars spent on unsuccessful oil exploration show.

One of the most famous non-predictive

explanations is the theory of evolution which specifies mechanisms such as natural selection and mutation which are seen to underlie the evolutionary process. Because evolution takes place within an open system it is not possible to predict its future.

Human behaviour takes place in open systems. Because of this it is not possible to predict its course with any degree of accuracy. There is no way of controlling all the variables which affect human action. However, from a realist viewpoint, this does not rule out a social science. It is still possible to explain human behaviour in terms of underlying structures and mechanisms, just as meteorologists, geologists and evolutionary biologists explain behaviour in the natural world.

Structures, mechanisms and consciousness From a realist point of view human behaviour operates within structures. Sayer defines structures as 'sets of internally related objects and practices' (1992, p92). He gives the following example using the landlord-tenant relation. The diagram illustrates the necessary relations for its existence. In Sayer's words, 'The landlord-tenant relation itself presupposes the existence of private property, rent, the production of economic surplus and so on; together they form a structure' (1992, p92). There are of course structures within structures. For example, the landlord-tenant structure forms part of the wider class structure in capitalist society.

Structures constrain human behaviour, they place limits on human action. However, this does not mean that human beings are simply directed by structural constraints. In the open system which is human society, they have varying degrees of freedom to direct their own actions. Realists include consciousness as part of the explanation for behaviour. They accept the interpretive view of social reality as socially constructed. And they also accept the Marxist view of false consciousness - that socially constructed meanings can distort reality (Blaikie, 1993, pp62, 89).

Mechanisms operate within structures. It is part of the scientist's job to identify these mechanisms and explain how they work. And in this respect the social scientist's job is the same as the natural scientist's. So just as an evolutionary biologist identifies mechanisms such as natural selection to account for biological change so a sociologist identifies mechanisms such as the class struggle to account for social change.

Realism, sociology and science From a realist viewpoint events in both the natural and social worlds are produced by structures and mechanisms. Given this, social science is based on the same principles as natural science. Both are concerned with the identification and explanation of structures and mechanisms.

Summary

1 There are many views of science and scientific methods.

2 As a result there are many views about the relationship between sociology and science and the appropriateness of applying the assumptions and methods of the natural sciences to the study of human society.

The landlord-tenant structure

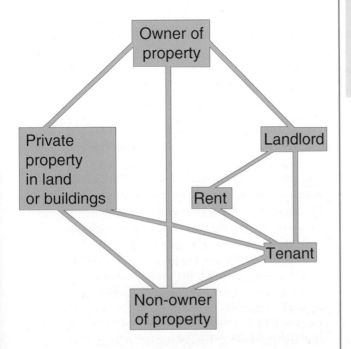

From A. Sayer, 1992, p93

Activity 10   Views of Science

Item A   *Suicide statistics*

Rate of suicides per million inhabitants in European countries

	Period 1866-70	Period 1871-75	1874-78	Numerical position in the 1 period	2 period	3 period
Italy	30	35	38	1	1	1
Belgium	66	69	78	2	3	4
England	67	66	69	3	2	2
Norway	76	73	71	4	4	3
Austria	78	94	130	5	7	7
Sweden	85	81	91	6	5	5
Bavaria	90	91	100	7	6	6
France	135	150	160	8	9	9
Prussia	142	134	152	9	8	8
Denmark	277	258	255	10	10	10
Saxony	293	267	334	11	11	11

From E. Durkheim *Suicide: A Study in Sociology*, 1970, p50

Item B   *An open system*

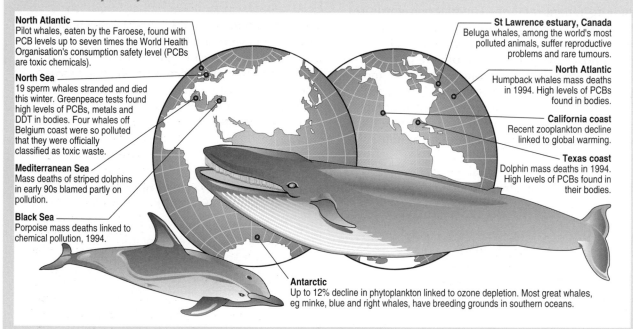

North Atlantic
Pilot whales, eaten by the Faroese, found with PCB levels up to seven times the World Health Organisation's consumption safety level (PCBs are toxic chemicals).

North Sea
19 sperm whales stranded and died this winter. Greenpeace tests found high levels of PCBs, metals and DDT in bodies. Four whales off Belgium coast were so polluted that they were officially classified as toxic waste.

Mediterranean Sea
Mass deaths of striped dolphins in early 90s blamed partly on pollution.

Black Sea
Porpoise mass deaths linked to chemical pollution, 1994.

St Lawrence estuary, Canada
Beluga whales, among the world's most polluted animals, suffer reproductive problems and rare tumours.

North Atlantic
Humpback whales mass deaths in 1994. High levels of PCBs found in bodies.

California coast
Recent zooplankton decline linked to global warming.

Texas coast
Dolphin mass deaths in 1994. High levels of PCBs found in their bodies.

Antarctic
Up to 12% decline in phytoplankton linked to ozone depletion. Most great whales, eg minke, blue and right whales, have breeding grounds in southern oceans.

Man-made pollution and climatic change are threatening the survival of the world's great whales, new scientific research reveals.

Nine years after commercial whaling was banned, the effects of global industrialisation now pose as great a threat to the world's largest mammals as the huge factory whaling fleets of the past. The hazards are outlined in scientific papers submitted to the International Whaling Commission, which meets in Dublin this week.

The authors argue that chemical pollution, ozone depletion and global warming are hindering the recovery of whale populations hunted almost to extinction in the 60s and 70s.

A separate report by biologist Dr Kevin Brown, commissioned by the London-based Environmental Investigation Agency, estimates that at least 150,000 man-made chemicals, increasing by 2,000 a year, are dumped in the oceans. He warns that damage to marine life caused by global warming and a thinning ozone layer could worsen the effects of chemicals through complex interactions which scientists are unable to predict.

'There are vast gaps in our knowledge ... but I wouldn't be surprised if there is a spiralling effect and whale numbers start crashing,' said Dr Brown, of Durham University.

His fears are echoed by Dr Mark Simmonds, of the University of Greenwich, who points out six mass deaths of seals and dolphins have been recorded since 1987 - all in highly contaminated waters such as the North Sea - compared with only four over the previous eight decades.

Although viruses were the immediate cause of death, he argues in a paper to the commission, that pollution must have played a major role.

Norway is pressing to be allowed to hunt minke whales in the north-east Atlantic where numbers have recovered slightly. But environmentalists argue the ban should not be lifted while the oceans' health is so uncertain.

Adapted from *Observer*, 28.5.95

Questions

1 Durkheim claimed that 'each society is predisposed to contribute a definite quota of voluntary deaths'.
 a) What support for this statement is provided by Item A?
 b) Use Item A to support Durkheim's claim that a science of society is possible.
2 Use Item B to support the realist view that:
 a) both the social and natural sciences operate in open systems
 b) conclusive verification or falsification are not possible in open systems
 c) in view of this, there are basic similarities between the methodologies of the natural and social sciences.

5 Interpretive Methodology

Key Issues

1 How significant are meanings for understanding social action?
2 What are the similarities and differences between the main interpretive perspectives?

Interpretive sociology covers a range of theoretical perspectives which see fundamental differences between the natural and social worlds. From an interpretive perspective the social world is essentially a world of meaning. Human beings construct their own social reality. Their actions are directed by meanings, their experience is based on meanings. Any understanding of human action must therefore involve an understanding of those meanings. And for many researchers this means employing methodologies which are very different from those used in the natural sciences.

5.1 Max Weber: social action

Social action Max Weber (1864-1920) defined sociology as 'a science which attempts the interpretive understanding of social action in order thereby to arrive at a causal explanation of its course and effects' (1964, p88). Social action is action which involves other members of society. It is based on meanings in the minds of social actors which direct their actions. Weber was particularly concerned with motives, the intentions and purposes which directed social actors to achieve certain goals.

Verstehen Motives are an important part of any explanation of social action. Weber's method of interpreting motives is known as *verstehen* which

roughly translates as empathetic understanding. Researchers put themselves in the place of social actors and attempt to see the world through their eyes. The problem of course is whether verstehen produces a true picture of the actor's world view. Weber's solution to this problem will be examined shortly.

The Protestant ethic Weber's methodology can be illustrated with his most famous work, *The Protestant Ethic and the Spirit of Capitalism* (see also pp504-505). Weber was interested in the meanings and motives - the 'spirit of capitalism' - which led to the rise of capitalism. On the basis of a wide range of historical documents he claimed that they developed from early forms of Protestantism which preceded capitalism. Weber identified a Protestant work ethic in terms of which work became a 'calling' which must be pursued with a single mind. Making money is an indication of success in one's calling, it shows that a person has not lost favour in God's sight. Weber argues that the Protestant work ethic is a major cause of the rise of capitalism.

The comparative method How does Weber know that his interpretation of motives - in this case the Protestant work ethic - is correct? His answer is to use the *comparative method* which compares different societies and different groups within the same society. In the absence of a laboratory in which variables can be manipulated and controlled, Weber attempts to find 'natural' laboratories which allow the influence of variables to be measured.

If Weber's interpretation of the Protestant work ethic is correct, then Protestants should have spearheaded the rise of capitalism. He produces evidence which indicates that early capitalism developed within predominantly Protestant rather than Catholic societies and within those societies the 'business leaders and owners of capital are overwhelmingly Protestant' (1958, p35). From this Weber claims that his interpretation of the motives of social actors is validated. (For further discussion of Weber's methodology, see pp665-667).

5.2 Herbert Blumer: symbolic interactionism

Weber investigated meanings on a wide canvas, often drawing on information from across the world and from different time periods. Symbolic interactionists tend to focus on meanings in the context of small scale interaction situations. From this point of view the meanings which direct action are developed and negotiated during the process of social interaction. The job of the sociologist is to discover these meanings.

Discovering meaning Herbert Blumer (1962) has developed a methodology for the study of social interaction. The first step is for researchers to immerse themselves in interaction situations, to observe and interpret the actions of others and attempt to see the world through their eyes. In Blumer's words, this involves 'feeling one's way inside the experience of the actor' in order to 'catch the process of interpretation through which they construct their action'. Blumer is refreshingly honest when discussing how this might be achieved. 'It is a tough job requiring a high order of careful and honest probing, creative yet disciplined imagination, resourcefulness and flexibility in study, pondering over what one is finding, and constant readiness to test and recast one's views and images of the area.'

Structure and meaning Symbolic interactionists accept that to some extent social interaction is structured. Meanings are not constantly reinvented, social interaction is often routine and repetitive rather than creative and spontaneous. But this does not mean that negotiation and interpretation aren't still important aspects of interaction. Nor does it mean that human action is shaped by the structures and mechanisms of the social system as some sociologists would argue.

Blumer gives the example of family structure and industrialisation to illustrate this point. It has been claimed that industrialisation leads to the replacement of extended families by nuclear families. Blumer objects to this view which tends to see human action as a product of structures and mechanisms. Where in the equation are the meanings people give to family life, where are the interpretations they place on industrialisation? Without these meanings and interpretations

sociologists have little chance of grasping social reality.

Blumer argues that the research process must be as systematic, rigorous and objective as possible. Equally important however are qualities such as sensitivity and sympathy. Both the tone and substance of Blumer's methodology are a long way from many of the views of science outlined in previous sections. (For further discussion of Blumer's methodology, see pp678-679).

5.3 Phenomenology

Phenomenological perspectives take the logic of a social reality to its furthest point. They argue that as human beings our only reality consists of meanings. The job of the sociologist is to discover these meanings and nothing more, for the logic of this argument states there is nothing more to discover. The methodology that results from this view will now be examined using the example of suicide.

Discovering suicide In *Discovering Suicide* J. Maxwell Atkinson's basic question is 'How do deaths get categorised as suicide?' When he has answered this question he can go no further because suicide is simply a meaning and has no reality beyond that meaning. Classifications of suicide are not right or wrong, they just are. For example, there is no such thing as a 'real' or objective suicide rate waiting to be discovered. The official statistics are the rate, full stop.

Atkinson's research attempts to discover the meanings used by coroners to classify deaths as suicide. He held discussions with coroners, attended inquests, observed a coroner's officer at work and analysed a coroner's records. He argues that coroners have a 'commonsense theory of suicide' which they use to both classify and explain deaths as suicide. In terms of this theory the following evidence is seen as relevant for reaching a verdict.

1 Whether suicide threats have been made or suicide notes left.
2 The type of death - hanging, gassing and drug overdose are seen as typical suicide deaths.
3 The location of death - death by gunshot at home is more likely to be seen as suicide than in the countryside where it may well be interpreted as a hunting accident.
4 The biography of the deceased - a recent divorce, the death of a close friend or relative, a history of depression, problems at work, financial difficulties, lack of friends are seen as typical reasons for suicide.

The closer the deceased fits this commonsense theory of suicide, the more likely his or her death will be defined as suicide. In Atkinson's words, coroners 'are engaged in analysing features of the deaths and of the biographies of the deceased according to a variety of taken-for-granted assumptions about what constitutes a "typical suicide", "a typical suicide biography", and so on'.

Having uncovered to his satisfaction the meanings used to classify death as suicide, Atkinson's research is finished. There are no more questions to ask.

Causation As outlined in a previous section, Durkheim's research on suicide was concerned with causation, in particular with the causes of variations in suicide rates. Phenomenologists see this as a pointless and misguided exercise. Suicides are not objective 'social facts' with causes that can be explained, they are meanings. To try and discover the 'causes' of suicide will simply result in uncovering

the meanings used to classify a death as suicide. Thus it comes as no surprise that the 'typical suicide biography' - the friendless, divorced loner - is very similar to Durkheim's socially isolated individual. Suicides, like any other aspect of social reality, are simply constructions of meaning.

Conclusion Phenomenology rejects the entire scientific enterprise as it is normally understood. It is a distortion of social reality to treat it as 'social facts', as 'things'. There are no 'structures' or 'mechanisms' operating in human society. There are no objective facts with causes which can be explained. There are only meanings to be uncovered and understood.

Activity 11 Suicide

Item A *Suicide in 1870*

SUICIDE OF TWO LOVERS BY LEAPING OVER THE TAFFRAIL OF THE AMERICAN PASSENGER SHIP "BLOOMENTHORPE" ON THE PASSAGE TO SAN LUIS.

DISTRESSING SUICIDE AFTER WARWICK RACES.

Item B *Retired coroner*

During the War it was something of an understanding that you didn't bring in suicide verdicts unless you really had to. 'Bad for National Morale' - and of course I think most people felt responsible for keeping morale up. I think with suicide at that time we felt it was a kind of 'defeatism', defeatism in the face of the enemy, and that was a cardinal sin, letting the side down, you know. So when there was a verdict of suicide lots of coroners couldn't resist reading a sermon about moral cowardice. I expect I did.

Quoted in P. Langley (ed) *Discovering Sociology*, 1988, p99

Item C *No more suicides*

Suicide has been officially abolished in the Irish Republic - not because people have stopped taking their own lives, but because coroners are forbidden to say that they did.

A decision by the High Court in Dublin last April means that verdicts of suicide cannot be brought in by coroners. As a result, the Republic has officially had a nil suicide rate since then.

This situation came about when relatives of a person recorded as having committed suicide challenged the coroner's verdict. The law has always prevented coroners from apportioning blame: verdicts on road accident victims, for example, could not say who was to blame.

The High Court ruled that this prohibition extended to suicide: coroners could not blame victims for their own deaths either.

Adapted from *Guardian*, 4.11.85

Questions

1 Use Items A, B and C to support a phenomenological view.
2 Do you believe there is a 'real', 'objective' suicide rate? Give reasons for your answer.

5.4 Two sociologies?

It is sometimes argued that there are 'two sociologies'. The first is based on 'scientific methodology', using 'hard' quantitative data and concerned with discovering causal relationships. This approach is sometimes labelled 'positivism'. The second is based on 'interpretive methodology', using 'soft' qualitative data and concerned with understanding the meanings which make up social reality. This approach is sometimes labelled 'phenomenology'.

This crude contrast - made even cruder here by simplification and brevity - distorts sociology as a discipline and gives a false picture of the relationship between theory, research methods and the actual practice of doing sociology. The discussion of methodology in the chapter so far should have made this apparent.

This view of the 'two sociologies' has been described by Ray Pawson (1989) as a 'methodological myth'. In other words the two sociologies don't exist. Instead there is a whole range of different views, different assumptions and different methodologies. As previous sections have shown, there are various views of science and its application to the study of human society. And sociologists who are primarily concerned with meanings use a variety of research methods and types of data and often start from different theoretical perspectives. This variety cannot be reduced to 'two sociologies'.

Summary

1 Interpretive perspectives emphasise the importance of meanings for understanding social action.

2 However, there are important differences between interpretive perspectives. Some look for causal explanations of social action, others seek only to discover the meanings used to construct social reality.

3 Given the variety of sociological perspectives and methodological assumptions, the idea of 'two sociologies' has been seen as a 'methodological myth'.

6 Sociology, Methodology and Values

Key Issues

1 Is an objective, value free sociology possible?

2 Is it desirable?

The section on reflexivity (see p633) made the point that what we see, the questions we ask and the way we interpret data are influenced by a range of social and personal factors. These include our class, gender, ethnicity, nationality and culture and our personalities, experiences and life histories. These points will now be developed focusing on the influence of values on social research.

Can the research process in particular and sociology in general be value free? And, going one step further, is a value free sociology desirable? These questions will first be examined in terms of feminist methodology. The focus will then widen to sociology as a whole.

6.1 Feminist methodology

Over the past 30 years 'women's studies' has become a major growth industry. In university bookshops, shelves are stacked with books about women and their place in history and society. And most of these books are written by women.

What does this mean? Clearly it means that women are seen as more important than before. And seeing women as more important is a value judgement. The growth of women's studies can be seen as a reflection of the rise of feminism and changes in perceptions of women's roles in Western society. There is little doubt that social change and the changes in values which accompany it influence choices about what to study. For many feminists, however, the effects of these changes are a lot more fundamental than simply choice of subject matter.

Feminism - the weak thesis

Ray Pawson (1992) distinguishes between the 'weak thesis' and the 'strong thesis' of feminist methods. In terms of the 'weak thesis', research methods in sociology are essentially sound. The problem is that in practice they are shot through with sexism. The solution is to purge them of sexism. Eichler's *Non-Sexist Research Methods* (1988) is an example of this approach. She identifies major areas of sexism which infuse the research process. These include:

Androcentricity This means viewing the world from a traditional male perspective, with its assumptions of male dominance and superiority - for example seeing women as passive objects rather than active subjects. As a result women are largely 'invisible', in Sheila Rowbotham's words they are 'hidden from history'.

Overgeneralisation Many studies deal only with men but present their findings as though they applied to both men and women. For example, until recently social mobility studies in Britain were based solely on men. Since women's social status was seen to derive from the status of their husbands, there seemed little point in looking at women in their own right. Their class position could be simply 'read off' from the position of their husband. (See pp141-147 for a discussion of women and social class).

Research methods According to Eichler the sexist assumptions outlined above infuse research methods. This can be seen from her examples of questions taken from questionnaires. The first is an example of a sex specific term when talking about people in general.

- If someone wanted to make a speech in your community claiming that blacks are inferior, should he be allowed to speak or not?

The next question reflects common assumptions about male dominance.

- It is acceptable for women to hold important political offices in state and national government. Yes/No.

The solution is to reformulate the questions in a non-sexist way.

Eichler's argument suggests reform rather than radical change. Research methods in and of themselves are not sexist. Once researchers learn to use them in a non-sexist way, then the problem will be solved.

Feminism - the strong thesis

The changes advocated by the strong thesis are more fundamental. Something of their flavour is provided by Ann Oakley's article 'Interviewing Women: A Contradiction in Terms' (1981).

Feminist interviewing Oakley argues that the standard approach to interviewing has the following characteristics. '(a) its status as a mechanical instrument of data-collection; (b) its function as a specialised form of conversation in which one person asks the questions and another gives the answers; (c) its characterisation of interviewees as essentially passive individuals and (d) its reduction of interviewers to a question asking and rapport-promoting role' (1981, pp36-7).

Oakley sees this approach as clinical, manipulative, exploitive and hierarchical. The interviewer 'uses' the respondent for 'his' purposes, controlling the content and direction of the interview. The relationship is unequal- the interviewer takes and the respondent gives. A feminist methodology would replace this by a non-hierarchical relationship, with the researcher giving as well as receiving. For example, an interviewer must 'be prepared to invest his or her personal identity in the relationship' which means honesty, sincerity, understanding and compassion between equals. It means that both parties have a say in the content and direction of the interview. Only with this personal involvement will 'people come to know each other and admit others into their lives'.

This example argues for a change in research methods - a new type of interviewing - rather than simply cleansing existing methods of sexism. It argues that research techniques are so imbued with male assumptions and practices that they must be radically changed. These changes are not only morally correct, they will also result in better data.

One reaction to Oakley's views is summed up by Ray Pawson's (1992) query, 'What's new?' There is a long tradition of interviewing which emphasises sensitivity and non-directive approaches. Whether Oakley's views are significantly different from this is questionable.

The struggle for truth Some feminists argue that the 'women's struggle' and feminist methodology are inseparable. 'Malestream' sociology is so saturated with assumptions of male dominance that a feminist alternative is required. Maria Miles (1993) provides an example of this approach. She argues that a feminist methodology must have the following features.

1 **Conscious partiality** The idea of so-called value free research has to be replaced by conscious partiality, which in practice means that female researchers must positively identify with the women they study.
2 **View from below** This replaces the 'view from above', with its assumptions of male dominance, which supports the existing power structure. Researchers must take the 'view from below' because it is more likely to reflect women's experiences and more likely to empower women in their struggle for liberation.
3 **Action research** Rather than being a detached spectator, a dispassionate observer, the researcher should actively participate in the struggle for women's liberation.
4 **Changing the status quo** From this involvement in their own emancipation, both researchers and the women they study will develop a better understanding of their situation. This is based on the idea, 'If you want to know a thing, you must

change it'. Only by challenging and changing patriarchy will its true nature be revealed.

5 **Raising consciousness** Both researchers and the researched must raise their consciousness - become aware of their oppression. In particular, it is the job of the researcher to give women the means to gain insight into and change their situation.

6 **Individual and social history** Part of the process of raising consciousness requires a study of women's individual and social history. This will allow women to reclaim their history from its appropriation by men.

7 **Collectivising experience** Women must collectivise their experience and join together and cooperate in their struggle for liberation. They must overcome the individualism, competitiveness and careerism which characterise the male world.

In terms of these propositions, Maria Miles is claiming that valid knowledge can only emerge from the struggles waged by the oppressed against their oppressors. Paradoxically the journey to truth involves just the opposite of value freedom. In Miles's case it requires a wholehearted commitment to women's liberation.

Miles's views are not new. Marxists have produced similar arguments for the liberation of the working class as have black Americans for black liberation in the USA. Whatever the virtues of this point of view, it is unlikely to offer a recipe for sociology as a whole since there is more to human society than oppressors and oppressed.

The primacy of experience

A number of feminists have argued that the only way to know something is to experience it. Given this, it is crucial for feminist research to capture the experience of women and to express it as directly as possible with a minimum of reinterpretation on the part of the researcher.

Too often researchers see the experience of others in terms of their values and preconceptions. In particular they force this experience into theoretical frameworks and categories which only serve to distort it. This argument was put forcibly by Kaluzynska (1980) when she rejected the whole Marxist debate about domestic labour - whether it was 'productive' or 'non-productive', whether it created 'surplus value', whether it was 'alienating' and so on. She objects to the imposition of concepts which she argues distort the experience of housework. In her words, 'Why did we have to get to grips with value theory to appreciate what a drag housework was?' (quoted in Pawson, 1992, p121).

There are, however, problems with giving primacy to personal experience. It makes the assumption that if we dig hard enough and deep enough we'll get to

the 'real thing' - the direct experience of others. But, as the section on reflexivity indicated, recording the experience of others will always to some degree be coloured by the values and theoretical concepts of the researcher.

Conclusion Many feminist researchers wear their hearts and values on their sleeves. Despite their differences, most would agree that:
1 Sociology is not and cannot be value free.
2 A recognition of this will result in changes to the research process and the discipline as a whole.
3 These changes will produce a more valid picture of social reality.

6.2 Sociology and values

The founding fathers of sociology believed that an objective, value free science of society was both possible and desirable. Despite their many differences, not least in terms of personal values, Comte, Marx and Durkheim each believed his work to be uncontaminated by value judgements. Today's sociologists are a lot less certain. A brief look at the debate about values and the study of deviance illustrates this.

Values and the study of deviance

In an article entitled 'Whose Side Are We On?' the American sociologist Howard Becker (1970) argues that it is impossible to conduct research 'uncontaminated by personal and political sympathies'. Becker's sympathies lie with the underdog, those who have been labelled deviant. He is critical of the agents of social control who, in his eyes, create deviance by selectively applying labels to the poor and powerless (see pp475-476). Becker argues that not only the research process but the theories which lie behind it - in his case interactionism - are infused with value judgements. From his standpoint 'interactionist theories look (and are) rather left'.

Like Becker, the American sociologist Alvin Gouldner (1975) believes that a value free sociology is impossible. However his values are a lot further to the left than Becker's. From his standpoint, Gouldner accuses the interactionists of adopting a 'bland liberal position' (liberalism advocates reform within the existing structure rather than radical social change). A more radical position would lead to a critical examination of the relationship between deviance and the unequal distribution of power in society.

Gouldner pictures Becker and his interactionist colleagues as white middle class liberals who 'get their kicks' from a 'titillated attraction to the underdog's exotic difference'. Their sympathies result in no more than a mild reproof of the agents of social control. Their bland liberalism prevents a radical critique of the structure of social inequality which creates deviance.

Looking at sociology from this point of view it is possible to see values underlying every sociological perspective.

Functionalism, Marxism and values

Functionalism has often been seen as reflecting a conservative position which advocates the maintenance of the status quo - the way things are. In doing so it is seen to justify existing social structures. With its view that order, stability and consensus are essential for the smooth running of society and its emphasis on the positive functions of social institutions, it implies that radical change is harmful to society.

Alvin Gouldner (1971) argues that in terms of the logic of functionalism, 'only "evil" - social disorder, tension or conflict - can come from efforts to remove the domination of man by man or make fundamental changes in the character of authority'. He attacks Davis and Moore's theory of stratification (see pp37-38) as a conservative doctrine which implies that 'the social world is for all time divided into rulers and ruled'. It therefore follows that 'equality is a dream'.

The values which underlie Marxism are plain for all to see. Marx was committed to socialism. His vision of communism is utopian - a perfect society. He looked forward to an egalitarian society free from the evils of capitalism - free from oppression, exploitation and alienation, with wealth and power shared by all rather than concentrated in the hands of the few. And it is partly in terms of this vision that Marxists see capitalist society. For example, J.C. Kincaid's solution to poverty states, 'Poverty cannot be abolished in a capitalist society but only in a socialist society under workers' control, in which human needs and not profits determine the allocation of resources'. Marxism replaces the functionalist commitment to the status quo with a commitment to revolutionary change.

The question of relativism

If we accept that to some degree value judgements underlie all sociological perspectives, where does this leave the search for 'truth'? Since all perspectives are value based it can be argued that there is no way - apart from our own value judgements - of deciding whether one is superior to another. Some would agree with this argument. They would take a *relativist* position seeing all knowledge as relative. In terms of this view there is no such thing as objective knowledge since everything is seen through the lens of our values and culture.

Others argue that just because a perspective is based on values does not necessarily negate its insights and its findings. Taking a relativist view is like dismissing the research findings of Greenpeace and the nuclear industry simply because of the differing values and vested interests of those organisations. And since any view of society can only be partial, differing perspectives in sociology may add breadth to that view. It is this breadth that allows Melvin Tumin (1967) to make the following statement about social stratification. 'The evidence regarding the mixed outcomes of stratification strongly suggests the examination of alternatives. The evidence regarding the possibilities of social growth under conditions of more equal rewarding is such that the exploration of alternatives seems eminently worthwhile.' And here Tumin is referring to evidence produced from a variety of sociological perspectives.

Views of reality

At one extreme there is the position that objectivity and value freedom are possible. At the other extreme all knowledge is seen as relative and there is no way of deciding between opposing views of reality. The most radical version of relativism rejects any possibility of objective knowledge seeing in its place only subjective experience. In this respect there is no reality outside human perception. What we see is what there is and there is nothing else.

Few, if any, sociologists accept this position - if they did there would be little point in doing sociology. Here is an elegant rejection of relativism by Julia O'Connell Davidson and Derek Layder.

'But the idea that there is no reality separate from the conceptual systems employed by people to grasp it accords quite ludicrous powers to human thought (Trigg, 1989). A tree that falls in a forest falls regardless of whether a person is there to witness and conceptualise the event, children in Somalia die of starvation regardless of whether the governments of the Western world believe that they are providing adequate aid. Many people in Britain and the United States fondly imagine that they live in a meritocratic, post-racist, post-sexist society, but this does not mean that a working-class child or a Black child or a female child is truly blessed with the same chances of obtaining wealth and social power as the middle-class, white, male child. Of course one person's freedom fighter is another person's terrorist. And of course you can never know with absolute certainty that another person understands what you say in *exactly* the same way that you understand it. And of course language, concepts and beliefs affect our *perception* of social reality. But this does not mean that there really is no solid world out there separate from human beings' concepts and beliefs. In practice, as King Canute is purported to have discovered, the object world has a nasty habit of intruding no matter what people may believe about it' (1994, p25).

Summary

1 There is evidence to suggest that values underlie every aspect of the sociological enterprise from the gathering of data to the construction of theories.

2 Many sociologists, while accepting that a value free sociology is not possible, still retain the ideal of objectivity. This means that research which is rigorous, systematic and reflexive is better than research which is sloppy, unsystematic and uncritical.

Activity 12 Thinking About Values

Item A *Taking sides*

To have values or not to have values: the question is always with us. When sociologists undertake to study problems that have relevance to the world we live in, they find themselves caught in a crossfire. Some urge them not to take sides, to be neutral and do research that is technically correct and value free. Others tell them their work is shallow and useless if it does not express a deep commitment to a value position.

This dilemma, which seems so painful to so many, actually does not exist; for one of its horns is imaginary. For it to exist, one would have to assume, as some apparently do, that it is indeed possible to do research that is uncontaminated by personal and political sympathies. I propose to argue that it is not possible and, therefore that the question is not whether we should take sides, since we inevitably will, but rather on whose side we are on.

Adapted from H. Becker 'Whose Side Are We On?' in H. Becker *Sociological Work*, 1970

Item C *The value of money – a Blackfoot view*

One day white men came into our camp to buy our land for dollar bills and put us on reservations with other Indians.

When the white chief had laid all of his money down on the ground and shown how much he would give all of us for signing a treaty with him, our chief took a handful of clay and made a ball of it and put it on the fire and cooked it. And it did not crack. Then he said to the white chief:

'Now, give me some of your money; we will put the money on the fire and the clay alongside of it, and whichever burns the quickest is the cheapest.'

The white chief said:

'My money will burn the quickest, because it is made of paper; so we can't do that.'

Our chief then reached down into his belt pocket and took out a little buckskin bag of sand, and he handed it to the white chief, and said: 'Give me your money. I will count the money, while you count the grains of sand. Whichever can be counted the quickest will be the cheapest.'

The white chief took the sand and poured it out into the palm of his hand, and as he looked at it, he said:

'I would not live long enough to count this, but you can count the money quickly.'

'Then,' our chief said, 'our land is more valuable than your money. It will last forever. It will not even perish by the flames of fire. As long as the sun shines and the waters flow, this land will be here to give life to men and animals. We cannot sell the lives of men and animals; therefore we cannot sell this land. It was put here for us by the Great Spirit, and we cannot sell it because it does not belong to us. You can count your money and burn it within the nod of a buffalo's head, but only the Great Spirit

Item B *Better ways of conducting research*

Social researchers draw on their everyday knowledge and on their political and moral values in the process of research; they use them to set the research agenda and to design classification systems; they use their social, as well as professional, skills to obtain information; they employ their knowledge as members of society and their political values to analyse and interpret their findings. But accepting this inevitable and indissoluble link between scientific and everyday thinking and between social theories and moral and political values does not make critical investigation impossible. As Geerz (1973, p30) comments in relation to ethnographic and anthropological work:

'I have never been impressed by the argument that, as complete objectivity is impossible ... one might as well let one's sentiments run loose. As Robert Solow has remarked, that is like saying that as a perfectly aseptic environment is impossible, one might as well conduct surgery in a sewer.'

Research that is rigorous and reflexive produces knowledge that is more objective than research which is sloppy and uncritical. Researchers who, as well as being technically competent, consider the impact of their own gender, 'racialised' and class identity upon the research process and who understand that research is itself a form of social interaction will produce a more reliable picture of the social world. In short, there are better and worse ways of conducting research.

From J. O'Connell Davidson and D. Layder *Methods, Sex and Madness*, 1994, p28 can count the grains of sand and the blades of grass on these plains. As a present to you, we will give you anything we have that you can take with you; but the land, never.'

From Chief Buffalo Child Long Lance *Long Lance*, 1956, pp182-3

Questions

1 Do you agree with Becker's view in Item A? Give reasons for your answer.
2 'There are better and worse ways of conducting research.' Discuss with reference to Item B.
3 It is useful to look at social life from a variety of standpoints and vantage points. Discuss with some reference to Item C.

Blackfoot Indians performing a religious ceremony

References

Arber, S. 'Designing Samples' in N. Gilbert (ed) 1993

Atkinson, J.M. *Discovering Suicide* (Macmillan, London, 1978)

Barker, E. *The Making of a Moonie* (Blackwell, Oxford, 1984)

Becker, H.S. 'Social Class Variations in the Teacher-Pupil Relationship' in B.R. Cosin et al (eds) *School and Society* (Routledge, London, 1971)

Becker, H.S. 'Whose Side Are We On?' in H. S. Becker *Sociological Work* (Transaction Books, New Brunswick, 1970)

Bhaskar, R. *A Realist Theory of Science* 2nd edition (Harvester, Hassocks, 1978)

Blaikie, N. *Approaches to Social Enquiry* (Polity Press, Oxford, 1993)

Blumer, H. 'Society as Symbolic Interaction' in A.M. Rose (ed) *Human Behaviour and Social Processes* (Routledge, London, 1962)

Bruce, S. 'Religion and the Sociology of Religion' in M. Haralambos (ed) *Developments in Sociology* vol 11 (Causeway Press, Ormskirk, 1995)

Chagnon, N. *Yanomamo* (Holt, Rinehart & Winston, New York, 1968)

Cicourel, A.V. *The Social Organisation of Juvenile Justice* (Heinemann, London, 1976)

Crossman, R.H.S. *The Diaries of a Cabinet Minister Volume 1* (Jonathan Cape, London, 1975)

Cumberbatch, G. and Negrine, R. *Images of Disability on Television* (Routledge, London, 1992)

Denscombe, M. *Sociology Update 1994* (Olympus Books, Leicester, 1994)

Denzin, N.K. *The Research Act in Sociology* (Butterworths, London, 1970)

Ditton, J. *Part-time Crime* (Macmillan, London, 1977)

Dobash, R.E. and Dobash, R. *Violence Against Wives* (Open Books, Wells, 1980)

Douglas, J.W.B. *The Home and the School* (MacGibbon & Kee, London, 1964)

Durkheim, E. *The Rules of Sociological Method* (The Free Press, New York, 1938)

Durkheim, E. *Suicide: A Study in Sociology* (Routledge, London, 1970)

Eichler, M. et al *Non-Sexist Research Methods* (Allen & Unwin, London, 1988)

Festinger, L. et al *When Prophecy Fails* (Harper Torchbooks, New York, 1964)

Fielding, N. 'Qualitative Interviewing' in Gilbert (ed) 1993

Gilbert, N. (ed) *Researching Social Life* (Sage, London, 1993)

Giles-Sim, J. *Wife-battering* (Guildford Press, Guildford, 1983)

Goffman, E. *Asylums* (Penguin, Harmondsworth, 1968)

Gouldner, A.W. *The Coming Crisis of Western Sociology* (Heinemann, London, 1971)

Gouldner, A.W. *For Sociology* (Penguin, Harmondsworth, 1975)

Griffin, J.H. *Black Like Me* (Signet, New York, 1960)

Gross, R.D. *Psychology* (Edward Arnold, London, 1987)

Haralambos, M. *Right On: From Blues To Soul in Black America* (Causeway Press, Ormskirk, 1994)

Hargreaves, D.H. *Social Relations in a Secondary School* (Routledge, London, 1967)

Hart, N. *When Marriage Ends* (Tavistock, London, 1976)

Hornsby-Smith, M. 'Gaining Access' in N. Gilbert (ed) 1993

Humphreys, L. *Tearoom Trade: Impersonal Sex in Public Places* (Aldine, Chicago, 1970)

Jowell, R. et al *British Social Attitudes: the 11th Report* (Dartmouth, Aldershot, 1994)

Kaluzynska, E. 'Wiping the Floor with Theory' *Feminist Review* no 7, 1980

Kincaid, J.C. *Poverty and Equality in Britain* (Penguin, Harmondsworth, 1973)

Kitzinger, J. 'Understanding AIDS' in J. Eldridge (ed) *Getting the Message: News, Truth and Power* (Routledge, London, 1993)

Kuhn, T.S. *The Structure of Scientific Revolutions* (University of Chicago Press, Chicago, 1962)

Langley, P. (ed) *Discovering Sociology* (Causeway Press, Ormskirk, 1988)

Lewis, O. *Life in a Mexican Village: Tepoztlan Restudied* (University of Illinois Press, Urbana, 1951)

Liebow, E. *Tally's Corner* (Little Brown, Boston, 1967)

Long Lance, Chief Buffalo Child *Long Lance* (Corgi, London, 1956)

Macdonald, K. and Tipton, D. 'Using Documents' in N. Gilbert (ed) 1993

Malinowski, B. *Sex and Repression in Savage Society* (Routledge, London, 1927)

Mars, G. *Cheats at Work: An Anthropology of Workplace Crime* (Allen & Unwin, London, 1982)

Miles, M. 'Towards a Methodology for Feminist Research' in M. Hammersley (ed) *Social Research: Philosophy, Politics and Practice* (Sage, London, 1993)

Moser, C.A. and Kalton, G. *Survey Methods in Social Investigation* 2nd edition (Heinemann, London, 1971)

Munck, R. and Rolston, W. *Belfast in the 30s: an Oral History* (Blackstaff Press, Belfast, 1987)

Newby, H. 'In the Field: Reflections on a Study of Suffolk Farm Workers' in C. Bell and H. Newby (eds) *Doing Sociological Research* (Allen & Unwin, London, 1977)

Newell, R. 'Questionnaires' in N. Gilbert (ed), 1993

Oakley, A. *The Sociology of Housework* (Martin Robertson, Oxford, 1974)

Oakley, A. 'Interviewing Women: A Contradiction in Terms' in H. Roberts (ed) *Doing Feminist Research* (Routledge, London, 1981)

O'Connell Davidson, J. and Layder, D. *Methods, Sex and Madness* (Routledge, London, 1994)

Okely, J. *The Traveller - Gypsies* (Cambridge University Press, Cambridge, 1983)

Pawson, R. 'Methodology' in M. Haralambos (ed) *Developments in Sociology* vol 5 (Causeway Press, Ormskirk, 1989)

Pawson, R. 'Feminist Methodology' in M. Haralambos (ed) *Developments in Sociology* vol 8 (Causeway Press, Ormskirk, 1992)

Pawson, R. 'Methods of Content/Document/Media Analysis' in M. Haralambos (ed) *Developments in Sociology* vol 11 (Causeway Press, Ormskirk, 1995)

Pearson, G. *Hooligan: A History of Respectable Fears* (Macmillan, London, 1983)

Platt, J. *Realities of Social Research* (Chatto & Windus, London, 1976)

Popper, K. *The Logic of Scientific Discovery* (Hutchinson, London, 1959)

Pryce, K. *Endless Pressure* (Penguin, Harmondsworth, 1979)

Redfield, R. *Tepoztlan: A Mexican Village* (University of Chicago Press, Chicago, 1930)

Sayer, A. *Method in Social Science: A Realist Approach* (Routledge, London, 1992)

Shaw, C. *The Jack Roller* (University of Chicago Press, Chicago, 1930)

Shipman, M.D. *The Limitations of Social Research* (Longman, London, 1988)

Stands In Timber, J. and Liberty, M. *Cheyenne Memories* (Yale University Press, New Haven, 1967)

Taylor, I., Walton, P. and Young, J. *The New Criminology* (Routledge, London, 1973)

Thomas, W.I. and Znaniecki, F. *The Polish Peasant in Europe and America* (Dover, New York, 1958)

Tumin, M. *Social Stratification: The Forms and Functions of Social Inequality* (Prentice-Hall, Englewood Cliffs, 1967)

Turnbull, C. *The Forest People* (Jonathan Cape, London, 1961)

Weber, M. *The Protestant Ethic and the Spirit of Capitalism* (Charles Scribner's Sons, New York, 1958)

Weber, M. *The Theory of Social and Economic Organisation* (The Free Press, New York, 1964)

Whyte, W.F. *Street Corner Society* 2nd edition (University of Chicago Press, Chicago, 1955)

Williams *Obscenity and Film Censorship* (Cambridge University Press, Cambridge, 1981)

Williams, J.A. Jr 'Interviewer - Respondent Interaction' in B.J. Franklin and H.W. Osborne (eds) *Research Methods* (Wadsworth, Belmont, 1971)

Introduction

Throughout this book you have been examining specific topics with the help of sociological theories. You will have considered, for example, functionalist theories of education, the family and deviance, or Marxist theories of class, power and religion. Whilst these theories certainly do have a lot to say about such specific issues, they do in fact comprise much more general theories about the nature of society, individuals and the relationship between the two. The aim of this chapter is to explore these general theories in a little more depth, and to evaluate their contribution to our understanding of the nature and development of human societies and the individuals who comprise them.

Chapter summary

- Part 1 outlines the **nature of sociological theory** and the ways in which sociological theories can be evaluated.
- Part 2 discusses the **origins of sociological theory** and the work of three major 19th century theorists whose work has been central to all subsequent developments within the discipline.
- Part 3 examines the **establishment of three**

major schools of sociological theory which emerged during the first half of the 20th century.
- Part 4 addresses a **tension** implicit within sociological theory, between **structure and action**.
- Finally, Part 5 outlines a number of recent **challenges to sociological theory**.

1 What is Sociological Theory?

Key Issues

1 What is sociological theory?
2 How can sociological theories be evaluated?

In studying the material presented in the previous chapters of this book you have been using sociological theory, perhaps without even noticing it. Many of the chapters looked at their topic from the point of view of such different *perspectives* as Marxism, functionalism and symbolic interactionism. These, together with several others, are sociological theories, and they are fundamental to the whole discipline of sociology. Before we go on to examine exactly what the various sociological theories say, it will be helpful if we try to explain what a sociological theory actually is. There are essentially two elements to this: sociological theories as *models* and sociological theories as *propositions*.

1.1 Sociological theories as models

If we try to create a model of something, we attempt to create a *representation* of it. The sorts of models

with which most of us are familiar are models of objects such as boats or aircraft. When we make models of such objects, we attempt to represent their main features in such a way that they are recognisable, without actually building another whole boat or aircraft. Inevitably when we build such a model, we emphasise some features of the real object at the expense of the others - one model of the Q.E.II might have a particularly realistic passenger deck, whilst another a very realistic funnel. When we see a good model of the Q.E.II, we recognise it as a model of the Q.E.II but do not mistake it for the real ship. We can also recognise two different models as being equally good models, even though each has different strengths and weaknesses.

Sociologists do something rather similar to this when they attempt to represent society. In creating models of society they attempt to represent its important features. Just as with the example of building a model ship, some features of society are inevitably emphasised at the expense of others. So for example, Marxism places particular emphasis on the conflicts in society whilst functionalists tend to emphasise the degree of consensus in society. Neither gives a complete representation of society, but each draws attention to some of its important features.

A common difficulty with this view of sociological theories as models concerns how we can choose between them. Although, as we shall see in the following section, sociological theories can often be directly compared with features of the society they represent, and judgements made about their accuracy, sometimes this is not the case. Some theories are rather like a hall of mirrors at a British seaside resort. A hall of mirrors is a collection of distorting mirrors, some of which make you appear very thin, some very fat and others which grossly distort the proportions of your body. Of course, we know that our bodies are being distorted by such mirrors because we have seen our reflections in ordinary mirrors.

Similarly, sociological theories can function like a hall of mirrors. Each provides a different representation of society, but since we do not know which mirror gives the true representation, it is very difficult, if not impossible, for us to select the most accurate image. It is for this reason that choosing between competing sociological theories can be one of the most challenging, but also the most interesting tasks facing the sociologist.

1.2 Sociological theories as propositions

Although it might often be difficult to choose which competing sociological theory gives us the best representation of society, it is important that we do try to find ways of doing so. If we did not, and simply decided to regard each theory as a different but equally valid representation of society, we would face some serious difficulties.

The idea that competing theories are merely different but equally valid views of some phenomenon is often called *relativism.* The chief difficulty with relativism is that it can lead to conclusions which are logically impossible. This is sometimes referred to as the problem of *incoherence.* Consider the following example of a relativist argument: 'the feminist claim that the most fundamental divisions in society are those of gender is a different but equally valid argument as the Marxist claim that the most fundamental divisions in society are those of class'.

The problem is this: the most fundamental divisions in society cannot be *both* those of class and gender. One must be, by definition, more fundamental than the other. That is not to say that we could not claim the following: 'divisions of class and gender are equally fundamental'. In so doing, however, we would in fact be contradicting both claims in the original argument, because each one insists that one division is more fundamental than the other. This shows us that when we are faced with mutually contradictory theories - theories which just cannot

both be right - we must reject either one of the theories or both of the theories. So in the case of this example, we either reject the claim that class is the most fundamental division, or that gender is the most fundamental division or conclude that neither class nor gender is the most fundamental division (ie that some division other than class or gender is the most fundamental). What we cannot say is that *both* class and gender divisions are most fundamental.

The question is, therefore, on what basis should we reject or accept any given sociological theory? To begin to see the answer to this, it is important to notice that sociological theories - like other types of theory - usually contain within them what we might call *propositions*. Essentially, a proposition is any statement which purports to say something which is true. Both of the theories we considered above purported to say something which was truthful: that gender was the most fundamental division in society and that class was the most fundamental division in society. Both theories therefore contained propositions. There are basically two ways in which we can evaluate propositions.

Logical evaluation The first of these we could call logical evaluation. This concerns the internal validity of the argument we are examining. Do the various elements of the theory fit together in a logically coherent way, or do they contradict each other? We saw above one example of logical evaluation. We saw that to simultaneously accept the different claims of Marxists and feminists about which divisions in society are the most fundamental is simply illogical, and therefore should be rejected before we even begin to examine the available evidence.

Sometimes a theory might be perfectly logical, but contradicted by some piece of evidence. Consider the following example:

All sociologists vote Labour.
Basil is a sociologist.
Therefore, Basil votes Labour.

Logically, the conclusion, 'Therefore Basil votes Labour' follows from the premises of this argument. It may well be, however, that each statement within the argument is untrue: not all sociologists vote Labour and Basil could be an accountant who votes for the Natural Law Party.

Similarly, some or all of the elements of an argument could be perfectly true, but the argument itself is logically flawed. Consider the following:

The first professor of sociology was French.
Durkheim was the first professor of sociology.
Therefore Durkheim wrote a book called *Suicide.*

Each one of these statements is perfectly true, but

taken together the conclusion simply does not follow from the premises. In fact, logically, this 'argument' is nonsense, even though each of its elements is perfectly true.

What these examples show us is that it is as important to pay attention to the *form* of an argument as to the truth of its various elements. Clearly, however, the logical validity of any particular sociological argument is not the only criterion by which it should be evaluated.

Empirical evaluation As well as a theory's logical validity we should also be concerned about the truth of the specific propositions it contains. If we cannot accept on logical grounds the argument that Marxism and feminism present equally valid views of which are the most fundamental social divisions, then we are still left with the need to decide which divisions are in fact most fundamental. Somewhat obviously, we need to do this by somehow comparing the various claims being made with the social reality they are purporting to describe. This general task we can call empirical evaluation.

As you will have seen in the chapter on methodology, sociologists have devised many ingenious methods of gathering data about social phenomena. Let us take just one to illustrate the example we are considering. Imagine we decide to try to settle the dispute between Marxists and feminists by conducting a series of interviews with a carefully selected sample of individuals. Imagine we ask a group of working class women which group they feel they have most in common with: working class men, or upper class women. If the majority choose the latter then we might conclude that the feminist theory is the most accurate, in that gender is being identified by the respondents as the most important variable. If the majority choose the former, then we would perhaps conclude that the Marxist

point of view is the most accurate, since class has been identified as the most important variable.

Whilst at first sight this appears to be a straightforward way of settling disputes between theories, there is in fact a serious problem with it. This is that Marxists faced with the evidence that most people regard gender as the most important line of division in society could easily argue that this result has arisen from the *false consciousness* of the respondents. In other words, those people interviewed falsely believed gender to be most important because such a belief serves the class interests of the bourgeoise. Marxists might therefore argue that in reality it is class which is most important, even though people do not generally recognise this.

This last example illustrates a very important point about the relationship between sociological theories and empirical evidence. Whilst theories certainly make statements about the real world which they claim to be true, they also often contain their own standards by which these statements should be evaluated. In other words, some piece of empirical evidence might be accepted as valid by supporters of one theory, but not by supporters of another. What this means is that sociological theories cannot always be straightforwardly tested by obtaining empirical evidence, as the validity and relevance of this evidence may always be challenged by supporters of the theory in question.

We have tried in this section to show that sociological theories need to be evaluated both logically and empirically, but that the latter may not always be straightforward because there exists a complex relationship between theories and empirical evidence. We now turn our attention to a consideration of the origins of sociological theory in the ideas of the Enlightenment, and the writings of Karl Marx, Emile Durkheim and Max Weber.

Activity 1 Life of Galileo

Brecht wrote *Life of Galileo* in 1938. Galileo was a 17th century scientist whose discoveries challenged the Ptolemaic model of the universe which placed earth at the centre of the universe, a view supported by the Church. Galileo's discoveries also challenged the ideas of the ancient Greek philosopher Aristotle which were still influential. In this extract from Scene 4, Galileo is trying to persuade court scholars of the significance of his discoveries.

GALILEO *at the telescope*: As your highness no doubt realises, we astronomers have been running into great difficulties in our calculations for some while. We have been using a very ancient system which is apparently consistent with our philosophy but not, alas, with the

facts. Would you gentlemen care to start by observing these satellites of Jupiter, the Medician stars?
ANDREA (the housekeeper's son) *indicating the stool by the telescope*: Kindly sit here.
PHILOSOPHER: Thank you, my boy. I fear things are not quite so simple. Mr Galileo, before turning to your famous tube, I wonder if we might have the pleasure of a disputation? Its subject to be: Can such planets exist?
MATHEMATICIAN: A formal dispute.
GALILEO: I was thinking you could just look through the telescope and convince yourselves?
ANDREA: This way, please.
MATHEMATICIAN: Of course, of course. I take it you are familiar with the opinion of the ancients that there can be no stars which turn round centres other than the

earth, nor any which lack support in the sky?

GALILEO: I am.

PHILOSOPHER: Moreover, quite apart from the very possibility of such stars, which our mathematicians - *he turns towards the mathematician* - would appear to doubt, I would like in all humility to pose the philosophical question: are such stars necessary? The universe of the divine Aristotle, with the mystical music of its spheres and its crystal vaults, the orbits of its heavenly bodies, the slanting angle of the sun's course, the secrets of the moon tables, the starry richness catalogued in the southern

Galileo displays his telescope to Florentine nobles.

hemisphere and the transparent structure of the celestial globe add up to an edifice of such exquisite proportions that we should think twice before disrupting its harmony.

GALILEO: How about your highness now taking a look at his impossible and unnecessary stars through this telescope?

MATHEMATICIAN: One might be tempted to answer that, if your tube shows something which cannot be there, it cannot be an entirely reliable tube, wouldn't you say?

GALILEO: What d'you mean by that?

MATHEMATICIAN: It would be rather more appropriate, Mr Galileo, if you were to name your reasons for assuming that there could be free-floating stars moving about in the highest sphere of the unalterable heavens.

PHILOSOPHER: Your reasons, Mr Galileo, your reasons.

GALILEO: My reasons! When a single glance at the stars themselves and my own notes makes the phenomenon evident? Sir, your disputation is becoming absurd.

MATHEMATICIAN: If one could be sure of not over-exciting you, one might say that what is in your tube and what is in the skies is not necessarily the same thing.

PHILOSOPHER: That couldn't be more courteously put.

FEDERZONI: They think we painted the Medicean stars on the lens.

GALILEO: Are you saying I'm a fraud?

PHILOSOPHER: How could we? In his highness's presence too.

MATHEMATICIAN: Let's not beat about the bush. Sooner or later Mr Galileo will have to reconcile himself to the facts. Those Jupiter satellites of his would penetrate the crystal spheres. It is as simple as that.

FEDERZONI: You'll be surprised: the crystal spheres don't exist.

PHILOSOPHER: Any textbook will tell you that they do, my good man.

FEDERZONI: Right, then let's have new textbooks.

PHILOSOPHER: Your highness, my distinguished colleague and I are supported by none less than the divine Aristotle himself.

GALILEO *almost obsequiously*: Gentlemen, to believe in the authority of Aristotle is one thing, tangible facts are another. You are saying that according to Aristotle there are crystal spheres up there, so certain motions just cannot take place because the stars would penetrate them. But suppose those motions could be established? Mightn't that suggest to you that those crystal spheres don't exist? Gentlemen, in all humility I ask you to go by the evidence of your eyes.

MATHEMATICIAN: My dear Galileo, I may strike you as very old-fashioned, but I'm in the habit of reading Aristotle now and again, and there, I can assure you, I trust the evidence of my eyes.

GALILEO: I am used to seeing the gentlemen of the various faculties shutting their eyes to every fact and pretending that nothing has happened. I produce my observations and everyone laughs. I offer my telescope so they can see for themselves, and everyone quotes Aristotle.

FEDERZONI: The fellow has no telescope.

MATHEMATICIAN: That's just it.

PHILOSOPHER *grandly*: If Aristotle is going to be dragged in the mud - that's to say an authority recognised not only by every classical scientist but also by the chief fathers of the church - then any prolonging of this discussion is in my view a waste of time.

Adapted from B. Brecht *Life of Galileo*, 1980, pp 38-43

Questions

1 What reasons does Galileo give for believing his model of the universe and what reasons do the court scholars give for rejecting this model?

2 When sociologists evaluate theories are they likely to draw upon the type of evidence Galileo uses or the type of evidence the court scholars use? Give reasons for your answers.

2 Classical Sociology and the Advent of Modernity

Key Issues

1 What are the origins of sociological theory?

2 How significant is the work of Marx, Durkheim and Weber to the development of sociological theory?

Sociology, as a distinct form of enquiry, emerged in the 19th century in the wake of 'the so-called "twin revolutions" - the Industrial Revolution of England (and later elsewhere) which occurred roughly between 1780 and 1840 and the Democratic Revolutions of the United States of America in 1776 and France in 1789' (Lee and Newby, 1983, p26). These revolutions signalled a radical transformation in society and the advent of modernity. Although the early sociologists characterised the transformation in different ways, they recognised that the modern world - which they saw emerging in their lifetimes - represented a significant break from the past.

There is now widespread agreement over the major features of modernity. They can be grouped under three headings - the economic; the political; and the cultural. Economically, modernity involves the dominance of industrial capitalism; politically, it involves the consolidation of the nation state and typically liberal democracy; culturally it involves a stress on reason as opposed to tradition (Jones, 1993).

The dramatic changes, which occurred in North America and Northern Europe in the second half of the 18th century and the first half of the 19th century and which signalled the advent of modernity, generated very different political responses. For liberals, the changes were welcome. Individuals are naturally rational and should be able to be free to pursue their own interests. The removal of traditional restraints and the emergence of governments which guaranteed the rights of individuals were therefore seen as progressive developments. For socialists, the changes were not unwelcome but were seen as not going far enough. Human beings are naturally communal and their interests can therefore only be met collectively. This necessitates the replacement of capitalism which divides people by socialism which enables people to cooperate. In contrast to these two optimistic responses to social change, conservatives exhibited horror. Human beings are naturally members of a social organism - unequal but dependent on each other. The revolutions, in their disregard for tradition and their rupture of the natural order, were seen as dangerous developments.

Liberalism, socialism and conservatism have all influenced the development of sociology. Much 19th century sociology took up the conservative concern with the threat to social order (Nisbet, 1967) and much subsequent sociology has involved a debate with the ghost of Marx, exhibiting in the process the influence of socialism (Zeitlin, 1971). Liberalism, however, was the most significant in the emergence of sociology as a distinct form of enquiry because this was the dominant political philosophy of the Enlightenment.

2.1 The Enlightenment

The Enlightenment refers to 'a period in European intellectual history which spans the time from roughly the first quarter to the last quarter of the 18th century. Geographically centred in France, but with important outposts in most of the major European states, the "Enlightenment" is composed of the ideas and writings of a fairly heterogeneous group, who are often called by their French name *philosophes'* (Hamilton, 1992, p24). Whatever differences there were between the philosophes, they recognised that they were engaged on a common project. This is evident in their cooperative enterprise - the publication over twenty years of the *Encyclopédie*. This work reflected two shared principles - confidence in the ability of human reason to provide an understanding of the world and faith in the ability of human beings to use this understanding to improve the world. The radical nature of these two principles should not be underestimated. For they constituted a direct challenge to the traditional conception of the world propagated by the Roman Church. Reason was no longer seen as subservient to divine revelation as interpreted through the teachings of the Roman Church. And history was no longer seen as 'synonymous with God working his purpose out' (Smart, 1992, p8). Instead stress was placed on the power of human reason to create knowledge, which in turn can be used to improve the human condition. In the process, the Enlightenment brought about a cultural change in what constitutes knowledge and what the purpose of knowledge is. A distinctly modern conception of knowledge was born.

The Enlightenment philosophes systematically developed and popularised among influential members of society ideas which had been originally formulated in an earlier era. Scientific discoveries in the 16th and 17th centuries challenged the traditional religious world view which placed the earth at the centre of the universe. The problem of deciding what constituted the truth was therefore raised in an acute form. Philosophers in the 17th century grappled with this question and came up with two broad answers. For the *rationalists*, true knowledge was logically deduced from a few basic premises which could not be doubted. Descartes, for example, concluded that however much he doubted, he could be sure of one thing, 'cogito ergo sum' (I think therefore I am). This constituted for him a firm foundation for knowledge. For the *empiricists*, true knowledge was induced from observations. Berkeley, for example, concluded that 'esse est percipi' (to exist is to be perceived). This constituted for him a firm foundation for knowledge. Although the rationalists and empiricists (and indeed many of the Enlightenment philosophes) continued to believe in a God, the basis of knowledge was no longer seen as the word of God (as interpreted through the Church) but reason or sensory observation. What the Enlightenment philosophes did was to synthesise these two traditions. 'An understanding or knowledge of natural and social reality was deemed to depend upon a unity of reason and observation, made possible by the practice of scientific methods of inquiry' (Smart, 1992, p9). Indeed when 18th century writers talk of the power of human reason they 'meant the scientific method: the deductive reasoning of the mathematical sciences and the inductive, empirical reasoning of the sciences of nature' (Dunthorne, 1991, p7).

The 17th century also witnessed a dispute between the 'ancients' and the 'moderns' over the respective merits of the works of classical antiquity and the more recent thinking of an emerging modern Europe. The view of the 'moderns' that knowledge had grown over time eventually gained ascendancy and paved the way for the Enlightenment to argue that there existed a more general process of social development and that knowledge could be used to promote further progress.

The Enlightenment belief that science was a force for enlightenment and progress generated tremendous optimism. The success of the natural sciences encouraged a belief 'that in the struggle of man against nature the balance of power was shifting in favour of man' (Gay, 1973, p3). Science would enable human beings to gain mastery over nature and the application of the scientific method to social arrangements would justify the reform of social institutions. In both cases the result would be the enhancement of human freedom.

The emergence of a sociological perspective can be detected in the Enlightenment. 'For the first time, man could "dare to know" about the social arrangements under which he lived, rather than have them presented to him through the obscuring haze of a religious ideology. By knowing about these social arrangements, their operation would become clear, and thus open to change' (Hamilton, 1992, pp55-56). The philosophes tended not to have a clearly worked out model of society, however. Wedded to the notion that individuals are essentially rational and self sufficient, society was seen as a collection of individuals. It was therefore left to later writers in the 19th century to develop more coherent models of society and to give birth to sociology as a distinct form of enquiry. What is significant is that these writers built on the cultural change which the Enlightenment brought in ways of thinking about society. It is to the work of the three who above all others have established the principal frames of reference of modern sociology - Marx, Durkheim and Weber - that we now turn.

Activity 2 The Individual and Society

Item A *A medieval model of the individual and society*

Society, like the human body, is an organism composed of different members. Each member has its own function - prayer or defence or merchandise or tilling the soil. Each must receive a means suited to its station and must claim no more. Within classes there must be equality. If one takes into his hand the living of two, his neighbour will go short. Between classes there must be inequality, or otherwise a class cannot perform its function or enjoy its rights.

Adapted from R. Tawney, *Religion and the Rise of Capitalism*, 1936, p22

Item B *The view of a sixteenth century writer*

God made all the parts of the body for the soul and with the soul to serve him and all the subjects in the kingdom to serve their King and with their King to serve him. If the head of the body ache, will not the heart be greatly grieved and every part feel his part of the pain of it. And if a King in his world be displeased then the heart of his kingdom (the hearts of his subjects) will have a feeling of it.

Nicholas Bretton, a 16th century writer

Item C *The rise of individualism*

The transformations which ushered in modernity tore the individual free from their stable moorings in traditions and structures. Since these were believed to be divinely ordained, they were held not to be subject to fundamental change. One's status, rank and position in the 'great chain of being' - the secular and divine order of things - overshadowed any sense that one was a sovereign individual. The birth of the 'sovereign individual' represented a significant break with the past.

The sovereign individual - the idea that the individual is the centre of the universe, that all things can be traced back to the individual, that the individual sets things in motion, makes the world go round and is the motor of social action and change - was a new idea which only gradually emerged.

Many major movements in Western thought and culture contributed to the emergence of this new conception: the Reformation and Protestantism, which set the individual conscience free from the religious institutions of the Church and exposed it directly to the eye of God; Renaissance humanism, which placed Man at the centre of the universe; the scientific revolutions, which endowed Man with the faculty and capacities to inquire into, investigate and unravel the mysteries of Nature; and the Enlightenment, centred on the image of rational, scientific Man, freed from dogma and intolerance, before whom the whole of human history was laid out for understanding and mastery.

Adapted from S. Hall 'The Question of Cultural Identity' in S. Hall et al *Modernity and its Futures*, 1992

Item D *An Enlightenment model of the individual and society*

Man was born free, and he is everywhere in chains. Those who think themselves the masters of others are indeed greater slaves than they. How did this transformation come about? I do not know. How can it be made legitimate? That question I believe I can answer. . . . The social order is a sacred right which serves as a basis for all other rights. And as it is not a natural right, it must be one founded on covenants [binding agreements]. The problem is to determine what those covenants are.

'How to find a form of association which will defend the person and goods of each member with the collective force of all, and under which each individual, while uniting himself with the others, obeys no one but himself, and remains as free as before.' This is the fundamental problem to which the social contract holds the solution.

Whichever way we look at it, we always return to the same conclusion: namely that the social pact establishes equality among the citizens in that they all pledge themselves under the same conditions and must all enjoy the same rights.

From J. Rousseau *The Social Contract* quoted in D. Held et al (eds) *States and Societies*, 1983, pp 71-5

Item E *Sir Isaac Newton*

William Blake's painting (dated 1795) of the scientist Sir Isaac Newton. Blake portrays him as a godlike figure drawing on a chart beside his underwater grotto.

Questions

1 Read Items A and B. How do they portray the relation between the individual and society?
2 Read Item C. How does the relation between the individual and society change with the rise of modernity?
3 Read Item D. How does this Enlightenment model of society differ from that presented in Items A and B?
4 Briefly comment on the painting of Sir Isaac Newton in the light of Items A to D.

2.2 Karl Marx (1818-1883)

Marx did not see himself as a sociologist but nonetheless his ideas have been extremely influential within sociology (as well as of course the wider society) and have in fact formed the basis for a distinct sociological perspective. This perspective is characterised by three central features. Firstly, the starting point for analysing society should always be the material conditions of production - the way people organise the production of goods and services. Secondly, the motor of social change is class conflict and it is such conflict which propels society forward from one production system to another. Thirdly, the conditions which will enable the working class to replace the modern oppressive productive system by a classless system can be scientifically identified. Marx's espousal of a scientific approach and his view that this approach can help society to progress indicate his debt to the Enlightenment.

The materialist conception of history

For Marx, the first priority of human beings is to ensure physical survival by producing the means of subsistence. Unless the provision of food and shelter is met, no other activity is possible. Hence, according to Marx, the way society organises its production is the most fundamental aspect of human existence and it is from this that all other aspects of human activity develop. Thus ideas, which other writers such as Hegel had seen as fundamental, are ultimately dependent upon the way people organise the production of their means of subsistence.

The economic base and social superstructure

In developing his materialist conception of history, Marx distinguished between the *base* and *superstructure* of society. The base consists of the *forces of production* (the tools and machinery, the knowledge and the raw materials which people use in order to produce goods and services) and the *relations of production* (the social relationships between people involved in the production process). Those parts of the forces of production which can be legally owned, for example land in feudal society and factories in capitalist society, are known as the *means of production.*

Together, the forces and relations of production define the way a society organises its production of goods or services, or *mode of production.* The economic base or dominant mode of production is the bedrock of society and all other social institutions and processes develop from it and are ultimately dependent upon it. As Marx put it, the economic base is 'the real foundation on which legal and political superstructures arise and to which definite forms of social consciousness correspond. The mode of production of material life determines the general character of the social, political and spiritual processes of life' (Bottomore and Rubel, 1961, p67).

Let us take an example of one mode of production, feudalism. In societies where this was the dominant mode of production, land was the chief means of production so that ownership of land put the lords in a position of dominance over the serfs who had to work the land in order to survive. Since the serfs did not own the land they were forced to hand over a proportion of what they produced as tithes to the lords. The rest of the social structure reflected the economic subordination of the serfs to the lords. The legal system obliged serfs to provide military service for their lords and the church justified their exploitation.

Class and social change

Marx was less concerned to offer a description of any particular mode of production than to put forward an account of how it changes and is eventually replaced by another. He distinguished four main modes of production which have succeeded each other. In chronological order they are primitive communism, ancient society, feudalism and capitalism. Apart from primitive communism where people only produce enough to subsist and there is no surplus for a particular group to appropriate, each mode of production is characterised by a particular set of class relations. Those who own the means of production exploit the labour of those who do not own the means of production. In ancient society masters exploited the labour of slaves whom they owned; in feudal society the lords exploited the labour of serfs who were tied to the land; and in capitalist society the bourgeoisie exploit the labour power of the proletariat who are forced to work for them in order to survive. In each case exploitation leads to class conflict and the eventual replacement of each mode of production.

Class conflict leads to the overthrow of a mode of production because of underlying contradictions which develop within the mode of production between the forces of production and relations of production. The forces of production develop as people discover new ways of mastering nature and generating wealth. There comes a point, however, when their full potential is held back by the existing relations of production. It is then that the conditions are conducive for the class who own the new means of production to rise up and overthrow the old mode of production. This process can be illustrated by the transition from feudalism to capitalism. Within feudalism the discovery of new sources of power such as steam allowed human beings to master nature more effectively. For this potential to be realised, however, it was essential that people were no longer tied to the land but free to work for those who owned the new sources of power. These were the conditions which encouraged the bourgeoisie to unite and overthrow the feudal relations of production and establish a new mode of production. In Marx's words, 'With the change of the economic foundation the entire immense superstructure is more or less rapidly transformed' (Bottomore and Rubel 1961, p68). Thus the bourgeoisie oust the feudal aristocracy from political power and the culture is transformed as concepts such as freedom replace the dominant concepts of feudalism such as loyalty. The resolution of old contradictions however, does not mean an end to contradictions. Contradictions develop within the new mode of production - the contradictions of capitalism will eventually lead to its replacement by communism.

The transition from capitalism to communism

Marx's primary concern was to analyse capitalism and identify the conditions which will bring about its downfall. Capitalism can be defined in terms of two interrelated features: a) the production of goods and services is primarily geared to the search for profits which accrue to those people who own the means of production and b) the process is organised in terms of a market in which commodities, including labour power itself, are bought and sold. As a consequence, capitalism is characterised by two classes - those who own the means of production (the bourgeoisie) and those who do not own the means of production (the proletariat) who are therefore forced to sell their labour power and work for the bourgeoisie. The relation between these classes is on the surface less exploitive than in a feuded society in which people were obliged, for example, to hand over a definite amount of produce to the lord of the manor or to work unpaid on the lord's land. In a capitalist society, workers hire out their energies and skills, in order to produce the goods and services which are eventually sold on the market, in exchange for wages. The exchange, however, is not on inspection a fair one. The wages invariably represent less in terms of value than the value realised through the sale of the products of proletarian labour and the difference between the two, which Marx called *surplus value*, is appropriated by the bourgeoisie as profit. For Marx, the relation between the bourgeoisie and proletariat is clearly one of exploitation, and has, as a consequence, the increasing alienation of the proletariat.

Alienation 'In what does this alienation consist?' Marx asked. 'First, that the work is external to the worker, that it is not a part of his nature, that consequently he does not fulfil himself in his work but denies himself, has a feeling of misery, not of wellbeing, does not develop freely a physical and mental energy, but is physically exhausted and mentally debased. The worker, therefore, feels himself at home during his leisure, whereas at work he feels homeless. His work is not voluntary but imposed, forced labour. It is not the satisfaction of a need, but only a means for satisfying other needs. Its alien character is clearly shown by the fact that as soon as there is no physical or other compulsion, it is avoided like the plague. Finally, the alienated character of work for the worker appears in the fact that it is not his work but work for someone else, that in work he does not belong to himself but to another person' (Bottomore and Rubel, 1961, p177).

Crisis and contradiction As capitalism develops, Marx argued, so the conditions for its transcendence become more apparent. Driven by the need to maintain the rate of profit, the bourgeoisie adopts increasingly sophisticated technology, thus creating the possibility for the population as a whole to enjoy a high standard of living and for its members to fulfil themselves. Such an outcome is, however, not possible so long as the bourgeoisie continues to appropriate surplus value for itself. In Marx's terms, the relations of production in a capitalist society prevent the promise of shared material abundance, which the developing forces of production point to, from being fully realised. What is more, the existence of a fundamental imbalance between production and consumption results in periodic crises when the market is unable to absorb all the goods and services which have been produced. The bourgeoisie, of course, responds to such crises by seeking new markets around the world thus encouraging in the process European colonial expansion. Economic crises, however, recur and invariably result in bankruptcies. In order to counteract these tendencies to overproduction, capital becomes more concentrated, thus making it increasingly possible for production to be centrally coordinated and orientated to people's needs. However, such an outcome is again not possible so long as the bourgeoisie compete with each other to make profits. For these possibilities, which emerge in a capitalist society, to be realised, the revolutionary action of the proletariat is needed.

Class polarisation At first the proletariat's resistance to bourgeois domination is only sporadic. Members are not united but struggle among each other as well as against the bourgeoisie. Over time however, a combination of circumstances promotes the *class consciousness* of the proletariat. The development of capitalism tends to mean the demise of classes characteristic of the former pre-industrial society - landowners and serfs - and therefore the emergence of a more simplified class structure as the last vestiges of the previous class structure disappear. The existence of a particularly vulnerable and unorganised sector of the labour force, which can be tapped during a boom but disposed of during a slump, described by Marx as 'a reserve army of labour,' tends to mean that wages remain around subsistence levels and the relative disparity in wealth between the bourgeoisie and proletariat increases. The introduction of machinery tends to mean the erosion of traditional craft skills and the elimination of skill divisions within the proletariat. In short, a process of *class polarisation* occurs, in which the proletariat, less divided and subject to increasing relative poverty, face a clearly distinct bourgeoisie. As they live through the economic crises of capitalism with their attendant increases in unemployment and decreases in wages and as they work concentrated together in large factories, so members of the proletariat communicate to each other their increasing dissatisfaction with bourgeois exploitation. They organise themselves to begin with on a local level, later on a national level, to improve their wages and conditions until finally they are strong enough to oust the bourgeoisie and set up a new society. In the process they transform themselves from a mere category of people who happen to share the same conditions, to a group of people who, realising they share the same conditions, organise to change them. In Marx's terms, they make the transition from a *class in itself* to a *class for itself.*

Revolutionary change The bourgeoisie of course does attempt to prevent the proletariat from making this transition from a class in itself to a class for itself. Although its power rests ultimately on ownership of the means of production, such economic dominance is translated into political dominance with the result that the bourgeoisie becomes a ruling class. The state, considered by Marx to be 'the executive committee for managing the common affairs of the whole bourgeoisie' represents the interests of the class as a whole, managing its common affairs in two major ways. The first relies on its control of the means of coercion and involves being repressive. Examples here include legislation inhibiting the formation of trade unions and the use of the army to quash strikes. The second depends on its significance in the dissemination of beliefs and values throughout society and involves propagating *ideologies* which purport to show the justice and necessity of bourgeois domination. Particularly because, as Marx put it, 'the ideas of the ruling class are, in every age, the ruling ideas: ie the class which is the dominant material force in society is at the same time its dominant intellectual force' (Bottomore and Rubel 1961, p93), the development of class consciousness may be delayed. Ultimately, Marx argued, the proletariat will see through the fog of bourgeois ideology and become revolutionary. For the revolution is inevitable. Marx went even further claiming that the proletarian revolution will be unique. For, whereas past revolutions have been made by a minority for the benefit of a minority, the proletariat's revolution will be made by the majority for the benefit of the majority. This will enable a classless society to be formed in which the ideals put forward during the French Revolution will be fully realised: freedom will replace oppression; fulfilment alienation; equality inequality; fraternity self-interest. Such a society Marx called *communism.*

Evaluation

Economic determinism While it is indisputable that Marx saw economic factors as crucial in any analysis of society, it is unlikely that he ever believed, as some argue, that all social development is caused by economic changes. His famous statement 'Men make history but not under circumstances of their own choosing' suggests rather that Marx believed human beings can have an influence on the outcome of events, but that this freedom of action is constrained by the limits set by the development of the economy. Whether Marx nonetheless placed an undue emphasis on economic factors still remains a contentious issue, however.

Social change The opening line of the *Communist Manifesto* states that 'the history of hitherto existing society is the history of class struggle'. This suggestion that history has an overall direction and that it is governed by a dynamic principle such as the class struggle is questioned by many contemporary sociologists, such as Giddens (1990). What's more, there is some dispute whether it's possible to talk of class divisions prior to the advent of capitalism and indeed whether other social divisions in modern societies are not at least as significant.

The transition to communism Capitalist societies have not developed in the direction Marx anticipated. Although the 20th century has witnessed the establishment of communist states following revolutions, these have occurred in non-capitalist societies and have failed to fulfil Marx's vision. What's more, the collapse of communist regions in Eastern Europe since 1989 has led some commentators to argue that Marx's ideas are no longer relevant. Needless to say, Marxists believe that they can explain why capitalist societies have remained resistant to revolution, why communist regimes have collapsed and why Marx's ideas remain as significant today as they ever were.

Activity 3   Class and Ideology

Item A *Clement Atlee, Labour Prime Minister 1945*
Now a new Parliament must be elected. The choice is between that same Conservative Party which stands for private enterprise, private profit and private interests and the Labour Party which demands that in peacetime as in war the interests of the whole people should come before that of a section.

Item B *Harold MacMillan, Conservative Prime Minister 1959*
This election has shown that the class war is obsolete.

Item C *Harold Wilson, Labour Prime Minister 1964*
Let us be understanding. Let us not condemn them too harshly. For remember that these are men who were sure at birth that they were ordained by providence to rule over their fellow citizens and to find themselves rudely deprived of the powers that they exercised cannot have been easy for them.

Item D *Ted Heath, Conservative Prime Minister 1970*
Our purpose is not to divide but to unite and where there are differences to bring reconciliation; to create one nation.

Item G *Your Country Needs You*

Item E *Margaret Thatcher, Conservative Prime Minister 1988*
In the world in which we now live, divisions into class are outmoded and meaningless. We are all working people who basically want the same things.

Item F *John Major, Conservative Prime Minister 1992*
I believe that in the next ten years we will have to continue to make changes that will genuinely produce across the whole of this country a genuinely classless society in which people can rise to whatever level that their own abilities and their own good fortune may take them from wherever they started.

Questions

1 Read items A to F. What similarities can you detect in these statements by postwar British Prime Ministers. How would Marx account for these similarities?

2 Look at Item G. How does this poster illustrate a similar ideology to that in Items A to F?

2.3 Emile Durkheim (1858-1917)

Although the word 'sociology', and many of the discipline's founding principles had been established by Auguste Comte (1798 - 1857), it was Emile Durkheim who finally established sociology as a serious and respectable academic discipline. In particular, it was Durkheim who first offered a formal statement of 'sociological method' in his book *The Rules of Sociological Method* (1964; first published in 1895) and exemplified in several other publications. Although, as we shall see, Durkheim's approach to the study of society can be subjected to a number of criticisms, its influence on sociology to this day should not be underestimated.

Durkheim's methodology: the study of 'social facts'

Durkheim's central methodological principle, first outlined in his *The Rules of Sociological Method*, was as follows: 'Consider social facts as things'. To understand what Durkheim meant by this, and to appreciate its significance, we need to begin by defining his concept of 'the social fact'. For Durkheim, social facts are characterised by two things: first, they must be *external* to the individual, and secondly they must *exercise constraint* over the individual. Some examples will help to clarify what is meant by this.

A very obvious example (when we think about it) of a social fact is language. Let us see how language fulfils Durkheim's two criteria. First, language is external to individuals. Although it is perfectly true that it is internal to us in the sense that we all possess an individual knowledge of the language(s) which we speak, it is external to us in the sense that the language we speak was in existence before any one of us was born, and will continue to be in existence after each of us has died. Language is not an individual characteristic or creation. It is shared by and produced by the social group. As such it is external to the individual.

Secondly, although we might not feel that language exercises a constraint over us, a moment's reflection will reveal that it certainly does in the sense that if we wish to say something to another speaker of the same language as us, we really have no choice but to use certain words as opposed to others. It is thus no use my using the word 'cheval' if I want to talk to a fellow English speaker about a horse; I have little choice but to use the word 'horse', if I want to be understood.

Perhaps Durkheim's best known example of a social fact can be seen in his analysis of suicide. In his book, *Suicide: A Study in Sociology* (1952; first published in 1897), Durkheim shows how the apparently highly individual act of suicide can be analysed as a social fact. First suicide, or rather the suicide rate, can be shown to be external to individuals by the fact that the suicide rate varies between different social groups, and that this variation remains fairly constant over time. For example, Durkheim noticed that suicide rates were consistently lower in Catholic countries than they were in Protestant countries and that this difference remained stable over relatively long periods of time. Suicide rates thus seemed to be products of social groups, rather than of individuals. Secondly, the suicide rate could be seen as constraining because the probability that any individual would commit suicide could be shown to vary according to which social groups they belong.

Of course, Durkheim does not claim that reference to the social fact of the suicide rate will tell us which members of a social group will commit suicide. This, he argued, was the proper province of the psychologist. The job of the sociologist was first to identify social facts - such as the suicide rates of various social groups - and secondly to explain them. (For further discussion of Durkheim's view of social facts, see pp636-637; for his study of suicide, see pp469-470; 636-637).

Cause and function

One of the more important arguments advanced by Durkheim in *The Rules of Sociological Method* - and one which many of his followers neglected - was that it in explaining social facts it is necessary to distinguish between their *causes* and their *social functions*. To understand what Durkheim meant by social functions we must consider his so-called 'organismic analogy', the idea that societies are like living organisms.

To see how this analogy works consider the following example. If I take a living organism, say a dog, each of its parts - its legs, its tail, its liver, its heart and so on - can be seen to make a contribution to the dog's overall functioning. However, by contrast, if I were to take any one of these parts in isolation, say its tail, it would 'do' very little, and I would be unable to see how it makes a contribution to the overall functioning of the dog. It only makes sense, as it were, in relation to all the other parts which go to make up the dog. Even if I took all the individual parts of a dog, and placed them in a box, I still would not have something we could meaningfully call 'a dog', which barked and wagged its tail. All I would have would be a pile of lifeless limbs and organs. Similarly, Durkheim argued that only by examining the contribution which each of a society's parts makes to its overall functioning can we arrive at a complete understanding of these parts. Sometimes this approach is known as *holism*, and can be summed up in the phrase: *the whole is greater than the sum of its parts*.

So for Durkheim, the study of any social fact's functions must be different from the study of its causes. This is because unless we were to say that a particular social fact was the result of deliberate intentions, its cause cannot be the same as its functional effects. The reason for this is obvious: since functional effects occur only *after* a phenomenon has come into existence, they cannot have caused that phenomenon to come into existence. Durkheim therefore claimed that the causes of social facts should be sought in other social facts which had occurred at an earlier point in time. If however, we wish to explain why a social fact persists over time, we should seek to discover the contribution it makes to the overall working of society, in short, its *function*.

The division of labour

At the centre of Durkheim's work is a concern with morality. Morality can be seen as a classic example of a social fact. Moral codes are external to individuals in the sense that they are properties of social groups, and they are constraining over individuals in that they plainly influence our behaviour. But for Durkheim morality is also central to his understanding of how social order is possible.

At the centre of Durkheim's analysis, as with most social theorists, are a set of assumptions about 'human nature'. For Durkheim, following the philosopher Rousseau, human beings possess an innate tendency towards limitless desire. If these desires remain unchecked then, Durkheim argued, human beings could never be happy, because their desires would always outstrip their ability to satisfy them. At the same time, such limitless desires would pose an obvious threat to social order. Durkheim thus argued that human happiness, social order and social solidarity could only be achieved by the regulation of human desires to within attainable limits. It is for this reason that morality - the social fact responsible for the regulation of individual desires - was so central to Durkheim's whole approach.

In his first major work, *The Division of Labour in Society* (1933; first published 1893) Durkheim set out to show how, as societies developed from simple, small scale pre-literate forms, to modern, complex and industrial forms, the basis of moral regulation, and hence of social solidarity, also underwent change. In the former type of society, Durkheim argued that social order was achieved by what he termed *mechanical solidarity*. In such societies the extent to which different individuals perform different tasks - the *division of labour* - was very limited. Therefore, since most people shared a common set of interests and problems, a single set of moral rules to guide them was sufficient. The source of such moral regulation was of course religious, and Durkheim assumed that members of such societies shared a common commitment to the authority of their religion which provided appropriate moral limits in any situation they were likely to face. This he called the 'conscience collective', which roughly translates as the 'collective conscience'.

The basis of the mechanical solidarity of small scale societies is similarity - the division of labour is limited and there is little role differentiation. As the division of labour becomes increasingly specialised and complex, mechanical solidarity is replaced by *organic solidarity*. This organic solidarity is based on difference. The different and specialised parts of the division of labour work together to maintain the social unit. Specialised occupational roles are interdependent - they need each other.

As societies became more complex, however, Durkheim argued that the ability of a single source of moral authority to regulate the increasingly divergent lives of society's members was gradually weakened. So much so, that modern societies, which are characterised by a very highly developed division of labour, faced a chronic state of crisis as far as moral regulation was concerned. Durkheim called this lack of moral regulation *anomie*, and this is closely linked to his belief in the growth of excessive individualism: people come to see themselves first and foremost as individuals rather than as member of social groups. Although Durkheim regarded anomie as a very significant feature of modern societies, he maintained that it could be overcome by the development of strong occupational associations which would become the source of moral regulation for their members. For example, they would regulate terms and conditions of employment and wages and salaries. These associations, Durkheim argued, would overcome the problems posed by modern societies in two principal ways: first they would counter the modern trend towards individualism by integrating their members into a social group, and secondly they would set limits on the rewards which members of society could expect to receive, and hence would serve to limit desires to within attainable bounds.

Evaluation

Although there can be little doubt about Durkheim's enormous influence on the development of sociology, we need to take account of a number of criticisms in our evaluation of his work.

Anomie and human nature It can be argued that Durkheim's view of human nature is unrealistically pessimistic. In many ways, his argument that human beings need to be morally regulated by society is the direct opposite of Marx's view that human nature is in fact corrupted by the social relations of production in capitalist societies. We shall return to this issue later in the chapter when we consider the impact of recent developments in evolutionary biology on our views of human nature.

Determinism It is sometimes said that Durkheim's approach represents an extreme form of determinism. That is, human actions are explained purely by the effects of external forces acting upon the individual. It has been argued that this can be seen in his analysis of suicide: apparently one of the most individual choices a human being can ever make, Durkheim claims that the suicide rate is in fact nothing more than a product of social forces over which individuals have absolutely no control. Many sociologists, most notably perhaps symbolic interactionists whose ideas we consider later in this chapter, have argued that this presents an inaccurate picture of human action. Instead, they argue that although social forces perhaps influence individual choices, they do not determine them in a straightforward way. Human beings, they argue, possess freedom of choice, and so can always resist the influences of social forces if they so choose.

Power and inequality Durkheim was extremely concerned about the consequences of the increasingly specialised division of labour - the inequalities which it entails and the anomie it generates. However, it is sometimes argued that he failed to grasp the extent to which modern capitalist societies are composed of groups with fundamentally opposing interests. Unlike Marx, who considered capitalist societies to be characterised by irresolvable class conflicts, Durkheim regarded such conflicts as did occur to be temporary anomalies which could be overcome by the development of new forms of moral regulation. At no

time, however, does he consider that the moral regulations which are central to all forms of social solidarity might be ideologies - that is, sets of beliefs which portray a false picture of reality and justify fundamentally unjust power relations.

Whilst each of these criticisms might be convincing to some sociologists, it is important to note that we cannot settle any of them simply by appealing to available evidence. Each point of view presented reflects, in large measure, simply different ways of 'seeing' society: it is as though, to return to our earlier analogy, each is viewing society in a different distorting mirror. They do, nevertheless, sensitise us to possible weaknesses in Durkheim's approach. We shall return to some of these later in the chapter when we consider the development of functionalism after Durkheim.

Activity 4 The Case of Robinson Crusoe

Item A *Shipwrecked*

In 1719 the novelist Daniel Defoe published a classic story about a man on his own, called Robinson Crusoe. Crusoe went out from England to make his fortune and had many adventures before being shipwrecked on a desert island. He was the only survivor of the wreck, and though he managed to salvage many things from it and to make himself some sort of life on the island, he survived entirely alone until he discovered a single footprint in the sand. This was the mark of a native whom he discovered, named 'Friday' (after the day on which he found him) and made him his servant. Crusoe was finally rescued and taken home.

Robinson Crusoe pictured in the first edition, 1719

Item B *Family*

Born in the city of York, of a good family, though not of that country, my father being a foreigner of Bremen, who first settled at Hull. He got a good estate by merchandise, and leaving off his trade lived afterwards at York, from whence he married my mother from a very good family in that country.

Item C *Education*

My father had given me a competent share of learning, as far as house education and a county free-school generally goes, and designed me for the law. Being the third son of the family and not bred to any trade, my head began to be filled with early rambling thoughts.

Item D *Religion*

I frequently sat down with thankfulness and admired the hand of God's providence, which had thus spread my table in the wilderness. These reflections made me very sensible of the goodness of Providence to me and very thankful for my present condition.

Item E *Power*

In a little time I began to speak to him and to teach him how to speak to me; and first I made him know his name should be Friday, which was the day I saved his life. I likewise taught him to say Master, and then let him know that was to be my name.

Item F *A social being*

Robinson Crusoe was indeed a unique individual, making his way in the world by his own efforts, 'master of all he surveys', as the poem puts it. But this is very different from saying that he can be understood and explained in individual terms. We can't fully explain who he is, where he comes from, what he thinks and does, how he behaves, by looking at him simply as an individual. This is the problem with individualist types of explanation.

Adapted from S. Hall 'The Idea of the Social' in *Social Structures and Social Divisions*, 1993

Questions
1 What 'social facts' influenced Robinson Crusoe?
2 Is there an argument for combining social and individual explanations to understand Robinson Crusoe's behaviour?

2.4 Max Weber (1864-1920)

Whilst Durkheim's approach to the study of society rested firmly upon his assumption of the effects of external and constraining social facts on individual behaviour, Weber emphasised the importance of taking into account the points of view of social actors, and the meanings which they attribute to their own behaviour and that of others. For this reason, Weber is often regarded as the founding father of *interpretive sociology*, or of the *social action approach* within sociology.

Meaning and the concept of verstehen

As we saw in the previous section, Durkheim regarded the proper task of sociology to be the identification of relationships between social facts. It is often argued, however, that this approach ignores the meaningful nature of human conduct. Let us examine what is meant by this.

If we are concerned to identify what it is that distinguishes human beings from either animals or inanimate objects, then perhaps the most crucial difference is that human beings are capable of intentional action. We do things on purpose, in order to reach some goal, and usually we have some choice both about the goal and the means we select to achieve it. For example, if asked why you are reading this chapter, you will probably answer with reference to some goal: to enable you to pass an examination in sociology perhaps. You will also, presumably, have some choice about both the goal and the means you have selected to achieve it: you could always decide not to take the examination, and you could always choose to read another book. It is for this reason that Weber would say that your action is meaningful: it is not merely the product of the operation of external forces over which you have no control, but is the result of your own interpretations of the world around you and of the conscious choices you make about your future.

Weber thus emphasised that it is not enough merely to note statistical correlations between social facts as Durkheim had done (although Weber certainly believed that such correlations were an important starting point for sociological analysis) but insisted in addition that explanations of human action should be adequately grasped on the level of meaning. Whilst, methodologically, it may not be difficult to explore the meanings of actors' conduct when one has the opportunity to interview them - although Weber did not himself practice this kind of sociological investigation - obvious difficulties are faced when one is dealing with social events which took place in the past. Since Weber's own preoccupation was with the origins of modern capitalism he had himself to overcome this difficulty, since the events he was concerned with had taken place several centuries before he was born. His solution was the method of *verstehen*.

Verstehen can be translated from the German as broadly meaning 'empathetic understanding'. In simple terms one attempts to imagine how the world would have looked from the point of view of the actors whose actions one wishes to understand, even where such a point of view is quite alien to one's own. The classic example of the application of verstehen can be found in Weber's account of the behaviour of early Calvinists in *The Protestant Ethic and the Spirit of Capitalism* (1958). (For further discussion of Weber's methodology, see pp641-642; for his study of Protestantism and capitalism, see pp504-506).

The ideal type

Before we move on to consider the ways in which Weber categorised social action, it will be helpful to briefly explain his concept of the ideal type. Ideal types are generalisations which help researchers to organise and classify their findings. Rarely, if ever, are they found in their pure form, but they provide us with a set of categories through which we can make sense of our observations. For example, Weber produced an ideal type of a bureaucracy (see p359). He lists six 'ideal' characteristics of bureaucracies, but it is unlikely that any actual bureaucratic organisation will possess all six characteristics in pure form. We can nevertheless identify it as a bureaucracy, because it comes closer to the ideal typical bureaucracy than to any other form of organisation.

Types of action

Both the concept of verstehen, and Weber's use of ideal types can be seen in his four-fold categorisation of types of action. These categories of action begin from the assumptions of verstehen in that they adopt the point of view of the actor. They are ideal types in that they are theoretically pure forms to which real instances of action only ever approximate.

Instrumentally rational action *(Zweckrational)* In this type of 'purely' rational action, the actor assesses both their goals and the means by which these should be achieved. For example, if it is my goal to win a marathon, then it would be instrumentally rational for me to undergo a strict regime of training and dieting prior to the race. By contrast, it would not be rational, in relation to this goal, for me to spend the weeks prior to the race indulging in an almost incessant orgy of drinking, smoking and over-eating. However, it would still be instrumentally rational for me to decide that the costs (in terms of pain and suffering) of dieting and training were not worth the benefit of winning the marathon. Under these circumstances, I would simply reject the goal of winning the marathon, thus making my over-indulgent behaviour rational in terms of my revised goal of gaining as much immediate pleasure as possible.

Value-rational action *(Wertrational)*. This type of rational action is similar to instrumentally rational action in that means are judged to be rational if they are thought to be successful in reaching the goal towards which they are directed. However, in this case, the goals cannot be abandoned even if they are immensely difficult to achieve. For example, a devoutly religious person who believed that they would only enjoy salvation if they lived a life of celibacy would, if acting in accordance with value-rationality, accept a life of celibacy no matter how difficult this might prove. To reject the goal as being simply too difficult to achieve, however, would be an example of instrumentally rational action.

Traditional action This form of action does not involve the assessment of either goals or means. Instead it is performed simply because tradition dictates that it should be. Although Weber felt that traditional action had declined in significance in modern societies, which he believed were characterised increasingly by rational action, examples of traditional conduct can still be found. In Britain, for example, it is still usual to celebrate Christmas by, amongst other things, purchasing and decorating a Christmas tree. The majority of people who engage in this behaviour, however, can give no other reason for doing so other than the fact that it is 'traditional'.

Affective action This final form of action can best be expressed as being a result of emotion. Again, Weber felt that this type of action was becoming less significant in modern societies, but examples can still be found. Someone hearing the news that a close relative had been killed in an accident might burst into tears out of grief. Or, a wife discovering her husband's infidelity might assault him out of anger. No well thought out goals are involved in such

actions, and since the circumstances are, by definition novel, the actions can clearly not be described as traditional. They are the direct result of the unusual emotional state of the actor.

Rationalisation and disenchantment

Weber argued that modern societies are characterised increasingly by a process of rationalisation. As the term suggests, this means that the world is increasingly governed by rationality, in which traditional and affective forms of action are replaced by predominantly rational forms. Organisations increasingly adopt a bureaucratic form (see pp358-360) and legitimate authority is predominantly rational legal (see pp192-193). Corresponding to this was a trend towards what is usually translated from the German as *disenchantment*, although a more literal translation of Weber would be *the driving out of magic from things*. This can be seen partly as secularisation, but is in fact broader than this and includes the progressive removal of non-rational elements from all spheres of life. Weber was fearful that in the process warmth and humanity might be driven out of social life, the very things which give meaning to human existence (see p526).

Evaluation

Psychologism Whilst Durkheim has often been accused of ignoring the role of psychological factors in human behaviour, it has sometimes been said that Weber over-emphasises the role of such factors. This criticism has two aspects to it. First, it has been suggested that in using the method of verstehen, Weber is forced to go beyond available evidence and attribute motives to social actors without any means of verifying them. Taken to its extreme, this could reduce sociological enquiry to little more than guesswork. Secondly, it can be argued that in giving such weight to individual motives, Weber underestimates the power of external social forces to constrain and determine behaviour.

Ambiguity Although Weber makes a great effort to be clear about exactly what he means by the ideal type, it can nevertheless be argued that the concept can lead to certain ambiguities, particularly when applied to types of action. Percy Cohen points out, for example, that many forms of traditional action may also conform to one or other type of rationality (Cohen, 1968). For instance, when people in small scale non-literate societies give gifts to the village headman, both because it is traditional to do so *and* because they hope to receive some benefits as a result. Similarly, whilst an outburst of rage might appear to be purely affective, it could be seen from the point of view of a psychoanalyst, as rational in that it could have been motivated by an unconscious desire to reduce one's level of stress.

Conclusion

In this part, we have considered some of the most important early influences on the development of sociological theory. Although each has been subjected to criticism, the ideas we have discussed have had an enduring influence on the ways in which sociologists seek to understand human societies. In the part which follows, we turn our attention to the ways in which these founding theorists' ideas have been developed by later generations of social theorists.

Summary

1 Sociology has its roots in the Enlightenment, where the notion that social theories could improve the human condition was first systematically articulated.

2 Marx, Durkheim and Weber were three founding fathers of the discipline of sociology who adopted a scientific approach towards the understanding of the nature and development of human societies.

3 Their characterisations of modern societies were different - Marx stressed capitalism and class conflict, Durkheim stressed industrialism and the division of labour and Weber stressed rationalisation and bureaucracy.

4 Although all three identified problems in modern society, Marx and Durkheim were generally optimistic about the future - believing that their theories could improve the human condition - while Weber was much more pessimistic.

Activity 5 Disenchantment

Item A *A religious point of view*

Modernity is the transition from fate to choice. At the same time it dissolves the commitments and loyalties that once lay behind our choices. Technical reason has made us masters of matching means to ends. But it has left us inarticulate as to why we should choose one end rather than another. The values that once led us to regard one as intrinsically better than another - and which gave such weight to words like good and bad - have disintegrated, along with the communities and religious traditions in which we learned them. Now we choose because we choose. Because it is what we want; or it works for us; or it feels right to me. Once we have dismantled a world in which larger virtues held sway, what is left are success and self-expression, the key values of an individualistic culture.

Max Weber delivered the famous prophetic warning that the cloak of material prosperity might eventually become an iron cage. It was already becoming an end in itself, and other values were left, in his words, 'like the ghost of dead religious beliefs'. Once capitalism consumed its religious foundations, he feared the consequences.

In the past, disadvantaged groups could find in religion what Karl Marx called 'the feeling of a heartless world'. A purely economic order offers no such consolations. A culture of success places little value on the unsuccessful.

The erosion of those bonds of loyalty and love which religion undergirded has left us increasingly alone in an impersonal economic and social system. Emile Durkheim was the first to give this condition a name. He called it anomie: the situation in which individuals have lost their moorings in a collective order. It is the heavy price we pay for our loss of communities of faith.

Adapted from J. Sachs 'The Persistence of Faith' *The Listener*, 15.11.90, p6

Item B *No religion; no future*

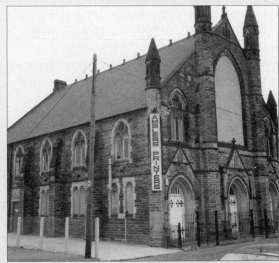

From prayer to print

A punk with NO FUTURE tattoed on her cheek

Item C *The logical song*
When I was young, it seemed that life was so wonderful,
A miracle, oh it was beautiful, magical.
And all the birds in the trees, well they'd be singing so happily,
Joyfully, playfully watching me.
But then they sent me away to teach me how to be sensible,
Logical, responsible, practical.
And they showed me a world where I could be so dependable,
Clinical, intellectual, cynical.

There are times when all the world's asleep,
The questions run too deep
For such a simple man.
Won't you please, please tell me what we've learned
I know it sounds absurd
But please tell me who I am.

From *Breakfast in America* by Supertramp, 1979, words and music by Roger Hodgson

Questions
1 How do Items A, B and C illustrate Weber's belief that rationalisation is resulting in disenchantment?
2 What similarities and differences are there between Weber's picture of modernity and those of Marx and Durkheim?

3 The Establishment of Sociological Theory

Key Issues
1 What are the main assumptions of functionalism, Marxism and symbolic interactionism?
2 How significant are these perspectives for the development of sociological theory?

There has never been one model of society on which all sociologists are agreed. In this section we shall be considering three competing models which have their origins in the work of Marx, Durkheim and Weber. The three models which we shall consider- functionalism, Marxism and symbolic interactionism - each make very different assumptions about the nature of human beings and the societies which they inhabit. Although these are not the only models which have emerged in sociology, and some sociologists straddle different models, they are nevertheless three of the most significant in the development of sociology as a discipline. This is evident both in this book, where continual references are made to these models, and in any of the major textbooks in sociology (see, for example, Haralambos and Holborn, 1995). Although as we shall see in later sections, matters are now more complex than a consideration of these three models suggests, they do nonetheless form the basis of the modern discipline.

3.1 Functionalism
During the first half of the twentieth century, functionalism became the dominant theoretical perspective in sociology. Functionalism has its origins in the work of such 19th century social theorists as Auguste Comte and Herbert Spencer, but owes most to the work of Emile Durkheim. Functionalism was subsequently adopted by sociologists, but much of its early impact was through the work of British social anthropologists such as Bronislaw Malinowski and A. R. Radcliffe-Brown.

Social systems Although the various formulations of functionalist sociologists differ considerably in detail, they share in common a concern with studying societies as *systems*. The idea that a society is a system has a number of implications, which are central to functionalist analysis. First, is the assumption that societies should be studied as wholes, rather than as agglomerations of independent parts. As we saw in connection with Durkheim's work, just as a living organism is more than merely the sum of its constituent parts, so societies need to be treated as entities in their own right with, as it were, a life of their own. Secondly, and following from this, is the assumption that the parts of society need to be understood in terms of the contribution which they make to the functioning of the whole. If, for example, we were to be interested in central heating systems, we could only understand the role of, say, the radiators, in relation to the system as a whole. On their own radiators do very little, and had we never seen one as part of a functioning central heating system, we would stand little chance of figuring out what they are for. In exactly the same way, functionalists assume that we can only understand the role of the constituent parts of societies in terms of their contribution to the functioning of the society as a whole. Thirdly, and more implicitly, is the assumption that parts of societies perform a primarily positive function in relation to the overall functioning of the society in which they are found. Just as we would not expect to find parts of central heating systems which either perform no function whatsoever, or actually impair the overall performance of the system, so functionalists would not expect to find parts of societies which either do not contribute to, or actually impair their overall functioning. This means that functionalist analysis tends always to search for positive functions of social institutions, whilst either denying or seriously underplaying, their negative or disruptive aspects.

Although by the 1950s, functionalism had become the dominant theoretical perspective in sociology, this dominance was not to last. From this time onwards, functionalism was subjected to a range of criticisms which ultimately led to its widespread rejection. Nevertheless, the influence of functionalism on modern sociological theory remains substantial.

Talcott Parsons (1902-1979)

Although Parsons' work is often criticised for what some see as its rather dry and obscure style, there can be no doubt that, taken as a whole, it represents the fullest and most systematic statement of functionalist theory available. For Parsons, as with Durkheim before him, the central problem for all social theory was what, after the 17th century philosopher Thomas Hobbes, is often called the 'Hobbesian problem of order'. Hobbes believed that human beings were driven by passions which, if left unrestrained, would lead to social chaos, or a 'war of all against all'. The problem, therefore, was how to explain the fact that this state of affairs does not routinely obtain in human societies. Indeed, not only does chaos not reign in human societies, but they are in fact, for most of the time, rather orderly and peaceful places. Hobbes' solution to this problem was to assume that, driven ultimately by the need for self-preservation, people voluntarily agree to restrain their passions and submit to the sovereign authority of the state.

As we saw in the discussion of Durkheim's work, he offered the rather different solution that social order is maintained by a shared commitment to a common morality. This, essentially, was Parsons' solution too, although his formulation is arguably both more detailed and systematic than that proposed by Durkheim.

The social system and its functional prerequisites

It was suggested in the introduction to this section that the assumption that societies are systems is fundamental to functionalist theory. This assumption is made most explicitly in the work of Parsons; indeed, his major statement of functionalist theory is presented in a book entitled *The Social System* (Parsons, 1951). For Parsons, any social system inevitably faces four problems, which must be solved if the system is to survive. Parsons calls these four problems *functional prerequisites*, and they are as follows: adaptation, goal attainment, integration and pattern maintenance or latency.

Adaptation The first, adaptation, refers to the need for any social system to adapt to its environment. In even the most simple societies, some mechanism must exist whereby food and shelter are obtained. This could involve, for example, hunting and gathering and the production of simple shelters against the elements. Such activities might strike us as straightforward in comparison with the complex arrangements which exist in our own societies for converting the raw materials of the natural environment into produced goods for consumption and use. They do nevertheless require social organisation, and crucially for Parsons, normative regulation. Whilst in simple societies this might be achieved by the existence of customs and norms, in advanced industrial societies it tends to be achieved by legally regulated economies.

Goal attainment The second of Parsons' functional prerequisites is goal attainment. This refers to the need for societies to set goals towards which the activities of their members and institutions are directed. In simple societies, this might revolve around the need to obtain sufficient food, whilst in complex societies such as our own, it involves more complex economic goals such as seeking profit. In such societies, goal attainment is fundamentally the responsibility of the political system, which establishes a legal and economic framework which regulates and directs the pursuit of such goals.

Integration The third functional prerequisite is integration. This refers to the need to maintain cohesion within the social system and to deal effectively with deviance which threatens the overall stability of the system. Whilst in simple societies this function would be fulfilled largely as a result of what Weber called traditional authority, in modern complex societies it is performed largely by the legal system - what Weber called rational legal authority.

Pattern maintenance The final functional prerequisite is pattern maintenance, or latency. This refers to the need to maintain the pattern of value commitments amongst a society's members. Crucial to this is the process of socialisation which takes place within institutions such as the family and the education system. Socialisation serves to internalise a society's values into the personalities of individual actors.

This framework allowed Parsons to classify all the parts of any given society into one of these four categories, and in doing so, to claim that each contributes in at least one of these four ways to the overall functioning of that society.

Social evolution and equilibrium

It is sometimes said that functionalism in general, and Parsons' theory in particular, emphasise social stability to such an extent that they are in danger of failing to account for social change. We shall return to this charge in our evaluation of functionalism. For the present it is important to note that Parsons does not ignore the issue of social change, but in fact makes its explanation a central facet of his general theory.

Equilibrium An important element of Parsons' analysis of social systems is that they exist in a state of *equilibrium*. Equilibrium is best defined as 'balance', and in relation to social systems, refers to the ways in which the four subsystems are interrelated. This means, for Parsons, that a change in one part of a social system, tends to produce changes elsewhere in the social system such that the system, overall, returns to a state of equilibrium. Social systems are therefore regarded as self-regulating, always tending to return to a state of equilibrium, albeit a changed one. In this way, Parsons explains social change as a dynamic and functionally necessary response to disturbances within the system. Although, for Parsons, social systems tend towards a state of equilibrium, a perfect equilibrium is never attained; instead societies are thought to exist in a state of 'moving equilibrium'.

Social evolution A second aspect of Parsons' approach to social change is his notion of *social evolution*. Heavily influenced by such 19th century social evolutionists as Herbert Spencer, Parsons believed that all social systems are involved in an evolutionary development from more simple to more complex forms. The central concept used by Parsons to explain the patterns of social evolution is *structural differentiation*. This refers to the tendency of social institutions to become more specialised. Thus, for example, prior to the industrial revolution, the household used to be not only a domestic space, but also a place where goods were produced. After the industrial revolution, factories replaced the household as a site of production and the household came to fulfil the more specialised role as a site of domestic activity only. This trend carries with it its own problems, however, which modern societies must solve. In particular, the development of increasingly specialised roles and institutions require the development of an increasingly broad and general set of values capable of regulating a wider range of activities. In modern industrial societies such values include a belief in *universalism* and in *achievement* - universal society-wide standards of achievement are applied to everyone and form the basis for allocating people to roles and fixing their rewards. Such general values are capable of regulating a very wide range of specialised activities in our societies.

Robert K. Merton

Parsons' work perhaps represents the height of functionalist theorising in sociology, and is certainly the most systematic and abstract of functionalist approaches. Parsons' desire to explain all aspects of all societies from within a single theoretical framework has led to his theory being described as a *grand* theory. One functionalist sociologist who attempted to refine functionalist analysis, but at the same time rejected the highly abstract approach developed by Parsons, was Robert K. Merton.

Merton's modification of functionalist theory begins with a critique of the notion - fundamental to Parsons' model - that societies exhibit 'functional unity'. This is the idea that all parts of a society are interconnected such that all parts of the system work together for the benefit of the whole, and that a change in one part of the system will necessarily produce change elsewhere. Merton suggests that whilst this may sometimes be the case, one cannot assume that it will be in advance. Rather, the degree to which parts of the social system are interconnected is a matter which should be empirically investigated in each case. Indeed, Merton suggests that in modern highly differentiated societies, a relatively high degree of *functional autonomy* will exist within parts of the social system.

Merton also challenges the idea of 'universal functionalism', that is, the idea that all parts of the social system fulfil some positive function. Again, as with the issue of functional unity, Merton suggests that whether or not a particular part of the social system fulfils a positive function is a matter for investigation and is not something which can be assumed in advance. For Merton, any part of the system might be either functional, dysfunctional or non-functional. In other words, its contribution to the social system may be positive, negative or non-existent.

Finally, Merton challenges what he terms the 'postulate of indispensability', the assumption that the institutions or roles which actually exist within a society are the only ones which could meet that society's functional prerequisites. In other words, he challenges the assumption made by many functionalists that social institutions and roles exist by necessity and are therefore inevitable parts of that society. Instead Merton argues that the same functional needs could just as well be met by different institutions and roles which are *functionally equivalent*.

These specific criticisms of grand theory advanced by Merton led him to suggest that social theorists should abandon their search for over-arching theoretical systems which specify the nature and functions of social institutions in advance. Instead, they should concentrate upon developing more concrete theories grounded in empirical evidence, which address specific social phenomena, rather than entire social systems. Such theories were called by Merton, *theories of the middle range*.

Evaluation

Despite Durkheim's early caution about confusing the cause of a phenomenon with its functions (see p662), this charge can be levelled at later functionalist theorists. In particular, functionalist theories may be accused of being *teleological*. A theory is said to be teleological if it explains a phenomenon's causes in terms of its effects. Thus if functionalists argue that the cause of social stratification is to allocate the most able individuals to the most important positions in society, then their argument is teleological - it explains causes in terms of effects. This can lead to some very strange explanations. For example, if it is argued that the family exists because it has the effect of stabilising adult personalities and of accomplishing the primary socialisation of children, then it seems difficult to avoid the assumption that this is because someone sat down and invented the family for this purpose. Of course this would be absurd. As we have seen, however, functionalist explanations tend to be of this type, and so can be criticised on the logical grounds that they confuse cause and effect.

A second criticism which can be levelled at functionalist theory is that it over-emphasises the degree of value consensus in societies. As Merton's critique of functionalism suggests, it can be argued that the degree of value consensus in a society is an empirical matter which cannot be presumed in advance. At the very least, it seems difficult to avoid the conclusion that the degree of value consensus which exists will undergo change over time, and will vary between different social groups. In addition, it has been suggested there is no reason to assume that even if a high degree of value consensus exists, it will necessarily promote social solidarity. Collective commitment to an ethic of individualism, for example, may produce exactly the opposite effect.

A third criticism of functionalism is that in its concentration on social order and value consensus, it largely ignores the existence of coercion and conflict in society. For example, David Lockwood has pointed out that Parsons' emphasis on social order and value consensus ignores the fact that competition for scarce resources, an inherent feature of modern societies, will inevitably lead to conflict over scarce resources.

Activity 6 Functions and Dysfunctions

Item A

Glastonbury pop festival

Item B

A 'joy rider' spins a stolen car on a wet Saturday night.

Item C

A birthday party

Item D

A soldier on patrol in Northern Ireland

Item E

Moki Indians of Arizona performing a raindance

Questions

1 Identify the functional features of the activities pictured in Items A to E.
2 Identify the dysfunctional features of these activities.

3.2 Marxism

Although Marxism has a long ancestry, it did not grow to prominence within sociology until the 1960s. That decade saw a range of social movements which challenged the dominant social order and made the functionalist picture of a consensual social system less plausible. In this context, Marxism gained

converts with its picture of society as inherently riven by social conflict.

Marxism, as a sociological perspective, does not slavishly follow Marx in every particular but rather accepts three of his central beliefs: a belief that in some sense the economy is of primary importance, that class conflict is consequently central and that ultimately this will result in a more desirable form of society. Where modern Marxists part company with Marx is over the question of whether it is possible to identify the conditions which will entail the demise of capitalism. Marx himself was somewhat ambivalent on this issue, given his stress on the fact that people make history, but a number of his followers adopted an economic determinist position whereby economic crises were seen as inevitably dooming capitalism to extinction.

The Marxists we shall be examining in this section completely reject this position. Impressed by the capacity of capitalism to survive crises, they pay particular attention to the role of the superstructure in maintaining it. We shall look in turn at two very different versions of Marxism: humanist Marxism and structuralist Marxism. The first develops Marx's early work and adopts as its starting point the assumption that human beings are able to transform their environment. The second develops Marx's late work and adopts as its starting point the assumption that human beings are the product of structures.

Humanist Marxism

Gramsci Gramsci's central contribution to Marxism is his development of Marx's ideas on ideology through a theory of *hegemony* (1971). The bourgeoisie, he argues, seeks to maintain its domination not only by using the state to coerce people but also increasingly by propagating ideologies, through the institutions of civil society such as the churches, in order to win people's consent. For the bourgeoisie to be ideologically dominant, or hegemonic, these ideologies need to be tied into the popular culture of the subordinate classes. The extent to which such hegemony is achieved varies over time but it is unlikely ever to be complete. There are two reasons for this. Firstly, the bourgeoisie are often divided and frequently need to forge alliances with other groups in order to constitute a *power bloc* and control the state. Secondly, the proletariat has a *dual consciousness*, one part of which reflects the ideas of the bourgeoisie and the other part of which reflects their everyday experience. The need to create a power bloc inhibits the propagation of a coherent ideology while the existence of dual consciousness means that workers will at least partially see through bourgeois ideology.

For Gramsci a proletarian revolution will not inevitably result from economic crises. What is needed is for the proletariat to make alliances with other groups and for Marxists to win the hearts and minds of the subordinate classes by connecting Marxist ideas to popular culture. Gramsci is optimistic that in the struggle for hegemony, people will eventually be persuaded of the need for revolution. The stress Gramsci places on popular culture as the site in which ideologies compete has

been taken up in cultural studies where youth subcultural styles are seen on the one hand as indicative of resistance to domination and on the other hand as an opportunity for marketing a new fashion for general consumption and profit. (For further discussion of Gramsci, see p210).

Critical theory What distinguishes critical theory is its attempt to identify what is distinctively human and to use this as a yardstick from which to criticise existing society. We shall look at two examples here - the Frankfurt School, and particularly its three main figures, Adorno, Horkheimer and Marcuse, and the chief heir to that inheritance, Habermas.

For the Frankfurt School there are two attributes which distinguish human beings from animals - the ability, which Marx highlighted, to transform the environment and the ability, which the Enlightenment stressed, to make rational decisions about our lives. Capitalist societies do not allow human beings to exercise their creativity and reason and thus warrant criticism for being oppressive and irrational. The Frankfurt School agrees with Gramsci that particular attention needs to be paid to ideology which is increasingly integrating people into the capitalist system. Two phenomena are highlighted as crucial here - the growth of *instrumental reason* which is seen as the dominant way of thinking in capitalist societies and the development of *mass culture*.

The stress on instrumental reason is reminiscent of Weber's emphasis on rationalisation as a central feature of modernity. It is a way of looking at the world which 'is concerned with discovering how to do things, not what should be done' (Craib, 1984, p187) According to the Frankfurt School, the search for the most efficient means to achieve ends not only generates an uncritical attitude towards the ends pursued in capitalist societies but also encourages us to treat people as means rather than ends in themselves. Reason does not, as the Enlightenment hoped, liberate people in capitalist societies but instead becomes a mechanism for oppressing people.

People's acceptance of instrumental reason is explained by the Frankfurt School in terms of the development of mass culture. Not only is culture now an industry but developments in technology have meant that through various media such as newspapers it reaches the mass of the population. Adorno and Horkheimer use the term 'culture industry' to refer to the products and processes of mass culture. Such an industry does not meet people's true needs but instead produces and satisfies false needs. Our true need - to make collective rational choices about our lives - is denied and instead we are encouraged as individuals to choose which standardised products to consume. We are discouraged in the process from thinking beyond the confines of the moment. Art or high culture is different because it embodies ideals which cannot be met within capitalist societies and therefore provides us with a vision of an alternative society. This function of art, however, is increasingly lost as the culture industry turns it into another cultural commodity. While at one stage, the music of Mozart provided a vision of a harmonious world at odds with existing disorder, now it has become incorporated into mass culture. The culture industry claims that the world is already harmonious so that the critical function of art now only resides at the margins, in the work of those who challenge this supposed harmony such as the music of Schoenberg.

Such an analysis leads the Frankfurt School to a very pessimistic conclusion. Hegemony in contemporary capitalist societies now seems almost complete. People are dominated not only at work but also in their leisure. What's more there seem to be few signs of resistance. Although Marcuse recognises that there are a few marginal groups such as ethnic minorities who are not fully integrated into the system, the overriding picture is of society as a mass of isolated individuals who are manipulated by big business. There seems to be no way out.

Habermas Habermas's starting point is different from that of the Frankfurt School. For Habermas, what distinguishes human beings is not only their ability to transform the environment but also language - the ability to use signs to communicate with each other. This has far reaching consequences. According to Habermas, when one person talks to another, that person implicitly claims that what is said is intelligible, true, justified and sincere. For there to be rational communication speakers need to be able to defend all four claims. This presumes various conditions, ie that 'there are no external constraints preventing participants from assessing evidence and argument, and in which each participant has an equal and open chance of entering the discussion' (Giddens, 1985, p131). Circumstances where these conditions are met Habermas calls an *ideal speech situation* and it is this which provides him with a yardstick against which to measure existing social arrangements.

Social evolution has witnessed increasing possibilities for rational communication and at the same time the emergence of legally sanctioned institutions such as state bureaucracies and markets. In a complex society it is not always possible for communication to settle competing claims. Instead power and money become major mechanisms for routinely settling issues ranging from an individual's welfare entitlement to the value of bananas. A problem arises, however, when power and money 'penetrate into areas of everyday life and practice

which requires communicative action' (Layder, 1994, p197). According to Habermas this has happened with politics. Whereas politics should involve discussion and debate over what are desirable ends, increasingly it has become simply a question of who can run the economy best. In other words communicative rationality has been displaced by instrumental rationality. Unlike the Frankfurt school, Habermas does see the glimmering of a way out, for he does not see capitalism as a stable system.

Habermas identifies four types of crisis through which the system moves. In early capitalism *economic crises* present the main problem. According to Habermas, the state reacts to economic crises by accepting an increasing level of responsibility for the management of the economy through such familiar strategies as the protection of home markets and promotion of public sector production. Such action, however, generates a *rationality crisis*. Government intervention in the economy requires heavy borrowing but this creates inflation and disrupts the normal working of the market. Government intervention ceases for a time but the shift between interventionist and laissez faire (non-interventionist) approaches to the management of the economy makes the state appear to be acting in an irrational manner. This leads to a *legitimation crisis*. The state finds it increasingly difficult to reconcile the conflicting demands placed upon it. The switch from an interventionist to a laissez faire approach means that people's expectations of improved welfare cannot be met. At this stage the state loses its legitimacy. This in turns leads to a *motivation crisis*. Increased state power coupled with the seeming irrelevance of which political party forms the government undermine people's motivation for participating in the system at all. There is a way out, however. For new social movements may emerge, such as the environmentalist and women's movements, to challenge instrumental rationality and inject back into politics a concern with values. Although critical theory questions the link which Marx saw between the rise of the proletariat and the advent of a free society, its search for 'an emancipatory alternative to the existing order' indicates its continuing commitment to the Enlightenment ideal (Bronner and Kellner, 1989, p2).

Structuralist Marxism

For structuralist Marxism the notion that we are the authors of our actions is mistaken. Rather we are the products of underlying structures. Despite its opposition to humanistic Marxism on this issue, there is agreement that economic determinism needs to be rejected. This is clear(ish) in the work of Althusser.

According to Althusser, societies - which he labels social formations - comprise three levels: the economic, the political and the ideological. Although the economy is 'determinant in the last instance', the political and ideological levels are not mere reflections of the economy but have 'relative autonomy' and do have effects on the economy.

To clarify what this means, it is helpful to think of an analogy - a three storey building comprising a shop on the ground, offices on the second and living quarters on the third. It does not make sense to say 'that the first and second floors are caused by the ground floor, even though they rest upon it' (Craib, 1984, p131). If we assume that the building is one enterprise, the office work which goes on on the first floor is obviously dependent upon the kind of trading conducted in the shop, but work relationships there may well develop in a quite different way. Similarly, if the owners live on the second floor their style of life is influenced by the nature of the business but their family life has its own dynamics. The economy in short does set limits on the political and ideological levels but the latter are not completely dependent upon the former. What's more these levels effect the economy. Returning to our example, new information systems in the office may increase turnover in the shop while a family bust up might force the business to close down. The interaction, in short, between the three levels is extremely complex.

Althusser's rejection of economic determinism is further apparent when he argues that different types of society can be distinguished according to the dominance of the different levels. What he means by this is that in the operation of a society, one particular level may become more important than the others. It is however, the economic level which determines which of the levels is dominant at any particular time. 'It is as if the economic level hands over its power to one of the other levels, or keeps it to itself, for the duration of that type of society' (Craib 1984, p134). Two examples illustrate this. Under feudalism, the landlords have to ensure that serfs hand over the surplus which they have produced. To do this they are reliant on the state forcing them to do so, or the church persuading them to do so. In this mode of production, the political and ideological levels are thus dominant. Under capitalism by contrast the bourgeoisie automatically receive the surplus produced by the proletariat. In this mode of production, the economic level is dominant.

Although this is the case, Althusser recognises that capitalist relations of production depend upon a number of conditions being fulfilled which cannot be guaranteed purely at the economic level. Workers need, for example, to be trained in the appropriate skills and persuaded to accept their role. For Althusser (1971) (and indeed for Poulantzas, see p211), it is above all the state which ensures that these conditions are met and that 'the reproduction of the relations of production' occurs. It does this in two ways - through 'repressive state apparatuses' such as the army and the police which coerce people and through 'ideological state apparatuses' such as education and the mass media which ensure that people are socialised to fill their allotted places in the relations of production. We may think that we are the authors of our own actions but in fact we are the products of pre-existing structures which map out our lives for us. Capitalism can be overthrown but this will depend not upon people changing their consciousness but rather upon contradictions at different levels coming together to reinforce each other. Althusser calls this process *overdetermination*. This is when capitalism is most vulnerable to revolution, as in the case of the Russian revolution.

Evaluation

What is most striking when looking at Marxism are the different approaches within it. We need really to evaluate each separately. Nonetheless there is some agreement that central to the analysis of modern society are the concepts of capitalism and class. The central concerns of Marxism are twofold: 1) to account for the unexpected stability of capitalism and 2) to identify the factors likely to lead to the demise of capitalism. While Marxists agree that the economy is in some sense fundamental and that class conflict is therefore central, in practice they often pay particular attention to the superstructure (the state and ideology) and acknowledge the importance of social movements not based on class. They therefore often find themselves on the horns of a dilemma. If they attempt to do justice to the complexity of the world and question for example the link between the proletariat and the demise of capitalism, aren't they abandoning Marxism? If they attempt to do justice to the complexity of the world and see, for example, the economy as only determinant in the last instance, aren't they putting forward a theory which is 'unfalsifiable' and in Popper's view as unscientific as the belief that God is all powerful?

Activity 7 A Crisis of Hegemony?

Item A *The Handsworth 'mugging'*

In March 1973, two boys were found guilty of robbing and inflicting grievous bodily harm on a man in Handsworth, Birmingham. The boys had stolen a total of 30p, some keys and five cigarettes. They had also returned to attack the victim two hours after the initial incident. Each boy received a ten year sentence. A third boy, the 'ringleader', according to the judge on the case, was found guilty of attempted murder and robbery with regard to the same victim. He was given a twenty year sentence. All three sentences were extremely long and, arguably, harsh for the type of crimes committed.

Item B *Press headline 17 August 1972*

As Crimes of Violence Escalate, a Word Common in The United States Enters the British Headlines: Mugging. To our Police, it's a frightening new strain of crime. (*Daily Mirror*)

Item C *Press editorial 13 October 1972*

WHAT ARE the British people most concerned about today? Wages? Prices? Immigration? Pornography? People are talking about all these things. But the *Sun* believes there is another issue which has everyone deeply worried and angry: VIOLENCE IN OUR STREETS... Nothing could be more utterly against our way of life, based on a common sense regard for law and order ... If punitive jail sentences help to stop the violence - and nothing else has done - then they will not only prove to be the only way. They will, regrettably, be the RIGHT way. *And the judges will have the backing of the public. (Sun)*

Item D *A judge's view*

Mugging is becoming more and more prevalent, certainly in London. As a result, decent citizens are afraid to use the Underground late at night, and indeed are afraid to use the underpasses for fear of mugging. We are told that in America people are even afraid to walk in the streets late at night for mugging. This is an offence for which deterrent sentences should be passed.

Judge Alexander Karmel, QC

Item E *A politician's view*

In my view it is absolutely essential to stop this rising tide of mugging in our cities. I have seen what happens in America where muggings are rife. It is absolutely horrifying to know that in all the big American cities, coast to coast, there are areas where people dare not go out after dark. I am extremely anxious that such a situation should never come to Britain.

Birmingham MP, Mrs Jill Knight (quoted in the *Birmingham Evening Mail*, 20.8.72)

Item F Social conflict

A Saracen armoured car backs up British troops as they move against rioters in the Bogside area of Derry in 1971. In 1972, the IRA stepped up its bombing campaign and tens of thousands of Catholics took part in civil rights marches. On 30 January 1972, soldiers opened fire on an illegal march in Derry killing 13 and injuring 29. On 22 February, seven people were killed in an IRA attack on the 16th Parachute Brigade at Aldershot. On 28 March, 100,000 Protestants marched against direct rule from Westminster.

Striking miners clash with police in February 1972 as they try to prevent trucks taking coke from the West Midland Gas Board coke depot in Birmingham. At Longannet, near Edinburgh, 2,000 miners fought with police to prevent deliveries of oil to the power station. Most power stations were working well below capacity and 12 were completely shut down by fuel shortages. The government called a state of emergency.

3.3 Symbolic interactionism

Although, as we have seen, there are significant differences between functionalist and Marxist theories of society, both emphasise the ways in which individual behaviour and consciousness are shaped by external forces in society. In their own ways, therefore, both may be regarded as to some extent *deterministic* theories, in which little scope is allowed for individuals to shape their own destinies by the exercise of their free will. Symbolic interactionists, by contrast, emphasise the ways in which society is actively shaped by the conscious and deliberate actions of its members. For this reason, symbolic interactionism is usually regarded as a *social action theory*, whilst functionalism and Marxism are regarded as *structural* theories.

Although a wide range of intellectual influences on the development of symbolic interactionism may be traced - including especially the work of such 18th century Scottish Moralists as Adam Ferguson, John Millar and Adam Smith, and in the 19th century, Charles Darwin's theory of evolution - perhaps the greatest influence was the late 19th century American philosophy of 'pragmatism' developed by such men as John Dewey, William James and Charles Pierce. At the heart of pragmatism, as with symbolic interactionism, was a concern with 'meaning'. For pragmatists, the meaning of an object was not intrinsic to that object, but depended upon the ways in which human beings behaved towards it. So, for example, there is nothing about a chair which intrinsically gives it its significance as something we sit upon - this significance derives entirely from the fact that this is indeed how human beings behave towards chairs. It would be entirely possible for us to treat chairs as objects of worship, as places for our pet canaries to perch, or as virtually anything else. And if we were to do so the meaning of 'chair' would be quite different even though the physical nature of the object remains unchanged. It is this pragmatist concern with the ways in which human beings actively make their environments meaningful that forms the starting point of symbolic interactionism.

George Herbert Mead

One of the most significant figures in the development of the symbolic interactionist tradition was the American philosopher and social psychologist, George Herbert Mead. Mead taught at the University of Chicago from 1893 until his death in 1931, and founded what, because of its continued association with the university and the city, became known as the 'Chicago School' of symbolic interactionism. During his lifetime Mead published very little, most of his work being published posthumously on the basis of lecture notes and fragmentary manuscripts. Probably his most significant book from the point of view of symbolic interactionism is *Mind Self and Society*, first published in 1934.

Human conduct versus animal behaviour What is the difference between the behaviour of animals and that of human beings? Mead's answer to this question gives us the clue to the whole approach of symbolic interactionism. For Mead, following the ideas of behaviourists such as John B. Watson, animal behaviour could be accounted for in terms of responses to stimuli. Such responses may either be directly instinctual, such as a cat's response to a physical threat, or learned, as was demonstrated by Ivan Pavlov in his famous experiments where he 'conditioned' a dog to salivate whenever a bell was rung, by repeatedly associating the sound of the bell with the arrival of food. Whilst Mead agreed that such processes could account for certain aspects of human behaviour, he argued that most needed to be characterised in a qualitatively different way.

To see Mead's point, consider the following situation. If I walk up to a dog belonging to one of my students and deliver a hefty kick to its rear end, its behaviour will be predictable. It will probably bark, turn around and snap at my ankles. It would do the same whoever was to deliver the kick, and under whatever circumstances. Of course, following Pavlov's principle, it is possible that if I repeat this often enough, the dog will come to associate my presence with being kicked, and will begin to bark and snap at my ankles even when I do not kick it. But even so, its behaviour remains entirely predictable. Now, imagine that instead of kicking the dog, I kick its owner, my student. How will the student respond? An initial response might be to say that he will kick me back, but a moment's reflection reveals that things are not so straightforward as at first they might seem. Will the student kick me back? He may, but this will depend upon how he has interpreted my kick. For example, he may interpret it as simply an act of gratuitous violence, in which case he would probably feel quite justified in returning the kick. However, there are a good many other ways in which my behaviour could be interpreted. He might judge that it was the result of mental instability on my part, in which case returning the kick begins to seem not merely inappropriate, but even callous - in our society, at least, assaulting the mentally ill is generally frowned upon. He might judge that my kick was merely an over-enthusiastic attempt to explain the principles of symbolic interactionism, in which case he might consider a verbal remonstration sufficient, as at least I had intended no harm.

The point is that how the student reacts will depend upon how he interprets my behaviour, or, in other words, what *meaning* he attributes to it. For Mead, this ability involves the distinctively human capacity to put oneself in the place of others, and to see oneself from the point of view of others. This he calls *role-taking*. In assessing how to respond to my kick, my student has to imagine the situation from my point of view - in short he has to 'take my role'.

The self In an attempt to understand this distinctively human ability to take the role of others, Mead developed the concept of the *self*. For Mead, the self is viewed as having two elements which he terms the *I* and the *Me*. To understand the distinction which Mead is making, consider the following example. Imagine that, in the course of a particularly dull lecture, you become aware of an impulse to leave the room and go for coffee. This impulse originates from the part of your personality which Mead calls the *I*: it is spontaneous and, as it were, uncensored. However, although such impulses may be common enough, they are in fact rarely acted upon. This is because as soon as you become aware of such a desire, you cannot avoid imagining what sort of response your walking out of the lecture would provoke in those around you, and especially perhaps the lecturer! This 'imagining' of the likely responses of others originates from the part of the personality which Mead calls the *Me*: this is the internalised points of view of other people, and acts as a sort of censor of the *I*'s plans.

Crucial to Mead's notion of the self, was the fact that it can only emerge as the result of social interaction. We have to learn the points of view of both specific other people (*significant others* in Mead's terminology) and of society in general (for Mead, the *generalised other*). Mead identified two principal stages by which the child acquires a social self. The first he calls the *play stage*. This phase, which begins as soon as the child starts to use language, is exemplified by the tendency of young children to pretend to be someone else. For example, children will play 'doctors and nurses' or 'teachers', or pretend to be their father or mother

chastising a younger sibling. Mead argues that, in doing this, children learn to see themselves from the point of view of significant others. The second stage is termed by Mead the *game stage*. This phase is exemplified by the playing of team games, in which the child has to see himself not only from the point of view of specific individuals, but of entire groups. For example, although the members of the opposing team in a game of football all have individual points of view, a player must be able to imagine himself from the collective point of view of that team, ie as their opponent. It is this process which, in Mead's view, completes the development of the social self because it engenders the ability to view oneself from the generalised point of view of one's society.

The significance of Mead's work Although Mead's work has important implications for both philosophy and social psychology, its importance to sociological theory lies principally in his view of human beings as socially self-conscious. They are not the mindless products of external social norms over which they have no control. Potentially, therefore, Mead's theory, or model, has the ability to explain how social order is maintained - by the fact that human beings possess an internalised representation of the point of view of their fellow members of society - whilst also recognising that human beings act self-consciously in possibly unpredictable ways.

Herbert Blumer

After Mead's death in 1931, the tradition which he had helped to establish at the University of Chicago was continued by the sociologist Herbert Blumer. Indeed, although his work clearly owed an immense amount to Mead's influence, it was in fact Blumer who coined the term *symbolic interactionism*. Perhaps Blumer's greatest contribution to the development of the tradition of symbolic interactionism was his working out of some of the major implications of symbolic interactionist theory for how sociologists should study society.

Blumer's critique of variable analysis As we have seen, a major assumption of a number of sociological approaches is that human behaviour can be understood in terms of the influences of external causes which are amenable to measurement. A classic example of this is Durkheim's study of suicide, in which a society's suicide rate is correlated with certain other features of that society, such as the degree of integration or regulation which prevails. Such explanations take the form, variable X (say a low level of integration) produces variable Y (say a high suicide rate). Individual consciousness as such is deliberately ignored in such explanations.

For Blumer this was unacceptable. First of all, he emphasises the fact that variables are in fact creations of sociologists, and can usually only be identified and measured if the sociologist makes some quite arbitrary assumptions. Consider the example of social class. Imagine that a sociologist wishes to demonstrate a relationship between being working class and experiencing relatively poor health. Before this can even be meaningful, the sociologist must define and operationalise 'social class'. He may employ the Registrar General's scale, in which case he classifies his population on the basis of occupation. Next he must define and operationalise the second variable, 'relatively poor health'. He may choose to use the incidence of longstanding illness. Finally, he must examine the relationship between the two variables: does being working class increase one's risk of experiencing poor health? The crucial point for Blumer, however, is that the answer to his question will depend almost entirely on how the variables have been defined and operationalised. They could, quite legitimately, have been defined and operationalised quite differently, and this would inevitably have produced a different answer to the question being addressed.

Secondly, and most importantly for Blumer, is the fact that even if social class does influence health, the process by which this occurs needs to be examined. Following Mead's theoretical lead, Blumer emphasises the fact that human behaviour does not result from the blind operation of external social forces (or, in other words, variables). Instead, behaviour (or *conduct*) results from how a social actor interprets or attributes meaning to a situation. Thus, to continue the same example, the central question would be, what meanings do people attach to their class position, and how do these meanings contribute to subsequent conduct which either promotes, or damages, their health? Crucially for Blumer, as for Mead, is the fact these meanings are not inevitable and pre-determined, but will change over time and vary between individuals.

Blumer therefore uses symbolic interactionist theory to challenge certain other sociological approaches on methodological grounds. In Blumer's view it is simply not legitimate to conceive of human behaviour as resulting from the operation of measurable variables. Instead individual actions need to be examined from the point of view of the actor's interpretation of the situation in which he finds himself. It is for this reason that sociologists of a symbolic interactionist persuasion have tended to rely upon such qualitative research techniques as participant observation in an attempt to elicit these meanings. (See p642 for further discussion of Blumer's methodology).

Erving Goffman: the dramaturgical analogy

All the world's a stage,
And all the men and women merely players;
They have their exits and their entrances,
And one man in his time plays many parts.

(*As You Like It,* Act II, Scene VII, Shakespeare)

Impression management Erving Goffman, the most influential symbolic interactionist, uses a dramaturgical analogy - society as drama - to illuminate social interaction and explore 'the way in which the individual in ordinary work situations presents himself and his activity to others, the ways in which he guides and controls the impression they form of him' (1959, Preface). Goffman argues that in everyday social interaction individuals are not only constantly expressing themselves to others but also are trying to create certain impressions of themselves in the mind of an audience. This process of *impression management* is central to our behaviour as social actors attempt to control the impressions others have of them.

Goffman pays most attention to the non-verbal aspects of interpersonal communication and this is illustrated by the example he quotes from his research into rural life in the Shetland Isles. The crofter's wife, when serving native dishes to tourists, would check on the stated feelings of liking the food by watching how quickly the tourists ate the food and how eagerly it was consumed. In social interaction, we constantly watch for these non-verbal 'signs given off' as the ways in which a person's true feelings might be revealed. We do not always take things at face value, but we check the whole performance for any discrepancies and for signs of the underlying motivations of the performer.

The idea of *performance* is very important to Goffman's analysis. It refers to any activity of a participant in a social interaction which influences other participants. When playing a part, the individual is implicitly asking the others in an interaction to believe in their performance. And to achieve this, the social actor must create the appropriate impression. For example, some teachers take the view that it is important to get the upper hand in a new class, starting out tough. And letting the students know who's boss. Any bumbling around or signs of weakness will not create the desired impression and the performance will fail, endangering future performances before that class. Goffman recognises that we can believe in the roles we play or perform them with no real conviction. Deluding an audience may be out of self-interest or it may be because the audience demands to be deluded. An illustration of the latter is the way doctors may give placebos (something which will have no medical effect) to hypochondriacal patients in the knowledge that there is nothing wrong with them, but simply because they demand treatment.

To be effective, performances need to be cohesive and sustained. Some of the techniques used to confirm an impression are considered next.

Front and regions Social actors employ the equivalent of theatrical 'props' to assist in the creation of a particular impression or definition of a situation. Anything which intentionally or unintentionally is used to enhance the effectiveness of a performance, Goffman refers to as 'front'. Furniture, decor and specialised equipment may be used to create the right setting for a performance and these are allied to the personal 'front' of clothing, speech, facial expressions and body language in order to create a cohesive impression consistent with the role being expressed. The budding young executive, keen to create an impression of dynamism, will go in for 'power dressing' and is likely to develop the leisure interests and activities associated with that image. Many of the 'props' we carry or utilise have an apparently practical purpose, but their real value lies in the way they contribute to creating a desired impression. Solicitors' case papers are usually tied with ribbon, ostensibly to prevent the contents from falling out, but the social impact is one of setting aside legal papers from other kinds of material, inferring a special and superior status to them and to the person carrying them.

Just as a theatre has a 'frontstage' where the performance takes place, and a 'backstage' where actors can relax out of their roles, so there are separate 'regions' in social interactions. A 'region' is any area which is bounded to some degree by barriers to perception. Performances take place in a 'front region' whilst in the 'back region', a performance can be knowingly contradicted by out-of-role behaviour. In a school or college, the classroom, corridors, dining areas, etc form the 'front region' for adults performing the role of teacher and for younger people presenting the role of student. However, both teachers and students can relax from their respective roles in either the staff room or in areas where teachers tend not to visit. Even in these 'back regions' however, a performance of a different kind has to be maintained as colleagues or friends now form a different audience to the 'frontstage' one. So the 'back region' for one performance becomes the 'front region' for another.

When performances fail Goffman notes that sometimes discrepancies appear in our performances which affect the audience's impressions of us. Sometimes an individual fails to maintain their expressive control, the mask slips and the whole performance can be jeopardised in the same way as a jarringly wrong chord can spoil an entire concert.

Goffman suggests that examining occasions when this happens tells us a great deal about the nature of performances. For example, an audience, or part of an audience, sometimes colludes with a role player to cover up or ignore discrepancies in a performance and this illustrates the way social actors can work in 'teams', helping to maintain expressive control. Sometimes, however, discrepant behaviour can be more damaging to attempted impression management, culminating in embarrassment and even retirement from that role.

Role distance Goffman creates a strongly humanistic version of social role. The roles we perform in social interaction are not scripted for us by society but are actively created and defined by our performances. Individuals often distance themselves from the role they are occupying by making communications out of character with the role, thus showing themselves to be more than the role being performed. Elements of the individual's 'self', made up from other roles they occupy, may appear in the performance of a role, and it is this which allows for spontaneity and creativity in a performance. In acting out the role of teacher for example, an individual may allow other roles - of parent, 'ordinary person' or friend - to enter their performance. Similarly a civil servant, even when turning down a request because it doesn't fit the rules, may show a 'human face', to indicate that they are more than the role they are performing. We are not programmed into a role, straight jacketing our behaviour, but through the use of 'role distance', actively create the roles we occupy.

Roles and power Analogies in sociology have to be used with care. It is one thing to point to apparent similarities between social behaviour and acting on a stage, and another to suggest that the two are identical. Goffman recognises the limitations of the dramaturgical analogy, pointing out that the stage presents activity which is imaginary and rehearsed whilst social behaviour is real and frequently unplanned. Furthermore, in social life the audience often takes a very much more active role than it does in the theatre. For Goffman, therefore, the dramatic analogy is only a framework with which to begin to understand behaviour and many parts of his analysis, for example the idea of role distance, go much further.

Unlike some of the early symbolic interactionists, Goffman does pay specific attention to the ways in which inequalities in power are played out in face-to-face interaction. Without attempting to analyse the structural location and causes of inequality, Goffman nevertheless identifies the way hierarchies create problems of self-respect and opportunity. In *Asylums*, a study of the experience of inmates in a mental hospital, Goffman (1968) explores the problem posed for individual social actors by the imposition on them of a complete regime in a 'total institution' (see pp380-381). Even in this, the most extreme case of apparent powerlessness, the individual is still capable of employing strategies which ensure that some self-determination can be retained. Inmates who fool the staff in such ways as getting extra food or cigarettes, are maintaining their sense of self-determination. In this respect, Goffman's work carries the important message that power is not merely the creation of a hierarchy of positions in society, but the constant acting out in face-to-face interaction of that inequality.

Whilst Goffman rejects the structural view that the individual is what their place in an organisation defines them to be, he does not, unlike some of the early symbolic interactionists, ignore the effect of external constraints. The individual's 'self' does not arise solely out of their interaction with others, but within the context of the limitations imposed by social institutions. The self constantly moves between the limitations of external society and the needs of inner individuality. Goffman concludes that, 'it is against something that the self can emerge'. That 'something' is society. From this it can be seen that Goffman is acknowledging the impact on our individuality of external social constraints. Our individual 'self' is created in the context of hierarchical organisations which, although they do not rigorously define the way we are, play a part in forging our individuality.

Evaluation

As has been noted above, symbolic interactionism has a number of strengths. First, it moves away from the deterministic assumptions of much sociological theory, and emphasises the conscious involvement of the actor in social life. Secondly, it recognises that human conduct is meaningful, and hence that a grasp of actors' meanings and interpretations is essential to an understanding of their conduct.

Equally, however, symbolic interactionism can be criticised. The most fundamental and persistent difficulty is its tendency to ignore the influence of social structures. It is possible to acknowledge Blumer's criticisms of variable analysis whilst still recognising that an individual's economic position

(their 'class', however this is defined) will affect their behaviour whether they recognise it or not. Poverty, for example, would seem to be real enough, and its effects will be obvious whether or not an actor defines himself as poor. A second, and related criticism, is that symbolic interactionism exaggerates the extent to which human actors do in fact consciously interpret their environments. It may be argued that whilst self-conscious interpretation does occur, this tends to be only when some unusual situation is encountered. For most of the time human beings seem to act as though on 'automatic pilot', or merely out of habit. The notion of habit seems closer to the view of action advanced by systems and structural theorists than to that advanced by symbolic interactionists.

Summary

1 Three major schools of sociology can be distinguished as significant in the establishment of sociology as a discipline - functionalism, Marxism and symbolic interactionism.

2 The primary concern of functionalism is with the problem of order in modern society. For functionalists particular attention needs to be paid to the role of consensus and the positive functions fulfilled by social institutions for the stability of society as a whole.

3 The central concerns of Marxism are to account for the unexpected stability of capitalism and to identify the factors likely to lead to its demise. For Marxists, particular attention needs to be given to the role of the economy and consequently to class conflict as the key engine of social change.

4 Symbolic interactionism differs from both functionalism and Marxism in that it is concerned with the level of micro-interaction rather than the structure of society as a whole. For symbolic interactionists, particular attention needs to be given to the fact that human beings are actors and that the meanings of actions are continually modified as people negotiate with each other.

Activity 8   Defining the Situation

Henderson Dores is out with his girlfriend Irene Stein. They are trying to locate his car after spending the evening in a restaurant. It is central New York, just after midnight and Henderson has just noticed four men coming towards them. Irene is searching in her handbag for a tissue and has noticed nothing.

Henderson looked round again in what he hoped was an unconcerned natural way. The figures - dark, lithe-looking - had crossed to their side of the street with what looked like more urgency.

Jesus Christ, Henderson thought, they say it happens to everybody sooner or later - like a car crash or a burglary. He felt a surging panic begin to overwhelm him. It's only when you haven't got any money that they kill you. Or pour petrol over you and set you alight. Or rape you. Gang-sodomise you. They were only ten yards away.

'RUN!' Henderson screamed, simultaneously flinging away the umbrella and giving Irene a mighty push. His hand closed around his wallet, fat with credit cards and dollars.

'You can have it, you bastards!' he yelled at the muggers and with all his strength bowled his wallet in their

direction. He saw it fly open and notes and cards shower out, then he turned and ran.

Henderson races off, pursued by two of the men who eventually catch up with him.

'OK,' he bellowed in mingled rage and terror as he was hauled to a stop, 'kill me, kill me, I don't care!'

Both his hands were firmly gripped. 'Sir,' a quiet voice came. 'Relax, please, sir. We have your wallet and your money here.'

Later, Henderson was able to reconstruct what happened. The four men were returning theatre-goers who had been surprised by Henderson suddenly throwing his girlfriend to the ground, throwing his wallet at them and running off in panic-stricken flight!

Adapted from W. Boyd *Stars and Bars*, 1985

Questions

1 Make a list of the ways in which meanings are transmitted in the situation described above.

2 How does this extract illustrate the view of one symbolic interactionist, W. I. Thomas, that 'if men define situations as real they are real in their consequences'?

4 Structure and Action in Sociology

Key Issues

1 What are the main assumptions of structuralism, ethnomethodology and structuration theory?

2 How have they seen the relation between structure and action?

Although functionalism, Marxism and symbolic interactionism have been central to the establishment of sociology as a discipline, alternative approaches have developed. In this part, we shall look at three which present very different ways of looking at the relation between 'structure' and 'action'.

4.1 Structuralism

As the name implies, structuralism is concerned with structures. It has been an influential way of looking at the world, not only in sociology and the social sciences, but also in the arts, literary studies and history. The origins of structuralism lie in linguistics -

the study of language - and in particular in the work of a Swiss linguist, Ferdinand de Saussure. In order to understand how structuralism has been of relevance as a sociological theory, it will be helpful to begin by considering the distinctive approach adopted by Saussure to the study of language.

Ferdinand de Saussure

Central to Saussure's analysis of language, and indeed to structuralism in general, is the observation that it is possible to study a language in two dimensions. First, we can study what individual people actually write and say. If a man utters a sentence like 'elephants are bigger than apples' we can pay attention to the meaning of this particular utterance, consider its truth, his reasons for saying it and so on. This dimension of language - the dimension of what people actually write and say - is called the *diachronic*. Contrasted with this, however, is the fact that it is only possible for anyone to utter this sentence, or indeed any other, because there are *rules* which go to make up the language which is being spoken. Most obviously, there are rules governing the relationship between words and things (or what Saussure calls *signifiers* and *signifieds*). In English, the word elephant (the signifier) is attached by convention to the large animals with trunks which are indigenous to Africa and India. Of course, there is no absolute reason why we should call them elephants (the word itself is quite arbitrary), but once the convention is established we must use it if we are to make sense. Secondly, there are rules of grammar. In English, for example, there are particular rules governing tenses. So the sentence 'elephants were bigger than apples' has a different meaning from our original sentence, 'elephants are bigger than apples', by virtue of the grammatical rules governing past and present tenses. Saussure's point is that we can also study language in this way, as a system of rules governing what we can and cannot say. This second dimension, which concerns itself with the structure of language itself, is called the *synchronic*.

This distinction between the diachronic and the synchronic is fundamental not only to structuralist linguistics, but to the whole structuralist approach. To see how the distinction works, let us consider an example of human activity. Let us take lunch. When we have a meal, we are most likely to be concerned with its diachronic dimension - that is, what we are actually going to eat, and in what order. Imagine we go into a restaurant. Our order may well look something like this: we begin with soup of the day; we then move on to roast chicken, with potatoes, carrots and peas, and finally we choose strawberries and cream followed by coffee and mints. However, as with uttering individual sentences, this meal as it appears in the diachronic dimension, depends upon rules which exist in the synchronic. First there are rules, often specific to cultures, about what we can and cannot eat. It is not generally permitted in our culture, for example, to eat parrots, whilst chickens are perfectly acceptable. Secondly, there are rules about what we can eat together from the same plate, and in what order - the grammatical rules of eating in fact. In our culture, for example, it is not really permissible to begin a meal with dessert and coffee, or to round it off with a bowl of soup. What is clear from this example, as with the example of language, is that the diachronic dimension - the element of action - depends upon the synchronic dimension - the element of structure. It is this concern with the synchronic, or structural elements of human activity, which is distinctive of structuralism.

Claude Lévi-Strauss

As you will by now have noticed, many of the sociological theorists considered in this chapter could be called structuralist. Certainly, Durkheim's concern with social facts, or Marx's emphasis on the underlying logic of capitalism, could win them the label of structuralist.

However, the theorist who did most to formulate the implications of the structuralist approach for the social sciences was the Belgian anthropologist Claude Lévi-Strauss. Lévi-Strauss was concerned to apply structuralist methods to the analysis of human culture. One of his most famous analyses was of myths. Myths exist in all societies. Although, superficially, the myths which different societies possess are quite different from each other, Lévi-Strauss's analysis emphasises that this is only so when considered in a diachronic sense. When viewed synchronically he argues that myths possess certain common structural features. One can, according to Lévi-Strauss, and indeed he spends much time attempting to demonstrate this, place a large number of myths (theoretically all myths) alongside each other, and detect a common set of underlying rules which govern their structure. Lévi-Strauss attempts to explain this deep structure in terms of fundamental properties of the human mind: the underlying structure of culture, he says, is ultimately produced by the biologically determined structures of the human brain.

Oppositions Here is a brief illustration of Lévi-Stauss's approach. Myths are based on *oppositions*. Typical oppositions are good/evil; male/female; life/death; night/day; land/sea. For example, these and many other oppositions are found in the creation myth in *Genesis* which tells the story of the creation of the world, of life, and of humans beings.

Many of these oppositions cause unwelcome contradictions for human beings. For example, death contradicts life. Myths can resolve this contradiction by stating that death is not a necessary consequence of life. They can introduce a new possibility, a new form of existence which is neither life nor death. Thus myths often contain 'mythical beings' such as angels, ghosts and other supernatural creatures who are neither alive nor dead as we normally understand these terms. In this way myths mediate between the opposition of life and death, they resolve the contradiction.

Lévi-Strauss argues that all myths have the same basic structure - opposition and mediation, or put another way, contradiction and resolution. Only when this structure is revealed are we in a position to interpret the function of myths. In Lévi-Strauss's words, 'the purpose of myth is to provide a logical model capable of overcoming a contradiction' (1965, p574).

Semiotics

Derived from the theoretical basis of structuralism, *semiotics*, or the study of signs, was developed most famously in the work of Roland Barthes. Semiotic analysis concentrates upon the central structuralist principle that the relationship between signifier and signified is arbitrary, and hence determined only by convention and applied according to rules. For example, consider a red rose. A red rose can be considered a signifier, in the sense that it has a meaning, beyond its mere physical existence as a flower. We know this from the fact that if a man gives a bunch of red roses to a woman, she will interpret this in a quite different way than if he had given her a bunch of daffodils. Red roses, in our culture, signify love, whilst daffodils do not. There is no necessary reason for this; it could just as easily be the other way round. The task of semiotics is to interpret the meanings of signs in our culture.

Barthes was also heavily influenced by Marxism, and one of his central tasks was to analyse the deep ideological meanings of signs in modern popular culture. He argued that very often such signs, whilst appearing on the surface trivial enough, betray deeper ideological 'myths', which are often invisible to ordinary people and can only be seen when subjected to semiological analysis. One of Barthes' own examples will serve to illustrate this point. The example is of a black soldier saluting the French flag on the cover of the magazine *Paris Match*. At face value, this is just what it appears to be: a black soldier saluting the French flag. However, at a deeper level, Barthes argues, this picture signifies a strongly ideological message, namely, 'that France is a great Empire, that all her sons, without colour discrimination, faithfully serve under her flag, and that there is no better answer to the detractors of an alleged colonialism than the zeal shown by this Negro in serving his so-called oppressors' (Barthes, 1973, pp,125-6). In other words, this seemingly straightforward picture of a black soldier saluting the flag, contains a hidden justification of French imperialism and a denial of racial discrimination.

As with other structuralist writers, Barthes' approach rests upon his analysis of the synchronic dimension, and specifically upon the systems of rules which govern the relationship between signifiers and that which they signify. It is only in relation to these systems of rules, which link certain signs with deeper ideological meanings, that the specific products (that is the diachronic dimension) of popular culture can be understood.

Evaluation

There can be no doubt that structuralism provides a powerful method for the analysis of virtually any aspect of human culture. More specifically, it has encouraged sociologists to recognise that 'what appears to us as solid, normal or natural, is in fact the end result of a process of production from some form of underlying structure' (Marshall, 1994, p516). It has nevertheless been subject to criticisms.

One is that in reducing the diachronic to the synchronic - or, interpreting actual utterances, myths, pictures or whatever in terms of underlying systems of rules - we are in danger of losing the uniqueness and subtlety of actual human action. Subtle differences in meaning between myths, for example, are in danger of being lost sight of in the eagerness of the structuralist to find some underlying pattern which all myths have in common.

Secondly, it can be argued that structuralism has an inevitable difficulty in explaining change. If particular instances of action are to be explained with reference to some underlying structure, then it is difficult to see how changes in that structure are to be explained.

Despite these criticisms, as we shall see, the insights of structuralism have nevertheless been important in shaping modern sociological theory.

Activity 9   Semiotics

Item A

Notting Hill carnival - the 'dancing policeman' is a theme often pictured by the media.

Item B

World War 1 poster from the USA

Item C

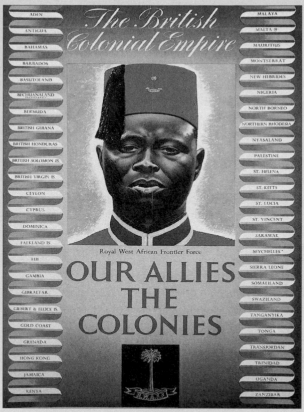

World War 2 poster from Britain

Question

Look at Items A, B and C and interpret the ideological significance of each.

4.2 Ethnomethodology

Ethnomethodology is an approach to sociological theorising developed during the 1960s by the American writer, Harold Garfinkel.

Ethnomethodology can be seen largely as a reaction to the highly structural and systematic theorising in sociology which reached its climax with the work of Garfinkel's teacher, Talcott Parsons. The philosophical underpinnings of ethnomethodology lie in a branch of European philosophy known as phenomenology, and in particular in the work of Edmund Husserl (1859-1938) and Alfred Schutz (1899-1959). Before we undertake an examination of ethnomethodology, therefore, it will be helpful to briefly consider the essence of phenomenology.

Phenomenology

The central point of phenomenology, first outlined by its founder Edmund Husserl, is that human beings do not experience the world at first hand, but rather interpret the world through their senses in a way which is meaningful to them. Imagine that you are

looking at a table. How do you know that it is a table? At first sight, of course, that sounds like an absurd question, but a moment's thought reveals that it is in fact more profound than it seems. What you are in fact looking at is not intrinsically a table, but a solid object of a certain shape and size. You only call it a table because you know about tables; in other words, because you possess the category of table in your mind, and when you see objects of a certain shape and size, you place them into this category. Had you never encountered the concept of table you would not - somewhat obviously - describe the object as a table; indeed to you, it would not be a table. It is this concern with how human actors make sense of the world around them that is at the centre of phenomenology.

This fundamental concern was applied specifically to the subject matter of sociology by Husserl's student, Alfred Schutz. Schutz emphasised the fact that the ways in which human beings classify objects in the world is not an individual process, but rather a collective process. The categories we use are not peculiar to ourselves, but are shared with other members of our society. Such categories are called by Schutz *typifications*. Typification refers to any shared concept - golf ball, democracy, Church, armchair, etc - and forms the basis of communication. Collectively, Schutz says that our typifications build up what he calls a stock of 'commonsense knowledge'. Of course, one consequence of this notion is that there is no guarantee that any two individuals will perceive the world in the same way, as there may always be differences in the typifications which they adopt as a result of different experiences of life. Yet Schutz argues that, in order for communication to be possible at all, we must assume that the typifications which we adopt are shared with others. We thus get by in the social world by creating and sustaining a sort of illusion of shared understanding.

Harold Garfinkel and ethnomethodology

An approximate meaning of the term 'ethnomethodology' is 'the methods used by people'. Specifically, it refers to the study of the methods which social actors (or 'members' as ethnomethodologists usually refer to them) use to make sense of their social world. It thus begins from the phenomenological assumption that the world does not present itself with an already meaningful and clearly demarcated order; rather this order is actively constructed through the activities of members. Ethnomethodology seeks to understand how they do this.

The documentary method For Garfinkel, members employ the *documentary method* to make sense of and account for the social world which they inhabit. The documentary method involves taking certain aspects of a situation from an infinite number which could have been selected, defining them in a particular way, and then using this definition to provide evidence for some underlying pattern. New situations are then themselves interpreted in relation to this underlying pattern. An example of this is Atkinson's study of the practices of coroners (see pp642-643). The underlying pattern here was the coroner's commonsense view of what constituted a suicide, and on this basis individual deaths were deemed either to be or not to be suicides. However, the very act of classifying deaths itself gives further support to the belief in the existence of an underlying pattern. Identifying particular examples of the pattern and the belief in the existence of the pattern itself are therefore mutually reinforcing. This mutual reinforcement was termed by Garfinkel *reflexivity*, and he felt that this was an essential element of social life. Members constantly seek to explain events in terms of underlying patterns, and use these explanations to justify and reinforce their initial belief in the existence of the underlying patterns. There is

no reason to believe, however, that these patterns refer in any direct way to some external social reality.

Indexicality A central part of Garfinkel's analysis was the observation that members make interpretations of situations on the basis of context. Two members, acting in precisely the same way, may be subject to quite different interpretations depending upon the contexts of their actions. For example, if the action concerned is telling an off-colour joke, then if it is performed by a comedian in a night club it is likely to elicit a different interpretation than if it is told by a nun in a convent. This is what Garfinkel meant by *indexicality*: the meaning of the action in each case is not derived from intrinsic features of the action, but rather from the social contexts in which it takes place.

Rules and social order Unlike Parsons and other sociologists who assumed that rules were simply learned in the process of socialisation and were capable of guiding conduct in any situation, Garfinkel emphasises that it is the assumption of the existence of rules, rather than rules themselves, which is responsible for the maintenance of social order. Garfinkel illustrates this with reference to a simple game. His point is that even in a simple game, where the rules are written down in an unambiguous fashion, it is easy to find what he calls 'monsters', or possibilities not covered by the rules. Here is his illustration of how easy it is to find such monsters in even the simplest of games:

> Say we are going to propose a game of ticktacktoe. Two persons play ticktacktoe. Any two persons? When, today? Tomorrow? Do we have to be in sight of each other? Can we play by mail? Can one player be dead (cited in Heritage, 1984).

The point of this illustration is that we assume that our activities are guided by clearly understood rules. However, in reality this is not the case. The extent to which the maintenance of social order is based upon such fragile assumptions is illustrated in Garfinkel's so-called 'breaching experiments'. Here he asked his students to go into familiar situations and behave in unexpected ways. For example, some went into a department store and started to haggle over the price of goods, whilst others went home to their families and behaved like lodgers. In each case the behaviour could not be easily accounted for, and produced such reactions as confusion and anger. What these experiments illustrate is that social order is in fact very fragile and only maintained by the mutual assumptions of members.

Ethnomethodology and sociology

As well as being a radically different approach to understanding social order, ethnomethodology also offers a general critique of sociological theory. Garfinkel argued that 'man' is usually represented by sociology as a 'cultural dope'; that is someone who unthinkingly and compliantly acts out the norms of their society. In contrast, ethnomethodology regards the individual as a skilled member of society, who is constantly engaged in interpreting and giving meaning to situations, and maintaining a sense of social order. For Garfinkel, then, social order is not an objective pre-given determinant of human action, but rather is the active accomplishment of members.

Ethnomethodologists have argued that conventional sociology employs very similar procedures as members living their everyday lives. Specifically, just as members employ the documentary method to identify and justify underlying patterns, so do professional sociologists. Social class is one example. Because sociologists assume that there is an underlying pattern of social class relationships, particular instances of behaviour - such as voting patterns, educational achievements and so on - are interpreted in the light of this underlying pattern. This interpretation, in turn, gives further credence to the existence of the underlying pattern. For ethnomethodologists, however, this would just be another example of a mutually reinforcing fiction.

The realities of sociologists, therefore, are seen as just as 'constructed' as those of any other members.

Evaluation

There can be no doubt that ethnomethodology constituted a radical critique of conventional sociology. Its emphasis upon interpretation and social order as the active accomplishment of members did indeed offer a new way of looking at social order. It can nevertheless be subjected to various criticisms.

First, Alvin Gouldner has accused ethnomethodology of being preoccupied with trivia. In concentrating upon the mundane elements of everyday life, it ignores the wider inequalities in power and wealth which prevail in modern societies. Even granting Garfinkel's emphasis on the active construction of social reality by members, he seems to ignore the ways in which different groups in society might find it easier than others to have their view of reality adopted by the majority.

Secondly, ethnomethodology's critique of mainstream sociology could very easily be directed back on itself. Surely, if all other actors - including sociologists - employ the documentary method, then why should ethnomethodologists themselves be exempt? If they are not, then ethnomethodology becomes just another self-reinforcing account of an ultimately unknowable social world.

Activity 10 Ethnomethodology

Item A *An experiment in counselling*

In an experiment conducted in a university department of psychiatry, students were invited to take part in what was described as a new form of psychotherapy. Students were told to summarise a personal problem, and then ask the counsellor a series of questions which could be answered either 'yes' or 'no'. The counsellor sat in an adjoining room, and communicated with the student by intercom. Unknown to the students, the 'counsellor' was not who they claimed to be, and the answers were randomly divided in a predetermined sequence between 'yes' and 'no'. Despite the fact that the answers were completely random, and indeed that some contradicted previous answers, the students felt that the advice received was helpful and sensible.

Adapted from H. Garfinkel *Studies in Ethnomethodology*, 1967

Item B *A streaker*

Questions

1. Read Item A. In what ways does this experiment demonstrate the documentary method?
2. Item B is a picture of a streaker. How does this statement illustrate Garfinkel's concept of indexicality?

4.3 The unification of structure and action

As we have seen in this chapter, sociological theories tend to come closer to one of two general approaches: one which emphasises social structure, and the other which emphasises social action. It would be wrong to say that any theory in sociology completely ignores either structure or action, but it would be fair to say that whilst Marxists, functionalists and structuralists tend to emphasise the role of social structures, Weber, symbolic interactionists and ethnomethodologists tend to emphasise the creative and interpretive nature of social action. This tendency for sociological theories to emphasise one aspect at the expense of the other, has led some writers on sociological theory to suggest that structure and action represent alternative ways of looking at society which cannot be brought together. In this section, we shall consider one influential approach to this problem, that of the British sociologist Anthony Giddens.

Anthony Giddens and the theory of structuration

The duality of structure At the centre of Giddens' concern to overcome the division between structural and action approaches within sociology is his concept of the *duality of structure*. In simple terms, action (or 'agency' as he usually calls it) and structure are just two ways of looking at the same thing. For Giddens, structures are produced by social action, and it is only through social action that they are maintained over time. However, at the same time, it is only by the existence of structures that actions are made possible. Let us take the example of speech and language to illustrate this.

Language can be regarded as a structure. It is a set of rules for communication which exists independently of any particular individual who uses it. It therefore exerts constraint over individual language users (like Durkheim's social facts) in that if I wish to say something, I am obliged to use certain words in a certain order - if I want to be understood that is. However, language (the structure) only exists because people use it correctly when they speak and write - in other words, through action. Indeed, it is *only* because people speak and write according to the rules of their language, that the language continues to exist. This should not be taken to imply that languages are simply reproduced by the act of

speaking and writing, however. Although this will usually be the case, it is quite possible for new words to be introduced, old ones to be forgotten and even new grammatical rules to enter the language as a result of the ways in which people write and speak. Thus for Giddens, although structure clearly influences action, action may also independently influence structure.

Structure, rules and resources Giddens identifies two important elements of structure: *rules* and *resources*. Rules refer to the range of regulatory principles which influence action. They could refer to unwritten rules such as how one proposes marriage, or to laws regulating how one is to drive a motor car. The second element of structure for Giddens is resources. Giddens identifies both *allocative* and *authoritative* resources. Allocative resources refer broadly to what Marx identified as the 'forces of production', whilst authoritative resources refer to the distribution of social power. For Giddens, each of these elements of structure may be reproduced through the agency of social actors, but equally it may be transformed by social actors.

Agency and the reproduction of structures Although Giddens allows the possibility that structures can be transformed through agency, he also seeks to explain their reproduction. According to Giddens, much human action is 'mundane', and draws upon stocks of shared commonsense knowledge which is routinely applied with little conscious thought. Agents draw upon their knowledge of rules, and make use of available resources to accomplish their goals. Giddens in fact suggests that human beings have an innate desire for predictability in their social lives. He believes that we share a basic need for what he calls 'ontological security': a confidence that the world is in fact as it appears to be. This tends to produce social stability and persistence rather than social change.

Although Giddens does emphasise the degree to which structures are reproduced through human agency, he also allows the possibility that they may change. Drawing on the insights of writers such as Goffman, Giddens points out that actors do not merely react to external stimuli, but engage in the 'reflexive monitoring of action'. This means that they can reflect upon their own actions and their consequences, and have the ability to choose new courses of action. However, Giddens acknowledges that structures do not only change as a result of deliberate actions by actors, but can change as the result of the unintended consequences of actions. For example, the decision by sufficient numbers of actors to visit a particular holiday resort may produce major changes in the local economy which no one intended, but which nevertheless resulted from these actions.

Evaluation

There can be no doubt that Giddens' work represents a major attempt to solve an apparently intractable problem in sociological theory: the relationship between structure and agency. Whilst Giddens' theory of structuration does indeed appear to offer a way out of this theoretical cul-de-sac, his work has nevertheless been subjected to criticism.

Margaret Archer has criticised Giddens for failing to give sufficient attention to the extent to which structures themselves influence the degree to which they can be changed through agency. She emphasises the fact that actors cannot simply change the world as they wish, and that very often structures will constrain action and systematically frustrate the transformative efforts of actors.

On a different theme, Ian Craib has argued that Giddens' model of the personality is in fact rather confused, and rests upon certain basic misunderstandings of psychoanalytic theory. Specifically, Craib suggests that the important notion of ontological security is based upon a 'fundamentally oversimplified notion of the individual' (Craib, 1992, p177).

Summary

1 Structuralism attempts to explain the nature of social phenomena by revealing underlying deep structures.

2 Ethnomethodology, by contrast, seeks to demonstrate that the apparently orderly and structured nature of social reality is in fact only sustained by the day-to-day accomplishments of members.

3 Anthony Giddens' theory of structuration attempts to bridge the gap between structure and agency.

5 Challenges to Sociological Theory

Key Issues
1 What are the main assumptions of sociobiology, globalisation and postmodernism?
2 How do they challenge more traditional sociological theories?

New approaches are constantly emerging which challenge the conventional wisdom of sociologists. Feminism, for example, questioned the male bias of the discipline and opened up new areas for investigation (see pp644-646). In this section we shall look at three recent approaches which challenge the taken for granted assumptions of most sociologists.

5.1 Sociobiology

An important and controversial challenge to conventional sociological theories emerged during the 1970s with the development of the discipline of sociobiology. In essence, sociobiology is an attempt to apply the theory of biological evolution to an explanation of human social behaviour. It therefore represents a significant departure from the usual assumption made by sociological theorists - of whatever persuasion - that human behaviour is principally the result of cultural rather than biological influences.

Darwinian evolution

The modern theory of biological evolution is derived from the work of Charles Darwin whose path-breaking book *On The Origin of Species* was published in 1859. Although Darwin proposed a highly complex set of arguments to account for biological evolution, the essence of his argument is quite straightforward. In short, Darwin proposed that all species contain variations which are capable of being inherited biologically. Some of these variations may make no difference to the survival chances of members of the species, other variations may make a real difference.

Consider the following example from human evolution. Inherited characteristics such as hair colour and texture do not appear to confer any significant advantages for human survival. However, there is considerable evidence that the evolution of the human brain over the last million years has been crucial for the development and survival of modern homo sapiens. In particular the frontal region of the brain which is associated with intelligence has grown steadily larger. Increased intelligence gives an important survival advantage as human beings rely increasingly on culture - a creation of intelligence - to adapt to a range of environments from the Arctic to the Sahara. In this respect the more intelligent will be more likely to survive, to reproduce, and to pass on their biologically based characteristics to their offspring. This, then, is the point of Darwinian evolution: those traits which evolve will be those which promote their own reproductive success to a greater extent than others in the population.

One of the reasons why sociobiology has been so controversial amongst sociologists is that reasoning such as this has led some sociobiologists to suggest that in human beings (and other mammalian species) certain biologically based differences in behaviour between the sexes will exist. A basic biological fact is that males are able to produce many more offspring than females. It has thus been suggested that evolution will select different sexual strategies in males and females. Whilst a female has to invest a great deal in each offspring (at least nine months, and probably considerably longer) the male only has to invest enough time as is necessary to complete the act of copulation. It has thus been suggested that evolution will select coyness in females, whilst in males it will select a more promiscuous approach to sexual relations.

The term *reproductive success* is now used by many sociobiologists to replace the more ambiguous term 'survival of the fittest' which, although often attributed to Darwin, was in fact coined by the sociologist Herbert Spencer.

Neo-Darwinism and the selfish gene

Whilst Darwin's essential insight into the mechanism of evolution remains at the centre of evolutionary theory, the modern theory differs from Darwin's original in that it incorporates the science of genetics. Darwin was unaware of genetics, and so indeed were most other people until the 1930s, despite the fact that the basic facts of genetic inheritance had been discovered by Gregor Mendel (1822-84) as early as 1865. Nevertheless, the fact remains that Darwin's own theory turned out to be remarkably compatible with what is now understood about the mechanisms of genetic inheritance, and it is this synthesis of Darwinian evolution and genetics on which modern evolutionary biology - and the discipline of sociobiology - rest.

According to modern genetics, the basic unit of biological inheritance is the gene. A gene is a sequence of DNA which contains coded information which is present in every cell of an organism's body. In human beings, 50% of an individual's genes are obtained from each parent. It follows from this that, because of common descent, full siblings share 50% of their genes in common, half-siblings 25% and first cousins 12.5%. This is the probability that any gene present in an individual will also be present in that relative. This is know in evolutionary biology as the *coefficient of relatedness* and is represented by the letter *r*. Whilst this may appear to be largely incidental to Darwin's theory, closer inspection

reveals that it has far reaching implications, especially for the predictions which evolutionary theory can make about human behaviour.

The problem of altruism Modern evolutionary biologists have pointed out that one important consequence of neo-Darwinian theory is that *altruistic* behaviour will *not* evolve. An altruistic act is defined by biologists as one 'whereby one organism promotes the reproductive success of another at its own expense' (Badcock, 1991, p289). Although the absence of altruism is a self-evident consequence of neo-Darwinian theory, it has surprisingly important implications for sociological theory. First, it suggests that sociological theories like Marxism, which imply that human beings possess an innate capacity for self-sacrifice in the interests of the group, rest upon an incorrect theory of human nature. Secondly, it suggests that the prevalent sociological assumption, that human beings are born 'blank slates' with few, if any, innate drives, is similarly misguided. Instead, it suggests that human beings, like all other species, possess innate tendencies which have evolved, ultimately, because they promote the reproductive success of the organism. It therefore places far less emphasis on culture as a determinant of human behaviour than other sociological theories, and far more emphasis on the role of biology.

Although, as we have seen, sociobiologists claim that altruistic behaviour cannot evolve, two forms of apparent altruism have been identified which have important implications for human behaviour: *kin altruism* and *reciprocal altruism*.

Kin altruism The idea of kin altruism is derived from the fact, noted above, that it is possible to calculate the degree of genetic relatedness between organisms. Consider that an organism possesses a gene which causes it to seek as many reproductive opportunities as possible. It is not difficult to see that such a gene will enjoy a high level of reproductive success; in other words, that it will leave many copies of itself in future generations. However, if we consider a rival organism which possesses a gene which causes it not only to seek reproductive opportunities for itself, but also for its siblings, then, because there is a 50% chance that the same gene will be present in these siblings, this organism will leave even more copies of its genes than the first. In short, because of genetic relatedness, it will pay an organism, in terms of reproductive success, to promote the reproduction of its relatives as well as of itself.

Now, it is important to notice that the degree of relatedness between relatives varies, and so, therefore, does the probability that they will share a gene in common. This means, for example, that whilst there is a 50% chance that full siblings will share a gene in common, there is only a 25% chance that half-siblings will. According to the theory of kin-altruism, therefore, evolution will select a greater degree of altruism between full siblings than half siblings - twice as much in fact.

This theory therefore implies that, irrespective of culture, human beings will be biologically predisposed to be more altruistic towards relatives than non-relatives.

Reciprocal altruism The second form of apparent altruism which can evolve is known as *reciprocal altruism*. This is derived from the fact that individuals may benefit by cooperating with each other reciprocally. If we imagine a simple, but no doubt common situation which would have faced our hunter-gatherer forebears, the evolutionary benefits of reciprocity are not hard to see. Imagine that one individual is particularly successful at hunting one week. Imagine that he kills two large buffalo. Of course, following the principle of kin altruism, we can expect that he will be evolutionarily selected to share this meat with his kin, favouring those to whom he is most closely related. However, assuming either that there is some left over when the needs of his kin have been met, or that there may be even more evolutionarily beneficial strategies open to him, what else might he do?

On the face of it, the suggestion that he should give some of his surplus to an unrelated neighbour, sounds most implausible - like an act of unqualified altruism in fact. However, if he could rely upon this neighbour returning this act of altruism at some future time, then it begins to look more plausible. Indeed, it is possible to see that, provided that the neighbour reciprocates by returning food of the same value as that donated, the actor might stand to gain a net benefit by the exchange. Imagine, for instance, that in the week following the one in which our hunter-gatherer made his apparently altruistic donation to his neighbour, he failed to kill any buffalo, whilst his neighbour this time killed two. In a world of pure selfishness, and in the absence of a donation from relatives, he and his family would starve. If he could call in a favour from his neighbour, however, he could feed his family.

Whilst such reciprocal exchanges can clearly be of benefit to both parties, Robert Trivers has pointed out that it will always pay an individual, in evolutionary terms, to cheat if he can get away with it (Trivers, 1986). Thus Trivers suggests that just as evolution will select for reciprocity, so it will also select for cheating. However, just as cheating will pay, so will the ability to detect cheating in others. Trivers suggests that this situation will create an 'evolutionary arms race' between the evolution of ever more subtle forms of cheating and ever more subtle abilities to detect cheating in others. He goes on to suggest that human beings may possess the innate characteristics

which they do as a result of this evolutionary process: we are expert cheats, but at the same time are expert at detecting cheating in others. He goes so far as to suggest that human beings have evolved the ability to deceive themselves about their true motives, so that they may more effectively deceive others. On this reading, much implicit sociological theorising about human altruism may just be evidence of our basic tendency towards self-deception.

Crude sociobiology versus evolutionary psychology

Sociobiologists such as E.O.Wilson have been criticised on the grounds that their theories make predictions about human behaviour which human beings simply do not exhibit. In particular, it has been pointed out that human beings often seem to exhibit far higher levels of altruism than the theory predicts. Kamikaze pilots, homosexuals and Roman Catholic priests, for example, all appear to forgo some or all of their potential reproductive success. It is therefore difficult to see how modern evolutionary theory could explain their behaviour.

Recently, however, a number of evolutionary writers have pointed out that this criticism does not necessarily invalidate evolutionary theory, because all behaviour is the outcome of an interaction between the individual's genetic make-up and the environment in which they exist. Thus, since human beings evolved in very different environments than those which exist today (specifically as primal hunter-gatherers) then we should not expect their behaviour in modern environments to be evolutionarily adaptive. Instead, we need only assume that we possess inherited *psychological mechanisms* which produced adaptive behaviours in the environments in which we evolved, but which do not necessarily do so in today's environment. This approach is known as *evolutionary psychology*, because it emphasises evolved psychological mechanisms, rather than the actual behaviour of individuals which it recognises to be a product of an interaction between genes and environment.

Such a view has been put forward by Christopher Badcock, who has attempted to synthesise the central insights of modern evolutionary biology with those of Freudian psychoanalysis (Badcock, 1994). Badcock has argued, for example, that the psychological mechanisms which promote much apparently inexplicable group behaviour, and altruism directed at non-kin - camaraderie on the battlefield, nationalism, membership of groups and clubs and so forth - might well result from a psychological process described by Freud as 'identification', which in simple terms amounts to favouring individuals who in some way remind us of ourselves. Badcock points out that identification would probably have produced adaptive behaviour in the primal hunter-gatherer situation because such similarity would most likely have been a reliable indicator of genetic relatedness (Badcock, 1986). Thus, whilst this psychological mechanism undoubtedly produces apparently inexplicable altruism in the modern world, its existence is explained by the advantages it conferred in terms of reproductive success in the past. This approach thus recognises that the environments in which we live change too rapidly for evolution to keep up, and so the current adaptive value of a piece of behaviour should not be taken as an indicator of its evolutionary benefits to those individuals in whom it first evolved.

Evaluation

One of the most powerful objections raised against the work of early sociobiologists such as E.O.Wilson (Wilson, 1975) was that it made predictions about behaviour which human beings simply did not display (Sahlins, 1976). In the minds of many sociologists this still remains their central objection. However, as we have seen, the emergence of evolutionary psychology removes the requirement that modern behaviour displays current adaptive value. Indeed the work of writers such as Trivers and Badcock demonstrates that evolutionary theory in fact predicts a highly complex and subtle human psychology, capable of deception and self-deception.

A second prominent objection to sociobiology is ideological. Many sociologists have objected to it on the grounds that because it seems to suggest that our behaviour is largely the product of our genes, it offers a justification for all manner of self-interested behaviour. Thus some feminists have claimed that the views of sociobiologists on gender roles are a thinly disguised justification for patriarchy, whilst other social scientists have suggested that it seems to justify the individualistic self-interest on which capitalism depends. (For criticisms of sociobiological approaches to gender, see p122; to 'race', see pp86-87).

Whilst these criticisms certainly deserve consideration, they do seem to rest upon the fundamentally mistaken assumption that to demonstrate that some behaviour has a genetic base is the same as condoning it morally. Such a position would in fact be as absurd as saying that because physicians recognise the biological basis of cancer, they necessarily claim that the disease is both unavoidable and morally good! There is of course no necessity for us to condone behaviour simply because it has a genetic base. And indeed, as the insights of evolutionary psychologists show, a common genetic base can in fact produce a very wide range of actual behaviour, much of which can be altruistic.

Sociobiology thus seems to present a considerable challenge to conventional sociological theories, both in the seriousness with which it takes our biological endowment, and the scepticism with which it regards the assumption that we are infinitely culturally malleable.

Activity 11 Whose Offspring?

Item A *Infanticide*

Infanticide - the killing of young - has been observed in a number of species, including langur monkeys. Langur monkeys travel in groups of roughly 10 - 20 adult females and their young, to which is attached a single dominant male. The other males travel in all-male groups, and dominant members of these groups sometimes attempt to displace the dominant male attached to a group of adult females. When such a displacement occurs, the new dominant male often starts to kill dependent offspring. In particular, he tries to kill infants up to about six months of age or older, but begins by concentrating on the youngest. Additionally he often kills infants that are born during the first months after the takeover, but not thereafter.

Adapted from R. Trivers *Social Evolution*, 1985

Langur monkeys with young in India

Item B *Step-parenting*

An interview study of middle class step-parents in Cleveland Ohio, who were not experiencing any particular kind of stress in relation to their step-children, found that only 53% of step-fathers and 25% of step-mothers claimed any 'parental feeling' towards their step-children, and fewer still professed to feel 'love' for them.

An American child living with one or more substitute parents in 1976 was approximately 100 times more likely to be fatally abused than was a child living with its natural parents.

Adapted from C. Badcock *Evolution and Individual Behaviour*, 1991

Questions

1 a) Why, according to evolutionary theory, might a male langur kill dependent offspring when he takes over a group of females?
   b) What behaviour would we expect to see in the mothers of these threatened offspring?
   c) Why should the male kill offspring born during the first few months of the takeover, but not thereafter?

2 a) How might the theory of kin-altruism help to explain the behaviour outlined in Item B?
   b) What explanations, other than those suggested by sociobiology, can you think of for the behaviour of the step-parents?

5.2 Globalisation

At various stages in this chapter we have talked about society and indeed, if pushed to define the subject matter of sociology, many sociologists would say 'modern society'. Society in turn is often visualised as a social system with distinct boundaries separating it from other social systems. And this 'society' is usually equated with the nation state. This is not surprising. For it reflects the nineteenth century origins of sociology when 'nation states become supreme because they won at war, were economically successful and, subsequently, achieved a significant degree of legitimacy in the eyes of their populations and other states' (Held, 1992, p103).

Beyond the nation state There are two problems with picturing the subject matter of sociology in this way. Firstly, human behaviour has never been explicable purely in terms of particular societies or nation states. The influence of major religions, patterns of trade and indeed war and conquest extend well beyond the boundaries of nation states. Secondly, we live in an increasingly 'shrinking' world. In this context, human behaviour is increasingly influenced by global forces. While *globalisation*, in the sense of the growing interconnectedness of societies, has always been a feature of modernity, a number of theorists have suggested that in the last two decades we have entered a qualitatively new phase of globalisation. One of its main features has been described as 'time-space compression', in recognition of the fact that our lives are increasingly, and remarkably quickly, influenced by distant events. David Harvey puts it well: 'As space appears to shrink to a "global" village of telecommunications and a "spaceship earth" of economic and ecological interdependencies - to use just two familiar and everyday images - and as time horizons shorten to the point where the present is all there is, so we have to learn to cope with an overwhelming sense of compression of our spatial and temporal words' (Harvey, 1989, p240).

Let us take each of these images of globalisation in turn. The Live Aid movement of the mid 1980s provides a good example of the way the world 'has come to seem like a village' (Tester, 1995). The movement, founded by the singer Bob Geldof, emerged in order to raise money to relieve an appalling famine in Ethiopia. It culminated in a day long concert, held at venues in Britain and America 3,000 miles apart but linked by satellite into one programme. The mass media was central. For it was television which allowed people in Britain and America to become aware in their living rooms of a famine miles away and it was television which broadcast the concert around the world.

A dramatic illustration of our ecological interdependence on 'spaceship earth' was the explosion in 1986 at the Chernobyl nuclear power station in the former Soviet Republic of Ukraine. The consequences were not foreseeable but were felt as far away as Cumbria. The explosion provides an example of the way globalisation is producing what Ulrich Beck (1992) calls a 'risk society', in which the survival of the planet is threatened by technological developments. While natural hazards such as floods, hurricanes and volcanoes threatened people in the past, the risk environment which now confronts us 'is structured mainly by humanly created risks' (Giddens, 1990, p 111).

Opposing tendencies While there is widespread agreement that we are living through a period of increasing globalisation, there is no agreement about what has brought it about or what it will lead to. Indeed some aspects of globalisation appear contradictory.

In Giddens' words, globalisation does not bring about 'a generalised set of changes acting in a uniform direction, but consists of mutually opposed tendencies' (1990, p64). Here are some examples of these opposed tendencies.

Firstly, cultural homogenisation versus differentiation. Globalisation does encourage cultural homogenisation so that we can now drink Coca Cola at McDonald's, wear jeans and trainers and watch Hollywood films on television across the world. At the same time there is a fascination with difference so that ethnic food, dress and music are also available around the world.

Secondly, old identities versus new identities. Globalisation makes us increasingly aware of cultural differences. For some this may be experienced as a threat to the familiar certainties of the past. Cultural racism and fundamentalism are examples. They can be seen as defensive reactions which attempt to preserve or recreate a perceived past. For others, however, an awareness of other cultures may be interpreted as an opportunity to construct new identities which fuse different cultural traditions.

Thirdly, centralisation versus decentralisation. Globalisation enables organisations to develop which transcend national boundaries. Transnational corporations and the European Union are examples. At the same time it generates a powerful decentralising dynamic as communities seek to control their own fate. Hence the resurgence of nationalism in Eastern Europe with the break up of the Soviet Union.

The effects of globalisation are not only complex but there is also an unevenness with which globalisation has been experienced across space and time. It has quickened up recently but its consequences are not uniform across the globe. 'In the latest form of globalisation, it is still the images, artifacts and identities of Western modernity, produced by the cultural industries of "Western" societies (including Japan) which dominate the global networks' (Hall, 1992, p 305).

Evaluation The concept of globalisation does capture an important phenomenon and it does challenge the idea of society as a well-bounded system. While this means that we need to be highly sceptical of sociological theories which visualise societies as discrete social systems, it does not mean that we should abandon the idea of society. For societies can still exist within the framework of a global society. They are still recognised as societies by their members. And their boundaries are sufficiently clear for sociologists to recognise and study them as social units. (For further discussion and examples of globalisation see pp218-221; 578-580).

Activity 12 Global Risks

Item A *The world's fish*
THE RAPE OF THE OCEANS

Last month a fleet's annual quota of fish was caught in eight minutes. The sea cannot stand it.

The world's fisheries are hurtling towards commercial extinction as hi-tech supertrawlers become ever more efficient at hoovering up their prey. The oceans, covering 70% of the globe, should - and could - adequately meet the needs of humanity without unbalancing the marine ecosystem. But greed, rather than commonsense or conservation, is driving exploitation of the seas.

The problem is that the prizes are still great. Consider the *Estai*, the Spanish trawler at the centre of the current fish war off Newfoundland. When the Canadian gunboat cut the *Estai's* nets and boarded her on 9 March, she had 400 tonnes of fish on board. That catch - which she had been gathering and freezing since last October - would fetch more than £1.5 million had it all been landed intact at her home port.

The rush for riches is both producing incalculable effects on the oceans' health and threatening the future of tens of millions of people worldwide. There are already signs that the switch from 'boom' to 'bust' is well under way. Last month the United Nations Food and Agriculture Organisation (FAO) warned 9 of the world's 17 major fishing grounds had been devastated by over-fishing, with four more under serious threat. The global fish catch, which rose five-fold between 1950 and 1989, has now levelled out at around 100m tonnes a year.

Some fishing fleets are now so efficient that they can

The British trawler 'Ocean Surf'

only fish for a few days or weeks a year before a quota is exhausted. Just last month, the trawler men of British Columbia set sail to catch roe herring - and reached their quota of 770 tonnes for the entire year in a single fishing session, lasting eight minutes.

It is these boats - the pride of large national fleets, such as the Spanish and Japanese - which are moving increasingly into the high seas and, sometimes illegally, into the territorial waters of developing countries, provoking conflicts there with traditional fishermen.

Similarly, South Indian fishermen have clashed repeatedly with foreign supertrawlers that can scoop up 2,000 tonnes in one catch - the equivalent to the collective load of 1,500 traditional boats.

Nobody knows for sure what effect chronic over-fishing will have on other marine wildlife. Just as worrying is the effect on the human beings who rely on fish to stay alive. But for the developing world, the disappearance of commercial fisheries would spell disaster. In Asia alone, a billion people rely on fish as their main source of animal protein. And apart from the spectre of starvation, a fishing crash would cost an enormous number of jobs.

Adapted from *Observer*, 2.4.95

Item B *Chernobyl*

Western governments and nuclear experts have repeatedly urged Ukraine to shut down the nuclear plant at Chernobyl. A fortnight ago - under intense diplomatic pressure following the latest safety reports - Ukraine's Prime Minister, Leonid Kuchma, pledged to do so by the year 2000.

But the cash strapped republic could only act, he said, if Western governments came up with $4.4 billion (£2.75bn) to build a replacement gas fired power station and to shore up the make-shift sarcophagus of concrete - now sporting ominous cracks - which covers the reactor which exploded in 1986.

His stance provoked predictable accusations of blackmail from Western diplomats.

Decontaminating the streets of Chernobyl after the nuclear reactor exploded in 1986.

Yet the Ukraine's dilemma is real - and it provides a stark lesson about the huge sum which a single major nuclear accident can cost the world.

Nine years after the radioactive cloud released from Chernobyl passed over Wales, long-suffering farmers 1,500 miles from the scene of the accident still face controls on their sheep flocks.

In the former Soviet republics of Ukraine and Belarus, which took the brunt of the radiation, 1.3m hectares of land is contaminated, and latest estimates put the final clean-up bill at between $200bn and $600bn (between £1.25bn and £3.75bn).

This figure includes resettlement of 2.5 million refugees living on contaminated land, medical treatment for victims, and the clean-up of the plant and surrounding irradiated countryside.

The trouble is that no matter how we generate energy, we create problems. The burning of coal, gas and oil plays havoc with our atmosphere, just as surely as the abuse of nuclear power devastates the ground.

It is an issue that transcends national borders. Global economic growth needs global energy planning. We do not have that, and there are precious few signs we will ever get it. The human mind seems almost incapable of dealing with the time scales and geography which are required when dealing with nuclear power. Yet we must face up to the issues. The alternative is short term manoeuvring, and long term disaster.

Adapted from *Observer*, 30.4.95

Questions

1 How do these items show time and space becoming compressed in the modern world?

2 Do these items indicate that globalisation is producing an 'environment of risk'?

3 Globalisation demands institutions for global government. Discuss with reference to Items A and B.

5.3 Postmodernism

Postmodernism is currently fashionable. The term is used, however, in a variety of bewildering ways and is difficult to pin down. Initially employed to describe a postwar movement, it has since been extended to depict changes in the arts and other cultural forms and most recently to characterise a critique of the Enlightenment 'project'. The challenge which postmodernism poses for sociological theory flows predominantly from this critique. For sociology shares the Enlightenment belief that human beings are not only capable of achieving a rational understanding of social reality but can also use their understanding to create a more rational and fair society. It is just this belief which one version of postmodernism challenges.

Postmodernism and architecture

Modernism in architecture came to fruition in the 1920s with a distinct mission - to create buildings according to rational principles. For advocates of this view, the machine epitomised such rationality, with Le Corbusier going as far as to argue that architecture should be concerned with producing 'machines for modern living'. Modernism met a positive reception in the postwar period, given the need for urban renewal. Planning became the order of the day, with the new materials of steel, concrete and glass being used to create a built environment with no ornamental frills. Functional high rise tower blocks became a common feature of the urban landscape and a monument to modernism. By the 1970s, however, such buildings were seen not so much as a celebration of advanced technology but as soulless. Postmodernism was born and the 'glass towers, concrete blocks and steel slabs that seemed set fair to steam roller over every urban landscape... have progressively given way to ornamental tower blocks, imitation medieval squares and fishing villages, custom designed or vernacular housing, renovated factories and warehouses, and rehabilitation landscapes of all kinds' (Harvey, 1989, p40). For postmodernism, urban environments are necessarily fragmented containing buildings from different periods. The search for an overarching style in the design of new buildings is abandoned. Styles from different historical periods are mixed and surfaces celebrated, with playful ornamentation replacing rational functionality. In the process the disdain expressed by the modernists towards vernacular architecture of places like Las Vegas is completely rejected. Anything goes.

Postmodernism and the arts

Modernism does not just refer to a movement in architecture. It has often been used 'to refer to the set of artistic, musical, literary, more generally aesthetic moments that emerged in Europe in the 1880s, flourished before and after the First World War and became institutionalised in the academies and art galleries of post-Second World War Europe and America' (Boyne and Rattansi, 1990, p7). Take, for example, artistic movements. 'Modernism struggled to penetrate the "deeper" reality to represent what has been made invisible for the convention bound eye. To attain such "better", correct, true representation, they sought the guidance of science: that recognised authority on what reality is really like. Thus the impressionists took inspiration (and legitimacy for their practices) from optics, cubists from relativity theory, surrealists from psychoanalysis. Contemporary artists, on the contrary, would overtly abandon all pretension, and denigrate all intention, of representation' (Bauman, 1992, p28). Pop artists such as Andy Warhol, who is renowned for his prints of famous popular cultural icons like Marilyn Monroe and everyday consumer items like Coca Cola bottles, recognise that their art has no such depth. In Warhol's words, 'There's nothing behind it' (quoted in Hebdidge, 1988, p35).

The condition of postmodernity

Changes in architectural and artistic styles, although interesting, are not sociologically very significant in themselves. What some writers would argue, however, is that the developments we have been pointing to indicate the advent of a new postmodern culture and the arrival of a new social condition of postmodernity. The rejection by architects of the overriding style of modernism illustrates widespread scepticism towards all general theories. And the abandonment by artists of any attempt to represent reality reflects common doubts about what the images all around us mean. The two writers who have been most influential in presenting the postmodern condition as one marked on the one hand by a crisis in the status of knowledge and on the other hand by a crisis of representation are Lyotard and Baudrillard respectively.

Lyotard Knowledge in the modern era meant science. Philosophers were, however, unable to agree upon the foundations for such knowledge. Science therefore needed to be justified in terms of a grand story or *metanarrative*. For the Enlightenment, science was justified on the grounds that it would lead to human emancipation. In view of the complicity of science in creating, for example, weapons of indiscriminate mass destruction, people are now sceptical towards this metanarrative and the status of science has consequently been questioned. And what is true of this metanarrative is true of others. None can be 'objectively' proved or rejected and so we need to be sceptical towards all metanarratives. Hence it is that Lyotard defines the condition of postmodernity as 'incredulity towards metanarratives' (Lyotard, 1992, p356).

This is not to say that knowledge is unimportant. We live in a post-industrial society where in fact it is central. Knowledge has, however, fragmented into a series of 'language games' where the rules governing what counts as knowledge differ. The central concern is 'performativity', whether the information produced is efficient and saleable rather than of intrinsic value or serving some human purpose. Lyotard welcomes the demise of metanarratives and the emergence of a plurality of language games. Grand stories, with their privileged truth to tell, rode roughshod over many groups and, in the case of Marxism, led to totalitarianism. In the postmodern era there is a chance to hear the voices of diverse groups previously on the margins, such as women and ethnic minorities.

Baudrillard Baudrillard agrees with Lyotard that we now live in a post-industrial society. His emphasis, however, is different and centres on the production and consumption of signs. Baudrillard's view is that although at one stage signs were a 'reflection of a basic reality' they now often 'bear no relation to any reality whatsoever' (Poster, 1988, p170). Such signs are known as 'simulations' and are characteristic of the images we see on our television screens, when stories and items that have no meaningful or logical connection to each other are juxtaposed. Baudrillard argues that news reporting often involves simulation. 'Watergate' for example was reported as a scandal to conceal the fact that political corruption is rife. Sometimes simulations can be experienced as more real that reality. This is the 'hyperreal' where, for example, people write to characters in soap operas. John Storey gives a good example : 'The riots, following the acquittal of the four Los Angeles police officers captured on video physically assaulting the black motorist Rodney King, were headlined in two British newspapers as "LA Lawless", and in another as "LA War"; the story anchored not by historical reference to similar disturbances in Watts Los Angeles in 1965, or to the implications of the words - "No justice, no peace" - chanted by demonstrators during the riots; the editors chose instead to locate the story within the fictional world of the American television series *LA Law*. Baudrillard calls this "the dissolution of TV into life, the dissolution of life into TV" '(Storey, 1993, p63).

Baudrillard's response to this situation where image and reality can no longer be distinguished is ambivalent. At times he suggests that we live in a society where we are able to construct our own identities in the process of consumption. Clothes and other items of consumption are not only material objects but also are signs which have meaning. By picking and mixing appropriate images we can distinguish ourselves from others. At other times he suggests the best we can do is to enjoy the meaningless spectacle produced for us and delight in the sensuous pleasure which images can offer us.

Postmodern theory and social change

The work of Lyotard, Baudrillard and other postmodern theorists has been stimulating in raising new questions about social change. Are we witnessing a shift to a new postmodern culture? Have Lyotard and Baudrillard correctly identified the central features of this new culture? Is it true that people increasingly find general theories implausible and are sceptical towards the old political philosophies of liberalism, socialism and social democracy? Do we live in an era where media images are so pervasive that we find it increasingly difficult to distinguish what is real? Does the advent of a postmodern culture signify a shift towards a new social condition of postmodernity? Have Lyotard and Baudrillard correctly identified the central features of this new condition? Is it true that we now live in a post-industrial society? Is this a society which allows an increasing diversity of lifestyles to flourish? Is it one where we have much greater freedom to construct our own individual and collective identities, or one which witnesses an increasing fragmentation of our identities? These questions , which were initially raised by postmodern theorists, are central to much contemporary sociology and have stimulated other theorists, including Marxists such as Jameson and Harvey, to develop their theories in order to account for the fact that we are clearly living through an era of massive social change (Thompson, 1992).

Postmodernism and the Enlightenment

The challenge, which postmodernism poses for sociological theory generally, results from its rejection of the Enlightenment 'project' - the promise which underpinned the emergence of sociology that human beings could use their reason to produce knowledge of the social world and on that basis promote human progress. Three central arguments have been put forward.

The first is known as *anti-foundationalism*. The search by philosophers for indisputable foundations to knowledge has been a failure. There are no general criteria which enable us to distinguish truth and falsity. We therefore have to accept that different communities will use different criteria to distinguish truth and falsity. What's more these communities will look at the world differently. For we are the subjects of language and other sign systems and can't step outside them to discover what things really mean. In short there is absolutely nothing to guarantee what is true or what things mean.

The second argument is known as *anti-totalisation*. In view of the fact that there are no indisputable foundations to knowledge or firm bases to meaning, it is extremely arrogant of us to put forward general theories which pretend to reveal *the* truth or *the* meaning of things. We need to abandon attempts to produce theories which seek to depict the structure and dynamics of society as a whole and tolerate the coexistence of a diversity of more limited theories.

The third argument is known as *anti-utopianism*. In practice, knowledge has not produced the utopia of human emancipation, but has been used to impose one truth and one meaning on others. Knowledge has not so much provided us with the power to do things that we could not otherwise do, as allowed some groups to exert power over others.

These arguments cannot be dismissed lightly. Firstly, we cannot attain certainty over questions of truth and meaning. Secondly, general theories which claim to reveal the inevitable development of society are flawed. There is no justification for believing that history has a purpose, or that we can predict the future. Thirdly, knowledge has often been used by Western societies to dominate others.

Evaluation

The Enlightenment project, and with it the possibility of sociological theory, cannot be so easily dismissed.

Firstly, the fact that there are no indispensable foundations to knowledge and meaning does not mean that there are no general criteria of truth and that there is not a connection between sign systems and the world. To presume otherwise is to fall into the trap of relativism (see p647). Presumably the postmodern theorists believe that what they say is meaningful and true or otherwise they would not bother to write books.

Secondly, the fact that different communities have different notions of what is true and what things mean does not mean that we should abandon the search for general theories which seek to show how they are interrelated. Indeed, somewhat inconsistently, postmodern theorists do provide such general theories.

Thirdly, the fact that reason has been used to dominate people does not mean that it did not play a progressive role in the past in combating 'the relative blinkeredness and backwardness of the epoch of pre-modernity' (McClennan, 1992, p334), and that we should abandon the Enlightenment ideal that knowledge might further human emancipation. The arguments of the postmodernist theories which challenge the very possibility of sociological theory are unconvincing.

Summary

1 Sociobiology challenges the view that culture rather than biology is more significant in the explanation of human behaviour.

2 Globalisation theorists challenge the view, that the subject matter of sociology - 'society' - is a social system with distinct boundaries.

3 Postmodernism challenges the view that it is possible to construct general sociological theories.

Activity 13 Postmodern Identities

Item A *Picking and mixing identities*

Item B *Changing identities*

The more social life becomes mediated by the global marketing of styles, places and images, by international travel, and by globally networked media images and communications systems, the more identities become detached - disembedded - from specific times, places, histories and traditions, and appear 'free-floating'. We are confronted by a range of different identities, each appealing to us, or rather to different parts of ourselves, from which it seems possible to choose. It is the spread of consumerism, whether as reality or dream, which has contributed to this 'cultural supermarket' effect.

Adapted from S. Hall 'The Question of Cultural Identity' in S. Hall et al (eds) *Modernity and its Futures*, 1992, p 303

Questions

1 Look at the pictures in Item A. How do these suggest that we can pick and mix our identities? What limits are evident to the choices we can make?

2 Read Item B. Why do some postmodernists believe that we have more freedom now to construct our own identities?

References

Althusser, L. *Lenin and Philosophy and Other Essays* (New Left Books, London, 1971)

Badcock, C. *The Problem of Altruism* (Basil Blackwell, Oxford, 1986)

Badcock, C. *Evolution and Individual Behaviour* (Basil Blackwell, Oxford, 1991)

Badcock, C. *PsychoDarwinism: The New Synthesis of Darwin and Freud* (Harper Collins, London, 1994)

Barthes, R. *Mythologies* (Paladin, London, 1973)

Bauman, Z. *Intimations of Postmodernity* (Routledge, London, 1992)

Beck, U. *Risk Society: Towards a New Modernity* (Sage, London 1992)

Bottomore, T. and Rubel, M. *Karl Marx : Selected Writings* (Penguin, Harmondsworth 1961)

Boyne, R. and Rattansi, A. (eds) *Postmodernism and Society* (Macmillan, London, 1990)

Bronner, S. E. and Kellner, D. M. (eds) *Critical Theory and Society* (Routledge, London, 1989)

Cohen, P. *Modern Social Theory* (Heinemann, London, 1968)

Craib, I. *Modern Social Theory* (Harvester Wheatsheaf, London, 1984)

Craib, I. *Anthony Giddens* (Routledge, London 1992)

Dunthorne, H. *The Enlightenment* (The Historical Association, London, 1991)

Durkheim, E. *The Division of Labour in Society* (The Free Press, New York, 1933)

Durkheim, E. *Suicide: A Study in Sociology* (Routledge and Kegan Paul, London, 1952)

Durkheim, E. *The Rules of Sociological Method* (The Free Press, New York, 1964)

Garfinkel, H. *Studies in Ethnomethodology* (Prentice-Hall, Englewood Cliffs, 1967)

Gay, P. *The Enlightenment : An Interpretation Vol 2 : The Science of Freedom* (Wildwood House, London, 1973)

Giddens, A. 'Jürgen Habermas' in Q. Skinner (ed) *The Return of Grand Theory in the Human Sciences* (Cambridge University Press, Cambridge, 1985)

Giddens, A. *The Consequences of Modernity* (Polity, Cambridge, 1990)

Goffman, E. *The Presentation of Self in Everyday Life* (Penguin, Harmondsworth, 1959)

Goffman, E. *Asylums* (Penguin, Harmondsworth, 1968)

Gramsci, A. *Selections from the Prison Notebooks* (Lawrence and Wishart, London, 1971)

Hall, S. 'The Question of Cultural Identity' in S. Hall et al (eds) *Modernity and its Futures* (Polity, Cambridge 1992)

Hamilton, P. 'The Enlightenment and the Birth of Social Science' in S. Hall and B. Gieben (eds), *Formations of Modernity* (Polity, Cambridge, 1992)

Haralambos, M. and Holborn, M. *Sociology: Themes and Perspectives* 4th edition (Collins Educational, London, 1995)

Harvey, D. *The Condition of Postmodernity* (Blackwell, Oxford, 1989)

Hebdidge, D. *Hiding in the Light* (Routledge, London, 1988)

Held, D. 'The Development of the Modern State' in S. Hall and B. Gieben (eds) *Formations of Modernity* (Polity, Cambridge 1992)

Heritage, J. *Garfinkel and Ethnomethodology* (Polity Press, Cambridge, 1984)

Jones, P. *Studying Society: Sociological Theories and Research Practices* (Collins Educational, London, 1993)

Layder, D. *Understanding Social Theory* (Sage, London, 1994)

Lee, D. and Newby, H. *The Problem of Sociology* (Hutchinson, London, 1983)

Lévi-Strauss, C. 'The Structural Study of Myth' in W. A. Lessa and E. Z. Vogt (eds) *Reader in Comparative Religion,* second edition (Harper & Row, New York, 1965)

Lyotard, J. F. 'Abandoning the Metanarratives of Modernity' in S. Hall et al (eds) *Modernity and its Futures* (Polity, Cambridge, 1992)

McClennan, G. 'The Enlightenment Project Revisited' in S. Hall et al (eds) *Modernity and its Futures* (Polity, Cambridge, 1992)

McGrew, A. 'A Global Society?' in S Hall et al (eds) *Modernity and its Futures* (Polity, Cambridge 1992)

Marshall, G. (ed) *The Concise Oxford Dictionary of Sociology* (Oxford University Press, Oxford, 1994)

Mead. G. H. *Mind, Self and Society* (University of Chicago Press, Chicago, 1934)

Nisbet, R. *The Sociological Tradition* (Heinemann, London, 1967)

Parsons, T. *The Social System* (The Free Press, New York, 1951)

Poster, M. (ed) *Jean Baudrillard : Selected Writings* (Polity, Cambridge, 1988)

Sahlins, M. *The Use and Abuse of Biology* (Tavistock, London, 1976)

Smart, B. *Modern Conditions, Postmodern Controversies* (Routledge, London, 1992)

Storey, J. *An Introductory Guide to Cultural Theory and Popular Culture* (Harvester Wheatsheaf, London, 1993)

Tester, K. 'Postmodernism' in M Haralambos (ed) *Developments in Sociology* vol 11 (Causeway Press, Ormskirk, 1995)

Thompson, K. 'Social Pluralism and Postmodernity' in S. Hall et al (eds) *Modernity and its Futures* (Polity, Cambridge, 1992)

Trivers, R. *Social Evolution* (Benjamin Cummings, Menlo Park, 1985)

Weber, M. *The Protestant Ethic and the Spirit of Capitalism* (Charles Scribner's Sons, New York, 1958)

Wilson, E. O. *Sociobiology: The New Synthesis* (Harvard University Press, Cambridge, Mass., 1975)

Zeitlin, I. *Ideology and Social Theory* (The Free Press, Glencoe Illinois, 1971)

Author Index

Abbott, P. 144, 146
Abel-Smith, B. 183
Abercrombie, N. 53, 55, 60
Abrams, M. 410
Abrams, P. 397
Acker, J. 143
Adorno, T.W. 673
Aglietta, M. 335
Ainley, P. 283
Akhtar, P. 556-7
Albrow, M. 360
Alexander, S. 121
Allan, G. 160, 249, 261, 263
Allport, G. 75
Allsopp, J.G. 227
Althusser, L. 196, 288, 674-5
Amin, K. 84, 111-12
Amos, V. 132
Anderton, A. 324
Anderson, B 387, 560
Anderson, D. 182
Anderson, M. 243, 245-7, 268
Anderson, R.J. 33
Anthias, F. 119, 131
Arber, S. 142, 144, 613
Archer, M. 689
Arensberg, G.M. 245
Aries, P. 409
Ashton, D. 346
Ashton, P. 173-4
Atkinson, J. 331, 335-6, 338, 686
Atkinson, J.M. 470, 642-3

Bachrach, P. 193
Backett, K.C. 242-3
Badcock, C. 690-3
Bagehot, W. 222
Bainbridge, S. 525, 527
Baker, M. 351
Bales, R.F. 237
Balint, M. 438
Ballard, R. 70, 256
Banton, M. 66-8, 75, 92, 98
Baratz, M. 193
Barker, D.J.P. 448
Barker, E. 524, 633-4
Barker, M. 73, 77
Barnett, A. 594
Barr, A. 37
Barrett, M. 130, 132, 157
Barron, R. 136
Barrow, J. 256
Barthes, R. 683-4
Baudrillard, J. 696-7
Bauman, Z. 696
Bazen, S. 333
Beackon, D. 91
Beard, H. 68
Beattie, G. 387, 398
Bechofer, F. 261, 326
Beck, U. 693
Becker, H.S. 291, 301, 476, 619, 646, 648
Beechey, V. 134, 329-31
Bell, C. 250, 262, 350
Bell, D. 56, 218, 320, 332-3
Bellah, R. 498
Bem, S. 123
Ben-Tovim, G. 107
Ben-Yehuda, N. 475

Bensman, J. 391
Benston, M. 239
Bentham, J. 382
Benyon, J. 291, 537
Beral, V. 446
Beresford, P. 51, 53
Berger, B. 240, 508
Berger, J. 630
Berger, P. 2-4, 15, 34, 240, 242, 507-8, 526, 572
Berkman, L. 447-8
Berle, A.A. 53, 322
Bernstein, B. 297
Beteille, A. 26
Beynon, H. 326, 340, 371, 377
Bhachu, P. 78, 112, 131-2, 256, 406-7
Bhaskar, R. 638
Bhavnani, K. 132
Bird, C. 300
Bird, F. 524
Birnbaum, N. 502
Bittner, E. 366
Blaikie, N. 639
Blau, P.M. 360, 362-3, 372
Blauner, R. 95, 325-6, 328
Blaxter, M. 446-7
Bleier, R. 86
Blumer, H. 475, 642, 678-9, 681
Bly, R. 150
Boden, D. 221
Bonnerjea, L. 249, 255-6
Bonnett, K. 219
Booth, M. 446
Bornat, J. 403
Bott, C. 391, 395
Bott, E. 259
Bottomley, A.K. 461
Bottomore, T. 197, 206, 658-60
Boudon, R. 297
Bourdieu, P. 297
Bourne, J. 119, 314-15
Bourne, R. 555
Bowles, S. 288-9
Boyd, W. 682
Boyne, R. 696
Bradley, I. 527
Braham, P. 353-4
Brandt, W. 568
Braverman, H. 55, 328-9, 332, 334, 343, 375-6
Brecht, B. 654
Breen, R. 28, 30, 39
Bremner, C. 302
Brenner, M.H. 350
Breslow, L. 447-8
Brett, E.A. 593
Britten, N. 143
Brittan, S. 200, 204
Broadbent, P. 399
Brockington, R. 283
Bronner, S.E. 674
Brown, C. 81, 84, 131, 179
Brown, D. 517
Brown, G.W. 451
Brownmiller, S. 126
Bruce, S. 522, 615, 617
Bruegel, I. 240
Brummer, A. 531
Bryan, B. 129-30, 134
Bryant, A. 521, 523
Budge, I. 207
Bulmer, M. 391, 397

Burch, M. 216
Burgess, R.G. 302, 307
Burgoyne, J. 252
Burns, T. 362-3, 372-3
Burrell, G. 383
Buswell, C. 283
Butler, D. 209
Butler, D.E. 222
Butler, G.A. 452
Butterworth, E. 185
Bygott, D. 80
Byrne, P.S. 439
Byson, L 169

Calvin, J. 504-5, 630
Campbell, B. 119, 125, 394, 403
Campbell, C. 524
Campbell, N. 484
Carby, H. 119, 130, 240
Carlen, P. 484
Carmichael, S. 84, 95
Carrigan, T. 149
Carrington, B. 315
Carroll, V. 234
Carson, G. 102
Cartwright, A. 439
Cartwright, F.F. 427
Carver, R. 603, 606
Cashmore, E. 61, 75, 78, 88, 112, 120, 217
Castells, M. 412-13
Castles, S. 107
Cerf, C. 68
Chagnon, N. 620
Chalfont, H.P. 437
Chambliss, W.J. 18
Chapman, T. 145-6
Cherlin, A. 251
Chester, R. 253, 267, 270
Chignell, H. 135
Christie, N. 458
Cicourel, A.V. 19, 22, 476, 626, 633
Clairborne, L. 95
Clark, D. 242-3, 252
Clark, S. 453
Clarke, J. 43, 352, 355, 399, 411, 473
Clarke, R. 488
Clatterbaugh, K. 124, 150
Cleaver, E. 96
Clegg, H.A. 369
Clegg, S. 378-9
Clinard, M. 468
Cloward, R. 471-2
Clutterbuck, D. 377
Coates, D. 211-12
Coates, K. 183, 185, 343
Cobb, J. 38
Cockburn, A. 61, 64, 576, 604
Cockburn, C. 343, 399
Cohen, A. 387, 409, 415, 471-4
Cohen, P. 283, 666
Cohen, R. 39, 253, 350-1
Cohen, S. 383, 478, 551
Cohn, N. 516
Cole, W.O. 498
Coleman, C.A. 461
Coleman, J. 369
Collard, J. 350
Comte, A. 570, 636, 646, 661, 668
Cooper, J. 28
Cooper, L. 218

Coote, A. 119, 125
Cornwell, J. 393, 403-4
Cosin, B.R. 301
Cotgrove, S. 30
Cotton, I. 520
Coulson, M. 132
Coward, R. 433
Craib, I. 673, 675, 689
Crawford, A. 489
Crenson, M. 195
Crewe, I. 43, 58, 222-4, 226-7, 537, 549-50
Critcher, C. 352, 355, 413
Croal, H. 475
Crompton, R. 30-31, 36, 49-50, 55 135, 137-8, 331
Crossman, R.H.S. 631
Cumberbatch, G. 629
Cumming, E. 410
Curtice, J. 225, 227, 229
Curtis, S.J. 274

Dahl, R. 193, 195, 199, 200, 207
Dahrendorf, R. 53, 61-2, 103-4, 322, 339
Dahya, B. 87
Dale, A. 142, 144
Dale, B. 138
Dale, J. 57, 117-18, 134, 138
Dalrymple, T. 422
Dalrymple, W. 27
Daly, M. 122
Daniel, W.W. 81, 339-40
Darwin, C. 689-90
Davidson, N. 39, 186, 443
Davies, M. 204
Davies, N. 462
Davis, E. 189
Davis, K. 37-8, 262, 468, 647
Davis, H. 29
Dawkins, R. 86
Day, G. 391, 414
de Mello, A. 36
Deem, R. 318, 352, 403
Deer, B. 510
Delamont, S. 366
Delphy, C. 144
Denney, D. 104
Dennis, N. 268, 394, 399, 402, 487
Denscombe, M. 294, 348, 626
Denver, D. 223-4, 226, 228
Denzin, N.K. 632
Devine, F. 249, 262, 396-7
Dex, S. 144
Dickinson, J. 459
Dickson, W.J. 371, 375
Ditton, J. 621
Djilas, M. 367
Dobash, Rebecca 240-41, 618
Dobash, Russell 240-41, 618
Donaldson, L. 374
Donnison, D. 172
Douglas, J.D. 470
Douglas, J.W.B. 295, 625
Douglass, F. 100
Downes, D. 455, 468, 471-2, 474, 483, 490
Doyle, C. 453
Drew, D. 311
Driver, G. 70, 256
Dubos, R. 421
Dunleavy, P. 43, 226
Dunthorne, H. 656
Durkheim, E. 18, 242, 287, 319, 389, 468-70, 493-5, 498, 500-1, 504, 525, 527, 570, 636, 638, 640, 643, 646, 653, 656, 661-6, 668-9, 671, 678, 683, 688

Durkin, K. 556-7
Dutton, B. 550, 556-7
Dworkin, A. 125

Eaton, M. 484
Edgell, S. 261, 264
Edholm, F. 233
Edwards, P.K. 341
Edwards, R. 329
Ehrenreich, B. 148
Eichler, M. 644-5
Eisenstadt, S. 409
Eldridge, J. 524, 539, 552, 555
Elias, N. 352
Elliott, B. 54-5
Ely, P. 104
Engels, F. 209-10, 238-40, 500-2
Erdos, J. 487
Eriksen, T. 387
Esland, G. 57
Etzioni, A. 56, 138, 388, 393
Eversley, D. 255-6
Eysenck, H.J. 294, 467, 563

Fagin, L. 349-50
Fallon, I. 53
Faludi, S. 120
Farrell, W. 152
Featherstone, M. 410
Ferriman, A. 449
Festinger, L. 621
Field, F. 62-3, 104, 182, 489
Field, S. 104
Fielding, N. 42, 189, 618-9, 623
Finch, J. 160, 162, 249, 263, 404
Finer, M. 252
Finn, D. 283
Firestone, S. 119
Fitzgerald, M. 227
Fitzpatrick, S. 368
Fleming, J. 149
Fletcher, D. 442
Fletcher, R. 236-7, 240, 265, 268
Forrest, R. 168
Forsdahl, A. 448
Fortes, M. 234
Foster, P. 57, 117-18, 134
Foster-Carter, A. 567, 578-9, 596
Foucault, M. 381-3
Frank, A.G. 575, 595
Frankenberg, R. 246
Franklin, B. 546-8
Fransella, F. 196
Frayman, H. 175-6
Frazer, E. 141
Freidan, B. 117, 120
Freidson, E. 434
French, J. 307
Freud, S. 691
Friedman, A. 329, 376
Friedman, M. 156, 161, 345
Frith, S. 409, 473-4
Frost, K. 196
Fryer, P. 67, 71, 98
Fukuyama, F. 29
Fuller, M. 129

Gabriel, J. 107
Galbraith, J.K. 322
Gallagher, M. 555
Gallie, D. 327
Gans, H. 412, 416-17
Garber, J. 409
Garfinkel, H. 365, 685-7
Garland, D. 383, 458, 466

Garrett, S. 139
Gathorne-Hardy, J. 125
Gavron, H. 139, 403
Gay, P. 656
George, V. 155
Geraghty, C. 398, 402
Gershuny, J.I. 317, 332-3
Giddens, A. 33, 46, 50-51, 194, 201, 207-8, 218-21, 353, 418, 455, 660, 674, 688-9, 693
Giddy, D. 274
Gilbert, G. 144
Gilder, G. 150
Giles-Sim, J. 617
Gillborn, D. 311-14
Gillis, J. 265
Gilpin, R. 221
Gilroy, P. 69-70, 77-8, 94, 99, 107, 217, 405
Ginsberg, N. 158
Gintis, H. 288-9
Gittins, D. 251
Glanvill, R. 417
Glasgow, D. 103
Glass, D.V. 48
Glasser, R. 398
Glendinning, C. 179
Glyn, A. 345
Goddard-Spear, M. 306
Goffman, E. 17, 22, 160, 380-1, 383, 440, 477, 620, 623, 679-81, 688
Gold, M. 605
Goldberg, E. 446
Goldberg, S. 122
Goldthorpe, J.H. 31, 33, 43-4, 48-50, 58-9, 143, 145-6, 248-9, 261, 326-7, 340, 396
Goode, E. 475
Goode, W. 150, 247, 267-8
Goodman, A. 188
Gordon, P. 72, 79, 81-2, 85, 94
Gouldner, A.W. 340, 361-4, 372, 646-7, 687
Graham, H. 404, 444
Gramsci, A. 34, 60, 210-12, 502-3, 673
Grant, M. 536, 551, 555
Grant, W. 202
Green, A. 110-12
Green, E. 353, 403
Green, D.G. 168
Greer, G. 117, 125
Griffin, C. 126, 137
Griffin, J.H. 80, 620, 635
Grigg, D. 573
Gross, R.D. 609-10
Groves, D. 160, 404
Gunter, B. 560-1

Habermas, J. 673
Hadfield, G. 32, 40, 45-6
Hakim, C. 332
Hall, C. 246, 258
Hall, E. 8-9
Hall, P. 54
Hall, R.H. 372
Hall, S. 69, 77-8, 81, 88, 107, 130, 405, 418, 479, 482, 487, 557, 657, 664, 694, 699
Halmos, P. 57
Halsey, A.H. 103, 186, 294-6
Hamilton, C. 84
Hamilton, P. 95, 655-6
Handy, C. 377
Handy, L.J. 339
Hannah, L. 323
Hansard Society 138
Haralambos, M. 95, 162, 224, 618, 621,

635, 668
Harbury, C.D. 51, 207
Hargreaves, D.H. 291, 300-1, 622
Harloe, M. 168
Harris, C. 249
Harris, N. 572-3
Harris, T. 451
Harrison, J. 345
Harrison, P. 399, 400, 413, 583, 590, 595, 600-1
Harrison, T. 494
Hart, N. 268, 427, 431, 434, 436, 439-40, 613
Hartley, J.F. 349
Hartmann, P. 558
Hartnett, O. 124
Harvey, D. 219, 412, 693, 696-7
Harwood, J. 68
Haskey, J. 39, 72-3, 132, 267-8
Hatcher, R. 81
Hay, D. 526
Hayek, F.A. 155
Healey, P. 417
Hearn, J. 121, 148
Heath, A. 143, 225-6, 228-9, 279, 294-6, 299
Hebdidge, D. 473, 696
Hebron, S. 353
Hegel, A.W.F. 658
Heidensohn, F. 455, 474, 484-5
Held, D. 220, 657, 693
Helman, C.G. 424-5, 429-30, 438
Henry, W. 410
Hepworth, M. 410
Herberg, W. 529-30
Heritage, J. 686
Hewitt, C.J. 201
Hickson, D. 372
Hillery, G. 386-7
Himmelweit, H.T. 223
Hiro, D. 87
Hitchens, D.M.W. 51
Hobbes, T. 669
Hobsbawm, E.S. 58, 345
Hoebel, E.A. 10
Hoggart, R. 394-5, 402
Holborn, M. 224, 668
Holdaway, S. 461-2
Holdsworth, A. 139
Hollender, M.H. 439
Holman, R. 185
Holme, A. 397
Hoogvelt, A. 574
Horkheimer, M. 673
Hornsby-Smith, M. 622
Horton, D. 401
Howitt, D. 559
Hudson, B. 486
Humphreys, L. 621
Humphries, J. 259
Hunt, S. 547-8
Husband, C. 558
Husserl, E. 685
Hutton, W. 52, 61
Hyman, R. 339-42

Ignatieff, M. 408
Illich, I. 57, 422
Illsley, R. 446
Ineichen, B. 269
Inglehart, R. 219

Jackson, M. 369
Jacobson, L. 299
Jacques, M. 29, 45
Jahoda, M. 349

Jeffcoate, R. 70, 83
Jenkins, C. 345
Jenkins, J. 503
Jenkins, P. 457
Jenkins, R. 110, 112
Jenkins, S. 285
Jenkins, S.P. 188
Jerrome, D. 411
Jessop, B. 28
Jewson, N. 405-6, 416
Johnson, D. 280
Johnson, M. 410
Johnson, N. 159, 162
Johnson, P. 79
Johnson, T. 439
Johnston, R.J. 227
Jones, G. 55, 331
Jones, K. 404
Jones, P. 655
Jones, T. 83-4, 112, 129, 309, 489
Jowell, R. 225, 229, 527, 614, 618
Jury, L. 448

Kalton, G. 612
Kaluzynska, E. 646
Katz, E. 538
Kaufert, J.M. 438, 441
Kavanagh, D. 209
Kealey, T. 281
Keesing, R.M. 234
Keil, C. 95
Keller, P. 614
Kelley, M.R. 336
Kellner, D.M. 674
Kellner, H. 242, 508
Kelly, J. 343
Kennedy, D. 510
Kennon, A. 215
Kerr, C. 339
Kerr, J. 479
Kershaw, A. 112
Keynes, J.M. 345
Keys, D. 576
Kimball, S.T. 245
Kincaid, J.C. 184, 647
King, A. 224
Kingdom, J. 393
Kitch, M.J. 506
Kitching, G.N. 577
Kitzinger, J. 628
Klein, J. 260
Knight, J. 676
Kosack, G. 107
Krausz, E. 87
Kuhn, T.S. 638
Kurtz, I. 128, 149
Kurtz, R.A. 437

Labov, W. 298
Lacey, C. 300
Lakatos, I. 638
Lambert, J. 74
Land, H. 157, 246, 258-9, 263
Lansley, S. 174
Lapping, B. 100
Laslett, P. 245, 247, 252
Lawless, P. 400
Layder, D. 612, 617, 619, 630, 647-8, 674
Layton-Henry, Z. 85, 216, 486
Lazarfield, P.F. 349, 538
Le Grand, J. 186-7
Le Play, F. 245
Lea, J. 104, 217, 462, 483, 489-90
Leach, E. 251
Lee, C. 151

Lee, D. 283, 655
Lee, G. 104
Leech, K. 409
Lees, S. 127, 141, 305-6
Lemert, E.M. 476
Lenin, V.I. 367-8
Leonard, D. 144
Levi, M. 462
Lévi-Strauss, C. 683
Lewis, O. 182-3, 622
Lewis, R. 77, 82
Liberty, M. 10, 624
Liebow, E. 620
Linhart, R. 327
Lipset, S.M. 369
Lister, R. 104
Little, M. 349-50
Littler, C. 376
Litwak, E. 249
Livingstone, J. 119
Lockwood, D. 55, 144, 248-9, 261, 326, 671
Lombroso, C. 467
Long, B.E. 439
Long Lance, Chief Buffalo Child 649
Longley, C. 503
Lowe, R. 274
Lowie, R.H. 10
Lucas, D. 168
Lukes, S. 193-4, 199, 200, 261
Lupton, T. 207
Lyotard, J.F. 696-7

Macdonald, K. 630, 633
MacIntyre, S. 446-7
Mack, J. 174
Madge, N. 183
Maduro, O. 502-3, 514
Maguire, M. 461-5
Maguire, S. 409
Makeba, M. 102
Malcolm X 3, 292
Malinowski, B. 497, 620, 668
Mama, A. 131
Mandel, E. 156, 333
Mangin, W. 182
Mankoff, M. 18
Mann, M. 194
Mann, N. 90
Marcuse, H. 673
Marmot, M.G. 446-7
Mars, G. 621
Marsh, D. 200
Marsh, P. 337
Marshall, G. 30, 43-4, 55-6, 59-60, 63, 142-3, 145, 147, 396, 684
Marshall, T.H. 155,
Marsland, D. 35, 156, 182, 185
Martin, D. 522, 527
Martin, J. 134, 139, 146, 262
Martin, P. 28
Martin, R. 369
Marx, K. 16, 33-6, 59, 61, 209-10, 238-9, 288, 319, 322, 325, 328, 345, 367-8, 375, 377, 389, 500-2, 504-5, 525, 541, 572, 574-5, 637, 646-7, 653, 655-60, 663-4, 668, 672-4, 683, 688
Mason, J. 249
Massey, D. 414, 418
Matza, D. 474
Maung, N.A. 461
Mayhew, P. 461-5, 488
Maynard, M. 129, 144, 148, 318
Mayo, E. 371
McAllister, I. 228
McClennan, G. 698
McCormick, J. 219

McCrudden, C. 92
McDowell, L. 187
McGrew, A. 417-18
McGuire, M.B. 500
McHugh, D. 379
McIntosh, M. 130, 132
McIntosh, S. 352
McKee, L. 262, 350
McKenzie, R. 222
McKeown, T. 426, 433
McLellan, D. 522
McLellan, J. 392
McMahon, P.C. 207
McRobbie, A. 127, 141, 409, 557
Meacher, M. 553
Mead, G.H. 677-9,
Mead, M. 122
Meadows, S. 446
Means, G.C. 53, 322
Mellors, C. 214
Melton, J.G. 517-8, 525, 529
Melville, J. 528
Mendel, G. 690
Merton, R.K. 361, 470-1, 474, 670-1
Mervin, D. 97
Meyenn, R.J. 300
Meyer, R. 363
Michels, R. 368-9, 624
Miles, R. 67, 74, 83, 108
Miles, M. 645-6
Miliband, R. 54, 106, 156, 210-11, 540-1
Millar, J. 179
Miller, W. 473
Millett, K. 240
Mills, C.W. 1, 206-7
Millward, N. 339-40, 342, 344
Mintzberg, H. 373, 377, 379
Mitchell, J. 116, 118, 120, 240
Modood, T. 69
Moore, R. 83
Moore, S. 130
Moore, W.H. 37-8, 647
Moran, M. 216,
Morgan, D. 121, 148
Morgan, D.H.J. 244, 255, 269
Morgan, G. 379
Morgan, L.H. 239
Morgan, M. 435
Morley, D. 418
Morris, D. 232-3
Morris, J. 124
Morris, L. 140
Morrison, S. 446
Morton, P. 239
Mosca, G. 206
Moser, C.A. 612
Mount, F. 236
Muncie, J. 459, 465, 474, 478-9
Munck, R. 633
Murdoch, J. 391, 414
Murdock, G.P. 233-5
Murie, A. 168
Murphy, L. 119
Murray, C. 62, 64, 104, 182, 184, 487
Murray, F. 377

Negrine, R. 629
Nelken, D. 475
Nelson, D. 91
Newburn, T. 564
Newby, H. 60, 387, 391, 412, 414-15, 611, 655
Newell, R. 615
Newman, D.M. 361
Newton, K. 537
Nias, D.K. 563
Nichols, T. 326, 371, 377

Nicholson, J. 306
Niebuhr, R. 510, 518-9
Nisbet, R. 383, 386-7, 389, 655
Nissel, M. 249, 627
Nitzova, P. 89
Norman, A. 410
Norris, C. 136
Norris, D. 158
Norris, P. 227
North, P.J. 392

O'Connell Davidson, J. 612, 617, 619, 630, 647-8
O'Connor, J. 156
O'Donnell, M. 408
O'Toole, R. 499
Oakley, A. 23, 118, 120-21, 136, 139-40, 248, 258, 262, 305, 613, 645
Offe, K. 156
Ohlin, L. 471-2
Okely, J. 621, 623
Oldfield, N. 172
Oppenheim, C. 62, 104, 111, 135, 168-9, 178-82, 410
Osler, A. 69, 133
Ouseley, H. 80, 187
Owen, D. 110-12

Page, C.H. 364
Page, R. 160
Paglia, C. 120
Pahl, J. 126, 261
Pahl, R.E. 43, 59, 139, 142, 317, 322, 346, 350, 395, 401, 412
Parekh, B. 92
Pareto, V. 206
Paris, C. 168
Parker, G. 160, 404
Parker, S. 352
Parker, T. 394
Parkin, F. 34, 55, 59-60, 103, 142
Parmar, P. 132
Parsons, T. 13, 194, 235-7, 245, 247, 258-9, 287-8, 319, 398, 433, 436-7, 439-40, 497-8, 669-71, 685-6
Pascall, G. 158
Patterson, O. 98-9
Patterson, S. 87
Pattie, C.J. 227
Pawson, R. 628, 644-6
Payne, G. 46, 49, 145
Peak, S. 535-6
Pearson, G. 398, 463, 630
Pease, K. 455
Perkin, J. 302-3
Philo, G. 539, 550, 554-5, 628
Phizacklea, A. 108
Phoenix, A. 69, 256
Piachaud, D. 174
Picardie, J. 528
Pietroni, P. 432
Pilger, J. 549
Pilkington, A. 105, 129, 187
Pines, M. 421
Piore, M.J. 335, 337
Platt, J. 261, 326, 619
Platt, S. 351
Plummer, K. 457
Pollert, A. 136-7, 327-8, 336
Polsby, N. 193
Popper, K. 637, 675
Poster, M. 697
Poulantzas, N. 211, 675
Procter, I. 396
Pryce, K. 78, 104, 315, 404-5, 623
Pugh, D. 372

Raban, J. 416
Radcliffe Richards, J. 118, 123, 125
Radcliffe-Brown, A.R. 234, 668
Raffe, D. 283
Rafiq, M. 112
Ramazanoglu, C. 129, 133
Randall, V. 214
Rapoport, Robert 352
Rapoport, Rhona 352
Rasumussen, J.S. 216
Rattansi, A. 472, 696
Redfield, R. 390, 412, 622
Reed, M. 365
Rees, T. 135
Reeves, F. 77
Reid, I. 30, 32, 42, 138
Reimer, B. 524
Reiner, R. 464-5, 476, 486, 490
Resler, H. 107, 175, 178, 186, 200, 202
Rex, J. 75, 83, 103-5
Rice, B. 277
Richardson, J. 74
Ridge, J.M. 294-6
Ridley, F.F. 351
Ritzer, G. 361
Roberts, C. 134, 139, 146, 262
Roberts, D. 198, 216,
Roberts, K. 54, 58, 283, 394, 399, 403
Roberts, R. 396
Robinson, O. 334
Rock, P. 455, 468, 471-2, 474, 483, 490, 551
Rodney, W. 99
Roethlisberger, F.G. 371, 375
Roiphe, K. 120
Rolston, W. 633
Rose, R. 228
Rosen, R. 401
Rosenberg, D. 79, 94
Rosenthal, R. 299
Rosser, R. 249
Rostow, W.W. 571-2
Rottman, D. 28, 30, 39
Rousseau, J. 657
Rowbotham, S. 120, 645
Rowntree, J. 349
Rowntree, S. 171, 173, 177-8
Rubel, M. 658-60
Runciman, W.G. 50, 54, 58
Runnymede Trust 72, 82, 84, 89, 104, 346
Rushdie, S. 69, 77, 407-8
Rutter, M. 183, 299

Sabel, C.F. 335, 337
Sachs, J. 667
Sachs, W. 567
Saggar. S. 109
Sahlins, M. 692
Saifullah-Khan, V. 132
Salaman, G. 318
Sampson, A. 208
Sanders, D. 603, 606
Sanderson, K. 135, 137
Sapsford, R. 146
Sarvlik, B. 223
Saunders, C. 43
Saunders, P. 38, 43, 49, 51, 55, 63, 103-4, 167-8, 389, 394, 412, 414
Saussure, F. de 682-3
Sauvain, P. 305, 320-21
Savage, M. 56
Saville, J. 156, 165
Sayer, A. 638-9
Scarman, The Rt Hon Lord 83, 217, 405

Scase, R. 28-29
Scheff, T. 446
Schlesinger, A. 4
Schlesinger, P. 459
Schonell, F.J. 277
Schumacher, E.F. 577, 583
Schutz, A. 2, 685-6
Schwartz, W. 57
Scott, J. 42, 51-4, 143, 208, 323, 630
Scraton, P. 490
Scraton, S. 353-4
Scull, A. 160, 383
Scullion, H. 341
Seabrook, J. 35, 91, 170, 380, 394, 396, 401
Searle, C. 314, 559
Segalman, R. 156
Seidler, V. 148
Seligman, M. 450
Semetko, H. 227
Sennett, R. 38, 417
Sewell, T.A. 216, 227
Seymour-Ure, C. 536-7, 549
Sharkey, P. 162, 168
Sharp, K. 86
Sharp, W. 363
Sharpe, S. 305
Shaw, C. 624
Sherlock, H. 415, 417
Sherman, B. 345
Shils, E. 496
Shipman, M.D. 610
Showler, B. 347
Siegel, A. 339
Silburn, R. 183, 185
Silver, A. 222
Silverman, D. 12, 364
Sim, A. 520
Simmel, G. 412
Sinfield, A. 346-7
Sivanandan, A. 85, 92, 104, 107, 314-15
Skellington, R. 94
Skelton, C. 303
Skipworth, M. 32, 40, 45-6
Smart, B. 418, 655-6
Smiles, S. 165
Smith, D. 81, 309-11, 314, 459, 486
Smith, M. 203
Smith, R. 253
Smith, S. 404
Solomos, J. 72, 77, 85, 88, 405
Souhami, D. 128, 137
Spencer, H. 182, 570, 668, 670, 690
Spender, D. 306-7
Spink, J. 354
Srinivasan, S. 112
Stacey, J. 120
Stacey, M. 390
Stainton Rogers, W. 428
Stalin, J. 367
Stalker, G.M. 362-3, 372-3
Stampp, K.M. 100
Stands In Timber, J. 10, 624
Stanworth, M. 143-4, 306-7
Stanworth, P. 201, 207
Stark, R. 518, 525, 527
Stern, J. 350
Stevens, M. 342
Stewart, A. 142
Stimson, G. 441
Stokes, D. 222
Stone, J. 86, 101, 106-7
Storey, J. 697
Stouffer, S.A. 4
Stradling, R. 205
Stratta, E. 138
Strauss, A. 364-5
Strinati, D. 401, 542

Sudjic, D. 417
Sutherland, E. 474-5
Szasz, T. 439, 442

Tawney, R.H. 186, 505, 656
Taylor, B. 121
Taylor, F.W. 328-9, 370-1, 374
Taylor, I. 482-3, 627
Taylor, L. 341
Taylor, S. 405, 438
Terkel, S. 96
Tester, K. 219, 693
Thirwall, T. 333
Thomas, D. 152
Thomas, K. 522
Thomas, R. 2,
Thomas, W.I. 17, 624
Thompson, E.P. 352
Thompson, J. 260
Thompson, K. 697
Thompson, P. 330, 379
Thornes, B. 350
Thorns, D. 416-17
Thrift, N. 397
Timmins, N. 180
Tipton, D. 630, 633
Titmuss, R. 157, 161, 164
Tizard, B. 69
Tolson, A. 149
Tomlinson, S. 103-5, 309-11, 314
Tonnies, F. 389, 570
Topham, T. 343
Townroe, C. 278
Townsend, P. 39, 173-5, 177-9, 183-4, 186, 443, 445-6
Tracey, M. 563
Trivers, R. 691-2
Troeltsch, E. 508-9
Trotsky, L. 367
Trow, M. 369
Troyna, B. 75, 81, 217, 315
Tuckett, D. 438, 441
Tumber, H. 459
Tumin, M. 38, 647
Tunstall, J. 555-6
Turnbull, C. 620
Turner, B. 36

Urry, J. 53, 55, 195, 353
Useem, M. 322
Utley, R.M. 517

Van den Berghe, P. 86
Van Dijk, T. 558-9
Veal, A.J. 353
Vidich, A. 391
Visram, R. 128

Waddington, P. 487
Wade, D. 528
Wagg, S. 535-6
Wainwright, M. 449
Walby, S. 145, 148, 336
Walford, G. 281
Walker, A. 403
Wallace, C. 144
Wallerstein, I. 575, 578
Wallis, R. 510, 512-3, 518, 522
Walsh, P. 227
Walton, P. 341, 627
Walvin, J. 71, 98-9, 128
Ward, R. 112
Warde, A. 334, 336
Warren, B. 572

Warrier, P. 130
Watson, J. 78
Watson, J.B. 677
Webb, B. 368, 441
Webb, S. 2, 166, 188, 368
Weber, M. 30, 35-6, 192-3, 196-7, 199, 320, 358-63, 365, 368, 370-3, 375, 377, 379, 382-3, 389, 434, 497, 500, 504-8, 525-6, 624, 630, 641, 653, 656, 665-6, 668, 673, 688
Weldon, F. 407
Wellman, B. 397
Wells, H.G. 275
Westergaard, J. 28-30, 33, 43, 59, 107, 175, 178, 186, 200, 202
Westwood, S. 132, 136-7, 149, 256, 472
Whale, J. 541
White, R. 283
Whitehead, M. 444-6
Whitley, R. 207-8
Whyte, W.F. 620-22, 633
Wicks, M. 39,
Widgery, D. 397, 400
Wilding, P. 57, 155
Williams, J.A. Jr 619
Williams, K.M. 518
Williams, P. 459
Williams, R. 397-8
Willis, P. 125, 289-91, 624, 632
Willmott, P. 22-3, 59, 139, 247-50, 258-59, 261-2, 394, 397, 401-3, 611
Wilson, A. 270
Wilson, B. 268
Wilson, B.R. 514, 519, 521-4, 526, 529
Wilson, D. 204
Wilson, E.O. 122, 691-2
Wilson, J.Q. 487
Wilson, S. 207
Wilson, W.J. 85-6, 96, 103
Winant, H. 472
Winkler, J. 322
Wirth, L. 71, 412, 416
Wohl, R. 401
Wolf, N. 120, 125
Wood, S. 329, 336, 338
Woodward, D. 353
Worpole, K. 416
Worrall, A. 484
Worsthorne, P. 47, 79, 177
Wrench, J. 104
Wright, C. 312-14
Wright, E.O. 55
Wright, R. 7-8

Yates, G. 278
Yeandle, S. 262
Yeo, A. 511
York, P. 37
Young, J. 104, 217, 462, 476, 483, 487, 489-91, 551, 611, 627
Young, K. 43
Young, M. 22-3, 47, 59, 139, 247-8, 258, 260-62, 394, 397, 401-3, 496
Yu A. 172
Yuval-Davis, N. 119

Zedner, L. 485
Zeisel, H. 349
Zeitlin, I. 655
Zimmerman, D. 365
Znaniecki, F. 624
Zubeida, S. 516

Subject Index

abolition, of slavery 99
abortion 117-118, 133-134, 219
absenteeism from work 339-341, 441
accumulation, state and 156, 211, 219
achieved status; see status
action; see social action
adaptation, as functional prerequisite 669
adaptations, in total institutions 381
adhocracy 373, 377
adolescence; see youth
advertising 31, 170
    and consumerism 401
    and images of women 125, 128
    political 548
    and postmodernism 542, 544
aetiology of disease 430
affirmative action 95-96
affluent workers; see workers, affluent
Africans 69, 98, 110
Afro-Caribbeans 69-70, 76, 87, 104; see also ethnicity
    and community 404-406
    and crime 482-483, 486, 490
    and education 309-315
    and employment/unemployment 81, 84, 110, 112, 179, 348
    families 132-134, 256-257
    voting behaviour 216, 227
    women 128-129, 131
age 408-411; see also youth, elderly
    discrimination 71
    of marriage and divorce 268-269
    and gender 119
    social construction of 408
    and stratification 9, 36, 42, 116, 144, 408
    and unemployment 282, 346, 348, 409-410
age structure
    of British population 410, 591
    of ethnic minorities 74, 83, 132, 256
    of Third World countries 589, 591
ageism 410
agency 688; see also social action
agenda management 193, 200, 215
agenda setting, and media 550, 552, 559
aggression, sex differences in 122
agriculture
    decline of employment in 332, 414
    effect on patterns of disease 425
    in feudal society 319
    industrialisation of 596, 599
    as a political issue 203
    and rural life 414
    in Third World 573-574, 577, 581-582, 596, 599
aid, and development 583-585, 603
AIDS 160, 437
alcohol, and health 426, 428, 446, 448, 450
alcoholism, as sickness 441
alienation
    and loss of community 398, 412, 567, 596
    masculinity as 151
    and religion 500-501
    and work 33, 59, 320, 325-326, 328, 659
altruism 38, 690-692
    kin 690
    and professions 57
    reciprocal 86, 691
ancient society 658
androcentricity 645

androgyny 121
animal behaviour 677
anomie 242
    and development 567, 596
    and deviance 470-471, 487
    division of labour and 319, 663-664, 667
    and religion 507, 516
    and suicide 469-470
anorexia 453
anti-collectivism; see market liberalism
anti-discrimination legislation 81, 83, 92, 124, 135, 217; see also
        Race Relations Acts; Sex Discrimination Act
anti-foundationalism 697-698
anti-racism 77, 79, 83, 91-96, 119, 216-217, 405
anti-school subculture; see culture, counter-school
anti-sexism, in education 307-308
anti-totalisation 698
anti-utopianism 698
apartheid 76-77, 98, 100-102
architecture, and postmodernism 696
aristocracy 51-52, 61, 212; see also upper class
art of mistrust 3
arts, and postmodernism 696
ascribed status; see status
Asians 70, 76, 103-104
    and community 406-408
    and crime 486
    East African 70-71, 84-85, 257, 406-407
    and education 309-314
    and employment/unemployment 81, 110-113, 179
    families 132-134, 256-257
    and voting behaviour 216, 227
    women 129, 131-134
assembly line 320, 325-328, 334
assimilation, of ethnic minorities 71, 87-88
Assisted Places Scheme 280-281
asylums; see hospitals, psychiatric
attitudes; see also culture; values
    of poor 182
    political 58
    racist 75-76, 80
    upper class 52
    to welfare state 168
    of young blacks 104
authority 192-195, 196
    charismatic 193-195
    in the family 239
    rational legal 193-195, 359, 666, 669
    traditional 193-195, 669
automation 46, 55, 325, 336; see also technology, continuous
        process
autonomy
    in work 56, 136, 373, 379
    of race from class 107

Bangladeshis 70, 84, 90, 93, 128, 131-132, 256-257, 346, 348
bargaining; see collective bargaining; negotiation
battered women; see violence, domestic
beauty myth 125
begging 488-489
behaviourism 677
belief systems 494
beliefs 210; see also attitudes; values
    about gender 196
    about health and illness 423-425, 430

racist 75-76
benefits; *see* welfare benefits
Benetton 338, 377
Beveridge Report 158, 164-165, 172
bias
    experimenter 609
    interviewer 614
    in media; *see* mass media, bias vs impartiality
    in sociology; *see* value freedom
bimodal pattern, of women's work 134
biology; *see also* sociobiology
    and crime 467
    and gender 121-122, 148, 303, 690
    and race 67
    and structure of human mind 683
biomedicine 428-431
birth control; *see* contraception
birth rate 74, 244, 260, 426
    and population growth 585-590
    outside marriage 232, 254, 265-266
black consciousness 405
black people 69, 72; *see also* Afro-Caribbeans; Asians; ethnic
        groups; ethnicity
    images of 69, 79-80
    men 149, 151
    women 128-134, 240
Black Report 186, 442-443
body
    and gender 121
    as a machine 430
    manipulation of 440
    punishment of 382-384
    social construction of 424-425
body language 17
Boer War 100, 164
boundary debate 55; *see also* class, boundaries
bourgeoisie 31, 33, 54, 55, 209-210, 658-660, 673, 675; *see also*
        capitalists, ruling class
British Crime Surveys 463-465
British Election Surveys 225
British Empire 67, 71; *see also* colonialism
British Nationality Acts 85
British National Party 90-93
bulimia 453
bureaucracy 36, 358-384; *see also* organisations
    advantages of 359
    characteristics of 359
    under communism 367-368
    and democracy 199, 360, 368-370, 373, 377, 379
    dysfunctions of 360-364
    and efficiency 359-362, 370, 371
    end of 377-380
    ideal type 359, 362, 665
    and leisure 352
    Marxism and 365, 367-368, 375-377, 383
    and personality 361
    and power 322, 358-359
    and rationality 193, 359-360, 506
    and red tape 363
    and the state 194, 196, 218, 220
    types of 372-373
    Weber on 358-361, 365, 370, 382-383, 665-666
    in welfare provision 155, 161
bureaucratic assets 56
bureaucratic control 329
bureaucratic personality 361
business; *see also* ownership and control of business
    class 53
    organisations 54
    ownership by ethnic minorities 112
    small 54; *see also* petty bourgeoisie

Calvinism 504-506, 526, 571, 665
capital 51, 53
capitalism
    and alienation 320, 325-326
    classes in 16, 28-29, 33-35, 43, 59-60, 658-660, 673-675
    contradictions of 16, 33, 156, 345, 502, 658-659
    and crime 18, 480, 483
    crisis of 34, 483, 659, 674
    definition 28
    and development 572, 574-575; *see also* development and
        industrialisation
    and health 433
    and education 288-289
    and the family 236, 238-240
    and gender roles 119-120, 130, 145, 151, 156, 239-240
    and immigration policy 85
    logic of 34, 89, 107, 329, 412
    and loss of community 389, 398, 401
    mercantile 574, 591
    monopoly 322
    and organisations 365, 368, 375-377
    overthrow of 34, 184, 210, 659-660, 673, 675
    and poverty 183-184
    power and the state 184, 196, 200-201, 204, 209-214, 660,
        673-675
    and protestant ethic 320, 504-506, 641, 665
    and racism 88-89, 106-107, 145
    and religion 500-502, 504-506
    and unemployment 345
    and welfare state 154-158, 164
    and work 319-320, 322, 325-326, 332, 335-336, 338, 340
capitalist class; *see* capitalists
capitalist society; *see* capitalism
capitalists 16, 33-34, 36, 51, 54-55, 240, 320; *see also*
        bourgeoisie; ruling class
    entrepreneurial 53
    finance 53, 208, 212
    industrial 212
    internal 53
carceral organisations 381-383
careers
    deviant 476
    women's 138, 141
Cartesian body-mind dichotomy 430, 432
case studies 624
cash nexus 59
caste system 26-28, 30, 46
casual employment; *see* work, casual and temporary
causation 609-610, 636-637, 643, 662
censorship 219, 407, 548
Census 73-74, 245, 626
centralisation and decentralisation 694
charities 163, 182; *see also* voluntary organisations
Chicago School 412, 677
child abuse 64, 148, 200, 441, 462, 484-485
Child Benefit 155, 165, 167, 178, 184
child care
    in kibbutzim 233-234, 240
    men and 139, 196, 262, 264, 350
    welfare state and 162, 237, 252
    women and 117, 134, 136, 139, 157, 215, 239-240, 259, 263-
        264, 268, 327, 331
Child Poverty Action Group 138, 160, 178, 182
Child Support Agency 252
childbearing 119, 259; *see also* birth rate; reproduction
    female investment in 122
children
    as asset/liability 587, 590
    feminist attitudes to 120
    and families 232-234, 237, 242-243, 246, 249-250, 252, 257
chiropractic 432

cholera 165-166, 170
churches 210
  black 94
  characteristics of 508
  and politics 514
  and poverty 163, 514
cinema 533
circumcision, female 130
cities; *see* urban sociology
Citizens Charter 63
citizenship 63, 104, 155-156, 197
  categories of British 85
City of London, and politics 203, 212
City Technology Colleges; *see* schools
civil rights 26, 63, 197
  legislation 95-96; *see also* anti-discrimination legislation
  movements 8, 92, 94-95, 219
civil service 197, 199, 207, 215, 363
civil society 210
civilising process 352
class, social 16, 25-65, 94, 116; *see also* bourgeoisie; capitalists;
      intermediate class; middle class; proletariat; ruling
      class; service class; subject class; underclass; upper class;
      working class
  analysis 43-44, 142-143, 145
  antagonisms 36
  boundaries 46, 50-64
  in capitalist societies 28-29, 658-661
  and community 391, 399-400
  conflict 15, 33-34, 36, 38, 43-44, 59-61, 78, 103, 106-107,
      155-156, 211, 219-220, 325-326, 399, 510, 639,
      658, 660, 664, 672
  consciousness 34, 43-44, 59-60, 141, 326, 394, 502, 659-660;
      see also false consciousness
  and consumption 30-31, 43-45
  contradictory locations 55
  and crime 19, 465, 475, 489-490
  definitions 28, 30
  descriptive approaches 30-32
  Dex's occupational scale 144
  and divorce 39
  and doctor-patient interaction 439
  and education 31, 39, 46, 52, 137, 186-187, 255, 273-281,
      283, 285, 287-290, 293-301, 309-310, 615
  and ethnicity 98-113, 141
  ethnomethodology and 687
  and family 22, 236, 239, 246-251, 255, 258-262, 264
  formation 46
  functionalism and 33, 37-39
  gender and 36, 42, 58, 119-121, 129, 141-147
  Goldthorpe scheme 31, 48, 142
  and health 5, 21, 39, 63, 186, 442-443, 446-449
  Heath et al scheme 225
  and housing 39, 58, 103, 187, 255
  and income 39-41; *see also* distribution of wealth and income
  interests 34
  and leisure 30, 39, 56, 353, 355, 394, 400-402, 534
  and life chances 25, 28, 30-31, 35, 39-43, 276
  and lifestyle 28, 31, 39, 43-45, 56, 58, 248, 395-397, 399-400,
      446
  measurement of 30-32
  maps 50-64
  Market Research classification 31, 225
  Marxist theory and 14, 33-36, 55, 59-60, 129, 220, 647, 657-
      661, 673-675
  mobility; *see* social mobility
  the new 367
  objective approaches 31-32
  and occupation 28, 31-32, 48, 51, 142-147
  organisation 60
  polarisation of 33-34, 659-660
  and poverty 175, 178
  Registrar-General's scale 31-32, 58, 141-143, 145, 679
  relationships 58-59
  in socialist societies 29-30
  structure 26, 223
  struggle; *see* class conflict
  subjective approaches 30-32
  Surrey Occupational Scale 144
  and unemployment 28, 49, 346, 349-350
  and voting behaviour 31, 43, 222-229
  Weberian theory and 35-37, 184
  and welfare state 186-189
  widening differences 63, 188-189
classification, occupational; *see* class and occupation
classlessness 42-45
closure
  of elites 207
  strategies 35, 142
coercion 13, 107, 192-193, 239, 288
coercive pacification 342
cohabitation 139, 232, 236, 252, 263, 265-266, 269
collective bargaining 339-344
collective conscience/consciousness 18, 495-496, 663
collectivism 59, 61, 342
  and education 280, 289
  and welfare 154, 164, 168, 335
colleges; *see* education, further and higher; schools, city
      technology colleges
colonialism 88, 130-131, 198, 218, 568, 572-573, 574-575, 592-
      593, 602, 659, 685
  neo- 574-575
Commission for Racial Equality 92, 187
commodities 33, 319, 659
  and Third World 581-582, 593
commonsense
  attitudes to class 30
  and suicide 642
  views of crime and deviance 458
  views on race 67, 75, 77
commonsense knowledge 365, 686, 688
Commonwealth Immigrants Acts 85
communications; *see also* language; mass media
  and compression of time and space 218, 579
  and extended family 249-250
  and interaction 679-680, 686
communism 16, 36
  and alienation 325
  and bureaucracy 367-368
  and communities 389
  and democracy 198
  the end of 29-30, 34, 60, 212, 376, 568, 575, 578, 660
  and the family 239-240
  primitive 209, 239, 658
  stratification under 29-30
  transition to 34, 659-660
community 77, 386-419
  action 403
  and age groups 408-411
  as agency of political socialisation 222
  class model 399-400
  decline/loss of 90-91, 182, 248, 389-391, 395, 397-398, 401,
      409-410, 415
  and ethnicity 131, 391, 393, 397, 404-408
  and family 245-249, 260, 394, 402
  and gender 394-395, 402-404
  gemeinschaft/gesellschaft and 389-390, 397, 411-412, 417,
      567
  and globalisation 417-419
  imagined 387
  and inner city 399-400, 404-406
  integration and strikes 339-340

and local politics 391
and locality 387, 391, 393-394, 412
mass society model 401-402
meaning and definitions of 386-388
myth of 390-391
pluralist model 400-401
postmodernism and 401
relevance of concept of 391-393
representations in TV soaps 401-402
and rural life 414-416
and small town myth 391
social/geographical mobility and 389, 391, 401
and social networks 391-392, 397, 403
and space 411-419
studies 393-394
and subcultures 387, 393
urbanisation and 389, 412-413, 415-417
virtual 392
working class 58, 247, 394-398, 401
community care 159-160, 162-163, 167, 249, 403-404, 410
comparative method 339, 372, 641
compression of time and space 218, 418, 693
computerisation 46, 55
and social control 382
and work 329-331, 335, 337, 361, 379
concentration ratio 323-324; see also ownership and control of
business, concentration of configurations, in organisations
373
conflict 9, 15-16, 288, 671
class 15, 33-34, 36, 38, 43-44, 59-61, 78, 103, 106-107,
155-156, 211, 219-220, 325-326, 399, 501, 639, 658,
660, 664, 672
in communities 399-400
over consumption issues 413
cultural 87-88
ethnic 15, 69, 75, 103, 217-218
gender 15, 34, 144, 402-403
industrial 325-328, 338-341, 375
new sources of 219
religious 16, 493
conflict theories 12-16, 651; see also Marxism
of community 399-400
of education 288-290
of family 238-242, 248
of organisations 375-377
of racism 88-89
of stratification 33-37
conformity 7
conjugal roles 22-23, 258-264
joint 259-260, 395
segregated 248, 259-261, 395, 403
conscious partiality 645
consciousness 639; see also class consciousness; collective
consciousness; false consciousness
consciousness raising 117, 119, 646
consensus 38, 287; see also value consensus
consensus theories 12-15, 87, 235-237, 287-288, 651; see also
functionalism
conservatism; see also New Right
and masculinity 150
and modernity 655
religious organisations and 514-515, 530-531
Conservative governments 201
and the family 236
and education 276, 278, 281, 284-285
and inner city 400
and official statistics 626-627
and welfare 156, 165, 167-168, 177, 182, 184
Conservative Party
and business organisations 203, 208
and ethnic minorities 69, 109, 218; see also New Right

and mass media 534, 536-537, 548-550
and voting behaviour 143, 222-229
constellation of interests 53, 323
consumer goods 30, 42, 58
consumer society 45, 401
consumption 139
cleavages 43
collective 413
globalisation and 418
and leisure 352-354
as a political issue 219
and post-Fordism 335
and post-industrial society 332-333, 697
privatisation of 167-168
styles 35, 43, 58, 142
content analysis, and the mass media 552, 554, 628-629
contingency theory 373-374
contraception 117-118, 133-134, 587
effect on mortality rates 426
and world population growth 586, 588, 590
contracts, flexibility in 335
contradictions of capitalism 16, 33, 156, 345, 502, 658-659
contradictory class locations 55
control, at work 320, 322-323, 325-326, 328-330, 335-336, 338,
340-341, 375-376; see also social control
control theory, and crime 488
conventional approach, to gender and class 142-143
convergence, of classes 59
convergence theory 29
cooperation 12, 15
core and periphery, and development 575
core workforce 335, 378-379
Coronation, and religion 495, 501-502
coroners, and suicide 470, 642-643, 686
corporations; see also transnational corporations
and crime 475, 480
growth in size 323
correlation 609, 614-615, 636-637, 665
correspondence theory, and education 288-289
councils; see local government
counterculture 116, 409; see also culture, counter-school
craft work 334-335; see also workers, skilled
crime 18, 455-491; see also deviance
biological explanations 467, 484
capitalism and 18, 480, 483
class and 19, 465, 475, 489-490
control of 7
dark figure of 461
definition 455
ethnicity and 79, 217, 465, 482-483, 486, 490
as functional 20, 468-469
gender and 465, 484-486
official statistics on 461-465, 484, 626-627
personality and 467
police and 461, 465, 463, 486
recording of 461, 463-464, 489
reporting of 461-464
trends in 462-464
in urban areas 464
in USA 96
and the underclass 64, 103, 158, 182
unemployment and 349-351487, 489
victim surveys 106, 463-465
waves 463
white collar 474-475, 480
youth and 409-410, 465; see also juvenile delinquency
criminal justice system, bias in operation of 476, 484, 486
criminology
and disciplinary power 382
radical 480-483, 490
critical theory 673-674

cross-class families 142-143
cross-cultural studies 121, 233-234
cult of man 495-496
cults 512-514
    characteristics of 510-511
    development of 518, 526
cultural capital 52, 56, 297, 407
cultural commodities 674
cultural deprivation theory, and education 295-296, 315; see also
        culture of poverty
cultural diversity; see cultural pluralism, multicultural society
cultural effects theory, and media 538-539
cultural homogenisation 693
cultural identity; see identity
cultural pluralism 88, 407, 566
cultural racism 75, 77, 87-89, 694
    in USA 94-95
cultural relativism 131
culture 6, 9, 34
    class and 51-52, 56, 62, 104, 295-296
    counter-school 289-290, 300, 624
    definitions of 6
    and definitions of poverty 172-173
    of dependency 62, 64, 154, 156, 182, 185
    dominant 297
    and education 287, 294-296, 314-315
    ethnicity and 34, 70, 77-79, 87-88, 95, 103, 119, 130-131,
        133, 314-315
    and family life 233-234
    of femininity 127
    and gender roles 34, 121-122, 130, 148
    globalisation and 218-219
    and health 446-447, 450-452
    mass 673-674; see also mass society theory
    and patriarchy 145
    popular 685; see also mass media
    postmodernism and 697
    of poverty 62, 64, 104, 182-183, 185-186, 296
    sociobiology and 690, 692
    structuralism and 682-685
culture industry 673-674
curriculum 285, 289, 299; see also National Curriculum
    gender and 301-303, 306
    widening of 275
Cypriots 81, 131, 257

data collection 21, 24
dealignment 222-229
    class 223
    partisan 222-224
death 5, 57; see also mortality
    and religion 497-498
debt, Third World 583-585
decarceration; see community care
decision making
    manipulation of 194, 200-202, 262
    non- 193, 195, 200, 202, 261-262
    and power 193, 195, 199-201, 212
    within marriage 261-262, 264
deductive method 637, 656
deferred gratification 295
deference 45
    in voting behaviour 222
definitions
    of situation by actors 17
    in sociology 20, 24
deindustrialisation 332-333, 345
delinquency; see crime; juvenile delinquency
demand side, explanations of women's employment 136
democracy
    African 198

and capitalism 34, 209
and bureaucracy 199, 366, 368-370, 373, 377, 379
definitions of 197-198
and development 572, 592, 595
elite theory and 206-207
and pressure groups 202, 204-205
liberal 29, 197-199, 206, 655
Marxist and socialist theory and 197-198
and mass media; see politics and mass media
participatory/direct 197-199
pluralist theories and 199, 204
representative/indirect 54, 197-199
and the state 196-197, 199
demographic transition 586, 588
demography; see also age structure; birth rate; immigration;
        migration; mortality; urbanisation
    and marriage/divorce 268-269
    natural increase 598
    overpopulation/population explosion 586-591
    population distribution 585
    reasons for population change 585
    and role of women 134, 259, 589, 605
demonstrations
    and anti-racism 92
    and class struggle 59
    and pressure groups 203
denominations
    characteristics of 510
    development from sects 518-519
deprivation 179; see also cultural deprivation theory; poverty
    cycle of 183
    and educational underachievement 294-296
    and ethnicity 83
    and poor health 447-448
    inner city 399-400
    multiple 103, 183
    relative 174-175, 177, 490
deprofessionalisation 56; see also deskilling, proletarianisation
deskilling 55-56, 328-331, 334-336, 375-376, 599
determinism 11, 15, 663, 677
    economic 210, 240, 660, 674-675
developing countries 247, 323; see also development; Third
        World
development 218, 566-606
    aid, loans and debt 583-585, 593, 605
    concept of 566-567
    and food/malnutrition 569, 576, 601-605
    and economic growth 567
    First/Second/Third World model and 568
    and globalisation 572, 574-575, 578-581
    and health 426, 566, 574, 601-606
    and industrialisation 567, 571, 575-577, 581, 591-597, 599
    Marxist theories 572; see also underdevelopment theory
    modernisation theory 219, 570-571, 573-574, 576, 578, 581,
        591, 594
    neo-populist theory 577, 591
    New Right theory 571-572, 574
    North/South model and 568
    and population 574, 585-591
    populist theory 570, 576-577
    and postmodernism 578-580
    and poverty 566-567, 569, 576, 578, 584, 587, 589, 598-599,
        601-602
    underdevelopment theory 570, 572-576, 581, 591, 594
    and urbanisation 571, 576-577, 597-600
    and world trade 581-582
    and work 566
Development Corporations 400
deviance 455-491; see also crime; juvenile delinquency
    amplification 478-480, 486
    anomie and 470-471, 487

control theory 488
definitions of 455
diversity of 455-456
feminist theories 484-485
fully social theory of 482-483
functionalist theories 468-471, 474-475
interactionist/labelling theories 450, 475-481, 483, 646
left realist theories 484, 487, 489-491
Marxist/radical theories 383, 473-474, 480-483
media representations of 458-461, 478-479, 483, 558
medicalisation of 440-442
normality of 458, 466-467
primary and secondary 476-478
public concern over 458-459
relativity of 457
right realist theories 484, 487-489
situational 457
as social construct 455-458, 461-462, 627
societal 457
structural theories of 470-474
subcultural theories of 471-474, 476-477, 490
deviant voters 222
devolution 197
diachronic 682-684
dictatorship 197-198, 206
of the proletariat 367
diet, and health 183, 426, 428, 446, 448-449, 453, 586, 601-605
direct action 92-93, 117, 203-204
directorships 51, 215
interlocking 53, 322-323
disability
and old age 410
physical 71
and politics 219
and poverty 178, 183-184
welfare state and 155, 159-160, 162, 167
class 61
discourse
analysis 558
racial 77
discrimination 71; see also age discrimination, racial
discrimination, sexual discrimination
disease 158, 165; see also health; illness
aetiology of 430
definition 422
degenerative 425-426
history of 425-427
infectious 425-427, 439, 601
physico-chemical model 433; see also biomedicine
stress and 430-431
theories of 428-433
in Third World; see development and health
welfare state and 154, 157, 153, 186, 235
disenchantment 506-507, 526, 666-668
distribution of income and wealth 2, 25-26, 30, 35, 38, 60, 63,
399; see also redistribution of income and wealth
in Britain 39-43, 180-181, 186, 188-189, 200, 211, 349
global 568, 576, 586
in socialist societies 29
welfare state and 155, 186, 189, 349
distribution of talents, and social mobility 49
divided working class model 107
division of labour 353; see also work
and bureaucracy 359-360, 363, 368, 379
domestic 232, 262-264, 394; see also housework; conjugal
roles
functionalism and 319, 663
and gender roles 22-23, 258
and industrialisation 319-320
new international 323, 575
and social stratification 33

and religion 496
specialisation of 319, 334-335, 663
and urban life 412
divorce 177, 239, 267-270
alternatives to 267, 270
and class 39
explanations of increase 267-269
and family diversity 251-255
legislation 267-268
and men's rights 150
rate 61, 232, 265, 267-270
and unemployment 350
doctors; see medical profession
documentary method 686-687
documents
historical 630-632
in research 628-630, 635
dole; see unemployment benefit
domestic role, of women 134-136, 138-141, 239-241, 246, 258-
264, 268, 350, 352, 403; see also childcare;
housework
domestic science 139
domestic sphere; see private sphere
domination, male 120-122; see also patriarchy
double standard, sexual 125, 127
dowry 132-134, 407
dramaturgical analogy 679-680
drift, delinquency and 474
drug abuse/addiction 64, 96, 182, 409, 441
dual class theory 145
dual labour market 136, 338
dysfunctions 670-672
of bureaucracy 360-364
of stratification 38
of racism 89

earnings; see pay; income; low pay; wages
Eastern Europe 34, 60
class in 29
revolutions in 34, 60, 221; see also communism, the end of
ecological theory, of urban life 412
ecology; see environment
economic base 16, 34; see also infrastructure
economic differences 58; see also pay; distribution of income
and wealth
economism 59
economy
communal 318
formal 317, 599-600
household 317; see also housework
informal 317, 352, 598-600
education 154, 158, 168, 273-315; see also educational
achievement; schools; training
academic-vocational divide in 283
assessment in 284; see also examinations
class and 31, 39, 46, 52, 186-187, 273-281, 283, 285, 287,
289, 293-301, 309-310
classroom interaction in 289-292, 299-301, 306-307, 610
comprehensive system 276-279, 286, 294, 299
and development 571
and discipline in schools 280-281, 301, 314
and the economy 273-275, 282, 287-289, 305
eleven plus in 275-276, 285, 303
of elites 207-209, 211, 279-280
ethnicity and 277, 308-315
feminism and 301, 305-308
functionalism and 287-288
further 159, 273, 296, 306
gender and 117, 124, 187, 279, 301-308
higher 159, 186-187, 273, 303-304
history of system in Britain 163-165, 273-286, 301-303

informal 273; see also socialisation
interactionism/interpretivism and 291, 299-301, 313-314
Marxism and 60, 288-290
mixed ability 286, 300; see also streaming
multicultural and anti-racist 83, 91, 217
opportunity and inequality; see educational achievement; equality of opportunity; meritocracy
parental choice in 280, 284-285, 287
primary 275, 285, 302, 313
private 161, 168, 275, 277-281; see also public schools
secondary 275-279, 285, 302, 313-314
socialisation and 273, 287-288, 305
standards in 277-279, 285-286
streaming and setting in 278, 285-287, 300-301, 312-313
tripartite system 275-279, 294, 299, 303
vocational 282-284; see also training
educational achievement
biological explanations 303
class and 137, 255, 276, 278-279, 288-290, 293-301, 309-310, 615
comprehensives and 277-279, 294
cultural factors and 295-298, 314-315
ethnicity and 83, 96, 103, 105, 288, 308-315
gender and 117, 135-136, 138, 187, 303-308
intelligence and 294, 314
language and 297-298, 315
lone parent families and 237, 255
material factors and 294-296
parental interest and 295, 315
positional theory and 297
poverty and 182-183, 185, 286
schools'/teachers' influence on 299-301, 306-308, 310-314
Education Acts 163, 274-276, 279-280, 301-303
Educational Priority Areas
Education Reform Act 276, 284-287
efficiency, in welfare provision 156, 161, 167
egalitarianism 45, 47
elaborated code 297-298
elderly; see also age; pensioners
and disengagement 410
and families/households 235, 246, 249-251, 255-256, 403
lifestyles 410-411
and poverty 178-179, 183-184
welfare services for the 154-155, 159-160, 161-165, 167, 186, 249, 403
elections 216, 222-229 see also voting behaviour
and democracy 54, 199, 202, 207, 222
race issues in 90-93, 109
elites 48, 51, 53-54, 195
in bureaucracies 368
circulation of 206
communism and 367-368
economic 53, 207-208
education of 207-209, 211, 279-280
integration of 207, 209, 211
military 207
political 54, 207-209
power 206-208
recruitment of 207, 209
women in 214-216
elite pluralist theories; see pluralism
elite theory 203, 206-209, 211
classical 206-207, 210, 369
fragmented 207-208
power 206-207
embourgeoisement 42, 58-59
emigration, statistics on 74; see also migration
empiricism 656
employment; see also work
female; see women, and employment
legislation 184, 188, 331, 336; see also anti-discrimination

legislation
racial discrimination in 81, 83
rights 131
end of history 29
Enlightenment 655-657, 674
postmodernism and 696-698
entrepreneurs 38, 51, 53-54
black 112
environment
and behaviour 691
and intelligence 294
and politics 195, 200, 203, 219-221
costs of industrialisation to 583, 596
Equal Opportunities Commission 118, 184
equal pay, for women 117, 135
Equal Pay Act 118, 142, 187
equality of opportunity 42, 47, 49, 63, 161, 198; see also inequality
and education 276, 285, 289, 293, 295, 297
legislation; see anti-discrimination legislation
for women 117-118, 187
equal rights, for women 118
equilibrium, in society 155, 235, 670
Establishment, the 51; see also elites, upper class
estate duties 51
estates, feudal 27
ethics
in professions 56
and research 609, 622-623
ethnic absolutism 70, 77
ethnic cleansing 89
ethnic diversity 66, 353
ethnic groups 66-67, 70-73, 83, 87, 98, 674; see also ethnicity
internal divisions in 69-70, 77-78
and nationalism 218-220
percentage born in UK 71
policies towards 71-72
sex distribution of 129
statistics on 72-74
ethnic minorities, see ethnic groups
ethnic monitoring 94
ethnicities, new 77
ethnicity 28, 36, 42, 46, 58, 66-113, 116
and citizenship rights 63
and class 98-113, 141
and community 131, 391, 393, 397, 404-408
and conflict 15, 69, 75, 103, 217-218
and crime 79, 217, 465, 482-483, 486, 490
and culture 34, 70, 77-79, 87-88, 103, 119, 130-131, 133, 314-315
and education 83, 96, 103, 105, 217, 277, 288, 308-315
and employment 83-84, 104, 134, 379
and family 132-133, 236, 240, 251, 255-257, 405-407
and gender 94, 110, 119, 126, 128-134, 256-257
and health 443-444, 451-452
and housing 81, 83-84, 103, 106, 187-188, 452
and identity 45, 217
and inequality 66, 72, 83-84, 144
and leisure 353-354
Marxism and 88-89, 98, 106-108
and mass media 79, 85, 94, 557-560
and poverty 28, 40, 83-84, 93, 96, 132, 151, 179, 183-184, 405
and power 66, 71, 83, 98, 200, 216-218
and religion 70, 406-408
and social control 7-8
sources of data on 72-74
terminology 66-68
and the underclass 61-62, 83, 103-106, 491
and unemployment 28-29, 66, 83-84, 90, 96-97, 105, 110-111, 179, 346, 348

in the USA 94-97
    and voting 109, 216, 227-228
    and the welfare state 104, 169, 187-188
ethnocentrism 74, 110, 129, 131
ethnographic studies 620-621, 624; see also participant
        observation
    of community 404
    of deviance 484, 633
    of education 314, 632
    of ethnicity 78, 104, 128, 623
    of family 244
    of work 136
ethnomethodology
    criticisms of 365, 687
    and organisations 365-366
    and sociological theory 685-688
European Community/Union
    and globalisation 218-220, 580, 694
    and immigration laws 85-86
evolution 232; see also sociobiology
    and altruism 691-692
    as explanation of racism 86
    and sex differences 122, 150
    social 671, 674; see also social change
    theory of 67, 677, 689
evolutionary psychology 691-692
examinations 276, 301
    league tables 285-286, 299, 314
    results and schools 277-279, 299; see also educational
        achievement
exclusion, from schools 314
exclusion strategy 142
exercise, and health 426, 446
experience, primacy of 646
experiments
    ethnomethodological 686-688
    field 609-610
    laboratory 608-6610
    on media effects 538, 557, 561, 563, 610
exploitation 13, 78
    colonial/global 572, 574-575
    class 16, 33, 36, 59, 209, 288-289, 326, 336, 340, 345, 375,
        500, 658-659
    of consumers 352
    racial 75
    of women 119, 129, 131, 141, 145, 240, 330, 394
extension pattern, of leisure 352

factory work 135-137, 321
false consciousness 16, 34, 60, 240, 326, 639, 653
    mass media and 540
    religion as 500, 502
falsification 86, 637, 675
family 232-270; see also kinship; marriage
    class and 22, 236, 239, 246-251, 255, 258-262, 264
    and community 245-249, 260, 394, 402
    decline of the 236-237, 253, 522
    diversity 233-234, 236, 240
    ethnicity and 132-133, 236, 240, 251, 255-257, 405, 406-407
    extended 132, 159-160, 233, 245-250, 256-257, 259, 268,
        319, 394-395, 406; see also kinship
    feminism and the 118, 120, 132, 235-237, 239-244, 246,
        248-249, 258-265, 268
    financial help and 249-250
    functionalism and the 15, 17, 233-242, 245, 248, 259, 261,
        263
    functions of the 3, 159, 232-238, 240, 242, 245, 247,
    gender roles in the 143, 232, 239-242, 248-249, 251, 258-264,
        268, 270, 327, 403-404
    industrialisation and 235, 238, 244-249, 258, 319, 642

interpretivism and 235-236, 240, 242-244
    life cycle and the 233, 250-253, 255, 263
    locality and 236, 251, 255-256
    lone parent 2, 40, 62, 64, 103, 132, 142, 177, 179, 184-185,
        236-237, 251-257, 296, 487
    Marxism and 196, 235-243, 246, 263
    matrilocal 131-132, 256
    neo-conventional 252-253
    New Right and the 182, 235-237, 240, 265, 487
    nuclear 132, 157, 159, 232-237, 239-240, 245, 247-249,
        251-253, 256-258, 265, 268
    and poverty 177-179, 184-185, 237, 252, 255, 259
    power and the 214, 243, 261-264
    in pre-industrial societies 233-235, 239, 245-248
    privatisation of 59, 247-249, 259, 395-396, 401, 416
    reconstituted 252
    social control and 7
    socialisation and 121, 222, 233, 235-237, 239, 242-243, 255
    sociobiology and the 232-233, 236
    structural isolation of 245
    symmetrical 22, 139-140, 239, 248, 258, 262, 403
    traditional values and 150, 187, 236-238, 240, 265-266, 487
    unemployment and 139-140, 237, 242, 255-256, 262, 350
    as unit of production 245-246, 248
    universality of the 232-234
    and welfare 156-157, 159-160, 162-163, 167, 182, 186-187,
        237, 245, 249
Family Allowances; see Child Benefit
Family Expenditure Survey 31, 39-40
family planning 134; see also contraception
family size 74, 259-260; see also birth rate; household size
    contraception and 117, 133, 426
family wage 157, 246
famine 554-555, 578, 693; see also development, and
        food/malnutrition
fascism 82, 85, 92-93, 197; see also British National Party;
    Nazism
fashion 125, 127
fatalistic attitudes 60, 104, 182, 295
female dependency 157, 258, 263
femininity
    feminist critique of 120
    social construction of 121-123, 187
feminisation
    of poverty 179
    of workforce 134, 137, 143
feminism 20, 690; see also gender; women's movement
    and beauty 125
    black 118-119, 129-131, 240
    and community 402-404
    and crime 484-485
    criticisms of 119-120, 150-151, 240-241
    definition 118
    and deskilling
    and education 301, 305-308
    and the family 118, 132, 235-237, 239-244, 246, 248-249,
        258-265, 268
    first wave 116
    liberal 118-119
    Marxist/socialist 118-119, 129, 157, 239-242, 259
    and masculinity 148
    and mass media 120, 555, 557
    men's reactions to 150-151
    and methodology 644-646, 653
    and politics 214, 219; see also power, and gender
    post 120
    power- 120
    radical 118-119, 122, 129, 144, 148, 240
    second wave 116
    and sexuality 125-128
    and sociobiology 692

and welfare 157-158, 160, 162, 249, 403-404
and work and leisure 327, 329-330, 336, 352
feminist mystique 120
fertility; see birth rate
feudalism 26-28, 30, 33, 46, 196, 319, 658, 675
fiddling, at work 317
Finer Report 252
fiscal crisis, of the state 156-157, 168, 413
flexibility in work 62, 130, 135, 331, 334-338, 342, 376-379
    numerical 335-336, 378
    functional 335, 378
folk devils 478
folk societies 390
food 261; see also development, and food; diet, and health
football hooliganism 479-480
forces of production; see means of production
Fordism 328, 334-335, 377-378
fragmentation
    of classes 56
    of life-worlds 507
    of work tasks 55
Frankfurt School 673-674
fraud 461-462, 465, 475
free will 11, 15
freedom, individual
    welfare state and 155, 161
freedom of speech 54, 63, 197, 407
Freudian theory
    and evolutionary psychology 692
    and masculinity 148
friendly societies 163, 434
fringe benefits 58, 178
functional differentiation 235, 237, 319
functional prerequisites 669-670
functionalism
    and citizenship rights 155
    criticisms of 15, 38, 236, 239, 288, 291, 647, 663-664,
        670-672
    and deviance 468-471, 474-475
    and education 287-288
    and the family 15, 17, 233-242, 245, 248, 259, 261, 263
    and host-immigrant model 87
    and professional power
    and religion 495-500, 514, 525-526, 663
    and sick role 436-437
    and social change 319, 670
    and social stratification 13, 37-39, 647
    and sociological theory 15, 647, 651, 661-664, 668-672, 688
    and youth culture 409
functions 15, 662, 669-671; see also functionalism
    of crime and deviance 20, 468-469
    of education 3, 287-288
    of families 3, 159, 232-238, 240, 242, 245, 247
    of political parties 199-200
    of religion 495, 497-498, 501, 504, 508, 514
    of stratification 37
fundamentalism; see religion fundamentalist

gangs, and deviance 471-473, 484-486
gatekeepers, and media 550
gay men 151, 213, 353; see also homosexuals
gemeinschaft and gesellschaft 389-390, 397, 411-412, 417, 567
gender 20, 34, 46, 116-151; see also men, women
    and age 119
    biology versus culture debate 121-123
    and class 36, 42, 58, 119-121, 129, 141-147
    and community 394-395, 402-404
    and crime 465, 484-486
    and culture 34, 121-122, 148
    definition 121

desirable characteristics 123
discrimination; see sexual discrimination
and doctor-patient interaction 439
and education 117, 124, 135-136, 138, 187, 279, 301-308
and employment; see women and employment
and ethnicity 94, 110, 119, 120-121, 126, 128-134, 256-257
and family 143, 232, 239-242, 248-249, 251, 258-264, 268,
    270, 327, 403-404
and health 443, 449-454, 602
ideal 124
inequalities 28, 63, 118
and leisure 263, 352-354, 394, 403
and mass media 1125, 127-128, 555-557
and poverty 178-179, 183-184
and power/politics 28, 125, 130, 148, 150-152, 179, 214-216,
    219, 261-264
roles 124-125, 258-264, 692
and sex 121
socialisation 121-122, 124, 148, 239, 305, 327, 450
and status 9, 125, 130, 142
and stratification 129, 141-147
and the underclass 62
and unemployment 135, 149, 347-349
and welfare 157-158, 162, 169, 187
General Household Survey 21, 31, 143, 293, 611, 626
General Medical Council 434
generation gap 409
genetics
    and distribution of talent 49, 294
    and gender roles 121-122
    and race 67, 86
    and sociobiology 690-691
gentrification 399
geographical mobility
    and community 389, 401
    and development 571
    of families 245, 249-250, 255, 259
    and religious belief 507, 526
    of women 138, 263
ghettoes 95-96, 104
girls; see also gender
    attitudes to class 141
    attitudes to education and employment 305
    ethnic minority 133
    and sexuality 127, 133
glass ceiling 135
global communication networks 418
global village 218, 417, 693
globalisation
    and community 417-419
    and development 572, 574-575, 578-581
    and mass media 218-219, 221, 418, 693
    and politics 218-221
    and sociological theory 693-695
goal attainment 669
goal displacement 361
Goldthorpe social classification; see class
grandparents 247
Grey Power 410
guestworkers 107

handicap, see disability
Hawthorne effect 609
Hawthorne studies 371, 375
health 421-453; see also disease, illness, medicine
    beliefs about 424, 430
    and class 5, 21, 39, 63, 186, 442-443, 446-449
    cultural-behavioural theories 445-447, 450-451
    definitions 421-422
    and development 426, 566, 574, 601-606

and ethnicity 443-444, 451-452
explanations of inequalities 445-453
and gender 443, 449-454, 602
materialist-structuralist theories 445, 448, 450-452
measurement of 422, 601
natural and social selection theories 445-446, 450-451
and old age 410
personal concepts of 423
and poverty 183, 349-350
primary care 605-606
private sector 161, 168, 170
public 164-166, 382, 586, 601-602; *see also* Public Health
  Acts
racism and 452
regional differences 179
as relative concept 421-424
services 154-155, 170, 187, 603; *see also* National Health
  Service
social construction of 423-424, 433-435
social constructionist theories 445-446, 449
and unemployment 349-351, 448, 451
Health Insurance Act 434
hegemony 60, 210, 502, 673-674, 676
heredity 67,
  and crime 467
  and intelligence 294
heterosexual chauvinism 125
heterosexuality 151
hierarchy 26, 45
  class 42,48, 184, 239
  in education 289
  patriarchy and 151
  of races 67
  in organisations 137, 329, 358-359, 363, 368, 382
Hindus 27, 70, 81, 133, 256, 406
historical research
  using documents 630-631
  and the family 245-247, 258, 265
holism 662, 668
Home Office
  figures on racial attacks 82
  victim surveys; *see* British Crime Surveys
home ownership 42-43, 165, 252
  and class 58, 61, 255
homelessness 63, 163, 170, 187, 256, 296, 409
homeworking 131
homosexuals/homosexuality 219, 236, 441; *see also* gay men;
lesbians
  as deviance 457
honour; *see* status
hospitals 163, 165, 167, 249
  private 161, 168
  health service trust 167
  and mortification of self 381, 440
  psychiatric 160, 162, 167, 364-365, 380-381, 383, 403, 441,
    477, 623
  in Third World 603-604
host-immigrant model 87
House of Lords 197
households; *see also* family
  ethnic differences in size 84, 132, 256
  in pre-industrial Britain 245-247
  size of 247
  types 251, 253, 255
  as unit of class analysis 142-143, 179
housework and housewives 23, 116, 119, 124, 131, 133-134,
    136, 139-140, 142, 157, 196, 239-241, 248, 258-
    264, 268, 305, 317-318, 327, 331, 350, 353, 394, 396, 403,
    646
  and health 451
housing; *see also* home ownership

council 81, 83, 165, 187-188, 255
  and class 39, 58, 103, 187, 255
  and educational achievement 295-296
  and ethnicity 81, 83-84, 90, 103, 106, 187-188, 452
  and health 452
  and inner city 399-400
  of lone parents 252
  and poverty 174, 185
  privatisation of 167-169, 187
  rented 81
  welfare state and 154-155, 158, 158, 165-166, 170, 185
Housing Benefit 167, 187
human relations theories 339, 371, 375-378
hunting and gathering societies 26, 33, 691
husbands; *see* marriage
hyperreality 353, 697
hypodermic syringe model, of media 538
hypothesis 21, 24, 608, 610-611
hysteria 441

ideal types
  of action 665-666
  of authority 193, 195
  of bureaucracy 359, 362, 665
  of community 389-390, 394
  sick role as 439
identity
  and community 387, 400
  and consumption 43, 353
  cultural 43, 45, 78
  ethnic 45, 217
  fragmentation and dislocation of 130
  globalisation and 694
  men's 149, 353
  political 143
  postmodernity and 353, 401, 697-699
  schools and pupils' 291
  sickness and 437
  and status 36-37
ideological state apparatuses 196, 626, 675
ideology 15-16, 35
  and definitions of poverty 175
  dominant class/ruling class 34, 60, 194, 210-211, 239,
    288-289, 399, 660-661, 673-675
  of the family 241, 246, 251
  feminist 118
  mass media and 540-541, 549, 556-558
  patriarchal 157, 196, 262, 304, 306, 556-557
  of professionalism 57
  racist 75-76, 107, 108, 558
  religion as 500-503, 656
  semiotics and 684-685
  socialist 34
  welfare 163
idleness; *see* unemployment
ignorance; *see* education
illegitimacy; *see* birth rate, outside marriage
illness; *see also* disease; health; mental illness; sickness
  chronic 437-440
  definition 422
  and poverty 183
  and social class 5, 186
immigrants 66-67, 71-74, 81, 91, 107; *see also* ethnic groups
immigration 90
  history of in Britain 71
  legislation 83, 85, 132, 187
  statistics on 74, 79
immiseration thesis 33
impression management 616-617, 679-680
incest 234

incoherence, problem of 652
income; *see also* pay; wages
    and class 39-41
    definition 39-40
    disposable 40
    distribution, *see* distribution of income and wealth
    low 2, 255; *see also* low pay, poverty
    original 40, 189
    post-tax 189
Income Support 40, 157, 165, 167, 170, 172, 179
    poverty lines based on 172-174, 180
Independent schools; see education, private
indexicality 686
Indians, North American 9-10, 517, 624, 648-649
Indians, South Asian 69, 81, 84, 112, 128, 132-133, 256-267,
    348
individual classifications, of occupations 143
individualism 198, 671
    and education 290
    and loss of community 390, 393, 401
    and modernity 656-657, 663
    and post-Fordism 335, 342
    and welfare 164
inductive method 637, 656
indulgency pattern, of organisation 362, 364
industrial accidents and diseases 178, 339
industrial conflict 325-327, 338-341
    institutionalisation of 338-339
    types of 339-341
industrial distribution, of ethnic minorities 110
industrial relations 338-344
    legislation 341-342
Industrial Revolution; *see* industrialisation
industrial sabotage 59, 339, 341
industrial society 196
    and bureaucracy 358-360
    and occupational status 9
    theories of 319-320, 332; *see also* post-industrial society
industrialists 51
industrialisation
    and community 389, 415, 596
    costs of 595-596
    and development 567, 571, 575-577, 581, 591-597, 599
    and disease 425
    and education system 273-275
    export-oriented 594-595
    and family 235, 238, 244-249, 258, 319, 642
    and gender roles 139, 258
    and modernity 655
    obstacles to 592-594
    import-substitution and 594
    and religion 516, 526
    and welfare state 163
    and work 244, 318-321, 332, 345
inequality
    and apartheid 101
    class; *see* class
    education and; *see* education
    gender; *see* gender
    global; *see* development
    income and wealth; *see* distribution of income and wealth
    natural 49
    of opportunity; *see* equality of opportunity
    and poverty 171, 175, 177, 181
    of power 206-221
    racial; *see* ethnicity, race
    social 25-26, 30; *see also* social stratification
    and the underclass 62
    welfare state and 154, 186-188
    widening of in Britain 161, 177-179, 180-181, 188-189
infant mortality, *see* mortality

infanticide 426
inflation, and unemployment 345
informal sector
    of economy; *see* economy
    of welfare 159-160, 187, 249-250, 403, 411
information technology
    and globalisation 221
    and leisure 354
infrastructure 16, 210-211, 238, 502
inheritance
    and class 42, 47, 51-52, 246
    and monogamy 239
    taxes 51
inner city
    and community 399-400, 404-406
    and crime 464
    and ethnic minorities 354, 404-406
    and families 251-252, 256
    religion in 527
    and unemployment 347
Inner City Programme 91
innovation, and deviance 471
instincts 6, 232
institutional model, of welfare 155
institutionalisation
    in total institutions 249, 381
instrumental rationality 673-674
instrumentalist attitudes 59-60, 326
instrumentalist theory of state 211
integration
    of ethnic minorities 95; *see also* assimilation
    as functional prerequisite 669
intelligence
    evolution and 690
    and educational achievement 294, 314
    quotient (IQ) 47
    testing and education 275-277, 299; *see also* education,
    11+ in
intelligentsia 29
interaction 11, 16-17, 22, 364, 608
    classroom 290-292, 299-300, 306-307, 366, 610
    doctor-patient 437, 439-440
    and impression management 679
    in marriage 242
    para-social 401
    power and 681
    in research 244, 648
    and self 678
interactionism; *see also* interpretivism
    and bureaucracy 364-366
    and deviance 450, 475-481, 483, 646
    criticisms of 17-18, 291, 365, 480, 646-647, 681
    and education 291, 299-301, 313-314
    and methodology 642, 646, 648, 678-679
    and organisations 364-366
    and sick role 437
    and sociological theory 16-19, 663, 677-682, 688
interest groups 35, 156, 199-203, 212, 339; *see also* pressure
    groups
    as communities 387, 401
intermediate class 33, 48-50, 142
International Labour Organisation, definition of unemployment
    346-348
international organisations 218-220
International Passenger Survey 71
International Typographical Union 369
interpretivism 11, 16, 291, 299-300, 364-366, 504, 665; *see also*
    social action theory, interactionism, phenomenology
    and family 235-236, 240, 242-244
    and methodology 639, 641-644, 678-679
    and official statistics 626

and organisations 364-365
and religion 506-508
interviewer bias 614, 616, 619
interviews 73, 81, 618-620
    active approaches to 619
    and domestic violence 620
    and education 298, 307, 313
    feminist 645
    non-directive 619, 645
    structured 21, 244, 614; *see also* questionnaires
    unstructured/in-depth 22, 242-244, 618-619, 621, 633, 635
    and workers' attitudes 326
intrapreneurship 377
Islam; *see* Muslims
Islington Crime Survey 464
issue method 193, 195, 199, 201-202

Japan 34, 126
Japanese organisations 334-335, 378-380
jet set 51
Jews 71, 90, 257
Jim Crow system 7-8, 94-95
jobs; *see* employment; occupations; work
job satisfaction; *see* work satisfaction
Jobseekers Allowance; *see* unemployment benefits
joint classifications, of occupations 143
joint stock companies 322
judiciary 197, 207
just in time system 378
juvenile delinquency
    labelling theories 19, 476
    and lone parent families 237, 255, 487
    and poverty 183
    subcultural theories 471-474

Kerner Report 95
kibbutz 233-234, 236, 240
kin altruism 690-691
kinship; *see also* family
    in Britain 247-250, 268, 411
    and community 389, 395
    in different societies 232-235
    in ethnic minorities 256-257
    and industrialisation 235-237, 245-247, 319
    in upper class 47, 52, 207-208, 211, 246
    selection and racism 86
knowledge, in post-industrial society 332

labelling 183
    of crime 476, 483
    of pupils in education 291, 299-301, 610
    of sick and disabled 437
labelling theory
    and deviance 19, 450, 475-481, 483, 646
    and education 299
    and health inequalities 445, 450
labour
    domestic; *see* housework
    migrant 85
    shortage 134
Labour Force Survey 73, 83, 110, 134-135, 308-309, 625
Labour governments 201
    and education 276
    and social inequality 200, 214
    and trade unions 203, 341
    and welfare state 165
labour market 33
    ethnicity and the 109-113

poverty and the 183-184, 188
sectors 110
segmentation 61
women in the 134-138, 143; *see also* dual labour market theory, women and employment
Labour Party
    and community values, 393
    and democracy 369
    and ethnic minorities 90, 103, 108, 216-217, 227
    and voting behaviour 143, 222-229
    and women 216
    and working class 59, 394
labour process 325, 328; *see also* work
labour theory of value 33
laissez faire 163
land reform 588
landowners 27, 51-52
language 6, 17
    and education 297-298, 315
    and cultural diversity 70
    and political correctness 68
    postmodernism and 697-698
    racist 77
    and sexual abuse 127
    social evolution and 674
    as a social fact 662, 688
    structuralism and 682-683
    upper class 52
language games 697
law 2, 20, 196-197
    changes in and crime statistics 463
    changes in the law and divorce statistics 267-268
    Marxist view of 480
    and order 18-19, 483-484
law enforcement; *see also* criminal justice system, police
    and crime statistics 463
    racialism in 80, 96
    selective 18, 480-481
learning 7
left realism 484, 487, 489-491
left wing politics 59
legal system 210; *see also* criminal justice system
legitimation
    crisis 674
    as function of democracy and the state 197, 210, 413
    as function of education 288-289, 297
    as function of racism 88
    as function of religion 497, 500-501
    as function of welfare state 156
leisure 352-355
    age and 352, 409-411, 534
    big business and 352, 355
    class and 30, 39, 56, 353, 355, 394, 400-402, 534
    definition of 318-319, 352
    ethnicity and 353-354
    gender and 263, 352-354, 394, 403
    home centredness in 248, 259-261, 395-397, 401, 410; *see also* privatisation in family life
    industrialisation and 352
    mass media and 534
    postmodernism and 353-354, 401
    unemployment and 345, 350, 353
    work and 352-353
lesbians 117, 125, 213
liberal democracy 29, 197-199, 206, 655
Liberal Democrat Party; *see* Liberal Party
Liberal Party 90, 222-224, 226-228
    and community values 393

liberalism
  and democracy 197
  and modernity 655
liberation theology 503
life chances
  and class 25, 28, 30-31, 35, 39-42, 43, 276
  and ethnicity 75, 96-97, 102
  and gender 129
life cycle
  and family; 233, 250-253, 255, 263
  and leisure 352
life expectancy
  and class 39, 443
  and ethnicity in USA 96
  and gender 150-151, 259-260, 443
  increase in 251, 268
life histories 624
  and social mobility 46
lifestyles; see also leisure
  and age 409-411
  and class 28, 31, 39, 43-45, 47, 56, 58, 248, 395-397,
    399-400, 446
  and consumption 43, 45
  of ethnic minorities 405
  and health 446, 453; see also health, cultural-behavioural
    theories
  and locality 412
  and mass media 534
  and postmodernity 353-354, 401, 697
  and poverty 174
  and status groups 35
  of women 129, 142
linguistics 682-683; see also language
living standards
  and capitalism 34-35, 219
  of working class 58, 248, 259, 396-397
lobbying, of MPs 208
local government 215
  and democracy 197
  and education 275-276, 285
  and welfare provision 159, 163, 166-168, 403
  and anti-racism 94, 216-217
locality; see also regional differences
  and community 387, 391. 393-394, 412
  and family 236, 251, 255-256
locality social system 390-391
log linear analysis, of voting behaviour 226
logic of capitalism; see capitalism
logic of industrialism 29, 219
longitudinal studies 625
loony left 94
low pay 341, 353
  black people and 88, 103
  women and 130-131, 135, 157, 179, 187
  part time work and 331
  poverty and 154, 178, 184
lower class; see working class
lumpenproletariat 61

magazines 79, 125, 128, 533, 541
  teenage 127, 555-557
malestream sociology 66, 116, 148, 645
management 51
  in Japanese organisations 378, 380
  and organisations 371, 373-375
  strategies 328-330, 336, 341, 376; see also scientific
    management
  and work 320
management theories
  and industrial relations 338-339

and organisations 370-375
managerial revolution thesis 53, see also separation of
    ownership and control
managers 328; see also management
  attitudes to ethnic minorities 110
  attitudes to women 137
  and class situation 31-32, 48, 54-56,
  and corporations 53, 322-323
manufacturing industry 46
  decline of 332-333, 342
  employment of ethnic minorities in 110
  employment of women in 135, 331
  and industrialisation 244, 319-321
  in Third World 573, 595
marginalisation 61, 71
  and crime 104, 405, 489
  and unemployment 351
  of youth 409
marijuana use, and labelling theory 476
market 28, 35, 36, 167, 659
market forces 29, 41, 57, 63, 120, 320, 345, 568
  and development 572
  and mass media 540
  and welfare state 154-157, 161-162, 164, 167
market liberal theories
  and poverty 175, 182, 185
  and unemployment 345
  and welfare 155-158, 160-161, 163-165, 167-168
market position; see market situation
market situation 35, 48, 55, 98, 142
marriage; see also family
  arranged 78, 132-133, 247, 406-407
  breakdown of 242, 267-270; see also divorce
  changes in 247-248, 252, 258-270
  and the construction of reality 242
  empty shell 267-268
  equality and inequality in 237, 258-264, 327
  expectations of 268
  feminist views on 118, 258-259, 261-265
  financial control in 261
  forced 130
  historical research on 247, 265
  second and subsequent 252, 265-266, 268-269
  teenage 268-269
  trends in popularity 259, 265-266, 523
Marxism
  and bureaucracy 365, 367-368, 375-377, 383
  and class 14, 33-35, 55, 59-60, 129, 220, 647, 657-661,
    673-675
  criticisms of 16, 34, 211-212, 240-241, 289, 291, 637, 660,
    690
  and development 572; see also underdevelopment theory
  and deviance 383, 473-474, 480-483
  and education 60, 288-290
  and the family 196, 235-243, 246, 263
  and feminism; see feminism, Marxist/socialist
  humanist 673-674
  and industrial society 219, 319-310
  and leisure 352, 355
  and mass media 54, 60, 196, 210, 540-541, 549, 552-554
  and official statistics 626
  and poverty 157, 175, 184, 647
  and power 194, 200, 202, 204, 206-207, 209-214, 297, 340,
    399
  and pressure groups 204
  and professional power 434
  and race and ethnicity 88-89, 98, 106-108
  and religion 34, 500-503, 514, 525
  and semiotics 684
  and social change 658-660
  and sociological theory 651-653, 657-661, 672-677, 688

and the state 54, 88, 156-157, 196, 209-212, 483, 540, 660, 673-675
structuralist 211, 674-675
and urban life 412-413
and unemployment 345
and the welfare state 156-158, 160, 212
and work 59, 319-320, 322-326, 332-333, 335-336, 339-340, 342
masculinity 116, 148-151, 260, 262; see also men
contradictions in 148-149
crisis of 148
hegemonic 149
postmodernism and 353
social construction of 121-123, 148
mass culture 395, 673-674; see also mass society theory
mass media 533-564; see also advertising, cinema, newspapers, magazines, radio, television, video
audience 533, 538, 541, 628
bias vs impartiality 534, 536-537, 544-546, 548-550, 552-554
cultural effects theory 538-539
definition 533-534
and deviance 458-461, 478-479, 483, 558
effects 79, 538-541, 549-550, 557-564
and ethnicity/race 79, 85, 94, 557-560
and Falklands War 544-546
and families 232
and feminism 120, 555, 557
and gender 125, 127-128, 555-557
and globalisation 218-219, 221, 418, 693
hypodermic syringe model 538, 561-562
and identity 45
and industrial conflict 338
Marxist theories 54, 60, 196, 210, 540-541, 549, 552-554
methods of research into 552, 554, 558, 561, 628-629
and New Right 79
and news 539, 544-546, 550-555, 628, 697
ownership and control of 533-537
pluralist theories 540-541
and politics 203, 223, 227-228, 536-538, 546-550, 553-554
and poverty 64
and pornography 125
postmodernism and 542-544, 697
and religion 522-523, 526-527, 529-530
two step flow model 538
and violence 64, 560-564, 610
mass production
decline of 334-336, 377
and development 577
mass society theory 401-402; see also mass culture
material factors
as cause of educational underachievement 294-296
as cause of racism 90
materialism 658; see also health, materialist-structural theories
maternity rights 240
matriarchy 129, 131, 152
matrilineal societies 234
McDonald's 218, 334, 342
McDonaldisation of society 360-361
meanings 11, 17, 22, 677, 680-681
of deviance 475
in education 291, 299
in family life 242-243
in organisations 364
in research 617-619, 622, 630-631, 636, 642-643, 665, 679
and religion 497, 504, 507, 526
semiotics and 685
of youth subcultures 409, 473-474
means testing 155-156, 164-165, 167-168, 179
means of production 16, 28, 36, 688
ownership of 36, 207, 319-320, 322, 325, 658-660; see also ownership and control of business

measurement, in research 21, 608, 636
mechanical solidarity 389, 663
mechanisation 244
mechanisms 639, 642
media; see mass media
medical profession
challenges to autonomy of 435
criticisms of 427
degrees of control over patients 439
functionalist theories of 433-434
historical development of 434-435
Marxist theories of 433
and patients 436-442
Weberian theories 434
Medical Registration Act 434
medical systems
civilised vs primitive 428
classification of 428-430
medicalisation of deviance 440-442
medicine 421-453; see also health; medical profession
alternative 423, 431-433
holistic 431-432
non-Western 428-429
preventative 434
source of power of 433-434
role in decline of disease 425-427, 587
in Third World 601-606
Western; see biomedicine
melting pot, USA as a 94-97
Members of Parliament 201, 203, 208-209
educational background 209
ethnic minority 108-109, 216
women as 214-216
men; see also gender, masculinity
feminist attitudes to 120
involvement in housework and childcare 23, 139-140, 240
new 148, 353
reaction to feminism of 150-151
sociological study of 148-149
men's rights movement 150
men's studies 148, 150
mental handicap; see disability
mental illness 183, 256, 350, 477; see also hospitals, psychiatric
and class 446
and community care 159-160, 162, 167, 403
and ethnicity 444
and gender 443, 450-451
mergers 322, 534
meritocracy 46-47, 50, 288-289
metanarratives, and postmodernism 578, 696-697
methodological pluralism 633-635
methodology 4, 21-24, 374, 608-649; see also case studies; documents; ethnographic studies; experiments; interviews; official statistics; participant observation; qualitative methods; quantitative methods; questionnaires; sampling; science of society; social surveys; sources
assessing 632-635, 653
and communities 394
Durkheim and 636-637, 661-663
and family life 22-23
feminist 644-646, 653
interpretivism and 639, 641-644, 678-679
science and 636-641
and voting behaviour 225-226
metropolis 389, 412, 416
and satellites 575
middle class, 26, 31, 34, 36, 42, 49, 50, 54-59, 137, 187, 207; see also service class; intermediate class
black 96, 108, 112
and consumption cleavages 43
divisions in 54-56, 223

and education; *see* education, and class; educational
achievement, and class
families 246, 250, 258-259, 262, 264
images of the 56
lifestyles 43, 56
lower 54-55, 143
middle 54
new and old 54, 219
and voting behaviour; *see* voting behaviour and class
upper 54-5
women 139
middle mass 59
middle range theory 671
migrant labour 108; *see also* immigrants
migration 587; *see also* immigration
net 585
and urbanisation 598-599
militancy, working class 59
millionaires 51-53, 113
mimetic function, of leisure 352
miners' strike 59, 219, 539, 676
minority groups 66-68, 71, 184, 219; *see also* ethnic groups
mixed parentage 69-70, 99
modernisation theory 219, 570-571, 573-574, 576, 578, 581, 591, 594
modernism, and arts/architecture 696
modernity 673
and emergence of sociology 655-668
and lifestyles 353
and the nation state 196, 218-220, 693-694
modes of production 33, 145, 209, 238, 319, 325, 658, 675
modes of regulation 335
mods and rockers 478
monarchy 196-197
monetarism; *see also* market liberalism
and unemployment 345
and welfare 155, 168
monogamy 3, 239
monopolisation, of business ownership 322
moral panics
and delinquency 478-479, 630
and immigration 72
and media violence 564
and mugging 81, 88, 482-483
morality, and social order 663, 669
morbidity; *see also* disease
class and 443-444, 446
ethnicity and 444
gender and 443-444
as measure of health 422
effect of modern medicine on 426-427, 601-602
mortality
and class 186, 443, 445-446
death rate and 244, 585
decline in Europe 585-587
effect of modern medicine on 426-427, 587
ethnicity 444
gender and 443
infant and child 5, 31, 445, 567, 587, 589, 601-602
as measure of health 422, 601, 679
regional differences 179, 350
in Third World 566-567, 589, 601-602
mortification of self 381, 440
motherhood
feminist views on 118, 120
unmarried; *see* family, lone parent
mugging 79, 81, 478-479, 557, 676
multicultural education 83, 91, 217
multicultural society 66, 70, 77, 79, 507
multinationals; *see* transnational corporations
murder 126

Muslims 70, 81, 87, 133, 256
and Rushdie affair 407-408
women 131
myths 683

names, significance of 3-4
nation state
end of the 219-221, 579, 693
rise of the 196, 218, 571
National Assistance; *see* Income Support
National Curriculum 279, 284-287, 300, 302
National Front 90, 92, 623
National Health Service 57, 154-155, 160, 163, 165, 168, 186, 223, 435, 442
charges 155
class differences in use 447
effectiveness of 427, 436
reforms 435
National Insurance scheme 157, 164-165
national project 212
nationalised industries 214
nationalism 34, 218-221, 415, 571, 694
nationality 73, 196
natural selection 86
Nazism 77, 94; *see also* fascism; 34
negotiation 17, 642
in classroom 291, 299
between doctors and patients 437, 441-442
in family life 242-243, 249
of order in organisations 364-366
of roles 11
of justice 19, 366
neo-Darwinism 690; *see also* sociobiology
neo-Fordism 335
neo-Marxism; *see* Marxism
neutralisation, techniques of
neutrality pattern, of leisure 352
New Age Travellers 457
New Commonwealth 70
immigration from 71-73, 85, 87, 88, 128
new international division of labour 323
new religious movements 219, 431, 508
evolution of 518-521
origins of 516-518
and politics 514-516
and secularisation 524-531
types 512-514
New Right
and development 571-572, 574
and deviance; *see* right realism
and the family 182, 235-237, 240, 265, 487
and mass media 79
and politics 200, 204
and race 77-78, 86, 94
and religion 515
and welfare 155-156, 158, 167, 182, 185; *see also* market liberal theories
new social movements; *see also* new religious movements; women's movement
for personal growth 149
political 219-221, 672, 674; *see also* pressure groups
urban 413
new vocationalism 282-284
news agencies 550
newspapers; *see also* mass media
and news selection 550-552
ownership 534-537
and politics 227-228, 534, 536-537, 548-550
and race 79, 94
readership 533-535

and images of women 125
normalisation 382
norms 8-9, 11, 13, 15, 243, 287-288, 315, 636
    and class 58-59
    for conversational distance 8
    and definition of deviance 455
    of poor 182-183
    religion and 497-500
North-South divide; see regional differences
nouveaux riches 52
nuclear weapons, feminism and 118, 121
numbers game 72
numerical control systems 330, 337
nutrition, and health; see diet and health

objectivity 20-21, 622; see also bias
obligations, in family life 249
observation methods; see also participant observation
    in education 289, 313
occupational crime 474
occupational structure
    and changes in class structure 56, 226, 228
    and social mobility 46, 49
occupations; see also workers
    of blacks and whites in USA 97
    and class; see class
    of ethnic groups in Britain 105
    and health risks 450-451; see also class and health
    manual 46
    nonmanual 46
    status of 9
    of women 134-138, 141-144
odds ratio, for class and voting 225-226, 229
official statistics 625-627, 634
    advantages and disadvantages of 626
    on class 30-32
    on crime 79, 461-465, 484, 626-627
    on domestic violence 241-242
    on education 293, 303-304, 308-309
    on ethnicity and immigration 72-74
    on income and wealth 39, 41-42
    parish records as 245
    on racial attacks 82
    on suicide 640, 642-643
    on unemployment 21, 346-349
old age; see elderly; pensioners
Old Commonwealth 71, 85
old money 51
oligarchy, iron law of 368-370, 624
ontological security 688
operationalising concepts 615
opinion polls 201, 224, 227-228
opportunity structures, and delinquency 472
opposition, in politics 197-199
opposition pattern, in leisure 352
oppositions, in myths 683
order, problem of 669
organic solidarity 389
organisations 358-384; see also bureaucracy
    Aston Group and 372
    configurations of 372-373
    conflict theories 375-377
    contingency theories 373-374
    control in 375-376, 379
    design of 371-374
    and environments 363, 372-374
    ethnomethodological theories 365-366
    human relations theories 371, 375-378
    industrial 319, 361-363, 376-377
    informal structures in 362, 364, 371, 373-375

interactionist theories 364-366
Japanese 334-335, 378-380
Marxist theories; see bureaucracy, Marxism and;
    organisations, conflict theories
managerial theories 370-375
mechanistic 362-363
organic 362-363, 373
post-Fordism and 377-378
postmodern 377-380
professionals and 364-365, 372-373
religious 508-521
scientific management theory and 370-371, 374-375
and social control 380-384
organisational effectiveness 194
organising out outsiders 200
organism, society as an 235, 662
osteopathy 431-432
outdoor poor relief 163
overloaded government 156, 200
ownership and control of business 206, 209
    concentration of 323-324, 377, 534-536, 659
    and mass media 533-537
    separation of 53, 211, 322-324
Oxbridge Universities 52, 207-209, 279, 303

Pakistanis 81, 84, 87, 128, 131-133, 256-257, 346, 348
panopticon 382, 384
paradigms 638
paramedical occupations 435
parasuicide 351
parents
    and family life 242-243, 249-250, 252
    interest and educational achievement 295, 315
    lone; see families, lone parent
parity of esteem, in education 275-276
part time work; see work
participant observation 22, 620-623, 633-634, 679
    advantages 621-622
    disadvantages 622-623, 632
    of religion 521, 623, 633
    of traveller-gypsies 623
    of work 326-327
participation in labour market
    by ethnic minorities 110
    by women 110, 134-135, 143
parties, political 35, 54, 182, 210, 214, 222; see also parties by
        name
    democracy in 368-370
    and pressure groups 202-203
    role of 199-200
party, Weberian concept of 35-36
paternity leave 240
patrials 85
patriarchy 123, 129, 144-145, 151, 692; see also ideology,
patriarchal
    debates over 120-121
    definition 119, 145
    in the family 143, 157, 239-240, 255-256, 258, 261-262, 265
    in education 301, 304-305
    in ethnic minorities 130-131
    in traditional working class communities 394
patriotism 77
pattern maintenance 669
pay, inequalities in; see also distribution of income and wealth;
        low pay; wages
    and ethnicity 97, 179
    and gender 135-136, 187, 259, 263
    and class 40-41, 54
peace movement 116, 118, 121, 200, 219
peasants 29, 245-246

peer group
  as agency of gender socialisation 121
pensioners, old age 62, 177; *see also* elderly; old age
pensions
  funds 53, 211
  occupational 40-42, 178
  private 161, 168
  state 40-41, 154, 164-165, 167, 178-179
performance, in interaction 17, 679-680
peripheral workforce 335-336, 379
periphery and core, and development 575
permissiveness 117, 236
perspectives, *see* sociological theory
personal as political 117, 214
personal service occupations 56-57, 332-333
personality traits, and gender 124
petty bourgeoisie 33, 55-56, 108, 212, 225; *see also* business,
  small
phenomenology; *see also* ethnomethodology; interpretivism
  and methodology 642-644
  and sociological theory 684-685
pilot studies 616, 624
planning 29, 156
plantation economy, and slavery 98-99
pluralism 199-202
  and community 400-401
  classical 199
  criticisms of 54, 200-202, 208-209
  and decision making 193, 199, 201-202, 261
  and ethnicity 71
  elite 200-201, 207
  of life-worlds 507-508
  and mass media 540-541
  and political parties 199-200
  and pressure groups 199-200, 204
  and power 54, 193, 206, 208, 209, 322
  religious 526
polarisation of social classes 33-34, 659-660
police 366; *see also* criminal justice system; law enforcement
  and crime statistics 461, 465, 483, 486
  left realism and 489
  and racism 79-80, 83, 217, 406, 483, 486, 557
policy communities 200, 203
policy networks 203-204
political attitudes; *see* attitudes
political correctness 68, 94
political economy, of urban life 412
political organisations; *see* parties, pressure groups
political parties; *see* parties
political society 210
political systems 196-198
politics 192-229; *see also* power, voting behaviour
  of difference 78
  of experience 139
  and globalisation 218-221
  and mass media 203, 223, 227-228, 536-537, 540
  of racial struggle 107, 216-218
  religion and 514-516, 530-531
pollution; *see* environment
polygamy 233-234, 267
Poor Law 163, 165
pop music 78, 127
population; *see* demography
populist theory, and development 576-577
pornography 64, 125
positive action, against racial discrimination 92
positivism 636, 644
post-Fordism 334-338, 377-378
post-industrial society 56, 320, 322, 332-333, 697
postmodernism
  and community 401

  criticisms of 698
  and development 578-580
  and leisure/lifestyles 56, 353-354, 401, 697
  and mass media 542-544, 697
  and the nation state 219-220
  and organisations 377-380
  and sociological theory 696-699
poverty 64, 90, 163, 171-186, 200; *see also* inequality
  absolute 171-173, 175, 177-178
  Breadline Britain studies 174-177
  and capitalism 34
  and class 175, 178
  and crime 487
  culture of 62, 182-183, 185-186
  dependency theories 182, 185
  deprivation standard 174-175, 177
  deserving and undeserving 62
  and ethnicity 28, 40, 83-84, 93, 96, 132, 151, 179, 183-184,
    405
  explanations of 181-186
  extent and distribution of 40, 61, 164, 170-171, 174, 177-181,
    219
  and families 177-179, 184-185, 237, 252, 255, 259
  and gender 178-179, 183-184
  and health 447-448, 601-602; *see also* health and class
  Income Support based definitions 172-174, 180
  individualistic theories 182
  low cost budget line 172
  market liberal theories 181-182, 185
  Marxist theories 157, 175, 184, 647
  primary and secondary 171
  regional differences 179
  relative 171-172, 177, 186
  Rowntree's research into 171-172, 177
  rural 415
  social democratic theories 155, 183-184
  situational constraints and 183
  and stratification 171, 183-184
  Third World 566-567, 569, 576, 578, 584, 587, 589, 598-599,
    601-602
  in traditional working class communities 397-398
  and the underclass 62, 104, 182, 184-185
  and unemployment 2, 39-40, 177-178, 183-184, 349-351
  welfare state and 154-155, 158, 164-165, 182, 184, 186, 188
  women and 178-179, 183-184
poverty trap 2, 155, 158, 182
power 26, 35-36, 54, 97, 185, 192-229, 291, 379, 688; *see also*
    authority
  bureaucracy and 322, 358-359
  definition and measurement of 30, 192-196, 199-202
  disciplinary 382
  and ethnicity 66, 71, 83, 98, 200, 216-218
  in the family 214, 243, 261-264
  functionalist theories 38, 194
  and gender 28, 125, 130, 148, 150-152, 179, 214-216,
    261-264
  and globalisation 218-221
  inequalities of 206-221
  interactionism and 680-681
  Lukes' three faces of 193-196, 200, 207, 210
  Marxist theories 194, 200, 202, 204, 206-207, 209-214, 297,
    340, 399
  pluralism and 199-202
  of professions 57, 433-434
  sovereign 381
  variable sum concept 194
  Weber on 192, 358-359
  and upper class 51
  zero sum concept 194
power blocs 54, 210-212, 673
pragmatism 677

predestination, doctrine of 504
pre-industrial societies
    age stratification in 408
    disease in 425
    the family in 139, 245-247
    and occupational status 9
    work in 318-320, 359, 659
prejudice; see also racial prejudice
    against women 118
presentation of self 17
press; see newspapers
pressure groups 35, 54, 160, 168, 199, 202-205, 212, 214,
        217-218, 219, 222, 236; see also new social movements
    and democracy 202, 204-205
    insider and outsider 201-205
    methods 203-204, 208
    protective and promotional 202
prestige, see status
primary sector, of employment 135
primitive communism 33
prisons 380
    Foucault on 381-383
    population by ethnic group 106
private property 18, 33, 99, 200, 210, 325
private sector
    of education; see education, private
    of welfare 156, 159, 161-162, 167-168, 403
private sphere; see also domestic role
    and marriage 242-243
    women and the 117, 139, 145, 215, 263, 484
private troubles and public issues 1-2, 44
privatisation
    of family and leisure 59, 247-249, 259, 395-396, 401, 416
    of religion 526
    of welfare 156, 167-168, 170, 187
    of industry 41-42, 112
privilege 61
production
    family as unit of 245, 248
    flexibility in 334-338
production relations 36
profeminism 150
professionalisation 56-57
professions; see also medical profession
    black people in 112-113
    and class 31-32, 48, 54, 56-57,
    definitions 56
    higher 138
    lower 56, 138
    in organisations 364-365, 372-373
    and post-industrial society 332
    as pressure groups 204
    welfare 57
    women in 138
    and work 320, 328
profit 28, 33-34, 202, 319, 322, 325-326, 345, 375, 659
proletariat 16, 31, 33, 55, 658-660, 673-675; see also working
        class
proletarianisation 55, 58, 329
promiscuity, sex differences in 122
property 56; see also capital
props, use of in impression management 17
prostitution, as functional 468
Protestant ethic 320, 504-507, 641-642, 665
psychology
    evolutionary 691-692
    and masculinity 148
    and prejudice 75
    and unemployment 349-350
public expenditure
    on education 273

growth in 165, 168, 168, 169, 204, 345
    cuts in 156, 158, 162, 167, 169
public hygiene, and health 426
Public Health Acts 163-164
public schools; see schools
public sphere, and the family 242-243
punishment 7
    capital 204
    changing methods of 381-384
    and deviance 455
    of slaves 99-100
    of white collar crime 475
purdah 78, 131
pyramid model of racial stratification 104-105

qualifications, educational; see educational achievement
qualitative methods 21-24, 372, 632, 679
quality circles 378-379
quantitative methods 21-24, 314, 608, 614-616, 618, 632, 634,
        636
    and organisations 372, 374
questionnaires 21-22, 614-617, 633-634
    advantages and disadvantages 616, 622
    on domestic violence 617
    on education 311, 314
    postal 616, 618
    on poverty 174-176
    on racial prejudice 75
    on religious belief 615, 633-634
    self-completion 614, 616
    sexism in 645
    on workers' attitudes 326
questions, open and closed 615

race; see also ethnicity
    biological classifications 67
    as a social definition 67-68
race relations 66, 86, 108
    effects of slavery on 99
    immigration legislation and 85
    industry 77
Race Relations Acts 68, 72, 80, 92, 187
racial attacks 81-82, 90-93, 126, 132, 311, 558
racial disadvantage 83-84, 217, 354; see also ethnicity, and
        inequality
racial discrimination 66, 69, 75, 80-81, 83, 87-88, 92, 98, 104,
        106, 110, 112, 187-188, 217, 240, 312, 314, 350,
        490; see also racialism
    definition 75
    direct and indirect 80
    PEP/PSI surveys 81, 83, 179
    in USA 94-97
racial groups, in South Africa 101
racial harassment 82, 132, 149, 240, 311
racial inequality; see ethnicity; racial disadvantage
racial minorities; see ethnic groups
racial prejudice 69, 74-76, 80, 91-92, 106; see also racism
racial segregation 80
racial stratification 97-98
racial types 67
racialisation 67, 108
racialised class fraction model 108
racialism 80-83, 85, 94-95; see also racial discrimination
racism 66, 68-69, 74-97, 129-130, 132-133, 137, 145, 151, 217,
        354, 405, 408
    in criminal justice system 486
    cultural 74-80, 83, 87-88, 94-95, 694
    definition 75
    in education 312-314
    in elections 90-91, 400

in education 311-314
explanations 86-91
feminism and 119, 240
functions of 88-89
and health inequalities 452
institutional 83-85, 87, 94-95
in media 557-560
new 76, 86, 94; see also New Right
scientific 75
sociobiology and 86-87
strategies for combating 91-97; see also anti-racism
structural theories 87-89
radical theories; see also criminology radical; Marxism
of race and class 106-107
of value free sociology 646-647
radio 533
rape 120, 126, 131, 148, 151
Rastafarians 70, 78, 133, 217, 517-518
rationalisation 193, 196, 320, 666-668, 673-674
and bureaucracy 359-360
and community 389
and religion 504-507, 516, 526
rationalism 655-656
reactive ethnicity 78
realism 638-639; see also left realism; right realism
reason 655-656, 673, 698
rebellion, and deviance 471
recession, economic
and unemployment 49, 62, 111, 345
and industrial relations 342
and voting behaviour 228
reciprocal altruism 691-692
red tape 362; see also bureaucracy
redistribution of income and wealth 58, 63, 155, 184, 186; see also distribution of income and wealth
reductionist explanations
economic 107
genetic 86
reflexive monitoring of action 688
reflexivity
ethnomethodology and 686
in social research 633, 644, 646, 648
refugees 71
regime of accumulation 335
region, and interaction 681
regional differences
and class 58
and family; see locality and family
and poverty 179
and unemployment 347-348
and voting behaviour 227
Registrar General's Social Class Scheme 31-32, 58, 141-143, 145, 679
regulationist theory 335-336
relations of production 209, 325, 658-659, 675
relative autonomy
of class and race 107
of state 211
relativism 647, 652, 698; see also cultural relativism
reliability 608, 632
religion
attitudes to contraception 133, 589
civil 498-500
definitions 493-495
discrimination on grounds of 71
and economy 500-507
and ethnicity 70, 406-408
functionalist theories 495-500, 514, 525-526, 663
fundamentalist 407-408, 528-531
interpretive theories 506-508
Marxist theories 34, 500-503, 514, 525

mass media and 522-523, 526-527, 529-530
new movements 219, 431, 508, 512-521, 524-531
pluralism 526
and politics 514-516, 530-531
sacred and profane 493-495
and secularisation 268, 521-531, 666-667
and social order 7, 495-503, 663
statistics on belief and membership 71, 522-523, 524-525, 527-529, 615
and supernatural 494
in USA 498-500, 515, 528-531
Weber on 504-505, 526, 641-642
religious organisations 508-521
repatriation 91
replication, in research 609-610, 622, 632
repressive state apparatuses 675
reproduction; see also childbearing
black women and 133-134
as a function of the family 233-234
social and cultural 297, 675
of structures 688
technology 119
as work 318
reproduction of labour power
education and 288-289
family and 239
reproductive success 690
research methods; see methodology
reserve army of labour 342, 659
black people as 88
women as 119, 240
residential segregation
and class 58
and race 94, 101
residual model, of welfare 155
resistance
class 59
politics of 77
to racism 354
religion and 502-503
by slaves 99
workers' 329-330
by youth 409, 473-474, 673
reskilling 329
resources, allocative and authoritative 688
response rates, in research 613-614, 616
responsible autonomy 329, 376
restricted code 297-298
restructuring of employment 112
retail revolution, and urban life 415
retreatism, and deviance 471
revisionist approach, to gender and class 143-144
revolution
Christian 503
democratic 655
Eastern European 221
industrial; see industrialisation
proletarian 34, 59, 164, 210, 345, 660, 673, 675
Russian 367-368
scientific 638
rich, the 50-53
right realism 484, 487-489
riots
in UK 104, 204, 217-218, 351, 405-406, 410, 491, 557
in USA 95-97, 491, 697
risk society 693-694
rite de passage 440
ritualism, and deviance 471
rituals, religious 495, 497-499, 526
robots, and work 321
role distance 681

role models, for black people 113
role taking 678
roles 9, 11-12, 679-681
    gender; *see* gender roles
    instrumental and expressive 258
    in marriage; *see* conjugal roles
    in organisations 364
romance 127, 133, 247
Roman Catholics 133
rules 6, 9; *see also* norms
    bargaining over
    and bureaucracy 196, 359, 361, 362
    and definition of deviance 455
    ethnomethodology and 686
ruling class 47-48, 50, 210; *see also* capitalists, bourgeoisie
    divisions in the 210-211
    hegemony 60, 210
    ideology; *see* ideology, dominant class
    Marxist theory and the 16, 54, 106, 156-157, 194, 196, 211, 660
    and religion 500, 502, 514
rural life 414-416
    changes in 412, 414-415
    and family 256
    problems of 415
rural-urban framework 411-412
Rushdie affair 407-408

sacred and profane 493-495
salariat 54, 225-226, 229
salaries; *see* wages
sampling 73, 81, 145, 290, 311, 314, 611-614, 616, 622, 626
    multistage cluster 612
    quota 612
    random 611
    snowball and volunteer 612-614
    stratified 612-613
    systematic 611
sampling frame 611
sanctions 7
    against South Africa 101
scapegoating, of black people 88, 90-91
school leaving age
    class and 295
    increases in 275, 282-283, 299
school meals 164
schools 163, 167, 213, 273; *see also* education
    church and charity 273, 275
    City Technology Colleges 284-285
    comprehensive 276-279, 286, 294, 299
    elementary 274-275
    grant maintained 159, 167, 284-285
    grammar 273-279, 285, 296
    independent; *see* education, private
    public 47, 52, 207-209, 273-275, 279-281
    secondary modern 275-276, 278, 296
    single sex 302, 306
    technical 275-276
science
    as a metanarrative 696
    natural 609, 636, 538-641, 656
    normal 638
    and racism 75
science of society, sociology as 21, 636-641, 657-658
scientific management 328-329, 370-371, 374
scientific method 608-609, 636-637
scientific revolutions 638
Second World War
    influence on education system 275
    influence on welfare state 164

sects 70
    characteristics of 508-509
    development of 518-519
    and politics 514-516
    and secularisation 526-527
    types of 514-515
secular voters 222
secularisation
    criticisms of 522, 524-529, 530-531
    definition 521
    evidence for 268, 521-525, 529-530
    explanations of 525-526, 666
    new religious movements and 524-525
    in USA 529-531
segregation of workforce 142
    horizontal 135
    vertical 135, 138
selection process, for employment
    and ethnic minorities 110
selectivity, in welfare provision 155-156, 167, 182; *see also*
means testing
self 678, 681
self-deception 691-692
self-employed 33, 54, 112, 599
self-fulfilling prophecy 148, 276, 291, 299
    and deviance 476
self-help 160, 163-166, 182, 216
self-recruitment
    and class 48
self report studies 465-466
self service economy 332-333
semi-autonomous wage earners 55
semi-professions; *see* professions, lower
semiotics 683-685
separation of conception from execution 329, 375
separatism, feminist 119, 125
serfs 27, 319
service class 48-50, 53, 56-57, 142, 145-146, 187
service sector 46, 56
    employment of ethnic minorities in 110
    employment of women in 135, 142, 331, 345, 347
    and post-industrial society 320, 332-333
setting; *see* streaming
sex; *see also* gender
    as biological difference 121
sex discrimination 71, 118-119, 150, 303, 306
Sex Discrimination Act 142, 187
sex objects, women as 125, 137
sex role system 124-125, 127
sex roles; *see* gender roles
sex war 119
sexism 119, 127, 129-131, 133, 137, 143, 307, 352, 408,
    644-645; *see also* gender; sexual discrimination
sexual abuse 126-127; *see also* child abuse
sexual behaviour; *see also* sexuality
    gender differences in 122
    historical changes in 265
sexual harassment 125, 129, 137, 215, 353, 403
sexual orientation 71
sexual revolution 125
sexual violence; *see* violence 125
sexual scripts 125
sexuality
    adolescent girls' 127
    advertising and 128
    family and 233-234, 237, 239
    self-determining 125
    women's 117, 120, 125-128, 145, 214
share ownership 42, 211, 213, 322, 324
shareholders 41, 51
    institutional 53, 322

mutual 323
shop stewards 340
sick role 422, 436-441
    and deviance 437, 440
    as dissent 441
    Parsons on 436-437
    and role avoidance 440
    and self identity 437
    and vulnerability 436
sickness; 422 see also disease; health; illness
signs 697
signifier and signified 683-684
Sikhs 70, 78, 112, 131, 133, 256-257, 406-407
simulations 697
single parents; see family, lone parent
sisterhood 119
situation tests 81
situational constraints 183
skill shortages 282
skinheads 35-36, 82, 409, 473-474
slags, women as 124, 127
slavery 26, 30, 33, 76, 88, 98-100, 131, 151, 405, 658
smokestack industries 110
smoking 39
    as deviance 457-458
    and health 426, 428, 446, 448, 450, 453
social action 55, 59, 641, 688
    Weber's typology of 665-666
social action theories 11-12, 16-19, 677, 688; see also
        interactionism; interpretivism
    and organisations 364-366
    Weber and 641-642, 665
    and workers' attitudes 326-327, 340
social class; see class
social change
    and the family 244-261
    functionalism and 670
    Marxism and 658-660
    postmodernism and 697
    religion and 504-505
    structuralism and 684
social closure 142
social construction
    of age 408
    of crime and deviance 455-458, 461-462, 627
    of educational attainment 291, 300
    of family and marriage 233, 241-243
    of gender 121-123, 187, 258
    of health 423-424, 433-435
    of individual 11
    of race 67-67
    of reality 2, 622, 639, 641-642, 647, 687
    of rules in organisations 365
    of suicide 470
Social Contract 341
social control 7-8, 11, 15, 18-19
    family and 7
    informal 455
    and labelling 476
    mass media and 540, 549
    medicine and 440-441
    organisations 380-384
    and race 7-8
    religion and 7, 497, 500-501
social democratic theories
    and poverty 175, 182-184
    and welfare 154-155, 157, 161, 164-165, 167, 186
Social Democratic Party 223
social disorder 15
social divisions; see age; class; ethnicity; gender; social
      stratification

social facts 636, 662, 665
Social Fund 167
social inequality; see inequality
social integration 637; see also social solidarity
social justice 63, 175
social mobility 26, 28, 34, 44, 46-50, 104, 145-147, 207-208, 222
    absolute and relative 49, 145
    black people and 112-113
    British patterns and trends 46, 48-49
    buffer zone thesis 48, 146
    closure thesis 48, 146
    and community 389, 401
    counterbalancing thesis 48, 146
    debates over 49
    definitions of 46
    and development 571
    and health 446
    into elites; see elite recruitment
    inflows and outflows 50, 147
    intergenerational and intragenerational 46, 48-49, 50, 146
    ladders to 46
    long range 48, 146
    occupational structure and 46, 49
    measurement of 48-50
    Oxford mobility study 48-49, 146, 186, 294-296
    People in Society study 145-146
    and religious belief 507, 526
    Scottish study 49, 145-146
    women and 145-147, 645
social networks
    and community 391-392, 397, 403
    and family 256, 259-260; see also family extended
social order 15, 365, 686-687; see also order, problem of
social policy; see also welfare state
    feminist theories 157-158
    market liberal theories 155-158
    Marxist theories 156-158
    social democratic theories 154-155, 157
    and values 154, 158
social pressures 11
social problems 19-20
    welfare state and 155
social security system 62, 155, 157, 167-169, 179, 251, 263,
      351; see also Income Support; welfare benefits; welfare
      state
social services 63, 164, 235; see also welfare state
social solidarity 9, 15, 663-664, 671
    crime and 468
    mechanical and organic 319, 663
    religion and 495
    threats to 319, 663
social strata, definition of 25-26
social stratification, 116; see also age; class; ethnicity; gender
    and age 9, 36, 42, 116, 144, 408
    definitions of 26, 30
    ethnic minorities and 98
    functionalist theory of 13, 37-39, 647
    and gender 141-149
    Marxist theory and 33-35, 647
    and poverty 171, 183-184
    slavery and 99
    types of system 26-30
    Weberian theory and 35-37, 184
social surveys 21-23, 73, 611-614; see also interviews;
      questionnaires; sampling
    official statistics from 626
    of racial prejudice 75-76
social system 11-12, 17, 291, 668-670, 693
    community as a 387
    theories 11-16; see also structural theories
socialisation 6-7, 16, 1-12, 15, 669-671

agencies of 7
education and 273, 287-288, 305
family and 121, 222, 233, 235-237, 239, 242-243, 255
gender 121-122, 124, 148, 239, 305, 327, 450
in organisations 379
mass media and 541
political 222, 228
primary 7, 235-236
secondary 7, 236
of upper class 52
and youth culture 409
socialism 60, 185, 345
and democracy 197, 199, 210
and development 577
and gender equality 119, 151, 240
and modernity 655
municipal 94, 166
myth of community under 391
and religion 514-516
Socialist Party of Germany (SPD) 369
Socioeconomic groups 31, 186; see also class
gender and ethnic distribution 105, 141
sociobiology
and family 232-233, 236
and gender 122, 150
and race 77, 86-88
and sociological theory 689-693
sociological consciousness 2-3
sociological imagination 1
sociological perspectives; see sociological theory
sociological problems 19-20, 24
sociological research; see methodology
sociological theory 11-19, 24, 651-699
classical 655-667
ethnomethodology and 685-688
evaluating 652-653
feminism and 118-120
functionalism and 15, 647, 651, 661-664, 668-672, 688
globalisation and 693-695
interactionism and 16-19, 663, 677-682, 688
Marxism and 651-653, 657-661, 672-677, 688
models and 651-652
postmodernism and 396-399
propositions and 652-653
sociobiology and 689-693
structuralism and 682-685
structure and action in 688-689
sociology as a science; see science of society
soft city 416
sophisticated control 341
sources
historical 630-631
primary 608-625
secondary 608, 625-631, 635
South Africa 76, 100-102
Soviet Union; see USSR
space 411-419
as attitude of mind 416
significance of 414
specialisation
and bureaucracy 359
in division of labour 319, 334-335
of role of the family 235-238, 245
and structural differentiation 671
speech codes 297-298
spiritual approach, to masculinity 150
squalor; see housing
stabilisation of adult personalities, and family 235-236
Standard Occupational Classifications 142
state 184, 669; see also nation state; welfare state
communism and the 367-368

definitions of 196
and democracy 196-197, 199
development of the modern 194, 196
globalisation and the 218-221
hegemony and the 210
instrumentalist view 210-211
Marxist theories of the 54, 88, 156-157, 209-212, 483, 540, 660, 673-675
and patriarchy 145
pluralism and the 199
structuralist view 211
state intervention 194
in the economy 212, 335, 345, 572
and welfare 155-156, 164-166, 184, 335
stateless societies 196
statistics; see official statistics; quantitative methods
status 9, 26, 28, 30, 35-37, 54, 58,
achieved and ascribed 9, 46, 142, 245, 287-288
circles in upper class 52
and ethnicity 66, 97, 103
and gender 125, 130, 142
master 440
of slaves 99
status groups 35-36, 103, 145
status situation 55; see also status
status symbols 35, 137
statutory sector of welfare; see welfare state
stereotypes
definition 75
of deviants 476
of elderly 410
gender 116, 118, 124-125, 128, 148, 555
in media 79, 555, 559
racial 66, 69, 75, 77, 79, 95, 99, 110, 131, 315, 559
in total institutions 381
stigmatisation
of divorce 268
of ethnic minorities 103
of poor 61-62, 155
of sick 437
of slaves 99
stocks and flows, in unemployment 346
strategy for equality 186, 188
stratified diffusion 248
streaming, in education
and ethnicity 312-313
and class 278, 300-301
and National Curriculum 285-287, 312
stress
and disease 431
religion and 497
strikes 59, 92, 142, 219, 326, 338-341, 375
causes of 339-340
definition of 339
in mass media 539, 553-554
measurement of 339, 343
structural break, in working class 103-104
structural differentiation 670; see also functional differentiation
structural position, of ethnic minorities 78
structural/structuralist theories 11, 291, 677, 681, 688; see also functionalism; Marxism
of deviance 471-474
of health 445-448, 450-452
and language/semiotics 682-685
of poverty 183-184
of racism 87-89
of religion 495-504
of the state 211
of the underclass 62-64, 104
structuration theory 688-689
structure

and action debate 289-290, 474, 688-689
of family 245, 246-247
interactionism and 642
realism and 639
social 1, 55, 59, 62, 242
struggle, class; *see* conflict, class
subcontracting, and work organisations 335, 337-338, 377-379
subcultures
as communities 387, 393
and deviance 471-474, 476-477, 490
and education 289-290; *see also* culture, counter-school
ethnicity and 354
and social stratification
youth 409, 673
subject class 16, 194, 210; *see also* working class
subordination, of women 120
subterranean values 474
suburbia 416-417
suffragettes 116
suicide
class differences in 448
Durkheim on 469-470, 636-637, 640, 662-663, 678
interpretivism/phenomenology and 470, 642-644, 678-679, 686
medicalisation of 441
sex differences in 151, 450
sunrise industries 46, 110
superstructure 16, 34, 210, 238, 433, 658
and religion 502
Supplementary Benefit; *see* Income Support
supply side, explanations of female employment 136
surplus value 239, 659
surveillance 382-384, 488
surveys; *see* social surveys
survival of the fittest 67
sus laws 72
Swann Report 308-309, 314-315
symbolic interactionsism; *see* interactionism
symbols 17, 77
and communities 387
religious 495, 499, 526
subcultural styles as 473-474
symmetry, in conjugal roles; *see* family, symmetrical
synchronic 683-684
systems; *see also* social system
open and closed 638-641

takeovers 323
target hardening, and crime 488
Taylorism; *see* scientific management
tax system 2, 40, 251, 317, 345
and welfare 156, 156, 161, 169, 181, 182, 186-189, 275
teachers 273
as agents of capital 289
expectations and pupils' performance 299-301, 306-309, 312-314
power and authority 291
pupils' attitudes to 290
women as 135
technical control 329
technical experts 56, 322-323, 332
technicians 31, 54, 225-226, 326
techniques of neutralisation, and deviance 474
technology 33
alienation and 325-326
alternative/intermediate 576-578
assembly line 320, 325-326
continuous process 325-327
craft 325
deskilling and 328-331

flexibility and 334-338
and industrialisation 320
machine 325
new 46, 328
and post-industrial society 332-334
and unemployment 345
teenagers; *see* youth
televangelism 515, 530
television 534; *see also* mass media
hours of viewing 533
and images of women 127, 555-557
and loss of community 401-402
news 539, 544-546, 560
and politics 227
and race 79, 560
soaps 401-402, 541
terrorism 196, 204
test tube fertilisation 119
textual analysis 628
Thatcher, Margaret 73, 147, 212, 214
Thatcherism 62, 167, 168, 212, 342
thematic analysis 628
theory, *see* sociological theory
Third World 85, 182, 322, 336, 418, 566-606; *see also* development
media coverage of 554-555
religion in 503, 526
time and motion studies; *see* work study
time and space, postmodernism and 542, 693
time-space paths 414
total institutions 380-381, 440, 477, 681
totalitarianism 197
totemism 495
tourism 353
trade, and development 581-582, 592
trade unions 35, 54, 182, 185, 327, 336
and ethnic minorities 92, 103, 109
and collective bargaining 339, 341-342, 344, 378
declining power of 335, 342-344
democracy in 201, 368-370
and inflation 345
in Japanese organisations 378
legislation on 188, 341-342
membership 342-344
and politics 201, 203, 210, 212
in Third World 595
and women 136, 215, 343
and workers' resistance 329-330
and the working class 58-59, 164, 339, 394
training 37-38
for unemployed 154, 346, 350
youth 282-284, 409
transition from childhood to adulthood 287, 409
transnational corporations 335
and development 85, 578, 580-581, 594-595, 603
and globalisation 218, 220, 418, 694
and mass media 534-536
power and control of 53, 322, 333, 390,
transport, public spending on 187
triangulation 632-635
triple systems theory 145
truancy 64
two step flow model, of media 538
typifications 686

underclass 26, 50, 61-64
and crime 64, 103, 158, 182
criticisms of concept 62, 104-105
culture and values 62
ethnic minorities and the 61-62, 83, 103-106, 491

poverty and the 62, 104, 182, 184-185
secretaries as an 137
underdevelopment theory 570, 572-576, 581, 591, 594
unemployment 61, 90, 200, 219, 344-351
age and 282, 346, 348, 409-410
causes of 344-345
class and 28, 49, 346, 349-350
crime and 349-351, 487, 489
definitions of 21, 346-348
distribution of 346-349
ethnicity and 28-29, 66, 83-84, 90, 96-97, 105, 110-111, 179, 346, 348
family life and 139-140, 237, 242, 255-256, 262, 350
frictional 344
gender and 135, 149, 347-349
health and 349-351, 448, 451
and inner city 399-400
Keynsian theory 345
and leisure 318, 350, 353-354
levels in Britain 282, 332, 344, 346-349
market liberal theory 345
Marxist theories 345
new technology and 345
and poverty 2, 39-40, 177-178, 183-184, 349-351
as a 'public issue' 1
and riots 405-406, 410
and region 179, 347-348
social consequences of 349-352
and trade unions 342
training 154, 282-284
and the underclass 62-63, 103, 105, 182
voluntary 344
welfare state and 154-155, 157, 163-165, 168-170, 185-186, 188
unemployment benefits 39, 167, 349
unions; see trade unions
unitary working class model 107
United States 34, 71, 322
anti-racism in the 94-97
religion in 498-500, 515, 528-531
universalism 670
universality, in welfare provision 155-156, 164-165, 168, 185
universities; see education, higher
upper class 26, 37, 50-54, 207; see also elites, ruling class
assets 51-53
changes in 51
culture of 51
decomposition of 322
family and kinship 47, 52, 207-208, 211, 246, 248
urban managerialism 412
urban myths 417
urban sociology 411-413
changes in cities and towns 415-416
urbanisation
and community 389-390, 412, 415-416
and development 571, 576-577, 597-600
and family 244
and religion 526-527
and welfare state 163
urban way of life 412, 415-416
postmodernism and 690
USSR 29, 34; see also Eastern Europe
break up of 580; see also communism end of
usurpation strategy 142

validity 21-22, 618-619, 621, 632-633
value consensus 13, 15, 87, 238, 287-288, 319, 671; see also consensus theories
value freedom 20-21, 35, 132, 154, 157, 188, 374, 644-649
values 8-9, 11, 13, 15-16, 35, 636; see also attitudes, culture

and class 43, 52, 62, 210, 295
and community 387, 397
and ethnicity 70, 315
and gender 142
of poor 182-183
religion and 497-500
in sociology; see value freedom
subterranean 474
traditional cultural 78
Victorian 187, 238
of lower working class subculture 473
vandalism 456, 463-464
variables 608-609, 611, 634, 637, 641, 678-679, 681
verstehen 641, 665-666
victim blaming theories 62, 64, 87, 104, 237, 283
victim surveys 106, 463-465, 489
victims
of crime 484-485, 489
ethnic minorities as 82, 94, 106
men as 149, 150-151
women as 120, 262
video
ownership 533
violence 563-564
violence
and crime 462-464
domestic 116-117, 126, 133, 148, 160, 200, 240-242, 461-462, 465, 484-485, 618, 620
and media 64. 560-564, 610
as political protest 204
racial 81-82; see also racial attacks
sexual 119, 125-126, 131, 145
in US ghettoes 96
virtual reality 353
volatility, in electorate 223
voluntary organisations 54, 138, 155-156, 159-161, 163, 167, 182, 318, 403, 411
and Third World 583
voting behaviour 222-229
absolute and relative measures 225-226, 229
and class 31, 43, 222-229
and dealignment 222-229
deviant voters 222
and ethnicity 109, 216, 227-228
and gender 227
and issues 223-225, 227-228
lifetime learning model 228
long and short term factors in 228
and mass media 223, 227-228, 536-537, 538, 548-550
and opinion polls 227
and partisan alignment 222
and party leaders 224, 228
and political socialisation 222, 228
racism and 90-91, 400
and region 227-228
tactical 227
trendless fluctuation in 225-226, 229
voting rights
universal 164, 209
for women 116

wage labour 317-318; see also work
wages 28, 33, 139, 209, 245; see also low pay
disputes over and strikes 340
increases in 41
Wages Councils, abolition of 184
want; see poverty
War Against Poverty 95
wealth 14, 25-26, 36, 47, 54, 66, 97
Cheyenne attitudes to 10

definition 41-42
distribution; *see* distribution of income and wealth
marketable 41-42
and upper class 51-53, 207
Weberian theory 665-668
  and bureaucracy 358-361, 365, 370-371, 373, 377, 379, 382-383, 506
  and class stratification 35-37, 184
  criticisms of 361-363, 505, 666-667
  and gender stratification 142
  and professional power 434
  and power and authority 192-193, 358-359
  and race and ethnicity 88, 98, 103-107
  and rationalisation 320, 359, 504-506, 666
  and religion 504-506, 526, 641-642
  of social action 641-642, 665-666
  and the state 196
welfare benefits 2, 40, 62, 64, 184, 186, 189, 237, 261
  cuts in 158, 164, 167, 178, 182, 188
welfare pluralism 159, 161-163, 167
welfare sectors 158-163
welfare state 154-170, 186-188, 213
  central and local services 159
  and class inequality 186-188
  competition in 156, 167
  contradictory functions of 156-157
  crisis of the 167-169
  and Beveridge's five evils 158-159, 164-165
  and dependency 62, 64, 104, 156, 182, 237, 487
  and development 571
  and ethnic minorities 104, 187-188
  expenditure on; *see* public expenditure
  and family 156-157, 159-160, 162-163, 167, 182, 186-187, 237, 245, 249
  feminist theories 157-158, 160, 162, 249, 403-404
  and gender inequalities 157-158, 187
  historical development 163-166
  market liberal theories 155-158, 160-161, 164
  Marxist theories 156-158, 160, 212
  neo-Fordism and 335
  and poverty 154-155, 158, 164-165, 182, 184, 186, 188
  privatisation of 156, 167-168, 170, 187
  social democratic theories 154-155, 157, 164, 186
West Indians; *see* Afro-Caribbeans
white collar workers; *see* workers, nonmanual
white collar crime 474-475, 480
wives; *see* marriage
women 116-126; *see also* gender
  birth rates and status of 589
  and employment 117, 134-138, 187, 214, 240, 252, 256, 258-260, 262-263, 268, 305, 327-334, 379
  ethnic minority 110, 119, 126, 128-134, 240
  and feminism 116-121
  and gender roles 121-123
  and housework 139-140, 239-240, 258-263; *see also* housewives
  invisibility of 128, 306, 484, 645
  and the sex role system 124-125
  and sexuality 125-128
  and social mobility 145-147
  and stratification 129, 141-145
women's movement 116-118, 133, 149-150, 200, 219; *see also* feminism
women's refuges 131
women's studies 644
work 317-355; *see also* housework; industrial conflict; workers
  alienation from 33, 59, 320, 325-326, 328, 659
  as a calling 504-506, 641
  casual and temporary 62, 112, 178, 188, 240, 332, 335
  changing patterns of 331-334
  collapse of 345

definition of 142, 317-319
degradation of 328; *see also* deskilling
deprivations at 174
education and training for 273-275, 282-284, 287-290
ethnicity and 83-84, 104, 134, 379
and health; *see* class and health; occupations and health; unemployment and health
industrialisation and 244, 318-321, 332, 345
Marxism and 59, 319-320, 322-326, 332-333, 335-336, 339-340, 342
non-; *see* leisure; unemployment
orientations to 136-137, 326-327
part time 112, 134-135, 142, 162, 179, 187-188, 240, 262, 331-336, 343, 347
and political attitudes 222
satisfaction 59, 289, 325-326
social action theories 326-327
technology and 325-338
voluntary; *see* voluntary organisations
women and 117, 134-140, 187, 214, 240, 252, 256, 258-260, 262-263, 268, 305, 327-334, 345, 379
work situation 48, 55, 142
work study 328, 361, 371
work to rule 339, 362
workers; *see also* work; working class
  affluent 58-59, 61, 212, 248-249, 260-261, 326, 340, 396-397
  attitudes and behaviour 136-138, 325-328, 340
  clerical 32, 54, 58, 137, 142, 330-331
  female; *see* work, women and
  manual 31-32, 38, 40, 48, 55, 58, 135, 142, 146; *see also* working class
  nonmanual 31-32, 40, 48, 54-56, 58, 142, 328-329, 332; *see also* middle class
  resistance 329
  secretarial 137
  skilled 31-31, 48, 59, 142-143, 328, 330, 394
  technical; *see* technicians
  unskilled 31-32, 48, 183, 320, 328-330
workhouses 160, 163-164
working class 26, 31, 33, 38, 42, 48-50, 50, 55, 58-61, 64, 106, 142-143, 225, 228; *see also* proletariat
  careers 58
  class consciousness of 59-60, 210, 339, 340, 394, 396, 502
  community 58, 247, 394-398, 401
  concessions to the
  and consumption cleavages 43
  divisions in the 58, 223
  and education; *see* education and class; educational achievement and class
  embourgeoisement 42, 58-59
  families 239, 246-250, 258-262
  Marxism and the 210, 328
  models of ethnic minorities in 107-108
  new 58, 223-224, 395-397; *see also* workers, affluent
  old/traditional 58, 223-224, 260, 394-395, 406. 409
  political attitudes 58, 222; *see also* voting behaviour, and class
  and power 198, 207, 212-213, 215, 368-369
  rough and respectable 394
  and the welfare state 156, 158, 164, 169, 186

young people; *see* youth
youth 408-410
  and ethnicity 92, 409
  and class 409, 411
  and crime 409-410
  and gender 127, 141, 409
  and sexuality 127
  subcultures 409, 673
  unemployment 282-283, 346, 348, 409
yuppies 56, 90, 400